PSYCHOLOGY

Cover illustration: *No Beginning*, digital art by Richard Stine/Jaz & Jaz

DAVID G. MYERS
PSYCHOLOGY

Fifth Edition

Hope College
Holland, Michigan

WORTH PUBLISHERS

to christine

with thanks for a decade of
wonderful support and friendship

PSYCHOLOGY, Fifth Edition

Copyright © 1998, 1995, 1992, 1989, 1986 by Worth Publishers, Inc.
All rights reserved.
Manufactured in the United States of America
Library of Congress Catalog Card Number: 97-060931
ISBN: 1-57259-590-6
        1-57259-207-9 (comp.)
Printing: 5 4
Year: 02 01 00 99 98

Executive editor: Catherine Woods
Development editor: Christine Brune
Design: Malcolm Grear Designers
Art director: George Touloumes
Project editor: Laura Rubin
Production supervisor: Stacey B. Alexander
Layout: Fernando Quiñones and Heriberto Lugo
Photo editor: Joan Meisel
Chapter-opening photo research: Silvia Dinale
Graphics art manager: Demetrios Zangos
Illustrations: Shawn Kenney, Bonnie Hofkin and Demetrios Zangos

Compositions and separations: TSI Graphics, Inc.
Printing and binding: Von Hoffmann Press, Inc.
Cover: *No Beginning*, digital art by Richard Stine/Jaz & Jaz

Credits begin on page C-1 and constitute an extension
of the copyright page.

All royalties from the sale of this book are assigned to the
David and Carol Myers Foundation, which exists to receive
and distribute funds to other charitable organizations.

Worth Publishers
33 Irving Place
New York, NY 10003

about the author

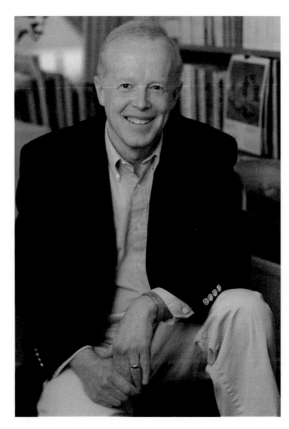

David G. Myers is professor of psychology at Michigan's Hope College, where he has spent his career and been voted "outstanding professor" by students. His writings have appeared in four dozen journals and magazines, from *Science* to *Scientific American*, and in ten books.

contents in brief

contents

x

preface

Like the human beings whom psychologists study, textbooks, too, develop with age. From its conception in 1982 to its birth in 1986 and through the first several editions of its childhood and youth, this book, like the field it reports, has matured. Today's psychological science is more attuned to evolutionary and genetic influences, to the neuroscience revolution, and to gender and cultural diversity. We today can also harness new ways to present information, both in books and via electronic media. These changes are exhilarating! Keeping up with new discoveries and technologies fills each day and connects me with many colleagues and friends.

The thousands of instructors and millions of students who have studied this book have contributed immensely to its development. Much of this has occurred spontaneously, through correspondence and conversations. For this edition, we also welcomed survey input and reviews from 4234 students and 240 instructors, from British Columbia to Florida, and from New Hampshire to New Zealand. I look forward to continued feedback as we strive, over future editions, to create an ever better book.

Throughout its five editions, however, my vision for *Psychology* has not wavered: *to merge rigorous science with a broad human perspective in a book that engages both mind and heart.* My aim has been to create a state-of-the-art introduction to psychology, written with sensitivity to students' needs and interests. I aspire to help students gain insight into, and appreciate the wonder of, important phenomena of their lives. I also want to convey the inquisitive, caring spirit in which psychologists *do* psychology. The study of psychology, I believe, enhances our abilities to restrain intuition with critical thinking, judgmentalism with compassion, and illusion with understanding.

Believing with Thoreau that "Anything living is easily and naturally expressed in popular language," I seek to communicate psychology's scholarship with crisp narrative and vivid storytelling. Writing as a solo author, I hope to tell psychology's story in a way that is warmly personal as well as rigorously scientific. I love to reflect on connections between psychology and other realms, such as literature, philosophy, history, sports, politics, and popular culture. And I love to provoke thought, to play with words, and to laugh.

Big Changes in the Fifth Edition

This new edition retains its predecessor's voice, and much of its content and organization. However, every page has been updated. The result is 664 new references and many new sections and examples reflecting the psychology of the late 1990s. This edition also *looks* new. Its reconceptualized illustrations, more effective chapter design, and many improved photos should help it *work* better than ever.

Increased Evolution and Behavior Genetics Coverage

The evolutionary and behavior genetics perspectives on psychology are now introduced in the first chapter, and coverage of these issues is now even more extensively integrated throughout the book (see the table on the following page). Chapter 2

Evolution and Behavior Genetics Coverage

The **evolutionary perspective** is covered on the following pages:

Aging, p. 130
Anxiety disorders, p. 464
Attraction, p. 582
Biological predispositions in learning, pp. 250–252, 261
Chapter 2, Neuroscience, Genetics, and Behavior
Charles Darwin, p. 2
Electromagnetic spectrum, sensitivity to, p. 154
Emotional expression, p. 401
Evolutionary perspective, defined, pp. 4–5
Fear, p. 404
Hearing, p. 164
Instincts, p. 364
Intelligence, pp. 358–359
Language, pp. 319, 322
Love, p. 137
Need to belong, p. 367
Overconfidence, p. 314
Sensation, pp. 148, 170

Sensory adaptation, p. 152
Signal detection theory, p. 149
Sleep, p. 215
Smell, pp. 174–176
Stress and the immune system, p. 524

Behavior genetics is covered on the following pages:

Abuse, intergenerational transmission of, p. 266
Adoption studies, pp. 110–111
Aggression, pp. 571–578
Behavioral effects of gender, p. 34
Behavior genetics perspective, defined, pp. 4–5
Biomedical therapies, pp. 507–512, 513
Body type, p. 431
Chapter 2, Neuroscience, Genetics, and Behavior
Development, pp. 77–78
 attachment, pp. 97-98

authoritative parenting, pp. 104–105
brain development, experience and, pp. 83–84
language development, pp. 322–326
motor development, p. 86
parental credit/ blame, 111–113
physical development, pp. 116–118
prenatal development, pp. 79–81
stranger anxiety, pp. 94–95
temperament, pp. 96–97
Depth perception, p. 186
Drives and incentives, pp. 364–365
Drug use, pp. 236–238
Emotion and cognition, pp. 415–417
Fear, pp. 404–405
Genetics of conception, p. 78
Happiness, p. 412

Intelligence, pp. 352–359
Learning, pp. 250–252, 261
Nature/ nurture debate, pp. 77–78
Obesity and weight control, pp. 539–546
Perception, pp. 194–200
Personality traits, p. 432
Psychological disorders:
 anxiety disorders, p. 464
 bio-psycho-social perspective, p. 456
 depression, pp. 471–472
 personality disorders, pp. 482–483
 schizophrenia, pp. 478–479
Romantic love, p. 137
Sex chromosomes and hormones, p. 79
Sexuality, pp. 375–378
Sexual orientation, pp. 380–382
Smell, p. 175
Stress, personality, and illness, pp. 516–524, 526–528
Twin studies, pp. 108–111

offers a new main section on "Genetics and Behavior," which includes subsections on evolutionary psychology and behavior genetics. This new section introduces students to basic concepts of evolution and behavior genetics that will recur throughout the book. I have retitled the chapter "Neuroscience, Genetics, and Behavior" to reflect the new content.

The integrated coverage of evolution and genetics appears in 16 of the book's 18 chapters. For example, Chapter 3 ("The Developing Child") discusses "The Genetics of Life," "Sex Chromosomes, Sex Hormones, and Gender," "Twin Studies," and "Adoption Studies." Chapter 11 ("Intelligence") includes a lengthy section on "Genetic and Environmental Influences on Intelligence."

New discoveries from the neuroscience frontier have also been added, building on Chapter 2's axiom that *"everything psychological is simultaneously biological."* Rather than pack all this information into an early chapter or two, much of it is more palatably disseminated throughout the book. Chapter 2, "Neuroscience, Genetics, and Behavior," thus aims not to overwhelm students with biology, but to introduce important concepts and to whet readers' appetite for more.

Fully Integrated Gender and Cultural Diversity Coverage

You asked for it. We listened. Here it is: The fourth edition's "Diversity and Community" chapter material is now integrated throughout the text, where all student readers will encounter it. This integrated material adds to existing coverage. Topics range from the first chapter's discussions of the social-cultural perspective, of cultural and gender variations, and of "human diversity and kinship," through the last chapter's discussion of cultural and gender roles. In between are dozens more gender- and culture-related topics, including those itemized on the next page.

For this and succeeding editions I also am working to offer a world-based psychology for our worldwide student readership. Thus, I continually search the world for research findings and text and photo examples, conscious that readers may be in Melbourne, Sheffield, Vancouver, or Nairobi. North American and European examples come easily, given that I reside in the United States, maintain contact with friends and colleagues in Canada, subscribe to several European periodicals, and live periodically in the United Kingdom. But

Coverage of the Psychology of Men and Women

Coverage of **the psychology of women and men** can be found on the following pages:

Coverage of Culture and Multicultural Experience

From the Introduction to Chapter 18, coverage of **culture and multicultural experience** permeates the book in the following discussions:

this edition also offers more than 50 mentions of Australia and New Zealand. We are all citizens of a shrinking world, thanks to increased migration and the growing global economy. Thus, American students, too, benefit from information and examples that internationalize their world-consciousness. And if psychology seeks to explain *human* behavior (not just American or Canadian or Australian behavior), the broader the scope of studies presented, the more accurate is our picture of this world's people. My aim is to expose all students to the world beyond their own country. Thus, I continue to welcome input and suggestions from all readers everywhere.

All-New Illustration Program and Design

A team of artists, designers, and psychologists worked together to reconceptualize each piece of art and to create new illustrations. Malcolm Grear Designers also created a new, more student-friendly design for this book, partly in response to the input from over 4000 student readers. The result is a visually more effective book that better reinforces the key concepts for students. The anatomical art, for example, is all new—redrawn (as illustrated below) to be optimally comprehensible and appealing.

New Electronic Teaching and Learning Opportunities

I am pleased to be part of an unprecedented collaborative effort to provide teaching resources and interactive learning opportunities for introductory psychology. A team of psychology educators and I have been working together with Peregrine Publishers to create a one-stop Web site, **The Psychology Place** (http://www.psychplace.com). Instructors will find continuously updated teaching resources, including news and teaching tips. Student resources include interactive learning activities, carefully reviewed "Best of the Web" links, and hyperlinked *Scientific American* articles. Please also visit Worth Publishers' Web site (www.worthpublishers.com) for other features designed to complement your teaching and learning experience.

Our new **student CD-ROM, *PsychQuest*** (by Thomas Ludwig, Hope College), provides active learning of important concepts for higher student interest and better retention. *PsychQuest* contains eight modules, each exploring a high-interest topic addressed in introductory psychology. The topics are depth perception in sports, psychoactive drugs, memory, weight regulation, depression, chronic stress, stereotyping, and mate selection. *PsychQuest* is an interactive tool that allows students to explore various psychological research topics, participate in experiments and simulations, quiz them-

Figure **2.13**

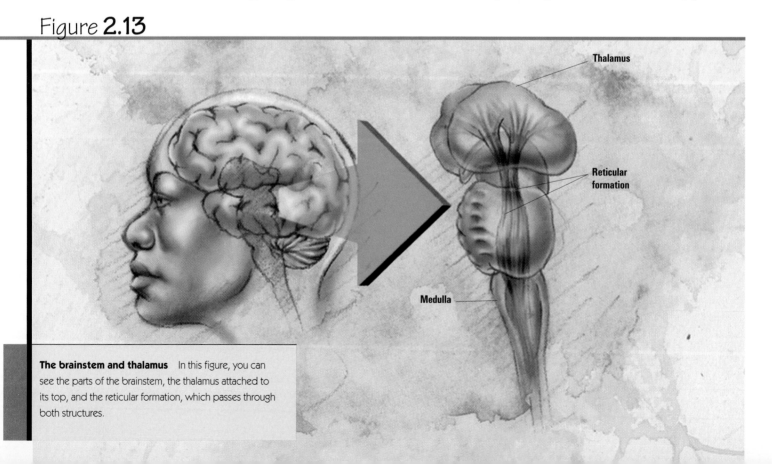

Thalamus

Reticular formation

Medulla

The brainstem and thalamus   In this figure, you can see the parts of the brainstem, the thalamus attached to its top, and the reticular formation, which passes through both structures.

selves on content, and link to the World Wide Web for additional information. Each module is designed to foster critical thinking and stimulate interest in key issues in psychology by relating psychological concepts to real-world issues.

Goals for the Fifth Edition

Throughout this revision, I have steadfastly followed eight principles:

1. **To exemplify the process of inquiry** I strive to show students not just the outcome of research, but how the research process works. Throughout, the book tries to excite readers' curiosity. It invites them to imagine themselves as participants in classic experiments. Several chapters introduce research stories as mysteries that progressively unravel as one clue after another falls into place. (See, for example, the historical story of research on the brain's processing of language—page 63.)

2. **To teach critical thinking** By presenting research as intellectual detective work, I exemplify an inquiring, analytical mind-set. Whether students are studying development, cognition, or statistics, they will become involved in, and see the rewards of, critical reasoning. Moreover, they will discover how an empirical approach can help them evaluate competing ideas and claims for highly publicized phenomena—ranging from subliminal persuasion, ESP, and facilitated communication to astrology, basketball streak-shooting, and repressed and recovered memories.

3. **To put facts in the service of concepts** My intention is not to fill students' intellectual file drawers with facts, but to reveal psychology's major concepts—to teach students how to think, and to offer psychological ideas worth thinking about. In each chapter I place emphasis on those concepts I hope students will carry with them long after they complete the course. Always, I try to follow Albert Einstein's dictum: "Everything should be made as simple as possible, but not simpler."

4. **To be as up-to-date as possible** Few things dampen students' interest as quickly as the sense that they are reading stale news. While retaining psychology's classic studies and concepts, I also present the discipline's most important recent developments. Fully 24 percent of the references in this edition are dated 1994 to 1997.

5. **To integrate principles and applications** Throughout—by means of anecdotes, case histories, and the posing of hypothetical situations—I relate the findings of basic research to their applications and implications. Where psychology can illuminate pressing human issues—be they racism and sexism, health and happiness, or violence and war—I have not hesitated to shine its light.

6. **To enhance comprehension by providing continuity** Many chapters have a significant issue or theme that links subtopics, forming a thread that ties the chapter together. Chapter 8, "Learning," conveys the idea that bold thinkers can serve as intellectual pioneers. Chapter 10, "Thinking and Language," raises the issue of human rationality and irrationality. Chapter 15, "Psychological Disorders," conveys empathy for, and understanding of, troubled lives. "The uniformity of a work," observed Edward Gibbon, "denotes the hand of a single artist." Because the book has a single author, other threads, such as behavior genetics and cultural diversity, weave throughout the whole book, and students hear a consistent voice.

7. **To reinforce learning at every step** Everyday examples and rhetorical questions encourage students to process the material actively. Concepts presented earlier are frequently applied, and thereby reinforced, in later chapters. For instance, in Chapter 5, "Sensation," students learn that much of our information processing occurs *outside* our conscious awareness. Ensuing chapters reinforce this concept. A marginal glossary, and end-of-section and end-of-chapter lists of key terms, help students master important terminology. Major sections begin with previews and end with summaries that highlight the organization and key concepts.

8. **To convey respect for human unity and diversity** Time and again, readers will see evidence of our human kinship—our shared biological heritage, our common mechanisms of seeing and learning, hungering and feeling, loving and hating. They will also better understand the dimensions of our diversity—our *individual* diversity in development and aptitudes, temperament and personality, and disorder and health; and our *cultural* diversity in attitudes and expressive styles, childrearing and care for the elderly, and life priorities.

The Supplements Package

Psychology is accompanied by widely acclaimed materials to enhance teaching and learning. For students who desire additional help mastering the text, there is Richard O. Straub's (University of Michigan, Dearborn) *Study Guide*. Each chapter follows the text's *PRTR: Preview/Read/Think Critically/Review* format to guide students at each step of their study. For each section of the text chapter, an explanation is provided of the idioms and other phrases potentially unfamiliar to students for whom English is a second language. Several new Internet activities, called "Web Sightings," have been included, along with new crossword puzzles and pedagogically effective new fill-in-the-blank flow charts. The study guide is also computerized in a highly interactive program for use in the Windows or Macintosh formats.

The *Instructor's Resources*, created by Martin Bolt (Calvin College) for *Psychology*, has been hailed as the finest set of psychology teaching resources ever assembled. With 20 percent new items in this edition, it features dozens of ready-to-use demonstration handouts, along with learning objectives, lecture/discussion ideas, student projects, classroom exercises, video and film suggestions, and Internet exercises. Martin Bolt's *Lecture Guides*, which come in both printed and easily modifiable WordPerfect formats, offer instructors an additional resource for lecture preparation.

PsychSim 4, the award-winning computer software developed by Thomas Ludwig (Hope College) brings some of psychology's most important concepts and methods to life. *PsychSim 4* (available on CD-ROM or floppies) contains 19 programs for use in the Windows or Macintosh format. Some simulations engage the student as experimenter—conditioning a rat, electrically probing the hypothalamus, or working in a sleep lab. Others engage the student as subject—responding to tests of memory or visual illusions, or interpreting facial expressions. Still others provide a dynamic tutorial/demonstration of, say, hemispheric processing or cognitive development principles. Student worksheets are provided. *PsychSim 4* is significantly enhanced over an earlier version that received the 1990 Educom/NCRIPTAL Higher Education Software Award for "Best Psychology Software"—marking the first time that software specifically designed for introductory psychology had been so honored. See also p. xx for a description of Ludwig's new *PsychQuest CD-ROM.*

The *Test Banks*, by John Brink (Calvin College), provide over 4000 multiple-choice questions, plus essay questions. Each question is keyed to a learning objective, page-referenced to the textbook, and rated in level of difficulty. (Optional questions are also included for the *PsychSim* programs and *The Brain, The Mind,* and *PsychQuest* modules; see below.) User-friendly computerized test generation is also available.

Our *Psychology Videodisc* will help you bring to life for your students all the major topics in *Psychology*, combining brief, exciting video clips and animated segments with a library of stills. This videodisc is accompanied by an extensive *Instructor's Guide*, by Martin Bolt and Richard O. Straub, complete with bar codes, descriptions of each item and suggestions for how to incorporate the material into your lecture, and a subject index that references and cross-references all items by topic. Thomas Ludwig's accompanying presentation software package, which includes a bar-code generator, is also available for use on IBM-PC or Macintosh computers.

For users of the *Discovering Psychology* telecourse, we have a *Discovering Psychology* Study Guide. This Study Guide is designed for use with this text and with the *Discovering Psychology* telecourse, narrated by Philip Zimbardo and produced by the Annenberg/CPB Project.

In addition, Worth Publishers has produced **38 video modules from *The Mind* series,** in association with WNET. These modules were edited by Frank J. Vattano (Colorado State University) with the consultation of Charles Brewer (Furman University) and myself. Rather than displace the instructor, as do longer films, these brief clips (which can be dubbed onto individual cassettes) dramatically enhance and illustrate lectures. They do so in ways that written and spoken words cannot—by introducing students to a split-brain patient being tested, a sleeping subject being monitored in a lab, a patient suffering the ravages of schizophrenia, and so forth. In addition to the 38 modules on videocassettes, Worth Publishers also offers a laser disc with 14 highlights from *The Mind* modules. The laser disc is accompanied by a bar-coded Faculty Guide.

The new **Second Edition of *The Brain* teaching modules** by Frank J. Vattano, Thomas L. Bennet, and Michelle Butler (all of Colorado State University) is also available with this text. Accompanied by a faculty guide keyed specifically to the chapters in the book, these video modules are the perfect complement to help capture students' interest and vividly illustrate the important role of biological processes underlying human behavior. There are 11 new and 12 significantly updated modules in addition to nine from the original series.

Finally, Worth Publishers has created the **Scientific American Frontiers Video Collection for Introductory Psychology**. The collection, approximately 25 video segments that are 8 to 25 minutes long, is an excellent resource to stimulate class discussion and interest on a variety of topics.

In Appreciation

If it is true that "whoever walks with the wise becomes wise," then I am wiser for all the wisdom and advice received from my colleagues. With the aid of several hundred consultants and reviewers over the last decade, this has become a better, more accurate book than one author alone (this author, at least) could write. My indebtedness continues to each of the teacher-scholars whose influence I acknowledged in the four previous editions.

My gratitude now extends to the colleagues who contributed criticism, corrections, and creative ideas to this new edition. For their expertise and encouragement, I thank the following reviewers:

Michael Akiyama, *University of Michigan—Dearborn*

Lynn Augsbach, *Morehead State University*

F. Samuel Bauer, *Christopher Newport University*

Gira Bhatt, *Camosun College*

Charles Brewer, *Furman University*

James Butler, *James Madison University*

Arnold Chamove, *Massey University*

Steve Charlton, *Kwantlen University College*

Donald V. Coscina, *Wayne State University*

Dianne Crisp, *Kwantlen University College*

Jadwiga Dolzycki, *Tennessee Technological University*

Marte Fallshore, *Utah Valley State College*

Deborah Finkel, *Indiana University Southeast*

Jody Fournier, *Ohio State University*

Randolph Grace, *University of New Hampshire*

Sergio Guglielmi, *Lake Forest College*

Diane Halpern, *California State University—San Bernardino*

Judith Rich Harris

Kathleen Hart, *Xavier University*

Joseph Horvat, *Weber State University*

Cheryl Hosley, *Ohio State University*

Robert Jensen, *California State University—Sacramento*

James A. Johnson, *Sam Houston State University*

Eric Landrum, *Boise State University*

Elizabeth Loftus, *University of Washington*

Karsten Look, *Columbus State Community College*

Alan Monat, *California State University—Hayward*

Joel Morgovsky, *Brookdale Community College*

Peter E. Nathan, *University of Iowa*

James O'Brien, *Tidewater Community College*

Elizabeth Weiss Ozorak, *Allegheny College*

Hal Pashler, *University of California—San Diego*

Michael J. Renner, *West Chester University*

Stephen Saunders, *Marquette University*

Christopher Taylor, *University of Arizona*

G. Patience Thomas, *Raymond Walters College*

Irving Tucker, *Shepherd College*

Robert Lee Williams, *Gallaudet University*

Through its first four editions, Charles Brewer (Furman University) enhanced this book with meticulous critiques, probing questions, and spirit-sustaining encouragement. In the planning of this new edition, he helped define priorities as a special consultant.

At Worth Publishers a host of people played key roles in creating this fifth edition. Christine Brune, chief editor for the last three editions, is a wonder worker. She offers just the right mix of encouragement, gentle admonition, attention to detail, and passion for excellence. An author could not ask for more.

Worth president Susan Driscoll, managing editor Suzanne Thibodeau, and psychology executive editor Catherine Woods helped construct and execute the plan for this new edition. Catherine also became a trusted sounding board as we faced the myriad discrete decisions along the way. Betty Probert and Penny Bice ably edited and produced the supplements, and Betty offered sage advice on the book as well.

Other Worth staff also played essential roles. Freelance copyeditor Nancy Fleming sensitively fine-tuned the final manuscript. Project editor Laura Rubin effectively guided the transformation of manuscript into book with the able assistance of Cele Gardner and Yuna Lee. Worth's gifted artistic and production team, led by George Touloumes and including Stacey Alexander, Demetrios Zangos, and Fernando Quiñones, plus Mary Marshall and photo researchers Joan Meisel and Silvia Dinale, took their game to a new level in creating this unprecedented new design and photo program. And psychology marketing manager Kate Steinbacher has led the effort to make this new edition available to psychology instructors. To all of them I am deeply grateful for an extraordinary effort.

At Hope College, the supporting team members for this edition included Gretchen Rumohr-Voskuil, who researched countless bits of information, proofed hundreds of pages, and prepared the name index. With infectious good cheer, Kathy Adamski composed my awkward dictation into letters to researchers. Typesetters Phyllis and Richard Vandervelde met or exceeded all deadlines, often by working into the wee hours to enter or revise every one of the more than 400,000 words, and finally to code them for electronic delivery.

Again, I gratefully acknowledge the influence of my writing coach, poet Jack Ridl, whose influence lingers in the voice you will be hearing in the pages that follow. He more than anyone cultivated my delight in dancing with the language, and taught me to approach writing as a craft that shades into art.

After hearing countless dozens of people say that this book's supplements have taken their teaching to a new level, I reflect on how fortunate I am to be a part of a team on which everyone has produced on-time work marked by the highest professional standards. For their remarkable talents, their dedication, and their friendship, I thank Martin Bolt, John Brink, Thomas Ludwig, and Richard O. Straub. Rick Straub also authored the critical thinking exercises that appear at the end of each chapter.

Finally, my gratitude extends to the students and instructors who have written to offer suggestions or just an encouraging word. It is for them, and for those about to begin their study of psychology, that I have done my best to introduce the field I love.

As soon as those who paint the Golden Gate Bridge finish, it is time to start over again. So it is with this book. The ink is barely dry before I begin envisioning the next edition. By the time you read this, I will be gathering information for the sixth edition. Your input will again influence how this book continues to evolve. So, please, do share your thoughts.

David Myers

Hope College
Holland, Michigan 49422-9000
USA
E-mail: myers@hope.edu

PSYCHOLOGY

Introduction

"What's it like being married to a psychologist?" people occasionally ask my wife. "Does he use his psychology on you?"

"So, does your Dad, like, analyze you?" my children have hundreds of times been asked by friends.

"What do you think of me?" asked one barber, hoping for an instant personality analysis after learning that I was a psychologist.

For these questioners, as for most people whose exposure to psychology comes from popular books, magazines, and TV, psychologists analyze personality, offer counseling, and dispense child-rearing advice.

Do they? Yes, and much more. Consider some of psychology's questions, questions that from time to time you may wonder about:

Have you ever found yourself reacting to something just as one of your parents would—perhaps in a way you vowed you never would—and then wondered how much of your personality you inherited? *To what degree are you really like your mother or your father? To what extent is your parents' influence transmitted through their genes? To what extent through the environment they gave you?*

Have you ever played peekaboo with a 6-month-old infant and wondered why the baby finds the game so delightful? The baby reacts as though, when you momentarily move behind a door, you actually disappear—only to reappear later out of thin air. *What do babies actually perceive and think?*

Have you ever awakened from a nightmare and, with a wave of relief, wondered why we have such crazy dreams? *How often, and why, do we dream?*

Have you ever wondered what makes for school and work success? Are some people just born smarter? *Does brute intelligence explain why some people get richer, think more creatively, or relate more sensitively?*

Do you ever get depressed or anxious and wonder whether you'll ever feel "normal"? *What triggers our bad moods—and our good ones?*

Have you ever worried about how to act among people of a different culture, race, or sex? *In what ways are we alike as members of the human family? How do we differ?*

A smile is a smile the world around Throughout this book, you will see examples of our cultural and gender diversity, but also of the similarities that define our shared human nature. Men and women in different cultures show differences in when and how often they smile, but a smile *means* the same thing anywhere in the world.

Such questions provide grist for psychology's mill, for psychology is a science that seeks to answer all sorts of questions about us all: how we think, feel, and act.

Psychology's Roots

Psychology has developed from international roots in biology and philosophy to become a science that aims to describe and explain how we think, feel, and act. This book shows how smart-thinking people can apply psychology's strategies, and it highlights psychology's most humanly significant findings.

To be human is to be curious about ourselves and the world around us. Psychology's ancestors therefore date to the world's early writings. Before 300 B.C., the Greek naturalist and philosopher Aristotle theorized about learning and memory, motivation and emotion, perception and personality. Today we chuckle at some of his guesses, like a meal making us sleepy by causing gas and heat to collect around the source of our personality, the heart. But credit Aristotle with asking the right questions.

At the dawn of modern science in the 1600s, British philosophers adopted a down-to-earth approach to knowledge, rooted in observation. One of them, John Locke, rejected the notion of inborn ideas. At birth, he said, the mind is but a "white paper," upon which experience writes.

In 1831, an indifferent student but ardent collector of beetles, mollusks, and shells set sail on what was to prove a historic round-the-world voyage. The 22-year-old voyager was Charles Darwin, and for some time afterward, he pondered the incredible species variation he had encountered, including tortoises on one island that would differ from those on other islands of the region. His 1859 *Origin of Species* explained this diversity of life by proposing an evolutionary process. From among chance variations in organisms, he believed, nature selects those that best enable an organism to survive and reproduce in a particular environment. Darwin's big idea—"the single best idea anyone has ever had," says philosopher Daniel Dennett (1996)—is called *natural selection*, and it is still with us 140 years later, having become an organizing principle of biology. Evolution also has become an important principle for psychology. This would surely have pleased Darwin, for he believed his theory explains not only animal structures (such as why polar bear coats are white) but also animal behaviors (such as the emotional expressions associated with lust and rage).

Thinking about thinking continued to evolve until the birth of psychology as we know it, on a December day in 1879. In a small room on the third floor of a shabby building at Germany's University of Leipzig, two young men were helping a long-faced, austere, middle-aged professor, Wilhelm Wundt (pronounced Vooont), create an experimental apparatus. Their machine measured the time lag between people's hearing a ball hit a platform and their pressing a telegraph key (Hunt, 1993). Later, they compared this to the time required for slightly more complex tasks. Wundt was seeking to measure the "atoms of the mind"—the fastest and simplest mental processes. Thus began what many consider psychology's first experiment, launching the first psychological institute, staffed by Wundt and psychology's first graduate students.

The young science of psychology thus evolved from the more established fields of biology and philosophy. Wundt was both a physiologist and a philosopher. Darwin was an English naturalist. Ivan Pavlov, who pioneered the study of learning, was a Russian physiologist. Sigmund Freud, renowned personality theorist, was an Austrian physician. Jean Piaget, this century's most influential observer of children, was a Swiss biologist. William James, author of an important 1890 psychology textbook, was an American philosopher. This list of pioneering psychologists—"Magellans of the mind," as Morton Hunt (1993) calls them—illustrates that psychology has its origins in many countries (Figure 1).

Psychology is a science that seeks to answer all sorts of questions about us all: how we think, feel, and act.

Figure 1

A timeline of psychology's pioneers, 1879–1913

Hermann Ebbinghaus in Germany reports the first experiments on memory (1885).

Alfred Binet (shown) and **Theodore Simon** devise the first intelligence test for use with Parisian schoolchildren (1905).

Wilhelm Wundt establishes the first psychology laboratory at the University of Leipzig, Germany (1879).

Edward L. Thorndike in the United States conducts the first experiments on animal learning (1898).

Margaret Floy Washburn, the first woman to receive a Ph.D. in psychology, synthesizes research on animal behavior in *The Animal Mind* (1908).

American Psychological Association is founded (1892).

1875   1880   1885   1890   1895   1900   1905   1910   1915

G. Stanley Hall, a student of Wundt's, establishes the first American psychology laboratory at Johns Hopkins University (1883).

Sigmund Freud in Austria introduces his psychoanalytic theory in *The Interpretation of Dreams* (1900).

John B. Watson in the United States champions psychology as the science of behavior (1913).

William James publishes the widely used *Principles of Psychology* in the United States (1890),

Mary Whiton Calkins creates paired-associates technique for studying memory; becomes president of American Psychological Association (1905).

Ivan Pavlov in Russia begins to publish his classic studies of animal learning (1906).

psychology
*the science of behavior and
mental processes.*

So what is psychology? With activities ranging from recording nerve cell activity to psychotherapy, psychology is not easily defined. Psychology began as the science of mental life. Wundt's basic research tool became introspection—self-examination of one's own emotional states and mental processes. Wundt focused on *inner* sensations, feelings, and thoughts. Thus, until the 1920s, psychology was defined as "the science of mental life."

From the 1920s into the 1960s, American psychologists, led by flamboyant and provocative John Watson, dismissed introspection and redefined psychology as "the science of observable behavior." After all, they said, science is rooted in observation. You cannot observe a sensation, a feeling, or a thought, but you *can* observe people's *behavior* as they respond to different situations.

In the 1960s, psychology began to recapture its initial interest in mental processes through studies of how our minds process and retain information. To encompass psychology's concern both with observable behavior and with inner thoughts and feelings, psychology has become *the science of behavior and mental processes*.

Let's unpack this definition. *Behavior* is anything an organism *does*—any action we can observe and record. Yelling, smiling, blinking, sweating, talking, and questionnaire-marking are all observable behaviors. *Mental processes* are the internal subjective experiences we infer from behavior—sensations, perceptions, dreams, thoughts, beliefs, and feelings.

For many psychologists, the key word in psychology's definition is *science*. Psychology, as I will emphasize in Chapter 1 and throughout this book, is less a set of findings than a way of asking and answering questions. As a science, psychology aims to sift opinions and evaluate ideas with careful observation and rigorous analysis. In its quest to describe and explain nature (human nature included), psychological science welcomes hunches and plausible-sounding theories. And it puts them to the test. If a theory works—if the data support its predictions—so much the better for it. If the predictions fail, the theory gets rejected or revised.

My aim in this text, then, is not merely to report results but to show you how we play the game. How do research psychologists sift contesting opinions and ideas? And how might all of us, whether scientists or simply curious people, think

Throughout this book, important concepts are underlined. As you study, you can find these terms with their definitions in a nearby margin and also at the end of the book in the Glossary section.

smarter when describing and explaining the events of our lives?

Of course, psychology also has content: Its scientific sifting of ideas has produced a smorgasbord of concepts and findings, from which we can only sample the fare. Once aware of psychology's well-researched ideas—about how body and mind connect, how a child's mind grows, how we construct our perceptions, how we remember (and misremember) our experiences, how people across the world differ (and are alike)—your mind may never again be quite the same.

> *"Once expanded to the dimensions of a larger idea, [the mind] never returns to its original size."*
>
> JURIST OLIVER WENDELL HOLMES, 1841–1935

Psychology's Perspectives

Although debates arise among psychologists working from differing perspectives, each addresses important questions.

We can simultaneously view any psychological event from multiple perspectives (Table 1). Let's consider anger, for example.

- Someone working from a *neuroscience perspective* might study the brain circuits that trigger the physical state of being "red in the face" and "hot under the collar."

- Someone working from an *evolutionary* perspective might analyze how anger has facilitated the survival of one's genes.

- Someone working from a *behavior genetics* perspective would study how heredity and experience influence our individual differences in temperament.

- Someone working from a *behavioral perspective* might study the facial expressions and body gestures that accompany anger, or might attempt to determine which external stimuli result in angry responses or aggressive acts.

- Someone working from a *cognitive perspective* might study how our interpretation of a situation affects our anger and how our anger affects our thinking.

- Someone working from a *social-cultural perspective* might explore which situations produce the most anger, and how expressions of anger vary across cultural contexts.

Psychology...is less a set of findings
than a way of asking and answering questions.

Psychology's Current Perspectives

Table 1

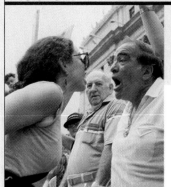

Perspective	Focus	Sample Questions
Neuroscience	How the body and brain create emotions, memories, and sensory experiences	How are messages transmitted within the body? How is blood chemistry linked with moods and motives?
Evolutionary	How natural selection favors traits that promote the perpetuation of one's genes	How does evolution influence behavior tendencies?
Behavior genetics	How much do our genes, and our environment, influence our individual differences	To what extent are psychological traits such as intelligence, personality, sexual orientation, and depression attributable to our genes? To our environment?
Behavioral	How we learn observable responses	How do we learn to fear particular objects or situations? What is the most effective way to alter our behavior, say, to lose weight or stop smoking?
Cognitive	How we process, store, and retrieve information	How do we use information in remembering? Reasoning? Solving problems?
Social-cultural	How behavior and thinking vary across situations and cultures	How are we—as Africans, Asians, Australians, or North Americans—alike as members of one human family? As products of different environmental contexts, how do we differ?

Such perspectives needn't contradict one another. Rather, they are complementary outlooks on the same biological state. It's like explaining why grizzly bears hibernate. Is it because their inner physiology drives them to do so? Because hibernation enhanced their ancestors' survival and reproduction? Because cold environments hinder food gathering during winter? Such perspectives are complementary, because "everything is related to everything else" (Brewer, 1996).

This important point—that different perspectives on the big issues can complement one another—is also true of the different academic disciplines. Each provides a particular perspective on nature and our place in it. The basic sciences investigate nature's building blocks, seeking principles based on objective observation. The humanities (including literature and philosophy) address questions of life's meaning and value, using more subjective methods. Psychology lies near the middle of this continuum; it uses scientific methods to explore our thoughts and actions.

Each perspective has its questions and its limits. Differing perspectives are like different two-dimensional views of a three-dimensional object (see Figure 2). Each two-dimensional perspective is helpful, but none by itself reveals the whole picture.

So bear in mind psychology's limits. Don't expect it to answer the ultimate questions posed by Russian novelist Leo Tolstoy (1904): "Why should I live? Why should I do anything? Is there in life any purpose which the inevitable death that awaits me does not undo and destroy?" Instead, expect that psychology will help you understand why people think, feel, and act as they do. Then you should find the study of psychology both fascinating and useful.

Figure 2

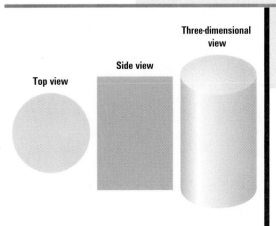

Top view

Side view

Three-dimensional view

Complementary Perspectives
What is this object? One person, looking down from the top, sees a disk. Another, looking at it from the side, sees a rectangle. Their differing perspectives seem contradictory. In fact, they are complementary, for we can assemble these images into a three-dimensional view of the object, a cylinder. The views offered by psychology's different perspectives are often like this: A lot depends on your point of view.

nature-nurture issue
the longstanding controversy over the relative contributions that genes and experience make to the development of psychological traits and behaviors.

Psychology's Big Issues

Several issues cut across psychology, the most persistent of which concerns the impact of biological nature and experienced nurture.

During its short history (which we will explore in more detail in chapters to come), psychology has wrestled with some issues that will reappear throughout this book. One such issue concerns *stability versus change*. Do our individual traits persist as we age? Do we become older versions of our same old selves? Does a reactive infant become a volatile adult? Or do people change? Can shy preschoolers become teenage class clowns? Can troubled teens become mature executives? Do our personalities change in different situations?

Another issue concerns human *rationality versus irrationality*. How deserving are we of our name *homo sapiens*—wise humans? We will see that in some ways—recognizing patterns, handling language, processing abstract ideas—we outstrip the smartest computers. The simple act of perceiving this book involves disassembling visual stimuli into millions of nerve impulses, distributing them for processing in different brain regions, and then, in an imperceptible instant, reassembling the information into a colorful image. As human observers we all have an urge to explain behavior, to attribute it to some cause. Indeed, using certain rules of thumb, we make snap judgments with amazing efficiency and sufficient rationality. "How noble in reason!" declared Shakespeare's Hamlet.

But we are prone to err. We sometimes shoehorn reality into our preconceptions. We deceive ourselves about the accuracy of our memories. We overestimate our judgments. We often are swayed more by compelling anecdotes than by statistical reality. We "see" causes and associations that don't exist. We treat others in ways that lead them to confirm our mistaken ideas about them. These lim-

its to human rationality—also spelled out in the pages to come—caused philosopher Bertrand Russell to lament that "most people would sooner die than think; in fact, they do so."

The biggest and most persistent issue, however, concerns the relative contributions of biology and experience. This nature-nurture debate is long-standing. The ancient Greek philosopher Plato assumed that character and intelligence are largely inherited and that certain ideas are inborn. Aristotle replied that there is nothing in the mind that does not first come in from the external world through the senses. In the 1600s, philosophers rekindled the debate. John Locke believed that the mind is blank at birth and that most knowledge comes in through the senses. René Descartes believed that some ideas are innate.

The nature-nurture debate weaves a thread from the distant past to our time. Today's psychologists have continued the debate by asking these and other questions:

- Are intelligence, personality, obesity, and psychological disorders more influenced by heredity or by environment?
- Is children's grammar innate or shaped by experience?
- Are eating and sexual behavior more "pushed" by inner biology or "pulled" by external incentives?
- Is depression a brain disorder or a thought disorder?
- How are humans alike (thanks to their common biology) and different (thanks to their differing cultures)?
- Are gender differences biologically predisposed or socially constructed?

Over and over again we will see the nature-nurture tension dissolve: Nurture works on what nature endows. Unlike reptiles, our species is biologically endowed with an enormous capacity to learn and adapt. Moreover, every psychological event (every thought, every emotion) is simultaneously a biological event. Thus depression can be *both* a thought disorder and a brain disorder.

Like peas in a pod Because identical twins have the same genes, they are ideal participants in studies designed to shed light on hereditary and environmental influences on temperament, intelligence, and other traits. Studies of identical and fraternal twins provide a rich array of findings—described in later chapters—that underscore the importance of both nature and nurture.

Psychology's Subfields

Psychology is a collection of diverse subfields. Some psychologists do basic research, some do applied research, and some provide professional services.

Picturing a chemist at work, you probably envision a white-coated scientist surrounded by glassware and high-tech equipment. Picture a psychologist at work and you would be right to envision

- a white-coated scientist probing a rat's brain.

- an intelligence researcher measuring how quickly an infant becomes bored with (looks away from) a familiar picture.

- an executive proposing a new "healthy life-styles" employee-training program.

- someone at a computer keyboard, analyzing data on whether adopted teens have temperaments more like their adoptive or biological parents.

- a traveler en route to collecting data on human values and behaviors in different cultures.

- a therapist listening carefully to a client's depressed thoughts.

The cluster of subfields that we call psychology has less unity than most other sciences. But there is a payoff: Psychology is a meeting ground for different disciplines, and thus a perfect home for those with wide-ranging interests. In their diverse activities, from biological experimentation to cultural comparisons, psychologists share a common quest: describing and explaining behavior and the mental processes that underlie it.

Some psychologists conduct <u>basic research</u> that builds psychology's knowledge base. In the pages to follow we will meet a wide variety of such researchers: *biological psychologists* exploring the links between brain and mind; *developmental psychologists* studying our changing abilities from womb to tomb; *personality psychologists* investigating our inner traits.

Other psychologists conduct <u>applied research</u> that tackles practical problems. For example, *industrial/organizational psychologists* study and advise on behavior in the workplace. They use psychology's concepts and methods to help organizations and companies select and train their employees, boost morale and productivity, and design products and implement systems and assess people's responses to them.

Although most psychology texts focus on the methods and results of psychological science, psychology is also a helping profession devoted to such practical issues as how to have a happy marriage,

"I'm a social scientist, Michael. That means I can't explain electricity or anything like that, but if you ever want to know about people I'm your man."

Drawing by Handelsman; ©1986 The New Yorker Magazine, Inc.

how to overcome anxiety or depression, and how to raise thriving children. <u>Clinical psychologists</u> study, assess, and treat troubled people. After graduate school training, they administer and interpret tests, provide psychotherapy, manage mental health programs, and conduct research. By contrast, <u>psychiatrists</u>, who also often provide psychotherapy, are medical doctors licensed to prescribe drugs and otherwise treat physical causes of psychological disorders. In both of these mental health professions, some practitioners are influenced by Sigmund Freud's *psychoanalytic perspective*, which saw problems arising from unconscious desires, repressed traumas, or unresolved childhood conflicts.

---

basic research
pure science that aims to increase the scientific knowledge base.

applied research
scientific study that aims to solve practical problems.

clinical psychology
a branch of psychology that studies, assesses, and treats people with psychological disorders.

psychiatry
a branch of medicine dealing with psychological disorders; practiced by physicians who sometimes provide medical (for example, drug) treatments as well as psychological therapy.

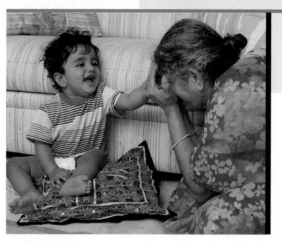

I see you! A biological psychologist might view this child's delighted response as evidence for brain maturation. A cognitive psychologist might see it as a demonstration of the baby's growing knowledge of his surroundings. For a cross-cultural psychologist, the role of grandparents in different societies might be the issue of interest. As you will see throughout this book, these and other perspectives offer complementary views of behavior.

Psychology: A science and a profession In their laboratories and consulting rooms, psychologists study and treat a wide range of human conditions. Here you see a psychologist testing a child, a laboratory experiment designed to test social judgment, and a face-to-face encounter typical of psychotherapy.

Information sources are cited in parentheses, with name and date, then provided fully in the References section at the book's end.

With perspectives ranging from the biological to the social, and with settings from the clinic to the laboratory, psychology has become a meeting place for many disciplines. More and more, psychology connects with fields ranging from mathematics and biology to sociology and philosophy. And more and more, psychology's methods and findings aid other disciplines. Psychologists teach in medical schools, law schools, and theological seminaries, and they work in hospitals, factories, and corporate offices. They engage in interdisciplinary studies, such as psychohistory (the psychological analysis of historical characters), psycholinguistics (the study of language and thinking), and sports psychology (the application of psychology to athletic performance and fan behavior).

Today, psychology's researchers and students, like its historic pioneers, are citizens of many lands. In the last few decades, psychology has flourished more in North America, where there are now about 200,000 psychologists, than in such countries as China (2000 psychologists), Nicaragua (500 psychologists), or Nigeria (fewer than 100 psychologists) (Akin-Ogundeji, 1991; Antaki, 1989; DeAngelis, 1988; Vetter, 1989). Nevertheless, the field is thriving, from Australia to Western Europe to the developing nations. Worldwide, the number of psychologists—now well over 500,000—has doubled since 1980 (Rosenzweig, 1992). Sixty-three nations, from Argentina to Zimbabwe, participate in the International Union of Scientific Psychology (Pawlik & d'Ydewalle, 1996).

Thanks to the tripling of psychologists in the work force and to women's increased professionalism, psychology now includes increasing numbers of women. In Britain, 51 percent of recent doctorates have gone to women, as have 61 percent in the United States (Cantor, 1995; Colley, 1995; NRC, 1995). In both countries, women earn more than 7 in 10 undergraduate psychology degrees. In Canada, 69 percent of students receiving professional training in psychology are women, as are 70 percent in The Netherlands, 73 percent in Denmark, and 89 percent in Spain (Adair & others, 1996; Foltved, 1996; Sanchez & others, 1996; van Drunen, 1996). What a change from the turn of the century, when Harvard University denied Mary Whiton Calkins the Ph.D. she had earned, because she was a woman. (Calkins refused Harvard's offer of a doctorate from its undergraduate sister school for women, and she went on to become the American Psychological Association's first woman elected president.)

Psychology's influence also penetrates into modern culture. Knowledge transforms. Learning to read, to understand the solar system, and to comprehend the germ theory of disease alters the way people think and act. Learning psychology's findings also changes people: They less often judge psychological disorders as a moral failing, treatable by punishment and ostracism. They less often regard and treat women as men's mental inferiors. They less often view and rear children as ignorant, willful beasts in need of taming. "In each case," notes Morton Hunt (1990, p. 206), "knowledge has modified attitudes, and, through them, behavior."

Studying Psychology

Although psychology has much to offer, mastering it requires active study. A preview-read-think-review study method, supplemented by other effective study principles, should boost your learning and performance.

The investment you are making in studying psychology should enrich your life and enlarge your vision. Although many of life's significant questions are beyond psychology, some very important ones are illuminated by even a first psychology course. Through painstaking research, psychologists have gained insights into brain and mind, depression and joy, dreams and memories. Even the unanswered questions can enrich us, by renewing our sense of mystery about "things too wonderful" for us yet to understand. What is more, your study of psychology can help teach you *how to ask and answer important questions*—how to think critically as you evaluate competing ideas and claims.

Having your life enriched and your vision enlarged (and getting a decent grade, too) requires effective study. As you will see in Chapter 9, to master any subject you must *actively process* it. Your mind is not like your stomach, something to be filled passively; it is more like a muscle, which grows stronger with exercise. Countless experiments reveal that people learn and remember material best when they put it in their own words, rehearse it, and then review and rehearse it again.

A simple study method incorporates these principles. You can remember it as PRTR: *P*review, *R*ead, *T*hink critically, and *R*eview.

First, *preview* what you're about to read. Note its organization (as hinted in the preview paragraph that begins most main sections). This provides a framework on which you can hang the information to come. We tend to remember organized information and to forget disorganized facts.

Second, *read* the section you have previewed. Usually a single main chapter section will be as much as you can absorb without tiring. Treat each main chapter section as if it were a whole chapter.

Third, *think actively and critically*. Ask questions. Make notes. Reflect on implications: How does what you've read support or challenge your assumptions? How convincing is the evidence? How does it relate to your own life?

Fourth, *review*. To drive a section's organization more deeply into your memory, rescan the section and the marginal definitions of key terms, or read its "Review" paragraphs. Glance over your notes or highlighting. Then stop and let it all sink in.

Preview, read, think, review. I have organized the chapters to facilitate your using the PRTR study method. Each chapter begins with an outline that helps you preview what is upcoming, and each main section begins with a two- or three-sentence preview. I have divided chapters into three to five main sections of readable length. To assist your reviewing, each main section ends with a summary (as if it were a little chapter). Then the whole chapter ends with an organized reminder of key terms and the page numbers where you can find their definitions. Preview, read, think, review.

Four additional study hints may further boost your learning:

1   **Distribute your study time.** One of psychology's oldest findings is that "spaced practice" promotes better retention than "massed practice." You'll remember material better if you space your time over several study periods—perhaps one hour a day, six days a week—rather than cram it into one long study blitz. Spacing your study sessions requires a disciplined approach to managing your time. (Richard O. Straub explains time management in *Discovering Psychology*, the study guide that accompanies this text.) For example, rather than trying to read a whole chapter in a single sitting, read just one of the chapter's main sections and then turn to something else.

2   **In class, listen actively.** As psychologist William James urged nearly 100 years ago, *"No reception without reaction, no impression without . . . expression."* Listen for the main idea and sub-ideas in lectures. *Write them down.* Ask questions during and after class. In class, as in your private study, process the information actively and you will understand and retain it better.

3   **Overlearn.** Psychology tells us that "overlearning improves retention." The more often students read a chapter and the fewer classes they miss, the better their exam scores are (Woehr & Cavell, 1993). Students frequently stop short of overlearning and overestimate how much they know. Really *learning* something requires more than momentarily understanding it. You may understand a chapter as you read it, but if you devote extra study time to rereading, to testing yourself, and to reviewing what you think you know, you will actually *learn* the material and retain your new knowledge further into the future.

4   **Be a smart test-taker.** If a test contains both multiple-choice questions and an essay question, turn first to the essay. Read the question carefully, noting exactly what the instructor is asking. On the back of a page, pencil in a list of points you'd like to make, and then organize them. Before writing, put the essay aside and work through the multiple-choice questions. (As you do so, you may continue to mull over the essay question. Sometimes the objective questions will bring pertinent thoughts to mind.) Then reread the essay question, rethink your answer, and start writing. When you finish, proofread your work to eliminate spelling and grammatical errors that make you look less competent than you are.

When reading multiple-choice questions, don't confuse yourself by trying to imagine how each choice might be the right one. Try instead to answer the question as if it were a fill-in-the-blank. First, cover the answers, recall what you know, and complete the sentence in your mind. Then read the answers on the test and find the alternative that best matches your own answer.

As you read psychology, you will learn much more than effective study techniques. Psychology teaches us how to ask important questions—how to think critically as we evaluate competing ideas and popular claims. It deepens our appreciation for how we humans perceive, think, feel, and act. By so doing it can enrich our lives and enlarge our vision. Through this book I hope to help guide you toward that end. As educator Charles Eliot said a century ago, "Books are the quietest and most constant of friends, and the most patient of teachers."

TERMS AND CONCEPTS TO REMEMBER

psychology (p. 4)	**applied research** (p. 7)
nature-nurture issue (p. 6)	**clinical psychology** (p. 7)
basic research (p. 7)	**psychiatry** (p. 7)

chapter *1*

Thinking Critically With Psychological Science

What good fortune for those in power that people do not think.

ADOLPH HITLER
1889–1945

Although in some ways we outsmart the smartest computers, our intuition often goes awry. To err is human. Enter psychological science. With its procedures for gathering and sifting evidence, science restrains error. As we familiarize ourselves with its strategies and incorporate its underlying principles into our daily thinking, we can think smarter.

Hoping to satisfy their curiosity about people and to remedy their woes, millions of people turn to "psychology." They listen to talk shows featuring over-the-air counseling, read magazine columns on harnessing psychic powers, attend seminars on how to stop smoking through hypnosis, and browse self-help books on the meaning of dreams, the secrets of ecstatic love, the roots of personal happiness.

Others, intrigued by claims of psychological truth, wonder: Do mothers and infants bond in the first hours after birth? Should we trust memories of childhood sexual abuse "recovered" in adulthood—and prosecute the alleged predators? Are first-born children more driven to achieve? Does handwriting give clues to personality? Does psychotherapy help?

In answering such questions, how can we separate pseudopsychology from the science of behavior and mental processes? Mere opinions from examined conclusions? *How can we use psychology to understand why people think, feel, and act as they do?*

The Scientific Attitude

A scientific approach to nature and to life is under-girded by curious *skepticism* and open-minded *humility*. The critical inquiry that flows from such attitudes helps winnow sense from nonsense.

Underlying all science is a hard-headed curiosity, a passion to explore and understand without fooling or being fooled. Some questions (Is there life after death?) are beyond science. To answer them either way requires a leap of faith. With many other ideas, the proof is in the pudding. No matter how sensible or crazy-sounding an idea, the hard-headed question is, Does it work? When put to the test, can its predictions be confirmed?

This scientific approach has a long history. How to evaluate a self-proclaimed prophet? Moses had an answer: Put the prophet to the test. If the predicted event "does not take place or prove true," then so much the worse for the prophet (Deuteronomy 18:22). Magician James Randi uses Moses' approach when testing those claiming to see auras around people's bodies:

Randi: Do you see an aura around my head?

Aura-seer: Yes, indeed.

Randi: Can you still see the aura if I put this magazine in front of my face?

Aura-seer: Of course.

Randi: Then if I were to step behind a wall barely taller than I am, you could determine my location from the aura visible above my head, right?

The Amazing Randi The magician James Randi, shown here with the "Alexander the Man Who Knows" machine, is an exemplar of skepticism. He has tested and effectively debunked a variety of psychic phenomena.

Randi tells me that no aura-seer has yet agreed to take this simple test.

When subjected to such scrutiny, crazy-sounding ideas sometimes find support. During the 1700s, scientists scoffed at the notion that meteorites had extraterrestrial origins. When two Yale scientists dared to deviate from the conventional opinion, Thomas Jefferson jeered, "Gentlemen, I would rather believe that those two Yankee Professors would lie than to believe that stones fell from heaven." Sometimes scientific inquiry refutes skeptics.

More often, it relegates crazy-sounding ideas to the mountain of forgotten claims of perpetual motion machines, miracle cancer cures, and out-of-body travels into centuries past. To sift reality from fantasy, sense from nonsense, therefore requires a scientific attitude: being skeptical but not cynical, humbly open but not gullible.

As scientists, psychologists aim to approach the world of behavior with a curious *skepticism*. They persistently ask two questions: What do you mean? and How do you know? Consider some familiar claims. Can a theater owner make you hungry by flashing an imperceptibly brief message—EAT POPCORN? Do lie detectors tell the truth? Can astrologers analyze your character and predict your future based on the position of the planets at your birth? As you will see in the chapters that follow, we can test all such claims. In the arena of competing ideas, skeptical testing can reveal which ones best match the facts. "To believe with certainty," says a Polish proverb, "we must begin by doubting."

"A skeptic is one who is willing to question any truth claim, asking for clarity in definition, consistency in logic, and adequacy of evidence."

PHILOSOPHER PAUL KURTZ
THE SKEPTICAL INQUIRER,
1994

Putting a scientific attitude into practice also requires *humility* because it means that we may have to reject our own ideas. In the last analysis, what matters is not my opinion or yours, but whatever truths nature reveals in response to our questioning. If animals or people don't behave as our ideas predict, then so much the worse for our ideas. As Agatha Christie's Miss Marple explained, "It wasn't what I expected. But facts are facts, and if one is proved to be wrong, one must just be humble about it and start again." This is the humble attitude expressed in one of psychology's early mottos: "The rat is always right."

Historians of science tell us that these attitudes of curious skepticism and open-minded humility helped make modern science possible. Many of its founders were people whose religious convictions made them humble before nature and skeptical of any human authority (Hooykaas, 1972; Merton, 1938). Of course, scientists, like anyone else, can have big egos and may cling stubbornly to their preconceptions. We all view nature through the spectacles of our preconceived ideas. Still, the ideal that unifies psychologists with all scientists is the skeptical yet humble scrutiny of competing ideas.

"My deeply held belief is that if a god anything like the traditional sort exists, our curiosity and intelligence are provided by such a god. We would be unappreciative of those gifts ... if we suppressed our passion to explore the universe and ourselves."

CARL SAGAN (1979A)

This attitude, armed with scientific principles for sifting reality from illusion, prepares us to think smarter. Smart thinking, called critical thinking, examines assumptions, discerns hidden values, evaluates evidence, and assesses conclusions. Whether reading news reports or listening to conversation, critical thinkers ask questions. They wonder, How do they know that? and What axe is this person grinding? Is the conclusion based on mere anecdote and gut feelings, or on trustworthy evidence? Does the evidence justify a cause-effect conclusion? What alternative explanations are possible? Carried to an extreme, healthy skepticism can degenerate into a negative cynicism that scorns any unproven idea. But a critical attitude can also produce humility—an awareness of our own vulnerability to error and an openness to surprises and new perspectives.

Has psychology's own critical inquiry indeed been open to surprising findings? The answer, as ensuing chapters illustrate, is plainly yes. Believe it or not ...

- massive losses of brain tissue early in life may have minimal long-term effects (see page 85).

- within days, newborns can recognize their mother's odor and voice (see pages 81–82).

- on average, any two children from the same family (children reared under the same parental philosophy and in the same schools, neighborhood, and social class) have personalities nearly as different as any two children picked from the population at random (see page 113).

- prolonged stress hinders the body's disease-fighting immune system, making people more vulnerable to physical illness (see Chapter 17).

- diverse groups—men and women, old and young, rich and working class, those with disabilities and without—report roughly comparable levels of personal happiness (see page 410).

- electroconvulsive ("shock") therapy is often a very effective treatment for severe depression (see page 510).

And has critical inquiry convincingly debunked popular presumptions? The answer, as ensuing chapters also illustrate, is again yes. The available evidence *contradicts* beliefs that . . .

- as part of their passage to middle adulthood, men in their early forties undergo a traumatic midlife crisis (see page 136).

- most mothers are depressed for a time after their children grow up and leave home (see page 138).

- some people seldom dream; sleepwalkers are acting out their dreams; sleeptalkers are verbalizing their dreams (see Chapter 7).

- our past experiences are all recorded in our brains; with brain stimulation or hypnosis, one can "play the tape" and relive long-buried or repressed memories (see Chapter 9).

- most people suffer from unrealistically low self-esteem (see pages 438–439).

- opposites attract (see Chapter 18).

The Limits of Intuition and Common Sense

Two reliable phenomena—hindsight bias and judgmental overconfidence—illustrate why Madeline L'Engle was right: "The naked intellect is an extraordinarily inaccurate instrument."

Skeptical inquiry and humility before nature are well and good for science. But don't intuition and plain common sense suffice for everyday life? In sifting reality from illusion, do we need the scientific attitude that drives critical thinking?

Some doubt it. They say psychology merely documents what people already know and dresses it in jargon: "So what else is new—you get paid for using fancy methods to prove what my grandmother knew?"

Others scorn a scientific approach because of their faith in human intuition. Advocates of "intu-

critical thinking
thinking that does not blindly accept arguments and conclusions. Rather, it examines assumptions, discerns hidden values, evaluates evidence, and assesses conclusions.

hindsight bias
the tendency to believe, after learning an outcome, that one would have foreseen it. (Also known as the I-knew-it-all-along phenomenon.)

itive management" urge us to tune into our hunches. When hiring, firing, and investing, we should distrust statistical predictors and listen to our premonitions. We should follow *Star Wars'* Luke Skywalker by trusting the force within.

Actually, intuition sometimes blunders. Consider, for example, two situations in which our statistical intuition might lead us astray. (See page 16 for the answers.)

- Imagine (or ask someone to imagine) folding a sheet of paper on itself 100 times. Roughly how thick would it then be?

- Given our year with 365 days, a group needs 366 people to ensure that at least two people share the same birthday; how big should a group be to have a 50 percent chance of finding a birthday match?

Our notions of common sense similarly err. We're all after-the-fact pundits, presuming we could have foreseen what we know happened.

The limits of intuition   Personnel interviewers tend to be overconfident of their gut feelings about job applicants. Their confidence stems partly from their recalling cases where their favorable impression proved right, and their ignorance about rejected applicants who succeeded elsewhere.

Did We Know It All Along? The Hindsight Bias

Psychologists Paul Slovic and Baruch Fischhoff (1977) and Gordon Wood (1979) have shown how scientific results and historical happenings can indeed *seem* like obvious common sense. They discovered that events that don't seem obvious beforehand seem so in hindsight. A curious thing happens once people learn the outcome of an experiment or a historical episode: It suddenly seems less surprising to them than to people asked to

guess the outcome. Finding out that something has happened makes it seem inevitable. After the next stock market swing, many investment gurus will say "the market was obviously overdue for a correction." Psychologists call this 20/20 hindsight vision the hindsight bias, also known as the *I-knew-it-all-along phenomenon.*

This phenomenon is easy to demonstrate by giving half the members of a group some purported psychological finding, and the other half an opposite result. For example, if you were in the first group, you might read, "Psychologists have found that separation weakens romantic attraction. As the saying goes, 'Out of sight, out of mind.'" Could you imagine why this might be true? Most people can, and nearly all will then regard the finding as unsurprising.

But what if you had read the opposite: "Psychologists have found that separation strengthens romantic attraction. As the saying goes, 'Absence makes the heart grow fonder.'" People given this result can also easily explain it, and they overwhelmingly see it as unsurprising common sense. Obviously, when both a supposed finding and its opposite seem like common sense, there is a problem.

Consider hindsight bias in a medical context. To doctors given case information plus an autopsy report, a cause of death may seem obvious—something they easily could have foreseen, knowing the symptoms. But it is not so obvious to doctors told the same symptoms without the autopsy report (Dawson & others, 1988).

We often experience hindsight bias while looking back on history. In contrast to other people's preelection uncertainty, people questioned *after* a presidential election exude confidence that they could have told you how it would turn out (Powell, 1988). Similarly, many people who had expected O. J. Simpson's first jury to declare him "guilty" found on reflection that the announced verdict was unsurprising (Bryant & Brockway, in press). How easy it is to seem astute when drawing the bull's eye after the arrow has struck.

> "Life is lived forwards, but understood backwards."
>
> **SØREN KIERKEGAARD**
> 1813–1855

From our vantage point, it may in hindsight seem obvious that Eastern European countries would exchange communism for democracy. But it wasn't obvious to United Nations ambassador Jeanne Kirkpatrick in 1980 when she warned,

Nevertheless, Grandmother is often right. As baseball great Yogi Berra once said, "You can observe a lot by watching." (We have Berra to thank for other gems, such as "Nobody ever comes here—it's too crowded," and "If the people don't want to come out to the park, nobody's gonna stop 'em.") Because we're all behavior-watchers, it would be surprising if many of psychology's findings had *not* been foreseen.

> Common sense describes what has happened more easily than it predicts what will happen.

But some research findings *do* jolt our common sense. Sometimes Grandmother's intuition has it wrong. Informed by countless casual observations, our intuition may tell us that familiarity breeds contempt, that dreams predict the future, and that emotional reactions coincide with menstrual phase. As we will see in later chapters, the available evidence suggests that these common sense ideas are wrong, wrong, and wrong. Throughout this book we will see how research has both inspired and overturned popular ideas—about aging, about sleep and dreams, about personality. And we will also see how it has surprised us with discoveries about how the brain's chemical messengers control our moods and memories, about animal abilities, about the effects of stress on our capacity to fight disease.

Overconfidence

Our everyday thinking is limited not only by our after-the-fact common sense but also by our human tendency toward overconfidence. As Chapter 10 explains, we tend to think we know more than we do. Asked how sure we are of our answers to factual questions (is Boston north or south of Paris?), we tend to be more confident than correct.[1] Or consider these three anagrams, which Richard Goranson (1978) asked people to unscramble.

WREAT → WATER

ETRYN → ENTRY

GRABE → BARGE

Reflect for a moment: About how many seconds do you think it would have taken you to unscramble each of these?

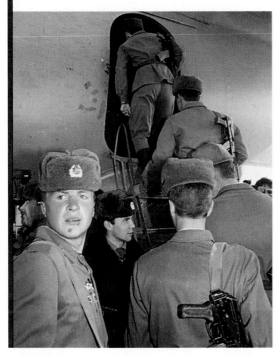

Looking backward   These Soviet troops were among the last to leave Afghanistan in 1989, after a decade-long, inconclusive military intervention. With the "wisdom" of hindsight, it is hard to see how experts in the former Soviet Union could have made such an "obvious" policy blunder. But then, after Pearl Harbor and the Vietnam War, people asked similar questions about U.S. foreign policy.

"The history of this century provides no grounds for expecting that radical totalitarian regimes will transform themselves." The point is *not* that common sense is usually wrong, but that it is after the fact. Common sense describes what has happened more easily than it predicts what will happen. As Dr. Watson said to Sherlock Holmes, "Anything seems commonplace, once explained."

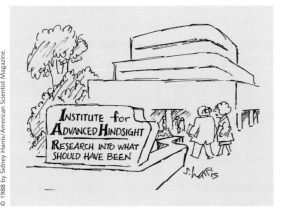

INSTITUTE for ADVANCED HINDSIGHT

RESEARCH INTO WHAT SHOULD HAVE BEEN

> "It ain't so much the things we don't know that get us into trouble. It's the things we know that just ain't so."
>
> **ARTEMUS WARD**
> 1834–1867

[1] Boston is south of Paris.

Once people know the target word, hindsight makes it seem obvious—so much so that they become overconfident. They think they would have seen the solution in only 10 seconds or so, when in reality the average subject spent 3 minutes, as you also might, given an anagram without the solution: OCHSA (see page 19 to check your answer).

Are we any better at predicting our social behavior? To find out, Robert Vallone and his associates (1990) had students predict at the beginning of the school year whether they would drop a course, vote in an upcoming election, call their parents more than twice a month, and so forth. On average, the students felt 84 percent confident in making these self-predictions. Later quizzes about their actual behavior showed their predictions were correct only 71 percent of the time. Even when they were 100 percent sure of themselves, their self-predictions erred 15 percent of the time.

Or consider the confidence of new collegians about their college future: As they begin college, only 2 percent of American students say there is a very good chance they will drop out permanently or temporarily (Sax & others, 1996). But the optimism of the other 98 percent is often unrealistic. Nearly half of the students entering a four-year college or university do not earn a degree within five years.

Overconfidence stems partly from our human tendency to seek information that *confirms* our ideas (a phenomenon that Chapter 10 will label *confirmation bias*). When assessing our ideas, we prefer to look at evidence that might confirm rather than disconfirm them. Reflecting on many experiments, P. C. Wason (1981) reports that once people have a wrong idea they often will not budge from their illogic: "Ordinary people evade facts, become inconsistent, or systematically defend themselves against the threat of new information relevant to the issue."

Our quest for positive instances of an idea biases our thinking even when we're neutral on an issue. In one study, people reflected on which pair of countries was most similar: East and West Germany, or Sri Lanka and Nepal. Scanning their memories for examples that would confirm similarity, most people answered East and West Germany. Others considered which of these same pairs of countries was most dissimilar. Again, after scanning their memories, most people answered East and West Germany (Tversky & Gati, 1978). Obviously, something was awry here: The same pair of countries couldn't be both more similar and more dissimilar. People in both groups had looked for—and found—more German examples that confirmed whatever idea they were assessing.

"We don't like their sound. Groups of guitars are on their way out."

DECCA RECORDS, IN TURNING DOWN A RECORDING CONTRACT WITH THE BEATLES

"Computers in the future may weigh no more than 1.5 tons."

POPULAR MECHANICS
1949

"They couldn't hit an elephant at this dist—."

GENERAL JOHN SEDGWICK'S LAST WORDS, UTTERED DURING A U.S. CIVIL WAR BATTLE, 1864

Answers to page 14: Given a 0.1-millimeter-thick sheet, the thickness after 100 folds would be 800 trillion times the distance between the earth and the sun (Gilovich, 1991). Only 23 people are needed to give better than even odds of any two people having the same birthday.

SUMMING UP

Scientific inquiry begins with an attitude—an eagerness to skeptically scrutinize competing ideas and an open-minded humility before nature. Putting ideas, even crazy-sounding ideas, to the test helps us winnow sense from nonsense. The curiosity that drives us to test ideas and to expose their underlying assumptions carries into everyday life as *critical thinking*.

If intuition and common sense were trustworthy, we would have less need for scientific inquiry and critical thinking. But without such thinking we readily succumb to *hindsight bias*, also called the I-knew-it-all-along phenomenon. Learning the outcome of a study (or of an everyday happening) can make it seem like obvious common sense. We also are routinely *overconfident* of our judgments, thanks partly to our bias to seek information that confirms them. Such biases lead us to overestimate our unaided intuition. Although limited by the testable questions it can address, a scientific approach helps us sift reality from illusion, taking us beyond the horizons of our intuition and common sense.

KEY TERMS AND CONCEPTS critical thinking, hindsight bias

Research Strategies: How Psychologists Ask and Answer Questions

Like all scientists, psychologists construct theories that organize observations and imply testable hypotheses. To describe, predict, and explain behavior and mental processes, psychologists use three methods: They describe behavior using case studies, surveys, and naturalistic observations. They predict behavior from correlational studies. And they seek cause-effect explanations through experiments that manipulate one or more factors under controlled conditions.

Psychologists arm their scientific attitude with the scientific method: They make observations, form theories, and then refine their theories in the light of new observations.

The Scientific Method

In everyday conversation, we tend to use "theory" to mean "mere hunch." In science, "theory" is linked with observation. A scientific <u>theory</u> *explains* through an integrated set of principles that *organizes* and *predicts* observable behaviors or events. By organizing isolated facts, a theory simplifies things. There are now so many known facts about behavior—Nobel-laureate psychologist Allen Newell (1988) estimated 3000 (including 29 that govern behavior while typing at a keyboard)—that we could never hope to remember them all. By linking observations and bridging them to deeper principles, a theory offers a useful summary. G. E. Morton (1994) likens theory construction to solving a connect-the-dots puzzle; as lines are drawn linking the isolated dots, a coherent picture emerges even before the dots are all connected.

A good theory of depression, for example, will first help us organize countless observations concerning depression into a much shorter list of principles. Say we observe over and over that depressed people describe themselves—their past, present, and future—in gloomy terms. We might therefore theorize that low self-esteem contributes to depression. So far so good: Our self-esteem principle neatly summarizes a long list of facts about depressed people.

Yet no matter how reasonable a theory may sound—and low self-esteem certainly seems a reasonable explanation of depression—we must put it to the test. A good theory doesn't just sound appealing. It must imply testable predictions, called <u>hypotheses</u>. By enabling us to test and reject or revise the theory, such predictions give direction to research. They specify in advance what results would support the theory and what results would disconfirm it. To test our self-esteem theory of depression, we might give people a test of self-esteem on which they respond to statements such as "I have good ideas." Then we could see whether, as we hypothesized, people who report poorer self-images are indeed more depressed (Figure 1.1).

In testing our theory, we should be aware that it can bias our observations. Having theorized that depression springs from low self-esteem, we may see what we expect to see. We may be tempted to perceive depressed people's comments as self-disparaging.

As one check on their biases, psychologists report their research precisely enough to allow others to <u>replicate</u> (repeat) their observations. If other researchers re-create the essence of a study with different subjects and materials and get similar results, then our confidence in the reliability of our finding grows. The first study of hindsight bias aroused psychologists' curiosity. Now, after many

theory
an explanation using an integrated set of principles that organizes and predicts observations.

hypothesis
a testable prediction, often implied by a theory.

replication
repeating the essence of a research study, usually with different subjects in different situations, to see whether the basic finding generalizes to other subjects and circumstances.

Figure **1.1**

generate or refine

Theories
Example: Low self-esteem feeds depression.

lead to

Research and Observations
Example: Administer tests of self-esteem and depresssion. See if a low score on one predicts a high score on the other.

Hypotheses
Example: People with low self-esteem are more apt to feel depressed.

lead to

The scientific method A self-correcting process for asking questions and observing nature's answer.

case study
an observation technique in which one person is studied in depth in the hope of revealing universal principles.

Good theories explain by
1. organizing and linking observed facts.
2. implying hypotheses which offer testable predictions and, sometimes, practical applications.

CORRELATION

EXPERIMENTATION

successful replications with differing people and questions, we feel quite sure of the phenomenon's power.

In the end, our theory will be useful if it (1) effectively *organizes* a range of observations and (2) implies clear *predictions* that anyone can use to check the theory or to derive practical applications. (If we boost people's self-esteem, will their depression lift?) Eventually, our research will probably lead to a revised theory (such as the one on page 474) that better organizes and predicts what we know about depression.

The alternative research strategies include descriptive, correlational, and experimental methods. We test hypotheses and refine our theories by making *observations* that *describe* behavior, detecting *correlations* that help *predict* behavior, and doing *experiments* that help *explain* behavior. To think critically about popularized psychology claims, we need to recognize these designs and to know how we can use them to sharpen our everyday thinking.

Description

The starting point of any science is description. In everyday life, all of us observe and describe people, often forming hunches about why they behave as they do. Professional psychologists are doing much the same, only more objectively and systematically.

The Case Study

Among the oldest research methods is the case study, in which psychologists study one or more individuals in great depth in the hope of revealing things true of us all. Some examples: Much of our early knowledge about the brain came from case studies of individuals who suffered a particular impairment after damage to a certain brain region.

Sigmund Freud constructed his theory of personality from a handful of case studies. Developmental psychologist Jean Piaget taught us about children's thinking after carefully observing and questioning his own three children. Studies of a few chimpanzees have revealed their capacity for understanding and language. Intensive case studies are sometimes very revealing.

> "'Well my dear,' said Miss Marple, 'human nature is very much the same everywhere, and of course, one has opportunities of observing it at closer quarters in a village.'"
>
> **AGATHA CHRISTIE**
> *THE TUESDAY CLUB MURDERS*
> 1933

Although case studies can also suggest hypotheses for further study, they sometimes have a problem: Any given individual may be atypical, making the case misleading. Our tendency to leap from unrepresentative information is a common source of mistaken judgment. Indeed, anytime a researcher mentions a finding ("Smokers die younger: 95 percent of men over 85 are nonsmokers") someone is sure to offer a contradictory case ("Well, I have an uncle who smoked two packs a day and lived to be 89"). Anecdotal cases—dramatic stories, personal experiences, even psychological case examples—have a way of overwhelming general truths. Numbers are numbing (in one study of 1300 dream reports concerning a kidnapped child, only 5 percent correctly envisioned the child as dead—see page 203). Anecdotes are alarming ("But I know a man who dreamed his sister was in a car accident, and two days later she was badly injured").

After 12-year-old Polly Klaas was kidnapped from her California bedroom and murdered, and after 2-year-old James Bulger was abducted from a Liverpool shopping mall and bludgeoned to death, children and parents in both countries became noticeably "scared" (as a 1994 *Newsweek* cover story put it)—much more scared than they were of car accidents or cancer, which cause child deaths hundreds of times more often than kidnapping does. The brutal kidnappings were impressed on people's memories, and people intuitively judge various risks based on how easily they remember examples of them. As psychologist Gordon Allport said, "Given a thimbleful of [dramatic] facts we rush to make generalizations as large as a tub."

So, individual cases can suggest fruitful ideas. But to discern the general truths that cover individual cases, we must turn to other methods of answering questions.

The case of the conversational chimpanzee In intensive case studies of chimpanzees, psychologists have explored the intriguing question of whether language is uniquely human. Here Nim Chimpsky signs "hug" as his trainer, psychologist Herbert Terrace, shows him the puppet Ernie. But is Nim really capable of using language? We'll explore that issue in Chapter 10.

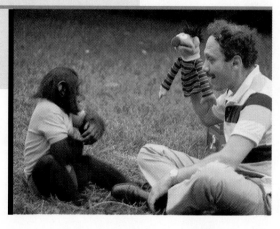

The Survey

The survey method, which is commonly used in both descriptive and correlational studies, looks at many cases in less depth. A survey asks people to report their behavior or opinions. Questions about everything from sexual practices to political opinions get put to the public. It's hard to think of a significant question that survey researchers have not asked. In the United States, for example, recent Harris and Gallup polls have revealed that 72 percent of people think there is too much TV violence, 84 percent favor equal job opportunities for homosexuals, 89 percent say they face high stress, 95 percent believe in God, and 96 percent would like to change something about their appearance.

Wording Effects

Asking questions is tricky, because even subtle changes in the order or wording of questions can have big effects. Should cigarette ads or pornography be allowed on television? People are much more likely to approve "not allowing" such things than "forbidding" or "censoring" them. In a recent national survey, only 27 percent of Americans approved of "government censorship" of media sex and violence, though 66 percent approved of "more restrictions on what is shown on television" (Lacayo, 1995). People are similarly much more approving of "aid to the needy" than of "welfare," of "affirmative action" than of "preferential treatment," and of "revenue enhancers" than of "taxes." Because wording questions is such a delicate matter, critical thinkers will reflect on how the phrasing of a question might have affected the opinions respondents expressed.

Sampling

In everyday experience we are exposed to a biased sample of people. We associate mostly with those who share our attitudes and habits. Thus, when we are guessing how many people hold a particular belief, those who think as we do come to mind most readily. This tendency to overestimate others' agreement with us is the false consensus effect (Ross & others, 1977). Vegetarians will think more people are vegetarians than will meat-eaters, and conservatives will perceive more support for conservative views than will liberals. To restrain this bias, we can gather a more representative sample of people.

Most surveys sample a target group. If you wished to survey the students at your college or university you could question them all, but probably there are too many to do so. Instead, you could survey a representative sample of the total student population—the whole group you wanted to study and describe. How could you make your sample representative of this population? By making it a random sample, one in which every person in the entire group has an equal chance of participating.

To sample the students at your institution randomly, you would *not* send them all a questionnaire. (The conscientious people who return it would not be a random sample.) Rather, you would aim for a representative sample by, say, using a table of random numbers to pick participants from a student listing and then making sure you get responses from as many as possible. Large, representative samples are better than small ones, but it is better to have a small, representative sample of 100 than a haphazard, unrepresentative sample of 500.

The random-sampling principle also works in national surveys. Imagine that you had a giant barrel containing 60 million white beans thoroughly mixed with 40 million red beans. A scoop that randomly sampled 1500 of them would contain about 60 percent white and 40 percent red beans, give or take 2 or 3 percent. Sampling voters in a national election survey is like sampling the beans; 1500 randomly sampled people, drawn from all areas of a country, provide a remarkably accurate snapshot of the opinions of a nation.

Because gathering a random sample can be a huge task, some survey takers don't make the effort. Shere Hite's book *Women and Love* reported survey findings based on only a 4.5 percent response rate from mailings to an unrepresentative sample of 100,000 women. The response was dou-

survey
a technique for ascertaining the self-reported attitudes or behaviors of people, usually by questioning a representative, random sample of them.

false consensus effect
the tendency to overestimate the extent to which others share our beliefs and behaviors.

population
all the cases in a group, from which samples may be drawn for a study.

random sample
a sample that fairly represents a population because each member has an equal chance of inclusion.

Solution to anagram on page 16: CHAOS.

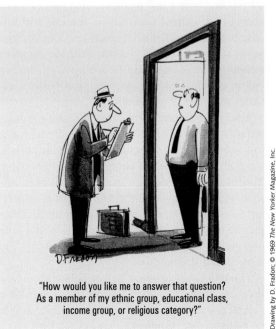

"How would you like me to answer that question? As a member of my ethnic group, educational class, income group, or religious category?"

Drawing by D. Fradon; © 1969 *The New Yorker Magazine, Inc.*

naturalistic observation
observing and recording behavior
in naturally occurring situations
without trying to manipulate
and control the situation.

THIS MODERN WORLD by Tom Tomorrow © 1991.

bly unrepresentative because not only did she have a modest, self-selected return, but the women initially contacted were members of women's organizations. Nonetheless, "It's 4500 people. That's enough for me," reported Hite. And it was apparently enough for *Time* magazine, which made a cover story of her findings—that 70 percent of women married five or more years were having affairs, and that 95 percent of women felt emotionally harassed by the men they love (Wallis, 1987). Evidently it didn't matter that on less publicized surveys, *randomly* sampled American women express much higher levels of satisfaction: Half or more report feeling "very happy" or "completely satisfied" with their marriage; only 3 percent say they are "not at all happy" (Peplau & Gordon, 1985). And only 1 in 7 reports having had an affair during their current marriage—a level of faithfulness replicated in British, French, and Danish surveys (Greeley, 1991, 1994). Without random sampling, large samples like Hite's—including call-in phone samples—merely give better estimates of a misleading number.

You can forecast the weather by taking a haphazard sample—by looking at the clouds and holding your finger in the wind—or you can look at weather maps based on comprehensive reporting. You can describe human experience using common sense, dramatic anecdotes, personal experience, and haphazard samples. But for an accurate picture of the experiences and attitudes of a whole population there's only one game in town—the representative survey.

The point to remember: Before believing survey findings, think critically: Consider the sample. You cannot compensate for an unrepresentative sample by adding more people.

We can extend this point to everyday thinking, as we generalize from samples we observe. We meet a few students and attend a few classes during a visit to a college and infer from those instances how friendly the campus is and how good the teaching is. We observe the weather during a week-long visit to Scotland and then tell our friends about the climate there.

It is often tempting to overgeneralize from such select samples, especially so when they are vivid cases. Given (a) a statistical summary of a professor's student evaluations and (b) the vivid comments of two irate students, an administrator's impression of the professor may be influenced as much by the two unhappy students as by the many favorable evaluations in the statistical summary. Driving into Chicago from the south, many people see the miles of tenement houses near the highway and think, "What an unfortunate city this is." Standing in the checkout line at the supermarket, George sees the woman in front of him pay with government-provided food stamps, and then watches with dismay as she drives away in a BMW. In each of these situations, the temptation to generalize from a few vivid but unrepresentative cases is nearly irresistible.

The point to remember: The best basis for generalizing is not from the exceptional cases one finds at the extremes, but from a representative sample of cases.

Naturalistic Observation

Watching and recording the behavior of organisms in their natural environment is known as naturalistic observation. Naturalistic observations range from watching chimpanzee societies in the jungle, to unobtrusive measures of parent-child interactions in different cultures, to recording students' self-seating patterns in the lunchrooms of multiracial schools.

Like the case study and survey methods, naturalistic observation does not *explain* behavior. It *describes* it. Nevertheless, description can be revealing. We once thought, for example, that only humans use tools. Then naturalistic observation revealed that chimpanzees sometimes insert a stick in a termite mound and withdraw it, eating the stick's load of termites. Chimps and baboons also use deception to achieve their aims. Psychologists Andrew Whiten and Richard Byrne (1988) repeatedly saw one young baboon pretending to have been attacked by another as a tactic to get its mother to drive the other baboon away from its food.

Naturalistic observation   By unobtrusively watching and recording behavior in natural environments, cross-cultural psychologists have discovered significant variations in human child-rearing patterns. Here in Zaire's rain forest, psychologist Gilda Morelli and her research assistant gather data on Efe children's involvement in community routines.

Through naturalistic observations we have also learned that Scandinavians, North Americans, and the British prefer more personal space than do Latin Americans, Arabs, and the French (Sommer, 1969). If someone invades our *personal space*— the portable buffer zone we like to maintain around our bodies—we feel uncomfortable. At a social gathering, a Mexican seeking a comfortable conversation distance may waltz around a room with a backpedaling American. (You can demonstrate this at a party by playing space invader as you talk with someone.) To the American, the Mexican may seem intrusive; to the Mexican, the American may seem cold and standoffish. reservado

DESCRIPTION
CORRELATION
EXPERIMENTATION

Correlation

Describing behavior is a first step toward predicting it. When surveys and naturalistic observations reveal that one trait or behavior accompanies another, we say the two correlate. A correlation is a statistical measure of relationship: It reveals how closely two things vary together and thus how well either one *predicts* the other. Knowing how much aptitude test scores *correlate* with school grades tells us how well the scores *predict* grades.

A *positive* correlation (between 0 and +1.00) indicates a *direct* relationship, meaning that two things increase together or decrease together. Some examples:

- According to some studies, the amount of violence viewed on television correlates about +.3 with aggressive social behavior; people's TV-viewing habits therefore modestly predict their aggressiveness (or vice versa).

- Genetically identical twins correlate about +.6 on tests of extraversion, which means that the outgoingness of either twin gives a reasonable clue to that of the other (Bouchard & others, 1990.)

- University of Michigan surveys of 71,000 representatively sampled high school seniors revealed that the more hours students worked on a job, the less they slept and exercised and the more they used cigarettes, alcohol, and other drugs (ISR, 1994).

A *negative* correlation—equally predictive—indicates an *inverse* relationship: As one thing increases, the other decreases. Our findings on self-esteem and depression illustrate a negative correlation: People who score *low* on self-esteem tend to score *high* on depression. Negative correlations could go as low as –1.00, which means that one set of scores goes down precisely as the other goes up.

Though informative, psychology's correlations usually leave most of the variation among individuals unpredicted. As we will see, there is a correlation between parents' abusiveness and their children's later abusiveness when they become parents. But this does not mean most abused children become abusive. The correlation simply indicates a statistical relationship: Although most abused children do not grow into abusers, nonabused children are even less likely to become abusive.

Likewise, early crime correlates with later crime. Boys arrested by age 14 are eighteen times more likely to become chronic offenders than boys who have not been arrested by that age, and chronic offenders are fourteen times more likely to commit violent offenses. Yet two-thirds of boys arrested only once do *not* go on to commit violent crime (Forgatch, 1995). Correlations point us toward predictions, but usually imperfect ones.

correlation
a statistical measure that indicates the extent to which two factors vary together and thus how well either factor predicts the other.

illusory correlation
the perception of a relationship where none exists.

Illusory Correlations

Correlations make visible relationships that the naked eye would miss. They also help us stop "seeing" relationships that actually don't exist. A perceived correlation that does not really exist is an illusory correlation. When we *believe* there is a relationship between two things, we are likely to *notice* and *recall* instances that confirm our belief (Troilier & Hamilton, 1986).

Illusory correlations help explain many a superstitious belief, such as the presumption that more babies are born when the moon is full or that infertile couples who adopt become more likely to conceive (Gilovich, 1991). Those who conceive after adopting capture our attention. We're less likely to notice those who adopt and never conceive, or those who conceive without adopting. In other words, illusory correlations occur when we over-rely on the top left cell of Figure 1.2, ignoring equally essential information in the other cells.

> We are, it seems, very, very good at detecting patterns, whether they're there or not, and not so good at testing our hypotheses.

Such illusory thinking helps explain why for so many years people believed (and many still do) that sugar made children hyperactive, that getting cold and wet predisposed a cold, and that weather changes trigger arthritis pain. Physician Donald Redelmeier, working with Amos Tversky (1996; Kolata, 1996), a psychologist who specialized in "debugging human intuition," followed 18 arthritis patients for 15 months. The researchers recorded both the patients' pain reports and the daily temperature, humidity, and barometric pressure.

Despite patients' beliefs, the weather was uncorrelated with their discomfort, either on the same day or up to two days earlier or later. Shown columns of random numbers labeled "arthritis pain" and "barometric pressure," even college students saw a correlation where there was none. We are, it seems, very, very good at detecting patterns, whether they're there or not, and not so good at testing our hypotheses.

Because we are sensitive to dramatic or unusual events, we are especially likely to notice and remember the occurrence of two such events in sequence—say, a premonition of an unlikely phone call followed by the call. When the call does not follow the premonition, we are less likely to note and remember the nonevent.

Likewise, instances of positive-thinking people being cured of cancer impress those who believe that positive attitudes counter disease. But to assess whether positive thinking actually affects cancer, we need three more types of information. First, we need an estimate of how many positive thinkers *were not* cured. Then we need to know how many people with cancer were and were not cured among those not using positive thinking. Without these comparison figures, positive examples of a few hope-filled people tell us nothing about the actual correlation between attitudes and disease. (As Chapter 17 explains, emotions do influence health and illness.)

The point to remember: When we notice random coincidences, we may forget that they are random and see them as correlated. Thus, we can easily deceive ourselves by seeing what is not there.

Perceiving Order in Random Events

Illusory correlations arise from our natural eagerness to make sense of our world. Given even random data, we look for order, for meaningful

Figure **1.2**

	Conceive	Do not conceive
Adopt	confirming evidence	disconfirming evidence
Do not Adopt	disconfirming evidence	confirming evidence

Illusory correlation in everyday life Many people believe infertile couples become more likely to conceive a child after adopting a baby. Their belief arises from their attention being drawn to such cases. The many couples who adopt without conceiving or conceive without adopting grab less attention. To determine whether there actually is a correlation between adoption and conception, we need data from all four cells in this figure. (From Gilovich, 1991)

Figure 1.3

Two random sequences Your chances of being dealt either of these hands is precisely the same: 1 in 2,598,960.

patterns. And we usually find it, because *random sequences often don't look random*. If someone flipped a coin six times, would one of the following sequences of heads (H) and tails (T) be most likely: HHHTTT or HTTHTH or HHHHHH?

Daniel Kahneman and Amos Tversky (1972) found that most people believe HTTHTH would be the most likely random sequence. Actually, all possible sequences are equally likely (or, you might say, equally unlikely) to occur. A bridge or poker hand of 10 through Ace, all of hearts, would seem extraordinary; actually, it would be no more or less likely than any other specific hand of cards (Figure 1.3).

Psychologists Thomas Holtgraves and James Skeel (1992) exposed people's perceptions of randomness in their bets placed in Indiana's Pick-3 Lottery. You can play, too: Pick any three-digit number from 0 to 999.

Did your number have a repeated digit (as in 525)? Probably not. Only 14 percent of 2.24 million number strings chosen in July 1991 had a repeated digit. Although repeated digits actually occur in 28 percent of the available numbers, such numbers *look* less random (and people prefer to bet random-looking series). In actual random sequences, seeming patterns and streaks (such as repeating digits) occur more often than people expect. Thus, shown random data, scientists and psychics alike can often "see" an interesting pattern (Guion, 1992). To demonstrate this phenomenon for myself (as you can do), I flipped a coin 51 times, with these results:

tosses 30 to 38 I had a "cold hand," with only one head in eight tosses. But my fortunes immediately reversed with a "hot hand"—seven heads out of the next nine tosses.

What explains these patterns? Was I exercising some sort of paranormal control over my coin? Did I snap out of my tails funk and get in a heads groove? No such explanations are needed, for these are the sort of streaks found in any random data. Comparing each toss to the next, 24 of the 50 comparisons yielded a changed result—just the sort of near 50-50 result we expect from coin tossing. Despite the seeming patterns in these data, the outcome of one toss gives no clue to the outcome of the next toss.

The failure to recognize random occurrences for what they are can predispose people to seek extraordinary explanations for ordinary events. Imagine that on one warm spring day 4000 college students gather for a coin-tossing contest. Their task is to

1. H	14. T	27. H	40. T
2. T	15. T	28. T	41. H
3. T	16. H	29. H	42. H
4. T	17. T	30. T	43. H
5. H	18. T	31. T	44. H
6. H	19. H	32. T	45. T
7. H	20. H	33. T	46. H
8. T	21. T	34. T	47. H
9. T	22. T	35. T	48. T
10. T	23. H	36. H	49. T
11. T	24. T	37. T	50. T
12. H	25. T	38. T	51. T
13. H	26. T	39. H	

Bizarre-looking, perhaps. But actually no more unlikely than any other number sequence.

Looking over the sequence, patterns jump out: Tosses 10 to 22 provided an almost perfect pattern of pairs of tails followed by pairs of heads. On flip heads. On the first toss, 2000 students do so and remain standing for a second round. As you might expect, about 1000 of these progress to a third round, 500 to a fourth, 250 to a fifth, 125 to a sixth, 62 to a seventh, 31 to an eighth, 15 to a ninth, and 8 amazing individuals, having flipped heads nine times in a row with ever-increasing displays of concentration and effort, remain standing for the tenth round.

The failure to recognize random occurrences for what they are can predispose people to seek extraordinary explanations for ordinary events.

By now, the crowd of losers is in awestruck silence as these expert coin tossers prepare to display their amazing ability yet again. The proceedings are temporarily halted so that a panel of impartial scientists can observe and document the incredible achievement of these gifted individuals. Alas, on succeeding tosses half of those remaining flip a tail, until all have sat down. "But, of course," their admirers say, "coin tossing is a highly sensitive skill. The tense, pressured atmosphere created by the scientific scrutiny has disturbed their fragile gift."

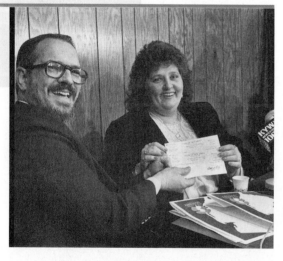

Given enough random events, something weird will happen
Evelyn Marie Adams was the beneficiary of one of those extraordinary, chance events when she won the New Jersey lottery a second time.

Some happenings, though, seem so extraordinary that we struggle to conceive an ordinary, chance-related explanation (as applies to our coin tosses). In such cases, statisticians often are less mystified. When Evelyn Marie Adams won the New Jersey lottery *twice*, newspapers reported the odds of her feat as 1 in 17 trillion. Bizarre? Actually, 1 in 17 trillion are the odds that a given person who buys a single ticket for two New Jersey lotteries will win both times. But statisticians Stephen Samuels and George McCabe (1989) report that, given the millions of people who buy U.S. state lottery tickets, it was "practically a sure thing" that someday, somewhere, someone would hit a state jackpot twice. Indeed, say fellow statisticians Persi Diaconis and Frederick Mosteller (1989), "with a large enough sample, any outrageous thing is likely to happen."

We all experience enough events that we're sure to feel astonished now and then. One day when my daughter bought two pairs of shoes, we later were astounded to discover that the two brand names were her first and last names. Checking out a photocopy counter from our library, I confused the clerk when giving him my six-digit department charge number—which just happened at that moment to be identical to the counter's one-in-a-million number on which the last user had finished. Ron Vachon was astounded while sitting among thousands of fans at a September 1990 baseball game in Boston. Oakland A's outfielder Rickey Henderson hit two foul balls right to him, on successive pitches. That something like that should have happened to Vachon (who dropped them both) was incredibly unlikely. That it sometime would happen to someone was not. An event that happens to but one in 1 billion people every day occurs about six times a day, 2000 times a year. For two provocative instances of random sequences that don't look random, see Thinking Critically About Hot and Cold Streaks in Basketball and the Stock Market.

Correlation and Causation

So far we've seen that correlations help us predict and restrain the illusions of our flawed intuition. Violence-viewing correlates with (and therefore predicts) aggression. But does it *cause* aggression? Does low self-esteem *cause* depression? If, based on the correlational evidence, you assume that they do, you have much company. Perhaps the most irresistible thinking error made both by laypeople and by professional psychologists is assuming that correlation proves causation. No matter how strong the relationship, it does not! If watching TV violence correlates positively with aggressiveness, does this mean that watching TV violence influences aggressive behavior? It may. Or does it mean that aggressive people prefer violent programs?

THINKING CRITICALLY ABOUT

Hot and Cold Streaks in Basketball and the Stock Market

Throughout this book, you will encounter Thinking Critically About . . . boxes. Each highlights careful thinking about some interesting or important issue.

Misinterpreting random sequences is common in sports and investing. In both arenas, the statistical facts collide with common sense intuition.

Basketball Players' "Hot Hands"
Every basketball player and every fan intuitively "knows" that players have hot and cold streaks. Players who have "hot hands" can't seem to miss. Those who have "cold" ones can't find the center of the hoop. When Thomas Gilovich, Robert Vallone, and Amos Tversky (1985) interviewed Philadelphia 76ers, the players estimated they were about 25 percent more likely to make a shot after they had just made one than after a miss. In one survey, 9 in 10 basketball fans agreed that a player "has a better chance of making a shot after having just *made* his last two or three shots than he does after having just *missed* his last two or three shots." Believing in shooting streaks, players will feed the ball to a teammate who has just made two or three shots in a row. Many coaches will bench the player who has just missed three in a row.

The only trouble is (believe it or not), it isn't true. When Gilovich and his collaborators studied detailed individual shooting records, they found that the 76ers—and the Boston Celtics, the New Jersey Nets, the New York Knicks, and Cornell University's men's and women's basketball players—were equally likely to score after a miss and after a basket. A typical 50 percent shooter averages 50 percent after just missing three shots, and 50 percent after just making three shots. It works with free throws, too. Celtics star Larry Bird made 88 percent of his free throws after making a free throw and 91 percent after missing. (Did this reduce Larry Bird to a mere puppet, manipulated by statistical laws? No, his skill was reflected in his 90 percent average.)

Why, then, do players and fans alike believe that players are more likely to score after scoring and to miss after missing? It's because streaks do occur, more than people expect in random sequences. In any series of 20 shots by a 50 percent shooter (or 20 flips of a coin), there is a 50-50 chance of four baskets (or heads) in a row, and it is quite possible that 1 person out of 5 will have a streak of five or six. Players and fans notice these random streaks and so form the myth that "when you're hot, you're hot" (Figure 1.4).

Mutual Funds: Does Past Performance Predict Future Returns?
The same misinterpretation of random sequences occurs when investors believe that a mutual fund that has had a string of good years will likely outperform one that has had a string of bad years. Based on that assumption, investment maga-zines report mutual funds' performance. But, as economist Burton Malkiel (1989, 1995) documents, past performances of mutual funds do *not* predict their future performance. If on January 1 of each year since 1980 we had bought the previous year's top-performing funds, our hot funds would not have beaten the next year's market average. Putting our money instead on the *Forbes* "Honor Roll" of funds each year would have gotten us an annual return since 1975 of 13.5 percent (compared with the market's overall 14.9 percent annual return). Of the top 81 Canadian funds during 1994, 40 performed above average and 41 below average during 1995 (Chalmers, 1995).

When funds have streaks of several good or bad years, we may nevertheless be fooled into thinking that past success predicts future success. "Randomness is a difficult notion for people to accept," notes Malkiel. "When events come in clusters and streaks, people look for explanations and patterns. They refuse to believe that such patterns—which frequently occur in random data—could equally well be derived from tossing a coin. So it is in the stock market as well."

The point to remember: Whether watching basketball, choosing stocks, or flipping coins, remember that our intuition often deceives us. Random sequences frequently don't look random. Expect streaks.

Figure 1.4

Who is the chance shooter?
Here are 21 consecutive shots, each scoring either a basket or a miss, by two players who each make 11. Within this sample of shots, which player's sequence looks more like what we would expect in a random sequence? (See page 26.) (Adapted from Barry Ross, *Discover*, 1987.)

Player A

Player B

Correlation need not mean causation Length of marriage correlates with hair loss in men. Does this mean that marriage causes men to lose their hair (or that balding men make better husbands)? In this case, as in many others, a third factor obviously explains the correlation: Golden anniversaries and baldness both accompany aging.

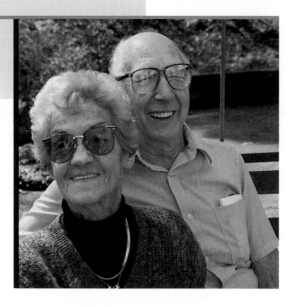

Answer to Figure 1.4 (page 25): Player B, whose outcomes may look more random, actually has fewer streaks than would be expected by chance. For these players, chance shooting, like chance coin tossing, should produce a change in outcome about 50 percent of the time. But 70 percent of the time (14 times out of 20) Player B's outcome changes on successive shots. Player A is scoring more, as we would expect from a 50 percent shooter; 10 times out of 20, Player A's next outcome is different.

And what about the negative correlation between self-esteem and depression? Perhaps low self-esteem does cause depression. But as Figure 1.5 suggests, we'd get the same coincidence of low self-esteem and depression if depression caused people to be down on themselves or if something else—a third factor such as heredity or brain chemistry—caused both low self-esteem and depression. Among men, length of marriage correlates positively with hair loss—because both are associated with a third factor, age.

The point to remember: Correlation may hint at possible cause-effect relationships. But it does not provide a causal explanation. Knowing that two events are correlated need not tell us anything about causation. *Correlation does not prove causation.* Remember this principle and you will be wiser as you see reports of scientific studies in the news and in this book.

Experimentation

Happy are they "who have been able to perceive the causes of things," remarked the Roman poet Virgil. We endlessly wonder and debate *why* people act as they do. As I write, the day's newspapers are filled with such wonderings: What caused two English schoolboys to bludgeon a 2-year-old to death? Why do people smoke? Have babies as unmarried teens? Do stupid things when drunk? Psychology can't answer these questions directly, but it has helped us to understand what influences aggression, drug use, sexual attitudes, and thinking when drinking.

In everyday life, many factors influence behavior. To isolate cause and effect—to explain what helps cause, say, depression—psychologists conduct experiments. Experiments enable a researcher to focus on the possible effects of one or more factors by (1) *manipulating the factors of interest* and (2) *holding constant ("controlling") other factors.* Imagine that some researchers wanted to study the effect of alcohol consumption on thinking ability. Before giving a thinking test, they would *manipulate* alcohol consumption (by giving some people a strong-tasting drink laced with alcohol, others the same-tasting drink without alcohol). By randomly assigning people to the two conditions, which otherwise are similar, they would hold all other factors constant. This would eliminate alternative explanations for why thinking might vary with drinking.

If behavior changes when we vary an experimental factor, such as alcohol, then the factor is having an effect. To repeat: Unlike correlational studies, which uncover naturally occurring relationships, an experiment manipulates a factor to see its effect. To illustrate, let's consider two actual experiments.

Figure **1.5**

Three possible cause-effect relationships People low in self-esteem tend to be more depressed than those high in self-esteem. One possible explanation of this negative correlation is that a bad self-image causes depressed feelings. But, as the diagram indicates, other cause-effect relationships are possible.

| Low self-esteem | → | Depression |

| Depression | → | Low self-esteem |

| Low self-esteem ← Distressing events or biological predisposition → Depression |

Do Black Sports Uniforms Affect Perceptions?

Cornell University psychologists Mark Frank and Thomas Gilovich (1988) noticed that in virtually all cultures from central Africa to Asia to Western Europe, the color black connotes evil. In movies, the bad guys wear black. It's a "black day" when we get "blackballed" or "blackmailed." Iran's Ayatollah Khomeini reportedly referred to the residence of the U.S. president as the "Black House."

Summarizing these varied observations, Frank and Gilovich proposed a simple, small-scale theory: Black garb suggests evil, cuing us to *perceive* people dressed in black as evil and cuing those who wear black to *act out* their evil image. Knowing that a useful theory must offer testable predictions, the researchers derived several hypotheses. First, they predicted that people unfamiliar with football and hockey would rate the black uniforms of National Football League and National Hockey League teams as seeming more evil than nonblack uniforms. Indeed, for both sports, people rated black uniforms as bad, mean, and aggressive.

Second, Frank and Gilovich hypothesized, and found, a positive correlation between black team uniforms and total penalties for aggressive play. In all but one of the 17 seasons between 1970 and 1986, the football teams with black uniforms were penalized a disproportionate number of yards. Likewise, in all 16 hockey seasons between 1970–1971 and 1985–1986, the teams wearing black uniforms spent more time in the penalty box. Moreover, when the Pittsburgh Penguins switched to black uniforms during the middle of the 1979–1980 season, their penalties increased from an average of 8 minutes per game to 12 minutes. So, in these two sports at least, there definitely has been a correlation between black uniforms and penalized play.

Remember, a correlation is simply a relationship between two factors—in this case, uniform color and penalties. Correlation cannot prove a cause-effect relationship. Maybe there is no cause-effect connection; maybe organizations wanting an aggressive image simply choose black outfits and hire aggressive players. (For the Hell's Angels, white outfits just won't do.) But can you imagine *possible* causes of this correlation? Frank and Gilovich suggested two: The correlation could occur because referees *perceive* acts by players in black as more violent than similar acts by players not wearing black. Or, players who wear black uniforms might *enact* the expected tough image.

In experimenting to evaluate these two possibilities, Frank and Gilovich found, first, that uniform color did indeed affect perceptions. They videotaped two staged football plays in which black- or white-clad defenders either drove the ball carrier back several yards and then threw him to the ground or hit the ball carrier violently in midair. The experimenters then manipulated the jersey-color factor. They randomly assigned people to either an experimental condition or a control condition. In the experimental condition, raters saw the same videotape in full color. With the color on, the raters (fans and professional referees) were more likely to judge the tackles as aggressive and illegal when committed by players wearing black (Figure 1.6). For comparison, the experimenters took the color out of the picture to create a control condition—a condition that contrasts with the experimental treatment. When all the players' jerseys appeared dull gray, raters judged the tackles of the white- and black-clad defenders as equally illegal. Thus, the control condition of an experiment provides a baseline against which we can compare the effect of the treatment used in the experimental condition.

Note that a key feature of experiments is random assignment. If enough individuals of different ages and opinions are randomly assigned to two groups, the random assignment will roughly equalize the two groups in age, opinion, and every other characteristic that could possibly affect the results. With random assignment, we can therefore say that if

experiment a research method in which the investigator manipulates one or more factors (independent variables) to observe their effect on some behavior or mental process (the dependent variable) while controlling other relevant factors by random assignment of subjects.

experimental condition the condition of an experiment that exposes subjects to the treatment, that is, to one version of the independent variable.

control condition the condition of an experiment that contrasts with the experimental treatment and serves as a comparison for evaluating the effect of the treatment.

random assignment assigning subjects to experimental and control conditions by chance, thus minimizing pre-existing differences between those assigned to the different groups.

Figure **1.6**

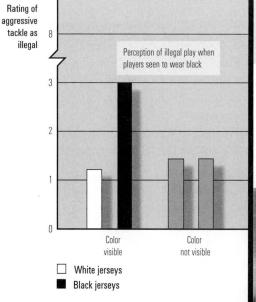

Rating of aggressive tackle as illegal

Perception of illegal play when players seen to wear black

Color visible   Color not visible

□ White jerseys
■ Black jerseys

Perceptions of violence People judged videotaped midair tackles as more likely illegal when the tackler was wearing black—but only when the color of the jersey was visible. When the same videos were shown with the original color (black or white) made to look a dull gray, there was no difference in the degree to which the tackles were judged illegal. (From Frank & Gilovich, 1988)

independent variable
the experimental factor that is manipulated; the variable whose effect is being studied.

dependent variable
the experimental factor—in psychology, the behavior or mental process—that is being measured; the variable that may change in response to manipulations of the independent variable.

operational definition
a statement of the procedures (operations) used to define research variables.

Note the distinction between random sampling in surveys and random assignment in experiments. Random sampling helps us generalize to a larger population. Random assignment controls extraneous influences, which helps us infer cause and effect.

Note the importance of random assignment. If people had chosen their jersey color, the results might merely reflect a greater natural aggressiveness among those who prefer black.

the two groups behave or feel differently at the end of the experiment, it very probably is due to the manipulated factor. Without random assignment, the groups might differ in ways that could affect the results. If the researchers asked people from one university dormitory to view the color video and asked people from another dormitory to view the no-color video, they wouldn't know whether the color or the dorm population made the difference.

In a second experiment, Cornell University students came to a study of "the psychology of competition." Frank and Gilovich randomly assigned them to wear either black or white jerseys and then invited them to choose some games. The students who donned black jerseys rather than white preferred more aggressive games. On average, wearing black affected not only perceptions but behavior as well.

The Frank and Gilovich experiments were fairly simple. They manipulated just one factor, jersey color. We call this experimental factor the independent variable because we can vary it independently of the other factors, such as the age or size of the players. Experimenters examine the effect of one or more independent variables on some measurable behavior, called the dependent variable because it can vary *depending* on what takes place during the experiment.

Both variables are given precise operational definitions. Operational definitions specify the procedures that manipulate the independent variable

or measure the dependent variable. Thus they answer the "what do you mean?" question with an exactness that allows others to repeat the study. In Frank and Gilovich's first experiment, the dependent variable was the subjects' ratings of illegal aggression. Table 1.1 shows the independent and dependent variables in their second experiment.

Let's recap: An experiment has at least two different conditions, a comparison or control condition and an experimental condition. Random assignment equates the conditions before any treatment effects. In this way, an experiment tests the effect of at least one independent variable (the experimental factor) on at least one dependent variable (the measured response).

Note, too, that in this series of studies a very simple theory, inspired by everyday observations, generated hypotheses. These predictions were confirmed by the correlation between uniforms and penalties, which in turn stimulated experiments that examined causation. Table 1.2 compares the features of psychology's research methods.

"In solving one discovery we never fail to get an imperfect knowledge of others of which we had no idea before, so that we cannot solve one doubt without creating several new ones."

JOSEPH PRIESTLY
EXPERIMENTS AND OBSERVATIONS ON DIFFERENT KINDS OF AIR
1775–1786

Table 1.1

The Design of the Second Frank and Gilovich Experiment

	Condition	Manipulation of Independent Variable	Measurement of Dependent Variable
Random assignment of subjects	Experimental	Wear black jerseys	Aggressiveness (game choice)
	Control	Not wear black jerseys (wear white)	Aggressiveness (game choice)

Comparing Research Methods

Table **1.2**

Research Method	Basic Purpose	How Conducted	What Is Manipulated
Descriptive	To observe and record behavior	Case studies, surveys, and naturalistic observations	Nothing
Correlational	To detect naturally occurring relationships; to assess how well one variable predicts another	Computing statistical association, sometimes among survey responses	Nothing
Experimental	To explore cause and effect	Manipulating one or more factors and using random assignment to eliminate preexisting differences among subjects	The independent variable(s)

How freely can we generalize Frank and Gilovich's findings? Surely we don't perceive Catholic priests and nuns as aggressive, nor does it seem that wearing black causes them to act aggressively. Frank and Gilovich wonder: Do the effects occur only in situations involving competition and aggressive confrontation? As often happens, answering one question has led to asking another. Scientific inquiry is a voyage of discovery toward a horizon, beyond which yet another horizon beckons.

These concepts—experimental and control conditions, independent and dependent variables, random assignment—are important, yet easily confused. So let's put them to work with another intriguing set of experiments.

Can Subliminal Tapes Improve Your Life?

A new generation of entrepreneurs would have you believe so. Mail-order catalogs, cable television ads, and bookstores offer tapes with imperceptibly faint messages that will "reprogram your unconscious mind for success and happiness." While underachieving students listen to soothing music, subliminal messages (below one's threshold for hearing) persuade the unconscious that "I am a good student. I love learning." Procrastinators can be similarly reprogrammed to think "I set my priorities. I get things done ahead of time!"

Is there *anything* to these wild and sometimes wacky claims? Might positive subliminal messages help us, even a little? In Chapter 5, we will see that subliminal sensation is for real. We do process much information without conscious

Scientific inquiry is a voyage of discovery toward a horizon, beyond which yet another horizon beckons.

awareness. And under certain conditions, a stimulus too weak to recognize can briefly affect us.

But does this subtle, fleeting effect extend to the powerful, enduring influence claimed by the subliminal tape merchants? Anthony Greenwald and his colleagues (1991) decided to find out. They randomly assigned eager university students to listen daily for five weeks to commercial subliminal tapes designed to improve either self-esteem or memory. Then the researchers manipulated an experimental factor. On half the tapes the researchers switched the labels. People given these tapes *thought* they were receiving affirmations of self-esteem when they actually were hearing the memory enhancement tape. Or they got the memory tape but *thought* their self-esteem was being recharged (Figure 1.7).

In this experiment, what was the independent variable? The dependent variable? (See page 30.)

Figure **1.7**

Subliminal tape content

Self-esteem   Memory

Tape label

Self-esteem

Memory

Design of the subliminal tapes experiment Students' self-esteem and memory abilities were assessed before and after listening to subliminal tapes purporting to increase either self-esteem or memory. Half the students, however, received deliberately mislabeled tapes.

placebo
[pluh-SEE-bo] an inert substance or condition that may be administered instead of a presumed active agent, such as a drug, to see if it triggers the effects believed to characterize the active agent.

double-blind procedure
an experimental procedure in which both the subject and the research staff are ignorant (blind) about whether the subject has received the treatment or a placebo. Commonly used in drug-evaluation studies.

Answer to question on page 29: In the subliminal tapes experiment, the primary independent variable was the type of subliminal message, self-esteem versus memory. (This experiment actually had a second independent variable as well: people's beliefs about which tape they received.) The primary dependent variable was improvement on the self-esteem and memory measures.

Were the tapes effective? Scores on both self-esteem and memory tests, taken before and after the five weeks, revealed no effects. Zilch. Nevertheless, those who *thought* they had heard a memory tape *believed* their memories had improved. Same for those who thought they had heard a self-esteem tape. Although the tapes had no effects, people *perceived* themselves receiving the benefits they expected. Reading this research, we can hear echoes of the testimonies that adorn the mail-order tape catalogs. Having bought something that is not supposed to be heard, and having indeed not heard it, many customers are impressed. "I really know that your tapes were invaluable in reprogramming my mind," wrote one thankful customer.

> ... whether or not a remedy is effective, enthusiastic users will probably endorse it. To find out whether it actually is effective, we must experiment.

Our natural tendencies to try new remedies when we are in an emotional down can further distort a testimony. When our emotions rebound to normal, we attribute the rebound to something we have done. If three days into a cold we start taking vitamin C tablets and find our cold symptoms lessening, the pills may seem more potent than they are (an illusion of control). If, after doing exceptionally poorly on the first exam, we listen to a "peak learning" subliminal tape and then improve on the next exam, we may be deceived into crediting the tape rather than realizing that our performance has simply returned to our average. In the 1700s, even blood-letting *seemed* effective. Sometimes people improved after the treatment; when they didn't, the practitioner inferred the disease was too far advanced to be reversed. So, whether or not a remedy is effective, enthusiastic users will probably endorse it. To find out whether it actually is effective, we must experiment.

And that is precisely how we evaluate new drug treatments and new methods of psychological therapy (see Chapter 16). In many of these studies, the subjects are *blind* (uninformed) about what treatment, if any, they are receiving. One group might receive the treatment (say, a particular subliminal message or a new drug). Others receive a pseudo-treatment—an inert placebo (a tape without the expected message, or a pill with no drug in it). Often

neither the subject nor the research assistant who collects the data will know which condition the subject is in. This double-blind procedure allows researchers to check a treatment's actual effects apart from their subjects' and their own enthusiasm for it. In one ten-year period, sixteen double-blind experiments evaluated subliminal self-help tapes. Their results were uniform: Not one found any therapeutic effect (Greenwald, 1992).

Among the general public there is surprising ignorance of the importance of controlled experiments. A 1995 science literacy survey asked people to imagine testing a new drug to combat high blood pressure (Miller & Pifer, 1996). Would it make more sense to give it to 1000 individuals and see what happened, or to give it to half of them and compare their reactions to those who got no drug? One third preferred to give the drug to all 1000 people, reasoning that the greater the number of people tested, the more reliable the finding. Among those who preferred the option with the control group, 30 percent did so to save lives: "If the drug kills people, it only kills half as many." Remember: Psychology's most powerful tool for sorting reality from wishful thinking and evaluating cause and effect is the control group.

Experiments can also help us evaluate social programs. Do early childhood education programs boost impoverished children's chances for success? What are the effects of different anti-smoking appeals? Do school sex education programs reduce teen pregnancies? To answer such questions, we can experiment: If a treatment is welcomed but resources are scarce, we could use a lottery to randomly assign some people (or regions) to experience the new program and others to a control condition. If later the two groups differ, there will be much less to argue about (Passell, 1993).

Using the principles discussed in this chapter can also help us think critically—to see more clearly what we might otherwise miss or misinterpret and to generalize more accurately from our observations. People do think smarter when they understand and use the principles of research methods and statistics (Fong & others, 1986; Lehman & others, 1988; VanderStoep & Shaughnessy, 1997). It requires training and practice, but developing the ability to think clearly and critically is part of becoming an educated person. The report of the Project on Redefining the Meaning and Purpose of Baccalaureate Degrees (1985) eloquently asserts why there are few higher priorities in a college education:

If anything is paid attention to in our colleges and universities, thinking must be it. Unfortunately, thinking can be lazy. It can be sloppy. . . . It can be fooled, misled, bullied. . . . Students possess great untrained and untapped capacities for logical thinking, critical analysis, and inquiry, but these are capacities that are not spontaneous: They grow out of wide instruction, experience, encouragement, correction, and constant use.

SUMMING UP

The Scientific Method Research stimulates the construction of *theories*, which organize the *observations* and imply predictive *hypotheses*. These hypotheses (predictions) are then tested to validate and refine the theory and to suggest practical applications.

Description Through individual case studies, surveys among random samples of a population, and naturalistic observations, psychologists observe and describe behavior and mental processes. In generalizing from observations, remember: Representative samples are a better guide than vivid examples.

Correlation The strength of relationship between one factor and another is expressed in their *correlation*. Correlations help us to see relationships that the naked eye might miss and to discount illusory correlations and random events that might otherwise look significant. Knowing how closely two things are positively or negatively correlated tells us how much one predicts the other. But correlation is only a measure of relationship; it does not reveal cause and effect.

Experimentation To discover cause-and-effect relationships, psychologists conduct *experiments*. By constructing a controlled reality, experimenters can manipulate one or more factors and discover how these independent variables affect a particular behavior, the dependent variable. In many experiments, control is achieved by randomly assigning people either to be experimental subjects, who are exposed to the treatment, or control subjects, who experience no treatment or a different version of the treatment.

KEY TERMS AND CONCEPTS theory, hypothesis, replication, case study, survey, false consensus effect, population, random sample, naturalistic observation, correlation, illusory correlation, experiment, experimental condition, control condition, random assignment, independent variable, dependent variable, operational definition, placebo, double-blind procedure.

Frequently Asked Questions About Psychology

A scientific approach can restrain our flawed intuition while satisfying our curiosity about what predicts or causes behavior. But for many thoughtful students the idea of applying science to human affairs raises concerns about how well experiments relate to life, whether they apply to all cultures and both genders, how experimenters treat human and animal subjects, and how psychologists' values influence their work and its applications.

We have seen how case studies, surveys, and naturalistic observations allow us to describe behavior. We have noted that correlational studies assess the relationship between two factors, indicating how well we can predict one thing, knowing another. We have examined the logic that underlies experiments, which use control conditions and random assignment of subjects to isolate the effects of an independent variable on a dependent variable. And we have reflected on how a scientific approach can restrain the biases of our unaided intuition.

This is reasonable preparation for understanding what lies ahead and for thinking critically about psychological matters. Yet, knowing this much, students often approach psychology with a mixture of curiosity and apprehension. So before we plunge in, let's confront some typical questions and concerns.

Can Laboratory Experiments Illuminate Everyday Life?

When you see or hear a report of psychological research, do you ever wonder whether people's behavior in the laboratory has "external validity"—whether it predicts their behavior in real life? Does detecting the blink of a faint red light in a dark room have anything useful to say about flying a plane at night? Does our tendency to remember best the first and last items in a list of unrelated words tell us anything about how we remember the names of people we meet at a party? After viewing a violent, sexually explicit film, does an angered man's increased willingness to push buttons he thinks electrically shock a woman really say anything about whether violent pornography makes

culture
the enduring behaviors, ideas, attitudes, and traditions shared by a large group of people and transmitted from one generation to the next.

men more likely to abuse women? Where on earth but in a psychological laboratory does someone squint at red lights in a dark room, watch unrelated words flash on a video screen, or push buttons that supposedly deliver electric shocks?

Before you answer, consider the intent of laboratory experiments. Far from considering artificiality a problem, the experimenter intends the laboratory environment to be a simplified reality—one in which important features of everyday life can be simulated and controlled. Just as an aeronautical wind tunnel enables an engineer to re-create atmospheric forces under controlled conditions, a laboratory experiment enables a psychologist to re-create psychological forces under controlled conditions.

> As psychologists, our concerns lie less with particular behaviors than with general principles that help explain many behaviors.

Obviously, deciding whether to push a button that delivers shock is not literally the same as slapping someone in the face. But the principle is the same. The experiment's purpose, notes Douglas Mook (1983), is not to re-create the exact behaviors of everyday life but to test theoretical principles. *It is the resulting principles—not the specific findings—that help explain everyday behaviors.* When psychologists apply laboratory research on aggression to actual violence, they are applying theoretical *principles* of aggressive behavior, principles refined through many experiments. Similarly, it is the principles of the visual system, developed from experiments in artificial settings (such as looking at red lights in the dark), that we apply to more complex behaviors such as night flying.

The point to remember: As psychologists, our concerns lie less with particular behaviors than with general principles that help explain many behaviors.

Doesn't Behavior Depend on One's Culture?

If culture shapes behavior, what can psychological studies done in one culture—often with white North Americans—really tell us about people in general? As we will see time and again, culture—shared ideas and behaviors that one generation passes on to the next—matters. Our culture influences our standards of promptness and frankness, our attitudes toward premarital sex and differing body shapes, our tendencies to be casual or formal, and much more. Being aware of such differences can restrain our assuming that others will—or should—think and act as we do. Given the growing mixing and clashing of cultures, the need for such awareness becomes urgent.

Yet our shared biological heritage unites us as members of a universal human family. The same underlying processes guide people everywhere. The variation in languages—spoken and gestured—may impede communication across cultures. Yet all languages share deep principles of grammar, and people from opposite sides of the globe can communicate with a smile or a frown. People in different cultures vary in feelings of loneliness, yet across cultures shyness and low self-esteem magnify loneliness (Jones & others, 1985). Japanese prefer their fish raw and North Americans prefer theirs cooked, but the same principles of hunger and taste influence both when they sit down to a meal. It is truly said that we are each in certain respects like all others, like some others, and like no other. Studying people of all races and cultures helps us discern our similarities and differences.

> *"All people are the same; only their habits differ."*
>
> CONFUCIUS
> 551–479 B.C.

The point to remember: Even when specific attitudes and behaviors vary across cultures, as they often do, the underlying processes are much the same. (See Close-Up: Human Diversity and Human Kinship.)

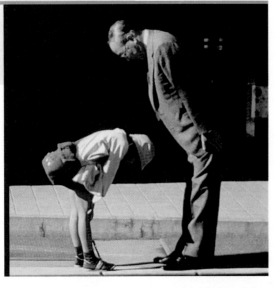

A cultured greeting Because culture shapes people's understanding of social behavior, actions that seem ordinary to us may seem quite odd to visitors from far away. Yet underlying these differences are powerful similarities. Schoolchildren everywhere greet their teachers with respect, although not necessarily with the formality of this young Japanese schoolchild.

CLOSE-UP

Human Diversity and Human Kinship

Whatever our differences, we are the leaves of one tree. We in the human family share not only a common biological heritage—cut us and we bleed—but also common behavioral tendencies. Our shared brain architecture predisposes us to sense the world, develop language, and feel hunger through identical mechanisms. Coming from opposite sides of the globe, we know how to read one another's smiles and frowns. Whether our last name is Wong, Nkomo, Gonzales, or Smith, we fear strangers beginning at about eight months of age and as adults prefer the company of individuals whose attitudes and attributes are similar to our own. Regardless of our culture or gender, we regard female features that signify youth and health—and reproductive potential—as attractive. Whether we live in the Arctic or the tropics, we prefer sweet tastes to sour, we divide the color spectrum into similar colors, and we feel drawn to behaviors that produce and protect offspring. As members of one species, we affiliate, conform, reciprocate favors, punish offenses, organize hierarchies of status, and grieve a child's death. A visitor from outer space could drop in anywhere and find humans dancing and feasting, singing and worshipping, playing sports and games, laughing and crying, living in families, and forming groups. To be human is to be more alike than different. Taken together, such universal behavioral tendencies define human nature.

These behavioral similarities arise from our biological similarity. Genetically, we are all very similar to one another. Of our genetic differences, only 6 percent is differences among races. Only 8 percent is differences among groups within a race. The rest—over 85 percent—is individual variation within local groups. The average genetic difference between two Icelandic villagers or between two Kenyans is much greater than the difference between the two groups. Thus, notes geneticist Richard Lewontin (1982), if after a worldwide catastrophe only Icelanders or Kenyans survived, the human species would suffer only "a trivial reduction" in its genetic diversity.

Among our similarities, the most important—the behavioral hallmark of our species—is our enormous capacity to learn and adapt. Ironically, this fundamental likeness enables human diversity. We all are driven to eat, but depending on our culturally learned tastes, we may have a yen for fish eyes, fried insects, or chicken legs. Go barefoot for a summer and you will develop toughened, calloused feet—a biological adaptation to friction. Meanwhile, your shoed neighbor will remain a tenderfoot. Is the difference between the two of you an effect of environment? Yes, of course. Is it also the product of a biological mechanism? Yes again. Our shared biology enables our adaptive diversity (Buss, 1991).

As citizens in a multicultural world, we need to appreciate our similarities. We also need to understand our differences. At various points throughout this book we will examine our *individual differences* in traits such as temperament, intelligence, personality, psychological disorder, and health. Depending on their experiences in particular environments, one person may become aggressive, another gentle; one may value freedom, another order and control; one may prize individuality, another the social ties that bind people together. We will also glimpse a second dimension of diversity—our *group differences* in tendencies ranging from concern about body weight, to expressing anger, to individualism. Here again, our shared biology enables our adaptive diversity: Where famine threatens, plump is beautiful; where food is abundant, slender is chic.

"Whatever I do or think as a black can never be more than a variant of what all people do and think. . . . All races are composed of human beings."

SHELBY STEELE
THE CONTENT OF OUR CHARACTER
1990

Doesn't Behavior Vary With Gender?

At your birth, people immediately wondered which of the two human types you were: male or female. Given how basic our gender is to our identity and to others' perceptions of us, do we need a different psychology for women and for men?

As you will see throughout this book, gender issues penetrate psychology. Researchers report gender differences in what we dream, in how we express and detect emotions, and in our risk of alcoholism, depression, and eating disorders. Studying such differences is not only interesting but also potentially beneficial. Many researchers believe, for example, that women converse more readily to build relationships, and that men talk more to give information and advice (Tannen, 1990). Knowing this difference can help prevent conflicts and misunderstandings on the job and in everyday relationships.

Nevertheless, it's important to remember that psychologically as well as biologically, women and men are overwhelmingly similar. Whether female or male, we learn to walk at about the same age; experience the same sensations of light and sound; feel the same pangs of hunger, desire, and fear; and exhibit similar overall intelligence and happiness. Moreover, we tend to exhibit and perceive the very behaviors our culture expects of males and females.

So, gender matters. Biology determines our sex, and then culture further bends the genders. But viewing life through the lens of gender can exaggerate the differences. The lesson of research embedded throughout this book is expressed by a children's song: "We're all the same and different."

> . . . psychologically as well as biologically, women and men are overwhelmingly similar.

Why Do Psychologists Study Animals?

Many psychologists study animals because they find them fascinating. Psychologists also study animals to learn about people, by doing experiments that are permissible only with animals. Human physiology resembles that of many other animals. That is why animal experiments have led to treatments for human diseases—insulin for diabetes, vaccines to prevent polio and rabies, transplants to replace defective organs.

Likewise, the processes by which humans see, exhibit emotion, and become obese operate in rats and monkeys. To discover more about the basics of human learning, researchers are even studying sea slugs. To understand how a combustion engine works, you would do better to study a lawn mower's engine than a Mercedes'. Humans, like Mercedes, are more complex. But it is precisely the simplicity of the sea slug's nervous system that makes it so revealing of the neural mechanisms of learning.

Is It Ethical to Experiment on Animals?

If we share important similarities with other animals, then should we not respect them? "We cannot defend our scientific work with animals on the basis of the similarities between them and ourselves and then defend it morally on the basis of differences," notes Roger Ulrich (1991). The animal protection movement protests the use of animals in psychological, biological, and medical research—some 20 million U.S. animals annually, according to the National Academy of Sciences (1991), plus 3 million British and 2 million Canadian animals (Mukerjee, 1997). Researchers remind us that these 25 million animals are less than 1 percent of the 6 billion animals killed annually in these countries as a source of food (which means the average person eats 20 animals a year). While researchers each year conduct experiments on some 200,000 dogs and cats cared for under humane regulations, humane animal shelters are forced to kill 50 times that many.

Mobilization for Animals, a network of animal protection organizations, has nevertheless been concerned. It has declared that animals used in psychological experiments are shocked "until they lose the ability to even scream in pain, . . . [are] deprived of food and water to suffer and die slowly from hunger and thirst, . . . [are] put in total isolation chambers until they are driven insane or even die from despair and terror," and are made "the victims of extreme pain and stress, inflicted upon them out of idle curiosity." Psychologists Caroline Coile and Neal Miller (1984) analyzed every animal research article published in the American Psychological Association's journals during the preceding five years. They found no study in which any of these allegations was true. Even when researchers used shock, it usually was of a mild intensity that humans can easily endure on their fingers. Only 7 percent of psychology's studies involved animals, 95 percent of which were rats, mice, rabbits, or birds. About 10 percent of these

Justifiable experimentation Is it right to use animals to advance our understanding of humans? For animal rights activists, no purpose justifies hurting, frightening, or (as here) manipulating an animal. For most psychologists and medical researchers, animal research is ethically justified so long as researchers observe strict standards and inflict no unnecessary pain.

animal studies involved electric shock (Coile & Miller, 1984; Gallup & Suarez, 1985). In British psychology departments, where animal use has dropped by two-thirds since 1977, electric shock has been used in only 4 percent of animal studies—all involving rats (Thomas & Blackman, 1991).

Animal protection organizations, such as Psychologists for the Ethical Treatment of Animals, advocate naturalistic observations of animals rather than laboratory manipulation. However, say researchers, this is not the morality of good versus evil but of compassion (for animals) versus compassion (for people). How many of us would have attacked Pasteur's experiments with rabies, which in causing some dogs to suffer led to a vaccine that spared millions of people, and dogs, from agonizing death? And would we really wish to have deprived ourselves of the animal research that led to effective methods of training retarded children; of relieving fears and depression; and of controlling obesity, alcoholism, and stress-related pain and disease?

> "I believe that to prevent, cripple, or needlessly complicate the research that can relieve animal and human suffering is profoundly inhuman, cruel, and immoral."
>
> **PSYCHOLOGIST NEAL MILLER (1983)**

Out of the heated debate on this subject, two issues emerge. The basic one is whether it is right to place the well-being of humans above that of animals. In experiments on stress and cancer, is it right that mice get tumors so that people might not? Should some monkeys be exposed to an HIV-like virus in the search for developing an AIDS vaccine? Is the human use of other animals as natural and moral as the behavior of carnivorous hawks, cats, and whales? (Animals themselves do not assign rights to other animals lower on the food chain.) Defenders of research on animals argue that anyone who has eaten a hamburger, worn leather shoes, tolerated hunting and fishing, or supported the extermination of crop-destroying or plague-carrying pests has already agreed that, yes, it is sometimes permissible to sacrifice animals for the sake of human well-being. After all, the most fundamental right is the right not to be eaten.

Scott Plous (1993) notes that our compassion for animals varies, as does our compassion for people, based on their perceived similarity to us. As Chapter 18 explains, we feel more attraction, give more help, and act less aggressively toward similar others. Likewise, we value animals according to their perceived kinship with us. Few people equate all animals, as did Ingrid Newkirk, the director of People for the Ethical Treatment of Animals: "A rat is a pig is a dog is a boy" (quoted by Baldwin, 1993). Primates and companion pets get top priority. (Western people raise or trap mink and foxes for their fur, but not dogs or cats.) Other mammals occupy the second rung on the privilege ladder, followed by birds, fish, and reptiles on the third rung, with insects at the bottom. In human-animal relations, a cockroach is not a crow is not a cow is not a collie is not a chimpanzee. In deciding which animals have rights, we must draw a cut-off line somewhere across the animal kingdom.

> "Please do not forget those of us who suffer from incurable diseases or disabilities who hope for a cure through research that requires the use of animals."
>
> **PARAPLEGIC PSYCHOLOGIST DENNIS FEENEY (1987)**

. . . our compassion for animals varies, as does our compassion for people, based on their perceived similarity to us.

> "The righteous know the
> needs of their animals."
>
> PROVERBS 12:10

If we give human life first priority, the second issue is the priority given the well-being of animals. What safeguards should protect animals? Most researchers today feel ethically obligated to enhance the well-being of captive animals and protect them from needless suffering. They also believe that humane care is good science, because pain and stress would distort animals' behavior during experiments. Thus, they welcomed national animal protection legislation updated by the United States in 1985 and by Britain in 1986, and they supported the accompanying regulations and laboratory inspections (Cherfas, 1990; Johnson, 1990).

Occasionally, though, researchers temporarily stress or deceive people. This is done only when judged essential to a justifiable end, such as understanding and controlling violent behavior or studying mood swings. Such experiments wouldn't work if the participants knew all there was to know about the experiment beforehand. Either the procedures would be ineffective or the participants, wanting to be helpful, might try to confirm the researchers' predictions.

Ethical principles developed by the American Psychological Association (1992) and the British Psychological Society (1993) urge investigators to (1) obtain the informed consent of potential participants, (2) protect them from harm and discomfort, (3) treat information about individual participants confidentially, and (4) fully explain the research afterward. Moreover, most universities today screen research proposals through an ethics committee that safeguards participants' well-being.

At its best, a psychology that is concerned for humans and sensitive to animals can serve the welfare of both.

> "The greatness of a nation
> can be judged by the way its
> animals are treated."
>
> MAHATMA GANDHI
> 1869–1948

Ironically, animals have themselves benefitted from animal research. Studies have helped improve their care and management in laboratories, zoos, and natural habitats. By revealing our behavioral kinship with animals and the remarkable intelligence of some animals, experiments have also increased our empathy with them. At its best, a psychology that is concerned for humans and sensitive to animals can serve the welfare of both.

Is It Ethical to Experiment on People?

If the image of animals or people receiving supposed electric shocks troubles you, you may find it reassuring that most psychological research involves no such stress. Blinking lights, flashing words, and pleasant social interactions are the rule.

Is Psychology Free of Value Judgments?

Psychology is definitely not value-free. Values affect what we study, how we study it, and how we interpret results. Consider: Researchers' values influence their choice of research topics—whether to study worker productivity or worker morale, sex discrimination or gender differences, conformity or independence. Values can also color "the facts." Our preconceptions can bias our observations and interpretations; sometimes we see what we want or expect to see (Figure 1.8). Even the words we use to describe a phenomenon can reflect our values. Whether we label the sex acts we do not practice as "perversions" or as "sexual variations" conveys a value judgment. The same holds true in everyday speech, as when one person's "terrorists" are another's "freedom fighters," or one person's "faith"

Figure **1.8**

What do you see? People interpret ambiguous information to fit their preconceptions. Did you see a duck or a rabbit? What influenced your first impression? (From Shepard, 1990.)

is another's "fanaticism." Our labeling someone as "firm" or "stubborn," "careful" or "picky," "discreet" or "secretive" reveals our feelings. Both in and out of psychology, labels describe and labels evaluate.

Popular applications of psychology also contain hidden values. When people defer to "professional" guidance about how to live—how to raise children, how to achieve self-fulfillment, what to do with sexual feelings, how to get ahead at work—they are accepting value-laden advice. A science of behavior and mental processes can help us reach our goals, but it cannot decide them. (See Thinking Critically About the Death Penalty.)

"It is doubtless impossible to approach any human problem with a mind free from bias."

SIMONE DE BEAUVOIR
THE SECOND SEX
1953

Is Psychology Potentially Dangerous?

If some people see psychology as mere common sense, others have an opposite concern—that it is becoming dangerously powerful. Is it an accident, someone once wondered, that astronomy is the oldest science and psychology the youngest? Exploring the external universe is one thing, but exploring our own inner universe is even more dangerous and threatening. Might psychology be used to manipulate people? Might it become the tool of someone seeking to create a totalitarian *Brave New World* or *1984?*

Knowledge is a power that, like all powers, we can use for good or evil. Nuclear power has been used to light up cities—and to demolish them. Persuasive power has been used to educate people—and to deceive them. The power of mind-altering drugs has been used to restore sanity—and to destroy it.

Although psychology has the power to deceive, it strives to enlighten. Psychologists are exploring ways to enhance learning, creativity, and compassion. And psychology speaks to many of the world's great problems—war, overpopulation, prejudice, family dysfunction, crime—all of which involve attitudes and behaviors. Psychology also speaks to humanity's deepest longings—for food and water, for love, for happiness. Psychology cannot address all the great questions of life, but it speaks to some mighty important ones.

SUMMING UP

Can Laboratory Experiments Illuminate Everyday Life? By intentionally creating a controlled, artificial environment in the lab, researchers aim to test theoretical principles. These principles help us to understand, describe, explain, and predict everyday behaviors.

Doesn't Behavior Depend on One's Culture? Although attitudes and behaviors vary across cultures, the principles that underlie them vary much less. Cross-cultural psychology explores both our cultural differences and the universal similarities that define our human kinship.

Doesn't Behavior Vary With Gender? Gender is a basic fact of life. Although gender differences tend to capture attention, it is important to remember our greater gender similarities.

Why Do Psychologists Study Animals? Some psychologists study animals out of an interest in animal behavior. Others do so because knowledge of the physiological and psychological processes of animals gives them a better understanding of the similar processes operating in humans.

Is It Ethical to Experiment on Animals? Only about 7 percent of all psychological experiments involve animals, and under ethical and legal guidelines these animals rarely experience pain. Nevertheless, animal rights groups raise an important issue: Is an animal's temporary suffering justified if it leads to the relief of human suffering?

Is It Ethical to Experiment on People? Occasionally researchers temporarily stress or deceive people in order to learn something important. Professional ethical standards provide guidelines concerning the treatment of human as well as animal participants.

Is Psychology Free of Value Judgments? Psychology is not value-free. Psychologists' own values influence their choice of research topics, their theories and observations, their labels for behavior, and their professional advice.

Is Psychology Potentially Dangerous? Knowledge is power that can be used for good or evil. Applications of psychology's principles have so far been mostly for the good, and psychology addresses some of humanity's greatest problems and deepest longings.

KEY TERMS AND CONCEPTS culture

THINKING CRITICALLY ABOUT

The Death Penalty: When Beliefs Collide With Psychological Science

An influential modern viewpoint, ironically called *postmodernism*, questions scientific objectivity. Rather than mirroring the real world, say postmodernists, scientific concepts are socially constructed fictions. "Intelligence," for instance, is a concept we created and defined. Because personal values guide theory and research, truth becomes personal and subjective. (What behaviors shall we call "intelligent"?) In questing for truth, we cannot help but follow our hunches, our biases, our cultural bent.

Psychological scientists agree that many important questions lie beyond the reach of science. And they agree that personal beliefs often shape perceptions. But they also believe that there is a real world out there, and that we advance truth by checking our hunches against it. Madame Curie did not just construct the concept of radium, she *discovered* radium. It really exists. In the social sciences, pure objectivity, like pure selflessness, may be unattainable, but should we not pursue it as an ideal? Better to humble ourselves before reliable evidence than to cling to our presumptions.

Letting go of presumptions is what the U.S. Supreme Court did, after considering pertinent social science evidence before deciding to disallow five-member juries and to end school desegregation. These decisions in turn helped inspire hundreds of studies that researchers hoped might similarly inform future judicial decisions. Recently, however, the Court has joined postmodernists in discounting social science research. In deciding whether the death penalty falls

under the Constitution's ban on "cruel and unusual punishment," the Court wrestled with whether society defines execution as cruel and unusual, whether courts inflict the penalty arbitrarily, whether they apply it with racial bias, and whether execution deters crime more than all other available punishments. The social science answers to each of these questions, note psychologists Mark Costanzo (1997) and Craig Haney and Deana Logan (1994), could hardly be clearer. On two issues—the fairness of the death penalty and its effectiveness—the Court has disregarded social science research.

Is the Death Penalty Fair? Should it be permissible to execute a person with mental retardation—someone having the mental age of a 6½-year-old, as in one case? Attitudes toward capital punishment tend to follow legal practice, and thus are now mostly favorable in the United States and opposed in most other nations (as readers in Canada, Western Europe, Australia, New Zealand, and most of South America will recognize). Nevertheless, public opinion surveys show Americans to be overwhelmingly opposed to executing people with mental retardation. Some justices have dismissed such surveys, preferring to trust state legislation and jury decisions as indicators of public attitudes. However, studies show that those eligible to serve as jurors in capital punishment cases—those who accept the death penalty—are unrepresentative of the greater population. Compared with people excluded by virtue of their qualms about capital

punishment, those chosen are less likely to be minorities and women. They are more likely to believe prosecution arguments, and they are more conviction-prone. *propenso*

The Court has accepted social science evidence that a 15-year-old is too immature emotionally and too vulnerable to peer pressure for the death penalty to be appropriate. Yet, without explanation, it ignored the same body of evidence when deciding that a 16-year-old, and even someone with the mental ability of a 6½-year-old, could be executed.

Does the Death Penalty Work— Does It Deter Crime? The evidence is impressively consistent: States with a death penalty do not have lower homicide rates. Their rates have not dropped after instituting the death penalty. And homicide has not risen when states abandoned the death penalty. People committing a crime of passion don't pause to calculate the consequences (and, if they did, would likely consider life in a prison cell an ample deterrent). But no matter, the Court persists in deciding that 16-year-olds and adults with the mental abilities of 6½-year-olds have sufficient judgment and perspective to be executable, that admitting only jurors who accept the death penalty provides a fair and representative jury of one's peers, and that "the death penalty undoubtedly is a significant deterrent."

Yes, beliefs *do* guide perceptions. And that, say psychological scientists responding to postmodernists, is why we *need* to think smarter— to restrain our hunches, our biases, and our cultural leanings by checking them against available evidence. Why not put our testable beliefs to the test? If they find support, so much the better for them. If they collide against a wall of observation, so much the worse for them. Such are the ideals of skeptical scrutiny and humility that fuel all scientific endeavor.

TERMS AND CONCEPTS TO REMEMBER

critical thinking (p. 13)

hindsight bias (p. 14)

theory (p. 17)

hypothesis (p. 17)

replication (p. 17)

case study (p. 18)

survey (p. 19)

false consensus effect (p. 19)

population (p. 19)

random sample (p. 19)

naturalistic observation (p. 20)

correlation (p. 21)

illusory correlation (p. 22)

experiment (p. 26)

experimental condition (p. 27)

control condition (p. 27)

random assignment (p. 27)

independent variable (p. 28)

dependent variable (p. 28)

operational definition (p. 28)

placebo [pluh-SEE-bo] (p. 30)

double-blind procedure (p. 30)

culture (p. 32)

CRITICAL THINKING EXERCISE
by Richard O. Straub

Now that you have read and reviewed Chapter 1, take your learning a step further by testing your critical thinking skills on this scientific problem-solving exercise. For an introduction to these exercises, turn to Appendix B before you begin working.

Philip, who teaches first grade, believes that educational television programs such as *Sesame Street* promote reading ability in young children. He announces his hunch to his students and tells their parents about his idea during a P.T.A. meeting. Some parents respond enthusiastically when he asks for volunteers to participate in a three-month experiment to test his hypothesis. Ten volunteers are assigned to the experimental group and instructed to have their children watch the one-hour *Sesame Street* program each day after school. The parents of ten other students, who are picked at random from the remaining members of the class, receive the same instructions, except that the program they watch is a one-hour non-educational cartoon. After the three-month period, Philip administers a standardized reading test to both groups. He is delighted to find that the average test score of the students in the experimental group is substantially higher than that of the students in the comparison group.

1. What is the focal behavior of the study?

2. What is Philip's hypothesis? *SESAME STREET PROMOTE READING ABILITY*

3. What is the independent variable? *SESAME STREET TV SHOW*

4. What is the dependent variable? *THE CHANGES IN READING ABILITY*

5. List three variables that are controlled in the experiment. *= PROGRAM*

6. List three variables that are not controlled and explain how *THE PREVIOUS ABILITY* they might have affected Philip's findings.

7. Was the research a valid test of Philip's hypothesis? Explain your reasoning. *NO, IS INCOMPLETE*

Check your progress on becoming a critical thinker by comparing your answers with the sample answers found in Appendix B.

chapter
2

Neuroscience, Genetics, and Behavior

No principle is more central to today's psychology, or to this book, than this: *Everything psychological is simultaneously biological.* Your every idea, every mood, every urge is a biological happening. You are a body. You think, feel, and act with your body. You relate to the world through your body. (Try laughing, crying, or loving without it.) Your body—your genes, your brain, your body chemistry, your inner organs, your appearance—is you. Without your body, you are, indeed, nobody. Although we find it convenient to talk separately of biological and psychological influences on behavior, let us not forget: To think, feel, or act without a body is as plausible as running without legs.

As we finish this century, scientific attention is riveted on the most amazing parts of our body—our brain, its component neural systems, and their genetic blueprints. The brain's ultimate challenge is to understand itself. How does the brain organize and communicate with itself? How does heredity prewire the brain and experience modify it? How do its parts process the information needed for a basketball player's jump shot? A poet's rhythm of words? A lover's memory of the first kiss?

To appreciate the excitement that has pervaded this "decade of the brain" (as declared by the U.S. Congress), consider the explosion in our understanding of how the brain enables the mind. Although the ancient philosopher Plato correctly located the mind in the spherical head—his idea of the perfect form—Aristotle believed the mind was in the heart, which pumps warmth and vitality to the body. The heart remains our Valentine symbol for love, but science has long overtaken philosophy on this issue. It's your brain, not your heart, that falls in love.

On the time scale of human existence, the last 150 years are only a few ticks of the clock. But that's how recently a scientific understanding of the brain-mind connection began to emerge. We have come far since the early 1800s, when a German physician named Franz Gall invented *phrenology*, an ill-fated theory that bumps on the skull could reveal our mental abilities and character traits. At one point, Britain had 29 phrenological societies, and phrenologists traveled North America giving skull readings (Hunt, 1993).

Despite its wrong-headedness, phrenology correctly focused attention on the idea that various brain regions have particular functions. In little more than a century, we have also realized that the body is composed of cells; that among these are nerve cells that conduct electricity and "talk" to one another by sending chemical messages across a tiny gap that separates them; that specific brain systems serve specific functions (though not the functions Gall supposed); and that from the information processed in these different brain systems, we construct our experience of sights and sounds, meanings and memories, pain and passion. You and I are privileged to live in a time when discoveries about the interplay of our biology and behavior are occurring at an exhilarating pace.

Throughout this book you will find examples of how our biology underlies our behavior and mental processes. By studying the links between biological activity and psychological events, biological psychologists are gaining a better understanding of sleep and dreams, depression and schizophrenia, hunger and sex, stress and disease. We therefore begin our study of psychology with a look at its biological roots.

Neural Communication

The body's information system is built from billions of interconnected cells called neurons. To fathom our thoughts and actions, memories and moods, we must first understand how neurons work and communicate.

Each of us is a system composed of subsystems which are in turn composed of even smaller subsystems. Cells organize to form body organs such as the stomach, heart, and brain, which form larger systems for digestion, circulation, and information processing, which are part of an even larger system—you, which in turn forms a part of your family, community, and culture. For a deep understanding of behavior, we must study how biological, psychological, and social systems work and interact. We are bio-psycho-social systems.

In this book we start small and build—up to the brain, in this chapter, and to the environmental and cultural influences that interact with our biology, in later chapters. At all levels, psychologists examine how we process information—how we get information in; how we organize, interpret, and store it; and how we use it. For scientists, it is a happy fact of nature that the information systems of humans and other animals operate similarly. So similarly, in fact, that you could not distinguish between small samples of brain tissue from a human and a monkey. This similarity allows researchers to study relatively simple animals, such as squids and sea slugs, to discover how their neural systems operate, and to study mammals' brains to understand the organization of our own. Human brains are more complex, but they follow principles that govern the rest of the animal world.

Neurons

Our body's neural information system is complexity built from simplicity. Its building blocks are neurons, or nerve cells. Each neuron consists of a cell body and its branching fibers (Figure 2.1). The fibers are of two types: The bushy dendrites receive information. The axon passes it along to other neurons or to muscles or glands. Unlike the short dendrites, axons may be short or may project through the body up to several feet. A neuron that carries orders to a leg muscle has a cell body and axon that are roughly on the scale of a basketball attached to a rope 4 miles long. A layer of fatty cells, called the myelin sheath, insulates the axons of some neurons and helps speed their impulses. The importance of the myelin sheath can be seen in the disease multiple sclerosis, in which the myelin sheath degenerates, with resulting slowdown of communication to muscles and loss of muscle control.

Depending on the type of fiber, the neural impulse travels at speeds ranging from a sluggish 2 miles per hour to, in some myelinated fibers, a breakneck 200 or more miles per hour. But even this top speed is 3 million times slower than the speed of electricity through a wire. We measure brain activity in milliseconds (thousandths of a second) and computer activity in nanoseconds (bil-

biological psychology
a branch of psychology concerned with the links between biology and behavior. (Some biological psychologists call themselves behavioral neuroscientists, neuropsychologists, behavior geneticists, physiological psychologists, or biopsychologists.)

neuron
a nerve cell; the basic building block of the nervous system.

dendrite
the bushy, branching extensions of a neuron that receive messages and conduct impulses toward the cell body.

axon
the extension of a neuron, ending in branching terminal fibers, through which messages are sent to other neurons or to muscles or glands.

myelin [MY-uh-lin] sheath
a layer of fatty cells segmentally encasing the fibers of many neurons; makes possible vastly greater transmission speed of neural impulses.

action potential
a neural impulse; a brief electrical charge that travels down an axon. The action potential is generated by the movement of positively charged atoms in and out of channels in the axon's membrane.

Figure **2.1**

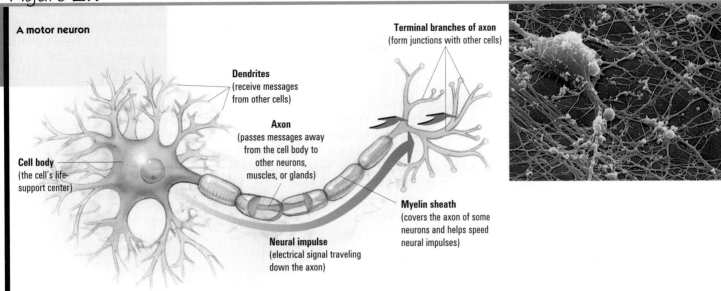

A motor neuron

Dendrites
(receive messages
from other cells)

Terminal branches of axon
(form junctions with other cells)

Axon
(passes messages away
from the cell body to
other neurons,
muscles, or glands)

Cell body
(the cell's life-
support center)

Myelin sheath
(covers the axon of some
neurons and helps speed
neural impulses)

Neural impulse
(electrical signal traveling
down the axon)

lionths of a second). That helps to explain why, unlike the nearly instantaneous reactions of a high-speed computer, it may take a quarter-second or more for you to react to a sudden event, such as a child darting in front of your car.

A neuron fires an impulse when stimulated by pressure, heat, light, or chemical messages from adjacent neurons. The impulse, called the action potential, is a brief electrical charge that travels down the axon, rather like a line of dominoes falling. Just as batteries generate electricity from chemical events, so does the neuron's electrical impulse arise from chemical events.

The chemistry-to-electricity process involves the exchange of electrically charged atoms, called *ions*. The fluid interior of a resting axon carries mostly negatively charged ions, while the fluid outside the axon membrane has mostly positively charged ions. This positive-outside/negative-inside polarization, called the *resting potential*, occurs because the cell's membrane is selectively permeable—it has gates that the positive ions cannot pass through. When a neuron fires, the first bit of the axon opens its gates, allowing the positively charged ions to rush in through a channel (Figure 2.2). This *depolarizes* that part of the axon, which causes the axon's next channel to open, and then the next, like dominoes falling. During a resting

Figure **2.2**

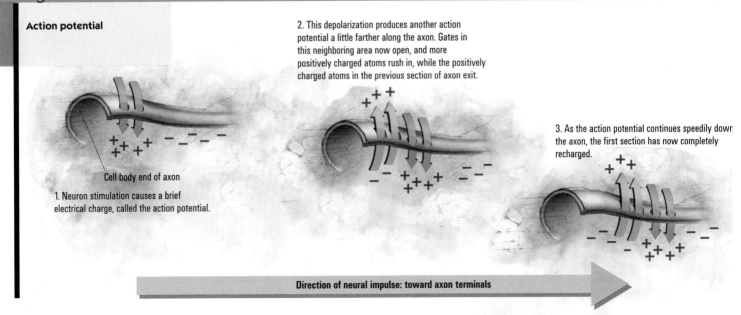

Action potential

2. This depolarization produces another action potential a little farther along the axon. Gates in this neighboring area now open, and more positively charged atoms rush in, while the positively charged atoms in the previous section of axon exit.

3. As the action potential continues speedily down the axon, the first section has now completely recharged.

Cell body end of axon

1. Neuron stimulation causes a brief electrical charge, called the action potential.

Direction of neural impulse: toward axon terminals

pause (the *refractory period*), the neuron pumps positively charged atoms back outside. Then it can fire again. The mind boggles when imagining this electrochemical process repeating 100 times a second. This is but the first of many astonishments.

The neuron, a miniature decision-making device, receives signals on its dendrites and cell body from hundreds or even thousands of other neurons. Some of these signals are *excitatory*, rather like pushing a neuron's accelerator. Other signals are *inhibitory*, rather like pushing its brake. The combined signals trigger an impulse if excitatory signals minus inhibitory signals exceed a minimum intensity, called the threshold. If excitatory inputs exceed the threshold, the neuron transmits an electrical impulse (the action potential) down its axon, which branches into junctions with hundreds or thousands of other neurons and with the body's muscles and glands.

Increasing the stimulus above the threshold, however, will not increase the impulse's intensity. (The neuron's reaction is an *all-or-none response*; like guns, neurons either fire or they don't.) Nor does the strength of the stimulus affect the impulse's speed.

How then do we detect the intensity of a stimulus? How do we distinguish a gentle touch from a firm hug? A strong stimulus cannot trigger a stronger or faster impulse in a neuron—squeezing a trigger harder won't make a bullet go faster. But a strong stimulus can trigger more neurons to fire, and to fire more often.

How Neurons Communicate

Neurons interweave so intricately that even with a microscope it is hard to see where one neuron ends and another begins. A hundred years ago many scientists believed that the branching axon of one cell fused with the dendrites of another in an uninterrupted fabric. But then British physiologist Sir Charles Sherrington (1857–1952) noticed that neural impulses were taking more time to travel a neural pathway than they should. Sherrington inferred there must be a brief interruption in the transmission.

We now know that the axon terminal of one neuron is indeed separated from the receiving neuron by a tiny gap less than a millionth of an inch wide. This junction Sherrington called the synapse, and the gap is called the *synaptic gap* or *cleft*. To the Nobel laureate, Spanish neuroanatomist Santiago Ramùn y Cajal (1832–1934), these near-unions of neurons—"protoplasmic kisses," he called them—

were another of nature's marvels. How does the nerve impulse execute the protoplasmic kiss? How does it cross the tiny synaptic gap? The answer is one of the important scientific discoveries of our age.

> "All information processing in the brain involves neurons 'talking to' each other at synapses."
>
> NEUROSCIENTIST SOLOMON H. SNYDER (1984)

When the action potential reaches the knoblike terminals at an axon's end, it triggers the release of chemical messengers, called neurotransmitters (Figure 2.3). Within 1/10,000th of a second, the neurotransmitter molecules cross the synaptic gap and bind to receptor sites on the receiving neuron—as precisely as a key fits a lock. For an instant, the neurotransmitter unlocks tiny channels at the receiving site. This allows ions to enter the receiving neuron, thereby either exciting or inhibiting its readiness to fire.

> "When it comes to the brain, if you want to see the action, follow the neurotransmitters."
>
> NEUROSCIENTIST FLOYD BLOOM (1993)

Most neurons have a resting rate of random firing that increases or decreases with input from other neurons and from chemicals that affect their sensitivity. Roughly speaking, the neuron is democratic: If it receives many more excitatory than inhibitory messages, the cell fires often. More electrical impulses flash down its axon, releasing more packets of neurotransmitters, which diffuse across their synaptic gaps to other neurons.

How Neurotransmitters Influence Us

The discovery of some 75 different neurotransmitters raises questions: Are certain neurotransmitters found only in specific places? What are their effects? Can we boost or diminish these effects through drugs or diet? Could such changes affect our moods, memories, or mental abilities?

Later chapters explain the role of neurotransmitters in depression and euphoria, hunger and thinking, addictions and therapy. For now, let's glimpse how neurotransmitters influence our motions and emotions. We now know that a particular neural

threshold
the level of stimulation required to trigger a neural impulse.

synapse [SIN-aps]
the junction between the axon tip of the sending neuron and the dendrite or cell body of the receiving neuron. The tiny gap at this junction is called the *synaptic gap* or *cleft*.

neurotransmitters
chemical messengers that traverse the synaptic gaps between neurons. When released by the sending neuron, neurotransmitters travel across the synapse and bind to receptor sites on the receiving neuron, thereby influencing whether it will generate a neural impulse.

acetylcholine [ah-seat-el-KO-leen] (ACh)
a neurotransmitter that, among its functions, triggers muscle contraction.

Figure **2.3**

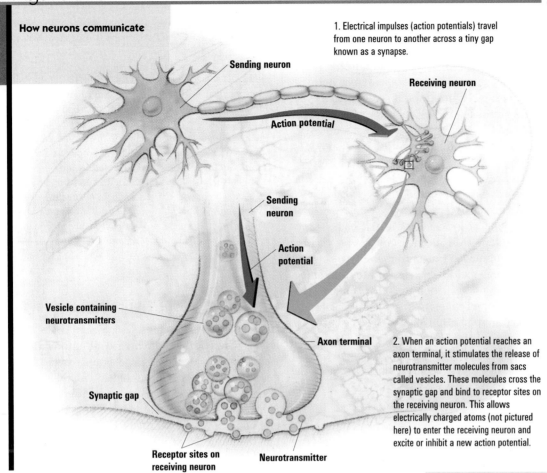

How neurons communicate

1. Electrical impulses (action potentials) travel from one neuron to another across a tiny gap known as a synapse.

Sending neuron

Action potential

Receiving neuron

Sending neuron

Action potential

Vesicle containing neurotransmitters

Axon terminal

2. When an action potential reaches an axon terminal, it stimulates the release of neurotransmitter molecules from sacs called vesicles. These molecules cross the synaptic gap and bind to receptor sites on the receiving neuron. This allows electrically charged atoms (not pictured here) to enter the receiving neuron and excite or inhibit a new action potential.

Synaptic gap

Receptor sites on receiving neuron

Neurotransmitter

pathway in the brain may use only one or two neurotransmitters, and that particular neurotransmitters may have particular effects on behavior and emotions. One of the best understood neurotransmitters, acetylcholine (ACh), is the messenger at every junction between a motor neuron and muscle. With powerful electron microscopes, neurobiologists can magnify thinly sliced specimens of tissue enough to see the sacs that store and release ACh molecules. When ACh is released to the muscle cells, the muscle contracts.

If the transmission of ACh is blocked, muscles cannot contract. Curare, a poison that certain South American Indians have put on the tips of their hunting darts, occupies and blocks ACh receptor sites, leaving the neurotransmitter unable to affect the muscles. Struck by one of these darts, an animal becomes paralyzed. Botulin, a poison that can form in improperly canned food, causes paralysis by blocking ACh release from the sending neuron. By contrast, the venom of the black widow spider causes a synaptic flood of ACh. The result? Violent muscle contractions, convulsions, and possible death.

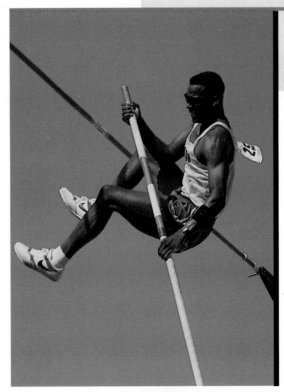

Molecules and muscles   When your body moves, a flood of acetylcholine molecules triggers the muscle action.

The Endorphins

An exciting discovery about neurotransmitters occurred when Candace Pert and Solomon Snyder (1973) attached a radioactive tracer to morphine, allowing them to see exactly where in an animal's brain it was taken up. (Morphine, an opiate drug, elevates mood and eases pain.) Pert and Snyder discovered that the morphine was taken up by receptors in areas linked with mood and pain sensations.

It was hard to imagine why the brain would contain these "opiate receptors" unless it had its own naturally occurring opiates. Why would the brain have a chemical lock, unless it also had a corresponding key? Researchers soon confirmed that the brain does indeed contain several types of neurotransmitter molecules similar to morphine. Named endorphins (short for *end*ogenous [produced within] m*orphine*), these natural opiates are released in response to pain and vigorous exercise (Farrell & others, 1982; Lagerweij & others, 1984). They may therefore help explain all sorts of good feelings, such as the "runner's high," the painkilling effects of acupuncture, and the indifference to pain in some severely injured people, such as David Livingstone reported in his 1857 *Missionary Travels*:

> I heard a shout. Starting, and looking half round, I saw the lion just in the act of springing upon me. I was upon a little height, he caught my shoulder as he sprang, and we both came to the ground below together. Growling horribly close to my ear, he shook me as a terrier does a rat. The shock produced a stupor similar to that which seems to be felt by a mouse after the first shake of the cat. It caused a sort of dreaminess in which there was no sense of pain nor feeling of terror, though [I was] quite conscious of all that was happening. . . . This peculiar state is probably produced in all animals killed by the carnivora; and if so, is a merciful provision by our benevolent Creator for lessening the pain of death.

How Drugs Alter Neurotransmission

If indeed the endorphins lessen pain and boost mood, why not flood the brain with artificial opiates, thereby intensifying the brain's own "feel-good" chemistry? One problem is that when flooded with opiate drugs such as heroin and morphine, the brain may stop producing its own natural opiates. When the drug is withdrawn, the brain may therefore be deprived of any form of opiate. For a drug addict, the result is agony that persists until the brain resumes production of its natural opiates or receives more artificial opiates. As we will see in later chapters, mood-altering drugs, from alcohol to nicotine to heroin, share a common effect: They trigger unpleasant, lingering aftereffects. For suppressing the body's own neurotransmitter production, nature charges a price.

The good news is that neurotransmitter research is enabling the creation of new therapeutic drugs, such as those used to alleviate depression and schizophrenia. *Agonists* work by mimicking a particular neurotransmitter (Figure 2.4b). An agonist is a drug molecule that is similar enough to the neurotransmitter to mimic its effects. This may, for example, produce a temporary "high" by amplifying normal sensations of arousal or pleasure (as with opiate drugs). *Antagonists* work by blocking neurotransmitters (Figure 2.4c). An antagonist is a drug molecule that is enough like the natural neurotransmitter to occupy its receptor site and block its effect but not similar enough to stimulate the receptor. Some poison and snake venoms paralyze by blocking acetylcholine receptors that produce muscle movement. Other drugs are neither agonists nor antagonists but work by hampering the neurotransmitter's natural breakdown or its reabsorption.

Figure **2.4**

Agonists and antagonists

Neurotransmitter molecule

Receiving cell membrane

receptor site on receiving neuron

(a)

This neurotransmitter molecule has a molecular structure that precisely fits the receptor site on the receiving neuron, much like a key fits a lock.

This agonist molecule is similar enough in structure to the neurotransmitter molecule that it mimics its effects on the receiving neuron. Morphine, for instance, mimics the action of endorphins by stimulating receptors in brain areas involved in mood and pain sensations.

Agonist mimics neurotransmitter

(b)

This antagonist molecule has a structure similar enough to the neurotransmitter to occupy its receptor site and block its action, but not similar enough to stimulate the receptor. An example is venom that paralyzes its victims by blocking ACh receptors involved in muscle movement.

Antagonist blocks neurotransmitter

(c)

Designing a drug can be harder than it sounds. A *blood-brain barrier* enables the brain to fence out unwanted chemicals circulating in the blood, and some chemicals don't have the right shape to slither through this barrier. Scientists know, for example, that the tremors of Parkinson's disease result from the death of nerve cells that produce a neurotransmitter called *dopamine*. Giving the patient dopamine as a drug doesn't help, though, because dopamine cannot cross the blood-brain barrier. But L-dopa, a raw material the brain can convert to dopamine, can sneak through. Given L-dopa, patients gain better muscular control.

SUMMING UP

The body's circuitry, the nervous system, consists of billions of individual cells called *neurons*. A neuron receives signals from other neurons through its branching dendrites and cell body, combines these signals in the cell body, and transmits an electrical impulse (the action potential) down its axon. When these signals reach the end of the axon, they stimulate the release of chemical messengers called *neurotransmitters*. These molecules pass on their excitatory or inhibitory messages as they traverse the synaptic gap between neurons and combine with receptor sites on neighboring neurons. Researchers are studying neurotransmitters to discern their role in behavior and emotion. Some drugs (agonists) mimic particular neurotransmitters; others (antagonists) block them.

KEY TERMS AND CONCEPTS biological psychology, neuron, dendrite, axon, myelin sheath, action potential, threshold, synapse, neurotransmitters, acetylcholine (ACh), endorphins

Neural and Hormonal Systems

To live is to take information in from the world and the body's tissues, to make decisions, and to send information and orders back to the body's tissues. Neurons are the elementary components of our nervous system, our body's speedy electrochemical information system. Hormones released by the endocrine glands form the body's slower information system.

Neurons communicating with other neurons form our body's primary information system, the nervous system (Figure 2.5). The brain and spinal cord form the central nervous system (CNS). The peripheral nervous system (PNS) links the central nervous system with the body's sense receptors, muscles, and glands. The sensory and motor axons carrying this information are bundled into the electrical cables that we know as nerves. The optic nerve, for example, bundles nearly a million axon fibers into a single cable carrying the information that each eye sends to the brain.

endorphins [en-DOR-fins] "morphine within"—natural, opiatelike neurotransmitters linked to pain control and to pleasure.

nervous system the body's speedy, electrochemical communication system, consisting of all the nerve cells of the peripheral and central nervous systems.

central nervous system (CNS) the brain and spinal cord.

peripheral nervous system (PNS) the sensory and motor neurons that connect the central nervous system (CNS) to the rest of the body.

nerves neural "cables" containing many axons. These bundled axons, which are part of the peripheral nervous system, connect the central nervous system with muscles, glands, and sense organs.

Figure **2.5**

The functional divisions of the human nervous system

sensory neurons
neurons that carry incoming in-formation from the sense recep-tors to the central nervous system.

interneurons
central nervous system neurons that internally communicate and intervene between the sensory inputs and motor outputs.

motor neurons
the neurons that carry outgoing information from the central nervous system to the muscles and glands.

skeletal nervous system
the division of the peripheral nervous system that controls the body's skeletal muscles.

Information travels in the nervous system through three types of neurons. The sensory neurons send information from the body's tissues and sensory organs inward to the brain and spinal cord, which process the information. This process-ing involves a second class of neurons, the central nervous system's own interneurons, which enable its internal communication. The central nervous system then sends instructions out to the body's tissues via the motor neurons. Our complexity, though, resides mostly in our interneuron systems. Our nervous system has a few million sensory neu-rons, a few million motor neurons, and billions and billions of interneurons.

The Peripheral Nervous System

Our peripheral nervous system has two compo-nents—skeletal and autonomic. The skeletal nervous system controls the voluntary movements of our skeletal muscles. As you reach the bottom of this page, the skeletal nervous system will report to your brain the current state of your skeletal mus-cles and carry instructions back, triggering your hand to turn the page.

Our autonomic nervous system controls the glands and the muscles of our internal organs. Like an automatic pilot, it may sometimes be con-sciously overridden. But usually it operates on its own (autonomously) to influence our internal func-tioning, including our heartbeat, digestion, and glandular activity.

The autonomic nervous system is a dual system (Figure 2.6). The sympathetic nervous system arouses us for defensive action. If something alarms or enrages you, the sympathetic system will accelerate your heartbeat, slow your digestion, raise your blood sugar, dilate your arteries, and cool you with perspiration, making you alert and ready for action. When the stress subsides, the parasympathetic nervous system produces oppo-

Figure **2.6**

The dual functions of the autonomic nervous system
The autonomic nervous system controls the more autonomous (or self-regulating) internal functions. Its sympathetic division arouses and expends energy. Its parasym-pathetic division calms and con-serves energy, allowing routine maintenance activity. For example, sympathetic stimulation acceler-ates the heartbeat, whereas para-sympathetic stimulation slows it.

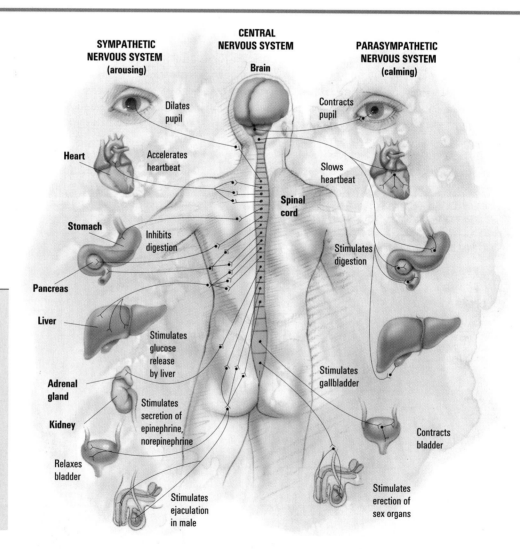

SYMPATHETIC NERVOUS SYSTEM (arousing)

CENTRAL NERVOUS SYSTEM
Brain

PARASYMPATHETIC NERVOUS SYSTEM (calming)

Dilates pupil

Contracts pupil

Heart — Accelerates heartbeat

Slows heartbeat

Spinal cord

Stomach — Inhibits digestion

Stimulates digestion

Pancreas

Liver — Stimulates glucose release by liver

Stimulates gallbladder

Adrenal gland — Stimulates secretion of epinephrine, norepinephrine

Kidney

Relaxes bladder

Stimulates ejaculation in male

Contracts bladder

Stimulates erection of sex organs

site effects. It conserves energy as it calms you by decreasing your heartbeat, lowering your blood sugar, and so forth. In everyday situations, the sympathetic and parasympathetic nervous systems work together to keep us in a steady internal state.

The Central Nervous System

From the simplicity of neurons "talking" to other neurons arises the complexity of the central nervous system that enables our humanity—our thinking, feeling, and acting. Tens of billions of neurons, each in communication with thousands of other neurons, yield an ever-changing wiring diagram that dwarfs a powerful computer.

Spinal Cord

The central nervous system's spinal cord is an information highway connecting the peripheral nervous system to the brain. Ascending neural tracts send up sensory information, and descending tracts send back motor-control information.

A look at the neural pathways governing our reflexes, our automatic responses to stimuli, illustrates the spinal cord's work. A simple spinal reflex pathway is composed of a single sensory neuron and a single motor neuron, which often communicate through an interneuron. The knee-jerk response is one example; a headless warm body could do it.

Another such pathway enables the pain reflex (Figure 2.7). When your fingers touch a hot stove, neural activity excited by the heat travels via sensory neurons to interneurons in your spinal cord. These interneurons respond by activating motor neurons to the muscles in your arm, causing you to jerk your hand away.

Because the simple pain reflex pathway runs through the spinal cord and out, you jerk your hand from a candle's flame *before* your brain receives and responds to the information that causes you to feel pain. Information travels to and from the brain by way of the spinal cord. Were the top of your spinal cord severed, you would not feel such pain. Or pleasure. Your brain would literally be out of touch with your body. Thus, you would lose all sensation and voluntary movement in body regions whose sensory and motor neurons connect with the spinal cord below its point of injury. Male paraplegics (whose legs are paralyzed) are usually capable of an erection (a simple reflex) if their genitals are stimulated. But, depending on where and how completely the spinal cord is severed, they may be genitally unresponsive to erotic images and have no genital feeling (Kennedy & Over, 1990). To produce bodily pain or pleasure, the sensory information must reach the brain.

autonomic [aw-tuh-NAHM-ik] **nervous system**
the part of the peripheral nervous system that controls the glands and the muscles of the internal organs (such as the heart). Its sympathetic division arouses; its parasympathetic division calms.

sympathetic nervous system
the division of the autonomic nervous system that arouses the body, mobilizing its energy in stressful situations.

parasympathetic nervous system
the division of the autonomic nervous system that calms the body, conserving its energy.

reflex
a simple, automatic, inborn response to a sensory stimulus, such as the knee-jerk response.

> "If the nervous system be cut off between the brain and other parts, the experiences of those other parts are nonexistent for the mind. The eye is blind, the ear deaf, the hand insensible and motionless."
>
> **WILLIAM JAMES**
> *PRINCIPLES OF PSYCHOLOGY*
> 1890

Figure **2.7**

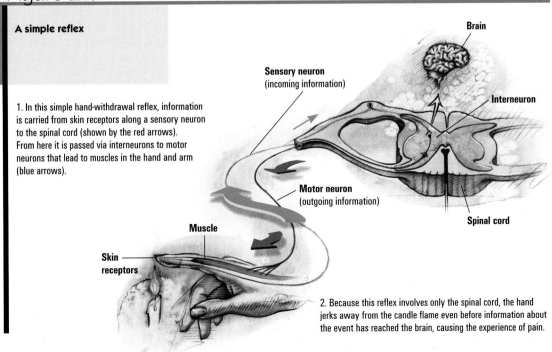

A simple reflex

1. In this simple hand-withdrawal reflex, information is carried from skin receptors along a sensory neuron to the spinal cord (shown by the red arrows). From here it is passed via interneurons to motor neurons that lead to muscles in the hand and arm (blue arrows).

Sensory neuron (incoming information)

Brain

Interneuron

Motor neuron (outgoing information)

Spinal cord

Muscle

Skin receptors

2. Because this reflex involves only the spinal cord, the hand jerks away from the candle flame even before information about the event has reached the brain, causing the experience of pain.

neural networks
interconnected neural cells. With experience, networks can learn, as feedback strengthens or inhibits connections that produce certain results. Computer simulations of neural networks show analogous learning.

endocrine [EN-duh-krin] system
the body's "slow" chemical communication system; a set of glands that secrete hormones into the bloodstream.

hormones
chemical messengers, mostly those manufactured by the endocrine glands, that are produced in one tissue and affect another.

Neural Networks

The other part of your central nervous system, your brain, receives information, interprets it, and decides responses. In doing so, the brain functions rather like a computing machine. It receives slightly differing images of an object from the two eyes, computes their difference, and instantly infers how far away the object must be to project such a difference. As Michael Jordan shoots a falling-away jump shot, his agile brain performs an incredible number of instant computations, adjusting for body position and movement, distance, and angle.

How do our brains perform such computations? First, our neurons cluster into work groups called neural networks. To understand why neurons tend to connect with nearby neurons, Stephen Kosslyn and Olivier Koenig (1992, p. 12) invite us to "think about why cities exist; why don't people distribute themselves more evenly across the countryside?" Like people networking with people, neurons network with nearby neurons with which they can have short, fast connections. As in Figure 2.8, the cells in each layer of a neural network connect with various cells in the next layer. Learning occurs as feedback strengthens connections that produce certain results. New computer models simulate neural networks, complete with excitatory and inhibitory connections that gain strength with experience—and mimic the brain's capacity for learning.

Of course, the system inside each of us is more complicated than the networks depicted in Figure 2.8. In our brains, one neural network is interconnected with other networks that do different things. There are no arrows to tell us where one network ends and the next begins; what distinguishes them is their specific functions. Each is a subnetwork, contributing its little bit of information to the whole information-processing system we call the brain.

The Endocrine System

Interconnected with the nervous system is the second of the body's communication systems, the endocrine system (Figure 2.9). The endocrine system's glands secrete hormones, chemical messengers that are produced in one tissue and travel through the bloodstream and affect other tissues, including the brain. Hormones acting on the brain influence our interest in sex, food, and aggression.

Some hormones are chemically identical to neurotransmitters (those chemical messengers that diffuse across a synapse and excite or inhibit an adjacent neuron). The endocrine system and nervous system are therefore kindred systems: They both secrete molecules that activate receptors elsewhere. But unlike the speedy nervous system, which zips messages from eyes to brain to hand in a fraction of a second, endocrine messages use the slow lane. If the nervous system's communication delivers messages rather like e-mail, the endocrine system is the body's snail mail. Several seconds or more may elapse before the bloodstream carries a hormone from an endocrine gland to its target tissue. But these endocrine messages are often worth waiting for, because their effects are usually longer-lasting than the effects of a neural message.

The endocrine system's hormones influence many aspects of our lives, from growth to reproduction, from metabolism to mood, keeping everything in balance while we respond to stress, exertion, and internal thoughts. In a moment of

Figure **2.8**

A simulated neural network
Neurons network with nearby neurons. Given feedback, the network can strengthen connections that produce a given output in response to a given pattern of inputs.

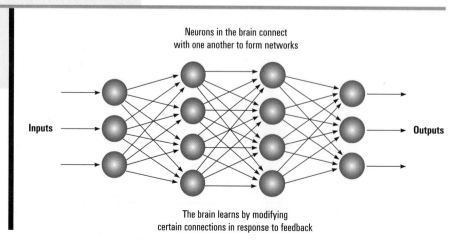

Neurons in the brain connect
with one another to form networks

Inputs

Outputs

The brain learns by modifying
certain connections in response to feedback

Figure **2.9**

The body's major endocrine glands

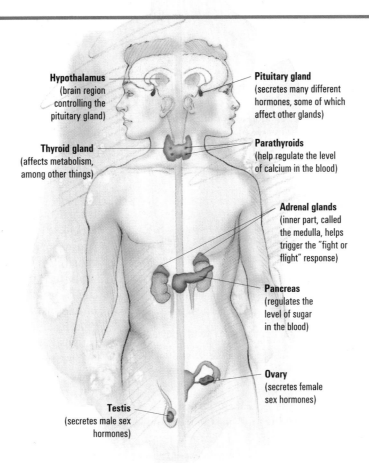

Hypothalamus
(brain region controlling the pituitary gland)

Pituitary gland
(secretes many different hormones, some of which affect other glands)

Thyroid gland
(affects metabolism, among other things)

Parathyroids
(help regulate the level of calcium in the blood)

Adrenal glands
(inner part, called the medulla, helps trigger the "fight or flight" response)

Pancreas
(regulates the level of sugar in the blood)

Ovary
(secretes female sex hormones)

Testis
(secretes male sex hormones)

adrenal [ah-DREEN-el] glands
a pair of endocrine glands just above the kidneys. The adrenals secrete the hormones epinephrine (adrenaline) and norepinephrine (noradrenaline), which help to arouse the body in times of stress.

pituitary gland
the endocrine system's most influential gland. Under the influence of the hypothalamus, the pituitary regulates growth and controls other endocrine glands.

danger, for example, the autonomic nervous system will order the adrenal glands on top of the kidneys to release *epinephrine* and *norepinephrine* (also called *adrenaline* and *noradrenaline*). These hormones increase heart rate, blood pressure, and blood sugar, providing us with a surge of energy. When the emergency passes, the hormones—and the feelings of excitement—linger a while.

The most influential endocrine gland is the pituitary gland, a pea-sized structure located in the base of the brain, where it can be controlled by an adjacent brain area called the hypothalamus. The pituitary releases hormones that influence growth. Its secretions also influence the release of hormones by other endocrine glands. This makes the pituitary a sort of master gland. For example, under the brain's influence, the pituitary triggers your sex glands to release sex hormones, which may in turn influence your brain and behavior.

This feedback system (brain → pituitary → other glands → hormones → brain) illustrates the intimate connection of the nervous and endocrine systems. The nervous system directs endocrine secretions, which affect the nervous system. The two systems are so closely connected that the distinction between them sometimes blurs. Researchers have discovered that neurotransmitters can drift in the brain's fluid to nerve receptors at distant sites, thereby affecting overall alertness or mood (Agnati & others, 1992; Pert, 1986). In such cases, the distinction between certain neurotransmitters and their chemical twins—which are called hormones when released by glands—is no longer so clear. Conducting and coordinating this whole electrochemical orchestra is that maestro we call the brain.

SUMMING UP

The central nervous system's neurons in the brain and spinal cord communicate with the peripheral nervous system's sensory and motor neurons. The peripheral nervous system has two main divisions. The skeletal nervous system directs voluntary movements and reflexes. The autonomic nervous system, through its sympathetic and parasympathetic divisions, controls our involuntary muscles and the glands of our endocrine system. Hormones released by endocrine glands travel through the bloodstream and affect other tissues, including the brain.

lesion [LEE-zhuhn]
tissue destruction. A brain lesion is a naturally or experimentally caused destruction of brain tissue.

electroencephalogram (EEG)
an amplified recording of the waves of electrical activity that sweep across the brain's surface. These waves are measured by electrodes placed on the scalp.

CT (computed tomograph) scan
a series of x-ray photographs taken from different angles and combined by computer into a composite representation of a slice through the body. Also called CAT scan.

PET (positron emission tomograph) scan
a visual display of brain activity that detects where a radioactive form of glucose goes while the brain performs a given task.

MRI (magnetic resonance imaging)
a technique that uses magnetic fields and radio waves to produce computer-generated images that distinguish among different types of soft tissue; allows us to see structures within the brain.

The human brain This small, wrinkled organ is far more complex than the most sophisticated computer. What you see here is only a portion of the brain's outer layer. Most of its surface lies hidden within its convoluted folds.

[1]Carl Sagan's *Broca's Brain* (1979a) inspired this question.

KEY TERMS AND CONCEPTS nervous system, central nervous system (CNS), peripheral nervous system (PNS), nerves, sensory neurons, interneurons, motor neurons, skeletal nervous system, autonomic nervous system, sympathetic nervous system, parasympathetic nervous system, reflex, neural networks, endocrine system, hormones, adrenal glands, pituitary gland

The Brain

The known universe's most amazing organ is being probed and mapped by a new generation of neural cartographers. Lower-level brain networks sustain basic life functions and enable memory, emotions, and basic drives. Atop the brain, neural networks within the cerebral hemispheres form specialized work teams that enable our perceiving, thinking, and speaking.

In a jar on a display shelf in Cornell University's psychology department resides the well-preserved brain of Edward Bradford Titchener, a great turn-of-the-century experimental psychologist and proponent of the study of consciousness. Imagine yourself gazing at that wrinkled mass of grayish tissue. Is there any sense in which Titchener is still in there?[1]

You might answer that without the living whir of electrochemical activity there could be nothing of Titchener in his preserved brain. Consider then an experiment about which the inquisitive Titchener himself might have daydreamed. Imagine that just moments before his death, someone removed Titchener's brain from his body and kept it alive by pumping enriched blood through it as it floated in a tank of cerebral fluid. Would Titchener now still be in there? Further imagine, to carry our fantasy to its limit, that someone transplanted the still-living brain into the body of a badly brain-damaged person. To whose home should the recovered patient return?

That we can imagine such questions illustrates how convinced we are that we live in our heads. And for good reason: As Woody Allen has said, the brain is a very important organ. The brain enables the mind: seeing, hearing, remembering, thinking, feeling, speaking, dreaming. Indeed, say neuroscientists, the *mind is what the brain does*. But precisely where and how are mind functions tied to the brain? Let's first see how scientists explore such questions.

The Tools of Discovery

It is exciting to consider how fast and how far the neurosciences have progressed within a lifetime. For centuries, the human brain lay largely beyond the reach of science. The neuron was too small to study with the naked eye, its impulses too faint to record with ordinary electrodes. We were able to feel bumps on the skull, dissect and analyze lifeless brains, and observe the effects of specific brain diseases and injuries. But there were no tools high-powered yet gentle enough to explore the living brain. Now, that has changed. Whether in the interests of science or medicine, we can selectively destroy tiny clusters of normal or defective brain cells, leaving their surroundings unharmed. We can probe the brain with tiny electrical pulses. We can snoop on the messages of individual neurons and on the mass action of billions. We can see color representations of the brain's energy-consuming activity. These new tools and techniques have made possible a neuroscientific revolution.

Clinical Observations

The oldest method of studying brain-mind connections is to observe the effects of brain diseases and injuries. Such observations were first recorded some 5000 years ago. But it was not until the last two centuries that physicians began systematically to record the results of damage to specific brain

THE FAR SIDE

"That's a lie, Morty! . . . Mom says you might have got the brains in the family, but I got the looks!"

areas. Some noted that damage to one side of the brain often caused numbness or paralysis on the body's opposite side, suggesting that the right side of the body is wired to the brain's left side, and vice versa. Others noticed that damage to the back of the brain disrupted vision, and that damage to the left front part of the brain produced speech difficulties. Gradually, the brain was being mapped. Today, records of more than 1500 brain-injured patients have been assembled by University of Iowa researchers into the largest-ever brain-damage registry.

Manipulating the Brain

Today's scientists need not wait for brain injuries. They can also electrically, chemically, or magnetically stimulate various parts of the brain, noting the effects. Or they can surgically lesion (destroy) tissue in specific brain areas in animals. For example, a lesion destroying the region of a rat's brain called the hypothalamus reduces eating, causing the rat to starve unless force-fed. A lesion in a nearby area produces *over*eating.

Recording the Brain's Electrical Activity

Modern researchers have also learned to eavesdrop on the brain. The tips of modern microelectrodes are so small they can detect the electrical pulse in a single neuron, making possible some astonishingly precise findings. For example, we can now detect exactly where the information goes after someone strokes a cat's whisker.

Electrical activity in the brain's billions of neurons sweeps in regular waves across its surface. The electroencephalogram (EEG) is an amplified tracing of such waves by an instrument called an electroencephalograph. Studying an EEG of the gross activity of the whole brain is like studying the activity of a car engine by listening to the hum of its motor. However, by presenting a stimulus repeatedly and having a computer filter out brain activity unrelated to the stimulus, one can identify the electrical wave evoked by the stimulus (Figure 2.10).

Brain-Imaging Techniques

Other new windows into the brain give us a Supermanlike ability to see inside the brain without lesioning it. For example, the CT (computed tomograph) scan examines the brain by taking x-ray photographs that can reveal brain damage. Even more dramatic is the PET (positron emission tomo-

Figure 2.10

An electroencephalograph providing amplified tracings of waves of electrical activity in the brain Here it is detecting brain response to sound, making possible an early evaluation of what may be a hearing impairment.

graph) scan (Figure 2.11). A PET scan depicts the activity of different brain areas by showing each area's consumption of its chemical fuel, the sugar glucose (see illustration, page 63). Active neurons burn more glucose. When a person is given a temporarily radioactive form of glucose, the PET scan locates and measures the radioactivity, thereby detecting where this "food for thought" goes. In this way, researchers can see which brain areas are most active as the person performs mathematical calculations, listens to music, or daydreams.

Another new way of looking into the living brain exploits the fact that the centers of atoms, including those in our brains, spin like tops. In MRI (magnetic resonance imaging) scans, the head is put in a strong magnetic field, which aligns the spinning atoms. Then a brief pulse of radio waves disorients the atoms momentarily. When the atoms return to their normal spin, they release detectable signals, which become computer-generated images of their concentrations. The result is a detailed picture of the brain's soft tissues. For example, MRI

> "I am a brain, Watson. The rest of me is a mere appendix."
>
> SHERLOCK HOLMES
> IN ARTHUR CONAN DOYLE'S
> "THE ADVENTURE OF THE MAZARIN
> STONE"

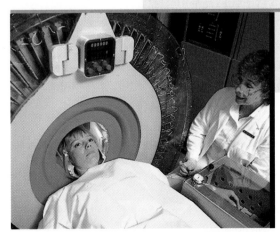

Figure 2.11

The PET scan To obtain a PET scan, researchers inject volunteers with a low and harmless dose of a short-lived radioactive sugar. Detectors around the subject's head pick up the release of gamma rays from the sugar, which has concentrated in active brain areas. A computer then processes and translates these signals into a map of the brain at work.

Figure **2.12**

MRI scan of a healthy individual (left) and a schizophrenia patient (right) Note the enlarged fluid-filled brain region in the image on the right.

scans reveal enlarged fluid-filled brain areas in some patients who have schizophrenia, a disabling psychological disorder (Figure 2.12).

By taking pictures less than a second apart, MRI scans can now show the brain lighting up (with increased oxygen-laden bloodflow) as a person performs different mental functions. As a person sees a light turn on, a *functional MRI* (also called *fast* or *dynamic MRI*) machine detects blood rushing to the back of the brain, which processes visual information (Figure 2.20, page 61). Ask the person to solve a verbal analogy problem, and the part of the brain's left side near the front will light up. Such snapshots of the brain's mind-making activity provide new insights into how and where the brain divides its labor.

These new brain-imaging instruments are doing for psychological science what the microscope did for biology and the telescope for astronomy—they are triggering a scientific revolution. To be learning about the neurosciences now is like studying world geography while Magellan was exploring the seas. Every year the explorers announce new discoveries, which also generate new interpretations of old discoveries. A small sampling of new revelations:

- PET scans show that the brain areas that light up when people silently say the name of an animal differ from those that light up when they say the name of a tool (Martin & others, 1996).

- MRI scans reveal a larger-than-average neural area in the left brain of musicians who display perfect pitch (Schlaug & others, 1995).

- Functional MRI scans reveal that, during a rhyming task, men's brains have a distinctively active left brain area, whereas women's brains are active on both sides (Shawitz & others, 1995).

Such data from different brain-imaging techniques are appearing faster than anyone can read and remember them. One recent Society for Neuroscience meeting offered the 23,000 attendees 12,000 scientific presentations. Researchers are now assembling this information in computer databases. This brain cartography will give all re-searchers instant access through electronic networks to PET or MRI studies that reveal activity in a particular brain area while a person, for example, solves math problems. Clearly, this is the decade of the brain, the golden age of brain science.

Lower-Level Brain Structures

If you could open the skull and look inside, the first thing you might notice is the brain's size. In dinosaurs, the brain represents 1/100,000th of the body's weight, in whales 1/10,000th, in elephants 1/600th, in humans 1/45th. It looks as though a principle is emerging. But keep on. In mice the brain is 1/40th the body's weight, and in marmosets 1/25th. So there are exceptions to the rule of thumb that the ratio of brain to body weight provides a clue to a species' intelligence.

More useful clues to an animal's capacities come from the brain's structures. In primitive vertebrate (backboned) animals, such as sharks, the brain primarily regulates basic survival functions: breathing, resting, and feeding. In lower mammals, such as rodents, a more complex brain enables emotion and greater memory. In advanced mammals, such as humans, the brain processes more information, enabling us to act with foresight.

THE FAR SIDE

"The picture's pretty bleak, gentlemen. . . . The world's climates are changing, the mammals are taking over, and we all have a brain about the size of a walnut."

Brain evolution has not greatly altered the basic mechanisms for survival. Rather, as the English neurologist John Hughlings Jackson recognized a century ago, evolution has elaborated new brain systems on top of the old, much as the earth's landscape covers the old with the new. Digging down, one discovers the fossil remnants of the past—brainstem components still performing much as they did for our distant ancestors. Let's now explore the brain, starting with the brainstem and working up.

The Brainstem

The brainstem is the brain's oldest and innermost region. It begins where the spinal cord enters the skull and swells slightly, forming the medulla. Here lie the controls for your heartbeat and breathing. If the top of a cat's brainstem is severed from the rest of the brain above it, the animal will still breathe and live—and even run, climb, and groom (Klemm, 1990). But cut off from the brain's higher region, it won't purposefully run or climb to get food.

Here in the brainstem is also the crossover point, where most nerves to and from each side of the brain connect with the body's opposite side. This peculiar cross-wiring is but one of many surprises the brain has to offer.

Inside the brainstem, the reticular ("netlike") formation, a finger-shaped network of neurons, extends from the spinal cord right up to the thalamus (Figure 2.13). As the spinal cord's sensory input travels up to the thalamus, some of it branches off to the reticular formation, which filters incoming stimuli and relays important information to other areas of the brain. Among its other functions, the reticular formation helps control arousal.

In 1949, Giuseppe Moruzzi and Horace Magoun discovered that electrically stimulating the reticular formation of a sleeping cat almost instantly produced an awake, alert animal. Magoun also severed a cat's reticular formation from higher brain regions without damaging the nearby sensory pathways. The effect? The cat lapsed into a coma from which it never awakened. Magoun could clap his hands by the cat's ear, even pinch it; still, no response. This established the reticular formation's involvement in arousal. Later researchers discovered that elsewhere in the brainstem are neurons whose activity is needed for sleep. (As we will see, the brain is not idle during sleep.)

The Thalamus

Atop the brainstem sits a joined pair of egg-shaped structures called the thalamus (Figure 2.13). This is the brain's sensory switchboard: It receives information from the sensory neurons and routes it to the higher brain regions that deal with seeing, hearing, tasting, and touching. We can think of the thalamus as being to neural traffic what London is to England's train traffic: Sensory input passes through it en route to various destinations. The thalamus also receives some of the higher brain's replies, which it directs to the cerebellum and medulla.

brainstem
the oldest part and central core of the brain, beginning where the spinal cord swells as it enters the skull; it is responsible for automatic survival functions.

medulla [muh-DUL-uh]
the base of the brainstem; controls heartbeat and breathing.

reticular formation
a nerve network in the brainstem that plays an important role in controlling arousal.

thalamus [THAL-uh-muss]
the brain's sensory switchboard, located on top of the brainstem; it directs messages to the sensory receiving areas in the cortex and transmits replies to the cerebellum and medulla.

Figure 2.13

Thalamus

Reticular formation

Medulla

The brainstem and thalamus
In this figure, you can see the parts of the brainstem, the thalamus attached to its top, and the reticular formation, which passes through both structures.

Figure **2.14**

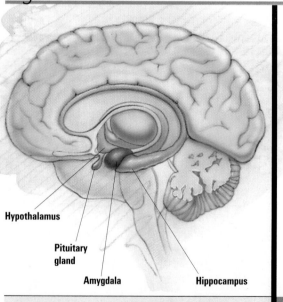

Cerebellum

Spinal cord

The cerebellum Hanging at the back of the brain, this "little brain" coordinates our movements.

The Cerebellum

Extending from the rear of the brainstem is the cerebellum, meaning little brain, which is rather what its two wrinkled hemispheres look like (Figure 2.14). As we will see in Chapter 9, the cerebellum influences one type of learning and memory. But its most obvious function is coordinating voluntary movement. If you injured your cerebellum, you would probably have difficulty walking, keeping your balance, or shaking hands. Your movements would be jerky and exaggerated.

Note that these lower brain functions all occur without any conscious effort. This illustrates another of this book's recurring themes: *Our brain processes much information outside of our awareness.* We are aware of the *results* of our brain's labor (say, our current visual experience) but not of *how* we construct the visual image. Likewise, whether we are asleep or awake, our brainstem manages its life-sustaining functions, freeing our higher brain regions to dream, to think, to talk, to savor a memory.

The Limbic System

At the border ("limbus") of the brain's older parts and the cerebral hemispheres is a doughnut-shaped neural system called the limbic system (Figure 2.15). We will see in Chapter 9 how one limbic system component, the *hippocampus*, processes memory. (When animals or humans lose their hip-

You can challenge your understanding of the essential functions of lower-level brain areas by considering these questions: Within what brain region would damage be most likely to disrupt your ability to skip rope? Your ability to sense tastes or sounds? In what brain region would damage perhaps leave you in a coma? Without the very breath and heartbeat of life? (See page 60.)

pocampus to surgery or injury, they become unable to lay down new memories of facts and experiences.) For now, let's look at the limbic system's links to emotions, such as fear and anger, and to basic motives, such as those for food and sex. As we will see, the limbic system's influence on emotions and motives occurs partly through its control of the body's hormones.

The Amygdala

Two almond-shaped neural clusters in the limbic system, called the amygdala, influence aggression and fear. In 1939, psychologist Heinrich Klüver and neurosurgeon Paul Bucy surgically lesioned part of a rhesus monkey's brain that included the amygdala. The operation transformed the normally ill-tempered monkey into the most mellow of creatures. Poke it, pinch it, do virtually anything that normally would trigger a ferocious response, and still the animal remained placid. In later studies with other wild animals, including the lynx, wolverine, and wild rat, researchers noted the same effect. What then might happen if we electrically stimulated the amygdala in a normally placid domestic animal, such as a cat? Do so in one spot and the cat prepares to attack, hissing with its back arched, its pupils dilated, its hair on end. Move the electrode only slightly within the amygdala and the cat cowers in terror when caged with a small mouse.

Figure **2.15**

Hypothalamus

Pituitary gland

Amygdala

Hippocampus

The limbic system Although part of the endocrine system, not the brain, the pituitary gland is controlled by the limbic system's hypothalamus, just above it.

These experiments testify to the amygdala's role in such emotions as rage and fear, not to mention the perception of such emotions in others (Adolphs & others, 1994). Still, we must be careful not to think of the amygdala as *the* control center for aggression and fear. The brain is *not* neatly organized into structures that correspond to our categories of behavior. Aggressive and fearful behavior involve neural activity in all levels of the brain. Even within the limbic system, stimulating neural structures other than the amygdala can evoke such behavior. Similarly, if you put a charge to your car's dead battery you can activate your car's engine, but that doesn't mean that the battery by itself runs the car. It is merely one link in an integrated system.

Given that amygdala lesions can change violent monkeys into mellow ones, might such lesions do the same in violent humans? Such *psychosurgery* has produced varied results (Mark & Ervin, 1970; Valenstein, 1986). In a few cases involving patients who suffered brain abnormalities, it reduced fits of rage, though sometimes with devastating side effects on the patient's everyday functioning. For ethical reasons, and because of the uncertainties involved, drastic psychosurgery is highly controversial and seldom used. Perhaps, though, as we learn more about how the brain controls behavior, we will learn to alleviate brain disorders without creating new ones.

The Hypothalamus

Another of the limbic system's fascinating structures lies just below (*hypo*) the thalamus, and so is called the hypothalamus. By lesioning or stimulat-

Aggression as a brain state Back arched and fur fluffed, this fierce cat is ready to attack. Electrical stimulation of a cat's amygdala provokes reactions such as the one shown here, suggesting its role in emotions like rage. Which division of the autonomic nervous system is activated by such stimulation? (See page 61.)

ing different areas in the hypothalamus, neuroscientists have isolated within it neural networks that perform specific bodily maintenance duties. Some of these neural clusters influence hunger; still others regulate thirst, body temperature, and sexual behavior.

The hypothalamus monitors blood chemistry and takes orders from other parts of the brain. Thinking about sex (in your brain's cerebral cortex) can stimulate your hypothalamus to secrete hormones. Through these hormones, the hypothalamus controls the adjacent "master gland," the pituitary, which influences hormone release by other glands, which the hypothalamus monitors (Figure 2.15). (Note again the interplay between the nervous and endocrine systems: The brain influences the endocrine system, which in turn influences the brain.) The powerful little hypothalamus also exerts control by triggering autonomic nervous system activity.

The story of a remarkable discovery about the hypothalamus illustrates how progress in scientific research often occurs—when curious, open-minded investigators make an unexpected observation. Two young McGill University neuropsychologists, James Olds and Peter Milner (1954), were trying to implant electrodes in the reticular systems of white rats when they made a magnificent mistake. In one rat, they incorrectly placed an electrode in what was later discovered to be a region of the hypothalamus (Olds, 1975). Curiously, the rat kept returning to the place on its tabletop enclosure where it had been stimulated by this misplaced electrode, as if it were seeking more stimulation. Upon discovering their mistake, the alert investigators recognized that they had stumbled upon a brain center that provides a pleasurable reward.

In a meticulous series of experiments, Olds (1958) then went on to locate other "pleasure centers," as he called them. (What the rats actually experience only they know, and they aren't telling.

The hypothalamus This small but important structure, colored red in this MRI brain scan photograph, helps keep the body's internal environment in a steady state by regulating thirst, hunger, and body temperature. Its activity also influences experiences of pleasureful reward.

cerebellum [sehr-uh-BELL-um] the "little brain" attached to the rear of the brainstem; it helps coordinate voluntary movement and balance.

limbic system a doughnut-shaped system of neural structures at the border of the brainstem and cerebral hemispheres; associated with emotions such as fear and aggression and drives such as those for food and sex. Includes the hippocampus, amygdala, and hypothalamus.

amygdala [ah-MIG-dah-la] two almond-shaped neural clusters that are components of the limbic system and are linked to emotion.

hypothalamus [hi-po-THAL-uh-muss] a neural structure lying below (*hypo*) the thalamus; it directs several maintenance activities (eating, drinking, body temperature), helps govern the endocrine system via the pituitary gland, and is linked to emotion.

Not wanting to attribute human feelings to the rat, today's scientists prefer "reward centers," not "pleasure centers.") When Olds allowed rats to trigger their own stimulation in these areas by pressing a pedal, they would sometimes do so at a feverish pace—up to 7000 times per hour—until they dropped from exhaustion. Moreover, they would do anything to get this stimulation, even cross an electrified floor that a starving rat would not cross to reach food (Figure 2.16).

Figure 2.16

Rat with an implanted electrode   With an electrode implanted in a reward center of its hypothalamus, the rat readily crosses an electrified grid, accepting the painful shocks, to press a lever that sends electrical impulses to its "pleasure centers."

Similar reward centers in or near the hypothalamus were later discovered in many other species, including goldfish, dolphins, and monkeys. In fact, animal research reveals both a general reward system that triggers the release of the neurotransmitter dopamine, and specific centers associated with the pleasures of eating, drinking, sex, and addictive drugs. Animals, it seems, come equipped with built-in reward systems for activities essential to survival.

These dramatic findings made people wonder whether humans, too, might have limbic centers for pleasure. Indeed they do. One neurosurgeon has used electrodes to calm violent patients. Stimulated patients report mild pleasure; unlike rats, they are not driven to a frenzy by it (Deutsch, 1972; Hooper & Teresi, 1986). Some researchers also believe that addictive disorders, such as alcoholism, drug abuse, and food binging, may stem from a *reward deficiency syndrome*—a genetically disposed deficiency in the natural brain systems for pleasure and well-being that leads people to crave substances that provide missing pleasure or to relieve negative feelings (Blum & others, 1996).

The Cerebral Cortex

The cerebral cortex is an intricate covering of interconnected neural cells that, like bark on a tree, forms a thin surface layer on the cerebral hemispheres. It is our body's ultimate control and information-processing center.

> "If you were designing a robot vehicle to walk into the future and survive, . . . you'd wire it up so that behavior that ensured the survival of the self or the species—like sex and eating—would be naturally reinforcing."
>
> CANDACE PERT (1986)

The people who first dissected and labeled the brain used the language of scholars—Latin and Greek. Their words are actually attempts at graphic description: For example, cortex means "bark," cerebellum is "little brain," and thalamus is "inner chamber."

> Animals, it seems, come equipped with built-in reward systems for activities essential to survival.

With the elaboration of the cerebral cortex, tight genetic controls relax and the organism's adaptability increases. Thus, frogs and other amphibians have a small cortex and operate extensively on preprogrammed genetic instructions; the larger cortex of mammals offers increased capacities for learning and thinking, enabling them to be more adaptable. Most of what makes us distinctively human arises from the complex functions of our highly developed cerebral cortex.

Structure of the Cortex

Opening a human skull and exposing the brain, we would see a wrinkled organ, shaped rather like the meat of an oversized walnut. Eighty percent of the brain's weight lies in the ballooning left and right cerebral hemispheres, which are mostly filled with axon connections between the brain's surface and its other regions. The thin surface layer of the cerebral hemispheres is the cerebral cortex, a one-eighth-inch-thick sheet of cells composed of some 30 billion nerve cells. (A square millimeter speck of cortical tissue is packed with nearly 150,000 neurons [Ornstein, 1991].) Supporting these billions of nerve cells are nine times as many glial cells—"glue cells" that guide neural connections, provide nutrients and insulating myelin, and mop up ions and neurotransmitters. Some researchers now believe that glial cells, by "chatting" with neurons, may also participate in information transmission and memory (Travis, 1994).

Each neuron connects with thousands of others. To get a feeling for the complexity of these interconnections, consider that you could join two 8-studded Lego bricks 24 ways, and six bricks nearly 103 million ways. With some 30 billion neurons, each having roughly 10,000 contacts with other neurons, we end up with something like 300 trillion cortical synaptic connections. Being human takes a lot of nerve.

The first thing you would notice about the cerebral cortex is its wrinkled appearance, which leaves only about one-third of it visible on the surface. These folds greatly increase the brain's surface area, which, if flattened out, would be roughly

Figure **2.17**

The cerebral cortex If flattened, a human cortex would cover about four pages of this book. A chimpanzee's would cover one page, a monkey's a postcard, and a rat's a postage stamp. (From *Scientific American*, October 1994, p. 102.)

cerebral [seh-REE-bruhl] cortex
the intricate fabric of interconnected neural cells that covers the cerebral hemispheres; the body's ultimate control and information-processing center.

glial cells
cells in the nervous system that are not neurons but that support, nourish, and protect neurons.

frontal lobes
the portion of the cerebral cortex lying just behind the forehead; involved in speaking and muscle movements and in making plans and judgments.

parietal [puh-RYE-uh-tuhl] lobes
the portion of the cerebral cortex lying at the top of the head and toward the rear; includes the sensory cortex.

occipital [ahk-SIP-uh-tuhl] lobes
the portion of the cerebral cortex lying at the back of the head; includes the visual areas, which receive visual information from the opposite visual field.

temporal lobes
the portion of the cerebral cortex lying roughly above the ears; includes the auditory areas, each of which receives auditory information primarily from the opposite ear.

the size of a newspaper page. In rats and other lower mammals, the surface of the cortex is much smoother, which means there is less of this neural fabric (Figure 2.17).

We can view each brain hemisphere as divided into four regions, or *lobes*. Starting at the front of your brain and going around over the top, there are the frontal lobes (behind your forehead), the parietal lobes (at the top and to the rear), the occipital lobes (at the back of your head), and the temporal lobes (just above your ears). These lobes are convenient geographic subdivisions separated by prominent folds (Figure 2.18). Each lobe carries out many functions, and some functions require the interplay of several lobes.

Functions of the Cortex

More than a century ago, autopsies of partially paralyzed or speechless people revealed damage to specific areas of the cortex. But this rather crude evidence did not prove that specific parts of the cortex perform specific functions. After all, if control of speech and movement were diffused across the cortex, damage to almost any area might pro-

duce the same effect. A television would go dead with its power cord cut, but we would be deluding ourselves if we were to think we had "localized" the source of the picture in the cord. This analogy suggests how easy it is to err when trying to localize brain functions.

Figure **2.18**

The basic subdivisions of the cortex

Frontal lobe

Parietal lobe

Occipital lobe

Temporal lobe

Figure **2.19**

Motor cortex
(Left hemisphere section
controls the body's right side)

Sensory cortex
(Left hemisphere section receives
input from the body's right side)

Left hemisphere tissue devoted to each body part in the motor cortex and the sensory cortex

As you can see, the amount of cortex devoted to a body part is not proportional to that part's size. Rather, the brain devotes more tissue to sensitive areas and to areas requiring precise control. Thus, the fingers have a greater representation in the cortex than does the upper arm. However, the neural wiring is complex. Individual muscles are linked with multiple neural clusters, which may also link with other muscles.

Answers to questions at bottom of page 56: the cerebellum, the thalamus, the reticular formation, and the medulla.

Motor Functions

In 1870, German physicians Gustav Fritsch and Eduard Hitzig applied mild electrical stimulation to the cortexes of dogs and made an important discovery: They could make different body parts move. The effects were selective: Stimulation caused movement only when applied to an arch-shaped region at the back of the frontal lobe, running roughly from ear to ear across the top of the brain. This arch we now call the motor cortex (Figure 2.19). Moreover, when the researchers stimulated specific parts of this region in the left or right hemisphere, specific body parts moved on the *opposite* side of the body.

A half century ago, neurosurgeons Otfrid Foerster in Germany and Wilder Penfield in Montreal mapped the motor cortex in hundreds of wide-awake patients. The surgeons needed to know the possible side effects of removing different parts of the cortex. So, before putting the knife to the brain, they would painlessly (the brain has no sensory re-

ceptors) stimulate different cortical areas and note body responses. Like Fritsch and Hitzig, they found that when they stimulated different areas of the motor cortex at the back of the frontal lobe, different body parts moved. They were therefore able to map the motor cortex according to the body parts it controlled (Figure 2.19). Interestingly, those areas of the body requiring precise control, such as the fingers and mouth, occupied the greatest amount of cortical space.

More recent research reveals that the precise muscle-to-brain connections are not so simple as the early brain stimulation studies suggested. In one study, researchers studied these connections using functional MRI scans to observe where the brain lights up when specific muscles are moved (Sanes & others, 1995). They found that a given finger or wrist movement, for example, would activate multiple and overlapping sites. Although it's true that certain areas of the cortex control certain

Figure **2.20**

New technology shows the brain in action In this composite sketch and photograph, a functional MRI scan shows the visual cortex activated (color representation of increased bloodflow) as researchers shine a light into a subject's eyes. If the light is switched off, the region instantly calms down.

areas of the body and that some areas require more brain tissue than others, the wiring pattern is complex—complex enough to enable the many different muscle combinations needed to produce specific gestures.

Neuroscientist José Delgado demonstrated the mechanics of motor behavior. In one monkey, he evoked a smiling response over 400,000 times. In a human patient, stimulation of a certain spot on the left motor cortex triggered the right hand to make a fist. Asked to keep the fingers open during the next stimulation, the patient, whose fingers closed despite his best efforts, remarked, "I guess, Doctor, that your electricity is stronger than my will" (Del-

gado, 1969, p. 114). More recently, scientists have been able to predict what a monkey will draw a tenth of a second before it does—by repeatedly measuring motor cortex activity preceding specific arm movements (Gibbs, 1996).

Sensory Functions

If the motor cortex sends messages out to the body, where do *incoming* messages reach the cortex? Penfield identified a cortical area that specializes in receiving information from the skin senses and from the movement of body parts. This area, parallel to the motor cortex and just behind it at the front of the parietal lobes, we now call the sensory cortex (Figure 2.19). Stimulate a point on the top of this band of tissue, and the person may report being touched on the shoulder; stimulate some point on the side, and the person may feel something on the face.

The more sensitive a body region, the greater the area of the sensory cortex devoted to it; your super-sensitive lips project to a larger brain area than do your toes (Figure 2.19). Similarly, rats have a large area of the brain devoted to whisker sensations, owls to hearing sensations, and so forth. If a monkey or a human loses a finger, the region of the sensory cortex devoted to receiving input from that finger branches to receive sensory input from the adjacent fingers, which now become more sensitive (Fox, 1984). As this illustrates, the brain is sculpted not only by our genes but also by our experience.

Further exploration identified areas where the cortex receives input from the other senses. At this moment you are receiving visual information in the occipital lobes at the very back of your brain (Figure 2.20). Stimulated there, you might see flashes of light or dashes of color. So, in a sense, we *do* have eyes in the back of our head. From your occipital lobes, the visual information you are now processing goes to other brain areas that specialize in tasks such as identifying words, detecting emotions, and recognizing faces.

Any sound you are hearing you processed with the auditory areas in your temporal lobes (Figure 2.21). Most of this auditory information travels a circuitous route from one ear to the auditory receiving area above your opposite ear. Stimulated there, you might hear a sound.

Association Functions

So far, we have pointed out small areas of the cortex that either receive sensory information or direct muscular responses. In humans, that leaves

motor cortex
an area at the rear of the frontal lobes that controls voluntary movements.

sensory cortex
the area at the front of the parietal lobes that registers and processes body sensations.

The cat on page 57 is aroused via its sympathetic nervous system.

Figure **2.21**

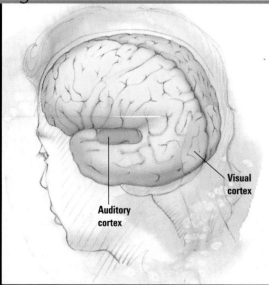

Visual cortex

Auditory cortex

The visual and auditory cortex The occipital lobes at the rear receive input from the eyes. An auditory area of the temporal lobes receives information from the ears.

Figure **2.22**

■ Motor areas
■ Sensory areas
■ Association areas

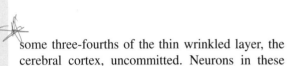

Rat

Cat

Chimpanzee

Human

Areas of the cortex in four mammals More intelligent animals have increased "uncommitted" or association areas of the cortex. These vast areas of the brain are responsible for integrating and acting on information received and processed by sensory areas.

association areas
areas of the cerebral cortex that are not involved in primary motor or sensory functions; rather, they are involved in higher mental functions such as learning, remembering, thinking, and speaking.

aphasia
impairment of language, usually caused by left hemisphere damage either to Broca's area (impairing speaking) or to Wernicke's area (impairing understanding).

Broca's area
an area of the left frontal lobe that directs the muscle movements involved in speech.

Wernicke's area
an area of the left temporal lobe involved in language comprehension.

some three-fourths of the thin wrinkled layer, the cerebral cortex, uncommitted. Neurons in these association areas (the gray areas in Figure 2.22) integrate information. They associate various sensory inputs with stored memories—an important part of thinking.

Electrically probing the association areas doesn't trigger any response. So, unlike the sensory and motor areas, we can't so neatly specify the functions of the association areas. Their silence seems to be what someone had in mind when formulating one of pop psychology's most widespread myths: that we ordinarily use only 10 percent of our brains. This myth—"one of the hardiest weeds in the garden of psychology," writes Donald McBurney (1996, p. 44)—implies that if we could activate our whole brain, we would be far smarter than those who drudge along on 10 percent brain power. But from observing surgically lesioned animals and brain-damaged humans, we know that the association areas are not dormant. (The brain has no appendix—no apparently purposeless tissue.) Rather, the association areas interpret, integrate, and act on information processed by the sensory areas.

Association areas in the frontal lobe enable judging and planning. People with damaged frontal lobes may have intact memories, score high on intelligence tests, and be well able to bake a cake—yet they may be unable to plan ahead to *begin* baking the cake for a birthday party.

Frontal lobe damage can also alter personality, removing a person's inhibitions. Consider the classic case of railroad worker Phineas Gage. One afternoon in 1848, Gage, then 25 years old, was packing gunpowder into a rock with a tamping iron. A spark ignited the gunpowder, shooting the rod up through his left cheek and out the top of his skull, leaving his frontal lobes massively damaged. To everyone's amazement, Gage was still able to

sit up and speak, and after the wound healed he returned to work. Although his mental abilities and memories were intact, his personality was not. The affable, soft-spoken Phineas Gage was now an irritable, profane, capricious person who eventually lost his job and ended up earning his living as a fairground exhibit. This person, said his friends, was "no longer Gage." With his frontal lobes ruptured, Gage had lost his moral compass.

The association areas of the other lobes also perform mental functions. For example, an area on the underside of the right temporal lobe enables us to recognize faces. If a stroke or head injury destroyed this area of your brain, you would still be able to describe facial features and to recognize someone's gender and approximate age, yet be strangely unable to identify the person as, say, Boris Yeltsin or your next-door neighbor or even your spouse. But by and large, complex mental functions such as learning and memory don't reside in any one place. There is no one spot in a rat's small association cortex that, when damaged, will obliterate its ability to learn or remember a maze. Such functions seem spread throughout much of the cortex.

Phineas Gage reconsidered Using measurements of his skull (which was kept as a medical record) and modern neuroimaging techniques, researcher Hanna Damasio and her colleagues (1994) have reconstructed the probable path of the rod through Gage's brain.

Language

Complex human abilities, such as language, result from the intricate coordination of many brain areas. For example, consider the curious finding that damage to any one of several cortical areas can cause aphasia, an impaired use of language. It is even more curious that some aphasic people can speak fluently but are unable to read (despite good vision), while others can comprehend what they read but are unable to speak. Still others can write but not read, read but not write, read numbers but not letters, or sing but not speak. These observations are puzzling because we think of speaking and reading, or writing and reading, or singing and speaking as merely different examples of the same general ability. Consider the clues that helped researchers solve this mystery of language:

Clue 1 In 1865, French physician Paul Broca reported that damage to a specific area of the left frontal lobe, later called Broca's area, left a person struggling to form words yet able to sing familiar songs and comprehend speech.

Clue 2 In 1874, German investigator Carl Wernicke discovered that damage to a specific area of the left temporal lobe (Wernicke's area) left people able to speak words but in a meaningless way. Asked to describe a picture that showed two boys stealing cookies behind a woman's back, one patient responded:"Mother is away her working her work to get her better, but when she's looking the two boys looking the other part. She's working another time" (Geschwind, 1979).

Clue 3 It was later discovered that reading aloud involves a third brain area. The *angular gyrus* receives the visual information from the visual area and recodes it into the auditory form from which Wernicke's area derives its meaning.

Clue 4 Nerve fibers interconnect these brain areas.

Norman Geschwind assembled these clues into an explanation of how we use language. When you read aloud, the words (1) register in the visual area, (2) are relayed to the angular gyrus, which then transforms the words into an auditory code that is (3) received and understood in the nearby Wernicke's area, and (4) sent to Broca's area, which (5) controls the motor cortex, creating the pronounced word (Figure 2.23). Depending on which link in this chain is damaged, a different form of aphasia occurs. Damage to the angular gyrus leaves the person able to speak and understand but unable to read. Damage to Wernicke's area disrupts understanding. Damage to Broca's area disrupts speaking. The general principle bears repeating: Complex abilities result from the intricate coordination of many brain areas.

Said differently, the brain operates by dividing its mental functions—speaking, perceiving, think-ing, remembering—into subfunctions. Our conscious experience *seems* indivisible. Right now you are experiencing a whole visual scene as if your eyes were video cameras projecting the scene into your brain. Actually, as we will see, your brain breaks vision into specialized subdimensions, such as color, depth, movement, and form. (After a localized stroke that destroys one of these neural work teams, people may lose just one aspect of vision, such as the ability to perceive movement.) These specialized neural networks, each having done its own thing, then feed their information to "higher-level" networks that combine the atoms of experience and relay them to progressively higher-level association areas, enabling us to recognize a face as "Grandmother." The same is true of reading a word: The brain computes the word's form,

(a) Hearing **(b) Seeing** **(c) Speaking**

Brain activity when hearing, seeing, and speaking words PET scans such as these detect the activity of different areas of the brain by measuring their relative consumption of a temporarily radioactive form of the brain's normal fuel, glucose. This series of side-view PET scans of left-facing patients shows levels of increased brain activity in specific areas: (a) when hearing a word—auditory cortex and Wernicke's area; (b) when seeing a word—visual cortex and angular gyrus; and (c) when repeating a word—Broca's area and the motor cortex. The red blotches show where the brain is rapidly consuming glucose.

Figure **2.23**

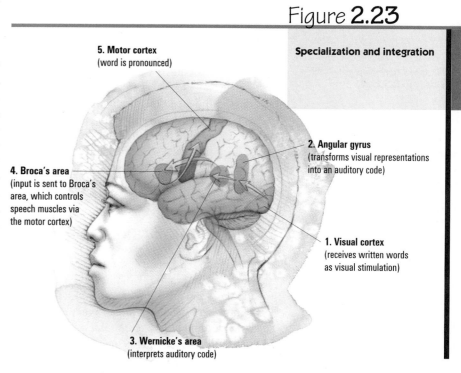

Specialization and integration

5. Motor cortex (word is pronounced)

4. Broca's area (input is sent to Broca's area, which controls speech muscles via the motor cortex)

2. Angular gyrus (transforms visual representations into an auditory code)

1. Visual cortex (receives written words as visual stimulation)

3. Wernicke's area (interprets auditory code)

Figure **2.24**

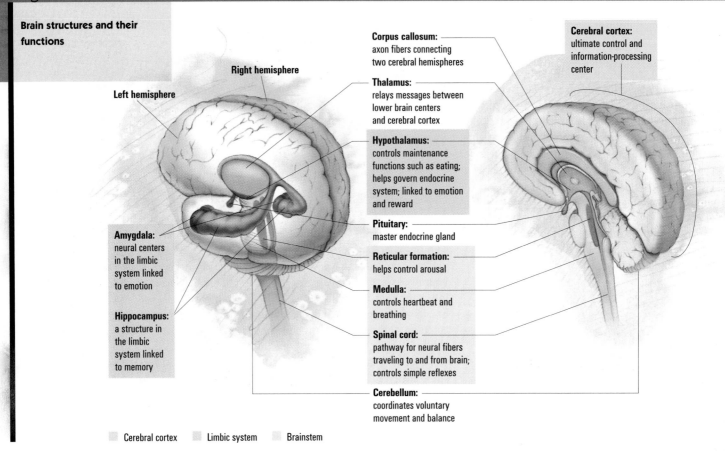

Brain structures and their functions

Right hemisphere

Left hemisphere

Corpus callosum: axon fibers connecting two cerebral hemispheres

Cerebral cortex: ultimate control and information-processing center

Thalamus: relays messages between lower brain centers and cerebral cortex

Hypothalamus: controls maintenance functions such as eating; helps govern endocrine system; linked to emotion and reward

Amygdala: neural centers in the limbic system linked to emotion

Pituitary: master endocrine gland

Reticular formation: helps control arousal

Medulla: controls heartbeat and breathing

Hippocampus: a structure in the limbic system linked to memory

Spinal cord: pathway for neural fibers traveling to and from brain; controls simple reflexes

Cerebellum: coordinates voluntary movement and balance

☐ Cerebral cortex ☐ Limbic system ☐ Brainstem

Question: If your Broca's area were damaged, could you write a letter? (See page 66.)

corpus callosum [KOR-pus kah-LOW-sum]
the largest bundle of neural fibers connecting the two brain hemispheres and carrying messages between them.

split brain
a condition in which the two hemispheres of the brain are isolated by cutting the connecting fibers (mainly those of the corpus callosum) between them.

sound, and meaning using different neural networks (Posner & Carr, 1992). Think about it: *What you experience as a continuous, indivisible stream of perception is actually but the visible tip of the information-processing iceberg, most of which lies beneath the surface of your conscious awareness.*

To sum up, the mind's subsystems are localized in particular brain regions (Figure 2.24), yet the brain acts as a unified whole. Moving your hand; recognizing faces; even perceiving color, motion, and depth all depend on specific neural networks. Yet complex functions such as language, learning, and loving involve the coordination of many brain areas. Both principles—specialization and integration—appear in research on the two brain hemispheres.

Our Divided Brains

For more than a century, clinical evidence has shown that the brain's two sides serve differing functions. Accidents, strokes, and tumors in the left hemisphere generally impair reading, writing, speaking, arithmetic reasoning, and understanding. Similar lesions in the right hemisphere do not have

such dramatic effects. Small wonder, then, that the left hemisphere became known as the "dominant" or "major" hemisphere, and its silent companion to the right as the "subordinate" or "minor" hemisphere. The left, verbal hemisphere is rather like the moon's facing side—the one easiest to observe and study. The other side is there, of course, but less visibly noticeable. (With some left-handers, speech is processed in the right hemisphere—see page 68.)

By 1960, the assumption of left hemisphere superiority was well accepted. But then the "minor" right hemisphere was found to be not so limited after all. As with the moon, we have observed and come to appreciate the other side. The story of this discovery is a fascinating chapter in psychology's history.

Splitting the Brain

In 1961, two Los Angeles neurosurgeons, Philip Vogel and Joseph Bogen, were considering surgery for several patients who suffered from epilepsy. The surgeons speculated that major epileptic seizures were caused by an amplification of abnormal brain activity that reverberated between the two hemispheres. They therefore wondered whether they might control severe epilepsy by cutting communication between the hemispheres. To do so, the surgeons would have to sever the corpus callosum, the wide band of axon fibers connecting the two hemispheres (Figure 2.25).

They had reason to believe such an operation would not be incapacitating. Psychologists Roger Sperry, Ronald Myers, and Michael Gazzaniga had divided the brains of cats and monkeys in this manner, without serious ill effects. So Vogel and Bogen operated. The result? The seizures were nearly eliminated and the patients were surprisingly normal, their personalities and intellect hardly affected. Waking from the surgery, one patient even managed to quip that he had a "splitting headache" (Gazzaniga, 1967).

If you chatted with one of these split-brain patients you probably would not notice anything unusual. You could understand why only a decade earlier neuropsychologist Karl Lashley had jested that maybe the corpus callosum served only "to keep the hemispheres from sagging." But surely a broad band of 200 million nerve fibers capable of transferring more than a billion bits of information per second between the hemispheres must have a more significant purpose. It does, and the ingenious experiments of Sperry and Gazzaniga revealed its purpose and provided a key to understanding the two hemispheres' special functions.

After one of the split-brain operations, the researchers placed an unseen object in a patient's left hand. He denied it was there. This came as no surprise to Sperry or Gazzaniga. They knew that information from the left hand went to the right hemisphere, and their animal experiments suggested that the right hemisphere would be unable to send this information to the left hemisphere (which in most humans controls speech). More extraordinary results came when Sperry and Gazzaniga conducted some perceptual tests.

Our eyes connect to our brains in such a way that, when we look straight ahead, the left half of our field of vision transmits through both eyes to our right hemisphere (Figure 2.26). Likewise, the right side of our field of vision transmits only to our left hemisphere. One woman, who had lost a vision-related part of her *right* hemisphere to a massive stroke but was otherwise normal, sometimes complained that nurses had not put dessert or coffee on her tray. A nurse would then turn the woman's head so that the tray came into view in the right half of her field of vision (where her *left* visual cortex could detect it). She then would say, "Oh, there it is—it wasn't there before" (Sacks, 1985, p. 73).

Figure 2.25

Corpus callosum

The corpus callosum This large band of neural fibers connects the two brain hemispheres. To photograph the half brain shown here, the hemispheres were separated by cutting through the corpus callosum and lower brain regions.

Figure 2.26

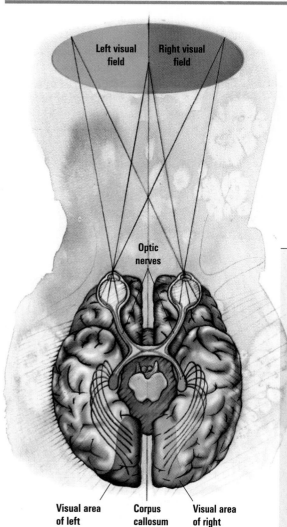

Left visual field

Right visual field

Optic nerves

Visual area of left hemisphere

Corpus callosum

Visual area of right hemisphere

The information highway from eye to brain Information from the left half of your field of vision goes to your right hemisphere, and information from the right half of your visual field goes to your left hemisphere. (Note, however, that each eye receives sensory information from both the right and left visual fields.) The data received by either hemisphere are quickly transmitted to the other across the corpus callosum. In a split-brain patient with a severed corpus callosum, this information sharing does not take place.

Most of the body's paired organs—kidneys, lungs, breasts—perform identical functions, providing a backup system should one side fail. Not so the brain's two halves, which form a biological odd couple, serving differing functions.

Answer to question on page 64: Yes. Broca's area produces a program for controlling the muscles of speech. If the area is damaged, a victim can still understand speech and communicate through gestures or writing.

In those of us with healthy, intact brains, information presented only to our right hemisphere is quickly sent to our left hemisphere, which names it. But what happens in a person whose corpus callosum has been severed? To find out, experimenters ask a split-brain patient to look at a designated spot. Then they send information to either the left or right hemisphere (by flashing it to the spot's right or left). Finally, they quiz each hemisphere separately.

See if you can guess the results of an experiment using this procedure (Gazzaniga, 1967). While the patients stared at a dot, the word HEART was flashed across the visual field with HE in the left visual field and ART in the right. First, what did the patients *say* they saw? Second, asked to identify with their *left* hands what they had seen, did they *point* to HE or ART?

As Figure 2.27 shows, the patients *said* they saw ART and so were startled when their left hands *pointed* to HE. When given an opportunity to ex-

press itself, each hemisphere reported only what it had seen.

Similarly, when a picture of a spoon was flashed to their right hemisphere, the patients could not say what they saw. But when asked to identify what they had seen by feeling with their left hands an assortment of objects hidden behind a screen, they readily selected the spoon (Figure 2.28). If the experimenter said, "Right!" the patient might reply, "What? Right? How could I possibly pick out the right object when I don't know what I saw?" It is, of course, the left hemisphere doing the talking here, bewildered by what its other half knows. It was as if the patients had "two separate inner visual worlds," noted Sperry (1968).

The left hemisphere, which acts as the brain's press agent, does mental gymnastics to rationalize reactions it does not understand. If the patient followed an order sent to the right hemisphere ("Walk"), the interpretive left hemisphere would offer a ready explanation ("I'm going into the house to get a Coke"). Thus, Michael Gazzaniga (1988) concludes that the left hemisphere is an "interpreter" that instantly constructs theories to explain our behavior.

These experiments demonstrate that the right hemisphere understands simple requests and easily perceives objects. In fact, the right hemisphere is superior to the left at copying drawings, recognizing faces, perceiving differences, and expressing emotion (through the more expressive left side of the face [Hauser, 1993; Metcalfe & others, 1995; Skinner & Mullen, 1991]). Most of the body's

Figure 2.27

Testing the divided brain When an experimenter flashes the word HEART across the visual field, the split-brain patient reports seeing the portion of the word transmitted to her left hemisphere. However, if asked to indicate with her left hand what she saw, she points to the portion of the word transmitted to her right hemisphere. (From Gazzaniga, 1983.)

"Look at the dot."

Two words separated by red dot appear projected in front of person.

"What word did you see?"

"art"

or

"Point with your left hand to the word you saw."

Figure **2.28**

"I don't know."

"What did you see?"

"With your left hand, select the object you saw from those behind the screen."

The nonverbal right hemisphere Seeing a spoon flashed on the screen, the right hemisphere directs the left hand to locate it among the objects hidden behind the screen. But the split-brain patient cannot say what he has seen. (From Gazzaniga, 1983.)

paired organs—kidneys, lungs, breasts—perform identical functions, providing a backup system should one side fail. Not so the brain's two halves, which form a biological odd couple, serving differing functions.

The right hemisphere's perceptual superiority is apparent in one of Sperry's films. A split-brain patient's left hand (directed by the right hemisphere) easily rearranges some blocks to match a drawing. When the right hand (directed by the left hemisphere) tries to perform the same perceptual task, it makes many errors. The bumbling performance frustrates the right hemisphere, which is observing all this. So it triggers the left hand to interrupt the bumbling right hand, but the persistent right hand pushes the left hand away. Outside the laboratory, a few split-brain patients have been for a time bothered by the unruly independence of their left hand, which would unbutton a shirt while the right hand buttoned it. It was as if each hemisphere was thinking "I've half a mind to wear my green (blue) shirt today." Indeed, said Sperry (1964), split-brain surgery leaves people "with two separate minds." (Reading these reports, I fantasize a split-brain person enjoying a solitaire game of "rocks, paper, and scissors"—left versus right hand.)

"Do not let your left hand know what your right hand is doing."

MATTHEW 6:3

Studying Hemispheric Differences in the Intact Brain

What about the 99.99+ percent of us with undivided brains? Have scientists found our hemispheres similarly specialized? They have indeed, in several different types of studies. For example,

when a person performs a *perceptual* task, brain waves, bloodflow, and glucose consumption reveal increased activity in the *right* hemisphere; when a person speaks or calculates, activity increases in the *left* hemisphere.

On occasion, hemispheric specialization has been even more dramatically shown by briefly sedating an entire hemisphere. To check for the locus of language before surgery, a physician may inject a sedative into the neck artery that feeds blood to the hemisphere on its side of the body. Before the drug is injected, the patient is lying down, arms in the air, conversing easily. Can you predict what happens when the drug flows into the artery going to the left hemisphere? Within seconds, the right

THE FAR SIDE

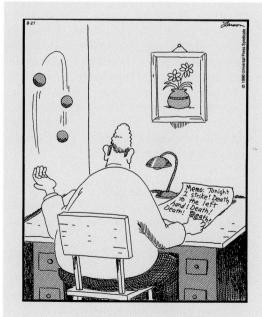

Innocent and carefree, Stuart's left hand didn't know what the right was doing.

Question: If we flashed a red light to the right hemisphere of a split-brain patient and a green light to the left hemisphere, would each observe its own color? Would the person be aware that the colors differ? What would the person verbally report seeing? (*Answers on page 69.*)

CLOSE-UP

Left-Handedness—Is Being a Lefty All Right?

Judging by our everyday conversation, left-handedness is not all right. To be "coming from left field" or to offer a "left-handed compliment" is hardly better than to be "gauche" or "sinister" (words derived from the French and Latin for left). On the other hand, right-handedness is "right on," which any "righteous" "right-hand man" "in his right mind" usually is.

How Many People Are Left-Handed? About 10 percent (somewhat more among males, somewhat less among females) of the human population is left-handed. Judging from cave drawings and the tools of prehistoric humans, this veer to the right occurred long ago in the development of our species. Thus, right-handedness prevails today in all human cultures (Corballis, 1989). Moreover, it appears prior to culture's impact: Ultrasound observations of fetal thumb-sucking reveal that more than 9 in 10 fetuses suck the right hand's thumb (Hepper & others, 1990). This right-hand bias is uniquely human; other primates are more ambidextrous.

Is Handedness Inherited? There is no simple genetic code for handedness, which is one of but a few traits that genetically identical twins aren't especially likely to share (Halpern & Coren, 1990).

Nevertheless, observing 150 babies during the first two days after birth, George Michel (1981) found that two-thirds consistently preferred to lie with their heads turned to the right. When he restudied a sample of these babies at age 5 months, almost all of the "head right" babies reached for things with their right hands, and almost all of the "head left" babies reached with their left hands. Such findings, along with the universal prevalence of right-handers, indicate that either genes or some prenatal factor influences handedness.

Is the Brain Organization of Left-Handers Opposite That of Right-Handers? Tests reveal that about 95 percent of right-handers process speech primarily in the left hemisphere (Springer & Deutsch, 1985). Left-handers are more diverse. More than half process speech in the left hemisphere, as right-handers do. About one-quarter process language in the right hemisphere; the other quarter use both hemispheres more or less equally. Such left-handers may therefore require better communication between the hemispheres. This might explain the discovery that the corpus callosum averages 11 percent larger in left-handers (Witelson, 1985).

So, Is It All Right to Be Left-Handed? Left-handers are more numerous among people with reading disabilities, allergies, and migraine headaches (Geschwind &

Behan, 1984). But left-handedness is also more common among musicians, mathematicians, professional baseball and cricket players, architects, and artists, including such luminaries as Michelangelo, Leonardo da Vinci, and Picasso.* Although left-handers must tolerate elbow-jostling at dinner parties, right-handed desks, and awkward scissors, it seems the pros and cons of being a lefty are roughly equal.

Lefties Famous left-handers include John McEnroe, Jimi Hendrix, and Bill Clinton.

---

*Strategic factors explain the higher-than-normal percentage of lefties in sports. For example, it helps a soccer team to have left-footed players play the left side of the field (Wood & Aggleton, 1989).

arm falls limp and, assuming the person's left hemisphere controls language, the subject becomes speechless until the drug wears off. When the drug goes into the artery to the right hemisphere, the *left* arm falls limp, but speech is still possible.

Other tests confirm hemispheric specialization. Most people recognize pictures faster and more accurately when the image is flashed to the right hemisphere. But they recognize words faster and more accurately when the word is flashed to the left hemisphere. If a word is flashed to your right hemisphere, perception takes a fraction of a second longer—the length of time it takes to send the information through the corpus callosum to the more verbal left hemisphere.

Finally, which hemisphere would you suppose enables sign language among the deaf? Is it the right hemisphere, because of its visual-spatial superiority? Or the left, because of its preparedness to process language? Studies reveal that just as hearing people use the left hemisphere to process speech, deaf people use the left hemisphere to read signs (Corina & others, 1992). A stroke in the left hemisphere therefore disrupts a deaf person's signing much as it would disrupt a hearing person's speaking. To the brain, language is language, whether spoken or signed.

So, a variety of observations—of people with split brains and people with normal brains—converge beautifully. There is now little doubt that we have unified brains with specialized parts. Although language requires the left hemisphere, the right hemisphere helps us modulate our speech to make meaning clear—as when we ask "What's that in the road ahead?" instead of "What's that in the road, a head?" (Heller, 1990). From looking at the two hemispheres, which look alike to the naked eye, who would suppose that they contribute so uniquely to the harmony of the whole?

We have glimpsed the truth of our overriding principle: Everything psychological is simultaneously biological. This chapter has focused on some ways in which our thoughts, feelings, and actions arise from our specialized yet integrated brain. Chapters to come will further explore the significance of the biological revolution in psychology. We will see, for example, how

- brain development underlies a child's mental development.
- the brain compensates for brain damage that occurs early in life.

> A stroke in the left hemisphere disrupts a deaf person's signing much as it would disrupt a hearing person's speaking. To the brain, language is language, whether spoken or signed.

- genes and experience jointly influence our personality, emotions, gender, and intelligence.
- our sense organs and our brain enable us to see and hear.
- the brain records memories.
- aberrant brain anatomy and chemistry influence depression and schizophrenia, and how biological treatments can alleviate these conditions.
- our brain and body work to create our experiences of hunger and sexuality, anger and fear, sleep and dreams.
- mind and body together influence our vulnerability to disease and our capacity for healing.
- our species' evolutionary history may predispose us to hurt, help, or love certain others.

Answers to questions on page 67: Yes. No. Green.

From nineteenth-century phrenology to today's neuroscience we have come a long way. Yet what is unknown still dwarfs what is known. We can describe the brain. We can learn the functions of its parts. We can study how the parts communicate. But how does this electrochemical whir give rise to a feeling of elation, a creative idea, or a memory of Grandmother's freshly baked cookies?

The mind boggles both at what is known and what is not comprehended. To judge from interviews with leading brain scientists, feelings of awe and wonder are commonplace. Others ponder philosophical mysteries: How does the material brain give rise to consciousness? And to what extent can a thing understand itself? The mind seeking to understand the brain—that is indeed the ultimate scientific challenge.

> "If the human brain were so simple that we could understand it, we would be so simple that we couldn't."
>
> **EMERSON M. PUGH, QUOTED BY GEORGE E. PUGH**
> *THE BIOLOGICAL ORIGIN OF HUMAN VALUES*
> 1977

> The mind seeking to understand the brain—that is indeed the ultimate scientific challenge.

THINKING CRITICALLY ABOUT

Left Brain/Right Brain

"Error flies from mouth to mouth, from pen to pen, and to destroy it takes ages."

VOLTAIRE 1694–1778

You've heard or read it many times: Some people are "left-brained," others "right-brained." Leaping from the new research on split and intact brains, educators, management advisers, and self-help writers urge us to harness our undeveloped half brain. Are you lacking in creativity, music appreciation, or emotional empathy? Well, get your brain in balance. Awaken your dormant right hemisphere. Advocate "whole brain" education in your schools. Unleash intuitive, right-brained management from the chains of cold logic and statistics. Try *Drawing on the Right Side of the Brain* (the title of a million-copy bestseller translated into 10 languages).

What should we make of all this? By calling my friend Elsie "right-brained" have I explained why she's such a zany free spirit? And why her "left-brained" husband Bill is so coolly analytical? We've seen that research does show that each hemisphere serves special functions. The left is more logical, verbal, and able to deal with things in sequence. The right is more emotionally intuitive and expressive, skilled at spatial relations, and able to deal with things all at once. But neuroscientists offer a caution flag: Beware the fad of locating complex human abilities such as science or art in either hemisphere. "The left-right dichotomy in cognitive mode is an idea with which it is very easy to run wild," warned Sperry (1982). Complex activities such as doing science or creating art require the integrated activity of both hemispheres. Even when we just read a story, both

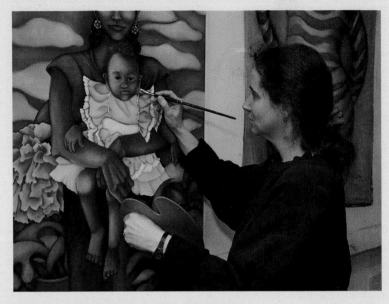

hemispheres are active—the left processing the words and finding meaning, the right appreciating humor, imagery, and emotional content (Hellige, 1993; Levy, 1985).

Why, then, do the popularizations of brain research so greatly exaggerate the findings? In *The Left-Hander Syndrome*, University of British Columbia psychologist Stanley Coren (1993) illustrates how journalism often oversimplifies and embellishes science. He recalls hearing a convention talk by Doreen Kimura, a psychologist at the University of Western Ontario in London, Ontario. Kimura reported that melodies fed to the left ear were more easily recognized than melodies fed to the right ear. Knowing that the left ear sends most of its information to the right hemisphere, she concluded that, among her right-handed student volunteers, the right brain was better at recognizing melodies.

A few days later, the *New York Times* reported that "Doreen Kimura, a psychologist from Lon-

don, Ontario, has found that *musical ability* is controlled by the right side of the brain" (italics highlight the embellishment). Apparently drawing from the *Times* story, a syndicated newspaper story then reported that "London psychologist, Dr. Doreen Kimura, claims that musicians are right-brained!" (But Kimura studied university students, not musicians.) Later, a follow-up newspaper article further distorted the study: "An English psychologist has finally explained why there are so many great left-handed musicians."

Knowing that Kimura is not English, did not study musicians, and did not study left-handers, Coren recalled the words of an American editor: "Everything you read in the newspaper is absolutely true, except for the rare story of which you happen to have first-hand knowledge."

What can happen is this: As information flows from scientist to reader, it gets simplified and embellished, much as gossip does in passing from one person to the next. A

Left brain/right brain Is the artist a "right-brained" person? Such notions distort scientific findings regarding the cerebral hemispheres. While some areas of each hemisphere specialize in different tasks, the brain's two sides cooperate to enable the person in whatever he or she does.

TV network picks up an interesting finding, then reduces it to a 30-second report with an 11-second sound bite from the researcher. This alerts a major newspaper to a story angle, which in turn gets picked up by popular science magazines and, eventually, by supermarket magazines and tabloids.

At each step, notes Coren, "Ideas become more speculative and more distant from the actual research. . . . After a while, the neuropsychologist is no longer even visible in the communication chain." Eventually, the rumors grow, accumulate, and evolve into scientific myths that become "'accepted truths,' which show up in conversation and writing in sentences that begin with, 'As everybody knows . . . ,' or 'Scientists have shown that . . . .'" In the end, sighs Coren, the public myth drowns the weak voices of dissenting scientists.

The moral is not to disbelieve everything you read. Surely Oscar Wilde was too cynical when expressing gratitude "for modern journalism. By giving us the opinions of the uneducated, it keeps us in touch with the ignorance of the community." (Although few journalists check the accuracy of their draft articles with those they've interviewed, some do.) Rather, beware that reporters want their stories to be newsworthy. At their best, their ideal (and mine, in writing this book) is to extract the essence—to simplify without oversimplifying. At their worst, they distort pretzel-shaped findings into a breadstick-shaped story: Some people are left-brained, others right-brained. . . .

SUMMING UP

The Tools of Discovery Clinical observations have long revealed the general effects of damage to various brain areas. But CT and MRI scans now reveal brain structures, and EEG, PET, and functional MRI recordings reveal brain activity. By surgically lesioning or electrically stimulating specific brain areas, by recording the brain's surface electrical activity, and by displaying neural activity with computer-aided brain scans, neuroscientists explore the connections among brain, mind, and behavior.

How the Brain Governs Behavior The brainstem begins where the spinal cord swells to form the medulla, which controls heartbeat and breathing. Within the brainstem, the reticular formation has control over arousal. Atop the brainstem is the thalamus, the brain's sensory switchboard. The cerebellum, attached to the rear of the brainstem, coordinates muscle movement.

Between the brainstem and cerebral cortex is the limbic system, which is linked to memory, emotions, and drives. One of its neural centers, the amygdala, is involved in aggressive and fearful responses. Another, the hypothalamus, is involved in various bodily maintenance functions, pleasurable rewards, and the control of the endocrine system.

Each hemisphere of the cerebral cortex—the neural fabric that covers the hemispheres—has four geographical areas: the frontal, parietal, occipital, and temporal lobes. Small, well-defined regions within these lobes control muscle movement and receive information from the body senses. However, most of the cortex—its association areas—is uncommitted to such functions and is therefore free to process other information.

Some brain regions serve specific functions. The brain divides its labor into specialized subtasks and then integrates the outputs from its neural networks. Thus human emotions, thoughts, and behaviors result from the intricate coordination of many brain areas. Language, for example, depends on a chain of events in several brain regions.

Our Divided Brains Clinical observations long ago revealed that the left cerebral hemisphere is crucial for language. Experiments on split-brain patients have refined our knowledge of each hemisphere's special functions. By testing the two hemispheres separately, researchers have confirmed that in most people the left hemisphere is the more verbal, and that the right hemisphere excels in visual perception and the recognition of emotion. Studies of healthy people with intact brains confirm that each hemisphere makes unique contributions to the integrated functioning of the brain.

KEY TERMS AND CONCEPTS lesion, electroencephalogram (EEG), CT (computed tomograph) scan, PET (position emission tomograph) scan, MRI (magnetic resonance imaging), brainstem, medulla, reticular formation, thalamus, cerebellum, limbic system, amygdala, hypothalamus, cerebral cortex, glial cells, frontal lobes, parietal lobes, occipital lobes, temporal lobes, motor cortex, sensory cortex, association areas, aphasia, Broca's area, Wernicke's area, corpus callosum, split brain

chromosomes
threadlike structures made of DNA molecules that contain the genes.

DNA (deoxyribonucleic acid)
a complex molecule containing the genetic information that makes up the chromosomes.

genes
the biochemical units of heredity that make up the chromosomes; a segment of DNA capable of synthesizing a protein.

evolutionary psychology
the study of the evolution of behavior using the principles of natural selection, which presumably favors behavior tendencies that contribute to the preservation and spread of one's genes.

More than 98 percent of our genes are identical to those of chimpanzees, making them as close to us as a fox is to a dog (de Waal, 1995). But what a difference that 2 percent makes—enabling not only our art and science but also our power to destroy all our achievements.

Genetics and Behavior

Our genes provide the blueprint for our biology, which predisposes our behaviors. Evolutionary psychologists look for clues to behaviors that might be universal. They study how natural selection favors behavioral tendencies that contribute to the survival and spread of our genes. Behavior geneticists study our individual differences. Their interdisciplinary research weighs genetic and environmental contributions to various traits.

Behind the story of our human brain—surely the most awesome thing on earth—are the blueprints that design both our universal human attributes and our individual traits. When egg and sperm unite, the 23 chromosomes carried in the egg pair up with the 23 chromosomes brought to it by the sperm. These 46 chromosomes contain the master plan for your development. Each chromosome is composed of a coiled chain of a molecule called DNA (deoxyribonucleic acid). DNA in turn is made of thousands of genes. Our genes are the biochemical units of heredity that—by synthesizing specific proteins—make each of us a distinctive human being. The genes we share are what make us people rather than dogs or tulips (Figure 2.29).

As we will see in chapters to come, one of psychology's really big questions concerns the extent to which our genes provide the blueprints not only for our bodies but for our behaviors. Clearly, genes do predispose certain behaviors. Dog breeders, as Robert Plomin and his colleagues (1997) remind us, have given us sheepdogs that herd, retrievers that retrieve, trackers that track, and pointers that point. They also have given us placid spaniels and aggressive bulldogs. Psychologists, too, have bred dogs, mice, and rats whose genes predispose them

to be serene or reactive, quick learners or slow learners.

Everyone agrees that the tight genetic leash that predisposes an ant's nest building, a dog's retrieving, or a cat's pouncing is looser on humans. Our genes endow us with a capacity to learn and to adapt to life on the tundra or in the jungle. But to what extent do our genetic predispositions explain both our shared human nature and our individual differences?

Evolutionary Psychology: Explaining Universal Behaviors

In some ways, we differ from others in our culture, and certainly we differ from people shaped by other cultures. Yet in the big picture, human lives are remarkably alike. We all face certain questions: Who is my ally, who my foe? What food should I eat? With whom should I mate?

At the dawn of human history, some individuals answered those questions more successfully than others. Those who ate food that nourished rather than poisoned them more often survived to contribute their genes to later generations. Similarly successful were those who mated with someone with whom they could produce and nurture offspring. Individuals who made less fortunate choices tended, over generations, to have their genes lost from the human gene pool. As further random variations occurred, those that gave an adaptive edge continued to be selected. The result, say evolutionary psychologists, produced not only the physical characteristics but also the behavioral tendencies and ways of thinking that prepared our stone age ancestors to survive, reproduce, and send their genes into the future. Nature selected the fittest adaptations.

Figure 2.29

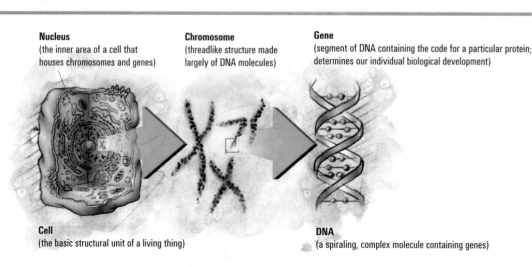

The genes: Their location and composition Contained in the nucleus of each of the trillions of cells in your body are chromosomes. Each chromosome contains a coiled chain of the molecule DNA. Genes are DNA segments that form templates for the production of proteins. By directing the manufacture of proteins, the genes determine our individual biological development.

Nucleus
(the inner area of a cell that houses chromosomes and genes)

Chromosome
(threadlike structure made largely of DNA molecules)

Gene
(segment of DNA containing the code for a particular protein; determines our individual biological development)

Cell
(the basic structural unit of a living thing)

DNA
(a spiraling, complex molecule containing genes)

As inheritors of this prehistoric genetic legacy, we therefore love the taste of sweets and fats, which once were hard to come by, but which prepared our ancestors to survive famines. Today, with famine rare in Western cultures, and sweets and fats beckoning us from store shelves, fast-food outlets, and vending machines, obesity is a growing problem. Evolution has been an important concept in the fields of anthropology and biology for a long time. Only recently, however, has psychology incorporated it as a major perspective that can increase our understanding of some very important issues. Darwin (1859) anticipated this "second Darwinian revolution"—the application of evolutionary principles to psychology. In concluding his book *Origin of Species*, he foresaw "open fields for far more important researches. Psychology will be based on a new foundation . . ." (p. 346).

Psychologists, as we shall see, have used evolutionary principles to explore questions such as these:

- Why at about the time they become mobile do infants come to fear strangers?

- Why are most parents so passionately devoted to their children?

- Why do we display greater empathy and helpfulness toward those who think, look, and act as we do?

- Why do men tend to find healthy-looking, younger women attractive, and why are men with status and resources appealing to women?

- Why are men quicker than women to perceive friendliness as sexual interest, to initiate sexual relations, and to feel jealous rage over their mate's having sex with someone else?

The answer to these and other questions, say evolutionary psychologists, is that nature selects behavioral tendencies that increase the likelihood of sending one's genes into the future. Nature predisposes us, as mobile gene machines, to have longings and make choices that worked for our ancestors. For possible explanations of *why* such behaviors were genetically successful, stay tuned. Future chapters will offer some answers.

Behavior Genetics: Explaining Individual Differences

Whereas evolutionary psychologists explore the behavioral implications of Darwin's big idea, in hopes of explaining our universal human tendencies, behavior geneticists explore the ways we differ from one another. How much are we shaped by our genetic blueprint? By our upbringing? By our culture and current circumstances—and by how our environment reacts to our genetic traits?

Studying the Genetic Factor

To answer such questions, behavior geneticists harness powerful methods such as these:

- **Twin studies** To discern the effect of heredity, it would be nice if we could hold shared environment constant while varying heredity. Happily for our purposes, nature has given us ready-made subjects for this experiment: identical versus fraternal twins. Identical twins, who develop from a single fertilized egg that splits in two, are genetically identical (Figure 2.30). Fraternal twins, who develop from separate eggs, are genetically no more similar than ordinary brothers and sisters. A person whose identical twin had Alzheimer's disease has a 60 percent risk of sharing the disease; with an affected fraternal twin, the risk is 30 percent (Plomin & others, 1997). Such a difference suggests a genetic influence. Behavior geneticists seek similar differences in personality and other traits. One study currently under way is following all twins born in England between 1994 and 1996. Behavior geneticists have also used the twin method to assess the effect of environment when heredity is constant, by comparing identical twins reared separately.

- **Adoption studies.** Another of nature's experiments, adoption, creates two groups of relatives: genetic relatives (biological parents and siblings) and environmental relatives (adoptive parents and siblings). Behavior geneticists therefore wonder whether adopted individuals are more like their adoptive parents, who contribute their rearing, or their biological parents, who contribute their genes. And how similar are adopted individuals to their adoptive and biological siblings?

Heritability

Using such methods, behavior geneticists can mathematically estimate the heritability of any trait—the extent to which variation among individuals is due to their differing genes. As emphasized in Chapter 11, if the heritability of intelligence (or happiness or temperament) is, say, 50 percent, this does *not* mean that your intelligence is 50 percent genetic. (If the heritability of height is 90 percent, this does not mean that a 60-inch-tall woman can credit her genes for 54 inches and her environment for the other 6 inches.) It means that we can attribute 50 percent of the observed variation among people to genetic influence.

So, to what extent are we the product of our genes? The answer varies with the trait. But we will see that on traits as widely varying as sleep needs, obesity, happiness, intelligence, personality, and sexual orientation, the genetic influence is

Figure 2.30

Identical twins | Fraternal twins

Same sex only | Same or opposite sex

Same egg, same genes; different eggs, different genes
Identical twins develop from a single fertilized egg, fraternal twins from two.

Curiously, twinning rates vary by race. The rate among Caucasians is roughly twice that of Asians and half that of Africans (Diamond, 1986).

behavior genetics
the study of the power and limits of genetic and environmental influences on behavior.

identical twins
twins who develop from a single zygote (fertilized egg) that splits in two, creating two genetic replicas.

fraternal twins
twins who develop from separate zygotes. They are genetically no closer than brothers and sisters, but they share the fetal environment.

heritability
the proportion of variation among individuals that we can attribute to genes.

considerable. Yet the bio-psycho-social perspective reminds us that genes always are expressed in a particular environment. Genes and environment, nature and nurture, work together like two hands clapping, with the environment reacting to and shaping what nature predisposes. Thus, asking whether your intelligence—or your personality—is more a product of your genes or environment is like asking whether the area of a field is more the result of its length or width.

We could, however, ask whether the differing areas of various fields result more from differences in their length or from differences in their width. For psychological traits, human differences are nearly always the result of both genetic and environmental influences. Thus (to give a preview of coming attractions) we now know that eating disorders are genetically influenced; some individuals are more at risk than others. But we also know that culture bends the twig, for eating disorders are a contemporary Western cultural phenomenon. Likewise, criminal and aggressive tendencies are known to be genetically influenced. Yet genetic changes cannot explain the explosion in juvenile violence since 1960.

If genetic influences help explain individual differences in traits such as aggressiveness, can the same be said of group differences between men and women, or between people of different races? Not necessarily. Individual differences in height and weight are highly heritable. Yet nutritional rather than genetic influences explain why, as a group, today's adults are taller and heavier than those of a century ago. As with height and weight, so with personality and intelligence scores: Heritable individual differences need not imply heritable group differences.

Molecular Genetics

Molecular biologists are teaming with psychologists in search of genes that put people at risk for genetically influenced disorders. As we will see, these include alcoholism, Alzheimer's disease, anxiety disorders, depression, Down syndrome, obesity, and schizophrenia. In Chapter 15, for example, we will take note of a worldwide research effort currently under way to sleuth the genes that

make one vulnerable to the emotional swings of "bipolar disorder" (formerly called *manic-depressive disorder*). To tease out which genes are implicated, molecular geneticists use *linkage analysis*. First, they find families that have had the disorder across several generations. Then they draw blood from both affected and unaffected family members and examine their DNA, looking for differences. The ultimate quest is to identify the aberrant genes causing the disease.

Such research can raise significant ethical issues. If scientists developed genetic tests that could reveal who is at risk for these and other disorders, would you want the test performed in uterus on your unborn offspring? Would society benefit or lose if such embryos were aborted? Should prospective parents take their egg and sperm to a genetics lab for screening before combining them to produce an embryo? Most significant human traits are influenced by many genes, making a simple genetic test unrealistic. But for some disorders, single-gene abnormalities may raise difficult ethical issues. As always, progress is a two-edged sword, raising new possibilities and new problems.

SUMMING UP

Genes are segments of complex DNA molecules. These biochemical units of heredity provide the blueprint for protein molecules, the building blocks of our physical and behavioral development. Evolutionary psychologists study how natural selection has shaped our universal behavioral tendencies. Behavior geneticists explore our individual differences. Using methods such as twin and adoption studies, they identify the heritability of various traits and disorders. Molecular biologists are teaming with psychologists in pursuit of genes that put people at risk for various psychological disorders.

KEY TERMS AND CONCEPTS chromosomes, DNA (deoxyribonucleic acid), genes, evolutionary psychology, behavior genetics, identical twins, fraternal twins, heritability

TERMS AND CONCEPTS TO REMEMBER

biological psychology, p. 42

neuron, p. 42

dendrite, p. 42

axon, p. 42

myelin [MY-uh-lin] sheath, p. 42

action potential, p. 43

threshold, p. 44

synapse [SIN-aps], p. 44

neurotransmitters, p. 44

acetylcholine [ah-seat-el-KO-leen] (ACh), p. 45

endorphins [en-DOR-fins], p. 46

nervous system, p. 47

central nervous system (CNS), p. 47

peripheral nervous system (PNS), p. 47

Lower-Level Brain Structure	How the Structure Is Involved in Musical Performance
1. _____	1. _____
2. _____	2. _____
3. _____	3. _____

Upper-Level Brain Structure	How the Structure Is Involved in Musical Performance
1. _____	1. _____
2. _____	2. _____
3. _____	3. _____

Check your progress in becoming a critical thinker by comparing your answers to the sample answers found in Appendix B.

FOR FURTHER INFORMATION

More information on **neuroscience** can be found on the following pages. (A similar listing for **evolution** and **behavior genetics** may be found in the Preface at the beginning of this text.)

CRITICAL THINKING EXERCISE

by Richard O. Straub

Now that you have read and reviewed Chapter 2, take your learning a step further by testing your critical thinking skills on this pattern recognition exercise.

Playing a musical instrument is a complicated skill that involves every major aspect of behavior and cognition. To be proficient, musicians must have honed their fine motor skills. In addition, many aspects of thinking come into play, including *memory* of how to play the instrument and of musical scales and time signatures, and the planning and *decision making* inherent in translating a piece of sheet music into sound. The musician's *motivation* and *emotion* are equally important influences on a musical performance.

In this exercise you will develop a map describing how various parts of the brain enable a musician to perform a piece of music. Identify three lower-level brain structures and three upper-level structures; then describe how each structure is involved in musical performance.

chapter

chapter

3

The Developing Child

In mid-1978, the newest astonishment in medicine, covering all the front pages, was the birth of an English baby nine months after conception in a dish. The older surprise, which should still be fazing us all, is that a solitary sperm and a single egg can fuse and become a human being. . . . This has been going on under our eyes for so long a time that we've gotten used to it; hence the outcries of amazement at this really minor technical modification of the general procedure—nothing much, really, beyond relocating the beginning of the process from the fallopian tube to a plastic container.

LEWIS THOMAS
THE MEDUSA AND SNAIL
1979

The developing person is no less a wonder after birth than in the womb. Physically, mentally, socially, we are always in the process of becoming. As we journey through life from womb to tomb, how and when do we change?

Usually we notice how we differ. To psychologists our commonalities are just as important. Virtually all of us began walking around age 1 and talking by age 2. As children we all engaged in social play in preparation for life's serious work. We all smile and cry, love and loathe, and occasionally ponder our inevitable death.

Developmental Issues

Unlike most other chapters in this book, this one and the next focus not so much on a topic—the brain, memory, thinking, personality, social behavior—as on a *perspective*. The developmental perspective examines how all such things *change* over the life span. Developmental psychologists study physical, mental, and social changes occurring throughout the life cycle. Much of their work centers on three major issues:

1 **Nature/nurture** How is our development influenced by our heredity (our *nature*) and by our experience (including the *nurture* we receive)? Does our individual

developmental psychology
a branch of psychology that studies physical, cognitive, and social change throughout the life span.

genetic makeup explain why one person is outgoing, another shy? Why one person is slow-witted and another smart? Do children in different cultures travel the same developmental highway, thanks to their shared human nature? Or do they travel different developmental roads, depending on their cultural nurture?

2   **Continuity/stages** Change happens: Adults are vastly different from infants. But do they differ as a giant redwood differs from its seedling—a difference created by gradual, cumulative growth? Or do they differ as a butterfly differs from a caterpillar—a difference of distinct stages? Is developmental change gradual and continuous? Or does it proceed through a sequence of separate stages?

3   **Stability/change** How much do we change? Do our individual traits persist? For much of this century, psychologists took the position that once a person's personality forms, it hardens like clay. Researchers are following lives through time to see how much our past reaches into our future. Are the effects of early experience enduring or temporary? Will the cranky infant grow up to be an irritable adult? Or is such a child as likely to become placid and patient? Do classmates' differences in aggressiveness, aptitude, or strivings for achievement persist across the life span? In short, do we grow into older versions of our early selves, or do we become new persons?

> Do children in different cultures travel the same developmental highway, thanks to their shared human nature? Or do they travel different developmental roads, depending on their cultural nurture?

At the end of this chapter and the next we will reflect on these three developmental issues. But first, our main agenda: to examine human development across the life span, from conception to death.

Prenatal Development and the Newborn

How, over time, did we come to be who we are? From the union of sperm and egg to birth of the newborn, development progresses in an orderly, though fragile, sequence. By birth, infants are equipped with perceptual and behavioral abilities that facilitate their survival.

The Genetics of Life

Nothing is more natural than a species reproducing itself. Yet nothing is more wondrous. Consider human reproduction. The process starts when a woman's ovary releases a mature egg, a cell roughly the size of the period at the end of this sentence, and the 200 million or more sperm deposited during intercourse begin their race upstream toward it. A girl is born with all the immature eggs she will ever have, although only 1 in 5000 will ever mature and be released. A boy, in contrast, begins producing sperm cells at puberty. The manufacturing process continues 24 hours a day for the rest of his life, although the rate of production—more than 1000 sperm during the second it takes to read this phrase—does slow down with age.

Like space voyagers approaching a huge planet, the sperm approach a cell 85,000 times their own size. The relatively few sperm that make it to the egg release digestive enzymes that eat away the egg's protective coating, allowing a sperm to penetrate (Figure 3.1). But the egg is hardly passive. Rather, as soon as one sperm begins to penetrate, the egg's surface blocks out all other sperm. Mean-

Human development Has John F. Kennedy, Jr.'s development been shaped more by his genetic nature or his experienced nurture? Has it been continuous or marked by stages? Will he in the future be the same person he is today? Such questions intrigue developmental psychologists.

Figure **3.1**

(a)

(b)

The union of egg and sperm   (a) A hoard of sperm cells surrounds a huge ovum. (b) As one sperm penetrates the egg's jellylike outer coating, a series of chemical events begins that will cause sperm and egg to fuse into a single cell. If all goes well, that cell will subdivide again and again to emerge 9 months later as a 100-trillion-cell human being.

while, fingerlike projections sprout around the successful sperm and pull it inward. The egg nucleus and the sperm nucleus move toward each other and, before half a day elapses, fuse. The two have become one.

Consider it your luckiest of moments. Among 200 million sperm, the one needed to make you, in combination with that one particular egg, won the race. A 7-year-old boy was overheard explaining the idea to a friend: "Robbie, do you know how many sperm were trying to be you? (Robbie shook his head.) Well, there were millions. I saw it on *Nova*. They were all racing against you, but *you* won. Anybody who is alive won. So you're a winner and I'm a winner; everybody's a winner" (Mahoney, 1989).

Sex Chromosomes, Sex Hormones, and Gender

Males and females are variations on a single form. Eight weeks after conception, they are anatomically indistinguishable. Then, your genes activated your biological sex. Your sex is determined by your twenty-third pair of chromosomes, the sex chromosomes. The member of the pair that came from your mother was an X chromosome. From your father, you received either an X chromosome, making you a girl, or a Y chromosome, making you a boy. The Y chromosome contains a single gene that throws a master switch triggering the testes to develop and produce the principal male hormone, testosterone, which in turn triggers the development of external male sex organs. The fourth and fifth months of prenatal development are a key time for sexual differentiation, which also involves differing brain-wiring patterns for males and females.

What do you suppose happens when glandular malfunction or hormone injections expose a female embryo to excess testosterone? These genetically female infants are born with masculine-appearing genitals, which can be corrected surgically. Until puberty, such females tend to act in more aggressive "tomboyish" ways than is typical of most girls, and they dress and play in ways more typical of boys than of girls (Berenbaum & Hines, 1992; Ehrhardt, 1987). Given a choice of toys, they (like boys) play with cars and blocks rather than with dolls and crayons. Some develop into lesbians, but most—like nearly all girls with traditionally feminine interests—become heterosexual.

Is their behavior due to the prenatal hormones? If so, may we conclude that biological sex differences produce behavioral gender differences? Experiments with many species, from rats to monkeys, confirm that female embryos given male hormones later exhibit more masculine appearance and more aggressive behavior (Hines & Green, 1991). But these girls frequently look masculine and are known to be "different," so perhaps people also treat them more like boys. Early exposure to sex hormones thus affects us both directly (physically) and indirectly—by influencing experiences that shape us. Biological appearances have social consequences.

Prenatal Development

Fewer than half of fertilized eggs, called zygotes, survive beyond the first 2 weeks (Grobstein, 1979). But for you and me, good fortune prevailed. Beginning as one cell, each of us became two cells, then four—each cell just like the first. Then, within the first week, when this cell division had produced a zygote of some 100 cells, the cells began to *differentiate*—to specialize in structure and function.

X chromosome
the sex chromosome found in both men and women. Females have two X chromosomes; males have one. An X chromosome from each parent produces a female.

Y chromosome
the sex chromosome found only in males. When paired with an X sex chromosome from the mother, it produces a male child.

testosterone
the most important of the male sex hormones. Both males and females have it, but the additional testosterone in males stimulates the growth of the male sex organs in the fetus and the development of the male sex characteristics during puberty.

gender
in psychology, the characteristics, whether biologically or socially influenced, by which people define male and female.

zygote
the fertilized egg; it enters a 2-week period of rapid cell division and develops into an embryo.

embryo
the developing human organism from about 2 weeks after fertilization through the second month.

fetus
the developing human organism from 9 weeks after conception to birth.

teratogens
agents, such as chemicals and viruses, that can reach the embryo or fetus during prenatal development and cause harm.

fetal alcohol syndrome (FAS)
physical and cognitive abnormalities in children caused by a pregnant woman's heavy drinking. In severe cases, symptoms include noticeable facial misproportions.

Prenatal development
zygote: conception to 2 weeks
embryo: 2 weeks through 8 weeks
fetus: 9 weeks to birth

"From the very moment that the sperm hits the egg, a precarious trip on the thin edge of biological extinction has begun."

RALPH BLAIR
NEVERTHELESS JOY!
1989

How identical cells do this—as if one decides "I'll become a head, you become intestines!"—is a scientific puzzle that developmental biologists are beginning to solve.

About 10 days after conception, the increasingly diverse cells attach to the mother's uterine wall, beginning approximately 37 weeks of the closest human relationship. When the zygote's outer part attaches to the uterine wall, it becomes the placenta, through which nourishment passes. In this second prenatal stage, the inner cells become the embryo (Figure 3.2). During the next 6 weeks, the embryo's body organs begin to form and function. The heart begins to beat and the liver begins to make red blood cells.

By two months after conception, the embryo looks unmistakably human and is now a fetus. By the end of the sixth month, internal organs such as the stomach have become sufficiently formed and functional to allow a prematurely born fetus a chance of survival. By that time, the developing fetus also becomes responsive to sound. Microphone readings taken inside the uterus reveal that the fetus is exposed to a muffled version of its mother's voice (Ecklund-Flores, 1992). Immediately after birth, infants prefer this familiar voice to another woman's voice or their father's voice (Bus-

nel & others, 1992; DeCasper & others, 1980, 1984, 1986).

At each prenatal stage, genetic *and* environmental factors affect development. The placenta screens out many potentially harmful substances, while allowing nutrients and oxygen to pass through. But nourishment isn't all that passes the placental screen. Devastating effects may follow when the placenta admits teratogens—harmful agents, such as certain viruses and drugs. A pregnant woman never smokes alone. When she puffs on a cigarette, she and her fetus both experience reduced blood oxygen and a shot of nicotine. If she is a heavy smoker, her newborn probably will be underweight, sometimes dangerously so. If she is a heroin addict, her baby will be born a heroin addict. If she carries the AIDS virus, her baby may also.

When a pregnant woman takes a drink, alcohol enters her bloodstream—and her fetus's—and depresses activity in both their central nervous systems. If she drinks heavily, her baby will be at risk for birth defects and mental retardation. For 1 in 750 infants, the effects are visible as fetal alcohol syndrome (FAS), which involves a small, misproportioned head and lifelong brain abnormalities, making it now the leading cause of mental retardation (Niccols, 1994; Streissguth & others, 1991). Although there is no known safe amount of alcohol for a pregnant woman—even moderate drinking can affect the fetal brain (Braun, 1996)—children of alcoholic mothers are especially at risk. About 4 in 10 alcoholic mothers who drink during pregnancy have babies who suffer the enduring damage

Figure **3.2**

Prenatal development

(a)
The embryo grows and develops rapidly. At 40 days, the spine is visible and the arms and legs are beginning to grow.

(b)
Five days later, the inch-long embryo's proportions have begun to change. The rest of the body is now bigger than the head, and the arms and legs have grown noticeably.

(c)
By the end of the second month, when the fetal period begins, facial features, hands, and feet have formed.

(d)
As the fetus enters the fourth month, its 3 ounces could fit in the palm of your hand.

rooting reflex
a baby's tendency, when touched on the cheek, to open the mouth and search for the nipple.

Pregnant women do not eat, drink, or smoke alone
When eating healthy, as this woman is, the usual result is a healthy baby.

of fetal alcohol syndrome. Where maternal drinking is common—as in France and among Native Americans—more children suffer from FAS (Dorozyaski, 1993; Dorris, 1989). "If women didn't drink anymore during pregnancy," notes researcher Ann Streissguth (1993), "there would *never* be another baby born with fetal alcohol syndrome."

"You shall conceive and bear a son.
So then drink no wine or strong drink."

JUDGES 13:7

The Competent Newborn

Having survived prenatal hazards, newborns come equipped with reflexes ideally suited for survival. Infants will withdraw a limb to escape pain. Put a cloth over their faces, interfering with their breathing, and they will turn their heads from side to side and swipe at it. New parents are often awed by the coordinated sequence of reflexes by which babies get food. The rooting reflex illustrates this: When something touches their cheeks, babies will open their mouths and vigorously "root" for a nipple. Finding one, they will automatically close on it and begin sucking—which itself requires a coordinated sequence of tonguing, swallowing, and breathing. Failing to find satisfaction, the hungry baby may cry—a behavior parents are predisposed to find highly unpleasant to hear and very rewarding to relieve.

The pioneering American psychologist William James (who once said, "The first lecture on psychology I ever heard was the first I ever gave") presumed that the newborn experiences a "blooming, buzzing confusion." Until the 1960s, few people disagreed. It was said that, apart from a blur of meaningless light and dark shades, newborns could not see. Then, just as new technology led to neuroscience progress, so too did new investigative techniques enhance infant studies. Scientists discovered that babies can tell you a lot—if you know how to ask. To ask, you must capitalize on what the baby can do—gaze, suck, turn the head. So, equipped with eye-tracking machines and pacifiers wired to electronic gear, researchers set out to answer parents' age-old questions: What can my baby see, hear, smell, and think?

They discovered that infants are born preferring sights and sounds that facilitate social responsiveness. Newborns turn their heads in the direction of human voices. They gaze longer at a drawing of a human face (Figure 3.3) than at a bull's-eye pattern; yet they gaze more at a bull's-eye pattern—which has contrasts much like that of the human eye—than at a solid disk (Fantz, 1961). They prefer to look at objects 8 to 12 inches away, which, wonder of wonders, just happens to be the approximate distance between a nursing infant's eyes and its mother's (Maurer & Maurer, 1988).

Figure **3.3**

Newborns' preference for faces
When shown these two stimuli in the first week of life, Italian newborns spent nearly twice as many seconds looking at the facelike image. (Johnson & Morton, 1991.)

Babies' perceptual abilities are continuously developing during the first months of life. Within days of birth, babies can distinguish their mothers' odor. The infant's brain is an absorbent sponge, its neural networks stamped immediately with the smell of its mother's body. Thus, a week-old nursing baby, placed between a gauze pad from its mother's bra and one from another nursing mother, will usually turn toward the smell of its own mother's pad (MacFarlane, 1978). At 3 weeks of age, an infant given a pacifier that sometimes turns

Babies can tell you a lot—if you know how to ask. To ask, you must capitalize on what the baby can do—gaze, suck, turn the head.

maturation
biological growth processes that enable orderly changes in behavior, relatively uninfluenced by experience.

on recordings of its mother's voice and sometimes that of a female stranger will suck more vigorously when it hears its now-familiar mother's voice (Mills & Melhuish, 1974). Newborns can also learn to turn their heads to the left or right to receive a sugar solution when their forehead is stroked (Lancioni, 1980). So not only can young infants see what they need to see, and smell and hear well, but they are already using their sensory equipment to learn. The "helpless infant" of a generation ago has become today's "amazing newborn."

SUMMING UP

Prenatal Development By studying the human life span from conception to death, developmental psychologists examine how we develop physically, cognitively, and socially. The life cycle begins when one sperm cell, out of the some 200 million ejaculated, unites with an egg to form a zygote. Attached to the uterine wall, the developing embryo begins to form body organs. The X (female) or Y (male) chromosome inherited from the father determines the child's sex. By two months, the fetus becomes recognizably human. Along with nutrients, teratogens ingested by the mother can reach the developing child and place it at risk.

The Competent Newborn With the aid of new methods for studying babies, researchers have discovered that newborns are surprisingly competent. They are born with sensory equipment and reflexes that facilitate their interacting with adults and securing nourishment. For example, they quickly learn to discriminate the smell and sound of their mothers.

KEY TERMS AND CONCEPTS developmental psychology, X chromosome, Y chromosome, testosterone, gender, zygote, embryo, fetus, teratogens, fetal alcohol syndrome (FAS), rooting reflex

Infancy and Childhood

During infancy, a baby grows from newborn to toddler, and during childhood from toddler to teenager. Beginning in this chapter with infancy and childhood and continuing in the next chapter with adolescence through old age, we will see how people of all ages develop—physically, cognitively, and socially.

Physical Development

Infants' biological development enables their psychological development. Experience, too, sculpts the brain's maturing neural networks. The developing brain also fosters developing motor skills.

Brain Development

While you resided in your mother's womb, your body was forming nerve cells at the rate of about one-quarter million per *minute*. On the day you were born, you had essentially all the brain cells you will ever have. However, at birth your nervous system was immature: After birth, the neural networks that enabled you to walk, talk, and remember had a wild growth spurt (Figure 3.4).

As a flower unfolds in accord with its genetic blueprint, so do we experience an orderly sequence of genetically designed biological growth processes called maturation. Maturation decrees many of our commonalities: standing before walking, using nouns before adjectives. Although extreme deprivation or abuse will retard development, the genetic growth tendencies are inborn. Maturation sets the basic course of development and experience adjusts it.

Maturation and Infant Memory

The lack of neural connections helps explain why our earliest memories seldom predate our third birthdays (Howe & Courage, 1993; Nelson, 1993). For example, children who gain a baby brother or sister at age 4 or later will usually recall the event as adults, but not if they were under age 3 when the

Figure **3.4**

Drawings of human cerebral cortex sections
In humans, the brain is immature at birth. As the child matures, the neural networks grow increasingly more complex.

| At birth | 3 months | 15 months |

baby was born. Preschoolers who experienced an emergency fire evacuation caused by a burning popcorn maker were able seven years later to recall the alarm and what caused it—*if* they were 4 to 5 years old at the time. Those who experienced the event as 3-year-olds could not remember the cause and usually misrecalled being already outside when the alarm sounded (Pillemer, 1995).

For parents, this "infantile amnesia," as Freud called it, can be disconcerting. After all the hours we spend with our babies—after all the frolicking on the rug, all the diapering, feeding, and rocking to sleep—what would they consciously remember of us if we died before they reached age 3? Virtually nothing!

But if little is consciously recalled, something has still been gained. Consider:

- Given occasional reminders, 3-month-old infants who learn that moving their leg propels a mobile will remember the association for at least a month (Figure 3.5).

- Eleven-month-olds who observe a researcher making a rattle by putting a button in a box will imitate the action if given the objects a day or even three months later (Mandler & McDonough, 1995).

- At age 2, children will spontaneously bottle-feed a teddy bear *if* they had observed and imitated this play behavior a year earlier (McDonough & Mandler, 1994).

- Shown an out-of-focus picture, 3-year-olds will more quickly recognize it if they saw a clear version of the picture three months earlier—despite having no conscious recall of seeing it before (Drummey & Newcombe, 1995).

Such memories are not of words. They appear rather to be "implicit" memories of images, sounds, and emotions. As with adults, repeated experiences and reminder cues boost recall (Bauer, 1996).

Animals such as guinea pigs, whose brains are mature at birth, more readily form permanent memories in infancy than do animals with immature brains, such as rats (Campbell & Coulter, 1976). These findings cast doubt on the idea that humans, whose brains are also immature at birth, subconsciously remember their prenatal life or the trauma of their birth.

Because of changes after age 5 in how memories are organized, most people also have few memories of their preschool years. Elizabeth Loftus and Leah Kaufman (1992) note that trying to access our preschool memories is like trying to read a diskette that was formatted by an earlier version of a computer operating system. As we will see in Chapter 9 (Memory), researchers have therefore critically evaluated children's recall and testimony regarding alleged traumatic preschool experiences.

Figure 3.5

Infant at work Babies only 3 months old can learn that kicking moves a mobile—and can retain that learning for a month. (From Rovee-Collier, 1989.)

Experience and Brain Development

Experience helps develop the brain's neural connections. Although "forgotten," early learning helps prepare our brains for thought and language, and also for later experiences.

How do early experiences leave their "marks" in the brain? Mark Rosenzweig and David Krech reared some young rats in solitary confinement and others in a communal playground (Figure 3.6). Rats living in the enriched environment usually developed a heavier and thicker brain cortex. Rosenzweig (1984; Renner & Rosenzweig, 1987) reported being so surprised by these effects of experience on brain tissue that he repeated the experiment several times before publishing his findings.

Impoverished environment

Enriched environment

Figure 3.6

Experience affects brain development Mark Rosenzweig and David Krech reared rats either alone in an environment without playthings or with others in an environment enriched with playthings that were changed daily. In 14 of 16 repetitions of this basic experiment, the rats placed in the enriched environment developed significantly more cerebral cortex (relative to the rest of the brain's tissue) than did those in the impoverished environment. An artist illustrates a typical brain cell from a rat reared in each condition. (From "Brain changes in response to experience" by M. R. Rosenzweig, E. L. Bennett, and M. C. Diamond. Copyright © 1972 Scientific American, Inc. All rights reserved.)

The effects are great enough that, shown brief video clips of rats in a novel situation, you could actually identify whether their rearing was impoverished or enriched (Renner & Renner, 1993). Such results have helped encourage improvement in the environments provided for laboratory, farm, and zoo animals—and for children in institutions.

Several research teams have found that infant rats and premature babies benefit from the stimulation of touch or massage (Field & others, 1986; Meaney & others, 1988). "Handled" infants of both species gain weight more rapidly and develop faster neurologically. William Greenough and his University of Illinois colleagues (1987) further discovered that repeated experiences modify a rat's neural tissue—at the very spot in the brain that processes the experience. After brain maturation provides an abundance of neural connections, experience preserves activated connections while allowing unused connections to degenerate. The result by puberty is a massive loss of unemployed connections.

> Throughout life our neural tissue is changing. Sights and smells, touches and tugs activate and strengthen some neural pathways while others weaken from disuse.

Here, then, at the juncture of nurture and nature, is where a child's enriched environment activates and preserves connections that, given impoverished experiences, might have died off from disuse. There is a biological reality to early childhood education. Consider:

- Children from impoverished environments score better on intelligence tests given at age 12, if given stimulating infant care (Ramey & Ramey, 1992).

- During early childhood—while the excess connections are still on call—youngsters can most easily master the grammar and accent of another language. Lacking any exposure to language (written or signed) before adolescence, the person will never master any language (see page 324).

- Lacking visual experience during the early years, people whose vision is restored by cataract removal never achieve normal perceptions (see page 195). The brain cells normally assigned to vision have died or been diverted to other uses.

- String musicians who started playing before age 12 have larger and more complex neuron circuits controlling the note-making left-hand fingers than do string musicians whose training started after age 13 (Elbert & others, 1995).

For optimum brain development, the early years are critical. The maturing brain seems governed by a rule: Use it or lose it.

The brain's development does not, however, end with childhood. Throughout life our neural tissue is changing. Sights and smells, touches and tugs activate and strengthen some neural pathways while others weaken from disuse. Like pathways through a forest, less traveled paths are abandoned, popular paths are broadened. Our genes dictate our overall brain architecture, but experience directs the details. If a monkey is trained to push a lever with a finger several thousand times a day, the brain tissue that controls the finger changes to reflect the experience. Human brains work similarly. The wiring of Eric Clapton's brain reflects the thousands of hours he has spent practicing guitar. Similarly, while learning to keyboard or roller-blade or perform a laboratory task, we perform with increasing skill as our brain incorporates the learning (Figure 3.7). Experience nurtures nature.

Figure 3.7

A trained brain A well-learned finger-tapping task activates more motor cortex neurons (orange area, right) than were active in the same brain before training (left).

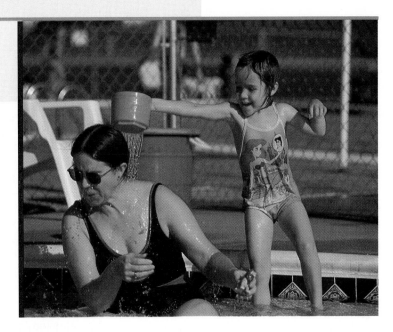

Brain plasticity Believe it or not, this 4-year-old is functioning with only half a brain. Her right hemisphere was surgically removed to eliminate seizures. Now neurons in her left brain have made countless new connections to take over the tasks once performed by her right brain.

Brain Reorganization

Nurture's sculpting of the ever-changing brain is evident in studies of the brain's plasticity. Most severed neurons will not regenerate (if your spinal cord is severed, you are permanently paralyzed). But neural tissue can reorganize in response to damage.

In one experiment, neuroscientists severed the neural pathways for incoming information from a monkey's arm. The area of the sensory cortex that formerly received this input gradually shifted its function and began to respond when researchers touched the animal's face (Pons & others, 1991). Similarly, if a laser beam damages a spot in a cat's eye, the brain area that received input from that spot will soon begin responding to stimulation from nearby areas in the cat's eye. If blind people use one finger to read Braille, the brain area dedicated to that finger expands (Barinaga, 1992a). PET scans also reveal activation of the *visual* cortex when blind people read Braille (Sadato & others, 1996). Among deaf people who communicate with sign language, it is the temporal lobe area normally dedicated to auditory information that waits in vain for stimulation. Finally, it looks for other signals to process, such as those from the visual system.

Thus, the brain may not be as "hard-wired" as once thought. Unlike fixed computer circuits, brain hardware changes with time. In response to changing stimulation, the brain can either rewire itself with new synapses or (according to another theory) select new uses for its prewired circuits (Gazzaniga, 1992). When one brain area is damaged, other areas may in time reorganize and take over some of its functions. If neurons are destroyed,

nearby neurons may partly compensate for the damage by making new connections that replace the lost ones. These new connections are one way the brain struggles to recover from a minor stroke. They are also the brain's way of compensating for the gradual loss of neurons with age.

Our brains are most plastic when we are young children (Kolb, 1989). Children are born with a surplus of neurons. If an injury destroys one part of a child's brain, the brain will compensate by putting other surplus areas to work. Thus, if the speech areas of an infant's left hemisphere are damaged, the right hemisphere will take over much of its language function. After age 5, left hemisphere damage permanently and severely disrupts language.

As an extreme example of plasticity, consider a 5-year-old boy whose severe seizures, caused by a deteriorating left hemisphere, require removing the *entire* hemisphere. What hope for the future would such a child have? Is there any chance he might attend school and lead a normal life, or would he suffer permanent retardation?

Astonishingly, one such individual was at last report an executive. Half his skull is filled with nothing but cerebrospinal fluid—functionally it might as well be sawdust—yet he has scored well above average on intelligence tests, has completed college, and has attended graduate school (Smith & Sugar, 1975; A. Smith, 1987). Although paralyzed on the right side, this man (along with other such cases of "hemispherectomy") testifies to the brain's extraordinary powers of reorganization when damaged before it is fully developed.

plasticity
the brain's capacity for modification, as evident in brain reorganization following damage (especially in children) and in experiments on the effects of experience on brain development.

Triumphant toddlers Roll, crawl, walk, run—the sequence of these motor development milestones is the same the world around, though babies reach them at varying ages.

Motor Development

As the infant's muscles and nervous system mature, more complicated skills emerge. With minor exceptions, the sequence of physical ("motor") development is universal. Babies roll over before they sit unsupported, and they creep on all fours before walking.

But there are individual differences in the timing of this sequence. In the United States, for example, one in four babies walks by age 11 months, half within a week after their first birthday, and 90 percent by age 15 months (Frankenburg & others, 1992). Nurture may influence motor development. Compared with babies who spend much of the day lying in a crib, Ugandan babies, who usually walk by 10 months, experience more intimate and rhythmic physical contact while being carried upright on the back (Bril, 1986).

Although cultural differences could be genetic, experiments reveal that experience does influence motor behavior. Two-week-old babies wave their arms more if they can see them, suggesting that they are learning to visually control their movements (van der Meer & others, 1995). Although 3-month-old infants still cannot efficiently reach and grab something, their seemingly spontaneous kicking movements become more purposeful and coordinated when they activate a mobile (Thelen, 1994, 1995).

But nature (genes) plays a major role, too. Identical twins typically begin sitting up and walking on nearly the same day (Wilson, 1979). Biological maturation—including the rapid development of the cerebellum at the brain's rear—creates a readiness to learn walking at about 1 year of age. Experience before that time has a limited effect. This is true for other physical skills, including bowel and bladder control. Until the necessary muscular and neural maturation occurs, no amount of pleading, harassment, or punishment will produce successful toilet training.

As a child's skills develop rapidly, so does the child's size. After a growth spurt during the first 2 years, children grow a steady 2 to 3 inches per year through childhood. With all the neurons and most of their interconnections in place, brain development after age 2 similarly proceeds at a slower pace. The sensory and motor cortex areas continue to mature, enabling fine motor skills to develop further (Wilson, 1978).

SUMMING UP

Brain Development Within the brain, nerve cells form before birth. Sculpted by experience, their interconnections multiply rapidly after birth. If one hemisphere is damaged early in life, the other will pick up many of its functions, thus demonstrating the brain's plasticity. The brain becomes less plastic later in life. Frequently, however, nearby neurons can partially compensate for damaged ones, as when a person recovers from a stroke or brain injury.

Motor Development Infants' more complex physical skills—sitting, standing, walking—develop in a predictable sequence whose actual timing is a function of individual maturation rate and culture. Childhood—from toddlerhood to the teen years—is a period of slow, steady physical development.

KEY TERMS AND CONCEPTS maturation, plasticity

Cognitive Development

As a newborn, you confronted a sea of sensations and began making sense of them with greater speed and ease than psychologists once believed possible. By 6 months you comprehended permanence, number, and simple physical laws. From these beginnings blossomed your capacity for taking another's perspective, for logic, and for all that defines the mature mind.

The association areas of the cortex—those linked with thinking, memory, and language—are the last brain areas to develop. As they do, the child's mental abilities surge ahead (Chugani & Phelps, 1986; Thatcher & others, 1987). Brain and mind, neural hardware and cognitive software, develop together. Cognition refers to all the mental activities associated with thinking, knowing, remembering, and communicating. Few questions intrigue developmental psychologists more than these concerning cognitive development: When and how do children begin to see things from another's point of view? Reason logically? Think symbolically? Simply put, how does a child's mind grow? Such were the questions posed by developmental psychologist Jean Piaget (pronounced Pee-ah-ZHAY).

Piaget became intrigued by children's wrong answers. Where others saw childish mistakes, Piaget saw intelligence at work.

"Who knows the thoughts of a child?" wondered poet Nora Perry. As much as anyone of his generation, Piaget knew. His interest began in 1920, when he was working in Paris to develop questions for children's intelligence tests. While administering tests to find out at what age children could answer certain questions correctly, Piaget became intrigued by children's *wrong* answers. Where others saw childish mistakes, Piaget saw intelligence at work. The errors made by children of a given age, he noted, were often strikingly similar.

The half century Piaget spent with children convinced him that the child's mind is not a miniature model of the adult's. Young children understand the world in radically different ways than adults do, a fact that we sometimes overlook when teaching children. Piaget was not the first to say this. The philosopher Jean Jacques Rosseau (1798) be-

lieved that "childhood has its own way of seeing, thinking, and feeling, and there is nothing more foolish than the attempt to put ours in its place." Just as Copernicus revolutionized our understanding of the solar system, Piaget revolutionized our understandings of children's minds, suggests William Damon (1995). Until Piaget, most people—forgetting their own preschool days—assumed children "simply knew less, not *differently*, than adults" (p. 100). Thanks partly to Piaget, we now understand that "children reason in wildly illogical ways about problems whose solutions are self-evident to adults" (Brainerd, 1996).

Piaget further believed that the child's mind develops through a series of stages, in an upward march from the newborn's simple reflexes to the adult's abstract reasoning power. An 8-year-old child therefore comprehends things that a 3-year-old cannot. An 8-year-old might grasp the analogy "getting an idea is like having a light turn on in your head," but trying to teach the same analogy to a 3-year-old would be fruitless.

How the Mind of a Child Grows

The driving force behind this intellectual progression is our unceasing struggle to make sense of our experience. Piaget's core idea is that "children are active thinkers, constantly trying to construct more advanced understandings of the world" (Siegler & Ellis, 1996). To this end, the maturing brain builds concepts, which Piaget called schemas. Schemas (or schemes) are mental molds into which we pour our experience. By adulthood we have built countless schemas that range from knowing how to tie a knot to our concept of love.

Piaget proposed two concepts to explain how we use and adjust our schemas. First, we interpret our experience in terms of our current understandings. In Piaget's terms, we use our schemas to incorporate, or assimilate, new experiences. Given a simple schema for *dog*, a toddler may call all four-legged animals *doggies*. But we also adjust, or accommodate, our schemas to fit the particulars of new experiences. The child soon learns that the

cognition
all the mental activities associated with thinking, knowing, and remembering.

schema
a concept or framework that organizes and interprets information.

assimilation
interpreting one's new experience in terms of one's existing schemas.

accommodation
adapting one's current understandings (schemas) to incorporate new information.

An impossible object Look carefully at the "devil's tuning fork" above. Now look away—no, better first study it some more—and then look away and draw it. . . . Not so easy, is it? Because this tuning fork is an impossible object, you have no schema into which you can assimilate what you see.

Two-year-old Gabriella has learned the schema for "cow" from her picture books.

Gabriella sees a moose and calls it a "cow." She is trying to assimilate this new animal into an existing schema. Her mother tells her, "No, it's a moose."

Gabriella accommodates her schema for large, shaggy animals and continues to modify that schema to include "mommy moose," "baby moose," etc.

Pouring experience into mental molds   We use our existing schemas to assimilate new experiences. But sometimes we need to accommodate (adjust) our schemas to include new experiences.

original *doggie* schema is too broad and accommodates by refining the category. As children interact with the world, they construct and modify their understandings.

Piaget's Theory and Current Thinking on Cognitive Stages

Piaget described cognitive development as occurring in four stages—sensorimotor, preoperational, concrete operational, and formal operational (Table 3.1). Developing children, he believed, experience spurts of change followed by greater stability as they move from one developmental plateau to the next. Each plateau has distinctive characteristics that permit specific kinds of thinking. To appreciate how the mind of a child grows, let's look at each of Piaget's stages in light of current thinking about cognitive development.

[handwritten: BY 1 YEAR THE DON'T DO THE AB ERROR]

lives in the present. What is out of sight is out of mind. By 8 months, infants begin to exhibit memory for things no longer seen. Hide the toy and the infant will momentarily look for it. Within another month or two, the infant will look for it even after being restrained for several seconds.

But today's researchers wonder: Do children's cognitive abilities really grow through distinct stages? Does object permanence in fact blossom by 8 months, much as a tulip blossoms in spring?

Jean Piaget   "If we examine the intellectual development of the individual or of the whole of humanity, we shall find that the human spirit goes through a certain number of stages, each different from the other" (1930).

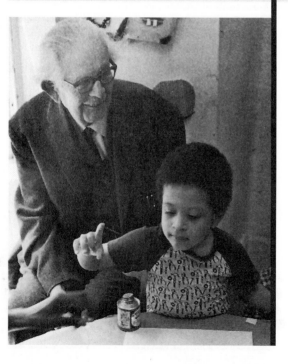

The infant lives in the present. What is out of sight is out of mind.

Sensorimotor Stage

During the sensorimotor stage, from birth to nearly age 2, babies understand the world through their sensory and motor interactions with objects— through looking, touching, mouthing, and grasping. At first they seem unaware that things continue to exist apart from their perceptions.

In one of his tests, Piaget would show an infant an appealing toy and then flop his beret over it to see whether the infant searched for the toy. Before the age of 6 months, they did not. They lacked object permanence—the awareness that objects continue to exist when not perceived. The infant

sensorimotor stage
in Piaget's theory, the stage (from birth to about 2 years of age) during which infants know the world mostly in terms of their sensory impressions and motor activities.

object permanence
the awareness that things continue to exist even when not perceived.

Piaget's Stages of Cognitive Development

Table **3.1**

Typical Age Range	Description of Stage	Developmental Phenomena
Birth to nearly 2 years	*Sensorimotor* Experiencing the world through senses and actions (looking, touching, mouthing)	• Object permanence • Stranger anxiety
About 2 to 6 years	*Preoperational* Representing things with words and images but lacking logical reasoning	• Pretend play • Egocentrism • Language development
About 7 to 11 years	*Concrete operational* Thinking logically about concrete events; grasping concrete analogies and performing arithmetical operations	• Conservation • Mathematical transformations
About 12 through adulthood	*Formal operational* Abstract reasoning	• Abstract logic • Potential for mature moral reasoning

Figure **3.8**

Today's researchers see development as more continuous than did Piaget. For example, they now view object permanence as unfolding gradually, beginning with young infants' looking for a toy where they saw it hidden a second before.

Researchers believe that Piaget and his followers underestimated young children's competence. Before age 2, Piaget assumed, infants cannot think. They can recognize things, smile at them, crawl to them, manipulate them. But they have no abstract concepts or ideas. Theirs is a life not thought about, only lived.

Consider, however, some simple experiments:

• Andrew Meltzoff and Richard Borton gave 1-month-old babies one of two pacifiers to suck on without letting them see the objects (Figure 3.8). When later shown both pacifiers, the infants *looked* mostly at the

nipple they had *felt* in their mouth. Follow-up studies revealed the same amazing result with infants as young as 12 hours old (Kaye & Bower, 1994).

• Infants look longer when viewing an unexpected scene of a car seeming to pass through a solid object or a ball stopping in midair (Bailargeon, 1992, 1994; Wellman & Gelman, 1992).

Infants can think   After sucking on one of these two pacifiers, babies looked longer at the nipple they had felt in their mouth. (From Meltzoff & Borton, 1979.)

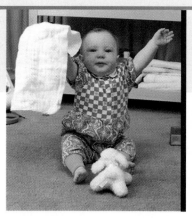

Object permanence   Infants younger than 6 months do not understand that things continue to exist when they are out of sight. But for this infant, out of sight is definitely not out of mind.

THINKING CRITICALLY ABOUT

Infants' Thinking

Can a newborn see well enough to distinguish shapes? Can a 3-month-old recognize faces? Does a 5-month-old have a concept of number? If only babies could talk, we would ask them.

Might there nevertheless be ways to ask such questions without words? Psychology, the science of behavior and mental processes, often lets behavior do the talking. Developmental researchers, for example, exploit a simple form of learning called habituation—decreasing responsiveness with repeated stimulation. A novel stimulus gets attention when first presented. But the more it is presented, the weaker the response becomes. This seeming boredom with familiar stimuli provides a way to assess what infants see and remember.

Alan Slater and his University of Exeter colleagues (1988) illustrated the strategy when they asked newborns as young as 7 hours old what they could see. When first shown a stimulus like the one within Figure 3.9, the newborns gazed intently for an average 41 seconds. With repeated presentations, their interest soon waned.

What if the figure were rotated 90° to a new position? Could the infants remember the initial stimulus and perceive it as different from the new one? As Figure 3.10 indicates, they could indeed. Shown a stimulus with lines oriented as already seen, plus another stimulus with the novel, rotated orientation, the infants looked three times longer at the new one. Their behavior indicated they could remember and discriminate between differing visual stimuli. Using the habituation phenomenon, other researchers report that infants can also discriminate colors, shapes, and sounds and can understand some basic concepts of numbers and physics (for example, that two solid objects cannot occupy the same space). In all these studies, researchers assume that infants' greater attention to some stimuli reveals their ability to distinguish different stimuli.

Given the elegant simplicity of such studies, why have they been done only recently? Researcher Slater (1994) explains: To recognize a new stimulus as different, an infant must remember the initial stimulus. Until the early 1980s, researchers assumed a newborn's brain was too immature to enable such memory. Thus, they never tested for habituation. Then, as appreciation for the newborn's abilities began to grow, investigators created new ways to test the scope of their cognition.

Figure **3.9**

Habituation Newborns become bored with (look less at) a repeatedly presented visual stimulus. (Data from Slater & others, 1988.)

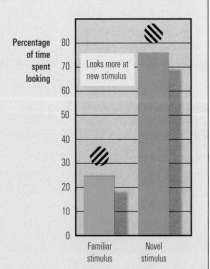

Figure **3.10**

Novelty preference Having habituated to the old stimulus, newborns preferred gazing at a new one. Their renewed attention to a slightly different stimulus reveals their visual ability. (Data from Slater & others, 1988.)

habituation

decreasing responsiveness with repeated stimulation. As infants gain familiarity with repeated exposure to a visual stimulus, their interest wanes and they look away sooner.

Figure **3.11**

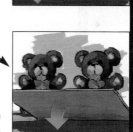

4. Possible outcome: Screen drops, revealing one object.

1. Objects placed in case. 2. Screen comes up. 3. One object is removed.

4. Impossible outcome: Screen drops, revealing two objects.

Baby mathematics Shown a numerically impossible outcome, infants stare longer. (From Wynn, 1992.)

- Babies exhibit not only an intuitive grasp of simple laws of physics, they also comprehend number. Karen Wynn (1992, 1995) showed 5-month-old infants one or two objects; then she hid the objects behind a screen, sometimes removing or adding one through a trap door (Figure 3.11). When she lifted the screen, the infants sometimes did a double take, staring longer when shown a wrong number of objects.

Clearly, infants comprehend more than Piaget realized.

Piaget's test of conservation This preoperational child does not yet understand the principle of conservation of substance. Closed beakers with identical volumes seem suddenly to hold different amounts after one is merely inverted.

Preoperational Stage

Piaget believed that during the preschool period and up to about age 6 or 7, children are in a preoperational stage—too young to perform mental operations. For a 5-year-old, the quantity of milk that is "too much" in a tall, narrow glass may become an acceptable amount if poured into a short, wide glass. This is because the child focuses only on the height dimension and is incapable of performing the *operation* of mentally pouring it back. The child lacks the concept of conservation—the principle that quantity remains the same despite changes in shape.

Although Piaget did not view the stage transitions as abrupt, the rudiments of conservation appear at an earlier age than he supposed. If questioned in a way that makes sense to them, 5- and 6-year-olds will exhibit some understanding of conservation (Donaldson, 1979). And earlier than Piaget realized, preoperational children are capable of thinking symbolically. Judy DeLoache (1987) discovered this when she showed a group of 2½-year-olds a model of a room and hid a model toy in it (say, a miniature stuffed dog behind a miniature couch). The children could easily remember where to find the miniature toy. But they could not readily use that model to locate an actual stuffed dog behind a couch in a real room. Only 6 months older, 3-year-olds usually went right to the actual stuffed animal in the real room, showing that they *could* think of the model as a symbol for the room.

Seen through the eyes of Piaget, preschool children are still unable to reason and to take another's point of view. Although aware of themselves, of time, and of the permanence of objects, they are, he said, egocentric: They cannot perceive things from another's point of view. Asked to "show Mommy your picture," 2-year-old Gabriella holds

Question: If most 2½-year-olds do not understand how miniature dolls and toys can symbolize real objects, should anatomically correct dolls be used when questioning such children about alleged physical or sexual abuse? Judy DeLoache (1995) reports that "very young children do not find it natural or easy to use a doll as a representation of themselves."

preoperational stage in Piaget's theory, the stage (from about 2 to 6 or 7 years of age) during which a child learns to use language but does not yet comprehend the mental operations of concrete logic.

conservation the principle (which Piaget believed to be a part of concrete operational reasoning) that properties such as mass, volume, and number remain the same despite changes in the forms of objects.

egocentrism in Piaget's theory, the inability of the preoperational child to take another's point of view.

the picture up facing her own eyes. Three-year-old Rebecca hides under a table, assuming that if she can't see someone's eyes they can't see her. Children's conversations also reveal their egocentrism, as one young boy demonstrated (Phillips, 1969, p. 61): *"Do you have a brother?" "Yes." "What's his name?" "Jim." "Does Jim have a brother?" "No."*

Preschool TV-watchers who block your view of the television assume that you see what they see. Preschoolers who ask a question while you are on the phone assume that you hear no more than they hear. When relating to a young child, remember that such behaviors reflect a cognitive limitation: The egocentric preschooler is not intentionally "selfish" or "inconsiderate" but rather has difficulty taking another's viewpoint.

Preschoolers also find it easier to follow positive instructions ("Hold the puppy gently") than negative ones ("Don't squeeze the puppy"). Parents who abuse their children generally have no understanding of these limits. They see their children as junior adults who are in control of their behavior (Larrance & Twentyman, 1983). Thus, they perceive children who stand in the way, spill food, disobey negative instructions, or cry as willfully malicious.

Private speech A badger starring in a series of children's books sings to herself—in this case, to help her cope with the jealousy she feels toward her younger sister, who is soon to celebrate a birthday.

Everybody makes a fuss
for birthday girls who are not us
Girls who take your pail away
Eat cake and q-p-m all day

Although Piaget's concept of egocentrism is important, preschoolers are not purely egocentric. Given very simple tasks, 4-year-olds will adjust their explanations to make them clearer to a blindfolded listener and will show a toy or picture with the front side facing the viewer (Gelman, 1979; Siegel & Hodkin, 1982). Preschoolers also acquire a "theory of mind." They seek to understand what made a playmate angry, when a sibling will share, and what might make a parent buy a toy. This growing ability to take another's perspective enables the preschooler's growing ability to tease, empathize, and persuade.

Between ages 3 and 5, for example, children come to realize that others may hold false beliefs. University of Toronto researchers Jennifer Jenkins and Janet Astington (1996) showed children a Band Aids (plasters) box and asked them what was inside. The children naturally expected Band Aids, and so they were surprised when they discovered that the box actually contained pencils. Asked what another child who had never seen the box would think was inside, 3-year-olds typically answered "pencils." By age 4 to 5, children's theory of mind had leapt forward, and they delighted in anticipating their friends' false belief that the box would hold Band Aids.

Even as adults, we never completely lose our early egocentrism. Once we know a problem's solution, we instantly find it difficult to appreciate how hard the problem may be for others. We also have a curious tendency to overestimate others' agreement with our opinions—a phenomenon that social psychologists call "the false consensus effect" (see page 19). And we imagine that others notice us more than they do. Thomas Gilovich (1996) demonstrated this "spotlight effect" by having individual Cornell University students don Barry Manilow T-shirts before entering a room with other students. Feeling self-conscious, the T-shirt wearers guessed that nearly half of their peers would take note of the shirt as they walked in. In reality, only 23 percent did. So, next time you have a bad hair day, relax. Fewer people notice than you imagine.

The abilities to perform mental operations, to think symbolically, and to take another's perspective are not absent in the preoperational stage—and then present at some later time. Rather, these abilities begin early and develop gradually.

By age 7, noted the Russian psychologist Lev Vygotsky (1896–1934), children also stop thinking aloud and instead rely on inner speech. By internalizing their culture's language, children become more capable of verbal thinking and of using it to work out solutions to problems. Second-graders who mutter to themselves while doing math problems grasp third-grade math better the following year (Berk, 1994). Whether out loud or inaudible, talking to themselves helps children control their behavior and emotions and master new skills. "I think I can, I think I can," says *The Little Engine That Could*, illustrating the commonality of private speech in children's literature.

Concrete Operational Stage

By about 6 or 7 years of age, said Piaget, children enter the concrete operational stage. Given concrete materials, they begin to grasp that a given quantity remains the same no matter how its shape changes. Children can mentally pour the milk back and forth between different-shaped glasses. They realize that change in shape does not mean change in quantity. They also enjoy jokes that allow them to use their new concepts, such as conservation:

> Mr. Jones went into a restaurant and ordered a whole pizza for his dinner. When the waiter asked if he wanted it cut into 6 or 8 pieces, Mr. Jones said, "Oh, you'd better make it 6, I could never eat 8 pieces!" (McGhee, 1976)

During the concrete operational stage, said Piaget, children fully gain the mental ability to comprehend mathematical transformations and conservation. When my daughter Laura was 6, I was astonished at her inability to reverse arithmetic operations—until considering Piaget. Asked, "What is eight plus four?" she required 5 seconds to compute "twelve," and another 5 seconds to then compute twelve minus four. By age 8, she could reverse the process and answer the second question instantly.

If Piaget was correct—if children construct their understandings and think differently than adults do—what are the implications for parents and teachers? Piaget contended that learning grows from children's *interactions* with the world. Thus, children are not passive receptacles waiting to be filled with a teacher's knowledge. Building on what children already know, teachers should engage children in concrete demonstrations and stimulate them to think for themselves. Future parents and teachers, remember: Young children are incapable of adult logic. Understand how children think. Realize that what is simple and obvious to you—that, say, subtraction is the reverse of addition—may be incomprehensible to a 6-year-old. Accept children's cognitive immaturity as adaptive—as nature's strategy for keeping children close to protective adults and providing time for learning and socialization (Bjorklund & Green, 1992).

Formal Operational Stage

By age 12, reasoning expands from the purely concrete (involving actual experience) to encompass abstract thinking (involving imagined realities and symbols). As they approach adolescence, said Piaget, many children become capable of solving hypothetical propositions and deducing consequences: *If* this, *then* that. Systematic reasoning, which Piaget called formal operational thinking, is now within their grasp.

But are younger children incapable of abstract logic? Consider this simple problem:

> If John is in school, then Mary is in school. John is in school. What can you say about Mary?

Many 7-year-olds have no trouble answering correctly (Suppes, 1982). This illustrates why, once again, critics say the rudiments of Piaget's cognitive stages begin earlier than he realized.

Reflections on Piaget's Theory

Piaget's stage theory is controversial. In some ways it gets high marks. Studies around the globe, from aboriginal Australia to Algeria to North America, reveal that human cognition everywhere unfolds basically in the sequence he proposed (Segall & others, 1990). Today's researchers do, however, see development as more continuous than did Piaget. By detecting the beginnings of each type of thinking at earlier ages, they have revealed conceptual abilities that Piaget missed. Moreover, they see formal logic as a smaller part of cognition than did Piaget.

concrete operational stage
in Piaget's theory, the stage of cognitive development (from about 6 or 7 to 11 years of age) during which children gain the mental operations that enable them to think logically about concrete events.

formal operational stage
in Piaget's theory, the stage of cognitive development (normally beginning about age 12) during which people begin to think logically about abstract concepts.

For more information on formal operational reasoning, see Chapter 4, Adolescence and Adulthood.

Dennis the Menace

"Cut it up into a LOT of slices, Mom. I'm really hungry!"

What remains of Piaget's ideas about the child's mind? Plenty. "Assessing the impact of Piaget on developmental psychology is like assessing the impact of Shakespeare in English literature," mused Harry Beilin (1992). Piaget identified important cognitive milestones and stimulated interest in how the mind develops. What Piaget emphasized was less the ages at which children typically reach specific milestones than their sequence—which is pretty much as he described (Lourenco & Machado, 1996). He would not be surprised that today we are adapting his ideas to accommodate new findings—as part of our own cognitive development.

SUMMING UP

Jean Piaget's observations of children convinced him—and almost everyone else—that the mind of the child is not that of a miniature adult. Piaget theorized that the mind develops by forming schemas that help us assimilate our experiences and that must occasionally be altered to accommodate new information. In this way, children progress from the sensorimotor simplicity of the infant to more complex stages of thinking. For example, by about 8 months, an infant becomes aware that things still exist even when out of sight.

Piaget believed that preschool children, in the preoperational stage, are egocentric and unable to perform simple logical operations. However, he thought that at about age 6 or 7 children enter the concrete operational stage, in which they become capable of performing concrete operations, such as those required to comprehend the principle of conservation. Finally, at about age 12, children enter the formal operational stage, in which systematic reasoning is within their grasp.

Recent research indicates that human cognition, regardless of culture, tends to unfold basically in the sequence Piaget proposed. Young children are more capable, and development more continuous, than Piaget believed, however. The cognitive abilities that emerge at each stage apparently begin developing in a rudimentary form in the previous stage.

KEY TERMS AND CONCEPTS cognition, schema, assimilation, accommodation, sensorimotor stage, object permanence, habituation, preoperational stage, conservation, egocentrism, concrete operational stage, formal operational stage

stranger anxiety
the fear of strangers that infants commonly display, beginning by about 8 months of age.

attachment
an emotional tie with another person; shown in young children by their seeking closeness to the caregiver and showing distress on separation.

Social Development

A human is, as Aristotle said, "a social animal," destined to live in close relationship with important others. How, then, do the bonds of attachment form? What happens when they form securely, or when they are missing or broken? And how do parents and culture influence a child's self-concept?

Babies are social creatures from birth. Almost from the start, parent and baby communicate through eye contact, touch, smiles, and voice. Even when interacting over life-size, closed-circuit TV, 9-week-old babies and their mothers have a comfortable synchrony. But if the tape of the mother is rewound and replayed, so that the same mother no longer responds to her child's actions, the baby turns away and fidgets. When real-time interaction resumes, the child cheers up again (Murray & Trevarthen, 1986). Parent-child interactions promote infants' survival and their emerging sense of self, so that they, too, eventually may bear and nurture a new generation.

Interactions shape us in ways understood by the Russian psychologist Lev Vygotsky, whose sociocultural theory influences many Western developmentalists. According to Vygotsky, parents and other teachers transmit to every child whatever skills, values, and perspectives that society needs. The skill might be, in an Alaska Native village, knowing how to catch and store salmon. Depending on the culture, the value might be modest self-effacement or brash self-assurance. The perspective might be that women are inferior, superior, or equal to men. From earliest infancy, the social context that surrounds us provides many of our thoughts, beliefs, and behaviors.

In all cultures, infants develop an intense bond with those who care for them. Beginning with newborns' attraction to humans in general, infants soon come to prefer familiar faces and voices and then to coo and gurgle when given their mother's or father's attention. Soon after object permanence emerges and children become mobile enough to crawl into danger, a curious thing happens: They develop a fear of strangers, called stranger anxiety. Watch how infants of different ages react when handed over to a stranger. Beginning at 8 or 9 months, they often will cry and reach for their familiar caregivers. After about 8 months of age, children have schemas for familiar faces; when they can't assimilate an approaching new face into these remembered schemas, they become distressed (Kagan, 1984). This illustrates an important principle: The brain, the mind, and social-emotional behavior develop together.

At 12 months, many infants cling tightly to a parent when frightened or expecting separation. Reunited, they shower the parent with smiles and hugs. No social behavior is more striking than this intense and mutual infant-parent bond, called attachment—a powerful survival impulse that keeps infants close to their caregivers.

Origins of Attachment

A number of elements work to create the parent-infant bond. Infants become attached to those—typically their parents—who are comfortable, familiar, and responsive to their needs.

Body Contact

For many years, developmental psychologists reasoned that infants became attached to those who satisfied their need for nourishment. It made perfect sense. But an accidental finding revealed that this explanation is incomplete. During the 1950s, University of Wisconsin psychologist Harry Harlow bred monkeys for his learning studies. To equalize the infant monkeys' experiences and to prevent the spread of disease, he separated the monkeys from their mothers shortly after birth and raised them in sanitary, individual cages, which included a cheesecloth baby blanket (Harlow & others, 1971). Surprisingly, the infants became intensely attached to their blankets: When the blankets were taken to be laundered, the monkeys became distressed.

Harlow soon recognized that this attachment to the blanket contradicted the idea that attachment derives from the association with nourishment. But could he show this more convincingly? To pit the drawing power of a food source against the contact comfort of the blanket, Harlow created two artificial mothers. One was a bare wire cylinder with a wooden head, the other a cylinder wrapped with terry cloth. He could associate either with nourishment by attaching a bottle.

When reared with both a nourishing wire mother and a nonnourishing cloth mother, the monkeys overwhelmingly preferred the cloth mother (Figure 3.12). Like human infants clinging to their mothers, the monkeys would cling to their cloth mothers when anxious. They also used her as a secure base from which to venture into the environment, as if attached to the mother by an invisible elastic band that stretches so far and then pulls the infant back. Further studies revealed that other qualities—rocking, warmth, and feeding—could make the cloth mother even more appealing.

Stranger anxiety A newly emerging ability to evaluate people as unfamiliar and possibly threatening helps protect babies during the second six months of life.

Human infants, too, become attached to parents who are soft and warm and who rock, feed, and pat. All this should reassure the fathers of breastfed infants: Attachment does not depend on feeding alone.

Moreover, for humans, too, attachment consists of one person providing another with a *secure base* from which to explore the world and a *safe haven* in times of stress. As we mature, our attachments change. Our secure base and safe haven shift from parents to peers and partners. But at all ages we are

Figure **3.12**

Harlow's mothers Psychologist Harry Harlow reared monkeys with two artificial mothers—one a bare wire cylinder with a wooden head and an attached feeding bottle, the other a cylinder with no bottle but covered with foam rubber and wrapped with terry cloth. Harlow's discovery surprised many psychologists: The monkeys much preferred contact with the comfortable cloth mother, even while feeding from the nourishing mother.

critical period
an optimal period shortly after birth when an organism's exposure to certain stimuli or experiences produces proper development.

imprinting
the process by which certain animals form attachments during a critical period very early in life.

temperament
a person's characteristic emotional reactivity and intensity.

Lee Kirkpatrick (1994) reports that for some people a perceived relationship with God functions as do other attachments—by providing a secure base for exploration and a safe haven when threatened.

THE FAR SIDE

When imprinting studies go awry . . .

"The Far Side" cartoon is reprinted by permission of Chronicle Features, San Francisco.

social creatures. We gain strength when someone says to us, by words and actions, "I am here. I will be here. I am interested in what you do and what you think and feel. I will actively support you" (Crowell & Waters, 1994). We are "happiest and able to deploy [our] talents to best advantage," said attachment researcher John Bowlby (1979), when we know that one or more trusted friends will stand behind us, come what may.

Familiarity

Another key to attachment is familiarity. As we noted earlier, nature opens windows of opportunity for wiring the brain for vision or language, then slams them shut. In many animals, attachments based on familiarity likewise form during a sensitive, critical period—an optimal period shortly after birth when certain events must take place if proper development is to occur (Bornstein, 1989). The first moving object a gosling, duckling, or chick sees during the hours shortly after hatching is normally its mother. Thereafter the young fowl follows her, and her alone.

Konrad Lorenz (1937) explored this rigid attachment process, called imprinting. He wondered what ducklings would do if *he* was the first moving creature they observed. What they did was follow him around: Everywhere that Konrad went, the ducks were sure to go. Further tests revealed that although baby birds imprint best to their own species, they also will imprint to a variety of moving objects—an animal of another species, a box on wheels, a bouncing ball (Colombo, 1982; Johnson, 1992). Once formed, this attachment is difficult to reverse.

Proponents of a critical "bonding" period argue that for humans, too, contact during the first hours after birth boosts parent-infant attachment (Kennell & Klaus, 1982). Believing this, many hospitals now have "bonding rooms" where staff members seek to ensure that bonding occurs before mother and infant leave. Is this very early contact essential? If so, are adoptive parents, and mothers who have had cesarean deliveries, poorly bonded with their children?

Developmental psychologists are unconvinced (Eyer, 1992). Human infants do prefer familiar faces and objects, but they *don't* have a precise critical period for becoming attached. Although

psychologists welcome the trend toward humanizing childbirth, parents who miss their child's birth needn't feel deficient. Attachment in humans develops more gradually, allowing plenty of time for parents and their infants to come to know and love each other. Maternity ward cuddling is but a small beginning.

Although children—unlike ducklings—do not imprint, they do become attached to what they've known. "Mere exposure" to people and things fosters fondness (see page 580). Thus, children like to reread the same books, rewatch the same movies, reenact the same family traditions. They prefer to eat familiar foods, live in the same familiar neighborhood, attend school with the same old friends. Familiarity breeds content.

Temperament

In studies the world over, some babies seem more disposed to forming a secure attachment. Placed in a strange situation (usually a laboratory playroom), about 60 percent of infants show *secure attachment*. In their mother's presence they play comfortably, happily exploring their new environment. When she leaves, they are distressed; when she returns, they seek contact with her. Other infants show *insecure attachment*. They are less likely to explore their surroundings and may even cling to their mother. When she leaves, they either cry loudly and remain upset or seem indifferent to their mother's going and returning (Ainsworth, 1973, 1989; Kagan, 1995; van IJzendoorn & Kroonenberg, 1988). What accounts for these differences?

Might the infants' differing behavior patterns be inborn? An infant's temperament includes the inborn rudiments of personality, especially the child's emotional excitability—whether reactive, intense, and fidgety or easygoing, quiet, and placid. From the first weeks of life, "difficult" babies are more irritable, intense, and unpredictable. "Easy" babies are cheerful, relaxed, and predictable in feeding and sleeping (Chess & Thomas, 1987).

Temperament endures. Consider these findings:

- The most emotionally reactive newborns tend also to be the most reactive 9-month-olds (Wilson & Matheny, 1986; Worobey & Blajda, 1989).

- Four-month-olds who react to changing scenes with arched back, pumping legs, and crying are usually fearful and inhibited in their second year. Those who react with relaxed smiles are usually fearless and sociable in their second year (Kagan, 1990).

- Exceptionally inhibited and fearful 2-year-olds often are still relatively shy as 8-year-olds; about half will become introverted adolescents (Kagan & others, 1992, 1994).

. . . nature opens windows of opportunity for wiring the brain for vision or language, then slams them shut.

- The most emotionally intense preschoolers tend to be relatively intense as young adults (Larsen & Diener, 1987).

In one study that is following more than 900 New Zealanders through time, emotionally reactive and impulsive 3-year-olds developed into somewhat more impulsive, aggressive, and conflict-prone 21-year-olds (Newman & others, 1997). Inhibited 3-year-olds, 18 years later, still tended to be more cautious and unassertive. With age, many shy, inhibited infants relax, but few fearless, spontaneous infants become shy.

Infant monkeys also vary in temperament. Some are timid and fearful, others more relaxed. When researcher Stephen Suomi (1987) placed infant monkeys who were genetically predisposed to be "uptight" or "easygoing" with foster mothers who were themselves uptight or easygoing, heredity overrode rearing. Compared with the easygoing monkeys, the uptight monkeys reacted more anxiously to the stress of separation from the mother, even when they were being raised by easygoing, nurturant foster mothers.

Heredity seems to predispose human differences, too. Physiological tests reveal that anxious, high-strung human infants have high and variable heart rates and a reactive nervous system (Kagan & others, 1992). They become more physiologically aroused when facing new or strange situations. Compared to nonidentical twins, twins who share identical genes are more likely to have similar temperaments (Emde & others, 1992; Gabbay, 1992; Robinson & others, 1992).

Genetic influences also seem to help explain why several studies find newborn and infant Asian infants calmer, more placid, and less reactive than Caucasian infants. That should not stun us, say Jerome Kagan and his colleagues (1994), because Europeans and Asians were "reproductively isolated for about 30,000 years, or about 1500 generations." In animal experiments, one can selectively breed obvious trait differences after "only 15 to 20 generations." There's a practical moral here, says Kagan (1995): We "should not automatically assume that every anxious child had an insensitive parent but should entertain the possibility that temperament" also makes the child.

Responsive Parenting

But there is more to infant attachment differences than inherited temperament. Another possible influence on attachment is the mother's behavior. Mary Ainsworth (1979) observed mother-infant pairs at home during their first 6 months and then later observed the 1-year-old infants in a strange

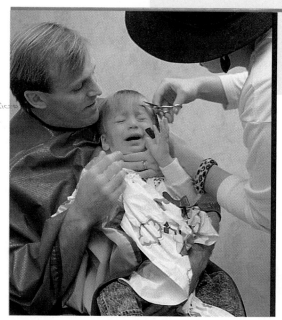

Temperament   Some babies are predisposed to be emotionally reactive, others to react calmly. Caregiving that is responsive to a child's needs usually enables the parent and child to form a secure bond.

situation without their mothers. Sensitive, responsive mothers—mothers who noticed what their babies were doing and who responded appropriately—had infants who usually became securely attached. Insensitive, unresponsive mothers—mothers who attended to their babies when they felt like doing so but ignored them at other times—had infants who often became insecurely attached. Harlow's monkey studies, in which the artificial mothers were the ultimate in unresponsiveness, produced even more striking effects. When put in strange situations without their artificial mothers, the deprived infants were more than distressed—they were terrified (Figure 3.13).

To see whether human infants' attachments are also a product of parenting and not just of biologically disposed temperaments, Dutch researcher Dymphna van den Boom (1990) varied parenting while controlling temperament. (Pause and think: If you were the researcher, how might you have done this?)

Figure **3.13**

Social deprivation and fear
Monkeys raised by artificial mothers were terror-stricken when placed in strange situations without their surrogate mothers. (Today's climate of greater respect for animal welfare precludes such primate studies.)

basic trust according to Erik Erikson, a sense that the world is predictable and trustworthy; said to be formed during infancy by appropriate experiences with responsive caregivers.

Van den Boom's solution was to randomly assign one hundred 6- to 9-month-old temperamentally difficult infants to either an experimental condition, in which mothers received personal training in sensitive responding, or to an untreated control condition. At age 1, 68 percent of the experimental condition infants were rated securely attached, as were only 28 percent of the control condition infants.

With time, children become familiar with a wider range of situations and communicate with strangers more freely as the attachments of early childhood eventually relax. Whether children are raised entirely at home or also in a day care center, whether they live in North America, Guatemala, or the Kalahari Desert, anxiety over separation from parents peaks at around 13 months and then gradually declines (Kagan, 1976). (See Figure 3.14.)

Figure 3.14

Infants' distress over separation from parents In an experiment, groups of infants who had and had not experienced day care were left by their mothers in an unfamiliar room. In both groups, the percentage who cried when the mother left peaked at about 13 months. (From Kagan, 1976.)

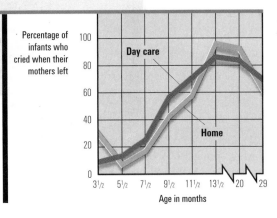

Does this mean that our need for and love of others also fades away? Hardly. In other ways our capacity for love grows, and our pleasure in touching and holding those we love never ceases. The power of early attachment nonetheless gradually relaxes, allowing children to move out into the world. One might even say that much of the life cycle story boils down to a poignant rhythm of attachment and separation—from the attachment of fetal life to the separation of birth, from infant attachment to adolescent separation, from the attachments of marriage and parenthood to the separation of death.

Effects of Attachment

Does a trusting, secure attachment have lasting benefits? And does the quality of an infant's attachment predict the child's social competence in the years that follow?

Secure Attachment Predicts Social Competence

At the University of Minnesota, Alan Sroufe and his colleagues (1983) identified infants who were securely attached at 12 to 18 months of age—those who used their mother as a base for comfortably exploring the world and as a haven when distressed. When Sroufe restudied these infants as 2- to 3-year-olds, he saw them functioning more confidently than other toddlers. Given challenging tasks, they were more enthusiastic and persistent. With other children they were more outgoing and responsive.

Developmental theorist Erik Erikson (1902–1994) said that securely attached children approach life with a sense of basic trust—a sense that the world is predictable and reliable. Erikson attributed basic trust not to one's continuing positive environment or inborn temperament, but to early parenting. He theorized that infants blessed with sensitive, loving caregivers form a lifelong attitude of trust rather than fear. Erikson would not have been surprised that as adults, our romantic love styles exhibit either secure, trusting attachment; insecure, anxious attachment; or the avoidance of attachment (Feeney & Noller, 1990; Shaver & Hazan, 1993; Simpson & others, 1992). Our early attachment styles, it seems, form a foundation for our future relationships. "What is learned in the cradle," says a French proverb, "lasts to the grave."

> *"Out of the conflict between trust and mistrust, the infant develops hope, which is the earliest form of what gradually becomes faith in adults."*
>
> **ERIK ERIKSON (1983)**

Deprivation of Attachment

If secure attachment nurtures social competence, what happens when circumstances prevent children from forming attachments? In all of psychology, no research literature is more saddening. Babies reared in institutions without the stimulation and attention of a regular caregiver, or locked away at home under conditions of abuse or extreme neglect, are often withdrawn, frightened, even speechless. Those who were abandoned in Romanian orphanages "look frighteningly like Harlow's monkeys" (Carlson, 1995). Adopted during infancy or childhood into a loving home, they usually progress rapidly, especially in their cognitive development. Nevertheless, they frequently bear scars from their early mistreatment (Malinosky-Rummell & Hansen, 1993; Rutter, 1979).

CLOSE-UP

Father Care

Perhaps you are wondering why mothers are the focus of so much developmental research. Why not fathers, too? The common assumption, long seen in child-custody decisions, has been that fathers are less interested and less competent than mothers in child care. Current increases in divorce and nonmarital births help foster this assumption: Half of today's American children and increasing numbers in other countries will spend time in a single-parent family, and seven out of eight such children do not live with their father and usually see him only rarely (Bureau of the Census, 1993; Whitehead, 1993). In subtle ways, psychologists, too, have sometimes assumed that fathers matter little. Infants who lack mother care are said to suffer "maternal deprivation"; those lacking father care are said merely to experience "father absence."

Across the world mothers do assume more responsibility for infant care, and young children more quickly turn to their mothers for comfort and support (Hartup, 1989). Moreover, a breast-feeding mother and nursing infant have wonderfully coordinated biological systems that predispose their responsiveness to one another.

Fathering a child Although fathers and mothers interact with their infants in distinctive ways, men, too, can provide sensitive infant care.

Breast-feeding, an intimate and pleasurable source of perfect nutrition for the infant, serves also to moderate lactating mothers' stress-hormone response to challenging situations (Altemus & others, 1995).

In contrast to this intimate situation, fathers are in close proximity to their infants only occasionally in 37 percent of 186 cultures studied; in another 20 percent, fathers are rarely or never with them (Hewlett, 1991). Nevertheless, in the remaining 43 percent of cultures, fathers are frequently with their infants. And as an increasing number of modern fathers have become more involved in infant care, researchers have become more interested in fathers.

One of the leading father-watchers, Ross Parke (1981), reports that fathers can be as interested in, sensitive to, and affectionate toward their infants as mothers typically are. Although most infants prefer their mothers when anxious, when left alone they are as distressed by their father's departure as by their mother's. Moreover, infants whose fathers have shared in their diapering, bathing, and feeding are more secure when left with a stranger. Preschoolers with involved fathers tend to become adults who are especially concerned with being kind, sensitive, and warmhearted (Koestner & others, 1990). On the down side, just as mothers' psychological problems correlate with problems among their children, so do fathers' problems (Phares & Compas, 1992).

Looking for caregiving differences, research psychologists have also uncovered several distinctive ways in which fathers and mothers interact with their infants. Fathers smile less at their babies. (Males smile less at everyone.) They spend more of their interaction in play rather than in caregiving (especially with sons). And their play is more physical (Parke, 1981).

However, fathers who are the primary caregivers interact with their babies as mothers typically do. Separated from their preschoolers, fathers report feeling as much anxiety as do mothers (Deater-Deckard & others, 1994). This suggests that father-mother differences are not biologically fixed but have social roots as well. Animal research supports this view. When Harlow caged monkey fathers with their infants, the fathers were protective and affectionate toward their infants.

Children raised in two-parent families may reap an additional benefit: Mothers and fathers who support one another and who sense this mutual support and agreement in child-rearing are more responsive to their infants and feel more competent as parents (Dickie, 1987).

Thanks partly to this research, the meaning of "fathering" is shifting. "Fathering a child" once meant impregnating; "mothering" meant nurturing. More and more these days, people appreciate that fathers are not just mobile sperm banks. Thus, fathering and mothering both mean parenting.

So, too, did Harlow's monkeys if reared in total isolation, without even an artificial mother. As adults they either cowered in fright or lashed out in aggression when placed with other monkeys their age. Upon reaching sexual maturity, most were incapable of mating. Artificially impregnated females often were neglectful, abusive, or even murderous toward their first-born offspring.

Most abusive human parents, too, report having been neglected or battered as children (Kempe & Kempe, 1978). Many condemned murderers report the same. One study of 14 young men awaiting execution for juvenile crimes found that all but two had histories of brutal physical abuse (Lewis & others, 1988). The unloved often become the unloving.

So, do most victims of child abuse become abusive? Is today's victim predictably tomorrow's predator? No. Most abused children do *not* later become violent criminals or abusive parents. But 30 percent of those abused do abuse their children—a rate four times higher than the national rate of child abuse (Kaufman & Zigler, 1987; Widom, 1989a,b). Moreover, young children terrorized through sexual abuse, physical abuse, or wartime atrocities (being beaten, witnessing torture, and living in constant fear) may suffer other scars—often nightmares, depression, and a troubled adolescence involving substance abuse, binge eating, or aggression (Kendall-Tackett & others, 1993; Polusny & Follette, 1995; Trickett & McBride-Chang, 1995).

Deep and longstanding attachments seldom break quickly; detaching is a process, not an event.

Such experiences can leave footprints on the brain. When normally placid golden hamsters are repeatedly threatened and attacked while young, the effects linger into their adult lives. They grow up to be cowards when caged with same-sized hamsters or bullies when caged with weaker ones (Ferris, 1996). Such animals show changes in the brain chemicals such as serotonin, which calms aggressive impulses. Abused children who become aggressive teens and adults have been found to have a similarly sluggish serotonin response.

Disruption of Attachment

What happens to an infant when attachment is disrupted? Separated from their families, both monkey and human infants become upset and, before long, withdrawn and even despairing (Bowlby, 1973; Mineka & Suomi, 1978). Fearing that such extreme stress might cause lasting damage (and when in doubt, acting to protect parents' rights), courts are usually reluctant to remove children from their homes.

If placed in a more positive and stable environment, most infants recover from the distress of separation. In studies of adopted children, Leon Yarrow and his co-workers (1973) found that when children between 6 and 16 months of age were removed from their foster mothers, they initially had difficulties eating, sleeping, and relating to their new mothers. But when these children were studied at age 10, little visible effect remained. Thus, they fared no worse than children placed before the age of 6 months (with little accompanying distress). Most year-old infants form new attachments without permanent emotional scars. Foster care that moves a child through a series of foster families and thereby prevents attachment can be very disruptive, however, as can repeated and prolonged removals from a mother and reunions with her.

For adults, too, severed attachment bonds, whether through death or separation, produce a predictable sequence of agitated preoccupation with the lost partner, followed by deep sadness and, eventually, the beginnings of emotional detachment and a return to normal living (Hazan & Shaver, 1994). Even newly separated couples who have long ago ceased feeling affection are often surprised at their desire to be near the former partner. Deep and longstanding attachments seldom break quickly; detaching is a process, not an event.

Does Day Care Affect Attachment?

During the fifties and sixties, when Mom-at-home was the social norm, researchers asked, "Is day care bad for children? Does it disrupt children's attachments to their parents?" For the high-quality day care programs usually studied, the answer was no (Belsky, 1990). In *Mother Care/Other Care*, developmental psychologist Sandra Scarr (1986) explained that children are "biologically sturdy individuals . . . who can thrive in a wide variety of life situations." Scarr speaks for many developmental psychologists, whose research has uncovered no major impact of maternal employment on children's development (Hoffman, 1989; Mott, 1991).

That issue settled, and with slightly more than half of all mothers of preschoolers now employed, the research questions have shifted to the effects of different forms of day care on different types and ages of children. We now know enough to distinguish good day care from poor. Scarr and Richard

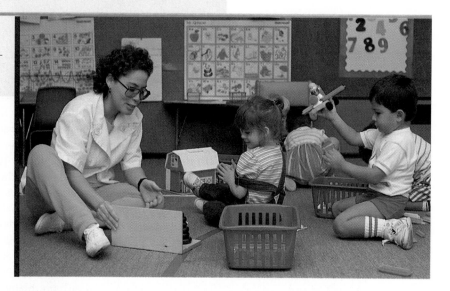

An example of high-quality day care
Forms of day care differ widely in philosophy and quality. Research has shown that in safe, stimulating environments like this day care center, young children thrive both socially and intellectually. A ratio of about one caregiver for every three or four children is especially important in producing this outcome.

Weinberg (1986) explain: "Good care means three or four infants and toddlers per caregiver and six to eight preschoolers. . . . Good care also means a cheerful, stimulating, and safe physical environment." The ideal, then, is a verbally stimulating environment in which any child frequently talks with a familiar adult caregiver. In this regard, quality day care offers a child more intellectual boost and opportunity for social development than does most home care with a sitter (Clarke-Stewart & others, 1994; Zaslow, 1991).

Parents of children 2 years of age and older may gain some relief from knowing that day care can mean high-quality child care. But the scientific jury is still debating infant day care. Developmental psychologists Jay Belsky (1988, 1994) and Edward Zigler (1986) express concern. In Belsky's words, "Children growing up in families using more than 20 hours per week of non-parental care in their first year of life are at heightened risk of seeming insecure as 1-year-olds and of being disobedient and aggressive at older ages." This is especially so when such care is early and extensive throughout the preschool years in centers with poorly trained and paid staff, who frequently change.

Many developmentalists believe, however, that *quality* infant day care does not hinder secure attachment. They find support in two studies of enriched infant day care in the United States and Sweden (Andersson, 1989; Field, 1991). In both, schoolchildren who had experienced quality day care during their first 6 months were more outgoing, popular, and academically successful than those who had no similar experience. Even routine day care seems not harmful for the children of sensitive, responsive parents. That's the preliminary

conclusion from an ongoing study following 1153 infants in ten cities from ages 1 month to 7 years. At the latest observation (age 15 months), the amount of time spent in day care had no influence on children's attaching securely (NICHD, 1996).

Children's ability to thrive under varied types of responsive caregiving should perhaps not surprise us, given how cultures vary in attachment patterns. Westernized attachment features one or two caregivers and their offspring. In other cultures, such as the Efe Pygmies of Zaire, multiple caregivers are the norm (Field, 1996). Even before the mother holds her newborn, the baby is passed among several women. In the weeks to come, the infant is constantly held and fed, often by other breast-feeding women. As the now-famous African proverb says, "It takes a village to raise a child." The result is multiple attachments.

A striking outcome of research on parent care and day care is how *little* quality time children receive from parents, employed or not. One national survey revealed that employed mothers average only 11 minutes and fathers only 8 minutes per weekday in child-centered activities such as reading, conversing, and playing with their children. Most homemaker mothers also devote little time to such activities—only about 30 minutes per day (Timmer & others, 1985–1986).

"Natural variation in child care practices around the world [indicates] there is no single way to care for children well."

JAY BELSKY (1994)

Children's ability to thrive under varied types of responsive caregiving should perhaps not surprise us, given how cultures vary in attachment patterns.

There is little disagreement that the half million preschool children actually left *alone* for part of the time their parents are at work deserve better. So do those children who merely exist for 9 hours a day in minimally equipped, understaffed centers. What all children need is a consistent, warm relationship with people whom they can learn to trust. What they often get in a society that places a much lower value on workers who care for its future citizens than on those who care for its leaky pipes is an annual staff turnover rate approaching 50 percent (Wingert & Kantrowitz, 1990). When the same society seldom permits parents to shift from full- to part-time work (with benefits preserved) and then to return to full-time work after their child's first year or two, one must conclude that children are a low priority.

Children and Divorce

Nearly half of marriages in Western countries (slightly more than half in the United States, somewhat less in Canada, Britain, and elsewhere) end in divorce. That's double the proportion of 30 years ago. This fact makes people wonder and worry: Are children casualties of divorce? Does the stress of divorce and its aftermath erode children's well-being?

To glimpse possible effects of divorce, a research team led by sociologist Andrew Cherlin and others (1991, 1995) compared children before and after divorce. This monumental study began when researchers interviewed 17,414 women—the mothers of 98 percent of all British children born during the first full week of March 1958. Knowing that some of the children would experience parental divorce, Cherlin and his co-workers studied them as 7-year-olds and again as 11-, 16-, and 23-year-olds. For example, when the children reached age 23, the intrepid researchers traced and interviewed 12,537 of the original sample. These follow-up interviews enabled them to focus on those who at age 7 had lived with two biological parents. The researchers could then compare children whose parents had divorced versus not divorced during the ensuing nine years. Their finding: Those whose parents had divorced experienced more problems.

Summing up dozens of studies, Patrick Davies and Mark Cummings (1994) note that "Destructive forms of marital conflict undermine children's feelings of emotional security." (Children can benefit when escaping with their custodial parent from a traumatic or abusive situation.) So, are children's postdivorce problems influenced solely by the pre-existing marital conflict (divorce or no), or also by the marriage breakup? Controlling for predivorce

family problems did *not* weaken the divorce effect, report Cherlin and colleagues. Even after adjusting for emotional problems and school achievement at age 7, the odds of scoring above the clinical cutoff for psychopathology were 39 percent greater among 16-year-olds whose parents had divorced in the intervening years. By launching children into "negative life trajectories through adolescence into adulthood," divorce predicted problems that were unexplained by predivorce family problems (Case-Lansdale & others, 1995). Curiously, a parental death (which can feel less rejecting and involves less conflict) had "a substantially weaker effect."

Typically, divorce provides children with a double dose of stress. The first occurs immediately following the parents' divorce, when many children feel angry, resentful, and depressed. Young children may blame themselves. Older children may exhibit heightened aggression and noncompliance. Within two or three years, life typically settles back to a more comfortable equilibrium. Then, often three to five years after the divorce, a second dose of stress may follow when the custodial parent remarries. Because 75 percent of divorced mothers and 80 percent of divorced fathers remarry, most children of divorce will gain a stepparent. Especially for girls, the new stepfather's entering the home may at first be an unwelcome event, disrupting the single-mother–daughter relationship and necessitating another period of readjustment.

Data amassed from 92 studies suggest that this double stress does leave its mark on some children (Amato & Keith, 1991; Wallerstein, 1991). Divorce places "children at increased risk for developing social, psychological, behavioral and academic problems," report Mavis Hetherington and her colleagues (1989, 1992). Compared with those who grew up in intact, two-parent families, children of divorce grow up with a diminished feeling of well-being. As adults they are more likely to divorce and less likely to say they are "very happy."

But are their problems caused by divorce per se? Consider the results of one study of more than 17,000 children by the U.S. Census Bureau for the National Center for Health Statistics (1991). The researchers knew that intact and divided families can differ in many ways (parental education, race, income, and so forth), so they statistically adjusted their results to remove such influences. Still, children of divided parents were about twice as likely to experience a variety of social, psychological, or academic problems (Figure 3.15). As that figure shows, however, although these children are more at risk for difficulty, most of them do fine—espe-

self-concept
a sense of one's identity and personal worth.

Figure **3.15**

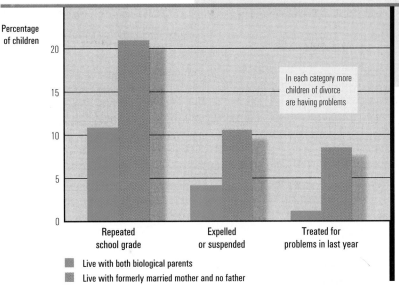

In each category more children of divorce are having problems

Percentage of children

- Live with both biological parents
- Live with formerly married mother and no father

Repeated school grade

Expelled or suspended

Treated for problems in last year

Percentage of children experiencing school problems in the previous year In this 1988 National Health Survey, children living with both their biological parents had fewer problems. Note, however, that these problems affected a minority of children. (Conducted by the U.S. Census Bureau for the National Center for Health Statistics, 1991.)

cially if endowed with an easygoing temperament and the love and support of relatives and friends.

Self-Concept

Infancy's number one social achievement is attachment. Childhood's major social achievement is a positive sense of self. By the end of childhood, at about age 12, most children have developed a self-concept—a sense of their own identity and personal worth. Parents wonder when and how this sense of self develops. "Is my baby aware of herself—does she know she is a person distinct from others?"

Although we cannot ask the baby directly, we can again capitalize on what she can do—letting her *behavior* provide clues to the beginnings of her self-awareness. In 1877, biologist Charles Darwin offered one idea: Self-awareness begins when a child recognizes herself in a mirror. By this indicator, self-recognition emerges gradually over about a year, starting in roughly the sixth month as the child reaches toward the mirror to touch her image as if it were another child (Damon & Hart, 1982, 1988).

How can we know when the child recognizes that the girl in the mirror is indeed herself and not just an agreeable playmate? In a simple variation of the mirror procedure, researchers sneakily dabbed rouge on children's noses before placing them in front of the mirror. Beginning by 15 to 18 months, children will touch their own noses when they see the red spot in the mirror (Butterworth, 1992; Gallup & Suarez, 1986). Apparently, 18-month-olds have a schema of how their faces

should look, wondering, "What is that spot doing on *my* face?"

Beginning with this simple self-recognition, the child's self-concept gradually becomes stronger. By school age, children begin to describe themselves in terms of their gender, their group memberships, and their psychological traits, and they compare themselves with other children (Newman & Ruble, 1988; Stipek, 1992). They come to see themselves as good and skillful in some ways but not others. They form a concept of which traits, ideally, they would like to have. By age 8 or 10, their self-images have become quite stable.

Children's views of themselves affect their actions. Children who form a positive self-concept are more confident, independent, optimistic, assertive, and sociable (Maccoby, 1980). This raises an important question: How can parents encourage a positive self-concept? How does parenting style affect children?

After prolonged exposure to mirrors, four other species—chimpanzees, orangutans, gorillas, and dolphins—have similarly demonstrated self-recognition of their mirror image (Marino & others, 1994; Wright, 1996).

Self-awareness Mirror images fascinate infants from the age of about 6 months. Only at about 18 months, however, does the child recognize that the image in the mirror is "me."

Child-Rearing Practices

Parenting styles vary. Some parents spank, some reason. Some parents are strict, some are lax. Some parents seem indifferent to their children, some liberally hug and kiss them. Do such differences affect children?

The most heavily researched aspect of parenting has been how, and to what extent, parents seek to control their children. Several investigators have identified four parenting styles:

1 *Authoritarian* parents impose rules and expect obedience: "Don't interrupt." "Don't leave your room a mess." "Don't stay out late or you'll be grounded." "Why? Because I said so."

2 *Authoritative* parents are both demanding and responsive. They exert control not only by setting rules and enforcing them but also by explaining the reasons and, especially with older children, encouraging open discussion and allowing exceptions when making the rules.

3 *Permissive* parents submit to their children's desires, make few demands, and use little punishment.

4 *Rejecting-neglecting* parents are disengaged. They expect little and invest little.

Studies by Stanley Coopersmith (1967), Diana Baumrind (1983, 1991), and John Buri and others (1988) reveal that children with the highest self-esteem, self-reliance, and social competence usually have warm, concerned, *authoritative* parents—parents who both control and communicate, who have standards yet respect a child's perspective. Although in most studies the subjects have been middle-class white families, studies with families of other races and in more than 200 cultures worldwide confirm the social and academic benefits of loving and authoritative parenting (Baumrind, 1991; Rohner, 1994).

What accounts for this finding? As later chapters will explain, people given *control* over their lives become motivated and self-confident. Those who experience little control more often see themselves as helpless and incompetent. Moreover, children who sense enough control to attribute their behaviors to their choices ("I obey because I am good") internalize their behaviors. Coerced children ("I obey or I get in bad trouble") tend not to internalize their actions.

Of the four parenting styles, authoritative parenting provides children with the greatest sense of control. Authoritative parents openly discuss family rules by explaining them to younger children and reasoning about them with older children. When rules seem more negotiated than imposed, older children feel more self-control (Baumrind, 1983; Lewis, 1981). And, when parents enforce rules with consistent, predictable consequences, the child controls the outcome.

Before jumping to conclusions about the results of different parenting styles, we must heed a caution. The evidence is correlational. It tells us that certain parenting styles (say, being firm but open) are associated with certain childhood outcomes (say, social competence). But remember: Correlation need not reveal cause and effect. Other explanations may be possible (Figure 3.16). Perhaps children's traits influence parenting more than vice versa. Perhaps socially mature, agreeable, easygoing children *elicit* greater trust and warmth from

Figure **3.16**

The correlation between authoritative parenting and social competence in children Three possible explanations are (1) parenting may influence children's competence; (2) children's social competence may influence parenting; or (3) both may be influenced by an underlying third factor.

(1) Parents' behavior may be influencing child.

Authoritative parents → Self-reliant, socially competent child

(2) Child's behavior may be influencing parents.

Self-reliant, socially competent child → Authoritative parents

(3) Some third factor may be influencing both parents and child.

High education, ample income, harmonious marriage, common genes → Authoritative parents / Self-reliant, socially competent child their parents than do less competent and less cooperative children—a possibility supported by twin studies (Kendler, 1996).

Or consider this: Authoritative parents are more often well educated and less often stressed by poverty or recent divorce, factors that can affect children's competence (Hetherington, 1979). Or maybe competent parents and their competent children share genes that predispose social competence.

When considering "expert" child-rearing advice we should also remember that all advice reflects the advice-giver's values. For those who prize unquestioning obedience from a child, an authoritarian style may have the desired effect. For those who value children's sociability and self-reliance, authoritative firm-but-open parenting is advisable. Different experts have different values, which helps explain their disagreements.

Parents struggle with conflicting advice and with the stresses of child-rearing. Indeed, the investment in raising a child buys many years not only of joy and love but of worry and irritation. Yet for most parents, a child is one's biological and social legacy—one's personal investment in the human future. To paraphrase psychiatrist Carl Jung, we reach backward into our parents and forward into our children, and through their children into a future we will never see, but about which we must therefore care.

. . . the investment in raising a child buys many years not only of joy and love but of worry and irritation. Yet for most parents, a child is one's biological and social legacy—one's personal investment in the human future.

care or nursery school, infants typically sleep with their mothers and spend their days close to a family member (Morelli & others, 1992; Whiting & Edwards, 1988). Children of communal cultures grow up with a stronger sense of "family self"—a feeling that what shames the child shames the family. Compared with Westerners, people in Japanese and Chinese cultures, for example, exhibit greater shyness toward strangers and greater concern for social harmony and loyalty (Bond, 1988; Cheek & Melchior, 1990; Triandis, 1994). "My parents will be disappointed in me" is a concern of 7 percent of American and Italian teenagers, 14 percent of Australian teens, but nearly 25 percent of teens in Taiwan and Japan (Atkinson, 1988).

Across place and time, children have thrived under various child-rearing systems. Upper-class British parents traditionally left routine caregiving to nannies, before sending their children off to boarding school. Their children generally grew up

Culture and Child-Rearing

Social values differ not only from expert to expert but also from one time and place to another. Do you prefer children who are independent or children who respect authority?

If you live in Western Europe or North America, the odds are you prefer the former. Most parents in Western societies want their children to think for themselves. "You are responsible for yourself," our families and schools tell us. "Follow your conscience. Be true to yourself. Define your gifts. Satisfy your personal needs." But cultural values change over time. A half century ago, Western parents placed greater priority on obedience, respect, and sensitivity to others (Alwin, 1990; Remley, 1988). "Be true to your traditions," they taught their children. "Be loyal to your heritage and country. Show respect toward your parents and superiors."

Unlike most Westerners, who now raise their children to be independent, many Asians and Africans live in communal cultures, which focus on cultivating emotional closeness. Rather than being given their own bedrooms and sent off to day

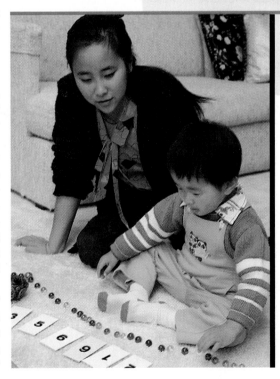

Parental involvement promotes development Parents in every culture facilitate their children's discovery of their world, but cultures differ in what they deem important. Asian cultures place more emphasis on school and hard work than does North American culture. This may help explain why Japanese and Taiwanese children get higher scores on mathematics achievement tests.

gender identity
one's sense of being male or female.

gender-typing
the acquisition of a traditional masculine or feminine role.

social learning theory
the theory that we learn social behavior by observing and imitating and by being rewarded or punished.

gender schema theory
the theory that children learn from their cultures a concept of what it means to be male and female and that they adjust their behavior accordingly.

to be pillars of British society, just like their parents. In some preindustrial societies, babies spend the day on their mother's back—with lots of body contact but little face-to-face and language interaction. When the mother becomes pregnant, the toddler is weaned and handed over to someone else, often an older sibling. Today's North American parents give their children lots of cuddles and hugs—more so than at the beginning of this century. Although children do better when treated warmly than when treated coldly, such diversity in child-rearing cautions us against presuming that our culture's way is the only way to rear successful children.

Gender and Child-Rearing

What biology initiates, environment accentuates. Society assigns each of us—even those few whose biological sex is ambiguous at birth—to a *gender*, the social category of male or female. The inevitable result is our strong gender identity, our sense of being male or female. To varying extents, we also become gender-typed. That is, some boys more than others exhibit traditionally masculine traits and interests, and some girls more than others become distinctly feminine.

Social learning theory assumes that children learn gender-linked behaviors by observing and imitating and by being rewarded or punished. "Nicole, you're such a good mommy to your dolls"; "Big boys don't cry, Alex." The modeling and rewarding is not done by parents alone, because differences in the way parents rear boys and

girls aren't enough to explain gender-typing (Lytton & Romney, 1991). Even when their families discourage traditional gender-typing, children organize themselves into "boy worlds" and "girl worlds," each guided by rules for what boys and girls do.

Gender schema theory combines social learning theory with cognition: Out of children's struggles to comprehend the world come concepts, or schemas, including a schema for their own gender (Bem, 1987, 1993). Gender becomes a lens (a schema) through which children view their experience (Figure 3.17). By age 3, language forces them to begin organizing their worlds on the basis of gender. English, for example, uses the pronouns *he* and *she*; other languages classify objects as masculine ("*le* train") or feminine ("*la* table"). Through language, dress, toys, and songs, social learning shapes gender schemas. Children then compare themselves with their concept of gender ("I am male—thus, masculine, strong, aggressive," or "I am female—therefore, feminine, sweet, and helpful") and adjust their behavior accordingly.

Developmental Similarities Across Groups

Mindful of how others differ from us, we often fail to notice the similarities predisposed by our shared biology. Cross-cultural research helps us appreciate both our cultural diversity *and* our human kinship. Compared with person-to-person differences within groups, differences between groups are small. Thus, regardless of our culture, we humans

Figure **3.17**

Two theories of gender-typing
Social learning theory proposes that gender-typing evolves through imitation and reinforcement. In gender schema theory, one's concept of maleness and femaleness influences one's perceptions and behavior.

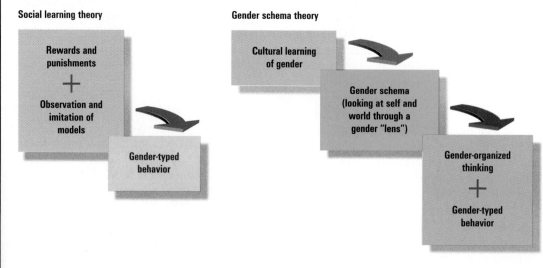

share the same life cycle. We all speak to our infants in similar ways and respond similarly to their coos and cries (Bornstein & others, 1992a,b). Across the world, parents who are warm and supportive have children who feel better about themselves and are less hostile than do punitive and rejecting parents (Rohner, 1986; Scott & others, 1991).

Within a larger culture, ethnic subgroups may differ in their behavior yet be influenced by the same underlying processes. Differences sometimes attributed to race may therefore actually result from other factors. David Rowe and his colleagues (1994, 1995) illustrate with an analogy: Black men tend to have higher blood pressure than white men. Suppose that (1) in both groups salt consumption correlates with blood pressure, and (2) blacks consume more salt than whites. What then might we expect? A blood pressure "race difference" that may actually be a *diet* difference.

And that, say Rowe and his colleagues, parallels psychological findings: Behavior differences, like blood pressure differences, can result from differing inputs to the same process. Or so they conclude after distilling data from six major investigations of ethnic differences in behavior. Although American Hispanic, Asian, black, and white ethnic groups differed in levels of school achievement and delinquency, the differences were "no more than skin deep." The factors that influenced adolescent behavior in different ethnic groups were "statistically indistinguishable." To the extent that variables such as family structure, peer influences, and parental education predicted behavior in one ethnic group, they did so for other groups as well.

The available data so far come from the United States. But "it bodes well," say the researchers, "that developmental processes are alike in many subgroups of *Homo sapiens*." In surface ways we may differ, but as members together of one species we seem subject to the same psychological forces. As members of different ethnic and cultural groups, our languages vary, yet they reflect universal principles of grammar (Chapter 10). Our tastes vary, yet they reflect common principles of hunger (Chapter 12). Our social behaviors vary, yet they reflect pervasive principles of human influence (Chapter 18).

"When someone has discovered why men on Bond Street wear black hats he will at the same moment have discovered why men in Timbuctoo wear red feathers."

G. K. CHESTERTON
1874–1936

SUMMING UP

Although the experiences of our infancy are not consciously remembered for long and their effects may be reversed by later experiences, they can nevertheless have a lasting influence on our social development.

Attachment style in infancy predicts later social development. Infants become attached to their mothers and fathers not simply because mothers and fathers gratify biological needs but, more important, because they are comfortable, familiar, and responsive. If denied such care, both monkey and human infants may become pathetically withdrawn, anxious, and eventually abusive. Once an attachment forms, infants who are separated from their caregivers will, for a time, be distressed. Human infants who display secure attachment to their mothers generally become socially competent preschoolers. Infants' differing attachment styles reflect both their individual temperaments and the responsiveness of their parents and child care providers. New research explores possible influences of different day care arrangements and family structures.

As with cognitive abilities, a self-concept develops gradually. By 18 months, infants will recognize themselves in a mirror. By age 8 or 10, children's self-images are quite stable and are linked with their independence, optimism, and sociability. Children who develop a positive self-image and a happy, self-reliant manner tend to have been reared by parents who are neither permissive nor authoritarian, but authoritative while allowing their children a sense of control. Decisions about child-rearing involve value judgments about what traits to encourage in children.

Cultural differences, such as between the communalism of Asian families and the individualism of Euro-American families, illustrate the impact of parental values. Cultural socialization through social learning and gender schemas helps explain why some children become more gender-typed than others. Cultural and ethnic differences in behavior may, however, arise from the same underlying forces.

KEY TERMS AND CONCEPTS stranger anxiety, attachment, critical period, imprinting, temperament, basic trust, self-concept, gender identity, gender typing, social learning theory, gender schema theory

Reflections on the Nature-Nurture Issue

To what extent is our development influenced by our genetically disposed nature? By our experienced nurture? And what does it mean to say that nature and nurture interact? Studies of twins and adoptees provide some answers.

Everyone agrees: We are all influenced by genes *and* experience. The question is, how important is each and how do their influences interact? For physical attributes such as hair color, the genetic factor predominates. For psychological attributes, the answer is less obvious. In Chapter 11, we will examine the thorny debate over genetic and environmental determinants of intelligence. Here we will consider some provocative findings on how nature and nurture influence the developing personality.

Twin Studies

Researchers have for years selectively bred animals in their studies of such traits as aggressiveness and obesity. Recently, scientists succeeded in *cloning*— genetically replicating—a sheep (Wilmut & others, 1997). "Are people next?" many wondered. "But you

"The good news is that you will have a healthy baby girl.
The bad news is that she is a congenital liar."

Drawing by Handelsman; © 1996 The New Yorker Magazine, Inc.

couldn't clone a *person*," said others, "because a person includes a unique bundle of experiences." Human cloning would raise major ethical issues, but it hardly raises new psychological issues. Millions of human clones already exist as identical twins, and twin studies are already revealing the genetic and environmental influences on the developing personality.

Researchers ask: Are identical twins, being genetic clones of one another, more similar than fraternal twins? Studies of nearly 13,000 pairs of Swedish identical and fraternal twins, of 7000 Finnish twin pairs, and of 3810 Australian twin pairs provide a consistent answer: On both extraversion (outgoingness) and neuroticism (emotional instability), identical twins are much more similar than fraternal twins. Genes matter.

If genes influence traits such as emotional instability, might they also influence the social effects of such traits? To find out, Matt McGue and David Lykken (1992) studied divorce rates among 1500 same-sex, middle-aged twin pairs. Their result: If you have a fraternal twin who has divorced, the odds of your divorcing go up 1.6 times (the same rate as for those whose parents have divorced). If you have an identical twin who has divorced, the odds of your divorcing go up 5.5 times. From such data McGue and Lykken estimated that people's differing divorce risk is about 50 percent attributable to genetic factors. Another study of 2315 twin pairs confirms that identical twins' recent troubles at home, work, and elsewhere are more alike than are fraternal twins' troubles (Kendler & others, 1993). Although identical twins also experience greater similarity in their childhood environments, the effect seems mostly genetic; twins who report more similar childhood environments are not more likely to have experienced similar upsets.

Other dimensions of personality also reflect genetic influences. John Loehlin and Robert Nichols (1976) gave a battery of questionnaires to 850 U.S. twin pairs. Once again, identical twins were much more similar, and in a variety of ways—in abilities, personality, even interests. However, the identical twins, more than fraternal twins, also reported being treated alike. So, did their experience rather than their genes account for their similarity? No, said Loehlin and Nichols. Identical twins whose parents treated them alike were *not* psychologically more alike than identical twins who were treated less similarly.

Separated Twins

Imagine a science fiction experiment in which a mad scientist decides to separate identical twins at birth and rear them in differing environments.

Affable by nature? Identical twins Gerald Levey and Mark Newman were separated at birth and raised in different homes. When reunited at age 31, they discovered they both volunteered as firefighters. Research has shown remarkable similarities in the life choices of separated identical twins, lending support to the idea that genes influence personality.

Would such twins differ from each other more than twins reared together? If so, one could only credit their differing environments.

In reality, circumstances occasionally set up just these conditions. In 1979 University of Minnesota psychologist Thomas Bouchard read a newspaper account of the reuniting of 39-year-old twins who had been separated from infancy. Seeing a scientific opportunity, he flew them to Minneapolis for extensive tests. Bouchard was looking for differences. What "the Jim twins," Jim Lewis and Jim Springer, presented were amazing similarities (Holden, 1980a,b). Both had married and divorced women named Linda and had later married women named Betty. One had a son James Alan, the other a son James Allan. Both had dogs named Toy, chain-smoked Salems, served as sheriff's deputies, drove Chevrolets, chewed their fingernails to the nub, enjoyed stock car racing, had basement workshops, and had built circular white benches around trees in their yards. They also had similar medical histories: Both gained 10 pounds at about the same time and then lost it. Both suffered what they mistakenly believed were heart attacks. Both began having late-afternoon headaches at age 18.

Identical twins Oskar Stohr and Jack Yufe presented equally striking similarities. One was raised by his grandmother in Germany as a Catholic and a Nazi, while the other was raised by his father in the Caribbean as a Jew. Nevertheless, they share traits and habits galore. They like spicy foods and sweet liqueurs, have a habit of falling asleep in front of the television, flush the toilet before using it, store rubber bands on their wrists, and dip buttered toast in their coffee. Stohr is domineering toward women and yells at his wife, as did Yufe before he and his wife separated.

Oblivious to their similarities, separated twins may each attribute their traits to their nurture, note Peter Neubauer and Alexander Neubauer (1990, pp. 20–21). Identical twin men, now age thirty, were separated at birth and raised in different countries by their respective adoptive parents. Both kept their lives neat—neat to the point of pathology. Their clothes were preened, appointments met precisely on time, hands scrubbed regularly to a raw, red color. When the first was asked why he felt the need to be so clean, his answer was plain.

"My mother. When I was growing up she always kept the house perfectly ordered. She insisted on every little thing returned to its proper place, the clocks—we had dozens of clocks—each set to the same noonday chime. She insisted on this, you see. I learned from her. What else could I do?"

The man's identical twin, just as much a perfectionist with soap and water, explained his own behavior this way: "The reason is quite simple. I'm reacting to my mother, who was an absolute slob."

Aided by publicity in magazine and newspaper stories, Bouchard and his colleagues (1990; Di-Lalla & others, in press) have located and studied 69 pairs of identical twins reared apart. They continue to be impressed by the similarities not only of tastes and physical attributes but also of personality, abilities, attitudes, interests, and even fears. In Sweden, which has a national registry of 25,000 pairs of adult twins, Nancy Pedersen and her co-workers (1988) identified 99 separated identical twin pairs and more than 200 separated fraternal twin pairs. Compared with equivalent samples of identical twins reared together, the separated identical twins had more dissimilar personalities. Still, separated twins were more alike when genetically identical rather than fraternal. And separation shortly after birth (rather than, say, at age 8) didn't amplify their personality differences.

The more bizarre similarities—such as flushing the toilet before using it—exist not because we have genes for specific behaviors, cautions Bouchard. Rather, presented with a similar range of options, similarly disposed people often make similar choices. Even on traits for which heredity strongly influences personality (such as "social potency"—having an assertive, take-charge nature), it does so not through a single gene but through a

"In some domains it looks as though our identical twins reared apart are . . . just as similar as identical twins reared together. Now that's an amazing finding and I can assure you none of us would have expected that degree of similarity."

THOMAS BOUCHARD (1981)

Coincidences are not unique to twins. Patricia Kern of Colorado was born March 13, 1941, and named Patricia Ann Campbell. Patricia DiBiasi of Oregon also was born March 13, 1941, and named Patricia Ann Campbell. Both had fathers named Robert, worked as bookkeepers, and have children ages 21 and 19. Both studied cosmetology, enjoy oil painting as a hobby, and married military men, within 11 days of each other. They are not genetically related. (From an AP report, May 2, 1983.)

complex combination of genes. Influencing a complex trait requires a very large number of genes, each having very small effects (Plomin, 1990a).

The cute stories do not impress Bouchard's critics. They contend that if any two strangers of the same sex and age were to spend hours comparing their behaviors and life histories, they would probably discover many coincidental similarities. Even the more impressive data from the personality assessments are clouded by the reunion of many of the separated twins for some years before being tested. Moreover, adoption agencies tend to place separated twins in similar homes. When environments are similar, the impact of environment looks smaller relative to heredity. As twins age, differing experiences often make their personality differences more noticeable (McCartney & others, 1990). Nevertheless, the twin studies illustrate why scientific opinion has shifted toward a greater appreciation of genetic influences.

Adoption Studies

Adoption studies offer additional clues. For any given trait we can ask whether adopted children are more like their adoptive parents, who contribute a home environment, or their biological parents, who contributed their genes. While sharing the same home environment, do adopted siblings come to share traits? The stunning finding from studies of hundreds of adoptive families in Minnesota, Texas, and Colorado is that people who grow up together do not much resemble one another in personality, whether biologically related or not (Rowe, 1990). As Sandra Scarr and her colleagues (1981) vividly stated,

It would have to be concluded that upper-middle-class brothers who attended the same school and whose parents took them to the same plays, sporting events, music lessons, and therapists and used similar child-rearing practices on them would be found to be only slightly more similar to each other in personality measures than to working-class or farm boys, whose lives would be totally different.

What we have here is developmental psychology's biggest puzzle: Why are children in the same family so different? Why do the shared genes and the shared family environment (the family's social class, the parents' personalities and marital status, day care versus home care, the neighborhood) have so little discernible effect on children's personalities? Is it because siblings—despite sharing half their genes—have very different combinations of genes (Lykken & others, 1992)? Is it because each sibling experiences a different environment—differing peer influences, birth orders, life events (Dunn & Plomin, 1990; Hetherington & others, 1993)?

"All parents are environmentalists—until the birth of their second child."

ANONYMOUS

Twin and adoption studies reveal that genetic influences account for nearly 50 percent of person-to-person differences in traits such as outgoingness and emotional instability. What accounts for the other 50 percent? Because siblings' extraversion and instability are *not* appreciably influenced by their shared home environment (shocking as that may sound), researchers assume they *are* influenced by their *non*shared experiences—their own unique experiences. Apparently what affects each child is not so much the parents per se as how the child interacts with and experiences them, plus other peer and cultural influences. The same parental influence may affect an easygoing child one way, a reactive child another. Family environment can matter, even if siblings differ, notes Lois Hoffman (1991). The same fire that tempers steel melts butter.

Adoption studies also show that, although the personalities of adopted children do not much resemble those of their adoptive parents, adoption has many effects (Brodzinsky & Schechter, 1990). First, the home environment influences adopted children's values, beliefs, and social attitudes. Second, in adoptive homes, child neglect and abuse and even parental divorce are rare. (Adoptive parents are carefully screened; natural parents are not.) So it is not surprising that, despite somewhat

Family ties Studies of adoptive families have provided new clues to hereditary and environmental influences. How similar would you expect adopted children to be to their adoptive parents? To their biological parents?

greater risk of psychological disorder, most adopted children thrive, especially when adopted as infants (Benson & others, 1994; Wierzbicki, 1993). They score higher than their biological parents on intelligence tests. Seven in eight report feeling strongly attached to one or both parents. And they generally become happier and more stable people than they would have in a stressed or neglectful environment. In a Swedish study, infant adoptees grew up with fewer problems than experienced by children raised by biological mothers who had registered them for adoption and then changed their mind (Bohman & Sigvardsson, 1990). Children need not resemble their adoptive parents to have benefited from adoption.

How Much Credit (or Blame) Do Parents Deserve?

Parents typically feel enormous pride in their children's successes, and guilt or shame over their failures. They beam when folks offer congratulations for the child who wins an award. They wonder where they went wrong with the child who is repeatedly called into the principal's or headmaster's office. Psychiatry and Freudian psychology have at times been the source of such ideas, by blaming problems from asthma to schizophrenia on "bad mothering." Society reinforces such parent-blaming: Believing that parents shape their children as a potter molds clay, people readily praise parents for their children's virtues and blame them for their children's vices. Even among chimpanzees, when one infant is hurt by another, the victim's mother will often attack the offender's mother (Goodall, 1968).

Given our readiness to praise or blame and to feel pride or shame, we should remember a simple principle: Within the normal range of environments, children's genetically predisposed tendencies will assert themselves. So, asks psychologist Judith Rich Harris (1995), "do parents have any important long-term effects on the development of their child's personality?" After examining the evidence, she challenges all the child-rearing recipe manuals and all the baby boomer complaints of overbearing mothers and distant fathers: "The answer is no." If we left a group of children with their same schools, neighborhoods, and peers, but switched the parents around, they "would develop into the same sort of adults" (Harris, 1996).

It may be scary to realize how risky is the business of having and raising children. In procreation, a woman and a man shuffle their gene decks and deal a life-forming hand to their child-to-be, who is then subjected to countless influences beyond their control. Keeping in mind that lives are formed by influences both under and beyond parents' control, we should, perhaps, be slower to credit parents for their children's achievements and slower still to blame them for their children's traits.

Predictably, other psychologists are now reminding us that there is some power to parenting (Baumrind, 1993). The extremes provide the sharpest examples—the abused who become abusive, the neglected who become neglectful, the loved but firmly handled children who become self-confident and socially competent. Recall, too, the effects of environmental deprivation versus enrichment on the developing neural network, and the effects of parental conflict and divorce on children's social and academic outcomes. Consider the remarkable academic and vocational successes of children of the refugee Asian boat people—successes attributed to close-knit, supportive, even demanding families (Caplan & others, 1992). And consider the parents of aggressive boys who, upon learning more effective communication and discipline skills, see their children behaving better (Patterson, 1995). Although genes do limit the family environment's influence on temperament and personality, parents more greatly influence their children's attitudes, values, faith, and politics. Parenting matters!

To say that genes and experience are *both* important is true but oversimplified. More precisely, their effects intertwine. Imagine two babies, one genetically predisposed to be attractive, sociable, and easygoing, the other less so. Assume further that the first baby attracts more affectionate and stimulating care than the second and so develops into a warmer and more outgoing person. As the two children grow older, the more naturally outgoing one seeks activities and friends that encourage further social confidence.

"If you want to blame your parents for your own adult problems, you are entitled to blame the genes they gave you, but you are not entitled—by any facts I know—to blame the way they treated you. . . . We are not prisoners of our past."

MARTIN SELIGMAN
(1994, pp. 232, 237)

CALVIN AND HOBBES

THINKING CRITICALLY ABOUT

"Dysfunctional Families"

Popular culture of the 1990s endlessly tells us of the psychological harm that parents inflict on their fragile children. "The major source of human misery" is the "neglected, wounded child" within each of us, claims author-lecturer John Bradshaw (1990, p. 7). Having survived our "toxic" parents, today's "adult children" have swarmed to "recovery groups." It's about time, contend some leaders of today's recovery movement, given that most of us come from "dysfunctional families." (If you think your family isn't or wasn't dysfunctional, they might add, that probably indicates you're "in denial.")

What should we make of all this? If parental slips—being occasionally shouted at or ignored—constitute "abuse," then, yes, we can hold our parents to blame for our resulting vices ("addictions"). And if we occasionally feel anxious, inadequate, or alienated, that might indicate we experienced emotional abuse or neglect. Given today's problem, we could infer a childhood cause.

But do parents produce future adults with a wounded child within by being (take your pick from the toxic lists) overbearing—or uninvolved? Pushy—or ineffectual? Overprotective—or distant? Are children indeed easily wounded by well-meaning but occasionally exhausted parents who don't successfully navigate the psychological tightrope? If so, should we blame our parents for our failings, and ourselves for our children's failings? Should we shame the parents of troubled children or pass city ordi-

nances that punish them for their children's misdeeds? Or does talk of wounding fragile children through normal parental mistakes trivialize the brutality of real abuse and the force of real addictions?

Consider: How might research shed light on these questions? To make the issue testable, we might ask whether parents' behaviors correlate with their children's traits. As we have seen, loving homes do produce outcomes noticeably different from those generated by abusive or neglectful homes. Likewise, differences are sometimes observed in the children of authoritarian and authoritative parents, and in the children of two-parent and father-absent homes. The social context matters.

But we must remember that correlations between parental behavior and child personality mirror not only parents' influence on children but children's influence on their parents (Bell & Harper, 1977). Children's easygoing or reactive dispositions influence their parents' child-rearing tactics.

The extreme environmentalism of 1990s pop psychology, say its critics, is also built on ignorance of a shocking but consistent finding. If millions of toxic, dysfunctional parents have predictably damaged their children, shouldn't children who grow up in the same home be noticeably alike? Shouldn't the children of "toxic" parents be wounded and the children of healthy parents be healthy?

That presumption is refuted by the most astonishing recent finding of developmental psychology. In

How much blame do parents deserve?
Although abuse and family collapse disturb many children, the differences among children raised in the same home reveal the limits of parental influence. Genetic predispositions and peer influences also shape children's lives.

the words of behavior geneticists Robert Plomin and Denise Daniels (1987), "Two children in the same family [are on average] as different from one another as are pairs of children selected randomly from the population." To developmental psychologist Sandra Scarr (1993), this implies that "parents should be given less credit for kids who turn out great and blamed less for kids who don't." Although environments matter, "Extreme environmentalism is cruel," contends Michael Gazzaniga (1992, p. 202), "because it suggests to the parents that their child has been warped by something they did."

What has caused their resulting personality difference? We cannot say simply that individual personalities are *x* percent due to genes and *y* percent to experience, for the gene-experience effect is also combined. Our genes influence our experiences. As we grow older we *select* environments well suited to our natures. Moreover, as in our imaginary example, our genetically influenced traits *evoke* significant responses in others. This helps explain why identical twins reared in *different* families recall their parents' warmth as remarkably similar—almost as similar as if they had the same parents (Plomin & others, 1988, 1991, 1994). Fraternal twins recall their early family life more differently—even if reared in the same family! "Children experience us as different parents, depending on their own qualities," notes Scarr (1990).

So, from conception onward, we are the product of a cascade of *interactions* between our genetic predispositions and our surrounding environments.

Our genes affect how our environment reacts to and influences us. Asking whether genes or experience is more important is therefore like asking whether a soccer field's area is due more to its length or its width. So, forget nature *versus* nurture, think nature *via* nurture.

> "Heredity deals the cards; environment plays the hand."
>
> CHARLES L. BREWER (1990)

SUMMING UP

Studies of the inheritance of temperament, and of twins and adopted children, provide scientific support for the idea that nature *and* nurture influence one's developing personality. Developmentalists generally agree that genes and environment, biological and social factors, direct our life courses as their effects intertwine.

TERMS AND CONCEPTS TO REMEMBER

developmental psychology, p. 77

X chromosome, p. 79

Y chromosome, p. 79

testosterone, p. 79

gender, p. 79

zygote, p. 79

embryo, p. 80

fetus, p. 80

teratogens, p. 80

fetal alcohol syndrome (FAS), p. 80

rooting reflex, p. 81

maturation, p. 82

plasticity, p. 85

cognition, p. 87

schema, p. 87

assimilation, p. 87

accommodation, p. 87

sensorimotor stage, p. 88

object permanence, p. 88

habituation, p. 90

preoperational stage, p. 91

conservation, p. 91

egocentrism, p. 91

concrete operational stage, p. 93

formal operational stage, p. 93

stranger anxiety, p. 94

attachment, p. 95

critical period, p. 96

imprinting, p. 96

temperament, p. 96

basic trust, p. 98

self-concept, p. 103

gender identity, p. 106

gender-typing, p. 106

social learning theory, p. 106

gender schema theory, p. 106

CRITICAL THINKING EXERCISE
by Richard O. Straub

Now that you have read and reviewed Chapter 3, take your learning a step further by testing your critical thinking skills on this perspective-taking exercise.

You have decided to open a baby-sitting service for children from 18 months to 12 years of age. Your advertising campaign is based on your intention to provide children with intellectually stimulating activities. To design activities that will be appropriate for children of different ages, you decide to follow Piaget's stage theory of cognitive development.

Your task in this exercise is to imagine the viewpoint of children at various stages of cognitive development. For the moment, set aside what you think about the intellectual abilities of children of various ages and try to identify with the unique ways in which they experience the world. Then describe two or three intellectually stimulating activities that would be appropriate for each group.

1. How does an 18-month-old child experience the world?
2. What activities would you plan for an 18-month-old child?
3. How does a 5-year-old child experience the world?
4. What activities would you plan for a 5-year-old child?
5. How does an 8-year-old child experience the world?
6. What activities would you plan for an 8-year-old child?
7. How does a 12-year-old child view the world?
8. What activities would you plan for a 12-year-old child?

Check your progress on becoming a critical thinker by comparing your answers to the sample answers found in Appendix B.

chapter

4

Adolescence and Adulthood

For much of this century, psychologists echoed poet Alexander Pope's sentiment that "as the twig is bent the tree's inclined." Developmental experts focused on the "critical" early years, reasoning that by the end of childhood our traits have nearly set, like clay. Life experiences might smooth the rough edges, but the pliable period is over. With our traits formed, the legacy of infancy and childhood will reach decades into the future.

Now, among a new generation of developmental psychologists, this view has given way to an awareness that development is *lifelong*. As today's life-span perspective emerged, psychologists began to look at how maturation and experience shape us in infancy and childhood—*and* in adolescence and beyond. At a five-year high school reunion, friends may be surprised at the divergence of their paths. A decade after college, two former soul mates may have trouble keeping a conversation going. As long as we live, we develop.

Adolescence

What defines adolescence? How are adolescents influenced by their physical maturation and their cognitive development? What tasks and challenges do they face en route to mature adulthood?

Adolescence is life between childhood and adulthood. It starts with the physical beginnings of sexual maturity and ends with the social achievement of independent adult status, a period that in the Western world roughly corresponds to the teen years.

Adolescence is a time of transition. At earlier times in Western societies (and in some developing countries today), adolescence was but a brief interlude between the dependence of childhood and the responsibilities of adulthood (Baumeister & Tice, 1986). Adult status and responsibilities were bestowed shortly after sexual maturity, often marked by an elaborate initiation. The new adult worked, married, and had children.

Figure **4.1**

Adolescence is being stretched from both ends In the 1890s the average interval between a woman's first menstrual period and marriage was about 7 years; today it is nearly 12 years. (Guttmacher, 1994.)

1890, WOMEN

7.2 - Year interval

Menarche
(First period)

Marriage

10   20   30

Age

1988, WOMEN

11.8 - Year interval

Menarche

Marriage

10   20   30

Age

How will you look back on your life 10 years from now? Are you making choices that someday you will recollect with satisfaction? In one survey, adults' most common regret was not having taken their education more seriously (Kinnier & Metha, 1989).

adolescence
the transition period from childhood to adulthood, extending from puberty to independence.

puberty
the period of sexual maturation, during which one first becomes capable of reproducing.

primary sex characteristics
the body structures (ovaries, testes, and external genitalia) that make sexual reproduction possible.

secondary sex characteristics
nonreproductive sexual characteristics, such as female breasts and hips, male voice quality, and body hair.

menarche [meh-NAR-key]
the first menstrual period.

But thanks to improved nutrition, sexual maturity began occurring earlier. And thanks to compulsory schooling, adult independence began occurring later. As a result, the brief interlude between biological maturity and social independence has widened to a considerable gap (Figure 4.1). That gap is adolescence.

What are the teen years like? To St. Augustine, these years were a time of fiery passions involving "the hot imagination of puberty. . . . Both love and lust boiled within me and swept my youthful immaturity over the precipice." In Leo Tolstoy's *Anna Karenina*, the teen years were, rather, "that blissful time when childhood is just coming to an end, and out of that vast circle, happy and gay, a path takes shape." In her diary, written when she and her family hid from the Nazis, teenager Anne Frank observed,

My treatment varies so much. One day Anne is so sensible and is allowed to know everything; and the next day I hear that Anne is just a silly little goat who doesn't know anything at all and imagines that she's learned a wonderful lot from books. . . . Oh, so many things bubble up inside me as I lie in bed, having to put up with people I'm fed up with, who always misinterpret my intentions.

To G. Stanley Hall (1904), one of the first psychologists to describe adolescence, the tension between biological maturity and social dependence created—no surprise to Augustine—a period of "storm and stress." Indeed, after age 30, many people look back on their teenage years as a time they would not like to relive, a time when the social approval of peers was imperative, one's sense of direction in life was in flux, and alienation from parents was deepest (Macfarlane, 1964). Humorist Dave Barry (1996) is one such person:

When my dad pulled up, wearing his poodle hat and driving his Nash Metropolitan—a comically tiny vehicle resembling those cars outside supermarkets that go up and down when you put in a quarter, except the Metropolitan looked sillier and had a smaller motor—I was mortified. I might as well have been getting picked up by a flying saucer piloted by some bizarre multi-tentacled stalk-eyed slobber-mouthed alien being that had somehow got hold of a Russian hat. I was horrified at what my peers might think of my dad; it never occurred to me that my peers didn't even notice my dad, because they were too busy being mortified by THEIR parents.

Of course eventually my father stopped being a hideous embarrassment to me, and I, grasping the Torch of Dorkhood, became a hideous embarrassment to my son.

Today's psychologists note that adolescence is, indeed, often marked by mood swings. Yet for many it is also as Tolstoy described it—a time of vitality without the cares of adulthood, a time of rewarding friendships, a time of heightened idealism and a growing sense of life's exciting possibilities (Coleman, 1980). These psychologists would not be surprised that 9 of 10 high school seniors agree with the statement, "On the whole, I'm satisfied with myself" (*Public Opinion*, 1987).

Physical Development

Adolescence begins with puberty, when one is becoming sexually mature. Puberty follows a surge of hormones, which may intensify moods and which trigger a two-year period of rapid physical development that usually begins in girls at about age 11 and in boys at about age 13. About the time of puberty, boys grow as much as 5 inches a year, compared with about 3 inches for girls—propelling the average male to greater height than the average female (Figure 4.2). During this growth spurt, the reproductive organs and external genitalia—the primary sex characteristics—develop dramatically. So do the secondary sex characteristics, the nonreproductive traits of females and males, such as enlarged breasts and hips in girls, facial hair and a deepened voice in boys, pubic and underarm hair in both sexes (Figure 4.3).

The landmarks of puberty are the first ejaculation in boys, which usually occurs by about age 14, and the first menstrual period in girls, by about age 13. (These events need not signify fertility; it may be another year or more before ejaculations contain sufficient live sperm and the menstrual cycle includes ovulation [Tanner, 1978].)

The first menstrual period, called menarche (meh-NAR-key), is a memorable event, one that is recalled by nearly all adult women. Most experience and later recall a mixture of feelings—pride, excitement, embarrassment, and apprehension (Greif & Ulman, 1982; Woods & others, 1983). For the first few months many keep it a secret from friends; while most discuss it with their mothers, very few discuss it with their fathers (Brooks-Gunn, 1989). Girls prepared for menarche usually experience it as a positive life transition. And a transition it is. Regardless of their age, girls afterward increasingly see and present themselves as different from boys and function more independently of their parents (Golub, 1983). Most men similarly recall their first ejaculation, which usually occurs as a nocturnal emission (Fuller & Downs, 1990). For both sexes, physical concerns

ranging from acne to weight gain contribute to adolescent self-consciousness. For some, an extreme result is eating disorders (see page 371).

As in the earlier life stages, the *sequence* of physical changes (for example, breast buds and visible pubic hair before menarche) is far more predictable than their *timing*. Some girls start their growth spurt at 9, some boys as late as age 16. Such variations have little effect on height at maturity, but they may have psychological consequences. Studies performed in the 1950s by Mary Cover Jones and her colleagues revealed that early

Figure **4.2**

Height differences Throughout childhood, boys and girls are similar in height. At puberty, girls surge ahead briefly, but then boys overtake them at about age 14. (Data from Tanner, 1978.)

Figure **4.3**

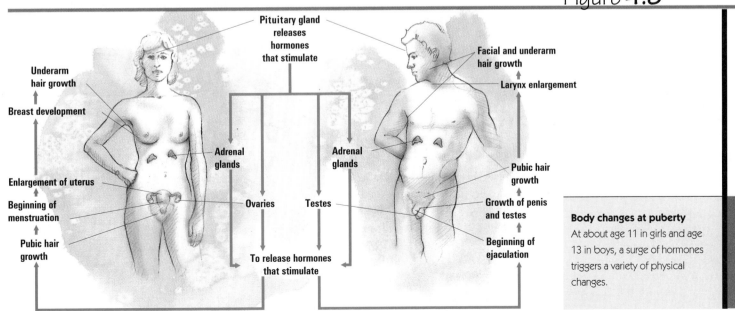

Body changes at puberty
At about age 11 in girls and age 13 in boys, a surge of hormones triggers a variety of physical changes.

maturation pays dividends for boys. Early-maturing boys, being stronger and more athletic during their early teen years, tend to be more popular, self-assured, and independent.

For girls, early maturation can be stressful. In Sweden, North America, and New Zealand, studies of girls whose menarche comes either early (before age 12) or late (age 14 or after) reveal that early maturation can amplify preexisting problems (Caspi & Moffitt, 1991; Simmons & Blyth, 1987; Stattin & Magnusson, 1990). If a young girl's body is out of sync with her emotional maturity and with what her friends are experiencing, she may begin associating with older friends and doing things considered out of bounds for girls her age. Moreover, the 11-year-old who towers over her classmates and becomes the object of sexual attention may temporarily suffer teasing and embarrassment (Petersen, 1987). But as her peers catch up, her postpubertal experience may help her to enjoy greater prestige and self-confidence.

For smooth adjustment it's not only when we mature that counts, but also how people around us react to our physical development. Remember: *Heredity and environment interact.* How the environment responds to the youngster depends on the genetically influenced timing of maturation.

Cognitive Development

Adolescents' developing ability to reason gives them a new level of social awareness and moral judgment. As young teenagers become capable of thinking about their thinking, and of thinking about other people's thinking, they begin imagining what other people are thinking about *them.* (Adolescents might worry less about what others think of them if they knew how similarly self-preoccupied their peers are.) As their cognitive abilities mature, many adolescents begin to think about what is ideally possible, and they begin to criticize their society, their parents, and even their own shortcomings.

Developing Reasoning Power

During the early teen years, reasoning is often self-focused. Adolescents may think their private experiences are unique. They may assume their parents just can't understand what it feels like to be dating or to hate school: "But, Mother, *you* don't really know how it feels to be in love" (Elkind, 1978).

Gradually, though, most achieve the intellectual summit that Piaget called *formal operations.* Preadolescents reason concretely, but adolescents

> *As young teenagers become capable of thinking about their thinking, and of thinking about other people's thinking, they begin imagining what other people are thinking about them.*

become more capable of abstract logic. They can reason hypothetically and deduce consequences: *If this, then that.* We can see this new abstract reasoning power as adolescents ponder and debate human nature, good and evil, truth and justice. Having perhaps envisioned God as an old man in the clouds when they were first capable of symbolic thinking in early childhood, they may now seek a deeper conception of God and existence (Elkind, 1970; Worthington, 1989). Adolescents' logical thinking also enables them to detect inconsistencies in others' reasoning and between their ideals and their actions. Indeed, their newfound ability to spot hypocrisy can lead to heated debates with parents and silent vows never to lose sight of their own ideals (Peterson & others, 1986).

Piaget (1972) may have underestimated the impact of culture and schooling and therefore overestimated the number of people who attain formal logic. If uneducated in the logic of science and mathematics, some adolescents and adults don't achieve formal operational reasoning. Consider this conversation between researcher Sylvia Scribner (1977) and an illiterate Kpelle farmer in a Liberian village:

"Ben is in his first year of high school, and he's questioning all the right things."

Drawing by Koren; ©1992 *The New Yorker Magazine, Inc.*

Demonstrating their reasoning ability Although on opposite sides of the abortion debate, these teens demonstrate their newfound ability to think logically about abstract topics. According to Piaget, they are in the final cognitive stage, formal operations.

Sylvia Scribner: All Kpelle men are rice farmers. Mr. Smith is not a rice farmer. Is he a Kpelle man?

Kpelle farmer: I don't know the man. I have not laid eyes on the man myself.

Kpelle villagers could, however, respond using formal logic if they had received formal schooling.

Developing Morality

A crucial task of childhood and adolescence is learning right from wrong and developing character—the psychological muscles for controlling impulses. To be a moral person is to *think* morally and *act* accordingly. "It is a delightful harmony when doing and saying go together," said the French essayist Montaigne. But such harmony often eludes us. "To put one's thoughts into action," noted the German poet Goethe, is "the most difficult thing in the world."

Moral Thinking

Piaget (1932) believed that children's moral judgments build on their cognitive development. Agreeing with Piaget, Lawrence Kohlberg (1981, 1984) sought to describe the development of *moral reasoning*, the thinking that occurs as we consider right and wrong. Kohlberg posed moral dilemmas to children, adolescents, and adults. He then analyzed their answers for evidence of stages of moral thinking. Ponder for a moment his best-known dilemma:

> In Europe, a woman was near death from a very bad disease, a special kind of cancer. There was one drug that the doctors thought might save her. It was a form of radium that a druggist in the same town had recently discovered. The drug was expensive to make, but the druggist was charging ten times what the drug cost him to make. He paid $200 for the radium and charged

$2,000 for a small dose of the drug. The sick woman's husband, Heinz, went to everyone he knew to borrow the money, but he could get together only about $1,000, which was half of what it cost. He told the druggist that his wife was dying and asked him to sell it cheaper or let him pay later. But the druggist said, "No, I discovered the drug and I'm going to make money from it." Heinz got desperate and broke into the man's store to steal the drug for his wife.

What do you think: Should Heinz have stolen the drug? Why was what he did right or wrong? Kohlberg would not have been interested in whether you judged Heinz's behavior as right or wrong—either answer could be justified—but rather in your reasoning. We all are moral philosophers, Kohlberg proposed, and our moral reasoning helps guide our judgments and behavior. Kohlberg himself discussed with a friend the moral dilemma of suicide before, nearing 60 and racked by pain, he committed suicide (Hunt, 1993).

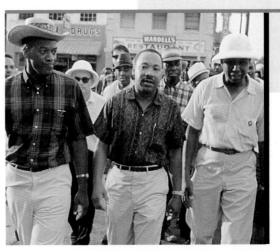

Martin Luther King, Jr. Those who conform to society's rules often do not take kindly to those who seek to change those rules. Kohlberg contended that postconventional moral thinking, embodied by Martin Luther King, Jr., may be rejected by those who do not comprehend it.

Kohlberg argued that as we develop intellectually we pass through as many as six stages of moral thinking, moving from the simplistic and concrete toward more abstract and principled reasoning. He clustered these six stages into three basic levels: preconventional, conventional, and postconventional.

Should we agree that Kohlberg's postconventional, Western morality is indeed the "highest" and most "mature" level? Would society benefit if we all disregarded conventions and followed our own perceptions of universal ethical principles?

- **Preconventional morality** Before age 9, most children have a preconventional morality of self-interest: They obey either to avoid punishment ("If you let your wife die, you will get in trouble") or to gain concrete rewards ("If you save your wife, you will be a hero").

- **Conventional morality** By early adolescence, morality usually evolves to a more conventional level that upholds laws and social rules simply because they are the laws and rules. Being able to take others' perspectives, adolescents may approve actions that will gain social approval or that will help maintain the social order ("If you steal the drug, everyone will think you are a criminal").

- **Postconventional morality** Those who develop the abstract reasoning of formal operational thought may come to a third level. Postconventional morality affirms people's agreed-upon rights ("People have a right to live") or follows what one personally perceives as basic ethical principles ("If you steal the drug, you won't have lived up to your own ideals").

Kohlberg's controversial claim was that these levels form a moral ladder (Figure 4.4). The rungs extend from a young child's immature, preconventional morality at the bottom to an adult's self-defined ethical principles at the top. As with all stage theories, the sequence does not vary. We begin on the bottom rung and ascend to varying heights.

Research confirms that children in various cultures do progress from the level Kohlberg called preconventional into the stages of his conventional level (Edwards, 1981, 1982; Snarey, 1985, 1987). And as our *thinking* matures, our *behavior* also becomes less selfish and more caring (Krebs & Van Hesteren, 1994; Miller & others, 1996). However, the postconventional level appears mostly in the European and North American educated middle class, which prizes individualism—giving priority to one's own goals rather than group goals (Eckensberger, 1994; Miller & Bersoff, 1995). Critics therefore contend that the theory is biased against the moral reasoning of those in communal societies such as China and India—and also against women, whose morality may be less a matter of abstract, impersonal principles and more a matter of caring relationships.

Figure **4.4**

Kohlberg's moral ladder Why is it wrong to steal or cheat on an exam? As moral development progresses, the focus of concern moves from the self to the wider social world.

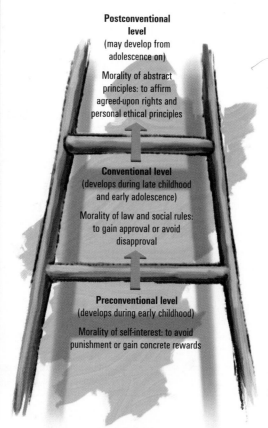

Postconventional level
(may develop from adolescence on)

Morality of abstract principles: to affirm agreed-upon rights and personal ethical principles

Conventional level
(develops during late childhood and early adolescence)

Morality of law and social rules: to gain approval or avoid disapproval

Preconventional level
(develops during early childhood)

Morality of self-interest: to avoid punishment or gain concrete rewards

"I am a bit suspicious of any theory that says that the highest moral stage is one in which people talk like college professors."

JAMES Q. WILSON
THE MORAL SENSE
1993

Moral Action

Our moral reasoning surely influences our moral talk, but sometimes talk is cheap. Morality is also *doing* the right thing, and what we do depends not only on our thinking but on social influences. As political theorist Hannah Arendt (1963) observed, many Nazi concentration camp guards during World War II were ordinary "moral" people who were corrupted by a powerfully evil situation.

Because of social influences, people's willingness to cheat, to discriminate racially, and to smoke marijuana are not neatly determined by their attitudes toward cheating, race, and drugs. The best predictor of whether a high school student smokes marijuana, for instance, is simply how many of the student's friends smoke it (Oetting & Beauvais, 1987). (Of course, adolescents also sort themselves into likeminded groups—the jocks, the nerds, the druggies, and so forth.)

"This might not be ethical. Is that a problem for anybody?"

Drawing by Victor; ©1987 The New Yorker Magazine, Inc.

Given the slack between thinking and acting, effective moral education must focus on both. We can stimulate children's moral reasoning through discussions of moral issues and their implications. We can teach children empathy for others' feelings. And we can teach them the self-discipline needed to restrain their impulses—to delay small gratifications now for the sake of bigger gratifications later. Those who learn to delay gratification become more socially responsible, academically successful, and productive (Funder & Block, 1989; Mischel & others, 1988, 1989).

We can also focus directly on just and caring moral commitments by teaching and modeling such behaviors. When parents set high moral standards and practice what they preach, their moral principles become forceful. Such was true of the caring parents of those morally courageous people who protected Jews in Nazi Europe (Oliner & Oliner, 1988).

Moral ideas grow stronger when acted on. As we will see in Chapter 18, our actions feed our attitudes. We are as likely to act ourselves into a way of thinking as to think ourselves into action. To develop deeper moral principles, people can act on the ones they have. To stand up and be counted, to explain and defend our convictions, to commit money and energy, is then to believe our convictions more strongly.

Social Development

Theorist Erik Erikson (1963) contended that each stage of life has its own "psychosocial" task, a crisis that needs resolution. Young children wrestle with issues of *trust* (page 98), then *autonomy* (independence), then *initiative* (Table 4.1). School-age children develop *competence*, the sense that

Erikson's Stages of Psychosocial Development

Table **4.1**

Approximate Age	Stage	Description of Task
Infancy (1st year)	Trust vs. mistrust	If needs are dependably met, infants develop a sense of basic trust.
Toddler (2nd year)	Autonomy vs. shame and doubt	Toddlers learn to exercise will and do things for themselves, or they doubt their abilities.
Preschooler (3–5 years)	Initiative vs. guilt	Preschoolers learn to initiate tasks and carry out plans, or they feel guilty about efforts to be independent.
Elementary school (6 years to puberty)	Competence vs. inferiority	Children learn the pleasure of applying themselves to tasks, or they feel inferior.
Adolescence (teen years into 20s)	Identity vs. role confusion	Teenagers work at refining a sense of self by testing roles and then integrating them to form a single identity, or they become confused about who they are.
Young adulthood (20s to early 40s)	Intimacy vs. isolation	Young adults struggle to form close relationships and to gain the capacity for intimate love, or they feel socially isolated.
Middle adulthood (40s to 60s)	Generativity vs. stagnation	The middle-aged discover a sense of contributing to the world, usually through family and work, or they may feel a lack of purpose.
Late adulthood (late 60s and up)	Integrity vs. despair	When reflecting on his or her life, the older adult may feel a sense of satisfaction or failure.

identity
one's sense of self; according to Erikson, the adolescent's task is to solidify a sense of self by testing and integrating various roles.

they are able and productive human beings. In adolescence, the task is to synthesize past, present, and future possibilities into a clearer sense of self. Adolescents wonder "Who am I as an individual? What do I want to do with my life? What values should I live by? What do I believe in?" Erikson called this quest to define one's sense of self more deeply the adolescent's "search for identity."

As sometimes happens in psychology, Erikson's interests were bred by his own life experience. As the son of a Jewish mother and a Danish father, Erikson was "doubly an outsider," reports Morton Hunt (1993, p. 391). He was "scorned as a Jew in school but mocked as a Gentile in the synagogue because of his blond hair and blue eyes" (from his Danish biological father). Such episodes fueled his interest in the adolescent struggle for identity.

Forming an Identity

To refine their sense of identity, adolescents in Western cultures usually try out different "selves" in different situations—perhaps acting out one self at home, another with friends, and still another at school and work. If two of these situations overlap—as when a teenager brings home friends with whom he is Joe Cool—the discomfort can be considerable. The teen asks, "Which self should I be? Which is the real me?" Often, this role confusion is resolved by the gradual reshaping of a self-definition that unifies the various selves into a consistent and comfortable sense of who one is—an identity.

But not always. Erikson noticed that some adolescents forge their identity early, simply by taking on their parents' values and expectations. (Traditional, less individualistic cultures tell adolescents who they are rather than letting them decide on their own.) Other adolescents may adopt a negative identity that defines itself in opposition to parents and society but in conformity with a particular peer group—complete, perhaps, with shaved head or

pierced body parts. Still others never quite seem to find themselves or to develop strong commitments. For most, the identity question—Who am I?—continues past the teen years and reappears at turning points during adult life.

The late teen years, when many people begin attending college or working full time, provide new opportunities for trying out possible roles. As seniors, many students have achieved a clearer identity than they had as first-year students (Waterman, 1988). Their identity typically incorporates an increasingly positive self-concept. In several nationwide studies, researchers have given young Americans tests of self-esteem. (Sample item: "I am able to do things as well as most other people.") Between ages 13 and 23, the self-concept usually becomes more positive, especially among boys and among those who belong to a satisfying peer group. A clearer, more self-affirming identity is forming, and with it comes a greater sense of control over one's future (Baumgardner, 1990; O'Malley & Bachman, 1983; Strange & Forsyth, 1993).

> "I am becoming still more independent of my parents; young as I am, I face life with more courage than Mummy; my feeling for justice is immovable, and truer than hers. I know what I want, I have a goal, an opinion, I have a religion, and love. Let me be myself and then I am satisfied. I know that I'm a woman, a woman with inward strength and plenty of courage."
>
> **ANNE FRANK**
> *DIARY OF A YOUNG GIRL*
> 1947

During these years, identity also becomes more personalized. Daniel Hart (1988) asked youths of various ages to imagine a machine that would clone *(a)* what you think and feel, *(b)* your appearance, or *(c)* your relationships with friends and

Who shall I be today? By varying the way they look, adolescents try out different "selves." Although we eventually form a consistent and stable sense of identity, the "self" we present may change with the situation.

family. He then asked (and you might pause to ask yourself) which of these clones "is closest to being you?" Among seventh-graders, three-fourths chose *(c)*, the one with the same social network. Among ninth-graders, three-fourths chose *(a)*, the clone with their individual thoughts and feelings.

Developing Intimacy

Erikson contended that the adolescent identity stage is followed in young adulthood by a developing capacity for intimacy, the ability to form emotionally close relationships. Once you have a clear and comfortable sense of who you are, said Erikson, you are ready for close relationships.

Gender and Social Connectedness

To Carol Gilligan and her colleagues (1982, 1990), the "normal" struggle to create one's separate identity describes individualist males more than relationship-oriented females. Gilligan believes females are less concerned than are males with viewing themselves as separate individuals, and are more concerned with "making connections."

This gender difference surfaces early, in children's play. Boys typically play in large groups with an activity focus and little intimate discussion. Girls play in smaller groups, often with one friend. Girls' play is less competitive than boys' and more imitative of social relationships (Lever, 1978). In play and in later achievement settings, females are more open and responsive to feedback than are males (Maccoby, 1990; Roberts, 1991). As teens, girls spend more time with friends and less time alone (Wong & Csikszentmihalyi, 1991).

The gender difference in connectedness carries into adulthood. Women, being more *interdependent*, use conversation to explore relationships; men use it to convey solutions (Tannen, 1990). Women emphasize caring and provide most of the care to the very young and the very old. Although 69 percent of people say they have a close relationship with their father, 90 percent say they're close to their mother (Hugick, 1989). Men, like empowered people generally, emphasize freedom and self-reliance. (That helps explain why at all ages men assign less importance to religion and pray less often than their female counterparts [Benson, 1992].)

Women also have closer relationships with each other. Study after study finds the bonds and feelings of support stronger among women than those among men (Rossi & Rossi, 1990). Women's ties, as mothers, daughters, sisters, and grandmothers, bind families together. As friends, women are more intimate than men; they talk more often and more openly (Berndt, 1992; Dindia & Allen, 1992). Women's more intense relationships don't always lead to liking, however. Women's friends, less often than men's, are friends with each other (Kashima & others, 1995).

When surveyed, women are far more likely than men to describe themselves as having empathy. If you are empathic, you identify with others. You rejoice with those who rejoice and weep with those who weep. You imagine what it must feel like to live with that problem, what it must be like to try so hard to impress people, what a thrill it must be to win that award. Physiological measures of empathy, such as one's heart rate while seeing an-

intimacy
in Erikson's theory, the ability to form close, loving relationships; a primary developmental task in late adolescence and early adulthood.

"What's the difference between a man and E.T.? E.T. phoned home."

ANONYMOUS

Gender and human bonds Empathy, social support, and talk about relationships often seem to come more "naturally" to females.

other's distress, reveal a much smaller gender gap than reported in surveys (Eisenberg & Lennon, 1983). Nevertheless, females are more likely to *express* empathy—to cry and to report distress when observing someone in distress.

Moreover, studies consistently find females better at reading people's emotional cues (Hall, 1987). Shown a silent, 2-second film clip of an upset woman's face, women are better than men at sensing whether she is criticizing someone for being late or discussing a divorce. Women's nonverbal sensitivity, perhaps a by-product of their roles, helps explain their greater emotional responsiveness in positive and negative situations (Grossman & Wood, 1993; Sprecher & Sedikides, 1993; Stoppard & Gruchy, 1993). It also helps explain why both men and women report their friendships with women to be more intimate, enjoyable, and nurturing (Rubin, 1985; Sapadin, 1988). When wanting understanding and someone with whom to share worries and hurts, both men and women usually turn to women.

Separating from Parents

As adolescents seek to form their own identities, they begin to separate themselves from their parents (Paikoff & Brooks-Gunn, 1991). The preschooler who can't be close enough to mother, who loves to touch and cling to her, becomes the 14-year-old who wouldn't be caught dead holding hands with mom. Arguments more often occur, usually over small things such as household chores, bed time, and homework (Tesser & others, 1989).

For a minority of parents and their adolescents, differences mean estrangement. But for most, disagreement at the level of bickering is not destructive.

- A study of 6000 adolescents in 10 countries, from Australia to Bangladesh to Turkey, found that most liked their parents (Offer & others, 1988). "We usually get along but . . . ," adolescents often report (Galambos, 1992; Steinberg, 1987).

- In one survey of 25,000 middle-class teens worldwide, more than 80 percent rated family relationships as an "important" guiding principle for their lives, and more than half said it was *most* important—more significant than their "relationship with friends," "having fun," or "making the world a better place" (Stepp, 1996).

- A Gallup poll (1996) of American teens reported that 97 percent said they got along "fairly" or "very" well with their parents. Most, however, reported getting along better with Mom than with Dad. Positive relations with parents support positive peer relations. High school girls who have the most affectionate relationships with their mothers tend also to enjoy the most intimate friendships with girlfriends (Gold & Yanof, 1985).

Moreover, most families easily bridge the generation gap, because it is rather narrow. Most adolescents closely reflect the social, political, and religious views of their parents (Gallatin, 1980). As often as not, "generation gaps" on such issues merely involve differences in the degree to which adolescents and their parents hold their shared views (Figure 4.5).

Figure **4.5**

High school seniors' attitudes versus those of their parents As this study found, high school seniors' attitudes appear to be in much closer agreement with those of their parents than many might suppose. Agreement is greater, however, on basic values than on life-style choices. (From Bachman & others, 1987.)

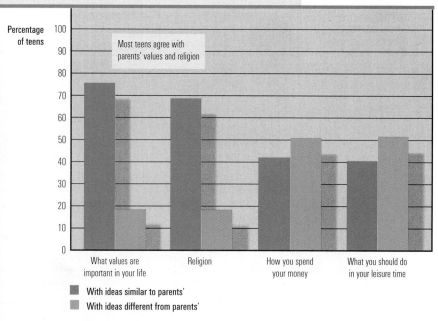

In Western cultures, adolescence is typically a time of growing peer influence and diminishing parental influence, especially on matters of personal taste and life-style. Asked in a 1997 survey if they "ever had a serious talk" with their child about illegal drugs, 85 percent of American parents answered yes. But the teens often tuned out their parents' earnest advice, for only 45 percent could recall such a talk (Morin & Brossard, 1997). Instead, what their friends are—what "everybody's doing"—they often become. One study asked teens to report their emotions when beeped by electronic pagers at random times. Most reported feeling more free and open with friends than with family (Larson & Bradney, 1988).

Peer influences on development may actually exceed parental influences, argued Judith Harris (1995). Consider:

- Preschoolers who disdain a certain food despite parents' urgings often will eat the food if put at a table with a group of children who like it.

- Children's (and monkeys') development seems less impaired by isolation from parents if close relationships with peers are available. One group of six Jewish children spent their first three years in a Nazi concentration camp, cared for by an ever-changing series of adults, none of whom survived. When the children arrived in England they cared only about one another, yet they grew up to become normal, effective adults.

- Direct parental influences on smoking are less important than many people suppose. Rather, teens who start smoking typically have friends who model smoking, who suggest its pleasures, and who offer cigarettes.

- Nazi youth group members mostly came from emotionally supportive, middle-class homes, according to behavior geneticist David Rowe (1990, 1994). What corrupted them was not bad parenting but the "heavier weight" of cultural change around them.

As people mature during the twenties, emotional ties between parents and children continue to loosen. During their early twenties, many still lean heavily on their parents. (From 1970 to 1994, the percentage of American 18- to 24-year-olds living with parents increased from 47 to 53 percent.) By their late twenties, most feel more comfortably independent of their parents and better able to empathize with them as fellow adults (Frank, 1988; White, 1983). As the twentieth century winds down, this graduation from adolescence to adulthood is taking longer. From Europe to Australia, adolescents are taking longer to finish college, to leave the nest, to establish their careers. Since 1960, Americans' average age at first marriage has increased nearly 4 years (to 26 for men, 24 for women).

Adolescent Sexuality and Pregnancy

Adolescents' physical maturation fosters a sexual dimension to their emerging identity. How and when sexuality is expressed differs with time and culture. In the United States, about half of ninth- to twelfth-graders report having sexual intercourse, as do 42 percent of Canadian 16-year-olds (Boroditsky & others, 1995; MMWR, 1995). Teen intercourse rates are higher in Western Europe but much lower in Arab and Asian countries. In one survey only 2.5 percent of 4688 unmarried Chinese students entering Hong Kong's six universities reported having had sexual intercourse (Meston & others, 1996). These varying sexual standards from country to country help explain culture differences in rates of nonmarital childbearing (Figure 4.6).

"Will your child learn to multiply before she learns to subtract?"

ANTI-TEEN-PREGNANCY POSTER
CHILDREN'S DEFENSE FUND

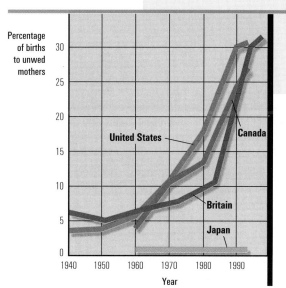

Figure 4.6

Births to unwed parents Since 1960, the percentage of babies born to unmarried Canadian, British, and American women—one-third of whom were teens—has more than quintupled. This increase stems from two trends: a decreasing birthrate among married women and a doubling of the birthrate among unmarried women. (Data from National Center for Health Statistics; Bureau of the Census [1996], Table 1330; and British Central Statistical Office, 1993.)

The increased adolescent pregnancy rate and the often impoverished futures of teen mothers and of children in father-absent homes have prompted new research on teen sexuality and adolescents' use of contraceptives. Short of "just saying no," contraceptives are the surest strategy of preventing pregnancy. Although the number of American teenagers using condoms doubled during the 1980s, half of teen sexual acts were unprotected. Only one-third of sexually active male teens used condoms consistently (Sonenstein, 1992). Why? Among the contributing factors are these:

1 **Ignorance** In eight surveys, fewer than half the adolescents could correctly identify the safe and risky times of the menstrual cycle (Morrison, 1985). Half of sexually active Canadian teen girls have mistaken ideas about which birth control methods will protect them from pregnancy and sexually transmitted diseases (STDs) (Immen, 1995). Thus, most unwed teens report surprise at finding themselves pregnant (Brooks-Gunn & Furstenberg, 1989).

2 **Guilt related to sexual activity** Although sexual inhibitions reduce sexual activity, they also result in lack of planned birth control for those who do engage in sex (Gerrard & Luus, 1995). Not wanting to appear deliberately sexual or promiscuous, teens may hesitate to carry and produce a condom. When, as sometimes happens, passion overwhelms intentions, the result may be conception.

3 **Minimal communication about birth control** Many teenagers are uncomfortable discussing contraception with parents, partners, and peers (Kotva & Schneider, 1990; Milan & Kilmann, 1987). Teens are more likely to use contraceptives if they talk freely with friends or parents and are in an exclusive relationship with a partner with whom they communicate openly.

4 **Alcohol use** Sexually active teens are typically alcohol-using teens (National Research Council, 1987). By depressing brain centers that control judgment, inhibition, and self-awareness, alcohol tends to break down normal restraints, a phenomenon well known to sexually coercive males (page 231).

5 **Mass media norms of unprotected promiscuity** The Planned Parenthood Federation (1986) has complained that television and movies help define sexual norms, which today are "Go for it *now*. . . ." An average hour of prime-time television on the three major U.S. networks contains approximately 15 sexual acts, words, and innuendos. Nearly all of these instances involve unmarried partners, and few communicate any concern for birth control or sexually transmitted disease (Sapolsky & Tabarlet, 1991). Planned Parenthood contends that repeated portrayals of unsafe sex, without consequence, amounts to a campaign of sex disinformation.

"All of us who make motion pictures are teachers, teachers with very loud voices."

FILM PRODUCER GEORGE LUCAS
ACADEMY AWARD CEREMONIES
1992

FEIFFER

SEX IN MOVIES.

SEX IN ROCK LYRICS.

SEX ON TV.

SEX IN ADVERTISING.

CONTRACEPTIVES IN SCHOOL—

TO PROTECT US FROM THE SEX EDUCATION WE GET IN THE MEDIA.

With teen pregnancy having risen despite increased sex education, the U.S. national health objectives for the year 2000 include a dual aim: increasing condom use to 90 percent among those sexually active, and reducing the proportion of 17-year-olds who have had intercourse from approximately 70 percent to under 40 percent (Centers for Disease Control, 1992). Sex education is similarly shifting toward a two-pronged emphasis on both contraception ("safe sex") and commitment ("saved sex").

The shift to include teen abstinence within comprehensive sex education is also a response to increased rates of sexually transmitted disease (STD)—in the U.S. 12 million cases annually, not including bacterial diseases such as chlamydia, syphilis, and gonorrhea (Guttmacher Institute, 1993). More than 60 percent of these new infections occur in persons under 25. Because of their less mature biological development and fewer protective antibodies, teenage girls seem to be especially vulnerable to STD and associated risks of becoming infertile and developing certain cancers (Guttmacher, 1994; Morell, 1995).

To comprehend the mathematics of sexually transmitted disease, imagine an island on which all people were virgins until one year ago, when they began having sex. Pat has sex with nine people, each of whom over the same time period has sex with nine other people, who in turn have sex with nine others. How many "phantom" sex partners (past partners of partners) will Pat have? Ohio State researchers Laura Brannon and Timothy Brock (1994) report that the actual number—511—is more than five times what the average student's guess is.

Given these odds, the rapid spread of STDs is not surprising. Condoms can reduce the risk of HIV transmission by two-thirds, although they do not always prevent transmission (condoms can leak HIV) (Weller, 1993). With certain other STDs, notably the human papilloma virus which is responsible for most genital cancers, condoms are virtually useless (Medical Institute, 1994).

Throughout history, the pendulum of sexual values has swung—from the European eroticism of the early 1800s to the conservative Victorian era of the late 1800s, from the libertine flapper era of the 1920s to the family values of the 1950s. With new 1990s voices decrying family disintegration and calling for a balance between sexual expression and restraint, the pendulum may have begun a new swing toward commitment. In West Germany, the percentage of teens who link sex with committed love is up significantly since 1970 (Schmidt & others, 1994). And would you agree or disagree that "if two people like each other, it's all right for them to have sex even if they've known each other for a very short time"? The percent of first-year American college and university students who agree dropped from 52 percent in 1987 to 42 percent in 1996 (Sax & others, 1996).

"We cannot renew our country when within a decade more than half of our children will be born into families where there is no marriage."

BILL CLINTON
STATE OF THE UNION ADDRESS, 1994

Social Development Erik Erikson theorized that a chief task of adolescence is solidifying one's sense of self—one's identity. For many people, this struggle continues into the adult years as new relationships emerge and new roles are assumed. Although adolescence has traditionally been viewed as a time of storm and stress, researchers have found that most teenagers relate to their parents reasonably well and generally affirm their parents' beliefs and attitudes. In the Western world, the last 35 years have been a time of changing sexual standards and increasing risk of teen pregnancy and sexually transmitted disease.

KEY TERMS AND CONCEPTS adolescence, puberty, primary sex characteristics, secondary sex characteristics, menarche, identity, intimacy

SUMMING UP

Due to earlier maturation and prolonged education, adolescence—the transition years between biological maturity and social independence—has lengthened in many countries.

Physical Development Adolescence begins with a growth spurt that heralds the period of sexual maturation we call puberty and ends with the achievement of adult independence. Depending on how other people react, early or late maturation can influence adjustment, which again illustrates how genes and environment interact in shaping us.

Cognitive Development Piaget theorized that adolescents develop the capacity for formal operations, which enables them to reason abstractly. However, some developmentalists believe that the development of formal logic depends on schooling as well, and that the rudiments of logic appear earlier than Piaget believed.

Following Piaget's lead, Lawrence Kohlberg contended that moral thinking likewise proceeds through a sequence of stages, from a preconventional morality of self-interest, to a conventional morality concerned with gaining others' approval or doing one's duty, to (in some people) a postconventional morality of agreed-upon rights or universal ethical principles. But morality also lies in actions, which are influenced by the social situation and inner attitudes as well as by moral reasoning. Moreover, say Kohlberg's critics, the postconventional level represents morality from the perspective of individualist, liberal-minded males.

Adulthood

As we age, our paths diverge. Yet we all continue to develop physically, cognitively, and socially. What sensory and neural changes mark the aging process? In what ways do memory and intelligence change? Is the journey from adolescence to death marked by stages that serve as developmental milestones?

At one time, psychologists viewed adulthood, especially the center-of-life years between adolescence and old age, as one long plateau. No longer. Those who follow the unfolding of people's adult lives now believe development continues. Physically, cognitively, and especially socially, people at age 50 differ from their 25-year-old selves.

It's harder to generalize about adulthood stages than about life's early years. During adulthood, age only modestly correlates with people's traits. If you know that James is a 1-year-old and Jamal is a 10-year-old, you could say a great deal about each child. Not so with adults who differ by a similar number of years. The boss may be 30 or 60; the marathon runner may be 20 or 50; your classmates may be teenagers or grandparents. Likewise, a 19-year-old can be a parent who supports a child or a child who gets an allowance. Yet our life courses are in some ways similar. Our bodies, our minds, and our relationships undergo some changes in common with those of childhood friends, who in other ways now seem so very different.

"I am still learning."

MICHELANGELO
1560, AT AGE 85

menopause
the time of natural cessation of menstruation; also refers to the biological changes a woman experiences as her ability to reproduce declines.

Physical Changes

Although few of us are aware of it at the time, our physical abilities peak in early adulthood. Muscular strength, reaction time, sensory keenness, and cardiac output all crest by the mid-twenties. Like the declining daylight after the summer solstice, declining physical prowess begins imperceptibly. Athletes are often the first to notice. World-class sprinters and swimmers peak in their teens or early twenties. Women, because they mature earlier than men, also peak earlier. But most people—especially those whose daily lives do not require peak physical performance—hardly perceive the early signs of decline.

Physical Changes in Middle Adulthood

Middle-aged athletes know all too well that physical decline gradually accelerates (Figure 4.7). As a 54-year-old who regularly plays full-court basketball, I now find myself occasionally wondering whether my team really needs me down court. But even diminished vigor is sufficient for normal activities. Moreover, during early and middle adulthood, physical vigor has less to do with age than with a person's health and exercise habits. Many of today's physically fit 50-year-olds run 4 miles with ease, while sedentary 25-year-olds find themselves huffing and puffing up two flights of stairs. Even many 70-year-olds don't yet feel old. How old does a person have to be before you think of them as old? The average 18- to 29-year-old says 67. The average person 60 and over says 76 (Yankelovich, 1995).

As in adolescence, the physical changes of adult life may trigger psychological responses, which vary depending on how one views growing older. In some Eastern cultures, where respect and power come with age, outward signs of advancing years are accepted and even welcomed. In Western cultures, where the perceived ideal is smooth skin and a slim torso, the wrinkles and bulges that frequently accompany middle age can threaten self-esteem. Billions are therefore spent in hopes of slowing the process. But nature will not be denied; inevitably the lines appear and the youthful form begins to change its shape.

For women, the foremost biological sign of aging is menopause, the ending of the menstrual cycle, usually beginning within a few years of age 50. Menopause and its physical symptoms, such as hot flashes in some women, accompany a reduction in the hormone estrogen. Like the stereotype of adolescent storm and stress, the image of menopausal emotionality and depression clashes with reality: Menopause usually does *not* create psychological problems for women. One survey of 2500 middle-aged Massachusetts women, another that followed 541 middle-aged Pennsylvania women for 3 years, and yet another that followed 3049 middle-aged women over 10 years all found them no more or less depressed if experiencing menopause (Busch & others, 1994; Matthews, 1992; McKinlay & others, 1987a,b).

A woman's expectations and attitudes regarding menopause influence its emotional impact. Does she see menopause as a sign that she is losing her femininity and sexual attractiveness and growing old? Or does she look on it as liberation from contraceptives, menstrual periods, fears of pregnancy, and children's demands?

To learn women's attitudes toward menopause, Bernice Neugarten and her colleagues (1963) did what, amazingly, no one had bothered to do: They questioned women whose experience of menopause had not led them to seek treatment. When asked whether it is true that after menopause "women generally feel better than they have for years," only one-fourth of the premenopausal women under age 45 guessed yes. Of the older women who had experienced menopause, two-thirds said yes. As one woman said, "I can remember my mother saying that after her menopause she really got her vigor, and I can say the same thing myself." Social psychologist Jacqueline Goodchilds (1987) quipped: "If the truth were known, we'd have to diagnose [older women] as having P.M.F.—Post-Menstrual Freedom."

Men experience no equivalent to the menopause—no cessation of fertility, no sharp drop in sex hormones. But they do experience a more gradual decline in sperm count, testosterone level, and speed of erection and ejaculation. Some may also experience psychological distress related to their perception of decreased virility and declining

After age 30, the risk of death doubles every 8 years. Although a 48-year-old's life expectancy is greater today than it was a century ago, his or her risk of dying is still twice as high as that of a 40-year-old (National Center for Health Statistics, 1992; Olshansky & others, 1993).

Figure **4.7**

The slow decline of the body's physical capacities during adulthood (Adapted from Insel & Roth, 1976.)

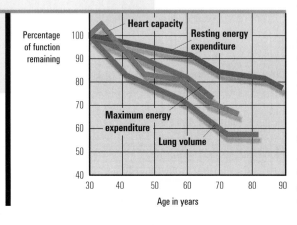

physical capacities. Nevertheless, after middle age most men and women remain capable of satisfying sexual activity.

Physical Changes in Later Life

Is old age "more to be feared than death" (Juvenal, *Satires*)? Or is life "most delightful when it is on the downward slope" (Seneca, *Epistulae ad Lucilium*)? What is it like to grow old? To gauge your own understanding, take the following true/false quiz:

1 By the year 2050, 1 in 10 people worldwide will be 65 or older (see page 130).

2 Older people become more susceptible to short-term illnesses (see page 131).

3 About one-fourth of people over age 65 live in nursing homes, hospitals, homes for the aged, or other institutions (see page 131).

4 During old age many of the brain's neurons die (see page 132).

5 If they live to be 90 or older, most elderly people eventually become senile (see page 132).

6 Recognition memory—the ability to identify things previously experienced—declines with age (see page 133).

7 Life satisfaction peaks in the fifties and then gradually declines after age 65 (see pages 140–141).

8 Among the elderly, there are twice as many widows as widowers (see page 141).

9 A fear of death preoccupies many older people (see page 141).

Life Expectancy

The above statements—all false—are among the myths about aging exploded by recent research on the world's most rapidly growing population group. The post–65-year-old population rose from fewer than 1 in 100 in 1900 to 1 in 16 in 1992, en route to 1 in 5 by 2050 (Figure 4.8). Worldwide, life expectancy increased from 49 years in 1950 to 67 in 1995 (Sivard, 1996).

The oldest known person ever to have lived was Shirechiyo Izumi of Japan, who died in 1986 at age 120 years, 237 days (National Institute on Aging, 1993).

Figure 4.8

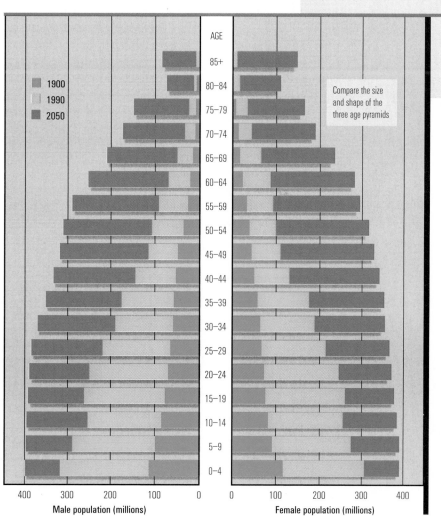

The aging world population
The age pyramid is becoming more rectangular, indicating a greater proportion of older people. (From Olshansky & others, 1993.)

Figure **4.9**

Australians' life expectancy, by age and sex   In Australia, as elsewhere, women have greater life expectancy at every age. (McLennan, 1995)

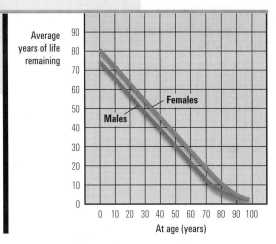

In developing countries, the proportionately small elderly population will double between 1980 and 2000. In China, where there were five children per elderly person in 1955, there will be but two children per elderly person in 2040 (Hugo, 1987). In Europe, the over-65 population will rise from 20 percent to 30 percent or more by 2025 (Pawlik & d'Ydewalle, 1996). Clearly, countries that depend on children to care for the aged are destined for major social changes.

Although 126 male embryos begin life for every 100 females who do so, males are more death-prone ever after (Strickland, 1992). By birth, the sex ratio is down to 105 males for every 100 females. During the first year, male infants' death rates exceed females' by one-fourth. Women outlive men by 3 years worldwide and by nearly 7 years in Canada, the United States, and Australia (Figure 4.9). (Rather than marrying a man older than themselves, 20-year-old women who want a husband who shares their life expectancy should wait for the 14-year-old boys to mature.) By age 100, females outnumber males 5 to 1.

But few of us live to 100, because even in the absence of a fatal disease or accident, the body senesces: It ages. Its cells stop reproducing. It becomes frail. It becomes vulnerable to tiny insults—hot weather, a fall, a mild flu bug—that would have been trivial at age 20. Even if no one died before age 50 and cancer, heart disease, and infectious illness were eliminated, life expectancy would still increase only to 85, by some estimates, or a few years beyond that, by other estimates (Barinaga, 1991).

But why do we age, eventually wearing out? Why don't we, like the bristlecone pine trees, rockfish, and some social insect queens, grow older without withering? One theory, proposed by evolutionary biologists, speculates that the answer relates to our survival as a species: We pass on our genes most successfully when we raise our young and then stop consuming resources. Moreover, once we've fulfilled our gene-reproducing task there are no natural selection pressures against genes that cause degeneration in later life (Olshansky & others, 1993; Sapolsky & Finch, 1991).

Sensory Abilities

As we have seen, physical decline begins in early adulthood, but not until later life do people become acutely aware of it. As visual sharpness diminishes and adaptation to changes in light level slows, older people have more accidents. Most stairway falls taken by older persons occur on the top step, precisely where the person typically descends from a window-lit hallway into the darker stairwell (Fozard & Popkin, 1978). By using what we know about aging when designing environments, we could reduce such accidents (National Research Council, 1990). Muscle strength, hearing, distance perception, reaction time, and stamina also diminish noticeably (Figure 4.10). In later life, the stairs

Figure **4.10**

The aging senses   Sight, smell, and hearing all decline in later life. (From Doty & others, 1984.)

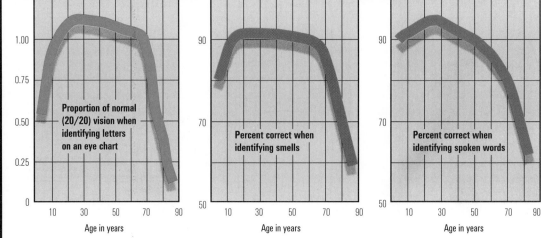

get steeper, the newsprint gets smaller, and people seem to mumble more. My 88-year-old father speaks for many nearing life's end: "Growing old is the nuts." After age 70, car accident rates per mile increase, reaching the relatively high teenage level by age 75 (National Research Council, 1990).

With age, the eye's pupil shrinks and its lens becomes less transparent, reducing the amount of light reaching the retina. In fact, a 65-year-old retina receives only about one-third as much light as its 20-year-old counterpart (Kline & Schieber, 1985). Thus, to see as well as a 20-year-old when reading or driving, a 65-year-old needs three times as much light—a reason for buying cars with untinted windshields. This also explains why older people sometimes ask younger people, "Don't you need better light for reading?"

Keeping the biological clock running smoothly How quickly people age depends in part on their health habits. As this cheerful group makes clear, the more active people remain, the more vigor they retain.

Health

For those growing older, there is both bad and good news about health. The bad news: The body's disease-fighting immune system weakens, making the elderly more susceptible to life-threatening ailments such as cancer and pneumonia. It's as if the very old have a very mild case of AIDS—the immune deficiency that hampers the body's ability to fight infections.

The good news: Thanks to a lifetime's accumulation of antibodies, older people *less* often suffer short-term ailments, such as common flu and cold viruses. For example, those over 65 are half as likely as 20-year-olds and one-fifth as likely as preschoolers to suffer upper respiratory flu each year (National Center for Health Statistics, 1990). This is one reason why older workers have lower absenteeism rates (Rhodes, 1983).

One survey revealed that most elderly people believe the majority of their peers suffer serious health problems. But when asked about their own

To see as well as a 20-year-old when reading or driving, a 65-year-old needs three times as much light.

health, fewer than one in four reported that *they* have such a problem (National Council on the Aging, 1976). So it shouldn't surprise us that only 5 percent of all those over 65 live in hospitals, nursing homes, and other such institutions.

By slowing neural processing, aging levies a tax on the brain. During the early years of life, up to the teen years, we process information more and more speedily (Fry & Hale, 1996; Kail, 1991). But compared with teens and young adults, older people take a bit more time to react, to solve perceptual puzzles, even to remember names (Bashore, 1994; Salthouse, 1992, 1994; and see Figure 4.11).

Figure **4.11**

Age and fatal accidents Slowing reactions contribute to increased accident risks among those 75 and older (Stock, 1995). Would you favor driver exams based on performance, not age, to screen out those whose slow reactions or mental confusion indicate accident risk?

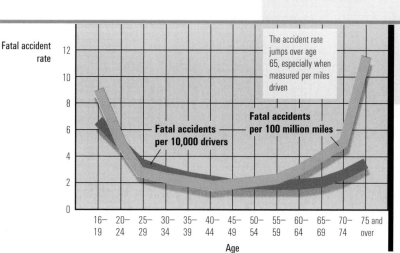

The accident rate jumps over age 65, especially when measured per miles driven

Fatal accidents per 10,000 drivers

Fatal accidents per 100 million miles

Age

Alzheimer's disease
a progressive and irreversible brain disorder characterized by gradual deterioration of memory, reasoning, language, and, finally, physical functioning.

If—as now seems likely—it becomes possible to discern by brain scans or genetic testing those likely to suffer Alzheimer's disease, would you want to take the test? If so, at what age would you take it?

Speed slows especially when the task becomes complex (Cerella, 1985; Poon, 1987). At video games, most 70-year-olds are no match for a 20-year-old. As we age, we become aware of a growing gap between what we were and what we are becoming.

During aging, brain regions important to memory begin to atrophy (Schacter, 1996). Beginning in young adulthood, there is also a small, gradual loss of brain cells, contributing to a 5 percent or so reduction of brain weight by age 80. But the proliferation of neural connections, especially in people who remain active, helps compensate for the cell loss (Coleman & Flood, 1986). This helps explain the common finding that adults who remain active—physically, sexually, and mentally—retain more of their capacity for such activities in later years (Jarvik, 1975; Pfeiffer, 1977). "Use it or lose it" is sound advice. We are more likely to rust from disuse than to wear out from overuse.

Dementia and Alzheimer's Disease

Some adults do, unfortunately, suffer a substantial loss of brain cells. A series of small strokes, a brain tumor, or alcoholism can progressively damage the brain, causing that mental erosion we call dementia (Figure 4.12). So, too, can the most feared of all brain ailments, Alzheimer's disease, which strikes 3 percent of the world's population by age 75. Alzheimer's symptoms are *not* the same as normal aging. (Occasionally forgetting where you laid the car keys or struggling over someone's name is no cause for alarm.) Up to age 95, the incidence of mental disintegration doubles roughly every 5 years.

Alzheimer's destroys even the brightest of minds. First memory, then reasoning and language deteriorate. Robert Sayre (1979) recalls his father shouting at his afflicted mother to "think harder" when she could not remember where she had put something, while his mother, confused, embarrassed, on the verge of tears, randomly searched the house. As the disease runs its course, after 5 to 20 years, the patient becomes emotionally flat, then disoriented, then incontinent, finally mentally vacant—a sort of living death, a mere body stripped of its humanity, as if extraterrestrials were nibbling away at the brain. If you lose it, you can't use it. Caregiving family members of increasingly confused and helpless sufferers themselves often become the disease's exasperated and exhausted victims.

> *Alzheimer's destroys even the brightest of minds. First memory, then reasoning and language deteriorate.*

Underlying the symptoms of Alzheimer's is a deterioration of neurons that produce the neurotransmitter acetylcholine. Deprived of this vital chemical messenger, memory and thinking suffer. An autopsy reveals two telltale abnormalities in these acetylcholine-producing neurons: shriveled protein filaments in the cell body and placques (globs of degenerating tissue) at the tips of neuron branches. Different forms of Alzheimer's disease have been linked to different chromosomes (Barinaga, 1995; Plomin & others, 1997).

With continuing advances in our understanding of the chemical, neural, and genetic roots of Alzheimer's, hopes grow for eventual control of this dread disease. One recent study examined 1124 elderly women who had taken an estrogen supplement which relieves menopause discomforts and reduces the risk of heart disease and osteoporosis (Davidson, 1996; Mayeux & others, 1996). Those who had taken the drug for at least a decade were 40 percent less likely to suffer Alzheimer's disease.

Cognitive Changes

One of the most controversial questions in the study of the human life span is whether adult cognitive abilities, such as memory, creativity, and in-

Figure **4.12**

Incidence of dementia (mental disintegration) by age Risk of mental loss due to Alzheimer's disease or a series of strokes doubles about every 5 years in later life. (From Jorm & others, 1987, based on 22 studies in industrial nations.)

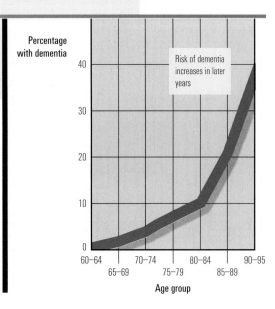

Percentage with dementia

Risk of dementia increases in later years

Age group

telligence, parallel the gradually accelerating decline of physical abilities. Employers, for example, may wonder whether they should encourage their senior workers to retire—or capitalize on their experience. People generally perceive the elderly as mentally less sharp (Kite & Johnson, 1988). Is this stereotype accurate? Is there truth in the proverb, "You can't teach an old dog new tricks"? Or does more truth lie with another proverb: "You're never too old to learn"?

Aging and Memory

Early adulthood is the peak time for some types of learning and remembering. In one experiment, Thomas Crook and Robin West (1990) invited 1205 people to learn some names. Fourteen videotaped people said their names, using a common format: "Hi, I'm Larry." Then the same individuals reappeared and said, for example, "I'm from Philadelphia"—thus providing a visual and voice cue for remembering the person's name. As Figure 4.13 shows, everyone remembered more names after a second and third replay of the introductions, but younger adults' recall for the names consistently surpassed that of older adults. Quicker learning by younger adults is not restricted to human beings. Aging monkeys, too, take progressively more time to master new tasks (Bachevalier & others, 1991, 1992).

But consider another experiment. David Schonfield and Betty-Anne Robertson (1966) asked adults of various ages to learn a list of 24 words. Without giving any clues, the researchers asked some to recall as many words as they could from the list. As Figure 4.14 shows, younger adults had better recall. Others, given multiple-choice questions that asked them simply to *recognize* the words they had seen, exhibited no memory decline with age. Recognition memory is especially good when older adults are tested early rather than late in the day (May & others, 1993). So, how well older people remember depends: Are they being asked simply to *recognize* what they have tried to memorize (minimal decline) or to *recall* it without clues (greater decline)?

Part of the memory difficulty older adults complain of may be normal forgetfulness. When a 20-year-old mislays her car keys, she gets frustrated; when her grandfather mislays his, he gets frustrated and blames his age. But forgetting seems also to depend on the type of information. If you are asked to recall meaningless information—nonsense syllables or unimportant events—then the older you are, the more errors you are likely to make. However, if the information is meaningful,

older people's rich web of existing knowledge helps them catch it. Thus, their capacity to learn and remember skills and *meaningful* material shows less decline (Graf, 1990; Labouvie-Vief & Schell, 1982; Perlmutter, 1983).

There also seems to be little decline with age in people's "prospective" memory—a type of memory involved in remembering to do something, such as taking a pill with meals or picking up bread on the way home (Einstein & McDaniel, 1990). And good news for intellectually active people comes from a study of aging college professors. Unlike most other aging people, their recall of taped prose passages did not slip with age (Shimamura & others, 1995).

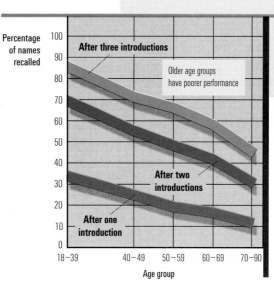

Figure 4.13

Tests of recall Recalling new names introduced once, twice, or three times is easier for younger adults than for older ones. (Data from Crook & West, 1990.)

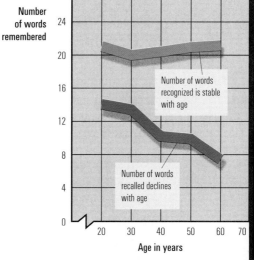

Figure 4.14

Recall and recognition in adulthood In this experiment, the ability to *recall* new information declined during early and middle adulthood, but the ability to *recognize* new information did not. (From Schonfield & Robertson, 1966.)

Given good health you're never too old to learn. At age 70, John Rock developed the birth control pill. At age 78, Grandma Moses took up painting, and she was still painting after age 100.

One other important complication: Right through their later years, people continue to diverge. If you think 20-year-olds differ widely in their abilities to learn and remember, consider this: 70-year-olds differ much more. Some 70-year-olds perform below nearly all 20-year-olds; other 70-year-olds match or outdo the average 20-year-old. Neuropsychologist Michela Gallagher (1990) has found that aging rats, too, vary much more than do young rats. Some old rats are as quick-witted as the smartest of young rats; others, for reasons related to brain deterioration, show their age.

Adults' learning skills can be seen in classrooms. In recent years, more and more adults have turned to leisure education programs or returned to school (including many of you reading this book). Despite occasional difficulties in adjusting to the demands of course work and testing, most older students do better than the typical 18-year-old, perhaps because they have clearer goals (Badenhoop & Johansen, 1980).

Aging and Intelligence

What happens to our broader intellectual powers as we age? Do they gradually decline, as does our ability to recall new material? Or do they remain constant, as does our ability to recognize meaningful material? The evolving answer to this question makes an interesting research story that illustrates psychology's self-correcting process (Woodruff-Pak, 1989).

Phase I: Cross-Sectional Evidence for Intellectual Decline

In cross-sectional studies, researchers test and compare people of various ages. When giving intelligence tests to representative samples of people, researchers consistently find that older adults give fewer correct answers than do younger adults. David Wechsler (1972), creator of the most widely used adult intelligence test, therefore concluded that "the decline of mental ability with age is part of the general [aging] process of the organism as a whole."

For a long time, this rather dismal view of mental decline went unchallenged. Many executives established mandatory retirement policies, assuming their companies would benefit by replacing aging workers with younger, presumably more capable, employees. As everyone "knew," you couldn't teach an old dog new tricks.

Phase II: Longitudinal Evidence for Intellectual Stability

Colleges began giving intelligence tests to entering students about 1920, making it possible to retest older people who had taken an intelligence test years earlier. Several psychologists saw their chance to study intelligence longitudinally, by retesting the same people over a period of years. What they expected to find was a decrease in intelligence after about age 30 (Schaie & Geiwitz, 1982). What they actually found was a surprise: Until late in life, intelligence remained stable (Figure 4.15). On some tests, it even increased.

How then are we to account for the findings from the cross-sectional studies? In retrospect, researchers saw the problem. When a cross-sectional study compares 70-year-olds and 30-year-olds, it compares people not only of two different ages but of two different eras. It compares generally less educated people (born, say, in the early 1900s) with more educated people (born after 1950), people raised in large families with people raised in smaller families, people growing up in less affluent families with people raised in more affluent families.

Figure 4.15

Cross-sectional versus longitudinal testing of intelligence at various ages In this test of one type of verbal intelligence (inductive reasoning), the cross-sectional method produced declining scores with age. The longitudinal method (in which the same people were retested over a period of years) produced a slight *rise* in scores well into adulthood. (Adapted from Schaie, 1994.)

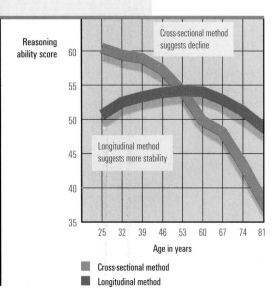

According to this more optimistic view, the myth that intelligence sharply declines with age is laid to rest. As everyone "knows," given good health you're never too old to learn. At age 70, John Rock developed the birth control pill. At age 78, Grandma Moses took up painting, and she was still painting after age 100. At age 81—and 17 years from the end of his college football coaching career—Amos Alozo Stagg was named coach of the year. At age 89, architect Frank Lloyd Wright designed New York City's Guggenheim Museum. Moreover, when people have kept alive their expertise—typing, playing chess, playing the piano—their abilities often remain intact well into their eighties (Schaie, 1987). As psychologist David Krech (1978) said, "He who lives by his wits, dies with his wits."

Phase III: It All Depends

But the controversy continues. For one thing, longitudinal studies have their own pitfalls. Those who survive to the end of longitudinal studies may be bright, healthy people whose intelligence is least likely to decline. (Perhaps people who died younger and got removed from the study had declining intelligence.) If so, such studies underestimate the average decline in intelligence.

Research is further complicated by the finding that intelligence is not a single trait (see Chapter 11). Intelligence tests that assess speed of thinking may place older adults at a disadvantage because of their slower neural mechanisms for processing information. But slower need not mean less intelligent. Given other tests that assess general vocabulary, knowledge, and ability to integrate information, older adults generally hold their own. Older Canadians surpass younger Canadians at answering questions such as, "Which province was once called New Caledonia?" (Told the right an-

swer on missed questions, younger Canadians, though, have the edge a week later at recalling these answers [Craik, 1986].)

German researcher Paul Baltes (1993, 1994) has developed "wisdom" tests that assess traits such as expertise and sound judgment on important matters of life. His results suggest that older adults more than hold their own on such tests. As we age, our neural networks store more and more of the decisions we've made and their associated results. This accumulation of experience enables us to generalize when making future decisions (Kosslyn & Koenig, 1992). Thus, despite 30-year-olds' quick-thinking smarts, we usually select older people to be president of the company, the college, or the country. To be growing older is, in some ways, to be still growing. Age is sage. To paraphrase one 60-year-old, "Forty years ago I had a great memory, but I was a fool."

> To be growing older is, in some ways, to be still growing. Age is sage.

So, whether intelligence increases or decreases with age depends on what type of intellectual performance we measure. Crystallized intelligence—one's accumulated knowledge as reflected in vocabulary and analogies tests—*increases* up to old age. Fluid intelligence—one's ability to reason speedily and abstractly, as when solving novel logic problems—*decreases* with age (Cattell, 1963; Horn, 1982). We can see this pattern in the intelligence scores of a national sample of adults. After adjusting for education, verbal scores (reflecting crystallized intelligence) held relatively steady from ages 20 to 74. Nonverbal, puzzle-solving intelligence declined (Figure 4.16).

cross-sectional study
a study in which people of different ages are compared with one another.

longitudinal study
research in which the same people are restudied and retested over a long period.

crystallized intelligence
one's accumulated knowledge and verbal skills; tends to increase with age.

fluid intelligence
one's ability to reason speedily and abstractly; tends to decrease during late adulthood.

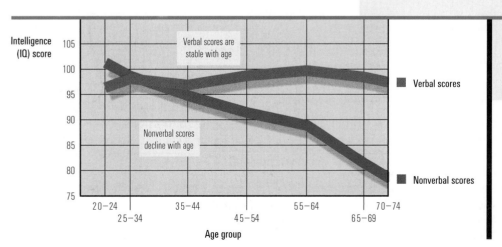

Figure **4.16**

Intelligence and age   After adjustments for education, verbal intelligence scores hold steady with age, while nonverbal intelligence scores decline. (Intelligence scores from standardization sample of the Wechsler Adult Intelligence Scale, based on norms for 25- to 34-year-olds.) (Adapted from Kaufman & others, 1989.)

This helps explain why mathematicians and scientists produce much of their most creative work during their late twenties or early thirties, while those in literature, history, and philosophy tend to produce their best work in their forties, fifties, and beyond, after accumulating more knowledge (Simonton, 1988, 1990). For example, poets (who depend on fluid intelligence) reach their peak output earlier than prose authors (who need a deeper knowledge reservoir)—a finding observed in every major literary tradition, for both living and dead languages. So, whether intellectual performance increases or decreases with age depends on how we assess it.

Mathematicians and scientists produce much of their most creative work during their late twenties or early thirties, while those in literature, history, and philosophy tend to produce their best work in their forties, fifties, and beyond, after accumulating more knowledge.

Social Changes

Many differences between younger and older adults are created not by the physical and cognitive changes that accompany aging but by life events associated with family relationships and work. A new job means new relationships, new expectations, and new demands. Marriage brings the joy of intimacy and the stress of merging your life with another's. The birth of a child introduces responsibilities and significantly alters your life focus. The death of a loved one creates an irreplaceable loss and a need to reaffirm your own life. Do these normal events of adult life shape a predictable sequence of life changes?

Adulthood's Ages and Stages

Some psychologists describe the human journey through adulthood by intensively studying small samples of people. Daniel Levinson and others (1978, 1996) conducted lengthy interviews with successful, middle-aged men and women. Based partly on their recollections, Levinson concluded that adults progress through periods of stability punctuated by times of upheaval and change. For

example, he has argued that as people enter their forties, they undergo a "midlife transition" to middle adulthood, which for many is a crisis, a time of great struggle or even of feeling struck down by life. They give up their dreams of fame and fortune (or the illusion that such bring happiness) and question their work and family commitments. The result, says Levinson, is often turmoil and despair. Fortyish people realize they no longer are starting out but rather are drawing closer to the end. When this painful growth period concludes at about age 45, they again settle into new or deepened attachments, set about completing their careers, and become more compassionate and reflective.

Many researchers are skeptical about such efforts to define adult life as a series of neatly packaged stages, especially stages based merely on interviews with a select few people. To generalize from their career-oriented lives or to use their "midlife crises" to explain or justify renouncing old relationships is misleading (Gilligan, 1982). The fact—from large samples of people—is that job dissatisfaction, marital dissatisfaction, divorce, anxiety, and suicide do *not* surge during the early forties (Hunter & Sundel, 1989). Divorce, for example, is most common among those in their twenties, suicide among those in their seventies and eighties.

Are these markers of crisis too crude to detect a more subtle midlife turmoil? National Institute of Aging researchers Robert McCrae and Paul Costa (1990) gave 350 men between the ages of 30 and 60 a "Midlife Crisis Scale," assessing sense of meaninglessness and mortality, job and family dissatisfaction, and inner turmoil and confusion. They could find "no evidence at all" that such concerns peak at midlife. Surprised, they gave their scale to a new group of 300 men and supplemented it with a measure of emotional instability, which they gave to nearly 10,000 men and women. "The results were an exact reconfirmation: There was not the slightest evidence" that distress peaks anywhere in the midlife age range (Figure 4.17).

There is another reason skeptics question age-linked stage theories. The social clock—the cultural prescription of "the right time" to leave home, get a job, marry, have children, and retire—varies

social clock
the culturally preferred timing of social events such as marriage, parenthood, and retirement.

LEVANTAMIENTO

from culture to culture and era to era. In Jordan, 40 percent of brides are in their teens; in Hong Kong, only 3 percent are (United Nations, 1992). In Western Europe, fewer than 10 percent of men over 65 remain in the work force, as do 16 percent in the United States, 36 percent in Japan, and 69 percent in Mexico (Davies & others, 1991). In contemporary Western nations, the 1950s sequence from student to worker to wife to at-home mom to older worker has loosened and the age of marriage has increased. Modern women occupy these roles in any order or all at once. Given variations in the social clock and individual experience, stage theory critics are suspicious of any neat timetable of adult ages and stages.

Figure **4.17**

Early-forties midlife crises?   Among 10,000 people responding to a national health survey, there was no early-forties increase in emotional instability ("neuroticism") scores. (From McCrae & Costa, 1990.)

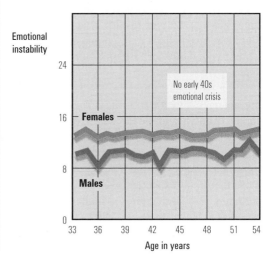

Life Events and Chance Encounters

More important than one's chronological age are life events. Marriage, parenthood, vocational changes, divorce, nest-emptying, relocation, and retirement mark transitions to new life stages whenever they occur—and increasingly they are occurring at unpredictable ages. The social clock is still ticking, but people feel freer to be out of sync with it.

Even chance events can have lasting significance, deflecting us down one road rather than another (Bandura, 1982). The influence of chance encounters on romantic attraction, for example, is implied by a recent study of identical twins and their spouses. Twins, especially identical twins, make similar choices of friends, clothes, vacations, jobs, and so on. So, if your identical twin became engaged to someone, wouldn't you (being in so many ways the same as your twin) expect to feel attracted to this person? Surprisingly, only half the identical twins recalled really liking their co-twin's selection, and only 5 percent said "I could have fallen for my twin's fiancée." Researchers David Lykken and Auke Tellegen (1993) surmise that romantic love is rather like ducklings' imprinting: Given repeated exposure to someone after childhood, you may form a bond (infatuation) with almost any available person who has a roughly similar background and level of attractiveness and who reciprocates your affections.

Adulthood's Commitments

Two basic aspects of our lives do, however, dominate adulthood. Erik Erikson called them *intimacy* (forming close relationships) and *generativity* (being productive and supporting future generations). Researchers have chosen various terms—*affiliation* and *achievement*, *attachment* and *productivity*, *commitment* and *competence*. But Sigmund Freud (1935) put it most simply: The healthy adult, he said, is one who can *love* and *work*. For most adults, love centers on family commitments toward partner, parents, and children. Work encompasses our productive activities, whether for pay or not.

Love

Across time and place, human societies have nearly always included a relatively monogamous bond between men and women and a bond between parents and their children. We flirt, fall in love, and marry—one person at a time. "Pair-bonding is a trademark of the human animal," notes anthropologist Helen Fisher (1993). The arrangement makes sense from an evolutionary perspective: Parents who cooperated to nurture their children to maturity were more likely to have their genes passed along to posterity than parents who didn't.

The bond of love is most satisfying and enduring when marked by a similarity of interests and values, a sharing of emotional and material support, and intimate self-disclosure (see Chapter 18). Women's marital satisfaction, even more than men's, is colored by their mate's social support (Acitelli & Antonucci, 1994). Happiness is having a reassuring, respectful, caring, and mutually confiding partner.

Resetting the social clock
The social clock once prescribed that university graduation should occur around age 22. For this proud graduate, "standard time" is no longer the only setting.

"One can live magnificently in this world if one knows how to work and how to love."

LEO TOLSTOY
1856

Love Intimacy, attachment, commitment—love by whatever name—is central to healthy and happy adulthood.

Thought question: Does marriage correlate with happiness because marital support and intimacy breed happiness, because happy people more often marry and stay married, or both?

Marriage bonds are usually lasting when couples also marry after age 20 and are well-educated. Compared with their counterparts of 30 years ago, people in Western countries are better educated and marrying later. Ironically, people are nevertheless divorcing more. When marrying, whether for the first time or the second, nearly everyone hopes for a satisfying, enduring bond. Yet marriages today are twice as likely to end in divorce as they were in 1960. To judge from the divorce rate— roughly 40 percent of Canadian marriages and half of U.S. marriages end in divorce—marriage has become a union that often defies management. In Europe, divorce is nearly as common, after increasing 400 percent since 1960 (Inglehart, 1990).

Although rocked by increased divorce and often replaced by cohabitation (page 139), the institution of marriage endures. More than 9 in 10 adults marry. Of those who divorce, 75 percent remarry—and their second marriages are virtually as happy as the average first marriage (Vemer & others, 1989). Although the relatively few people who feel trapped in an unhappy marriage typically feel miserable, most married Europeans and North Americans generally feel happier than those who are unmarried, especially when compared with others who are separated and divorced (Inglehart, 1990). In the United States, for example, fewer than 25 percent of unmarried adults, but nearly 40 percent of married adults, have reported being "very happy" (Lee & others, 1991). Lesbian women in couples, too, report greater well-being than those who are alone (Wayment & Peplau, 1995).

Marriages that last are not always devoid of conflict. Some couples fight but also shower one another with affection afterwards. Other couples never raise their voices yet also seldom praise or nuzzle. Both styles can last. After observing the interactions of 2000 couples, John Gottman (1994) reports a better indicator of likely marital success: at least a 5 to 1 ratio of positive to negative interactions. Stable marriages provide five times more smiling, touching, complimenting, and laughing than sarcasm, criticism, and insults. And if you want to predict which newlyweds will stay together, don't pay attention to how passionately they are in love. The couples who make it are more often those who restrain the number of putdowns that, unchecked, can take over a relationship (Notarius & Markman, 1993). To prevent a cancerous negativity, successful couples learn to fight fair (to state feelings without insulting) and to steer conflict away from chaos with comments like "I know it's not your fault" or "Be quiet for a moment and listen."

Often, love bears children. The most enduring of life changes, having a child, is for most people a happy event. As children begin to absorb time, money, and emotional energy, however, satisfaction with the marriage itself may decline. This is especially likely among employed women who, more than they expected, also bear the traditional burden of increased chores at home (Belsky & others, 1986; Hackel & Ruble, 1992). Efforts to create an equitable relationship can pay double dividends, making for more satisfying marriages, which also breed better parent-child relations (Erel & Burman, 1995).

Another significant event in family life happens when children leave home. If you have left home, consider your parents' experience: Did they suffer an "empty nest syndrome"—a feeling of distress focusing on a loss of purpose and relationship? Or did your parents discover renewed freedom, relaxation, and satisfaction with their own relationship?

Seven national surveys reveal that the empty nest is for most people a happy place (Adelmann & others, 1989; Glenn, 1975). Compared with middle-aged women who still have children at home, those whose nest has emptied report greater happiness and greater enjoyment of their marriage. Many parents therefore experience what sociologists Lynn White and John Edwards (1990) call a

Seven national surveys reveal that the empty nest is for most people a happy place.

THINKING CRITICALLY ABOUT

Trial Marriages–Do They Reduce Divorce?

Changing sexual values are evident in changing norms regarding cohabitation. In 1958, the University of Illinois fired a professor who suggested, through the student newspaper, the desirability of young people testing their love relationship before venturing into marriage. When Barnard College sophomore Linda Leclair in 1968 moved in with her boyfriend, a Columbia University junior, a student-faculty committee debated Leclair's fate for several months. They eventually decided that she could remain a student, but they denied her the use of the cafeteria, snack bar, and recreation room.

Today, most universities look the other way. Cohabitation has become commonplace. The number of cohabiting unmarried couples in the United States tripled during the 1970s and has more than doubled again since 1980 (Bureau of the Census, 1996). Similar trends have occurred since 1960 throughout much of Western Europe. In Australia, 56 percent of couples who married in 1992 had lived together before marrying—nearly four times the percentage who did so in 1975 (McLennan, 1995).

Many people see premarital cohabitation as a trial period that serves to weed out unsuccessful unions before marriage occurs. In one survey of nearly 300,000 first-year American college students, 51 percent agreed that "a couple should live together before marriage" (Astin & others, 1989). Might those who are sexually experienced and thoroughly familiar with the living habits of their partner indeed be less likely to stumble into an ill-fated marriage? Does test-driving life together before committing reduce the risk of divorce?

It seems not. Eight studies concur that, compared with couples who don't cohabit with their spouses-to-be, those who do have *higher* divorce rates. A U.S. survey of 13,000 adults found that couples who lived together before marriage were one-third more likely to separate or divorce within a decade (Bumpass & Sweet, 1989). A 1990 Gallup survey of still-married Americans also found that 21 percent of those who had not cohabited before marrying, and 40 percent of those who had, said they might divorce (Greeley, 1991). A Canadian national survey of 5300 women found that those who cohabited were 54 percent more likely to divorce within 15 years (Balakrishan & others, 1987). And a Swedish study of 4300 women found cohabitation linked with an 80 percent greater risk of divorce (Bennett & others, 1988).

Can you imagine why? (Remember: A *correlation* between cohabitation and divorce risk need not imply that cohabitation is a *cause* of future divorce.) William Axinn and Arland Thornton (1992) report data that support two explanations.

First, cohabitation attracts people who are more open to terminating unsatisfying relationships. The very idea of cohabitation presumes that intimate relationships need not be permanent. It sees love as conditional rather than committed. If either partner becomes dissatisfied, he or she can seek bliss elsewhere. People who cohabit therefore bring a more individualistic ethic to marriage, are more likely to see close relationships as temporary and fragile, and are more accepting of divorce.

Second, the experience of cohabitation increases acceptance of divorce. Over time, those who cohabit tend to become more approving of dissolving an unfulfilling union. This divorce-accepting attitude increases the odds of later divorce.

Percentage of 25-year-olds who have

U.S. rates of cohabitation and marriage by age 25
From the U.S. National Survey of Families and Households. (From Bumpass & Sweet, 1989.)

"post-launch honeymoon," especially if they maintain close relationships with their children. One such mother, 50-year-old Phoebe, explains: "Our family is very close. When my two sons come home I can't wait till they get here, I stay excited throughout their stay, and I'm in tears after they leave. Yet within a day or two we're back to enjoying our freedom—our time is ours!"

Work

For most adults, a large part of the answer to "Who are you?" depends on the answer to "What do you do?" For most adults, to feel productive and competent is to raise children and to undertake a career.

Because settling on an occupation takes time and because the impact of chance encounters can be very great, career choices are hard to predict. During the first two years of college or university, most students cannot predict their later career path. Most shift from their initially intended majors, many find their postcollege employment in fields not directly related to their majors, and most will change careers (Rothstein, 1980). To many career counselors, this unpredictability means that the best education is not a narrow vocational training, but rather a broad liberal education, an education that fosters "the critical qualities of mind and the durable qualities of character that will serve [people] in circumstances we cannot now even predict" (Gardner, 1984).

Does work, including a career, indeed contribute to self-fulfillment and life satisfaction, as Freud supposed? One approach to answering this question has been to compare the roughly equal numbers of North American women who are or are not employed. From their studies at the Wellesley College Center for Research on Women, Grace Baruch and Rosaline Barnett (1986) conclude that what matters is not which roles a woman occupies—whether it be as paid worker, wife, and/or mother—but the quality of her experience in those roles. Happiness is about having work that fits your interests and provides you with a sense of competence and accomplishment; having a partner who is a close, supportive companion and who sees you as special; and/or having loving children whom you like and feel proud of.

Well-Being Across the Life Span

To live is to grow older, which means that we all can look backward with satisfaction or regret, and forward with hope or dread. When people are asked what they would do differently if reliving their lives, their most common answer is "taken my education more seriously and worked harder at it." Other regrets—"I should have told my father I loved him," "I regret that I never went to Europe"—also focus less on mistakes made than on the things one *failed* to do (Gilovich & Medvec, 1995).

In later life, income shrinks, work is taken away, the body deteriorates, recall fades, energy wanes, family members and friends die or move away, and the great enemy, death, looms ever closer. Small wonder that many presume the over-65 years to be the worst of times (Freedman, 1978). But they are not. People of all ages report similar feelings of happiness and satisfaction with life. Ronald Inglehart (1990) confirmed this when he amassed interviews conducted during the 1980s with representative samples of nearly 170,000 people in 16 nations. As Figure 4.18 illustrates, older people report as much happiness and satisfaction with life as younger people do. Given that growing older is one sure consequence of living, an outcome most of us prefer to its alternative, we can all take comfort in this finding.

The astonishing stability of well-being across the life span obscures some interesting age-related emotional differences. As the years go by, feelings mellow (Costa & others, 1987; Diener & others, 1986). Highs become less high, lows less low. Thus, although the *average* feeling level may remain stable, with age we find ourselves less often feeling excited, intensely proud, and on top of the world, but also less often depressed. Compliments provoke less elation and criticisms less despair as

Job satisfaction and life satisfaction Work provides people with a sense of identity and competence and opportunities for accomplishment. Perhaps this is why a challenging and interesting occupation enhances people's happiness.

Figure **4.18**

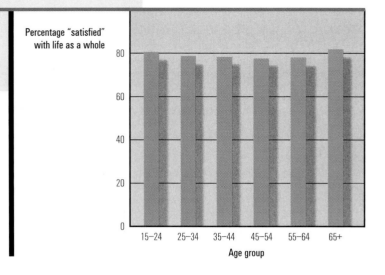

Age and life satisfaction   With early adult tasks behind them, many older adults have more time to pursue personal interests. No wonder their satisfaction with life remains high, especially if they are healthy and active. As this graph based on multinational surveys shows, age differences in life satisfaction are trivial. (Data from Inglehart, 1990.)

both become merely additional feedback atop a mountain of accumulated praise and blame. Psychologists Mihaly Csikszentmihalyi (pronounced chick-SENT-me-hi) and Reed Larson (1984) mapped people's emotional terrain by periodically signaling them with electronic beepers to report their current activities and feelings. They found that teenagers typically come down from elation or up from gloom in less than an hour. Adult moods are less extreme but more enduring. For most people, old age offers less intense joy but greater contentment, especially for those who remain socially engaged (Harlow & Cantor, in press). As we age, life's emotional roller coaster provides a smoother ride.

Death and Dying

Most of us will suffer and cope with the deaths of relatives and friends. Usually, the most difficult separation is from one's spouse—a loss suffered by five times more women than men. Grief is especially severe when the death of a loved one comes suddenly and before its expected time on the social clock. The accidental death of a child or the sudden illness that claims a 45-year-old spouse may trigger a year or more of mourning flooded with memories, eventually subsiding to a mild depression that sometimes continues for several years (Lehman & others, 1987). AIDS, which so often strikes down people in midlife and younger, has left countless grief-stricken partners whose bereavement is similar to that of spouses whose mates have died of other causes (Folkman & others, 1996).

The normal range of reactions to a loved one's death is wider than most people suppose. Some cultures encourage public weeping and wailing; others hide grief. Within any culture some individuals grieve more intensely and openly. Contrary to a popular myth, those who express the strongest grief immediately do not resolve their grief more quickly (Bonanno & others, 1995; Wortman & Silver, 1989).

Those who suffer a terminal illness live with the awareness of their impending death. In analyzing how people cope with the prospect of death, the stage theorists have once again arrived ahead of us. From her interviews with dying patients, Elisabeth Kübler-Ross (1969) proposed that the terminally ill pass through a sequence of five stages: *denial* of the terminal condition; *anger* and resentment ("Why me?"); *bargaining* with God (or physicians) for more time; *depression* stemming from the impending loss of everything and everyone; and, finally, peaceful *acceptance* of one's fate.

Others propose similar stages for coping with a sudden physical impairment—disbelief, protest, depression, recovery (Fitzgerald, 1970).

Critics question the generality of all such stages, stressing that each person's experience is unique. Real people, they say, don't fit into these neat boxes. Moreover, they argue, the simplified stages ignore many important factors—for example, that older people usually view death with less fear and resentment than younger people (Wass & others, 1978–1979). Critics also voice concern about the eagerness with which courses and books have popularized the death-and-dying formula. The danger, they fear, is that rather than having their feelings respected, dying people may be analyzed or ma-

> "Do not go gentle into that good night,
> Old age should burn and rave at close of day;
> Rage, rage against the dying of the light."
>
> **DYLAN THOMAS**
> *"DO NOT GO GENTLE INTO THAT GOOD NIGHT"*
> 1952
> POEM WRITTEN TO HIS FATHER AS HE LAY DYING PEACEFULLY

> Grief is especially severe when the death of a loved one comes suddenly and before its expected time on the social clock.

> "How many of us older persons have really been . . . prepared for the second half of life, for old age, death and eternity?"
>
> **CARL JUNG**
> *MODERN MAN IN SEARCH OF A SOUL*
> 1933

hospice
an organization whose largely volunteer staff provides support for dying people and their families either in special facilities or in people's own homes.

"Consider, friend, as you pass by, as you are now, so once was I. As I am now, you too shall be. Prepare, therefore, to follow me."

SCOTTISH TOMBSTONE EPITAPH

nipulated in terms of the stereotyped stages: "She's just going through the anger stage."

Nevertheless, the death-education movement has enabled us to deal more openly and humanely with death and grief. A growing number of individuals are aided by hospice organizations, whose staff and volunteers work in special facilities and in people's homes to support and comfort the terminally ill and their families. Hospice aims to help make dying a more comfortable and meaningful time "when good-byes can be said, when broken relationships can be healed, when forgiveness can be given or received" (Magno, 1989).

We can be grateful for the waning of death-denying attitudes. Facing death with dignity and openness helps people complete the life cycle with a sense of life's meaningfulness and unity—the sense that their existence has been good and that life and death are parts of an ongoing cycle. Although death may be unwelcome, life itself can be affirmed even at death. This is especially so for people who review their lives not with despair but with what Erik Erikson called a sense of *integrity*—a feeling that one's life has been meaningful and worthwhile.

SUMMING UP

During early life, we sail a narrow channel, constrained by biological maturation. As the years pass, the channel widens, allowing us to diverge more and more. By adulthood, age no longer neatly predicts a person's life experience and traits. Yet in some ways our bodies, minds, and relationships still undergo predictable changes. As long as we live, we adapt.

Physical Changes The barely perceptible physical declines of early adulthood begin to accelerate during middle adulthood. For women, a significant physical change of adult life is menopause, which generally seems to be a smooth rather than rough transition. After 65, perceptual acuity, strength, and stamina decline, but short-term ailments are fewer. Neural processes slow, but the brain remains healthy, except for those who suffer brain disease, such as the progressive deterioration of Alzheimer's disease.

Cognitive Changes As the years pass, recognition memory remains strong, although recall begins to decline, especially for meaningless information. Research on how intelligence changes with age has progressed through several phases: cross-sectional

studies suggesting a steady intellectual decline after early adulthood; longitudinal studies suggesting intellectual stability until very late in life; and today's view that fluid intelligence declines in later life, but crystallized intelligence does not.

Social Changes From close study of small samples of individuals, some theorists maintain that adults pass through an orderly sequence of life stages. Some theorists have contended that moving from one stage to the next entails recurring times of crisis, such as the transition to midlife during the early forties. But people are not so predictable. Adult life is influenced in unanticipated ways, not only by life events involving love and work but also by chance occurrences. Since 1960, marriage has been in decline, as reflected in later marriages, increased cohabitation, and doubled divorce rates.

Although few people grow old gratefully, most age gracefully, retaining a sense of well-being throughout life. Those who live to old age must, however, cope with the deaths of friends and family members and with the prospect of their own deaths. Those left behind when a loved one dies or who await their own impending death may experience some or all of the phases described by stage theorists. Our experience with death is, however, influenced by our experiences in life.

KEY TERMS AND CONCEPTS menopause, Alzheimer's disease, cross-sectional study, longitudinal study, crystallized intelligence, fluid intelligence, social clock, hospice

Reflections on Life-Span Development

We conclude our womb-to-tomb journey where we began in Chapter 3, with two of developmental psychology's big questions: Does life unfold through predictable stages? And as we develop, do our traits typically change or remain consistent?

Our survey of developmental psychology began in Chapter 3 by identifying three pervasive issues: (1) Is development steered more by genes or experience? (2) Is development a gradual, continuous process or a series of distinct stages? and (3) Is the life span marked more by stability over time or by change? We noted there how genes and experience jointly affect human development. Let's now take stock of current thinking on the latter two issues.

Continuity and Stages

We have considered several stage theorists: Jean Piaget on cognitive development, Lawrence Kohlberg on moral development, and Erik Erikson and Daniel Levinson on psychosocial development. And we have seen their stage theories criticized: Young children have some abilities that Piaget attributed to later stages. Kohlberg assumed a worldview characteristic of educated males in individualistic cultures. The ideas of Erikson and Levinson are challenged by research showing that adult life does not progress through a fixed, predictable series of steps.

Although research casts doubt on the idea that life proceeds through neatly defined, age-linked stages, the concept of stage remains useful. There are spurts of brain growth during childhood and puberty that correspond roughly to Piaget's stages (Thatcher & others, 1987). And stage theories contribute a developmental perspective on the whole life span. They show the order in which abilities develop and suggest how people of one age think and act differently when they arrive at a later age.

Stability and Change

This leads us to the final question: Over time, are people's personalities and social skills consistent, or do they change? If reunited with a long-lost grade-school friend, would you instantly recognize that "it's the same old Andy"? Or is a person likely to seem like a different person at a later period?

Obviously, either extreme is false: If there were no stability, we could not hope that the person we marry today would be the same person a decade later, or that the promising management trainee would remain suited for management. If there were no change, all juvenile delinquents would become career criminals; all alcoholics would drink themselves into the grave; life would be one long rut.

Still, the issue is real: Do infants' traits predict their childhood characteristics? Is the troubled adolescent likely to have a rocky adulthood? Will the assertive young woman still be noticeably assertive at age 60? Researchers who follow lives through time are debating the extent to which our past reaches into our future.

A generation ago, most psychologists and lay people assumed that the footprints of our genes and early experience are set in cement. Then, during the 1960s and 1970s, new findings suggested that throughout much of life personality evolves.

For example, Jean Macfarlane (1964) followed 166 people from babyhood to age 30 and discovered that "many of our most mature and competent adults had severely troubled and confusing childhoods and adolescences." Often, the unhappy, rebellious adolescent became a stable, successful, happy adult. Alexander Thomas and Stella Chess (1986) similarly followed 133 people from infancy to early adulthood and found that the troubled children among them usually became stable adults.

Some researchers have found that even adults frequently undergo surprising and unpredictable changes. Reflecting on her studies of such changes during the life cycle, Bernice Neugarten (1980) reported that "the primary consistency we have found is a lack of consistency." After following college students from age 20 to 42, Susan Krauss Whitbourne and her colleagues (1992) were similarly impressed by how much more self-confident they had become. Many a professor, too, has been amazed at the 20-year-old goof-offs who mature into 40-year-old business and cultural leaders.

Shall we then conclude that later experience writes over our early experience, erasing the voices of the past? If so, we can counsel parents of difficult babies and teenagers to be patient and hopeful. We can reassure the depressed, lonely young adult that development never ends: The struggles of the present may lay the base for a happier future.

But what do we make of recent research that reveals a consistency to personality? After painstakingly comparing people in their forties with ratings of the same people as junior high students, Jack Block (1981) concluded that there is an underlying stability to our basic social and emotional style.

> "In most of us, by the age of thirty, the character has set like plaster, and will never soften again."
>
> **WILLIAM JAMES**
> *PRINCIPLES OF PSYCHOLOGY*
> 1890

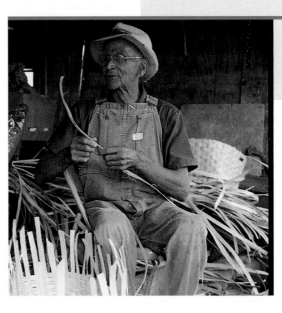

Stability yet change   Although our lives have continuity over decades, we each evolve as we age and confront new challenges.

The troubled adolescent often turned out better than we would have guessed, but it was usually a cheerful teenager who became the very cheerful 40-year-old.

Similarly, Avshalom Caspi and his colleagues (1987) found that, compared with milder-mannered boys, 9-year-old boys with explosive temper tantrums are more likely as adults to have trouble keeping good jobs and are twice as likely to have divorced by age 40. Leonard Eron (1987) and others found that the most physically aggressive 8-year-olds tended to become the most aggressive (and potentially violent) 30-year-olds (Figure 4.19). And David Magnusson and L. R. Bergman (1990) found that hyperaggressive Swedish 13-year-olds often developed adult records of crime and alcohol abuse.

Once people reach adulthood, their dispositions become even more stable. From their periodic retesting of adults in the Boston and Baltimore areas, Robert McCrae and Paul Costa (1982) concluded, "For the great majority of people, the self-concept at age 30 is a good guide to personality at age 80." During the adult years, people's outgoingness, emotional stability, openness, agreeableness, and conscientiousness are persistent (Conley, 1985; Costa & McCrae, 1993; Finn, 1986). Part of our consistency comes from our selecting environments and marrying people who help sustain our traits (Caspi & Herbener, 1990). Outgoing people, for instance, are more likely to seek social encounters that nourish their outgoingness and to marry sociable people.

So, should we conclude that throughout life we change, but our basic social and emotional styles become more stable as we grow older? Whatever their apparent disagreements, researchers agree that:

1   The first two years of life provide a poor basis for predicting a person's eventual traits. As people grow older, predictability increases. Compared with infant temperament, a child's temperament gives a better clue to adult temperament. There is also less stability from age 14 to 18 than from 18 to 22 (Stein & others, 1986) and less stability from 20 to 30 than from 30 to 40 (Costa & McCrae, 1989).

2   The greater the span of years between assessments, the greater the likelihood that personality will have changed. From assessing the traits of 25-year-olds, psychologists can better predict their personalities as 26-year-olds than as 40-year-olds (Schuerger & others, 1989).

3   Some characteristics, such as temperament, are more stable than others, such as social attitudes (Moss & Susman, 1980). But attitudes, too, become more stable with age (Krosnick & Alwin, 1989).

4   In some ways, we all change with age. Most shy, fearful toddlers begin opening up by age 4, and during adulthood most of us mellow. In the years after college, most people become calmer and more self-disciplined (McCrae & Costa, 1994). Such changes can occur without changing a person's position *relative* to others of the same age. The hard-driving young adult may mellow by later life yet still be a relatively hard-driving senior citizen.

Figure 4.19

The stability of aggressiveness

Leonard Eron and Rowell Huesmann (1984) found that the aggressiveness displayed by 8-year-old boys (low, medium, or high) helped predict their aggressiveness two decades later, as revealed by their wives' reports and by their criminal convictions.

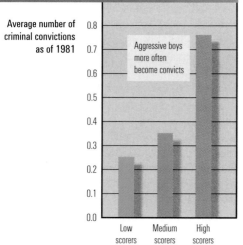

"At 70, I would say the advantage is that you take life more calmly. You know that 'this, too, shall pass!'"

ELEANOR ROOSEVELT
1954

SUMMING UP

Chapters 3 and 4 touch on three pervasive issues in developmental psychology: nature and nurture, continuity and discrete stages, and stability and change in personality. Although the stage theories of Piaget, Kohlberg, and Erikson have been modified in light of later research, each theory usefully alerts us to differences among people of different ages and helps us keep the life-span perspective in view. Research findings that people's traits continue to change in later life have helped create a new emphasis on lifelong development. Nevertheless, there is also an underlying consistency to most people's temperaments and personality traits, especially after age 30.

Finally, we should remember that life contains *both* stability and change. Stability enables us to depend on others. It motivates our concern for children's healthy formation. And it provides our identity. Change motivates our concerns about present influences. It sustains our hope for a brighter future when we are depressed. And it enables us to adapt and grow with experience.

TERMS AND CONCEPTS TO REMEMBER

adolescence, p. 115

puberty, p. 116

primary sex characteristics, p. 117

secondary sex characteristics, p. 117

menarche [meh-NAR-key], p. 117

identity, p. 122

intimacy, p. 123

menopause, p. 128

Alzheimer's disease, p. 132

cross-sectional study, p. 134

longitudinal study, p. 134

crystallized intelligence, p. 135

fluid intelligence, p. 135

social clock, p. 136

hospice, p. 142

CRITICAL THINKING EXERCISE

by Richard O. Straub

Now that you have read and reviewed Chapter 4, take your learning a step further by testing your critical thinking skills on the following psychological reasoning exercise.

Since he retired as a college professor five years ago, 65-year-old Bentley has suffered numerous health problems, including high blood pressure, chest pains, and muscle tremors. Once very active physically, Bentley has not been able to take his daily 30-minute jog for the past three years.

For the first time in his life, Bentley takes several prescription drugs daily, including one that controls his muscle tremors by blocking the neurotransmitter acetylcholine. Bentley's biggest complaint, however, is that he is bored and misses the intellectual stimulation of his former students and colleagues.

Bentley's daughter Mary recently read a magazine article on Alzheimer's disease and is worried that something may be seriously wrong with her father's mind. For a man who once prided himself on his infallible memory and the quickness of his thinking, Bentley's memory now occasionally falters, and his reactions are slower. Fearing that her father may be suffering from Alzheimer's disease, Mary decides to conduct an experiment. Pretending that she is stumped while working on a "brain teaser," she asks her father to help her identify the next letter in the series *d, f, i, m, r, x, e*. When Bentley becomes flustered and cannot quickly come up with the answer, Mary is crestfallen, certain that her father is in the early stages of a devastating disease.

1. State Mary's argument in your own words.

2. Describe the evidence on which Mary has based her argument.

3. State three reasons why Mary's evidence is not strong enough to support her argument.

Check your progress on becoming a critical thinker by comparing your answers to the sample answers found in Appendix B.

chapter

5

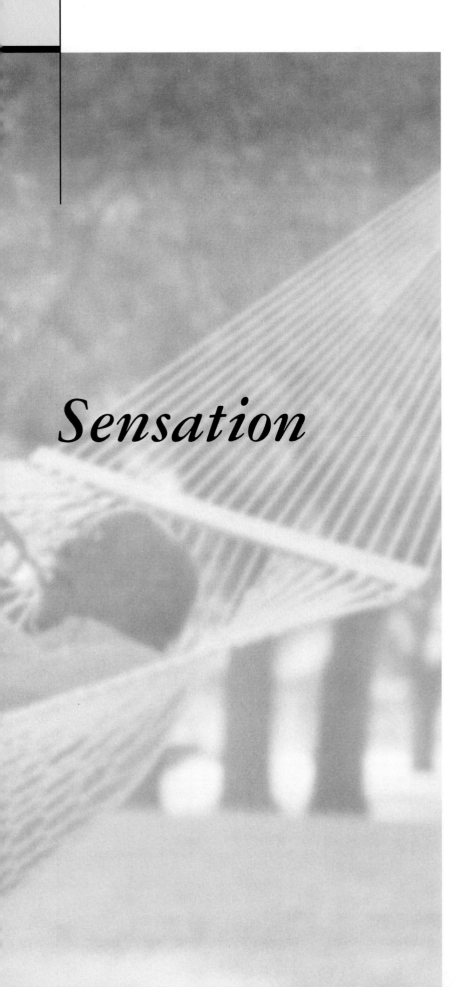

Sensation

In the outer world, innumerable stimuli bombard your body. In a silent, cushioned, inner world of utter darkness floats your brain. These facts raise a question that predates psychology by thousands of years and helped inspire its beginnings a century ago: *How does the world out there get in?*

To modernize the question: How do we construct our representations of the external world? How do we represent a campfire's flicker, crackle, and smoky scent as patterns of active neural connections? And how from this living neurochemistry do we create our conscious experience of the fire's motion and temperature, its aroma and beauty?

To represent the world in our head, we must detect physical energy from the environment and encode it as neural signals, a process traditionally called sensation. And we must select, organize, and interpret our sensations, a process traditionally called perception. In our everyday experiences, sensation and perception blend into one continuous process. In Chapters 5 and 6, we slow down that process to study its parts.

In this chapter we start with the sensory receptors and work up to higher levels of processing. Psychologists refer to sensory analysis that starts at the entry level as bottom-up processing. The next chapter focuses on how our minds interpret what our senses detect. We construct perceptions drawing not only on sensations coming "up" to the brain but also on our experience and expectations. Psychologists call this top-down processing.

Failures of perception may occur anywhere between sensory detection and perceptual interpretation. For example, the eyes of a person born with cataracts may be unable to detect light, rendering the brain's higher-level visual processing equipment useless. Brain-damaged patients reveal the importance of other links in the sensation-perception chain. After losing a temporal lobe area essential to recognizing faces, patient "E. H." suffers from a condition called *prosopagnosia*. She has complete sensation but incomplete perception. She can sense visual information—indeed may accurately report the features of a face—yet she cannot recognize it. Shown an unfamiliar face, she is unreactive. Shown a familiar face, her autonomic nervous system responds with measurable perspiration. Still, she hasn't a clue who the person is. Shown her own face in a mirror, she is again stumped. Because of her brain damage, she is unable to process top down—she cannot relate her stored knowledge to the sensory input.

Sensing the World: Some Basic Principles

We begin with questions that cut across all our sensory systems: What stimuli cross our threshold for conscious awareness? Could we unknowingly be influenced by *subliminal* stimuli that are too weak to be perceived? Why are we unaware of unchanging stimuli, such as the watch pressing against our wrist?

Sensory systems enable organisms to obtain needed information. Consider:

- A frog, which feeds on flying insects, has eyes with receptor cells that fire only in response to small, dark, moving objects. A frog could starve to death knee-deep in motionless flies. But let one zoom by and the frog's "bug detector" cells snap awake.
- A male silkworm moth has receptors so sensitive to the odor of the female sex-attractant that a single female silkworm moth need release only a billionth of an ounce per second to attract every male silkworm moth within a mile. Which is why there continue to be silkworms.
- We humans are similarly designed to detect what are, for us, the important features of our environments. Our ears are most sensitive to the sound frequencies of the human voice.

Nature's sensory gifts suit each recipient's needs.

Thresholds

We exist in a sea of energy. At this moment, you and I are being struck by x-rays and radio waves, ultraviolet and infrared light, and sound waves of very high and very low frequencies. But to all of them we are blind and deaf. The shades on our senses are open just a crack, allowing us only a restricted awareness of this vast sea. <u>Psychophysics</u> is the study of how this physical energy relates to our psychological experience. What stimuli can we detect? At what intensity? How sensitive are we to changing stimulation?

Our shaded senses   A mosquito's buzz can sound like a dive-bomber, thanks to our low threshold for sounds at its pitch. But a shrieking, dive-bombing bat will seem silent, its cries too high-pitched. Our ears are most sensitive to the pitch range of human speech.

<u>sensation</u>
the process by which our sensory receptors and nervous system receive and represent stimulus energies from our environment.

<u>perception</u>
the process of organizing and interpreting sensory information, enabling us to recognize meaningful objects and events.

<u>bottom-up processing</u>
analysis that begins with the sense receptors and works up to the brain's integration of sensory information.

<u>top-down processing</u>
information processing guided by higher-level mental processes, as when we construct perceptions drawing on our experience and expectations.

Absolute Thresholds

To some kinds of stimuli we are exquisitely sensitive. Standing atop a mountain on an utterly dark, clear night, we can, given normal senses, see a candle flame atop another mountain 30 miles away. In a silent room, we can hear a watch ticking 20 feet away. We can feel the wing of a bee falling on our cheek. We can smell a single drop of perfume in a three-room apartment (Galanter, 1962).

Our awareness of these faint stimuli illustrates our absolute thresholds—the minimum stimulation necessary to detect a particular stimulus (light, sound, pressure, taste, odor). Psychologists usually measure absolute threshold by recording the stimulation needed for detection 50 percent of the time. To test your absolute threshold for sounds, a hearing specialist would expose each of your ears to varying sound levels. For each pitch, the hearing test defines where half the time you correctly detect the sound and half the time you do not. For each of the senses, that 50–50 point defines your absolute threshold.

Signal detection How soon would you notice the radar blips of an approaching object? Fairly quickly if (1) you expect it, (2) it's important that you detect it, and (3) you are alert.

Signal Detection

Detecting a weak stimulus, or signal, depends not only on the signal's strength (such as the tone on a hearing test), but also on our psychological state—our experience, expectations, motivation, and fatigue. Signal detection theory predicts when we will detect weak signals. Signal detection theorists observe that absolute thresholds vary. Exhausted parents of a newborn will notice the faintest whimper from the cradle, while failing to notice louder, unimportant sounds. Responsiveness also increases in a horror-filled wartime situation, where failure to detect an intruder may mean death. A sentry standing guard alone at night may therefore notice—and fire at—an almost imperceptible noise. With heightened responsiveness come more false alarms. In peacetime, when survival is not threatened, the same sentry requires a stronger signal before sensing danger.

Signal detection theorists seek to understand why people respond differently to the same stimuli, and why the same person's reactions vary as circumstances change. Signal detection can have life-or-death consequences when people are responsible for detecting blips on a radar screen, watching for weapons at an airport security checkpoint, or monitoring equipment at an intensive care nursing station. Signal detection studies have shown, for example, that people's vigilance diminishes after about 30 minutes of judging when a faint signal appears. But this diminishing response depends on the task, on the time of day, and even on whether the participants periodically exercise (Warm & Dember, 1986).

Subliminal Stimulation

In 1956, controversy erupted over a false report that New Jersey movie audiences were unwittingly being influenced by imperceptible flashed messages to DRINK COCA-COLA and EAT POP-CORN (Pratkanis, 1992).

Many years later, the controversy erupted anew. Advertisers were said to manipulate consumers by imperceptibly printing the word *sex* on crackers and by embedding erotic images in liquor ads. Rock recordings were said to contain "satanic messages" that could be heard if the recordings were played backwards and that, even when played in a forward direction, could unconsciously persuade the unwitting listener.

In a more straightforward effort to trespass on our unconscious, entrepreneurs offer to help us lose weight, stop smoking, or improve our memories with audiotapes. These tapes contain soothing ocean sounds that mask unheard messages such as, "I am thin," "Smoke tastes bad," or "I do well on tests. I have total recall of information." Claims like these make two assumptions: that unconsciously we can sense subliminal (literally, "below threshold") stimuli, and that, without our awareness, these stimuli have extraordinary suggestive powers. Can we? Do they?

psychophysics
the study of relationships between the physical characteristics of stimuli, such as their intensity, and our psychological experience of them.

absolute threshold
the minimum stimulation needed to detect a particular stimulus.

signal detection theory
predicts how and when we detect the presence of a faint stimulus ("signal"). Assumes that there is no single absolute threshold and that detection depends partly on a person's experience, expectations, motivation, and level of fatigue.

subliminal
below one's absolute threshold for conscious awareness.

Can we sense stimuli below our absolute thresholds? In one sense, the answer is clearly yes. Remember that the "absolute" threshold is merely the point at which we detect a stimulus half the time (Figure 5.1). At or slightly below this threshold we will still detect the stimulus some of the time. The answer is yes in another sense, too. People who plead total ignorance when asked to make some perceptual judgment—for example, when deciding which of two very similar weights is heavier—usually beat chance. Sometimes we know more than we think we do.

Figure **5.1**

Absolute threshold Do I smell it or not? When stimuli are detectable less than 50 percent of the time they are "subliminal." Absolute threshold is the intensity at which we can detect a stimulus half the time.

How to think uncritically without psychology: James Vicary, an unemployed marketing researcher, masterminded the EAT POPCORN subliminal advertising hoax with the help of uncritical reporters and broadcasters. Vicary reportedly collected big fees from advertising firms for his promised services—and then disappeared (Rogers, 1993, 1994).

Can we be affected by stimuli too weak for us *ever* to notice? Recent experiments hint that, under certain conditions, the answer may again be yes. One experiment subliminally flashed either emotionally positive scenes (such as kittens or a romantic couple) or negative scenes (such as a werewolf or a dead body) an instant before participants viewed slides of nine people (Krosnick & others, 1992). Although the participants consciously perceived only a flash of light, they gave more positive ratings to people whose photos had been associated with positive scenes. People somehow looked nicer if their photo immediately followed unperceived kittens rather than an unperceived werewolf. Chinese characters, too, seem nicer if preceded by a flashed but unperceived smiling face rather than a scowling face (Murphy & Zajonc, 1993).

Consider, too, how invisible words can briefly *prime* your response to a later question. In a typical experiment, a word is quickly flashed, then replaced by a "masking" stimulus that interrupts the brain's processing before conscious perception. For example, if the imperceptible word *bread* were flashed and masked, you might then detect a related word such as *butter* faster than unrelated words such as *bottle* or *bubble* (Bornstein & Pittman, 1992; Carr & others, 1987; Marcel, 1983). This subliminal priming lasts only for a flicker of time (Greenwald & others, 1996). Yet the effect is intriguing: Sometimes we *feel* what we do not know and cannot describe.

So, we *can* process information without being aware of it. An imperceptibly brief stimulus evidently triggers a weak response that evokes a feeling, though not a conscious awareness of the stimulus. What the conscious mind can't recognize, the heart may know.

> "The heart has its reasons which reason does not know."
>
> **PASCAL**
> *PENSEES*
> 1670

But does the fact of subliminal *sensation* verify entrepreneurial claims of subliminal *persuasion*? Can advertisers really manipulate us with "hidden persuasion"? The near-consensus among research psychologists is no. Their verdict is like that of astronomers who say that, yes, astrologers are right that stars and planets are out there, but no, they don't directly affect us. The laboratory research reveals a *subtle, fleeting* effect on *thinking*, but the subliminal tape hucksters claim something different: a *powerful, enduring* effect on *behavior*. Experiments, such as one described in Chapter 1, show that commercial subliminal tapes have no effect beyond a placebo effect—an effect of one's belief in them (Moore, 1988; Pratkanis & others, 1994; Smith & Rogers, 1994).

Shortly after news of the supposed EAT POPCORN effect swept North America, the Canadian Broadcasting Corporation used a popular Sunday night TV show to flash a subliminal message 352 times (*Advertising Age*, 1958). Asked to guess the message, none of the almost 500 letter-writers did so. Nearly half, however, did report feeling strangely hungry or thirsty during the show. But this was merely an effect of expectations. The actual message was TELEPHONE NOW. The effect of these 352 subliminal messages on Canadian telephone usage? Zilch. All the evidence considered, say researchers Anthony Pratkanis and Anthony Greenwald (1988), "Subliminal procedures offer little or nothing of value to the marketing practitioner."

THINKING CRITICALLY ABOUT

Unconscious Influence: Backward Messages in Rock Albums

The influences on how we think and act are often subtle, even unrecognized. Might it therefore be possible for unperceived backward messages, implanted on rock albums, to corrupt unwitting listeners? In the 1980s, concerns about such messages led to political efforts in the Canadian parliament and several U.S. states to contain the supposed powers of "backmasking."

Are such concerns warranted? Assuming that backward messages exist, could they have any influence? If indeed people are unconsciously influenced by a message they can't perceive, how might psychologists detect such influence?

Confronted with such questions and armed with the methods of psychological science, University of Lethbridge psychologists John Vokey and Don Read (1985) decided to investigate. They began by recording some simple sentences from Lewis Carroll's "Jabberwocky" and from the Twenty-third Psalm and then rerecorded them in reverse. This recording retained the pauses and pitches, producing a string of sounds rather like a foreign language.

But it was gibberish. Listeners could not detect whether a given word was or wasn't present, whether they had heard a declarative sentence or a question, or whether the sentence was meaningful or nonsensical. When simple messages such as "Jesus loves me, this I know" were played backward, people couldn't surpass chance when guessing whether the words were satanic, Christian, pornographic, advertising, or from a nursery rhyme.

Might meaningless backward information nevertheless have a subtle influence? Research psychologists have invented clever methods for uncovering such influences, including one that uses homophones—words that sound alike but differ in spelling and meaning. Imagine, for example, hearing the sentence, "Climbing a mountain is a remarkable *feat*." Later, even after you had forgotten the sentence, you would be more likely to spell the italicized word as f-e-a-t rather than f-e-e-t. This effect occurs without people realizing why they have chosen a particular spelling. But you must hear the homophone normally, not backward. When Vokey and Read buried the homophone in a backward message, the unconscious influence disappeared.

In continued quest of unconscious influence, Ian Begg and his McMaster University colleagues (1993) adapted "the illusory truth effect"—the tendency for repeated statements, such as "The most prevalent infection in the world today is cholera," to seem true. The phenomenon disappears, Begg and McMaster found, when the statements are played backwards.

So, once again, a popular idea collapsed when tested experimentally. Those concerned about backward messages in rock music can relax. Rock's influence doesn't leak through as messages played backwards.

Difference Thresholds

To function effectively, we need absolute thresholds low enough to allow us to detect important sights, sounds, textures, tastes, and smells. We also need to detect small differences among stimuli. A musician must detect minute discrepancies in an instrument's tuning. A wine taster must detect the slight flavor difference between two vintage wines. Parents must detect the sound of their own child's voice amid other children's voices.

The difference threshold (also called the *just noticeable difference*, or *jnd*) is the minimum difference a person can detect between any two stimuli 50 percent of the time. The difference threshold increases with the magnitude of the stimulus. Thus, if you add 10 grams to a 100-gram weight, you will detect the difference; add 10 grams to a 1-*kilogram* weight and you will not, because the difference threshold has increased. More than a century ago, Ernst Weber noted that regardless of their magnitude, two stimuli must differ by a constant proportion for their difference to be perceptible. This principle—that the difference threshold is

difference threshold
the minimum difference that a subject can detect between two stimuli 50 percent of the time. We experience the difference threshold as a just noticeable difference. (Also called just noticeable difference, or jnd.)

Weber's law
the principle that, to perceive their difference, two stimuli must differ by a constant minimum percentage (rather than a constant amount).

sensory adaptation
diminished sensitivity as a consequence of constant stimulation.

not a constant amount but some constant *proportion* of the stimulus—is so simple and so widely applicable that we still refer to it as Weber's law. The exact proportion varies, depending on the stimulus. For the average person to perceive their differences, two lights must differ in intensity by 8 percent. Two objects must differ in weight by 2 percent. And two tones must differ in frequency by only 0.3 percent (Teghtsoonian, 1971).

Weber's law is a rough approximation that works well for nonextreme sensory stimuli. It also parallels some of our life experiences. If the price of a 50-cent chocolate bar goes up by 5 cents, shoppers might notice the change; similarly, it might take a $5000 price hike in a $50,000 Mercedes to raise the eyebrows of its potential buyers. In both cases, the price went up by 10 percent. Weber's principle: Our thresholds for detecting differences are a roughly constant proportion of the size of the original stimulus.

unnoticed by us, our eyes are always moving, quivering just enough to guarantee that retinal stimulation continually changes.

What if we could stop our eyes from moving? Would sights seem to vanish, as odors do? To find out, psychologists have devised ingenious instruments for maintaining a constant image on the retina. Imagine that we fitted a volunteer, Mary, with one of these instruments—a miniature projector mounted on a contact lens (Figure 5.2a). When Mary's eye moves, the image from the projector moves as well. Thus, everywhere that Mary looks the scene is sure to go.

If we project the profile of a face through such an instrument, what will Mary see? At first she will see the complete profile. But within a few seconds, as her sensory receptors begin to fatigue, things get weird. Bit by bit, the image vanishes, only later to reappear and then disappear—in recognizable fragments or as a whole (Figure 5.2b). Interestingly, the disappearance and reappearance of an image occurs in meaningful units. If a person is shown a word, it will disappear, and new words made up of parts of that word will appear and then vanish. This phenomenon anticipates the next chapter's major conclusion: Our perceptions are organized by the meanings that our minds impose.

The difference threshold In this computer-generated copy of the Twenty-third Psalm, each line of the typeface changes imperceptibly. How many lines are required for you to experience a just noticeable difference?

The LORD is my shepherd;
    I shall not want.
He maketh me to lie down
        in green pastures:
    he leadeth me
        beside the still waters.
He restoreth my soul:
    he leadeth me
        in the paths of righteousness
            for his name's sake.
Yea, though I walk through the valley
        of the shadow of death,
    I will fear no evil:
    for thou art with me;
        thy rod and thy staff
        they comfort me.
Thou preparest a table before me
    in the presence of mine enemies:
    thou anointest my head with oil,
        my cup runneth over.
Surely goodness and mercy
        shall follow me
        all the days of my life:
    and I will dwell
        in the house of the LORD
        for ever.

"My suspicion is that the universe is not only queerer than we suppose, but queerer than we can suppose."

J. B. S. HALDANE
POSSIBLE WORLDS
1927

Sensory Adaptation

"We need above all to know about changes; no one wants or needs to be reminded 16 hours a day that his shoes are on."

NEUROSCIENTIST DAVID HUBEL (1979)

For 9 in 10 people—but, curiously, for only 1 in 3 schizophrenia patients—this eye flutter turns off when the eye is following a moving target (Holzman & Matthysse, 1990).

Entering your neighbor's living room, you smell an unpleasant odor. You wonder how she tolerates the stench, but within minutes you no longer notice it. Jumping into a swimming pool, you shiver and complain how cold it is. A short while later a friend arrives and you exclaim, "C'mon in. Water's fine!" These examples illustrate sensory adaptation—our diminishing sensitivity to an unchanging stimulus. (To experience this phenomenon, move your watch up your wrist an inch: You will feel it—but only for a few moments.) After constant exposure to a stimulus, our nerve cells fire less frequently.

Why, then, if we stare at an object without flinching, does it not vanish from sight? Because,

Although sensory adaptation reduces our sensitivity, it offers an important benefit: It enables us to focus our attention on *informative* changes in our environment without being distracted by the uninformative constant stimulation of garments, odors, and street noise. Our sensory receptors are alert to novelty; bore them with repetition and they free our attention for more important things. This reinforces a fundamental lesson: We perceive the world not exactly as it is, but as it is useful for us to perceive it.

Sensory thresholds and adaptation are not the only commonalities among the senses. All the senses receive sensory stimulation, transform it into neural information, and deliver that information to the brain. How do the senses work? How do we see? Hear? Smell? Taste? Feel pain? Let's start with vision, the sense people tend to prize the most.

Figure 5.2

(a)

(b)

SUMMING UP

To study sensation is to study an ageless question: How does the world out there get represented inside our heads? Put another way, how are the external stimuli that strike our bodies transformed into messages that our brains comprehend?

Thresholds Each species comes equipped with sensitivities that enable it to survive and thrive. We sense only a portion of the sea of energy that surrounds us, but to this portion we are exquisitely sensitive. Our absolute threshold for any stimulus is the minimum stimulation necessary for us to detect it. Signal detection researchers report that our individual absolute thresholds vary with our psychological state.

Can we react to stimuli that are not only subthreshold (subliminal) but so weak that we could never consciously perceive them? Experiments reveal that we *can* process some information from stimuli too weak to recognize. But the restricted conditions under which this occurs would not enable unscrupulous opportunists to exploit us with subliminal messages. Nor is there any evidence or plausible theory that we can effortlessly "reprogram" our minds with subliminal tapes.

To survive and thrive, an organism must also have difference thresholds low enough to detect minute changes in important stimuli. In humans, difference thresholds (also called *just noticeable differences*, or *jnd's*) increase in proportion to the size of the stimulus—a principle known as Weber's Law.

Sensory Adaptation The phenomenon of sensory adaptation focuses our attention on changing stimulation by diminishing our sensitivity to constant or routine odors, sounds, and touches.

KEY TERMS AND CONCEPTS sensation, perception, bottom-up processing, top-down processing, psychophysics, absolute threshold, signal detection theory, subliminal, difference threshold (just noticeable difference, or jnd), Weber's law, sensory adaptation

> Our sensory receptors are alert to novelty; bore them with repetition and they free our attention for more important things.

Vision

One of nature's greatest wonders is neither bizarre nor remote, but commonplace: How does our material body construct our conscious visual experience? How do we transform particles of light energy into colorful sights?

Part of your taken-for-granted genius is your body's ability to convert one sort of energy to another. Sensory <u>transduction</u> is the process by which our sensory systems convert stimulus energy into neural messages. Your eyes, for example, receive light energy and manage an amazing feat: They transduce (transform) the energy into neural messages that the brain processes into what you consciously see. Let's consider how that happens.

> "The most commonplace crime is often the most mysterious. . . . Life is infinitely stranger than anything which the mind of man could invent."
>
> **SHERLOCK HOLMES, IN ARTHUR CONAN DOYLE'S**
> *A STUDY IN SCARLET*
> 1888

transduction
conversion of one form of energy into another. In sensation, the transforming of stimulus energies into neural impulses.

wavelength
the distance from the peak of one light or sound wave to the peak of the next. Electromagnetic wavelengths vary from the short blips of cosmic rays to the long pulses of radio transmission.

hue
the dimension of color that is determined by the wavelength of light; what we know as the color names blue, green, and so forth.

intensity
the amount of energy in a light or sound wave, which we perceive as brightness or loudness, as determined by the wave's amplitude.

The Stimulus Input: Light Energy

Scientifically speaking, what strikes our eyes is not color but pulses of electromagnetic energy that our visual system experiences as color. What we see as visible light is but a thin slice of the whole spectrum of electromagnetic radiation. As Figure 5.3 illustrates, this *electromagnetic spectrum* ranges from the imperceptibly short pulses or waves of gamma rays to the narrow band that we see as visible light to the long waves of radio transmission. Other organisms are sensitive to differing portions of the spectrum. For instance, bees cannot see red but can see ultraviolet light (see photos).

Two physical characteristics of light and sound help determine our sensory experience of them. Light's wavelength—the distance from one wave peak to the next (Figure 5.4a)—determines its hue (the color we experience, such as blue or green). Intensity, the amount of energy in light waves (determined by a wave's *amplitude*, or height), influences brightness (Figure 5.4b). To understand *how* we transform physical energy into a sensation of color, we first need to understand our mind's window, the eye.

Differing eyes When it comes to vision, humans and bees are on a different wavelength. Compare the way a flower is registered by a human and a bee's eye. The bee detects reflected ultraviolet wavelengths, enabling it to see the pollen landing field. The differing ecological niches occupied by different species demands sensitivity to different stimuli.

Human Eye **Bee's Eye**

Figure **5.3**

The spectrum of electromagnetic energy This spectrum ranges from gamma rays as short as the diameter of an atom to radio waves over a mile long. The narrow band of wavelengths visible to the human eye (shown enlarged) extends from the shorter waves of blue-violet light to the longer waves of red light.

Figure **5.4**

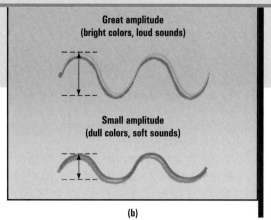

(a)   (b)

The physical properties of waves
(a) Waves vary in wavelength, the distance between successive peaks. Frequency, the number of complete wavelengths that can pass a point in a given time, depends on the wavelength. The shorter the wavelength, the higher the frequency. (b) Waves also vary in amplitude, the height from peak to trough. Wave amplitude determines the intensity of colors and sounds.

The Eye

Light enters the eye through the *cornea*, a transparent protector, then travels through the pupil, a small adjustable opening (Figure 5.5). The pupil's size, and therefore the amount of light entering the eye, is regulated by the iris, a colored muscle surrounding the pupil. Behind the pupil is a lens that focuses the incoming rays into an image on a light-sensitive surface. It does so by changing its curvature in a process called accommodation. The eyeball's light-sensitive surface on which the rays focus is the retina, a multilayered tissue.

For centuries, scientists have known that when the image of a candle passes through a small opening, its mirror image appears inverted on a dark wall behind (as in Figure 5.5). This fact had scholars baffled. If the retina receives an upside-down image, how can we see the world right side up? One idea was that the eye's sensing device is the lens. Realizing this wasn't so, the ever-curious Leonardo da Vinci had another idea: Perhaps the eye's watery fluids bent the light rays, reinverting the image to the upright position as it reached the retina. But in 1604, the astronomer and optics expert Johannes Kepler showed that the retina did receive upside-down images of the world (Crombie, 1964). And how could we understand such a world? "I leave it," said the befuddled Kepler, "to natural philosophers."

The "natural philosophers," who eventually included research psychologists, discovered that the retina doesn't read the image as a whole. Rather, its millions of receptor cells convert light energy into neural impulses. These impulses are sent to the brain and constructed *there* into a perceived, upright-seeming image.

pupil
the adjustable opening in the center of the eye through which light enters.

iris
a ring of muscle tissue that forms the colored portion of the eye around the pupil and controls the size of the pupil opening.

lens
the transparent structure behind the pupil that changes shape to focus images on the retina.

accommodation
the process by which the eye's lens changes shape to focus the image of near objects on the retina.

retina
the light-sensitive inner surface of the eye, containing the receptor rods and cones plus layers of neurons that begin the processing of visual information.

Figure **5.5**

The eye

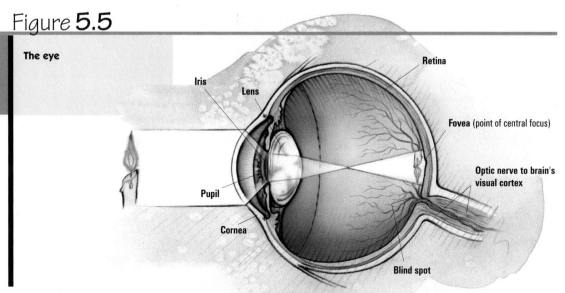

Iris
Lens
Retina
Fovea (point of central focus)
Optic nerve to brain's visual cortex
Pupil
Cornea
Blind spot

Figure **5.6**

Vision

(a)
Normal vision
Rays of light converge on the retina of a normal eye. This occurs for both nearby objects and, with appropriate readjustments in the curvature of the lens, for objects that are far away.

(b)
Nearsighted vision
In the eye of a person with nearsighted vision, the eyeball is longer than normal and the light rays from distant objects are focused in front of the retina. When their image reaches the retina, the rays are spreading out and the image is blurred.

(c)
Farsighted vision
In the eye of a person with farsighted vision, the eyeball is shorter than normal, and light rays from nearby objects come into focus behind the retina, resulting in blurred images.

Acuity, or sharpness of vision, can be affected by small distortions in the shape of the eye. Normally the lens focuses the image of any object on the retina (Figure 5.6a). In nearsightedness, where the eyeball is longer than normal in relation to its lens, or where the cornea is too sharply curved, the light rays from distant objects converge in front of the retina (Figure 5.6b). Generally, perception of near objects is clearer than that of distant objects, but people who are extremely nearsighted see nothing clearly. Farsightedness is a sort of opposite of nearsightedness. Here, the light rays from near objects entering through the cornea and lens reach the retina before they have converged, producing a blurred image (Figure 5.6c). In children, the eye's ability to accommodate usually makes up for this problem, and they rarely need glasses—but they may suffer eyestrain from overused eye muscles, and some get headaches. People who are only mildly farsighted often do not discover their condition until middle age, when the lens loses its ability to change shape rapidly, and they begin to have trouble seeing near objects clearly.

When viewing an eye chart, people with normal 20/20 vision can read material of a certain size from a distance of 20 feet. If you're standing 20 feet away and can discriminate only what people with normal vision can see at 50 feet, then you have 20/50 vision.

The Retina

If we were to follow a single particle of light energy into the eye, we would see that it first makes its way through the retina's outer layer of cells to its buried receptor cells, the rods and cones (Figure 5.7). Light energy striking the rods and cones produces chemical changes that generate neural signals. These signals activate the neighboring *bipolar cells*, which in turn activate the neighboring *ganglion cells*. The axons from the network of ganglion cells converge like the strands of a rope to form an optic nerve that carries information to the brain. Nearly a million messages can be sent by the optic nerve at once, through nearly 1 million ganglion fibers. (The auditory nerve, which enables hearing, carries much less information through its mere 30,000 fibers.) Where the optic nerve leaves the eye there are no receptor cells—creating a blind spot (Figure 5.8).

Rod-shaped rods and cone-shaped cones   As the scanning electron microscope shows, rods and cones are well named. Rods are more sensitive to light than are the color-sensitive cones, which is why the world looks colorless at night. Some nocturnal animals, such as toads, mice, rats, and bats, have retinas made up almost entirely of rods, allowing them to function well in dim light. These creatures probably have very poor color vision.

Figure **5.7**

The retina's reaction to light

2. Chemical reaction in turn activates bipolar cells.

1. Light entering eye triggers photochemical reaction in rods and cones at back of retina.

Light

Cross section of retina

Light

Ganglion cell

Bipolar cell

Cone

Neural impulse

Rod

Optic nerve

To visual cortex

3. Bipolar cells then activate the ganglion cells, the axons of which converge to form the optic nerve. This nerve transmits information to the visual cortex in the brain's occipital lobe.

acuity
the sharpness of vision.

nearsightedness
a condition in which nearby objects are seen more clearly than distant objects because the lens focuses the image of distant objects in front of the retina.

farsightedness
a condition in which faraway objects are seen more clearly than near objects because the image of near objects is focused behind the retina.

rods
retinal receptors that detect black, white, and gray; necessary for peripheral and twilight vision, when cones don't respond.

cones
receptor cells that are concentrated near the center of the retina and that function in daylight or in well-lit conditions. The cones detect fine detail and give rise to color sensations.

optic nerve
the nerve that carries neural impulses from the eye to the brain.

blind spot
the point at which the optic nerve leaves the eye, creating a "blind" spot because no receptor cells are located there.

fovea
the central focal point in the retina, around which the eye's cones cluster.

Most cones are clustered around the fovea, the retina's area of central focus (Figure 5.5). In fact, the fovea contains only cones, no rods. Unlike rods, many cones have their own bipolar cells to help relay their individual messages to the cortex, which devotes a large amount of its area to impulses from the fovea. This preserves the cones' precise information, making them better able to detect fine detail. (Rods have no such hotline to the brain; they share bipolar cells with other rods, so their individual messages get combined.) To illustrate, if you pick a word in this sentence and stare directly at it, focusing its image on the cones in your fovea, you will see that words a few inches off to the side appear blurred. This is because their image strikes the more peripheral region of your retina, where the rods predominate (Table 5.1).

Rods enable black-and-white vision; cones enable you to see color. As illumination diminishes, the cones become ineffectual. The rods, however, remain sensitive in dim light, because several rods will funnel their faint energy from dim light onto a single bipolar cell. That is why you don't see colors in dim light. When you enter a darkened theater or turn off the light at night, your pupils dilate to allow more light to reach the rods in the retina's periphery. Typically it takes 20 minutes or more before our eyes fully adapt.

Figure **5.8**

The blind spot Where the optic nerve leaves the eye (Figure 5.7), there are no receptor cells. This creates a blind spot in our vision. To demonstrate, close your left eye, look at the spot, and move the page to a distance from your face (about a foot) at which the car disappears. In everyday vision the blind spot doesn't impair your vision because your eyes are moving and because one eye catches what the other misses.

Table 5.1

Receptors in the Human Eye

	Cones	Rods
Number	6 million	120 million
Location in retina	Center	Periphery
Sensitivity in dim light	Low	High
Color sensitive?	Yes	No

You can demonstrate dark adaptation by closing or covering one eye for up to 20 minutes, then making the room light not quite bright enough to read this book with your open eye. Now open the dark-adapted eye and read. This period of dark adaptation is yet another instance of the remarkable adaptiveness of our sensory systems, for it parallels the average natural twilight transition between the sun's setting and darkness.

Knowing just this much about the eye, can you imagine why a cat sees so much better at night than you do? There are at least two reasons: A cat's pupils can open much wider than yours, letting in more light; and a cat has a higher proportion of light-sensitive rods (Moser, 1987). But there is a trade-off: With fewer cones, a cat can't see details or color as well as you do.

> Visual information percolates through progressively more abstract levels.

Visual Information Processing

Visual information percolates through progressively more abstract levels. At the entry level, the retina—which is actually a piece of the brain that migrates to the eye during early fetal development—processes information before routing it to the cortex. The retina's neural layers are not just passing along electrical impulses; they also help to encode and analyze the sensory information. The third neural layer in a frog's eye, for example, contains the "bug detector" cells that fire only in response to flylike stimuli.

In human eyes, the information from the retina's nearly 130 million receptor rods and cones is received and transmitted by the million or so gan-

feature detectors
nerve cells in the brain that respond to specific features of the stimulus, such as shape, angle, or movement.

glion cells, whose fibers make up the optic nerve. A typical ganglion cell responds to light/dark contrasts revealed by its receptor cells. This helps the brain detect edges and other important features of the visual world. But most information processing occurs in the brain. Any given area of the retina relays its information to a corresponding location in the occipital lobe—the visual cortex at the back of the brain (Figure 5.9).

The sensitivity that enables retinal cells to fire messages can lead them to misfire as well. Turn your eyes to the left, close them, and then gently rub the right side of your right eyelid with your fingertip. Note the patch of light to the left, moving as your finger moves. Why do you see light? Why at the left?

Your retinal cells are so responsive that even pressure triggers them. But your brain interprets their firing as light. Moreover, it interprets the light as coming from the left—where light normally comes from when it activates the right side of the retina.

Figure 5.9

How the visual cortex receives information from the eyes A brain scan shows visual cortex activity corresponding to a person's view of either half of a pattern.

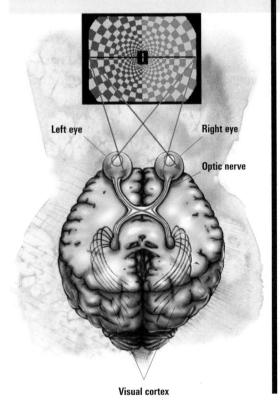

Left eye

Right eye

Optic nerve

Visual cortex

Cell's responses

Stimulus

Figure **5.10**

Electrodes record how individual cells in this monkey's visual cortex respond to different visual stimuli Hubel and Wiesel won the Nobel prize for their discovery that most cells in the visual cortex respond only to particular features—for example, to the edge of a surface, or to a line at a 30-degree angle in the upper right part of the field of vision. More complex features trigger higher-level detector cells, which integrate information from these simpler ones.

Feature Detection

When individual ganglion cells register information in their region of the visual field, they send signals to the visual cortex. Nobel prize winners David Hubel and Torsten Wiesel (1979) demonstrated that when certain cortical neurons, called feature detectors, receive this information, they respond to specific features of a scene—to particular edges, lines, angles, and movements. From these elements the brain assembles the perceived image.

For example, Hubel and Wiesel report that a given brain cell might respond maximally to a line flashed at a 2 o'clock tilt (Figure 5.10). If the line is tilted further—say, to a 3 o'clock or 1 o'clock position—the cell quiets down. Thus, the feature detection cells record amazingly specific features taken in by the eye. Feature detection cells pass this information to other cells that respond only to more complex patterns. The basic idea is that perceptions arise from the interaction of many neuron systems, each performing a simple task.

The visual cortex passes this information along to the temporal and parietal cortex, which includes higher-level brain cells that respond to specific visual scenes, such as a face or an arm movement in a particular direction. Psychologist David Perrett and his colleagues (1988, 1992, 1994) report that for biologically important objects and events, monkey brains (and surely ours as well) have a "vast visual encyclopedia" distributed as cells that respond to one stimulus but not to others. Perrett has identified nerve cells that specialize in responding to a specific gaze, head angle, posture, or body movement. Other supercell clusters integrate this information and fire only when the cues collectively indicate the direction of someone's attention and approach. This instant analysis, which aided our ancestors' survival, also helps a goalie anticipate the direction of an impending soccer kick and a pedestrian anticipate another pedestrian's next movement.

Researchers also have identified nerve cells that activate or not, depending on how a monkey *perceives* a given image (as "reported" by the monkey's eye movements) (Logothetis & Schall, 1989). Such studies remind us that our visual system works both bottom up and top down. Although our visual pathway faithfully represents retinal stimulation, our brain's representation also incorporates our assumptions, interests, and expectations (Maunsell, 1995). The higher-level brain activity that underlies perception combines sensory input and cognition.

Researchers debate the precise nature of the features and patterns that brain cells detect. New research suggests that any image, such as a face, can be broken down into patterns of changing light intensity that can be described mathematically. Thus, in seeing, the brain may actually be processing mathematical-like codes that represent a perceived image (Kosslyn & Koenig, 1992; Marr, 1982). Neuroscientists working with computer experts are

Going left or right? In the semifinal game of the 1996 European Cup, German goalie Andreas Kopke anticipates the direction of Gareth Southgate's tiebreaker kick for England. Before Southgate's foot connects with the ball, Kopke's visual system has processed information from Southgate's eyes, posture, and movement, activating "going right" supercells. Kopke blocks the kick and Germany wins.

parallel processing
the processing of several aspects of a problem simultaneously; the brain's natural mode of information processing for many functions, including vision. Contrasts with the step-by-step (serial) processing of most computers and of conscious problem solving.

Young-Helmholtz trichromatic (three-color) theory
the theory that the retina contains three different color receptors—one most sensitive to red, one to green, one to blue—which when stimulated in combination can produce the perception of any color.

Parallel processing Studies of brain-damaged patients suggest that the brain delegates the work of processing color, motion, form, and depth to different areas. After taking a scene apart, how does the brain integrate these subdimensions into the perceived image? The answer to this question is the Holy Grail of vision research.

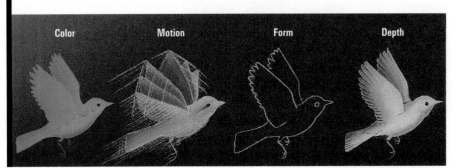

simulating the activity of the brain's interconnected, multilevel neural networks. Their goal is to build artificial vision systems that respond as our own visual system responds. For example, their simulated neural networks respond as humans do to the illusory image of a triangle, like that in Figure 5.11. Both the human and the simulated neural network activity respond as if they were reacting to a real triangle (Finkel & Sajda, 1994).

Parallel Processing

Neural impulses travel a million times slower than a computer's internal messages, yet the brain humbles any computer by recognizing a familiar face instantly. Unlike most computers, which do step-by-step serial processing, our brains engage in parallel processing, which means we can do several things at once. The brain divides a visual scene into subdimensions such as color, depth, movement, and form and works on each aspect simultaneously (Livingstone & Hubel, 1988). As David Rumelhart (1989) explains, this division of labor to specialized but overlapping neural networks more than makes up for the brain's slowness:

> Although the brain has *slow* components, it has *very many* of them. The human brain contains billions of such processing elements. Rather than organize computation with many, many serial steps, as we do with [computer] systems whose steps are very fast, the brain must deploy many, many processing elements cooperatively and in parallel to carry out its activities.

Thus the retina projects not just to one visual cortex area but to several areas, each of which becomes active in response to retinal stimulation. When the brain integrates this visual information, further processing in another cortex area, the temporal lobe, enables us to recognize an image as, say, Whoopi Goldberg. The whole process of facial recognition requires tremendous brain power—30 percent of the cortex, 10 times the area the brain devotes to hearing. The computations required for sensorimotor coordination dwarf even those involved in reasoning. We now have computers that

Figure **5.11**

Illusory contours Simulated neural networks respond to the illusory triangles as humans do—as if they were real triangles, and not just three Pacman faces.

can play chess with champion Garry Kasparov, but we're a long way from computer-driven robots that can play tennis with Monica Seles, much less dust the house.

The distribution of visual tasks to different neural work teams explains a strange phenomenon. After a stroke, people may lose just one aspect of vision. A person may perceive color but not movement. If something moves, it disappears until it stops. Other brain-damaged patients can tell you all about the subdimensions of an object or person (a rose's color or a woman's height) but cannot name the object or the person.

Still others have lost a neural area involved in consciously perceiving some aspect of their field of vision. One such woman was shown two drawings of a house—identical except that the house's left side was on fire in one drawing. Asked to select the house she would prefer to live in, she thought the question silly, "because they're the same." Yet she consistently chose the house that was not burning (Marshall & Halligan, 1988; Milner, 1995). This uncanny ability to respond to something not consciously perceived, called *blindsight*, reminds us once again of the startling truth: Our brains do many things at once, automatically and without our awareness.

Senses other than vision also process information with similar speed and intricacy. Opening the back door, you recognize the aroma wafting from the kitchen even before you step inside. Answering the phone, you recognize the friend calling from the moment she says "Hi." Within a fraction of a second after such events stimulate the senses, millions of neurons have simultaneously coordinated in extracting the essential features, comparing them with past experience, and identifying the stimulus (Freeman, 1991).

This scientific understanding of sensory information processing illustrates neuropsychologist Roger Sperry's (1985) reflection: The "insights of science give added, not lessened, reasons for awe, respect, and reverence." Think about it: As you look at someone, the visual information is sent to your brain as millions of neural impulses, then constructed into its component features, and finally, in some as yet mysterious way, composed into a meaningful perceived image, which is then compared with previously stored images and recognized as, for example, your grandmother. The whole process (Figure 5.12) is as complex as taking a car apart, piece by piece, transporting it to a different location, then having specialized workers reconstruct it. That all of this happens instantly, effortlessly, and continuously is indeed awesome.

"I am fearfully and wonderfully made."

KING DAVID
PSALMS 139:14

Color Vision

People talk as though objects possess color. We say, "The tomato is red." Perhaps you have pondered the old question, "If a tree falls in the forest and no one hears it, does it make a sound?" We can ask the same of color: If no one sees the tomato, is it red?

The answer is no. First, the tomato is everything *but* red, because it *rejects* (reflects) the long wavelengths of red. Second, the tomato's color is our mental construction. As Isaac Newton (1704) noted, "The [light] rays are not coloured." Color, like all aspects of vision, resides not in the object but in the theater of our brains. Even while dreaming, we may perceive things in color.

In the study of vision, one of the most basic and intriguing mysteries is how we see the world in color. How, from the light energy striking the retina, does the brain manufacture our experience of color—and of such a multitude of colors? Our difference threshold for colors is so low that we can discriminate some 7 million different color variations (Geldard, 1972).

At least most of us can. For about 1 person in 50, vision is color-deficient—and that person is usually male, because the defect is genetically sex-linked. To understand why some people have color-deficient vision we must first understand how normal color vision works.

Modern detective work on the mystery of color vision began in the nineteenth century when Hermann von Helmholtz built on the insights of an English physicist, Thomas Young. Young and Helmholtz recognized that any color can be created by combining the light waves of three primary colors—red, green, and blue (Figure 5.13). So, they inferred that the eye must have three types of receptors, one for each primary color of light.

Many years later, researchers measured the response of various cones to different color stimuli and confirmed the Young-Helmholtz trichromatic (three-color) theory, which simply states that the retina has three types of color receptors, each especially sensitive to one of three colors. And surprise! Those colors are, indeed, red, green, or blue. When we stimulate combinations of these cones, we see other colors. For example, there are no receptors especially sensitive to yellow. Yet when both red- and green-sensitive cones are stimulated, we see yellow.

Figure 5.12

A simplified summary of visual information processing

Abstraction:
Brain's higher-level cells respond to combined information from feature-detector cells

Feature detection:
Brain's detector cells respond to elementary features—bars, edges, or gradients of light

Recognition:
Brain matches the constructed image with stored images

Retinal processing:
Receptor rods and cones→ bipolar cells→ ganglion cells

Scene

"Only mind has sight and hearing; all things else are deaf and blind."

EPICHARMUS
FRAGMENTS
550 B.C.

Figure 5.13

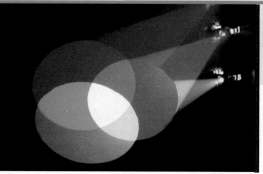

The three primary colors of light
The primary colors of light mix to create other colors. For example, red and green combine to create yellow. All three—red, green, and blue— combine to create white.

Figure 5.14

Color-deficient vision   People who suffer red-green blindness have trouble perceiving the number within the design.

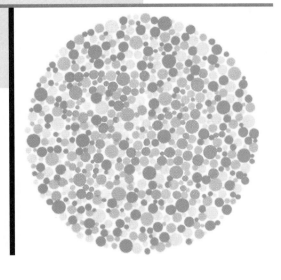

> "Is it not stirring to understand how the world actually works—that white light is made of colors, that color measures light waves, that transparent air reflects light . . . ? It does no harm to the romance of the sunset to know a little about it."
>
> CARL SAGAN
> *SKIES OF OTHER WORLDS*
> 1988

Most color-deficient people are not actually "colorblind." Rather, they simply lack functioning red- or green-sensitive cones. Their vision is dichromatic instead of trichromatic, making it difficult to distinguish red and green, as in Figure 5.14 (Boynton, 1979). Dogs, too, lack receptors for the wavelengths of red, giving them only limited, dichromatic color vision (Neitz & others, 1989).

Soon after Young and Helmholtz proposed the trichromatic theory, physiologist Ewald Hering pointed out that other parts of the color vision mystery remained unsolved. For example, we see yellow when mixing red and green light. But how is it that those blind to red and green can often still see yellow? And why does yellow appear to be a pure color and not a mixture of red and green, as purple does of red and blue?

Hering found a clue in the well-known occurrence of *afterimages*. When you stare at a green square for a while and then look at a white sheet of paper, you see red, green's *opponent color*. Stare at a yellow square and you will later see its opponent color, blue, on the white paper (as in the flag demonstration in Figure 5.15). Hering surmised

that there were two additional color processes, one responsible for red versus green perception, and one for blue versus yellow.

A century later, researchers confirmed Hering's opponent-process theory. *After* leaving the receptor cells, visual information is analyzed in terms of the opponent colors red and green, blue and yellow, and also black and white. In the retina and in the thalamus (where impulses from the retina are relayed en route to the visual cortex) some neurons are turned "on" by red but turned "off" by green. Others are turned on by green but off by red (DeValois & DeValois, 1975). So if you detect one of these colors at a particular point on the retina, you cannot simultaneously detect the opposing color at the same point; you therefore cannot see a greenish red.

Opponent processes explain afterimages, such as in the flag demonstration, in which we tire our green response by staring at green. When we then stare at white (which contains all colors, including red), only the red part of the green/red pairing will fire normally.

The present solution to the mystery of color vision is therefore roughly this: Color processing occurs in two stages. The retina's red, green, and blue cones respond in varying degrees to different color stimuli, as the Young-Helmholtz trichromatic theory suggested. Their signals are then processed by the nervous system's opponent-process cells, en route to the visual cortex.

Color Constancy

Our experience of color depends on something more than the wavelength information received by our trichromatic cones and transmitted through the opponent-process cells.

That something more is the surrounding *context*. If you view only part of a tomato, its color will seem to change as the light changes. But if you see the whole tomato as one item in a bowl of fresh vegetables, its color will remain roughly constant

Figure 5.15

Afterimage effect   Stare at the center of the flag for a minute and then shift your eyes to the dot in the white space beside it. What do you see? (After tiring your neural response to black, green, and yellow, you should see their opponent colors.)

as the lighting and wavelengths shift—a phenomenon known as color constancy. Dorothea Jameson (1985) notes that a chip colored blue under indoor lighting matches the wavelengths reflected by a gold chip in the sunlight. Yet bring a bluebird indoors and it won't look like a goldfinch. Likewise, a green leaf hanging from a brown branch may, when the illumination changes, now reflect the same light energy that formerly came from the brown branch. Yet to us the leaf stays greenish and the branch stays brownish. Put on yellow-tinted ski goggles and the snow, after a second, looks as white as before.

We take this color constancy for granted, but the phenomenon is remarkable. It demonstrates that our experience of color comes not just from the object—the color is not in the isolated leaf—but from everything around it as well. You and I see color thanks to our brains' computations of the light reflected by any object *relative to its surrounding objects*.

In an unvarying context, we maintain color constancy. But what if we change the context? Because the brain computes the color of an object relative to its context, the perceived color changes (as is dramatically apparent in Figure 5.16). This principle—that we perceive objects not in isolation but in their environmental context—is especially significant for artists, interior decorators, and clothing designers. The perceived color of a wall or of a swatch of paint on a canvas is determined not just by the paint in the can but by the surrounding colors.

Figure **5.16**

Color depends on context In this painting by Joseph Albers (1975), the unchanging line seems to vary from gray to yellow as its surrounding context changes.

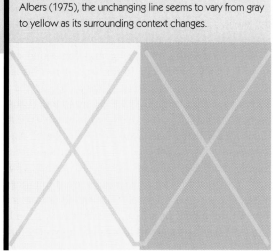

SUMMING UP

The task of our visual sense, as of each of our senses, is to receive stimulation, transduce it into neural signals, and send these neural messages to the brain.

The Stimulus Input: Light Energy The energies we experience as visible light are a thin slice from the broad spectrum of electromagnetic radiation. Their perceived hue and brightness of light depend on the wavelength and intensity.

The Eye After entering the eye through a camera-like lens, light waves strike the retina. The retina's light-sensitive rods and color-sensitive cones convert the light energy into neural impulses, which are coded by the retina before traveling up the optic nerve to the brain.

Visual Information Processing In the cortex, individual neurons, called feature detectors, respond to specific features of a visual stimulus, and their information is pooled for interpretation by higher-level brain cells. Subdimensions of vision (color, movement, depth, and form) are processed separately and simultaneously, illustrating the brain's capacity for parallel processing. The visual pathway faithfully represents retinal stimulation, but the brain's representation incorporates our assumptions, interests, and expectations.

Color Vision Research on how we see color supports two nineteenth-century theories. First, as the Young-Helmholtz three-color theory suggests, the retina contains three types of cones. Each is most sensitive to the wavelengths of one of the three primary colors (red, green, or blue). Second, as opponent-process theory maintains, the nervous system codes the color-related information from the cones into pairs of opponent colors, as demonstrated by the phenomenon of afterimages and as confirmed by measuring opponent processes within visual neurons of the thalamus. As illustrated by the phenomenon of color constancy under varying illumination, our brains construct our experience of color.

KEY TERMS AND CONCEPTS transduction, wavelength, hue, intensity, pupil, iris, lens, accommodation, retina, acuity, nearsightedness, farsightedness, rods, cones, optic nerve, blind spot, fovea, feature detectors, parallel processing, Young-Helmholtz trichromatic (three-color) theory, opponent-process theory, color constancy

opponent-process theory
the theory that opposing retinal processes (red-green, yellow-blue, white-black) enable color vision. For example, some cells are stimulated by green and inhibited by red; others are stimulated by red and inhibited by green.

color constancy
perceiving familiar objects as having consistent color, even if changing illumination alters the wavelengths reflected by the object.

audition
the sense of hearing.

frequency
the number of complete wave-lengths that pass a point in a given time (for example, per second).

pitch
a tone's highness or lowness; depends on frequency.

Hearing

Somewhat less mysterious, but still pretty amazing, is another aspect of our ordinary experience: the process by which we convert air pressure waves into neural messages that the brain interprets as a meaningful symphony of sound. How do we do it? What breaks in the system typically cause hearing loss? What is it like to live without hearing?

Like our other senses, our hearing, or audition, is highly adaptive. We hear a wide range of sounds, but we are best able to hear sounds having frequencies within a range that corresponds to the range of the human voice. We also are remarkably sensitive to faint sounds, an obvious boon to our ancestors' survival when hunting or being hunted. (If our ears were much more sensitive, we would hear a constant hiss from the movement of air molecules.) Moreover, we are acutely sensitive to differences in sounds. We can easily detect differences among thousands of human voices, which helps us instantly recognize the voice of almost anyone we know.

For hearing as for seeing, one fundamental question remains—How do we do it? How do we transduce sound energy into neural messages that the brain interprets as a particular sound coming from a particular place?

The sounds of music A violin's short, fast waves create a high pitch, an accordion's longer, slower waves a low pitch. Differences in the wave's height or amplitude create differing loudness.

The Stimulus Input: Sound Waves

Hit a piano key and the resulting stimulus energy is sound waves—jostling molecules of air, each bumping into the next, like a shove being transmitted through the crowded exit tunnel of a concert hall. The resulting waves of compressed and expanded air are like the ripples on a pond circling out from where a tossed stone has broken the surface of the water. The strength, or amplitude, of sound waves determines their *loudness*. Waves also vary in length, and therefore in frequency (recall Figure 5.4, page 155). Their frequency determines their pitch: The longer the waves (the lower their frequency), the lower the pitch; the shorter the waves (the higher their frequency), the higher the pitch. A piccolo produces much shorter sound waves than does a kettledrum.

Decibels are the measuring unit for sound energy. The absolute threshold for hearing is arbitrarily defined as 0 decibels. Every 10 decibels correspond to a tenfold increase in sound. Thus, normal conversation (60 decibels) is about 10,000 times louder than a soft whisper (20 decibels). And a tolerable 90-decibel sound is a trillion times louder than the faintest detectable sound. (For light, too, we can tolerate a stimulus a trillion times more intense than a barely noticeable glimmer.) When prolonged, however, exposure to sounds above 85 decibels can produce hearing loss (Figure 5.17).

Figure **5.17**

The intensity of some common sounds

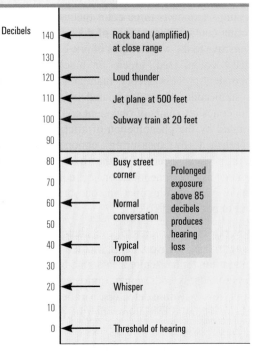

Decibels	
140	Rock band (amplified) at close range
130	
120	Loud thunder
110	Jet plane at 500 feet
100	Subway train at 20 feet
90	
80	Busy street corner
70	Prolonged exposure above 85 decibels produces hearing loss
60	Normal conversation
50	
40	Typical room
30	
20	Whisper
10	
0	Threshold of hearing

The Ear

To hear, we must somehow convert sound waves into neural activity. The human ear accomplishes this feat through an intricate mechanical chain reaction (Figure 5.18). First, the visible outer ear channels sound waves through the auditory canal to the *eardrum*, a tight membrane that vibrates with the waves. The middle ear transmits the eardrum's vibrations through a piston made of three tiny bones (the *hammer, anvil*, and *stirrup*) to a snail-shaped tube in the inner ear called the cochlea (KOHK-lee-uh). The incoming vibrations cause the cochlea's membrane (the *oval window*) to vibrate the fluid that fills the tube. This motion causes ripples in the *basilar membrane*, which is lined with *hair cells*, so named because of their tiny hairlike projections. At the end of this sequence, the rippling of the basilar membrane bends these hair cells, rather like the wind bending a wheat field. This hair cell movement triggers impulses in the adjacent nerve fibers, which converge to form the auditory nerve. Through this mechanical chain of events, sound waves cause the hair cells of the inner ear to send neural messages up to the temporal lobe's auditory cortex. From vibrating air to moving piston to fluid waves to electrical impulses to the brain: We hear.

How Do We Perceive Pitch?

How do we know whether a sound is the high-frequency, high-pitched chirp of a bird or the low-frequency, low-pitched roar of a truck? Current thinking on how we discriminate pitch, like current thinking on how we discriminate color, combines two theories.

Place theory presumes that we hear different pitches because different sound waves trigger activity at different places along the cochlea's basilar membrane. Thus, the brain can determine a sound's pitch by recognizing the place on the membrane from which it receives neural signals. When Georg von Békésy (1957) cut holes in the cochleas of guinea pigs and human cadavers and looked inside with a microscope, he discovered that high-frequency waves triggered activity mostly near the beginning of the cochlea's membrane, a discovery that contributed to his 1961 Nobel prize.

middle ear
the chamber between the eardrum and cochlea containing three tiny bones (hammer, anvil, and stirrup) that concentrate the vibrations of the eardrum on the cochlea's oval window.

inner ear
the innermost part of the ear, containing the cochlea, semicircular canals, and vestibular sacs.

cochlea
[KOHK-lee-uh] a coiled, bony, fluid-filled tube in the inner ear through which sound waves trigger nerve impulses.

place theory
in hearing, the theory that links the pitch we hear with the place where the cochlea's membrane is stimulated.

Figure **5.18**

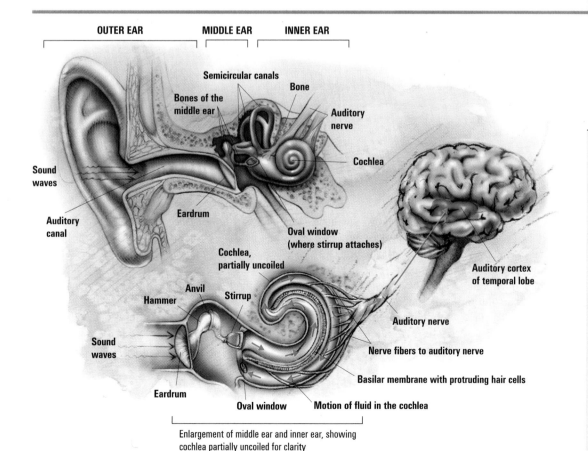

OUTER EAR | MIDDLE EAR | INNER EAR

Semicircular canals
Bone
Bones of the middle ear
Auditory nerve
Cochlea
Sound waves
Eardrum
Auditory canal
Oval window (where stirrup attaches)
Auditory cortex of temporal lobe
Cochlea, partially uncoiled
Anvil
Hammer
Stirrup
Sound waves
Auditory nerve
Nerve fibers to auditory nerve
Eardrum
Oval window
Motion of fluid in the cochlea
Basilar membrane with protruding hair cells

Enlargement of middle ear and inner ear, showing cochlea partially uncoiled for clarity

How we transform sound waves into nerve impulses that our brain interprets (a) The outer ear funnels sound waves to the eardrum. The bones of the middle ear amplify and relay the eardrum's vibrations through the oval window into the fluid-filled cochlea. (b) The resulting pressure changes in the cochlear fluid cause the basilar membrane to ripple, bending the hair cells on the surface. Hair cell movements trigger impulses at the bases of the nerve cells, whose fibers converge to form the auditory nerve. (For clarity, the cochlea is shown partially uncoiled.)

CLOSE-UP

Noise

Urban life is noisy. Traffic roars. Factory machines clatter. Jackhammers tear up pavement. Escaping to more pleasant sounds, runners stride to the beat of intense music on their headsets.

But the intensity of that sound may cause a problem. Brief exposure to extremely intense sounds, such as gunfire near one's ear, and prolonged exposure to intense sounds, such as amplified music, can damage receptor cells and auditory nerves (Backus, 1977; West & Evans, 1990). Although rock and roll may be here to stay, the sad truth for some rock musicians is that their hearing may not be.

Noise affects not only our hearing but also our behavior. On tasks requiring alert performance, people in noisy surroundings work less efficiently and make more errors (Broadbent, 1978). People who live with continual noise in factories, in homes near airports, and in apartments next to trains and highways suffer elevated rates of stress-related disorders; high blood pressure, anxiety, and feelings of helplessness are common (Evans & others, 1995).

But is it the noise that causes the stress? Laboratory experiments on the psychological effects of noise suggest an answer. In one such experiment, David Glass and Jerome Singer (1972) re-created the noise of city life by tape recording the chattering of office machines and of people speaking various languages. While working at various tasks, people heard this noise, played either loudly or softly, either at predictable or unpredictable intervals. Regardless of the conditions, the people soon adapted to the noise and performed well on most tasks. However, having coped with the noise, those exposed to the *unpre-*

The stress of noise
If prolonged, unpredictable noise can increase frustration and stress-related disorders.

dictable loud noise later made more errors on a proofreading task and reacted more quickly to frustration.

The conclusion: Noise is especially stressful when unanticipated or uncontrollable. That explains why the unpredictable and uncontrollable blaring of someone else's stereo can be so much more upsetting than the same decibels from your own. At such times we may wish that, as our eyes have eyelids, so our ears had earlids.

---

frequency theory
in hearing, the theory that the rate of nerve impulses traveling up the auditory nerve matches the frequency of a tone, thus enabling us to sense its pitch.

conduction deafness
hearing loss caused by damage to the mechanical system that conducts sound waves to the cochlea.

nerve deafness
hearing loss caused by damage to the cochlea's receptor cells or to the auditory nerves.

Although place theory explains how we hear high-pitched sounds, it doesn't explain how we hear low-pitched sounds, because the neural signals they generate are not so neatly localized on the basilar membrane. Frequency theory suggests an alternative solution to the pitch-discrimination mystery. The basilar membrane vibrates with the incoming sound wave. This vibration triggers neural impulses to the brain at the same rate as the sound wave. If the sound wave has a frequency of 100 waves per second, then 100 pulses per second travel up the auditory nerve. Thus, the brain can read pitch from the frequency of neural impulses.

Frequency theory can explain how we perceive low-pitched sounds. But it, too, has a problem: Individual neurons cannot fire faster than 1000 times per second. How then can it explain our sensing sounds with frequencies above 1000 waves per second (roughly the upper third of a piano keyboard and above)? Enter the *volley principle*: Like soldiers who alternate firing so that some can shoot while others reload, neural cells can alternate firing and thereby achieve a combined frequency well above 1000 times per second.

Thus, place theory best explains how we sense the higher pitches, and frequency theory best explains how we sense the low pitches. Some combination of place and frequency seems to handle the intermediate-range pitches.

How Do We Locate Sounds?

The slightly different messages sensed by the two microphones used in creating a stereophonic recording mimic the slightly different sound messages received by our two ears. As the placement of our eyes allows us to sense depth visually (page 187), the placement of our two ears allows us to enjoy stereophonic ("three-dimensional") hearing.

For at least two reasons, two ears are better than one. If a car to the right honks, your right ear receives a more *intense* sound slightly *sooner* than your left ear. Because sound travels 750 miles per hour and our ears are but 6 inches apart, the loudness difference and time lag are extremely small. But our sensitive auditory system can detect such minute differences (Brown & Deffenbacher, 1979; Middlebrooks & Green, 1991). A just noticeable difference in the direction from which two sounds come corresponds to a time difference of just 0.000027 second!

With auditory as with visual information, the brain uses parallel processing—by putting specialized neural teams to work simultaneously on different subtasks. Owls (and probably humans, too) process timing differences in one neural pathway and intensity differences in another before merging their information to pinpoint a sound's location (Konishi, 1993).

So how well do you suppose we do at locating a sound that is equidistant from our two ears, such as those that come from directly ahead, behind, overhead, or beneath us? Not very well, because such sounds strike the two ears simultaneously. You can experience this by sitting with closed eyes while a friend snaps fingers at various locations around your head. You will easily point to the sound when it comes from either side, but you will probably make mistakes when it comes from directly ahead, behind, above, or below. That is why, when trying to pinpoint a sound, you cock your head, so that your two ears receive slightly different messages.

Hearing Loss and Deaf Culture

The ear's intricate and delicate structure makes it vulnerable to damage. Problems with the mechanical system that conducts sound waves to the cochlea cause conduction deafness. If the eardrum is punctured or if the tiny bones of the middle ear lose their ability to vibrate, the ear's ability to conduct vibrations diminishes. A hearing aid may restore hearing by amplifying the vibrations.

Damage to the cochlea's hair cell receptors or their associated nerves can cause nerve deafness. Occasionally, disease causes nerve deafness, but more often biological changes linked with aging (Figure 5.19) and prolonged exposure to ear-splitting noise or music are the culprits. Once destroyed in the human ear, these tissues remain dead, though a hearing aid may amplify sound to stimulate other hair cells. In other animals, however, such as sharks and birds, hair cells can regenerate. Scientists have recently discovered ways to chemically stimulate hair cell regeneration in guinea pigs and rat pups (Forge & others, 1993; Warchol & others, 1993). This finding raises hopes that a way might someday be found to trick the human cochlea into regenerating hair cells—and thereby to restore hearing among those with nerve deafness.

Until then, the only game in town for restoring hearing among nerve-deafened people is a sort of bionic ear—a *cochlear implant*. This electronic device translates sounds into electrical signals, which are wired into the cochlea's nerves, conveying some information about sound to the brain.

How owls localize sounds The barn owl hardly has to cock its head to ensure that each ear receives a different message. The right ear and its opening are directed slightly upward; the left ear and its opening, slightly downward. The built-in asymmetry enables it to pinpoint the location of a sound both horizontally and vertically, making this species the successful nighttime hunter that it is. Even the faint sound of a field mouse scurrying through grass allows the owl to locate its prey with deadly accuracy.

Figure 5.19

Amplitude required for perception relative to 20–29-year-old group

1 time
10 times
100 times
1000 times

20–29 years old
30–39 years old
40–49 years old
50–59 years old
60 years old and up

32 64 128 256 512 1024 2048 4096 8192 16384

Frequency of tone in waves per second

Low ◄——— Pitch ———► High

Older people tend to hear low frequencies well but suffer hearing loss for high frequencies This high-frequency loss results from nerve degeneration near the beginning of the basilar membrane. This finding supports place theory's assumption that different pitches activate different places on the basilar membrane. (From Wever, 1949.)

CLOSE-UP

Living in a Silent World

Those who live with hearing loss are a diverse group. Some are profoundly deaf; others have limited hearing. Some were deaf "prelingually" (before developing language); others have known the hearing world. Some communicate with sign language and identify with the language-based culture of deafness; others, especially those postlingually deaf, are "oral" and converse with the hearing world by reading lips. Still others move between the deaf and hearing cultures. Those who grow up around other deaf people more often identify with the deaf community and feel positive self-esteem. Deaf children raised in a signing household, whether by deaf or hearing parents, also express higher self-esteem and feel more accepted (Bat-Chava, 1993, 1994).

Among deaf children, about one-fourth attend residential schools, half attend special education programs in public schools, and the remaining fourth are partially or wholly mainstreamed into regular classrooms, sometimes aided by sign language interpreters (Kirk & Gallagher, 1989). Among the deaf as among the hearing, some of these students are slow learners, others are brilliant. Essentially all children, whether deaf or hearing, whether signers or speakers, display a remarkable ability to learn language (Meier, 1991).

Still, all deaf people face challenges (Braden, 1994). Because academic subjects are rooted in spoken languages, school achievement may suffer. The social challenges are even greater. Unable to communicate in customary ways, deaf children and their playmates struggle to coordinate their play. Adolescents may experience social exclusion and resulting low self-confidence. Even adults whose hearing becomes impaired later in life may find the difficulties of social interaction producing a sort of shyness. "It's almost universal among the deaf to want to cause hearing people as little fuss as possible," reports Henry Kisor (1990, p. 244), a Chicago newspaper editor and columnist who lost his hearing at age 3. "We can be self-effacing and diffident to the point of invisibility. Sometimes this tendency can be crippling. I must fight it all the time."

I know. My 88-year-old mother, with whom we communicate by writing notes on an erasable "magic pad," lives in a silent world, long ago having withdrawn from the stress and strain of trying to interact with people outside a small circle of family and old friends. With my own hearing now declining on a trajectory toward hers, I find myself sitting front and center at plays and meetings, seeking quiet corners in restaurants, asking my wife to make necessary calls to friends whose accents differ from ours, using a special volume-controllable telephone. But the greatest frustration comes when, with or without a hearing aid, I can't hear the joke that everyone else is guffawing over; when, after repeated tries, I just can't catch that exasperated person's question and can't fake my way around it; when I can't hear the low frequencies of

Cracking the code With the help of a computer at the Lexington Center in New York, this profoundly deaf young man is learning to speak. The computer screen displays for him the position of his teacher's tongue, the vibration of her nose, and the intensity of her voice. By matching her speech patterns, this boy will learn to speak more clearly.

the bass that my son is playing in the school orchestra; when family members give up and say, "Oh, never mind" after trying three times to tell me something unimportant.

As my mother aged, she came to feel that seeking social interaction was just not worth the effort. But for newspaper columnist Kisor, communication is worth the effort. "So, for the most part, I will grit my teeth and plunge ahead" (p. 246). To reach out, to connect, to communicate with others, even across a chasm of silence, is to affirm our humanity as social creatures.

Learning to make sense of sound may take two or more years for a child who has never before heard sound (Fryauf-Bertschy & Gantz, 1994). The result often is a rough approximation of hearing—usually not enough to understand sentences with eyes closed but sufficient to assist lipreading and to hear a dog's bark or a horn's honk. With the implant, children may also become less distractable and impulsive (Quittner & others, 1994).

More than 90 percent of deaf children have hearing parents, most of whom want to give their children this window on the world of sound and talk. The National Association of the Deaf, which takes pride in deaf language and culture, does not always agree: The association objects to using the implants on children deafened before learning to speak, arguing that deafness is *not* a disability. Native signers, for example, are not linguistically disabled. Gallaudet University linguist William Stokoe confirmed this in his 1960 book, *Sign Language Structure*. He showed what native signers, like the proverbial fish who are the last to recognize water, had not fully understood: Sign is a complete language with its own grammar, syntax, and semantics.

Some deaf-culture advocates further contend that deafness could as well be considered "vision enhancement" as "hearing impairment." People who lose one channel of sensation seem to compensate with a slight enhancement of their other sensory abilities (Backman & Dixon, 1992; Levy & Langer, 1992). As a result of her lifelong blindness and deafness, Helen Keller's brain had regions normally dedicated to visual and auditory inputs available for other uses, such as discriminating touch sensations. Although deaf people don't generally have superior reading ability, visual compensation may help explain why so many of them are visually skilled engineers, architects, and mathematicians.

Of the 9 percent of people who experience hearing loss, the National Center for Health Statistics estimates that only about 1 percent were born deaf. Losses that develop with age are greatest in the higher frequencies. To older adults, birds seem to chirp more softly and whispered conversation becomes frustratingly unintelligible. Those of us whose hearing has diminished with age or illness—who live outside the deaf culture and have known, then lost, hearing—are more likely to describe ourselves as having an impairment or disability.

Indeed, for those who have never learned sign, the loss of hearing can be socially disabling. Helen Keller said she "found deafness to be a much greater handicap than blindness. . . . Blindness cuts people off from things. Deafness cuts people off from people." Those whose hearing is impaired needn't think of themselves as disabled *people* (which labels the person) to acknowledge that they are persons with a disability (describing the impairment). Thus, the celebrated 1992 civil rights act was called not the Disabled Americans Act but the Americans with Disabilities Act.

"By placing my hand on a person's lips and throat, I gain an idea of many specific vibrations, and interpret them: a boy's chuckle, a man's 'Whew!' of surprise, the 'Hem!' of annoyance or perplexity, the moan of pain, a scream, a whisper, a rasp, a sob, a choke, and a gasp."

HELEN KELLER (1908)

Good vibrations Scotland's Evelyn Glennie, who has been profoundly deaf since she was 12 years old, is a full-time percussion soloist. In performance she relates to her instruments through her sense of touch and to the conductor through her keen visual sense.

SUMMING UP

The Stimulus Input: Sound Waves The pressure waves we experience as sound vary in frequency and amplitude, and correspondingly in perceived pitch and loudness.

The Ear Through a mechanical chain of events, sound waves traveling through the auditory canal cause minuscule vibrations in the eardrum. Transmitted via the bones of the middle ear to the fluid-filled cochlea, these vibrations create movement in tiny hair cells, triggering neural messages to the brain.

Research on how we hear pitch supports both the place theory, which best explains the sensation of high-pitched sounds, and frequency theory, which best explains the sensation of low-pitched sounds. We localize sound by detecting minute differences in the loudness and timing of the sounds received by each ear.

Hearing Loss and Deaf Culture Hearing losses linked to conduction and nerve disorders can be caused by prolonged exposure to loud noise and by diseases and age-related disorders. Those who live with hearing loss face social challenges. Cochlear implants can enable some hearing by deaf children. But deaf-culture advocates, noting that sign is a complete language, question the enhancement.

KEY TERMS AND CONCEPTS audition, frequency, pitch, middle ear, inner ear, cochlea, place theory, frequency theory, conduction deafness, nerve deafness

The Other Senses

Extraordinary happenings are hidden within four other ordinary senses: touch, taste, smell, and our sense of body position and movement. What are these happenings? And what happens if we restrict input from any or all the senses?

For humans, seeing and hearing are the major senses. We depend on them, particularly for communication. Our brains give these two senses priority in the allocation of cortical tissue. For other animals, the priorities differ. Sharks and dogs rely on their extraordinary senses of smell, aided by the large segment of their cortexes devoted to it. Nevertheless, without our sense of touch, our senses of taste and smell, and our senses of body motion and position, we humans would be seriously handicapped, and our capacities for enjoying the world would be devastatingly diminished.

Touch

If you had to give up one sense, which would it be? If you could retain only one sense, which would it be?

Touch would be a good candidate for retention. Right from the start, touch is essential to our development. As we noted in Chapter 3, premature babies gain weight faster and go home sooner if stimulated by hand massage. Infant rats deprived of their mothers' grooming touch produce less growth hormone and have a lower metabolic rate—a good way to keep alive until the mother returns, but a reaction that stunts growth if she's delayed. Infant monkeys allowed to see, hear, and smell—but not touch—their mothers are desperately unhappy; much less so are those separated by a screen with holes that allow touching. As lovers, we yearn to touch—to kiss, to stroke, to snuggle.

Dave Barry is perhaps right to say of the skin that it "keeps people from seeing the inside of your body, which is repulsive, and it prevents your organs from falling onto the ground." But skin does more. Our "sense of touch" is actually a mix of at least four distinct skin senses—pressure, warmth, cold, and pain. Touching various spots on the skin with a soft hair, a warm or cool wire, and the point of a pin reveals that some spots are especially sensitive to pressure, others to warmth, others to cold, still others to pain. Within the skin are different types of specialized nerve endings. Does that mean that each type is a receptor for one of the basic skin

The precious sense of touch As William James wrote in his *Principles of Psychology* (1890), "Touch is both the alpha and omega of affection."

senses, much as the eye's cone receptors correspond to light's basic colors?

Surprisingly, there is no simple relationship between what we feel at a given spot and the type of specialized nerve ending found there. Only pressure has identifiable receptors. The relationship between warmth, cold, and pain and the receptors that respond to them remains a mystery. Other skin sensations are variations of the basic four (pressure, warmth, cold, and pain):

- Stroking adjacent pressure spots creates a tickle.
- Repeated gentle stroking of a pain spot creates an itching sensation.
- Touching adjacent cold and pressure spots triggers a sense of wetness, which you can experience by touching dry, cold metal.
- Stimulating nearby cold and warmth spots produces a feeling of "hot." Cold spots respond either to very low or very high temperatures. We sense hot when a stimulus activates both warm and cold spots (Figure 5.20).

Pain

Be thankful for occasional pain. Pain is your body's way of telling you that something has gone wrong. It draws your attention to a burn, a break, or a rupture and tells you to change your behavior immediately. The rare people who are born without the ability to feel pain may experience severe injury without ever being alerted by pain's danger signals. Usually, they die by early adulthood. Without the discomfort that makes us occasionally shift position, their joints fail from excess strain. Without pain, the effects of unchecked infections and injuries accumulate (Neese, 1991). More numerous are those who endure chronic pain. The suffering of people with persistent or recurring backaches, arthritis, headaches, and cancer-related pain prompts two questions: What is pain? How might it be controlled?

"When belly with bad pains doth swell,
It matters naught what else goes well."

SADI
THE GULISTAN
1258

What Is Pain?

Pain is a property not only of the senses—of the region where we feel it—but of the brain as well. As the dreamer may see with eyes closed and the listener may hear a ringing during utter silence, so some 7 in 10 amputees may feel pain or movement in their nonexistent limbs (Melzack, 1992, 1993).

Figure **5.20**

Warm + cold = hot When ice-cold water passes through one coil and comfortably warm water through another, we perceive the combined sensation as burning hot.

> Be thankful for occasional pain. Pain is your body's way of telling you that something has gone wrong.

(An amputee may also try to step off a bed onto a phantom limb or to lift a cup with a phantom hand.) These *phantom limb sensations* indicate that with pain, as with sights and sounds, the brain can misinterpret the spontaneous central nervous system activity that occurs in the absence of normal sensory input. To see, hear, and feel, we require not a body but a brain.

Oh, my aching feet Vigorously rubbing sore feet helps reduce pain sensations, perhaps by stimulating the spinal cord's large fibers and closing the pain "gate" described in gate-control theory.

gate-control theory
theory that the spinal cord contains a neurological "gate" that blocks pain signals or allows them to pass on to the brain. The "gate" is opened by the activity of pain signals traveling up small nerve fibers and is closed by activity in larger fibers or by information coming from the brain.

Unlike vision, however, the pain system is not located in a simple neural cord running from a sensing device to a definable area in the brain. Moreover, there is no one type of stimulus that triggers pains (as light triggers vision), and there are no special receptors (like the retina's rods and cones) for pain. At low intensities, the stimuli that produce pain cause other sensations, including warmth or coolness, smoothness or roughness.

Although no theory of pain explains all the available findings, psychologist Ronald Melzack and biologist Patrick Wall's (1965, 1983) gate-control theory provides a useful model. Melzack and Wall believe that the spinal cord contains a sort of neurological "gate" that either blocks pain signals or allows them to pass on to the brain. The spinal cord contains small nerve fibers that conduct most pain signals, and larger fibers that conduct most other sensory signals. When tissue is injured, the small fibers activate and open the neural gate, and you feel pain. Large-fiber activity closes the pain gate, turning pain off.

Thus, one way to treat chronic pain is to stimulate (electrically, by massage, or even by acupuncture) "gate-closing" activity in the large neural fibers. Rubbing the area around your stubbed toe creates competing stimulation that will block some of the pain messages. Placing ice on a bruise serves not only to control swelling but also to trigger cold messages that close the gate on the pain signals. Some arthritic patients wear a small portable electrical stimulation unit next to a painful area. When the unit stimulates nerves in the area, the patient feels a vibrating sensation rather than pain (T. Murphy, 1982).

Melzack and Wall believe the pain gate can also be closed by information from the brain. These brain-to-spinal-cord messages help explain some striking psychological influences on pain. When distracted from pain signals and soothed by the release of endorphins, our experience of pain may be greatly diminished. Sports injuries may be unnoticed, until taking the after-game shower. During a 1989 basketball game, Ohio State University player Jay Burson broke his neck—and kept playing. Clearly, there is more to pain than what stimulates the sense receptors.

There is also more to our memories of pain than the pain we experience. In experiments, and after medical procedures, people overlook a pain's duration. Their memory snapshots instead record its peak moment and how much pain they felt at the end. Daniel Kahneman and his co-researchers (1993) discovered this when they asked people to immerse one hand in painfully cold water for 60 seconds, and then the other hand in the same

painfully cold water for 60 seconds followed by a slightly less painful 30 seconds more. Curiously, when asked which trial they would prefer to repeat, most preferred the longer trial, with more net pain—but less pain at the end. When patients recalled the pain of a colon examination a month later, their memories were similarly dominated by the final (and the worst) moments, not by how long the pain lasted.

For medical personnel, the implication is clear: It's better to taper down a painful procedure than to switch it off abruptly. In one experiment, a physician did this for some patients undergoing colon exams—lengthening the discomfort by a minute, though with milder pain (Kahneman, in press). Although this discomfort added to the net pain experience, patients given the "taper down" treatment later recalled the exam as less painful than those whose pain ended abruptly.

"Pain is increased by attending to it."

CHARLES DARWIN
EXPRESSION OF EMOTIONS IN MAN AND ANIMALS
1872

"From there to here, from here to there, funny things are everywhere."

DR. SEUSS
ONE FISH, TWO FISH, RED FISH, BLUE FISH
1960

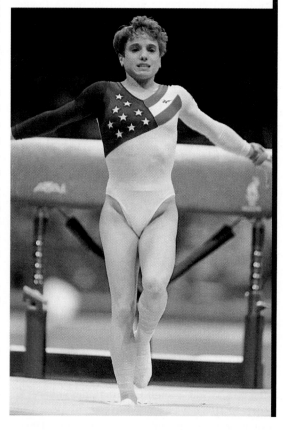

Putting pain out of mind   Kerri Strug had just sprained her left ankle so severely she could not do gymnastics for months afterwards. Yet with this near-perfect vault, she helped carry her team to a 1996 Olympic gold medal. Because pain is a phenomenon of the conscious brain, athletes sometimes endure serious injuries while focusing their attention outside their bodies.

THINKING CRITICALLY ABOUT

Matter Over Mind: Firewalking

The popular media have at times made the phenomenon of firewalking a hot topic. For a fee we can take a "mind over matter" class

Some like it hot At a New Zealand skeptics' meeting, University of Canterbury physicist John Campbell explained heat-diffusion principles that permit firewalking, then put his feet where his mouth was by leading 80 people across 12 feet of hot coals.

that supposedly enables us to alter our body's chemistry. The "proof": walking on red-hot coals without feeling pain or being burned. The psychological result: a newfound capacity to conquer one's fears. "If I can do something that's supposed to be impossible," says the elated firewalker, "I can do almost anything."

Skeptical scientists have taken a cool look at firewalking (Leikind & McCarthy, 1985, 1988). The secret, they report, lies not in any mental power to alter the senses but in the poor heat conductivity of the wood coals. Think of a cake baking in a 350° oven. Touch the aluminum cake tin and you'll get burned; touch the cake—like wood, a poor heat conductor—and you'll be

okay. Cakes and coals do conduct some heat, so you'd better not stay in touch with them too long or you will get burned. Some have learned the hard way that they who hesitate are lost. But the two seconds or less that it takes to quick-step across hot embers puts each foot in contact with the coals for only a fraction of a second and for less than a second in total time per foot. Wetting the feet on damp grass or in water before the firewalk provides further insulation (a phenomenon familiar to anyone who has used wet fingers to snuff a candle or test a hot iron). Confident of these facts, skeptical scientists have themselves performed the feat without the "mind over matter" training.

Pain Control

If pain is where body meets mind—if it is indeed a physical and a psychological phenomenon—then it should be treatable both physically and psychologically. Depending on the type of symptoms, pain control clinics select one or more therapies from a list that includes drugs, surgery, acupuncture, electrical stimulation, massage, exercise, hypnosis, relaxation training, and thought distraction.

The widely practiced Lamaze method of childbirth combines several of these pain control techniques. Among them are relaxation (through deep breathing and muscle relaxation), counterstimulation (through gentle massage), and distraction (through focusing attention on, say, a pleasant photograph). After Everett Worthington and his colleagues (1983) trained women in the use of such pain control techniques, the women could more easily tolerate the pain of having their hand in ice water. The women's pain tolerance was even greater when a trusted "coach" encouraged them,

as husbands or an intimate friend encourage Lamaze-trained women during childbirth.

Distracting people with pleasant images ("Think of a warm, comfortable environment") or drawing their attention away from the painful stimulation ("Count backward by 3's") is an especially effective way to increase pain tolerance (Fernandez & Turk, 1989; McCaul & Malott, 1984). The principle works in health care situations. A well-trained nurse may distract needle-shy patients by chatting with them and asking them to look away when inserting the needle. For hospitalized patients, a pleasing window view of natural vegetation may have a similarly relaxing and distracting effect. In examining the records of one Pennsylvania hospital, Roger Ulrich (1984) discovered that surgery patients assigned to rooms looking out on trees required less pain medication and had shorter stays than did those assigned to identical rooms overlooking a brick wall.

Although Lamaze training reduces labor pain, most Lamaze patients request a local anesthetic during labor. Some—having expected a "natural, painless birth"—feel needless guilt and failure (Melzack, 1984). Melzack therefore advocates—as does the Lamaze program itself—childbirth training that prepares a woman "to cope with an event which is often extremely painful and, at the same time, one of the most fulfilling peak experiences in her life."

> Although taste buds are essential for taste, there is more to taste than meets the tongue.

Taste

Like touch, our sense of taste involves four basic sensations—sweet, sour, salty, and bitter (McBurney & Gent, 1979). All other tastes are mixtures of these. Investigators have, however, been frustrated in their search for specialized nerve fibers for each of the four basic taste sensations.

Taste is a chemical sense. Inside the little bumps on the top and sides of your tongue are 200 or more taste buds. Each contains a pore that catches food chemicals. These molecules are sensed by 50 taste receptor cells that project antennalike hairs into the pore. Some of these receptors respond mostly to sweet-tasting molecules, others to salty-, sour-, or bitter-tasting ones. It doesn't take much to trigger a response. When a stream of water is pumped across the tongue, the addition of a concentrated salty or sweet taste for but one-tenth of a second gets noticed (Kelling & Halpern, 1983). When a friend asks for "just a taste" of your soft drink, you can squeeze off the straw after a mere fraction of a second.

Taste receptors reproduce themselves every week or two, so if you burn your tongue with hot food it matters little. However, as you grow older, the number of taste buds decreases, as does taste sensitivity (Cowart, 1981). (No wonder adults enjoy strong-tasting foods that children resist.) Smoking and alcohol use accelerate the decline in taste buds and sensitivities.

Although taste buds are essential for taste, there is more to taste than meets the tongue. Hold your nose, close your eyes, and have someone feed you various foods. A piece of apple may then be indistinguishable from a piece of raw potato; a piece of steak may taste like cardboard. To savor a taste, we normally breathe the aroma through our nose—which is why eating is not much fun when you have a bad cold, and why people who lose their sense of smell may think they have also lost their sense of taste. Smell not only adds to our perception of taste, it also changes it. A drink's strawberry odor enhances our perception of its sweetness. This is sensory interaction at work—the principle that one sense may influence another. Smell plus taste equals flavor. Similarly, we correctly perceive the location of the voice directly in front of us partly because we also *see* that the person is in front of us, not behind, above, or beneath us.

Taste researcher Linda Bartoshuk (1993) offers other fascinating facts about taste:

- Our emotional responses to taste are hard-wired. Put a sweet or bitter substance on a newborn's tongue and the baby's tongue and face react like an adult's.

- People without tongues can still taste—through receptors in the back and roof of the mouth.

- If you lose taste sensation from one side of your tongue, you probably won't notice. That's because the other side will become correspondingly supersensitive. Also, the brain doesn't localize taste well: Although the middle of the tongue has few taste receptors, we perceive taste as coming from the whole tongue.

- We can neither taste nor smell most nutrients—fat, protein, starch, and food vitamins. (Sugar is an exception.) But we do quickly associate the taste and smell of other food components with a food's nutritional or poisonous significance (see pages 250–251).

Smell

Breaths come in pairs—inhale, exhale—except at two moments: birth and death. Each day, as you inhale and exhale nearly 20,000 breaths of life-sustaining air, you bathe your nostrils in a stream of scent-laden molecules. More than you may realize, your resulting experiences of smell (*olfaction*) are intimate ones. To smell someone you inhale something of the person.

Like taste, smell is a chemical sense. We smell something when air-carried molecules of a substance reach a tiny cluster of 5 million receptor cells at the top of each nasal cavity (Figure 5.21). These olfactory receptor cells, waving like sea anemones on a reef, respond selectively to the aroma of cake baking, to a wisp of smoke, to a friend's fragrance, and they instantly alert the brain through their axon fibers. Even nursing infants and mothers have a literal chemistry to their relationship, as they quickly learn to recognize each other's scents (McCarthy, 1986). Aided by smell, a mother fur seal returning to a beach crowded with

The joy of taste Four taste sensations—salty, sweet, sour, and bitter—combine with odors to produce a multitude of flavors.

Figure **5.21**

Olfactory nerve

Olfactory bulb

Receptor cells in olfactory membrane

Nasal passage

The sense of smell To smell a rose, airborne molecules of its fragrance must reach receptors at the top of the nose. Sniffing swirls air up to the receptors, enhancing the aroma.

pups will find her own. Our own sense of smell is less impressive than the acuteness of our seeing and hearing. Looking out across a garden we see its forms and colors in exquisite detail and hear its singing birds, yet smell little of it without jamming our nose into the flowers.

Precisely how olfactory receptors work is a mystery. Unlike light, which can be separated into its spectral colors, an odor cannot be separated into more elemental odors. Thus, the olfaction system has no parallel to the retina, which detects myriad colors with sensory cells dedicated to red, green, or blue. Olfactory receptors recognize odors individually.

Odor molecules come in so many shapes and sizes that it takes lots of different receptors to detect them. A large family of 1000 genes—some 1 percent of all our genes—design receptor proteins that recognize particular molecules (Axel, 1995). As a key slips into a lock, so odor molecules slip into these receptors. Yet we seem not to have a distinct receptor for each of the some 10,000 odors we can detect. This suggests that some odors trigger a combination of receptors, whose activity the olfactory cortex interprets.

The ability to identify scents peaks in early adulthood and gradually declines thereafter (Figure 5.22). Despite our skill at discriminating scents, we aren't nearly so good at describing them. Words more readily portray the sound of a piccolo than the aroma of coffee. Compared with how we experience and remember sights and sounds, smells seem more primitive and harder to describe (Richardson & Zucco, 1989).

Figure **5.22**

Number of correct answers

Women and young adults have best sense of smell

Women

Men

4

3

2

0
10–19 20–29 30–39 40–49 50–59 60–69 70–79 80–89 90–99

Age group

Age, sex, and sense of smell Among the 1.2 million people who responded to a *National Geographic* scratch and sniff survey, women and younger adults most successfully identified six sample odors. (From Wysocki & Gilbert, 1989.)

Each day, as you inhale and exhale nearly 20,000 breaths of life-sustaining air, you bathe your nostrils in a stream of scent-laden molecules.

As any dog or cat with a good nose could tell us, we each have our own identifiable chemical signature. (One noteworthy exception: A dog will follow the tracks of one identical twin as though they had been made by the other [Thomas, 1974].) Animals that have many times more olfactory receptors than we do also use their sense of smell to communicate and navigate. Long before the shark can see its prey, or the moth its mate, odors direct the way.

Odors also have the power to evoke memories and feelings. They do so thanks to a hotline between the brain area that gets information from the nose and the brain's ancient limbic centers associated with memory and emotion. Smell is primitive. Eons before the elaborate analytical areas of our cerebral cortex had fully evolved, our mammalian ancestors were sniffing for food and predators.

In *Remembrance of Things Past*, the French novelist Marcel Proust described how the aroma and flavor of a bit of cake soaked in tea resurrected long-forgotten memories of his aunt's bedroom in the old family house. "The smell and taste of things," he noted, "bears unfaltering, in the tiny and almost impalpable drop of their essence, the vast structure of recollection."

Laboratory studies confirm that, though it's difficult to recall odors by name, we do indeed have a remarkable capacity to recognize long-forgotten odors and their associated personal episodes (Engen, 1987; Schab, 1991). Students who do a word exercise while smelling the aroma of chocolate remember the words better the next day if the chocolate aroma is again present (Schab, 1990). And pleasant odors evoke pleasant memories (Ehrlichman & Halpern, 1988). The smell of the sea, the scent of a perfume, or an aroma like the floorwax smell in Grandma's kitchen bring to mind happy times. Such is the power of odors to switch on memories and to retrieve associated emotions.

Pleasant moods produced by pleasant scents may also give a boost to workers' performance. That's what Robert Baron (1990) surmised after having students work in rooms with or without pleasant air scents. Pleasant scents boosted their moods and self-confidence, leading them to set slightly higher work goals on a clerical task and to negotiate more aggressively on a bargaining task.

The olfactory brain   Information from the taste buds (orange arrow) travels to an area of the temporal lobe not far from that where olfactory information is received. The brain's circuitry for smell (magenta arrow) also connects with areas involved in memory storage, which helps explain why a smell can trigger a memory explosion.

Body Position and Movement

With only the five familiar senses we have so far considered, we would be helpless. We could not put food in our mouths, stand up, or reach out and touch someone. To know just how to move your arms to grasp someone's hand, you first need to know the current position of your arms and hands and then be aware of their changing positions as you move them. To take just one step requires feedback from and instructions to some 200 muscles.

Humans come equipped with millions of such position and motion sensors. They are all over our bodies—in the muscles, tendons, and joints—and they are continually providing our brains with information. If we twist our wrists one degree, the sensors immediately report it. This sense of our body parts' position and movement is kinesthesis (kin-ehs-THEE-sehs).

Have you ever considered life without kinesthesis, without, say, being able to sense the positions of your limbs when awakening during the night? Such is the experience of Christina, whose nerve fibers carrying information from muscles, tendons, and joints were destroyed by disease, leaving her floppy as a rag doll (Sacks, 1985). What does it feel

The intricate vestibular sense   Thank your inner ears for the information that enables your brain to monitor your body's position.

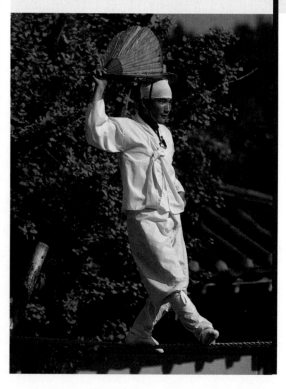

like? Like she is disembodied, her body dead, not real, not hers. Against all odds, Christina has, however, learned to walk and eat—by visually attending to her limbs and directing them accordingly.

A companion vestibular sense monitors the head's (and thus the body's) position and movement. The biological gyroscopes for this sense of equilibrium are in the inner ear. In the *semicircular canals*, which look like a three-dimensional pretzel (Figure 5.18*a*, page 165), and the *vestibular sacs*, which connect the canals with the cochlea, are substances that move when the head rotates or tilts. This movement stimulates hairlike receptors in these organs of the inner ear. The receptors then send to the brain messages that enable us continually to sense our body position and maintain our balance.

If you've been twirling around and come to an abrupt halt, the fluid in your semicircular canals and your kinesthetic receptors does not immediately return to its neutral state. The aftereffect fools your dizzy brain with the sensation that you're still spinning. This illustrates a principle that underlies the next chapter's discussion of perceptual illusions. Mechanisms that normally give us an accurate experience of the world can, under special conditions, fool us. Understanding how we get fooled provides clues to how our perceptual system works.

SUMMING UP

Touch Our sense of touch is actually four senses—pressure, warmth, cold, and pain—that combine to produce other sensations, such as "hot." One theory of pain is that a "gate" in the spinal cord either opens to permit pain signals traveling up small nerve fibers to reach the brain or closes to prevent their passage. Because pain is both a physiological and a psychological phenomenon, it often can be controlled through a combination of medical and psychological treatments.

Taste Taste, a chemical sense, is likewise a composite of four basic sensations—sweet, sour, salty, and bitter—and of the aromas that interact with information from the taste buds. The influence of smell on our sense of taste is an example of sensory interaction.

Smell Like taste, smell is a chemical sense, but there are no basic sensations for smell, as there are for touch and taste. Unlike the retina's receptor cells, the 5 million olfactory receptor cells recognize individual odor molecules, with some odors triggering a combination of receptors. Like other stimuli, odors can spontaneously evoke memories and feelings.

Body Position and Movement Finally, our effective functioning requires a kinesthetic sense, which notifies the brain of the position and movement of body parts, and a sense of equilibrium, which monitors the position and movement of the whole body.

KEY TERMS AND CONCEPTS gate-control theory, sensory interaction, kinesthesis, vestibular sense

Sensory Restriction

When deprived of one of their senses, or when experiencing sensory monotony, how do people respond?

Imagine that one of your sensory windows on the world snapped shut. Could your other senses partially make up for the loss? People with sensory deficits show us the rich potential of each sense. Blind people cope by making greater use of their hearing—for example, by locating obstacles while attending to echoes bouncing off them. Helen Keller, blind *and* deaf, vividly experienced life's aromas, tastes, and touches.

Close your eyes and immediately you, too, will notice your attention being drawn to your other senses. When kissing, lovers minimize distraction and increase their touch sensitivity by closing their eyes. People with aphasia—having lost the ability to comprehend language—typically become acutely sensitive to nonlanguage cues. You and I might miss the meaning conveyed by someone's intonation and gestures, but a person with aphasia reads these messages readily.

The loss of a sense is but one type of sensory restriction. Another is sensory monotony—the relatively unchanging sensory input experienced by prisoners in solitary confinement, by nighttime truck drivers and airline pilots, and by animals in barren zoos.

kinesthesis [kin-ehs-THEE-sehs] the system for sensing the position and movement of individual body parts.

vestibular sense the sense of body movement and position, including the sense of balance.

As living creatures we require sensory stimulation, but there are also times when we benefit from the peace and relaxation of restricted stimulation.

Sensory compensation *"Ears are eyes to the blind," wrote Sophocles. Cortney Glonk, blind since birth, uses her clicker's echoes to navigate the hallways at her Detroit school.*

To investigate how sensory restriction affects us, experimenters have put thousands of people through controlled, temporary simulations of such conditions. Some have spent several days in monotonous environments—small rooms in which light and sound are unchanging. Others have passed time in dark, silent rooms, deprived of normal sensory input. Initial "sensory deprivation" experiments produced bizarre and widely publicized findings (Heron, 1957). The volunteers, lying on beds and wearing translucent goggles to diffuse the light, typically began the experiment in good spirits. Here was a chance to make some easy money while enjoying a time for relaxation and creative thinking. Before long, however, they became disoriented. Many experienced hallucinations, and some became susceptible to piped-in messages arguing for the reality of ghosts.

As often happens in science, manipulating one factor simultaneously changes other factors. Are the effects of a monotonous environment caused by the sensory restriction or by the social isolation or stress of confinement? The dramatic reports from early experiments prompted many more investigations, most of which produced less newsworthy results (Suedfeld & Kristeller, 1982).

In fact, sensory restriction does not disturb most people. More often, it reduces stress and helps people become more open to positive influence. In experiments with smokers and overweight people at the University of British Columbia, Peter Suedfeld (1980) found that restricted sensory input helps people modify their behavior. People wanting to alter their behavior were often able to increase their self-control after 24 hours of what he aptly calls REST—restricted environmental stimulation therapy.

In one such experiment conducted by Allan Best and Suedfeld (1982), smokers listened to antismoking messages while spending 24 hours lying on beds in quiet, dark rooms (rising only to drink a liquid diet available through tubes or to use toilets next to the beds). In the week that followed, none relapsed to smoking. A year later, two-thirds were still abstaining—double the number of abstainers who had received the instruction without the day of REST.

Shorter REST periods can also pay dividends. In one experiment, heavy-drinking college students spent 2½ hours in REST. After 1½ hours, a 5-minute message gave factual information about alcohol's negative effects. Unlike those in control conditions, the REST-plus-message group decreased their alcohol consumption by 55 percent during the ensuing 6 months (Cooper & others, 1988).

In other times and places, periods of solitude and sensory restriction have fostered human fulfillment. Sensory restriction is a traditional component of the "quiet therapies" of Japan (Reynolds, 1982, 1986). For example, Morita therapy for depressed or anxious people sometimes begins with a week of bed rest and meditation and then progresses to assigned light tasks. The religious visions of Moses, Mohammed, and Buddha reportedly occurred during times of solitude and contemplation. As living creatures we require sensory stimulation, but there are also times when we benefit from the peace and relaxation of restricted stimulation.

REST *Restricted environmental stimulation therapy can provide healing relaxation.*

SUMMING UP

People temporarily or permanently deprived of one of their senses typically compensate by becoming more acutely aware of information from the other senses. Temporary experiences of sensory restriction often evoke a heightened aware-ness of all forms of sensation. Under supervision, sensory restriction may provide a therapeutic boost for those seeking control over problems such as smoking.

In this chapter we have taken a "bottom-up" look at how we experience the world, starting with how our ingenious sense receptors transduce phys-ical energy into neural messages sent to our brain.

We've also taken a "top-down" look at how our mind, too, shapes our experiences. Pain, for exam-ple, is a response to information coming both up the spinal cord's small nerves and down from what our mind is paying attention to. Our experiences are in the brain—so much so that the brain can choose how to interpret neural activity, or may even conjure up perceived sights, sounds, and pains without external stimulation. Sensation and perception are different aspects of one whole fabric—how we experience the world around us.

TERMS AND CONCEPTS TO REMEMBER

sensation, p. 147

perception, p. 147

bottom-up processing, p. 147

top-down processing, p. 147

psychophysics, p. 148

absolute threshold, p. 149

signal detection theory, p. 149

subliminal, p. 149

difference threshold, p. 151

Weber's Law, p. 152

sensory adaptation, p. 152

transduction, p. 153

wavelength, p. 154

hue, p. 154

intensity, p. 154

pupil, p. 155

iris, p. 155

lens, p. 155

accommodation, p. 155

retina, p. 155

acuity, p. 156

nearsightedness, p. 156

farsightedness, p. 156

rods, p. 156

cones, p. 156

optic nerve, p. 156

blind spot, p. 156

fovea, p. 157

feature detectors, p. 159

parallel processing, p. 160

Young-Helmholtz trichromatic (three-color) theory, p. 161

opponent-process theory, p. 162

color constancy, p. 163

audition, p. 164

frequency, p. 164

pitch, p. 164

middle ear, p. 165

inner ear, p. 165

cochlea [KOHK-lee-uh], p. 165

place theory, p. 165

frequency theory, p. 166

conduction deafness, p. 167

nerve deafness, p. 167

gate-control theory, p. 172

sensory interaction, p. 174

kinesthesis [kin-ehs-THEE-sehs], p. 176

vestibular sense, p. 177

CRITICAL THINKING EXERCISE
by Richard O. Straub

Now that you have read and reviewed Chapter 5, take your learning a step further by testing your critical thinking skills on the following psychological reasoning exercise.

Carlos, who is determined to quit smoking, today purchased a subliminal persuasion audio/videotape package. The book-let accompanying the tapes claims that subliminal sugges-tions "harness the power of the unconscious mind to [help you increase motivation to] quit smoking." Carlos is skepti-cal, but he decides to try the demonstration included on the videotape. The instructions are to turn off room lights, start the videotape, and stare at a fixation point (a plus sign that appears in the center of the television screen) until the screen goes blank. During the demonstration, which lasts about 5 minutes, Carlos occasionally perceives a flash of light on the screen just above the fixation point. Shortly after the screen goes blank, several geometric figures, including a square, a circle, a triangle, and a rectangle, appear above the question, "Which of these figures is most pleasing to you?" Although he is not sure why, Carlos picks the triangle. The tape ends with the following message: "If you picked the triangle, sub-liminal persuasion will work for you! During the demonstra-tion, what appeared to be flashes of light were actually subliminal presentations of triangles. The triangles, which appeared too briefly to be perceived by your conscious mind, *were* perceived by your unconscious mind. Since familiarity breeds fondness, your unconsciousness persuaded you that smoking is unhealthy, unflattering, and something you defi-nitely do not want to continue doing."

1. What assertions about subliminal persuasion are made in the booklet and videotape? Be sure to define all important con-cepts and terms as they are used in this example.

2. What evidence is presented that the subliminal suggestions will help Carlos quit smoking? Is this evidence trustworthy?

3. How else could you explain Carlos's preference for the triangle?

Check your progress on becoming a critical thinker by compar-ing your answers to the sample answers found in Appendix B.

chapter

6

Perception

Some 2400 years ago, the philosopher Plato rightly discerned that we perceive objects through the senses, with the mind. To construct the world in our heads we must detect physical energy from the environment and encode it as neural signals (a process traditionally called *sensation*). And we must select, organize, and interpret our sensations (a process traditionally called *perception*). We not only sense raw sights and sounds, tastes and smells, we *perceive*. We hear not just a mix of pitches and rhythms but a child's cry of pain, the hum of distant traffic, a symphony. In short, we transform meaningless sensations into meaningful perceptions.

Selective Attention

At any moment, our awareness focuses, like a flashlight beam, on a limited aspect of our experience.

Perceptions come to us moment by moment, one perception vanishing as the next appears. Note how Figure 6.1 evokes more than one perception. The circles can be organized into several coherent images, each equally plausible, and the mind switches back and forth from one to the next. Although you *know* that alternative interpretations of this figure, known as a "Necker Cube," are possible, you can consciously experience only one of them at any moment. This illustrates an important principle: Our conscious attention is *selective*.

Selective attention means that at any moment we focus our awareness on only a limited aspect of all that we are capable of experiencing. Until reading this sentence, you have been unaware that your shoes are pressing against your feet or that your nose is in your line of vision. Now, suddenly, your attentional spotlight shifts and your feet feel encased, your nose stubbornly intrudes on the page before you. While attending to these words, you've also been blocking from awareness information coming from your peripheral vision. But you can

selective attention
*the focusing of conscious aware-
ness on a particular stimulus, as
in the cocktail party effect.*

Figure **6.1**

Selective attention What do
you see: circles with gray lines, or a
cube? If you stare at the cube, you
may notice that it reverses location,
moving the tiny X in the center from
the front edge to the back. At times
the cube may seem to float in front
of the page, with circles behind it;
other times the circles may become
holes in the page through which the
cube appears, as though it were
floating behind the page. Because
attention is selective, you see only
one interpretation at a time. (From
Bradley & others, 1976.)

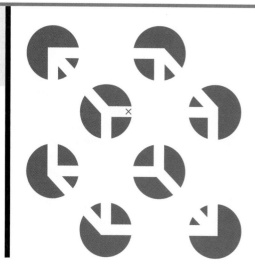

change that. While staring at the X below, notice
what surrounds the book (the edges of the page,
your desk top, and so forth).

X

Another example of selective attention is the
cocktail party effect—the ability to attend selectively to only one voice among many. Imagine
hearing two conversations over a headset, one in
each ear, and being asked to repeat the left-ear
message as it is spoken. When you pay attention to
what's being said in your left ear, you won't perceive what is said in your right ear. If later you are
asked what language your right ear heard, you may
draw a blank (though you could report the speaker's

gender and loudness). At the level of conscious
awareness, whatever has your attention pretty
much has your undivided attention.

It's true of other senses, too. From the immense
array of visual stimuli that are constantly before
us, we can select only a few for processing. Ulric
Neisser (1979) and Robert Becklen and Daniel
Cervone (1983) demonstrated this dramatically.
They showed people a one-minute videotape in
which the images of three men in black shirts tossing a basketball were superimposed over the images of three men in white shirts doing the same
thing. They asked the viewers to press a key every
time the black-shirted players passed the ball. Midway through the tape, a young woman carrying an
umbrella sauntered across the screen (Figure 6.2).
Most of the viewers focused their attention so
completely on the black-shirted players that they
failed to notice the woman. When the researcher
replayed the tape for them, they were astonished to
see her.

Can unnoticed stimuli affect us? Indeed yes. In
one experiment, women students listened through
headphones as a prose passage played in one ear.
Their task was to repeat its words out loud and to
check them against a written transcript (Wilson,
1979). Meanwhile, some simple, novel tunes
played in the other ear. The tunes were not subliminal—the women could hear them easily. But with
their attention selectively focused on the passage,
the women were no more aware of the tunes than
you normally are of your shoes. Thus, when they
later heard these tunes interspersed among new
ones, they could not recognize them (just as people
cannot recall a conversation to which they paid no
attention). Nevertheless, when asked to rate their

Figure **6.2**

Testing selective attention
In this experiment, viewers who
were attending to basketball
tosses among the black-shirted
players usually failed to notice the
umbrella-toting woman sauntering
across the screen. (From Neisser,
1979.)

fondness for each tune, they *preferred* the ones previously played. Their preferences revealed what their conscious memories could not.

In other experiments, listeners attend to a message piped into one ear (such as, "We stood by the bank"). When a pertinent word (*river* or *money*) is simultaneously sent to the other ear—the unattended one—the listeners do not consciously perceive it. Yet the word influences their interpretation of the ambiguous sentence (Baars & McGovern, 1994). Although perception requires attention, even unattended stimuli sometimes have subtle effects.

SUMMING UP

At any moment we are conscious of a very limited amount of all that we are capable of experiencing. One example of this selective attention is the cocktail party effect—attending to only one voice among many.

KEY TERM AND CONCEPT   selective attention

Perceptual Illusions

Once we have attended to certain stimuli, how do we organize them into meaningful perceptions? During the late 1800s, when psychology was emerging as a distinct discipline, perceptual illusions fascinated scientists. And they still do, because illusions reveal the ways we normally organize and interpret our sensations. Consider five such perceptual puzzles:

> **Puzzle 1** Below is an adaptation of a classic illusion created in 1889 by Franz Müller-Lyer. Does either line segment—AB or BC—appear longer? To most people the two segments appear the same length. Surprise! They are not. As your ruler can verify, line AB is a full one-third longer than line BC. Why do our eyes deceive us? (On page 191 you will discover one explanation.)

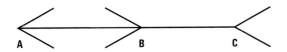

Puzzle 2 Below we have two unretouched photos of the same two girls, in the same room. The camera shows you these scenes much as you would see them if you were looking into the room through a single peephole. Why do the girls seem to change size when they switch places? (Pages 192–193 will reveal why.)

Puzzle 3 Is the St. Louis Gateway Arch taller than it is wide? Or vice versa? To most it appears taller. In truth, its height and width are equal. Once again, seeing is deceiving. Why? (On page 188 we will meet this phenomenon again.)

Morning fog

Midday sunshine

Ross's distance judgment experiment

Puzzle 4 Aircraft pilots, ship captains, and car drivers perceive their surroundings under varying visibility. When their perceptions or reactions err—as happens in most commercial airplane accidents (Adler, 1989)—the results can be devastating. To simulate distance judgments, psychologist Helen Ross (1975) asked passersby to estimate the distances of white disks she had placed on the lawn at Britain's Hull University. Those who judged the distance in the thick morning fog perceived the disks to be farther away than did those who made their estimates in the midday sunshine (see above). What does this suggest about how we normally judge distances? (Pages 191–192 explain distance perception.)

Puzzle 5 Illusions occur with the other senses, too, as the German psychologist Wilhelm Wundt pointed out more than a century ago. Wundt was puzzled by people's hearing the steady beat of a metronome or clock as if it were a repeating rhythm of two, three, or four beats. Rather than hearing an unaccented click-click-click-click, one might, for example, hear CLICK-click CLICK-click CLICK-click. Although a steady beat strikes the ear, each listener unconsciously shapes an auditory pattern. What perceptual principle is at work here? (See page 193 to find out.)

Psychology's emphasis on *visual* illusions reflects vision's preeminence among our senses. When there is conflict between vision and other sensations, vision usually dominates—a phenomenon called visual capture. People wearing prisms that displace the visual world to one side perceive their hand as where they *see* it, not where it physically is. When the sound of a movie comes from a projector behind us, we nevertheless perceive it as coming from the screen, where we *see* the actors talking (much as we perceive a voice from the ventriloquist's dummy). While viewing a roller coaster ride on a wraparound movie screen, we may brace ourselves, though our other senses tell us we're not moving. In all three cases, vision *captures* the other senses.

Perceptual Organization

To transform sensory information into meaningful perceptions, we must organize it: We must perceive objects as distinct from their surroundings, see them as having a meaningful and constant form, and discern their distance and motion. The brain's rules for constructing perceptions explain some puzzling illusions.

Early in this century, a group of German psychologists became intrigued with how the mind organizes sensations into perceptions. Given a cluster of sensations, the human perceiver organizes them into a gestalt, a German word meaning a "form" or a "whole." The Gestalt psychologists provided compelling demonstrations of gestalt perception and described principles by which we organize our sensations into perceptions. For example, look again at Figure 6.1 on page 182. Note that the individual elements of the figure are really nothing but eight blue circles, each containing three converging gray lines. But when we view them all together, we see a *whole* form, a "Necker cube."

As the Gestalt psychologists were fond of saying, in perception the whole may exceed the sum of its parts. Combine sodium, a corrosive metal, with chlorine, a poison gas, and something very different emerges—table salt. Likewise, a unique perceived form emerges from an object's components (Rock & Palmer, 1990). There is far more to perception than meets the senses.

Our human yen for assembling visual features into complete forms involves *bottom-up* processing, starting with entry-level sensory analysis, as well

visual capture
the tendency for vision to dominate the other senses. For example, in a movie theater we perceive voices as coming from the images on the screen we see rather than from the projector behind us.

gestalt
an organized whole. Gestalt psychologists emphasize our tendency to integrate pieces of information into meaningful wholes.

figure-ground
the organization of the visual field into objects (the figures) that stand out from their surroundings (the ground).

grouping
the perceptual tendency to organize stimuli into coherent groups.

as *top-down* processing that uses our experiences and expectations to interpret those sensations. The more we learn about this information-processing system, the fuzzier the distinction grows between *sensation* and *perception*. Sensation is not just bottom-up processing, and perception is not just top-down processing. Sensation and perception blend into one continuous process, progressing upward from specialized detector cells and downward from our assumptions. The cortex of a monkey's brain, for example, has specialized cells that respond to *illusory contours* similar to those shown in Figure 6.3 (Wenderoth, 1992; Winckelgren, 1992). Surprisingly, these cells are in a visual cortex area that receives signals from the eyes before much cognitive processing could have occurred (Grosof & others, 1993).

As you read about the Gestalt psychologists' organizational principles, keep in mind the fundamental truth they illustrate: Our brains do more than merely register information about the world. Perception is not just opening a shutter and letting a picture print itself on the brain. Always, we are filtering sensory information and inferring perceptions in ways that make sense to us. Mind matters.

Form Perception

Imagine that you wanted to design a video/computer system that, like your eye/brain system, could read handwritten addresses or recognize faces at a glance. (Postal services are, in fact, hoping to develop such a scanner.) What abilities would it need?

Figure and Ground

To start with, the system would need to recognize the addresses and faces as distinct from their backgrounds. Likewise, our first perceptual task is to perceive any object, called the *figure*, as distinct from its surroundings, called the *ground*. Among the voices you hear at a party, the one you attend to becomes the figure, all others part of the ground. As you read, the words are the figure; the white paper, the ground. In Figure 6.4, the figure-ground relationship continually reverses—but always we organize the stimulus into a figure seen against a ground. (Is it a vase, or profiles of a younger Prince Phillip and Queen Elizabeth?) Such reversible figure and ground illustrations demonstrate again that the same stimulus can trigger more than one perception. Curiously, though, if you do not *know* the figure is reversible, it likely will not reverse (Rock & others, 1994).

Figure **6.3**

Illusory contours You have to look closely to see there is no vertical line down the middle of this figure. The primary visual cortex of monkey brains contains cells that respond to such "subjective contours."

Grouping

Having discriminated figure from ground, we (and our video/computer system) must then organize the figure into a meaningful form. Some basic features of a scene—such as color, movement, and light-dark contrast—we process instantly and automatically (Treisman, 1987). To bring order and form to these basic sensations, our minds follow certain rules for grouping stimuli together (Figure 6.5). These rules, identified by the Gestalt psychologists, illustrate their idea that the perceived whole differs from the mere sum of its parts (Rock & Palmer, 1990):

Figure **6.4**

Reversible figure and ground

Figure **6.5**

Organizing stimuli into groups There are many ways we could perceive the stimuli shown here, and yet people everywhere see them similarly. The Gestalt psychologists believed this shows that the brain uses "rules" to order sensory information into wholes.

Proximity

Similarity

Continuity

Closure

Connectedness

Figure **6.6**

Grouping principles You probably perceive this doghouse as a gestalt—a whole (though impossible) structure. Actually, your brain imposes this sense of wholeness on the picture. As the photo on page 194 shows, gestalt grouping principles such as closure and continuity are at work here. (Reprinted from GAMES Magazine [810 Seventh Avenue, New York, NY 10019]. Copyright © 1983 PSC Games Limited Partnership.)

depth perception
the ability to see objects in three dimensions although the images that strike the retina are two-dimensional; allows us to judge distance.

visual cliff
a laboratory device for testing depth perception in infants and young animals.

binocular cues
depth cues, such as retinal disparity and convergence, that depend on the use of two eyes.

monocular cues
distance cues, such as linear perspective and overlap, available to either eye alone.

retinal disparity
a binocular cue for perceiving depth: the greater the disparity (difference) between the two images the retina receives of an object, the closer the object is to the viewer.

convergence
a binocular cue for perceiving depth; the extent to which the eyes converge inward when looking at an object.

Proximity We group nearby figures together. We see not six separate lines, but three sets of two lines.

Similarity Figures that are similar to each other we group together. We see the triangles and circles as vertical columns of similar shapes, not as horizontal rows of dissimilar shapes.

Continuity We perceive smooth, continuous patterns rather than discontinuous ones. This pattern could be a series of alternating semicircles, but we perceive it as two continuous lines—one wavy and one straight.

Closure We fill in gaps to create a complete, whole object. We easily fill the gaps in this figure's outline and see a complete triangle.

Connectedness We perceive spots, lines, or areas as a single unit when uniform and linked.

These grouping principles usually help us perceive reality. Sometimes, however, they can lead us astray, as when viewing the doghouse in Figure 6.6.

Depth Perception

From the two-dimensional images that fall on our retinas we somehow organize three-dimensional perceptions. Seeing objects in three dimensions, called depth perception, allows us to estimate their distance from us. At a glance, we estimate the distance of an oncoming car or the height of a cliff. This ability is partly innate. Eleanor Gibson and Richard Walk (1960) discovered this using a miniature cliff with a drop-off covered by sturdy glass. The inspiration for these experiments occurred to Gibson as she was eating a picnic lunch on the rim of the Grand Canyon. She wondered: Would a toddler peering over the rim perceive the dangerous drop-off and draw back?

Back in their Cornell University laboratory, Gibson and Walk placed 6- to 14-month-old infants on the edge of a safe canyon—a visual cliff (Figure 6.7). Their mothers then coaxed them to crawl out on the glass. Most refused to do so, indicating that they could perceive depth. Perhaps by crawling age they had *learned* to perceive depth. Yet newborn animals with virtually no visual experience—including young kittens, a day-old goat, and newly hatched chicks—respond similarly. Each species, by the time it is mobile, has the perceptual abilities it needs. What is more, during the first month of life, human infants turn to avoid objects coming directly at them but are unbothered by objects approaching at an angle that would not hit them (Ball & Tronick, 1971).

Although biological maturation predisposes our wariness of heights, experience amplifies it. Infants' wariness increases with crawling experience, at whatever age crawling begins. Given the enhanced locomotion made possible by a walker, infants become even more wary of heights (Campos & others, 1992).

How do we do it? How do we transform two-dimensional retinal images into three-dimensional perceptions? Some depth cues—binocular cues—require both eyes. Others—monocular cues—are available to each eye separately.

Figure **6.7**

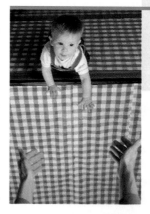

Visual cliff Eleanor Gibson and Richard Walk devised this miniature cliff with a glass-covered drop-off to determine whether crawling infants and newborn animals can perceive depth. Even when coaxed, infants are reluctant to venture onto the glass over the cliff.

Figure **6.8**

The floating finger sausage
Hold your two index fingers about 5 inches in front of your eyes, with their tips half an inch apart. Now look beyond them and note the weird result. Move your fingers out farther and the retinal disparity—and the finger sausage—will shrink.

Binocular Cues

Because our eyes are about 2½ inches apart, our retinas receive slightly different images of the world. When the brain compares these two images, the difference between them—their retinal disparity—provides an important cue to the relative distance of different objects. When you hold your finger directly in front of your nose, your retinas receive quite different views. (You can see this if you close one eye and then the other, or create a finger sausage as in Figure 6.8.) At greater distance—say, when you hold your finger at arm's length—the disparity is smaller.

The creators of three-dimensional (3-D) movies simulate retinal disparity by photographing a scene with two cameras placed a few inches apart (a feature we might want to build into our seeing computer). When viewed through spectacles or a device that allows the left eye to see only the image from the left camera and the right eye only the image from the right camera, the 3-D effect mimics normal retinal disparity. Computer-generated 3-D images do the same.

Can you find the three-dimensional Greek letter psi (Ψ) in the stereogram in Figure 6.9? Cross your eyes slightly (or look at a pencil tip three inches or so above the page). As the two dots at the top of the stereogram become three, the psi image will appear (at which point you will no longer feel that your eyes are crossed). The image looks so real you may be able to measure its distance from the page with a ruler.

But note that you cannot trace the outline of the 3-D image on the page—because it isn't on the page. Note also that if you close one eye, the image immediately disappears, again illustrating that it doesn't really exist, except in your brain. The perceived depth, from two slightly different images lying one on top of the other, occurs as each eye focuses on one image and the brain integrates the two versions into a single 3-D image. This dramatically illustrates this chapter's fundamental lesson: Perception is not merely projecting the world onto our brains. Rather, sensations are disassembled into information bits that the brain reassembles into its own functional model of the external world. *Our brains construct our perceptions.*

Another binocular cue to distance is convergence, a neuromuscular cue from the greater inward turn when the eyes view a near object. By noting the angle of convergence, the brain can compute whether you are focusing on this printed page or on the person across the room.

If you could pull out your eyeballs and switch their positions (leaving their neural wiring intact), you would reverse the retinal disparity, making all objects reversed in depth. Close objects would appear distant, and distant objects would appear close (Wolf, 1996).

Figure **6.9**

Two Eyes + Brain = Depth If you are having trouble seeing the 3-D image, try holding the picture close to your face, so that the center of it touches your nose, then slowly move it backward without changing the focus of your eyes. About a foot from your face, the 3-D image should emerge. The image appears because the picture contains two views of the Greek letter psi, from slightly different angles. When the brain fuses these two into one, you see the image in three dimensions.

Relative size

Monocular Cues

Try this: With both eyes open, hold two pens or pencils in front of you and touch their tips together. Now do so with one eye closed. Does the task become noticeably more difficult? This demonstrates the importance of binocular cues in judging the distance of nearby objects. Two eyes are better than one. How then do we judge whether a person is 10 or 100 meters away? In both cases, the retinal disparity while looking straight ahead is slight. At such distances we depend on monocular cues such as the following:

Relative size If we assume that two objects are similar in size, we perceive the one that casts the smaller retinal image as farther away.

Interposition If one object partially blocks our view of another, we perceive it as closer. The painting below purposely confuses figure and ground by interposition.

Interposition

Relative clarity Because light from distant objects passes through more atmosphere, we perceive hazy objects as farther away than sharp, clear objects. (Recall from Puzzle 4, page 184, the effects of fog on judging distance.)

Texture gradient A gradual change from a coarse, distinct texture to a fine, indistinct texture signals increasing distance. Far objects appear smaller and more densely packed.

Relative height We perceive objects higher in our field of vision as farther away. (This reverses above the horizon, as when we perceive a higher bird as closer.) Relative height may contribute to the illusion that vertical dimensions are longer than identical horizontal dimen-

Relative height

sions (as we saw in Puzzle 3, page 183, the St. Louis Gateway Arch). Is the vertical line here longer, shorter, or equal in length to the horizontal line? Measure and see.

Relative motion As we move, stable objects appear to move relative to us. If while riding in a train you fix your gaze on some object—say, a house—the objects closer than the house (the fixation point) appear to move backward. The nearer an object is, the faster it seems to move.

Objects beyond the fixation point appear to move with you at a decreasing speed as the object gets farther away. Your brain uses these speed and direction clues to compute the objects' relative distances.

Texture gradient

• **Fixation point**

Relative motion   **Direction of passenger's motion** ➡

Linear perspective

Relative brightness
(From "Perceiving Shape from Shading" by Vilayanur S. Ramachandran.
Copyright © 1988 by Scientific American, Inc. All rights reserved.)

Linear perspective Parallel lines, such as railroad tracks, appear to converge with distance. The more the lines converge, the greater their perceived distance. Linear perspective can contribute to rail-crossing accidents, by leading people to overestimate a train's distance (Leibowitz, 1985). (A train's massive size also makes it appear to be moving more slowly than it is.)

Relative brightness Nearby objects reflect more light to our eyes. Thus, given two identical objects, the dimmer one seems farther away. This illusion also contributes to accidents, as when a fog-shrouded vehicle, or one with only its parking lights on, seems farther away than it is. Shading, too, produces a sense of depth consistent with the assumed light source. Invert the illustration above and the hollow becomes a hill, because we assume that light comes from above.

To convey depth on a flat canvas (Figure 6.10), artists use such monocular cues, as do people who must gauge depth with but one eye. In 1960, the University of Washington football team won the year's biggest game, thanks partly to the superb ball throwing of Bob Schloredt. Schloredt, who was obviously skilled at judging his receiver's distance, used monocular cues for distance because he is blind in his left eye.

Figure **6.10**

Perspective techniques By the time that "Bristol, Broad Quay" was painted (c. 1730, Anonymous), techniques for depicting three dimensions on a flat surface were well established. Note the effective use of distance cues such as texture gradient, interposition, linear perspective, and relative size and height.

phi phenomenon
an illusion of movement created when two or more adjacent lights blink on and off in succession.

perceptual constancy
perceiving objects as unchanging (having consistent lightness, color, shape, and size) even as illumination and retinal images change.

Recall the famous EAT POPCORN/ DRINK COCA-COLA subliminal persuasion hoax described on page 149. For several reasons, we know that such an experiment could never have occurred. We know this not only because the reported site—the Fort Lee, New Jersey, theater—could not have held the number of people supposedly tested, and not only because the theater manager at the time denied such an experiment was ever conducted, but also because of what we know about stroboscopic movement. The briefest possible movie image, a 1/24th-second frame, would not have been subliminal (Rogers, 1994).

Motion Perception

Imagine that you could perceive the world as having color, form, and depth but that you could not see motion. Not only could you not play tennis or drive a car, you might have trouble writing, eating, and walking.

But you can perceive motion and depth, and if you are a skilled baseball, softball, or cricket player you can do it with astounding speed and accuracy. As the ball leaves a pitcher's hand, the batter's brain detects the ball's speed, spin, and direction, computes in a literal eyeblink of time where it is going to be 4/10ths of a second later, and, before 0.15 seconds elapse, directs the arms not to swing or to meet it with the bat. As a well-hit ball flies out, the fielder's brain now unconsciously computes the ball's trajectory, enabling the fielder to run through the point of its return precisely as it arrives (McBeath & others, 1995). A mathematical physicist working on a supercomputer could hardly compute more quickly or accurately.

Our brain computes motion based partly on its assumption that shrinking objects are retreating (not getting smaller) and enlarging objects are approaching. But the changing size and position of a retinal image isn't our only clue to motion. Nod your head and the visual field's retinal position changes, but nothing appears to move. (Close one eye and gently move your other eyeball by pushing on the upper eyelid. Now the brain reads the changing retinal image as a moving world.)

As film animation artists know well, the brain will also interpret a rapid series of slightly varying images as movement (a phenomenon called *stroboscopic movement*). By flashing 24 still pictures each second, a motion picture creates perceived movement. The motion we see is not in the film, which is just a superfast slide show, but is constructed in our heads.

Theater and restaurant marquees sometimes create another illusion of movement, using the phi phenomenon. When two adjacent stationary lights blink on and off in quick succession, we perceive a single light moving back and forth between them. Lighted signs exploit the phi phenomenon with a succession of lights that create the impression of, say, a moving arrow.

Perceptual Constancy

So far we have noted that our video/computer system must first perceive objects as we do—as having a distinct form, location, and perhaps motion. Its next task is even more challenging: to rec-

ognize the object without being deceived by changes in its size, shape, brightness, or color. Perceptual constancy allows us to perceive an object as unchanging even though the stimuli we receive from it change. Thus, we can identify things regardless of viewing angle, distance, and illumination. You glance at someone ahead of you on the sidewalk and instantly recognize a classmate. In less time than it takes to draw a breath, information reaching your eyes has been sent to your brain, where work teams comprising millions of neurons have extracted the essential features, compared them with stored images, and identified the person. Replicating this human perceptual feat, which has intrigued perception researchers for decades, provides a monumental challenge for our seeing computer.

Shape and Size Constancies

Sometimes an object's actual shape is unchanging, but the object *seems* to change shape with our viewing angle (Figure 6.11). More often, thanks to *shape constancy*, we perceive familiar objects as having a constant form even while our retinal images of them change. When a door opens, it casts a changing shape on our retinas, yet we manage to perceive the door as having a constant doorlike shape (Figure 6.12).

Thanks to *size constancy* we perceive objects as having a constant size, even while our distance from them varies. Size constancy allows us to perceive a car as big enough to carry people, even when we see its tiny image from two blocks away.

Figure **6.11**

Perceiving shape Do the tops of boxes A and B have different dimensions? They appear to. But—believe it or not—they are identical. (Measure and see.) With both boxes we adjust our perceptions relative to our viewing angle. (From Shepard, 1981.)

Box A   **Box B**

Figure **6.12**

Shape constancy A door casts an increasingly trape-zoidal image on our retinas as it opens, yet we still per-ceive it as rectangular.

This illustrates the close connection between an object's perceived *distance* and perceived *size*. Perceiving an object's distance gives us cues to its size. Likewise, knowing its general size—that the object is, say, a car—provides us with cues to its distance.

Size-Distance Relationship

The marvel of size perception is how effortlessly it occurs. Given the perceived distance of an object and the size of its image on our retinas, we instantly and unconsciously infer the object's size. Although the monsters in Figure 6.13(*a*) cast the same retinal images, the linear perspective tells our brain that the monster in pursuit is farther away. We therefore perceive it as larger.

This interplay between perceived size and perceived distance helps explain several well-known illusions. For example, can you imagine why the moon looks up to 50 percent larger near the horizon than when high in the sky? For at least 22 centuries, scholars have wondered and argued about reasons for the *moon illusion* (Hershenson, 1989). One reason is that cues to objects' distances at the horizon make the moon behind them seem farther away (Kaufman & Rock, 1962). Thus, the moon on the horizon seems larger, like the distant monster in Figure 6.13(*a*) and the distant bar in the *Ponzo illusion* in Figure 6.13(*b*). Take away these distance cues—by looking at the horizon moon (or each monster or each bar) through a paper tube—and it immediately shrinks.

The size-distance relationship helps us understand two illusions demonstrated earlier. Puzzle 1, the Müller-Lyer illusion concerning the lengths of straight lines between arrow tips, has been the subject of more than 1250 scientific publications, yet psychologists still debate its explanation. One is that our experience with the corners of rooms or buildings prompts us to interpret the vertical line on the ticket booth in Figure 6.14(*a*) as closer to us and therefore shorter, and the vertical line by the

Figure **6.13**

(a)   **(b)**

The interplay between perceived size and distance
(a) The monocular cues for distance make the pursuing monster look larger than the pursued. It isn't. (From Shepard, 1990.)

(b) This visual trick, called the Ponzo illusion, is based on the same principle as the fleeing monsters. The two orange bars cast identical-sized images on our retinas. But experience tells us that a more dis-

tant object can create the same-sized image as a nearer one only if it is actually larger. As a result, we perceive the bar that seems more distant as larger.

Figure **6.14**

The Müller-Lyer illusion

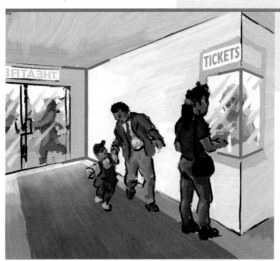

(a)

Richard L. Gregory (1968) suggested that the corners in our rectangularly carpentered world teach us to interpret "outward" or "inward" pointing arrowheads at the

ends of a line as a cue to the line's distance from us and so to its length. The red line defined by the corner at the ticket booth looks shorter than the red line defined by

the corner to the left. But if you measure them, you will see that both are the same length.

(b)

There is more to the Müller-Lyer illusion than size constancy, however, for if we replace the arrowheads with circles and judge whether the black or blue line seg-

ment seem longer, we still get much the same effect. Here the two line segments are equal. Most people judge the black line as longer, apparently because they

perceptually adjust the lengths of the lines toward the distance separating the figures. (From Day, 1984.)

More than we realize, our taken-for-granted perceptions of the world depend on our experience. We perceive the world not just as it is, but as we are.

door as farther away and therefore longer. Thus, what appears as an illusion when isolated in a line drawing actually enables correct depth perception in our three-dimensional world.

Supporting this theory, people are more susceptible to the Müller-Lyer illusion if, unlike some rural Africans, they have lived in a carpentered world of rectangular shapes (Segall & others, 1990). The phenomenon reflects cultural experience, not race, for the same study showed that Africans who live in carpentered cities are more vulnerable to the illusion than Africans in uncarpentered environments. Our experience in carpentered contexts provides a perspective that helps us construct our perceptions top-down.

Anthropologist Colin Turnbull (1961, p. 252) noted another effect of experience on perception when he took an African Pygmy guide, Kenge, on his first trip out of the dense forest. As they were crossing a wide plain, buffalo loomed several miles away. Kenge, unaccustomed to judging size over unbroken distances, wondered, "What insects are those?" "When I told Kenge that the insects were buffalo, he roared with laughter and told me not to tell such stupid lies," Turnbull reported. As they drove on, the mystified Kenge became frightened as the buffalo grew bigger and bigger.

Anthropologists, missionaries, and cross-cultural psychologists also report that people who have never before seen photos or drawings may initially find them confusing (Deregowski, 1989). Shown a painting or a black-and-white picture of a familiar animal such as a tortoise, the inexperienced person may at first just not get it. More than we realize, our taken-for-granted perceptions of the world depend on our experience. We perceive the world not just as it is, but as we are.

Size-distance relationships also explain Puzzle 2, the shrinking and growing girls. As Figure 6.15 reveals, the room is distorted. Viewed with one eye through a peephole, its trapezoidal walls produce the same images as those of a normal rectangular room viewed with both eyes. Presented with the camera's one-eyed view, the brain makes the reasonable assumption that the room *is* normal and that each of the girls is therefore the same distance from us. But given the different sizes of the images on the retina, our brain ends up calculating that the girls are very different in size.

Our occasional misperceptions demonstrate the workings of our normally effective perceptual processes. The perceived relationship between distance and size is generally valid, but under special circumstances it can lead us astray—as when helping to create the moon illusion, the Müller-Lyer illusion, and the distorted-room illusion. Using distance cues to assess perceived size triggers illusions only if we aren't familiar with the object or if the distance cues are misleading. When we correctly interpret the distance cues—which we normally do—we perceive the size of objects correctly.

Culture and depth perception

The spear points at which animal? People who have never seen two-dimensional drawings or photos of three-dimensional scenes often have difficulty seeing depth in a figure such as this. (Adapted from Jean B. Deregowski, "Pictorial Perception and Culture," November 1972, p. 83. Copyright 1972 by Scientific American, Inc. All rights reserved.)

Figure **6.15**

The illusion of the shrinking and growing girls   This distorted room, designed by Adelbert Ames, appears to have a normal rectangular shape when viewed through a peephole with one eye. The girl in the near corner appears disproportionately large because we judge her size based on the false assumption that she is the same distance away as the girl in the far corner.

Lightness Constancy

White paper reflects 90 percent of the light falling on it; black paper, only 10 percent. In sunlight the black paper may reflect 100 times more light than does the white paper indoors, but it still looks black (McBurney & Collings, 1984). This illustrates *lightness constancy* (also called *brightness constancy*); we perceive an object as having a constant lightness even while its illumination varies. Perceived lightness depends on *relative luminance*—the amount of light an object reflects relative to its surroundings. If you view sunlit black paper through a narrow tube so nothing else is visible, it may look gray, because in bright sunshine it reflects a fair amount of light. View it without the tube and it is again black, because it reflects much less light than the objects around it. The phenomenon is similar to that of color constancy (pages 162–163). A red apple in a fruit bowl retains its redness as the light changes, because our brain computes the light reflected by any object relative to its surrounding objects.

If perceived lightness stays roughly constant, given an unchanging context, what happens when the surrounding context changes? As Figure 6.16 shows, the brain computes brightness and color relative to surrounding objects. Thus, perceived lightness changes with context.

Form perception, depth perception, motion perception, and perceptual constancy illustrate how we organize our visual experiences. Perceptual or-ganization applies to other senses, too. It explains why we group the clock's steady clicks into patterns (Puzzle 5, page 184). Listening to an unfamiliar language, we have trouble hearing where one word stops and the next one begins. Listening to our own language, we automatically hear distinct words. This, too, is a form of perceptual organization. But it is more, for we even organize

Figure **6.16**

Brightness contrast   Although the interior rectangles are in fact identical, we perceive the right one as lighter because of the contrast with its dark surroundings. Like the effect of context on color perception (Figure 5.16), this phenomenon has great significance for artists and interior designers.

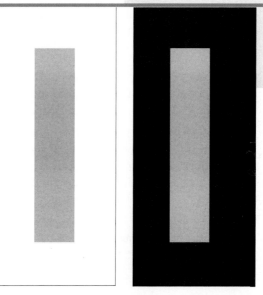

The solution Another view of the impossible doghouse in Figure 6.6 (page 186) reveals the secrets of this illusion. From the photo angle in Figure 6.6, the grouping principle of closure leads us to perceive the boards as continuous. (Reprinted from GAMES Magazine [810 Seventh Avenue, New York, NY 10019]. Copyright © 1983 PSC Games Limited Partnership.)

a string of letters—THEDOGATEMEAT—into words that make an intelligible phrase, more likely "The dog ate meat" than "The do gate me at" (McBurney & Collings, 1984). This process involves not only organization but interpretation—finding meaning in what we perceive.

SUMMING UP

From a top-down perspective, we see how, aided by knowledge and expectations, we transform sensory information into meaningful perceptions.

Perceptual Illusions Visual and auditory illusions were fascinating scientists even as psychology emerged. Explaining illusions required an understanding of how we transform sensations into meaningful perceptions, so the study of perception became one of psychology's first concerns. Conflict between visual and other sensory information is usually resolved with the mind accepting the visual data, a tendency known as *visual capture*.

Perceptual Organization The early Gestalt psychologists were impressed with the seemingly innate way in which we organize fragmentary sensory data into whole perceptions. Our minds structure the information that comes to us in several demonstrable ways:

> **Form Perception** To recognize an object, we must first perceive it (see it as a figure) as distinct from surrounding stimuli (the ground). We must also organize the figure into a meaningful form. Several Gestalt princi-

ples—proximity, similarity, continuity, closure, and connectedness—describe this process.

Depth Perception Research on the visual cliff reveals that many species perceive the world in three dimensions at, or very soon after, birth. We transform two-dimensional retinal images into three-dimensional perceptions by using binocular cues, such as retinal disparity, and monocular cues, such as the relative sizes of objects.

Motion Perception Our brain computes motion as objects move across or toward the retina. A quick succession of images, as in a motion picture or on a lighted sign, can also create an illusion of movement.

Perceptual Constancy Having perceived an object as a coherent figure and having located it in space, how do we recognize it—despite the varying images that it may cast on our retinas? Size, shape, and lightness constancies describe how objects appear to have unchanging characteristics regardless of their distance, shape, or motion. These constancies explain several of the well-known visual illusions. For example, familiarity with the size-distance relationships in a carpentered world of rectangular shapes makes people more susceptible to the Müller-Lyer illusion.

KEY TERMS AND CONCEPTS visual capture, gestalt, figure-ground, grouping, depth perception, visual cliff, binocular cues, monocular cues, retinal disparity, convergence, phi phenomenon, perceptual constancy

Interpretation

To what extent do we learn to perceive? If our eyes were covered with blinders or cataracts during our early years, would we enjoy normal perceptions when such were removed? If given glasses that displaced or inverted the world, could we adapt? To what extent do our assumptions and beliefs shape our interpretations, and thus our perceptions?

Philosophers have debated the origins of our perceptual abilities: Is it nature or nurture? German philosopher Immanuel Kant (1724–1804) maintained that knowledge comes from our *inborn* ways of organizing sensory experiences. Indeed, we come equipped to process sensory information. But British philosopher John Locke (1632–1704) argued that through our experiences we also *learn* to perceive the world. Indeed, we learn to link an object's distance with its size. But just how important is experience? How radically does it shape our perceptual interpretations?

Sensory Restriction and Restored Vision

Writing to John Locke (1690), William Molyneux wondered whether "a man *born* blind, and now adult, taught by his *touch* to distinguish between a cube and a sphere" could, if made to see, visually distinguish the two. Locke's answer was no, because the man would never have *learned* to see the difference.

Molyneux's hypothetical case has since been put to the test with dozens of adults who, though blind from birth, have gained sight (Gregory, 1978; von Senden, 1932). Most were people born with cataracts—clouded lenses that enabled them to see only diffused light, rather as you or I might see a diffuse fog through a Ping-Pong ball sliced in half. When their cataracts were surgically removed, the patients could distinguish figure from ground and could sense colors—suggesting that these aspects of perception are innate. But much as Locke supposed, the formerly blind patients often could not visually recognize objects that were familiar by touch.

> "Let us then suppose the mind to be, as we say, white paper void of all characters, without any ideas: How comes it to be furnished? . . . To this I answer, in one word, from EXPERIENCE."
>
> **JOHN LOCKE**
> *AN ESSAY CONCERNING HUMAN UNDERSTANDING*
> 1690

Perhaps in these cases the surgery didn't completely restore the patients' visual equipment. Seeking to gain more control than is provided by clinical cases, researchers have conducted Molyneux's imaginary experiment with infant kittens and monkeys. In one experiment, they outfitted them with goggles through which the animals could see only diffuse, unpatterned light (Wiesel, 1982). After infancy, when their goggles were removed, these animals exhibited perceptual limitations much like those of humans born with cataracts. They could distinguish color and brightness, but not the form of a circle from that of a square. Their eyes had not degenerated; their retinas still relayed signals to their visual cortex. But lacking stimulation, the cortical cells had not developed normal connections. Thus, the animals remained functionally blind to shape.

In both humans and animals, a similar period of sensory restriction does no permanent harm if it occurs later in life. Cover the eye of an animal for several months during adulthood, and vision will be unaffected after removing the eye patch. Remove cataracts that develop after early childhood, and a human, too, will enjoy normal vision. The effects of visual experiences during infancy in cats, monkeys, and humans suggest there is a *critical period* (page 96) for normal sensory and perceptual development. Experience guides the organization of the brain's neural connections.

We can also see the profound effects of early visual experience in experiments with young animals who were reared with severely restricted visual input. Cambridge University researchers Colin Blakemore and Grahame Cooper (1970) reared kittens in darkness, except for 5 hours each day during which they were placed in a horizontally or vertically striped environment (as in Figure 6.17). Remarkably, kittens raised without exposure to horizontal lines later had difficulty perceiving horizontal bars, and those raised without vertical lines had difficulty seeing vertical bars. While two of these kittens played, a researcher playfully shook a long black rod. The kitten reared in a world of vertical lines would play with the rod only when it was held upright. When the rod was held flat, that kitten ignored it while its companion—reared in a world of horizontal lines—ran to play with it. Eventually, their selective blindness diminished, but the kittens never regained normal sensitivity. By sampling the activity of the kittens' feature-detecting brain cells, Blakemore and Cooper found that whether such cells responded mostly to horizontal or vertical lines depended on the kittens' early visual experience.

Figure **6.17**

The experimental apparatus for the Blakemore and Cooper studies   From the time their eyes first opened, and until the age of 5 months, these kittens were removed from darkness each day to spend 5 hours alone in a black-and-white striped cylinder with a clear glass floor. A stiff collar prevented the kittens from seeing anything else, even their own bodies. Afterward, these kittens had difficulty perceiving horizontal forms, compared with other kittens exposed only to horizontal forms. (From Blakemore & Cooper, 1970.)

perceptual adaptation
in vision, the ability to adjust to an artificially displaced or even inverted visual field.

perceptual set
a mental predisposition to perceive one thing and not another.

Believe it or not, kittens, monkeys, and humans can adapt to an inverted world.

These experiments on perceptual limitations produced by early sensory deprivation provide a partial answer to a question debated in Chapter 4: Does the effect of early experience last a lifetime? For some aspects of visual perception, the answer is clearly yes: "Use it *soon* or lose it." We retain the imprint of early visual experiences far into the future.

Perceptual Adaptation

Given a new pair of glasses, we may feel slightly disoriented and dizzy. Within a day or two, we adjust. Our perceptual adaptation to changed visual input makes the world seem normal again. Now imagine a far more dramatic new pair of glasses— one that shifts the apparent location of objects 40 degrees to the left. When you first put them on and toss a ball to a friend, it sails off to the left. Walking forward to shake hands with the person, you veer to the left.

Could you adapt to this distorted world? Chicks cannot. When fitted with such lenses, they continue to peck where food grains *seem* to be (Hess, 1956; Rossi, 1968). But humans adapt to distorting lenses quickly. Within a few minutes your throws would again be accurate, your stride on target. Remove the lenses and you would experience an aftereffect: At first your throws would err in the *opposite* direction, sailing off to the right; but again, within minutes you would readapt.

Now imagine an even more radical pair of glasses—one that literally turns the world upside down. The ground is up, the sky is down. Could you adapt? Fish, frogs, and salamanders cannot. When Roger Sperry (1956) surgically turned their eyes upside down, they thereafter reacted to objects by moving in the wrong direction. But, believe it or not, kittens, monkeys, and humans can adapt to an inverted world. Turn-of-the-century psychologist George Stratton (1896) experienced this when he invented, and for 8 days wore, optical headgear that flipped left to right *and* up to down, making him the first person to experience a right-side-up retinal image while standing upright.

At first, Stratton was disoriented. When he wanted to walk, he had to search for his feet, which were now "up." Eating was nearly impossible. He became nauseated and depressed. But Stratton persisted, and by the eighth day he could comfortably reach for something in the right direction and walk without bumping into things. When Stratton finally removed the headgear, he readapted quickly.

Later experiments replicated Stratton's experience (Dolezal, 1982; Kohler, 1962). After a period of adjustment, people wearing the optical gear have even been able to ride a motorcycle, ski the Alps, and fly an airplane. Is this because through experience they perceptually reinvert their upside-down world to an upright position? No, the street, ski slopes, and runway still seem above their heads. But by actively moving about in this topsy-turvy world, they adapt to the context and learn to coordinate their movements.

Perceptual Set

As everyone knows, to see is to believe. As many people also know, but do not fully appreciate, to believe is to see. Our experiences, assumptions, and expectations may give us a perceptual set, or mental predisposition, that greatly influences what we perceive. Is the image in the center picture of Figure 6.18 a man playing the saxophone or a woman's face? What we see in such a drawing can be influenced by first viewing either of the two unambiguous versions (Boring, 1930).

Knowing this much, see if you can explain the results of another experiment. A slightly blurred picture was identified correctly by 73 percent of first-time viewers, but by only 25 percent of those who had previously been shown a *badly* blurred version of the same picture (Bruner & Potter, 1964). Why do you suppose the second group had such trouble perceiving the image?

It's because people cannot resist imposing a pattern on unpatterned stimuli. Shown a hopelessly blurred picture, people automatically form a preliminary hunch (perceptual set), which then interferes with their later perceptions. Thus, it is much harder to recognize a photo coming into focus than to "hang on" to the same photo going out of focus. Once we have formed a wrong idea about reality,

Perceptual adaptation "Oops, missed," thinks Hubert Dolezal as he views the world through inverting goggles. Remarkably, people can learn to adapt to an upside-down visual world.

we have more difficulty seeing the truth. Even scientists, striving for objectivity, perceive reality through the lenses of their theories. When first viewing the "canals" on Mars through telescopes, some astronomers and writers perceived them as the product of intelligent life. They were—but the intelligence was on the viewing end of the telescope.

> "The temptation to form premature theories upon insufficient data is the bane of our profession."
>
> SHERLOCK HOLMES IN ARTHUR CONAN DOYLE'S
> *THE VALLEY OF FEAR*
> 1914

Everyday examples of perceptual set abound. In 1972, a British newspaper published genuine, unretouched photographs of a "monster" in Scotland's Loch Ness—"the most amazing pictures ever taken," stated the paper. If this information creates in you the same perceptual set it did in most of the paper's readers, you, too, will see the monster in the photo reproduced in Figure 6.19(*a*). But when Steuart Campbell (1986) approached the photos with a different perceptual set, he saw a curved tree trunk—very likely the same tree trunk others had seen in the water the day the photo was shot. Moreover, with this different perceptual set, you may now notice that the object is floating motionless, without any water disturbance or wake around it—hardly what we would expect of a lively monster.

Our perceptual set can influence what we hear as well as what we see. Witness the kindly airline pilot who, on a takeoff run, looked over at his depressed co-pilot and said, "Cheer up." The co-pilot heard the usual "Gear up" and promptly raised the

Figure **6.18**

Perceptual set   What do you see in the center picture: a male saxophonist or a woman's face? Glancing first at one of the two unambiguous versions of the picture is likely to influence your interpretation. (From Shepard, 1990.)

wheels—before they had left the ground (Reason & Mycielska, 1982). When listening to rock music played backward, people often perceive an evil message *if* specifically told what to listen for (Vokey & Read, 1985). When observing political campaign debates, most people perceive their favorite candidate as being the better debater (Gallup, 1992). Clearly, much of what we perceive comes not just from the world "out there" but also from what's behind our eyes and between our ears.

Even when listening to Disney movies, sex-preoccupied viewers have perceived supposedly subliminal messages, such as the letters S-E-X in a cloud of dust stirred up by Simba in *The Lion King,* or "All good teenagers take off your clothes," murmured by a voice in *Aladdin.* The latter message was first perceived by a testosterone-laden male university student, who told his sister, who told her mother, who wrote to *Movie Guide*, whose report (later retracted), was picked up by the American Life League newsletter, whose allegation was reported by Virginia's *Newport News*, from which it was picked up by the Associated Press. "If somebody is seeing something, that's their perception," responded Rick Rhoades, a spokesperson for Disney, which was inundated with protest letters. "There's nothing there" (Bannon, 1995). Some things must be believed to be seen.

What determines our perceptual set? Through experience we form concepts, or *schemas*, which organize and interpret unfamiliar information. Our preexisting schemas for male saxophonists and

Figure **6.19**

Believing is seeing   What do you perceive in these photos? (a) Is this Nessie, the Loch Ness monster, or a log? (b) Are these flying saucers or clouds? We often perceive what we expect to see.

(a)

(b)

women's faces, for monsters and tree trunks, for airplane lights and UFOs, all help us interpret ambiguous sensations with top-down processing. Confronted with an ambiguous moving object in the sky, different people may therefore apply different schemas: "It's a bird." "It's a plane." "It's Superman!"

Children's drawings allow us to glimpse their developing perceptual schemas. A preschooler can draw circles and angled lines but cannot combine them to create an elaborate human figure. The child's problem is not clumsiness. A right-handed adult asked to draw with the left hand will create an awkward drawing, but it will be unlike the child's drawing in Figure 6.20. Part of the difference lies in children's difficulty representing visually what they see. The main difference, however, lies in the child's simplified schema for essential human characteristics. To a 3-year-old, a face is a more essential human feature than a body. From ages 3 to 8, children's schemas for bodies become more elaborate, and so do their drawings.

Our schemas for faces prime us to see facial patterns in cartoonists' caricatures and even in random configurations, such as the lunar landscape. Peter Thompson (1980) at the University of York discovered that our face recognition is especially attuned to the expressive eyes and mouth. Thus, we have trouble imagining what Madonna's inverted eyes and mouth will look like when we turn her face upright (Figure 6.21).

Figure **6.21**

Face schemas Which of these is the real Madonna? Slowly rotate the page to find out. As you do so you will reach a point where you suddenly cannot assimilate her mouth and eyes into your schema for faces.

Context Effects

A given stimulus may trigger radically different perceptions, partly because of our differing schemas, but also because of the immediate context. Some examples:

- Imagine hearing a noise interrupted by the words "eel is on the wagon." Likely, you would actually perceive the first word as *wheel*. Given "eel is on the orange," you would hear *peel*. This curious phenomenon, discovered by Richard Warren, suggests that the brain can work backward in time to allow a later stimulus to determine how we perceive an earlier one. The context creates an expectation that, top-down, influences our perception as we match our bottom-up signal against it (Grossberg, 1995).

- Did the pursuing monster in Figure 6.13(a) on page 191 look aggressive? Did the pursued one seem frightened? If so, you are experiencing a context effect. The two monsters are the same.

- Is the "magician's cabinet" in Figure 6.22 sitting on the floor or hanging from the ceiling? How we perceive it depends on the context defined by the bunnies.

- Did the speaker say "cults and sects" or "cults and sex"? Did the critic advocate "attacks" or "a tax" on our politicians? In both instances, we must discern the meaning from the surrounding words.

Figure **6.20**

Schemas Children's drawings reflect their schemas of reality, as well as their abilities to represent what they see. This drawing by a 3-year-old illustrates that the face has far greater importance than the body in young children's schemas of essential human characteristics.

Figure **6.22**

Context effects: the magician's cabinet Is the box in the far left frame lying on the floor or hanging from the ceiling? What about the one on the far right? In each case, the context defined by the inquisitive bunnies guides our perceptions. (From Shepard, 1990.)

CLOSE-UP

The Human Factor in Operating Machines

I love our VCR, though I still haven't figured out how to make it "express record." Our stove is wonderful, except for the moments I spend puzzling over which control works which burner. The push-bar doors on our campus buildings are safe and easy, though occasionally frustrating when I push the wrong end. The extra buttons on my computer-linked phone are handy, though when transferring a call I still must look up which button to press.

Human factors psychologists help to design appliances, machines, and work settings that harness rather than confound our natural perceptions. Psychologist Donald Norman (1988) suggests how simple design changes could reduce some of our frustrations. For example, by exploiting "natural mapping," we could design stove controls that require no labels.

Understanding human factors can do more than design for reduced frustration; it can help avoid disaster. After beginning commercial flights in the late 1960s, the Boeing 727 was involved in several landing accidents caused by pilot error. Psychologist Conrad Kraft (1978) noted a common setting for these accidents: All took place at night, and all involved landing short of the runway after crossing a dark stretch of water or unilluminated ground. Kraft reasoned that, beyond the runway, city lights would project a larger retinal image if on a rising terrain. This would make the ground seem farther away than it was. By re-creating these conditions in flight simulations, Kraft discovered that pilots were deceived into thinking they were flying safely, higher than their actual altitudes (Figure 6.23). Aided by Kraft's finding, the airlines began corrective measures (such as requiring the co-pilot to monitor the altimeter and call out altitudes) and the accidents diminished.

(a) Traditional labeling
With traditionally positioned stove controls, a person must read the labels to figure out which knob works which burner.

(b) Natural map
By positioning the controls in a natural map, which the brain understands at a glance, we can eliminate the need to ponder written instructions just to boil water.

Figure **6.23**

Human factors solution
Lacking distance cues when approaching a runway from over a dark surface, pilots simulating a night landing tended to fly too low. (From Kraft, 1978.)

Culture and context effects
What is above the woman's head? In one study, nearly all those questioned from East Africa thought she was balancing a metal box or can on her head and that the family was sitting under a tree. Westerners, to whom corners and boxlike architecture are more common, were more likely to perceive the family as being indoors, with the woman sitting under a window. (Adapted from Gregory & Gombrich, 1973.)

Soviet film director Lew Kulechov believed that skilled directors create audience emotion by defining a context in which viewers interpret an actor's expressions. He once produced three short films, each depicting one of three contexts, followed by identical clips of an actor with a neutral expression (Wallbott, 1988). Shown a film of a dead woman, viewers of the clip were struck by the actor's sadness. Shown a dish of soup, viewers judged the actor thoughtful. Shown a playing child, viewers said the actor appeared happy. Even hearing sad rather than happy music can predispose people to perceive spoken homophone words with their sad meanings—*mourning* rather than *morning*, *die* rather than *dye*, *pain* rather than *pane* (Halberstadt & others, 1995).

In Seattle's county hospital where I was once an orderly, we occasionally faced the task of transporting a dead body through crowded hallways without alarming the patients or their visitors. Our solution was to exploit the "Kulechov effect" by creating a context that matched people's schemas for sleeping and sedated patients: With the body's face uncovered and the sheet turned down in normal fashion, we could wheel an apparently "sleeping" body past the unsuspecting.

In everyday life, perceptual sets—for example, stereotypes about gender or culture—can color the context. Without the obvious clues of pink or blue, people will struggle over whether to call the new baby a "he" or a "she." But told an infant is "David," people (especially children) may perceive "him" as bigger and stronger than if the same infant is called "Diana" (Stern & Karraker, 1989).

Some gender differences, it seems, exist merely in the eyes of their beholders.

The effects of perceptual sets and context show how experience helps us construct perception. "We hear and apprehend only what we already half know," said Thoreau. The river of perception is fed by two streams, sensation and cognition. To return to the question—is perception innate or learned?—we can answer simply: It's both. "Simple" perceptions are the brain's creative products.

SUMMING UP

The most direct tests of the nature-nurture issue come from experiments that modify human perceptions.

Sensory Restriction and Restored Vision For many species, infancy is a critical period during which experience must activate the brain's innate visual mechanisms. If cataract removal restores eyesight to adults who were blind from birth, they remain unable to perceive the world normally. Generally, they can distinguish figure from ground and can perceive colors, but they are unable to distinguish shapes and forms. In controlled experiments, infant kittens and monkeys have been reared with severely restricted visual input. When their visual exposure is returned to normal, they, too, suffer enduring visual handicaps.

Perceptual Adaptation Human vision is remarkably adaptable. Given glasses that shift the world slightly to the left or right, or even turn it upside down, people manage to adapt their movements and, with practice, to move about with ease.

Perceptual Set Clear evidence that perception is influenced by our experience—our learned assumptions and beliefs—as well as by sensory input comes from the many demonstrations of perceptual set and context effects. The schemas we have learned help us to interpret otherwise ambiguous stimuli, a fact that helps explain why some of us "see" monsters, faces, and UFOs that others do not.

KEY TERMS AND CONCEPTS perceptual adaptation, perceptual set

Is There Perception Without Sensation?

Can we perceive only what we sense? Or, without sensory input, are we capable of extrasensory perception?

Half of Americans say they believe in extrasensory perception (ESP), and another quarter aren't sure—beliefs similar to those expressed by Japanese university students (Gallup & Newport, 1991; George, 1996; Nishizawa, 1996). The media overflow with reports of psychic wonders: crimes solved, dreams come true, futures foretold. Paranormal television (such as "Unsolved Mysteries" and "X-Files") and movies (such as *Close Encounters* and *The Exorcist*) are big business. The dial-a-psychic industry now tops $100 million a year (Emery, 1995; *Fortune*, 1995). Are there indeed people who can read minds, see through walls, or foretell the future?

In laboratory experiments, parapsychologists—those who study paranormal (literally, beyond the normal) happenings—have sometimes been astonished at psychics who seem capable of discerning the contents of sealed envelopes, influencing the roll of a die, or drawing a picture of what someone else is viewing at an unknown remote location. But other research psychologists and scientists—including 96 percent of scientists in the National Academy of Sciences—are skeptical (McConnell, 1991). If ESP is real, we would need to overturn the scientific understanding that we are creatures

whose minds are tied to our physical brains and whose perceptual experiences of the world are built of sensations. Sometimes new evidence does overturn our scientific preconceptions. So let's look at some claims for ESP, and then see why scientists remain dubious.

Claims of ESP

Claims of paranormal phenomena include astrological predictions, psychic healing, reincarnation, communication with the dead, and out-of-body frequent-flyer programs. Of these, the most respectable, testable, and—for a chapter on perception—relevant claims are for three varieties of ESP:

> *Telepathy,* or mind-to-mind communication—one person sending thoughts to another or perceiving another's thoughts.

> *Clairvoyance,* or perceiving remote events, such as sensing that a friend's house is on fire.

> *Precognition,* or perceiving future events, such as a political leader's death or a sporting event's outcome.

Closely linked with these are claims of *psychokinesis,* or "mind over matter," such as levitating a table or influencing the roll of a die.

On stage, the "psychic," like a magician, controls what the audience sees and hears. In the laboratory, the experimenter controls what the psychic sees and hears. Consider one careful experiment conducted by Bruce Layton and Bill Turnbull (1975) at the University of North Carolina. Layton and Turnbull had a computer generate a randomized 100-item list of the digits *1, 2, 3, 4,* and *5* for each of their 179 participants. They gave each student such a list in a sealed envelope and asked the student to guess which number was in each of the 100 positions.

By chance, 1 guess in 5, or 20 guesses out of the 100, should be correct. When told beforehand that ESP was beneficial, subjects averaged 20.66 correct out of 100. When told that ESP was harmful, they averaged only 19.49 correct. The difference might seem trivial—indeed, you would never notice so small an effect while observing an experiment. But a statistical analysis revealed that a difference that large among so many participants would seldom occur by chance. So Layton and Turnbull concluded that an ESP effect had occurred.

Bolstered by such experiments, believers in ESP accuse research psychologists of the same sort of skepticism that led eighteenth-century scientists to scoff at the idea that meteorites come from outer

extrasensory perception (ESP) the controversial claim that perception can occur apart from sensory input. Said to include *telepathy, clairvoyance, and precognition.*

parapsychology the study of paranormal phenomena, including ESP and psychokinesis.

> *"A man does not attain the status of Galileo merely because he is persecuted; he must also be right."*
>
> **STEPHEN JAY GOULD**
> *EVER SINCE DARWIN*
> 1973

space. Novelist Arthur Koestler, who on his death in 1983 left more than £500,000 ($800,000 American) to fund a British professorship in parapsychology, registered similar complaints. He once commented that today's skeptical scientists resemble the Italian philosophers who refused to look at Jupiter's moons through Galileo's telescope—because they "knew" that such moons did not exist. Stubborn skepticism sometimes blinds people to surprising truth.

Skepticism About ESP

The skeptics reply that an uncritical mind is a gullible mind. Time and again, they point out, so-called psychics have exploited unquestioning audiences with amazing performances in which they *appeared* to communicate with the spirits of the dead, read minds, or levitate objects—only to have it revealed that their acts were a hoax, nothing more than the illusions of stage magicians. Indeed, many psychic deceptions have been exposed by magicians, who resent the exploitation of their art in the name of psychic powers.

People's gullibility illustrates how tempting it is to label phenomena *they* don't understand as beyond explanation: "What other explanation could there possibly be but ESP?" asks the awestruck observer. Thus, before bats' echolocation ability was discovered, many people attributed bats' ability to avoid wires in complete darkness to clairvoyance (Gibson, 1979). When the bats were blinded, when their noses were sealed, when their wings were coated with varnish, they still could navigate, so what other explanation could there be but ESP?

Premonitions or Pretensions?

Can psychics see into the future? Although one might wish for a psychic stock forecaster, the tallied forecasts of "leading psychics" reveal meager accuracy. Between 1978 and 1985, the New Year's predictions of the *National Enquirer*'s favorite psychics yielded 2 accurate predictions out of 486 (Strentz, 1986). During the early 1990s, tabloid psychics were all wrong in predicting surprising events (Madonna did not become a gospel singer, Bill Cosby has not become an ambassador to South Africa, Queen Elizabeth did not abdicate her throne to enter a convent). And they missed all the big-news unexpected events, such as specific terrorist bombings, Saddam Hussein's assault on Kuwait, and the O. J. Simpson case. Before 1994, psychics offered many other predictions about

Michael Jackson—that he would marry Oprah Winfrey, become a traveling evangelist, and undergo a "complete sex change operation and insist that everyone call him Michelle"—but they missed their chance to predict his marriage to Lisa Marie Presley (CSICOP, 1994).

Analyses of psychic visions offered to police departments reveal that these, too, are no more accurate than guesses made by others (Reiser, 1982). Psychics working with the police do, however, generate dozens or even hundreds of predictions. This increases the odds of an occasional correct guess, which psychics can then report to the media. As a Spanish proverb says, "A person who talks a lot is sometimes right." Moreover, vague predictions can later be interpreted ("retrofitted") to match events, which provide a perceptual set for interpreting them. Nostradamus, a sixteenth-century French psychic, explained in an unguarded moment that his ambiguous prophecies "could not possibly be understood till they were interpreted after the event and by it." Police departments are wise to all this. When Jane Ayers Sweat and Mark Durm (1993) asked the police departments of America's 50 largest cities whether they ever used psychics, 65 percent said they never had. Of those that had, not one had found it helpful.

Are the spontaneous "visions" of ordinary people any more accurate? Consider our dreams. Do they foretell the future, as about half of university students believe (Messer & Griggs, 1989)? Or do they only seem to because we are more likely to re-

In 1996, Psychic Friends Network owner Michael Lasky spent $500,000 to purchase Eddie Murray's 500th home-run baseball (Dodd, 1996). One couldn't help but wonder not only about the poor souls whose money Lasky was spending, but why his psychics hadn't just told him when and where to sit to catch it himself.

BIZARRO

Which supposed psychic ability does Psychic Pizza claim?

call or reconstruct dreams that seem to have come true? Sixty years ago, two Harvard psychologists (Murray & Wheeler, 1937) tested the prophetic power of dreams. After aviator Charles Lindbergh's baby son was kidnapped and murdered but before the body was discovered, the researchers invited the public to report their dreams about the child. Of the 1300 dream reports submitted, how many accurately envisioned the child dead? A mere 5 percent. And how many also correctly anticipated the body's location—buried among trees? Only 4 of the 1300. Although this number was surely no better than chance, to those 4 dreamers the accuracy of their *apparent* precognitions must have seemed uncanny.

Every day each of us imagines many events. Occasionally an unlikely imagined event is bound to occur and to astonish us when it does. If you tell everyone in a group of 100 people to think "heads" before each tosses six coins, someone is likely to get all heads (whether thinking heads or not) and to feel eerie afterwards. As Chapter 1 explained, random sequences will sometimes contain weird conjunctions or streaks. Given the billions of events that occur in the world each day, and given enough days, some stunning coincidences are sure to occur. "Time converts the improbable to the inevitable," notes Stephen Jay Gould.

Finally, consider this, say the skeptics: If ESP existed, then surely someone out there could, when feeling the psychic spirit stirring, occasionally pick winning lottery numbers or blackjack outcomes (becoming fabulously wealthy or generous over time). And why doesn't some psychic make billions playing the stock market? But after tens of thousands of experiments, *there has never been discovered a reproducible ESP phenomenon, nor any individual who can convincingly demonstrate psychic ability*. A National Research Council investigation of ESP similarly concluded that "the best available evidence does not support the contention that these phenomena exist" (Druckman & Swets, 1988). And in 1995, a CIA-commissioned report evaluated ten years of military testing of psychic spies (a program previously abandoned by the CIA for having produced nothing). After $20 million was invested, the program had again produced nothing. After so many disappointing laboratory results and vague or erroneous psychic visions, the psychic spy program was scrapped (Hyman, 1996; Waller, 1995).

One skeptic, magician James Randi, has offered $10,000 to anyone who can demonstrate "*any paranormal ability*" before a group of competent experts. With pledges from others, that offer—"to anyone who proves a genuine psychic power under proper observing conditions"—has now been upped to over $1 million (Randi, 1996). Large as this sum is, the scientific seal of approval would be worth far more to anyone whose claims could be authenticated. So far, no winners have emerged, though Randi's offer has been publicized for three decades and dozens of people have been tested, sometimes under the scrutiny of an independent panel of judges.

To refute those who say there is no ESP, one need only produce a single person who can demonstrate a single reproducible ESP phenomenon. As yet, no one has exhibited any such power. Lacking such, and faced with increasing skepticism, the Parapsychological Association has lost membership, and several major parapsychological laboratories lost their funding and closed during the 1980s (Hess, 1993).

Thinking Critically About ESP

In times past, there have been all kinds of crazy ideas—that bumps on the head reveal character traits, that bloodletting is a cure-all, that each sperm cell contains a miniature person inside. When faced with such claims—or with claims of mind reading or out-of-body travel or communication with the dead—how can we separate crazy ideas from those that sound crazy but are true? At the heart of science we find a simple answer: Test them to see if they work. If they do, so much the worse for our skepticism. If they don't, so much the worse for the ideas.

This scientific attitude appears in the agreement of believers and skeptics that what parapsychology needs to give it credibility is a reproducible phenomenon and a theory to explain it. Could the Layton and Turnbull clairvoyance experiment (in which students beat chance in guessing numbers in sealed envelopes) provide such a reproducible phenomenon? The skeptical editor of the *Journal of Experimental Social Psychology*, to which Layton and Turnbull submitted their results for publication, wondered. So he and the authors reached an unusual agreement: The researchers would repeat their experiment, and the journal would then publish the results of both, regardless of the new outcome. (As this illustrates, both ESP researchers and skeptics genuinely seek truth.) The result of the second experiment? Layton and Turnbull summarized honestly and succinctly: "No [statistically] significant effects were present."

> "At the heart of science is an essential tension between two seemingly contradictory attitudes— an openness to new ideas, no matter how bizarre or counterintuitive they may be, and the most ruthless skeptical scrutiny of all ideas, old and new."
>
> **CARL SAGAN (1987)**

The ganzfeld procedure
Hoping to detect faint telepathy signals, some parapsychologists use sensory deprivation to minimize distractions.

Knowing how easily people are deceived, and lacking reproducible results, most research psychologists remain skeptical. Indeed, they are dismayed by all the shows, books, and magazines on paranormal topics. But some are newly intrigued by findings recently published by social psychologist Daryl Bem and parapsychologist Charles Honorton (1994) using the *ganzfeld procedure.* The procedure would place you in a reclining chair, play hissing white noise through headphones, and shine diffuse red light through Ping-Pong ball halves strapped over your eyes. Ostensibly, this reduction of external distractions would put you in an ideal state to receive others' thoughts, which you may hear as small voices from within. Building on earlier studies using this procedure, Bem and Honorton isolated a "sender" and "receiver" in separate, shielded chambers and had the sender concentrate for half an hour on one of four randomly selected visual images. The receivers were then asked which of four images best matched the images they experienced during the session. Over 11 studies, the receivers beat chance (25 percent accurately matched) by a small but reliable margin (32 percent accurately matched). University of Edinburgh parapsychologist Richard Morris and his students (1995, 1996) have reported similar results.

Recall that psychology-based critical inquiry asks two questions: What do you mean? And how do you know (what's your evidence)? Parapsychologists say these ganzfeld tests of ESP offer clear answers to both questions. Skeptic Ray Hyman (1994, 1996) grants that their methodology surpasses that of previous ESP experiments, but he questions certain procedural details that may have introduced bias. Intrigued, other researchers are now at work replicating these experiments. Will this be the first reliable ESP phenomenon? Or one more dashed hope, one more "phenomenon" that later will be refuted and abandoned? Stay tuned, and remember: The scientific attitude blends curious skepticism with open-minded humility. It demands that extraordinary claims be supported by clear and reliable evidence. (If at 5'7" and age 54 I claim to be able to dunk a basketball, the burden of proof would be on me to show that I can do it, not on you to prove that I couldn't.) Given such evidence, science is open to nature's occasional surprises.

As critical thinkers, we can share this attitude. We can be open to new ideas without being gullible, be discerning without being cynical. We can be critical thinkers, yet—knowing that our understanding of nature is incomplete—we can agree with Shakespeare's Hamlet that "there are more things in heaven and earth, Horatio, than are dreamt of in your philosophy."

Some things that we assume to be true—the reality of another's love, the existence or nonexistence of God, the finality of death or the reality of life after death—are beyond science. That is one reason why, after clearing away tested and rejected pseudomysteries, we can retain a humble sense of wonder regarding life's untestable mysteries.

Why are so many people predisposed to believe that ESP exists? In part, such beliefs may stem from understandable misperceptions, misinterpretations, and selective recall. But for some people there also exists an unsatisfied hunger for wonderment, an itch to experience the magical. In Britain and the United States, the founders of parapsychology were mostly people who, having lost their religious faith, were searching for a scientific basis for believing in the meaningfulness of life and the possibility of life after death (Alcock, 1985; Beloff, 1985). In the upheaval since the collapse of autocratic rule in Russia, there has come an "avalanche of the mystical, occult and pseudoscientific" (Kapitza, 1991). "Extrasensorial" healers, astrologers, and seers fascinate the awestruck public.

To feel awe and to gain a deep reverence for life, we need look no further than our own perceptual system and its capacity for organizing formless nerve impulses into colorful sights, vivid sounds, and evocative smells. Within our ordinary perceptual experiences lies much that is truly extraordinary—surely much more than has so far been dreamt of in our psychology. A century of research has revealed many of the secrets of sensation and perception, but for future generations of researchers there remain profound and genuine mysteries to solve.

We have now examined the first steps in our processing of information, from receiving sensory input to constructing meaningful perceptions. But our skull's three-pound information-processing system does much more: Under the influence of sleep, hypnosis, or drugs, it will construct unreal images (Chapter 7). It learns from our experiences, recalling them long afterward (Chapters 8 and 9). It thinks and makes intelligent plans (Chapters 10 and 11). Between our sensing and acting lies an unimaginably complex information system that, more than ever, beckons explorers of our mind's inner space.

SUMMING UP

Many people believe in or claim to experience extrasensory perception. Parapsychologists have tried to document several forms of ESP—telepathy, clairvoyance, and precognition. But for several reasons, especially the lack of a reproducible ESP effect, most research psychologists remain skeptical. New studies using the ganzfeld procedure have recently raised hopes of a possible telepathy phenomenon. Follow-up studies should soon indicate the phenomenon's reliability.

KEY TERMS AND CONCEPTS extrasensory perception (ESP), parapsychology

---

TERMS AND CONCEPTS TO REMEMBER

selective attention, p. 181

visual capture, p. 184

gestalt, p. 184

figure-ground, p. 185

grouping, p. 185

depth perception, p. 186

visual cliff, p. 186

binocular cues, p. 186

monocular cues, p. 186

retinal disparity, p. 187

convergence, p. 187

phi phenomenon, p. 190

perceptual constancy, p. 190

perceptual adaptation, p. 196

perceptual set, p. 196

extrasensory perception (ESP), p. 201

parapsychology, p. 201

CRITICAL THINKING EXERCISE
by Richard O. Straub

Now that you have read and reviewed Chapter 6, take your learning a step further by testing your critical thinking skills on the following practical problem-solving exercise.

The World Wide Web has become a distinct publishing genre with its own language and set of evolving rules and conventions. Although Web sites come in nearly every conceivable shape, size, and style, some are more informative, entertaining, or persuasive than others. Successful sites are visually pleasing, easy to navigate, and convey information efficiently.

As with the perception of any complex visual stimulus, our brains construct our perception of a Web site according to basic principles of perceptual organization and interpretation. These principles include those by which we group stimuli together into recognizable forms, those that enable the perception of depth and distance, and those by which our brains compute motion. The principle of stroboscopic movement, for example, states that our brains will interpret a rapid series of slightly varying images as movement. On a Web site such images form the basis for animation and video, which adds visual appeal and offers another venue for transmitting information. Motion on a Web page, such as a blinking "new" button, also attracts attention and conveys importance.

Now, suppose you have been commissioned by a local company to consult on the design of their home page. You are the "psychology expert" and need to explain how the following five major perceptual principles are involved in designing an effective Web site. First indicate what the principle enables the brain to perceive, and then explain how it can be exploited to enhance the effectiveness of a Web site.

Figure and ground:

Similarity:

Relative brightness:

Size–distance relationship:

Culture and perception:

Check your progress on becoming a critical thinker by comparing your answers to the sample answers in Appendix B.

chapter

7

States of Consciousness

Now playing at an inner theater near you: the premiere showing of some sleeping person's vivid dream. This never-before-seen mental movie features captivating characters wrapped in a plot so original and unlikely, yet so intricate and real-seeming, that the viewer later marvels at its creation. Awakening from a troubling dream, wrenched by its emotions, who among us has not wondered about this weird state of consciousness? How does our brain so creatively, colorfully, and completely construct this alternative conscious world? In the shadowland between our dreaming and waking consciousness, we may even wonder for a moment which realm represents reality. And what shall we make of other altered states of consciousness—of daydreaming, hypnosis, and drug-altered hallucinations?

But first questions first: What is consciousness? In every science there are concepts so fundamental they are nearly impossible to define. Biologists agree on what is alive but not on precisely what life is. In physics, matter and energy elude simple definition. To psychologists, consciousness is similarly a fundamental yet slippery concept.

Waking Consciousness

Psychologists have long explored consciousness, at first eagerly, then warily, and now with renewed vigor. What explains these swings of interest? And what are the levels and functions of consciousness?

At its beginning, psychology was sometimes defined as "the description and explanation of states of consciousness" (Ladd, 1887). But the difficulty of scientifically studying consciousness led many psychologists during the first half of this century to turn to direct observations of behavior—an approach favored by an emerging school of psychology called *behaviorism* (page 246). At midcentury, psychology was no longer defined as the study of consciousness or "mental life" but rather as the science of behavior. Psychology had nearly lost con-

As two behaviorists pass in the hall, one says: "You feel fine this morning. How do I feel?"

sciousness. Consciousness was viewed as resembling a car's speedometer: "It doesn't make the car go, it just reflects what's happening" (Seligman, 1991, p. 24).

By 1960, mental concepts began to reenter psychology. Advances in neuroscience made it possible to relate brain activity to various mental states—waking, sleeping, dreaming. Researchers were also beginning to study consciousness altered by hypnosis and drugs. Psychologists of all persuasions were affirming the importance of mental processes (cognition). Psychology was regaining consciousness.

For most psychologists today, consciousness is our awareness of ourselves and our environment. When we learn a complex concept or behavior—say, driving a car—consciousness focuses our concentration on the car and the traffic. This awareness varies with our attentional spotlight. With practice, driving becomes automatic and does not require our undivided attention—freeing our consciousness to focus on other tasks. If I call your attention to the weight of your body pressing on your buttocks as you sit reading, you will momentarily stop reading.

Beneath the surface, subconscious information processing occurs simultaneously on many parallel tracks.

Levels of Information Processing

Conscious awareness enables us to exert voluntary control and to communicate our mental states to others, yet consciousness is but the tip of the information-processing iceberg. Several of this book's other chapters (Perception, Learning, Memory, Thinking and Language, Emotion) reveal that we process much information outside our awareness. We register and react to stimuli we do not consciously perceive. We perform well-learned tasks automatically, as when keyboarding without attending to where the letters are. We change our attitudes and reconstruct our memories with no awareness of doing so. Our past influences us in ways we don't know (Greenwald & Banaji, 1995).

Beneath the surface, subconscious information processing occurs simultaneously on many parallel tracks. When we look at a flying bird, we are consciously aware of the result of our cognitive processing but not of our subprocessing of the bird's color, form, movement, distance, and identity. When we meet someone, we instantly and unconsciously react to their gender, race, and appearance, and then become aware of our response.

Stephen Kosslyn and Olivier Koenig (1992) suggest that brain events are to consciousness what a guitar's individual notes are to a chord. As a chord emerges from the interaction of different notes, so consciousness emerges from the interaction of individual brain events. As we experience the chord an instant *after* all the notes are present, so consciousness is known to lag the brain events that evoke it (Libet, 1985). (When people lift a fin-

Consciousness Our conscious awareness of ourselves and our environment is but the visible surface of our brain's information processing.

ger at will, their brain waves jump about 0.3 seconds ahead of their conscious perception of the decision.)

Unlike the parallel processing of subconscious information, conscious processing takes place in sequence (serially). Moreover, consciousness is relatively slow and has limited capacity. Consciousness is like a chief executive officer, whose many assistants automatically take care of routine business. Consider your hands. When not under conscious control, they have a life of their own, scanning your body for imperfections, grooming, gesturing. Traveling a familiar route, your hands do the driving while your mind engages in conversation. Running on automatic pilot allows consciousness—the mind's CEO—to monitor the whole system and deal with new challenges.

Novel tasks require our conscious attention. When we first arrive in a country where people drive on the other side of the road, driving commands our full attention. Or try this: If you are right handed, you can move your right foot in a smooth counterclockwise circle, and you can write the number 3 repeatedly with your right hand—but not at the same time. (If you are musically inclined, try something equally difficult: Tap a steady three times with your left hand while tapping four times with your right hand.) Both tasks require conscious attention, which can be in only one place at a time. If time is nature's way of keeping everything from happening at once, then consciousness is nature's way of keeping us from thinking and doing everything at once.

Daydreams and Fantasies

In James Thurber's classic story "The Secret Life of Walter Mitty," the bland existence of mild-mannered Walter Mitty is spiced with gratifying fantasies. As he drives past a hospital, Mitty imagines himself as Dr. Mitty, rushing to an operating room where two renowned specialists plead for his help. Again and again, the bumbling Walter Mitty relieves the tedium of his life by imagining himself as the triumphant Walter Mitty—now the world's greatest target shooter, now a heroic pilot.

Thurber's story became a classic because most of us can identify with Walter Mitty. From interview and questionnaire studies with hundreds of adults, clinical psychologist Jerome L. Singer (1975) reported that nearly everyone has daydreams or waking fantasies every day—on the job, in the classroom, walking down the street—in fact, almost anywhere at any time. Compared with older adults, young adults spend more time daydreaming

and admit to more sexual fantasies (Cameron & Biber, 1973; Giambra, 1974). About 95 percent of both men and women say they have had sexual fantasies. But men (whether gay or straight) fantasize about sex more often, more physically, and less romantically—and prefer books and videos accordingly (Leitenberg & Henning, 1995). Sexual fantasies do *not* indicate sexual problems or dissatisfaction. (If anything, sexually active and satisfied people have more sexual fantasies.)

Not all daydreaming is as overtly escapist or dramatic as Walter Mitty's. Mostly it involves the familiar details of our lives—perhaps imagining an alternative approach to a task we are performing, or picturing ourselves explaining to an instructor why a paper will be late, or replaying in our minds personal encounters that we relish or wish had gone differently.

Some individuals—perhaps 4 percent of the population—fantasize so vividly they are called fantasy-prone personalities. One study of 26 such women found that as children they had enjoyed unusually intense make-believe play with their dolls, stuffed animals, or imaginary companions (Wilson & Barber, 1983). As adults, they reported spending more than half their time fantasizing. They would relive experiences or imagine scenes so vividly that occasionally they later had trouble sorting out their remembered fantasies from their memories of actual events. When watching or imagining violent or scary scenes, they sometimes felt ill. Many reported profound mystical or religious experiences. Three-fourths had experienced orgasms solely by sexual fantasy.

consciousness
our awareness of ourselves and our environments.

fantasy-prone personality
someone who imagines and recalls experiences with lifelike vividness and who spends considerable time fantasizing.

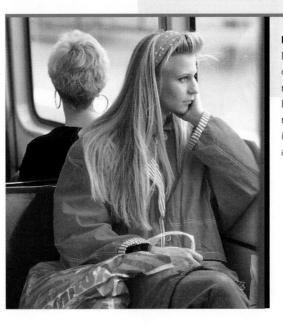

Looking into the inner world
Daydreams and fantasies are a constructive part of everyone's repertory of behavior. For these Dutch commuters, daydreams may release tension, increase creativity, illuminate solutions to problems—and even lessen boredom.

circadian rhythm
[ser-KAY-dee-an] the biological clock; regular bodily rhythms (for example, of temperature and wakefulness) that occur on a 24-hour cycle.

REM sleep
rapid eye movement sleep, a recurring sleep stage during which vivid dreams commonly occur. Also known as *paradoxical sleep* because the muscles are relaxed (except for minor twitches) but other body systems are active.

"The art of living requires us to steer a course between the two extremes of external and internal stimulation."

PSYCHOLOGIST JEROME L. SINGER (1976)

Are the hours we spend in fantasy merely a way of escaping rather than facing reality? Sometimes. But daydreaming can also be adaptive. Some daydreams help us prepare for future events by keeping us aware of unfinished business and serving as mental rehearsals. Playful fantasies enhance the creativity of scientists, artists, and writers. For children, daydreaming in the form of imaginative play feeds social and cognitive development—a fact that makes the diversion of television watching a matter of concern to some developmental psychologists (Singer, 1986).

"When I examined myself, and my methods of thought, I came to the conclusion that the gift of fantasy has meant more to me than my talent for absorbing positive knowledge."

ALBERT EINSTEIN

Daydreams may also substitute for impulsive behavior. People who are prone to delinquency and violence or who seek the artificial highs of dangerous drugs have fewer vivid fantasies (Singer, 1976). Perhaps Walter Mitty's imaginative reveries not only rescued him from boredom but also allowed him to indulge his impulses within the safety of his inner world.

Consciousness occurs in varied states. We have not only normal seeing and hearing, reasoning and remembering, daydreams and fantasies, but also the altered consciousness of sleep, hypnotic states, chemically induced hallucinations, and near-death visions.

SUMMING UP

Psychology began as the study of consciousness, then turned to the study of observable behavior. Today, scientific investigation of states of mind is again one of psychology's pursuits. Speedy, parallel processing handles subconscious information; conscious processing is serial and much slower.

Virtually everyone daydreams, especially fantasy-prone people and especially in times when attention can be freed from the tasks at hand. Daydreaming can be adaptive; it can help us prepare for future events and may substitute for impulsive behavior.

KEY TERMS AND CONCEPTS consciousness, fantasy-prone personality

Sleep and Dreams

Sleep—sweet, renewing, mysterious sleep. Sleep—the irresistible tempter to whom we must all succumb. Sleep—the mantle that covers human thought. What is it? Why must we have it? Why do we spend a third of our lives—some 25 years, on average—sleeping? What and why do we dream?

Sleep's age-old mysteries have intrigued humans for centuries. Now, some of these mysteries are being solved. In laboratories throughout the world, thousands have slept attached to recording devices while others observe. By recording sleepers' brain waves and muscle movements, by observing and awakening them from time to time, the sleep-watchers glimpse things that a thousand years of common sense never told us. Perhaps you can anticipate some of their discoveries. Are the following statements true or false?

1 When people dream of performing some activity, their limbs often move in concert with the dream (pages 212–213).

2 Older adults sleep more than young adults (Figure 7.6).

3 After two or three sleepless days, a person's performance on a brief but demanding intellectual task suffers (page 215).

4 Sleepwalkers are acting out their dreams (pages 212–213).

5 Sleep experts recommend treating insomnia with an occasional sleeping pill (page 217).

6 Some people dream every night; others seldom dream at all (page 214).

All these statements (adapted from Palladino & Carducci, 1983) are false. Let's see why.

"I love to sleep. Do you? Isn't it great? It really is the best of both worlds. You get to be alive and unconscious."

COMEDIAN RITA RUDNER
1993

The Rhythm of Sleep

The rhythm of the day parallels the rhythm of life—from our waking to a new day's birth to our nightly return to what Shakespeare called "death's counterfeit." Our bodies synchronize with the 24-hour cycle of day and night through a biological clock called the circadian rhythm (from the Latin *circa*, "about," and *dies*, "day"). Our body temperature, for example, rises as morning approaches, peaks during the day, dips for a time in early afternoon (when many people take siestas), and then begins to drop again before we go to sleep. Awake at 4:00 A.M., with a depressed body, we may fret over concerns: Does a lovers' spat signal a split? Does a child's moodiness mean more trouble ahead? By midday, our body energized, we fret less. Pulling an all-nighter, we feel groggiest about 4:00 A.M., but we feel a second wind as our normal wake-up time arrives.

Recent evidence suggests that thinking is sharpest and memory most accurate when people are at their daily peak in circadian arousal. University students often are "evening persons," report Cynthia May and Lynne Hasher (1997). Their performance typically improves across the day. Older adults tend to be "morning persons," with performance declining as the day wears on.

A transcontinental flight disrupts our circadian rhythm and we experience jet lag, mainly because we are awake when our circadian rhythm cries, "Sleep!" If we stay up late and sleep in on weekends, our biological clock begins to reset itself. When the weekend ends, the result may be "Sunday night insomnia" and "Monday morning blues." (Those who sleep till noon on Sunday and then go to bed just 11 hours later in preparation for the new workweek often find sleep elusive.)

Mysteriously, young adults isolated without clocks or daylight typically adopt a 25-hour day. This helps explain why many people find it easier to jet west, with an extended day, than east; why rotating shift workers adapt better to progressively later shifts than to earlier shifts; why until our later years we must discipline ourselves to get to bed on time and force ourselves to get up. When placed under constant illumination, most animals, too, exceed a 24-hour day.

There is also a biological rhythm during our sleep. About every 90 or 100 minutes we pass through a cycle of five distinct sleep stages. This elementary fact was unknown until 8-year-old Armond Aserinsky went to bed one night in 1952. His father, Eugene, a University of Chicago graduate student, needed to test an electroencephalograph he had been repairing during the day (Aserinsky, 1988; Seligman & Yellen, 1987). He placed electrodes near Armond's eyes to record the rolling eye movements believed to occur during sleep. Before long, the machine went wild, tracing deep zigzags on the graph paper. Aserinsky thought the machine was still broken. But as the night proceeded, the activity periodically recurred, indicating, Aserinsky finally realized, fast, jerky eye movements accompanied by energetic brain

activity. When he awakened Armond during one such episode, the boy reported he was having a dream. Aserinsky had discovered what we now know as REM sleep (rapid *eye movement* sleep).

To find out if similar cycles occur during adult sleep, Nathaniel Kleitman (1960) and Aserinsky pioneered procedures that have now been used with thousands of volunteers. To appreciate both their methods and findings, imagine yourself as a participant. As the hour grows late, you yawn in response to reduced brain metabolism. Yawning stretches your neck muscles and increases your heart rate, thus increasing the bloodflow to your brain and your alertness (Moorcroft, 1993). When you are ready for bed, the researcher glues electrodes to your scalp (to detect your brain waves), just outside the corners of your eyes (to detect eye movements), and on your chin (to detect muscle tension) (Figure 7.1). Other devices allow the researcher to record your heart rate, your respiration rate, and even the degree of your genital arousal.

If our natural circadian rhythm was attuned to a 23-hour cycle, would we instead need to discipline ourselves to stay up later at night and sleep in longer in the morning? Do older adults, who typically prefer an earlier bedtime than university students, have a shorter circadian rhythm?

Figure **7.1**

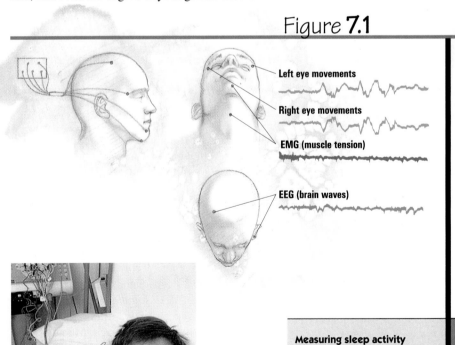

Measuring sleep activity

Sleep researchers measure brain-wave activity, eye movements, and muscle tension by electrodes that pick up weak electrical signals from the brain, eye, and facial muscles. (From Dement, 1978.)

Figure 7.2

Brain waves and sleep stages
The regular alpha waves of an awake, relaxed stage are quite different from the slower, larger delta waves of deep Stage 4 sleep. Although the rapid REM sleep waves resemble the near-waking Stage 1 sleep waves, the body is more aroused during REM sleep than during Stage 1 sleep. (From Dement, 1978.)

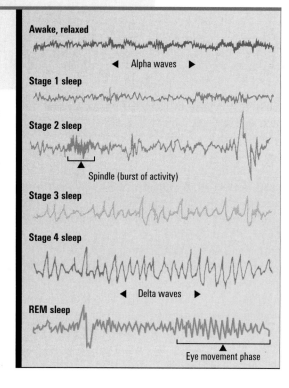

Awake, relaxed

◄ Alpha waves ►

Stage 1 sleep

Stage 2 sleep

Spindle (burst of activity)

Stage 3 sleep

Stage 4 sleep

◄ Delta waves ►

REM sleep

Eye movement phase

alpha waves
the relatively slow brain waves of a relaxed, awake state.

hallucinations
false sensory experiences, such as seeing something in the absence of an external visual stimulus.

delta waves
the large, slow brain waves associated with deep sleep.

When you are in bed with your eyes closed, the researcher in the next room sees on the EEG the relatively slow alpha waves of your awake but relaxed state (Figure 7.2). As you adapt to all this equipment and grow tired, you slip into sleep and begin your dive toward deeper and deeper levels. Your breathing rate slows and your brain waves slow further and show the irregular waves of Stage 1 sleep. During this light sleep, which lasts about 2 minutes, you may experience fantastic images, which are like hallucinations—sensory experiences that occur without a sensory stimulus. You may have a sensation of falling (at which moment your body may suddenly jerk) or of floating weightlessly. Such "hypnogogic" sensations may later be incorporated into memories. People who claim to have been abducted by aliens, for example, commonly recall being floated off their beds.

Soon, you relax more deeply and begin about 20 minutes of Stage 2 sleep, characterized by the periodic appearance of *sleep spindles*—bursts of rapid, rhythmic brain-wave activity. Although you can still be awakened without too much difficulty during this phase, you are now clearly asleep. Sleeptalking—usually garbled or nonsensical—can occur during this or any other sleep stage (Mahowald & Ettinger, 1990).

Then for the next few minutes you go through the transitional Stage 3 to the deep sleep of Stage 4. First in Stage 3, and increasingly in Stage 4, your brain emits large, slow delta waves. These

stages together are therefore called *slow-wave sleep*. They last for about 30 minutes, during which you are hard to awaken. Curiously, it is at the end of the deep sleep of Stage 4 that children may wet the bed or begin walking in their sleep. About 20 percent of 3- to 12-year-olds have at least one episode of sleepwalking, usually lasting 2 to 10 minutes; some 5 percent have repeated episodes (Giles & others, 1994).

Even when you are deeply asleep, your brain somehow processes the meaning of certain stimuli. You move around on your bed, but you manage not to fall out of it. If you sleep with your babies, you will not roll over and suffocate them. The occasional roar of passing vehicles may leave deep sleep undisturbed, but the cry from a baby's nursery quickly interrupts it. So does the sound of your name—a stimulus humans are ever alert for. EEG recordings confirm that the brain's auditory cortex responds to sound stimuli even during sleep (Kutas, 1990). All this reminds us of one of this book's basic lessons: We process most information outside of conscious awareness.

About an hour after you first fall asleep, a strange thing happens. Rather than continuing in deep slumber, you ascend from your initial sleep dive. Returning through Stage 3 and Stage 2 (where you spend about half your night), you enter the most intriguing sleep phase of all—REM sleep (Figure 7.3). For about 10 minutes, your brain waves become rapid and saw-toothed, more like those of the nearly awake Stage 1 sleep. But unlike Stage 1 sleep, REM sleep is a time when your heart rate rises, your breathing becomes rapid and irregular, and every half minute or so your eyes dart around in a momentary burst of activity be-

"Boy are my eyes tired! I had REM sleep all night long."

Figure **7.3**

The stages in a typical night's sleep Most people pass through the 5-stage sleep cycle several times, with the periods of Stage 4 sleep and then Stage 3 sleep diminishing and REM sleep periods increasing in duration. The second graph plots this increasing REM sleep and decreasing deep sleep based on data from 30 young adults. (Cartwright, 1978; Webb, 1992.)

hind closed lids. Because anyone watching a sleeper's eyes can notice these REM bursts, it is amazing that science was ignorant of REM sleep until 1952.

During REM sleep, your genitals become aroused and you have an erection or increased vaginal lubrication. The common "morning erection" stems from the night's last REM period, often just before waking. Except during very scary dreams, genital arousal always occurs, regardless of whether the dream's content is sexual (Karacan & others, 1966). In young men, sleep-related erections outlast REM periods, lasting 30 to 45 minutes on average (Karacan & others, 1983; Schiavi & Schreiner-Engel, 1988). A typical 25-year-old man therefore has an erection during nearly half his night's sleep, a 65-year-old man for one-quarter. Many men troubled by "erectile disorder" (impotence) have morning erections, which suggests that their problem is not with their genitals.

Although your brain's motor cortex is active during REM sleep, your brainstem blocks its mes-

sages, leaving your muscles relaxed—so relaxed that, except for an occasional finger, toe, or facial twitch, you are essentially paralyzed. Moreover, you cannot easily be awakened. Thus, REM sleep is sometimes called *paradoxical* sleep; internally the body is aroused while externally it appears calm.

Even more intriguing than the paradoxical nature of REM sleep is what the rapid eye movements announce: the beginning of a dream. Even those who claim they never dream will, more than 80 percent of the time, recall a dream after being awakened during REM sleep. Unlike the fleeting images of Stage 1 sleep, REM sleep dreams are often emotional and usually storylike. (People oc-

. . . those who say, "I never dream" actually spend about 600 hours a year experiencing some 1500 dreams . . .

casionally recall dreams when awakened from stages other than REM sleep, but these dreams usually contain a single vague image, such as, "I was trying to borrow something from someone.")

Are the eye movements linked to a dream's visual aspects? Is the dreamer "watching" the dream as if it were a private movie projected in the mind's inner theater? Most researchers believe not: The darting eyes, like the occasional twitching of muscles, may merely reflect the overflow of the dreamer's active nervous system (Chase & Morales, 1983).

As the night wears on, this sleep cycle repeats itself about every 90 minutes. Curiously, small animals have shorter sleep cycles (rats, 10 minutes) than big animals (elephants, 100+ minutes) (Hobson, 1989). During the night, deep Stage 4 sleep gets progressively briefer and then disappears, and the REM sleep period gets longer. By morning, 20 to 25 percent of our average night's sleep—some 100 minutes—has been REM sleep. This means that those who say, "I never dream" actually spend about 600 hours a year experiencing some 1500 dreams, or more than 100,000 dreams over a typical lifetime—dreams they rarely remember.

People rarely snore during dreams. When REM starts, snoring stops.

Why Do We Sleep?

Sleep commands roughly one-third of our lives. Deprived of it, we begin to feel terrible; our bodies yearn for it. It takes an alarm to awaken; sleep beckons while we listen to a lecture; we lack the vigor needed for peak functioning.

Obviously, we need sleep—enough, says sleep researcher William Moorcroft (1993), so you will not feel tired the next day. But why? It seems an easy question to answer: Just keep people awake for several days and note how they deteriorate. If

you were a volunteer in such an experiment, how do you think it would affect your body and mind?

Of course, you would become terribly drowsy at times—especially during the hours when your biological clock programs you to sleep. But could lack of sleep physically damage you? Would it noticeably alter your biochemistry or body organs? Would you become emotionally disturbed? Intellectually disoriented?

Owing to modern light bulbs, shift work, and social diversions, people in industrialized nations are able to sleep less than they did a century ago. Thomas Edison (1948, pp. 52, 178), inventor of the light bulb, was pleased to accept credit for this. For him, lost sleep meant more time and opportunity.

> When I went through Switzerland in a motor-car, so that I could visit little towns and villages, I noted the effect of artificial light on the inhabitants. Where water power and electric light had been developed, everyone seemed normally intelligent. When these appliances did not exist, and the natives went to bed with the chickens, staying there till daylight, they were far less intelligent.

Actually, a major effect of lessened sleep, as fatigued college students know, is sleepiness, and sometimes a general malaise (Mikulincer & others, 1989). People today more than ever suffer from sleep patterns that thwart their having an energized feeling of well-being. Teenagers typically need 8 or 9 hours sleep, but they now average nearly 2 hours less sleep a night than their counterparts of 80 years ago (Holden, 1993; Maas, 1998). Many fill this need by using homeroom for their first siesta and after-lunch study hall for a slumber party. As sleep researcher William Dement (1990) laments, "The national sleep debt is larger and more important than the national debt." (To test whether you are one of the many sleep-deprived college students, see Table 7.1.)

Some sleep-loss effects are more subtle. One such effect is suppression of the disease-fighting immune system (Beardsley, 1996; Irwin & others, 1994). In rats, sleep deprivation increases the pathogens normally suppressed by the immune system. In humans, sleep deprivation suppresses immune cells that fight off viral infections. When infections do set in, immune-boosting sleep typically increases.

Other sleep-loss effects include impaired creativity and concentration, slight hand tremors, irritability, slowed performance, and occasional misperceptions on monotonous tasks (Horne, 1989; Koslowsky & Babkoff, 1992). These effects can be devastating for some tasks, such as driving and piloting. Some 30 percent of Australian high-

Sleepless and suffering This fatigued, sleep-deprived person may also experience a depressed immune system, impaired concentration, and greater vulnerability to accidents.

Are You Sleep Deprived?

Table **7.1**

Cornell University psychologist James Maas reports that most college students suffer the consequences of less than needed sleep. To see if you are in that group, answer the following true-false questions:

True	False	
☐	☐	1. I need an alarm clock in order to wake up at the appropriate time.
☐	☐	2. It's a struggle for me to get out of bed in the morning.
☐	☐	3. Weekday mornings I hit the snooze bar several times to get more sleep.
☐	☐	4. I feel tired, irritable, and stressed out during the week.
☐	☐	5. I have trouble concentrating and remembering.
☐	☐	6. I feel slow with critical thinking, problem solving, and being creative.
☐	☐	7. I often fall asleep watching TV.
☐	☐	8. I often fall asleep in boring meetings or lectures or in warm rooms.
☐	☐	9. I often fall asleep after heavy meals or after a low dose of alcohol.
☐	☐	10. I often fall asleep while relaxing after dinner.
☐	☐	11. I often fall asleep within five minutes of getting into bed.
☐	☐	12. I often feel drowsy while driving.
☐	☐	13. I often sleep extra hours on weekend mornings.
☐	☐	14. I often need a nap to get through the day.
☐	☐	15. I have dark circles around my eyes.

If you answered "true" to three or more items, you probably are not getting enough sleep. To determine your sleep needs, Maas recommends that you "go to bed 15 minutes earlier than usual every night for the next week—and continue this practice by adding 15 more minutes each week—until you wake without an alarm clock and feel alert all day." (Quiz reprinted with permission from James B. Maas, *The sleep advantage: Preparing your mind for peak performance* [New York: Villard, 1998].)

way deaths occur when drivers fall asleep on long, monotonous roads (Maas, 1998). "Rest. That's what I need is rest," said Eastern Airlines Captain James Reeves to the control tower on a September 1974 morning—30 minutes before crashing his airliner at low altitude, killing the crew and all 68 passengers (Moorcroft, 1993). Consider also the *Exxon Valdez* oil spill; Union Carbide's Bhopal, India, disaster; and the Three Mile Island and Chernobyl nuclear accidents—they all occurred after midnight, when operators were likely to be drowsiest. Apparently asleep, the *Exxon Valdez* mate at the helm was unresponsive to clear signals to turn his vessel back into the shipping lanes.

On short, highly motivating tasks, however, sleep deprivation has little effect. When 17-year-old Randy Gardner made his way into the *Guinness Book of World Records* by staying awake for 11 days, he suffered hallucinations and speech and movement problems, and at times had to keep moving to stay awake. Nevertheless, during his final night of sleeplessness, Gardner managed to beat researcher Dement 100 straight times in a pinball game. He then slept 15 hours and awoke feeling fine (Coren, 1996; Gulevich & others, 1966).

Why, then, must we sleep? We have few answers, but sleep may have evolved for at least two reasons: First, sleep suits our ecological niche. When darkness precluded our ancestors' hunting and food gathering and made travel treacherous, they were better off asleep in a cave, out of harm's way. Animals with the least reason to fear predation or the most need to graze tend to sleep less. Elephants and horses sleep 3 to 4 hours a day, gorillas 12 hours, cats 15 hours, and bats 20 hours.

Second, sleep helps us recuperate. It helps restore body tissues, especially those of the brain. As we sleep, our brain is actively repairing and reorganizing itself and consolidating memories. Our lowered body temperature during sleep also conserves energy for the daytime hours.

Sleep may also play a role in the growth process. During deep sleep, the pituitary gland releases a growth hormone. As adults grow older, they release less of this hormone, and they spend less time in deep sleep (Pekkanen, 1982). These physiological discoveries are only beginning to solve the ongoing riddle of sleep. As researcher Dement (1978, p. 83) deadpanned, "We have miles to go before we sleep."

A few of the unanswered questions about sleep: Why do we sleep more when we are young? Why do some animals sleep most of the day, others not at all? Why, when REM sleep paralyzes our muscles, do we twitch and jerk? Most important, what is sleep's function? (Adapted from UCLA Brain Research Institute, 1989)

The current record holder, Robert ("Ramblin Rob") McDonald, reportedly stayed awake for 18 days and 22 hours in a 1986 rocking chair marathon.

1993 Time/CNN poll:
"How many hours do you sleep each night?"

Under six	12%
Six	26
Seven	30
Eight	28
Over eight	3

Sleep Disorders

The idea that "everyone needs 8 hours of sleep" is untrue. Newborns spend nearly two-thirds of their day asleep, most adults no more than one-third. Age-related differences in average time spent sleeping are rivaled by differences in the normal amount of sleep among individuals at any age. Some people thrive with fewer than 6 hours of sleep per night; others regularly sleep 9 hours or more. Sleep patterns may be genetically influenced. When Wilse Webb and Scott Campbell (1983) checked the pattern and duration of sleep among fraternal and identical twins, only the identical twins were strikingly similar.

Allowed to sleep unhindered, most humans will sleep 9 to 10 hours a night, reports Stanley Coren (1996). Given such sleep, they do not become groggy. Rather, long sleepers awake refreshed, sustain better moods, and perform more efficient and accurate work than people who get less sleep.

> Allowed to sleep unhindered, most humans will sleep 9 to 10 hours a night.

People who sleep less than 7 hours often show signs of sleep deprivation—depressed immune systems, poorer judgments, irritability, and more accidents. As a demonstration of the costs of widespread sleep deprivation among today's adolescents and adults, Coren capitalized on a naturally occurring experiment that manipulates sleep length—the "spring forward" to daylight time and "fall backward" to standard time. Searching millions of records, he found that in both Canada and the United States, accidents increase immediately after the shortened sleep associated with the spring time change. In Canada, for example, traffic accidents during 1991 and 1992 were 7 percent higher the Monday after the spring time change than on the Monday before, and they were 7 percent *lower* on the Monday following the extra sleep bestowed by the fall time change (Figure 7.4).

Whatever their normal need for sleep, some 10 to 15 percent of adults complain of insomnia— persistent problems in falling or staying asleep. True insomnia is not the occasional inability to sleep that we experience when anxious or excited. For a stressed organism, alertness is natural and adaptive. Moreover, from middle age on, sleep is seldom uninterrupted. Occasional awakenings become the norm, not something to fret over or treat with medication.

> "The lion and the lamb shall lie down together, but the lamb will not be very sleepy."
>
> **WOODY ALLEN**
> IN THE MOVIE *LOVE AND DEATH*
> 1975

Sometimes people fret unnecessarily about their sleep. Scientists have learned to doubt people's fretful sleep reports (Coren, 1996). In laboratory studies, insomnia complainers do get less sleep than others, but they typically overestimate, by about double, how long it took them to fall asleep, and they underestimate by nearly half how long they actually slept. Even if we've been awake only an hour or two, we may *think* we've had little sleep, because it's the waking part we remember. When researchers awaken people repeatedly during the night, some recall having slept soundly.

Figure **7.4**

Canadian traffic accidents, 1991 and 1992 The Monday after the spring time change, when people lose sleep, accidents increased as compared with the Monday before. After the fall time change, they dropped. (Adapted from Coren, 1996.)

The most common quick fixes for true insomnia, sleeping pills and alcohol, can aggravate the problem. Both reduce REM sleep and can leave a person with next-day blahs. With continued use, one needs bigger doses to get an effect, and when the drug is discontinued, the insomnia may worsen. Scientists are searching for natural chemicals that are abundant during sleep and might be synthesized as a sleep aid without side effects. In the meantime, sleep experts offer other natural alternatives:

- Relax before bedtime, using dimmer light.

- Avoid caffeine (this includes chocolate) after late afternoon and avoid rich foods before bedtime. A glass of milk may help. (Milk provides raw materials for the manufacture of serotonin, a neurotransmitter that facilitates sleep.)

- Sleep on a regular schedule (rise at the same time even after a restless night) and avoid naps. A regular sleep schedule boosts daytime alertness, too, as shown in a recent experiment in which University of Arizona students slept 7.5 hours a night on either a varying or consistent schedule (Manber & others, 1996).

- Exercise regularly but not in the late evening (late afternoon is best).

- Reassure yourself that the temporary loss of sleep causes no great harm, certainly nothing worth losing sleep over. "Sleep is like love or happiness," notes Wilse Webb (1992, p. 170). "If you pursue it too ardently it will elude you."

- If nothing else works, aim for less sleep; go to bed later or get up earlier.

"In 1757 Benjamin Franklin gave us the axiom, 'Early to bed, early to rise, makes a man healthy, wealthy, and wise.' It would be more accurate to say 'consistently to bed and consistently to rise . . .'"

JAMES B. MAAS
*THE SLEEP ADVANTAGE:
PREPARING YOUR MIND
FOR PEAK PERFORMANCE
1998*

More rare but also more severe than insomnia are the sleep disorders narcolepsy and sleep apnea. People with narcolepsy (from *narco*, "numbness," and *lepsy*, "seizure") suffer periodic, overwhelming sleepiness. This usually lasts less than 5 minutes, but sometimes occurs at the most inopportune times, perhaps just after taking a terrific swing at a softball or when laughing loudly or shouting angrily (Dement, 1978). In severe cases, the person may collapse directly into a brief period of REM sleep, with its accompanying loss of muscular tension. Those who suffer from narcolepsy—1 in 2000 people, estimates the Stanford University Center for Narcolepsy (1996)—must live with

extra caution. As a traffic menace, "snoozing is second only to boozing," says the American Sleep Disorders Association, and those with narcolepsy are especially at risk (Aldrich, 1989).

The National Heart, Lung, and Blood Institute reports that 1 in 25 people (mostly overweight men) suffer from sleep apnea—a disorder that was unknown before modern sleep research. They intermittently stop breathing during sleep. (*Apnea* means "stopping respiration.") After an airless minute or so, decreased blood oxygen arouses the sleeper to awaken and snort in air for a few seconds. The process can repeat more than 400 times a night, depriving the person of slow-wave sleep. Apart from complaints of sleepiness and irritability during the day—and their mates' complaints about their loud "snoring"—apnea sufferers are often unaware of their disorder.

Other sleepers, mostly children, experience night terrors. The person might sit up or walk around, talk incoherently, experience a doubling of heart and breathing rates, and appear terrified (Hartmann, 1981). The night-terror sufferer seldom awakens fully and recalls little or nothing the next morning—at most, a fleeting, frightening image. Night terrors are not nightmares (which, like other dreams, typically occur during early morning REM sleep). As with sleepwalking, night terrors usually occur during the first few hours of sleep and begin during Stage 4 sleep (Figure 7.5). Family members usually guide a sleepwalker back to bed or try to awaken and reassure the person with night terrors. As we grow older, we have less of the deep Stage 4 sleep, but this also usually means an end to night terrors and sleepwalking.

insomnia
a sleep disorder involving recurring problems in falling or staying asleep.

narcolepsy
a sleep disorder characterized by uncontrollable sleep attacks. The sufferer may lapse directly into REM sleep, often at inopportune times.

sleep apnea
a sleep disorder characterized by temporary cessations of breathing during sleep and consequent momentary reawakenings.

night terrors
a sleep disorder characterized by high arousal and an appearance of being terrified; unlike nightmares, night terrors occur during Stage 4 sleep, within 2 or 3 hours of falling asleep, and are seldom remembered.

Figure 7.5

Night terrors and nightmares
Night terrors occur within 2 or 3 hours of falling asleep, during Stage 4 sleep. Nightmares occur toward morning, during REM sleep. (From Hartmann, 1984.)

"I do not believe that I am now dreaming, but I cannot prove that I am not."

PHILOSOPHER BERTRAND RUSSELL
1872–1970

Would you suppose that people dream if blind from birth? Studies of blind people in France, Hungary, and Egypt all found them dreaming of using their nonvisual senses—hearing, touching, smelling, tasting (Buquet, 1988; Taha, 1972; Vekassy, 1977).

A popular sleep myth: If you dream you are falling and hit the ground (or if you dream of dying), you die. (Unfortunately, those who could confirm these ideas are not around to do so. Some people, however, have had such dreams and are alive to report them.)

Dreams

Discovering the link between REM sleep and dreaming opened a new era in dream research. Instead of relying on someone's hazy recall hours or days after having a dream, researchers could catch dreams as they happened. They could awaken people during a REM sleep period, or within 3 minutes afterward, and hear a vivid dream account.

What Do We Dream?

REM dreams—"hallucinations of the sleeping mind"—are vivid, emotional, and bizarre. Several times a night, you are the creator and producer of a surrealistic mental movie, in which events frequently occur in a jumbled sequence, scenes change suddenly, people appear and disappear, and physical laws, such as gravity, may be violated. Yet dreams are so vivid we may confuse them with reality. Occasionally, we may be sufficiently aware during a dream to wonder whether we are, in fact, dreaming. When experiencing such *lucid dreams*, some people are able to test their state of consciousness. If they can perform some absurd act, such as floating in the air, then they know they are dreaming.

Although we are more likely to be awakened by our most emotional dreams and to remember them, many dreams are rather ordinary. When awakened during REM sleep, people report dreams with sexual imagery less often than you might think. In one study, only 1 in 10 dreams among young men and 1 in 30 among young women had sexual overtones (Hall & Van de Castle, 1966).

More commonly, we dream of daily life events, such as a meeting at work or taking an exam. In the month after the San Francisco earthquake, 4 in 10 college students in the area (but only 1 in 20 students elsewhere) had one or more nightmares about an earthquake (Wood & others, 1992). Six years of our life we spend dreaming, most of which is anything but sweet: People commonly dream of repeatedly failing in an attempt to do something; of being attacked, pursued, or rejected; or of experiencing misfortune (Hall & others, 1982).

Across the world, people of all ages show a curious gender difference in dream content. Women dream of males and females equally often, whereas 65 percent of the characters in men's dreams are males. No one is sure why. Whatever its significance, dream researcher Calvin Hall (1984) believed we can add this fact to the short list of psychological gender differences.

"For what one has dwelt on by day, these things are seen in visions of the night."

MENANDER OF ATHENS
342–292 B.C.
FRAGMENT

The story line of our dreams—what Sigmund Freud called their manifest content—often incorporates experiences and preoccupations from the day's events, especially in our first dreams of the night. The sensory stimuli of our sleeping environment may also intrude. A particular odor or the telephone's ringing may be instantly and ingeniously woven into the dream story. In one experiment, William Dement and Edward Wolpert (1958) lightly sprayed cold water on dreamers' faces. Compared with sleepers who did not get the cold water treatment, these sleepers were more likely to dream about water—about a waterfall, a leaky roof, or even about being sprayed by someone. Even while in REM sleep, focused on internal stimuli, we maintain some awareness of changes in our external environment.

So, could we learn a foreign language by listening to tapes during sleep? If only it were so easy. While sleeping we can learn to associate a sound with a mild electric shock (and to react to the sound accordingly). But we do not remember taped information played while we are soundly asleep (Eich, 1990; Wyatt & Bootzin, 1994). In fact, experiences that occur during the 5 minutes just before falling asleep are typically lost from memory (Roth & others, 1988). This explains why sleep apnea patients, who repeatedly awaken with a gasp and then immediately fall back to sleep, do not recall the episodes. It also explains why dreams that momentarily awaken us are mostly forgotten by morning. To remember a dream, get up and stay awake for a while.

Why Do We Dream?

In his landmark book *The Interpretation of Dreams*, published in 1900, Freud offered "the most valuable of all the discoveries it has been my good fortune to make." He argued that by fulfilling wishes, a dream provides a psychic safety valve that discharges otherwise unacceptable feelings. According to Freud, a dream's manifest content is but a censored, symbolic version of its latent content, which consists of unconscious drives and wishes that would be threatening if expressed directly. Although most dreams have no overt sexual imagery, Freud nevertheless believed that most adult dreams can be "traced back by analysis to *erotic wishes*." In Freud's view, a gun, for example, might be a disguised representation of a penis.

Although Freud considered dreams the key to understanding our inner conflicts, his critics say that it's time to wake up from Freud's dream theory, which actually is one of his greatest failures. Dream interpretation leads down a blind alley, say the critics. Some contend that even if dreams were symbolic, they could be interpreted as one wishes. Others maintain that there is nothing hidden in dreams. A dream about a gun, they say, is a dream about a gun. Legend has it that even Freud, who loved to smoke cigars, remarked that "sometimes, a cigar is just a cigar."

Freud's theory of dreams is giving way to newer theories. One of these sees dreams as *information processing*: Dreams may help sift, sort, and fix in memory our day's experiences. Following stressful experiences or intense learning periods, REM sleep increases (Palumbo, 1978). What is more, there is "consistent and compelling evidence" that REM sleep facilitates memory (McGrath & Cohen, 1978). In experiments, people have heard unusual phrases or learned to find hidden visual images before bedtime. If awakened every time they began REM sleep, they remembered less the next morning than if awakened during other sleep stages (Empson & Clarke, 1970; Karni & Sagi, 1994). A night of solid sleep (and dreaming) does, it seems, have an important place in a student's life. As we sleep, our bodies are consolidating the day's important memories.

Another explanation of dreams proposes that

they may also serve a physiological function. Perhaps dreams—or the associated brain activity of REM sleep—provide the sleeping brain with periodic stimulation. As you may recall from Chapter 3, stimulating experiences develop and preserve the brain's neural pathways. This theory makes sense from a developmental point of view. Infants, whose neural networks are just developing, spend a great deal of time in REM sleep (Figure 7.6).

Figure 7.6

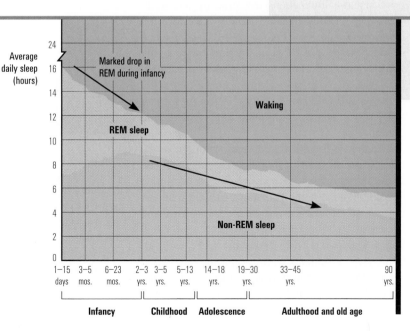

Sleep across the life span As we age, our sleep patterns change. During our first few months, we spend progressively less time in REM sleep. During our first 20 years, we spend progressively less time asleep. (Adapted from Snyder & Scott, 1972.)

REM rebound
the tendency for REM sleep to increase following REM sleep deprivation (created by repeated awakenings during REM sleep).

Still other physiological theories propose that dreams erupt from neural activity that spreads upward from the brainstem (Antrobus, 1991; Hobson, 1988). According to one version, this neural activity is random, and dreams are the brain's attempt to make sense of it. Much as a neurosurgeon can produce hallucinations by stimulating different parts of a patient's cortex, so can stimulation originating within the brain. Psychologists Martin Seligman and Amy Yellen (1987) note that the seconds-long bursts of rapid eye movements dur-

> A night of solid sleep (and dreaming) does, it seems, have an important place in a student's life. As we sleep, our bodies are consolidating the day's important memories.

ing REM sleep coincide with bursts of activity in the visual cortex. If awakened during one of these bursts of brain activity, people report vivid experiences, usually dramatic hallucinations.

Given these visual scenes, how does our cognitive machinery react? It does what it usually does with meaningless stimuli—it imposes meaning. (Recall from Chapter 2 how split-brain patients instantly "explain" puzzling actions commanded by their right hemisphere.) Thus, say Seligman and Yellen, our ever-active brain weaves a story line from whatever is available—residues from the day's experiences, the alarm clock's ringing, or the brief visual hallucinations triggered by the brainstem. The emotion-related limbic system also becomes active during REM sleep. PET scans taken of sleeping people (if you can imagine sleeping while lying in a brain-scanning machine) reveal increased activity in several brain areas, especially the amygdala (Maquet & others, 1996). Add its activity to the brain's commotion and—voila!—we dream.

The theory, then, is that dreams spring from the mind's relentless effort to make sense of unrelated visual bursts, which are given their emotional tone by the limbic system. This helps explain many of our dream experiences, such as the sudden and bizarre changes in scene (triggered by a new visual burst). Dream reports by Seligman's University of Pennsylvania students confirm that the most vivid dream images are the surprising, discontinuous aspects of the dream; the other, less vivid images are those we presumably conjure up to string the visual bursts together.

The function of dreams provokes vigorous debate, but the disputants all agree that we *need* REM sleep. Deprived of it by repeated awakenings, people return more and more quickly to the REM stage after falling back to sleep. When finally allowed to sleep undisturbed, they literally sleep like babies, with increased REM sleep—a phenomenon called REM rebound. The withdrawal of REM-suppressing sleeping medications also increases REM sleep, but with accompanying nightmares.

Most other mammals also experience REM sleep and REM rebound. Animals' need for REM sleep suggests that its causes and functions are deeply biological. That REM sleep occurs in mammals (and not in animals such as fish, whose behavior is less influenced by learning) also fits the information-processing theory of dreams. All of which serves to remind us once again of another basic lesson: Biological and psychological explanations of behavior are partners, not competitors.

But if dreams serve physiological functions and lack the disguised meanings that Freud supposed, are they psychologically meaningless? Are they as nonsensically random as Alice's dreams of Wonderland? Not necessarily. Every psychologically meaningful experience involves an active brain. Moreover, say advocates of dream reflection, dreams may be akin to abstract art—amenable to more than one meaningful interpretation, yet illuminating to ponder.

> "When people interpret [a dream] as if it were meaningful and then sell those interpretations, it's quackery."
>
> **SLEEP RESEARCHER J. ALLAN HOBSON (1995)**

SUMMING UP

The Rhythm of Sleep Our daily schedule of waking and sleeping is timed by a body clock known as circadian rhythm. Each night's sleep also has a rhythm of its own, running from transitional Stage 1 sleep to deep Stage 4 sleep and back up to the more internally active REM sleep stage. This cycle repeats several times during a normal night's sleep, with periods of Stage 4 sleep progressively shortening and of dream-laden REM sleep lengthening.

Why Do We Sleep? Depriving people of sleep has not conclusively revealed why, physiologically, we need sleep. Recent research reveals that sleep is linked with the release of pituitary growth hormone and that it may help to restore brain tissues and consolidate memories.

Sleep Disorders The disorders of sleep include insomnia (recurring wakefulness), narcolepsy (sudden uncontrollable sleepiness or lapsing into REM sleep), and sleep apnea (the stopping of breathing while sleeping).

Dreams Although conscious thoughts can occur during any sleep stage, awakening people during REM sleep yields predictable "dreamlike" reports; awakening during other sleep stages yields a fleeting image only occasionally. Our dreams are mostly of ordinary events; they often relate to everyday experiences and involve anxiety or misfortune more frequently than triumphant achievements.

Freud believed that a dream's manifest content, or story line, is a censored version of its latent content, which gratifies our unconscious wishes. Newer explanations of why we dream suggest that dreams (1) help process information from the day and fix it in memory, (2) serve a physiological function, and/or (3) are the brain's efforts to string periodic hallucinations (from activity bursts in the visual cortex) into a story line. Despite their differences, most theorists agree that REM sleep and its associated dreams serve an important function, as shown by the REM rebound that occurs following REM deprivation.

KEY TERMS AND CONCEPTS circadian rhythm, REM sleep, alpha waves, hallucinations, delta waves, insomnia, narcolepsy, sleep apnea, night terrors, manifest content, latent content, REM rebound

laxed. . . . Your breathing is now deep and regular. . . . Your muscles are becoming more and more relaxed. Your whole body is beginning to feel like lead."

After a few minutes of this hypnotic induction, your eyes are probably closed and you may undergo hypnosis—a social interaction in which one person (the hypnotist) suggests to another (the subject) that certain perceptions, feelings, thoughts, or behaviors will spontaneously occur. When the hypnotist suggests, "Your eyelids are shutting so tight that you cannot open them even if you try," your eyelids may seem beyond your control and may remain closed. Told to forget the number 6, you may be puzzled when you count 11 fingers on your hands. Invited to smell a sensuous perfume that is actually ammonia, you may linger delightedly over its pungent odor. Asked to describe a nonexistent picture the hypnotist claims to be holding, you may talk about it in detail. Told that you cannot see a certain object, such as a chair, you may indeed report that it is not there, although, curiously, you manage to avoid the chair when walking around.

And if instructed to forget all these happenings once you are out of the hypnotic state, you may later report posthypnotic amnesia, a temporary memory loss rather like being unable to recall a familiar name. Although people *say* they don't remember "forgotten" material, subtle tests lead skeptics to doubt their reported amnesia (Coe, 1989a). The material must be "in there," for it can affect later behavior and be recalled at a prearranged signal (Kihlstrom, 1985; Spanos & others, 1985). A critical issue, then, is whether people are genuinely *unable* to recall the "forgotten" material, or whether people distract themselves or withhold information to meet the hypnotist's expectations.

Hypnotic techniques have been used since antiquity, but credit for their modern popularity goes to

hypnosis
a social interaction in which one person (the hypnotist) suggests to another (the subject) that certain perceptions, feelings, thoughts, or behaviors will spontaneously occur.

posthypnotic amnesia
supposed inability to recall what one experienced during hypnosis; induced by the hypnotist's suggestion.

Hypnosis

What is it like to be hypnotized? What powers does hypnosis have? And what really is hypnosis—a special state of consciousness? Or an extension of normal consciousness?

Imagine you are about to be hypnotized. The hypnotist invites you to sit back, fix your gaze on a spot high on the wall, and relax. In a quiet, low voice the hypnotist suggests, "Your eyes are growing tired. . . . Your eyelids are becoming heavy . . . now heavier and heavier. . . . They are beginning to close. . . . You are becoming more deeply re-

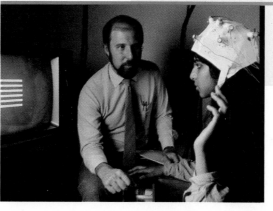

Subject to influence As a deeply hypnotized woman sits before a TV screen, researcher David Spiegel asks her to imagine that a cardboard box is blocking the screen. When a stimulus appears on the screen, her brain waves do not display the normal response. Such findings, Spiegel argues, suggest that hypnosis can alter brain functioning.

an Austrian physician, Anton Mesmer (1734–1815), who mistakenly thought he had discovered an "animal magnetism." With great flourish, Mesmer passed magnets over the bodies of ailing people, some of whom would lapse into a trancelike ("mesmerized") state and awaken much improved. A French commission chaired by Benjamin Franklin found no evidence of animal magnetism and attributed Mesmer's "cures" to "mere imagination." Thus, hypnosis—or mesmerism, as it was then called—became linked with quackery.

Also working against the respectability of hypnosis were the grand claims made by its practitioners. Supposedly, mesmerized people could see with the backs of their heads, perceive others' internal organs, and communicate with the dead. Researchers now agree that hypnotized persons can perform no such feats. Like unhypnotized people, those under hypnosis cannot leap tall buildings, run faster than a speeding bullet, or display superhuman strength. In experiments, their strength, stamina, learning, and perceptual abilities are like those of motivated unhypnotized people (Druckman & Bjork, 1994). Hypnotized people may surprise you by, say, extending their arms for 6 minutes straight—but so can unhypnotized people. (See Figure 7.7.)

Before considering whether the hypnotic state is actually an *altered* state of consciousness, let's first consider some areas of general agreement. Then, with the facts of hypnosis in mind, we can ponder two perplexing questions: What is hypnosis? And what does hypnosis tell us about human consciousness?

Facts and Falsehoods

Can Hypnosis Work for Anyone?

Those who study hypnosis agree that its power resides not in the hypnotist but in the subject's openness to suggestion (Bowers, 1984). To some extent, nearly everyone is suggestible. When people standing upright with their eyes closed are told repeatedly that they are swaying back and forth, most will indeed sway a little. In fact, postural sway is one of the items on the Stanford Hypnotic Susceptibility Scale that assesses a person's hypnotizability. During the assessment, a hypnotist gives a brief hypnotic induction and then presents a series of suggested experiences that range from easy (one's outstretched arms will move together) to difficult (with eyes open one will see a nonexistent person).

Those who are highly hypnotizable—say, the 20 percent who can carry out a suggestion not to smell or react to a bottle of ammonia held under the nose—are still likely to be the most hypnotizable 25 years later (Piccione & others, 1989). These hypnotically susceptible people, like the fantasy-prone people described earlier, frequently become deeply absorbed in imaginative activities (Lynn & Rhue, 1986; Silva & Kirsch, 1992). Typically, they have rich fantasy lives and easily become absorbed in the imaginary events of a novel or movie. Many researchers therefore refer to hypnotic "susceptibility" as hypnotic *ability*, a label with more positive connotations. Few of us would care to be "susceptible" to hypnosis, but most of us would be glad to have the "ability" to focus our attention totally on a task, to become imaginatively absorbed in it, to entertain fanciful possibilities. And that is what fantasy-prone people with hypnotic ability can do.

Actually, anyone who can turn attention inward, relax, and imagine is able to experience some degree of hypnosis—because that's what hypnosis is. And virtually anyone will experience hypnotic responsiveness if led to *expect* it. To convince even skeptical University of Connecticut students that they were hypnotizable, Cynthia Wickless and Irving Kirsch (1989) played a clever stunt on them. After a standard hypnotic induction, they suggested to the students that they would see red, then see green, then hear music, and so forth. After each suggestion, the merry prankster experimenters subtly projected appropriate stimuli—a very faint red or green light, or faint eerie music. Fooled by this weird experience of seeing and hearing what the hypnotist suggested, there were no doubters left. Thus, unlike those in control conditions not

Figure 7.7

The "amazing" hypnotized "human plank"   Actually, unhypnotized people can also perform this feat.

Those who study
hypnosis agree that
its power resides not
in the hypnotist but in
the subject's openness
to suggestion.

similarly persuaded, most scored as *highly* hypnotizable when later given the suggestions of the Stanford Hypnotic Susceptibility Scale.

Any real-life hypnotist does much the same in suggesting that "your eyes are growing tired . . . your eyelids are becoming heavy" after having people strain their eyes by staring at a high spot. Anyone's eyes would get tired. But if the hypnotist is successful, the subject will attribute the heavy eyelids to the hypnotist's powers.

Can Hypnosis Enhance Recall of Forgotten Events?

Can hypnotic procedures enable people to relive earlier experiences? To recall kindergarten classmates? To retrieve forgotten or suppressed details of a crime? Should testimony obtained under hypnosis be admissible in court?

Most people believe—wrongly, as Chapter 9 will explain—that our experiences are all "in there," that everything that happens to us gets recorded in our brains and can be recalled if only we are able to break through our own defenses (Loftus, 1980). Most university students, for example, agree that "under hypnosis a person [can] recall childhood events with very high accuracy" (Furnham, 1993). Testimonies to this come from *age regression* demonstrations, in which people supposedly relive experiences from their childhood. But 60 years of research dispute claims of age regression: Hypnotized people are *not* more genuinely childlike than unhypnotized people who are asked to feign childlike behavior (Nash, 1987). Age-regressed people act as they *believe* children would, but they typically miss the mark by outperforming real children of the specified age (Silverman & Retzlaff, 1986). Age-regressed people may, for example, *feel* childlike and may print much as they know a 6-year-old would, but they sometimes do so with perfect spelling and typically without any change in their adult brain waves, reflexes, and perceptions.

On rare occasions, the relaxed, focused state of hypnosis has enabled witnesses to produce leads in criminal investigations. One instance occurred in 1977, when 26 children and their bus driver, Ed Ray, were kidnapped and forced into an abandoned trailer truck buried 6 feet underground. After their rescue, Ray, under hypnosis, recalled all but one digit of the kidnapper's license plate. With this crucial information, police tracked down the abductors. This anecdote is atypical, and it is unclear whether hypnosis enabled the memory retrieval. Nevertheless, many researchers believe that hypnotic procedures may have some value—or at least do little harm—when used as an investigative tool.

The problem comes in putting on the witness stand someone whose memories are "hypnotically refreshed." Researchers have found that hypnotically refreshed memories combine fact with fiction. Thus, American, Australian, and British courts increasingly ban testimony from witnesses who have been hypnotized (Druckman & Bjork, 1994; Gibson, 1995; McConkey, 1995).

Hypnosis has unpredictable effects. Sometimes the relaxed reflection boosts recall. But often hypnosis contaminates memory with false recollections or increases confidence in false memories (McConkey, 1992). When pressed under hypnosis to recall details, perhaps to "zoom in on your visual memory screen," people use their imaginations to construct their memories. Without either person being aware of what is going on, the hypnotist's hints—"Did you hear loud noises?"—can become the subject's pseudomemory. Previously hypnotized witnesses may end up testifying confidently to events they never experienced (Laurence & Perry, 1988). And whether hypnotized or not, highly hypnotizable (fantasy-prone) people are especially vulnerable to false memory suggestions (Barnier & McConkey, 1992).

So, hypnosis cannot change the rules by which we form, store, and retrieve memories. "Hypnosis is not a psychological truth serum," concludes researcher Kenneth Bowers (1987), "and to regard it as such has been a source of considerable mischief."

It distresses memory researchers that many therapists do not appreciate the unreliability of hypnotically induced memories. When hypnosis researcher Michael Yapko (1994) surveyed 869 therapists attending various therapy conventions, 47 percent agreed that "psychotherapists can have

. . . hypnotically refreshed memories
combine fact with fiction.

posthypnotic suggestion
a suggestion, made during a hypnosis session, to be carried out after the subject is no longer hypnotized; used by some clinicians to help control undesired symptoms and behaviors.

greater faith in details of a traumatic event when obtained hypnotically than otherwise." And 54 percent agreed that "hypnosis can be used to recover memories of actual events as far back as birth." Such ignorance "of the facts" left Yapko aghast: "I am deeply concerned that psychotherapy patients will be led to believe destructive ideas that are untrue . . . all in the name of 'psychotherapy.'"

Striking examples of memories created under hypnosis come from the tens of thousands of people who since 1980 reported being abducted by UFOs, abused in satanic cults, or adulated during a past life. Under hypnosis, one woman

> remembered a light and a voice calling her out of bed. She obeyed against her will and went to a muddy field as a saucer-shaped craft neared the ground. Through the windows she saw beings and a piercing sound prevented her from moving. A warm beam of light then pulled her inside the craft. She found herself inside a white hospital room. Two small beings with tiny mouths and compelling eyes, dressed as if in motorcycle jackets, told her without speaking to undress and lie down on a table. She resisted but eventually gave in . . . at last the doctor entered and gave her an injection. He then inserted a needle into her navel. . . . One being . . . undressed himself and rubbed her with a jelly. It warmed her [and he] then raped her. (Bullard, 1987)

Studies reveal that most reports of UFOs have come from people who are predisposed to believe in aliens, are fantasy prone, and have undergone hypnosis (Newman & Baumeister, 1996; Nickell, 1996). Consider one hypnotic session with another supposed abductee:

Dr. Fiore: Now you're going to let yourself know if they put a needle in any part of your body, other than the rectum.

Sandi: No. They were carrying needles around, big ones, and I was scared for a while they were going to put one in me, but they didn't. [*Body tenses.*]

Dr. Fiore: Now just let yourself relax. At the count of three you're going to remember whether they put one of those big needles in you. If they did, know that you're safe. . . . And if they didn't you're going to remember that, too, at the count of three. One . . . two . . . three.

Sandi: They did. (Fiore, 1989, p. 26)

Can Hypnosis Force People to Act Against Their Will?

Researchers Martin Orne and Frederick Evans (1965) demonstrated that hypnotized people *could* be induced to perform an apparently dangerous act. For example, the participants followed a request to dip a hand briefly in fuming acid and then throw the "acid" in a research assistant's face. When interviewed a day later, they exhibited no memory of their acts and emphatically denied they

would follow orders to commit such actions.

Had hypnosis given the hypnotist a special power to control these people against their will? To find out, Orne and Evans unleashed that enemy of so many illusory beliefs—the control group: Orne asked some additional people to *pretend* they had been hypnotized. The laboratory experimenter, unaware that these control subjects had not been hypnotized, treated all participants in the same manner. The result? All the *un*hypnotized participants (perhaps believing that the laboratory context assured safety) performed the same acts as the hypnotized ones. Similarly, most hypnotized subjects can be induced to deface a sacred book, and a few will even cooperate in stealing an exam or selling illegal drugs. But people asked to simulate hypnosis are no less likely to perform the same acts (Levitt, 1986).

This illustrates a principle that Chapter 18 emphasizes: An authoritative person in a legitimate context can induce people—hypnotized or not—to perform some unlikely acts. Hypnosis researcher Spanos (1982) put it simply: "The overt behaviors of hypnotic subjects are well within normal limits."

Can Hypnosis Be Therapeutic?

Hypnotherapists do nothing magical. Rather, they try to help patients harness their own healing powers (Baker, 1987). Posthypnotic suggestions (suggestions to be carried out after the hypnosis session has ended) have helped alleviate headaches, asthma, warts, and stress-related skin disorders. One woman, who suffered open sores all over her body for more than 20 years, was asked to imagine herself swimming in shimmering, sunlit liquids that would cleanse her skin and to experience her skin as smooth and unblemished. Within three months her sores had disappeared (Bowers, 1984).

When hypnosis is applied to self-control problems such as nail biting and smoking, the most hypnotizable people show no greater benefit than those least hypnotizable. This suggests that the benefits are not a result of the hypnosis per se (Bowers & LeBaron, 1986). Should we also then question whether hypnosis is the therapeutic agent when we hear of improvements in problems unrelated to willpower, such as skin disorders? Do the benefits of hypnosis surpass those of merely encouraging people to relax and form positive images? The answer remains in doubt. For example, hypnosis speeds the disappearance of warts, but in controlled studies, so do the same positive suggestions given without hypnosis (Spanos, 1991, 1996).

Most reports of UFOs have come from people who are predisposed to believe in aliens, are fantasy prone, and have undergone hypnosis.

THINKING CRITICALLY ABOUT

Hypnotic Age Regression: A True Story

Remembrances of Christmases Past? What shall we make of a clever study by Robert True (1949)? He regressed hypnotized volunteers back to their Christmases and birthday parties at ages 10, 7, and 4. In each case, he asked them what day of the week it was. Without hypnosis, the odds that a person could name offhand the day of a long-ago date are but 1 in 7. Remarkably, the hypnotized subjects' answers were 82 percent correct.

Other investigators were unable to replicate True's results. When Martin Orne (1982) asked True why, he replied that *Science*, the journal that published his article, had shortened his key question to "What day is this?" Actually, he had asked his age-regressed subjects, "Is it Monday? Is it Tuesday?" and so forth until the subject stopped him with a yes. When Orne asked True if he knew the actual day of the week while posing the questions, True granted that he did but was puzzled why Orne would ask.

Can you see why? True's experiment appears to be a beautiful example of how hypnotists can subtly influence their subjects' memories (and, more generally, of how experimenters can subtly communicate their expectations). "Given the eagerness of the hypnotized subject to fulfill the demands placed upon him," surmised Orne, it takes only the slightest change of inflection (in asking "Is it Wednesday?") for the subject to respond, "Yes."

The final blow to True's experiment came when Orne simply asked ten 4-year-olds what day of the week it was. To his surprise, none knew. If 4-year-olds typically do not know the day of the week, then True's adults were reporting information they probably didn't know when they were 4.

Remembrances of Lives Past? If people's hypnotic regressions to childhood are partly imagined, then how believable are claims of hypnotic "regression to past lives"? Can the 20 to 30 percent of Americans who believe in reincarnation (Gallup & Newport, 1991; *George*, 1996) find support in such reports? Were 36 percent of university students correct to agree, in a survey by Scott Brown and others (1996), that "certain people can be age regressed to recall past lives"?

Nicholas Spanos (1987–1988; Spanos & others, 1991) reported that, when hypnotized, fantasy-prone people who believe in reincarnation will offer vivid details of "past lives." But they nearly always report being their same race—unless the researcher has informed them that different races are com-

Will the real King Henry VIII please stand up? Under hypnosis, people who claim to remember a past life too often report being someone famous.

mon. They often report being someone famous rather than one of the countless "nobodies." Some contradict one another by claiming to have been the same person, such as King Henry VIII (Reveen, 1987–1988). Moreover, they typically do not know things that any person of that historical time would have known. One subject who "regressed" to a "previous life" as a Japanese fighter pilot in 1940 could not name the emperor of Japan and did not know that Japan was already at war. Hypnotic regressions to past lives thus offer no credible evidence of reincarnation.

MY NAME IS EUNICE. I HAVE LIVED MANY PAST LIVES, MOST OF THEM IN TRENTON, NEW JERSEY,....

CHANNELLING ON THE CHEAP

Drawing by M. Stevens; © 1987 The New Yorker Magazine, Inc.

dissociation
a split in consciousness, which allows some thoughts and behaviors to occur simultaneously with others.

Can Hypnosis Alleviate Pain?

Yes, hypnosis *can* relieve pain (Druckman & Bjork, 1994; Kihlstrom, 1985). When unhypnotized subjects put their arms in an ice bath, they feel intense pain within 25 seconds. When hypnotizable subjects do the same after being given suggestions to feel no pain, they indeed report feeling little pain. As some dentists know, even light hypnosis can reduce fear, and thus hypersensitivity to pain. Nearly 10 percent of us can become so deeply hypnotized that even major surgery can be performed without anesthesia. And half of us can gain some pain relief from hypnosis.

How can this be? One theory of hypnotic pain relief involves dissociation, a split between different levels of consciousness. Hypnosis, it suggests, dissociates the sensation of the pain stimulus (of which the subject is still aware) from the emotional suffering that defines our pain experience. The ice water therefore feels very cold but not painful.

Another theory proposes that hypnotic pain relief is due to selective attention, as when an injured athlete, caught up in the competition, feels little or no pain until the game ends. Support for this view comes from several studies showing that hypnosis relieves pain no better than does merely relaxing and distracting people (Chaves, 1989). With their attention distracted during hypnosis, some women can experience childbirth with minimal pain; but so can some women without hypnosis, especially if given childbirth training (D'Eon, 1989).

Both views of pain assume that at some level a hypnotized person does experience the pain stimulus. Indeed, people who report feeling no pain nevertheless may respond to electric shock or a surgeon's knife with a pounding heart. Similar disparities between self-reports and behavior involve seeing and hearing. Following a suggestion of deafness, hypnotized people will deny being able to hear their own voices. But when they hear their voice over a headset with a half-second delay, they respond as unhypnotized people do: The delayed feedback disrupts their ability to speak fluently. If told they are colorblind, hypnotized people do not respond to colorblindness tests as do people with actual color-deficient vision. In each of these cases, the hypnotized subjects *report* perceiving no pain, sound, or color. Yet the stimuli have quite obviously registered within their sensory systems. Thus, hypnosis does *not* block sensory input. What people *say* they experience just doesn't fit with their behavior.

The unanswered question of how hypnosis relieves pain—by *dissociating* the pain sensation from conscious awareness, or merely by focusing *attention* on other things—brings us to the basic issue: Is hypnosis a unique psychological state?

Is Hypnosis an Altered State of Consciousness?

We have seen that hypnosis involves heightened suggestibility. We have also seen that hypnotic procedures do not endow a person with special powers. But they can sometimes enhance recall of real (and unreal) past events, aid in overcoming psychologically influenced ailments, and help alleviate pain. So, just what is hypnosis? Does it qualify as an altered—out-of-the-ordinary—state of consciousness?

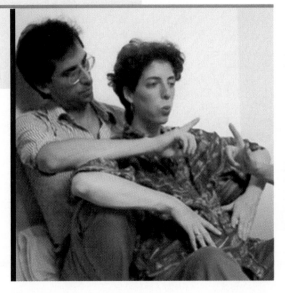

The Lamaze method of childbirth
Like hypnosis, the Lamaze method involves breathing and concentration techniques that draw attention away from pain. Women for whom the method works tend to have high hypnotic ability (Venn, 1986).

Hypnosis as a Social Phenomenon

Skeptics note that hypnosis is not a unique physiological state. Moreover, behaviors produced through hypnotic procedures can also be produced without them. This suggests that hypnotic phenomena may reflect the workings of normal consciousness (Lynn & others, 1990; Spanos & Coe, 1992).

In Chapter 6 we saw how powerfully our interpretations influence ordinary perceptions. Especially in the case of pain, for which the effects of hypnosis seem most dramatic, our perceptions follow our attention. Moreover, imaginative people can manufacture vivid perceptions without hypnosis. Perhaps, then, "hypnotized" people are just acting the role of "good hypnotic subjects" and allowing the hypnotist to direct their fantasies.

It's not that people are consciously faking hypnosis. Rather, they're doing and reporting what's expected of them. Like actors who get caught up in their roles, they begin to feel and behave in ways appropriate to the hypnotic role. The more they like and trust the hypnotist and feel motivated to demonstrate hypnotic behavior, the more they do so (Gfeller & others, 1987). If told later to scratch their ear when they hear the word *psychology*, subjects will likely do so only if they think the experiment is still under way (and scratching is therefore expected). If an experimenter eliminates the motivation for acting hypnotized—by stating that hypnosis reveals "gullibility"—subjects become unresponsive.

Based on such findings, advocates of the *social influence theory* contend that hypnotic phenomena are *not* unique to hypnosis. They argue that hypnotic phenomena—like behavior associated with other supposed altered states, such as dissociative identity disorder (page 466) and spirit or demon possession—are an extension of everyday social behavior (Spanos, 1994, 1996). Hypnotic subjects, say skeptics, are imaginative actors caught up in playing the role of hypnotic subject.

Hypnosis as Divided Consciousness

Most hypnosis researchers grant that normal social and cognitive processes play a part in hypnosis, but they believe hypnosis is more than imaginative acting. For one thing, hypnotized subjects will *sometimes* carry out suggested behaviors on cue, even when they believe no one is watching. Their doing so shows that more may be at work than merely trying to be a "good subject." Moreover, many practitioners remain convinced that certain phenomena *are* unique to hypnosis. What else explains hypnotic experiences such as pain reduction and compelling hallucinations (Bowers, 1990)? Skeptics reply that hypnotists' livelihoods depend on maintaining an aura of mysterious power (Coe, 1989b).

To veteran researcher Ernest Hilgard (1986, 1992), hypnosis involves not only social influence but also a special state of dissociated consciousness. Hilgard views hypnotic dissociation as a vivid form of everyday mind splits. Putting a child to bed, we might read *Goodnight Moon* for the fourteenth time while mentally organizing a busy schedule for the next day. Under the influence of my dentist's nitrous oxide—a real gas—I hear her ask me to "open wide." As my conscious self contemplates her request, my mouth, much to my surprise, immediately obeys. As she says, "Turn toward me," my head instantly complies, as if controlled by some strange force.

With practice, it is even possible to read and comprehend a short story while copying dictated words, much as you can doodle while listening to a lecture, or much as a skilled pianist can converse while playing a familiar piece (Hirst & others, 1978). Thus, when hypnotized subjects write answers to questions about one topic while talking or reading about a different topic, they display an accentuated form of normal cognitive dissociation.

"The total possible consciousness may be split into parts which co-exist but mutually ignore each other."

WILLIAM JAMES
PRINCIPLES OF PSYCHOLOGY
1890

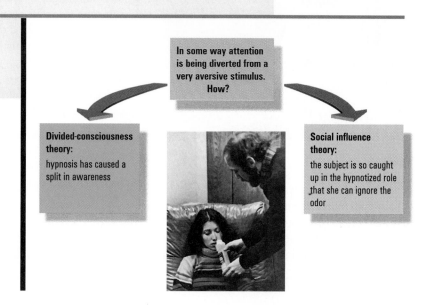

Explaining hypnosis How can she do it? How can this hypnotized young woman show no reaction to the terrible smell of ammonia? Divided-consciousness theory and social influence theories offer possible explanations.

In some way attention is being diverted from a very aversive stimulus. How?

Divided-consciousness theory: hypnosis has caused a split in awareness

Social influence theory: the subject is so caught up in the hypnotized role that she can ignore the odor

hidden observer
Hilgard's term describing a hypnotized subject's awareness of experiences, such as pain, that go unreported during hypnosis.

So, when today's researchers refer to a "hypnotic state," note Irving Kirsch and Steven Jay Lynn (1995), they merely refer to the subjective experience of hypnosis and not to a unique trance state.

Hilgard's discovery of hypnotic dissociation occurred dramatically. During a class demonstration of hypnosis, he induced deafness in someone and then set about showing the class that the person was now utterly unresponsive to questions, taunts, and even sudden loud sounds. When a student asked whether some part of the person might still be able to hear, Hilgard decided to show that the answer was no. He quietly asked the person to raise his right index finger if some part of him could still hear. To everyone's surprise—including Hilgard's and the subject's—the finger rose. When the person's hearing was restored, he explained that "it was a little boring just sitting here . . . when I suddenly felt my finger lift; that is what I want you to explain to me."

The divided-consciousness theory of hypnosis provoked controversy, because what the "hidden observer" reports varies with what the experimenter seems to want. But this much seems clear: You and I process much information without conscious awareness. We have seen other examples of unconscious information processing in the chapters on sensation and perception, and we will see more in later chapters on learning, memory, and thinking. Without doubt, there is much more to thinking and acting than we are conscious of. Our information processing *is* divided into simultaneous conscious and subconscious realms.

Then again, there is also little doubt that social influences do play an important role in hypnosis. So, might the two views—social influence and divided consciousness—be bridged? Researchers John Kihlstrom and Kevin McConkey (1990) believe there is no contradiction between the two approaches, which are converging toward a "unified account of hypnosis." Hypnosis, they suggest, is an extension *both* of normal principles of social influence *and* of everyday splits in consciousness.

Demonstrating the "hidden observer"   A hypnotized subject being tested by Ernest Hilgard exhibits no pain when her arm is placed in an ice bath. But asked to press a key if some part of her feels the pain, she does so. To Hilgard, this suggests that hypnosis divides consciousness into one part that is unaware of pain and another part— a "hidden observer"—that is aware of it.

This phenomenon spurred further inquiry. Hypnotized subjects, as we noted earlier, report far less pain than others when they place their arms in ice water. But when asked to press a key if "some part" of them does feel the pain, they invariably press the key. To Hilgard, this suggests that a dissociated consciousness, a hidden observer, is passively aware of what is happening.

SUMMING UP

Facts and Falsehoods
Although hypnosis was historically linked with quackery, it has more recently become the subject of serious research. Psychologists now agree that hypnosis is a state of heightened suggestibility to which people are subject in varying degrees, and that, although hypnotic procedures may help someone to recall past events, the hypnotist's beliefs frequently work their way into the subject's recollections. They also agree that hypnotized people can no more be made to act against their will than can nonhypnotized people. Hypnosis can be at least temporarily therapeutic, and hypnotizable people can enjoy significant pain relief.

Is Hypnosis an Altered State of Consciousness?   Hypnosis is at least partly a by-product of normal social and cognitive processes. Many researchers believe it also is an altered state of consciousness, perhaps involving a dissociation between levels of consciousness.

KEY TERMS AND CONCEPTS   hypnosis, posthypnotic amnesia, posthypnotic suggestion, dissociation, hidden observer

Drugs and Consciousness

What types of drugs influence consciousness? Do they work by changing the user's brain chemistry? The user's expectations? Both? Why do some people become regular users of consciousness-altering drugs?

If there is controversy about whether hypnosis alters consciousness, there is little dispute that drugs do. Psychoactive drugs are chemicals that change perceptions and moods. An imaginary drug user's day dramatizes the widespread use of legal psychoactive drugs: It begins with a wake-up cup of strong coffee. By midday, several cigarettes and a prescription tranquilizer have calmed the nerves. An early exit from work makes time for a happy-hour drink, providing a relaxing and sociable prelude to a dental appointment, where nitrous oxide makes an otherwise painful experience mildly pleasurable. A diet pill before dinner helps stem the appetite, and its stimulating effects can later be partially offset with a sleeping pill. Before drifting off into REM-depressed sleep, our hypothetical drug user is dismayed by a news report of "rising drug abuse."

Dependence and Addiction

Continued use of a psychoactive drug produces tolerance: The user requires larger and larger doses to experience the drug's effect. A person who rarely drinks alcohol might get tipsy on one can of beer, but an experienced drinker may not get tipsy until the second six-pack (Figure 7.8). Despite the connotations of "tolerance," alcoholics' brains, hearts, and livers suffer damage from the excessive alcohol they are "tolerating."

Users who stop taking psychoactive drugs may experience the undesirable side effects of withdrawal. As the body responds to the drug's absence, the user may feel physical pain and intense cravings. This indicates a physical dependence on the drug. People can also develop psychological dependence, particularly for stress-relieving drugs. Although such drugs may not be physically addictive, they nevertheless become an important part of the user's life, often as a way of relieving negative emotions. With either physical addiction or psychological dependence, the user's primary focus becomes obtaining and using the drug.

"Just tell me where you kids got the idea to take so many drugs."

© 1992 by Sidney Harris.

Misconceptions About Addiction

An "addiction" has traditionally meant a craving for a substance, with physical symptoms such as aches, nausea, and distress following sudden withdrawal. In recent pop psychology, the supposedly irresistible seduction of addiction has been extended to cover many behaviors formerly considered bad habits or even sins. Has the concept been stretched too far? Are addictions as irresistible as commonly believed? Many drug researchers believe the following three myths about addiction are false:

1. *Addictive drugs quickly corrupt; for example, morphine taken to control pain is powerfully addictive and often leads to heroin abuse.* After taking a psychoactive drug, some people—perhaps 10 percent—do indeed have a hard time using it in moderation or stopping altogether. However, there are many more controlled, occasional users than

psychoactive drug
a chemical substance that alters perceptions and mood.

tolerance
the diminishing effect with regular use of the same dose of a drug, requiring the user to take larger and larger doses before experiencing the drug's effect.

withdrawal
the discomfort and distress that follow discontinuing the use of an addictive drug.

physical dependence
a physiological need for a drug, marked by unpleasant withdrawal symptoms when the drug is discontinued.

psychological dependence
a psychological need to use a drug, such as to relieve negative emotions.

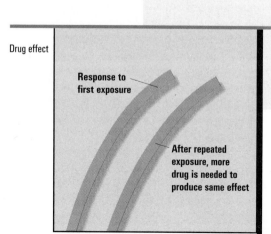

Drug effect

Response to first exposure

After repeated exposure, more drug is needed to produce same effect

Drug dose ⟶

Figure **7.8**

Drug tolerance With repeated exposure to a psychoactive drug, the drug effect lessens. Thus, it takes bigger doses to get the desired effect.

addicts of drugs such as alcohol, marijuana, and cocaine (Gazzaniga, 1988; Siegel, 1990). Moreover, people typically don't become addicted when using drugs medically. Those given morphine to control pain rarely develop the cravings of the addict who uses morphine as a mood-altering drug (Melzack, 1990).

2. *Addictions can't be overcome voluntarily; therapy is a must.* Some addicts do benefit from treatment programs. Alcoholics Anonymous, for example, has supported many people in overcoming their alcohol dependence. But, say critics, the recovery rates of treated and untreated groups differ less than one might suppose.

Moreover, viewing addiction as a disease, as diabetes is a disease, can undermine self-confidence and the will to change cravings that, without treatment, "one can't fight." And that, critics say, would be unfortunate, for many people do voluntarily stop using addictive drugs, without treatment. Some 70 percent of smokers who seek treatment for their addiction later return to smoking, whereas most of America's 41 million ex-smokers kicked the habit on their own (see Chapter 17). Half of the U.S. soldiers in Vietnam tried heroin or opium, and 20 percent became regular users. And, of nearly 500 men whose urine revealed narcotic use upon their departure from Vietnam, one-third did try narcotics again (Robins and others, 1974). Yet, removed from the war's stressful setting and all the stimulus cues associated with their drug use (the place, the friends, the circumstances), only 7 percent of the 500 became readdicted.

3. *We can extend the concept of addiction to cover not just drug dependencies, but a whole spectrum of repetitive, pleasure-seeking behaviors.* We can, and we have, but should we? The addiction-as-disease-needing-treatment idea has been suggested for a host of driven behaviors, including overeating, shopping, exercise, gambling, work, and sex. Initially, we may use the term metaphorically ("I'm a ski addict"), but when people begin taking the metaphor as reality, addiction becomes an all-purpose excuse. Those who embezzle to feed their "gambling addiction," or who abuse or betray to indulge their "sex addiction" can then seek sympathy and treatment rather than judgment and jail. As Washington, D.C., Mayor Marion Barry replied when asked why he lied about being "chemically dependent," "That was the disease talking. I did not purposely do that to you. I was a victim" (Leo, 1991).

Bookstores now carry whole sections of books on addictive relationships, also known as "codependence." A supposedly co-dependent person—usually a woman—is said to be addicted to, or dependent on, a dysfunctional partner, at the cost of losing her own identity and self-fulfillment. Indeed, daughters of alcoholic parents may learn to meet exploitive people's expectations (Lyon & Greenberg, 1991). And women who live with a substance abuser do experience great stress and sometimes help hide the abuser's addiction from public view. But, say critics, our individualistic culture often stretches "co-dependence" to include the lost freedoms of normal, mutually dependent wife-husband or parent-child relationships (Kaminer, 1992). Moreover, the co-dependent person often is *blamed*, and the dysfunctional partner's shame becomes hers as well. If people derive meaning from supporting and loving a troubled family member, are they really blameworthy or socially ill?

Sometimes, though, behaviors such as gambling do become compulsive and dysfunctional, much like abusive drug-taking. Is there justification for stretching the addiction concept to cover social behaviors? Debates over the addiction-as-disease model continue.

> People typically don't become addicted when using drugs medically. Those given morphine to control pain rarely develop the cravings of the addict who uses morphine as a mood-altering drug.

CALVIN AND HOBBES

Psychoactive Drugs

There are at least three categories of psychoactive drugs:

- Depressants, or "downers," calm neural activity and slow body functions.
- Stimulants, or "uppers," temporarily excite neural activity and arouse body functions.
- Hallucinogens distort perceptions and evoke sensory images in the absence of sensory input.

Drugs in all three categories do their work at the brain's synapses, by stimulating, inhibiting, or mimicking the activity of neurotransmitters, the brain's chemical messengers.

Depressants

Let's look first at drugs such as alcohol, barbiturates (tranquilizers), and opiates, which slow body functions.

Alcohol

True or false? In large amounts, alcohol is a depressant; in small amounts, it is a stimulant.

False. Small doses of "spirits" may, indeed, enliven a drinker, but they do so by slowing brain activity that controls judgment and inhibitions. If provoked, people under alcohol's influence respond more aggressively than usual. If asked to help, people under alcohol's influence respond more helpfully than usual. In everyday life, alcohol *increases* both harmful tendencies—as when sexually coercive college men try to disinhibit their dates by getting them to drink (Abbey, 1991; Mosher & Anderson, 1986)—and helpful tendencies—as when restaurant patrons tip more when tipsy (M. Lynn, 1988). Thus, alcohol makes us more aggressive or helpful or more self-disclosing or more sexually daring—when such tendencies are already present. The urges you feel when sober are the same ones you are more likely to act upon when intoxicated.

Low doses of alcohol relax the drinker by slowing sympathetic nervous system activity. With larger doses, alcohol can become a staggering problem: Reactions slow, speech slurs, and skilled performance deteriorates. These physical effects, combined with the lowering of inhibitions, contribute to alcohol's worst consequences—to several hundred thousand lives claimed worldwide in alcohol-related accidents and violent crime each year. Accidents occur despite drinkers' belief (when sober) that driving impaired is wrong and despite their insisting they wouldn't do so. Yet

under alcohol's influence, people's moral judgments become more immature, their qualms about drinking and driving lessen—and virtually all will drive home from a bar, even if given a breathalyzer test and told they are intoxicated (Denton & Krebs, 1990; MacDonald & others, 1995).

Alcohol not only affects judgment, it affects memory. It impairs neither short-term recall for what just happened nor existing long-term memories. Rather, it disrupts the *processing* of recent experiences into long-term memories. Thus, the day after being intoxicated, heavy drinkers may not recall whom they met or what they said or did the night before. This memory blackout stems partly from an inability to transfer memories from the intoxicated to the sober state (Eich, 1980). Blackouts after drinking may also result from alcohol's suppression of REM sleep. (Recall that people deprived of REM sleep have difficulty fixing their day's experiences into permanent memories.)

Alcohol has another intriguing effect on consciousness: It reduces self-awareness (Hull & others, 1986). Compared with people who feel good about themselves, those who want to suppress their awareness of failures or shortcomings are more likely to drink. The Nazi doctors who selected "unfit" concentration camp inmates for the gas chambers often did so while drunk, or got drunk afterwards (Lifton, 1986).

Alcohol also focuses attention on the immediate situation and away from future consequences. This facilitates urges that the individual might otherwise resist (Steele & Josephs, 1990). Thus, sexually active university students are less likely to use condoms when intoxicated (MacDonald & others, 1996; in press). And in surveys, over half of rapists acknowledge drinking before committing their offense (Seto & Barbaree, 1995).

As with other psychoactive drugs, alcohol's behavioral effects stem not only from its alteration of brain chemistry but also from the user's expectations. Many studies have found that when people *believe* that alcohol affects social behavior in cer-

depressants
drugs (such as alcohol, barbiturates, and opiates) that reduce neural activity and slow body functions.

stimulants
drugs (such as caffeine, nicotine, and the more powerful amphetamines and cocaine) that excite neural activity and speed up body functions.

hallucinogens
psychedelic ("mind-manifesting") drugs, such as LSD, that distort perceptions and evoke sensory images in the absence of sensory input.

A University of Illinois campus survey showed that before sexual assaults, 80 percent of the male assailants and 70 percent of the female victims had been drinking (Camper, 1990).

Fact: College and university students drink more alcohol than their nonstudent peers, and spend more on alcohol than on books and other beverages combined. Fraternity and sorority members drink three times as much as other students (Atwell, 1986; Malloy & others, 1994). Although few university students believe they have an alcohol problem, many meet the criteria for alcohol abuse (Marlatt, 1991). As students mature with age, they drink less.

Alcohol *increases* both harmful tendencies—as when sexually coercive college men try to disinhibit their dates by getting them to drink—and helpful tendencies—as when restaurant patrons tip more when tipsy.

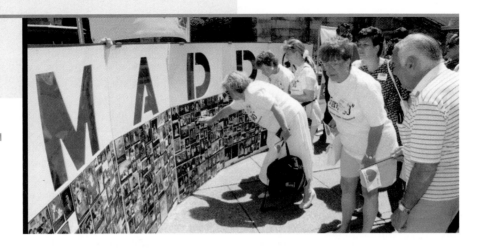

Don't drink and drive   With billboards like this one that shows the appalling consequences of driving under the influence of alcohol, Mothers Against Drunk Driving (MADD) has vigorously promoted awareness of the dangers of alcohol abuse. They have also lobbied for stiffer penalties for drunk drivers.

Fact: In a Harvard School of Public Health survey of 18,000 students at 140 colleges and universities, almost 9 in 10 students reported abuse by intoxicated peers, including sleep and study interruption, insults, sexual advances, and property damage (Wechsler & others, 1994).

Fact: Ten percent of U.S. drinkers account for half of the alcohol consumed (Centers for Disease Control, 1989).

Fact: Alcohol kills more people than all illegal drugs combined. So does tobacco (Siegel, 1990).

tain ways, and *believe*, rightly or wrongly, that they have been drinking alcohol, they will behave accordingly (Leigh, 1989). In a driving simulator, sensation-seeking people drive more recklessly when they *believe* they have consumed alcohol (McMillen & others, 1989).

Another example: Although alcohol decreases sexual inhibitions, people become even more responsive to sexual stimuli if they *believe* alcohol promotes arousal and *believe* they have been drinking. From their review of research, Jay Hull and Charles Bond (1986) concluded that for some people alcohol serves "as an excuse to become sexually aroused."

Consider one such experiment by David Abrams and Terence Wilson (1983). They gave Rutgers University men who volunteered for a study on "alcohol and sexual stimulation" either an alcoholic or a nonalcoholic drink. (Both drinks had a strong taste that masked any alcohol.) In each group, half the participants thought they were drinking alcohol and half thought they were not. After being shown an erotic movie clip, the men who *thought* they had consumed alcohol were more likely to report having strong sexual fantasies and feeling guilt-free. Being able to *attribute* their sexual responses to alcohol released their inhibitions—whether they actually had drunk alcohol or not. If, as commonly believed, liquor is the quicker pick-her-upper, the effect lies partly in that powerful sex organ, the mind.

This research illustrates an important principle: A drug's psychological effects are powerfully influenced by the user's expectations. And that explains why drug experiences vary with cultures (Ward, 1994). If one culture assumes that a particular drug produces euphoria (or aggression or sexual arousal) and another does not, each culture may find its expectations fulfilled.

Barbiturates

The barbiturate drugs, or *tranquilizers*, mimic the effects of alcohol. Because they depress sympathetic nervous system activity, barbiturates such as Nembutal and Seconal are sometimes prescribed to induce sleep or reduce anxiety. In larger doses, they can lead to impaired memory and judgment. In combination with alcohol—as when people take a sleeping pill after an evening of heavy drinking—the total depressive effect on body functions can be lethal. With sufficient doses, barbiturates by themselves can also cause death, which makes them the drugs often chosen by those attempting suicide.

Opiates

The opiates—opium and its derivatives, morphine and heroin—also depress neural functioning. The pupils constrict, the breathing slows, and the user becomes lethargic. For a few hours, blissful pleasure replaces pain and anxiety. But for pleasure one pays a price, which for the heroin user is the gnawing craving for another fix, the need for progressively larger doses, the week-long physical anguish of withdrawal—and for some, the ultimate price: death by overdose.

The pathway to addiction is treacherous. When repeatedly flooded with artificial opiates, the brain eventually stops producing its own opiates, the endorphins. If the drug is then withdrawn, the brain lacks the normal level of these painkilling neurotransmitters. The result is the agony of withdrawal.

Stimulants

The most widely used stimulants are caffeine, nicotine, the powerful amphetamines, and the even more powerful cocaine. Stimulants speed up body functions, hence the nickname "speed" for amphetamines. Strong stimulants increase heart and breathing rates. The pupils dilate, appetite diminishes (because blood sugar rises), and energy and self-confidence rise. For these reasons, people use stimulants to stay awake, lose weight, or boost mood or athletic performance. As with other drugs, the benefits come with a price. When drug stimulation ends, the user experiences a compensating slowdown and may "crash" into tiredness, headaches, irritability, and depression. Like the depressants, stimulants, including coffee, can be addictive (Silverman & others, 1992). (For information on nicotine addiction, see Chapter 17.)

In national surveys, 3 percent of adults and 4 percent of high school seniors reported having tried cocaine during the past year (Johnston & others, 1996; National Institute on Drug Abuse, 1992). Of the seniors, 2 percent said they had smoked *crack*, a potent form of cocaine. By the early 1990s the decade-long cocaine epidemic began subsiding. Credit goes partly to increased treatment and awareness but also to the impoverishment, imprisonment, and deaths of so many cocaine victims (Hamid, 1992).

Cocaine addiction is a fast track from euphoria to crash. When animals and people chew coca leaves, only small amounts of cocaine enter the bloodstream, and they do so gradually, without seeming ill effects (Siegel, 1990). But when extracted cocaine is sniffed ("snorted"), and especially when injected or smoked ("free-based"), it enters the bloodstream quickly. The result: a "rush" of euphoria that lasts 15 to 30 minutes. Because the rush depletes the brain's supply of the neurotransmitters dopamine, serotonin, and norepinephrine, a crash of agitated depression occurs as the drug's effect wears off (Figure 7.9). Crack works even faster and produces a briefer but more intense high, a more intense crash, and a craving for more crack, which wanes after several hours and then returns several days later (Gawin, 1991).

To explore dopamine's role in cocaine addiction, researchers created a strain of mice in which they had "knocked out" the gene for a protein that mops up and recycles the excess dopamine released by a nerve cell (Giros & others, 1996). Like cocaine-hyped mice, these mice became hyperactive. They passed through a photocell beam five times as often as other mice. Moreover, cocaine did not affect the "knockout" mice. This suggests that cocaine raises dopamine concentrations by binding to the mop-up site, thus blocking its reuptake of dopamine.

Regular cocaine users become addicted. Monkeys have become so strongly addicted that they will press a lever more than 12,000 times to gain each cocaine injection (Siegel, 1990). Human and animal cocaine users may experience emotional disturbance, suspiciousness, convulsions, cardiac arrest, or respiratory failure. In situations that trig-

barbiturates
drugs that depress the activity of the central nervous system, reducing anxiety but impairing memory and judgment.

opiates
opium and its derivatives, such as morphine and heroin; they depress neural activity, temporarily lessening pain and anxiety.

amphetamines
drugs that stimulate neural activity, causing speeded-up body functions and associated energy and mood changes.

The recipe for Coca-Cola originally included an extract of the coca plant, creating a cocaine tonic for tired elderly people. Between 1896 and 1905, Coke was indeed "the real thing."

Figure **7.9**

Cocaine euphoria and crash

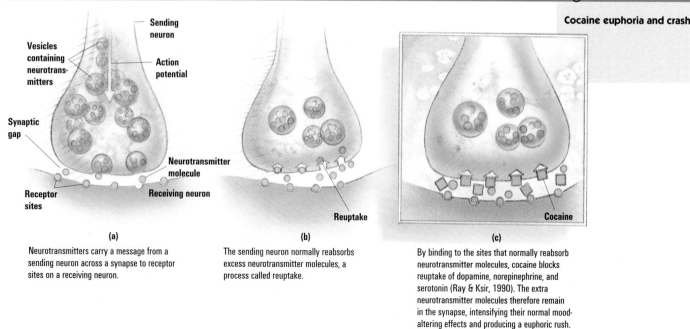

(a)
Neurotransmitters carry a message from a sending neuron across a synapse to receptor sites on a receiving neuron.

(b)
The sending neuron normally reabsorbs excess neurotransmitter molecules, a process called reuptake.

(c)
By binding to the sites that normally reabsorb neurotransmitter molecules, cocaine blocks reuptake of dopamine, norepinephrine, and serotonin (Ray & Ksir, 1990). The extra neurotransmitter molecules therefore remain in the synapse, intensifying their normal mood-altering effects and producing a euphoric rush. When the cocaine level drops, the absence of these neurotransmitters produces a crash.

LSD
a powerful hallucinogenic drug; also known as acid (*lysergic acid diethylamide*).

THC
the major active ingredient in marijuana; triggers a variety of effects, including mild hallucinations.

ger aggression, ingesting cocaine may increase aggressive reactions. Caged rats fight when given foot shocks, and they fight even more when given cocaine and foot shocks. Asked to determine how much electric shock one's opponent will receive in a laboratory competition, cocaine users who have ingested high-dose cocaine rather than a placebo set higher levels (Licata & others, 1993).

As with all psychoactive drugs, cocaine's psychological effects depend not only on the dosage and form in which one takes the drug but also on one's expectations, one's personality, and the situation—a mix of factors. Given a placebo, cocaine users who *think* they are taking cocaine often have a cocainelike experience (Van Dyke & Byck, 1982).

Hallucinogens

Hallucinogens are psychoactive drugs that distort perceptions and evoke vivid images in the absence of sensory input (which is why these drugs are also called *psychedelics*, meaning "mind-manifesting"). Some hallucinogens are natural substances, such as marijuana, a mild hallucinogen. Others are synthetic. Of the synthetics, the two best known are PCP ("angel dust"), a potent and illegal painkiller that has highly unpredictable and sometimes devastating psychological effects, and LSD.

LSD

The first "acid trip" was taken in 1943 by chemist Albert Hofmann, the creator of LSD (*lysergic acid diethylamide*). After accidentally ingesting some of the chemical, Hofmann reported that he "perceived an uninterrupted stream of fantastic pictures, extraordinary shapes with intense, kaleidoscopic play of colors" (Siegel, 1984). LSD and other powerful hallucinogens are chemically similar to (and therefore block the actions of) a subtype of the neurotransmitter serotonin (Jacobs, 1987). The emotions of an LSD trip vary from euphoria to detachment to panic.

As with all drug use, a person's current mood and expectations color the LSD experience. Despite emotional variations, the resulting perceptual distortions and hallucinations have commonalities. Psychologist Ronald Siegel (1982) reports that whether you provoke your brain to hallucinate by loss of oxygen, extreme sensory deprivation, or drugs, "it will hallucinate in basically the same way." The experience typically begins with simple geometric forms, such as a lattice, a cobweb, or a spiral (Figure 7.10). The next phase consists of more meaningful images; some may be superim-

posed on a tunnel or funnel, others may involve the replay of past emotional experiences. When the hallucinogenic experience peaks, people frequently feel separated from their bodies and experience dreamlike scenes as if they were real—so real that users may become panic-stricken or may harm themselves.

Marijuana

Marijuana consists of the leaves and flowers of the hemp plant, which for 5000 years has been cultivated for its fiber. Marijuana's major active ingredient is THC, the everyday name of the complex organic molecule delta-9-tetrahydrocannabinol. Whether smoked or eaten in such foods as chocolate brownies, THC produces a mix of effects that makes the drug difficult to classify. (Smoking gets the drug into the brain in about 7 seconds; this produces a greater effect than does eating the drug, which causes its peak concentration to be reached at a slower, unpredictable rate.) Like alcohol, marijuana relaxes, disinhibits, and may produce a euphoric high. But marijuana also acts as a mild hallucinogen by amplifying sensitivity to colors, sounds, tastes, and smells.

As with other drugs, the marijuana user's experience varies, depending on the situation. If the person feels anxious or depressed, taking the drug may intensify these feelings. In other situations,

Figure **7.10**

Hallucinationlike patterns Geometric forms, similar to those experienced by drug users during drug-induced hallucinations, can be seen in the embroidery of the Huichol. These Mexican Indians used peyote, from which the hallucinogen mescaline derives.

using marijuana can be not only pleasurable but therapeutic. For those who suffer the pain of glaucoma (caused by pressure within the eyeball) or the nausea that sometimes accompanies cancer chemotherapy, marijuana may spell relief. Such benefits have motivated legislation legalizing the drug for such patients.

A review of marijuana research published by the National Academy of Sciences (1982) also identified some not-so-pleasant consequences. Like alcohol, marijuana impairs the motor coordination, perceptual skills, and reaction time necessary for safe driving and machine operation. "THC causes animals to misjudge events," reports Ronald Siegel (1990, p. 163). "Pigeons wait too long to respond to buzzers or lights that tell them food is available for brief periods; and rats turn the wrong way in mazes." Marijuana also disrupts memory formation and interferes with immediate recall of information learned only a few minutes before. Such cognitive effects outlast the period of smoking (Pope & Yurgelun-Todd, 1996; Smith, 1995). Clearly, being stoned is not conducive to learning.

Unlike alcohol, which the body eliminates within hours, THC and its by-products linger in the body for a month or more. Thus, contrary to the usual tolerance phenomenon, regular users may achieve a high with smaller amounts of the drug than occasional users would take to get the same effect.

Uncertainty persists about marijuana's physical effects, but medical research suggests that long-term marijuana use may depress male sex hormone and sperm levels and damage the lungs more than does cigarette smoking (Wu & others, 1988). Large doses hasten the loss of brain cells (Landfield & others, 1988). Although marijuana is not as addictive as cocaine or nicotine, one study that followed 654 junior high students into their early twenties found that adolescents who heavily used marijuana developed more health and family problems than did nonusers (Newcomb & Bentler, 1988).

Despite their differences, the psychoactive drugs summarized in Table 7.2 share a common feature: They trigger negative aftereffects that offset their immediate positive effects. The aftereffects illustrate a more general principle that emotions tend to produce opposing emotions, which linger after the original emotions disappear. With repetition, the opposing emotions grow stronger (page 408). This emotions-trigger-opposing-emotions principle parallels that of drug-induced pleasures; the pleasures wane as the drug exacts its compensatory price. That helps explain both tolerance and withdrawal. As the opposing, negative aftereffects get stronger, it takes larger and larger doses to produce the desired high (tolerance), causing the aftereffects to worsen in the drug's absence (withdrawal). This in turn creates a need to switch off the withdrawal symptoms by taking yet more of the drug.

> "How strange would appear to be this thing that men call pleasure! And how curiously it is related to what is thought to be its opposite, pain! . . . Wherever the one is found, the other follows up behind."
>
> **PLATO**
> *PHAEDO*
> FOURTH CENTURY B.C.

A Guide to Selected Psychoactive Drugs

Table **7.2**

Drug	Type	Pleasurable Effects	Adverse Effects
Alcohol	Depressant	Initial high followed by relaxation and disinhibition	Depression, memory loss, organ damage, impaired reactions
Heroin	Depressant	Rush of euphoria, relief from pain	Depressed physiology, agonizing withdrawal
Cocaine	Stimulant	Rush of euphoria, confidence, energy	Cardiovascular stress, suspiciousness, depressive crash
Nicotine	Stimulant	Arouses and relaxes, sense of well-being	Heart disease, cancer (from tars)
Marijuana	Mild hallucinogen	Enhances sensation, relieves pain, distorts time, relaxed high	Lowered sex hormones, disrupted memory, lung damage

Influences on Drug Use

Drug use by North American youth increased during the 1970s. Then, thanks to drug education and the media's deglamorization of drug use, it declined sharply until the early 1990s. Since then, with the cultural anti-drug voice softened and countered by the reglamorization of drugs in some music and films, drug use has rebounded, renewing public concern. Consider the trends:

- In the University of Michigan's annual survey of 16,000 high school seniors, the proportion who believed there is "great risk" in regular marijuana use rose from 35 percent in 1978 to 79 percent in 1991, then retreated to 60 percent in 1996 (Johnston, 1996).

- After peaking in 1978, marijuana use by this age group declined until 1992, but has been rising since then (Figure 7.11).

- In the UCLA/American Council on Education annual survey of new college and university students, support for the legalization of marijuana dropped from 53 percent in 1977 to 17 percent in 1989, and rebounded to 33 percent in 1996 (Sax & others, 1996).

Similar attitude and usage changes since the late 1970s appear in surveys of Canadian teens (Smart & others, 1991).

Figure **7.11**

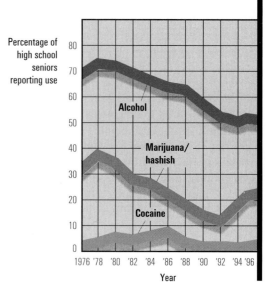

Trends in drug use The percentage of high school seniors who report having used alcohol, marijuana, or cocaine during the past 30 days declined from the late 1970s to 1992. Since then drug use has been increasing and drug merchandise has become more openly available in stores and at concerts. (From Johnston & others, 1996.)

> Evidence accumulates that heredity influences alcoholic tendencies.... Such findings have fueled the search for a better understanding of genetic and biochemical influences on addiction.

Other studies reveal a changing national attitude toward alcohol. More than at any time since prohibition, health- and safety-conscious people see alcohol less as a cheerful beverage than as a drug to be shunned. The number of new U.S. collegians who reported abstinence from beer during the past year increased from 25 percent in 1981 to 47 percent in 1996. For any given month, 49 percent of Americans report having abstained from all alcohol use (National Institute on Drug Abuse, 1991). Hard liquor consumption per person dropped 40 percent from 1980 to 1994 in the United States, and has similarly declined in Canada (Bureau of the Census, 1996; Statistics Canada, 1996). When the alcohol industry started substituting wine coolers for wine, and nonalcoholic beer for alcoholic, you knew attitudes were changing.

Cigarette smoking, though addictive, has similarly plummeted among the general population, but has recently rebounded among teens (see Chapter 17). The drop is especially great among highly educated people, most of whom either never started or have stopped. Effectively inform people about the health hazards of using cocaine, marijuana, alcohol, or tobacco and—without therapy, support groups, or medicines—many will simply stop.

Why, then, do some people continue to use psychoactive drugs, and why is teen drug use increasing? Why, for example, do 40 percent of American high school seniors report having tried an illegal drug during the past year (Johnston & others, 1996)? For some adolescents, occasional drug use represents thrill-seeking. Why do other adolescents become regular drug users?

In the case of alcohol, some people may be biologically vulnerable. For example, evidence accumulates that heredity influences alcoholic tendencies:

- Adopted individuals are more susceptible to alcoholism if one or both of their biological parents has a history of alcoholism (Mirin & Weiss, 1989).

- Having an alcoholic identical twin puts a male at especially increased risk for alcohol problems (Heath & others, 1989; McGue & others, 1992; Prescott & others, 1994).

- Compared with children of nonalcoholics, children of alcoholics have a higher tolerance for multiple alcoholic drinks taken over an hour or two (Schuckit & Smith, 1996). They also show a smaller evoked brain response to certain types of sensory stimulation (Polich & others, 1994).

- Researchers have bred rats and mice that prefer alcoholic drinks to water (Azar, 1995; Holden, 1991; Goldman, 1996).

- Molecular geneticists have recently identified a gene on chromosome 11 that is more common among alcoholics, especially severe alcoholics (Noble, 1993).

Such findings have fueled the search for a better understanding of genetic and biochemical influences on addiction. The biggest study yet—a $25 million, 5-year analysis of 600 alcoholics and their relatives—is under way. If biological markers of addiction-proneness can be found, then perhaps young people at risk for specific addictions can be identified and counseled.

Psychological and social factors may also have an important influence. In their studies of youth and young adults, Michael Newcomb and L. L. Harlow (1986) found that one psychological factor is the feeling that one's life is meaningless and directionless, a common feeling among school dropouts who subsist without job skills, without privilege, with little hope.

Other studies reveal that heavy users of alcohol, marijuana, and cocaine often have experienced significant stress or failure and are depressed. By temporarily dulling the pain of self-awareness, alcohol may offer a way to avoid having to cope with depression, anger, anxiety, or insomnia. The relief may be temporary, but as Chapter 8 explains, behavior is often controlled more by its immediate than by its later consequences.

Especially for teenagers, drug use also has social roots, evident in differing rates of drug use across cultural groups. Alcohol and other drug addiction rates are extremely low among the Amish, Mennonites, Mormons, and Orthodox Jews (Trimble, 1994). And what do you suppose is the rate of drug usage among African-American students— low or high? One of psychology's best-kept secrets is that, contrary to popular stereotypes, African-American high school seniors "report the lowest rates of use for virtually all drugs" (Johnston &

others, 1994, 1996). For example, nearly a third of white seniors, but only 13 percent of black seniors, report recent heavy drinking. Monthly smoking rates are 38 percent among white seniors but only 14 percent among black seniors. Although these data exclude high school dropouts, independent government studies of drug use in households nationwide and among 12,272 high schoolers in all 50 states confirms the finding: African-American teens have sharply lower rates of drinking, smoking, and cocaine use (Bass & Kane-Williams, 1993; Kann & others, 1993). (Curiously, however, cocaine-related arrests and emergency room visits occur more often among African-Americans [Bennett & DiIulio, 1996].)

Social influences are transmitted largely through the peer culture. By their words and examples, peers influence attitudes about drugs. They also provide the drugs and the parties for their use. If an adolescent's friends use drugs, the odds are that he or she will, too. If the friends don't, the temptation may not even arise. Indeed, the peer factor is so powerful that other predictors of adolescent drug use, such as family strength, religiousness, and school adjustment, seem to operate through their effects on peer associations.

Peer influence is a matter not just of what friends do and say but also of what adolescents *believe* their friends are doing and favoring. Young adolescents consume more alcohol when, as often happens, they overestimate their friends' use (Aas & Klepp, 1992; Graham & others, 1991). At the university level, drinking dominates social occasions partly because students overestimate their fellow students' enthusiasm for alcohol use (Prentice & Miller, 1993; Self, 1994). Thinking that few students share their concerns about the risks associated with alcohol, most students surrender to the perceived norm.

Those who use drugs are more likely to stop if their drug use was peer influenced (Kandel & Raveis, 1989). When the friends stop or the social network changes, usage typically ceases. As noted earlier, more than 9 in 10 soldiers who became drug-addicted while in Vietnam ceased their drug use after returning home. Teenagers who come

... contrary to popular stereotypes, African-American high school seniors "report the lowest rates of use for virtually all drugs."

Some warning signs of alcoholism:

- Drinking binges
- Regretting things done or said when drunk
- Feeling low or guilty after drinking
- Failing to honor a resolve to drink less
- Drinking to alleviate depression or anxiety
- Avoiding family or friends when drinking

In the real world, alcohol accounts for one-sixth or less of beverage use. In television's world, alcohol drinking occurs more often than the combined drinking of coffee, tea, soft drinks, and water (Gerbner, 1990).

Annual Beer and Wine Consumption, Litres per Person

	Beer	Wine
France	41	67
Germany	143	25
Italy	23	57
New Zealand	110	15
Australia	102	19
U.K.	106	12
United States	87	7
Sweden	59	12

Source: Australian Social Trends, 1995.

from happy families and do well in school seldom use drugs, largely because they rarely associate with those who do (Oetting & Beauvais, 1987, 1990). As always with correlations, the traffic between friends' and one's own drug use may be two way: Our friends influence us, but we also select as friends those who share our likes and dislikes.

The findings suggest three possible channels of influence for drug prevention and treatment programs: (1) education about the long-term costs of a drug's temporary pleasures, (2) efforts to boost people's self-esteem and purpose in life, and (3) attempts to modify peer associations or to "inoculate" youth against peer pressures, by training "refusal skills." Said differently, people rarely abuse drugs if they understand the physical and psychological costs, feel good about themselves and the direction their lives are taking, and are in a peer group that disapproves of drug use.

SUMMING UP

Psychoactive drugs, including depressants, stimulants, and hallucinogens, also alter consciousness.

Dependence and Addiction Drugs often trigger withdrawal symptoms—negative aftereffects that oppose and offset their temporary pleasure. Such symptoms can lead to physical or psychological dependence. Medical use of drugs rarely creates addictions, however, and many who do suffer drug addictions overcome them when their social context changes.

Psychoactive Drugs Alcohol, barbiturates, and the opiates act by *depressing* neural functioning. Each offers its pleasures, but at the cost of impaired memory and self-awareness or other physical consequences.

Caffeine, nicotine, the amphetamines, and cocaine act by *stimulating* neural functioning. As with nearly all psychoactive drugs, they act at the synapses by influencing the brain's neurotransmitters, and their effects depend on dosage and the user's personality and expectations.

LSD and marijuana can distort the user's judgments of time and, depending on the setting, can alter sensations and perceptions.

Influences on Drug Use Drug use among teenagers and young adults declined during the 1980s, as attitudes changed, and began a rebound during the mid-1990s. Psychological factors (such as stress, depression, and hopelessness) and social factors (such as peer pressure) combine to lead many people to experiment with—and become dependent on—drugs. Some people also appear to have a greater biological susceptibility to dependence on drugs such as alcohol.

KEY TERMS AND CONCEPTS psychoactive drug, tolerance, withdrawal, physical dependence, psychological dependence, depressants, stimulants, hallucinogens, barbiturates, opiates, amphetamines, LSD, THC

Near-Death Experiences

What should we make of the reports of people who describe mystical experiences after close brushes with death? Do they prove that we can look forward to bliss on the other side of death? Do they confirm Plato's doctrine that mind—or soul—is separable from body? Do those facing death reliably experience such flights of mind?

A man . . . hears himself pronounced dead by his doctor. He begins to hear an uncomfortable noise, a loud ringing or buzzing, and at the same time feels himself moving very rapidly through a long dark tunnel. After this, he suddenly finds himself outside of his own physical body . . . and sees his own body from a distance, as though he is a spectator. . . . Soon other things begin to happen. Others come to meet and to help him. He glimpses the spirits of relatives and friends who have already died, and a loving, warm spirit of a kind he has never encountered before—a being of light—appears before him. . . . He is overwhelmed by intense feelings of joy, love, and peace. Despite his attitude, though, he somehow reunites with his physical body and lives. (Moody, 1976, pp. 23, 24)

This passage from Raymond Moody's bestselling book, *Life After Life*, is a composite description of a near-death experience. Near-death experiences are more common than you might suspect. Several investigators each interviewed a hundred or more people who had come close to death through such physical traumas as cardiac arrest. In each study, 30 to 40 percent of such patients recalled a near-death experience (Ring, 1980; Schnaper, 1980). When George Gallup, Jr. (1982; Gallup & O'Connell, 1986) interviewed a national sample of Americans, 15 percent reported having experienced a close brush with death. One-third of these people—representing some 8 million people by Gallup's estimate—reported an accompanying mystical experience. Some claimed to recall things said while they lay unconscious and near death. (But then, anesthetized surgical patients in a "controlled coma" are sometimes not as out cold for the count as surgical teams might suppose. Occasionally, they can later recall operating room conversation or obscure facts or words presented over headphones [Bonke & others, 1986; Merikle & Daneman, 1996; Jelicic & others, 1992].)

Did Moody's description of the "complete" near-death experience sound familiar? The parallels with Ronald Siegel's (1977) descriptions of the typical hallucinogenic experience are striking: replay of old memories, out-of-body sensations, and visions of tunnels or funnels and bright lights or beings of light (Figure 7.12). In short, the content of the near-death experience is just what one would expect from a knowledge of hallucinations. Moreover, oxygen deprivation and other insults to the brain are known to produce hallucinations. As oxygen deprivation turns off the brain's inhibitory cells, neural activity increases in the visual cortex, notes Susan Blackmore (1991, 1993). The result is a growing patch of light, which looks much like what you would see moving through a tunnel.

Perhaps, then, the brain under stress manufactures the near-death experience. Patients who have experienced temporal lobe seizures have also reported profound mystical experiences, as have solitary sailors and polar explorers while enduring monotony, isolation, and cold (Suedfeld & Mocellin, 1987). Recall that the twilight state between waking and sleeping may similarly produce sensations of floating up off the bed. Fantasy-prone persons are especially susceptible to near-death and other out-of-body experiences, such as believing one has encountered aliens or been abducted by them (Ring, 1992; Wilson & Barber, 1983).

Siegel (1980) concluded that the near-death experience is best understood "as a dissociative hallucinatory activity of the brain": When external input dims, the brain's own interior activity becomes perceptible. He illustrates with an analogy: When gazing out a window at dusk, we begin to see the reflected interior of the room as if it were outside, either because the light from outside is dimming (as in the near-death experience) or because the inside light is being amplified (as with LSD). When projected on our perceptual window, says Siegel, our mind's internal images appear real. Those having a near-death experience, like those on an LSD trip, explore "the beyond within."

Some investigators of near-death experiences object. People who have experienced both hallucinations and the near-death phenomenon typically deny their similarity. Moreover, a near-death experience may change people in ways that a drug trip doesn't. Those who have been "embraced by the light" may become kinder, more spiritual, more believing in life after death. Skeptics reply that these effects stem from the death-related context of the experience. Near death, people worldwide sometimes report visions of another world, though the content of that vision often depends on the culture (Kellehear, 1996).

near-death experience
an altered state of consciousness reported after a close brush with death (such as through cardiac arrest); often similar to drug-induced hallucinations.

Figure **7.12**

Near-death vision or hallucination? Psychologist Ronald Siegel (1977) reports that people under the influence of hallucinogenic drugs often see "a bright light in the center of the field of vision. . . . The location of this point of light create[s] a tunnel-like perspective." (From "Hallucinations" by R. K. Siegel. Copyright © 1977 Scientific American, Inc. All rights reserved.)

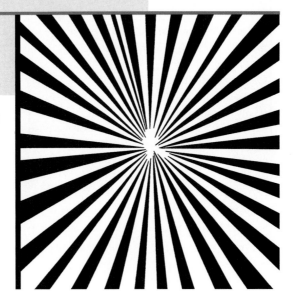

dualism
the presumption that mind and body are two distinct entities that interact.

monism
the presumption that mind and body are different aspects of the same thing.

"The mind seems to act independently of the brain in the same sense that a programmer acts independently of his computer."

NEUROSCIENTIST WILDER PENFIELD (1975)

The controversy over interpreting near-death experiences raises a basic mind-body issue: Is the mind immaterial? Can it exist separate from the body? Dualists answer yes. They believe that the mind and body are interacting but distinct entities—the mind nonphysical, the body physical. As Socrates says in Plato's *Phaedo*, "Does not death mean that the body comes to exist by itself, separated from the soul, and that the soul exists by herself, separated from the body? What is death but that?" For Socrates, as for those today who believe that near-death experiences are proof of immortality, death is not really the death of the person. Death is merely a person's liberation from the bodily prison, an occasion for rejoicing. (Carried to its extreme, this dualist view has given rise to glorifications of the afterlife trip under such titles as "The Thrill of Dying" and "The Wonderful World of Death.")

THE FAR SIDE

THE FAR SIDE © 1992 FARWORKS, INC./Dist. by UNIVERSAL PRESS SYNDICATE.
Reprinted by permission. All rights reserved.

"You, your joys and sorrows, your memories and your ambitions, your sense of personal identity and free will, are in fact no more than the behavior of a vast assembly of nerve cells and their associated molecules."

GENETICIST SIR FRANCIS CRICK
THE ASTONISHING HYPOTHESIS
1994

Monists answer no to the separation of mind and body. They contend that mind and body are different aspects of the same thing. The mind is what the brain does. In the Western world, monists include both scientists who assume the inseparability of mind and brain and theologians who hold to an afterlife that involves some form of bodily resurrection. Such monists generally believe that death is real and that without bodies we truly are nobodies.

As debates over the significance of dreams, fantasy, hypnotic states, drug-induced hallucinations, and near-death experiences illustrate, science informs our wondering about human consciousness and human nature. Although there remain questions that it cannot answer, science nevertheless helps fashion our image of who we are—of our human potentials and our human limits.

SUMMING UP

About one-third of those who have survived a brush with death, such as through cardiac arrest, later recall visionary near-death experiences. Dualists interpret these experiences as evidence of human immortality. Monists point out that reports of such experiences closely parallel reports of hallucinations.

KEY TERMS AND CONCEPTS   near-death experience, dualism, monism

TERMS AND CONCEPTS TO REMEMBER

consciousness, p. 208

fantasy-prone personality, p. 209

circadian rhythm [ser-KAY-dee-an], p. 210

REM sleep, p. 211

alpha waves, p. 212

hallucinations, p. 212

delta waves, p. 212

insomnia, p. 216

narcolepsy, p. 217

sleep apnea, p. 217

night terrors, p. 217

manifest content, p. 218

latent content, p. 218

REM rebound, p. 220

hypnosis, p. 221

posthypnotic amnesia, p. 221

posthypnotic suggestion, p. 224

dissociation, p. 226

hidden observer, p. 228

psychoactive drug, p. 229

tolerance, p. 229

withdrawal, p. 229

physical dependence, p. 229

psychological dependence, p. 229

depressants, p. 231

stimulants, p. 231

hallucinogens, p. 231

barbiturates, p. 232

opiates, p. 232

amphetamines, p. 232

LSD (*lysergic acid diethylamide*), p. 234

THC, p. 234

near-death experience, p. 238

dualism, p. 240

monism, p. 240

CRITICAL THINKING EXERCISE

by Richard O. Straub

Now that you have read and reviewed Chapter 7, take your learning a step further by testing your critical thinking skills on the following creative problem solving exercise.

Rapid eye movement, or REM sleep, is the recurring stage during which vivid dreaming occurs. Theories of why people dream range from Freud's belief that dreams are a psychic safety valve, to the role that dreaming may play in information processing, to the possibility that dreams merely erupt from random neural activity in the brain. Although *why* we dream continues to be debated, that people *need* REM sleep is not. Periods of REM deprivation are invariably followed by increased amounts of REM sleep.

In this exercise, imagine that your middle-aged aunt is worried about her sleep. She claims that she sleeps only three or four hours a night, feels alert only in the morning, and has stopped dreaming altogether. Fearing that her loss of sleep and dreaming will lead to psychological problems, she has tried napping during the day to "catch up," late-night aerobics to tire herself out, and even having a "nightcap or two" before going to bed. Although she claims her insomnia is affecting her health and mood, you haven't noticed any changes in either. Moreover, she seems to have no difficulty concentrating while conversing.

1. Are your aunt's concerns valid? Should she be worried about her insomnia?

2. If your aunt would like to improve her sleep patterns, what steps should she take?

3. Is it likely that your aunt has stopped dreaming altogether? How can she find out for sure?

4. Suppose that your aunt *is* correct in her belief that she has stopped dreaming. What are some of the probable effects of such a condition according to Freud? According to a physiological psychologist? A cognitive psychologist?

Check your progress on becoming a critical thinker by comparing your answers to the sample answers found in Appendix B.

FOR FURTHER INFORMATION

More information on **drugs** can be found on the following pages:

Alcohol
and aggression, pp. 572–573
and memory, p. 285

Alcoholism treatment, pp. 250, 548–549

Classical conditioning in drug therapy, p. 252

Drugs and the fetus, pp. 80–81

Drugs and neurotransmission, pp. 46–47

Drug therapies, pp. 507–510

Nausea conditioning in chemotherapy patients, pp. 251–252

Opiates and endorphins, p. 46

Opponent-process theory, p. 408
and immediate reinforcement
in drug use, p. 257

Smoking (nicotine), pp. 536–539

chapter 8

Learning

All animals, especially humans, adapt to their environments aided by learning. The process of learning associations between events is called conditioning. Through classical conditioning, we learn to anticipate important events, such as the arrival of food or pain. Through operant conditioning, we learn to repeat acts that bring rewards and to avoid acts that bring punishment. Through observational learning, we learn from the experience and example of others.

When a chinook salmon first emerges from its egg in the gravel bed of a stream, its genes provide many of the behavioral instructions it needs for life. It instinctively knows how and where to swim, what to eat, and how to protect itself from predators. Following this built-in plan, the young salmon soon begins a trek to the sea. After some four years in the ocean, the mature salmon returns to its birthplace. It navigates hundreds of miles to the mouth of its home river and then, guided by the scent of its home stream, begins an upstream odyssey to its ancestral spawning ground. Once there, the salmon seeks out the exact conditions of temperature, gravel, and water flow that will facilitate its breeding, and then mates and dies.

Unlike the salmon, we are not born with a genetic blueprint for life. Much of what we do we must learn from experience. Although we struggle to find the life direction a salmon is born with, our learning gives us more flexibility. We can learn how to build grass huts or submarines or space stations and thereby adapt to almost any environment. Indeed, nature's most important gift to us may be our *adaptability*—our capacity to learn new behaviors that enable us to cope with changing circumstances.

No topic is closer to the heart of psychology than learning, *a relatively permanent change in an organism's behavior due to experience*. In earlier chapters we considered the learning of moral ideas, of visual perceptions, of a drug's expected effect. In later chapters we will consider how learning shapes our thought and language, our motivations and emotions, our personalities and attitudes.

learning
a relatively permanent change in an organism's behavior due to experience.

associative learning
learning that certain events occur together. The events may be two stimuli (as in classical conditioning) or a response and its consequences (as in operant conditioning).

Learning in all such realms breeds hope. What is learnable we can potentially teach—a fact that encourages parents, educators, coaches, and animal trainers. What has been learned we can potentially change by new learning—an assumption that underlies counseling, psychotherapy, and rehabilitation programs. No matter how unhappy, unsuccessful, or unloving we are, that need not be the end of our story.

By definition, experience is key to learning. More than 200 years ago, philosophers such as John Locke and David Hume echoed Aristotle's conclusion from 2000 years earlier: We learn by association. Our minds naturally connect events that occur in sequence: We *associate* them. If, after seeing and smelling freshly baked bread, you eat some and find it satisfying, then the next time you see and smell fresh bread, your experience will lead you to expect that eating some will be satisfying again. And if you associate a sound with a frightening consequence, then your fear may be aroused by the sound itself. As one 4-year-old ex-

claimed after watching a TV character get mugged, "If I had heard that music, I wouldn't have gone around the corner!" (Wells, 1981).

> "Learning is the eye of the mind."
>
> THOMAS DRAKE
> *BIBLIOTHECA SCHOLASTICA INSTRUCTISSIMA*
> 1633

Simpler animals can learn simple associations. When disturbed by a squirt of water, the sea snail *Aplysia* will protectively withdraw its gill. If the squirts continue, as happens naturally in choppy water, the withdrawal response diminishes. (The snail's response "habituates.") But if the sea snail repeatedly receives an electric shock just after being squirted, its withdrawal response to the squirt alone becomes stronger. The animal associates the squirt with the impending shock. More complex animals can learn more complex associations, especially those that bring favorable consequences. Seals in an aquarium will repeat behaviors, such as slapping and barking, that prompt people to toss them a herring.

By linking two events that occur close together, both the sea snail and the seal exhibit associative learning. The sea snail associates the squirt with impending shock; the seal associates slapping and barking with receiving a herring (Figure 8.1). In both cases, the animals learned something important to their survival: to associate the past with the immediate future.

Learned associations influence people, too, sometimes in weird ways. In one experiment, people rated neutral stimuli (Chinese characters) more positively when pressing their arms upward (as when lifting food) rather than when pressing them downward (as when pushing something or someone away). The positive associations of upward flexion imbued the stimuli with more positive overtones (Cacioppo & others, 1993). (Can you feel a subtle emotional difference while lifting a table edge with upturned hands rather than pressing it down?)

Figure **8.1**

Associative learning: Learning to associate two events

EVENT 1

EVENT 2

Sea snail associates splash with a tail shock

Seal learns to expect a snack for its showy antics

Learning . . . breeds hope.
What is learnable
we can potentially teach. . . .
What has been learned
we can potentially change.

Figure **8.2**

Classical conditioning

Two related events:

Stimulus 1
Lightning

Stimulus 2
Thunder

Result after repetition:

Stimulus
We see
lightning

Response
We wince
anticipating
thunder

Conditioning is the process of learning associations. In *classical conditioning*, we learn to associate two stimuli. We learn that a flash of lightning signals an impending crack of thunder, and start to brace ourselves when lightning flashes nearby (Figure 8.2).

In *operant conditioning*, we learn to associate a response and its consequence. We learn that pushing a vending machine button relates to the delivery of a candy bar (Figure 8.3).

To simplify things, we will consider these two types of associative learning separately. Often,

Figure **8.3**

Operant conditioning

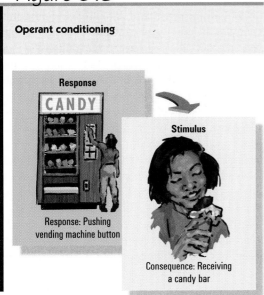

Response

CANDY

Response: Pushing
vending machine button

Stimulus

Consequence: Receiving
a candy bar

Of all the world's creatures, we humans are the most capable of changing our behavior through learning.

though, they occur together in the same situation. A clever Japanese rancher reportedly herds cattle by outfitting them with electronic pagers, which he calls from his portable phone. After a week of training, the cows learned to associate two stimuli—the beep on their pager and the arrival of food (classical conditioning). But they also learned to associate their hustling to the food trough with the pleasure of eating (operant conditioning).

This, however, leaves many questions: What principles influence the learning and the loss of associations? How can we apply these principles? And what really are the associations: Do associations form between neurons that are simultaneously active, such that firing one neuron cluster activates another? If so, does the first event also trigger a mental representation of the second? Does the beep on the cow's pager evoke a cognitive representation of food, to which the cow responds by coming to the trough? Or does it make little sense to explain conditioned associations in terms of cognitive processes?

Conditioning is not the only form of learning. Complex animals, such as chimpanzees, sometimes learn behaviors merely by observing others perform them. If one animal watches another learn to solve a puzzle that gains a food reward, the observing animal may perform the trick more quickly. In all these ways—by classical and operant conditioning and by observation—we humans learn and adapt to our environments. As this chapter will explain, we learn to expect and prepare for significant events such as food or pain (classical conditioning). We also learn to repeat acts that bring good results and to avoid acts that bring bad results (operant conditioning). By watching others, we gain new behaviors indirectly (observational learning). And, through language, we also learn things we have neither experienced nor observed. Of all the world's creatures, we humans are the most capable of changing our behavior through learning.

In searching for laws underlying learning, psychologist John B. Watson (1913) urged his colleagues to discard reference to inner thoughts, feelings, and motives. Psychology should instead study how organisms respond to stimuli in their

Which type of conditioning does the sea snail illustrate? What about the seal?

Most of us would be unable to name the order of the songs on our favorite CD. Yet hearing the end of one piece cues (by association) an anticipatory mental representation of the next. Likewise, when singing your national anthem, you associate the end of each line with the beginning of the next. (Pick a line out of the middle and notice how much harder it is to recall the previous line.)

Conditioned fear Because of pain experienced during previous visits to the dentist chair, this young patient has learned to expect discomfort.

behaviorism
the view that psychology (1) should be an objective science that (2) studies behavior without reference to mental processes. Most research psychologists today agree with (1) but not with (2).

classical conditioning
a type of learning in which an organism comes to associate stimuli. A neutral stimulus that signals an unconditioned stimulus (UCS) begins to produce a response that anticipates and prepares for the unconditioned stimulus. (Also called *Pavlovian conditioning*.)

unconditioned response (UCR)
in classical conditioning, the unlearned, naturally occurring response to the unconditioned stimulus (UCS), such as salivation when food is in the mouth.

unconditioned stimulus (UCS)
in classical conditioning, a stimulus that unconditionally—naturally and automatically—triggers a response.

Ivan Pavlov *"Experimental investigation . . . should lay a solid foundation for a future true science of psychology" (1927).*

environments, said Watson. "Its theoretical goal is the prediction and control of behavior. Introspection forms no essential part of its methods." Simply said, psychology should be an objective science based on *observable behavior*. This view, which influenced North American psychology during the first half of this century, Watson called behaviorism.

"[Psychology's] factual and theoretical developments in this century—which have changed the study of mind and behavior as radically as genetics changed the study of heredity—have all been the product of objective analysis— that is to say, behavioristic analysis."

PSYCHOLOGIST DONALD HEBB (1980)

Classical Conditioning

Russian physiologist Ivan Pavlov explored one important form of learning in his classic experiments on conditioning dogs. Pavlov showed how scientific research can reveal learning principles that apply across species. Others have modified Pavlov's understandings by asserting the importance of cognition and of biological predispositions to learn certain associations.

Although the idea of learning associations had long generated philosophical discussion, it was only in the early twentieth century that psychology's most famous research verified it. For many people, the name Ivan Pavlov rings a bell. His experiments are classics, and the phenomenon he explored we justly call classical conditioning (or *Pavlovian conditioning*).

Pavlov's Experiments

Pavlov was driven by a lifelong passion for research. After receiving a medical degree at age 33, he spent the next two decades studying the digestive system, work that earned him Russia's first Nobel prize in 1904. But it was his novel experiments on learning, to which he devoted the last three decades of his life, that earned this feisty scientist his place in history.

Pavlov's new direction came when his creative mind seized on an incidental finding. After studying salivary secretion in dogs, he knew that when he put food in a dog's mouth the animal would invariably salivate. He also noticed that when he worked with the same dog repeatedly, the dog began salivating to stimuli associated with food— to the mere sight of the food, to the food dish, to the presence of the person who regularly brought the food, or even to the sound of that person's approaching footsteps. Because these "psychic secretions" interfered with his experiments on digestion, Pavlov considered them an annoyance—until he realized they pointed to a simple but important form of learning. From that time on, Pavlov studied learning, which he hoped might enable him to understand better the brain's workings.

At first, Pavlov and his assistants tried to imagine what the dog was thinking and feeling as it drooled in anticipation of the food. This only led them into fruitless debates. So to attack the phenomenon more objectively, they experimented. They paired various neutral stimuli with food in the mouth to see if the dog would begin salivating to the neutral stimuli alone. To eliminate the possible influence of extraneous stimuli, they isolated the dog in a small room, secured it in a harness, and attached a device that diverted its saliva to a measuring instrument (Figure 8.4). From an adjacent room they could present food—at first by sliding in a food bowl, later by blowing meat powder into the dog's mouth at a precise moment. If a neutral stimulus—something the dog could see or hear—now regularly signaled the arrival of food, would the dog associate the two stimuli? If so, would it begin salivating to the neutral stimulus in anticipation of the food?

The answers proved to be yes. Just before placing food in the dog's mouth to produce salivation, Pavlov sounded a tone. After several pairings of tone and food, the dog began salivating to the tone alone, in anticipation of the meat powder. Using this procedure, Pavlov conditioned dogs to salivate to other stimuli—a buzzer, a light, a touch on the leg, even the sight of a circle.

Because salivation in response to food in the mouth was unlearned, Pavlov called it an unconditioned response (UCR). Food in the mouth automatically, *unconditionally*, triggers a dog's salivary reflex (Figure 8.5). Thus, Pavlov called the food stimulus an unconditioned stimulus (UCS).

Salivation in response to the tone was *conditional* upon the dog's learning the association between the tone and the food. This learned response

Figure **8.4**

Pavlov's device for recording salivation The dog's saliva was collected drop by drop in a tube. (Adapted from Goodwin, 1991.)

conditioned response (CR) in classical conditioning, the learned response to a previously neutral conditioned stimulus (CS).

conditioned stimulus (CS) in classical conditioning, an originally neutral stimulus that, after association with an unconditioned stimulus (UCS), comes to trigger a conditioned response.

we therefore call the conditioned response (CR). The previously neutral tone stimulus that now triggered the conditional salivation we call the conditioned stimulus (CS). It's easy to distinguish these two kinds of stimuli and responses. Just remember: conditioned = learned; *un*conditioned = *un*learned.

If this demonstration of associative learning was so simple, what did Pavlov do for the next three decades? He and his associates explored the causes and effects of classical conditioning. Their experiments identified five major conditioning processes: acquisition, extinction, spontaneous recovery, generalization, and discrimination.

Figure **8.5**

Pavlov's classic experiment Pavlov presented a neutral stimulus (a tone) just before an unconditioned stimulus (food in mouth). The neutral stimulus then became a conditioned stimulus, producing a conditioned response.

The unconditioned stimulus is repeatedly presented just after the neutral stimulus. The unconditioned stimulus continues to produce an unconditioned response.

The neutral stimulus alone now produces a conditioned response (CR), thereby becoming a conditioned stimulus (CS).

acquisition
the initial stage of learning, during which a response is established and gradually strengthened. In classical conditioning, the phase in which a stimulus comes to evoke a conditioned response. In operant conditioning, the strengthening of a reinforced response.

extinction
the diminishing of a conditioned response; occurs in classical conditioning when an unconditioned stimulus (UCS) does not follow a conditioned stimulus (CS); occurs in operant conditioning when a response is no longer reinforced.

spontaneous recovery
the reappearance, after a rest period, of an extinguished conditioned response.

generalization
the tendency, once a response has been conditioned, for stimuli similar to the conditioned stimulus to evoke similar responses.

Acquisition

To understand the acquisition, or initial learning, of the stimulus-response relationship, Pavlov and his associates first had to confront the question of timing: How much time should elapse between presenting the neutral stimulus (the tone, the light, the touch, or whatever) and the unconditioned stimulus? They found that, in most cases, the answer was not much. With many species and procedures, half a second works well. What do you suppose would happen if the food (UCS) appeared *before* the tone (CS) rather than after? Would conditioning occur?

Not likely. Although there are exceptions, conditioning seldom occurs when the CS comes after the UCS. This finding fits the presumption that classical conditioning is biologically adaptive. It helps organisms *prepare* for good or bad events. Pavlov's tone (CS) signals an important biological event—the arrival of food (UCS). To a deer in the forest, the sound of a snapping twig (CS) may come to signal a predator (UCS). If the good or bad event had already occurred, the CS would not likely signal anything significant.

Michael Domjan (1992, 1994) showed how this works by conditioning the sexual arousal of male Japanese quail. The researchers turned on a red light before presenting an approachable female. Over time, as the red light continued to herald a female's impending arrival, it caused the male quail to become excited (and to copulate with her more

quickly when she arrived). Moreover, the male quail developed a general liking for their cage's red-light district.

In humans, too, objects, smells, and sights associated with sexual pleasure become conditioned stimuli for sexual arousal. Psychologist Michael Tirrell (1990) recalls: "My first girlfriend loved onions, so I came to associate onion breath with kissing. Before long, onion breath sent tingles up and down my spine. Oh what a feeling!" (Questions: What is the unconditioned stimulus here? What is the conditioned response? See the diagram below.) In laboratory experiments, even a geometric figure can become sexually arousing if repeatedly associated with an erotic stimulus (Byrne, 1982). (Note that in this case the figure is a CS, which gains its power to arouse by repeated pairing with a naturally erotic stimulus.)

Extinction and Spontaneous Recovery

After conditioning, what happens if the CS occurs repeatedly without the UCS? Will the CS continue to elicit the CR? Pavlov found that when he sounded the tone again and again without presenting food, the dogs salivated less and less. Their declining salivation illustrates extinction, the diminished responding that occurs when the CS (tone) no longer signals an impending UCS (food).

Pavlov found, however, that if he allowed several hours to elapse before sounding the tone again, the salivation to the tone would reappear spontaneously (Figure 8.6). This spontaneous recovery—the reappearance of a (weakened) CR after a rest pause—suggested to Pavlov that extinction was suppressing the CR rather than eliminating it.

After breaking up with his fire-breathing heartthrob, Tirrell also experienced extinction and spontaneous recovery. He recalls that "the smell of onion breath (CS), no longer paired with the kissing (UCS), lost its ability to shiver my timbers. Occasionally, though, after not sensing the aroma for a long while, smelling onion breath awakens a small version of the emotional response I once felt."

An unexpected CS Onion breath does not usually produce sexual arousal. But when repeatedly paired with a passionate kiss it can become a CS and do just that.

UCS (passionate kiss)
UCR (sexual arousal)

CS (onion breath)
+
UCS (passionate kiss)
UCR (sexual arousal)

CS (onion breath)
CR (sexual arousal)

. . .classical conditioning is biologically adaptive. It helps organisms prepare for good or bad events.

Figure 8.6

Idealized curve of acquisition, extinction, and spontaneous recovery The rising curve shows that the CR rapidly grows stronger as the CS and UCS are repeatedly paired (acquisition), then wanes as the CS is presented alone (extinction). After a rest pause, the CR reappears (spontaneous recovery).

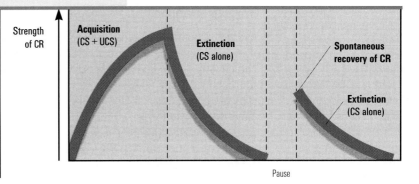

Generalization

Pavlov and his students noticed that a dog conditioned to the sound of one tone also responded somewhat to the sound of a different tone never paired with food. Likewise, a dog conditioned to salivate when rubbed would also salivate some when scratched (Windholz, 1989) or when stimulated on a different body part (Figure 8.7). This tendency to respond to stimuli similar to the CS is called generalization.

Generalization can be adaptive, as when toddlers taught to fear moving cars in the street respond similarly to trucks and motorcycles, or as when a child bitten by one dog may fear all dogs. So automatic is the process that one tortured Argentine writer still recoils with fear when he sees black shoes—his first glimpse of his torturers when they approached his cell. And a year after being shot in the shoulder and ribs during the 1995 massacre of 16 five-year-olds and their teacher in

Dunblane, Scotland, Matthew Birnie similarly showed evidence of generalization. Matthew still responded with terror to the sight of toy guns and the sound of balloons popping, festive trappings that were excluded from his sixth birthday party (Craig & Shields, 1996).

Because of generalization, stimuli that are similar to naturally disgusting or appealing objects will, by association, evoke some disgust or liking. Normally desirable foods, such as fudge, are unappealing when presented in a disgusting form, as when shaped to resemble dog feces (Rozin & others, 1986). We perceive adults with childlike facial features (round face, large forehead, small chin, large eyes) as having childlike warmth, submissiveness, and naiveté (Berry & McArthur, 1986). In both cases, people's emotional reactions to one stimulus generalize to similar stimuli.

Remember:
UCS = UnConditioned Stimulus
UCR = UnConditioned Response
CS = Conditioned Stimulus
CR = Conditioned Response

Check yourself: If the aroma of cake baking sets your mouth to watering, what is the UCS? The CS? The CR? (See page 250.)

Figure 8.7

Generalization Pavlov demonstrated generalization by attaching miniature vibrators to various parts of a dog's body. After conditioning salivation to stimulation of the thigh, he stimulated other areas. The closer a stimulated spot was to the thigh, the stronger the conditioned response. (From Pavlov, 1927.)

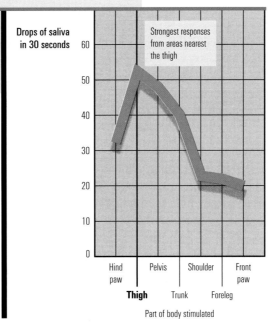

Answer to questions on page 249: the cake (and its taste) are the UCS. The associated aroma is the CS. Salivation to the aroma is the CR.

John Garcia As the laboring son of California farmworkers, Garcia attended school only in the off-season during his early childhood years. After entering junior college in his late twenties, and earning his Ph.D. in his late forties, he received the American Psychological Association's Distinguished Scientific Contribution Award "for his highly original, pioneering research in conditioning and learning" and was elected to the National Academy of Sciences.

Discrimination

Pavlov's dogs also learned to respond to the sound of a particular tone and *not* to other tones. This learned ability to *distinguish* between a conditioned stimulus and other stimuli is discrimination. Like generalization, discrimination has survival value. Slightly different stimuli are at times followed by vastly different consequences. Being able to recognize these differences is adaptive. Confronted by a pit bull, your heart may race; confronted by a cocker spaniel, it does not. Facing an approaching group of skinheads, you may cross the street to avoid them; approaching some bald gentlemen, you don't.

Updating Pavlov's Understanding

Pavlov's and Watson's disdain for "mentalistic" concepts such as consciousness has given way to a growing realization that they underestimated the importance of cognitive processes (thoughts, perceptions, expectations) and of biological constraints on an organism's learning capacity.

Cognitive Processes

The early behaviorists believed that the learned behaviors of various organisms could be reduced to mindless mechanisms. The idea that rats and dogs exhibit cognition therefore struck many psychologists as unnecessary. No longer. Robert Rescorla and Allan Wagner (1972) argued that when two significant events occur close together in time, an animal learns the *predictability* of the second event. If a shock always is preceded by a tone, and then sometimes also by a light that accompanies the tone, a rat will react with fear to the tone but not the light. Although the light always is followed by the shock, the tone better predicts impending shock. The more predictable the association, the stronger the conditioned response.

It's as if the animal learns an *expectancy*, an awareness of how likely it is that the UCS will occur. Rescorla (1988) surmised that classical conditioning "is not a stupid process by which the organism willy-nilly forms associations between any

"All brains are, in essence, anticipation machines."

DANIEL C. DENNETT
CONSCIOUSNESS EXPLAINED
1991

two stimuli that happen to occur." Conditioning occurs best when the CS and UCS have just the sort of relationship that would lead a scientist to conclude that the CS *causes* the UCS.

This principle helps explain why classical conditioning treatments that ignore cognition often have limited success. For example, therapy for alcoholics sometimes includes giving them alcohol spiked with a nauseating drug. Will they then associate alcohol with sickness? If classical conditioning were merely a matter of "stamping in" stimulus associations, we might hope so, and—to some extent—this does occur (as we will see on page 494). However, alcoholics are aware that they can blame their nausea on the drug, not on the alcohol. This cognition often weakens the association between alcohol and sickness. So, even in classical conditioning, it is not only the simple CS–UCS association but also the thought that counts.

Biological Predispositions

Ever since Darwin, scientists have assumed that animals share both a common evolutionary history and resulting commonalities in their makeup and functioning. Pavlov and Watson, for example, believed the basic laws of learning were essentially similar in all animals. So it should make little difference whether one studied pigeons or people. Moreover, it seemed that any natural response could be conditioned to any neutral stimulus. As learning researcher Gregory Kimble proclaimed in 1956, "Just about any activity of which the organism is capable can be conditioned and . . . these responses can be conditioned to any stimulus that the organism can perceive" (p. 195).

Twenty-five years later, Kimble (1981) humbly acknowledged that "half a thousand" scientific reports had proven him wrong. More than the early behaviorists realized, an animal's capacity for conditioning is constrained by its biology. The biological predispositions of each species dispose it to learn the particular associations that enhance its survival. Environments are not the whole story.

The person most responsible for challenging the prevailing behaviorist environmentalism was John Garcia. While researching the effects of radiation on laboratory animals, Garcia and Robert Koelling (1966) noticed that rats began to avoid drinking water from the plastic bottles in the radiation chambers. They wondered whether classical conditioning might be the culprit. Might the rats have linked the plastic-tasting water (a CS) to the sickness (UCR) induced by the radiation (UCS)?

To test their hunch, Garcia and Koelling gave the rats a particular taste, sight, or sound (CS) and later also gave them radiation or drugs (UCS) causing nausea (UCR). Two startling findings emerged: First, even if sickened as late as several hours after tasting a particular flavor, the rats thereafter avoided that flavor. This appeared to violate the notion that for conditioning to occur, the UCS must follow the CS immediately.

Second, the sickened rats developed aversions to the tastes but not to the sights or sounds. This contradicted the behaviorists' idea that any perceivable stimulus could serve as a CS. But it made adaptive sense, because for rats the easiest way to identify tainted food is to taste it. (If sickened after sampling a new food, they thereafter avoid the food—which makes it difficult to eradicate a population of "bait shy" rats by poisoning.) Birds, which hunt by sight, appear biologically primed to develop aversions to the *sight* of tainted food (Nicolaus & others, 1983).

Humans, too, seem biologically prepared to learn some things rather than others. If you get violently ill four hours after eating poisoned sardines, you will likely develop an aversion to the taste of sardines, but not to the sight of the associated restaurant, its plates, the people you were with, or the music you heard there. Similarly, we learn an aversion to alcohol better by associating its taste with nausea than with something unrelated to consumption, such as electric shock. We also more readily learn to fear snakes and spiders than to fear flowers (Cook & others, 1986). Again, it makes sense: Such animals harm us more frequently than do flowers.

All these cases support Darwin's principle that natural selection favors traits that aid survival. Nature prepares the members of each species to learn those things crucial to their survival. Someone who readily learns a taste aversion is unlikely to eat the same toxic food again and is more likely to survive and leave descendants. Indeed, all sorts of bad feelings, from nausea to anxiety to pain, serve good purposes. Like the low-oil light on a car dashboard, each alerts the body to a threat (Neese, 1991).

The philosopher Schopenhauer once said that important ideas are first ridiculed, then attacked, and finally taken for granted. So it was with Garcia's findings on taste aversion. At first, the leading journals refused to publish his work. The findings were impossible, said some critics. But as often happens in science, Garcia and Koelling's provocative findings stimulated new research, which confirmed their surprising findings and extended them to other species. In one well-known study, coyotes and wolves that were tempted into eating sheep carcasses laced with a sickening poison developed an aversion to sheep meat (Gustavson & others, 1974, 1976). Two wolves that were later penned with a live sheep seemed actually to fear it.

Such research suggests possible humane ways for controlling predators and agricultural pests. This is but one instance in which psychological research that began with the discomfort of some laboratory animals enhanced the welfare of many more animals. In this case, the research saved the sheep from the coyotes. The coyotes in turn were saved from angry ranchers and farmers who, with their livestock no longer endangered, were less adamant about destroying the coyotes. Later experiments revealed that conditioned taste aversion could successfully prevent baboons from raiding African gardens, racoons from attacking chickens, and ravens and crows from feeding on crane eggs—all while preserving predators who occupy an important ecological niche (Garcia & Gustavson, 1997).

Has research on biological constraints compelled researchers to abandon the search for universal principles of learning that generalize across species? No, biological predispositions affirm a deeper principle: *Learning enables animals to adapt to their environments.* Adaptation shows us why animals would be responsive to stimuli that announce significant events, such as food or pain. Animals are predisposed to associate a CS with a UCS that follows predictably and immediately—for causes often immediately precede effects.

Adaptation also helps explain exceptions, such as the taste-aversion finding. In this case, effect need not follow cause immediately—bad food usually causes sickness quite a while after it has been consumed. Similarly, cancer patients who suffer nausea and vomiting beginning more than an hour following chemotherapy often develop classically conditioned nausea to stimuli associated with taking the drug. (Under normal circumstances, such revulsion to sickening stimuli is adaptive.) The conditioned stimuli evoke the associated nausea. Thus, merely returning to the clinic's waiting room or seeing the nurses can provoke sick feelings (Burish & Carey, 1986; Davey, 1992).

Pavlov's Legacy

What, then, remains of Pavlov's ideas about conditioning? A great deal. All the researchers we have met so far in this chapter agree that classical conditioning is a basic form of learning. Judged by today's knowledge of cognitive processes and biological predispositions, Pavlov's ideas were in-

"Once bitten, twice shy."

G. F. NORTHALL
FOLK-PHRASES
1894

Taste aversion If you became violently ill after eating mussels, you likely would have a hard time eating them again. Their smell and taste would have become a CS for nausea. This learning occurs readily because our biology prepares us to learn taste aversions to toxic foods.

Nausea conditioning among cancer patients

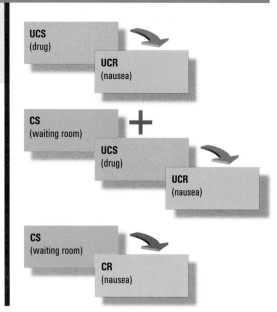

when they again encounter cues (people, places) associated with previous highs. Thus, drug counselors advise addicts to steer clear of settings associated with the euphoria of previous drug use. And, as we will see, counselors also attempt to give alcoholics experiences that reverse their positive associations with alcohol (page 494). Classical conditioning even works on the body's disease-fighting immune system. When, say, a particular taste accompanies a drug that influences immune responses, the taste by itself may come to produce an immune response (pages 525–528).

Pavlov's work provided a basis for John Watson's idea that human behavior, though biologically influenced, is mainly a bundle of conditioned responses. In one famous study, Watson and Rosalie Rayner (1920; Harris, 1979) showed how specific fears might be conditioned. Their subject was an 11-month-old infant named Albert. Like most

John B. Watson Watson (1924) admitted to "going beyond my facts" when offering his famous boast: "Give me a dozen healthy infants, well-formed, and my own specified world to bring them up in and I'll guarantee to take any one at random and train him to become any type of specialist I might select—doctor, lawyer, artist, merchant-chief, and, yes, even beggar-man and thief, regardless of his talents, penchants, tendencies, abilities, vocations, and race of his ancestors."

complete. But if we see further than Pavlov did, it is because we stand on his shoulders.

Why is Pavlov's work so important? If he had taught us only that old dogs can learn new tricks, his experiments would long ago have been forgotten. Why should anyone care that a dog can be conditioned to drool at the sound of a tone? The importance lies first in this fact: Many other responses to many other stimuli can be classically conditioned in many other organisms—in fact, in every species tested, from earthworms to fish to dogs to monkeys to people (Schwartz, 1984). Thus, classical conditioning is one way that virtually all organisms learn to adapt to their environment.

Second, Pavlov showed us how an internal process such as learning can be studied objectively. Pavlov was proud that his methods involved virtually no subjective judgments or guesses about what went on in the dogs' minds. The salivary response is an overt behavior measurable as so many drops or cubic centimeters of saliva. Pavlov's success therefore suggested a scientific model for how the young discipline of psychology might proceed—by isolating the elementary building blocks of complex behaviors and studying them with objective laboratory procedures.

Applications of Classical Conditioning

In later chapters on motivation, emotion, psychological disorders, therapy, and health, we will see how Pavlov's principles of classical conditioning apply to human health and well-being. For example, former crack cocaine users often feel a craving

Little Albert's conditioning The pairing of a laboratory rat with a terribly loud noise gave Little Albert a conditioned fear (the CR) of both rats (the CS) and similar furry things (generalization).

CLOSE-UP

Rape as Classical Conditioning

"A burnt child dreads the fire," says a medieval proverb. Experiments with dogs reveal that, indeed, if a painful stimulus is sufficiently powerful, a single event is sometimes enough to traumatize the animal when it again faces the situation. The human counterparts to these experiments can be tragic, as illustrated by one woman's experience of being attacked and raped, and thereby conditioned to a life of fear. Her fear (CR) is most powerfully associated with particular locations and people (CS), but it generalizes to other places and people. Note, too, how her traumatic experience has robbed her of the normally relaxing associations with such stimuli as home and bed.

> Four months ago I was raped. In the middle of the night I awoke to the sound of someone outside my bedroom. Thinking my housemate was coming home, I called out her name. Someone began walking slowly toward me, and then I realized. I screamed and fought, but there were two of them. One held my legs, while the other put a hand over my mouth and a knife to my throat and said, "Shut up, bitch, or we'll kill you." Never have I been so terrified and helpless. They both raped me, one brutally. As they then searched my room for money and valuables, my housemate came home. They brought her into my room, raped her, and left us both tied up on my bed.
>
> We never slept another night in that apartment. We were too terrified. Still, when I go to bed at night—always with the bedroom light left on—the memory of them entering my room repeats itself endlessly. I was an independent person who had lived alone or with other women for four years; now I can't even think about spending a night alone. When I drive by our old apartment, or when I have to go into an empty house, my heart pounds and I sweat. I am afraid of strangers, especially men, and the more they resemble my attackers the more I fear them. My housemate shares many of my fears, and is frightened when entering our new apartment. I'm afraid to stay in the same town, I'm afraid it will happen again, I'm afraid to go to bed. I dread falling asleep.

Eleven years later this woman could report that her conditioned fears are gradually extinguishing:

> The frequency and intensity of my fears have subsided. Still, I remain cautious about personal safety and occasionally have nightmares about my experience. But more important is my renewed ability to laugh, love, and trust—both old friends and new. Life is once again joyful. I have survived.

(From personal correspondence, with permission.)

---

infants, "Little Albert" feared loud noises but not white rats. Watson and Rayner presented him with a white rat and, as he reached to touch it, struck a hammer against a steel bar just behind his head. After seven repetitions of seeing the rat and then hearing the frightening noise, Albert burst into tears at the mere sight of the rat (making this an ethically troublesome study by today's standards). What is more, five days later Albert showed generalization of his conditioned response by reacting with fear to a rabbit, a dog, and a sealskin coat, but not to dissimilar objects such as toys.

Although Little Albert's fate is unknown, Watson's is not. After losing his professorship at Johns Hopkins University over an affair with Rayner (whom he later married), he became the J. Walter Thompson advertising agency's resident psychologist. There he used his knowledge of associative learning to conceive many successful campaigns, including one for Maxwell House that helped make the "coffee break" an American custom (Hunt, 1993).

Although some psychologists had difficulty repeating Watson and Rayner's findings with other children, the work with Little Albert has had legendary significance for many psychologists. Some have wondered if each of us might not be a walking repository of conditioned emotions. Might our less adaptive emotions be controlled by the application of extinction procedures or by conditioning new responses to emotion-arousing stimuli? One therapist told a patient, who for 30 years had feared going into an elevator alone, to force himself to enter 20 elevators a day. Within 10 days, his fear nearly vanished (Ellis & Becker, 1982). In Chapter 16 we will see more examples of how psychologists use behavioral techniques to treat emotional disorders.

In Watson and Rayner's experiment, what was the UCS? The UCR? The CS? The CR? (See page 254.)

operant conditioning
a type of learning in which behavior is strengthened if followed by reinforcement or diminished if followed by punishment.

respondent behavior
behavior that occurs as an automatic response to some stimulus; Skinner's term for behavior learned through classical conditioning.

operant behavior
behavior that operates on the environment, producing consequences.

law of effect
Thorndike's principle that behaviors followed by favorable consequences become more likely, and that behaviors followed by unfavorable consequences become less likely.

Skinner box
a chamber containing a bar or key that an animal can manipulate to obtain a food or water reinforcer, with attached devices to record the animal's rate of bar pressing or key pecking. Used in operant conditioning research.

shaping
an operant conditioning procedure in which reinforcers guide behavior toward closer and closer approximations of a desired goal.

Answer to question on page 253: The UCS was the loud noise; the UCR was the startled fear response; the CS was the rat; the CR was fear.

SUMMING UP

Although learning by association had been discussed for centuries, it remained for Ivan Pavlov to capture the phenomenon in his classic experiments on conditioning.

Pavlov's Experiments Pavlov repeatedly presented a neutral stimulus (such as a tone) just before an unconditioned stimulus (UCS, food) triggered an unconditioned response (UCR, salivation). After several repetitions, the tone alone (now the conditioned stimulus, CS) began triggering a conditioned response (CR, salivation). Further experiments on acquisition revealed that classical conditioning was usually greatest when the CS was presented just before the UCS, thus preparing the organism for what was coming. Other experiments explored the phenomena of extinction, spontaneous recovery, generalization, and discrimination.

Pavlov's work laid a foundation for John B. Watson's emerging belief that psychology, to be an objective science, should study only overt behavior, without considering unobservable mental activity. Watson called this position *behaviorism*.

Updating Pavlov's Understanding The behaviorists' optimism that learning principles would generalize from one response to another and from one species to another has been tempered. Conditioning principles, we now know, are cognitively influenced and biologically constrained. In classical conditioning, animals learn when to "expect" an unconditioned stimulus. Moreover, animals are biologically predisposed to learn associations between, say, a peculiar taste and a sickness-producing drink, which they will then avoid. But they don't learn to avoid a sickening drink announced by a noise.

Pavlov's Legacy Pavlov taught us that principles of learning apply across species, that significant psychological phenomena can be studied objectively, and that conditioning principles have important practical applications.

KEY TERMS AND CONCEPTS learning, associative learning, behaviorism, classical conditioning (Pavlovian conditioning), unconditioned response (UCR), unconditioned stimulus (UCS), conditioned response (CR), conditioned stimulus (CS), acquisition, extinction, spontaneous recovery, generalization, discrimination

Operant Conditioning

Through classical (Pavlovian) conditioning, an organism associates different stimuli that it does not control. Through operant conditioning, the organism associates its behaviors with consequences. Behaviors followed by reinforcers increase; those followed by punishment decrease. This simple but powerful principle has many applications, but also several important qualifications.

Classical conditioning associates neutral stimuli with important stimuli that produce responses which often are automatic. It's one thing to teach an animal to salivate at the sound of a tone or a child to fear cars in the street; it's something else to teach an elephant to walk on its hind legs or a child to say *please*. Another type of associative learning explains—and trains—such behaviors. Through operant conditioning subjects associate behaviors with their consequences. Thus, they become more likely to repeat rewarded (reinforced) behaviors and less likely to repeat punished behaviors.

Both classical and operant conditioning involve acquisition, extinction, spontaneous recovery, generalization, and discrimination. Yet their difference is straightforward: Classical conditioning forms associations between stimuli (a CS and the UCS it

DENNIS THE MENACE

"I think Mom's using the can opener."

signals). It also involves <u>respondent behavior</u>—behavior that occurs as an *automatic* response to some stimulus (such as salivating in response to meat powder and later in response to a tone). Operant conditioning involves <u>operant behavior</u>, so-called because the act *operates* on the environment to produce rewarding or punishing stimuli. We can therefore distinguish classical from operant conditioning by asking: *Is the organism learning associations between events that it doesn't control (classical conditioning)? Or is it learning associations between its behavior and resulting events (operant conditioning)?*

A discriminating creature
University of Windsor psychologist Dale Woodyard uses a food reward to train this manatee to discriminate between objects of different shapes, colors, and sizes. A manatee can remember such responses for as long as a year.

Skinner's Experiments

B. F. Skinner (1904–1990) was a college English major and an aspiring writer who, seeking a new direction, entered graduate school in psychology. He went on to become modern behaviorism's most influential and controversial figure. Skinner's work elaborated a simple fact of life that turn-of-the-century psychologist Edward L. Thorndike called the <u>law of effect</u>: Rewarded behavior is likely to recur. Using Thorndike's law of effect as a starting point, Skinner developed a "behavioral technology" that enabled him to teach pigeons such unpigeonlike behaviors as walking in a Figure 8, playing Ping-Pong, and keeping a missile on course by pecking at a target on a screen.

For his pioneering studies with rats (and later with pigeons), Skinner designed the now famous <u>Skinner box</u> (Figure 8.8). The box is typically a soundproof chamber with a bar or key that an animal presses or pecks to release a food or water reward, and with a device that records these responses.

Experiments by Skinner and other operant researchers did far more than teach us how to pull habits out of a rat. They explored the precise conditions that foster efficient and enduring learning.

Shaping

In his experiments, Skinner used <u>shaping</u>, a procedure in which rewards, such as food, gradually guide an animal's behavior toward a desired behavior. Imagine that you wanted to condition a rat to press a bar. After observing how the animal naturally behaves before training, you would build on its existing behaviors. You might give the rat a food reward each time it approaches the bar. Once the rat is approaching regularly, you would require it to move closer before rewarding it, then closer still; finally, you would require it to touch the bar before you gave it the food. With this method of *successive approximations*, you reward responses that are ever-closer to the final desired behavior, and you ignore all other responses. In just this way, researchers and animal trainers gradually *shape* complex behaviors.

By shaping nonverbal organisms to discriminate between stimuli, a psychologist can also determine what they perceive. Can a dog distinguish colors? Can a baby discriminate sounds? If we can shape them to respond to one stimulus and not to another, then obviously they can perceive the difference. Experiments show that some animals are remarkably capable of forming concepts; they demonstrate this by discriminating between classes of events or objects. If an experimenter reinforces a pigeon for pecking after seeing a human face, but not after seeing other images, the pigeon will learn to recognize a face (Herrnstein & Loveland, 1964).

Figure **8.8**

A Skinner box Inside the box, the rat presses a bar for a food reward. Outside, a measuring device records the animal's accumulated responses.

After being trained to discriminate between flowers, people, cars, and chairs, pigeons can usually identify in which of these categories a new pictured object belongs (Bhatt & others, 1988; Wasserman, 1993). With training, pigeons have even been taught to discriminate between Bach's music and Stravinsky's (Porter & Neuringer, 1984).

HI AND LOIS

Parents may use rewards to shape good table manners by praising eating behavior that is more and more adultlike. This sounds simple, but let's compare the essential features of shaping to what often happens at home and at school. In the shaping procedure, the trainer builds on the individual's existing behaviors by expecting and immediately rewarding successively closer approximations of a desired behavior. In everyday life, too, we continually reward and shape the behavior of others, said Skinner, but we often do so unintentionally. Sometimes we unthinkingly reward behaviors we find annoying. Billy's whining, for example, annoys his mystified parents, but look how they typically deal with Billy.

Billy: *Could you tie my shoes?*

Father: *(Continues reading paper.)*

Billy: *Dad, I need my shoes tied.*

Father: *Uh, yeah, just a minute.*

Billy: *DAAAAD! TIE MY SHOES!*

Father: *How many times have I told you not to whine? Now, which shoe do we do first?*

Or consider the way some teachers use rewards. On a wall chart, the teacher pastes gold stars after the names of children scoring 100 percent on spelling tests. All children take the same tests. As everyone can then see, some children, the academic all-stars, easily get 100 percent. The others, no matter how hard they try or how much they improve, get no reward. The teacher would be better advised to apply the principles of operant conditioning—to reward all spellers for gradual improvements (successive approximations toward fulfilling their own potential).

reinforcer
in operant conditioning, any event that strengthens the behavior it follows.

Principles of Reinforcement

So far, we have referred rather loosely to the power of "rewards." This idea gains a more precise meaning in Skinner's concept of the reinforcer, any event that increases the frequency of a preceding response. A reinforcer may be a tangible reward. It may be praise or attention. Or it may be an activity—being able to use the car when the dishes are done, or to have a break after an hour of study.

Most people think of reinforcers as rewards. Actually, there are two basic kinds of reinforcers. One type (positive reinforcer) strengthens a response by *presenting* a stimulus after a response. Food is a positive reinforcer for animals; attention, approval, and money are positive reinforcers for most people. The other type (negative reinforcer) strengthens a response by reducing or *removing* an aversive stimulus. (Negative reinforcers, like negative numbers, subtract something.) Imagine that alien invaders put you in an electrified cage, but that you could reduce or remove the electric shock by pressing a bar. You would surely press the bar, and be (negatively) reinforced for doing so. When a barely awake person pushes the snooze button, the silencing of the annoying alarm is similarly a reinforcer. When someone stops nagging or whining, that, too, is a reinforcer. (Note that contrary to popular usage, a negative reinforcer is not a punishing event; it is the *removal* of a punishing event.)

So imagine that whenever Billy throws a tantrum, his parents give in for the sake of peace and quiet. The child's tantrums will be reinforced when the parents give in. And the parents' behavior will be reinforced when Billy stops screaming. Or imagine a worried student who, after goofing off and getting a bad exam grade, studies harder for the next exam. The student may be reinforced by reduced anxiety and by a better grade. Whether it works by giving something positive or by reducing something negative, *a reinforcer is any consequence that strengthens behavior.*

Positive reinforcement
A high grade positively reinforces this boy's effort, as do his classmates' smiles and his teacher's praise.

Primary and Secondary Reinforcers

Primary reinforcers—getting food or being relieved of electric shock—are innately satisfying. Secondary reinforcers are learned. They get their power through association with primary reinforcers. If a rat in a Skinner box learns that a light reliably signals that food is coming, the rat will work to turn on the light. The light has become a secondary reinforcer associated with food. Our lives are filled with secondary reinforcers—money, good grades, a pleasant tone of voice, a word of praise—each of which has been linked with more basic rewards. Secondary reinforcers greatly enhance our ability to influence one another.

Immediate and Delayed Reinforcers

Let's return to the imaginary shaping experiment in which you were conditioning a rat to press a bar. Before performing this "wanted" behavior, the hungry rat will engage in a sequence of "unwanted" behaviors—scratching, sniffing, and moving around. Whichever of these behaviors immediately precedes the food reinforcer becomes more likely to recur. If you delay the reinforcement of bar pressing for longer than 30 seconds, allowing other behaviors to intervene and be reinforced, virtually no learning of the bar pressing will occur.

Unlike rats, humans do respond to reinforcers that are greatly delayed: the paycheck at the end of the week, the grade at the end of the semester, the trophy at the end of the season. Indeed, to function effectively we must learn to postpone immediate rewards for greater long-term rewards. Four-year-old children who in laboratory testing show an ability to delay gratification—who'd sooner have a big reward tomorrow than a small one right now—become more socially competent and more likely to be high achievers as adolescents (Mischel & others, 1989). A big part of maturity—and of gaining the most rewarding life—is learning to delay gratification.

But to our detriment, small but immediate reinforcements are sometimes more alluring than big but delayed reinforcements. Smokers, alcoholics, and other drug users may know that their immediate pleasure—the kick that often comes within seconds—is more than offset by future ill effects. Still, immediate reinforcement prevails. Thus, hangovers do not prevent further drinking, and drugs such as nicotine and cocaine that provide the most immediate reinforcement are the most strongly addictive (Marlatt, 1991). Likewise, for many teens the immediate gratification of risky, unprotected sex in passionate moments prevails over the delayed gratifications of safe sex or saved sex (Loewenstein & Furstenberg, 1991). And the

hour-long enjoyment of staying up to watch another TV show may seem to outweigh the prospect of tomorrow's day-long sluggishness.

Reinforcement Schedules

So far, most of our examples assume continuous reinforcement: The desired response is reinforced every time it occurs. Under such conditions, learning occurs rapidly. But when the reinforcement stops—when we disconnect the food delivery chute—extinction also occurs rapidly. The rat soon stops pressing the bar. If a normally dependable candy machine fails to deliver a chocolate bar twice in a row, we stop putting money into it (although a week later we may exhibit spontaneous recovery by trying again).

In real life, continuous reinforcement is rare. A salesperson does not make a sale with every pitch, nor does an angler get a bite with every cast. But they persist because their efforts have occasionally been rewarded. Researchers have explored several partial reinforcement schedules in which responses are sometimes reinforced, sometimes not (Nevin, 1988). Initial learning is typically slower with partial reinforcement, which makes continuous reinforcement preferable until a behavior is mastered.

"Oh, not bad. The light comes on, I press the bar, they write me a check. How about you?"

Drawing by Cheney; © 1993 The New Yorker Magazine, Inc.

But partial reinforcement produces greater persistence—greater *resistance to extinction*—than is found with continuous reinforcement. Imagine a pigeon that has learned to peck a key to obtain food. When the experimenter gradually fades out the delivery of food until it occurs only rarely and unpredictably, pigeons may peck 150,000 times without a reward (Skinner, 1953). With partial reinforcement, hope springs eternal.

primary reinforcer
an innately reinforcing stimulus, such as one that satisfies a biological need.

secondary reinforcer
a conditioned reinforcer; a stimulus that gains its reinforcing power through its association with a primary reinforcer.

continuous reinforcement
reinforcing the desired response every time it occurs.

partial reinforcement
reinforcing a response only part of the time; results in slower acquisition of response but much greater resistance to extinction than does continuous reinforcement.

> "The charm of fishing is that it is the pursuit of what is elusive but attainable, a perpetual series of occasions for hope."
>
> SCOTTISH AUTHOR JOHN BUCHAN
> 1875–1940

With partial reinforcement, hope springs eternal.

fixed-ratio schedule
in operant conditioning, a schedule of reinforcement that reinforces a response only after a specified number of responses.

variable-ratio schedule
in operant conditioning, a schedule of reinforcement that reinforces a response after an unpredictable number of responses.

fixed-interval schedule
in operant conditioning, a schedule of reinforcement that reinforces a response only after a specified time has elapsed.

variable-interval schedule
in operant conditioning, a schedule of reinforcement that reinforces a response at unpredictable time intervals.

punishment
an aversive event that *decreases* the behavior that it follows.

Question: Airline frequent-flyer programs that offer a free flight after every 25,000 miles of travel use which reinforcement schedule? Door-to-door salespeople are reinforced by which schedule? (See page 260.)

Corresponding human examples come readily to mind. Slot machines reward gamblers occasionally and unpredictably. This partial reinforcement affects them much as it affects pigeons: They keep trying, sometimes interminably. There is also a valuable lesson here for parents. *Occasionally* giving in to children's tantrums for the sake of peace and quiet puts the child on a partial reinforcement schedule. That's the very best procedure for making a behavior persist.

Skinner (1961) and his collaborators compared four schedules of partial reinforcement. Some are rigidly fixed, some unpredictably variable.

Fixed-ratio schedules reinforce behavior after a set number of responses. Like people paid on a piecework basis—say, for every 30 pieces—laboratory animals may be reinforced on a fixed ratio of, say, one reinforcer for every 30 responses. Once conditioned, the animal will pause only briefly after a reinforcer and will then return to a high rate of responding (Figure 8.9). Because resting while on a fixed-ratio schedule reduces rewards, employees often find such arrangements tiring. Unions have therefore pressured employers to replace piecework pay with hourly wage schedules.

Variable-ratio schedules provide reinforcers after an unpredictable number of responses. This is what gamblers and fly casters experience—unpredictable reinforcement—and what makes gambling and fishing behavior so hard to extinguish. Like the fixed-ratio schedule, it produces high rates of responding, because reinforcers increase as the responding increases.

Fixed-interval schedules reinforce the first response after a fixed time period. Like people checking more frequently for the mail as the delivery time approaches, pigeons on a fixed-interval schedule peck a key more frequently as the anticipated time for reward draws near, producing a choppy stop-start pattern (see Figure 8.9).

Variable-interval schedules reinforce the first response after *varying* time intervals. Like the unpredictable pop quiz that reinforces studying or the "Hello" that finally rewards persistence in redialing a busy phone number, variable-interval schedules tend to produce slow, steady responding. This makes sense, because there is no knowing when the waiting will be over. Should the pop quiz become predictable, students will begin the stop-start work pattern that characterizes fixed-interval schedules.

Animal behaviors differ, yet Skinner (1956) contended that these reinforcement principles of operant conditioning are universal. It matters little, he said, what response, what reinforcer, or what species you use. The effect of a given reinforcement schedule is pretty much the same: "Pigeon, rat, monkey, which is which? It doesn't matter. . . . Behavior shows astonishingly similar properties."

Punishment

The effect of punishment is opposite that of reinforcement. Reinforcement increases a behavior; punishment decreases it. Thus, a punisher is an aversive consequence that *decreases* the frequency of a preceding behavior. Swift and sure punishers

Figure **8.9**

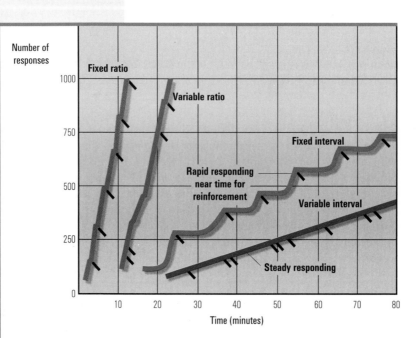

Partial reinforcement schedules
Skinner's laboratory pigeons produced these response patterns to each of four reinforcement schedules. (Reinforcers are indicated by diagonal marks.) For people, as for pigeons, reinforcement linked to number of responses (a ratio schedule) produces a higher response rate than reinforcement linked to amount of time elapsed (interval schedule). But the predictability of the reward also matters. A predictable (fixed) schedule produces a higher response rate than an unpredictable (variable) schedule. (Adapted from "Teaching Machines" by B. F. Skinner. Copyright © 1961, *Scientific American*, Inc. All rights reserved.)

can powerfully restrain unwanted behavior. The dog that learns to come running at the sound of the electric can opener will learn to hide if its master starts running the can opener to attract and catch it for banishment to the basement. The rat that is shocked after touching the forbidden object and the child who loses a treat after running into the street will learn not to repeat the behavior.

Boys Town psychologist Robert Larzelere (1994, 1996) notes a problem with human punishment studies, which often find that spanked children are at increased risk for aggression, depression, and low self-esteem. Well, yes, says Larzelere, just as people who have received radiation treatments are more likely to die of cancer, and people who have undergone psychotherapy are more likely to suffer depression—because they had preexisting problems that triggered the treatments. If one adjusts for preexisting cancer or depression—or antisocial behavior—then radiation, psychotherapy, or an occasional single swat or two of misbehaving 2- to 6-year-olds looks more effective, if the swat is combined with a generous dose of reasoning and positive parenting.

Nevertheless, say advocates of nonviolent parenting, punishment has drawbacks. Punished behavior is not forgotten; it is suppressed. This temporary suppression may (negatively) reinforce the punishing behavior. The child swears, the parent swats, the parent hears no more swearing from the child, and the parent feels the punishment was successful in stopping the behavior. But was it? If the punishment is avoidable, the punished behavior may reappear in safe settings. The child may simply learn not to swear around the house but to swear elsewhere. The driver who is hit with a couple of speeding tickets may buy a radar detector and speed freely when no radar patrol is around.

Punishment may also increase aggressiveness by demonstrating that aggression is a way to cope with problems. This helps explain why so many aggressive delinquents and abusive parents come from abusive families (Straus & Gelles, 1980). Moreover, punishment can create fear; the person receiving the punishment may associate the fear not only with the undesirable behavior but also with the person who administers it or with the situation in which it occurs. Thus, a child may come to fear the punitive teacher and want to avoid school. Worse, when punishments are unpredictable and inescapable, both animals and people may develop the sense that events are beyond their control. As a result, they may come to feel helpless and depressed. For these reasons, most European countries have banned hitting children in schools and child care institutions (Leach, 1993, 1994). The

Punishment tells you what not to do; reinforcement tells you what to do.

Scandinavian countries and Austria have further outlawed physical punishment by parents, thereby extending to children the same legal protection given to spouses.

Even when punishment suppresses unwanted behavior, it often does not guide one toward more desirable behavior. Punishment tells you what *not* to do; reinforcement tells you what *to* do. (Recall that children more easily understand positive instructions than negative ones—see page 92.) Thus, punishment combined with reinforcement is usually more effective than punishment alone. This approach has been used with children who bite themselves or bang their heads. They may be mildly punished (say, with a squirt of water in the face) whenever they bite themselves, but also be rewarded with positive attention and food when they behave well. The approach also works in the classroom. The teacher whose feedback on a paper says, "No, but try this . . ." and "Yes, that's it!" reduces unwanted behavior by reinforcing alternative behaviors.

Parents of delinquent youth often lack this awareness of how to reinforce desirable behavior without screaming or hitting (Patterson & others, 1982). Training programs for such parents help them reframe contingencies from dire threats to positive incentives—from "You clean up your room this minute or no dinner!" to "You're welcome at the dinner table after you get your room cleaned up." When you stop to think about it, many threats of punishment are just as forceful, and perhaps more effective, if rephrased positively. Thus, "If you don't get your homework done, there'll be no TV" would better be phrased as. . . .

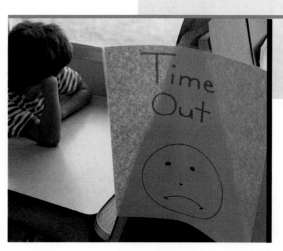

The problem with punishment
Swift and sure punishment can decrease unwanted behavior, but it can also evoke undesired responses, such as anger, fear, or resistance.

cognitive map
a mental representation of the layout of one's environment. For example, after exploring a maze, rats act as if they have learned a cognitive map of it.

latent learning
learning that occurs but is not apparent until there is an incentive to demonstrate it.

Answer to question on page 258: Frequent-flyer programs use a fixed-ratio schedule. Door-to-door salespeople are reinforced on a variable-ratio schedule (after varying numbers of rings).

To sum up, swift and sure punishment can be effective, and it may on occasion cause less pain than does the self-destructive behavior it suppresses. However, punished behavior may reappear if the threatened punishment can be avoided. (What punishment often teaches, said Skinner, is how to avoid it.) Punishment can also have undesirable side effects, such as creating fear and teaching aggression, and it often fails to teach how to act positively. Most psychologists therefore favor an emphasis on reinforcement rather than on punishment. Catch people doing something right and affirm them for it.

Updating Skinner's Understanding

Although Skinner granted the existence of private processes and the biological underpinnings of behavior, many psychologists criticized him for discounting the importance of these factors.

Cognition and Operant Conditioning

A mere eight days before dying of leukemia, Skinner (1990) stood before the American Psychological Association convention for one final critique of "cognitive science," which he viewed as a throwback to turn-of-the-century introspectionism. Skinner died resisting the growing belief that cognitive processes—thoughts, perceptions, expectations—have a necessary place in the science of psychology and even in our understanding of conditioning.

Yet we have seen several hints that cognitive processes might be at work in operant learning. For example, animals on a fixed-interval reinforcement schedule respond more and more frequently as the time approaches when a response will produce a reinforcer. The animals behave as if they expect that repeating the response will soon produce the reward. To a behaviorist, however, talk of "expectations" is unnecessary; it is enough to say that responses that are reinforced under certain conditions recur when those conditions recur.

Latent Learning

Other evidence of cognitive processes comes from studies of rats in mazes. Rats exploring a maze, with no obvious reward, are like people driving around a new town. The rats develop a cognitive map, a mental representation of the maze. This occurs even if the rats are carried passively through the maze in a wire basket. When an experimenter then places a reward in the maze's goal box, the rats immediately perform as well as rats that have been reinforced with food for running the maze (Figure 8.10).

During their explorations, the rats seemingly experience latent learning—learning that becomes apparent only when there is some incentive to demonstrate it. The unavoidable conclusion: Learning can occur without reinforcement. As the cognitive mapping experiments suggest, there is more to learning than associating a response with a consequence. There is also cognition. In Chapter 10 we will encounter striking evidence of animals' cognitive abilities in solving problems and using aspects of language.

Figure **8.10**

Latent learning Animals, like people, can learn from experience, with or without reinforcement. After exploring a maze for 10 days, rats received a food reward at the end of the maze. They quickly demonstrated their prior learning of the maze—by immediately doing as well as (and even better than) rats that had been reinforced for running the maze. (From Tolman & Honzik, 1930.)

Overjustification

The cognitive perspective has also led to an important qualification concerning the power of rewards: Unnecessary rewards sometimes carry hidden costs. Most people think that offering tangible rewards will boost anyone's interest in a task (Boggiano & others, 1987). Actually, promising children a reward for a task they already enjoy can backfire. People who begin to see the reward as their motive for performing the task may lose their intrinsic interest in it. This phenomenon is called the overjustification effect, because an already justifiable activity becomes *over*justified by the promise of added reward.

In experiments, children promised a payoff for playing with an interesting puzzle or toy later play with the toy less than do children who are not paid to play (Tang & Hall, 1995). It is as if the children think, "If I have to be bribed into doing this, then it must not be worth doing for its own sake."

Wendy Grolnick and Richard Ryan (1987) showed how overjustification can affect teaching and learning. They invited fifth graders to read a passage from a social studies book. Some they instructed in a controlling way: "I'll be grading you on the test to see if you're learning enough." Others, treated in a less controlling manner ("You won't be graded on . . . I'm just interested in what children can remember"), learned as much *and found the passage more interesting.*

Interest also survives when rewards are used not to bribe or control but to signal a job well done (Boggiano & others, 1985). If a reward boosts your feeling of competence after doing good work, your liking of the task may increase. Rewards, rightly administered, have positive effects (Eisenberger & Cameron, 1996).

Biological Predispositions

As with classical conditioning, an animal's natural predispositions constrain its capacity for operant conditioning. When you reinforce a hamster's behavior with food, you can easily condition it to dig or to rear up, because these are among the animal's natural behaviors when searching for food. But it is harder to use food reinforcers to shape hamster behaviors, such as face washing, that aren't normally associated with food or hunger (Shettleworth, 1973). Similarly, pigeons easily learn to flap their wings to avoid shock and to peck to obtain food, because they naturally flee with their wings and eat with their beaks. But they have a hard time learning to peck to avoid shock or to flap to obtain food (Foree & LoLordo, 1973). Biological constraints predispose organisms to learn associations that are naturally adaptive.

Skinner's former associates, Keller Breland and Marian Breland (1961), came to appreciate biological predispositions while using operant procedures to train animals for circuses, TV shows, and movies. The Brelands had originally assumed that operant principles would work on almost any response that any animal could make. But after training 6000 animals of 38 different species, from chickens to whales, they concluded that biological predispositions were more important than they had supposed. In one act, they trained pigs to pick up large wooden "dollars" and deposit them in a piggy bank. After learning this behavior, however, the animals began to drift back to their natural ways. They would drop the coin, push it with their snouts as pigs are prone to do, pick it up again, and then repeat the sequence—delaying their food reinforcer. As this "instinctive drift" illustrates, "misbehaviors" occurred when the animals reverted to their biologically predisposed patterns.

overjustification effect *the effect of promising a reward for doing what one already likes to do. The person may now see the reward, rather than intrinsic interest, as the motivation for performing the task.*

For more information on animal behavior, see books by (I am not making this up) Robin Fox and Lionel Tiger.

"Never try to teach a pig to sing. It wastes your time and annoys the pig."

MARK TWAIN

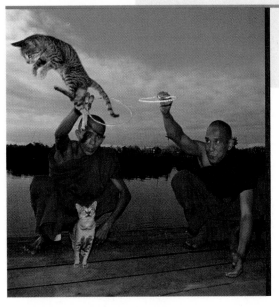

Natural athletes Animals can most easily learn and retain behaviors that draw on their biological predispositions, such as cats' inborn tendency to leap high and land on their feet.

Skinner's Legacy

B. F. Skinner was one of the late twentieth century's most controversial intellectual figures. He stirred a hornet's nest by repeatedly insisting that external influences, not internal thoughts and feelings, shape behavior and by urging the use of operant principles to influence people's behavior at school, work, and home. To help or manage people effectively, Skinner said, we should worry less about their illusions of freedom and dignity. Recognizing that behavior is shaped by its consequences, we should administer rewards in ways that promote more desirable behavior.

Skinner's critics objected, saying that he dehumanized people by neglecting their personal freedom and by seeking to control their actions. Skinner's reply: People's behavior is already haphazardly controlled by external consequences, so why not administer those consequences for human betterment? In place of the punishments used in homes, schools, and prisons, would not reinforcers be more humanitarian? And if it is humbling to think that we are shaped by our histories, this very idea also gives us hope that we can shape our future.

Applications of Operant Conditioning

We have seen applications of operant conditioning principles, and in later chapters we will see how psychologists apply these principles to problems ranging from high blood pressure to social withdrawal. Reinforcement technologies are also at work in schools, businesses, and homes.

At School

A generation ago, Skinner and others advocated teaching machines and textbooks that would shape

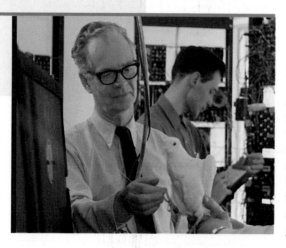

B. F. Skinner "I am sometimes asked, 'Do you think of yourself as you think of the organisms you study?' The answer is yes. So far as I know, my behavior at any given moment has been nothing more than the product of my genetic endowment, my personal history, and the current setting" (1983).

learning in small steps and provide immediate reinforcement for correct responses. These machines and texts, they said, would revolutionize education and free teachers to concentrate on their students' special needs.

To envision Skinner's dream, imagine two math teachers. Faced with a class of academically diverse students, Teacher A gives the whole class the same math lesson. The teacher knows that some students already understand the concepts and that others will be frustrated by their inability to comprehend. But with so many different children, how can one teacher guide them individually? When test time comes, the whiz kids breeze through unchallenged, and the slower learners again experience failure. Faced with a similar class, Teacher B paces the material according to each student's rate of learning and provides prompt feedback with positive reinforcement to slow and fast learners. Does the individualized instruction of Teacher B sound like an impossible ideal?

Although the predicted revolution has not occurred, to the end of his life Skinner (1986, 1988, 1989) believed the ideal was achievable. "Good instruction demands two things," he said. "Students must be told immediately whether what they do is right or wrong and, when right, they must be directed to the step to be taken next." To do this, and to free teachers for uniquely human tasks, computers were his final hope. For reading and math drills, the computer could be Teacher B—engaging the student actively, pacing material according to the student's rate of learning, quizzing the student to find gaps in understanding, providing immediate feedback, and keeping flawless records for the supervising teacher. With online testing systems improving and more and more interactive student software and Internet resources becoming available, we are closer than ever before to achieving Skinner's ideal.

Reinforcement principles can also enhance sports abilities. Again, the secret is to shape behavior, first by reinforcing small successes, and then gradually increasing the challenge. Thomas Simek and Richard O'Brien (1981, 1988) applied these principles to teaching golf and baseball by starting with responses that are easily reinforced. Golf students begin with very short putts. As they build mastery, they eventually step back farther and farther until taking full swings off the tee. Likewise, novice baseball players begin with half swings at an oversized ball pitched from 10 feet away, which immediately gives them the pleasure of smacking the ball. As their confidence builds with success and they achieve mastery at each level, the pitcher gradually moves back to 15 feet, then 22 feet, 30

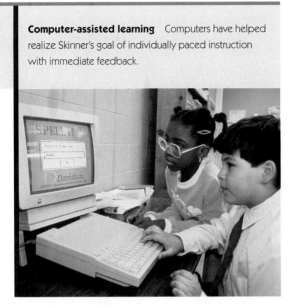

Computer-assisted learning   Computers have helped realize Skinner's goal of individually paced instruction with immediate feedback.

feet, and 40.5 feet, and eventually introduces a regular ball. Compared with children taught by conventional methods, those trained by this behavioral method show faster skill improvement in both testing and game situations.

At Work

Believing that reinforcers influence productivity, business managers have capitalized on psychological research. Many companies now enable their employees to share profits, or even to participate in company ownership. When workers' productivity boosts rewards for all, their motivation, morale, and cooperative spirit often increase (Deutsch, 1991). Reinforcement for jobs well done is especially effective in boosting productivity when the desired performance is *well-defined and achievable*. Reward specific behaviors, not vaguely defined merit. Criticism, too, triggers the least resentment and the greatest performance boost when it is considerate and specific (Baron, 1988).

It's also a good idea to make the reinforcement *immediate*. Thomas Watson, who led IBM during its tremendous growth, would write out a check on the spot for achievements he observed (Peters & Waterman, 1982). But rewards need not be material, nor should they be so big that they become political and a source of discouragement to those who don't receive them. An effective manager may simply walk the floor and praise people for good work, or write unexpected notes of appreciation for a completed project. As Skinner said, "How much richer would the whole world be if the reinforcers in daily life were more effectively contingent on productive work?"

Animals, too, can be trained to perform useful work. Imagine a self-propelled marine vehicle with a sonar system and on-board computer suitable for detecting, classifying, and manipulating targets. That pretty well describes how the U.S. Navy once viewed its dolphins and sea lions, which at various times have been trained to perform salvage duties, serve as watch dogs around a submarine base, or seek out explosive mines in the Persian Gulf. The animals' training used food reinforcements to shape them toward ever-closer approximations of the desired behavior (Holing, 1988; Morrison, 1988).

At Home

Many economists and psychologists view people's spending behavior as controlled by its consequences (its costs and benefits). Compared with people who rent apartments in buildings where energy costs are paid by the landlord, those who live in comparable buildings but pay their own energy costs (therefore reaping the rewards of their own energy savings) use about 20 percent less energy. Similarly, home electricity users on an "energy diet" are helped by frequent feedback that shows their current usage compared with their past consumption (Darley & others, 1979). In homes, as elsewhere, immediate consequences most effectively influence behavior. Al Gore (1992, p. 348) suggests how tax policies might harness the power of consequences:

> There is an economic rule of thumb: whatever we tax, we tend to get less of; whatever we subsidize, we tend to get more of. Currently, we tax work and we subsidize the depletion of natural resources—and both policies have contributed to high unemployment and the waste of natural resources. What if we lowered the tax on work and simultaneously raised it on the burning of fossil fuels?

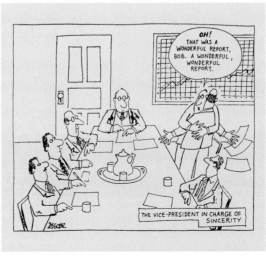

OH! THAT WAS A WONDERFUL REPORT, BOB. A WONDERFUL, WONDERFUL REPORT.

THE VICE-PRESIDENT IN CHARGE OF SINCERITY

Drawing by Ziegler; © 1989 *The New Yorker Magazine, Inc.*

We can use operant conditioning on ourselves, by reinforcing our most desired behaviors and extinguishing those undesired.

We can also use operant conditioning in parenting. Parent training researchers Michelle Wierson and Rex Forehand (1994) remind us that when parents say "get ready for bed" and then concede to protesting or defiance, they reinforce unwanted behaviors. Eventually, exasperated, they may yell at the child or make a menacing gesture, at which point the child's fearful compliance reinforces the parents' angry behavior. Over time, a destructive parent-child relationship develops. To disrupt this cycle, they recommend that parents

- give children attention and other reinforcers when they are behaving *well*. Target a specific behavior, reward it, and watch it increase.

- ignore whining. If whining has triggered attention in the past, it may temporarily increase when ignored. Over time, if not reinforced, it will diminish.

- when children misbehave or are defiant, don't yell or hit. Simply explain the misbehavior and give them "time-out"—remove them from reinforcing surroundings for a specified time.

Finally, we can use operant conditioning on ourselves, by reinforcing our most desired behaviors and extinguishing those undesired. To take charge of your own behavior, psychologists suggest these step-by-step procedures:

1 State your goal—say, to stop smoking, eat less, or study or exercise more—in measurable terms, and make your intention public. You might, for example, aim to boost your study time by an hour a day, and announce that goal to your friends.

2 Record how often you engage in the behavior you wish to promote and note how this behavior is being reinforced. You might log your current study time, noting under what conditions you do and don't study. (When I began writing textbooks, I logged my time and was astonished to discover how much time I was wasting.)

3 Begin systematically to reinforce the desired behavior. To increase your study time, allow yourself a snack (or some other reinforcing activity) only after specified periods of study. Agree with your friends that you will join them for weekend activities only if you have met your weekly studying goal.

4 As your new behaviors become more habitual, gradually reduce the incentives while giving yourself a mental pat on the back.

SUMMING UP

Through operant conditioning, organisms learn to produce behaviors that are followed by reinforcing stimuli and to suppress behaviors that are followed by punishing stimuli.

Skinner's Experiments When placed in a Skinner box, rats or pigeons can be shaped to display successively closer approximations of a desired behavior. Researchers have also studied the effects of primary and secondary reinforcers, and of immediate and delayed reinforcers. Partial reinforcement schedules (fixed-ratio, variable-ratio, fixed-interval, and variable-interval) produce slower acquisition of the target behavior than does continuous reinforcement, but they also create more resistance to extinction. Punishment is most effective when it is strong, immediate, and consistent. However, it can have undesirable side effects.

Updating Skinner's Understanding Skinner's emphasis on external control of behavior made him an influential but controversial figure. Many psychologists criticized Skinner (as they did Pavlov) for underestimating the importance of cognitive and biological constraints. For example, research on latent learning and overjustification further indicates the importance of cognition in learning.

Skinner's Legacy Skinner stimulated vigorous intellectual debate regarding the nature of human freedom and strategies and ethics of managing people. Nevertheless, his operant principles are being applied in schools, the workplace, and homes. For example, computer-assisted instruction can embody the operant ideal of individualized shaping and immediate positive reinforcement.

Contrasting Conditioning Techniques The last three decades of research have changed psychologists' views of both classical and operant conditioning (summarized in Table 8.1). Learning, like so much else, depends on both nature and nurture. As we have seen, biological predispositions make learning some associations easier than learning others. Yet animals exhibit more sophisticated cognitive processes than once seemed likely. And rewarding people to do what they already enjoy may undermine their interest.

KEY TERMS AND CONCEPTS operant conditioning, respondent behavior, operant behavior, law of effect, Skinner box, shaping, reinforcer, primary reinforcer, secondary reinforcer, continuous reinforcement, partial reinforcement, fixed-radio schedule, variable-ratio schedule, fixed-interval schedule, variable-interval schedule, punishment, cognitive map, latent learning, overjustification effect

"O! This learning, what a thing it is."

WILLIAM SHAKESPEARE
TAMING OF THE SHREW
1597

Comparison of Classical and Operant Conditioning

Table **8.1**

	Classical Conditioning	Operant Conditioning
The Response	Involuntary, automatic	"Voluntary," operates on environment
Acquisition	Associating events; CS announces UCS.	Associating response with a consequence (reinforcer or punisher).
Extinction	CR decreases when CS is repeatedly presented alone.	Responding decreases when reinforcement stops.
Cognitive processes	Subjects develop expectation that CS signals the arrival of UCS.	Subjects develop expectation that a response will be reinforced or punished; they also exhibit latent learning, without reinforcement.
Biological predispositions	Natural predispositions constrain what stimuli and responses can easily be associated.	Organisms best learn behaviors similar to their natural behaviors; unnatural behaviors instinctively drift back toward natural ones.

Learning by Observation

Learning occurs not only through conditioning but also from our observations of others. Lord Chesterfield (1694–1773) had the idea: "We are, in truth, more than half what we are by imitation."

From drooling dogs, running rats, and pecking pigeons we have learned much about the basic processes of learning. But conditioning principles alone do not tell us the whole story. Among higher animals, especially humans, learning need not occur through direct experience. Observational learning, in which we observe and imitate others' behaviors, also plays a big part.

"Children need models more than they need critics."

JOSEPH JOUBERT
PENSÉES
1842

The process of observing and imitating a specific behavior is often called modeling. By observing and imitating models we learn all kinds of social behaviors. By 9 months of age, infants will imitate novel play behaviors, and by age 14 months will imitate acts modeled on television (Meltzoff, 1988a,b,c). To persuade children to smoke, expose them to parents and older youth who smoke. To encourage children to read, read to them and surround them with books and people who read them. To increase the odds of your children practicing your religion, worship and attend other religious activities with them.

Learning from observation
This 14-month-old boy in Andrew Meltzoff's laboratory is imitating behavior he has seen on TV. In the top photo the infant leans forward and carefully watches the adult pull apart a toy. In the middle photo he has been given the toy. In the bottom photo he pulls the toy apart, imitating what he has seen the adult do.

Bandura's Experiments

Picture this scene from a famous experiment devised by Albert Bandura, the pioneering researcher of observational learning (Bandura & others, 1961). A preschool child is at work on a drawing.

observational learning
learning by observing and imitating the behavior of others.

modeling
the process of observing and imitating a behavior.

prosocial behavior
positive, constructive, helpful behavior. The opposite of antisocial behavior.

Albert Bandura
"Learning would be exceedingly laborious, not to mention hazardous, if people had to rely solely on the effects of their own actions to inform them what to do" (1977).

A model grandma This boy is learning to cook by observing his grandmother. As the sixteenth-century proverb states, "Example is better than precept."

An adult in another part of the room is working with some Tinker Toys. The adult then gets up and for nearly 10 minutes pounds, kicks, and throws a large inflated Bobo doll around the room, while yelling such remarks as, "Sock him in the nose. . . . Hit him down. . . . Kick him."

After observing this outburst, the child is taken to another room where there are many appealing toys. Soon the experimenter interrupts the child's play and explains that she has decided to save these good toys "for the other children." She now takes the frustrated child to an adjacent room containing a few toys, including a Bobo doll. Left alone, what does the child do?

Compared with children not exposed to the adult model, children who observed the aggressive outburst were much more likely to lash out at the doll. Apparently, observing the adult model beating up the doll lowered their inhibitions. But something more than lowered inhibitions was at work, for the children also imitated the very acts they had observed and used the very words they had heard.

Applications of Observational Learning

The bad news from such studies is that antisocial models—in one's family or neighborhood, or on TV—may have antisocial effects (pages 573–578). This helps us understand how abusive parents might have aggressive children and why men who beat their wives often had wife-battering fathers. The lessons we learn as children are not easily unlearned as adults, and they are sometimes visited on future generations. Critics note that the intergenerational transmission of abuse could be genetic. But with monkeys, at least, we know it can be environmental. In study after study, young monkeys that received high levels of aggression when reared apart from their mothers grew up to be perpetrators of aggression (Chamove, 1980). Monkey see, monkey do.

The good news is that prosocial (positive, helpful) models can have prosocial effects. People who exemplify nonviolent, helpful behavior can prompt similar behavior in others. Mahatma Gandhi and Martin Luther King, Jr., both drew on the power of modeling, making nonviolent action a powerful force for social change. Parents are powerful models. Research indicates that European Christians who risked their lives to rescue Jews from the Nazis, like the civil rights activists of a generation ago, usually had a close relationship with at least one parent who modeled a strong moral or humanitarian concern (London, 1970; Oliner & Oliner, 1988).

Models are most effective when their actions and words are consistent. Sometimes, however, models say one thing and do another. Many parents seem to operate according to the principle "Do as I *say*, not as I do." Experiments suggest that children learn to do both (Rice & Grusec, 1975; Rushton, 1975). When exposed to a hypocrite, they tend to imitate the hypocrisy by doing what the model did and saying what the model said.

What determines whether we will imitate a model? Bandura believes part of the answer is reinforcements and punishments—those received by the model as well as by the imitator. We look and we learn. By looking, we learn to anticipate a behavior's consequences in situations like those we are observing. By watching TV programs, children may "learn" that physical intimidation is an effective way to control others, that free and easy sex brings pleasure without the misery of unwanted pregnancy or disease, or that men are supposed to be tough and women gentle. We are especially likely to imitate those we perceive as similar to ourselves, as successful, or as admirable.

Although our knowledge of learning principles comes from the work of thousands of investigators, this chapter has focused on the ideas of a few pioneers—Pavlov, Watson, Skinner, and Bandura. They illustrate the impact that can result from single-minded devotion to a few well-defined problems and ideas. These researchers defined the issues and impressed on us the importance of learning. As their legacy demonstrates, intellectual history is often made by people who, at the risk of overstatement, pursue ideas to their limits.

SUMMING UP

Another important type of learning, especially among humans, is what Albert Bandura and others call *observational learning*. In experiments, children tend to imitate what a model both does and says, whether the behavior is prosocial or antisocial. Such experiments have stimulated research on social modeling in the home, on television, and within peer groups. We are especially likely to imitate those we perceive to be like us, successful, or admirable.

KEY TERMS AND CONCEPTS observational learning, modeling, prosocial behavior

TERMS AND CONCEPTS TO REMEMBER

learning, p. 243

associative learning, p. 244

behaviorism, p. 246

classical conditioning, p. 246

unconditioned response (UCR), p. 246

unconditioned stimulus (UCS), p. 246

conditioned response (CR), p. 247

conditioned stimulus (CS), p. 247

acquisition, p. 248

extinction, p. 248

spontaneous recovery, p. 248

generalization, p. 249

discrimination, p. 250

operant conditioning, p. 254

respondent behavior, p. 255

operant behavior, p. 255

law of effect, p. 255

Skinner box, p. 255

shaping, p. 255

reinforcer, p. 256

primary reinforcer, p. 257

secondary reinforcer, p. 257

continuous reinforcement, p. 257

partial reinforcement, p. 257

fixed-ratio schedule, p. 258

variable-ratio schedule, p. 258

fixed-interval schedule, p. 258

variable-interval schedule, p. 258

punishment, p. 258

cognitive map, p. 260

latent learning, p. 260

overjustification effect, p. 261

observational learning, p. 265

modeling, p. 265

prosocial behavior, p. 266

CRITICAL THINKING EXERCISE
by Richard O. Straub

Now that you have read and reviewed Chapter 8, take your learning a step further by testing your critical thinking skills on the following pattern recognition exercise.

Psychologists believe that children learn to control their bladders during sleep through classical conditioning, a type of learning in which an organism comes to associate different events. Normally, a wet bed or diaper causes a child to awaken. Through repeated pairings, bladder tension becomes associated with the sensation of wetness and children wake up when they sense that the bladder is full.

Imagine that you are baby-sitting a 6-year-old bed-wetter who has not yet learned the connection between bladder tension and wetness. In desperation, the child's parents consult a behavioral psychologist who has developed a classical conditioning technique for controlling bed-wetting, using a special sheet containing fine electric wires. When a sleeping child wets the bed, the urine (which conducts electricity) immediately completes an electrical circuit and causes a loud bell to ring, awakening the child. Over time, bladder tension becomes associated with the bell and the child is conditioned to wake up before actually wetting the bed.

Although the parents have read a pamphlet that explains the basic principles underlying the conditioning technique, they are seeking your help in understanding exactly *why* it works.

1. Can you identify the components of classical conditioning for children who learn to wake up before they wet the bed *without* special training?

Unconditioned stimulus → FULL BLADDER

Unconditioned response urine

Conditioned stimulus — Bell

Conditioned response — UR

2. Can you identify the components of classical conditioning for children who are conditioned to wake up through use of the special sheet and bell?

Unconditioned stimulus

Unconditioned response

Conditioned stimulus

Conditioned response

3. Does the classical conditioning explanation of how children learn on their own to wake up before wetting the bed make sense? Can you explain this learning, using principles of operant conditioning?

Check your progress on becoming a critical thinker by comparing your answers to the sample answers found in Appendix B.

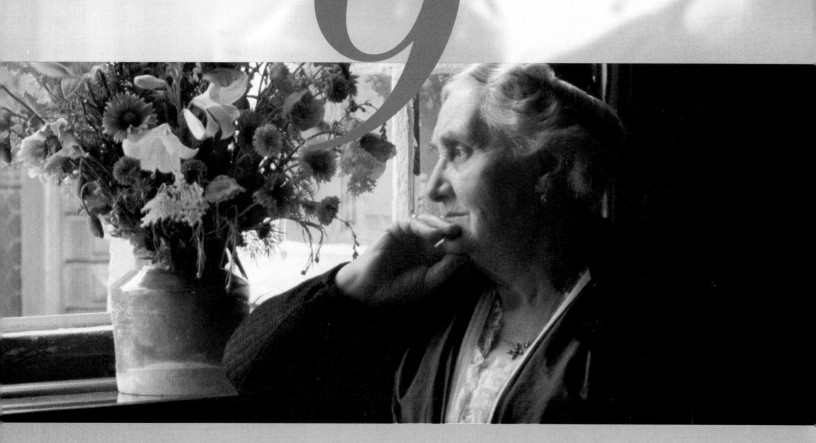

chapter

9

Memory

Imagine your life without memory. There would be no savoring the remembrances of joyful moments, no guilt or misery over painful recollections. Each moment would be a fresh experience. But each person would be a stranger, every language foreign, each task—dressing, cooking, biking—a novel challenge.

Your memory is your mind's storehouse, the reservoir of your accumulated learning. To the Roman statesman Cicero, memory was "the treasury and guardian of all things." To a psychologist, memory is any indication that learning has persisted over time. It is our ability to store and retrieve information.

The Phenomenon of Memory

The range of human memory is evident in some fascinating cases that stimulate our wonderings: How does the memory system work? What types of memory does it contain?

Conversing with John, a former graduate student, you would be impressed by his wit, his intelligence (he might explain his master's thesis), and his skill at tasks such as typing. It might be some time before you noticed that John suffers a tragic defect, caused by a brain injury suffered in a motorcycle accident. John cannot form new memories. Although he remembers his life before the accident, John otherwise lives in an eternal present. Each morning when his rehabilitation therapist greets him she must reintroduce herself. She must listen patiently as over and over he retells anecdotes from his preaccident life. Each time the need arises, he inquires, "Where is the bathroom?" and is told anew.

At the other extreme are some special people who would be medal winners in a memory Olympics. One woman, whom psychologist Ulric

Memory lost and found Larry Treadgold, an engineer, invented a paging system that serves as a kind of artificial memory for his son Adrian. Brain-injured in an auto accident, the young man can speak, understand, and retain information for as long as he pays attention. But as soon as he is distracted, the information fades away. The paging system allows a central computer to take over memory functions, reminding him, for example, to "take your 8:00 A.M. medications; call 123–4567 to confirm." If Adrian fails to confirm, the computer continues to page him and eventually contacts an emergency number.

Which is more important—your experiences or your memories of them?

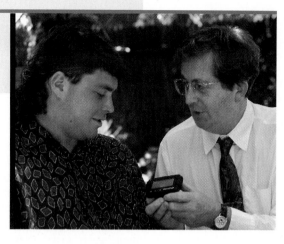

Neisser (1982) calls MZ, would have been the envy of every student. Until suffering a severe illness at age 29, MZ could recall anything her teachers wrote on the board and whole sections from her textbooks. When she worked as a biology technician, her employer began each day by giving her detailed instructions on the exact order in which to mount some 150 insects, which MZ then did without writing anything down.

The gold medalist of our memory Olympics would probably be a Russian journalist, Shereshevskii, or S, as psychologist Alexander Luria (1968) called him. S's memory not only allowed him merely to listen while other reporters were scribbling notes, it also earned him a place in virtu-

memory
the persistence of learning over time via the storage and retrieval of information.

flashbulb memory
a clear memory of an emotionally significant moment or event.

ally every modern book on memory. You and I can repeat back a string of about seven digits—almost surely no more than nine. S could repeat up to 70 digits or words, provided they were read about 3 seconds apart in an otherwise silent room. Moreover, he could recall them backward as easily as forward. His accuracy was unerring, even when he was asked to recall a list as much as 15 years later, after having memorized hundreds of other lists. "Yes, yes," he might recall. "This was a series you gave me once when we were in your apartment. . . . You were sitting at the table and I in the rocking chair. . . . You were wearing a gray suit and you looked at me like this. . . ."

Do these memory feats make your own memory seem feeble? If so, consider your capacity for remembering countless voices, sounds, and songs; tastes, smells, and textures; faces, places, and happenings. Imagine viewing more than 2500 slides of faces and places, for only 10 seconds each, and later seeing 280 of these slides one at a time, paired with a previously unseen slide. If you are like the subjects in this experiment by Ralph Haber (1970), you would recognize 90 percent of those you saw before.

Or consider the vividness of your memories of unique and highly emotional moments in your past—perhaps a car accident, your first romantic kiss, your first day as an immigrant in a new country, or your surroundings when you heard some tragic news. One vivid memory of mine is of my only hit in an entire season of Little League baseball. Most Americans over 50 feel sure of exactly what they were doing when they heard the news of President Kennedy's assassination (Brown & Kulik, 1982). Few San Francisco Bay Area residents will hesitate in recalling exactly where they were when the 1989 earthquake struck. This clarity for our memories of surprising, significant events leads some psychologists to call them flashbulb memories, because it's as if the brain commands, "Capture this!"

How do we accomplish such memory feats? How can we remember things we have not thought about for years, yet forget the name of someone we met a minute ago? How are memories stored in our brains? Why can even our flashbulb memories sometimes prove dead wrong? (Hours after the space shuttle *Challenger* explosion, people recalled where they had heard the news. Yet they were sometimes wildly inaccurate when again recalling their whereabouts 1 to 3 years later [McCloskey & others, 1988; Neisser & Harsch, 1992].) How can we improve our memories? These will be our questions as we review a century of research on memory.

THE FAR SIDE

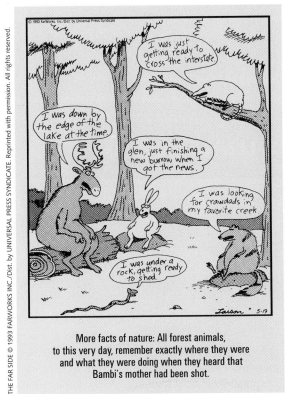

More facts of nature: All forest animals,
to this very day, remember exactly where they were
and what they were doing when they heard that
Bambi's mother had been shot.

Forming Memories: An Example

History is sometimes determined by what people can remember about events. On June 17, 1972, police caught five men trying to tap the telephones of the Democratic National Committee in the Washington, D.C., Watergate Office Building. In 1973, when President Nixon's legal counsel, John Dean, testified before a U.S. Senate committee investigating White House involvement in what came to be called "the Watergate scandal," his recall of conversations with the President was so impressive that some writers called him "the human tape recorder." Ironically, it was later revealed that a secret taping system had actually recorded the conversations that Dean recounted, providing a rare opportunity to compare an eyewitness's recollections with the actual event. Dean's recollection of the essentials proved correct. The highest-ranking members of the White House staff went to prison for doing what John Dean said they did, and President Nixon was forced to resign.

However, when Ulric Neisser (1981) compared the details in the tapes with the testimony, he discovered that John Dean was far from a human tape recorder. For example, Dean recalled that entering a September 15 meeting with President Nixon and his chief-of-staff, Robert Haldeman,

> the president asked me to sit down. Both men appeared to be in very good spirits and my reception was very warm and cordial. The president then told me that Bob—referring to Haldeman—had kept him posted on my handling of the Watergate case. The president told me I had done a good job and he appreciated how difficult a task it had been and the president was pleased that the case had stopped with [his reelection committee's attorney] Liddy.

But almost every detail Dean recalled was wrong. The tape of the meeting revealed that the president did not ask Dean to sit down. He did not say Dean had done a good job. He did not say anything about Liddy or the indictments.

Dean's memory was better for a March 15 conversation during which he delivered a well-prepared report to the president on the unraveling of the White House cover-up. The tape caught Dean actually saying, "We have a cancer within, close to the presidency, that is growing. It is growing daily . . . because (1) we are being blackmailed, (2) people are going to start perjuring themselves. . . ." In his later congressional testimony, Dean *recalled* "telling the president that there was a cancer growing on the presidency and . . . that it was important that this cancer be removed immediately because it was growing more deadly every day."

How could John Dean have been so right in his basic understanding of the Watergate discussions, yet, except for the March 15 conversation, so wrong in recalling the details of most conversations? Why are you likely later in this chapter to misrecall this sentence: *"The angry rioter threw the rock at the window"*? To understand Dean's memory (and our own), we need a model of memory.

A human tape recorder? John Dean is shown here testifying before the Senate Watergate Committee. When his testimony was compared with the White House tapes, Dean's memory was found to be accurate for the substance of most conversations but not for the details.

encoding
the processing of information into the memory system, for example by extracting meaning.

storage
the retention of encoded information over time.

retrieval
the process of getting information out of memory storage.

long-term memory
the relatively permanent and limitless storehouse of the memory system.

short-term memory
activated memory that holds a few items briefly, such as the seven digits of a phone number while dialing, before the information is stored or forgotten.

Memory as Information Processing

Human memory is in some ways like a computer information-processing system. To remember any event requires that we *get information into our brain* (encoding), *retain* that information (storage), and later *get it back out* (retrieval). Consider how a computer encodes, stores, and retrieves information. First, it translates input (keystrokes) into an electronic language, much as the brain encodes sensory information into a neural language. The computer permanently stores vast amounts of information on a disk. From this information storehouse it can retrieve a file or document into a working memory, which also can receive new information from the keyboard. Part of this working memory is visible on the screen.

Similarly, we store vast amounts of information in long-term memory. (Our memories are, however, less literal and more fragile than a computer's.) From our memory storehouse we can retrieve information into an active working memory, part of which is displayed on our mental screen as short-term memory. And, just as a computer's screen-saver program blanks the screen after a period of inactivity, activated human memories rapidly decay unless used or rehearsed.

Like orchestra conductors, we can't focus on everything at once. So we shine the flashlight beam of attention on certain incoming stimuli, often novel or changing stimuli that fill our on-screen, short-term memory (Figure 9.1).

SUMMING UP

Memory is the persistence of learning over time. The computer is one convenient model for thinking about human memory. Both systems must encode, store, and retrieve information. Both feature long-term storage, from which we can activate information into a working memory, part of which is displayed on screen. On-screen memory is similar to our short-term memory; unless used or rehearsed, it quickly disappears.

KEY TERMS AND CONCEPTS memory, flashbulb memory, encoding, storage, retrieval, long-term memory, short-term memory

Figure 9.1

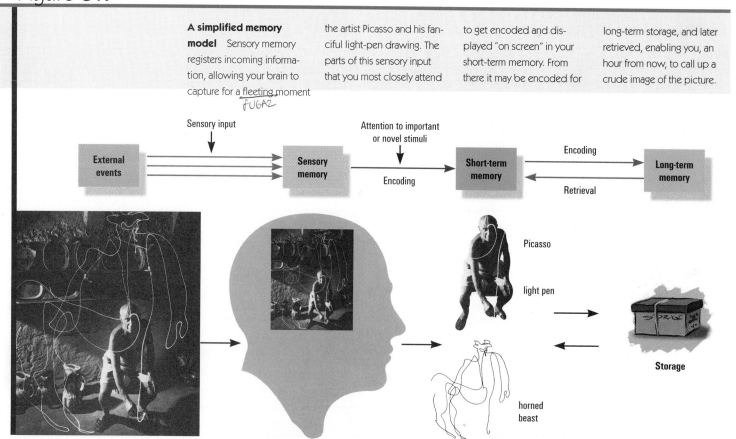

A simplified memory model Sensory memory registers incoming information, allowing your brain to capture for a fleeting moment the artist Picasso and his fanciful light-pen drawing. The parts of this sensory input that you most closely attend to get encoded and displayed "on screen" in your short-term memory. From there it may be encoded for long-term storage, and later retrieved, enabling you, an hour from now, to call up a crude image of the picture.

Encoding: Getting Information In

How does sensory information, once registered, get encoded and transferred into the memory system? What types of information do we absorb incidentally? What types require intentional effort? Is the failure to encode information an important factor in forgetting?

How We Encode

Some encoding occurs automatically, freeing your attention to simultaneously process information that requires effort. Thus, your memory for the route you walked to class yesterday you handled by automatic processing. Your learning this chapter's concepts requires effortful processing (Figure 9.2).

Automatic Processing

With little or no effort, you encode an enormous amount of information about *space*, *time*, and *frequency*: During an exam, you may recall the place on the textbook page where the forgotten material appears. To guess where you left your coat, you can recreate a sequence of the day's events. You may realize that "this is the third time I've run into you this afternoon." Memories like these form almost automatically. In fact, not only does automatic processing occur effortlessly; it is also difficult to shut off. When you hear or read a word in your native language, whether an insult or a compliment, it is virtually impossible not to register its meaning automatically.

Some types of automatic processing we learn. For example, learning to read reversed sentences at first requires effort:

.citamotua emoceb nac gnissecorp luftroffE

After practice, effortful processing becomes more automatic, much as reading from right to left becomes easy for students of Hebrew (Kolers, 1975).

Automatic processing occurs with little or no effort, without our awareness, and without interfering with our thinking about other things. (This is another example of our brain's capacity for parallel processing of multiple information streams.) If such processing requires no special attention, then asking people to attend to information they encode automatically, such as judging the frequency of words presented during an experiment, should be of little benefit. Lynn Hasher and Rose Zacks (1979, 1984) have shown that this is often the case. Although memory for such material may be modestly boosted by effort, our encoding is mostly automatic: We cannot switch it on and off at will.

Effortful Processing

We encode and retain vast amounts of information automatically, without any intentional effort. Other types of information we remember only with effort and attention. When learning novel information such as names, we can boost our memory through rehearsal, or conscious repetition. This was shown long ago by the pioneering researcher of verbal memory, German philosopher Hermann Ebbinghaus (1850–1909). Ebbinghaus did for the study of memory what Ivan Pavlov did for the study of conditioning. Impatient with philosophical speculations about memory, Ebbinghaus wanted to study it scientifically. To do so, he decided to study his own learning and forgetting of novel verbal materials.

Where could Ebbinghaus find verbal material that was not familiar? His solution was to form a list of all possible nonsense syllables created by sandwiching a vowel between two consonants. Then, for a particular experiment, he would randomly select a sample of the syllables. To get a feel for how Ebbinghaus tested himself, rapidly read aloud, eight times over, the following list (from Baddeley, 1982). Then recall the items:

JIH, BAZ, FUB, YOX, SUJ, XIR, DAX, LEQ, VUM, PID, KEL, WAV, TUV, ZOF, GEK, HIW.

automatic processing
unconscious encoding of incidental information, such as space, time, and frequency, and of well-learned information, such as word meanings.

effortful processing
encoding that requires attention and conscious effort.

rehearsal
the conscious repetition of information, either to maintain it in consciousness or to encode it for storage.

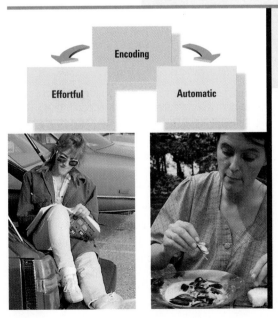

Figure **9.2**

Automatic versus effortful processing Some information, such as this chapter's concepts, requires effort to encode and remember. Other information, like what you ate for dinner yesterday, you process automatically.

Figure **9.3**

Ebbinghaus's retention curve
Ebbinghaus found that the more times he practiced a list of nonsense syllables on day 1, the fewer repetitions he required to relearn it on day 2. Said simply, the more time we spend learning novel information, the more we retain. (From Baddeley, 1982.)

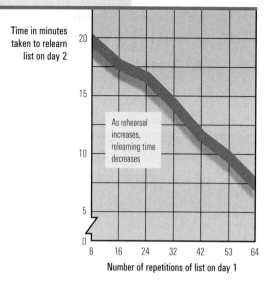

Time in minutes taken to relearn list on day 2

As rehearsal increases, relearning time decreases

Number of repetitions of list on day 1

After learning such a list, Ebbinghaus could recall few of the syllables the following day. But were they entirely forgotten? As Figure 9.3 portrays, the more frequently he repeated the list aloud on day 1, the fewer repetitions he required to relearn the list on day 2. Here, then, was a simple beginning principle: *The amount remembered depends on the time spent learning.* Even after we learn material, additional rehearsal (*overlearning*) increases retention. Thus, John Dean almost perfectly recalled his "cancer on the presidency" remarks because he had written them out and rehearsed them several times before uttering them to President Nixon.

The point to remember is that for novel verbal information, practice—effortful processing—does indeed make perfect. And that helps us understand some other interesting phenomena:

- The *next-in-line effect*: When people go around a circle reading words or saying their names, their poorest memories are for what was said by the person just before them (Bond & others, 1991; Brenner, 1973). When we are next in line, we focus on our own performance and often fail to process the last person's words.

- Information presented in the seconds just before sleep seldom is remembered (Wyatt & Bootzin, 1994). When our consciousness fades before we've processed the information, all is lost.

- Taped information played during sleep is registered by the ears but is not remembered (Wood & others, 1992). Without opportunity for rehearsal, "sleep learning" doesn't occur.

We also retain information better when rehearsal is distributed over time (as when learning classmates' names), a phenomenon called the spacing effect (Dempster, 1988). Harry Bahrick and Lynda Hall (1991) noted the effect of spaced rehearsal in a study of adults' memory of high school algebra.

spacing effect
the tendency for distributed study or practice to yield better long-term retention than is achieved through massed study or practice.

serial position effect
our tendency to recall best the last and first items in a list.

Those who took algebra only once forgot most of what they learned over the next half century. Others—after doing no better in high school—rehearsed their algebra knowledge while taking higher-level math courses. For the rest of their lives these people remembered most of their high school algebra, especially if their college math was spaced over several semesters rather than massed into a single year.

In a 9-year experiment, Bahrick and three of his family members (1993) practiced foreign language word translations for a given number of times, at intervals ranging from 14 to 56 days. Their consistent finding: The longer the space between practice sessions, the better their retention, up to 5 years later. Reflecting on the spacing effect, Bahrick saw a practical implication: Restudying material for comprehensive final exams, capstone review courses, and senior examinations will enhance lifelong retention. Spreading out learning—say, over a semester or a year, rather than over shorter terms—should also help. In the first century, the Roman philosopher Seneca anticipated the finding that spaced study beats cramming: "The mind is slow in unlearning what it has been long in learning."

That makes adaptive sense, note John Anderson and Lael Schooler (1991). In our environments, events that are spaced out *are* more likely to recur. Compared with a name we've heard or read five times in one month, the name we've read once a month for five months is a name we're more likely to read again. (They confirmed this by looking at such things as word frequencies in 730 consecutive *New York Times* headlines.) In this and other ways, our memory system, like so much else about us, is optimally designed to support our functioning and survival.

A phenomenon you have surely experienced further illustrates the benefits of rehearsal. Experimenters have shown people a list of items (words, names, dates) and then immediately asked them to recall the items in any order. As people struggle to recall the list, they often demonstrate the serial position effect: They remember the last and first

Seneca anticipated the finding that spaced study beats cramming: "The mind is slow in unlearning what it has been long in learning."

items better than they do those in the middle (Figure 9.4). Perhaps because they are still in short-term memory, the last items are briefly recalled especially quickly and well. But after a delay—after attention has shifted from the last items—recall is best for the first items. As an everyday parallel, imagine that as you are being introduced to several people, you repeat (rehearse) all their names from the beginning as you meet each person. By the end, you will have spent more time rehearsing the earlier names than the later names; thus, the next day you will probably recall the earlier names better. Also, learning the first few names may interfere with your learning the later ones.

Rehearsal will not encode all information equally well. Sometimes merely repeating information, such as the new phone number we are about to dial, is not enough to store it for later recall (Craik & Watkins, 1973; Greene, 1987). How, then, do we process information into long-term memory? Processing our sensory input is like sorting through the day's mail: Some items we instantly discard. Others we process more thoughtfully: We open, read, and retain them. Our memory system processes information not just by repetitive rehearsal, but by encoding its significant features.

What We Encode

We process information in three key ways—by encoding its meaning, by visualizing it, and by mentally organizing it. To some extent we do these things automatically. But in each case there are effortful strategies for enhancing memory.

Encoding Meaning

Do you recall (from page 271) the sentence about the rioter? Can you complete the sentence: "The angry rioter threw . . . "?

When processing verbal information for storage, we usually encode its meaning. For example, we associate it with what we already know or imagine. Whether we hear "eye-screem" as "ice cream" or "I scream" depends on how the context and our experience guide us to interpret the sounds.

Perhaps, then, like the subjects in an experiment by William Brewer (1977), you recalled the rioter sentence as the meaning you encoded when you read it (for example, "The angry rioter threw the rock through the window") and not as written ("The angry rioter threw the rock *at* the window"). As such recall indicates, we tend not to remember things exactly as they were. Rather, *we remember what we encoded*. Studying for an exam, you may

Figure 9.4

The serial position effect graph showing Percentage of words recalled (vertical axis, 0 to 90) versus Position of word in list (horizontal axis, 1 through 12). "Immediate recall: last items best" and "Later recall: only first items recalled well."

The serial position effect After being presented with a list of words or names, people immediately recall the last items well (perhaps because they are still "on screen"), and quite often the first few items nearly as well. But later they recall the first items best. (From Craik & Watkins, 1973.)

remember your lecture notes rather than the lecture itself. Likewise, as we hear or read about a situation, our minds construct a model of it. Gordon Bower and Daniel Morrow (1990) liken our minds to theater directors who, given a raw script, imagine a finished stage production. Asked later to recall what we heard or read, we recall not the literal text but the mental model we constructed from it. This helps us understand John Dean's misrecollections of precisely what President Nixon said and did, and Dean's better recall of the *meaning* that he encoded from his conversations with the president.

What kind of encoding do you think yields the best memory of verbal information? <u>Semantic encoding</u> of meaning? <u>Acoustic encoding</u> of sound? <u>Visual encoding</u> of images? To find out, Fergus Craik and Endel Tulving (1975) flashed a word at people. Then they asked a question that required the people to process the words (1) visually (the appearance of the letters), (2) acoustically (the sound of the words), or (3) semantically (the meaning of the words). To experience the task yourself, rapidly answer the following questions:

Sample Questions to Elicit Processing	Word Flashed	Yes	No
1. Is the word in capital letters?	chair	____	____
2. Does the word rhyme with train?	BRAIN	____	____
3. Would the word fit in this sentence:			
The girl put the ____ on the table.	gun	____	____

Which type of processing would best prepare you to recognize the words at a later time? In Craik and Tulving's experiment, the deeper, semantic encoding—question 3—yielded much better memory

Here is another sentence I will ask you about later: The fish attacked the swimmer.

How many Fs are in the following sentence?
FINISHED FILES ARE THE RESULTS OF YEARS OF SCIENTIFIC STUDY COMBINED WITH THE EXPERIENCE OF YEARS. *(See page 279.)*

semantic encoding
the encoding of meaning, including the meaning of words.

acoustic encoding
the encoding of sound, especially the sound of words.

visual encoding
the encoding of picture images.

Figure **9.5**

Levels of processing Processing a word deeply—by its meaning (semantic encoding)—produces better recognition of it at a later time than does shallow processing by attending to its appearance or sound. (From Craik & Tulving, 1975.)

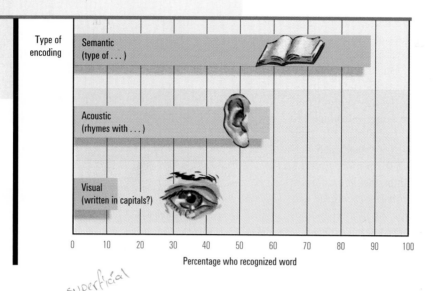

Type of encoding

Semantic (type of . . .)

Acoustic (rhymes with . . .)

Visual (written in capitals?)

0   10   20   30   40   50   60   70   80   90   100

Percentage who recognized word

than the "shallow processing" elicited by question 2 and especially by question 1 (Figure 9.5). *[superficial]*

To experience the importance of meaning for verbal memory, put yourself in the place of the students whom John Bransford and Marcia Johnson (1972) asked to remember the following recorded passage:

> The procedure is actually quite simple. First you arrange things into different groups. Of course, one pile may be sufficient depending on how much there is to do. . . . After the procedure is completed one arranges the materials into different groups again. Then they can be put into their appropriate places. Eventually they will be used once more and the whole cycle will then have to be repeated. However, that is part of life.

When the students heard the paragraph you have just read, without a meaningful context, they remembered little of it. When told that the paragraph was about washing clothes (something meaningful to them), they remembered much more of it—as you probably could now after rereading it.

Such research suggests the benefits of rephrasing what we read and hear into meaningful terms. From his experiments on himself, Ebbinghaus estimated that, compared with learning nonsense material, learning meaningful material required but one-tenth the effort. As memory researcher Wayne Wickelgren (1977, p. 346) noted, "The time you spend thinking about material you are reading and relating it to previously stored material is about the most useful thing you can do in learning any new subject matter."

We therefore have excellent recall for information we relate to ourselves. If asked how well certain adjectives describe another person, people will often forget them; if asked to rate how well the adjectives describe themselves, they remember the words well—a phenomenon called the *self-reference effect* (Symons & Johnson, 1997). Thus, you can profit from taking time to find personal meaning in what you are studying. Information deemed "relevant to me" is more likely to be processed deeply and to be accessible in memory.

Encoding Imagery

We struggle to memorize formulas, definitions, and dates, yet we can easily picture where we were yesterday, who was with us, where we sat, and what we wore. Your earliest memories—probably of something that happened at around age 3 or 4—almost surely involve visual imagery, or mental pictures.

> "A thing when heard, remember, strikes less keen on the spectator's mind than when 'tis seen."
>
> **HORACE**
> *ARS POETICA*
> 8 B.C.

In a variety of experiments, researchers have documented the benefits of mental images. For example, we remember words that lend themselves to picture images better than we remember abstract, low-imagery words. (When I quiz you later, which three of these words will you most likely recall: *typewriter, void, cigarette, inherent, fire, process*?) Similarly, you probably still recall the sentence about the rock-throwing rioter, not only because of the meaning you encoded but also because the sentence lent itself to a visual image. As the example suggests, and as some memory experts believe, memory for concrete nouns is aided by encoding them *both* semantically and visually (Marschark & others, 1987; Paivio, 1986). Two codes are better than one.

imagery
mental pictures; a powerful aid to effortful processing, especially when combined with semantic encoding.

The imagery principle Abstract ideas become memorable when carried by visual images. Numerical facts about the power of today's nuclear weapons are forgettable; tie them to an image that visually illustrates the trend and the message is more memorable. (From Sivard, 1996.)

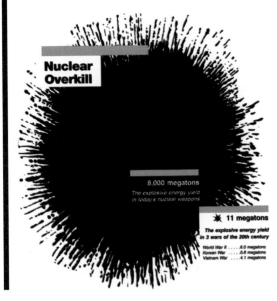

Nuclear Overkill

8,000 megatons
The explosive energy yield
in today's nuclear weapons

☀ 11 megatons
The explosive energy yield
in 3 wars of the 20th century
World War II . . . . . 6.0 megatons
Korean War . . . . . . 0.8 megatons
Vietnam War . . . . . . 4.1 megatons

Thanks to the durability of our most vivid images, we recall our experiences with mental snapshots of their best or worst moments. Thus, the best moment of a pleasure or joy, and the worst moment of a pain or frustration, often colors our memories more than does its duration (Fredrickson & Kahneman, 1993). Recalling the high points while forgetting the mundane moments may explain a phenomenon that Terrence Mitchell and Leigh Thompson (1994) call "rosy retrospection": People tend to recall events such as a camping holiday more positively than they evaluated them at the time. The visit to Disney World is remembered less for the muggy heat and long lines than for the exciting rides, fun foods, and enchanting surroundings.

Imagery is at the heart of many memory aids. Mnemonic devices (so named after the Greek word for memory) were developed by ancient Greek scholars and orators as aids to remembering lengthy passages and speeches. Using the "method of loci," they imagined themselves moving through a familiar series of locations, associating each place with a visual representation of the to-be-remembered topic. Then, when speaking, the orator would mentally revisit each location and retrieve the associated image.

A variation on this method uses vivid stories to organize words to be memorized. Gordon Bower and Michael Clark (1969) used lists of unrelated nouns, asking one group simply to study the lists and another group to invent stories using the nouns. (A sample made-up story: "A LUMBER-JACK DARTed out of a forest, SKATEd around a HEDGE past a COLONY of DUCKs. He tripped on some FURNITURE, tearing his STOCKING while hastening toward the PILLOW where his MISTRESS lay.") After working through 12 lists of 10 words each, the group that merely studied each list struggled to recall 13 percent of the words; the group that invented vivid stories recalled an astounding 93 percent.

Other mnemonic devices involve both acoustic and visual codes. For example, the "peg-word" system requires that you first memorize a jingle:

One is a bun; two is a shoe;
Three is a tree; four is a door;
Five is a hive; six is sticks;
Seven is heaven; eight is a gate;
Nine is swine; ten is a hen.

Without much effort, you will soon be able to count by peg-words instead of numbers: bun, shoe, tree . . . and then to visually associate the peg-words with to-be-remembered items. Now you are ready to challenge anyone to give you a grocery list to remember. Carrots? Imagine them stuck into a bun. Milk? Fill the shoe with it. Paper towels?

mnemonics
[nih-MON-iks] memory aids, especially those techniques that use vivid imagery and organizational devices.

Thanks to the durability of our most vivid images, we recall our experiences with mental snapshots of their best or worst moments.

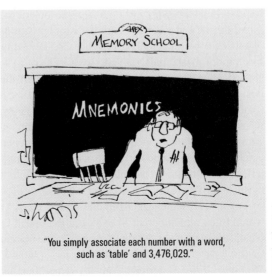

MEMORY SCHOOL

MNEMONICS

"You simply associate each number with a word, such as 'table' and 3,476,029."

chunking
organizing items into familiar, manageable units; often occurs automatically.

Drape them over the tree branch. Think "bun, shoe, tree" and you see their associated images: carrots, milk, paper towels. With few errors (Bugelski & others, 1968), you will be able to recall the items in any order and to name any given item. Such mnemonic systems are often the secret behind the feats of memory experts who repeat long lists of names and objects.

Organizing Information for Encoding

Meaning and imagery enhance memory partly by helping us organize information. When Bransford and Johnson's laundry paragraph (page 276) became meaningful, its sentences formed a sequence. Mnemonic devices help organize material for later retrieval. To experience the importance of organization, glance for a few seconds at row 1 of Figure 9.6, then look away and try to reproduce what you saw. It's nearly impossible. But you can easily reproduce the second row, which is no less complex. Similarly, row 4 is much easier to remember than row 3, although both contain the same letters. And the sixth cluster is more easily remembered than the fifth, although both contain the same words.

Chunking

As this demonstrates, we organize easily remembered information into meaningful units, or chunks. Chunking information into meaningful units occurs so naturally that we take it for granted. Consider your ability to reproduce perfectly the 150 or so line segments that make up the sixth cluster of phrases in Figure 9.6. Surely it would astonish an illiterate person or someone unfamiliar with English.

You or I might feel similar admiration for the ability of someone literate in Chinese to glance at Figure 9.7 and then to reproduce all the strokes; or for chess masters who, after a 5-second look at the board during a game, can recall the exact positions of most of the pieces (Chase & Simon, 1973); or for varsity basketball players who, given a 4-second glance at a basketball play, can recall the positions of the players (Allard & Burnett, 1985). Like the experienced chess masters and athletes, we all remember information best when we can organize it into personally meaningful arrangements.

Chunking also aids our recall of unfamiliar material. One mnemonic technique organizes it into a more familiar form by creating words (called *acronyms*) or sentences from the first letters of words to be remembered. Should you ever need to recall the names of North America's five Great Lakes, just remember HOMES (*H*uron, *O*ntario, *M*ichigan, *E*rie, *S*uperior). Want to remember the colors of the rainbow in order of wavelength?

Figure 9.6

Effects of chunking on memory   When we organize information into meaningful units, such as letters, words, and phrases, we recall it more easily. (From Hintzman, 1978.)

1.	◁ ⊃ ⯗ ∾ ⊓ ⊏
2.	K L C I S N E
3.	KLCISNE NVESE YNA NI CSTTIH TNDO
4.	NICKELS SEVEN ANY IN STITCH DONT
5.	NICKELS SEVEN ANY IN STITCH DONT SAVES AGO A SCORE TIME AND NINE WOODEN FOUR YEARS TAKE
6.	DONT TAKE ANY WOODEN NICKELS FOUR SCORE AND SEVEN YEARS AGO A STITCH IN TIME SAVES NINE

Think of ROY G. BIV (*r*ed, *o*range, *y*ellow, *g*reen, *b*lue, *i*ndigo, *v*iolet).

With chunking, you can increase your recall of digits, too. An impossible string of 16 numbers—1-4-9-2-1-7-7-6-1-8-1-2-1-9-4-1—becomes easy for an American when chunked into 1492, 1776, 1812, 1941 (as would 1066, 1688, 1815, and 1914 for those familiar with British history). After more than 200 hours of practice in the laboratory of Anders Ericsson and William Chase (1982), two Carnegie-Mellon University students even managed to increase their memory span from the typical 7 digits to more than 80. In another testing session, student Dario Donatelli heard the researcher read one digit per second in a monotonous voice: "15185937655021578416658506120094885 686772731418186105462974801294974965928." Motionless while learning the numbers, Donatelli then sprang alive. He whispered numbers, rubbed his chin, tapped his feet, counted on his fingers, and ran his hands through his hair. "Okay," he announced almost 2 minutes later. "The first set is 1518. Then 5937. . . ." He repeated all 73 digits, in groups of 3 and 4.

How did he do it? By increasing the capacity of his short-term memory? No. When asked to remember letters, Donatelli fell back to about a seven-item capacity. Rather, he had developed a sophisticated strategy for number chunking. "First set was a 3-mile time," reported Donatelli, an All-American cross-country runner. "Second set was a 10-mile time. Then a mile. Half-mile. Two-mile time. An age. . . . Two mile. Age. Age. Age. Two-mile. . . ." (Wells, 1983).

Figure 9.7

An example of chunking—for those who read Chinese   After looking at these characters, can you reproduce them exactly? If so, you are literate in Chinese.

蝶

千

種

Figure **9.8**

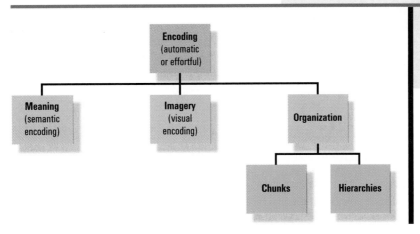

Organization benefits memory
When we organize words or concepts into hierarchical groups, as here, we remember them better than when we see them presented randomly.

Hierarchies

For Donatelli to reach his peak—106 digits—he retrieved the chunks of numbers by clustering them as a hierarchy (Waldrop, 1987). First came "three groups of four," he might think, and so forth. When people develop expertise in an area, they process information not only in chunks but also in hierarchies composed of a few broad concepts divided and subdivided into narrower concepts and facts. By organizing their knowledge in such ways, experts can retrieve information efficiently. This chapter therefore aims not only to teach you the elementary facts of memory but also to help you organize these facts around broad principles, such as encoding; subprinciples, such as automatic and effortful processing; and still more specific concepts, such as meaning, imagery, and organization (Figure 9.8).

Gordon Bower and his colleagues (1969) demonstrated the benefits of hierarchical organization by presenting words either randomly or grouped into categories. When the words were hierarchically organized, recall was two to three times better. Such results show the benefits of organizing what you study—of giving special attention to chapter outlines, headings, topic sentences, and summary paragraphs. If you can master a chapter's concepts with their overall organization, your recall should be good at test time. Taking lecture and text notes in outline format—a type of hierarchical organization—may also prove effective.

Forgetting as Encoding Failure

Amidst all the applause for memory—all the efforts to understand it, all the books on how to improve it—have any voices been heard in praise of forgetting? William James (1890, p. 680) was such a voice: "If we remembered everything, we should on most occasions be as ill off as if we remembered nothing." To discard the clutter of useless or out-of-date information—where we parked the car yesterday, a friend's old phone number, restaurant orders already cooked and served—is surely a blessing (Bjork, 1978). The Russian memory whiz S, whom we met at the beginning of the chapter, was haunted by his junk heap of memories, which continually dominated his consciousness. He had difficulty thinking abstractly—generalizing, organizing, evaluating. A good memory is helpful, but so is the ability to forget.

What causes forgetting? One answer is that we failed to encode the information (Figure 9.9). Thus, it never entered the memory system. Brain areas that jump into action when young adults are encoding new information are less responsive among older adults. This impaired encoding helps explain age-related memory decline (Grady & others, 1995).

But no matter how young we are, we cannot attend to more than a few of the myriad sights and sounds that continually bombard us. Thus, much of

"Happiness is nothing more than health and a poor memory."

PHYSICIAN ALBERT SCHWEITZER
1875–1965

Answer to question on page 275: Partly because your initial processing of the letters was primarily acoustic rather than visual, you probably missed some of the six Fs, especially those that sound like a V rather than an F.

Figure **9.9**

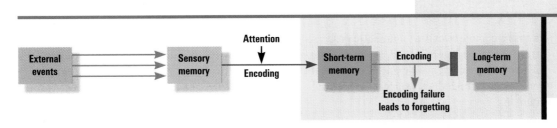

Forgetting as encoding failure

"Each of us finds that in [our] own life every moment of time is completely filled. [We are] bombarded every second by sensations, emotions, thoughts... nine-tenths of which [we] must simply ignore. The past [is] a roaring cataract of billions upon billions of such moments: any one of them too complex to grasp in its entirety, and the aggregate beyond all imagination.... At every tick of the clock, in every inhabited part of the world, an unimaginable richness and variety of 'history' falls off the world into total oblivion."

ENGLISH NOVELIST-CRITIC C. S. LEWIS 1967

what we sense we never notice. Consider something you've looked at countless times: What letters accompany the number 5 on your telephone? Or where is the number 0 on your calculator? For most people these are surprisingly difficult questions.

If you live in North America, Britain, or Australia, you have probably also looked at thousands of pennies in your lifetime. You can surely recall the features (color and size) you use to distinguish coins. But can you recall what the side with the head looks like? If not, let's make the memory test easier: If you are familiar with U.S. coins, can you recognize the real thing in Figure 9.10? Raymond Nickerson and Marilyn Adams (1979) discovered that most people cannot. Likewise, few British people can draw from memory the one-pence coin they have seen thousands of times (Richardson, 1993). The details of a penny are not very meaningful—nor are they essential for distinguishing pennies from other coins—and few of us have made the effort to encode them. As we noted earlier, we encode some information automatically; other types of information require effortful processing. Without effort, many memories never form.

Figure **9.10**

Test your memory Which one of these pennies is the real thing? (If you live outside the United States, try drawing your own country's penny.) (From Nickerson & Adams, 1979.) (See page 282.)

(a) (b) (c)

(d) (e) (f)

(g) (h) (i)

(j) (k) (l)

(m) (n) (o)

sensory memory
the immediate, initial recording of sensory information in the memory system.

iconic memory
a momentary sensory memory of visual stimuli; a photographic or picture-image memory lasting no more than a few tenths of a second.

echoic memory
a momentary sensory memory of auditory stimuli; if attention is elsewhere, sounds and words can still be recalled within 3 or 4 seconds.

SUMMING UP

Some types of information, notably information concerning space, time, and frequency, we encode mostly automatically. Other types of information, including much of our processing of meaning, imagery, and organization, require effort. Mnemonic devices depend on the memorability of visual images and of information that is organized into chunks. Organizing information into chunks and hierarchies also aids memory.

One explanation of forgetting is that we fail to encode information for entry into our memory system. Without effortful processing, much of what we sense we never notice or process.

KEY TERMS AND CONCEPTS automatic processing, effortful processing, rehearsal, spacing effect, serial position effect, semantic encoding, acoustic encoding, visual encoding, imagery, mnemonics, chunking

Storage: Retaining Information

At the heart of memory is storage. Our sensory memory, short-term memory, and long-term memory retain information for varying time periods. What is the capacity and duration of each? How and where does the brain physically store memories?

If you experience something that you later recall, you must, somehow, have stored and retrieved it. What is stored in long-term memory lies dormant, waiting to be reawakened by a cue. What is our memory storage capacity? Let's start with the first memory store noted in Figure 9.1, our fleeting sensory memory.

Sensory Memory Storage

Consider what one intriguing memory experiment revealed about our sensory memory—the initial recording of sensory information in the memory system. As part of his doctoral research, George Sperling (1960) showed people three rows of three letters each for only 1/20th of a second (Figure 9.11). It was harder than reading by flashes of lightning. After the nine letters disappeared from the screen, the subjects could recall only about half of them.

Why? Was it because they had insufficient time to glimpse them? No. Sperling cleverly demonstrated that even at faster than lightning-flash speed, people actually *can* see and recall all the letters, but only momentarily. Rather than ask them to recall all nine letters at once, Sperling would sound a high, medium, or low tone immediately *after* flashing the nine letters. This cue directed the subject to report only the letters of the top, middle, or bottom row, respectively. Now the subjects rarely missed a letter, showing that all nine letters were momentarily available for recall.

Sperling's experiment revealed that we have a fleeting photographic memory called iconic memory. For an instant, the eyes register an exact representation of a scene and we can recall any part of it in amazing detail—but only for a few tenths of a second. If Sperling delayed the tone signal by as much as a second, the iconic memory was gone and the subjects once again recalled only about half the letters. The visual screen clears quickly, as it must, lest new images be superimposed over old ones.

We also have an impeccable, though fleeting, memory for auditory sensory images, called echoic memory (Cowan, 1988; Lu & others, 1992). However, if partially interpreted, the auditory echo disappears more slowly. The last few words spoken seem to linger for 3 or 4 seconds. Sometimes, just as you ask, "What did you say?" you can hear in your mind the echo of what was said.

Short-Term Memory Storage

Among the vast amounts of information registered by our sensory memory, we illuminate some with our attentional flashlight. We also retrieve information from long-term storage for "on-screen" display. But unless we meaningfully encode or rehearse that information, it quickly disappears. During your finger's trip from the phone book to the phone, your memory of a telephone number will disappear unless you work to maintain it in consciousness.

Figure **9.11**

K	Z	R
Q	B	T
S	G	N

Momentary photographic memory When George Sperling flashed a group of letters similar to this for 1/20th of a second, people could recall only about half of the letters. But when signaled to recall a particular row *immediately* after the letters had disappeared, they could do so with near-perfect accuracy.

For an instant, the eyes register an exact representation of a scene and we can recall any part of it in amazing detail—but only for a few tenths of a second.

To find out how quickly a short-term memory will disappear, Lloyd Peterson and Margaret Peterson (1959) asked people to remember three consonants, such as *CHJ*. To prevent subjects' rehearsal of the letters, the researchers asked them to count aloud backwards by threes from some number. With the help of a friend, you can demonstrate the result shown in Figure 9.12. After 3 seconds people recalled the letters only about half the time; after 12 seconds they seldom recalled them at all.

How many of the six quiz words on page 276 can you now recall? Of these, how many are high-imagery words? How many are low-imagery?

Figure **9.12**

Percentage who recalled consonants

Rapid decay with no rehearsal

Time in seconds between presentation of consonants and recall request (no rehearsal allowed)

Short-term memory decay Unless rehearsed, verbal information may be quickly forgotten. (From Peterson & Peterson, 1959.)

Answer to question on page 280: The first penny (a) is the real penny.

Without active processing, short-term memories have a limited life.

The short-term memory store is limited not only in duration but also in capacity. It typically stores but seven or so chunks of information (give or take two). This recall capacity has been enshrined in psychology as "the Magical Number Seven, plus or minus two" (Miller, 1956).

Actually, people's short-term memory spans—the amount of information they can immediately recall correctly 50 percent of the time—vary. Short-term recall is slightly better for random digits (such as those of a phone number) than for random letters, which sometimes have similar sounds. It is slightly better for information we hear than for images we see. Both children and adults have short-term recall for roughly as many words as they can speak in 2 seconds (Cowan, 1994; Hulme & Tordoff, 1989). The basic principle: At any given moment, we can consciously process only a very limited amount of information.

Long-Term Memory Storage

In Arthur Conan Doyle's *A Study in Scarlet*, Sherlock Holmes offers a popular theory of memory capacity:

> I consider that a man's brain originally is like a little empty attic, and you have to stock it with such furniture as you choose. . . . It is a mistake to think that that little room has elastic walls and can distend to any extent. Depend upon it, there comes a time when for every addition of knowledge you forget something that you knew before.

Contrary to Sherlock Holmes's belief, our capacity for storing long-term memories is essentially limitless. By one careful estimate, the average adult has about a billion bits of information in memory. Allowing for all the brain must do to encode, store, retrieve, and manipulate this information, its storage capacity is probably a thousand to a million times greater (Landauer, 1986). So our brains are *not* like attics, which once filled can store more only by discarding old items.

The point is vividly illustrated by those whose efforts have enabled phenomenal memory feats. Consider Rajan Mahadevan, a Florida State University graduate student from India. Give him any string of 10 digits from the first 30,000 or so digits of pi and, after a few moments of mental search for the string, he'll pick up the series from there, firing numbers like a machine gun. He also can repeat 50 random digits—backwards (Thompson & others, 1993). It's no genetic gift, he says; anyone could learn to do it. But given the genetic influence on so many human traits, and knowing that Rajan's father memorized Shakespeare's complete works, one wonders.

How precise and durable are our stored memories? Ebbinghaus (1885) learned lists of nonsense syllables and measured how much he retained when relearning each list, from 20 minutes to 30 days later. His famous "forgetting curve" (Figure 9.13) indicates that much of what we learn we may quickly forget. Many later experiments allow us to state the forgetting curve as one of psychology's laws: The course of forgetting is initially rapid, then levels off with time (Wixted & Ebbesen, 1991).

Figure **9.13**

Ebbinghaus's forgetting curve   After learning lists of nonsense syllables, Ebbinghaus studied how much he retained up to 30 days later. He found that memory for novel information fades quickly, then levels out. (Adapted from Ebbinghaus, 1885.)

Clark's Nutcracker Among animals, one contender for champion memorist would be a mere birdbrain—the Clark's Nutcracker—which during winter and early spring can locate up to 6000 caches of buried pine seeds (Shettleworth, 1993).

Harry Bahrick (1984) confirmed Ebbinghaus's finding. He examined the forgetting curve for Spanish vocabulary learned in school. By using the cross-sectional method (page 134), he compared the knowledge of Spanish among people who had just taken Spanish with the knowledge of those who had studied it up to 50 years before. Compared with those just completing a high school or college Spanish course, those who had been out of school for 3 years had forgotten much of what they had learned (Figure 9.14). However, after roughly 3 years, forgetting leveled off; what people remembered then, they still remembered 25 years later, even if they had not used their Spanish at all.

Storing Memories in the Brain

For a time, it was thought that brain stimulation during surgery provided evidence that our past is "in there," in complete detail, just waiting to be relived. Even today, 6 in 10 university students agree that "everything we learn is permanently stored, although sometimes inaccessible" (Brown & others, 1996). Perhaps some of them have heard of the brain surgery experiments described on page 60. To predict possible side effects of such surgery, Wilder Penfield helped map the brain's motor cortex by electrically stimulating wide-awake patients. Occasionally, Penfield's patients would report hearing things, such as "a mother calling her little boy." Penfield (1969) assumed he was activating long-lost experiences etched permanently on the brain.

Scrutinizing these famous reports, memory researchers Elizabeth Loftus and Geoffrey Loftus (1980) discovered that these flashbacks were extremely rare, occurring in only a handful of Penfield's 1100 stimulated patients. Moreover, the content of these few recollections suggested that the experiences were not being relived but were being invented. As if they had been dreaming, people would recall being in locations they had never visited. Although the brain's storage capacity may be essentially unlimited, Penfield's evidence did *not* suggest that we store most information with the exactness of a tape recorder. Rather, say memory researchers, forgetting occurs as new experiences interfere with our retrieval (pages 291–292) and as the physical memory trace gradually decays.

"Our memories are flexible and superimposable, a panoramic blackboard with an endless supply of chalk and erasers."

ELIZABETH LOFTUS AND KATHERINE KETCHAM
THE MYTH OF REPRESSED MEMORY
1994

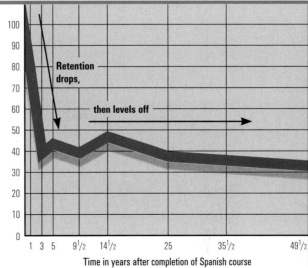

Percentage of original vocabulary retained

Retention drops,

then levels off

Time in years after completion of Spanish course

Figure **9.14**

The forgetting curve for Spanish learned in school Compared with people just completing a Spanish course, those 3 years out of the course remembered much less. Compared with the 3-year group, however, those who studied Spanish even longer ago did not forget much more. (Adapted from Bahrick, 1984b.)

long-term potentiation (LTP)
an increase in a synapse's firing potential after brief, rapid stimulation. Believed to be a neural basis for learning and memory.

But what exactly is the "memory trace"? Since 1980, new clues to the physical basis of long-term memory have surfaced rapidly. While cognitive psychologists study our memory "software," neuroscientists are gaining new insights into our memory "hardware"—how and where we physically store information in our brains.

For several decades, neuroscientists have searched the brain for physical evidence of memory. The search has at times been exasperating. One psychologist, Karl Lashley (1950), trained rats to solve a maze, then cut out pieces of the rats' cortexes and retested their memory of the maze. Eventually, he hoped to locate where memory of the maze was stored. Alas, no matter what part of the cortex he removed, the rats retained at least a partial memory of how to solve the maze. Lashley's conclusion: Memories do not reside in single, specific spots.

> While cognitive psychologists study our memory "software," neuroscientists are gaining new insights into our memory "hardware"—how and where we physically store information in our brains.

Are memories instead rooted in the brain's ongoing electrical activity? If so, then temporarily shutting down that activity should eliminate them, much as a power failure eliminates the settings on an electronic clock. To test this, Ralph Gerard (1953) trained hamsters to turn right or left to get food. Then he lowered their body temperature until the brain's electrical activity ceased. When the hamsters were revived and their brains were active again, would they remember which way to turn? Yes. Their long-term memories survived the electrical blackout. "I must admit that memories are more of a spiritual than a physical reality," said one memory researcher in commenting on the elusiveness of the memory trace with tongue only partly in cheek. "When you try to touch them, they turn to mist and disappear" (Loftus & Ketcham, 1994, p. 4).

Recently, the search for the physical basis of memory has focused on the firing potential of the synapses.

Synaptic Changes

Other neuroscientists are, however, beginning to touch memories by exploring changes within and between single neurons. Memories begin as impulses whizzing through brain circuits, somehow leaving permanent neural traces. Where does the neural change occur? The available clues point to the synapses—the sites where nerve cells communicate with one another through their neurotransmitter messengers (Alkon & others, 1991). Recall from Chapter 3 how experience modifies the brain's neural networks. Given increased activity in a particular pathway, neural interconnections form or strengthen.

Eric Kandel and James Schwartz (1982) observed actual changes in the sending neurons. Their subjects were among the simpler animals, the California sea snail, *Aplysia*. Its mere 20,000 or so nerve cells are unusually large and accessible, enabling the researchers to observe synaptic changes during learning. Chapter 8 noted how the sea snail can be classically conditioned (with electric shock) to reflexively withdraw its gills when squirted with water, much as a shell-shocked soldier jumps at the sound of a snapping twig. By observing sea snails' neural connections before and after conditioning, the researchers pinpointed changes. When learning occurs, the snail releases more of the neurotransmitter serotonin at certain synapses, and these synapses become more efficient at transmitting signals.

What's next?   In the early stages of Alzheimer's disease, a loss of brain tissue that secretes important neurotransmitters results in considerable mental impairment. In recent years, social agencies have begun offering day care services. At centers like the one shown here, patients are kept busy and their caretakers get a break.

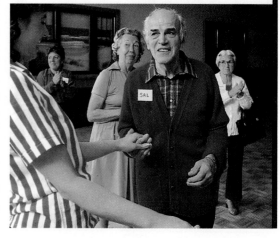

Increased synaptic efficiency makes for more efficient neural circuits. In experiments, rapidly stimulating certain memory-circuit connections has increased their sensitivity for hours or even weeks to come. (The sending neuron now needs less prompting to release its neurotransmitter, and receptor sites may increase.) This prolonged strengthening of potential neural firing, called long-term potentiation (LTP), provides a neural basis for learning and remembering associations. We know now that drugs that block LTP interfere with learning (Lynch & Staubli, 1991). Mutant mice engineered to lack an enzyme needed for LTP can't learn their way out of a maze (Silva & others, 1992). And rats given a drug that enhances LTP will learn a maze with half the usual number of mistakes (Service, 1994). These findings raise hopes that researchers may someday discover a drug to enhance human memory, especially for those whose memory is fading.

Passing an electric current through the brain won't disrupt old memories after long-term potentiation has occurred. But the current will wipe out very recent experiences. Such is the experience both of laboratory animals and of depressed people given electroconvulsive therapy (page 510). A blow to the head can do the same. When football players who have been dazed or momentarily knocked unconscious are interviewed a few minutes later, they typically cannot recall the name of the play during which the incident occurred (Yarnell & Lynch, 1970). Likewise, a boxer knocked out in round 2 may have no memory of the round. (They are like sleepers who can't remember what they heard just before losing consciousness.) The information in short-term memory before the blow just didn't have time to consolidate into long-term memory.

Drugs that block neurotransmitters also disrupt information storage (Squire, 1987). For example, alcohol impairs memory formation by disrupting serotonin's messenger activity (Weingartner & others, 1983). The morning after a night of heavy drinking, a person may have trouble remembering the previous evening.

Stress Hormones and Memory

The naturally stimulating hormones that humans and animals produce when excited or stressed also affect learning and retention—they boost it. When a rat receives an arousing hormone and then a mild foot shock, it forms an indelible memory—like the one it forms when an *intense* foot shock naturally triggers release of the same hormone (Gold, 1987, 1992; Martinez & others, 1991). By making more glucose energy available to fuel brain activity, the

Stress hormones and memory
When we are greatly aroused, our stress hormones help make memories indelible.

hormone surge signals the brain that something important has happened. The arousal sears the events onto the brain. Conversely, people who are given a drug that blocks the effects of stress hormones will later have more trouble remembering the details of an upsetting story (Cahill, 1994). No emotion means weaker memories.

Emotion-triggered hormonal changes help explain why we long remember exciting or shocking events, such as our first kiss, a political assassination, or an earthquake. People who have suffered traumatic experiences often relive the experience with vivid flashbacks. And people who experienced the 1989 San Francisco Bay earthquake had perfect recall a year and a half later of where they were and what they were doing (as they had recorded within a day or two). Others' memories for the circumstances under which they *heard* about the quake were prone to errors (Neisser & others, 1991; Palmer & others, 1991). (A second reason for the durability of dramatic experiences is our reliving and rehearsing them.) The point to remember, according to James McGaugh (1994), is that "stronger emotional experiences make for stronger, more reliable memories." After traumatic experiences—a wartime ambush, a house fire, a rape—vivid recollections of the horrific event intrude again and again, as if they were burned in.

Emotion-triggered hormonal changes help explain why we long remember exciting or shocking events, such as our first kiss, a political assassination, or an earthquake.

amnesia
the loss of memory.

implicit memory
retention without conscious recollection (of skills and dispositions). (Also called nondeclarative memory.)

explicit memory
memory of facts and experiences that one can consciously know and "declare." (Also called declarative memory.)

The two-track memory system reinforces an important principle introduced in Chapter 5's description of parallel processing: Mental feats such as vision, thinking, and memory may seem to be single abilities, but they are not. Rather, we split information into different components for separate and simultaneous processing.

Storing Implicit and Explicit Memories

After a memory-to-be enters the cortex through the senses, it wends its way into the brain's depths. Where it goes depends on the type of information, as dramatically illustrated in the special amnesic patients similar to John, whom we met at the beginning of this chapter.

Neurologist Oliver Sacks (1985, pp. 26–27) describes another such patient. Jimmie, a brain-damaged man, had no memories—thus, no sense of elapsed time—beyond his brain damage in 1945. Asked to name the U.S. president, he replied, "FDR's dead. Truman's at the helm."

When Jimmie gave his age as 19, Sacks thrust a mirror at him: "Look in the mirror and tell me what you see. Is that a 19-year-old looking out from the mirror?"

Jimmie turned ashen, gripped the chair, cursed, then became frantic: "What's going on? What's happened to me? Is this a nightmare? Am I crazy? Is this a joke?" When his attention was diverted to some children playing baseball, his panic ended, the dreadful mirror swiftly forgotten.

Flipping through a *National Geographic*, Sacks showed Jimmie a photo. "What is this?" he asked.

"It's the moon," Jimmie replied.

"No, it's not," Sacks answered. "It's a picture of the earth taken from the moon."

"Doc, you're kidding? Someone would've had to get a camera up there!"

"Naturally."

"Hell! You're joking—how the hell would you do that?" Jimmie's wonder was that of a bright young man from 50 years ago reacting with amazement to his travel back to the future.

Careful testing of these unique people reveals something even stranger: Although incapable of recalling new facts or anything they have recently done, Jimmie and other similarly amnesic people can learn. They can be classically conditioned. Shown hard-to-find figures in pictures (where's Waldo?), they can quickly spot them again later. They can learn to read mirror-image writing or do a jigsaw puzzle, and they have even been taught complicated job skills (Schacter, 1992, 1996; Squire, 1987). *They do all these things with absolutely no memory of having learned them.*

Consider what happens when such patients have learned to solve a Tower of Hanoi puzzle, which requires moving rings from one pole to another until they are stacked in order of size. Amnesia victims will deny having seen the puzzle before, insist it is silly for them to try, and then, like practiced experts, proceed to solve it. They are in some ways like the brain-damaged people who cannot consciously recognize faces, but whose physiological responses to familiar faces reveal an implicit (unconscious) recognition.

These curious findings make it hard to argue that memory is a single, unified system. Instead, we seem to have two memory systems operating in tandem (Figure 9.15). Whatever has destroyed the amnesics' conscious recall has not destroyed their unconscious capacity for learning. They can learn *how* to do something—called implicit memory (*nondeclarative memory*). But they cannot know and declare *that* they know—called explicit memory (*declarative memory*). Having read a story once, they will read it faster a second time, showing implicit memory. But there will be no explicit memory, for they cannot recall having seen the story before. Having played golf on a new course,

Figure 9.15

Memory subsystems We process and store our explicit and implicit memories separately. Thus, one may lose explicit memory (becoming amnesic), yet display implicit memory for material one cannot consciously recall.

Figure **9.16**

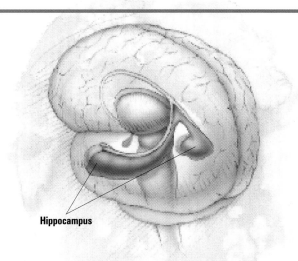

Hippocampus

The hippocampus Explicit memories for facts and episodes are processed in the hippocampus (circled red in the MRI scan) and fed to other brain regions for storage.

We seem to have two memory systems operating in tandem.

they will forget it completely, yet their game will improve with experience on the course. If repeatedly shown the word *perfume*, they wouldn't recall having seen it. But if asked the first word that comes to mind in response to the letters *per*, they surprise themselves by readily displaying their learning. Strangely, they retain their past but do not explicitly recall it. The memory system's operating without producing conscious recall is rather like a company's workers doing their job but not reporting such to the CEO.

These remarkable patients provoke our wondering: Do our explicit and implicit memory systems involve separate brain regions? Scans of the brain in action, and autopsies of amnesic patients, reveal that new explicit memories of names, images, and events are layed down via a limbic system structure called the hippocampus (Figure 9.16). When people recall words (using explicit memory) the hippocampus lights up on a PET scan (Squire, 1992). Chickadees and other birds can store food in hundreds of places and return to these unmarked caches months later, but not if their hippocampus has been removed (Sherry & Vaccarino, 1989). Like the cortex, the hippocampus is lateralized, and damage to the left and right sides seems to produce different results. Patients with left hippocampus damage have trouble remembering verbal information, but they have no trouble recalling visual designs and locations. Those with right hippocampus damage have the reverse problem (Schacter, 1996).

When monkeys lose their hippocampus to surgery, they also lose most of their recall for things learned during the preceding month (Squire & Zola-Morgan, 1991). Older memories remain intact, suggesting that the hippocampus is not the permanent storehouse, but is instead a way station that feeds new information to other brain circuits for permanent storage (McClelland & others, 1995). The hippocampus seems rather like a library's "new books" shelf, which holds new material for a while before transferring it to permanent storage elsewhere.

Our neural library assigns different information to different regions. Brain scans reveal that, once stored, our mental encores of past experience activate various parts of the frontal and temporal lobes (Fink & others, 1996; Gabrieli & others, 1996; Markowitsch, 1995). Calling up a telephone number and holding it in working memory activates a region of the left frontal cortex; recall of a birthday scene would more likely activate the right hemisphere.

Although your hippocampus is a temporary processing site for your explicit memories, you could lose it and still lay down memories for skills and conditioned associations. Hoping to locate such implicit memories, psychologist Richard Thompson and his fellow sleuths David Krupa and Judith Thompson studied how a rabbit's brain learns to associate a tone with an impending air puff in the eye (and thus to blink in anticipation of the puff). First, they traced the pathway connecting the brain's reception of the tone with the blink response. They discovered that it runs to the brainstem through a part of the cerebellum (at the back of the head), and that if they cut this pathway, the learned response would be lost. That was like cutting the cords to your stereo speakers, which would confirm the cord's part in the electronic path but might still leave you wondering where the

"[Brain scanning] technologies are revolutionizing the study of the brain and mind in the same way that the telescope revolutionized the study of the heavens."

ENDEL TULVING (1996)

hippocampus
a neural center located in the limbic system that helps process explicit memories for storage.

recall
a measure of memory in which the person must retrieve information learned earlier, as on a fill-in-the-blank test.

recognition
a measure of memory in which the person need only identify items previously learned, as on a multiple-choice test.

relearning
a memory measure that assesses the amount of time saved when relearning previously learned information.

priming
the activation, often unconsciously, of particular associations in memory.

music is stored. Their next step was to administer a drug during the rabbits' eye-blink training, temporarily deadening different parts of the neural pathway. This pinpointed the implicit memory—in the cerebellum. The rejuvenated rabbits failed to display the learned response only when the cerebellum was deactivated during training (Krupa & others, 1993). Human patients with a damaged cerebellum are likewise incapable of eye-blink conditioning (Daum & Schugens, 1996).

This dual explicit-implicit memory system helps explain infantile amnesia: The reactions and skills we learned during infancy reach far into our future, yet as adults we recall nothing (explicitly) of our first three years. Our conscious minds are blank, not only because we index so much of our explicit memory by words that nonspeaking children have not learned, but also because the hippocampus is one of the last brain structures to mature.

SUMMING UP

Sensory Memory Storage Information first enters the memory system through the senses. We register and briefly store visual images via iconic memory, and sounds via echoic memory.

Short-Term Memory Storage Our short-term memory span for information just presented is very limited—a seconds-long retention of up to about seven or eight items, depending on the information and how it is presented.

Long-Term Memory Storage Our capacity for storing information permanently is essentially unlimited.

Storing Memories in the Brain How and where we store information is uncertain. The search for the physical basis of memory has recently focused on the synapses and their neurotransmitters and on the long-term potentiation of brain circuits, such as those running through the hippocampus. Studies of brain-damaged patients reveal two types of memory—explicit (declarative) memories processed by the hippocampus, and implicit (nondeclarative) memories processed by more ancient brain regions. The differing types of memory loss reveal that there is no single function called "memory." Rather, the brain processes and stores information in differing ways.

KEY TERMS AND CONCEPTS sensory memory, iconic memory, echoic memory, long-term potentiation (LTP), amnesia, implicit (nondeclarative) memory, explicit (declarative) memory, hippocampus

Retrieval: Getting Information Out

To remember an event requires not only getting it in (encoding) and retaining it (storage), but getting it out. Retrieval is aided by cues associated with the event, including those in the context where we encoded it.

To most people, memory is recall, the ability to retrieve information not in conscious awareness. To a psychologist, memory is any sign that something learned has been retained. So *recognizing* or more quickly *relearning* information also indicates memory.

Long after you cannot recall most of the people in your high school graduating class, you may still be able to recognize their yearbook pictures from a photographic lineup and pick their names from a list of names. Harry Bahrick and his colleagues (1975) reported that people who graduated 25 years earlier could not *recall* many of their old classmates, but they could *recognize* 90 percent of their pictures and names.

Relearning speed can reveal memory. If you once learned something and then forgot it, you probably will relearn it more quickly than when you learned it originally. When you study for a final exam or resurrect a language used in early childhood, the relearning is easier. Tests of recognition and of time spent relearning reveal that we remember more than we can recall. Although older people often find it increasingly difficult to *recall* names and information, they have fewer difficulties *recognizing* such (see page 283).

Remembering things past Even if Madonna and Paul Newman had not become famous, their high school classmates would most likely still recognize their yearbook photos.

The speed and vastness of our recognition memory dwarfs any librarian's ability to call up information. "Is your friend wearing a new or old outfit?" "Old." "Is this seconds-long movie clip from a film you've ever seen?" "Yes." "Have you ever before seen this person—this minor variation on the same old human features (two eyes, one nose, and so on)?" "No." Before the mouth can form our answer to any of millions of such questions, the mind knows, and knows that it knows.

Retrieval Cues

To retrieve a fact from a library, you need a way to access it. In recognition tests, retrieval cues (such as photographs) provide reminders of information (classmates' names) we could not otherwise recall. Retrieval cues also are guides to where to look. If you want to know what the pyramid on the back of an American dollar signifies, you might look in *Collier's Encyclopedia* under "dollar," "currency," or "money." But your efforts would be futile. To get the information you want, you would have to look under "Great Seal of the United States" (Hayes, 1981). Like information stored in encyclopedias, memories are inaccessible unless we have the right cues for retrieving them. Do you recall the gist of the second sentence I asked you to remember (on page 275)? If not, does the word *shark* help? Experiments show that *shark* more readily retrieves the image you stored than does the sentence's actual word, *fish* (Anderson & others, 1976).

You can think of a memory as held in storage by a web of associations. To retrieve a specific memory, you first need to identify one of the strands that leads to it, a process called priming. Philosopher-psychologist William James referred to priming as the "wakening of associations." Often our associations are activated, or primed, without our awareness. As Figure 9.17 indicates, seeing or hearing the word *rabbit* primes associations with *hare* even though we may not recall having seen or heard *rabbit*.

Priming has been called "memory without remembering." If, walking down a hallway, you see a missing-child poster, you will then be more likely to interpret an ambiguous adult-child interaction as a possible kidnapping (James, 1986). Although you don't consciously remember the poster, it primes your interpretation. (As we saw in Chapter 5, even subliminal stimuli can briefly prime responses to later stimuli.)

Retrieval cues often prime our memories for earlier experiences. Mnemonic devices provide us with handy retrieval cues: ROY G. BIV; HOMES; bun, shoe, tree. The best retrieval cues come from the associations formed at the time we encode a memory. Before the Watergate hearings, John Dean refreshed his memory "by going through every single newspaper article outlining what had happened and then placing myself and what I had done in a given sequence in time" (Neisser, 1981). This helped activate associations that were specific to the encoded memory.

Context Effects

It does help to put yourself back in the context where you experienced something. Duncan Godden and Alan Baddeley (1975) discovered this by having scuba divers listen to a list of words in two different settings, either 10 feet underwater or sitting on the beach. As Figure 9.18 illustrates, the divers recalled more words when they were retested in the same place.

Figure 9.17

Priming—awakening associations
After seeing or hearing *rabbit*, we are later more likely to spell the spoken word as *h-a-r-e*. The spreading of associations unconsciously activates related associations. This phenomenon is called priming. (Adapted from Bower, 1986.)

Multiple-choice questions test our
a. recall.
b. recognition.
c. relearning.
Fill-in-the-blank questions test our _____.
(See page 291.)

Figure 9.18

The effects of context on memory
Words heard underwater are best recalled underwater; words heard on land are best recalled on land. (Adapted from Godden & Baddeley, 1975.)

Figure 9.19

Familiar context activates memory After learning to move a mobile by kicking, infants had their learning reactivated most strongly when retested in the same rather than a different context. (From Butler & Rovee-Collier, 1989.)

You have probably experienced similar context effects. Returning to where you once lived or to the school you once attended may flood you with retrieval cues and memories. Taking an exam in the same room where you are taught may help a little. In several experiments, Carolyn Rovee-Collier (1993) found that a familiar context activates memories even in 3-month-olds. After learning that kicking would move a crib mobile (via a connecting ribbon from the ankle), the infants kicked more when again tested in the same crib with the same bumper (Figure 9.19).

déjà vu
that eerie sense that "I've experienced this before." Cues from the current situation may subconsciously trigger retrieval of an earlier experience.

mood-congruent memory
the tendency to recall experiences that are consistent with one's current good or bad mood.

Sometimes, being in a context similar to one we've been in before may trigger the experience of déjà vu (French for "already seen")—that eerie sense that "I've been in this exact situation before." People often wonder, "How could I recognize a situation that I'm experiencing for the first time?" Those who suppose something paranormal is occurring may think of reincarnation ("I must have experienced this in a previous life") or precognition ("I viewed this scene in my mind before experiencing it"). If we pose the question differently ("Why do I feel as if I recognize this situation?"), we can see how our memory system might produce déjà vu (Alcock, 1981). If we have previously been in a similar situation, the current situation may be loaded with cues that unconsciously retrieve the earlier experience. Thus, if in such a context you see a stranger who looks and walks like one of your friends, the similarity may give rise to an eerie feeling of recognition. Because the feeling conflicts with your knowing that the person is a stranger, you may think, "I've seen that person in this situation before."

Moods and Memories

Associated words, events, and contexts are not the only retrieval cues. Events in the past may have aroused a specific emotion, which later can prime us to recall its associated events. Cognitive psychologist Gordon Bower (1983) explained it this way: "A specific emotional state is like a specific room in a library into which the subject places memory records, and he can most easily retrieve those records by returning to that same room or emotional state." The things we learn in one state—be it joyful or sad, drunk or sober—are sometimes more easily recalled when we are again in the same state, a subtle phenomenon called *state-dependent memory*. What is learned when depressed, high, or drunk is not recalled well in *any* state (depression and certain drugs interfere with encoding), but it's recalled slightly better when again drunk, high, or depressed. Someone who hides money when drunk may forget the location until drunk again.

More striking is the way our memories are biased by our moods (Eich, 1995; Ellis & Ashbrook, 1989; Matt & others, 1992). We seem to associate good or bad events with their accompanying emotions. Thus, the emotions become retrieval cues; when again feeling good or bad, we more easily recall associated good or bad times. If people are put in a buoyant mood—whether under hypnosis or just by the day's events (a World Cup soccer victory for the German subjects of one study)—they

CALLAHAN

"I wonder if you'd mind giving me directions. I've never been sober in this part of town before."

Distributed by Levin Represents.

recall the world through rose-colored glasses (Forgas & others, 1984; Schwarz & others, 1987). They judge themselves to be competent and effective, other people to be benevolent, life in general to be wonderful. Put in a bad mood by negative events, the very same people suddenly recall and predict everything more negatively.

So it shouldn't surprise us that in some studies *currently* depressed people recall their parents as having been rejecting, punitive, and guilt-promoting, whereas *formerly* depressed people describe their parents much as do those who have never suffered depression (Lewinsohn & Rosenbaum, 1987; Lewis, 1992). Our memories are somewhat <u>mood-congruent</u>. Being depressed sours memories by priming negative associations, which we use to explain our current mood. No wonder Robert Bornstein and others (1991) report that adolescents' ratings of parental warmth give little clue to how the same adolescents will rate their parents six weeks later. When teenagers are down, their world, including their parents, seems inhuman; as their mood brightens, their parents metamorphose from devils into angels. (The phenomenon is worth remembering the next time you hear someone in a bad mood recalling bitter memories, and someone giddy with love recalling only good times.) You and I may nod our heads knowingly. Yet, in a good or bad mood, we persist in attributing to reality our own changing judgments and memories.

> "When a feeling was there, they felt as if it would never go; when it was gone, they felt as if it had never been; when it returned, they felt as if it had never gone."
>
> **GEORGE MACDONALD**
> *WHAT'S MINE'S MINE*
> 1886

Moods also influence how we *interpret* other people's behavior. In a bad mood, we read someone's look as a glare; in a good mood we encode the same look as interest. How we perceive the world depends on our mood. Passions exaggerate.

Finally, our moods affect how attentive we are to new information. Sad people are often preoccupied—less attentive to new information and more focused on their aches and woes (Salovey & Birnbaum, 1989; Wood & others, 1990). In some respects, that's healthy. A negative mood signals that all's not well, motivating people to ruminate and reassess—and to have impaired memory for unrelated events (Hertel, 1994). But very happy moods

can also trigger distracting thoughts, impairing memory for the task at hand (Seibert & Ellis, 1991).

Your mood's effect on encoding and retrieval helps explain why moods persist. When happy, you recall happy events, which helps prolong the good mood. When depressed, you recall sad events, which in turn darkens your interpretations of current events. As we will see in Chapter 15, this process maintains depression's vicious cycle.

Forgetting as Retrieval Failure

We have seen that forgetting occurs when we fail to encode information and when our stored memories decay. Forgotten events are like books you can't find in your library—some because you never acquired them, others because they were discarded.

There is a third possibility: Even if the book is stored and available, it may be inaccessible. Perhaps you don't have the information needed to look it up and retrieve it. Information sometimes gets into our brain and, though we know it is there, we cannot get it out (Figure 9.20). A person's name may lie poised on the tip of the tongue, waiting to be retrieved. When people who cannot recall information get retrieval cues ("It begins with an *M*"), they often remember what they could not recall. Retrieval problems lie behind the occasional memory failures of older adults. (As Chapter 4 noted, older people tend to recall less than younger adults do, but they usually remember as well as younger people when given reminders or a recognition test.)

Interference

Learning some items may interfere with retrieving others, especially when the items are similar. If someone gives you a phone number to remember, you may be able to recall it later. But if two more people give you their numbers, each successive number will be more difficult to recall. Such

Mood and memory   Elated, we remember other happy times. Mood serves as a retrieval cue, activating other memories tinged with the same emotion. These memories help sustain the current mood.

Answers to questions on page 289: Multiple-choice questions test recognition. Fill-in-the-blank questions test recall.

Figure **9.20**

Retrieval failure   Forgetting can result from failure to retrieve information from long-term memory.

External events	→	Sensory memory	Attention / Encoding →	Short-term memory	Encoding →	Long-term memory

Retrieval

Retrieval failure leads to forgetting

proactive interference
the disruptive effect of prior learning on the recall of new information.

retroactive interference
the disruptive effect of new learning on the recall of old information.

proactive (*forward-acting*) interference occurs when something you learned earlier disrupts recall of something you experience later. As you collect more and more information, your mental attic never fills, but it certainly gets cluttered.

For example, after buying a new combination lock or receiving a new phone number, the old one may interfere. Benton Underwood (1957) found that people who learn different lists of words on successive days have more and more difficulty remembering each new list the next day. This proactive interference explains why Ebbinghaus, after memorizing countless lists of nonsense syllables during his career, could remember only about one-fourth of a new list of syllables on the day after he learned it—far fewer than you as a novice could remember after learning a single list.

Retroactive (*backward-acting*) interference occurs when new information makes it harder to recall something you learned earlier (Figure 9.21). For example, the learning of new students' names typically interferes with a professor's recall of names learned in previous classes.

You can minimize retroactive interference by re-ducing the number of interfering events—say, by going to sleep shortly after learning new information. This is what John Jenkins and Karl Dallenbach (1924) found in a classic experiment. Day after day, two people each learned some nonsense syllables, then tried to recall them after up to 8 hours of being awake or asleep at night. As Figure 9.22 shows, forgetting occurred more rapidly after being awake and involved with other activities. The investigators surmised that "forgetting is not so much a matter of the decay of old impressions and associations as it is a matter of interference, inhibition, or obliteration of the old by the new" (1924, p. 612). Later experiments have confirmed that the hour before a night's sleep (but not the minute before sleep) is a good time to commit information to memory (Fowler & others, 1973).

Although interference is an important cause of forgetting, we should not overstate the point. Sometimes old information facilitates our learning of new information. Knowledge of Latin may help us to learn French—a phenomenon called *positive transfer*. It's when the old and new information compete with each other that interference occurs.

Figure **9.21**

Proactive and retroactive interference

French, learned beforehand, interferes proactively

Study French — papier, livre, plume, école

Study Spanish — papel, libro, pluma, escuela

Spanish 101 Mid-term exam

proactive interference

Spanish, learned afterward, interferes retroactively

Study French — papier, livre, plume, école

Study Spanish — papel, libro, pluma, escuela

French 101 Mid-term exam

retroactive interference

Figure **9.22**

Percentage of syllables recalled

Without interfering events, recall is better

After sleep

After remaining awake

Hours elapsed after learning syllables

Retroactive interference More forgetting occurred when a person stayed awake and experienced other new material. (From Jenkins & Dallenbach, 1924.)

Motivated Forgetting

The huge cookie jar in our kitchen was jammed with freshly baked chocolate chip cookies. Still more spread across the cooling racks on the counter. Twenty-four hours later, not a crumb was left. Who had taken them? My wife, three children, and I were the only people in the house during that time. So while memories were still fresh, I conducted a little memory test. Andy acknowledged wolfing down as many as 20. Peter admitted eating 15. Laura guessed that she had stuffed her then-6-year-old body with 15 cookies. My wife, Carol, recalled eating 6, and I remembered consuming 15 and taking 18 more to the office. Collectively, we sheepishly accepted responsibility for 89 cookies. Still, we had not come close; 160 cookies had been baked.

In experiments that parallel the cookie-memory phenomenon, Michael Ross and his colleagues (1981) found that people unknowingly revise their own histories. After Ross persuaded a group of people that frequent tooth brushing is desirable, they (more than other people) recalled having frequently brushed their teeth in the last 2 weeks. Having taken a highly touted study skills course, students later inflated their estimates of self-improvement. By *de*flating their evaluations of their previous study habits they convinced themselves that they had really benefited (Conway & Ross, 1984). To remember our past is often to revise it. By recalling events in a desired manner we protect and enhance our self-images.

Why do our memories fail us? Why did my family and I not encode, store, and retrieve all the instances of our cookie-eating? As Figure 9.23 reminds us, we automatically encode sensory information in amazing detail. So was it a storage problem? Might

"[It is] necessary to remember that events happened in the desired manner. And if it is necessary to rearrange one's memories . . . then it is necessary to forget that one has done so. The trick of doing this can be learned like any other mental technique. . . . It is called doublethink."

GEORGE ORWELL
NINETEEN EIGHTY-FOUR
1948

Figure **9.23**

Information bits

Sensory memory
The senses momentarily register amazing detail.

Short-term memory
A few items are both noticed and encoded.

Long-term storage
Some items are altered or lost.

Retrieval from long-term memory
Depending on interference, retrieval cues, moods, and motives, some things get retrieved, some don't.

When do we forget? Forgetting can occur at any memory stage. As we process information, we filter, alter, or lose much of it.

repression
in psychoanalytic theory, the basic defense mechanism that banishes anxiety–arousing thoughts, feelings, and memories from consciousness.

misinformation effect
incorporating misleading information into one's memory of an event.

our memories of cookies, like Ebbinghaus's memory of nonsense syllables, have vanished almost as fast as the cookies themselves? Or might the information still be intact but irretrievable because it would be embarrassing to remember?[1]

With his concept of repression, Sigmund Freud proposed that with painful information our memory systems are indeed self-censoring. To protect our self-concepts and to minimize anxiety, we supposedly repress painful memories. But the submerged memory still lingers, said Freud, and with patience and effort may be retrieved during therapy or by some later cue. One reported case involved a woman with an intense, unexplained fear of running water. An aunt solved the mystery one day by whispering, "I have never told." The words cued the woman's memory of an incident when, as a disobedient young child, she wandered away from a family picnic and became trapped under a waterfall—until being rescued by her aunt, who promised not to tell her parents (Kihlstrom, 1990). Such stories have fed the now-common belief, shared by 9 in 10 university students, that "memories for painful experiences are sometimes pushed into the unconsciousness" (Brown & others, 1996). Repression is central to Freud's psychology and has been part of psychology's lore. Therapists assume it. People believe it. Yet increasing numbers of memory researchers think repression rarely, if ever, occurs. As we will see, people do forget negative (and positive) experiences. Do they repress them? Stay tuned.

SUMMING UP

Retrieval Cues To be remembered, information that is "in there" must be retrieved, with the aid of associations (cues) that prime the memory. Retrieval is sometimes aided by returning to the original context. Mood affects memory, too. While in a good or bad mood, we often retrieve memories congruent with that mood.

Forgetting as Retrieval Failure Forgetting that is related to retrieval failures may be caused by proactive or retroactive interference or even by motivated forgetting.

KEY TERMS AND CONCEPTS recall, recognition, relearning, priming, déjà vu, mood-congruent memory, proactive interference, retroactive interference, repression

[1]One of my cookie-scarfing sons, on reading this in his father's textbook years later, confessed that he also had fibbed a little.

Memory Construction

Memory retrieval is partly memory construction and sometimes involves "source amnesia." With surprising ease, people therefore form and feel certain of false memories, a phenomenon that raises questions about the accuracy of some eyewitness memories.

Picture yourself having this pleasant experience:

> You go to a fancy restaurant for dinner. You enter the restaurant and are seated at a table with a white tablecloth. You study the menu. You tell the waiter that you want prime rib, medium rare, a baked potato with sour cream, and a salad with blue cheese dressing. You also order some red wine from the wine list. A few minutes later the waiter returns with your salad. Later he brings the rest of the meal, which you enjoy, except that the prime rib is a bit overdone.

Were I immediately to quiz you on this paragraph (from Hyde, 1983), you could surely retrieve considerable detail. For example, without looking back, answer the following questions:

1 What kind of salad dressing did you order?

2 Was the tablecloth red checked?

3 What did you order to drink?

4 Did the waiter give you a menu?

You were probably able to recall exactly what you ordered, and maybe even the color of the tablecloth. Does retrieval therefore consist merely of "reading" the information stored in our brain's library? We do have an enormous capacity for storing and reproducing the incidental details of our daily experience. But we often construct our memories as we encode them, and we may also alter our memories as we withdraw them from the memory bank. Like a scientist who infers a dinosaur's appearance from its remains, we infer our past from stored information plus what we now assume. Did the waiter give you a menu? Not in the paragraph given. Nevertheless, many people answer yes. By filtering information and filling in missing pieces, our schemas for restaurants direct our memory construction.

Misinformation and Imagination Effects

In many dozens of experiments, involving more than 20,000 people, Elizabeth Loftus has shown how eyewitnesses similarly reconstruct their memories when questioned. In one experiment with John Palmer, Loftus showed a film of a traffic accident and then quizzed the viewers about what they saw (Loftus & Palmer, 1974). Those asked, "How fast were the cars going when they *smashed* into each other?" gave higher speed estimates than those asked, "How fast were the cars going when they *hit* each other?" A week later, the researchers asked the viewers if they recalled seeing any broken glass. Compared with those who had been asked the question with *hit*, those asked the question with *smashed* were more than twice as likely to recall broken glass (Figure 9.24). In fact, the film showed no broken glass.

In many follow-up experiments around the world, people have witnessed an event, received or not received misleading information about it, and then taken a memory test. The repeated result is a misinformation effect: After exposure to subtle misinformation, many people misremember. They have misrecalled a yield (give way) sign as a stop sign, hammers as screwdrivers, Coke cans as peanut cans, *Vogue* magazine as *Mademoiselle*, "Dr. Henderson" as "Dr. Davidson," breakfast cereal as eggs, and a clean-shaven man as a man with a mustache (Loftus & others, 1992). As a memory fades with time following an event, the injection of misinformation becomes easier (Loftus, 1992).

So unwitting is the misinformation effect that people later find it nearly impossible to discriminate between their memories of real and suggested events (Schooler & others, 1986). This difficulty was strikingly true among those who three years later misrecalled their whereabouts on hearing of the space shuttle *Challenger*'s explosion (Neisser & Harsch, 1992). When shown their own handwritten accounts from the day after, many were surprised. Some were so sure of their false memories that they insisted their original version must have been flawed.

As people recount an experience, they fill in their memory gaps with plausible guesses and assumptions. After more retellings, they often recall these guessed details, now absorbed into their memories, as if they actually observed them (Roediger & others, 1993). Others' vivid retellings may also implant false memories.

Even repeatedly *imagining* nonexistent events can create false memories. In one experiment by Maryanne Garry and others (1996), university students noted whether they had experienced certain childhood events, such as breaking a window with their hand. Two weeks later, half were asked to imagine themselves experiencing four of these events—for example, running, tripping, falling, and cutting their hand as it crashed through a win-

Figure **9.24**

Accident

Leading question:
"About how fast were the cars going when they *smashed* into each other?"

Memory construction

Memory construction When people who saw the film of a car accident were asked a leading question, they recalled a more serious accident than they had witnessed. (From Loftus, 1979.)

dow. After vividly imagining the fictional event, one-fourth of them became more likely to believe that such may actually have happened during their childhood.

In similar experiments, Ira Hyman and his co-workers (1995, 1996) invited Western Washington University students to recall actual childhood events (reported to the researchers by their parents), along with a suggested false event, such as spilling a punch bowl at a wedding. By a third interview (after encouragement to think about the events between interviews), one-fourth of the students had constructed false memories. They were asked, for example, to recall something that hap-

"Memory is insubstantial. Things keep replacing it. Your batch of snapshots will both fix and ruin your memory . . . . You can't remember anything from your trip except the wretched collection of snapshots."

ANNIE DILLARD
"TO FASHION A TEXT"
1988

Like a scientist who infers a dinosaur's appearance from its remains, we infer our past from stored information plus what we now assume.

pened "when you were six years old and you were attending a wedding." One student recalled, "It was an outdoor wedding and I think we were running around and knocked something over like the punch bowl or something and made a big mess and of course got yelled at for it." Elizabeth Loftus and Jacqueline Pickrell (1995) confirmed this result. When they asked students to recall one false and three actual childhood events, one-fourth remembered the suggested nonevent. The take-home point: Given time, the mind's search for a fact may create a fiction.

Psychologists are not immune to memory construction:

- Frederick Bartlett, a pioneer in studies of memory construction, recalled two decades later the "brilliant afternoon in May 1913" when the Cambridge University experimental psychology lab was opened. His colleague, Sir Godfrey Thompson, remembered that it poured rain (Ross, 1996).

- Another memory researcher, Ulric Neisser (1982), vividly recalls hearing the announcement of the bombing of Pearl Harbor as an interruption to a baseball game broadcast. Years later he realized that American baseball games aren't played in December, when the bombing occurred. Although he knows the memory is false, he still "recalls" the incident.

- The psychologist Jean Piaget was startled as an adult to learn that his vivid, detailed memory of his nursemaid's thwarting his kidnapping was utterly false. Piaget apparently constructed the memory from the many retellings of the story he had heard (later confessed by the nursemaid to have been false).

Source Amnesia

Note that Piaget remembered, but attributed his memory to the wrong source (to his own experience rather than to his nursemaid's stories). When we encode memories, we distribute different aspects of them to different parts of our brains. One of the frailest parts of a memory is its source. Thus, we may recognize someone but have no idea where we have seen the person. We retain the image, but not the context in which we acquired it.

Debra Poole and Stephen Lindsay (1995) replicated Piaget's source amnesia (also called *source misattribution*) by having preschoolers interact with "Mr. Science," who engaged them in demonstrations such as blowing up a balloon with baking soda and vinegar. Three months later, their parents on three successive days read them a story about themselves and Mr. Science. The stories described some things they had experienced and some they had not. When asked by a new interviewer what Mr. Science had done with them, 4 in 10 children spontaneously recalled Mr. Science doing things that were only mentioned in the story.

Ronald Reagan's occasional source misattributions illustrate how fiction can be remembered as fact. During his three U.S. presidential campaigns, he told and retold a story of heroic sacrifice. A World War II B-1 gunner was terrified when his plane was hit by anti-aircraft fire and he could not eject from his seat. "Never mind, son," said his commander, "we'll ride it down together." With

DOONESBURY

misty eyes, Reagan would conclude by telling how the brave commander received the Congressional Medal of Honor posthumously. A curious journalist later checked the 434 World War II Congressional Medal recipients. Finding no similar story, he kept digging until he found the episode—in a 1944 movie, *A Wing and a Prayer* (Loftus & Ketcham, 1994).

Discerning True Memories from False Ones

Because memory is reconstruction as well as reproduction, we can't be sure whether a memory is real by how real it feels. Unreal memories feel like real memories.

We also can't be sure whether a memory is real by how persistent it is. Memory researchers Charles Brainerd and Valerie Reyna (Brainerd & others, 1995) note that memories we derive from experience have more detail than memories we derive from imagination. Memories of imagined experiences contain more of the gist of the supposed event—the meanings and feelings we associate with it. Because gist memories are durable, children's false memories often outlast their true memories.

Although false memories created by suggested misinformation and misattributed sources may *feel* as real as true memories and may be very persistent, brain scans have revealed telltale signs of false memories. Imagine that I were to read aloud a list of words such as *candy, sugar, honey,* and *taste.* Later, I ask you to recognize the presented words from a larger list. If you are like the individuals tested by Henry Roediger and Kathleen McDermott (1995), you would err three times in four— falsely remembering a nonpresented similar word such as *sweet.* In a follow-up study, PET scans revealed that the hippocampus is equally active whether the subject is truly or falsely recalling a word (Schacter & others, 1996). But only when correctly remembering a spoken word such as *candy* did the brain light up in a left temporal lobe area that processes speech sounds. Because the false recognized word (*sweet*) was never heard, there was no sensory record to be activated from the temporal lobe. (There currently is no way to use this technique as a truth detector for memories of one's more distant past.)

In experiments on eyewitness testimony, researchers have repeatedly found that the most con-

fident and consistent eyewitnesses are the most persuasive, but they often are not the most accurate. Eyewitnesses, whether right or wrong, express roughly similar self-assurance (Bothwell & others, 1987; Cutler & Penrod, 1989; Wells & Murray, 1984). Confidence also gives little clue to accuracy in studies of "earwitness" identifications of a previously heard voice among a lineup of voices (Yarmey, 1991).

Memory construction helps explain why John Dean's recollections of the Watergate conversations were a mixture of real and imagined events. It explains why "hypnotically refreshed" memories of crimes so easily incorporate errors, some of which originate with the hypnotist's leading questions. ("Did you hear loud noises?") It explains why dating partners who fall in love *over*estimate their first impressions of one another, while those who break up *under*estimate their earlier liking (McFarland & Ross, 1987). And it explains why people who are asked how they felt ten years ago about marijuana or gender issues recall attitudes closer to their current views than those they actually reported a decade earlier (Markus, 1986).

Australian psychologist Donald Thompson found his own work on memory distortion haunting him when authorities brought him in for questioning about a rape. Although he was a near-perfect match to the victim's memory of the rapist, he had an airtight alibi. Just before the rape occurred Thompson was being interviewed on live television, and he could not possibly have made it to the crime scene. Then it came to light that the victim had been watching the interview—ironically about face recognition—and had experienced source amnesia, confusing her memories of Thompson and the rapist (Schacter, 1996).

Recognizing that the misinformation effect can occur as police and attorneys ask questions framed by their own understandings of an event, Ronald Fisher, Edward Geiselman, and their colleagues (1987, 1989) train police interviewers to ask less suggestive, more effective questions. To activate retrieval cues, the detective first asks witnesses to visualize the scene—the weather, time of day, lighting, sounds, smells, positions of objects, and their mood. Then the witness tells in detail, and without interruption, every point recalled, no matter how trivial. Only then does the detective ask evocative follow-up questions: "Was there anything unusual about the person's appearance or clothing?" When this "cognitive interview" technique is used, Fisher and Geiselman report, accurate recall increases by some 50 percent.

Authors and songwriters sometimes suffer source amnesia. They think an idea came from their own creative imagination, when in fact they are unintentionally plagiarizing something they earlier read or heard.

> "Memory isn't like reading a book; it's more like writing a book from fragmentary notes."
>
> PSYCHOLOGIST JOHN F. KIHLSTROM (1994)

Eyewitness recollections Our memories of witnessed events are fallible, especially when prompted by misleading questions. Even our relatively good memories of faces are not photographic, as this police sketch and photo of accused Unabomber Theodore Kaczynski show.

Children's Eyewitness Recall

If memories can be sincere, yet so sincerely wrong, might children's recollections of sexual abuse err? A vigorous emotional debate has arisen between those who would protect two different groups of potential victims. The question boils down to this: Who is most often victimized—abused children whose recollections are disbelieved, or those falsely accused whose reputations are ruined? Both sides in this debate agree on the following:

- Child sexual abuse does occur, and it can leave a person scarred—more vulnerable to low self-image, sexual promiscuity, anxiety, and depression (Briere & Runtz, 1993; Trickett & Putnam, 1993). (One cannot, however, reliably infer the reverse—that anxious or depressed people have probably been sexually abused.)

- Some innocent people, occasionally those caught in a child-custody conflict, suffer the injustice of false accusations.

- Some perpetrators hide their guilt by casting doubt on their truth-telling accusers.

At issue is the credibility of children's reports. As we have seen, interviewers who ask leading questions can plant false memories of a story they expect to hear. We also know that children sometimes are credible eyewitnesses in criminal cases, but that they tend to be suggestible. In 15 of 18 studies, preschoolers were more suggestible than were older children or adults. In one study of nearly 2000 people who had watched a film clip while visiting a San Francisco science museum, younger children were especially susceptible to the misinformation effect (Loftus & others, 1992). But the belief that children routinely confuse reality with fantasy is not supported by research. If questioned about their experiences in words they understand, children often freely recall what happened and who did it (Goodman & others, 1990). Children are especially credible when involved adults have not talked with them prior to the interview and when their disclosure is made in a first interview with a neutral person who asks nonleading questions.

Studies of children's recollections of physical examinations illustrate both reasonable accuracy and occasional lapses. Lynne Baker-Ward and her colleagues (1993) tested children's memories with general questions ("Tell me what the doctor did to check you") and specific questions ("Did the doctor shine a light in your eyes?"). Three to six weeks after the exam, 3-year-olds recalled about 60 percent and 7-year-olds about 90 percent of what the doctor did. Asked about things that didn't happen ("Did the doctor cut your hair?" "Did the nurse sit on top of you?"), 3-year-olds gave wrong answers nearly 30 percent of the time; 7-year-olds erred only about 15 percent of the time.

As a father of a young child, Stephen Ceci (1993) thinks "it would be truly awful to ever lose sight of the enormity of child abuse." Yet Ceci and Maggie Bruck's (1993a, 1995) studies of children's memories have sensitized them to children's suggestibility. In one study, they asked 3-year-olds to show on anatomically correct dolls where a pediatrician had touched them. Fifty-five percent of the children who had not received genital examinations showed either genital or anal touching.

In another study, Ceci and Bruck had a child choose a card from a deck of possible happenings and an adult then read from the card. For example, "Think real hard, and tell me if this ever happened to you. Can you remember going to the hospital with the mousetrap on your finger?" After 10 weekly interviews, with the same adult repeatedly asking children to think about several real and fictitious events, a new adult asked the same question. The stunning result: 58 percent of preschoolers produced false (often vivid) stories regarding one or more events they had never experienced. Here is one from a boy who initially had denied the mousetrap incident (Ceci & others, 1994):

> My brother Colin was trying to get Blowtorch [an action figure] from me, and I wouldn't let him take it from me, so he pushed me into the wood pile where the mousetrap was. And then my finger got caught in it. And then we went to the hospital, and my mommy, daddy, and Colin drove me there, to the hospital in our van, because it was far away. And the doctor put a bandage on this finger.

Given such detailed stories, professional psychologists who specialize in interviewing children were often fooled. They could not reliably separate real from false memories. Nor could the children themselves. The above child, reminded that his parents had several times told him that the mousetrap incident never happened—that he had only imagined it—protested, "But it really did happen. I remember it!"

"[The] research leads me to worry about the possibility of false allegations. It is not a tribute to one's scientific integrity to walk down the middle of the road if the data are more to one side."

STEPHEN CECI (1993)

Repressed or Constructed Memories of Abuse?

In 1974, 4-year-old Rachel (not her real name) and two others were molested by Rachel's uncle. Rachel told her mother, who informed the mother of one of the others, who proceeded to stab and kill the uncle. Seventeen years later, psychologist Linda Meyer Williams (1995) tracked down Rachel and 128 other women who were recorded as having experienced child sex abuse (sexual intercourse or fondling). When asked whether she had ever been sexually abused as a child or whether any family members had ever gotten into trouble for their sexual behavior, Rachel calmly said no, then added: "Oh wait a minute. . . . My uncle sexually assaulted someone. . . . I never met my uncle (my mother's brother), he died before I was born. You see, he molested a little boy. When the little boy's mother found out that her son was molested, she took a butcher knife and stabbed my uncle in the heart, killing him." Rachel was but one of 49 victims—38 percent of those interviewed—who did not spontaneously recall the specific reported incident of their own abuse. (Most did recall other traumatic sexual experiences.)

So forgetting such events does happen. What does this mean for the scores of alleged victims who have come forward claiming to have *recovered* memories of abuse? Since 1991 in the state of Washington, for example, 682 people who claim repressed memories of sexual abuse and other crimes have sought money for their therapy bills from the state's victim compensation fund (Hallinan, 1997).

Writers Ellen Bass and Laura Davis (1988), authors of the popular incest-recovery manual *The Courage to Heal*, encouraged people's recovering and reporting such memories. They offered a long list of incest survivor characteristics, including feelings of shame, powerlessness, unworthiness, vulnerability, perfectionism, and deficient goals and motivation. If you have some of these feelings, some therapists have said, don't be surprised if you have no memory of sexual abuse, because "denial" and "repression" are common. "If you are unable to remember any specific instances. . . but still have a feeling that something abusive happened to you, it probably did," say Bass and Davis (pp. 21–22). "If you think you were abused and your life shows the symptoms, then you were."

Believing this, some therapists have reasoned with patients that "people who've been abused often have your symptoms, so you probably were abused. Let's see if, aided by hypnosis or drugs, or

helped to dig back and visualize your trauma, you can recover it." In one recent survey of British and American doctoral-level therapists, 7 in 10 said they had used such techniques to help clients recover suspected repressed memories of childhood sexual abuse (Poole & others, 1995).

As we might expect from the research on source amnesia and the misinformation effect, many patients exposed to such techniques do form an image of a threatening person. With further visualization, the image grows more vivid, leaving the patient stunned, angry, and ready to confront or sue the equally stunned and devastated parent or other relative, who, as the therapist has predicted, vigorously denies the accusation. One woman in her 32nd therapy session recalled that her father had abused her at age 15 months. After such aided recall, actress Roseanne Barr Arnold (1991) claimed to recall sexual abuse beginning in infancy.

Persuading adult women that their fathers or mothers were incestuous is understandably tearing families apart. Thousands of such families have sought advice from the False Memory Syndrome Foundation. The Foundation takes its name from the term John Kihlstrom (1996) defines as a disruptive condition in which a person's identity and relationships center around a false but strongly believed memory of traumatic experience. The person resists disconfirming information and may become so focused on the memory as to avoid coping with the real problems. In the mid-1990s, the False Memory Syndrome Foundation was tracking 700 suits against accused parents and 200 against therapists (Freyd, 1996). Seven in ten accused people report their accusers are women ages 31 to 50; of those accusers, 71 percent have siblings who do not believe the accusation (FMS, 1996).

Without questioning the professionalism of most therapists, the skeptics say that the uncorroborated accusations suggested by some therapists are a 1990s reenactment of the 1700s witch trials. Consider Connie Sievek, a 30-year-old teacher who swore under oath that she recalled her father, Larry Stegman, and another man raping, murdering, and disembowelling a woman. Sievek, however, was 3 years old at the time of the alleged

In one recent survey of British and American doctoral-level therapists, 7 in 10 said they had [helped] clients recover suspected repressed memories of childhood sexual abuse.

crime, and she recovered her memories with the help of a therapist whose help she had sought when depressed (Ahuja, 1996). (The case was therefore dismissed.) Clinicians who use "memory work" techniques such as "guided imagery," hypnosis, and dream analysis to recover such memories "are nothing more than merchants of mental chaos, and, in fact, constitute a blight on the entire field of psychotherapy," say some scientific critics (Loftus & others, 1995). Irate clinicians respond that those who dispute recovered memories of abuse are adding to abused women's trauma and playing into the hands of child molesters.

The trouble with inferring child abuse from adult symptoms is that the symptom list is "general enough to include everybody at least sometimes," notes Carol Tavris (1993). People feel unworthy, ashamed, and perfectionistic for so many reasons that the symptoms hardly prove any one cause.

In an effort to find a sensible common ground that might resolve this ideological battle, study panels have been convened and public statements made by the American Medical, Psychological, and Psychiatric Associations; the Australian Psychological Society; the British Psychological Society; and the Canadian Psychiatric Association. Those committed to protecting abused children and those committed to protecting wrongly accused adults agree on the following:

- *Incest happens.* And it happens more often than we once supposed. Although there is no characteristic "survivor syndrome" (Kendell-Tackett & others, 1993), sexual abuse can leave its victims predisposed to problems ranging from sexual dysfunction to depression.

- *Forgetting happens.* Like Rachel, notes Elizabeth Loftus (1995), many of the women interviewed by Linda Meyer Williams either were very young when abused or may not have understood the meaning of their experience—circumstances under which forgetting is "utterly common." Forgetting of isolated past events, both negative and positive, is an ordinary part of everyday life.

- *Recovered memories are commonplace.* Cued by a remark or an experience, we recover memories of long-forgotten events, both pleasant and unpleasant. What is debated is whether the unconscious mind sometimes forcibly represses painful experiences and, if so, whether these can be retrieved by certain therapist-aided techniques.

- *Memories "recovered" under hypnosis or the influence of drugs are especially unreliable.* (Recall from Chapter 7 the ease with which "age-regressed" hypnotized subjects incorporate suggestions into their memories, even memories of "past lives.")

- *Memories of things happening before age 3 are also unreliable.* People don't reliably recall happenings of any sort from their first 3 years—a phenomenon called *infantile amnesia.*

- *Memories, whether real or false, can be emotionally upsetting.* If a false memory of abuse becomes a real part of one's history, the client as well as the family may suffer. Like real traumas, such experiences can then cause lasting suffering.

Without knowing a person's initial experience (as we do in memory experiments) it is difficult to assess the validity of a person's memory. As Mark Pendergrast (1996) notes, "It is ironic that no one can ethically conduct an experiment to replicate what is happening throughout the UK and the US in private therapy settings." Nevertheless, to many memory researchers, the idea that people literally record, then repress, then recover painful experiences is scientifically naive. All the ingredients for cooking false memories are potentially present in the therapy setting, notes Stephen Lindsay (1995): a credible authority, repeated suggestions, imagination-enhancing techniques, affirmation for one's budding suspicions.

> "Spend time imagining that you were sexually abused, without worrying about accuracy, proving anything, or having your ideas make sense. As you give rein to your imagination, let your intuitions guide your thoughts"
>
> **WENDY MALTZ**
> *THE SEXUAL HEALING JOURNEY*
> 1991

To more closely approximate therapist-aided recall, Elizabeth Loftus and her colleagues (1996) have experimentally implanted false memories of childhood traumas. In one study, she had a trusted family member recall for a teenager three real childhood experiences and a false one—a vivid account of the child's being lost for an extended time in a shopping mall at age 5 until being rescued by an elderly person. Two days later, one subject, Chris, said, "That day I was so scared that I would never see my family again." Two days after that he began to visualize the flannel shirt, bald head, and glasses of the old man who supposedly had found him. Told the story was made up, Chris was incredulous: "I thought I remembered being lost . . . and looking around for the guys. I do remember that, and then crying, and Mom coming up and saying, 'Where were you? Don't you . . . ever do that again.'"

Such is the memory construction process by which people can recall being abducted by UFOs, victimized by a satanic cult, molested in a crib, or living a past life. Thousands of seemingly healthy people, notes Loftus, "speak in terror-stricken voices about their experience aboard flying saucers. They *remember*, clearly and vividly, being abducted by aliens. Or consider the fact that thou-

Elizabeth Loftus "People in general and jurors in particular have a lot of misconceptions about the way memory works" (quoted by Monaghan, 1992).

TODAY'S SPECIAL GUEST

BRUNDAGE MORNALD, OF
BATTLE CREEK, MONTANA

UNDER HYPNOSIS, MR. MORNALD
RECOVERED LONG-BURIED
MEMORIES OF A PERFECTLY
NORMAL, HAPPY CHILDHOOD.

Drawing by Lorenz; © 1993 *The New Yorker Magazine*, Inc.

sands of reasonable, normally functioning human beings relate in calm voices and with deeply felt conviction their past-life experiences. They *remember* having lived before" (Loftus & Ketcham, 1994, p. 66). There are likewise cases of medically certified virgins who *remember* being raped during satanic ritual abuse, and many thousands more who *remember* seeing babies murdered and eaten (but where, wonder skeptics, including the FBI, are the police reports of the missing babies?) (Pendergrast, 1996; Spanos & others, 1994).

Loftus knows firsthand the phenomenon she studies. At a recent family reunion, an uncle told her that at age 14, she found her mother's drowned body. Shocked, she denied it. But the uncle was adamant, and over the next three days she began to wonder if *she* had a repressed memory. "Maybe that's why I'm so obsessed with this topic." As the now-upset Loftus pondered her uncle's suggestion, she "recovered" an image of her mother lying in the pool, face down, and of herself finding the body. "I started putting everything into place. Maybe that's why I'm such a workaholic. Maybe that's why I'm so emotional when I think about her even though she died in 1959."

Then her brother called and said there was a mistake. The uncle had remembered what other relatives now confirmed. It was Aunt Pearl, not Loftus, who had found the body (Loftus & Ketcham, 1994; Monaghan, 1992).

But then again, after being molested by a male baby-sitter at age 6 (and not forgetting), Loftus also knows firsthand the reality of sexual abuse. And that makes her wary of those whom she sees as trivializing real abuse by suggesting and seeking out uncorroborated traumatic experiences, then accepting them uncritically as fact. The enemies of the truly victimized are not only those who prey and those who deny, she says, but those whose writings and allegations "are bound to lead to an increased likelihood that society in general will disbelieve the genuine cases of childhood sexual abuse that truly deserve our sustained attention" (Loftus, 1993).

So, does repression ever occur? Or is this concept—the cornerstone of Freud's theory and of so much popular psychology—a myth? In Chapter 14, we return to this hotly debated issue. As we will see, this much now appears certain: The most common response to a traumatic experience (witnessing the murder of a parent, experiencing the horrors of a Nazi death camp, being terrorized by a hijacker or wartime battle) is not banishment of the experience into an active but inaccessible unconscious. Rather, such experiences are typically etched on the mind as vivid, persistent, haunting memories. "The things we remember best," noted Baltasar Gracian in 1647, "are those better forgotten."

SUMMING UP

Memories are not stored as exact copies, and they certainly are not retrieved as such. Rather, we construct our memories, using both stored and new information. Thus, when child or adult eyewitnesses are subtly exposed to misinformation after an event, they often believe they saw the misleading details as part of the event. People also exhibit source amnesia, by attributing something heard, read, or imagined to a wrong source. Because false memories feel like true memories and are equally durable, sincerity need not signify reality.

Memory researchers are especially suspicious of claims of long-repressed memories of sexual abuse, UFO abduction, or other traumas that are "recovered" with the aid of a therapist or suggestive book. More than we once supposed, incest and abuse happen. But unless the victim was a child too young to remember life experience, such traumas are usually vividly remembered, not banished into an active but inaccessible unconscious.

KEY TERMS AND CONCEPTS misinformation effect, source amnesia (source misattribution)

There are ... cases of medically certified virgins who remember being raped during satanic ritual abuse, and many thousands more who remember seeing babies murdered and eaten (but where, wonder skeptics, including the FBI, are the police reports of the missing babies?).

Improving Memory

To recap the chapter, let's consider how we might apply memory principles. What can we do in everyday situations to better remember a person's name, or even the material of this chapter?

Now and then we are dismayed at our forgetfulness—at our embarrassing inability to recall someone's name, at forgetting to bring up a point in conversation, at forgetting to bring along something important, at finding ourselves standing in a room unable to recall why we are there (Herrmann, 1982). What can we do to minimize such lapses? Much as biology benefits medicine and botany benefits agriculture, so can the psychology of memory benefit education. Sprinkled throughout this chapter and summarized here for easy reference are concrete suggestions for improving memory. The PRTR—*P*review, *R*ead, *T*hink critically, *R*eview—study technique introduced in the Introduction incorporates several of these strategies.

> **Study repeatedly to boost long-term recall.** Overlearn. To learn a name, say it to yourself after being introduced; wait a few seconds and say it again; wait longer and say it again. To provide many separate study sessions, make use of life's little intervals—riding on the bus, walking across campus, waiting for class to start.
>
> **Spend more time rehearsing or actively thinking about the material.** Speed-reading (skimming) complex material—with minimal rehearsal—yields little retention. Rehearsal and critical reflection help more. It pays to study actively!
>
> **Make the material personally meaningful.** To build a network of retrieval cues, take thorough text and class notes in your own words. Mindlessly repeating information is relatively ineffective. Better to form images, understand and organize information, relate the material to what you already know or have experienced, and put it in your own words. Without such cues, you may be stuck when a question uses phrasing different from the rote forms you memorized. To increase retrieval cues, form as many associations as possible.
>
> **To remember a list of unfamiliar items, use mnemonic devices.** Associate items with pegwords. Make up a story that incorporates vivid images of the items. Chunk information into acronyms.
>
> **Refresh your memory by activating retrieval cues.** Mentally recreate the situation and the mood in which the original learning occurred. Return to the same location. Jog your memory by allowing one thought to cue the next.
>
> **Recall events while they are fresh, before you encounter possible misinformation.** If you are an eyewitness to an important event, record your memory before allowing others to suggest what may have occurred.
>
> **Minimize interference.** Study before sleeping. Don't study in close proximity topics that are likely to interfere with each other, such as Spanish and French.
>
> **Test your own knowledge, both to rehearse it and to help determine what you do not yet know.** If you must later *recall* information, do not be lulled into overconfidence by your ability to *recognize* it. Test your recall. Outline sections on a blank page. Define concepts listed at each chapter's end *before* turning back to their definitions. Take practice tests; the study guides that accompany many texts, including this one, can help.

Without self-testing, one can easily suffer overconfidence, as John Shaughnessy and Eugene Zechmeister (1992) found in an experiment with two groups of students. A "reread group" repeatedly read dozens of factual statements, then judged the likelihood that they would remember each fact, and then were tested on their recall. Students in

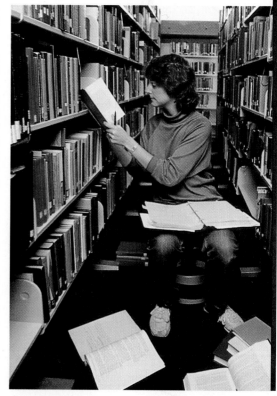

Thinking and memory   Most of what we know is not the result of efforts to memorize. We learn because we're curious and because we spend time thinking about our experiences. Actively thinking as we read, by rehearsing and relating ideas, yields the best retention.

"Knit each new thing on to some acquisition already there."

WILLIAM JAMES
PRINCIPLES OF PSYCHOLOGY
1890

this group felt fairly confident of their knowledge, even on the questions they later missed. Students in a "practice test group" also read the statements, but they then spent the rest of the time responding to tests requiring them to retrieve the facts. Compared with the "reread" group, the practice-test group did just as well on the final recall test. What is more, they could better discriminate what they did and did not know. Thus, self-testing enhances recall and can help you to know what you know—and thus to focus your study time on what you don't yet know. As former British Prime Minister Benjamin Disraeli once said, "To be conscious that you are ignorant is a great step to knowledge."

SUMMING UP

The psychology of memory suggests concrete strategies for improving memory. These include spaced study; active rehearsal; encoding of well-organized, vivid, meaningful associations; mnemonic techniques; the return to contexts and moods that are rich with associations; recording memories before misinformation can corrupt them; minimizing interference; and self-testing and rehearsal.

TERMS AND CONCEPTS TO REMEMBER

memory, p. 269

flashbulb memory, p. 270

encoding, p. 272

storage, p. 272

retrieval, p. 272

long-term memory, p. 272

short-term memory, p. 272

automatic processing, p. 273

effortful processing, p. 273

rehearsal, p. 273

spacing effect, p. 274

serial position effect, p. 274

semantic encoding, p. 275

acoustic encoding, p. 275

visual encoding, p. 275

imagery, p. 276

mnemonics [nih-MON-iks], p. 277

chunking, p. 278

sensory memory, p. 281

iconic memory, p. 281

echoic memory, p. 281

long-term potentiation (LTP), p. 285

amnesia, p. 286

implicit memory, p. 286

explicit memory, p. 286

hippocampus, p. 287

recall, p. 288

recognition, p. 288

relearning, p. 288

priming, p. 289

déjà vu, p. 290

mood-congruent memory, p. 291

proactive interference, p. 292

retroactive interference, p. 292

repression, p. 294

misinformation effect, p. 295

source amnesia, p. 296

CRITICAL THINKING EXERCISE
by Richard O. Straub

Now that you have read and reviewed Chapter 9, take your learning a step further by testing your critical thinking skills on the following practical problem-solving exercise.

Naomi happened to be driving into the parking lot of a mall just as another shopper was being carjacked. She caught a quick glimpse of a running man who seemed to be carrying a handgun. When the police arrived at the scene, Naomi couldn't say much about the gunman's appearance. Nevertheless, they took her to headquarters and showed her hundreds of mug-book photographs. After many frustrating hours during which Naomi was repeatedly shown a photo of a man named Raymond but was unable to identify anyone conclusively, the investigator handed her Raymond's photo and said, "We know this man visited the mall the night of the crime. Did you see him running in the parking lot?" When Naomi said she wasn't sure, she was allowed to leave and asked to think more carefully about what she had seen that night.

Three weeks later, Naomi was asked to pick the aggressor from a five-man lineup that included Raymond. Although she remembered feeling uncertain of the identity of the man when she was first questioned, Naomi was surprised at how easily and confidently she picked Raymond from the lineup now.

1. What's going on in this situation? What problem are the police trying to solve?

2. Why couldn't Naomi identify the gunman right after she witnessed the crime?

3. What is wrong with the police questioning procedures?

Check your progress on becoming a critical thinker by comparing your answers to the sample answers found in Appendix B.

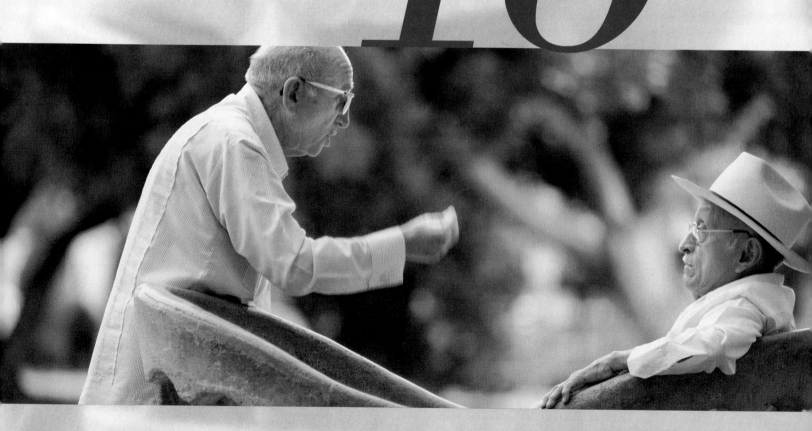

chapter

10

Thinking and Language

Throughout history, we humans have deplored our foolishness and celebrated our wisdom. In a moment of humility the psalmist wondered, "What are human beings that you are mindful of them?" but in the next breath rhapsodized that we were "little lower than God." The poet T. S. Eliot was struck by "the hollow men . . . Headpiece filled with straw." But Shakespeare's Hamlet extolled the human species as "noble in reason! . . . infinite in faculties! . . . in apprehension how like a god!" In the preceding chapters, we, too, have sometimes marveled at our capabilities, sometimes at our propensity to err.

We have studied the human brain—a mere three pounds of tissue containing circuitry more complex than the planet's telephone networks. We have marveled at the competence of newborn infants. We have appreciated the human sensory system, which disassembles visual stimuli into millions of nerve impulses, distributes them for parallel processing, and then reassembles them into clear and colorful perceived images. We have acknowledged the seemingly limitless capacity of human memory and the ease with which we process information, consciously and unconsciously. Little wonder, then, that our species has the genius to invent the camera, the car, and the computer; to unlock the atom and crack the genetic code; to travel into space and probe the oceans' depths.

At the same time, we have seen that our species is kin to the other animals, influenced by principles that produce learning in rats and pigeons. We have noted that we assimilate reality into our preconceptions and succumb to perceptual illusions. We have seen how easily we deceive ourselves about pseudopsychic claims, hypnotic regression, and false memories. Little wonder, then, that we sometimes imagine we can read minds and travel outside our bodies; that we form distorted images of other ethnic, age, and gender groups; that we operate on the same biological principles as other creatures.

In this chapter, we encounter further instances of these two images of the human condition—the rational and the irrational. We will see how we form concepts, solve problems, and make judgments. We will look at our flair for language and ask whether our species alone is capable of language. In the end, we

cognition
the mental activity associated with processing, understanding, and communicating information.

concept
a mental grouping of similar objects, events, or people.

prototype
the best example of a category; matching new items to the prototype provides a quick and easy method for including items in a category (as when comparing feathered creatures to a prototypical bird, such as a robin).

Cognition Cognitive psychologists study the mental activity by which we process and communicate information.

will reflect on how deserving we are of our name, *Homo sapiens*—wise human.

By thinking about thinking, and alerting us to common errors in our thinking, cognitive psychologists aspire to help us think smarter. Their research also suggests educational experiences that could help us to appreciate the powers and limits of our intuition, and to reason more effectively when making practical decisions and everyday judgments. (That is my aim in this chapter and in Appendix A, Statistical Reasoning.)

Thinking

To think is to form concepts that organize our world, to solve problems, and to make efficient decisions and judgments. As we do so, what strategies do we typically use? What biases put us at risk for error? And what are the relative advantages of artificial intelligence and human intelligence?

Previous chapters explained how we receive, perceive, store, and retrieve information. Now we consider how our cognitive system uses this information. Thinking, or cognition, is the mental activity associated with processing, understanding, and communicating information. *Cognitive psychologists* study these mental activities, including the logical and sometimes illogical ways in which we create concepts, solve problems, make decisions, and form judgments. We begin this chapter with the building blocks of thinking.

Concepts

To think about the countless events, objects, and people in our world, we simplify things. We group them into concepts—mental groupings of similar objects, events, and people. The concept *chair* sums up a variety of items—a baby's high chair, a reclining chair, the chairs around a dining room table, a dentist's chair.

Imagine life without concepts. We would need a different name for every object and idea. We could not ask a child to "throw the ball" because there would be no concept of *ball*. Instead of saying, "They were angry," we would have to describe facial expressions, vocal intensities, gestures, and words. Concepts such as *ball* and *angry* provide much information with a minimum of cognitive effort.

Animals, too, are capable of feats of concept formation. Pigeons demonstrate the surprising intelligence of bird brains by sorting objects according to their perceptual or functional similarity. Shown pictures of cars, cats, chairs, and flowers, they readily learn to identify the categories. Shown a picture of a never-before-seen chair, the pigeon will reliably peck a key that represents "chairs" (Wasserman, 1995).

To simplify things further, humans organize concepts into hierarchies. Cab drivers organize their cities into geographical sectors, which subdivide into neighborhoods and again into blocks. The earliest naturalists simplified and ordered the overwhelming complexity of some 5 million living species by clustering them into two basic categories—the plant and animal kingdoms. Then they divided these basic categories into smaller and smaller subcategories—vertebrates, bony fish, and Atlantic salmon, for instance.

We form some concepts by definition. Told the rule that a triangle has three sides, we thereafter classify all three-sided geometric forms as triangles. By definition, a bird is an animal that has wings and feathers and hatches from an egg. More often, we form our concepts by developing prototypes—a best example of a particular category (Rosch, 1978). The more closely something matches our prototype of a concept, the more readily we recognize it as an example of the concept. A robin and a goose both satisfy our rule for *bird*. Yet people agree more quickly that "A robin is a bird" than that "A goose is a bird." For most of us, the robin is the birdier bird; it more closely resembles our bird prototype. Likewise, "maternal love" and "self-love" both qualify as love. But people more instantly agree that "maternal love is a type of love," because it better matches their love prototype (Fehr & Russell, 1991).

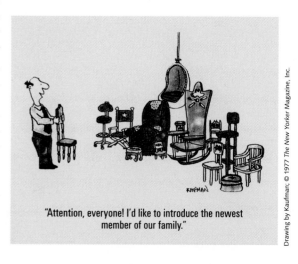

"Attention, everyone! I'd like to introduce the newest member of our family."

Drawing by Kaufman; © 1977 *The New Yorker Magazine, Inc.*

A bird and a . . .? If asked to imagine a bird, most people quickly come up with a mental picture that is something like this robin. It takes them a bit longer to conceptualize a penguin as a bird because it doesn't match their prototype of a small, feathered, flying creature.

algorithm
a methodical, logical rule or procedure that guarantees solving a particular problem. Contrasts with the usually speedier—but also more error-prone—use of heuristics.

heuristic
a rule-of-thumb strategy that often allows us to make judgments and solve problems efficiently; usually speedier but also more error-prone than algorithms.

insight
a sudden and often novel realization of the solution to a problem; it contrasts with strategy-based solutions.

If something fails to match our prototype, we may have trouble classifying it. Thus, we might be slow to recognize nonflying penguins and kiwis as birds. Similarly, we are slow to perceive an illness when our symptoms don't fit one of our disease prototypes (Bishop, 1991). People whose heart attack symptoms don't match their prototype of a heart attack may not seek help. And when discrimination doesn't fit our prejudice prototypes—of white against black, male against female, young against old—we often fail to notice it. People more easily detect male prejudice against female than female against male or female against female (Inman & Baron, 1996).

Solving Problems

One tribute to our rationality is our ability to form and use concepts. Another is our skill at solving problems as we cope with novel situations. Some problems we solve through trial and error—Thomas Edison tried thousands of light bulb filaments before stumbling upon one that worked. For other problems, we may follow an algorithm, a step-by-step procedure that guarantees a solution. Told to find another word using all the letters in SPLOYOCHYG, we could try each letter in each position, but generating and examining the 907,208 resulting combinations would take too long. Because step-by-step algorithms can be laborious (well-suited to computers), we often solve problems with simple rule-of-thumb strategies, called heuristics. Thus, in rearranging the letters of SPLOYOCHYG, we might exclude letter combinations such as two y's together. By using rule-of-thumb heuristics and then applying trial and error, you may hit upon the answer (page 308).

Sometimes we are unaware of using any problem-solving strategy; the answer just comes to us. We can all recall occasions when we puzzled over a problem for some time. Then, suddenly, the

pieces fell together and we perceived the solution. This facility for sudden flashes of inspiration we call insight. Ten-year-old Johnny Appleton displayed insight in solving a problem that had stymied construction workers: how to rescue a young robin that had fallen into a narrow 30-inch-deep hole in a cement block wall. Johnny's solution: to slowly pour in sand, giving the bird enough time to keep its feet on top of the constantly rising sand (Ruchlis, 1990). A tougher problem, "Fermat's Last Theorem," tantalized Princeton mathematician Andrew Wiles. After seven years of progress but still short of the elusive proof, he "saw in a flash" a "simple and elegant" solution (Cipra, 1995). This insight, which Wiles recalls as a "wonderful revelation," solved a problem that had stymied brilliant minds for 350 years.

We humans aren't the only creatures that display insight. German psychologist Wolfgang Köhler (1925) observed apparent insight while studying chimpanzees placed on an island off the coast of Africa. In one experiment with a caged chimp named Sultan, Köhler placed a piece of fruit and a long stick well beyond reach, and a short stick inside the cage. Spying the short stick, Sultan grabbed it and tried to reach the fruit with it. But

Heuristic searching To search for horseradish in a supermarket you could search every aisle (an algorithm) or check the mustard, spice, and gourmet sections (heuristics). The heuristic approach is often speedier, but an algorithmic search is exhaustive.

Chimpanzee inventiveness After learning that he could see himself on TV, "Austin" apparently wanted to see his throat better. So he picked up a flashlight and shined it in his throat, facing the camera. (Adapted from Rumbaugh & Savage-Rumbaugh, 1986.) And, at right, a wild chimp shows ingenuity by using a stick to catch termites.

Answer to SPLOYOCHYG anagram on page 307: PSYCHOLOGY.

confirmation bias
a tendency to search for information that confirms one's preconceptions.

fixation
the inability to see a problem from a new perspective; an impediment to problem solving.

mental set
a tendency to approach a problem in a particular way, especially a way that has been successful in the past but may or may not be helpful in solving a new problem.

functional fixedness
the tendency to think of things only in terms of their usual functions; an impediment to problem solving.

the stick, by design, was too short. After several unsuccessful attempts, the chimp dropped the stick and paused to survey the situation. Then suddenly, as if thinking "Aha!" Sultan jumped up, seized the short stick again and used it to pull in the longer stick—which he then used to reach the fruit. Sultan's actions displayed animal cognition, claimed Köhler, and showed that there is more to learning than conditioning.

Thanks to problem solving shaped by reinforcements, forest-dwelling chimpanzees have become natural tool users (Boesch-Achermann & Boesch, 1993). They can select appropriate branches or stones to use as hammers in cracking nuts. They can also break off a reed or a stick, strip the twigs and leaves, carry it to a termite mound, fish for termites by twisting it just so, and then carefully remove it without scraping off many termites. One anthropologist, trying to mimic the chimpanzee's deft termite fishing, failed miserably. Tool use has been observed in 32 African chimpanzee populations, each of which has developed its own variations of tool use. Such group differences, along with differing dialects and hunting styles, are the chimpanzee equivalent of cultural diversity (Gibbons, 1992).

In human experience, insight provides a sense of satisfaction. After solving a difficult problem or discovering how to resolve a conflict, we feel happy. The joy of a joke may similarly lie in our capacity for insight—our sudden comprehension of an unexpected ending or a double meaning. We find double meaning in the story of Professor Smith, who complained to his colleagues that student interruptions had become a problem: "The minute I get up to speak, some fool begins to talk."

Obstacles to Problem Solving

Inventive as we can be in solving problems, two cognitive tendencies—*confirmation bias* and *fixation*—often interfere.

Confirmation Bias

A major obstacle to problem solving is our eagerness to search for information that confirms our ideas, a phenomenon known as confirmation bias. In an experiment with British university students, Peter Wason (1960) demonstrated our reluctance to seek information that might disprove our beliefs. Wason gave students the three-number sequence 2-4-6 and asked them to guess the rule he had used to devise the series. (The rule was simple: any three ascending numbers.) Before submitting their answers, the students generated their own sets of three numbers, and each time Wason told them whether or not their sets conformed to his rule. Once they had done enough testing to feel *certain* they had the rule, they were to announce it.

The result? Seldom right but never in doubt: Most people convinced themselves of a wrong rule. Typically, they formed a wrong idea ("Maybe it's counting by twos") and then searched only for confirming evidence (by testing 6-8-10, 100-102-104, and so forth). Such experiments reveal that we seek evidence that will verify our ideas more eagerly than we seek evidence that might refute them (Klayman & Ha, 1987; Skov & Sherman, 1986). Business managers, for example, are more likely to follow the successful careers of those they once hired than to track the achievements of those they rejected, which helps them confirm their perceived hiring ability.

> "The human understanding, when any proposition has been once laid down . . . forces everything else to add fresh support and confirmation."
>
> **FRANCIS BACON**
> *NOVUM ORGANUM*
> 1620

Fixation

Try your hand at these brainteasers drawn from classic experiments:

> Arrange the six matches shown in Figure 10.1 so they will form four equilateral triangles.
>
> Suppose that you have a 21-cup jug, a 127-cup jug, and a 3-cup jug. Using these three jugs to draw and discard as much water as you like, how will you measure out exactly 100 cups of water? Solve the other problems presented in Figure 10.2, too.
>
> How can you use the box of matches, thumbtacks, and candle shown in Figure 10.3 to mount the candle on a bulletin board? (Read on after trying these problems.)

A major obstacle to problem solving is fixation—the inability to see a problem from a fresh perspective. Once we incorrectly represent the problem, it's hard to restructure how we approach it. If your attempts to solve the matchstick problem were fixated on two-dimensional solutions, then the three-dimensional solution shown in Figure 10.4 (page 310) will have eluded you.

We become fixated on certain solutions for good reason: Solutions that worked in the past often work on new problems. Consider:

> Given the sequence O-T-T-F-?-?-?, what are the final three letters?

Most people have difficulty recognizing that the three final letters are F(ive), S(ix), and S(even). But solving this problem may make the next one easier:

> Given the sequence J-F-M-A-?-?-?, what are the final three letters?
> (If this one proved difficult, too, ask yourself what month it is.)

Although past success can help solve present problems, it may also interfere with our finding new solutions. This tendency to repeat solutions that have worked in the past is a type of fixation called mental set. Mental set is like perceptual set (pages 196–198), except it affects problem solving rather than perception. You probably ran into mental set in the water jug problems. For the first jug problem, you probably developed the following formula:

$$B - A - 2C = \text{desired amount of water}$$

This same formula works for all seven problems. Once you developed this mental set, you probably solved the later problems faster. But did this mental set cause you to miss the much simpler solutions for problems 6 and 7? (See Figure 10.5, p. 310.)

Flexible, rational thinking becomes even more difficult in times of stress and tension (Janis, 1989). During international crises, views of an enemy become fixed in simplified good-versus-bad terms. During personal crises, too, thinking often becomes rigid. One Korean War paratrooper readying for a mission was given the last parachute—a left-handed one. "It's the same as the others," explained the ordnance sergeant, "but the rip cord hangs on the left side of the harness." At 8000 feet, the soldiers jumped one by one, and all went well—except for this one man who fell straight to his death. Investigators discovered that under the stress of the jump the man had become fixated on the familiar way to open a chute. The right side of his uniform, where normally he found the rip cord, was completely torn off. Even his chest flesh had been gouged by his bloody right hand. Inches to the left was the rip cord, apparently untouched (Csikszentmihalyi, 1990).

Another type of fixation goes by the awkward but appropriate label functional fixedness. This is our tendency to perceive the functions of objects as

Figure **10.1**

The matchstick problem
How would you arrange six matches to form four equilateral triangles? (From "Problem Solving" by M. Scheerer. Copyright © 1963 by Scientific American, Inc. All rights reserved.)

Figure **10.3**

The candle-mounting problem   Using these materials, how would you mount the candle on a bulletin board? (From Duncker, 1945.)

Figure **10.2**

The three-jugs problems
Using jugs A, B, and C with the capacities shown in the table, how would you measure out the volumes indicated in the right-hand column? (From Luchins, 1946.)

Problem	Given jugs of these sizes:			Measure out this much water:
	A	B	C	
1	21	127	3	100
2	14	46	5	22
3	18	43	10	5
4	7	42	6	23
5	20	57	4	29
6	23	49	3	20
7	15	39	3	18

Figure 10.4

Solution to the matchstick problem To solve this problem, you must break the fixation of limiting your considerations to two-dimensional solutions. (From "Problem Solving" by M. Scheerer. Copyright © 1963 by Scientific American, Inc. All rights reserved.)

Figure 10.5

Solution to the three-jugs problems (a) All seven problems can be solved by the equation shown in (a): B – A – 2C = desired volume. (b) But simpler solutions exist for problems 6 and 7, such as A – C for problem 6. Did your mental set cause you to miss it? (From Luchins, 1946.)

(a)

(b)

Figure 10.6

Solution to the candle-mounting problem Solving this problem requires recognizing that a box need not always serve as a container. (From Duncker, 1945.)

Bulletin board

Thumbtacks pushed through empty matchbox

fixed and unchanging. A person may ransack the house for a screwdriver when a dime would have done the job. Perhaps you experienced functional fixedness when you tried to solve the candle-mounting problem. If you thought of the matchbox as having only the function of holding matches, you may have overlooked its use shown in Figure 10.6. Perceiving and relating familiar things in new ways is part of creativity.

Making Decisions and Forming Judgments

When making each day's hundreds of tiny judgments and decisions—Is it worth the bother to take an umbrella? Can I trust this person? Should I shoot the basketball or pass to the player who's hot?—we seldom take the time and effort to reason systematically. Usually, we follow our intuition. After interviewing policymakers in government, business, and education, social psychologist Irving Janis (1986) concluded that they "often do not use a reflective problem-solving approach. How do they usually arrive at their decisions? If you ask, they are likely to tell you . . . they do it mostly by the *seat of their pants*."

Using and Misusing Heuristics

Those mental shortcuts we call heuristics often help us make reasonable seat-of-the-pants decisions. Thanks to the mind's automatic information processing, intuitive judgments are instantaneous. But the price we pay for this efficiency can sometimes be costly bad judgments. To gain an idea of how heuristics determine our intuitive judgments—and how they occasionally lead smart people into dumb decisions—consider two heuristics identified by cognitive psychologists Amos Tversky and Daniel Kahneman (1974): *representativeness* and *availability*.

> "In creating these problems, we didn't set out to fool people. All our problems fooled us, too."
>
> **AMOS TVERSKY (1985)**

The Representativeness Heuristic

To judge the likelihood of things in terms of how well they represent particular prototypes is to use the representativeness heuristic. To illustrate, consider:

A stranger tells you about a person who is short, slim, and likes to read poetry, and then asks you to guess whether this person is more likely to be a professor of classics at an Ivy League university or a truck driver. Which would be the better guess? (Adapted from Nisbett & Ross, 1980)

If you are like most people, you answered "professor" because the description seems more *representative* of Ivy League scholars than of truck drivers. The representativeness heuristic enabled you to make a snap judgment. But it also led you to ignore other relevant information, such as the total number of classics professors versus the number of truck drivers. When I help people think through this question, their own reasoning usually leads them to an answer that contradicts their immediate intuition. The typical conversation goes something like this:

Question: First, let's figure out how many professors fit the description. How many Ivy League universities do you suppose there are?

Answer: Oh, about 10, I suppose.

Question: How many classics professors would you guess there are at each?

Answer: Maybe four.

Question: Okay, that's 40 Ivy League classics professors. What fraction of these are short and slim?

Answer: Let's say half.

Question: And, of these 20, how many like to read poetry?

Answer: I'd say half—10 professors.

Question: Okay, now let's figure how many truck drivers fit the description. How many truck drivers do you suppose there are?

Answer: Maybe 400,000.

Question: What fraction are short and slim?

Answer: Not many—perhaps 1 in 8.

Question: Of these 50,000, what percentage like to read poetry?

Answer: Truck drivers who like poetry? Maybe 1 in 100—oh, oh, I can see where this is going—that leaves me with 500 short, slim, poetry-reading truck drivers.

Question: Yup. So, although the person I've described may be much more representative of classics professors than of truck drivers, this person is still (even if we accept your stereotypes) 50 times more likely to be a truck driver than a classics professor.

This illustrates people's illogical use of the representativeness heuristic. To judge the likelihood of something, we intuitively compare it with our mental representation of that category—of, say, what truck drivers are like. If the two match, then that fact usually overrides other considerations of statistics or logic.

The Availability Heuristic

The availability heuristic operates when we base our judgments on the availability of information in our memories. If instances of an event are easily available—if they come to mind readily—we presume such events are common. The faster people can remember an instance of some event ("a broken promise"), the more they expect it to recur (MacLeod & Campbell, 1992). Usually, cognitively available events *are* more likely to recur—but not always. To see this, make a guess: Does the letter *k* appear more often as the first or third letter in English words?

Because words beginning with *k* come to mind more easily than words having *k* as their third letter, most people guess that *k* occurs more frequently as the first letter. Actually, *k* is two to three times more likely to appear as the third letter. So far in this chapter, words such as *know, kingdom,* and *kin* are outnumbered 46 to 21 by words such as *make, likely, asked,* and *acknowledged.*

The judgmental errors influenced by the availability heuristic are frequently harmless, but not always. Many important decisions involve judgments of risk. Whether we favor using nuclear power or burning coal to produce energy depends partly on our judgments of the risks to health and environment. Our efforts to prevent various deadly diseases depend on our judgments of the likelihood of their occurrence. Our choice to spend or not to spend money on state lotteries (which return in prizes only about half of each dollar bet) depends on our hunch of the odds of striking it rich. (Based on the roughly 10 million to 1 odds against a bet winning a state Lotto jackpot, our chances are not much better than the odds of being struck by lightning.) Casinos entice our gambling by signaling even small wins with bells and lights—making them vividly memorable—while keeping big losses soundlessly invisible. In such ways, hucksters can manipulate the hopes and risk perceptions of statistically naive people.

"The information-processing shortcuts—called heuristics—which are normally both highly efficient and immensely time-saving in day-to-day situations, work systematically against us in the market-place. . . . The tendency to underestimate or altogether ignore past probabilities in making a decision is undoubtedly the most significant problem of intuitive predictions."

DAVID DREMAN
*CONTRARIAN INVESTMENT STRATEGY:
THE PSYCHOLOGY OF STOCK MARKET SUCCESS*
1979

representativeness heuristic
a rule of thumb for judging the likelihood of things in terms of how well they seem to represent, or match, particular prototypes; may lead one to ignore other relevant information.

availability heuristic
estimating the likelihood of events based on their availability in memory; if instances come readily to mind (perhaps because of their vividness), we presume such events are common.

THINKING CRITICALLY ABOUT

Risks—When Statistics Clash With Heuristics

"Most people reason dramatically, not quantitatively," said Oliver Wendell Holmes. With horrific television and magazine images of air crashes in mind, many people, petrified of air travel, prefer the safety of their own cars. One Gallup study (*Gallup Report*, 1989) found that, of those who do fly, 44 percent reported feeling fearful and 63 percent had "lost confidence" in airline safety.

Ironically, the statistical reality is that air travel is safer than ever. Mile for mile, U.S. travelers during the 1980s were 26 times more likely to die in a car crash than on a commercial flight (National Safety Council, 1991). In the 27 months following March 22, 1992, major U.S. airlines carried more than 1 billion passengers on *16 million* flights without a single death (Tolchin, 1994). For most air travelers, the most dangerous part of the journey is the drive to the airport. When a friend tells me of revising her will before flying, I cannot resist saying, "Much better to have done so before you drove to Kansas." For even if she were to board a random jet every day, she would (if her experience matched the average) have to live 21,000 years before crashing to her death (Barnett, 1996).

Still, when overall statistics vie with vivid images of helpless crash victims, many people find the memorable instances more persuasive. It's like judging the likelihood of shark attacks after watching the movie *Jaws*: Regardless of statistics, memorable images have a way of heightening swimmers' feelings of risk. People may *know* their fears are irrational, but no matter. The available images of a plane death—which is 6900 times more likely to make the *New York Times* front page than a cancer death (Barnett, 1990)—protrude into consciousness. Even smokers (whose habit shortens their lives by about 5 years) may senselessly fret before flying (which shortens the average person's life by one day).

The 1988 terrorist bomb that exploded Pan Am Flight 103 and the 1996 fiery explosion of TWA flight 800 caused many would-be international vacationers to stay home and brave the more dangerous highways. The same fearful public continues to smoke billions of cigarettes a year, guzzle alcohol, and devour foods that put people at risk for the greatest of killers—heart disease. All because people's *perceptions* of risk are virtually unrelated to actual risk (Slovic, 1987)—a phenomenon due partly to our greater fear of things we cannot control and partly to our overestimating the likelihood of dreaded, publicized, and cognitively available events. Thus, the public dreads a catastrophic nuclear accident (which after Chernobyl we can readily visualize). Yet it accepts the less dramatic risks of coal-generated power, which quietly fuels acid rain and global warming.

The point to remember: Whether making travel plans or choosing foods, defining safety standards or evaluating environmental hazards, smart thinkers should define risks based not on mentally available media images but on statistical reality.

Vivid events are more available to memory   Photos of this July 1994 crash etched a sharper image in many minds than did the 16 million consecutive fatality-free flights on U.S. airlines during the preceding 27 months. Because such vivid happenings are more available to memory, they seem more common than they really are.

Those who sell life and theft insurance sometimes exploit our tendency to believe that events are more likely if we can picture them readily (Cialdini & Carpenter, 1981). By having people imagine their families in mourning or their possessions stolen, salespeople may cause the images of these disasters to linger, making their occurrence seem more likely and the corresponding need for insurance more intense. In one experiment, Larry Gregory and his colleagues (1982) gave Arizona residents promotional information about cable TV; they asked others to picture themselves enjoying movies on cable instead of spending money on baby-sitters and gas. The latter group, having readily available images of themselves as subscribers, were more than twice as likely to subscribe.

The availability heuristic also affects our social judgments, as Ruth Hamill and her co-workers demonstrated (1980). They presented people with a single, vivid case of welfare abuse, in which a long-term welfare recipient had several unruly children. Statistically, this case was exceptional: Most people who receive welfare did so for four years or less (Duncan & others, 1988). Yet when the statistical reality was pitted against the single vivid case, the memorable case had greater influence on people's opinions about welfare recipients.

> "The human understanding is most excited by that which strikes and enters the mind at once and suddenly, and by which the imagination is immediately filled and inflated. It then begins almost imperceptibly to conceive and suppose that everything is similar to the few objects which have taken possession of the mind."
>
> **FRANCIS BACON**
> *NOVUM ORGANUM*
> 1620

In everyday life, too, a memorable picture sometimes overwhelms a thousand statistics. When a little girl named Jessica McClure fell into a Texas well, the attention of hundreds of millions of people worldwide was riveted on her three-day rescue. During those three days, more than 100,000 invisible children—mere statistics on some world health ledger—died of preventable starvation, diarrhea, and disease (Gore, 1992).

Overconfidence

Our use of intuitive heuristics when forming judgments, our eagerness to confirm the beliefs we already hold, and our knack for explaining away failures combine to create overconfidence, a tendency to overestimate the accuracy of our knowledge and judgments.

Kahneman and Tversky (1979) asked people to answer obscure factual questions with a wide enough range to surely include the actual answer. For example, "I feel 98 percent certain that the number of nuclear power plants operating in the world in 1980 was more than _____ but fewer than _____." Nearly one-third of the time, people's estimates, made with 98 percent confidence, failed to include the correct answer (189 nuclear power plants, in this instance). Although very sure of themselves, people were often wrong. Warning people against overconfidence and urging them to broaden their estimates doesn't much reduce overconfidence. Exposing them to others' widely differing estimates does (Plous, 1996).

People are also more confident than correct when answering such questions as, "Is absinthe a liqueur or a precious stone?" On questions where only 60 percent of people answer correctly, they typically feel 75 percent confident. Even when people feel 100 percent certain of their answers to such questions, they err about 15 percent of the time (Fischhoff & others, 1977). (Absinthe is a licorice-flavored liqueur.)

Overconfidence plagues decisions outside the laboratory, too. It was an overconfident Hitler who invaded Russia, an overconfident Lyndon Johnson who waged war with North Vietnam, an overconfident Saddam Hussein who marched into Kuwait. Stockbrokers and investment managers market their services with confidence that they can outperform the market average in picking stocks, despite overwhelming evidence to the contrary (Malkiel, 1985, 1995). A purchase of stock X, recommended by a broker who judges this to be the time to buy, is always balanced by a sale made by someone who judges this to be the time to sell. Despite their confidence, they can't both be right.

To check people's confidence in making social judgments, David Dunning and his colleagues (1990) asked Stanford University students to guess a stranger's answers to 20 two-choice questions. Topics included whether the person studied for exams alone or with others, kept neat or messy lecture notes, and would pocket $5 found in a restaurant or turn it in. Knowing the type of questions (but not the actual questions), the students were first given a chance to interview the target person about academic interests, hobbies, family background, aspirations, strengths and weaknesses, astrological sign, and anything else they thought might prove helpful. Then the target person answered the 20 questions, while the student interviewers predicted the answers.

overconfidence
the tendency to be more confident than correct—to overestimate the accuracy of one's beliefs and judgments.

The result? The interviewers were "markedly overconfident." Although they guessed right on 63 percent of their predictions, they felt, on average, 75 percent sure. When guessing their own roommates' responses to the 20 questions, students were somewhat more accurate—68 percent. But, again, their 78 percent confidence exceeded their accuracy. And the most confident people were the most *over*confident.

Roger Buehler and his colleagues (1994) were struck by how routinely planners exhibit overconfidence in estimating how quickly and inexpensively they can do a project. In 1957, planners predicted the Sydney Opera House would be completed in 1963 for $7 million. A reduced version actually opened in 1973 at a cost of $102 million. (Even as I write this we are moving into a new kitchen that our architect estimated would take one month, our contractor estimated would take three months, and that actually took five months.) Buehler reports that students, too, are routinely overconfident of how quickly they can do assignments and write papers. Students typically expect to finish projects ahead of schedule. But projects generally get finished after about twice as many days as predicted. Although people know they have often underestimated completion times, they remain overly confident of their next prediction.

Overconfidence has adaptive value. Failing to appreciate one's potential for error when making military, economic, or political judgments can have devastating consequences, but so can lack of self-confidence. People who err on the side of overconfidence live more happily and find it easier to make tough decisions (Baumeister, 1989; Taylor, 1989). Moreover, when given prompt and clear feedback on the accuracy of their judgments—as weather forecasters are after each day's predictions—people soon learn to assess their accuracy more realistically (Fischhoff, 1982). The wisdom to know when we know a thing and when we do not is born of experience.

Framing Decisions

A further test of rationality is whether the same issue, presented in two different but logically equivalent ways, will elicit the same answer. For example, whether a surgeon tells someone that 10 percent of people die while undergoing a particular surgery or that 90 percent survive, the information is the same. But the effect is not. The risk seems greater to people who hear that 10 percent will die (Marteau, 1989). This impact of the way we present an issue is called <u>framing</u>.

Similarly, consumers respond more positively to ground beef described as "75 percent lean" rather than "25 percent fat" (Levin & Gaeth, 1988). People are more bothered by some students cheating if told that 65 percent of their class had cheated than if told that 35 percent had not cheated (Levin & others, 1988). People express more surprise when a "1 in 20" event happens than when an equivalent "10 in 200" event happens (Denes-Raj & others, 1995). And 9 in 10 college students rate a condom as effective if it has a supposed "95 percent success rate" in stopping the AIDS virus; only 4 in 10 think it successful when given a "5 percent failure rate" (Linville & others, 1992).

Consider how the framing effect influences economic and business decisions:

- Merchants mark up their "regular prices" to appear to offer huge savings on "sale prices." A $100 coat marked down from $150 by Store X can seem like a better deal than the same coat priced regularly at $100 by Store Y (Urbany & others, 1988).

- Many people find taking a 7 percent pay cut in a period of zero inflation much more objectionable than a 5 percent pay raise when inflation is 12 percent (Kahneman & others, 1986).

- Federal Express doesn't charge extra to pick up at your door; instead, they offer a "drop-off discount." Likewise, my dentist doesn't charge more if we don't pay on the spot, though she does offer a 5 percent discount for immediate cash payment. FedEx and my dentist both understand that a fee framed as a forfeited discount irritates customers less than one framed as a surcharge, although they add up to the same thing.

That people's judgments flip-flop so dramatically is startling. It suggests that our judgments and decisions may not be well reasoned, and that those who understand the power of framing can use it to influence important decisions—for example, by framing survey questions to support or reject a particular viewpoint. (Recall from Chapter 1 the potentially powerful effects of subtle wording differences.)

Predict your own behavior
When will you finish reading this chapter?

"When you know a thing, to hold that you know it; and when you do not know a thing, to allow that you do not know it; this is knowledge."

CONFUCIUS (551–479 B.C.)
ANALECTS

framing
the way an issue is posed; how an issue is framed can significantly affect decisions and judgments.

"This CD player costs less than players selling for twice as much."

Drawing by Weber; © 1989 The New Yorker Magazine, Inc.

Belief Bias

We have seen that part of psychology's new thinking about thinking emphasizes that we are prone to bias—from seeking confirmation of our hunches, from reliance on efficient but fallible heuristics, from overconfidence, and from the effects of framing. Through brute logic, can we escape the bias inflicted by our beliefs?

Logic helps, but we still find it easier to accept conclusions that agree with our opinions. Consider this logical argument:

Premise 1:	Some communists are golfers.
Premise 2:	All golfers are Marxists.
Conclusion:	Some communists are Marxists.

In experiments, nearly everyone correctly recognized that the conclusion logically follows from the premises (Oakhill & others, 1989). But now consider this argument:

Premise 1:	Some communists are golfers.
Premise 2:	All golfers are capitalists.
Conclusion:	Some communists are capitalists.

Many people had a harder time seeing that, given the premises, this conclusion is equally valid. Judge this next conclusion for yourself (adapted from Hunt, 1982):

Premise 1:	Democracy supporters believe in free speech.
Premise 2:	Dictators do not believe in democracy.
Conclusion:	Dictators do not believe in free speech.

If that conclusion seems logical, you are experiencing belief bias—the tendency for our beliefs to distort our logic (Oakhill & others, 1990). (Premise 1 did not exclude the possibility that others, even dictators, can believe in free speech.) Consider another set of statements with *identical form and logic* and note how much easier it feels to refute the conclusion:

Premise 1:	Robins have feathers.
Premise 2:	Chickens are not robins.
Conclusion:	Chickens do not have feathers.

Thus, belief bias: We more easily see the illogic of conclusions that run counter to our beliefs than those that agree with our beliefs.

"God is love.
Love is blind.
Ray Charles is blind.
Ray Charles is God."

ANONYMOUS GRAFFITI

The Belief Perseverance Phenomenon

An additional source of irrationality is our tendency, called belief perseverance, to cling to our beliefs in the face of contrary evidence. Belief perseverance often fuels social conflict. Charles Lord and his colleagues (1979) revealed how this happens when they studied people with opposing views of capital punishment. People on both sides studied two supposedly new research findings, one supporting and the other refuting the claim that the death penalty deters crime. Each side was more impressed by the study that supported its beliefs, and each readily disputed the other study. Thus, showing the pro– and anti–capital-punishment groups the *same* mixed evidence actually *increased* their disagreement.

For those who wish to rein in the belief perseverance phenomenon, a simple remedy exists: *Consider the opposite.* When Lord and his colleagues (1984) repeated the capital-punishment study, they asked some of their participants to be "as *objective* and *unbiased* as possible." The plea did nothing to reduce the biased evaluation of evidence. They asked another group to consider "whether you would have made the same high or low evaluations had exactly the same study produced results on the *other* side of the issue." Having imagined and pondered *opposite* findings, these people were much less biased in their evaluations of the evidence.

If ambiguous evidence gets interpreted as supporting a person's preexisting belief, would the belief be demolished by information that clearly discredits its basis? Not necessarily. Craig Anderson and Lee Ross discovered that it can be surprisingly difficult to change a false belief once a person has ideas that support it. In one study with Mark Lepper (1980), they asked people to consider whether risk-prone people or cautious people are better fire fighters. Then they told half the people about a risk-taker who was an excellent fire fighter and about a cautious person who was a poor fire fighter. From these cases, the participants surmised that risk-prone people tend to be better fire fighters. "Risk-takers are braver," was a typical explanation. The researchers gave the other participants two cases suggesting the opposite conclusion, that cautious people are better fire fighters. These participants typically reasoned, "Cautious people think before they act. They're less likely to make foolish mistakes."

The researchers then discredited the basis for the beliefs by truthfully informing both groups that the cases were simply made up for the experiment. Did discrediting the evidence undermine the participants' newly formed beliefs? Not by much, be-

belief bias
the tendency for one's preexisting beliefs to distort logical reasoning, sometimes by making invalid conclusions seem valid, or valid conclusions seem invalid.

belief perseverance
clinging to one's initial conceptions after the basis on which they were formed has been discredited.

"Once you have a belief, it influences how you perceive all other relevant information. Once you see a country as hostile, you are likely to interpret ambiguous actions on their part as signifying their hostility."

POLITICAL SCIENTIST ROBERT JERVIS (1985)

Belief perseverance Do risk-prone or cautious people make better fire fighters? Once we've formed opinions on a question like this and developed reasons for our views, we tend to cling to our beliefs—even if the basis for our opinion is undermined.

cause they held on to their explanations for why these new beliefs made sense. Although the evidence was gone, their theory survived.

The more we come to appreciate why our beliefs might be true, the more tightly we cling to them. Once people have explained to themselves why they believe that a child is "gifted" or "learning disabled," or that candidate X or Y will be more likely to preserve peace or start a war, or that women or men are naturally superior, they tend to ignore evidence undermining that belief. Prejudice therefore persists.

Belief perseverance applies even to our beliefs about ourselves. Lepper and Ross, with Richard Lau (1986), encountered it after showing California high school students either an effective or a confusing instructional film. Each film demonstrated how to solve some reasoning problems. Those shown the effective film did well on a later test, felt successful, and surmised that they were good at such problem solving. Those shown the useless film did poorly, felt like failures, and surmised that they weren't very competent on such problems. Even when the researchers then explained that the *film* was responsible for their success or failure and showed them the other film as evidence, the students persisted in seeing themselves as either good or incompetent at that type of reasoning problem. (To prevent people from leaving the experiment feeling incompetent, the researchers more extensively debriefed and reassured them.)

And that, say the researchers, helps explain why early school failures can be so damaging. Even clearly demonstrating to children that their poor school performance "may well have been the consequence of an inept or biased teacher, a substandard school, or even prior social, cultural, or economic disadvantages" may fail to dent their feelings of incompetence. Once the belief that "I'm not very smart" forms, it tends to persist.

The belief perseverance phenomenon does not rule out people's changing their beliefs. It's just that once beliefs form and get justified, it takes more compelling evidence to change them than it did to create them.

We have seen how our irrational thinking can plague our efforts to solve problems, make wise decisions, form valid judgments, and reason logically. From this we might conclude that our heads are indeed filled with straw. All in all, these and many other findings suggest "bleak implications for human rationality" (Nisbett & Borgida, 1975). Still, let us not forget that our cognition is effective and wonderfully efficient: It enables our survival and our inventive genius.

"I'm happy to say that my final judgment of a case is almost always consistent with my prejudgment of the case."

One reason we function as well as we do is that in many real-life situations flawed reasoning *can* lead to correct conclusions (Funder, 1987). Physicians, for example, recognize the similarity between a patient's symptoms and those typical of a particular disease and then proceed to check out the hunch. In effect, their reasoning goes like this (Hunt, 1982):

- Symptoms A, B, and C indicate disease X.
- This patient has symptoms A, B, and C.
- Therefore, I presume this patient has disease X.

The physician's conclusion is not necessarily logical. (Other diseases may also have symptoms A, B, and C.) Yet it is efficient and plausible, perhaps even probable. We reason, then, not so much by formal logic as by simplified, speedy heuristics, such as, "This situation reminds me of situations I have faced before, so what was true in those situations should be true here." Experts in other fields—even avid racetrack bettors who intuitively calculate the odds on horses (Ceci & Liker, 1986)—are similarly shrewd without necessarily knowing exactly how they reason.

Still, we should not underestimate the worth of sound reasoning. When we are deriving scientific hypotheses, playing chess, or debating political issues, it helps to have the powers of reason at our disposal. This is why many college courses, including this one, aim to enhance critical thinking. This is also why psychologists study obstacles to problem solving, and biases in reasoning. By learning about our irrational tendencies, we hope to steer smart people away from dumb decisions.

Simulating Thinking: Artificial Intelligence

A tribute to human cognition comes from attempts to simulate human thinking on computers. Artificial intelligence (AI) is the science of designing computer systems to perform operations that mimic human thinking and do "intelligent" things. AI systems rely on massive stored information and rules for retrieving it. A hybrid of cognitive psychology and computer science, AI has two facets, one practical, the other theoretical.

The practical side of AI creates industrial robots that can "sense" their environment; "expert systems" that can carry out chemical analyses, offer tax planning advice, forecast weather, and help physicians diagnose their patients' diseases; and chess programs that now challenge the world's top chess masters. Using voice-recognition software, I can talk to my deaf mother—the words appearing on a screen, correctly spelled as, say, *too, two,* or *to,* depending on the grammatical context.

The theoretical side of AI was pioneered by psychologist Herbert Simon, and it studies, by trying to design computer systems that mimic or rival human thought processes, how humans think. The goal is a "unified theory of cognition" embodied in a computer system that can process information, solve problems, learn from experience, and remember, much as humans do.

Can computers mimic our thinking powers? In those areas where humans seem to have the most difficulty—manipulating huge amounts of numerical data, retrieving detailed information from memory, making decisions using specified rules—computers shine. Indeed, these areas of proficiency make computers indispensable to banks, libraries, and scientific laboratories. But even the most sophisticated computers are dwarfed by the most ordinary of human mental abilities—recognizing a face, distinguishing a cat from a dog, knowing whether the word *line* refers to a rope or a fragment of poetry or a social come-on, and exercising common sense. "Human minds do more than process information," notes Donald Griffin (1984); "we experience beliefs, desires, fears, expectations, and many other subjective mental states."

Compare computer operations with the brain's. Electricity races through the computer's microcircuits millions of times faster than neural impulses travel through our systems. Yet most computers process information serially—one step at a time. By contrast, the human brain does many things at once. One part of the brain analyzes speech while other parts recognize pictures, detect smells, or plan action. As Chapter 5 explained, the visual system splits information about color, depth, movement, and form into separate channels, processes each channel simultaneously, and reassembles the information into a recognized image. Through this capacity for parallel processing, the brain outclasses the serial computer. Computer processing exceeds our thinking at tasks that use its unique strengths—vast memory and precise logic and retrieval. But computers have not duplicated the wide-ranging intelligence of a human mind, which can *all at once* converse naturally, recognize a caricaturized face, use common sense, experience emotion, and consciously reflect on its own existence.

Researchers who met in 1956 to chart AI never imagined that 40 years later they would still be struggling to simulate so many tasks that people find easy (Lenat, 1995). We still must learn computer languages, because they haven't learned ours. Despite the "hype and bust" cycle of unfulfilled promises, excitement has grown over neural networks—computer systems designed to mimic the brain's interconnected neural units (McClelland & Rumelhart, 1988). As the brain has bil-

Discerning the difference between these two ads is much easier for a human than for a computer (from Schnitzer, 1984):

1. Car for sale. A classic! Lemon yellow coupe. Exterior is completely rustproof. Can be delivered upon request. No engine runs better. If the sun is out, you can remove the roof for the feel of the wind in your hair. Go ahead and kick the tires.

2. Car for sale. A classic lemon. Yellow coupe exterior is completely rust. Proof can be delivered upon request! No engine. Runs better if the sun is out. You can remove the roof. For the feel of the wind in your hair, go ahead and kick the tires.

> "Even though I am not religious, the amazement and wonder I have about the human mind is closer to religious awe than dispassionate analysis."
>
> **BILL GATES**
> 1997

artificial intelligence (AI) *the science of designing and programming computer systems to do intelligent things and to simulate human thought processes such as intuitive reasoning, learning, and understanding language. Includes practical applications (chess playing, industrial robots, expert systems) and efforts to model human thinking inspired by our current understanding of how the brain works.*

neural networks *computer circuits that mimic the brain's interconnected neural cells, performing tasks such as learning to recognize visual patterns and smells.*

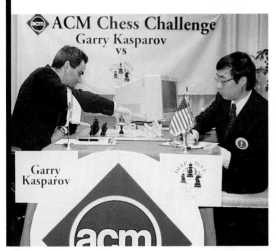

Artificial chess intelligence In 1996, IBM's Deep Blue computer challenged world chess champion Garry Kasparov to a six-game match. Deep Blue's 256 processor chips, enabling it to explore 100 billion possible board positions 13 moves ahead, defeated Kasparov in game 1. But Kasparov's own billions of processors (neurons) responded by winning three of the remaining games and tying the other two. "The main distinction" between his brain and the computer's, Kasparov later reflected, is that "I learned a lot from game 1 and game 2" (Guterl, 1996; Peterson, 1996). In a 1997 rematch, a doubly powerful Deep Blue dethroned Kasparov in a close match.

Artificial reasoning William McCune of Argonne National Laboratory has created a computer reasoning program. In 1996 it solved a problem that had stumped mathematicians for 60 years, offering a proof that would have been called creative if a human had thought of it (Kolata, 1996).

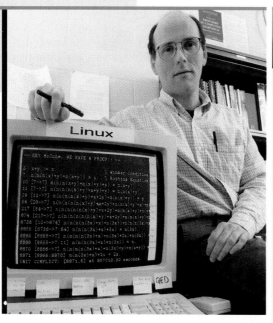

lions of neurons, each connected to thousands of others, so each computer processing unit can be connected to many others. The computer's electronic "neural network" can be programmed to execute rules that mimic how the brain's neurons communicate—with positive (excitatory) or negative (inhibitory) messages that fire when the signal strength reaches a certain threshold. As in the brain, the "neural" connections are programmed to gain strength with experience. The computer system's complex interaction is mind-boggling, but the basic idea is that simple.

The most exciting feature of artificial neural networks is their capacity to learn from experience as some interconnections strengthen and others weaken. This feature, together with their capacity for parallel processing, enables neural network computers to learn to recognize particular shapes, sounds, and smells, tasks conventional computers find extremely difficult. The hoped-for payoffs are twofold. Neural network systems provide neuroscientists with new ways to test models of how living neural systems process sensations and memories. And they provide computer scientists with new insights into how to mimic the brain's thinking power. The dream is that someday we may better understand how our own brains function—*and* benefit from robots that can learn and from telephone systems that can understand and translate speech, allowing, for example, an English speaker and a Spanish speaker to converse without an interpreter. The more we understand about our own brain, the more we realize what a grand model it provides of how future computers might work.

SUMMING UP

Our cognitive system receives, perceives, and retrieves information, which we then use to think and communicate, sometimes wisely, sometimes foolishly. This chapter has so far explored how we form concepts, solve problems, and make judgments and decisions.

Concepts Concepts simplify and order the world by organizing it into a hierarchy of categories. Concepts often form around prototypes, or best examples of a category. Matching objects and ideas with prototypes is an efficient way of making snap judgments about what belongs to a specific concept.

Solving Problems When faced with a novel situation for which no well-learned response will do, we may use any of several strategies, such as trial and error, algorithms, and rule-of-thumb heuristics. Sometimes the solution comes in a flash of insight. We do, however, face obstacles to successful problem solving. The confirmation bias predisposes us to verify rather than challenge our hypotheses. And fixations, such as mental set and functional fixedness, may prevent our taking a needed fresh perspective on a problem.

Making Decisions and Forming Judgments Our use of heuristics, such as representativeness and availability, provide highly efficient but occasionally misleading guides for making quick decisions and forming intuitive judgments. Our tendencies to seek confirmation of our hypotheses and to use quick and easy heuristics can blind us to our vulnerability to error, a phenomenon known as overconfidence. And the way someone poses, or frames, a question affects our responses.

Belief Bias People show a belief bias in their reasoning, accepting as more logical those conclusions that agree with their beliefs. We also exhibit belief perseverance, clinging to our ideas because the explanation we accepted as valid lingers in our minds, even after the basis for the ideas has been discredited. Yet despite our capacity for error and our susceptibility to bias, human cognition is remarkably efficient and adaptive. As we gain expertise in a field, we grow adept at making quick, shrewd judgments.

Simulating Thinking: Artificial Intelligence Experimental computers and robots are performing operations that mimic human thinking. The most notable AI successes focus computer capacities for memory and precise logic on specific tasks, such as playing chess or diagnosing illnesses. For now, the brain's capacity for processing unrelated information simultaneously and the wide range of its abilities dwarf those of the most sophisticated computer. But hopes grow that a new generation of computer neural networks, mimicking the brain's neural networks, will produce more humanlike capabilities.

KEY TERMS AND CONCEPTS cognition, concept, prototype, algorithm, heuristic, insight, confirmation bias, fixation, mental set, functional fixedness, representativeness heuristic, availability heuristic, overconfidence, framing, belief bias, belief perseverance, artificial intelligence (AI), neural networks

Language

Language, the form taken by so much of our thinking, is built of various elements that emerge as a child matures. What are the elements of language? How and why do they develop? Are humans the only species capable of language?

The most tangible indication of our thinking power is language—our spoken, written, or gestured words and the ways we combine them as we think and communicate. Humans have long and proudly proclaimed that language sets us above all other animals. "When we study human language," asserted linguist Noam Chomsky (1972), "we are approaching what some might call the 'human essence,' the qualities of mind that are, so far as we know, unique" to humans. To cognitive scientist Steven Pinker (1990), language is "the jewel in the crown of cognition." When the human vocal tract evolved the capacity to utter vowels, our capacity for language exploded, catapulting our species forward (Diamond, 1989). Whether spoken, written, or signed, language enables us to communicate complex ideas from person to person and to transmit civilization's accumulated knowledge across generations.

Language Structure

Consider how we might go about inventing a language. For a spoken language, we would need three building blocks. First, we would need a set of basic sounds, which linguists call phonemes. To say *bat* we utter the phoneme sounds *b, a,* and *t*. *Chat* also has three phonemes—*ch, a,* and *t*. Languages have varying numbers of phonemes. English has about 40; other languages have anywhere from half to twice that many.

Changes in phonemes produce changes in meaning. Variations in the vowel sound between *b* and *t* create 12 different meanings: *bait, bat, beat/beet, bet, bit, bite, boat, boot, bought, bout,* and *but* (Fromkin & Rodman, 1983). Generally, though, consonant phonemes carry more information than do vowel phonemes. The treth ef thes stetement shed be evedent frem thes bref demenstretien.

People who grow up learning one set of phonemes usually have difficulty pronouncing the phonemes of another language. The native English speaker may smile at the native German speaker's difficulties with the *th* sound, which often makes *this* sound like *dis*. But the German speaker can smile at the problems English speakers have rolling the German *r* or pronouncing the breathy *ch* in *Ich*, the German word for the personal pronoun *I*.

language
our spoken, written, or gestured words and the ways we combine them to communicate meaning.

phoneme
in a spoken language, the smallest distinctive sound unit.

Language transmits culture The actual words and grammar may differ from culture to culture, but every society has a history that it transmits in story form to its children. Here, a group of Ivory Coast boys listen as an elder retells a tribal legend.

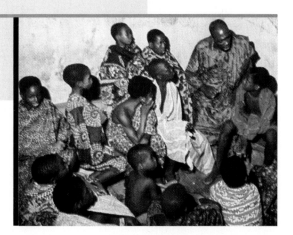

morpheme
in a language, the smallest unit that carries meaning; may be a word or a part of a word (such as a prefix).

grammar
a system of rules in a language that enables us to communicate with and understand others.

semantics
the set of rules by which we derive meaning from morphemes, words, and sentences in a given language; also, the study of meaning.

syntax
the rules for combining words into grammatically sensible sentences in a given language.

How many morphemes are in the word cats? (See page 322)

A cultural universal: In every language, the commonest words are the shortest. As a word or phrase is used more and more, it often gets shortened. Television becomes TV, compact disc becomes CD (Triandis, 1994).

Although you probably know 80,000 words, you use only 150 words for about half of what you say.

Sign language also has phonemelike building blocks defined by hand shapes and movements. Like speakers, native signers of one language may have difficulty with the phonemes of another. Chinese native signers who come to America and learn sign usually "sign with an accent," notes researcher Ursula Bellugi (1994).

The second building block is the morpheme, the smallest unit of language that carries meaning. In English, a few morphemes are also phonemes—the personal pronoun *I* and the article *a*, for instance. But most are combinations of two or more phonemes. Some morphemes, like *bat*, are words, but others are only parts of words. Morphemes include prefixes and suffixes, such as the *pre* in *preview* or the *–ed* that shows past tense. *Undesirables* has four morphemes—*un, desir, able*, and *s*—each of which adds to the word's total meaning.

Finally, our new language must have a grammar, a system of rules (called *semantics* and *syntax*) that enables us to communicate with and understand others. Semantics is the set of rules we use to derive meaning from morphemes, words, and even sentences. A semantic rule tells us that adding *ed* to *laugh* means that it happened in the past. Syntax refers to the rules we use to order words into sentences. One rule of English syntax says that adjectives usually come before nouns, so we say *white house*. Spanish adjectives usually come after nouns, so a Spanish speaker says *casa blanca*. The English rules of syntax allow the sentence *They are hunting dogs*. Given the context, semantics will tell us whether it refers to dogs seeking animals or people seeking dogs.

All 5000 human languages are intricately complex. "There are 'stone age' societies," says lin-

guist Steven Pinker (1995), "but they do not have 'stone age' languages." Contrary to the illusion that less educated people speak ungrammatically, they simply speak a different dialect. To a linguist, "ain't got no" is grammatically equal to "doesn't have any."

Note, however, that language becomes more complex as you move from phoneme to morpheme to word to sentence. In English, the relatively small number of 40 or so phonemes can be combined to form more than 100,000 morphemes, which alone or in combination produce the 616,500 word forms in the *Oxford English Dictionary* (including 290,500 main entries such as *meat* and 326,000 subentries such as *meat-eater*). We can then use these words to create an infinite number of sentences, most of which (like this one) are original. Like life itself constructed from the genetic code's simple alphabet, language is complexity built of simplicity.

Language Development

Make a quick guess: How many words did you learn in one average day during the years between your first birthday and your high school graduation?

The average secondary school graduate knows some 80,000 words (Miller & Gildea, 1987). That averages (after age 1) to nearly 5000 words learned each year, or 13 each day! How you did it—how the 5000 words a year you learned could so far outnumber the roughly 200 words a year that your schoolteachers consciously taught you—is one of the great human wonders. Before children can add 2 + 2, they are creating their own original and grammatically appropriate sentences. Most parents would have trouble stating the rules of syntax. Yet their preschoolers comprehend and speak with a facility that puts to shame a college student struggling to learn a foreign language or a scientist struggling to simulate natural language on a computer. How does our astonishing facility for language unfold, and how can we explain it?

Acquiring Language

Children's language development mirrors language structure—by moving from simplicity to complexity. Infants start without language (*in fantis* means "not speaking"). Yet by 4 months of age, babies can read lips and discriminate speech sounds. They prefer to look at a face that matches a sound, so we know they can recognize that *ah* comes from wide open lips and *ee* from a mouth with corners pulled back (Kuhl & Meltzoff, 1982). At about this age, babies enter a babbling stage in

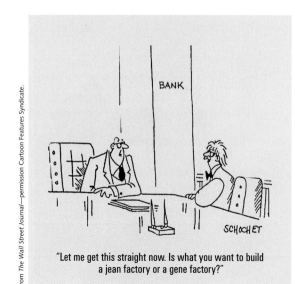

"Let me get this straight now. Is what you want to build a jean factory or a gene factory?"

From *The Wall Street Journal*—permission Cartoon Features Syndicate.

which they spontaneously utter a variety of sounds such as *ah-goo*.

Babbling is not an imitation of adult speech, for it includes sounds from various languages, even sounds that do not occur in the household's language. From this early babbling, a listener could not identify an infant as being, say, French, Korean, or Ethiopian. Deaf infants babble (repeat syllablelike gestures), too (Petitto & Marentette, 1991). It seems, then, that before nurture molds our speech, nature enables a wide range of possible phonemes.

Babbling eventually comes to resemble the characteristic sounds and intonations of the household language. By the time infants are about 10 months old, their babbling has changed so that a trained ear can identify the language of the household (de Boysson-Bardies & others, 1989). Phoneme sounds outside the infant's native tongue begin to disappear. And infants gradually lose their ability to discriminate sounds they never hear. Clever experiments by Janet Werker (1989) reveal that at 6 months infants can perceive subtle phoneme differences from other languages, but by 12 months they cannot (Figure 10.7). Without exposure to other languages, we became functionally deaf to speech sounds not found in our native language. Thus, by adulthood those who speak only English cannot discriminate certain Japanese phonemes. Nor can Japanese adults with no training in English distinguish between the English *r* and *l* (Japanese has a consonant midway between *r* and *l*). Thus, *la-la-ra-ra* may sound like the same repeated syllable to a Japanese adult (believe it or not). Japanese also has no *p* or *f*. So, *please* sounds very much like *freeze*, which may explain why Yoshihiro Hattori, a Japanese exchange student mistaken for a burglar, failed to understand a gun-toting Louisiana homeowner's order to *freeze* and was tragically shot to death.

Around the first birthday (the exact age varies from child to child), most children enter the one-word stage. Having already learned that sounds carry meanings, they begin to use sounds to communicate meaning. Their first words usually contain only one syllable—*ma* or *da*, for instance—and may be barely recognizable. But family members quickly learn to understand the infant's language, and gradually it conforms more and more to the family's language.

Most of the child's first words refer to things that move or can be played with—a dog or a ball, for example, rather than the table or crib that just sits there (Nelson, 1973). At this one-word stage, an inflected word may equal a sentence. "Doggy!" may mean "Look at the dog out there!"

Children typically use more and more single words during the second year. Before their second birthday, they usually enter the two-word stage,

babbling stage
beginning at 3 to 4 months, the stage of speech development in which the infant spontaneously utters various sounds at first unrelated to the household language.

one-word stage
the stage in speech development, from about age 1 to 2, during which a child speaks mostly in single words.

two-word stage
beginning about age 2, the stage in speech development during which a child speaks mostly two-word statements.

Figure **10.7**

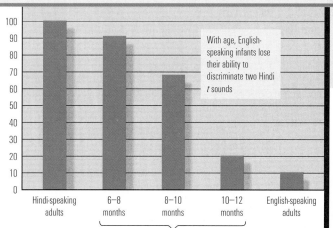

Percentage able to discriminate Hindi *t*'s

With age, English-speaking infants lose their ability to discriminate two Hindi *t* sounds

| Hindi-speaking adults | 6–8 months | 8–10 months | 10–12 months | English-speaking adults |

Infants from English-speaking homes

Testing for phoneme perception
We are all born with the ability to recognize speech sounds from all the world's languages. In Janet Werker's lab, an infant is reinforced with applause and by activating toy animals when he looks to the right after hearing a changed sound (as in *ba, ba, ba, ba, da, da*). Adult Hindi-speakers and young infants from English-speaking homes can easily discriminate two Hindi *t* sounds not spoken in English. By about age 1, however, English-speaking listeners rarely perceive the sound difference. (Adapted from Werker, 1989.)

telegraphic speech
early speech stage in which the child speaks like a telegram—"go car"—using mostly nouns and verbs and omitting "auxiliary" words.

"Got idea. Talk better. Combine words. Make sentences."

© 1994 by Sidney Harris.

Answer to question on page 320: Two—cat and -s.

when they start uttering two-word sentences (Table 10.1). Language at this stage is characterized by telegraphic speech: Like telegrams (TERMS AC-CEPTED. SEND MONEY), this early form of speech contains mostly nouns and verbs (*Want juice*). Also like telegrams, it follows rules of syntax; the words are in a sensible order. The English-speaking child typically says adjectives before nouns—*big doggy* rather than *doggy big*.

There seems to be no "three-word stage." Once children move out of the two-word stage, they quickly begin uttering longer phrases (Fromkin & Rodman, 1983). Although the sentences may still sound like a telegraphed message, they continue to follow the rules of syntax (*Mommy get ball*). By early elementary school, the child understands complex sentences and begins to enjoy the humor conveyed by double meanings: "You never starve in the desert because of all the sand-which-is there."

Table 10.1

Summary of Language Development

Month (approximate)	Stage
4	Babbles many speech sounds.
10	Babbling reveals household language.
12	One-word stage.
24	Two-word, telegraphic speech.
24+	Language develops rapidly into complete sentences.

Explaining Language Development

Those who study language acquisition inevitably wonder how we do it. Attempts to answer this question have sparked a spirited intellectual controversy. The controversy parallels the debate we noted in Chapter 8 over the behaviorist view of the malleable organism versus the view that each organism comes biologically prepared to learn certain associations. The nature-nurture debate surfaces again and, here as elsewhere, appreciation for innate predisposition has grown.

Behaviorist B. F. Skinner (1957) believed we can explain language development with familiar learning principles, such as association (of the sights of things with the sounds of words); imitation (of the words and syntax modeled by others); and reinforcement (with success, smiles, and hugs when the child says something right). Thus, Skinner (1985) argued, babies learn to talk in many of the same ways that animals learn to peck keys and press bars: "Verbal behavior evidently came into existence when, through a critical step in the evolution of the human species, the vocal musculature became susceptible to operant conditioning."

Linguist Noam Chomsky (1959, 1987) thinks Skinner was naive. Surely, says Chomsky, a Martian scientist observing children in a single-language community would conclude that language is almost entirely inborn. It isn't, because children do learn the language used in their environment. But the rate at which they acquire words and grammar without being taught is too extraordinary to be explained solely by learning principles. Children create all sorts of sentences they have never heard and, therefore, could not be imitating. They begin using morphemes in a predictable order. They begin adding –*ing* to words. Then they start using the prepositions *in* and *on*. Then come *a* and *the*, followed by *is* (Brown, 1973). There are 3,628,800 ways to arrange this sentence's ten words. Only a handful of them make any sense. Yet any 4-year-old could pick them out from among the 3,628,700+ nonsensical orderings.

Moreover, many of the errors young children make result from overgeneralizing logical grammatical rules, such as adding -*ed* to make the past tense (from de Cuevas, 1990):

Child: My teacher holded the baby rabbits and we petted them.
Mother: Did you say your teacher held the baby rabbits?
Child: Yes.
Mother: What did you say she did?
Child: She holded the baby rabbits and we petted them.
Mother: Did you say she held them tightly?
Child: No, she holded them loosely.

Chomsky (1987) likens the behaviorist view of how language develops to filling a bottle with water. He instead views language development as "helping a flower to grow in its own way." It is, he believes, akin to sexual maturation: Given adequate nurture, it just "happens to the child." All human languages have the same grammatical building blocks such as nouns and verbs, subjects and objects, negations and questions, singular and plural word forms. Our 5000 human languages are therefore dialects of the "universal grammar" for which our brains are prewired. Thanks to our inborn universal grammar, we readily learn whatever language we hear. It happens so naturally—as naturally as birds learning to fly—that training hardly helps. Just expose children to language and they will soak it up. If not exposed to a language, a group of children will make up their own. Without exposure to language, deaf children, too, will spontaneously create one with gestures, complete with sophisticated grammar (Horgan, 1995; Pinker, 1995).

Other worlds may have languages that, for us humans, are unlearnable, but our world does not. Chomsky maintains that our language acquisition capacity is like a box—a "language acquisition device"—in which grammar switches are thrown as children experience their language. Thus, English-speaking children learn to put the object of a sentence last ("She ate an apple"). Japanese-speaking children put the object before the verb ("She an apple ate"). We are born with the hardware and an operating system; experience writes the software (Figure 10.8).

Cognitive scientists still debate how much of our language capacity is inborn (Shanks, 1993). With experience (but with no "inborn" linguistic rules), computer neural networks can learn to form past-tense verbs appropriately. They can learn, for example, to change words ending in *ow* to *ew*, as in *throw/threw*. To some scientists, this suggests the brain could be a blanker slate than Chomsky believes.

The scholars agree, however, that life's first years are critical. Those who learn a second language as adults usually speak it with the accent of

> Thanks to our inborn universal grammar, we readily learn whatever language we hear. It happens so naturally—as naturally as birds learning to fly—that training hardly helps.

Figure 10.8

Nature and nurture Genes design the mechanisms for a language, and experience fills them as it modifies the brain. Grow up in Paris and you will speak French (environment matters), but not if you are a cat (genes matter).

Figure **10.9**

New language learning gets harder with age Young children have a readiness to learn language. Ten years after coming to the United States, Asian immigrants took a grammar test. Those who arrived before age 8 understood grammar as well as native speakers. Those who arrived later did not. (From Johnson & Newport, 1991.)

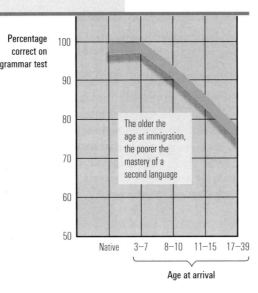

Percentage correct on grammar test

The older the age at immigration, the poorer the mastery of a second language

Native 3–7 8–10 11–15 17–39

Age at arrival

> "Childhood is the time for language, no doubt about it. Young children, the younger the better, are good at it; it is child's play. It is a onetime gift to the species."
>
> **LEWIS THOMAS**
> *THE FRAGILE SPECIES*
> 1992

their first language. Do they master the foreign grammar better than the accent? To find out, Jacqueline Johnson and Elissa Newport (1991) gave Korean and Chinese immigrants to the United States a grammar test, requiring them to identify each of 276 sentences ("Yesterday the hunter shoots a deer") as grammatically correct or incorrect. Some of the test-takers had immigrated in early childhood, others as adults. Regardless of their age at immigration, each had been in the United States for approximately 10 years. Nevertheless, as Figure 10.9 reveals, those who learned their second language early learned it best. Chomsky would say that once the grammar switches are thrown during a child's developing years, mastering another grammar becomes more difficult.

Learning is already throwing switches during the first year. When you or I listen to an unfamiliar language, the syllables all run together. Someone unfamiliar with English might, for example, hear the "United Nations" as the Uneye Tednay Shuns. Before our first birthday, our brains were discerning word breaks by statistically analyzing which syllables most often go together. Jenny Saffran and her colleagues (1996) showed this by exposing 8-month-old infants to a computer voice speaking an unbroken, monotone string of nonsense syllables (*bidakupadotigolabubidaku . . .*). After just two minutes of exposure, the infants were able to recognize (as indicated by their attention) three-syllable sequences that appeared repeatedly.

As a flower's growth is stunted without nourishment, so, too, are children linguistically stunted when isolated from language during the critical period for its acquisition. Consider Genie, who spent

most of her early years tied to a chair without being spoken to. When discovered by Los Angeles authorities in 1970 at age 13, she was mute and uncomprehending (Curtiss, 1977, 1981). In the years that followed, Genie learned some individual words but not how to construct grammatically correct sentences. Today, she lives in a home for mentally impaired adults (Rymer, 1993).

The impact of early experience is also evident among the deaf. Hearing children of hearing-speaking parents, and deaf children of deaf-signing parents, have much in common. Both groups babble as infants—hearing children by repeating sounds, deaf children by repeating elementary sign gestures (Petitto & Marentette, 1991). Both groups develop vocabularies, at comparable rates (Meier, 1991). For both groups, later-than-usual exposure to language (at age 2 or 3) unleashes their brain's idle language capacity, producing a rush of language. But consider the 90+ percent of deaf children born to hearing-nonsigning parents. These children typically do not experience language during their early years. Compared with deaf children exposed to sign language from birth, those who learn to sign as teens or adults are like immigrants who learn English after childhood. They can master the basic words and how to order them, but they never become as fluent as native signers in producing and comprehending subtle grammatical differences (Newport, 1990).

No means NO! No matter how you say it Deaf children of deaf-signing parents and hearing children of hearing parents have much in common. They develop language skills at about the same rate, and they are equally effective at opposing parental wishes and demanding their way.

To summarize, children's genes design complex brain wiring that prepares them to learn language as they interact with their caregivers. Skinner's emphasis on learning helps explain why infants acquire the language they hear and how they add new words to their vocabularies. Chomsky's emphasis on our built-in readiness to learn grammar rules helps explain why preschoolers acquire language so readily and use grammar so well. Once again, we see biology and experience working together.

Returning to our debate about humanity's thinking powers, let's pause to issue a report card. On decision making and judgment, our error-prone species might rate a C+. On problem solving, where humans are inventive yet vulnerable to fixation, we would probably receive better marks, perhaps a B+. On cognitive efficiency, our fallible but quick heuristics earn us an A. And when it comes to learning and using language, the awestruck experts would surely award the human species an A+.

Can Animals Exhibit Language?

If in our use of language we humans are, as the psalmist rhapsodized, "little lower than God," where do other animals fit in the scheme of things? Are they "little lower than human"? In part, the answer lies in the extent to which animals share our capacity for language.

Without doubt, animals communicate. Vervet monkeys have different alarm cries for different predators: a barking call for a leopard, a coughing for an eagle, and a chuttering for a snake. Hearing the leopard alarm, other vervets climb the nearest tree. Hearing the eagle alarm, they rush into the bushes. Hearing the snake chutter, they stand up and scan the ground (Byrne, 1991). Whales also communicate, with clicks and wails. But do animals' communications make up a language?

The Case of the Honeybee

More than 2000 years ago, the Greek philosopher Aristotle observed that once a lone honeybee discovers a source of nectar, other bees soon leave the hive and go straight to the newfound food source. Aristotle surmised that the original explorer must return to the hive and lead other bees back to the food. He was wrong. In 1901, a clever German researcher followed the explorer bee back to the hive and trapped it as it left to return to the food source. Although deprived of their guide, the new recruits still flew straight to the nectar.

Smart bird brain Alex, an African gray parrot trained and tested by University of Arizona professor Irene Pepperberg (1994), displays numerical competence when shown novel assortments of objects. Asked, for example, "How many red blocks?" or "How many blue balls?" Alex answers correctly more than 80 percent of the time.

How did the bees know where to go? Intrigued, Austrian biologist Karl von Frisch (1950) undertook experiments for which he later shared the Nobel prize. The experiments revealed that the explorer bee communicates with the other worker bees by means of an intricate dance. The direction and duration of the dance, Frisch discovered, informs other bees of the direction and distance of the food source (Figure 10.10). Using robotic honeybees that perform a credible song and dance act, experimenters have since discovered that it takes a combination of dance and sound to tell nestmate bees where to fly to find food (Kirchner & Towne, 1994).

Impressive as they are, the honeybees' song and dance hardly challenge the complexity, flexibility, and power of human language. The honeybee communicates, but not with the elements of language.

Figure **10.10**

Direction of nectar source

The dance of the honeybee The straight-line part of the dance points in the direction of a nectar source relative to the sun, and the duration of the dance indicates the distance. The other bees, who cannot see the dance in the dark hive, huddle close to feel what is going on. (From von Frisch, 1974.)

But is this language? The ability of chimpanzees to express themselves in American Sign Language (ASL) raises questions about the very nature of language. Here, the trainer is asking, "What is this?" The sign in response is "Baby." Does the response constitute language?

The Case of the Apes

The greatest challenge to humanity's claim to be the only language-using species has come from reports of apes that "talk" with people. Genetically speaking, our closest relatives are the chimpanzees, and the chimpanzees' closest relatives are not other apes, but us (Sagan & Druyan, 1992). Knowing that chimpanzees could not vocalize more than a few words, University of Nevada researchers Allen Gardner and Beatrice Gardner (1969) tried to teach sign language words to a chimp named Washoe, as though she were a deaf human child. After four years, Washoe could use 132 signs. By age 27, Washoe had a vocabulary of 240 signs (Geranios, 1993). The Gardners' announcement of the success of their efforts aroused enormous scientific and public interest. One *New York Times* reporter, having learned sign language from his deaf parents, visited Washoe and exclaimed, "Suddenly I realized I was conversing with a member of another species in my native tongue."

Seeing a doll floating in her water, Washoe signed, "Baby in my drink."

During the 1970s, further evidence of "ape language" surfaced. Although apes usually signed just single words, they sometimes strung signs together to form intelligible sentences. Washoe signed, "You me go out, please." Apes even appeared to combine words creatively. Washoe designated a swan as a "water bird." Koko, a gorilla trained by Francine Patterson (1978) in California, reportedly described a long-nosed Pinocchio doll as an "elephant baby." Lana, a chimpanzee that "talks" by punching buttons wired to a computer that translates her punchings into English, wanted her trainer's orange. She had no word for *orange*, but she did know her colors and the word for *apple*, so she improvised: "?Tim give apple which-is orange" (Rumbaugh, 1977).

As ape language reports accumulated, it seemed that apes might indeed be "little lower than human." Their vocabularies and sentences are simple, rather like those of a 2-year-old child. Yet the apes do seem to share what we humans have considered our unique ability.

But Can Apes Really Talk?

By the late 1970s, fascination with "talking apes" turned toward cynicism: Were the chimps language champs or were the researchers chumps? The ape language researchers were making monkeys out of themselves, said the skeptics, who raised the following arguments:

- Apes gain their limited vocabularies only with great difficulty. They are hardly like speaking or signing children, who effortlessly soak up dozens of new words a week. Saying that apes can learn language because they can sign words is like saying humans can fly because they can jump.

- Chimps can make signs or push buttons in sequence to get a reward, just as Moscow circus bears can learn to ride unicycles. But pigeons, too, can peck a sequence of keys to get grain (Straub & others, 1979). No one says the pigeon is "talking."

- Apes can certainly use symbols meaningfully. But "Give orange me give eat orange me eat orange . . ." is a far cry from the exquisite syntax of a 3-year-old (Pinker, 1995). To the child, "you tickle" and "tickle you" communicate different ideas. A chimp might sign the phrases interchangeably.

- After training a chimp whom he named Nim Chimsky, Herbert Terrace (1979) concluded that much of chimpanzees' signing is nothing more than imitation of their trainers' signs.

- Presented with ambiguous information, people tend to see what they want or expect to see. (Recall the demonstrations of perceptual set in Chapter 6.) Interpreting chimpanzee signs as language may be little more than wishful thinking on the part of their trainers, claimed Terrace. (When Washoe signed *water bird*, she perhaps was separately naming *water* and *bird*.)

Another "talking" chimpanzee Lana has learned to speak by punching word symbols on a computer keyboard. When she presses a key, the symbol lights up.

"Although humans make sounds with their mouths and occasionally look at each other, there is no solid evidence that they actually communicate with each other."

Although apes usually signed just single words, they sometimes strung signs together to form intelligible sentences. Washoe signed, "You me go out, please."

"Chimps do not develop language," surmises linguist Steven Pinker (1995). "But that is no shame on them; humans would surely do no better if trained to hoot and shriek like chimps, to perform the waggle-dance of the bee, or any of the other wonderful feats in nature's talent show."

In science as in politics, controversy stimulates progress. The provocative claim that "apes share our capacity for language" and the skeptical rejoinder that "apes no use language" (as Washoe might have put it) have moved psychologists toward a greater appreciation of apes' remarkable capabilities, and of our own. Everyone agrees that humans alone possess language, if by the term we mean verbal or signed expression of complex grammar. If we mean, more simply, the ability to communicate through a meaningful sequence of symbols, then apes are indeed capable of language.

Although chimpanzees do not have our facility for language, their thinking and communicating abilities continue to impress their trainers. After her second infant died, a depressed Washoe repeatedly asked "Baby?" and became withdrawn when told "Baby dead, baby gone, baby finished." Two weeks later, caretaker Roger Fouts (1992) had better news for Washoe: "I have baby for you." Washoe reacted to the signed news with instant excitement, her hair on end, swaggering and panting while signing over and again, "Baby, my baby." When Fouts then introduced the foster infant, Loulis, it took several hours for them to warm to each other, whereupon Washoe broke the ice by signing, "Come baby" and cuddling Loulis. In the months that followed, Loulis picked up 68 signs

"[Our] egocentric view that [we are] unique from all other forms of animal life is being jarred to the core."

DUANE RUMBAUGH AND SUE SAVAGE-RUMBAUGH (1978)

simply by observing Washoe and three other language-trained chimps.

Moreover, Washoe, Loulis, and the others now sign spontaneously, as when asking one another to *chase, tickle, hug, come,* or *groom.* People who sign can eavesdrop on these chimp-to-chimp conversations with near-perfect agreement about what the chimps are saying, 90 percent of which pertains to social interaction, reassurance, or play (Fouts & Bodamer, 1987). The chimps are even modestly bilingual; they can translate spoken English words into signs (Shaw, 1989–1990).

Most stunning, however, is the discovery by Sue Savage-Rumbaugh and her colleagues (1993) that pygmy chimpanzees can learn to comprehend the semantic nuances of spoken English. Kanzi, one such chimp with the grammatical abilities of a 2½-year-old, happened onto language while observing his adoptive mother being language trained. Kanzi behaves intelligently whether asked, "Can you show me the light?" or "Can you bring me the [flash]light?" or "Can you turn the light on?" Kanzi also knows the spoken words *snake, bite,* and *dog.* Given stuffed animals and asked, for the first time, to "make the dog bite the snake," he put the snake to the dog's mouth. For chimps as for humans, early life is a critical time for learning language. If raised without early exposure to speech or word symbols, the chimps are unable as adults to gain language competence (Rumbaugh & Savage-Rumbaugh, 1994).

So, trained apes' language capabilities are modest by human standards. Yet their impressive cognitive powers seem indeed to make them "little lower than human." If Kanzi "had a vocal tract, he would be talking," exclaims Duane Rumbaugh (1994). Realizing this, we see once again how animal research can increase our respect for the creatures studied. Believing that animals could not think, Descartes and other philosophers argued that they were living robots without moral rights. Animals, it has been said at one time or another, cannot plan, conceptualize, count, use tools, show compassion, or use language (Thorpe, 1974). Today, we know better. We have seen primates exhibit insight, show family loyalty, communicate with one another, display altruism, transmit cultural patterns across generations, and comprehend the syntax of human speech. Working out the moral implications of all this is an unfinished task for our own thinking species.

SUMMING UP

Language—our words and how we combine them to communicate meaning—facilitates and expresses our thoughts.

Language Structure Language is built of basic speech sounds, called *phonemes*; elementary units of meaning, called *morphemes*; and the *semantics* (meaning) and *syntax* (rules for word order) that make up grammar.

Language Development Among the marvels of nature is a child's ability to acquire language. The ease with which children progress from the babbling stage through the one-word stage to the telegraphic speech of the two-word stage and beyond has sparked a lively debate concerning how they do it. Behaviorist Skinner explained that we learn language by the familiar principles of imitation and reinforcement. Challenging this claim, linguist Noam Chomsky argued that children are biologically prepared to learn words and use grammar. For mastery of grammar, the learning that occurs during life's first few years is, however, critical.

Can Animals Exhibit Language? Another vigorously debated issue is whether language is uniquely human. Animals obviously communicate. Bees, for example, communicate the location of food through an intricate combination of dance and sound. And several teams of psychologists have taught various species of apes, including a number of chimpanzees, to communicate with humans by signing or by pushing buttons wired to a computer. Apes have developed considerable vocabularies. They string words together to express meaning and to make and follow requests. Skeptics point out important differences between apes' and humans' facilities with language, especially in their respective abilities to order words using proper syntax. Nevertheless, these studies reveal that apes have considerable cognitive ability.

KEY TERMS AND CONCEPTS language, phoneme, morpheme, grammar, semantics, syntax, babbling stage, one-word stage, two-word stage, telegraphic speech

linguistic relativity
Whorf's hypothesis that language determines the way we think.

Thinking and Language

A world without language would be a world without the concepts and cultures we hang on language. Language influences what we think, perceive, and remember. Education therefore aims to increase our word (and thinking) power. Yet much thinking involves no words.

Thinking and language intricately intertwine. Asking which comes first is one of psychology's chicken-and-egg questions. Do our ideas come first and wait for words to name them? Or are our thoughts conceived in words and unthinkable without them?

Language Influences Thinking

Linguist Benjamin Lee Whorf contended that language determines the way we think. According to Whorf's (1956) linguistic relativity hypothesis, different languages impose different conceptions of reality: "Language itself shapes a man's basic ideas." The Hopi, Whorf noted, have no past tense for their verbs. Therefore, he contended, a Hopi could not so readily *think* about the past.

Whorf's relativity hypothesis would probably not occur to people who speak only one language and view that language as simply a vehicle for thought. But to those who speak two dissimilar languages, such as English and Japanese, it seems obvious that a person thinks differently in different languages (Brown, 1986). Unlike English, which has a rich vocabulary for self-focused emotions such as anger, Japanese has many words for interpersonal emotions such as sympathy (Markus & Kitayama, 1991). Many bilinguals report that they even have a different sense of self, depending on which language they are using (Matsumoto, 1994). After immigrating from Asia to North America, bilinguals may reveal different personalities when taking the same personality test in their two languages (Dinges & Hull, 1992). Learn a language and you learn about a culture. When a language becomes extinct—the likely fate of most of the world's 5000 remaining languages—the world loses the culture and thinking that hangs on that language.

"All words are pegs to hang ideas on."

HENRY WARD BEECHER
PROVERBS FROM PLYMOUTH PULPIT
1887

It is too strong to say that language *determines* the *way* we think. A New Guinean without our words for shapes and colors nevertheless perceives them much as we do (Rosch, 1974). But our words do influence *what* we think (Hardin & Banaji, 1993). We therefore do well to choose our words carefully. When people referred to women as *girls*—as in "the girls at the office"—it perpetuated a view of women's having lower status, did it not? Or consider the generic use of the pronoun *he*. Does it make any difference whether I write "A child learns language as *he* interacts with *his* caregivers" or "Children learn language as *they* interact with *their* caregivers"? Some argue that it makes no difference because every reader knows that "the masculine gender shall be deemed and taken to include females" (as the British Parliament declared in 1850).

But is the generic *he* always taken to include females? Twenty studies have consistently found that it is not (Henley, 1989). For example, Janet Hyde (1984) asked children to finish stories for which she gave them a first line, such as "When a kid goes to school, _____ often feels excited on the first day." When Hyde used *he* in the blank, the children's stories were nearly always about males. "He or she" in the blank resulted in female characters about one-third of the time. Studies with adolescents and adults in North America and New Zealand have found similar effects of the generic *he* (Hamilton, 1988; Martyna, 1978; Ng, 1990). Sentences about "the artist and his work" tend to conjure up images of a man. Similarly, ambiguous actions taken by a "chairman of the board" seem to reveal an assertive and independent personality. The same actions taken by a "chairperson of the board" seem to reveal a more caring and warm personality (McConnell & Fazio, 1996).

Consider, too, that people use generic pronouns selectively, as in "the doctor . . . he" and "the secretary . . . she" (MacKay, 1983). If *he* and *his* were truly gender-free, we shouldn't skip a beat when hearing that "a nurse must answer his calls" or that "man, like other mammals, nurses his young." That we are startled indicates that *his* carries a gender connotation that clashes with our idea of *nurse*.

The power of language to influence thought makes vocabulary building a crucial part of education. To expand language is to expand the ability to think. In young children, thinking develops hand in hand with language (Gopnik & Meltzoff, 1986). What is true for preschoolers is true for everyone: *It pays to increase your word power.* That is why most textbooks, including this one, introduce new words—to teach new ideas and new ways of thinking.

Increased word power helps explain what McGill University researcher Wallace Lambert (1992; Lambert & others, 1993) calls the "bilingual advantage." Bilingual children in Canada, Switzerland, Israel, South Africa, and Singapore outperform monolinguals on intelligence tests. Knowing this, Lambert helped devise a Canadian program that enables English-speaking children to be immersed in French. (From 1981 to 1991, the number of non-Quebec Canadian children immersed in French quadrupled from 65,000 to 250,000—Columbo, 1994.) For most of their first three school years, the English-speaking children are taught by a French-speaking teacher; not until the fifth and sixth grades do they receive half their instruction in English. Not surprisingly, the children attain a natural French fluency unrivaled by other methods of language teaching. Moreover, compared with similarly capable children in control conditions, they do so without detriment to their English fluency, and with increased aptitude scores, math scores, and appreciation for French Canadian culture.

So, for English-speaking Canadians, immersion followed by bilingual education pays dividends. Does bilingual education for children in a linguistic minority also pay dividends? Advocates of "English-only" education doubt it. They argue that bilingual programs are expensive, ineffective, and detrimental to non–English-speaking children's assimilation into their English-based cultures. But studies find that such children benefit from bilingual education, especially in "two-way" schools where they, together with English-speaking children, experience half their classes in English and half in their native language. Compared with non–English-speaking children dropped into English-only schools, those in the two-way schools tend to develop higher self-esteem. They drop out less frequently. And they eventually attain higher levels of academic achievement and English proficiency (Hamers & Blanc, 1989; Padilla & Benavides, 1992; Thomas & Collier, 1997).

Increasing word power through sign language has also had great benefits for deaf people, who for thousands of years were viewed as incompetent to inherit property, marry, be educated, or have challenging work (Sacks, 1990). Since the spread of signed instruction, the deaf have shown that, when

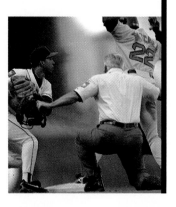

A safe sign We have outfielder William Hoy to thank for baseball sign language. The first deaf player to join the major leagues in 1892, he invented hand signals for "Strike!" "Safe!" (shown here) and "Yerr Out!" (Pollard, 1992). Such gestures worked so well that referees in all sports now use invented signs, and fans are fluent in sports sign language.

"To call forth a concept, a word is needed."

ANTOINE LAVOISIER
ELEMENTS OF CHEMISTRY
1789

Do our ideas come first and wait for words to name them? Or are our thoughts conceived in words and unthinkable without them?

exposed to signing as preschoolers and then schooled in their language, they become fully literate. Deaf children with native sign fluency—learned, for example, as children of signing deaf parents—outperform other signing deaf children on measures of intelligence and academic achievement (Isham & Kamin, 1993). For both the deaf and the hearing, language transforms experience. Language connects us to the past and the future. Language fuels our imagination. Language links us to one another.

Thinking Without Language

When you are alone, do you talk to yourself? Is "thinking" simply conversing with yourself? Without a doubt, words convey ideas. But are there not times when ideas precede words? To turn on the cold water in your bathroom, in which direction do you turn the handle?

To answer this question, you probably thought not in words but with a mental picture. Indeed, we often think in images. Artists think in images. So do composers, poets, mathematicians, athletes, and scientists. Albert Einstein reported that he achieved some of his greatest insights through visual images and only later put them into words.

Liu Chi Kung placed second in the 1958 Tchaikovsky competition—the piano Olympics—and was imprisoned a year later during China's cultural revolution. Soon after his release, after seven years without touching a piano, he was back on tour and critics judged his musicianship better than ever. How did he do it without practice? "I did practice," said Liu, "every day. I rehearsed every piece I had ever played, note by note, in my mind" (Garfield, 1986).

For Olympic athletes, "mental practice has become a standard part of training," reports Richard Suinn (in press). Golf great Jack Nicklaus has said that he would "watch a movie" in his head before each shot. Georgia Nigro (1984) demonstrated the wisdom of mental practice in a laboratory test. She had people make 24 actual dart throws at a target, then had half the people throw 24 darts mentally, and, finally, had all the people again make 24 throws. Only those who had mentally practiced showed any improvement. A National Research Council committee of psychologists investigated claims of performance-enhancement techniques for the U.S. Army and concluded that most techniques (including ESP) were of no value (Druckman & Swets, 1988). Based on experiments such as Nigro's, however, they deemed the mental practice of motor skills useful.

Moreover, remember a lesson from earlier chapters: Much information processing occurs outside of consciousness, beyond language. Inside the ever-active brain, many streams of activity flow in parallel, functioning automatically, remembered implicitly, only occasionally surfacing as conscious words. So, yes, there is much cognition without language.

What, then, should we say about the relationship between thinking and language? We have seen that language influences thinking. But if thinking did not also affect language, there would never be any new words. New words express new ideas. The basketball term *slam dunk* was coined after the act itself had become fairly common. So, let us simply say that *thinking affects our language, which then affects our thought.*

Psychological research on thinking and language mirrors the mixed reviews given our species in literature and religion. The human mind is simultaneously capable of striking intellectual failures and of vast intellectual power. Some misjudgments have disastrous consequences, so we do well to appreciate our capacity for error. Yet our heuristics often serve us well, and they certainly are efficient. Moreover, our ingenuity at problem solving and our extraordinary power of language surely, among the animals, rank humankind as almost "infinite in faculties."

A thoughtful art Piano playing engages thinking without language. In the absence of a piano, mental practice can sustain one's skill.

What time is it now? On page 314, did you underestimate or overestimate how quickly you would finish the chapter?

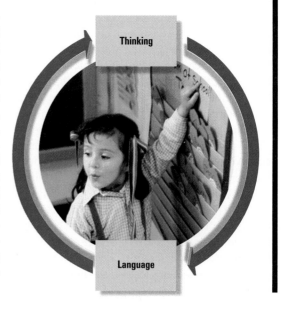

The interplay of thought and language The traffic runs both ways between thinking and language. Thinking affects our language, which affects our thought.

SUMMING UP

We consider thinking and language in the same chapter, for they are hard to separate.

Language Influences Thinking Words convey ideas, and different languages embody different ways of thinking. Although the linguistic relativity hypothesis suggested that language *determines* thought, it is more accurate to say that language *influences* thought. Studies of the effects of the generic pronoun *he* and the ability of vocabulary enrichment to enhance thinking reveal the influence of words.

Thinking Without Language Some ideas, such as the ability to perceive and remember different colors, do not depend on language. We sometimes think in images rather than in words, and we invent new words to describe new ideas. So we might say that our thinking affects our language, which then affects our thought.

KEY TERMS AND CONCEPTS linguistic relativity

TERMS AND CONCEPTS TO REMEMBER

cognition, p. 306 ✓

concept, p. 306 ✓

prototype, p. 306 ✓

algorithm, p. 307 ✓

heuristic, p. 307 ✓

insight, p. 307 ✓

confirmation bias, p. 308 ✓

fixation, p. 309 ✓

mental set, p. 309 ✓

functional fixedness, p. 309 ✓

representativeness heuristic, ✓
p. 310

availability heuristic, p. 311 ✓

overconfidence, p. 313 ✓

framing, p. 314 ✓

belief bias, p. 315 ✓

belief perseverance, p. 315 ✓

artificial intelligence (AI), ✓
p. 317

neural networks, p. 317 ✓

language, p. 319 ✓

phoneme, p. 319 ✓

morpheme, p. 320 ✓

grammar, p. 320 ✓

semantics, p. 320 ✓

syntax, p. 320 ✓

babbling stage, p. 320 3 to 4 M.

one-word stage, p. 321 from 1-2

two-word stage, p. 321 2

telegraphic speech, p. 322

linguistic relativity, p. 328

CRITICAL THINKING EXERCISE
by Richard O. Straub

Now that you have read and reviewed Chapter 10, take your learning a step further by testing your critical thinking skills on the following perspective-taking exercise.

Attempts to explain language development have sparked a spirited intellectual controversy. At the heart of this controversy is the nature-nurture debate. Behaviorist B. F. Skinner believed that we can explain how babies acquire language entirely with principles of learning, such as the *association* of objects with the sounds of words, the *imitation* of language modeled by others, and the *reinforcement* of correct use of words and syntax by parents and teachers. Linguist Noam Chomsky, who favors the nature position, believes that much of our language capacity is inborn. According to this perspective, just as "learning" to walk is programmed according to a timetable of biological maturation, so children are prewired to begin to babble and talk.

In this exercise, review each of the following examples of language use by children and decide whether it *best* supports the position of B. F. Skinner or Noam Chomsky. Then explain your reasoning.

Explanation:

1. While Marie and her mother are looking at a book together, Marie's mother shows her a picture of an animal and says "cow." Marie says "cow," and her mother praises her for her correct utterance. Two pages later, Marie spontaneously points to a picture and correctly identifies it as a *cow*.
Position supported:

Explanation:

2. When his day care teacher asks 2-year-old Jack what he did last Saturday, he responds with "We goed to the zoo." His teacher smiles, marveling at the fact that all children Jack's age make this type of grammatical error.
Position supported:

Explanation:

3. Nicole, who is deaf and was not exposed to sign language until age 3, lacks the manual linguistic skills of deaf children born to deaf-signing parents.
Position supported:

Explanation:

4. Twelve-year-old Malcolm, who emigrated to the United States at age 4, understands English grammar much better than 20-year-old Maya, who was first exposed to English at age 12.
Position supported:

Check your progress on becoming a critical thinker by comparing your answers to the sample answers found in Appendix B.

chapter 11

Intelligence

After testing Larry and six other African-American children, California school officials assigned them to special education classes for those with mental retardation. Their parents and the San Francisco Bay Area Black Psychology Association were unconvinced by the psychologists' judgments. They suspected the tests were biased. In 1979, Federal District Court Judge Robert Peckham agreed. Intelligence tests, he ruled, are "racially and culturally biased, have a discriminatory impact on black children, and have not been validated for the purpose of [putting] black children into educationally dead-end, isolated, and stigmatizing classes" (Opton, 1979). In 1986, Judge Peckham reiterated his complete prohibition against using IQ tests in California "as part of an assessment . . . placing black pupils in special education" (Landers, 1986).

In the last decade, three huge controversies have sparked debate in and beyond psychology. First is the "memory war," over whether traumatic experiences get repressed and can later be recovered, with therapeutic benefit (Chapters 9 and 14). The second great controversy is the "gender war," over the extent to which nature and nurture shape our behaviors as men and women (Chapters 3 and 18). In this chapter, we focus on the "intelligence war": Does each of us have an inborn general mental capacity (intelligence), and can we quantify this capacity as a meaningful number (an IQ score)?

School boards, courts, and scientists debate the usefulness and fairness of intelligence tests—tests for assessing a person's mental abilities and comparing them with the abilities of other people, by means of numerical scores. Should we use such tests to rank people and admit them to a particular college or to hire them for a particular job? If so, what *is* intelligence? How can we best assess it? To what extent does it result from nature (heredity) rather than nurture (environment)? What do test score differences among individuals and groups really mean? Is intelligence testing a positive way to guide people toward suitable opportunities? Or is it a potent, discriminatory weapon camouflaged as science? This chapter aims to help you gain a deeper understanding of these hotly debated issues.

The Origins of Intelligence Testing

"People are trapped in history," wrote James Baldwin in *Notes of a Native Son*, "and history is trapped in them." Recognizing that our concept of intelligence is a product of the history of intelligence testing, we begin with a look at why psychologists created intelligence tests and how they have used them.

Some societies concern themselves less with promoting individual opportunity than with promoting the collective welfare of the family, community, and society. Other societies emphasize the individual over the group. A pioneer of this individualist tradition, Plato wrote more than 2000 years ago in *The Republic* that "no two persons are born exactly alike; but each differs from the other in natural endowments, one being suited for one occupation and the other for another." As heirs to Plato's individualism, people in Western societies ponder how and why individuals differ.

About a century ago, Western attempts to assess individual differences in mental ability began in earnest. We can better understand the concept of intelligence if we first review the history of intelligence testing. The story illustrates an important lesson: Although science strives for objectivity, scientists are affected by their own attitudes.

Francis Galton: Quantifying Superiority

In the history of the testing movement, no one measured and ranked people with greater enthusiasm than the English scientist Sir Francis Galton (1822–1911). Galton's fascination with quantification led him to invent methods for measuring boredom, even-temperedness, the beauty of British women, the effects of prayer, and much more.

When his cousin Charles Darwin proposed that nature selects successful traits through the "survival of the fittest," Galton concluded that he could scientifically apply the principle. Why not measure human traits, he reasoned, and then selectively breed superior people? Those with the greatest "natural ability" could be encouraged to mate with each other, and those not so well endowed could be discouraged or prevented from reproducing. To promote his plan for human betterment, Galton founded the "eugenics" movement (from the Greek word *eugenes*, which means "well-born").

Galton assumed that human traits are inherited. He supported this assumption by noting that social prominence, like height, tends to run in families. Not surprisingly, Galton himself was an eminent child of a well-known upper-class family, and he married a "suitable" woman (though, ironically, his marriage was childless). Furthermore, although he popularized the phrase "nature and nurture," he was oblivious to the advantages enjoyed by the upper class in Victorian England (Fancher, 1979). A British male, he instead believed in the *natural* superiority of well-born white men over women, the poor, and members of other races.

Committed to quantifying human superiority, Galton set about trying to measure innate mental capacity. In his 1869 book, *Hereditary Genius*, he toyed with the idea of assessing intelligence by measuring head size, and over the next few years he developed various measures of what he presumed were the biological underpinnings of genius. Galton put his ideas to the test at London's 1884 International Exposition. Over 10,000 exposition visitors paid to receive his assessment of their "intellectual strengths," based on such things as reaction time, sensory acuity, muscular power, and body proportions.

How did the tests turn out? Did "superior" individuals (eminent adults and excellent students) outscore those supposedly not so bright? Did they, for instance, process information more swiftly on the tests of reaction time? They did not. Nor did the various measures correlate with one another. Nor did men consistently outscore women.

Although Galton failed in his efforts to invent simple measures of general mental ability, he was an innovative researcher who created some statistical techniques that we still use. Galton was also the first proponent of an idea that survives to this day—that we can quantitatively measure people's mental abilities.

Alfred Binet: Predicting School Achievement

The modern intelligence-testing movement began when the pioneering French psychologist Alfred Binet (1857–1911) successfully applied Galton's idea of measuring intellectual abilities. When the French government passed a law requiring that all children attend school, teachers soon faced a distressing range of individual differences. Some children seemed incapable of benefiting from the regular school curriculum and in need of special classes. But how could the schools objectively identify children with special needs?

Francis Galton "I have no patience with the hypothesis occasionally expressed, and often implied, especially in tales written to teach children to be good, that babies are born pretty much alike, and that the sole agencies in creating differences between boy and boy, and man and man, are steady application and moral effort. It is in the most unqualified manner that I object to pretensions of natural equality" (1892).

The government was justifiably reluctant to trust teachers' subjective judgments of children's learning potential. Academic slowness might merely reflect inadequate prior education. Also, teachers might prejudge children on the basis of their social backgrounds. To minimize bias, France's minister of public education in 1904 commissioned Binet and others to study the problem. In response, Binet and his collaborator, Théodore Simon, decided to develop an objective test to identify children who were likely to have difficulty in the regular classes.

Binet and Simon began by assuming that all children follow the same course of intellectual development but that some develop more rapidly. "Dull" children, they presumed, were merely "retarded" in their development. On tests, therefore, a "dull" child should perform as does a typical younger child, and a "bright" child as does a typical older child.

Binet and Simon set out to measure what came to be called a child's <u>mental age</u>, the chronological age that typically corresponds to a given level of performance. The average 9-year-old has a mental age of 9. But many 9-year-olds have mental ages below or above 9. Children below average, such as 9-year-olds who perform at the level of a typical 7-year-old, would struggle with schoolwork considered normal for their age.

To measure mental age, Binet and Simon theorized that mental aptitude, like athletic aptitude, is a general capacity that shows up in various ways. They then developed varied reasoning and problem-solving questions that might predict school achievement. By testing "bright" and "backward" Parisian schoolchildren on these questions, Binet and Simon succeeded: They found items that did predict how well the children handled schoolwork.

Note that Binet and Simon made no assumptions concerning *why* a particular child was slow, average, or precocious. Binet personally leaned toward an environmental explanation. To raise the capacities of low-scoring children, he recommended "mental orthopedics" that would train them to develop their attention span and self-discipline. He

refused to speculate about what the test was actually measuring, but he insisted that it did not measure inborn intelligence as a meterstick measures height. Rather, the test had a single practical purpose: to identify French schoolchildren needing special attention. Binet hoped his test would be used to improve children's education, but he also feared it would be used to label children and limit their opportunities (Gould, 1981).

Lewis Terman: The Innate IQ

What Binet viewed as merely a practical guide for identifying slow learners who needed special help was soon seen by others to be what Galton sought: a numerical measure of inherited intelligence. After Binet's death in 1911, Stanford University professor Lewis Terman (1877–1956) decided to use Binet's test. He soon found, however, that the Paris-developed age norms worked poorly with California schoolchildren. So Terman revised the test. He adapted some of Binet's original items, added others, established new age norms, and extended the upper end of the test's range from teenagers to "superior adults." Terman gave his revision the name it retains today—the <u>Stanford-Binet</u>.

For such tests, German psychologist William Stern derived the famous <u>intelligence quotient</u>, or <u>IQ</u>. The IQ was simply a person's mental age divided by chronological age and multiplied by 100 to get rid of the decimal point:

$$IQ = \frac{\text{mental age}}{\text{chronological age}} \times 100$$

Thus, an average child, whose mental and chronological ages are the same, has an IQ of 100. But an 8-year-old who answers questions as would a typical 10-year-old has an IQ of 125.

Most current intelligence tests, including the Stanford-Binet, no longer compute an IQ. The original IQ formula works fairly well for children but not for adults. Consider: Should a 40-year-old who does as well on the test as an average 20-year-old be assigned an IQ of only 50? Obviously, something is out of whack. Today's intelligence tests therefore produce a mental ability score based on the test-taker's performance relative to the average performance of others the same age. As on the original Stanford-Binet, current tests define this score so that 100 is average, with about two-thirds of all people scoring between 85 and 115. Although there is no longer any intelligence *quotient*, the term "IQ" still lingers in everyday vocabulary as a shorthand expression for "intelligence test score."

Alfred Binet "The scale, properly speaking, does not permit the measure of intelligence, because intellectual qualities . . . cannot be measured as linear surfaces are measured" (Binet & Simon, 1905).

"The IQ test was invented to predict academic performance, nothing else. If we wanted something that would predict life success, we'd have to invent another test completely."

SOCIAL PSYCHOLOGIST ROBERT ZAJONC (1984B)

mental age
a measure of intelligence test performance devised by Binet; the chronological age that most typically corresponds to a given level of performance. Thus, a child who does as well as the average 8-year-old is said to have a mental age of 8.

Stanford-Binet
the widely used American revision (by Terman at Stanford University) of Binet's original intelligence test.

intelligence quotient (IQ)
defined originally as the ratio of mental age (*ma*) to chronological age (*ca*) multiplied by 100 (thus, IQ = *ma/ca* × 100). On contemporary intelligence tests, the average performance for a given age is assigned a score of 100.

© 1982 by Sidney Harris; American Scientist magazine.

"You did very well on your IQ test. You're a man of 49 with the intelligence of a man of 53."

Lewis Terman "The children of successful and cultured parents test higher than children from wretched and ignorant homes for the simple reason that their heredity is better" (1916, p. 115)

"Science must be understood as a social phenomenon, a gutsy, human enterprise, not the work of robots programmed to collect pure information."

STEPHEN JAY GOULD (1981)

Terman shared Galton's belief that intelligence was measurable, and he promoted the widespread use of intelligence testing. His motive was to "take account of the inequalities of children in original endowment" by assessing their "vocational fitness." In sympathy with the eugenics movement, Terman (1916, pp. 91–92) lamented what he believed was the "dullness" and "unusually prolific breeding" of certain ethnic groups. He envisioned that the use of intelligence tests would "ultimately result in curtailing the reproduction of feeblemindedness and in the elimination of an enormous amount of crime, pauperism, and industrial inefficiency" (p. 7).

With Terman's help, the U.S. government developed new tests to evaluate 1.7 million World War I army recruits and newly arriving immigrants. To some psychologists, the results indicated the inferiority of people not sharing their Anglo-Saxon heritage. Following his 1913 study of arriving immigrants, psychologist Henry Goddard claimed that 83 percent of the Jewish immigrants, 80 percent of the Hungarians, 79 percent of the Italians, and 87 percent of the Russians were "feebleminded" (Eysenck & Kamin, 1981). Such findings were part of the cultural climate that led to the 1924 immigration law, which reduced immigration quotas for southern and eastern Europe to less than a fifth of those for northern and western Europe.

Binet surely would have been horrified at his test being adapted and used to draw such conclusions. Indeed, such sweeping judgments eventually became an embarrassment to most of those who championed testing. Terman, for instance, came to appreciate that test scores reflect not only people's innate mental abilities but also their education and their familiarity with the culture assumed by the test. Nevertheless, abuses of the early intelligence tests serve to remind us that science can be value-laden. Influenced by his ideology, Terman (1916, pp. 91–92) had expected "enormously significant racial differences in intelligence." Behind the screen of scientific objectivity, ideology sometimes hides.

SUMMING UP

Among the most controversial issues in psychology is the debate over intelligence testing: whether tests can measure and quantify a person's abilities and how widely the results can be used fairly.

More than a century ago in Great Britain, Francis Galton sought to measure individual mental abilities. Although Galton failed to develop simple, quantifiable measures of mental ability, Alfred Binet developed questions that helped predict children's future progress in the Paris school system. Like Galton, Lewis Terman of Stanford University believed intelligence was inherited. And like Binet, Terman believed his test (the Stanford-Binet) could help guide people toward appropriate opportunities. During the early part of the twentieth century, intelligence tests were sometimes used in ways that, in hindsight, even their designers regretted—to "document" a presumed innate inferiority of certain ethnic and immigrant groups.

KEY TERMS AND CONCEPTS intelligence test, mental age, Stanford-Binet, intelligence quotient (IQ)

What Is Intelligence?

Intelligence is one of psychology's slippery concepts. Although psychologists generally agree that intelligence is a concept, not a concrete thing, they debate the issues surrounding this topic: Should we consider intelligence as culturally defined or culture-free? As one aptitude or many? As linked to cognitive speed? As neurologically assessable?

We use the term *intelligence* as though we all agree on what it means. We don't. Psychologists debate whether we should define intelligence as an inherent cognitive capacity, an achieved level of intellectual performance, or an ascribed quality that, like beauty, is in the eye of the beholder. Reading all the conflicting ideas about intelligence can leave you feeling as Alice in Wonderland felt after reading "Jabberwocky": "Somehow it seems to fill my head with ideas—only I don't exactly know what they are."

Intelligence experts agree on this much: Intelligence is not a "thing." When we refer to someone's "IQ" as if it were a fixed and objectively real trait like height, we commit a reasoning error called *reification*—viewing an abstract, immaterial concept as if it were a real, concrete thing. To reify is to invent a concept, give it a name, and then convince ourselves that such a thing objectively exists in the world. When someone says, "She has an IQ of 120," they are reifying IQ; they are imagining IQ to be a thing one *has*, rather than a score once obtained on a particular test.

Intelligence is a socially constructed concept—one we invented to explain why some people perform better than others on cognitive tasks. In the *Handbook of Human Intelligence*, Robert Sternberg and William Salter (1982, p. 3) reported that most experts view intelligence as *a person's capacity for "goal-directed adaptive behavior."* Intelligent behavior reflects a capacity to adapt, by learning from experience, solving problems, and reasoning clearly.

Despite this general agreement about the concept, three controversies remain.

1   Should we consider intelligence as whatever abilities are adaptive in one's culture, or as a culture-free ability to solve problems?

2   Is intelligence a single overall ability or several specific abilities?

3   With the tools of modern neuroscience, can we now fulfill Galton's dream of measuring intelligence as the brain's information-processing speed?

Is Intelligence Culturally Defined?

According to one view, intelligent behavior varies with the situation. For Binet and the later intelligence testers, intelligence meant children's ability to adapt successfully to academic demands. For islanders in the South Pacific, it might mean the ability to excel at fishing and navigating. For a business manager or salesperson, it might mean the ability to achieve goals through social skills. For an inner-city resident, it might mean the ability to use street smarts to ensure a family's safety and well-being.

Those who view intelligence as people's successful adaptation to their environment are skeptical about the prospects for a *culture-free* test of intelligence—a test uninfluenced by one's culture. They believe that those who hope for such a test fail to understand that *intelligence* is whatever abilities your culture deems important. It might make sense to talk about a *culture-free* measure of height, but not of intelligence. As intelligence researcher Howard Gardner noted, a basketball superstar may not be considered exceptionally intelligent when in school, but in a society of keen-eyed hunters and spear-throwing warriors he would be the gifted one. Believing that intelligence is always expressed in a particular context, Gardner (1995) prefers to observe it at work—among such people as racetrack bettors, musicians, tailors, and negotiators.

Other researchers view intelligence as a basic cognitive ability that helps people solve problems in *any* environment (Baron, 1985). According to this view, the abstract and novel questions asked on intelligence tests evaluate our abilities to solve

intelligence
the capacity for goal-directed and adaptive behavior. Involves the abilities to profit from experience, solve problems, and reason effectively.

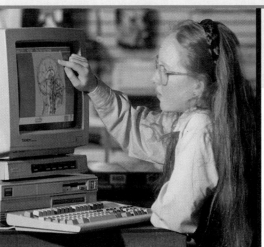

A common challenge   While their crafts look as different as their clothing and setting, these children have much in common: They are working to perfect skills their societies deem important—to become "intelligent" in their culture's terms.

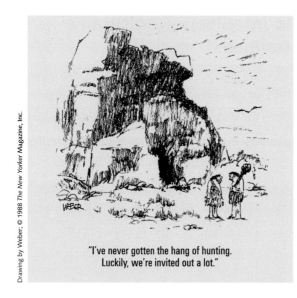

"I've never gotten the hang of hunting. Luckily, we're invited out a lot."

Drawing by Weber; © 1988 The New Yorker Magazine, Inc.

Charles Spearman (1863–1945), who helped develop factor analysis, believed there is also a general intelligence, or g, factor that underlies the specific factors. People often have special abilities that stand out, Spearman allowed. But those who score high on one factor, such as verbal intelligence, typically score higher than average on other factors, such as spatial or reasoning ability. So there is at least a small tendency for different abilities to come in the same package. Spearman believed that this commonality, the g factor, underlies all of our intelligent behavior, from excelling in school to navigating the sea.

This idea of a general mental capacity expressed by a single intelligence score was controversial in Spearman's day, and it remains so in our own. Opposing Spearman, L. L. Thurstone (1887–1955) gave 56 different tests to people. By analyzing the results mathematically, he identified eight clusters of "primary mental abilities," such as word fluency, memory, and reasoning. Thurstone did not rank his subjects on a single scale of general aptitude. But when other investigators studied the profiles of his subjects, they detected a small tendency for those who excelled in one of the eight clusters to score well on the others. So, they concluded, there was still some evidence of a g factor.

We might, then, liken mental abilities to physical abilities. Athleticism is not one thing but many. The ability to run fast is distinct from brute strength, which is distinct from the eye-hand coordination required to throw a ball on target. A champion weightlifter rarely has the potential to be a skilled ice skater. Yet there remains some tendency for good things to come packaged together—for running speed and throwing accuracy to correlate, thanks to general athletic ability. Likewise, intelligence involves several distinct abilities, which cluster together in the same individual often enough to define a small general intelligence factor.

various problems effectively, regardless of our cultural backgrounds. If a person can recite a string of eight digits in reverse order on an intelligence test, or can find the missing element in a picture, that person probably will also have an edge at solving all sorts of other problems, from taking tests in school to navigating the sea to growing corn.

Is Intelligence One General Ability or Several Specific Abilities?

We all know some people talented in science, others in creative writing, and still others in art, music, or dance. Perhaps you have known a talented artist who is dumbfounded by the simplest mathematical problems, or a brilliant math student who has little aptitude for literary discussion. We may therefore wonder whether people's mental abilities are too diverse to justify labeling them with the single word *intelligence* or quantifying them with a number from some single scale.

The Factor-Analysis Approach

To find out whether there might be a general ability factor that runs throughout our specific mental abilities, psychologists study how various abilities relate to one another. A statistical method called factor analysis allows researchers to identify clusters of test items that measure a common ability. For example, people who do well on vocabulary items often do well on paragraph comprehension. This cluster helps define a verbal intelligence factor. Other clusters include a spatial ability factor and a reasoning ability factor.

Contemporary Theories of Multiple Intelligences

Howard Gardner (1983, 1993a,b, 1995) supports Thurstone's idea that intelligence comes in different packages. He notes that brain damage may diminish one type of ability but not others. Gardner also studies reports of people with exceptional abilities, including those who excel in only one. People with savant syndrome, for example, score at the low end on intelligence tests but have an island of brilliance—some incredible ability, as in computation, drawing, or musical memory (Figure 11.1). These people may have virtually no lan-

factor analysis
a statistical procedure that identifies clusters of related items (called *factors*) on a test; used to identify different dimensions of performance that underlie one's total score.

general intelligence (*g*)
a general intelligence factor that Spearman and others believed underlies specific mental abilities and is therefore measured by every task on an intelligence test.

savant syndrome
a condition in which a person otherwise limited in mental ability has an amazing specific skill, such as in computation or drawing.

Figure **11.1**

guage ability, yet may be able to compute numbers as quickly and accurately as an electronic calculator, or identify almost instantly the day of the week that corresponds to any given date in history.

Using such evidence, Gardner argues that we do not have *an* intelligence, but instead have *multiple* intelligences, each independent of the others. In addition to the verbal and mathematical aptitudes assessed by the standard tests, he identifies distinct aptitudes for musical accomplishment, for spatially analyzing the visual world, for mastering movement skills (as in dance), and for insightfully understanding ourselves, others, and our natural environment. As exemplars of these alternative intellects he offers poet T. S. Eliot, scientist Albert Einstein, composer Igor Stravinsky, artist Pablo Picasso, dancer Martha Graham, psychiatrist Sigmund Freud, leader Mahatma Gandhi, and naturalist Charles Darwin. According to Gardner, the computer programmer, the poet, the street-smart adolescent who becomes a crafty executive, and the point guard on the basketball team exhibit different kinds of intelligence. A general intelligence score is therefore like the overall rating of a city—which doesn't give you much specific information about its schools, roads, or nightlife.

Wouldn't it be wonderful if the world were so just, responds intelligence researcher Sandra Scarr (1989), that being weak in any area would be compensated by genius in some other area? Alas, the world is not just, for there remains some tendency for different skills to correlate. For example, people with mental disadvantages often have lesser physical abilities as well; thus, we hold Special Olympics to give them a chance to enjoy fair competition.

Moreover, Gardner's critics question, does it really make sense to lump all sorts of abilities under the concept of intelligence? Are not some, such as verbal and reasoning skills, really more crucial than others? Intelligence is *mental* ability, they say. The abilities that we can manage without, as in music and athletics, are better considered *talents* than intelligences. If people lack physical talent, do we consider them as lacking an *intelligence*? Gardner believes all forms of intelligence have intrinsic value—it is one's culture and context that place greater value on some capacities than on others.

Practical Intelligence

Robert Sternberg, Richard Wagner, and their colleagues (1993, 1995) agree with Gardner's idea of multiple intelligences, but they distinguish more simply among three intelligences:

- **Academic problem-solving skills** These are the skills assessed by intelligence tests, which present well-defined problems having a single right answer.

- **Practical intelligence** This type of intelligence is often required for everyday tasks, which are frequently ill-defined, with multiple solutions.

- **Creative intelligence** This type of intelligence is demonstrated in reacting to novel situations.

Intelligence tests predict school grades reasonably well but predict vocational success less well. Managerial success, for example, depends less on the academic abilities assessed by an intelligence test score (assuming the score is average or above) than

Drawing by Reilly; © 1988 The New Yorker Magazine, Inc.

"You're wise, but you lack tree smarts."

on a shrewd ability to manage oneself, one's tasks, and other people. Sternberg and Wagner's test of practical managerial intelligence measures whether the test-taker knows how to write effective memos, how to motivate people, when to delegate tasks and responsibilities, how to read people, and how to promote their own careers. Business executives who score high on this test tend to earn higher salaries and receive better performance ratings than do those who score low. People who demonstrate keen practical intelligence may or may not have distinguished themselves in school. In a similar finding, Stephen Ceci and Jeffrey Liker (1986) report that racetrack fans' expertise in handicapping horses—a practical but complex cognitive task—is unrelated to their intelligence test scores.

Emotional Intelligence

Also distinct from academic intelligence is what Nancy Cantor and John Kihlstrom (1987) first called *social intelligence*—the know-how involved in comprehending social situations and managing oneself successfully. Seymour Epstein and Petra Meier (1989) agreed. If academic aptitude signifies social competence, they asked, why then are high-aptitude people "not, by a wide margin, more effective . . . in achieving better marriages, in successfully raising their children, and in achieving better mental and physical well-being?" Consistent with this distinction between academic and social intelligence is the repeated finding that college grades only modestly predict later work achievement (Bretz, 1989; Dye & Reck, 1989).

A critical part of social intelligence is what Peter Salovey and John Mayer (1990; Mayer & Salovey, 1993, 1995, 1997) call emotional intelligence—the ability to perceive, express, understand, and regulate emotions. Emotionally intelligent people are self-aware. They can manage their emotions with-

out being hijacked by overwhelming depression, anxiety, or anger. They can delay gratification in pursuit of big rewards, rather than being overtaken by their impulses. Their empathy allows them to read others' emotions. They handle others' emotions skillfully, and thus manage conflicts well. Simply said, they are emotionally smart, and thus they often succeed in careers, marriages, and parenting where other academically smarter (but emotionally less intelligent) people fail.

Given the significance of practical and emotional intelligence, researchers are now wondering: Can we assess these success-enabling alternative intelligences? Can we teach practical and emotional intelligence to schoolchildren? Can we stimulate their creative problem-solving abilities and their abilities to read and manage emotions (Goleman, 1995)? These questions define a new frontier in the study of intelligence (the capacity for goal-directed, adaptive behavior).

In defense of academic smarts—the *g* factor—other researchers point to studies in which intelligence scores *do* predict both occupational status and job performance (Hunt, 1995; Jensen, 1993; Schmidt & Hunter, 1993). Intelligence matters most in mentally demanding jobs. Meteorology more than meter reading requires intelligence to excel. However, once admitted to a vocation, those who become highly successful have other traits as well—they are conscientious, well-connected, and doggedly energetic. Thus, high intelligence does more to get you into a profession (via the schools and training programs that take you there) than it does to make you successful, once there.

So it seems that the academic aptitude tapped by intelligence tests is indeed central to our lives. Yet personal competence in everyday living requires much that traditional intelligence tests do not measure.

Is Intelligence Neurologically Measurable?

Using today's neuroscience tools, might we link differences in people's intelligence test performance to dissimilarities in the heart of smarts—the brain? Might there soon, as some have predicted, be neurological tests of intelligence?

Does this have a familiar ring? More than a century after Francis Galton's futile attempts to gauge intelligence in terms of head size, reaction times, and sensory abilities, his urge to reduce intelligence to simple brain measures still lives. Today's efforts ask whether intelligence scores correlate with brain anatomy or brain functioning.

emotional intelligence
the ability to perceive, express, understand, and regulate emotions.

Brain Size and Intelligence

Even before Galton, the phrenologist Franz Gall realized that human intelligence surpasses animal intelligence because the human cortex is more developed. He therefore wondered whether intelligence differences among humans might similarly be due to differing brain structures, detectable in skull protrusions. Although his efforts to gauge mental abilities failed, as did Galton's, 25 modern studies do reveal a slight +.15 correlation between head size (relative to body size) and intelligence score (Jensen & Johnson, 1994).

Maybe the correlation from modern studies of brain size and intelligence is so near zero (and was therefore undetectable in the nineteenth-century analyses) because head size is a weak proxy for brain size. There is, after all, more inside the skull than cortical tissue. Newer studies that directly measure brain volume using MRI scans reveal a more significant correlation of +.44 between brain size (adjusted for body size) and intelligence score (Rushton & Ankney, 1996). Moreover, as adults age, brain size and nonverbal intelligence test scores fall in concert (Bigler & others, 1995).

Efforts to link brain structure with cognition continue. One ongoing project is giving tests of abilities and personality to cancer patients with poor prognoses, and then collecting their brains for study after their deaths (Witelson & McCulloch, 1991). Should intelligence correlate with brain size, the cause could be differing genes, nutrition, environmental stimulation, some combination of these, or who knows what else. Recall from earlier chapters that experience alters the brain. Rats raised in a stimulating rather than deprived environment develop thicker, heavier cortexes. And learning leaves detectable traces in our brain's neural connections.

Brain Function and Intelligence

Even if the modest correlations between brain anatomy and intelligence prove reliable, they hardly explain intelligence differences. Searching for other explanations, neuroscientists are studying the brain's functioning. R. J. Haier (1993) and Randolph Parks and his colleagues (1988) have done PET scans while people with high or low abilities perform cognitive tasks. High performers' brains are *less* active (they guzzle less glucose energy). This link between ability on a task and neurological efficiency holds true whether one compares more intelligent people with less intelligent people, or one compares those who have had more opportunity to master the task with those who have had less opportunity.

Are more intelligent people literally more quick-witted? On some tasks they seem to be. Earl Hunt (1983) found that verbal intelligence scores are predictable from the speed with which people retrieve information from memory. Those who recognize quickly that *SINK* and *wink* are different words, or that *A* and *a* share the same name, tend to score high in verbal ability. Extremely precocious 12- to 14-year-old college students are especially quick in responding to such tasks (Jensen, 1989).

Across many studies, the correlation between the speed of intake of perceptual information and intelligence score tends to be about +.4 (Deary & Stough, 1996). A typical experiment flashes an incomplete stimulus, as in Figure 11.2. Its lingering afterimage is immediately masked by a stimulus that overrides it. Then the subject is asked whether the long side appeared on the right or left. How much stimulus inspection time would you need to answer correctly 80 percent of the time? Perhaps .01 second? Or .02 second? People who perceive quickly tend to score somewhat higher on intelligence tests, particularly tests based on perceptual rather than verbal problem solving.

Do the quicker perceptions of highly intelligent people reflect greater neurological speed? Repeated studies have found that their brain waves register a simple stimulus (such as a flash of light or a tone beep) more quickly and with greater complexity (Caryl, 1994; Deary & Caryl, 1993; Reed & Jensen, 1992). The evoked brain response also tends to be slightly faster when people with high intelligence scores perform a simple task, such as pushing a button when an *X* appears on a screen (McGarry-Roberts & others, 1992).

Neural processing speed on a simple task seems far removed from the untimed responses to complex intelligence test items, such as "In what way are *wool* and *cotton* alike?" As yet, notes intelligence expert Nathan Brody (1992), we have no firm understanding of *why* speedy reactions on simple tasks should predict intelligence test performance.

Recall from Chapter 1 that the lowest correlation, –1.0, represents perfect disagreement between two sets of scores—as the first score goes up, the second goes down. A correlation of zero represents no consistency. The highest correlation, +1.0, represents perfect consistency—as the first score goes up, so does the second.

Figure **11.2**

An inspection time task People who can perceive the stimulus very quickly tend to score somewhat higher on intelligence tests. (Adapted from Deary & Stough, 1996.)

Stimulus   Mask

Question: Long side on left or right?

aptitude test
a test designed to predict a person's future performance; aptitude is the capacity to learn.

achievement test
a test designed to assess what a person has learned.

Philip Vernon (1983) has speculated that "faster cognitive processing may allow more information to be acquired." Perhaps people who more quickly process information accumulate more information—about wool, cotton, and millions of other things.

The neurological approach to understanding intelligence (and so many other things in psychology) is currently in its heyday. Will this new research achieve Galton's aim of reducing what we now call the *g* factor to simple measures of underlying brain activity? Or are these efforts totally wrongheaded because what we call intelligence is not a single general trait but several culturally adaptive skills? The controversies surrounding the nature of intelligence are a long way from resolution.

SUMMING UP

It is misleading to reify concepts such as "intelligence" and "giftedness"—to regard these abstract concepts as if they were real, concrete things. To most psychologists, intelligence is the capacity for goal-directed and adaptive behavior.

Is Intelligence Culturally Defined? Some psychologists argue that intelligent behavior (say, a person's ability to adapt successfully to the demands of school or work) is culturally relative; others contend that intelligence is a culture-free ability to solve all sorts of problems.

Is Intelligence One General Ability or Several Specific Abilities? Psychologists agree that people have specific abilities, such as verbal and mathematical aptitudes. However, they debate whether a general intelligence (*g*) factor runs through them all. Factor analysis and studies of special conditions, such as the savant syndrome, have identified clusters of mental aptitudes.

Is Intelligence Neurologically Measurable? Galton's efforts to gauge intelligence in terms of simple brain measures have been reborn in today's efforts to correlate intelligence scores with brain anatomy and functioning. Several studies report a very slight correlation between head size (adjusted for body size) and intelligence test score, and a slightly greater (though still modest) correlation between brain size and intelligence test score. Other studies suggest that the brains of highly skilled people require less glucose energy while performing certain cognitive tasks. Highly intelli-

gent people also tend to take in information more quickly and to show faster brain wave responses to simple stimuli such as a flash of light. Time will tell whether these new neurological approaches to intelligence will bear important fruit. If they do, researchers will surely debate the extent to which nature and nurture affect the brain's structure and functioning.

KEY TERMS AND CONCEPTS intelligence, factor analysis, general intelligence (*g*), savant syndrome, emotional intelligence

Assessing Intelligence

What is the difference between an aptitude test and an achievement test? What does it mean for such tests to be standardized, reliable, and valid?

Modern Tests of Mental Abilities

What is intelligence? Movie hero Forrest Gump's answer, "Stupid is as stupid does," catches the spirit of psychology's simplest answer: Intelligent is as intelligent does, on an IQ test. In other words, intelligence is whatever intelligence tests measure. So, what are these tests, and what makes a test credible?

By this point in your life, you've faced dozens of abilities tests: elementary school tests of basic reading and math skills, course examinations, intelligence tests, driver's license examinations, and college entrance examinations, to name just a few. Psychologists classify such tests as either aptitude tests, intended to *predict* your ability to learn a new skill, or achievement tests, intended to *reflect* what you have learned. Thus, a college entrance exam, which seeks to predict your ability to do college work, is an aptitude test. Exams covering what you have learned in this course are achievement tests.

The actual differences between aptitude tests and achievement tests are not so clear-cut. Your achieved vocabulary influences your score on most aptitude tests. Similarly, your aptitudes for learning and test-taking influence your grades on tests of your course achievement. Most tests, whether labeled aptitude or achievement, assess both ability and its development. Practically speaking, how-

Matching patterns Block design puzzles test the ability to analyze patterns. Wechsler's individually administered intelligence test comes in forms suited for adults (WAIS) and children (WISC).

Wechsler Adult Intelligence Scale (WAIS)
the WAIS is the most widely used intelligence test; contains verbal and performance (nonverbal) subtests.

ever, aptitude tests predict future performance and achievement tests assess current performance.

Today's most widely used intelligence test, the Wechsler Adult Intelligence Scale (WAIS), was created by psychologist David Wechsler, who, as a 6-year-old Romanian boy, was among the supposedly feeble-minded Eastern European immigrants of the early 1900s. Later he developed a similar test for school-age children, called the Wechsler Intelligence Scale for Children (WISC), and still later a test for preschool children. The WAIS con-

sists of 11 subtests, as illustrated in Figure 11.3. It yields not only an overall intelligence score, as does the Stanford-Binet, but also separate "verbal" and "performance" (nonverbal) scores. Striking differences between the two scores alert the examiner to possible learning problems. For example, a verbal score much lower than the same person's performance score might indicate a reading or language disability. The tests also provide clues to cognitive strengths that a teacher or an employer might build upon.

Figure **11.3**

Sample items from the Wechsler Adult Intelligence Scale (WAIS) subtests (From Thorndike & Hagen, 1977.)

VERBAL

General Information
What day of the year is Independence Day?

Similarities
In what way are *wool* and *cotton* alike?

Arithmetic Reasoning
If eggs cost 60 cents a dozen, what does 1 egg cost?

Vocabulary
Tell me the meaning of corrupt.

Comprehension
Why do people buy fire insurance?

Digit Span
Listen carefully, and when I am through, say the numbers right after me.

7   3   4   1   8   6

Now I am going to say some more numbers, but I want you to say them backward.

3   8   4   1   6

PERFORMANCE

Picture Completion
I am going to show you a picture with an important part missing. Tell me what is missing.

'85

SUN	MON	TUE	WED	THU	FRI	SAT
1	2	3	4	5	6	7
8	9	10	11	12	13	14
15	16	17	18	19	20	21
22	23	24	25	26	27	28
29	30					

Picture Arrangement
The pictures below tell a story. Put them in the right order to tell the story.

Block Design
Using the four blocks, make one just like this.

Object Assembly
If these pieces are put together correctly, they will make something. Go ahead and put them together as quickly as you can.

Digit-Symbol Substitution

Code

△	○	⟋	✕	8
1	2	3	4	5

Test

△	8	✕	○	△	⟋	8	✕	△	8

standardization
defining meaningful scores
by comparison with the
performance of a pretested
"standardization group."

normal curve
the symmetrical bell-shaped
curve that describes the distribution of many physical and
psychological attributes. Most
scores fall near the average,
and fewer and fewer scores
lie near the extremes.

Principles of Test Construction

To be widely accepted, psychological tests must meet three criteria: They must be *standardized, reliable*, and *valid*. The Stanford-Binet and Wechsler tests meet these requirements.

Standardization

Knowing how many questions you got right on an intelligence test would tell us almost nothing. To evaluate your performance, we need a basis for comparing it with others' performance. To enable meaningful comparisons, test-makers first give the test to a representative sample of people. When other individuals take the test, we can then compare their scores with the standards defined by this group. This process of defining meaningful scores relative to a pretested group is called standardization.

Recall that Terman and his colleagues recognized that items developed for Parisians did not provide a satisfactory standard for evaluating Americans. So they revised the test and standardized the new version by testing 2300 native-born, white Americans of differing socioeconomic levels. Ironically, they then evaluated nonwhite American and immigrant groups based on this standard (Van Leeuwen, 1982).

Standardized test results typically form a *normal distribution*, a bell-shaped pattern of scores that forms the normal curve (Figure 11.4). Whether we are measuring people's heights, weights, or mental aptitudes, most scores tend to cluster around the average. On an intelligence test, we call this average score 100. As we move out from the average (toward either extreme) we find fewer and fewer people. Within each age group, the Stanford-Binet and the Wechsler tests assign any person a score according to how much that person's performance deviates above or below the average. As Figure 11.4 shows, a performance higher than all but 2 percent of all scores earns an intelligence score of 130. A raw score that is comparably *below* 98 percent of all the scores earns an intelligence score of 70.

The Stanford-Binet and the Wechsler scales are periodically restandardized to keep the average score near 100. If you took the revised WAIS recently, your performance was compared with a standardization sample who took the test between 1976 and 1980, not to David Wechsler's initial 1930s sample. When we compare the performance of the most recent standardization sample with that of the 1930s sample, do you suppose we find rising or declining test performance? Amazingly—given that college entrance aptitude scores were dropping during the 1960s and 1970s—intelligence test performance has been *improving*. This worldwide phenomenon is called the *Flynn effect* in honor of New Zealand researcher James Flynn (1987, 1996), who first calculated its magnitude. As Figure 11.5 indicates, if we assign a recent average performance a score of 100, then on the same scale the average performance 70 years earlier was a 76. Such rising performance has been observed in 20 countries. The increase seems real and is now widely accepted as an important phenomenon, because it suggests either a problem with the tests or that intelligence is changeable. Moreover, it counters the belief among Galton's modern-day followers that higher birthrates among those with lower IQ scores are taking human intelligence downward.

What an intriguing puzzle: Are aptitudes decreasing, as some have inferred from the decline in college aptitude test scores, or are they rising, as intelligence test data suggest? The college aptitude

Figure **11.4**

The normal curve Scores on aptitude tests tend to form a normal, or bell-shaped, curve. For example, the Wechsler scale calls the average score 100.

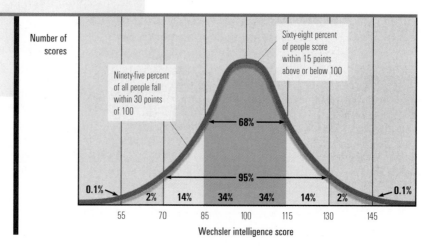

Number of scores

Ninety-five percent of all people fall within 30 points of 100

Sixty-eight percent of people score within 15 points above or below 100

68%

95%

0.1%   2%   14%   34%   34%   14%   2%   0.1%

55   70   85   100   115   130   145

Wechsler intelligence score

decline is due partly to the greater academic diversity of the students who began taking the test during the 1960s. The WAIS, however, has always been standardized on a more diverse and broadly representative group. Such people—people in general—have become more literate and better educated since the 1930s. These facts help explain why performance on the more complex college aptitude tests dropped while performance rose on the basic skills tested by the WAIS. Others have speculated the gains may result from improved nutrition, experience with testing, or some unknown factor. Mysteriously, the gains are greatest on nonverbal tests that improved schooling should least affect. (Perhaps playing with Legos, mazes, and video games like Tetris has helped, though the increase started before all these were popular.) Flynn finds it hard to imagine that his generation is so much smarter than his grandparents', yet he also finds the data hard to dismiss. "I'm baffled," he says.

Reliability

Comparing your test scores to those of the standardizing group still won't tell us much about you unless the test has reliability. A good test must yield dependably consistent scores. To check a test's reliability, researchers retest people using the same test or another form of it. If the two scores generally agree, or *correlate*, the test is reliable. Alternatively, the researcher may split a test in half and see whether scores derived from odd and even questions agree.

The higher the correlation between the *test-retest* or the *split-half* scores, the higher the test's reliability. The tests we have considered so far—the Stanford-Binet, the WAIS, and the WISC—all

What an intriguing puzzle: Are aptitudes decreasing, as some have inferred from the decline in college aptitude test scores, or are they rising, as intelligence test data suggest?

have reliabilities of about +.9, which is very high. In retests, people's scores tend to match their first score closely.

Validity

High reliability does not ensure a test's validity—the extent to which the test actually measures what it is supposed to measure or predicts what it is supposed to predict. If you use a shrunken tape measure to measure people's heights, your data would have high reliability (consistency) but low validity. How, then, can we determine whether a test is valid? For some tests, it is enough that they have content validity, which means the test taps the pertinent behavior. The road test for a driver's license has content validity because it samples the tasks a driver routinely faces. Your course exams have content validity if they assess your mastery of a representative sample of course material.

We evaluate other tests in terms of how well they agree with some criterion, an independent measure of what the test aims to assess. For some tests, the criterion is future performance. For example, aptitude tests must have predictive validity (also called criterion-related validity), which means they predict future achievement.

reliability the extent to which a test yields consistent results, as assessed by the consistency of scores on two halves of the test, on alternate forms of the test, or on retesting.

validity the extent to which a test measures or predicts what it is supposed to. (See also *content validity* and *predictive validity*.)

content validity the extent to which a test samples the behavior that is of interest (such as a driving test that samples driving tasks).

criterion the behavior (such as college grades) that a test (such as the SAT) is designed to predict; thus, the measure used in defining whether the test has predictive validity.

predictive validity the success with which a test predicts the behavior it is designed to predict; it is assessed by computing the correlation between test scores and the criterion behavior. (Also called *criterion-related validity*.)

Figure 11.5

Getting smarter? In every country studied, intelligence test performance has been rising, as shown here with American Wechsler and Stanford-Binet test performance between 1918 and 1989. In Britain, test scores have risen 27 points since 1942. (From Hogan, 1995.)

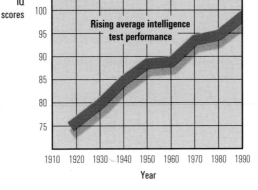

THINKING CRITICALLY ABOUT

Test-Preparation Courses

Suppose that after taking the Scholastic Assessment Test (SAT), the Law School Aptitude Test (LSAT), the Medical College Admission Test (MCAT), or the Graduate Record Examination (GRE), you were disappointed by your score. By enrolling in one of the widely advertised test-preparation courses, could you count on increasing your score when retaking the test? Or is your score on the test likely to be stable?

Being familiar with a test and knowing how to pace yourself on it does help. But the test-makers themselves offer you a sample test that is easily available. Beyond this, does it pay to sign up for a crash test-preparation course? These courses help people brush up on their academic knowledge, especially in mathematics. They may also provide a few useful tips about how to take the test. For instance, on the first questions in a section, which 80 percent or more people get right, the most obvious answer is usually correct; on the final questions, which more than 75 percent typically get wrong, the "obvious" answer is often wrong.

Despite the test-relevant teaching and the test-taking clues that SAT-preparation courses provide, and contrary to advertised claims, sev-

eral research reviews have concluded that a 20-hour coaching course increases math and verbal scores by an average of only about 15 points and 10 points, respectively, on the 200- to 800-point scale (Bond, 1989; ETS, 1994). This small boost is greatest on test items that have complex and possibly confusing formats (Powers, 1986). So, for the SAT at least, the best advice is to take rigorous academic

courses, brush up on algebra and geometry, and familiarize yourself with the test. "Hard work in demanding courses still seems the best way to prepare" for academic aptitude tests, advises Nancy Cole (1995), president of Educational Testing Service, which develops the tests. Having done that, you need not feel intimidated by those who have also taken a test-preparation course.

"I'm studying for my IQ test."

Are general aptitude tests as predictive as they are reliable? As critics are fond of noting, the answer is plainly no. The predictive power of aptitude tests is fairly strong in the early grades, but later it weakens. Academic aptitude test scores are reasonably good predictors of achievement in elementary school, where the correlation between intelligence score and grades is about +.60 (Jensen, 1980). The Scholastic Assessment Test (SAT), used in the United States as a college entrance exam, is less successful in predicting first-year college grades; here, the correlation is less than +.50

Figure 11.6

Diminishing predictive power Let's imagine a correlation between football linemen's body weight and their success on the field. Note how insignificant the relationship becomes when we narrow the range of weights to 250 to 290 pounds. As the range of data under consideration narrows, its predictive power diminishes.

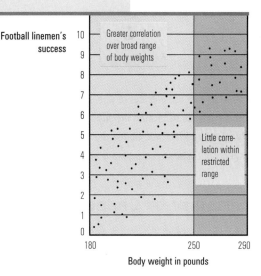

(Willingham & others, 1990). By the time we get to the Graduate Record Examination (GRE) (an assessment test similar to the SAT but for those applying to graduate school), the correlation with graduate school grades is an even more modest +.30 (GRE, 1990).

Why does the predictive power of aptitude scores diminish as students move up the educational ladder? Consider a parallel situation: Among all football linemen, body weight correlates with success. A 270-pound player tends to overwhelm a 190-pound opponent. But within the narrow 250- to 290-pound range typically found at the professional level, the correlation between weight and success becomes negligible (Figure 11.6). The narrower the *range* of weights, the lower the predictive power of body weight becomes.

Likewise, if Harvard takes only students with really high assessment scores, their hardly-varying scores can't possibly predict much. A similar narrowing of range explains why the GRE is only a modest predictor of graduate school grades. If a graduate school admits only those students whose assessment scores fall within a narrow range, it should not surprise us that their assessment scores will not closely predict their grades. This will be true even if the test has excellent predictive validity with a more diverse sample of students. So, when we validate a test using a wide range of people but then use it with a restricted range of people, it loses much of its predictive validity. A narrowed range of grades—as in graduate school departments that award mostly A's and B's—similarly reduces predictive validity.

SUMMING UP

Modern Tests of Mental Abilities Tests are commonly classified as either aptitude tests (designed to predict learning ability, as is the Wechsler) or achievement tests (designed to assess current competence).

Principles of Test Construction A good test must be *standardized*, so that any person's performance can be meaningfully compared to others'; *reliable*, so it yields dependably consistent scores; and *valid*, so it measures what it is supposed to measure. Test scores usually fall into a bell-shaped distribution, the normal curve. The average score is assigned an arbitrary number (such as 100 on an intelligence test). Aptitude tests tend to be highly reliable, but they are weak predictors of success in life. Their predictive validity for academic success is fairly strong in the early grades, however. Test validity weakens for predicting grades in college and even more so in graduate school, as the range of student abilities becomes more restricted.

KEY TERMS AND CONCEPTS aptitude test, achievement test, Wechsler Adult Intelligence Scale (WAIS), standardization, normal curve, reliability, validity, content validity, criterion, predictive validity (criterion-related validity)

mental retardation
a condition of limited mental ability, as indicated by an intelligence score below 70, that produces difficulty in adapting to the demands of life; varies from mild to profound.

Down syndrome
a condition of retardation and associated physical disorders caused by an extra chromosome in one's genetic makeup.

The Dynamics of Intelligence

We now can answer some age-old questions about the dynamics of human intelligence—about its stability over the life span, about the extremes of intelligence, and about that special ability called creativity.

Stability or Change?

If we retested people periodically throughout their lives, would their intelligence scores be stable? Chapter 4 explored the stability of intelligence in later life. What about the stability of intelligence scores early in life?

How smart is this baby? Infants' preference for novel stimuli is a moderate predictor of future intelligence. This researcher in Joseph Fagan's laboratory briefly shows an infant a previously seen picture alongside a new picture, recording how many seconds the child looks at each.

The search for indicators of infants' later intelligence has left few stones unturned. Unable to talk with infants, developmental researchers have assessed what they can observe—everything from birth weight, to whether the third toe was longer than the second, to age of sitting up alone. None of these measures provides any useful prediction of intelligence scores at much later ages (Bell & Waldrop, 1989; Broman, 1989). Perhaps, as developmental psychologist Nancy Bayley reflected in 1949, "we have not yet found the right tests." Someday, she speculated, we might find "infant behaviors which are characteristic of underlying intellectual functions" and which will predict later intelligence.

Such a test may have been found. Two dozen studies by Joseph Fagan, Marc Bornstein, John

Ironically, SAT and GRE scores correlate better with each other than either does with its intended criterion, school achievement. Thus, their reliability far exceeds their predictive validity. If either test was much affected by coaching, luck, or how one feels on the test day (as so many people believe), such reliability would be impossible.

Columbo, and others reveal that 2- to 7-month-old babies who quickly grow bored with a picture—who, given a choice, prefer to look at a new one—score higher on intelligence tests up to 11 years later (McCall & Carriger, 1993; Neisser & others, 1996). Although the prediction is crude, the tests can help identify children likely to be extremely below or above average.

So, can everyday observations or intelligence test scores now predict preschoolers' future performance and educational needs? The question is especially interesting to new parents wondering about their baby's intelligence and to educators wanting an early identification of children with special needs. Those anxious about comparing their baby with others can relax. Except for extremely impaired or very precocious children, casual observation and intelligence tests before age 3 predict children's future aptitudes only minimally (Humphreys & Davey, 1988). For example, children who are early talkers—talking in sentences typical of 3-year-olds by age 20 months—are *not* especially likely to be reading by age 4½ (Crain-Thoreson & Dale, 1992). (A better predictor of early reading is having parents who have read lots of stories to you.) Even Albert Einstein was slow in learning to talk (Quasha, 1980).

By age 3, however, children's performances on intelligence tests begin to predict their adolescent and adult scores. Moreover, high-scoring adolescents tend to have been early readers. One study surveyed the parents of 187 seventh- and eighth-graders who had taken a college aptitude test as part of a seven-state talent search and had scored considerably higher than most high school seniors. If their parents' memories can be trusted, more than half of this precocious group of adolescents began reading by age 4 and more than 80 percent were reading by age 5 (Van Tassel-Baska, 1983). Not surprisingly, then, intelligence tests given in kindergarten begin to predict school achievement (Tramontana & others, 1988).

After about age 7, intelligence test scores, though certainly not fixed, become even more stable (Bloom, 1964). Thus, the consistency of scores over time increases with the age of the child. The

> "My dear Adele, I am 4 years old and I can read any English book. I can say all the Latin Substantives and Adjectives and active verbs besides 52 lines of Latin poetry."
>
> **FRANCIS GALTON**
> *LETTER TO HIS SISTER*
> 1827

remarkable stability of aptitude scores by late adolescence is seen in an Educational Testing Service study of 23,000 students who took the SAT and then later took its more advanced counterpart, the GRE, which is taken by many college seniors (Angoff, 1988). On either test, verbal scores correlate only modestly with math scores—revealing that these two aptitudes are distinct. Yet scores on the SAT verbal test correlated +.86 with the scores on GRE verbal tests taken four to five years later. An equally astonishing +.86 correlation occurred between the two math tests. In view of the time lapse and differing educational experiences of these 23,000 students, the stability of their aptitude scores is remarkable—surely beyond what any of us would have predicted.

Extremes of Intelligence

One way to glimpse the validity and significance of any test is to compare people who score at the two extremes of the normal curve. The two groups should differ noticeably, and they do.

The Challenged

At one extreme are people whose intelligence test scores fall below 70. To be labeled as having mental retardation, a child must have both a low test score *and* difficulty adapting to the normal demands of living independently. Only about 1 percent of the population meets both criteria, with males outnumbering females by 50 percent (American Psychiatric Association, 1994). As Table 11.1 indicates, most such mentally challenged individuals can, with support, live in mainstream society.

Mental retardation sometimes results from known physical causes. One such case is Down syndrome, a disorder caused by an extra chromosome in the person's genetic makeup. Most people with Down syndrome are not severely retarded.

During the last two centuries, the pendulum of opinion about how best to care for the mentally challenged has made a complete swing. Until the mid-nineteenth century, they were cared for at home. Many of those with the most severe disabilities died, but people with milder forms of retardation often found a place in a farm-based society.

> Those anxious about comparing their baby with others can relax. Except for extremely impaired or very precocious children, casual observation and intelligence tests before age 3 predict children's future aptitudes only minimally.

Degrees of Mental Retardation

Table 11.1

Level	Typical Intelligence Scores	Percentage of the Retarded	Adaptation to Demands of Life
Mild	50–70	85%	May learn academic skills up to sixth-grade level. Adults may, with assistance, achieve self-supporting social and vocational skills.
Moderate	35–49	10	May progress to second-grade level academically. Adults may contribute to their own support by labor in sheltered workshops.
Severe	20–34	3–4	May learn to talk and to perform simple work tasks under close supervision but are generally unable to profit from vocational training.
Profound	Below 20	1–2	Require constant aid and supervision.

Source: Reprinted with permission from the Diagnostic and Statistical Manual of Mental Disorders, Fourth Edition. Copyright 1994 American Psychiatric Association.

A young man with Down syndrome In the past, people with this condition were often institutionalized. We now know that with a supportive and stimulating family environment and special education, many people with Down syndrome can achieve IQs in the mildly retarded range and are capable of learning to take care of themselves and holding a job.

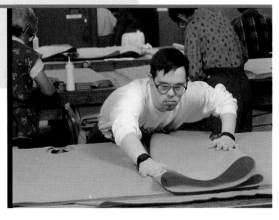

A gifted child At age 10, Lenny Ng became the youngest child to score a perfect 800 on the SAT math test. At age 16, his math project won a $20,000 scholarship in the 1993 Westinghouse Science Talent Search. Contrary to the myth that such precocious children suffer socially, high-aptitude children are typically well adjusted.

Then, residential schools for slow learners were established. By the twentieth century, many of these institutions had become warehouses, providing residents no privacy, little attention, and no hope. Parents often were told to separate themselves permanently from their impaired child before they became attached.

In the last half of the twentieth century, the pendulum swung back to normalization—allowing mentally impaired people to live in their own communities as normally as their functioning permits. We educate children with mild retardation in less restrictive environments, and we integrate, or *mainstream*, many into regular classrooms. Most grow up with their own families and then move into a protected living arrangement, such as a group home. The hope, and often the reality, is a happier and more dignified life.

The Gifted

In one famous project begun in 1921, Lewis Terman studied more than 1500 California schoolchildren with IQ scores over 135. Contrary to the popular myth that intellectually gifted children are frequently maladjusted because they are "in a different world" from their nongifted peers, Terman's high-scoring children were unusually healthy, well adjusted, and academically successful. When restudied over the next six decades, most of these people had attained high levels of education (Goleman, 1980). Their vocational success varied, yet the group included many doctors, lawyers, professors, scientists, and writers. Terman's whiz kids remind one of Jean Piaget, who by age 7 was devoting his free time to studying birds, fossils, and machines; who by age 15 began publishing scientific articles on mollusks; and who later went on to become this century's most famous developmental psychologist (Hunt, 1993).

Critics nevertheless question many of the assumptions of currently popular "gifted child" programs, such as the belief that only 3 to 5 percent of children are gifted and that it pays to identify and label these special few—to segregate them and give them academic enrichment not available to the 95 percent who are "ungifted." This is one example of "tracking"—placing students in separate classes with others who share their level of aptitude score. Many research studies conclude that students tracked by aptitude have academic achievement scores hardly higher than similar untracked students. Moreover, ability tracking tends to lower students' self-esteem and sometimes creates a self-fulfilling prophecy, which influences those labeled "ungifted" to become so (Lipsey & Wilson, 1993; Slavin & Braddock, 1993).

A report of the Carnegie Council on Adolescent Development (1989) therefore condemned academic tracking as "one of the most divisive and damaging school practices in existence." Denying "low-ability" students opportunities for enriched education serves to widen the achievement gap between the two groups and to increase their social isolation from one another, one reason why there is no tracking in the elementary schools of Japan and China (Stevenson & Lee, 1990). Because minority and low-income youth are more often placed in lower academic groups, tracking can also promote segregation and prejudice—hardly a healthy preparation for working and living in a multicultural society.

Sorting children into gifted and nongifted groups often presumes that giftedness is a single trait—measured by an intelligence test—rather than one of many potentials. Newspaper and magazine articles advise parents on how to spot "the signs of giftedness" in their children, as if giftedness were an objective quality, like blue eyes, that a child either has or lacks. This reifies giftedness—by creating the concept and then presuming that it has a concrete reality. It ignores the fact that we, not nature, are deciding the criteria of giftedness.

"Alpha children wear grey. They work much harder than we do, because they're so frightfully clever. I'm really awfully glad I'm a Beta, because I don't work so hard. And then we are much better than the Gammas and Deltas. Gammas are stupid."

ALDOUS HUXLEY
BRAVE NEW WORLD
1932

Everyone held up their crackers as David threw the cheese log into the ceiling fan.

Reprinted with permission of Paul Soderblom.

Critics and proponents of gifted education agree on this much, however: Children have differing gifts. Some are especially good at math, others at verbal reasoning, others at art, still others at social leadership. It is a maxim of biology that nature prefers diversity. By packaging different gifts in different bodies, nature enhances a group's welfare and the odds that some will survive environmental challenges. Educating children as if all were alike is as naive as assuming that giftedness is something you either have or don't have. One needn't hang value-laden labels on children to affirm their special talents and to challenge all at the frontiers of their own abilities and understandings.

Creativity and Intelligence

Creativity is the ability to produce ideas that are both novel and valuable. The outlets for creativity vary by culture. Samoan culture encourages creativity in dance, Balinese culture in music, the African Ashanti culture in wood carvings (Lubart, 1990). In each, creativity means expressing familiar themes in novel ways.

Results from tests of intelligence and creativity suggest that a certain level of aptitude is necessary but not sufficient for creativity. In general, people with high intelligence scores do well on creativity tests. ("How many uses can you think of for a brick?") But beyond a certain level—a score of about 120—the correlation between intelligence

scores and creativity disappears. Exceptionally creative architects, mathematicians, scientists, and engineers usually score no higher on intelligence tests than do their less creative peers (MacKinnon & Hall, 1972). So there is clearly more to creativity than intelligence scores. Studies of creative people suggest five other components of creativity (Sternberg, 1988; Sternberg & Lubart, 1991, 1992):

- **The first is *expertise*—a well-developed base of knowledge.** "Chance favors only the prepared mind," observed Louis Pasteur. The more ideas, images, and phrases we have to work with, through our accumulated learning, the more chances we have to combine these mental building blocks in novel ways.

- ***Imaginative thinking skills* provide the ability to see things in new ways, to recognize patterns, to make connections.** To be creative you must first master the basic elements of a problem, then redefine or explore the problem in a new way. Copernicus first developed expertise regarding the solar system and its planets and then defined the system as revolving around the Sun, not the Earth.

- **A *venturesome personality* tolerates ambiguity and risk, perseveres in overcoming obstacles, and seeks new experiences rather than following the pack.** Inventors, for example, have a knack for persisting after failures, as Thomas Edison did in trying countless substances for his light bulb filament.

- **The *intrinsic motivation* principle of creativity is the fourth component.** As psychologist Teresa Amabile points out, "People will be most creative when they feel motivated primarily by the interest, enjoyment, satisfaction, and challenge of the work itself—rather than by external pressures" (Amabile & Hennessey, 1992). Creative people focus not so much on extrinsic motivators—meeting deadlines, impressing people, or making money—as on the intrinsic pleasure and challenge of their work.

- **A *creative environment* sparks, supports, and refines creative ideas.** After studying the careers of 2026 prominent scientists and inventors, Dean Keith Simonton (1992) noted that the most eminent among them were not lone geniuses. Rather they were mentored, challenged, and supported by their relationships with colleagues. Such people often have the emotional intelligence needed to network effectively with peers.

creativity
the ability to produce novel and valuable ideas.

On his way home from picking up a Nobel prize in Stockholm, physicist Richard Feynman stopped in Queens, New York, to look at his high school record. "My grades were not as good as I remembered," he reported, "and my IQ was [a good, though unexceptional] 124" (Faber, 1987).

Creative people focus not so much on extrinsic motivators—meeting deadlines, impressing people, or making money—as on the intrinsic pleasure and challenge of their work.

Amabile's (1983, 1987) experiments have demonstrated that creative environments also free people from concern about social approval. In one experiment, she asked college students to make paper collages, telling half beforehand that experts would evaluate their work. Those unaware that their work would be evaluated produced collages that judges later rated as more creative. Unworried about being evaluated, they felt freer to be creative.

Managers who wish to foster innovation at work should keep the intrinsic motivation principle in mind, observed Amabile (1988). They should set employees to work on activities that naturally interest them. And they can emulate managers who have successfully nurtured creativity—by providing their subordinates with time, freedom, and support to attain set goals. So it is at the 3M company, which has encouraged researchers to spend 15 percent of their time pursuing creative projects that don't have immediate payoff and where the Eleventh Commandment is "Thou shalt not kill a new product idea." From this creativity-nurturing environment have come such products as the removable Post-it notes found in most offices today (Kreitner, 1992).

More on intrinsic motivation in the next chapter.

SUMMING UP

Stability or Change? The stability of intelligence test scores increases with age, with practical predictive value beginning by age 3 and scores becoming fairly stable by age 7. Among infants, those who quickly become bored with a picture, preferring to look at a new one, tend to score well on later intelligence tests.

Extremes of Intelligence Comparing those who score extremely low (the "challenged," or mentally retarded) with those who score extremely high (the "gifted") magnifies a test's apparent validity.

Creativity and Intelligence Intelligence correlates weakly with creativity. Increases in intelligence beyond a necessary threshold level are not linked with increased creativity.

KEY TERMS AND CONCEPTS mental retardation, Down syndrome, creativity

Genetic and Environmental Influences on Intelligence

Studies of twins and adopted children, and of children raised in enriched or neglectful environments, indicate that both genes and environment contribute to individual differences in intelligence scores. What, then, explains group differences? And do such differences mean that tests are biased? These are among psychology's most controversial issues.

Having considered the nature, assessment, and dynamics of intelligence, we cannot resist asking: What determines intelligence—genes or environment? As Francis Galton recognized, intelligence seems to run in families. Moreover, we have seen that intelligence seems modestly predictable from infants' boredom with familiar pictures or from the complexity and speed of a person's brain-wave responses to a flash of light. But why? Are intellectual abilities mostly inherited? Or primarily molded by one's environment?

Few of psychology's issues arouse such passion or have such serious political implications. Consider: If we mainly inherit our differing mental abilities, and if success reflects those abilities, then people's socioeconomic standing will correspond to their inborn differences. Thus, those on top may believe their innate mental superiority justifies their social positions.

If, on the other hand, mental abilities are primarily nurtured by the environments that raise and school us, then children from disadvantaged environments can expect to lead disadvantaged lives. In this case, people's standing will result from their unequal opportunities, a situation that many regard as basically unjust. Setting aside such political implications as best we can, let's examine the evidence.

> *"I am, somehow, less interested in the weight and convolutions of Einstein's brain than in the near certainty that people of equal talent have lived and died in cotton fields and sweatshops."*
>
> **STEPHEN JAY GOULD**
> *THE PANDA'S THUMB*
> 1980

Genetic Influences

Do people who share the same genes also share comparable mental abilities? As you can see from Figure 11.7, which summarizes many studies, the answer is clearly yes. In support of the genetic contribution to intelligence, researchers cite two sets of findings:

- The IQ scores of identical twins reared together are virtually as similar as those of the same person taking the same test twice. Fraternal twins, who share only half their genes, are much less similar in IQ scores.

- Even identical twins whose parents do not dress or treat them identically are virtual carbon copies of one another in IQ score (Loehlin & Nichols, 1976). Likewise, identical twins who have been reared separately have similar IQ scores—similar enough to lead twin researcher Thomas Bouchard (1996) to estimate that "about 70 percent" of intelligence score variation "can be attributed to genetic variation." (Other researchers have offered estimates nearer 50 percent.)

But there is also some evidence pointing to an effect of environment. Fraternal twins, who are genetically no more alike than any other siblings, but who are treated more alike because they are the same age, tend to score more alike than other siblings.

Seeking to disentangle genes and environment, researchers have also asked whether adopted children and their siblings, thanks to their shared environment, share similar aptitudes. During childhood, the intelligence test scores of adoptive siblings correlate modestly. But with age, their mental similarities disappear as the effect of common rearing wanes; by adulthood, the correlation is roughly zero (McGue & others, 1993). Such findings contradict the widely held belief that, as we accumulate life experience, the environmental influence on traits such as intelligence increases. In fact, the opposite seems true: With age, genetic influences become more apparent (Bouchard, 1995, 1996a; Plomin, 1986).

Researchers have also compared the intelligence test scores of adopted children with those of their biological parents, from whom they received their

> As Sandra Scarr (1989) noted, being reared "together in the same adoptive home does not make you intellectually similar to your brothers and sisters; being genetically related by half of your genes does."

Figure **11.7**

Intelligence: nature and nurture
The most genetically similar people have the most similar intelligence scores. Remember: 1.0 indicates a perfect correlation; zero indicates no correlation at all. (Data from McGue & others, 1993.)

Figure **11.8**

The correlations of intelligence test scores between 245 adopted Colorado children and their adoptive and biological parents By age 7, the adopted children had intelligence test scores more like those of their biological parents. (From Fulker & others, 1988.)

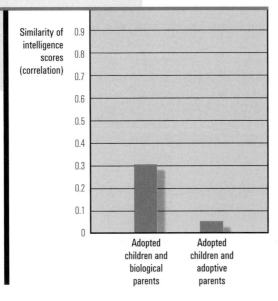

Think about it: As society succeeds in creating equality of opportunity, it will also increase the heritability of achievement. Perfect environmental equality would create 100 percent heritability—because genes alone would have to account for any remaining human differences.

Our genes shape the experiences that shape us.

heritability
the proportion of variation among individuals that we can attribute to genes. The heritability of a trait may vary, depending on the range of populations and environments studied.

genes, and those of their adoptive parents, who provided their home environment. As Figure 11.8 illustrates, adopted children's scores more closely resemble those of their biological parents than those of their adoptive parents. It matters whether one is adopted into an impoverished environment or an enriched one (Turkheimer, 1991). Yet as Sandra Scarr (1989) noted, being reared "together in the same adoptive home does not make you intellectually similar to your brothers and sisters; being genetically related by half of your genes does."

Recall from Chapter 2 the meaning of heritability. To say that the heritability of intelligence—the variation in intelligence test scores attributable to genetic factors—is roughly 50+ percent does *not* mean that your genes are responsible for 50+ percent of your intelligence and your environment for the rest. Rather, it means that we can attribute to heredity 50+ percent *of the variation in intelligence within a group of people*. This point is so often misunderstood that I repeat: We can never say what percentage of an *individual's* intelligence is inherited. Heritability refers instead to the extent to which *differences among people* are attributable to genes.

Even this conclusion must be qualified, because heritability can vary from study to study. If we were to follow Mark Twain's proposal to raise

boys in barrels to age 12, feeding them through a hole, they would emerge with lower-than-normal intelligence scores. Yet, given their equal environments, their individual IQ score differences at age 12 could be explained only by their heredity. In other words, heritability for their differences would be near 100 percent. *As environments become more equal, heredity as a source of differences necessarily becomes more important.* On the other hand, compare people with similar heredities who are raised in drastically different environments (barrels versus advantaged homes), and heritability—differences due to genes—will be low.

Remember, too, that genes and environment interact. For example, students with a natural aptitude for mathematics are more likely to select math courses in high school, and later to score well on math aptitude tests—thanks *both* to their natural math aptitude *and* to their math experience. Our genes shape the experiences that shape us.

Environmental Influences

We have seen that our genes make a difference. Even if we were all raised in the same intellectually stimulating environment, we still would not have the same aptitudes. But we have also seen that heredity doesn't tell the whole story. Within the limits dictated by our genes, our life experiences matter. The environment that siblings share doesn't much influence their aptitudes, but it significantly influences their scholastic achievement (Thompson & others, 1991).

Human environments are rarely as impoverished as the dark and barren cages inhabited by deprived rats that develop thinner-than-normal brain cortexes (see Chapter 3). Yet severe life experiences also leave marks on humans, as psychologist J. McVicker Hunt (1982) observed in a destitute Iranian orphanage in Tehran, where the typical child could not sit up unassisted at age 2 or walk at age 4. What care the infants received was not in response to their crying, cooing, or other behaviors. The infants were therefore not developing any sense of personal control over their environment, and so were becoming passive "glum lumps." Extreme deprivation was bludgeoning native intelligence.

Aware of the benefits of responsive caregiving, Hunt began a program of "tutored human enrichment." For instance, he trained caregivers to play vocal games with the infants. First, they imitated the babies' babbling. Then they led the babies in vocal follow-the-leader by shifting from one familiar sound to another. Then they began to teach sounds from the Persian language.

The results were dramatic. All 11 infants who received these language-fostering experiences could name more than 50 objects and body parts by 22 months. So charming had the infants become that most were adopted—an unprecedented success for the orphanage.

Hunt's findings testify to the importance of environment. There is no doubt that severe disadvantage takes a toll on children (Ramey & Ramey, 1992). And when the infant malnutrition associated with severe poverty is relieved with nutritional supplements, poverty's effect on physical and cognitive development lessens (Brown & Pollitt, 1996).

But do such findings indicate a way to "give your child a superior intellect"? Some popular books claim that with intensive preschool training this is possible, but most experts are doubtful (Phillips & Stipek, 1993). Although Sandra Scarr (1984) agrees that neglectful upbringing can have grave long-term consequences, she points out that "as long as an infant has normal human contact and normal exposure to sights, sounds, human speech, and so forth, the baby will thrive." As for future intelligence, "Parents who are very concerned about providing special educational lessons for their babies are wasting their time." Parents of children with high intelligence test scores may have been more likely to hang crib mobiles, take the children to the theater, or whatever. Did such experiences boost the children's scores a notch or

two? We don't know, stated Scarr (1986). Parents supply their children with both genes and environments. So even if the environments of children with high intelligence test scores are noticeably different from those with low scores, we can't be sure how much difference their environments make.

Hunt would probably agree with Scarr that extra instruction has little effect on the intellectual development of children from stimulating environments. But he was optimistic when it came to children from disadvantaged environments. Indeed, his 1961 book, *Intelligence and Experience*, helped launch Project Head Start in 1965. Head Start is a U.S. government–funded preschool program serving some 750,000 children, most of whom come from families below the poverty level. It aims to enhance children's chances for success in school and beyond by boosting their cognitive and social skills.

Does it succeed? Researchers study Head Start and other preschool programs by comparing equivalent children who do experience the program with those who don't. Their findings indicate that high-quality programs for disadvantaged children produce at least short-term cognitive gains, even on intelligence tests (Haskins, 1989). Quality programs also increase school readiness, decreasing the likelihood of a child's repeating a grade or being placed in special education. The aptitude benefits dissipate over time (reminding us that life experience *after* Head Start matters, too). The effect of education doesn't end with the preschool years. Psychologist Edward Zigler, the program's first director, believes there are other long-term benefits (Zigler & Muenchow, 1992). High-quality preschool programs improve emotional intelligence—creating better attitudes toward learning and reducing school dropouts and criminality.

"There is a large body of evidence indicating that there is little if anything to be gained by exposing middle-class children to early education."

DEVELOPMENTAL PSYCHOLOGIST
EDWARD F. ZIGLER (1987)

Getting a head start To increase readiness for schoolwork and expand children's notions of where school might lead them, Project Head Start offers educational activities. Here children in a classroom learn about colors and those on a field trip learn what fire fighters do.

Group Differences in Intelligence Test Scores

If there were no group differences in aptitude scores, psychologists could politely debate hereditary and environmental influences in their ivory towers. But there are group differences. What are they? And what shall we make of them?

Ethnic Similarities and Differences

Fueling this discussion are two disturbing but agreed-upon facts:

- Racial groups differ in their average scores on intelligence tests.

- High-scoring people (and groups) are more likely to attain high levels of education and income.

A statement by 52 intelligence researchers explains: "The bell curve for whites is centered roughly around IQ 100; the bell curve for American blacks roughly around 85; and those for different subgroups of Hispanics roughly midway between those for whites and blacks" (Avery & others, 1994). Comparable results come from other academic aptitude tests, such as the SAT. The black-white difference has diminished somewhat in recent years, and among children has dropped to 10 points in some recent studies (Neisser & others, 1996). Yet the test score gap persists.

There are differences among other groups as well. European New Zealanders outscore native Maori New Zealanders. Israeli Jews outscore Israeli Arabs. Most Japanese outscore the stigmatized Japanese minority, the Burakumin. And hearing people outscore those born deaf (Braden, 1994; Steele, 1990a; Zeidner, 1990).

Everyone further agrees that such *group* differences provide little basis for judging individuals. Women outlive men by six years, but knowing someone's sex doesn't tell us with any precision how long that person will live. Even Charles Murray and Richard Herrnstein (1994), whose writings have drawn attention to black-white differences, remind us that "millions of blacks have higher IQs than the average white."

If heredity contributes to individual differences in intelligence, does it also contribute to group differences? It's conceivable, and a few psychologists speculate that different climates and survival challenges could have led to racial differences in aptitudes (Lynn, 1991; Rushton, 1990, 1995). But it's also clear that, as in our earlier barrel-versus-home-reared boys example, group differences in a heritable trait may be entirely environmental. Consider one of nature's experiments: Allow some children to grow up hearing their culture's dominant language, while others, born deaf, do not. Then give them an intelligence test rooted in that language, and (no surprise) those with expertise in the test's language will score highest. Although individual performance differences may be substantially genetic, the group difference is not (Figure 11.9).

Consider: If each identical twin were exactly as tall as his or her co-twin, heritability would be 100 percent. Imagine that we then separated some young twins and gave only half of them a nutritious diet, and that the well-nourished twins all grew to be exactly 3 inches taller than their counterparts—an environmental effect comparable to that actually observed in both Britain and America, where adolescents are several inches taller than their counterparts were half a century ago (Angoff, 1987; Lynn, 1987). What would the heritability of height be now for our well-nourished twins? Still

Figure 11.9

Group differences and environmental impact Even if the variation between members within a group reflects genetic differences, the average difference between groups may be wholly due to the environment. Imagine that seeds from the same mixture are sown in poor and fertile soil. Although height differences within each pot will be genetic, the height difference between the two groups will be environmental. (From Lewontin, 1976.)

100 percent, because the variation in height within the group would remain entirely predictable from the heights of their malnourished identical siblings. So even perfect heritability within groups would not eliminate the possibility of a strong environmental impact on the group differences.

So, is there evidence that the racial gap may be similarly environmental? Consider these findings:

- Genetics research reveals that under the skin, the races are remarkably alike (Cavalli-Sforza & others, 1994; Lewontin, 1982). Individual differences within a race are much greater than between-race differences. The average genetic difference between two Icelandic villagers or between two Kenyans greatly exceeds the difference between Icelanders and Kenyans. Moreover, looks can deceive. Europeans and Africans are genetically closer than are Africans and Aboriginal Australians.

- Asian students outperform North American students on math achievement and aptitude tests. But this difference appears to be a recent phenomenon and may reflect conscientiousness rather than competence. Asian students also attend school 30 percent more days per year and spend much more time in and out of school studying math (Geary & others, 1996; Stevenson, 1992).

- The IQ test performance of today's better-fed and better-educated population exceeds that of the 1930s population (the Flynn effect) by the same margin that the average white today exceeds the average black. No one attributes the generational group difference to genetics.

- White and black infants have scored equally well on an infant intelligence measure (preference for looking at novel stimuli—a predictor of future intelligence scores [Fagan, 1992]).

- In different eras, different ethnic groups have experienced golden ages—periods of remarkable achievement. Twenty-five hundred years ago it was the Greeks and the Egyptians, then the Romans; in the eighth and ninth centuries, genius seemed to reside in the Arab world; 500 years ago it was the Aztec Indians and the peoples of northern Europe. Today, people marvel at Asians' technological genius. Cultures rise and fall over centuries; genes do not. That fact makes it difficult to attribute a natural superiority to any race.

As educational opportunities moved toward more equality between 1977 and 1996, the black-white difference in combined SAT scores (verbal + math) shrank 23 percent (College Board, 1987, 1996). Motivate children with rewards for correct

"Do not obtain your slaves from Britain, because they are so stupid and so utterly incapable of being taught."

CICERO (106–43 B.C.)

answers on intelligence tests and the racial difference shrinks even more (Bradley-Johnson & others, 1984).

Gender Similarities and Differences

In science, as in everyday life, differences, not similarities, excite interest. Compared with the anatomical and physiological similarities between men and women, our sex differences are relatively minor. Yet it is the differences we find exciting. Similarly, in the psychological domain, gender similarities dwarf gender differences, but the differences often capture our attention. To some, it is news that there is no gender gap in average verbal ability as assessed by tests of vocabulary, reading comprehension, and solving analogies (Hyde & Linn, 1988). But most people find differences more newsworthy. Girls are better spellers: At the end of high school, only 30 percent of males spell better than the average female (Lubinski & Benbow, 1992). Boys outnumber girls at the low extremes. Boys tend to talk later and stutter more often. In remedial reading classes, boys outnumber girls three to one (Finucci & Childs, 1981). In high school, underachieving boys outnumber girls by two to one (McCall & others, 1992).

The culture of scholarship
The children of Indochinese refugee families studied by Nathan Caplan, Marcella Choy, and James Whitmore (1992) typically excel in school. On weekday nights after dinner, the family clears the table and begins homework. Family cooperation is valued, and older siblings help younger ones.

In science, as in everyday life, differences, not similarities, excite interest.

Math and Spatial Aptitudes

In math grades, the average girl typically equals or surpasses the average boy (ETS, 1992; Kimball, 1989). And on math tests given to more than 3 million representatively sampled people in 100 independent studies, males and females obtained nearly identical average scores (Hyde & others, 1990). But again—despite greater diversity within the genders than between them—group differences make the news. Although females have an edge in math computation, males in various cultures score higher in math problem solving (Hedges & Nowell, 1995; Lummis & Stevenson, 1990). For example, male high school seniors average 45 points higher on the 200- to 800-point SAT math test (literally meaning that they average four more correct answers on the 60-question test). Because U.S. National Merit Scholarships are based on SAT scores, only about 35 percent of these awards have gone to girls (despite girls' generally higher grades).

World Math Olympics champs
After outscoring 350,000 of their U.S. peers, these boys all had perfect scores in competition with math whizzes from 68 other countries.

The score differences are sharpest at the extremes. Among precocious 12-year-olds scoring extremely high on SAT math, boys have outnumbered girls 13 to 1 (Lubinski & Benbow, 1992). In other Western countries, virtually all math prodigies participating in the International Mathematics Olympiad have been males. Female math prodigies have, however, reached the top levels in non-Western countries such as China (Halpern, 1991). The average male edge seems most reliable in tests like the one shown in Figure 11.10, which involve speedily rotating three-dimensional objects in one's mind (Masters & Sanders, 1993; Voyer & others, 1995). Such spatial ability helps when fitting suitcases into a car trunk, playing chess, or doing certain types of geometry problems.

Working from an evolutionary perspective, David Geary (1995, 1996) and Irwin Silverman and Marion Eals (1992) speculate that skills in navigating within three-dimensional space also helped our ancestral fathers in tracking their prey and navigating their way home. In contrast, the survival of our ancestral mothers was enhanced by keen memory for the location of edible plants—a legacy that lives today in women's superior memory for objects and their location.

In studies of over 100,000 American adolescents, girls also modestly surpassed boys in memory for picture associations (Hedges & Nowell, 1995). And among nearly 200,000 students taking Germany's Test for Medical Studies, young women year after year have surpassed men in remembering facts from short medical cases (Stumpf & Jackson, 1994). (My wife, who remembers many of my experiences for me, tells me that if she died I'd be a man without a past.)

Do natural sex differences therefore explain why most mathematicians and more than 9 in 10 rated chess players and American architects, engineers, and mapmakers are men? Or why the world chess body has therefore found it necessary to hold separate competitions for men and women? Exposure to high levels of male sex hormones during the prenatal period does enhance spatial abilities (Berenbaum & others, 1995). But social expectations also shape boys' and girls' interests and abilities (Crawford & others, 1995; Eccles & others, 1990). Traditionally, math and science have been considered masculine subjects. For example, many parents send their sons to computer camps and give their daughters more encouragement in English. Thus, the male edge in math problem solving grows with age, becoming detectable only after elementary school. But as more and more girls are encouraged to develop their abilities in math and science, the gender gap is narrowing. Among representative national samples of high school juniors taking the Preliminary Scholastic Assessment Test (PSAT), the male edge has nearly disappeared since 1960 (Linn & Hyde, 1991).

Emotion-Detecting Ability

Recall that part of emotional intelligence is empathic accuracy in reading others' emotions. Some of us are more sensitive to emotional cues. Robert Rosenthal, Judith Hall, and their colleagues (1979) discovered this by showing hundreds of people brief film clips of portions of a person's emotionally expressive face or body, sometimes with a garbled voice added. For example, after a two-second scene revealing only the face of an upset woman, the researchers asked whether the woman was criticizing someone for being late or was talking about her divorce. Rosenthal and Hall reported that some people are much better emotion detectors than others are, and that women are better at it than men.

Figure **11.10**

The mental rotation test   This is a test of spatial abilities. Which two responses show a different view of the standard? (From Vandenberg & Kuse, 1978.) (See page 360 for answers.)

Which two circles contain a configuration of blocks identical to the one in the circle at the left?

Standard

Responses

Some psychologists speculate that women's emotion-detecting ability helped our ancestral mothers read emotions in their infants and would-be lovers, which may in turn have fueled cultural tendencies to encourage women's empathic skills. Such skills may, as Chapter 4 noted, explain women's somewhat greater responsiveness in both positive and negative emotional situations.

An intelligence test measures a person's developed abilities at a particular time. These abilities necessarily reflect that person's experiences and environment.

The Question of Bias

Knowing about group differences in intelligence test scores leads us to wonder whether intelligence tests are biased. The answer depends on how we define *bias*. One meaning is that the tests detect not only innate differences in intelligence but also differences caused by cultural experiences. In this sense, everyone agrees that intelligence tests are biased. No one claims that heritability is 100 percent responsible for any test score. An intelligence test measures a person's developed abilities at a particular time. These abilities necessarily reflect that person's experiences *and* environment.

You may have read examples of intelligence test items that make middle-class assumptions (for example, that a cup goes with a saucer, or, as in one of the sample test items from the WAIS [Figure 11.3, page 343], that people buy fire insurance to protect the value of their homes and possessions). Do such items bias the test against those who do not use saucers and whose meager possessions hardly warrant the cost of fire insurance? Could such questions explain racial differences in test performance? If so, are tests a discriminatory vehicle, consigning potentially capable children to dead-end classes and jobs (as the judge argued in the case of Larry and the six other children noted at this chapter's beginning)?

Defenders of aptitude testing have in turn observed that racial group differences occur on non-verbal items, such as counting digits backward, as well as on verbal items, such as vocabulary knowledge (Jensen, 1983). Moreover, blaming the test for a group's lower scores is like blaming a messenger for bad news, they add. Why blame the tests for exposing unequal experiences and opportunities? If, because of malnutrition, people were to suffer stunted growth, would one blame the measuring stick that reveals it? If unequal past experiences predict unequal future achievements, a valid aptitude test will detect such inequalities.

Another meaning of *bias* hinges on whether a test is less valid for some groups than for others. If the SAT accurately predicts the college achievement of one race but not that of another, then the test would be biased. The near-consensus among psychologists, as summarized by the National Research Council's Committee on Ability Testing, is that the major aptitude tests are *not* biased in this statistical meaning of the term (Rowe & others, 1994; Wigdor & Garner, 1982). The predictive validity of the SAT or of a standard intelligence test is roughly the same for blacks and whites and for rich and poor. If an intelligence test score of 95 predicts C grades, the rough prediction usually applies equally to all ethnic and economic groups.

To predict school performance accurately, an aptitude test must mirror any gender or racial bias in school teaching and testing. Among students given a difficult math test by Steven Spencer and his colleagues (1997), men outperformed equally capable women—except when the women had been led to expect that women usually do as well as men on the test. Otherwise, the women apparently felt apprehensive and despairing when the going got tough. Claude Steele and Joshua Aronson (1996) observed the same self-fulfilling effect of negative beliefs. They found black students' verbal aptitude scores were lower when they took tests under conditions designed to make black students feel threatened. Steele (1995, 1997) concluded that if you tell students they probably won't succeed (as remedial "minority support" programs often do), this stereotype will eventually erode their performance both on aptitude tests and in school. Over time, such students may "disidentify" with school achievement and look for self-esteem elsewhere. University programs that instead challenge minority students to believe in their potential produce markedly higher grades and lower dropout rates.

If unequal past experiences predict unequal future achievements, a valid aptitude test will detect such inequalities.

So what can we conclude about aptitude tests and bias? The tests do seem biased in one sense—sensitivity to performance differences caused by cultural experience. But they are not biased in another—statistical prediction for different groups.

Does this mean the tests are discriminatory? Again, the answer can be yes or no. In one sense, yes, their purpose is to discriminate—to distinguish among individuals. In another sense, their purpose is to reduce discrimination by reducing reliance on subjective criteria for school and job placement—criteria such as who you know, what you look like, or how much the interviewer happens to like "your kind of person." Banning aptitude tests would force the people who decide on admissions and jobs to rely more on other considerations, such as their personal opinions. Civil service tests, for example, were devised to discriminate more fairly and objectively, by reducing the political, racial, and ethnic discrimination that preceded their use.

Perhaps, then, our aim should be threefold. First, we should realize the benefits that Alfred Binet foresaw for intelligence tests—to enable schools to recognize who might best benefit from early intervention. At the same time, we must remain alert to Binet's fear that test scores may be misinterpreted as literal measures of a person's worth and fixed potential. And finally, we must remember that *intelligence test scores reflect only one aspect of personal competence.* Our practical and emotional intelligence matter, too, as do other forms of talent and character. The competence that intelligence tests sample is important but far from all-inclusive. The spatial ability of the carpenter differs from the logical ability of the computer programmer, which differs from the verbal ability of the poet. Differences are not deficits. Because there are many ways of being successful, our personal and cultural differences—regardless of their origins—are variations on the human theme of adaptability.

Answers to the mental rotation test on page 358: the first and fourth alternatives.

"Almost all the joyful things of life are outside the measure of IQ tests."

MADELEINE L'ENGLE
A CIRCLE OF QUIET
1972

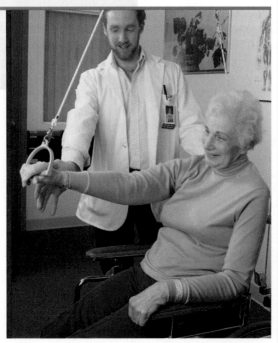

Untestable compassion Intelligence test scores are only one part of the picture of a whole person. They don't measure the abilities, talent, and commitment of, for example, people who devote their lives to helping others.

SUMMING UP

Because of its political and racial overtones, the debate over the nature and nurture of intelligence is an ongoing controversy.

Genetic Influences Studies of twins, family members, and adopted children together point to a significant hereditary contribution to intelligence scores. Heritability, the proportion of person-to-person variation attributable to genes, can vary, depending on the range of populations and environments studied.

Environmental Influences These same studies, plus others that compare children reared in extremely impoverished or enriched environments or in different cultures, indicate that life experiences also significantly influence intelligence test performance.

Group Differences in Intelligence Test Scores Like individuals, groups vary in intelligence test scores. Hereditary variation *within* a group need not signify a hereditary explanation of *between*-group differences. In the case of the racial gaps in test scores, the evidence suggests that environmental differences are largely, perhaps entirely, responsible. Girls have tended to outscore boys on spelling tests and in assessments of emotion detection, while boys have outscored girls on mental rotation tests and math aptitude tests with a spatial component. Psychologists debate evolutionary and cultural explanations of such differences.

The Question of Bias Aptitude tests aim to predict how well a test-taker will perform in a given situation. So they are necessarily "biased," in the sense that they are sensitive to performance differences caused by cultural experience. But "bias" can also mean what psychologists commonly mean by the term—that a biased test predicts less accurately for one group than for another. In this sense of the term, most experts do not consider the major aptitude tests to be significantly biased.

KEY TERMS AND CONCEPT heritability

TERMS AND CONCEPTS TO REMEMBER

intelligence test, p. 333

mental age, p. 335

Stanford-Binet, p. 335

intelligence quotient (IQ), p. 335

intelligence, p. 337

factor analysis, p. 338

general intelligence (g), p. 338

savant syndrome, p. 338

emotional intelligence, p. 340

aptitude test, p. 342

achievement test, p. 342

Wechsler Adult Intelligence Scale (WAIS), p. 343

standardization, p. 344

normal curve, p. 344

reliability, p. 345

validity, p. 345

content validity, p. 345

criterion, p. 345

predictive validity, p. 345

mental retardation, p. 349

Down syndrome, p. 349

creativity, p. 351

heritability, p. 354

CRITICAL THINKING EXERCISE
by Richard O. Straub

Now that you have read and reviewed Chapter 11, take your learning a step further by testing your critical thinking skills on the following creative problem-solving exercise.

Carlton, who owns a publishing company that employs copy-editors, personnel managers, and acquisitions editors, is fascinated by individual differences in intelligence. He believes that in each person there exists a measurable general mental capacity that forms the basis for all cognitive skills. Over the years, Carlton has made a study of the job performance of the people he hires. All applicants are required to take an intelligence test of his own invention: They are given a lengthy passage full of spelling, grammar, and punctuation errors, which they are expected to correct. To calculate the intelligence score, the number of proofreading errors the applicant misses is subtracted from the number of errors he or she corrects. Over lunch with a friend one day, Carlton confides that he has had mixed results in predicting employee success. An applicant's future success as an employee seems to depend more on the type of job the person is assigned to than on the individual's pre-employment test score.

1. What does Carlton mean by "intelligence"? What does his test actually measure?

2. Why doesn't Carlton's test measure what he wants it to measure?

3. What would be a more sensible way for Carlton to test potential employees?

Check your progress on becoming a critical thinker by comparing your answers to the sample answers found in Appendix B.

chapter

12

Motivation

In everyday conversation, the question "What motivated you to do that?" is a way of asking "What *caused* your behavior? *Why* did you act that way?" To psychologists, a <u>motivation</u> is a need or desire that serves to *energize* behavior and to *direct* it toward a goal. Like intelligence, motivation is a hypothetical concept. We infer motivation from behaviors we observe. Consider motivation in these situations:

- David Mandel (1983), a former Nazi concentration camp inmate, recalls how a starving "father and son would fight over a piece of bread. Like dogs." One father, whose 20-year-old son stole his bread from under his pillow while he slept, went into a deep depression, asking over and again how his son could do such a thing. The next day the father died. "Hunger does something to you that's hard to describe. I can't believe it myself today, so how can I expect anyone else to understand it?"

- In the Old Testament's *Song of Solomon* love poems, a man and a woman express their intense sexual passion for one another. "I am sick with love," she declares. "O that his left hand were under my head, and that his right hand embraced me!" He, in turn, pronounces her "delectable." "You are stately as a palm tree, and your breasts are like its clusters. I say I will climb the palm tree and lay hold of its branches."

- In Texas, a school truant officer discovers Alfredo Gonzales, age 14, picking fruit and sends him off to the first day of school in his life. Although placed at the lowest skill level and paddled for asking questions in Spanish—he knows no English—Alfredo decides "I could do better." Indeed, today he is a highly educated college administrator who works to motivate youth to wake up, as he did, to "their own potential and to gain a desire to achieve it."

In this chapter, we explore motivation by focusing on these three motives—hunger, sex, and achievement. Although other identifiable motives exist (including thirst, curiosity, and a need for approval), a close look at these three reveals the interplay between nature (the physiological "push") and nurture (the cognitive and cultural "pulls").

motivation
a need or desire that energizes
and directs behavior.

instinct
a complex behavior that is rigidly
patterned throughout a species
and is unlearned.

drive-reduction theory
the idea that a physiological
need creates an aroused tension
state (a drive) that motivates
an organism to satisfy the need.

Motivational Concepts

**Before considering hunger, sex, and achievement,
let's step back and see how psychologists have understood motivation. Three perspectives have been
influential: instinct theory (now replaced by an evolutionary perspective), drive reduction theory (emphasizing the interaction between inner pushes and
external pulls), and arousal theory (emphasizing the
urge for an optimum level of stimulation).**

Instincts

Early in this century, as the influence of Charles
Darwin's evolutionary theory grew, it became fashionable to classify all sorts of behaviors as instincts. If people criticized themselves, it was
because of their "self-abasement instinct." If they
boasted, it reflected their "self-assertion instinct."
After scanning five hundred books, one sociologist
compiled a list of 5759 supposed human instincts!
Before long, the instinct-naming fad collapsed
under its own weight. For rather than *explaining*
human behaviors, the early instinct theorists were
simply *naming* them. It was like "explaining" a
bright child's low grades by labeling the child an
"underachiever." To name a behavior is *not* to explain it.

To qualify as an instinct, a complex behavior
must have a fixed pattern throughout a species and
be unlearned (Tinbergen, 1951). Such behaviors
are common in other species (recall imprinting in
birds and the return of salmon to their birthplace).
Human behavior, too, exhibits certain innate tendencies, including simple fixed patterns such as an
infant's rooting and sucking. Most psychologists,
though, view human behavior as directed by physiological needs *and* psychological wants.

Although instinct theory failed to explain human
motives, the underlying assumption that genes predispose species-typical behavior is as strong as
ever. We saw this in Chapter 8's discussion of our
biological predisposition to learn certain aversions.
And we will see this in later discussions of how
evolution might influence our helping behaviors,
our romantic attractions, and our gender differences. Evolutionary psychology (the study of how
natural selection shaped our motivations and behaviors) is now in its heyday.

Drives and Incentives

When the original instinct theory of motivation
collapsed, it was replaced by drive-reduction
theory—the idea that a physiological need creates
an aroused psychological state that *drives* the organism to reduce the need by, say, eating or drinking. With few exceptions, when a physiological
need increases, so does a psychological drive—an
aroused, motivated state.

Same motive; different wiring The more complex the
nervous system, the more adaptable the organism. Both the
weaver bird and the woman satisfy their need for shelter
in ways that reflect their inherited capacities. The bird's
behavior pattern is fixed; it can build only this kind of nest.
The woman's behavior is flexible; she can learn whatever
skills she needs to build a house.

Not only are we pushed by our "need" to reduce drives, we also are pulled by incentives . . .

The physiological aim of drive reduction is homeostasis—the maintenance of a steady internal state. An example of homeostasis (literally "staying the same") is the body's temperature-regulation system, which works like a thermostat. Both systems operate through feedback loops: Sensors feed room temperature to a control device. If room temperature cools, the control device switches on the furnace. Likewise, if body temperature cools, blood vessels constrict to conserve warmth, and we feel driven to put on more clothes or seek a warmer environment. Similarly, if the water level in our cells drops, sensors detect our need for water and we feel thirsty.

Not only are we *pushed* by our "need" to reduce drives, we also are *pulled* by incentives—positive or negative stimuli that lure or repel us. This is one way our individual learning histories influence our motives. Depending on our learning, the aroma of fresh roasted peanuts (or toasted ants), the sight of someone we find attractive, and the threat of disapproval can all motivate our behavior. Our internal needs energize and direct our behavior, but so do these external incentives. The lure of money may energize us quite apart from any need-based drive.

When there is both a need and an incentive, we feel strongly driven. The food-deprived person who smells baking bread feels a strong hunger drive. In the presence of that drive, the baking bread becomes a compelling incentive. For each motive, we can therefore ask, "How is it pushed by our inborn physiological needs and pulled by incentives in the environment?"

Optimum Arousal

Rather than reducing a physiological need or minimizing tension, some motivated behaviors *increase* arousal. Well-fed animals will leave their shelter to explore, seemingly in the absence of any need-based drive. For taking such risks, animals may, however, gain information and resources (Renner, 1992).

Curiosity drives monkeys to monkey around trying to figure out how to unlock a latch that opens nothing, or how to open a window that allows them to see outside their room (Butler, 1954). It drives the 9-month-old infant who investigates every accessible corner of the house. It drives the scientists whose work this text discusses. And it drove the voyagers who first ventured across and beneath the oceans. Asked why he wanted to climb Mount Everest, George Mallory answered, "Because it is there." Those who, like Mallory, enjoy high arousal are most likely to enjoy intense music, novel foods, and risky behaviors (Zuckerman, 1979).

Recall, too, the experiments on sensory restriction described in Chapter 5. The peace and quiet of hour after hour isolated in a monotonous chamber sensitized the subjects to any available stimulation. Despite having all our biological needs satisfied, we feel driven to experience stimulation. Without it, we feel bored and look for a way to increase arousal to some optimum level. With too much stimulation, we feel stressed and look for a way to decrease arousal.

homeostasis
a tendency to maintain a balanced or constant internal state; the regulation of any aspect of body chemistry, such as blood glucose, around a particular level.

incentive
a positive or negative environmental stimulus that motivates behavior.

Driven by curiosity Baby monkeys and small people are fascinated by things they've never handled before. Their drive to explore the relatively unfamiliar is one of several motives that do not fill any immediate physiological need.

hierarchy of needs
Maslow's pyramid of human needs, beginning at the base with physiological needs that must first be satisfied before higher-level safety needs and then psychological needs become active.

A Hierarchy of Motives

Some needs take priority over others. At this moment, with your needs for air and water satisfied, other motives—such as your desire to achieve—energize and direct your behavior. Let your need for water go unsatisfied and your thirst will preoccupy you. But if you were deprived of air, your thirst would disappear.

Abraham Maslow (1970) described these priorities as a hierarchy of needs (Figure 12.1). At its base are our physiological needs, such as for food and water. Only if these needs are met are we prompted to meet our need for safety, and then to meet the uniquely human needs to give and receive love and to enjoy self-esteem. Beyond this, said Maslow (1971), lies the highest of human needs: to actualize one's full potential. (More on self-esteem and self-actualization in Chapter 14.)

Maslow's hierarchy is somewhat arbitrary. Moreover, the order of such needs is not universally fixed. People have starved themselves to make a political statement. Nevertheless, the simple idea that some motives are more compelling than others does provide a framework for thinking about motivation.

Let's now consider the three representative motives, beginning at the basic, physiological level with hunger and working up through sexual motivation to the higher-level need to achieve. At each level, we shall see how environmental factors interact with what is physiologically given.

Figure **12.1**

Maslow's hierarchy of needs
Once our lower-level needs are met, we are prompted to satisfy our higher-level needs. (From Maslow, 1970.)

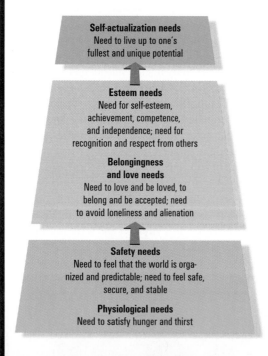

Self-actualization needs
Need to live up to one's
fullest and unique potential

Esteem needs
Need for self-esteem,
achievement, competence,
and independence; need for
recognition and respect from others

Belongingness
and love needs
Need to love and be loved, to
belong and be accepted; need
to avoid loneliness and alienation

Safety needs
Need to feel that the world is organized and predictable; need to feel safe,
secure, and stable

Physiological needs
Need to satisfy hunger and thirst

SUMMING UP

Motivation is the energizing and directing of behavior, the force behind our yearning for food, our longing for sexual intimacy, and our desire to achieve.

Instincts Under Darwin's influence, early theorists viewed behavior as controlled by biological forces, such as specific instincts. This approach fell into disfavor when it became clear that people were naming, not explaining, various behaviors by calling them instincts. The underlying idea—that genes predispose species-typical behavior—is still influential in evolutionary psychology.

Drives and Incentives Most physiological needs create aroused psychological states that drive us to reduce or satisfy those needs. The aim of drive reduction is internal stability, or homeostasis. Thus, drive reduction motivates survival behaviors, such as eating and drinking. Not only are we pushed by our internal drives, we are pulled by external incentives. Depending on our personal and cultural experiences, some stimuli (for example, certain foods or erotic images) will arouse our desires.

Optimum Arousal Rather than reducing a physiological need or tension state, some motivated behaviors increase arousal. Curiosity-driven behaviors, for example, suggest that too little as well as too much stimulation can motivate people to seek an optimum level of arousal.

A Hierarchy of Motives Maslow's hierarchy of needs expresses the idea that, until satisfied, some motives are more compelling than others.

KEY TERMS AND CONCEPTS motivation, instinct, drive-reduction theory, homeostasis, incentive, hierarchy of needs

The Need to Belong

We humans feel motivated to eat and have sex. Being what Aristotle called "the social animal," we also have a need to affiliate with others and even to become strongly attached to certain others in enduring, close relationships. Human beings, contended the personality theorist Alfred Adler, have an "urge to community" (Ferguson, 1989). Roy Baumeister and Mark Leary (1995) assemble evidence for this deep *need to belong*.

Aiding Survival Social bonds boosted our ancestors' survival rate. By keeping children close to their caregivers, attachments served as a powerful survival impulse. As adults, those who formed attachments were more likely to come together to reproduce and to stay together to nurture their offspring to maturity.

Cooperation in groups also enhanced survival. In solo combat, our ancestors were not the toughest predators. But as hunters they learned that six hands were better than two. Those who foraged in groups also gained protection from predators and enemies. If those who felt a need to belong survived and reproduced most successfully, their genes would in time predominate. The inevitable result: an innately social creature. People in every society on earth belong to groups (and, as Chapter 18 explains, prefer and favor "us" over "them").

Wanting to Belong The need to belong colors our thoughts and emotions. People spend much time thinking about their actual and hoped-for relationships. When relationships form, we often feel joy. Falling in mutual love, people have been known to get cheek-aches from their irrepressible grins. Asked, "What is necessary for your happiness?" or "What is it that makes your life meaningful?" most people mention—before anything else—satisfying close relationships with family, friends, or romantic partners (Berscheid, 1985). Happiness hits close to home.

Increasing Social Acceptance

Much of our social behavior aims to increase our belonging—our social acceptance and inclusion. To avoid rejection, we generally conform to group standards and seek to make favorable impressions. (More on this in Chapter 18.) To win friendship and esteem, we monitor our behavior, hoping to create the right impressions. Seeking love and belonging, we spend billions on clothes, cosmetics, and diet and fitness aids—all motivated by our quest for acceptance.

Like sexual motivation, which feeds both love and exploitation, the need to belong feeds both deep attachments and menacing threats. Out of our need to define a "we" come loving families, faithful friendships, and team spirit, but also teen gangs, ethnic rivalries, and fanatic nationalism.

Maintaining Relationships

People resist breaking social bonds. For most of us, familiarity breeds liking, not contempt. Thrown together at school, at summer camp, on a vacation cruise, people resist the group's dissolution. Hoping to maintain the relationships, they promise to call, to write, to come back for reunions. Parting, they feel distress. Attachments can even keep people in abusive relationships; the fear of being alone may seem worse than the pain of emotional or physical abuse.

When something threatens or dissolves our social ties, negative emotions overwhelm us. Exile, imprisonment, and solitary confinement are progressively more severe forms of punishment. Recently bereaved people often feel that life is empty and pointless. Children reared in institutions without a sense of belonging to anyone, or locked away at home under extreme neglect, become pathetic creatures—withdrawn, frightened, speechless. Adults who are denied others' acceptance and inclusion may feel depressed. Anxiety, jealousy, loneliness, and guilt all involve threatened disruptions of our need to belong. People suffer even when bad relationships break. In one 16-nation survey, separated and divorced people were half as likely as married people to declare themselves "very happy" (Inglehart, 1990). After such separations, feelings of loneliness and anger are commonplace. Such evidence supports Baumeister and Leary's (1995) contention that "human beings are fundamentally and pervasively motivated by a need to belong."

The need to belong

Separated from friends or family—isolated in prison, alone at a new school, living in a foreign land—most people feel keenly their lost connections with important others. Wrenched from the only family she has ever known by a 1993 court decision in an adoption dispute, 2½-year-old Jessica DeBoer sobs en route to her biological parents' home hundreds of miles away. As social animals, we all have something of Jessica within us—a sense of who we belong to, of who is "us."

Hunger

Hunger, like so much of our experience, reflects the interplay of our physiology and our learning. Blood sugar levels are monitored by the brain's hypothalamus, which regulates hunger and body weight. But there's more to hunger than the hypothalamus, for some people are especially responsive to external food cues, and others suffer eating disorders.

A vivid demonstration of the supremacy of physiological needs followed reports of starvation in World War II prison camps and occupied areas. To learn more about the results of semistarvation, scientist Ancel Keys and his colleagues (1950) solicited volunteers for an experiment. From among the more than 100 conscientious objectors to the war who applied, the researchers selected 36 men. First, they fed the men just enough to maintain their initial weight. Then, for six months, they cut this food level in half.

The effects soon became visible. Without thinking about it, the men began conserving energy; they appeared listless and apathetic. Their body weights dropped rapidly, eventually stabilizing at about 25 percent below their starting weights. The psychological effects were even more dramatic. Consistent with Maslow's idea of a needs hierarchy, the men became obsessed with food. They talked food. They daydreamed food. They collected recipes, read cookbooks, and feasted their eyes on delectable forbidden foods. Meanwhile, they lost their former interests in sex and social activities. They became preoccupied with their unfulfilled basic needs. As one participant reported, "If

"You're my best student, Beth, but I think this diet is having a negative effect on your work."

we see a show, the most interesting part of it is contained in scenes where people are eating. I couldn't laugh at the funniest picture in the world, and love scenes are completely dull."

The Physiology of Hunger

Keys's semistarved subjects felt hunger in response to a homeostatic system designed to maintain normal body weight and an adequate nutrient supply. But precisely what is it that triggers hunger? Is it the pangs of an empty stomach? So it feels. And so it seemed after A. L. Washburn, working with Walter Cannon (Cannon & Washburn, 1912), intentionally swallowed a balloon. When inflated in his stomach, the balloon transmitted his stomach contractions to a recording device (Figure 12.2). While his stomach was being monitored, Washburn pressed a key each time he felt hungry. The result: Washburn was having stomach contractions when-

"Nobody wants to kiss when they are hungry."

DOROTHEA DIX (1801–1887)

Figure **12.2**

Monitoring stomach contractions
Using this procedure, Washburn showed that stomach contractions (transmitted by the stomach balloon) accompany our feelings of hunger (indicated by a key press). (From Cannon, 1929.)

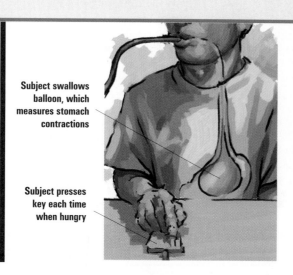

Subject swallows balloon, which measures stomach contractions

Subject presses key each time when hungry

Stomach contractions

Hunger pangs

0 1 2 3 4 5 6 7 8 9 1

Time in minutes

ever he felt hungry. Some diet aids reduce this empty stomach feeling by filling the stomach with indigestible fibers that swell as they absorb water.

Alas, there is more to hunger than the pangs of an empty stomach. Researchers discovered this a quarter-century later when they removed some rats' stomachs and attached their esophagi to their small intestines (Tsang, 1938). Without stomach pangs, did hunger persist? Did the rats continue to eat regularly? Indeed they did. Hunger persists similarly in humans whose ulcerated or cancerous stomachs have been removed. In fact, one can feel hungry even on a full stomach. Animals that fill their stomachs by eating low-calorie food will eat more than animals that consume a less filling, high-calorie diet (McHugh & Moran, 1978). If the pangs of an empty stomach are not the only source of our hunger, what else matters?

> "The full person does not understand the needs of the hungry."
>
> IRISH PROVERB

Body Chemistry

Changes in body chemistry also affect hunger. People and other animals automatically regulate their caloric intake to maintain a stable body weight. This suggests that the body is somehow, somewhere, keeping tabs on its available resources. One such resource is the blood sugar glucose. Increases in the hormone insulin diminish blood glucose, partly by converting it to stored fat. When the blood glucose level drops, hunger increases.

Body chemistry also influences taste preferences. When feeling tense or depressed, do you crave sweet or starchy carbohydrate-laden foods? Carbohydrates help boost levels of the neurotransmitter serotonin, which has calming effects. Given the drug fenfluramine, which similarly increases serotonin, carbohydrate cravers lose their cravings. This suggests that stress-related cravings might be treatable by providing food substitutes that mimic biochemical effects (Hall, 1987).

The Brain and Set Point

Low blood glucose triggers hunger. But you do not consciously feel your blood chemistry. Rather, the brain automatically monitors information on your body's internal state. Signals from the stomach, the intestines, and the liver (indicating whether glu-

Figure **12.3**

The hypothalamus   As we saw in Chapter 2, the hypothalamus performs various body maintenance functions, including control of hunger. Blood vessels supply the hypothalamus, enabling it to respond to our current blood chemistry as well as to incoming neural information about the body's state.

cose is being deposited or withdrawn) all signal the brain to motivate eating or not. But where in the brain are these messages integrated? During the 1940s and 1950s, researchers located hunger controls within the hypothalamus, a small but complex neural traffic intersection buried deep in the brain (Figure 12.3).

Actually, there are two distinct hypothalamic centers that help control eating. Experiments during the 1960s suggested that activity along the sides of the hypothalamus, known as the *lateral hypothalamus*, brings on hunger. When electrically stimulated there, a well-fed animal would begin to eat; when the area was destroyed, even a starving animal had no interest in food. Activity in the lower middle of the hypothalamus, known as the *ventromedial hypothalamus*, depresses hunger. Stimulate this area and an animal will stop eating; destroy it and the animal's stomach and intestines will process food more rapidly, causing it to eat more often and to become grossly fat (Duggan & Booth, 1986; Hoebel & Teitelbaum, 1966). This discovery explained why certain patients, with tumors near the base of the brain (in what we now realize is the hypothalamus), will eat excessively and become fat (Miller, 1995).

> Hunger persists in humans whose ulcerated or cancerous stomachs have been removed.

How do these complementary areas of the hypothalamus work? One theory is that they influence how much glucose is converted to fat and how much is left available to fuel immediate activity (and minimize hunger). After ventromedial lesions, rats produce more fat and use less fat for energy, rather like a miser who runs a bit of extra money to the bank and resists taking any out

glucose
the form of sugar that circulates in the blood and provides the major source of energy for body tissues. When its level is low, we feel hunger.

set point
the point at which an individual's "weight thermostat" is supposedly set. When the body falls below this weight, an increase in hunger and a lowered metabolic rate may act to restore the lost weight.

metabolic rate
the body's base rate of energy expenditure.

Evidence for the brain's control of eating A lesion near the ventromedial (middle) area of the hypothalamus caused this mouse's weight to triple. At 92.05 grams, it weighs about three times more than normal.

(Pinel, 1993). Recent experiments also suggest that a distributed brain system monitors the body's state and reports to the hypothalamus, which processes the information and sends it along to the frontal lobes, which decide behavior (Winn, 1995).

An older theory is that manipulating these two areas of the hypothalamus alters the body's "weight thermostat," which predisposes us to keep our body at a particular weight level, called its set point (Keesey & Corbett, 1983). When semistarved rats fall below their normal weight, biological pressures act to restore the lost weight: Hunger increases and energy expenditure decreases. If body weight rises—as happens when rats are force-fed—hunger decreases and energy expenditure increases. This stable weight toward which semistarved and overstuffed rats return is their set point.

Some researchers believe that slow, sustained changes in body weight can, however, alter one's set point. As we will see in Chapter 17's discussion of obesity and weight control, our heredity influences our body type and set point. Other researchers doubt that the body has a precise set point that drives hunger. Hunger, they say, is determined by too many factors, including learned incentives, for that to be true. Body weight settles around a level at which all these factors reach an equilibrium.

Despite the day-to-day variations in our eating, our bodies are astonishingly good at regulating our weight, much better than we could be through conscious efforts to control food intake precisely. Over the next forty years you will eat about twenty tons of food. If during those years you increase your daily intake by just .01 ounce more than required for your energy needs, you will gain 24 pounds (Martin & others, 1991). With astonishing precision, our bodies automatically balance energy intake and expenditure.

Our bodies regulate weight much as rats' bodies do—through the control of food intake and energy output. If our body weight rises above our set point, we tend not to feel so hungry; if our weight drops below, we tend to eat more. To maintain its set-point weight, the body also adjusts its metabolic rate—its resting rate of energy expenditure. By the end of their 24 weeks of semistarvation, the subjects in the World War II experiment had stabilized at three-quarters of their normal weight—while eating half what they previously did. The stabilization resulted from reduced energy expenditure, achieved partly by physical lethargy and partly by a 29 percent drop in their resting metabolic rate.

The Psychology of Hunger

Our eagerness to eat is both pushed by our physiological state—our body chemistry and hypothalamic activity—and pulled by our learned responses to external incentives.

Psychologists have studied how we eat and what we like to eat. As hunger diminishes, eating behavior changes. Eliot Stellar (1985) discovered this after outfitting people with a special dental retainer engineered to record each chew and swallow. The device answers questions about human eating that you may never have thought to ask. During a meal of sandwich snacks, how often does the average person swallow? Every 14 seconds. How many chews per swallow? On average, 19. How fast do people chew? Some 1.8 chews per second. As the meal progresses and both hunger and food tastiness decrease, people chew more. Ironically, the better a food tastes, the *less* time we leave it in our mouth.

Culture and Hunger

Our preferences for sweet and salty tastes are genetic and universal. Other tastes are conditioned, as when people given highly salted foods develop a liking for excess salt (Beauchamp, 1987) or when people develop an aversion to a food eaten before becoming violently ill. (The frequency of children's illnesses provides many chances for them to learn food aversions.)

An acquired taste For Alaskan Eskimos, but not for most other North Americans, whale blubber is a tasty treat. People everywhere learn to enjoy the fatty, bitter, or irritating foods that are prescribed by their culture.

Culture affects taste, too. Bedouins enjoy eating the eye of a camel, which most North Americans would find repulsive. Similarly, most North Americans and Europeans shun dog, rat, and horse meat, all of which are prized elsewhere, but welcome beef, which Hindus wouldn't think of eating. Such preferences vary with exposure (Pliner & Pelchat, 1991; Rozin, 1976). We humans have a natural dislike of many things unfamiliar, including novel foods (especially novel animal-based rather than vegetarian foods). Rats, too, prefer long-familiar foods (Sclafani, 1995). This "neophobia" surely was adaptive for our ancestors, serving to protect them from potentially toxic substances. In experiments, people have tried novel fruit drinks or ethnic foods. With repeated exposure, their appreciation for the new taste typically increases; moreover, exposure to one set of novel foods increases willingness to try another (Pliner, 1982; Pliner & others, 1993).

External Incentives and Hunger

Like Pavlov's dogs, people learn to salivate in anticipation of appealing foods. Some people are especially responsive to appealing foods. When food is abundant, such people tend to gain the most weight.

Consider the 9- to 15-year-old girls studied by Judith Rodin and Joyce Slochower (1976) at an eight-week summer camp. During the first week of camp, some girls could not resist munching readily visible M&M's, even after a full meal. These girls were typical of a category the researchers called *externals*—people whose eating is triggered more by the presence of food than by internal factors. In the seven weeks that followed, the "external" girls gained the most weight.

In a delicious demonstration of how internal and external factors interact, Rodin (1984) invited other research subjects to her laboratory for lunch after they had gone 18 hours without food. While blood samples were being taken, a large, juicy steak was wheeled in, crackling as it finished grilling. As the hungry subjects sat watching, hearing, and smelling the soon-to-be-eaten steak, Rodin monitored their rising blood insulin levels and their accompanying feelings of hunger. When stimulated by the sight, sound, and aroma of the steak, "externals" had the greatest insulin increase and accompanying hunger response. This illustrates how certain individuals' psychological experience of an external incentive (the steak) can affect their internal physiological state.

Eating Disorders

Psychological influences on eating behavior are strikingly evident in those for whom normal homeostatic pressures are overwhelmed by a motive for abnormal thinness. Consider two eating disorder cases.

Mary is a 5′ 3″ 15-year-old who, having reached 100 pounds, decided she needed to lose weight to enhance her attractiveness. After gradually reducing her food intake to a few vegetables a day and then adding a vigorous exercise program, she now weighs a mere 80 pounds. Yet she still feels "fat" and plans to continue dieting. Mary has been having difficulty sleeping, has at times been depressed, and no longer has regular menstrual periods. She is socially inactive, but she is very successful academically. Mary does not regard herself as ill or needing treatment.

Alice is a 5′ 9″, 160-pound 17-year-old who says she has always been a little chubby. For the last five years, she has often eaten in binges, followed by vomiting. She will eat a quart of ice cream or an entire pie and then, to control her weight, make herself vomit in secret. Alice wants to date, but she doesn't, partly because she is so self-conscious about her looks. She has at times taken diet pills to try to lose weight.

Mary is diagnosed as having anorexia nervosa— a disorder in which a person becomes significantly underweight (typically, 15 percent or more) yet feels fat and is obsessed with losing weight. Even when emaciated, the person continues to limit food

anorexia nervosa
an eating disorder in which a normal-weight person (usually an adolescent female) diets and becomes significantly (15 percent or more) underweight, yet, still feeling fat, continues to starve.

PEANUTS

Drawing by Charles Schulz; © 1989 United Feature Syndicate, Inc. Reprinted by permission of UFS, Inc.

bulimia nervosa
an eating disorder characterized by private, "binge-purge" episodes of overeating, usually of highly caloric foods, followed by vomiting or laxative use.

In a 1993 national survey, nearly one-half of U.S. women reported feeling negative about their appearance and preoccupied with being or becoming overweight (Cash & Henry, 1995).

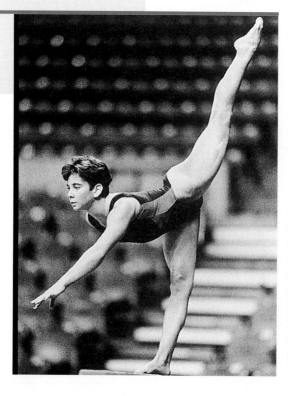

Dying to be thin Champion U.S. gymnast Christy Henrich, shown here at the 1989 World Games, was plagued by anorexia and bulimia. She was at times training nine hours a day and eating one apple. "My life is a horrifying nightmare. It feels like there's a beast inside of me," she explained before dying in 1994, a 60-pound tragedy who barely dented her hospital mattress (Deardorff, 1994).

intake. The disorder usually develops in adolescence, 9 times out of 10 in females.

Alice's condition, which is more common, is bulimia nervosa—a disorder marked by repeated binge-purge episodes of overeating followed by vomiting or laxative use. Bulimia patients eat as some alcoholics drink—in spurts, sometimes under the influence of friends who also are binging (Crandall, 1988). Most binge-purge eaters are women in their late teens or twenties. Like those with anorexia, they are preoccupied with food (craving sweet and high-fat foods), are fearful of becoming overweight, and are depressed or anxious (Hinz & Williamson, 1987). The depression and shame are felt most keenly during and following binges. About half of those with anorexia also display the binge-purge-depression symptoms of bulimia. But unlike anorexia, bulimia is marked by weight fluctuations within or above normal ranges. This makes the condition easy to hide.

Researchers report that the families of bulimia patients have a higher-than-usual incidence of alcoholism, obesity, and depression. Anorexia patients often come from a family that is competitive, high-achieving, and protective (Pate & others, 1992; Yates, 1989, 1990). They set high standards, fret about falling short of expectations, and are intensely concerned with how others perceive them (Heatherton & Baumeister, 1991; Striegel-Moore & others, 1993). Eating disorders do *not*, however,

provide (as some have speculated) a telltale sign of childhood sexual abuse (Kinz & others, 1994; Pope & others, 1992, 1994; Rorty & others, 1994).

Genetics also may influence susceptibility to eating disorders. When one twin has bulimia, the chances of the other twin's sharing the disorder are much greater if they are identical rather than fraternal twins (Fichter & Noegel, 1990). People with eating disorders may also have abnormal supplies of certain neurotransmitters that put them at risk for anxiety or depression (Fava & others, 1989).

There is, however, a cultural explanation for the fact that anorexia and bulimia occur mostly in women and mostly in weight-conscious cultures. Mothers of girls with eating disorders are themselves often focused on their own weight and on their daughters' weight and appearance (Pike & Rodin, 1991). Anorexia nervosa always begins as a weight-loss diet, and the self-induced vomiting of bulimics nearly always begins after a dieter has broken diet restrictions and gorged. Facing a diet, the bulimic's body revolts, overcoming willpower as it demands food to restore lost fat. Those whose natural set-point weight is well above their thin-ideal weight are especially vulnerable (Seligman, 1994).

Although ideals of beauty have varied over the centuries, women in every era have struggled to make their bodies conform to the ideal of their day. Thus, the sickness of today's eating disorders lies not just within the victims but also within their weight-obsessed culture—a culture that says, in countless ways, "Fat is bad," that motivates millions of women to be "always dieting," and that encourages eating binges by pressuring women to live in a constant state of semistarvation. "You can't be too rich or too thin," declared the Duchess of Windsor. As obesity researchers Susan Wooley and Orland Wooley (1983) noted, "An increasingly stringent cultural standard of thinness for women has been accompanied by a steadily increasing incidence of serious eating disorders in women."

Part of the cultural pressure is surely transmitted by the view of women pictured in fashion magazines, advertisements, and some toys. Expose young women to magazine models of ultra-thin models, report Eric Stice and Heather Shaw (1994), and they will feel more ashamed, depressed, and dissatisfied with their own bodies—the very attitudes that predispose eating disorders. But even the ultra-thin models don't define the impossible standard of the Barbie fashion doll. Adjusted to a 5' 7" height, her 32-16-29 figure (in centimeters, 82 bust, 41 waist, and 73 hips) defines a body shape approximated by fewer than 1 in 100,000 women (Norton & others, 1996).

Figure 12.4

Thinnest   **Women's ideal**   **What women believed men preferred**   **What men actually preferred**   **Women's current body image**   **Fattest**

Women's body images   Many U.S. women students tend to idealize—and misperceive men as idealizing—a body shape considerably thinner than their actual shape. (Adapted from Fallon, 1990; Fallon & Rozin, 1985.)

Women's distorted perceptions also extend to their impression of the body shapes that men find attractive. In one study of nearly five hundred University of Pennsylvania students, April Fallon and Paul Rozin (1985) found not only that women's ideal body weight was less than their current weight, but also that the weight they thought men preferred was less than the weight men actually preferred (Figure 12.4). The researchers found no such discrepancies in the men's self-ratings. Men more often judged their current weight, their ideal weight, and the weight they thought women preferred as all quite similar. Women's greater self-dissatisfaction stems from their perceiving their cheeks, waist, and hips as looking larger than they do (Thompson, 1986).

Women with low self-esteem are particularly likely to have a negative body image and are especially vulnerable to eating disorders (Mintz & Betz, 1986; Strauman & others, 1991; Striegel-Moore & others, 1986).

Body ideals vary across culture and time. In India, women students rate their ideals as close to their actual shape. In Western cultures, however, the rise in eating disorders has coincided with a dramatic increase over the last fifty years in women having a poor body image (Feingold & Mazzella, 1996). Moreover, eating disorders have plagued mainly *white* women (Dolan, 1991).

example, we are likely to feel hungry when our glucose levels are low. This information is integrated by the hypothalamus, which regulates the body's weight as it influences our feelings of hunger and satiety. To maintain weight, the body also adjusts its metabolic rate of energy expenditure.

The Psychology of Hunger   Our preferences for certain tastes are partly genetic and universal, but also partly learned in a cultural context. Especially in "external" people, the sight and smell of food can trigger hunger and eating, partly by stimulating a rise in insulin level. The impact of psychological factors, such as challenging family settings and weight-obsessed societal pressures, on eating behavior is dramatic in people with anorexia nervosa, who keep themselves on near-starvation rations, and in those with bulimia nervosa, who binge and purge in secret. A dramatic increase in poor body image has coincided with a rise in eating disorders among women in Western cultures in the past half-century.

KEY TERMS AND CONCEPTS   glucose, set point, metabolic rate, anorexia nervosa, bulimia nervosa

SUMMING UP

The Physiology of Hunger   Hunger's inner push primarily originates not from the stomach's contractions but from variations in body chemistry. For

Women in every era have struggled to make their bodies conform to the ideal of their day. Thus, the sickness of today's eating disorders lies not just within the victims but also within their weight-obsessed culture.

Sexual Motivation

The psychology of sexual motivation seeks to describe and explain sexually motivated behaviors and to treat sexual disorders. Sex is a physiologically based motive, like hunger, but it is more affected by learning and by one's values. New evidence suggests that sexual orientation is subject to genetic influences via prenatal hormones and the brain.

Sex is part of life. Had this not been so for all your ancestors, you would not be reading this book. Sexual motivation is nature's clever way of making people procreate, thus enabling our species' survival. When two people feel attracted, they hardly stop to think of themselves as guided by their genes. As the pleasure we take in eating is nature's inventive method of getting our body nourishment, so the pleasure of sex is our genes' way of preserving and spreading themselves.

Describing Sexual Behavior

Before looking at what energizes and directs sexual arousal, let's consider the behavior patterns that a theory of sexual motivation must explain.

Unable to answer his students' questions about people's sexual practices, Indiana University biologist Alfred Kinsey and his colleagues (1948, 1953) set out to find some answers. Kinsey's confidential interviews with 18,000 people—85 percent conducted by himself or his associate Wardell Pomeroy—asked more than 350 rapid-fire questions. Social scientists were quick to point out what Kinsey readily acknowledged—that his nonrandom sample contained an overrepresentation of well-educated, white urbanites. Nevertheless, his statistics-laden volumes became bestsellers. Here readers learned the surprising news that most of the men and nearly half the women reported having had premarital sexual intercourse; that most women and virtually all men reported masturbating; and that women who reported masturbating to

"Maybe . . .
it starts with a kiss."

PRENATAL PHOTOGRAPHER
LENNART NILLSON,
ANSWERING THE QUESTION "WHEN
DOES LIFE BEGIN?"

Alfred Kinsey The controversial biologist, shown here conducting one of his interviews, did not begin with sexually explicit questions. Rather, he first helped people feel at ease by asking nonthreatening questions about family background, health, and education.

As the pleasure we take in eating is nature's inventive method of getting our body nourishment, so the pleasure of sex is our genes' way of preserving and spreading themselves.

orgasm before marriage seldom had difficulties experiencing orgasm after marriage. One could also find evidence that sexual behavior is enormously varied. Kinsey found some men and women who said they had never had an orgasm, and others who said they had four or more a day. For those who evaluate themselves by comparisons with others, Kinsey's findings—and others showing wide variations in "normal" sexual behavior around the world—are reassuring. Given the range of sex drives and the variety of sexual behaviors, our own sexual interests probably fall well within the range of "normal."

Because we do not know whether Kinsey's sample accurately represented the nation's sexual practices in the 1940s, let alone those of today, it can be misleading to report his precise findings. Moreover, Kinsey and Pomeroy's questioning encouraged (some say, demanded) admission of sexual activity. They never asked subjects *whether* they had engaged in a particular activity, they asked them *when* they had first engaged in it (thus making it easier for people to divulge their behavior). Pomeroy (1972, pp. 113, 124, 127) reported that he and Kinsey "went on the broad assumption that everybody had done everything." If Kinsey or Pomeroy doubted a subject's denial, they might respond, "Yes, I know you have never done that, but how old were you the *first* time you did it?" or even "Look, I don't give a damn what you've done, but if you don't tell me the straight of it, it's better that we stop this history right here. Now, how old were you the first time this or that happened?"

By today's standards of random sampling and nonleading questioning, Kinsey's tactics, and thus his results, are suspect. Yet his surveys were surely less misleading than some of the haphazard sexual surveys that have been reported more recently in the popular press. Recall from Chapter 1 that when popular "sex reports" begin with a biased sample of people (such as subscribers to selected magazines) and receive replies from only 3 percent of this nonrandom sample, there is good reason to doubt the generality of their findings.

Better information is now becoming available. Despite the media image of rampant marital infidelity—an image reinforced by media psychologist Joyce Brothers' (1990) pronouncement that two-thirds of married men and half of married women have affairs—four recent surveys of randomly sampled U.S. adults provide a different view (Greeley, 1991; Laumann & others, 1994; Leigh & others, 1993; Smith, 1990). Nearly 9 in 10 married adults claim (even when responding anonymously) to have had sex only with their spouse during their present marriage. And 94 to 98 percent say they have been faithful during the past year. Apparently faithful attractions greatly outnumber fatal attractions. Moreover, disapproval of extramarital sex, at 91 percent, runs as high as ever among adult Americans (Smith, 1994).

Information should soon be available from new sex surveys. The World Health Organization, for example, is conducting the first-ever global survey of human sexuality, based on interviews with some 2000 people in each of 20 countries. Researchers hope that results from such surveys will help us better understand the behaviors that spread AIDS and other sexually transmitted diseases, and why some groups are especially vulnerable.

The Physiology of Sex

Like hunger, sexual arousal depends on the interplay of internal and external stimuli. To understand sexual motivation, we must consider both.

The Sexual Response Cycle

The headlines created by Kinsey's 1940s surveys reappeared after some 1960s studies in which scientists recorded the physiological responses of volunteers who masturbated or had intercourse. With the help of 382 female and 312 male volunteers—a somewhat atypical sample, consisting only of people able and willing to display arousal and orgasm while being observed in a laboratory—gynecologist-obstetrician William Masters and his collaborator Virginia Johnson (1966) monitored or filmed more than 10,000 sexual "cycles."

Their description of the sexual response cycle identified four stages, similar in men and women. During the initial *excitement phase*, the genital areas become engorged with blood, causing the man's penis to become partially erect and the woman's clitoris to swell and the inner lips covering her vagina to open up. Her vagina also expands and secretes lubricant, and her breasts and nipples may enlarge.

In the *plateau phase*, excitement peaks as breathing, pulse, and blood pressure rates continue to increase. The penis becomes fully engorged and some fluid (frequently containing enough live sperm to enable conception) may appear at the tip of the penis. Vaginal secretion continues to increase, the clitoris retracts, and orgasm feels imminent.

Masters and Johnson observed muscle contractions all over the body during *orgasm*; these were accompanied by further increases in breathing, pulse, and blood pressure rates. A woman's arousal and orgasm facilitate conception by helping propel semen from the penis, positioning the uterus to receive sperm, and drawing the sperm further inward. A woman's orgasm therefore not only reinforces intercourse, which is essential to natural reproduction, it also increases retention of deposited sperm (Furlow & Thornhill, 1996). In the excitement of the moment, men and women are hardly aware of all this but are more aware of their rhythmic genital contractions that create a pleasurable feeling of sexual release. The feeling apparently is much the same for both sexes. In one study, a panel of experts could not reliably distinguish between descriptions of orgasm written by men and those written by women (Vance & Wagner, 1976).

After orgasm, the body gradually returns to its unaroused state as the engorged genital blood vessels release their accumulated blood—relatively quickly if orgasm has occurred, relatively slowly otherwise. (It's like the nasal tickle that goes away rapidly if you have sneezed, slowly otherwise.) During this *resolution phase*, the male enters a refractory period, lasting from a few minutes to a day or more, during which he is incapable of another orgasm. A female does not have so lengthy a refractory period, which may make it possible for her to have another orgasm if restimulated during or soon after resolution (Figure 12.5).

sexual response cycle
the four stages of sexual responding described by Masters and Johnson—excitement, plateau, orgasm, and resolution.

refractory period
a resting period after orgasm, during which a man cannot achieve another orgasm.

A nonsmoking 50-year-old male has about a 1 in a million chance of a heart attack during any hour. This increases to merely 2 in a million during the hour following sex (with no increase for those who exercise regularly). Compared with risks associated with heavy exertion or anger (see Chapter 17), this risk seems not worth losing sleep (or sex) over (Muller & others, 1996).

Figure **12.5**

The sexual response cycle in men and in women. (Adapted from Masters & Johnson, 1966.)

Hormones and Sexual Behavior

Sex hormones have two effects: They direct the development of male and female sex characteristics, and (especially in nonhuman animals) they activate sexual behavior. In most mammals, nature neatly synchronizes sex with fertility. The female becomes sexually receptive ("in heat") when production of the female hormone estrogen peaks at ovulation. (In experiments, researchers simulate receptivity by injecting female animals with estrogen.) Male hormone levels are more constant, and researchers cannot so easily manipulate the sexual behavior of male animals by hormone treatments (Feder, 1984). Nevertheless, castrated male rats—having lost their testes, which manufacture the male sex hormone testosterone—gradually lose much of their interest in receptive females, and they gradually regain it if injected with testosterone.

"Fill'er up with testosterone."

Drawing by Mankoff; 1993 The New Yorker Magazine, Inc.

Hormones don't so neatly control human sexual behavior. Women's sexual desire is only slightly higher at ovulation (Harvey, 1987; Meuwissen & Over, 1992). Women's sexuality also differs from that of other mammalian females in being more responsive to testosterone level than to estrogen level (Andersen & Cyranowski, 1995).

In men, normal fluctuations in testosterone levels, from man to man and hour to hour, have little effect on sexual drive (Byrne, 1982). Indeed, hormone fluctuations are partly a response to sexual stimulation. When James Dabbs and his colleagues (1987) had male collegians converse separately with a male and with a female student, the men's testosterone levels rose with the social arousal, but especially after talking with the female. Like the effect of the crackling steak on insulin level, sexual arousal can be a cause as well as a consequence of increased testosterone levels.

Although normal short-term hormonal changes have little effect on desire, large hormone shifts have a bigger effect over the life span. A person's interest in dating and sexual stimulation usually increases with the pubertal surge in sex hormones. If the hormonal surge is precluded—as happened with prepubertal boys who were castrated during the 1600s and 1700s to preserve their soprano voices for Italian opera—the normal development of sex characteristics and sexual desire does not occur (Peschel & Peschel, 1987). Among adult men who suffer castration, sex drive typically falls along with declining testosterone levels (Hucker & Bain, 1990). Likewise, male sex offenders lose much of their sexual urge when voluntarily taking Depo-Provera, a drug that reduces testosterone levels to that of a prepubertal boy (Money & others, 1983). And in later life, the typical frequency of sexual fantasies and intercourse declines as sex hormone levels decline (Leitenberg & Henning, 1995).

Hormones influence sexual arousal via the hypothalamus, which both monitors variations in blood hormone levels and activates the appropriate neural circuits. In rats, destroying a key area of the hypothalamus may end sexual activity; stimulating this area, either electrically or by directly inserting minute quantities of hormones, may activate sexual behavior.

To summarize, we might compare human sex hormones, especially testosterone, to the fuel in a car. Lacking fuel, the car will not run. But if the fuel level is minimally adequate, adding more fuel to the gas tank won't change how the car runs. The analogy is imperfect, because the interaction between hormones and sexual motivation is two-way. However, the analogy correctly suggests that biology is a necessary but not sufficient explanation of human sexual behavior. The hormonal fuel is essential, but so are the psychological stimuli that turn on the engine, keep it running, and shift it into high gear.

The Psychology of Sex

Hunger and sex are different sorts of motives. Hunger responds to a *need*. If we do not eat, we die. Sex is not in this sense a need. If we do not have sex, we may feel like dying, but we do not die. There are nevertheless similarities between hunger and sexual motivation. Both depend on internal physiological factors. And both are influenced by external stimuli.

External Stimuli

Many studies confirm that men become aroused when they see, hear, or read erotic material. More surprising to many people (because sexually explicit materials are sold mostly to men) is that most women—at least the less inhibited women who volunteer to participate in such studies—report nearly as much arousal to the same stimuli (Stockton & Murnen, 1992).

In one such study, psychologist Julia Heiman (1975) had sexually experienced university volunteers attach instruments that detected arousal (changes in penis circumference or in vaginal color). Then the students listened to one of four tapes: a sexually explicit erotic tape, a romantic tape (of a couple expressing love without physical contact), a combined erotic-romantic tape, or a neutral control tape. Which do you suppose the men were most aroused by? And the women? Both found the tape of explicit sex most arousing, especially when a woman initiated the sex and the depiction centered on her responses.

People may find such arousal either pleasing or disturbing. (Those who find it disturbing often limit their exposure to such materials, just as those wishing to control hunger limit their exposure to tempting cues.) With repeated exposure, the emotional response to any erotic stimulus often "habituates" (lessens). During the 1920s, when women's hemlines first reached the knee, the exposed leg was a mildly erotic stimulus, as were once modest (by today's standards) two-piece swim suits and movie scenes of a mere kiss.

Some sexually explicit materials can have adverse effects. Depictions of women being sexually coerced—and enjoying it—tend to increase viewers' acceptance of the false idea that women enjoy rape, and they tend to increase male viewers' willingness to hurt women (see pages 576–577). Images of sexually attractive women and men may also lead people to devalue their own partners and relationships. After male collegians view TV or magazine depictions of sexually attractive women, they often find an average woman, or their own girlfriends or wives, less attractive (Kenrick & others, 1989; Kenrick & Gutierres, 1980; Weaver & others, 1984). Viewing X-rated sex films similarly tends to diminish people's satisfaction with their own sexual partners (Zillmann, 1989). Some sex researchers fear that reading or viewing erotica may create expectations that few men and women can hope to live up to.

Imagined Stimuli

Sexual motivation arises from the interplay of physiology and environment. But the stimuli inside our heads—our imaginations—also influence sexual arousal and desire (Figure 12.6). The brain, it has been said, is our most significant sex organ. People who, because of a spinal cord injury, have no genital sensation, can still feel sexual desire (Willmuth, 1987). Consider, too, the erotic potential of dreams. As noted in Chapter 7, genital arousal accompanies all types of dreams, even though most dreams have no sexual content. But in nearly all men and some 40 percent of women (Wells, 1986), dreams sometimes do contain sexual imagery that leads to orgasm. In men, these nocturnal emissions ("wet dreams") are more likely when orgasm has not occurred recently.

Figure 12.6

Forces affecting sexual motivation
Sexual motivation results from the interplay of physiology, environment, and imagination. (From Byrne, 1982.)

Diagram labels: Imaginative stimuli; External stimuli; Physiological readiness

Wide-awake people become sexually aroused not only by memories of prior sexual activities but also by fantasies. Fantasies need not correspond to actual behavior. In one survey of masturbation-related fantasies (Hunt, 1974), 19 percent of women and 10 percent of men reported imagining being taken by someone overwhelmed with desire for them. Fantasy is not reality, however. To paraphrase Susan Brownmiller (1975), for women there's a big difference between fantasizing that Fabio just won't take no for an answer and having a hostile stranger actually force himself on you. (See page 577 for a discussion of the "rape myth.")

"Ours is a society which stimulates interest in sex by constant titillation. . . . Cinema, television, and all the formidable array of our marketing technology project our very effective forms of titillation and our prejudices about man as a sexy animal into every corner of every hovel in the world."

GERMAINE GREER (1984)

"There is no difference between being raped and being run over by a truck except that afterward men ask if you enjoyed it."

MARGE PIERCY
"RAPE POEM"
1976

sexual disorder
a problem that consistently impairs sexual arousal or functioning.

SALLY FORTH

About 95 percent of both men and women say they have had sexual fantasies. But men (whether gay or straight) fantasize about sex more often, more physically, and less romantically—and prefer less personal and faster-paced sex content in books and videos (Leitenberg & Henning, 1995). Sexual fantasies do *not* indicate sexual problems or dissatisfaction. (If anything, sexually active people have more sexual fantasies.)

Sexual Disorders and Therapy

Masters and Johnson sought not only to describe the human sexual response cycle but also to understand and treat the inability to complete it. Sexual disorders are problems that consistently impair sexual functioning. Some involve sexual motivation, especially lack of sexual energy and arousability. Men, for example, may experience *premature ejaculation* (before they or their partners wish) or *impotence* (the inability to have or maintain an erection). Women more often than men experience low sexual desire or *orgasmic disorder* (infrequently or never experiencing orgasm).

What causes such problems? The idea that personality disorders are to blame has been largely discounted. Men who experience premature ejaculation are similar, even in their sexual arousal patterns, to men who do not; they simply ejaculate at lower levels of sexual arousal—something that often occurs with young men who have had long periods of sexual abstinence (Grenier & Byers, 1995; Spiess & others, 1984).

When Barbara Andersen (1983) reviewed research on the diagnosis and treatment of orgasmic disorder in women, she, too, could find no associated personality traits. Furthermore, she reported that treating orgasmic disorder through traditional psychotherapy (as though it were a disorder of per-

sonality) has been unsuccessful. She did, however, report a nearly 100 percent success rate with a behavioral treatment that trains women to enjoy their bodies and to give themselves orgasms, with a vibrator if necessary. Women who undergo such training are then sometimes able to generalize their new sexual responsiveness to interactions with their mates (Rosen & Leiblum, 1995; Wakefield, 1987). Some success has also been reported in training men to control their premature ejaculations by repeatedly stimulating the penis and then stopping stimulation (or even firmly squeezing the head of the penis) when the urge to ejaculate arises. Alternatively, men can reduce their excitability by simply having more orgasms (LoPicolo & Stock, 1986).

Gender and Sexuality

"With few exceptions anywhere in the world," report cross-cultural psychologist Marshall Segall and his colleagues (1990, p. 244), "males are more likely than females to initiate sexual activity." Across 177 studies of some 130,000 people, men are much more accepting of casual sex and they report masturbating much more often (Oliver & Hyde, 1993). This is among the largest of gender differences. A few examples:

- In a Canadian survey of 2350 adults-only video store customers, 80 percent were males (though half claimed to engage a partner in watching the movies—Jenish, 1993). Similarly, if you guessed that a hard-core pornography reader was male and a romance novel reader was female, you would usually be right (Malamuth, 1996).

- In a 1996 survey of 251,000 entering American college students, 54 percent of men but only 32 percent of women agreed that "if two people really like each other, it's all right for them to have sex even if they've known each other for a very short time" (Sax & others, 1996).

- In a careful survey of 3432 U.S. 18- to 59-year-olds, 48 percent of the women but only 25 percent of the men cited affection as a reason for first intercourse. And how often do they think about sex? "Every day" or "several times a day," acknowledged 19 percent of the women and 54 percent of the men (Laumann & others, 1994).

- Such gender differences characterize both heterosexual and homosexual people, as does a similar mating psychology. Like heterosexual men, gay men report more interest in uncommitted sex than lesbians report, and also more responsiveness to visual sexual stimuli, and more concern with their partner's physical attractiveness (Bailey & others, 1994).

Gender differences in attitudes carry over to differences in behavior. Casual hit-and-run sex is most frequent among males with traditional masculine attitudes (Pleck & others, 1993). Russell Clark and Elaine Hatfield (1989) observed the striking gender difference in sexuality when in 1978 they sent some average-looking student research assistants strolling across the Florida State University quadrangle. Spotting an attractive person of the other sex, a researcher would approach and say, "I have been noticing you around campus and I find you to be very attractive. Would you go to bed with me tonight?" The women all declined, some with obvious irritation ("What's wrong with you, creep, leave me alone"). But 75 percent of the men readily agreed, often with comments such as "Why do we have to wait until tonight?" Somewhat astonished by their result, Clark and Hatfield repeated their study in 1982 and twice more during the late-1980s AIDS era (Clark, 1990). Each time, virtually no women, but half or more of the men, agreed to go to bed with a stranger.

Men also have a lower threshold for perceiving someone's warmth as a sexual come-on. In study after study, men more often than women attribute a woman's friendliness to sexual interest (Abbey, 1987; Johnson & others, 1991). Such "misattribution" of a woman's cordiality as a "come-on" helps explain men's greater sexual assertiveness (Kenrick & Trost, 1987). The unfortunate results can range from sexual harassment to date rape (Kanekar & Nazareth, 1988; Muehlenhard, 1988; Shotland, 1989).

As Chapter 18 will explain, there is a possible evolutionary explanation for women's more relational and men's more recreational approach to sex. Compared with eggs, sperm are cheap. Moreover, while a woman incubates and nurses one infant, a male can spread his genes by impregnating other females. Our natural yearnings, argue psychologists working from an evolutionary perspective, are our genes' way of reproducing themselves. In our ancestral history, females

most often sent their genes into the future by pairing wisely, men by pairing widely. "Humans are living fossils—collections of mechanisms produced by prior selection pressures," says David Buss (1995). But remember, say critics, cultural expectations also bend the genders. If socialized to value lifelong commitment, men may sexually bond with one partner; if socialized to accept casual sex, women may willingly have sex with many partners.

Sexual Orientation

To motivate is to energize and direct behavior. So far, we have considered the energizing of sexual motivation but not its direction. We express the direction of our sexual interest in our sexual orientation—our enduring sexual attraction toward members of a particular gender. Cultures vary in their attitudes toward homosexuality. Yet as far as we know, all cultures in all times have been predominantly heterosexual (Bullough, 1990). Whether a culture condemns and punishes homosexuality or views it as an acceptable alternative, homosexuality survives and heterosexuality prevails.

Homosexual people often recall childhood play preferences like those of the other sex (Bailey & Zucker, 1995). But most homosexual people report not becoming aware of same-gender sexual feelings until during or shortly after puberty, and not thinking of themselves as gay or lesbian until around age 20 (Garnets & Kimmel, 1990).

How many people are exclusively homosexual? Until recently, the popular press assumed a homosexuality rate of 10 percent. But in both Europe and the United States, more than a dozen national surveys in the early 1990s explored sexual orientation, using methods that protected the respondent's anonymity. Their results agree in suggesting that a more accurate figure is about 3 or 4 percent of men and 1 percent of women (Laumann & others, 1994; National Center for Health Statistics, 1991; Rogers & Turner, 1991). Less than 1 percent of the respondents reported being actively bisexual, but a larger number of adults reported having had an isolated homosexual experience. And most people said they had had an occasional homosexual fantasy.

Although health experts find it helpful to know sexual statistics, numbers don't decide issues of human rights. Similarly, it's helpful in manufacturing school desks to know that about 10 percent of people are left-handed. But whether left-handers are 3 percent or 10 percent of the population doesn't answer the moral question of whether lefties should enjoy equal rights.

sexual orientation
an enduring sexual attraction toward members of either one's own gender (homosexual orientation) or the other gender (heterosexual orientation).

"It has been maintained for years that we each use only about 10 percent of our brain capacity; that the condom failure rate is 10 percent; and until just last year, that 10 percent of Americans are homosexual. Such statistics are partly artifacts, I suspect, of our decimal system; in a base 12 system, we'd no doubt show a similar affinity for statistics that were multiples of 8.333 percent."

JOHN ALLEN PAULOS
"COUNTING ON DYSCALCULIA"
1993

What does it feel like to be homosexual in a heterosexual culture? One way for heterosexual people to understand is to imagine how they would feel if they were to be ostracized or fired for openly admitting or displaying their feelings toward someone of the other sex; if they were to overhear people making crude jokes about heterosexual people; if most movies, TV shows, and advertisements portrayed (or implied) homosexuality; and if their family members were pleading with them to change their heterosexual life-style and to enter into a homosexual marriage.

Facing such reactions, homosexual people often struggle with their sexual orientation. At first, they may try to ignore or deny their desires, hoping they will go away. But they don't. Then they may try to change, through psychotherapy, willpower, or prayer. But the feelings typically persist, as do those of heterosexual people—who are similarly incapable of becoming homosexual (Haldeman, 1994). Eventually, homosexuals may accept their orientation—by electing celibacy (as do some heterosexuals); by engaging in promiscuous sex (a choice more commonly made by men than by women); or by entering into a committed, long-term love relationship (a choice more often made by women than by men) (Peplau, 1982; Weinberg & Williams, 1974).

Most psychologists today view sexual orientation as neither willfully chosen nor willfully changed. Sexual orientation in some ways is like handedness: Most people are one way, some the other. A very few are truly ambidextrous. Regardless, the way one is endures. Nor is sexual orientation linked with psychological disorder or sexual crime. "Child molester" is not a sexual orientation. Some homosexuals do abuse children, but most child molesters are heterosexual males (Gonsiorek, 1982). These facts led the American Psychiatric Association in 1973 to drop homosexuality from its list of "mental illnesses."

Understanding Sexual Orientation

If our sexual orientation is indeed something we do not choose and cannot change, then where do these preferences come from? How do we move toward either a heterosexual or a homosexual orientation? See if you can anticipate the consensus that has emerged from hundreds of research studies by responding yes or no to the following questions:

1   Is homosexuality linked with problems in a child's relationships with parents, such as with a domineering mother and an ineffectual father, or a possessive mother and a hostile father?

2   Does homosexuality involve a fear or hatred of people of the other gender, leading individuals to direct their sexual desires toward members of their own sex?

3   Is sexual orientation linked with levels of sex hormones currently in the blood?

4   As children, were many homosexuals molested, seduced, or otherwise sexually victimized by an adult homosexual?

Contrary to widely held ideas about homosexuality, the answer to all these questions is no (Storms, 1983). Consider the findings of lengthy Kinsey Institute interviews with nearly 1000 homosexuals and 500 heterosexuals (Bell & others, 1981; Hammersmith, 1982). The investigators assessed nearly every imaginable psychological cause of homosexuality—parental relationships, childhood sexual experiences, peer relationships, dating experiences. Their findings: Apart from homosexuals' somewhat greater nonconformity, the reported backgrounds of homosexuals and heterosexuals were similar. Homosexuals were no more likely to have been smothered by maternal love, neglected by their father, or sexually abused. More recent studies have also found that sons of homosexual men were *not* more likely to become gay if they lived with their gay dad, and that 9 in 10 children of lesbian mothers developed into heterosexuals (Bailey & others, 1995; Golombok & Tasker, 1996). If even being reared by a homosexual parent has no appreciable influence on sexual orientation, then having a gay or lesbian teacher or bus driver also seems unlikely to have an appreciable influence.

Homosexual people do, however, appear more often in certain populations:

- In America's dozen largest cities, the percentage of men identifying themselves as gay jumps to 9 percent, compared with only 1 percent in rural areas (Binson & others, 1995; Laumann & others, 1994).

- One study of the biographies of 1004 eminent people found homosexual and bisexual people overrepresented (11 percent of the sample), especially among poets (24 percent), fiction writers (21 percent), and artists and musicians (15 percent) (Ludwig, 1995).

- For uncertain reasons, men who have older brothers are somewhat more likely to be gay, report Ray Blanchard and his colleagues (1995, 1996a,b). Assuming the odds of homosexuality are roughly 3 percent among first sons, they rise to 4 percent among second sons and 5 percent for third sons.

So, what determines sexual orientation? One theory proposes that people develop same-sex erotic attachments if segregated by gender at the time their sex drive matures (Storms, 1981). But even in a tribal culture in which homosexual behavior is expected of all boys before marriage, heterosexuality

Note that the scientific question is not "What causes homosexuality?" (or "What causes heterosexuality?") but "What causes differing sexual orientation?" In pursuit of answers, psychological science compares the backgrounds and physiology of people whose sexual orientations differ.

Erick has two moms Maria Christina Vlassidis (left) and Marie Tatro (center) tell playmates of their son Erick, 8, that they are both his moms. Both women, who are lesbians, attend school conferences and support other aspects of his life. Studies suggest that being reared by lesbian or gay parents does not appreciably affect a child's sexual orientation.

prevails (Money, 1987). (As this illustrates, homosexual *behavior* does not always indicate a homosexual *orientation*.) Another theory proposes the opposite: that people develop romantic attachments to those who *differ* from, and thus are more fascinating than, the peers they associated with while growing up (Bell, 1982). The bottom line from a half-century's theory and research: If there are environmental factors that influence sexual orientation, we do not yet know what they are. If someone were to ask me, "What can I do to influence my child's sexual orientation?" my answer would have to be "I haven't a clue."

The Brain and Sexual Orientation

New research indicates that sexual orientation is at least partly physiological. Researcher Simon LeVay (1991) discovered this while studying sections of the hypothalamus taken from deceased heterosexual and homosexual people. As a gay scientist, LeVay wanted to do "something connected with my gay identity," but he knew he had to avoid biasing the results. So he did the study "blind," without knowing which donors were gay. After nine months of peering through his microscope at a cell cluster he thought might be important, LeVay sat down one morning and broke the codes. His discovery: The cell cluster was reliably larger in

heterosexual men than in women and homosexual men. As the brain difference became apparent, "I was almost in a state of shock. . . . I took a walk by myself on the cliffs over the ocean. I sat for half an hour just thinking what this might mean" (LeVay, 1994).

It should not surprise us that brains differ with sexual orientation. Remember our maxim: Although we find it convenient to talk separately of psychological and biological explanations, *everything psychological is simultaneously biological.* The critical question is, when did the brain difference begin? At conception? In the womb? During childhood or adolescence? Did experience produce the difference? Or did genes or prenatal hormones (or genes via prenatal hormones)?

LeVay does not view this little neural center as a sexual orientation center; rather, he sees it as an important part of the neural pathway engaged in sexual behavior. Moreover, he acknowledges that it's possible that sexual behavior patterns influence the brain's anatomy. (In fish, birds, and humans, brain structures are known to vary with experience.) But he believes it more likely that brain anatomy influences sexual orientation. Laura Allen and Roger Gorski (1992) offered a similar conclusion after discovering that a section of the fibers connecting right and left hemispheres is one-third larger in homosexual men than in heterosexual men. "The emerging neuroanatomical picture," notes Brian Gladue (1994), "is that, in some brain areas, homosexual men are more likely to have female-typical neuroanatomy than are heterosexual men."

Genes and Sexual Orientation

The evidence suggests that genetic influence plays a role (Whitam & others, 1993). One research team studied the twin brothers of homosexual men. Among their identical twin brothers, 52 percent were homosexual, as were 22 percent of fraternal twin brothers (Bailey & Pillard, 1991, 1995). In a follow-up study of homosexual women, a similar 48 percent of their identical twins were homosexual, as were 16 percent of their fraternal twins (Bailey & others, 1993). With half the identical twin pairs differing, we know that genes aren't the whole story. Moreover, a new study using a diverse sample of Australian twins found somewhat lower rates of sexual similarity—although, again, identical twins were more likely than fraternal twins to share homosexual feelings (Bailey & others, 1997). This is the sort of pattern we expect to see when genes are having an *influence*. Moreover, with a single transplanted gene, scientists can now cause male fruit flies to display homosexual behavior (Zhang & Odenwald, 1995).

"Gay men simply *don't* have the brain cells *to be* attracted to women."

SIMON LEVAY
THE SEXUAL BRAIN
1993

"Studies indicate that male homosexuality is more likely to be transmitted from the mother's side of the family."

ROBERT PLOMIN, JOHN DEFRIES, GERALD MCCLEARN, AND MICHAEL RUTTER
BEHAVIORAL GENETICS
1997

Prenatal Hormones and Sexual Orientation

The elevated rate of homosexual orientation even in fraternal twins might also result from their sharing the same prenatal environment. In animals and some exceptional human cases, sexual orientation has been altered by abnormal prenatal hormone conditions. German researcher Gunter Dorner (1976, 1988) pioneered this research by manipulating a fetal rat's exposure to male hormones, thereby "inverting" its sexual behavior toward rats of the other sex. Female sheep will likewise show homosexual behavior if their pregnant mothers are injected with testosterone during a critical gestation period (Money, 1987).

With humans, a critical period for the brain's neural-hormonal control system may exist between the middle of the second and fifth months after conception (Ellis & Ames, 1987; Gladue, 1990; Meyer-Bahlburg, 1995). It seems that exposure to the hormone levels typically experienced by female fetuses during this time may predispose the person (whether female or male) to be attracted to males in later life. Some tests reveal that homosexual men have spatial abilities like those typical of heterosexual women—a pattern consistent with the hypothesis that homosexuals were exposed to atypical prenatal hormones (Gladue, 1994; McCormick & Witelson, 1991). Curiously, gay men also have fingerprint patterns rather like those of heterosexual women. Most people have more fingerprint ridges on their right hand. Jeff Hall and Doreen Kimura (1994) observed that this right-versus-left difference is less true of females and gay males than of heterosexual males—a difference that these researchers believe is due to prenatal hormones.

Because the physiological evidence is preliminary and controversial, some scientists remain skeptical. Rather than specifying sexual orientation, perhaps biological factors predispose a temperament that influences sexuality "in the context of individual learning and experience" (Byne & Parsons, 1993). Perhaps, theorizes Daryl Bem (1996), genes code for prenatal hormones and brain anatomy, which predispose *temperaments* that lead children to prefer sex-typical or sex-atypical activities and friends. These preferences may lead children later to feel attracted to whichever sex feels different. The dissimilar-seeming sex (whether one's own or the other sex) becomes associated with anxiety and other forms of arousal, which eventually gets transformed into romantic arousal. The exotic becomes erotic.

Regardless of the process, the consistency of the genetic, prenatal, and brain findings has swung the pendulum toward a physiological explanation. Nature more than nurture, most psychiatrists now believe, predisposes sexual orientation (Vreeland & others, 1995). If biological influences prove critical (perhaps especially in certain environmental contexts), it would explain why sexual orientation is so difficult to change.

Still, some people wonder: Should the cause of sexual orientation matter? Maybe it shouldn't, but people's assumptions matter. Those who believe, as do most homosexual people, that sexual orientation is a biological given—an enduring identity, not a choice—express more accepting attitudes toward homosexual persons (Allen & others, 1996; Furnham & Taylor, 1990; Whitley, 1990). In American surveys, agreement that homosexuality is "something that people are born with" doubled from 16 to 31 percent between 1983 and 1993. Over roughly the same period, support for equal job rights for homosexuals increased from 59 to 80 percent (Moore, 1993). And agreement "that homosexuality should be an acceptable alternative lifestyle" increased between 1982 and 1996 from 34 to 44 percent (Gallup, 1996). Accepting attitudes are most common among women and those with a gay or lesbian friend or relative (Herek & Capitanio, 1996; Kite & Whitley, 1996).

To gay and lesbian activists, the new biological research is a double-edged sword (Diamond, 1993). If sexual orientation, like skin color and sex, is genetically influenced, that offers a further rationale for civil rights protection. Moreover, it may alleviate parents' concerns about their children having gay teachers and role models. It does, however, raise the haunting possibility that genetic markers of sexual orientation could someday be identified through fetal testing, and the fetus aborted.

Sex and Human Values

Recognizing that values are both personal and cultural, most sex researchers and educators strive to keep their writings on sexuality value-free.

But can the study of sexual behavior and what motivates it really be free of values? Those who think not say that the very words we use to describe behavior often reflect our personal values. When sex researchers label sexually restrained individuals as "erotophobic" and as having "high sex guilt," they express their own values. Whether we label sexual acts we do not practice as "perversions," "deviations," or part of an "alternative sexual life-style" depends on our attitudes toward the behaviors. Labels both describe and evaluate.

"Were it not for delicately balanced combinations of genetic, neurological, hormonal, and environmental factors, largely occurring prior to birth, each and every one of us would be homosexual."

LEE ELLIS AND M. ASHLEY AMES (1987)

"Biological theories of sexual orientation are far more promising than any current alternatives."

J. MICHAEL BAILEY AND RICHARD C. PILLARD (1994)

A sharing of love For most adults, a sexual relationship fulfills not only a biological motive, but a social need for intimacy.

about sex—that the initial spasms of male and female orgasm come at 0.8-second intervals, that the female nipples expand 10 millimeters at the peak of sexual arousal, that systolic blood pressure rises some 60 points and the respiration rate to 40 breaths per minute—but fail to understand the human significance of sexual intimacy.

Surely one significance of sexual intimacy is its expression of our deeply social nature. Sex is a socially significant act. Men and women can achieve orgasm alone, yet most people find greater satisfaction while embracing their loved one. There is a yearning for closeness in sexual motivation. Sex at its human best is life-uniting and love-renewing.

When education about sex is separated from the context of human values, some students may get the idea that sexual intercourse is merely recreational activity. Diana Baumrind (1982), a University of California child-rearing expert, has observed that adolescents interpret sex education that pretends to be "value-free" as meaning that adults are neutral about adolescent sexual activity. Such an implication is unfortunate, she added, because "promiscuous recreational sex poses certain psychological, social, health, and moral problems that must be faced realistically."

Researchers have found that teenagers who have had formal sex education are no more likely to engage in premarital sex than those who have not (Furstenberg & others, 1985; Zelnik & Kim, 1982). Moreover, we enrich our lives by knowing ourselves, by realizing that others share our feelings, by understanding what is likely to please or displease our loved one. Witness the crumbling of falsehoods about homosexuality. Witness the growing realization that some types of sexually explicit material can lead people to devalue or hurt others.

Perhaps we can agree that the knowledge provided by sex research is preferable to ignorance, yet also agree that researchers' values should be stated openly, enabling us to debate them and to reflect on our own values. We might also remember that scientific research on sexual motivation does not aim to define the personal meaning of sex in our own lives. One can know every available fact

> "The relationship between women and men should be characterized not by patronizing behavior or exploitation, but by love, partnership, and trustworthiness. . . . Sexuality should express and reinforce a loving relationship lived by equal partners."
>
> **TOWARDS A GLOBAL ETHIC,**
> **1993 PARLIAMENT OF THE WORLD'S RELIGIONS**

SUMMING UP

Describing Sexual Behavior Sexual behaviors vary across both place and time. The range of "normal" sexual interests and behaviors remains broad.

The Physiology of Sex Physiologically, the human sexual response cycle normally follows a pattern of excitement, plateau, orgasm, and resolution, followed in males by a refractory period, during which renewed arousal and orgasm are not possible. Sex hormones, in combination with the hypothalamus, help our bodies develop and function as either male or female. In nonhuman animals, hormones also help stimulate sexual activity. In humans, they influence sexual behavior more loosely, especially once sufficient hormone levels are present.

The Psychology of Sex External stimuli can trigger sexual arousal in both men and women. Sexually explicit materials may also lead people to perceive their partners as comparatively less appealing and to devalue their relationships. In combination with the internal hormonal push and the external pull of sexual stimuli, fantasies (imagined stimuli) influence sexual arousal.

Sexual Disorders and Therapy Sexual disorders, such as premature ejaculation and female orgasmic disorder, are being successfully treated by new methods, which assume that people learn and can modify their sexual responses.

Gender and Sexuality One of the largest reported gender differences is women's generally greater disapproval of and lesser willingness to engage in casual, uncommitted sex.

The mathematics of sexually transmitted disease: Imagine an island on which, up to now, all people are virgins. Now assume that Pat has sex with nine people, each of whom over the same time period has sex with nine people, who in turn have sex with nine others. How many "phantom" sex partners (past partners of partners) will Pat have? Laura Brannon and Timothy Brock (1994) report that the actual number—511—is more than five times the average student's guess.

achievement motivation
a desire for significant accomplishment: for mastery of things, people, or ideas; for attaining a high standard.

What is your greatest achievement to date? What is your greatest future ambition—to attain fame? Fortune? Creative accomplishment? Security? Love? Power? Wisdom? Spiritual wholeness?

Figure **12.7**

What is this boy daydreaming about? By analyzing responses to ambiguous photos like this, motivation researchers have sought clues to people's levels of achievement motivation.

Sexual Orientation One's heterosexual or homosexual orientation seems neither willfully chosen nor willfully changed. Preliminary new evidence links sexual orientation with genetic influences, prenatal hormones, and certain brain structures.

Sex and Human Values Sex research and education are not value-free. Some say that sex-related values should therefore be openly acknowledged, recognizing the emotional significance of sexual expression.

KEY TERMS AND CONCEPTS sexual response cycle, refractory period, estrogen, sexual disorder, sexual orientation

Achievement Motivation

With their basic needs met, humans to varying degrees also feel motivated to display competence and to reach goals. Who has the greatest need to achieve? Why? And how can effective leaders motivate higher levels of achievement?

The biological perspective on motivation—the idea that physiological needs drive us to satisfy those needs—provides only a partial explanation of what energizes and directs our behavior. Hunger and sex have both social and physiological components. Moreover, there are motives that, unlike hunger and sex, seem not to satisfy any physical need. Billionaires may be motivated to make ever more money, movie stars to become ever more famous, politicians to achieve ever more power, daredevils to seek ever greater thrills. Such motives seem not to diminish when they are fed. The more we achieve, the more we may need to achieve.

Identifying Achievement Motivation

Think of someone you know who strives to succeed by excelling at any task where evaluation is possible. Now think of someone who is less disciplined and driven. Psychologist Henry Murray (1938) defined the first person's high need for achievement, or achievement motivation, as a desire for significant accomplishment, for mastering skills or ideas, for control, and for rapidly attaining a high standard.

To study this motive, we first need a way to measure it. But how? Recall from the semistarvation studies that people driven by hunger begin to fantasize about food. Our sexual orientation is similarly reflected in our prevalent sexual fantasies. Do these examples suggest a way to assess a person's need to achieve?

Murray and investigators David McClelland and John Atkinson presumed that people's fantasies would reflect their achievement concerns. So they asked subjects to invent stories about ambiguous pictures. If, when shown the daydreaming boy in Figure 12.7, a subject commented that the boy was preoccupied with his pursuit of a goal, that he imagined himself performing a heroic act, or that he was feeling pride in some success, the story was scored as indicating achievement concerns. McClelland and Atkinson regarded people whose stories consistently included such themes as having a high need for achievement.

Would you expect people whose stories express high achievement to prefer tasks that are easy, moderately challenging, or very difficult? People whose stories suggest low achievement motivation tend to choose either very easy or very difficult tasks, where failure is either unlikely or not embarrassing (Geen, 1984). Those whose stories express high achievement motivation tend to prefer moderately difficult tasks, where success is attainable yet attributable to their skill and effort. In a ring toss game they often stand at an intermediate distance from the stake; this enables some successes, yet provides a suitable challenge. When things get difficult people with a strong need to achieve persist more (Cooper, 1983). By contrast, high school underachievers persist less in completing college degrees, holding on to jobs, and maintaining their marriages (McCall, 1994).

As you might expect from their persistence and eagerness for realistic challenge, people with high achievement motivation do achieve more. One study followed the lives of 1528 California children whose intelligence scores were in the top 1 percent. When researchers forty years later compared those whose were most and least successful professionally, they found a motivational difference. Those most successful were more ambitious, energetic, and persistent. As children, they had more active hobbies. As adults, they participated in more groups and favored participating in sports over passively watching (Goleman, 1980). Another study of outstanding athletes, scholars, and artists found that all were highly motivated and self-disciplined, willing to dedicate hours every day to the pursuit of their goals (Bloom, 1985). These superstar achievers were distinguished not so much by their extraordinary natural talent as by their extraordinary daily discipline. When their preparation met an opportunity, the result was success.——

Analyses of the life histories of great scientists, philosophers, political leaders, writers, and musicians confirms the importance of disciplined motivation. Great achievers, consumed by a passion to perfect their gift, often are continuously productive from an early age, notes Dean Keith Simonton (1994). So much so that a small proportion of contributors to any field produce most of its achievements. Although intelligence is distributed like a bell curve, achievements are not—and that tells us that achievement involves much more than raw ability.

The image of achievement What motivates a person to study to the level of a Ph.D., learn five languages, and become a leading expert in international issues—as did Madeleine Albright, before becoming the U.S. United Nations representative and then secretary of state?

Sources of Achievement Motivation

Why, despite similar potentials, does one person become more motivated to achieve than another? Highly motivated children often have parents who encourage their independence from an early age and praise and reward them for their successes (Teevan & McGhee, 1972). Such parents encour-

> *Superstar achievers were distinguished not so much by their extraordinary natural talent as by their extraordinary daily discipline. When their preparation met an opportunity, the result was success.*

age them to dress and feed themselves and to do well in school, and they express delight when their children achieve. Theorists speculate that the high achievement motivation displayed by such children has *emotional* roots, as children learn to associate achievement with positive emotions. There may also be *cognitive* roots, as children learn to attribute their achievements to their own competence and effort, raising their expectations (Dweck & Elliott, 1983).

These parental influences also help explain a fascinating finding—that birth order correlates with achievement. In North America and China, first-born and only children do slightly better in school and on intelligence tests and are more likely to achieve admission to prestigious colleges than are their later-born brothers and sisters (Falbo & Polit, 1986; Falbo & Poston, 1993). These findings may partly reflect the generally higher socioeconomic status of small families, which have fewer later-born children (Blake, 1989). However, in separate studies of eminent people, 64 percent of "distinguished Americans" from two-child families were first-born, as were 61 percent of Rhodes scholars, 66 percent of National Merit scholars, 64 percent of those in *Who's Who*, and 21 of the 23 astronauts chosen for the first U.S. space program.

It is fun to speculate about differences between the experiences of first-born and later-born children. One difference might be the greater parental attention given to first-borns during their years as solo children. Perhaps parents have invested more in a first-born child. They may take more pictures of their first child and provide that child with more encouragement and higher expectations. But the later-born often have noteworthy social strengths. They tend to be more socially relaxed and popular. Having less power than one's older siblings—less size, strength, verbal ability, and experience—apparently fosters more effective social skills (Miller & Maruyama, 1976).

> "They can because they think they can."
>
> **VIRGIL**
> *AENEID*
> 19 B.C.

Remember the two people you chose on page 384, one who consistently strives to succeed, the other who is less concerned with achievement? Is either a first-born (or only) child?

Figure **12.8**

Birth order and acceptance of new ideas Later-born scientists like Charles Darwin have been more likely to propose and support controversial new ideas than their first-born peers. (Data from Sulloway, 1990.)

Tiger Woods "I remember a daily ritual that we had: I would call Pop at work to ask if I could practice with him. He would always pause a second or two, keeping me in suspense, but he'd always say yes. . . . In his own way, he was teaching me initiative. You see, he never pushed me to play" (quoted in *USA Weekend*, 1977).

Throughout history later-born scientists have also been more supportive of new ideas—including bad new ideas, such as phrenology and mesmerism, and good new ideas, such as the Earth's orbit around the Sun. Copernicus, who proposed that orbital path, was the second of four children; Tycho Brahe, who defended the traditional view that the Sun and stars revolve around the Earth, was an only child. Charles Darwin, the fifth of six children, found his new ideas supported by most later-born scientists but rejected by his first-born peers (see Figure 12.8). Science historian Frank Sulloway (1996) reports that most leaders of radical scientific revolutions were later-borns. Among the 3881 scientists who participated in 28 controversies, 37 percent of the first-borns and 62 percent of the later-borns were supportive of the new ideas. The same was true of the Protestant Reformation, which later-born religious leaders more often supported. First-borns, it seems, are more conscientious and tradition-respecting, later-borns more freewheeling and creative.

Intrinsic Motivation and Achievement

In the classroom, at the workplace, and on the athletic field, two types of achievement motivation operate. Intrinsic motivation is the desire to be effective and to perform a behavior for its own sake. Intrinsically motivated people approach work or play seeking enjoyment, interest, self-expression, or challenge. Extrinsic motivation is seeking external rewards and avoiding punishments.

To sense the difference between extrinsic and intrinsic motivation, you might reflect on your own current experience. Are you feeling pressured to get this reading finished before a deadline? Worried about your course grade? Eager for rewards that depend on your doing well? If yes, then you are extrinsically motivated (as, to some extent, almost all students are). Are you also finding the course material interesting? Does learning it enable you to feel more competent? If there were no grade at stake, might you be curious enough to want to learn the material for its own sake? If yes, intrinsic motivation also fuels your efforts.

In sports, as in other activities, excessive external pressures and incentives can undermine intrinsic enjoyment. Researcher Dean Ryan (1980) studied university football players. He found that those on athletic scholarships (who were, in a sense, playing for pay) enjoyed their play less than did the non-scholarship players. Apparently, pay and pressure turn play into work. However, rewards can increase intrinsic motivation if their effect is to inform the players of their athletic competence (as with a "most improved player" award).

So, should coaches emphasize extrinsic pressures, rewards, and competition? Studies by motivation researchers Edward Deci and Richard Ryan indicate that it depends on the goal (1985, 1992). For some, as for legendary football coach Vince Lombardi, "Winning isn't everything; it's the only thing." If so, it may pay to control the players with pressures and rewards for winning. But what if the goal is—as it should be for most programs of physical education, fitness, and amateur sports—the promotion of an enduring interest and participation in physical activity? In that case, as Deci and Ryan observed, "External pressures, competitive emphasis, and evaluative feedback are in contradiction to this goal." Thus, if children's soccer coaches want their players to continue playing in the future, they should focus not on the urgency of winning but on the joy of playing one's best.

Researchers in the psychology of religion have also explored intrinsic versus extrinsic motivation (Bergin, 1991; Gorsuch, 1988). Some religiously active people score high on tests of extrinsic religious motivation, by reporting their religion is a means to other ends. (They might agree, for example, that "a primary reason for my interest in religion is that my church is a congenial social activity.") Others score high on *intrinsic* religious motivation, by reporting their religion is an end in itself. ("My religious beliefs are what really lie behind my whole approach to life.") Compared with the extrinsically religious, intrinsically religious people tend to score lower on tests of prejudice and anxiety. They also tend to live with a greater sense of control over their lives and a clearer sense of purpose (Wulff, 1991).

Motivating People

The growing field of industrial/organizational psychology includes studies of how managers might best:

- promote teamwork and group achievement.
- match people with jobs, by identifying motivated, well-suited personnel.
- make jobs suit people, by creating work environments that boost morale and output.
- evaluate performance and create incentives for excellence.

What every leader (manager, coach, or teacher) wants to know is "How can I manage in ways that enhance people's motivation, productivity, satisfaction?" (Satisfied workers aren't always more productive, but they are less likely to be absent or to quit.) Effective leaders cultivate intrinsic motivation, attend to people's motives, set goals, and choose an appropriate leadership style.

Cultivate Intrinsic Motivation

Given that intrinsic motivation stimulates achievement, especially in situations where people work independently (as students, executives, and scientists often do), how might we encourage it? The consistent answers, from hundreds of studies:

First, provide tasks that challenge and trigger curiosity (Malone & Lepper, 1986). Second, avoid snuffing out people's sense of self-determination with an overuse of controlling extrinsic rewards (Deci & Ryan, 1987).

Note that we can use extrinsic rewards in two ways: to *control* ("If you clean up your room, you can have some ice cream") or to *inform* someone of successes ("That was outstanding—we congratulate you"). Attempts to *control* people's behaviors through rewards and surveillance may be successful as long as these controls are present. If taken away, interest in the activity often drops. Ironically, teachers who try hardest to boost their students' achievement on competency tests tend to be most controlling, thus undermining their students' intrinsic interest. (Recall from Chapter 8 that unnecessary or excessive rewards can undermine intrinsic interest by overjustifying an activity.)

On the other hand, rewards that *inform* people that their efforts are paying off can boost their feelings of competence and intrinsic motivation. In one experiment, Thane Pittman and his colleagues (1980) asked college students to work on puzzles. Those given informative compliments ("Compared with most of my subjects, you're doing really well") usually continued playing with the puzzles when left alone. Those given either no praise or a controlling form of praise ("If you keep it up, I'll be able to use your data") were less likely to continue. So, depending on whether we use rewards to control or inform, they can either raise or lower intrinsic motivation.

There is an important practical principle here. Because the controlling use of rewards undermines

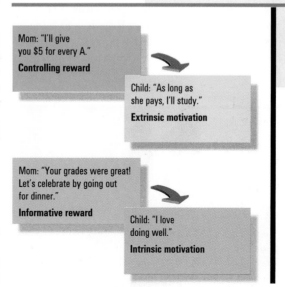

Rewards The type of reward affects motivation.

Mom: "I'll give you $5 for every A."
Controlling reward

Child: "As long as she pays, I'll study."
Extrinsic motivation

Mom: "Your grades were great! Let's celebrate by going out for dinner."
Informative reward

Child: "I love doing well."
Intrinsic motivation

task leadership
goal-oriented leadership that sets standards, organizes work, and focuses attention on goals.

social leadership
group-oriented leadership that builds teamwork, mediates conflict, and offers support.

intrinsic motivation (and creativity—see page 357), parents, teachers, and managers should take care not to be overcontrolling. It is important to expect, support, challenge, and inform, but if you want to encourage internally motivated, self-directed achievements, do not overly control.

Attend to People's Motives

Effective managerial styles vary with the people managed. To motivate people, Martin Maehr and Larry Braskamp (1986; Braskamp, 1987) have advised managers to assess their people's motives and adjust their managerial style accordingly. Challenge employees who value *accomplishment* to try new things and to exhibit excellence. Give those who value *recognition* the attention they desire. Place those who value *affiliation* in a unit that has a family feeling and shares decision making. Motivate those who value *power* with competition and opportunities for triumphant success. Different strokes for different folks, but for each a way to motivate.

What workers value—and the management style to which they respond best—also varies from culture to culture. In cultures where work is less intrinsically valued than in, say, Japan, personal relationships are more often a key to motivating workers (England & Misumi, 1986). As we noted in the Chapter 3 discussion of culture and child-rearing, human societies differ in whether they socialize children primarily toward social harmony and loyalty or toward thinking and achieving for themselves. The greater individualism of Europe and North America surfaced in surveys among 116,000 IBM employees in 40 countries. Individualism—for example, people's valuing their private lives outside of the company and wanting to adopt their own approach to their job—was highest in the United States, Australia, Britain, and Canada, somewhat lower in Scandinavia, and much lower in Asia and South America (Hofstede, 1980). Such

cultural differences have implications for multicultural business ventures. A study for the Dutch Ministry of Economic Affairs, for example, found that Norwegian and Swedish businesspeople shared the same cluster of values important to the Dutch. As a result, Scandinavian management styles have worked better in The Netherlands than have those of American managers (Hofstede, 1980).

Set Specific, Challenging Goals

In study after study, specific, challenging goals have motivated higher achievement, especially when combined with progress reports (Locke & Latham, 1990; Mento & others, 1987; Tubbs, 1986). Clear objectives, such as those you might set in planning your course work, serve to direct attention, promote effort, and stimulate creative strategies. When people find a goal reasonable, their reaching it or not impacts their self-evaluation (White & others, 1995). So, to motivate high productivity, effective leaders work with people to define explicit goals and elicit commitments, and they provide feedback on progress.

> *"Good leaders don't ask more than their constituents can give, but they often ask—and get—more than their constituents intended to give or thought it was possible to give."*
>
> **JOHN W. GARDNER**
> *EXCELLENCE*
> 1984

Choose an Appropriate Leadership Style

Whether a directive or a democratic leadership style works best depends on the situation and the leader. The best leadership style for leading a discussion is not the best style for leading troops on a charge (Fiedler, 1981). Moreover, different leaders are suited to different styles. Some excel at task leadership—setting standards, organizing work, and focusing attention on goals. Being goal-oriented, task leaders are good at keeping a group centered on its mission. Typically, they have a directive style, which can work well if the leader is bright enough to give good orders (Fiedler, 1987).

Other managers excel at social leadership—mediating conflicts and building the sort of team spirit that makes for high performance (Evans & Dion, 1991). Social leaders often have a democratic style: They delegate authority and welcome the

Toys "R" everywhere Hiring Japanese top executives who know their own culture and listening to what they have to say has enabled Toys "R" Us and some other Western firms to succeed in Japanese markets.

participation of team members. Many experiments show that social leadership is good for morale. Subordinates usually feel more satisfied and motivated when they can participate in decision making (Burger, 1987; Spector, 1986).

John Williams and Deborah Best (1990, p. 15) have suggested an imaginary scenario in which we hear about two people: One is "adventurous, autocratic, coarse, dominant, forceful, independent, and strong." The other is "affectionate, dependent, dreamy, emotional, submissive, and weak." Did you picture the first person as a man and the second as a woman? If so, you are not alone. The world around, people perceive the first set of traits as more descriptive of men, the second set as more descriptive of women. As leaders, men indeed tend to be directive, even autocratic, and women tend to be more democratic (Eagly & Johnson, 1990). When people interact, men are more likely to utter opinions, women to express support (Aries, 1987; Wood, 1987). In everyday behavior, men are more likely to act as powerful people do—to talk assertively, to interrupt, to initiate touching, to smile less, to stare (J. Hall, 1987; Major & others, 1990). Thus, women more often excel at social leadership, men at task leadership (Eagly & Karau, 1991).

Because effective leadership styles vary with the situation and the person, the once-popular "great person" theory of leadership—that all great leaders share certain traits—fell out of favor. However, Peter Smith and Monir Tayeb (1989) have compiled data from studies in India, Taiwan, and Iran indicating that effective managers in coal mines, banks, and government offices often exhibit a high degree of *both* task and social leadership. As achievement-minded people, effective managers care about how work is progressing, yet they are sensitive to their subordinates' needs. Effective leaders of laboratory groups, work teams, and large corporations also tend to exude a self-confident "charisma" (House & Singh, 1987; Shamir & others, 1993). Their charisma involves a *vision* of some goal, an ability to *communicate* it clearly and simply, and enough optimism and faith in their group to *inspire* others to follow. Such leadership motivates others to identify with and commit themselves to the group's mission.

Whether managers favor a participative/democratic approach depends not only on their personality but also on their assumptions about human motivation. Douglas McGregor (1960) identified two contrasting views. Theory X managers assume that workers are basically lazy, error-prone, and extrinsically motivated by money. Thus, they need simple tasks, close monitoring, and incentives to

work harder. Theory Y managers make opposite assumptions—that people are intrinsically motivated to work for reasons beyond money—for example, to promote self-esteem, enjoy satisfying relations with others, and fulfill their potential. Thus, given enough freedom and challenge, employees will strive to demonstrate their competence and creativity. Theory Y managers are more likely to give employees control over work procedures, to welcome employee participation in decision making, and to have creative and satisfied subordinates (Deci & others, 1989).

Theory Y is one guiding force behind the contemporary move by many businesses to increase employee participation in making decisions, a management style common in Sweden and Japan (Naylor, 1990; Sundstrom & others, 1990). Ironically, a major influence on the "Japanese-style participative management" now increasingly popular in North America was MIT social psychologist Kurt Lewin. Lewin and his students demonstrated the effects of worker participation on productivity in laboratory and factory experiments. Shortly before World War II, Lewin visited Japan and explained his findings to industrial and academic leaders (Nisbett & Ross, 1991).

Back in the United States, some companies quietly began implementing Lewin's participative management. One of these pioneer companies was Michigan's Herman Miller, Inc., now the world's second-largest manufacturer of office furniture. That success may be attributable in part to the belief of Herman Miller's now-retired chairman, Max DePree (1987), who invested in the idea that workers want to be effective and productive, to feel they are making a meaningful contribution, to have control over their own destinies, and to be appreciated. When workers share in corporate profits and become part owners, they become invested in their

Theory X
assumes that workers are basically lazy, error-prone, and extrinsically motivated by money and, thus, should be directed from above.

Theory Y
assumes that, given challenge and freedom, workers are motivated to achieve self-esteem and to demonstrate their competence and creativity.

Participative management The employees of Herman Miller, Inc., share in decision making, are highly productive, and have made the firm very profitable.

company's success. When workers participate in decision making and know that they and their managers are mutually accountable, a shared commitment to corporate and personal goals replaces labor-versus-management hostility. When workers feel respected, cared about, and involved, they find work more satisfying. And, thanks to their productivity, their company benefits. Between 1974 and 1996 Herman Miller's annual sales grew from $40 million to $1.3 billion.

In this chapter we have seen that identifiable physiological mechanisms drive some motives, such as hunger (though external incentives and learned tastes matter, too). Other motives, such as achievement, are more obviously driven by psychological factors, such as an intrinsic quest for mastery and the external rewards of recognition. What unifies all such motives is their common effect: the energizing and directing of behavior. Without motivation—without hunger, thirst, sex, curiosity, an urge to belong, a drive to achieve—life would be dull and aimless. Motivation adds purpose—and zing—to life.

SUMMING UP

Some human behaviors are energized and directed without satisfying any obvious physiological need. Achieving personal goals, for example, may be motivated by a person's need for competence and self-determination.

Identifying Achievement Motivation People with a high need to achieve tend to prefer moderately challenging tasks and to persist in accomplishing them.

Sources of Achievement Motivation Many achievement-oriented children have parents and teachers who encourage and affirm independent achievement rather than overly controlling them with rewards and threats. First-born children tend to be higher achievers, but later-borns tend to have greater social skills and to be more accepting of new ideas.

Intrinsic Motivation and Achievement Intrinsic motivation is the desire to be effective and to perform a behavior for its own sake. Extrinsic motivation is seeking external rewards and avoiding punishments.

Motivating People Industrial/organizational psychologists explore how best to create a motivated, productive, and satisfied work force. Rewards may increase intrinsic motivation if used not to control people but to boost their sense of competence or to inform them of improvement. It also helps to adjust one's managerial style in response to workers' motives; to set specific, challenging goals; and to combine goal-oriented task leadership with group-oriented social leadership.

KEY TERMS AND CONCEPTS achievement motivation, intrinsic motivation, extrinsic motivation, industrial/organizational psychology, task leadership, social leadership, Theory X, Theory Y

TERMS AND CONCEPTS TO REMEMBER

motivation, p. 363

instinct, p. 364

drive-reduction theory, p. 364

homeostasis, p. 365

incentive, p. 365

hierarchy of needs, p. 366

glucose, p. 369

set point, p. 370

metabolic rate, p. 370

anorexia nervosa, p. 371

bulimia nervosa, p. 372

sexual response cycle, p. 375

refractory period, p. 375

estrogen, p. 376

sexual disorder, p. 378

sexual orientation, p. 379

achievement motivation, p. 384

intrinsic motivation, p. 386

extrinsic motivation, p. 386

industrial/organizational psychology, p. 387

task leadership, p. 388

social leadership, p. 388

Theory X, p. 389

Theory Y, p. 389

CRITICAL THINKING EXERCISE
by Richard O. Straub

Now that you have read and reviewed Chapter 12, take your learning a step further by testing your critical thinking skills on the following pattern-recognition exercise.

Rochelle has always felt very competitive with other people, especially her older and only sibling, Doreen. Doreen is less competitive than Rochelle and is motivated more by a desire to perform to the best of her ability than by comparing herself with others. Rochelle has always received lower grades in school than Doreen, who receives consistently high scores. Rochelle claims this is because she intentionally selects more difficult classes and instructors than her sister's. Doreen responds that she picks instructors who are challenging yet fair, while her sister picks either impossibly difficult or ridiculously easy instructors.

Rochelle has often followed in her older sister's footsteps as Doreen developed new interests. For example, Doreen recently took up the guitar. On her own initiative, she began taking lessons and diligently practicing for an hour each day. Her proud parents frequently praised her for her discipline and musical progress. Not to be outdone, Rochelle decided to start playing the guitar as well. After a week or two, however, her interest in practicing began to wane. To increase their daughter's motivation, Rochelle's parents announced that for one month they would reward both daughters' efforts by giving them one dollar for each hour they practiced. The additional incentive seemed effective for Rochelle, who increased her practice time to nearly match Doreen's. Much to her parents' surprise, however, Doreen's interest level and practice time actually decreased when they offered the monetary incentive. At the end of the month, the puzzled parents withdrew the reward for practicing. Three weeks later, neither Rochelle nor Doreen seemed very interested in playing the guitar.

1. What principles of motivation might help explain why Rochelle and Doreen differ in the level of their school performance?

2. What principles of motivation might help explain why the monetary reward for practicing influenced Rochelle and Doreen differently?

3. What advice would you offer to Doreen's and Rochelle's parents if they wished to renew their daughters' interest in playing the guitar?

Check your progress on becoming a critical thinker by comparing your answers to the sample answers found in Appendix B.

FOR FURTHER INFORMATION

More information on **industrial/organizational psychology** can be found on the following pages:

chapter 13

Emotion

Feelings—powerful, spontaneous, sometimes unforgettable. No one needs to tell you that feelings add color to your life, that in times of stress they can disrupt your life or save it. Of all the species, we humans seem the most emotional (Hebb, 1980). More often than any other creature, we express fear, anger, sadness, joy, and love.

Fiction characters help us imagine life without emotion. *Star Trek's* Mr. Spock embodied cool, rational, emotionless intelligence. So did Data, the human-appearing android in *Star Trek: The Next Generation*. Data's brilliance and cool logic give him superhuman analytical intelligence. Yet he realizes something is missing. He can write poetry, but without the passions of the heart it falls flat. Data's intellectual curiosity makes him wonder about fear, anger, and joy. Try as he might, he cannot create such feelings, for Data is all cognition, no emotion.

Where do emotions come from? What are their ingredients? Imagine that, while walking home along a deserted street late at night, you hear the rumble of an engine and think that someone on a motorcycle is stalking you. Your heart begins to race, your pace quickens, you wonder about the cyclist's intent, and you feel scared. As this illustrates, emotions are a mix of (1) physiological arousal (heart pounding), (2) expressive behaviors (quickened pace), and (3) conscious experience (interpreting the person's intent and feeling fearful). The puzzle is how these three pieces fit together: Did you first notice your heart racing, your speeded-up walking, and then feel afraid? Or did your sense of fear come first, stirring your heart and legs to respond? Before trying to answer these questions, let's examine the individual pieces of the emotion puzzle—its physiology, expression, and conscious experience.

Not only emotion, but most psychological phenomena (vision, sleep, memory, sex, and so forth) can be approached these three ways—physiologically, behaviorally, and cognitively.

One explanation of sudden death caused by a voodoo "curse" is that the terrified person's parasympathetic nervous system, which calms the body, overreacts to the extreme arousal by slowing the heart to a stop (Seligman, 1974).

The Physiology of Emotion

Emotions involve physiological arousal. Does this arousal differ with specific emotions? And can a person's arousal accurately indicate whether the person is telling a lie or the truth?

Arousal

Emotion physically arouses you. Some physical responses are so obvious that you easily notice them. As you hear the motorcycle's rumble, your muscles tense, your stomach develops butterflies, your mouth becomes dry.

Your body also mobilizes for action in less noticeable ways. To provide energy, your liver pours extra sugar into your bloodstream. To help burn the sugar, by supplying needed oxygen, your respiration increases. Your digestion slows, diverting blood from your internal organs to your muscles. With blood sugar driven into the large muscles, it becomes easier to run. Your pupils dilate, letting in more light. To cool your stirred-up body, you perspire. If you were wounded, your blood would clot more quickly. Think of this after your next crisis: Without any conscious effort, your body's response to danger was wonderfully coordinated and adaptive—preparing you to fight or flee.

As we learned in Chapter 2, our *autonomic nervous system* controls our arousal (Figure 13.1). Its sympathetic division activates arousal by directing the adrenal glands atop the kidneys to release the stress hormones epinephrine (adrenaline) and norepinephrine (noradrenaline). The surge in epineph-

rine and norepinephrine increases heart rate, blood pressure, and blood sugar levels. When the crisis passes, the parasympathetic neural centers become active, calming the body. Even after the parasympathetic division inhibits further release of stress hormones, those already in the bloodstream linger awhile, so arousal diminishes gradually.

Prolonged arousal, produced by sustained stress, taxes the body (more on this in Chapter 17). Yet in many situations arousal is adaptive. Too little arousal (say, sleepiness) can be as disruptive as extremely high levels of arousal. When you're taking an exam, it pays to be moderately aroused—alert but not trembling with nervousness.

Although performance is usually best when arousal is moderate, the level of arousal for optimal performance varies for different tasks. With easy or well-learned tasks, peak performance comes with relatively high arousal, which enhances the dominant, usually correct, response. With more difficult or unrehearsed tasks, the optimal arousal is somewhat less (Figure 13.2). Runners, who are performing a well-learned task, usually achieve their peak performances when highly aroused by competition. Basketball players shooting free throws—a not-so-automatic skill—may perform slightly less well if a packed fieldhouse makes them hyperaroused (Sokoll & Mynatt, 1984). Likewise, students who feel great anxiety during exams perform more poorly than equally able but more confident students. Training anxious students how to relax before an exam often enables them to perform better (Hembree, 1988).

"Fear lends wings to his feet."

VIRGIL
AENEID
19 B.C.

Emotional arousal Elated excitement and panicky fear involve similar physiological arousal. That allows us to flip rapidly between the two emotions.

Figure **13.1**

Emotional arousal

Autonomic nervous system controls physiological arousal

Sympathetic division (arousing)		Parasympathetic division (calming)
Pupils dilate	**EYES**	Pupils contract
Decreases	**SALIVATION**	Increases
Perspires	**SKIN**	Dries
Increases	**RESPIRATION**	Decreases
Accelerates	**HEART**	Slows
Inhibits	**DIGESTION**	Activates
Secrete stress hormones	**ADRENAL GLANDS**	Decrease secretion of stress hormones

Figure **13.2**

Arousal and performance   Performance peaks at lower levels of arousal for difficult tasks, and at higher levels for easy or well-learned tasks.

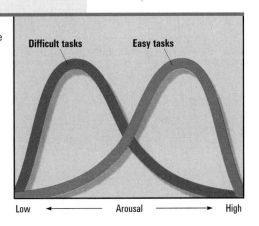

Performance level

Difficult tasks   Easy tasks

Low ⟵ Arousal ⟶ High

Physiological States Accompanying Specific Emotions

Imagine conducting an experiment exploring physiological signs of arousal. In each of four rooms, you have someone watching a movie: In the first is a horror show; in the second, an anger-provoking film; in the third, a sexually arousing film; in the fourth, an utterly boring film. From the control center you monitor each person's physiological responses. By examining the perspiration, breathing, and heart rates of the viewers, could you tell who was frightened, who was angry, who was sexually aroused, and who was bored? With training, you

could probably pick out the bored viewer from the other three. Discerning physiological differences among fear, anger, and sexual arousal is much harder (Cacioppo & others, 1997; Zillmann, 1986).

Fear, anger, and sexual arousal certainly *feel* different (and, as we shall see, cognitively they *are* different). A terrified person may feel a clutching, sinking sensation in the chest and a knot in the stomach. An angry person may feel "hot under the collar" and will probably experience a pressing, inner tension. The sexually stimulated person will experience a genital response. Despite their similar arousal, frightened and angered people also *look* different—"paralyzed with fear" and "ready to explode." Knowing this, can we pinpoint some distinct physiological indicators of each emotion?

"No one ever told me that grief felt so much like fear. I am not afraid, but the sensation is like being afraid. The same fluttering in the stomach, the same restlessness, the yawning. I keep on swallowing."

C. S. LEWIS
A GRIEF OBSERVED
1961

THINKING CRITICALLY ABOUT

Lie Detection

Given the physical indicators of emotion, might we, like Pinocchio, give some telltale sign whenever we lie? The *lie detector*, or polygraph, was once used mainly in law enforcement and national security work. But by the mid-1980s, 2 million Americans annually were reportedly being tested, usually by corporations trying to screen applicants for honesty or to uncover employee theft (Holden, 1986a).

Just what does the polygraph do?

It does not literally detect lies. Rather, it measures several of the arousal responses that accompany emotion, such as changes in breathing, pulse rate, blood pressure, and perspiration. While you try to relax, the examiner measures your physiological responses as you answer questions. Some of these, called control questions, are designed to make anyone a little nervous. If asked, "In the last twenty years, have you ever taken some-

thing that didn't belong to you?" many people will tell a white lie and say no, causing arousal that the polygraph would detect. If your physiological reactions to the critical questions ("Did you ever steal anything from your previous employer?") are weaker than to the control questions, the examiner infers you are telling the truth. The assumption is that only a thief becomes agitated when denying a theft (Figure 13.3).

Figure 13.3

Physiological responses to a lie detector test   (a) This is the record of a witness who supported an accused murderer's alibi. She reacted more strongly when answering no to a control question, "Up to age 18, did you ever deceive anyone?" than when answering yes to the rel-

evant question, "Was [the accused] at another location at the time of the murder?" As a result, the examiner concluded she was telling the truth. (b) This is the record of an accused murderer judged to be lying when he pleaded self-defense. He reacted less strongly in answering no to

the control question, "Up to age 18, did you ever physically harm anyone?" than when answering yes to the relevant question, "Did [the deceased] threaten to harm you in any way?" (From Raskin, 1982.)

polygraph
a machine, commonly used in attempts to detect lies, that measures several of the physiological responses accompanying emotion (such as perspiration, heart rate, blood pressure, and breathing changes).

But there is a problem: An innocent person might also respond with heightened tension to the accusations implied by the relevant questions. When a Yakima, Washington, mother of a 4-year-old boy was accused by her ex-husband's new wife of sexually abusing her son, she gladly accepted a police offer of a polygraph test "to prove her innocence." Asked, "Did you take Tommy's penis in your mouth?" the accused mother understandably reacted with greater perspiration and blood pressure than when asked "Have you ever told a lie to get out of trouble?" (Physiologically, the fear of being disbelieved looks a lot like the fear of being caught lying.) This revealed her guilt, explained the police-sergeant-turned-polygrapher to the jury. (Fortunately for the mother, her attorney managed to locate a scientific expert who persuaded the jury that, by itself, this was not credible evidence of guilt.) Many rape victims similarly "fail" lie detector tests when reacting emotionally while telling the truth about their assailant (Lykken, 1992).

The major adversary of lie detector tests is University of Minnesota psychologist David Lykken (1983, 1991). He notes that because physiological response is much the same from one emotion to another, the polygraph cannot distinguish among anxiety, irritation, and guilt—they all appear as arousal. Thus, these tests err about one-third of the time. They more often label the innocent guilty—when the relevant question upsets the honest person—than the guilty innocent (Figure 13.4). Good advice, then, would be never to take a lie detector test if you are innocent.

Though more accurate than a 50–50 coin toss, polygraph tests have been deemed too inaccurate for about half of U.S. state courts (Patrick & Iacono, 1991). More than a decade ago, the congressional Office of Technology Assessment (U.S. Congress, 1983, p. 4) warned that "the available research evidence does not establish the scientific validity of the polygraph test for personnel security screening." The American Psychological Association (1986) similarly voiced great reservations about the use of polygraph

tests to detect deception, as did the British Psychological Society (1986). The U.S. Congress acted on such warnings when it passed the Employee Polygraph Protection Act of 1988, prohibiting most nongovernmental polygraph testing. The truth is that lie detectors can lie.

Although too error-prone for use in testing applicants and employees, the polygraph can serve more appropriately as a tool in criminal investigation. Police sometimes use the polygraph to induce confessions by criminals whom they scare into thinking that any lies will be transparent. A more honest approach uses the *guilty knowledge test*, which assesses a suspect's physiological responses to details of a crime known only to the police and the guilty person. If a camera and money were stolen, the polygraph examiner could see whether the suspect reacts strongly to such details as the specific brand name of the camera and the dollar amounts. Presumably, only a guilty person would have such responses. Given enough such specific probes, an innocent person will seldom be wrongly accused.

Figure **13.4**

How often do lie detectors lie? Benjamin Kleinmuntz and Julian Szucko (1984) had polygraph experts study the polygraph data of 50 theft suspects who later confessed to being guilty and 50 suspects whose innocence was later established by someone's confession. Had the polygraph experts been the judges, more than one-third of the innocent would have been declared guilty, and almost one-fourth of the guilty would have been declared innocent.

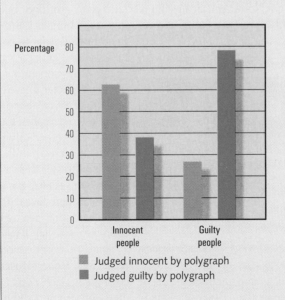

Percentage

Innocent people   Guilty people

■ Judged innocent by polygraph
■ Judged guilty by polygraph

Who's lying? Can polygraph tests like this identify liars, or are its promoters putting something over on a gullible public? To learn more about this disputed issue, read these two pages.

In 1966, a young man named Charles Whitman killed his wife and mother and then climbed to the top of a tower at the University of Texas and shot 38 people. An autopsy later revealed a tumor in his limbic system.

The physical accompaniments of emotion appear innate and universal— the same in a Sumatran village as in a North American village.

Fear and rage are sometimes accompanied by differing finger temperatures and hormone secretions (Ax, 1953; Levenson, 1992). Different emotions also arise through different brain circuits (Kalin, 1993; Panksepp, 1982). As we saw on page 56, stimulate one area of a cat's limbic system and it will pull back in terror at the sight of a mouse. Stimulate another limbic area and the cat will look enraged—pupils dilated, fur and tail erect, claws out, hissing furiously.

As people experience negative emotions, such as disgust, the right hemisphere becomes more electrically active. One man, having lost part of his right frontal lobe in brain surgery, became, his not-unhappy wife reported, less irritable and more affectionate (Goleman, 1995). The left hemisphere activates when processing positive emotions (Davidson & others, 1990, 1992). For some infants and adults, the left frontal lobe shows more activity than the right. These individuals are typically more cheerful and less readily threatened or depressed than those with more active right frontal lobes. Perhaps, speculates researcher Richard Davidson (1991), "people with more left frontal activity are better able to turn off upsetting feelings."

So, although emotions as varied as fear and anger involve a similar general autonomic arousal (thanks to the sympathetic nervous system), there are real, if subtle, physiological differences that help explain why we experience them so differently. Moreover, the physical accompaniments of emotion appear innate and universal—the same in a Sumatran village as in a North American village (Levenson & others, 1991).

SUMMING UP

Arousal Emotions are psychological responses that involve physiological arousal controlled by the autonomic nervous system. Our performance on a task is usually best when arousal is moderate, though this varies with the difficulty of the task.

Physiological States Accompanying Specific Emotions The physiological arousal that occurs with one emotion is, in most ways, indistinguishable from arousal that occurs with another. However, scientists have discovered subtle differences in the brain pathways and hormones associated with different emotions.

The polygraph measures several physiological indicators of emotion. The polygraph detects lies better than chance, but not nearly well enough to justify its widespread use in business and government.

KEY TERMS AND CONCEPTS   emotion, polygraph

Expressing Emotion

Emotions are revealed not only in our bodily arousal but also in our expressive behavior. Does nonverbal language vary with culture, or is it universal? Do our expressions influence our experienced emotions?

There is another, simpler method of deciphering people's emotions: We read their bodies, listen to their tone of voice, and study their faces.

Nonverbal Communication

All of us communicate nonverbally as well as verbally. If irritated, we may tense our bodies, press our lips together, and turn away. With a gaze, an averted glance, or a stare we can communicate intimacy, submission, or dominance (Kleinke, 1986). Among couples passionately in love, eye-gazing is typically prolonged and mutual (Rubin, 1970). Would intimate gazes stir such feelings between strangers? To find out, Joan Kellerman, James Lewis, and James Laird (1989) asked unacquainted male-female pairs to gaze intently for two minutes either at one another's hands or into one another's eyes. After separating, the eye-gazers reported feeling a greater tingle of attraction and affection.

Most of us are good enough at reading nonverbal cues to decipher the emotions in an old silent film. We are especially good at detecting nonverbal threats. In a crowd of faces, a single angry face will "pop out" faster than a single happy one (Hansen & Hansen, 1988). By exposing different parts of emotion-laden faces, Robert Kestenbaum (1992) discovered that we read fear and anger mostly from the eyes, happiness from the mouth.

Some of us are more sensitive than others to these cues. Robert Rosenthal, Judith Hall, and their colleagues (1979) discovered this by showing hundreds of people brief film clips of portions of a

"Your face, my thane, is a book where men may read strange matters."

WILLIAM SHAKESPEARE'S LADY MACBETH TO HER HUSBAND

person's emotionally expressive face or body, sometimes with a garbled voice added. For example, after a two-second scene revealing only the face of an upset woman, the researchers would ask whether the woman was criticizing someone for being late or was talking about her divorce. Rosenthal and Hall reported that some people are much better emotion detectors than others are. Introverts tend to do better at reading others' emotions, though extraverts are themselves easier to read (Ambady & others, 1995). As we noted in Chapter 11, women also are better at it than men.

Women and men also differ in which emotions they express best, as Erik Coats and Robert Feldman (1996) demonstrated. They asked students to recall and talk about times when they were happy, sad, and angry. They then showed silent five-second videos of their reports of the three emotional states to participants who acted as judges. The judges correctly discerned women's happy recall nearly two-thirds of the time, but they were able to spot it less than half the time when observing men. Men, however, slightly surpassed women in conveying their anger.

Armed with high-tech equipment, psychologists are now linking various emotions with specific facial muscles (Figure 13.5). Hard-to-control facial muscles reveal signs of emotions you may be trying to conceal. Lifting just the inner part of your eyebrows, which few people do consciously, reveals distress or worry. Eyebrows raised and pulled together signal fear. A feigned smile, such as one we make for a photographer, often continues for more than four or five seconds, by which time most authentic expressions have faded. Feigned smiles also get switched on more abruptly and off more abruptly than a genuine smile (Bugental, 1986).

Unless trained in recognizing such subtle signals, most people find it difficult to detect deceiving expressions. For example, Paul Ekman and Maureen O'Sullivan (1991) videotaped university students for a minute each as they watched either a nature film or an upsetting gruesome film. Regardless of which film they watched, the subjects were asked to talk and act as if they were watching and enjoying the nature film. Telltale signs of lying, such as a raised voice pitch, enabled the researchers to classify correctly 86 percent of the subjects as lying or truth-telling. But could the rest of us do as well, using only our intuition? Not likely. Ekman and O'Sullivan challenged 39 college students, 67 psychiatrists, 110 court judges, 126 police officers, and 90 federal polygraphers to spot the liars. All five groups' guesses were near chance (50 percent). Only a sixth group of experienced crowd-scanners—U.S. Secret Service

agents—beat chance, though still with only 64 percent correct.

When people aren't seeking to deceive us, we do much better. In fact, our brains are rather amazing emotion-detectors. Elisha Babad, Frank Bernieri, and Robert Rosenthal (1991) discovered just *how* amazing after videotaping teachers talking to unseen schoolchildren. A mere ten-second clip of either the teacher's voice or face provided enough clues for both young and old viewers to determine whether the teacher liked and admired the child he or she was addressing. Although teachers may think they can conceal their feelings and stay objective, their students can sense what their expressions and gestures reveal.

Subtle facial indicators of emotion may someday enable a new behavioral approach to lie detection.

Figure 13.5

Smiles as indicators of emotions
Paul Ekman's system for classifying a particular smile consists of a specific code for each of the 80 facial muscles used to create it. Notice how different these smiles are. (a) A smile that masks anger (the woman has just been told she is being dismissed). (b) An overly polite smile (the man is telling a patient to enjoy her hospital stay). (c) A smile softening verbal criticism ("I'd appreciate it if you wouldn't come to rehearsal drunk"). And (d) a reluctant, compliant smile ("I guess I don't have any choice, so OK").

A silent language of emotion
The art of nonverbal communication reached a pinnacle early in the century as silent films became widely available. For a nickel, enraptured audiences could watch performers mime a wide range of unmistakable emotions. Here Chester Conklin woos a woman on horseback while Louise Fazenda fumes.

For example, given mild emotional stimuli, electrodes attached to your facial muscles can now detect your hidden reactions (Tassinary & Cacioppo, 1992). Your face may not look any different, but voltage changes on the skin reveal underlying micromuscular smiles or frowns.

The growing awareness that we communicate through the body's silent language has led to studies of how job applicants and interviewers communicate (or miscommunicate) nonverbally. Popular guidebooks and articles offer advice on how to interpret nonverbal signals when negotiating a business deal, selling a product, or flirting with someone. It pays to be able to read feelings that "leak through" via subtle facial expressions, body movements, and postures. Fidgeting, for example, may reveal anxiety or boredom. More specific interpretations of postures and gestures are risky. Different expressions may convey the same emotion: Either a cold stare or the avoidance of eye contact may signify hostility. And a given expression can convey very different emotions: Folded arms, for example, can signify either irritation or relaxation.

Such gestures, facial expressions, and tones of voice are all absent in computer-based communication. E-mail communications sometimes include sideways "emoticons," such as ;-) for a knowing wink and :-(for a frown. But e-mail letters and Internet discussions otherwise lack nonverbal cues to status, personality, age, and emotion. Nobody knows what you look or sound like, or anything about your background—you are judged solely on your words. Thus, when first meeting an e-mail pen pal face to face, people are often surprised at the person they encounter.

Culture and Emotional Expression

The meaning of gestures varies with the culture. Some years ago, psychologist Otto Klineberg (1938) observed that in Chinese literature people clapped their hands to express worry or disappointment, laughed a great "Ho-Ho" to express anger, and stuck out their tongues to show surprise. Similarly, the North American "thumbs up" and "A-OK" signs would be interpreted as insults in certain other cultures. (When U.S. President Nixon made the latter sign in Brazil, he didn't realize he was saying "Let's have sex.") Just how important cultural definitions of gestures can be was demonstrated in 1968, when North Korea photographed supposedly happy officers from a captured U.S. Navy spy ship. In the photo, three of the men made the obscene middle-finger gesture; they had explained to their captors it was a "Hawaiian good luck sign" (Fleming & Scott, 1991).

Do facial expressions also have different meanings in different cultures? To find out, two investigative teams—one led by Paul Ekman and Wallace Friesen (1975, 1987, 1994), the other by Carroll Izard (1977, 1994)—showed photographs of different facial expressions to people in different parts of the world and asked them to guess the emotion. You can try this yourself. Match the six emotions with the six faces of Figure 13.6.

You probably did pretty well regardless of your ethnic background. A smile's a smile the world around. Ditto for the other basic expressions. (There is no culture where people frown when they are happy.) Despite some differences (Russell,

Understanding gestures
Volunteers working with international visitors during the 1996 Olympics were briefed on the cultural meanings of gestures.

Open palm Greece: an insult dating to ancient times; West Africa: You have five fathers, an insult akin to calling someone a bastard

Thumbs-up Australia: up yours; Germany: the number one; Japan: the number five; Saudi Arabia: I'm winning; Ghana: an insult; Malaysia: the thumb is used to point rather than the finger

Thumb and forefinger Most countries: money; France: something is perfect; Mediterranean: a vulgar gesture

OK Sign France: you're a zero; Japan: please give me coins; Brazil: an obscene gesture; Mediterranean countries: an obscene gesture

Figure **13.6**

Culture-specific or culturally universal expressions?
As people of differing cultures and races, do our faces speak differing languages? Which face expresses disgust? Anger? Fear? Happiness? Sadness? Surprise? The answers are on page 402. (From Matsumoto & Ekman, 1988.)

1991, 1995), cultures and languages also share many similarities in how they categorize emotions—as anger, fear, and so on. The physiological indicators of emotion also cross cultural boundaries (Levenson & others, 1992; Mesquita & Frijda, 1992).

"For news of the heart, ask the face."

GUINEAN PROVERB

Do people from different cultures make and interpret facial expressions similarly because they experience similar influences, such as American movies, the BBC, and CNN? Apparently not. Ekman and his team asked isolated people in New Guinea to display various emotions in response to such statements as, "Pretend your child has died." When the researchers showed videotapes of the New Guineans' facial reactions to North American collegians, the students could easily read them. Children's facial expressions—even those of blind children who have never seen a face—are also universal (Eibl-Eibesfeldt, 1971). The world over,

children cry when distressed, shake their heads when defiant, and smile when happy.

The discovery that the facial muscles speak a fairly universal language would have come as no surprise to pioneering emotion researcher Charles Darwin (1809–1882). He speculated that in prehistoric times, before our ancestors communicated in words, their ability to convey threats, greetings, and submission with facial expressions helped them survive. That shared heritage, he believed, is why all humans express the basic emotions with similar facial expressions. A sneer, for example, retains elements of an animal's teeth-baring snarl.

Smiles, too, are social phenomena, not just emotional reflexes. Bowlers don't smile when they score a strike—they smile when they turn to face their companions (Jones & others, 1991; Kraut & Johnston, 1979). Even euphoric winners of Olympic gold medals typically smile not when awaiting their ceremony but when interacting with officials and facing the crowd and cameras (Fernández-Dols & Ruiz-Belda, 1995).

It has also been adaptive for us to *interpret* faces in particular contexts. (Recall the aggressive or frightened monster from pages 191 and 198.) People judge an angry face set in a frightening situation as afraid. They judge a fearful face set in a painful situation as pained (Carroll & Russell, 1996). Movie directors harness the phenomenon by creating contexts and mood music that amplify our perceptions of particular emotions.

Emotional expressions may enhance survival in other ways, too. Surprise raises the eyebrows and widens the eyes, which take in more information. Disgust wrinkles the nose, closing the nose from foul odors.

Although cultures share a universal facial language for basic emotions, they differ in how, and how much, they express emotion. In cultures that encourage individuality, as in Western Europe, Australia, New Zealand, and North America, emotional displays often are intense and prolonged. People focus on their own goals and attitudes and express themselves accordingly. Watching a film of someone's hand being cut, Americans grimace (whether alone or with other viewers). In contrast, Japanese viewers hide their emotions in the presence of others (Triandis, 1994). Asians rarely and briefly display negative or self-aggrandizing emotions that might disrupt communal feeling within close-knit groups (Markus & Kitayama, 1991; Matsumoto & others, 1988). Moreover, in Asian and other cultures that emphasize social connections and interdependence, displays of emotions such as sympathy, respect, and shame are more common than in the West.

While weightless, astronauts' fluids move toward their upper body and their faces become puffy. This makes nonverbal communication more difficult, increasing the risks of misunderstanding, especially among multinational crews (Gelman, 1989).

The Effects of Facial Expressions

Expressions not only communicate emotion, they also amplify and regulate it. In his 1872 book, *The Expression of the Emotions in Man and Animals*, Darwin contended that "the free expression by outward signs of an emotion intensifies it. . . . He who gives way to violent gestures will increase his rage."

Was Darwin right? I was driving in my car one day when the song "Put On a Happy Face" came on the radio. How phony, I thought. But I tested Darwin's hypothesis anyway, as you can, too. Fake a big grin. Now scowl. Can you feel the difference?

The subjects in dozens of experiments have felt a difference. For example, James Laird and his colleagues (1974, 1984, 1989) subtly induced students to make a frowning expression by asking them to "contract these muscles" and "pull your brows together" (supposedly to help the researchers attach facial electrodes). The results? The students reported feeling a little angry. Students similarly induced to smile felt happier, found cartoons more humorous, and recalled happier memories than did the frowners. People instructed to mold their faces in ways that mimicked expressions of other basic emotions also experienced those emotions. For example, they reported feeling more fear than anger, disgust, or sadness when made to construct an expression of fear: "Raise your eyebrows. And open your eyes wide. Move your whole head back, so that your chin is tucked in a little bit, and let your mouth relax and hang open a little" (Duclos & others, 1989). Going through the motions awakens the emotions.

The effect is subtle, yet detectable in the absence of competing emotions. Consider these findings:

- If subtly manipulated into furrowing their brows (see Figure 13.7), people feel sadder while looking at sad photos.

Answers to the question in Figure 13.6: From left to right, top to bottom: happiness, surprise, fear, sadness, anger, disgust.

Which smile makes Paul Ekman feel happy? The smile on the right, which engages the face muscles of a natural smile.

- Saying the phonemes *e* and *ah*, which activate smiling muscles, puts people—believe it or not—in a better mood than saying the German *ü*, which activates muscles associated with negative emotions (Zajonc & others, 1989).

- Just activating one of the smiling muscles by holding a pen in the teeth (rather than with the lips, which activates a frowning muscle) is enough to make cartoons seem more amusing (Strack & others, 1988). A heartier smile, made not just with the mouth but with raised cheeks as well, works even better (Ekman & others, 1990). Smile warmly on the outside and you feel better on the inside. Scowl and the whole world seems to scowl back.

Why might this be so? Paul Ekman and his colleagues (1983) designed an experiment to find out. Their subjects were professional actors trained in the Stanislavsky method, in which they physically (and psychologically) "become" the characters they are playing. The actors were asked to assume an expression and then hold it for 10 seconds while the researchers measured their heart rates and finger temperatures. When they made a fearful expression, their heart rate increased some 8 beats per minute and finger temperature was steady. When making an angry expression, both heart rate and finger temperature increased as though the actor were indeed "hot-headed." Our facial expressions, it seems, send signals to our autonomic nervous system, which then responds accordingly. This experiment also confirms that subtly different body states do underlie different emotions.

Sara Snodgrass and her associates (1986) observed the behavior feedback phenomenon with walking behavior. You can duplicate her subjects' experience: Walk for a few minutes while taking short, shuffling steps, keeping your eyes downcast. Now walk around taking long strides, with your

Figure 13.7

How to make people frown without telling them to frown
Randy Larsen, Margaret Kasimatis, and Kurt Frey's (1992) solution: Attach two golf tees above the eyebrows and ask the subjects to make the tee tips touch. With "sad face" muscles activated, subjects felt sadder while viewing scenes of war, sickness, and starvation.

arms swinging and your eyes looking straight ahead. Can you feel your mood shift?

If assuming an emotional expression triggers a feeling, then imitating others' expressions should help us feel what they are feeling. Again, the laboratory evidence is supportive. Kathleen Burns Vaughn and John Lanzetta (1981) asked some students but not others to make a pained expression whenever an electric shock was apparently delivered to someone they were watching. With each apparent shock, the grimacing observers perspired more and had a faster heart rate than the other observers. So one small way to become more empathic—to feel what others feel—is to let your own face mimic the other person's expression. Acting as another acts helps us feel what another feels.

SUMMING UP

Nonverbal Communication Much of our communication is through the body's silent language. Psychologists have studied people's abilities to detect emotion, even from thin slices of behavior.

Culture and Emotional Expression Is nonverbal language universal? Although some gestures are culturally determined, facial expressions, such as those of happiness and fear, are common the world over. In communal cultures that value interdependence, intense displays of potentially disruptive emotions are infrequent.

The Effects of Facial Expressions Expressions not only communicate emotion, they also amplify the felt emotion and signal the body to respond accordingly.

Experiencing Emotion

The ingredients of emotion include not only physiological arousal and expressive behavior but also our conscious experience. We will consider three of the basic emotions: fear, anger, and happiness. What influences each?

Our feelings are "obscure and confused," noted Benjamin Constant de Rebecque in 1816. To cut through the obscurity, psychologists have asked people to report their experiences of different emotions. Estonians, Poles, Greeks, Chinese, and Canadians all seem to place emotions along two dimensions—pleasant versus unpleasant, and intensely aroused versus sleepy (Russell & others, 1989). On the intensity scale, for example, *terrified* is more frightened than *afraid*, *enraged* is angrier than *angry*, *delighted* is happier than *happy*. To these two dimensions, we might add a third: duration. Among Americans and Japanese, at least, the emotions of joy and sadness typically endure longer than anger and guilt, which outlast fear and disgust (Matsumoto & others, 1988).

Psychologists have sought to identify emotions that are facially and experientially distinct. Carroll Izard (1977) isolated 10 such basic emotions (joy, interest-excitement, surprise, sadness, anger, disgust, contempt, fear, shame, and guilt), most of which are present in infancy (Figure 13.8). Izard reported that other emotions are combinations of these 10. Love, for instance, is a mixture of joy and interest-excitement.

In this chapter, we focus on three important emotions: fear, anger, and happiness. What functions do they serve? And what influences our experience of them?

Figure 13.8

Infants' naturally occurring emotions To identify the emotions present from birth, Carroll Izard analyzed the facial expressions of very young infants. Shown here are (a) joy (mouth forming smile, cheeks lifted, twinkle in eye); (b) anger (brows drawn together and downward, eyes fixed, mouth squarish; (c) interest (brows raised or knitted, mouth softly rounded, lips may be pursed); (d) disgust (nose wrinkled, upper lip raised, tongue pushed outward; (e) surprise (brows raised, eyes widened, mouth rounded in oval shape); (f) sadness (brow's inner corners raised, mouth corners drawn down); and (g) fear (brows level, drawn in and up, eyelids lifted, mouth corners retracted).

(a)　　(b)

(c)　　(d)

(e)　　(f)　　(g)

Fear

Fear can be a poisonous emotion. It can torment us, rob us of sleep, and preoccupy our thinking. People can be literally scared to death. Fear can also be contagious. In 1903, someone yelled "Fire!" as a fire broke out in Chicago's Iroquois Theater. Eddie Foy, the comedian on stage at the time, tried to reassure the crowd by calling out, "Don't get excited. There's no danger. Take it easy!" Alas, the crowd panicked. During the 10 minutes it took the fire department to arrive and quickly extinguish the flames, more than five hundred people perished, most of them trampled or smothered in a stampede. Bodies were piled 7 or 8 feet deep in the stairways, and many of the faces bore heel marks (Brown, 1965).

More often, fear is an adaptive response. Fear prepares our bodies to flee danger. Fear of real or imagined enemies binds people together as families, tribes, and nations. Fear of injury protects us from harm. Fear of punishment or retaliation constrains us from harming one another. Fear triggers worry, which focuses the mind on a problem and rehearses coping strategies.

"He who fears all snares falls into none."

PUBLIUS SYRUS
SENTENTIAE
43 B.C.

Figure **13.9**

The amygdala—a neural key to fear learning

Amygdala

People can be afraid of almost anything—"afraid of truth, afraid of fortune, afraid of death, and afraid of each other," observed Ralph Waldo Emerson. Why so many fears? Psychologists note that we can learn to fear almost anything. Recall from Chapter 8 that dogs learn to fear neutral stimuli associated with shock, that infants come to fear furry objects associated with frightening noises, and that adults can become terrified of incidental stimuli linked with traumatic experiences such as rape. As infants become mobile they experience falls and near-falls—and become increasingly afraid of heights (Campos & others, 1992). Through such conditioning, the short list of naturally painful and frightening events can multiply into a long list of human fears—fear of driving or flying, fear of mice or cockroaches, fear of closed or open spaces, fear of failure, fear of another race or nation.

Learning by observation extends the list. Susan Mineka (1985) sought to explain why nearly all monkeys reared in the wild fear snakes, yet lab-reared monkeys do not. Surely, most wild monkeys do not actually suffer snake bites. Might they learn their fear through observation? To find out, Mineka experimented with six wild-reared monkeys (all strongly fearful of snakes) and their lab-reared offspring (virtually none of which feared snakes). After repeatedly observing their parents or peers refusing to reach for food in the presence of a snake, the younger monkeys developed a similar strong fear of snakes. When retested three months later, their learned fear persisted. This suggests that our fears reflect not only our own past traumas but also the fears of our parents and friends.

Moreover, we may be biologically prepared to learn some fears more quickly than others. Monkeys learn to fear snakes even by watching videotapes of monkeys reacting fearfully to a snake; but they *don't* learn to fear flowers when video-splicing transposes the seemingly feared stimulus into a flower (Cook & Mineka, 1991). We humans quickly learn to fear snakes, spiders, and cliffs—fears that probably helped our ancestors survive. We are less predisposed to fear cars, electricity, bombs, and global warming, which are now far more dangerous (Lumsden & Wilson, 1983; McNally, 1987). Stone age fears leave us unprepared for high-tech dangers.

A key to fear-learning lies in the amygdala, a limbic system neural center deep in the brain (Figure 13.9). The amygdala plays a key role in associating various emotions, including fear, with certain situations (Barinaga, 1992). Rabbits learn to react with fear to a tone that predicts an impending small shock—unless their amygdala is damaged. If rats have their amygdala deactivated by a drug that blocks the strengthening of neural connections, they, too, show no fear-learning. Not only does the amygdala link situations with fear responses, its output is wired to all the parts of the brain that produce the bodily symptoms of extreme fear, such as diarrhea and shortness of breath.

The amygdala is similarly involved in human fears. If an experimenter repeatedly blasts someone with a blaring horn after showing a blue slide, people will begin to react emotionally to the slide (as measured by their perspiring skin conducting electricity). If they have suffered hippocampus damage, they still show the emotional reaction but won't be able to remember why. If they have suffered amygdala damage, they will remember the conditioning but show no emotional effect of it (Schacter, 1996).

Of course, some people's fears are greater than others'. For a few people, intense fears of specific objects or situations disrupt their ability to cope. Furthermore, some people are very fearful of threatening or embarrassing situations. To be ever-attentive to potential threats is to be chronically anxious (Mineka & Sutton, 1992).

Others—courageous heroes and remorseless criminals—are less fearful. Astronauts and adventurers who have "the right stuff"—who can keep their wits and can function coolly and effectively in moments of severe stress—seem to thrive on risk. So, too, do con artists and killers who charm their intended victims without a hint of nervousness, and who in laboratory tests exhibit little fear of a tone that predictably precedes a painful electric shock. Experience helps shape such fearfulness or fearlessness, but so do our genes. (Recall from Chapter 3 that genes influence our temperament—our emotional reactivity.) Even among identical twins reared separately, one twin's level of fearfulness is similar to the other's (Lykken, 1982).

Anger

Anger is said by the sages to be "a short madness" (Horace, 65–8 B.C.) that "carries the mind away" (Virgil, 70–19 B.C.) and that can be "many times more hurtful than the injury that caused it" (Thomas Fuller, 1654–1734). But other sages say "noble anger" (William Shakespeare, 1564–1616) "makes any coward brave" (Cato, 234–149 B.C.) and "brings back . . . strength" (Virgil).

What makes us angry? To find out, James Averill (1983) asked many people to recall or keep careful records of their experiences with anger. Most reported becoming at least mildly angry several times a week; some became angry several times a day. Often the anger was a response to friends' or loved ones' perceived misdeeds. Anger was especially common when another person's act seemed willful, unjustified, and avoidable. But blameless annoyances—foul odors, high temperatures, a traffic jam, aches and pains—also have the power to make us angry (Berkowitz, 1990).

What do people do with their anger? And what *should* they do with it? When anger fuels physically or verbally aggressive acts that we later regret, it is maladaptive. But Averill's subjects recalled that when they were angry they often reacted assertively rather than hurtfully. Their anger frequently led them to talk things over with the offending person, thereby lessening the aggravation. Such controlled expressions of anger are more adaptive than either hostile outbursts or internalizing the angry feelings.

Popular books and articles on aggression sometimes advise that even hostile outbursts can be better than keeping anger pent up. When irritated, should we go ahead and curse, tell a person off, or retaliate? Was Ann Landers (1969) right that "youngsters should be taught to vent their anger"? Are "recovery movement" leaders right to encour-

Chapters 15 and 16 discuss how phobias develop and are treated.

One problem with chronic hostility is its link with heart disease (page 522).

"Anger will never disappear so long as thoughts of resentment are cherished in the mind."

THE BUDDHA
500 B.C.

A cool culture Caregivers who turn abusive against other family members are rare in Micronesia. This photo of community life on Pulap Island suggests one possible reason: Family life takes place in the open in the South Pacific. Relatives and neighbors who witness angry outbursts can step in before the emotion gets out of hand and turns into child, spouse, or elder abuse.

age our raging at our dead parents, imaginatively cursing the former boss, or confronting our childhood abuser? "Catharsis is magnificent to experience and impressive to behold," notes Martin Seligman (1994, p. 239).

Encouragement to vent your rage typifies individualized cultures, but it would seldom be heard in cultures where people's identity is more group-centered. People who keenly sense their *inter*dependence see anger as a threat to group harmony (Markus & Kitayama, 1991). In Tahiti, for instance, people learn to be considerate and gentle. From infancy on in Japan, expressions of anger are less common than in Western cultures.

The "vent your anger" advice presumes that emotional expression provides emotional release, or catharsis. The catharsis hypothesis maintains that we reduce anger by releasing it through aggressive action or fantasy. Experimenters report that this sometimes occurs. When people retaliate against someone who has provoked them, they may indeed calm down—*if* their counterattack is directly against the provoker, *if* their retaliation seems justifiable, and *if* their target is not intimidating (Geen & Quanty, 1977; Hokanson & Edelman, 1966). In short, expressing anger can be *temporarily* calming *if* it does not leave us feeling guilty or anxious.

Despite the afterglow—people sometimes feel better for hours afterward—catharsis usually fails to cleanse one's rage. More often, expressing anger breeds more anger. For one thing, it may provoke retaliation, thus escalating a minor conflict into a major confrontation. For another, expressing anger can magnify anger. (Recall Darwin's suggestion that violent gestures increase anger.) Ebbe Ebbesen and his colleagues (1975) saw this when they interviewed 100 frustrated engineers and technicians just laid off by an aerospace company. Some were asked questions that released hostility, such as, "What instances can you think of where the company has not been fair with you?" When these people later filled out a questionnaire that assessed their attitudes toward the company, did this opportunity to "drain off" their hostility reduce it? Quite the contrary. Compared with those who had not vented their anger, those who had let it all out exhibited *more* hostility.

Thus, although "blowing off steam" may temporarily calm an angry person, it may also amplify

underlying hostility. When angry outbursts do calm us, they may be reinforcing and therefore habit forming. If stressed managers can drain off some of their tension by berating employees, then the next time they feel tense with irritation they may be more likely to explode again. Similarly, the next time you are angry you are likely to do whatever has relieved your anger in the past.

So what's the best way to handle anger? Experts have offered two suggestions. First, bring down the level of physiological arousal of anger by waiting. "It is true of the body as of arrows," noted Carol Tavris (1982), "what goes up must come down. Any emotional arousal will simmer down if you just wait long enough." Second, deal with anger in a way that involves neither being chronically angry over every little annoyance nor passively sulking, which is merely rehearsing your reasons for anger. Don't be like those who, stifling their feelings over a series of provocations, finally overreact to a single incident (Baumeister & others, 1990). Vent the anger by exercising, playing an instrument, or confiding your feelings to a friend or a diary.

Anger can benefit relationships when it expresses a grievance in ways that promote reconciliation rather than retaliation. Civility means not only keeping silent about trivial irritations but also communicating important ones clearly and assertively. A nonaccusing statement of feeling—perhaps letting one's housemate know that "I get irritated when you leave your dirty dishes for me to clean up"—can help resolve the conflicts that cause anger.

Happiness

"How to gain, how to keep, how to recover happiness is in fact for most men at all times the secret motive for all they do," observed William James (1902, p. 76). Understandably so, for one's state of happiness or unhappiness colors everything else. People who are happy perceive the world as safer (Johnson & Tversky, 1983), make decisions more easily (Isen & Means, 1983), rate job applicants more favorably (Baron, 1987), and report greater satisfaction with their whole lives (Schwarz & Clore, 1983). When your mood is gloomy, life as a whole seems depressing. Let your mood brighten, and suddenly your relationships, your self-image, and your hopes for the future all seem more promising.

Moreover—and this is one of psychology's most consistent findings—when we feel happy we are more willing to help others. In study after study, a mood-boosting experience (such as find-

Although "blowing off steam" may temporarily calm an angry person, it may also amplify underlying hostility.

ing money, succeeding on a challenging task, or re-calling a happy event) made people more likely to give money, pick up someone's dropped papers, volunteer time, and so forth. It's called the feel-good, do-good phenomenon (Salovey, 1990).

Despite the significance of happiness, psychology has more often focused on negative emotions. From 1967 through 1995, *Psychological Abstracts* (a guide to psychology's literature) included 5119 articles mentioning anger, 38,459 mentioning anxiety, and 49,028 mentioning depression. For every 21 articles on these topics, only one dealt with the positive emotions of joy (402 articles), life satisfaction (2357), or happiness (1710). There is, of course, good reason to focus on negative emotions, which can make our lives miserable and drive us to seek help. But researchers are becoming increasingly interested in subjective well-being, assessed either as feelings of happiness (sometimes defined as a high ratio of positive to negative feelings) or as a sense of satisfaction with life. During the 1980s, annual research output on subjective well-being nearly quadrupled (Myers, 1993).

On this subject, as on so many others, whatever psychological research reveals will have been anticipated by someone. The sages of the ages have given us any number of contradictory maxims: that happiness comes from knowing the truth, and from preserving illusions; from living for the present, and from living for the future; from being with others, and from living in peaceful solitude (Tatarkiewicz, 1976). The list goes on, but the scientific task is clear: to ask which of these competing ideas fit reality. Sifting the actual predictors of happiness from the merely plausible hunches requires research.

"Everything important
has been said before."

PHILOSOPHER ALFRED NORTH
WHITEHEAD (1861–1947)

In their research on happiness, psychologists have studied influences upon both our temporary moods and our long-term life satisfaction. Studying people's reports of daily moods confirms that stressful events—an argument, a sick child, a car problem—trigger bad moods. No surprise there. But by the next day, the gloom nearly always lifts (Affleck & others, 1994; Bolger & others, 1989; Stone & Neale, 1984). If anything, people tend to rebound from bad days to a *better*-than-usual good mood the following day. When in a bad mood, can you usually depend on rebounding within a day or two? Are your times of elation similarly hard to sustain? In the long run, our emotional ups and downs tend to balance.

Faced with adversity In 1995, an accident transformed *Superman* actor Christopher Reeve into an immobile person needing others to feed, dress, and care for him. "Maybe I should just check out," he told his wife shortly after the accident. But within four months he reported in a Barbara Walters interview "genuine joy in being alive."

Apart from prolonged grief over the loss of a loved one or lingering anxiety after a trauma (such as child abuse, rape, or the terrors of war), even tragedy is not permanently depressing. The finding is surprising but reliable. People who become blind or paralyzed usually recover near-normal levels of day-to-day happiness. Consider these findings:

- Able-bodied University of Illinois students described themselves as happy 50 percent of the time, unhappy 22 percent of the time, and neutral 29 percent of the time. To within 1 percentage point, students with disabilities rated their emotions identically (Chwalisz & others, 1988).

- Students perceive their friends with disabilities as just as happy as their other friends (Allman, 1989).

- In one survey of 128 people with all four limbs paralyzed, most acknowledged having considered suicide after their injury. To suffer a disability is to live daily with the frustrations of an uncooperative body. Nevertheless, more than a year later, only 10 percent rated their quality of life as poor; most described it as good or excellent (Whiteneck & others, 1985). When 233 emergency room caregivers imagined how they would feel about themselves years after such an injury, only 39 percent guessed they would feel "satisfied with myself, on the whole." But that is how 95 percent of the actual patients felt (Gerhart & others, 1994). And 98 percent of them agreed that "I feel I am a person of worth."

- Learning that one is HIV-positive is devastating. Yet after five weeks of adapting to the grim news, those who tested positive felt less emotionally distraught than they expected (Sieff & others, 1997). As this finding illustrates, people seem to overestimate the long-term emotional consequences of very bad news.

"Weeping may tarry
for the night, but joy comes
with the morning."

PSALMS 30:5

"If I couldn't know the joy
of dancing, I could know the
ecstasy of creating."

CHRISTY BROWN
MY LEFT FOOT
1954

When your mood is gloomy, life as
a whole seems depressing. Let your mood
brighten, and suddenly your relationships,
your self-image, and your hopes for the
future all seem more promising.

CLOSE-UP

Opponent-Process Theory of Emotion

The adaptation-level phenomenon helps explain why, in the long run, our emotional ups and downs tend to balance. University of Pennsylvania psychologist Richard Solomon (1980) showed that emotions balance in the short run as well, and he developed a theory to explain why. Solomon was intrigued by the emotional price tag that so often follows pleasure and by the emotional dividends that can compensate for past suffering. For the pleasure of a drug high, one pays the price of discomfort when the drug wears off. For the pain of hard exercise or a hot sauna bath, one afterward receives the dividend of a pleasurable feeling of well-being.

Solomon proposed, with support from laboratory studies of human and animal emotions, that *every emotion triggers an opposing emotion.* He called this the *opponent-process theory* of emotion. Imagine that you are about to take your first parachute jump. Solomon said that the primary emotion you experience before the jump—fear—triggers an opposing emotion— elation—as you land. Once the opposing emotion activates, perhaps

to keep the initial emotion under control, you experience a diminishing of the initial emotion's intensity. This happens because you experience the primary emotion minus the opposing emotion. As the primary emotion subsides, the opposing emotion lingers a while (Figure 13.10a). After parachutists survive their first free-fall, which for many is a terrifying experience, the fear switches off and they feel elated. For some women, the pain and fear of labor and childbirth may enhance a sense of euphoric relief afterward.

Repetitions of the emotion-arousing event strengthen the opposing emotion. Thus, the primary emotional experience, such as the pleasure derived from drug use or the fear aroused by parachuting, diminishes. This helps explain drug tolerance: with repetition, the initial high lessens.

With repetition, the after-reaction, such as the pain of drug withdrawal, remains strong or becomes stronger (Figure 13.10b). This helps explain both drug hangovers (the opponent feelings that knock down the initial pleasure and linger after-

ward) and drug addiction (the craving for more of the drug to switch off the pain of withdrawal).

As Solomon wisely noted, opponent-process theory and the research that supports it are good news for puritans and bad news for hedonists: Those who seek pleasure pay for it later. With every kick comes a kickback, and with repetition even their pleasure will lose much of its intensity. "Take what you want," says an old Spanish saying. "Take it, and pay for it." But those who suffer will receive their reward. With most pain comes a gain.

Looking over the whole of psychology, we can see a deep principle emerging: Human nature is a battlefield of opposing tendencies. Our sympathetic and parasympathetic nervous systems, our neural balance between excitation and inhibition, our endorphin responses to pain, our opponent neural processes that create color and negative afterimages, our regulation of hunger and satiety, and our experiences of pleasure and misery—all involve carefully negotiated truces between opposing forces.

Figure **13.10**

Opponent processes in emotion (a) A primary emotional response to a stimulus triggers an opposing emotion. What we experience is the primary emotion minus the opposing emotion. (b) With repeated stimulation, the opponent emotion becomes stronger, weakening the experience of the primary emotion and lingering on. (From Solomon, 1980.)

Figure **13.11**

Are today's collegians materialistic? From 1970 through most of the 1980s, annual surveys of more than 200,000 entering U.S. college students revealed an increasing desire for wealth. (From Sax & others, 1996; Dey & others, 1991.)

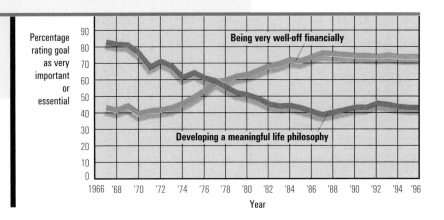

The effect of dramatically positive events is similarly temporary. Once their rush of euphoria wears off, state lottery winners typically find their overall happiness unchanged (Brickman & others, 1978). Other research confirms that there is much more to well-being than being well-off. Many people (including most new collegians, as Figure 13.11 suggests) believe they would be happier if they had more money. They probably would be—temporarily. But in the long run, increased affluence hardly affects happiness. Within most affluent countries, people with lots of money are not much happier than those with just enough to afford life's necessities. Wealth is like health: Its utter absence breeds misery, yet having it is no guarantee of happiness.

Although most people agree that money can't buy happiness, they do believe that a *little* more money would make them a *little* more secure, comfortable, and happy. So, over time, does our happiness grow, little by little, with our paychecks? It does not. During the last four decades, the average U.S. citizen's buying power doubled. The 1957 per-person income, inflated to 1995 dollars, was about $9000; by 1996, thanks partly to the rich getting richer and to women's increasing employment, it was almost $20,000. Did this doubled wealth—enabling twice as many cars per capita, and color TVs, VCRs, personal computers, air conditioning, and answering machines galore—also buy more happiness? As Figure 13.12 shows, the average

Figure **13.12**

Does money buy happiness? It surely helps us to avoid certain types of pain. Yet, though buying power has doubled since the 1950s, the average American's reported happiness has remained almost unchanged. (Happiness data from Niemi & others, 1989, and T. Smith, 1997; income data from *Historical Statistics of the U.S.* and *Economic Indicators.*)

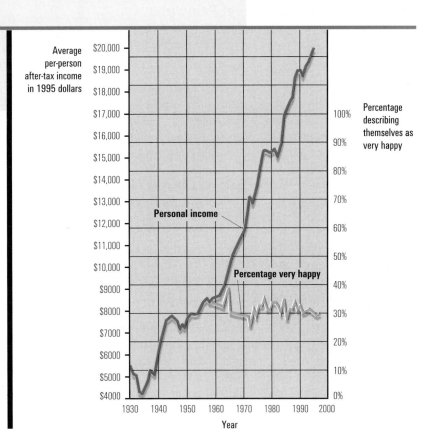

Economic growth in affluent countries has provided no apparent boost to morale or social well-being.

American is now twice as rich but no happier. In 1957, some 35 percent said they were "very happy," as did slightly fewer—30 percent—in 1996. Indeed, judging by the doubled divorce rate, tripled teen-suicide rate, quintupled juvenile violence, and mushrooming depression (page 468), contempory Americans seem to be more often miserable. The same is true of the European countries and Japan: In all these countries, people enjoy better nutrition, health care, education, and science, and are somewhat happier than people in very poor countries, yet increasing real incomes have *not* produced increasing happiness. The findings lob a bombshell at modern materialism: *Economic growth in affluent countries has provided no apparent boost to morale or social well-being.*

Two psychological principles explain why, for all but the very poor, more money buys no more than a temporary surge of happiness, and why our emotions seem attached to elastic bands that pull us back from highs or lows. In its own way, each principle suggests that happiness is relative.

The Adaptation-Level Principle: Happiness Is Relative to Our Prior Experience

The adaptation-level phenomenon describes our tendency to judge various stimuli relative to what we have previously experienced. As psychologist Harry Helson explained, we adjust our "neutral" levels—the points at which sounds seem neither loud nor soft, temperatures neither hot nor cold, events neither pleasant nor unpleasant—based on our experience. We then notice and react to variations up or down from these levels. Adaptation researcher Allen Parducci (1995) recalls a striking example: "On the Micronesian island of Ponope, which is almost on the equator, I was told of a bitter night back in 1915 when the temperature dropped to a record-breaking 69 degrees [Fahrenheit; 21 degrees Celsius]!"

Thus, if our income, grade-point average, or social prestige increases, we feel an initial surge of pleasure. We then adapt to this new level of achievement, come to see it as normal, and require something even better to give us another surge of happiness. From my childhood, I can recall the thrill of watching my family's first 12-inch, black-

and-white television set. Now, if the color goes out on our 25-inch TV, I feel deprived. Having adapted upward, I perceive as negative what I once experienced as positive. Yesterday's luxury has become today's necessity. The point to remember: Satisfaction and dissatisfaction, success and failure—all are relative to our recent experience.

So, could we ever create a permanent social paradise on earth? Donald Campbell (1975) answered no: If you woke up tomorrow to your utopia—perhaps a world with no bills, no ills, all A's, someone who loves you unreservedly—you would, for a time, feel euphoric. But before long, you would soon recalibrate your adaptation level. Before long you would again sometimes feel gratified (when achievements surpass expectations), sometimes feel deprived (when they fall below), and sometimes feel neutral. That helps explain why, despite the realities of triumph and tragedy, million-dollar lottery winners and paraplegics report similar levels of happiness. It also explains why material wants can be insatiable—why many a child "needs" just one more Nintendo game. Or why Imelda Marcos, surrounded by poverty while living in splendor as wife of the Philippines' president, bought 1060 pairs of shoes, more than she could ever wear. When the victor belongs to the spoils and the possessor is possessed by possessions, adaptation level has run amuck.

Seeking happiness through material achievement requires an ever-increasing abundance of things. At the end of his *Chronicles of Narnia*, writer C. S. Lewis depicts heaven as a place where good things do continually increase, where life is a never-ending story "in which every chapter is better than the one before." Here on Earth the unavoidable ups and downs of real life preclude a perpetual high.

adaptation-level phenomenon
our tendency to form judgments (of sounds, of lights, of income) relative to a "neutral" level defined by our prior experience.

The Relative Deprivation Principle: Happiness Is Relative to Others' Attainments

Happiness is relative not only to our past experience, but also to our comparisons with others. We are always comparing ourselves with others. And whether we feel good or bad depends on who those others are. We are smart or agile only when others are slow-witted or clumsy.

An example: To explain the frustration expressed by U.S. Air Corps soldiers during World War II, researchers formulated the concept of relative deprivation—the sense that we are worse off than others with whom we compare ourselves. Despite a relatively rapid promotion rate for the group, many soldiers were frustrated about their own promotion rates (Merton & Kitt, 1950). Apparently, seeing so many others being promoted inflated the soldiers' expectations. And when expectations soar above attainments, the result is disappointment. When the Oakland Athletics signed baseball outfielder Jose Canseco to a $4.7 million annual salary, his fellow outfielder Rickey Henderson became openly dissatisfied with his $3 million salary and refused to show up on time for spring training (King, 1991).

Such comparisons help us understand why the middle- and upper-income people in a given country, who can compare themselves with the relatively poor, tend to be slightly more satisfied with

"Our poverty became a reality.
Not because of our having less,
but by our neighbors having more."

WILL CAMPBELL
BROTHER TO A DRAGONFLY
1977

life than their less fortunate compatriots. Nevertheless, once a person reaches a moderate income level, further increases do little to increase happiness. Why? Because as people climb the ladder of success they mostly compare themselves with peers who are at or above their current level (Gruder, 1977; Suls & Tesch, 1978). For Rickey Henderson, Jose Canseco was the standard of comparison. For average people, athletes' salaries are emotionally irrelevant. "Beggars do not envy millionaires, though of course they will envy other beggars who are more successful," noted Bertrand Russell (1930, p. 90). Thus "Napoleon envied Caesar, Caesar envied Alexander, and Alexander, I daresay, envied Hercules, who never existed. You cannot, therefore, get away from envy by means of success alone, for there will always be in history or legend some person even more successful than you are" (pp. 68-69).

By "counting our blessings" when we compare ourselves with those less fortunate, we can, however, increase our satisfaction. As comparing ourselves with those who are better-off creates envy, so comparing ourselves with those less well-off boosts contentment. Marshall Dermer and his colleagues (1979) demonstrated this by asking University of Wisconsin-Milwaukee women to study others' deprivation and suffering. After viewing vivid depictions of how grim life was in Milwaukee in 1900, or after imagining and then writing about various personal tragedies, such as being burned and disfigured, the women expressed greater satisfaction with their own lives. Similarly, when mildly depressed people read about someone who is even more depressed, they feel somewhat better (Gibbons, 1986).

relative deprivation
the perception that one is worse off relative to those with whom one compares oneself.

*"I wish I came
in first more often."*

MICHAEL JORDAN
NEWSWEEK
FEBRUARY 17, 1992

The effect of comparison with others helps us understand why students of a given level of academic ability tend to have a higher academic self-concept if they attend a school where most other students are not exceptionally able (Marsh & Parker, 1984). If you were near the top of your class in high school, you might feel inferior upon entering a college where everyone was near the top of their class.

As comparing ourselves with those who are better-off creates envy, so comparing ourselves with those less well-off boosts contentment.

"I've got the bowl, the big yard, I know I should be happy."

Drawing by M. Twohy; © 1992 The New Yorker Magazine, Inc.

Predictors of Happiness

If, as the adaptation-level phenomenon implies, our emotions tend to balance around normal, then why do some people seem so filled with joy and others so gloomy day after day? What makes one person normally happy and another less so? Research reveals several predictors of happiness (Table 13.1).

Table **13.1**

Happiness Is . . .

Researchers Have Found That Happy People Tend to	However, Happiness Seems Not Much Related to Other Factors, Such as
Have high self-esteem	Age
Be optimistic and outgoing	Race
Have close friendships or a satisfying marriage	Gender (women are more often depressed, but also more often joyful)
Have work and leisure that engage their skills	Educational level
Have a meaningful religious faith	Parenthood (having children or not)
Sleep well and exercise	Physical attractiveness

Source: Summarized from Myers (1993) and Myers & Diener (1995, 1996).

Remember, though, that knowing that two variables correlate does not tell us whether one causes the other. For example, many studies indicate that religiously active people tend to report greater happiness and life satisfaction. Is happiness conducive to faith? Or does faith enhance happiness?

Whether at work or leisure, most of us derive greatest enjoyment from engaging, challenging activities. Mihaly Csikszentmihalyi (pronounced chick-SENT-me-hi, 1990) and his colleagues discovered this after giving research volunteers a pager. When beeped, the people would note what they were doing and how they were feeling. Usually, they felt happier if mentally engaged by work or active leisure than if passively vegetating. Ironically, the less expensive (and usually more involving) a leisure activity is, the more absorbed and happy people are while doing it. People are happier when gardening than when sitting on a power boat. They're happier when talking to friends than when watching TV. Happy adolescents and young adults also are more likely to be focused on personal strivings and close relationships than on

money and prestige (Kasser & Ryan, 1996; Perkins, 1991). So, happy are those whose work and leisure, and friendships absorb them, enabling them unself-consciously to "flow" in focused activity.

Satisfying tasks and relationships impact our happiness, but within limits imposed by our genetic leash. From their study of 254 identical and fraternal twins, David Lykken and Auke Tellegen (1996) estimated that 50 percent of the difference among people's happiness ratings is heritable. Even identical twins raised apart often are similarly happy. Depending on our outlooks and recent experiences, our happiness fluctuates around our "happiness set point," which disposes some people to be ever upbeat, and others down.

SUMMING UP

Among various human emotions, we looked closely at how we experience three: fear, anger, and happiness.

Fear Fear is an adaptive emotion, but it can be traumatic. Although we seem biologically predisposed to acquire some fears, what we learn through experience and observation best explains the variety of human fears.

Anger Anger is most often aroused by events that not only are frustrating or insulting but also are interpreted as willful, unjustified, and avoidable. Other negative emotions, such as depression, can also feed anger. Although blowing off steam may be temporarily calming, it does not, in the long run, reduce anger. Expressing anger can actually arouse more anger.

Happiness A good mood boosts people's perceptions of the world and their willingness to help others. The moods triggered by the day's good or bad

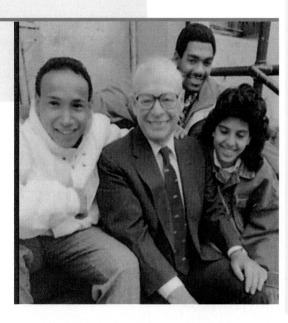

When downward comparisons lead upward Comparing ourselves with those worse off can sometimes prompt us not only to count our blessings but to share them. Self-made millionaire Eugene Lang (center) did just that during an address to the graduating class of the public grade school he had attended in Harlem. After reflecting on their poverty, he suddenly offered to pay the college costs of any who graduated from high school. (With his active support during the next four years, most did graduate from high school and over half went on to college.)

events seldom last beyond that day. Even significant good events, such as a substantial raise in income, seldom increase happiness for long. We can explain the relativity of happiness with the adaptation-level phenomenon and the relative deprivation principle. Nevertheless, some people are usually happier than others, and researchers have identified factors that predict such happiness.

KEY TERMS AND CONCEPTS catharsis, feel-good, do-good phenomenon, subjective well-being, adaptation-level phenomenon, relative deprivation

Figure **13.13**

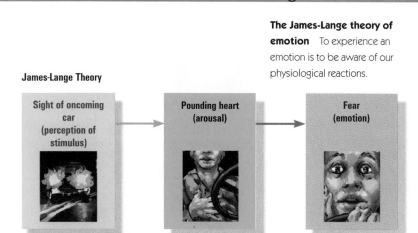

The James-Lange theory of emotion To experience an emotion is to be aware of our physiological reactions.

Theories of Emotion

We have seen that emotions arise from the interplay of physiological arousal, expressive behavior, and conscious experiences. But there are two controversies over this interplay. The first is an old debate: Does your heart pound because you are afraid, or are you afraid because you feel your heart pounding? The second concerns the link between our thinking and feeling: Does cognition always precede emotion?

The James-Lange and Cannon-Bard Theories

Common sense tells most of us that we cry because we are sad, lash out because we are angry, tremble because we are afraid. To pioneering psychologist William James this commonsense view of emotion was 180 degrees out of line. According to James, "We feel sorry because we cry, angry because we strike, afraid because we tremble" (1890, p. 1066). After you evade an oncoming car in your lane, you may notice your racing heart and *then* feel shaken with fright. Your feeling of fear follows your body's response (Figure 13.13).

James's idea, which was also proposed by Danish physiologist Carl Lange and is therefore called the James-Lange theory, struck U.S. physiologist Walter Cannon (1871–1943) as implausible. Cannon thought the body's responses were not distinct enough to evoke the different emotions. Does a racing heart signal fear, anger, or love? Also, changes in heart rate, perspiration, and body temperature seemed too slow to trigger sudden emotion. Cannon, and later another physiologist, Philip

Bard, concluded that physiological arousal and the emotional experience occur simultaneously: The emotion-arousing stimulus is routed simultaneously to the cortex, causing the subjective awareness of emotion, and to the sympathetic nervous system, causing the body's arousal. Thus, this Cannon-Bard theory implies that your heart begins pounding *as* you experience fear; one does not cause the other (Figure 13.14).

As long as the evidence suggested that the arousal of one emotion is much the same as another, the James-Lange assumption that we experience our emotions through differing body states seemed improbable. With new evidence showing subtle physiological distinctions among the emotions, the James-Lange theory became more plau-

Figure **13.14**

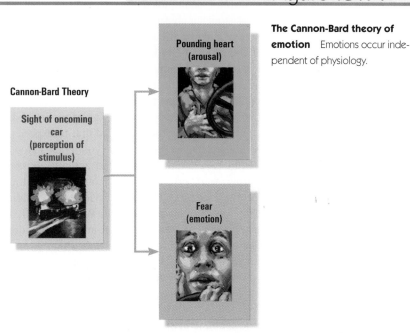

The Cannon-Bard theory of emotion Emotions occur independent of physiology.

James-Lange theory
the theory that our experience of emotion is our awareness of our physiological responses to emotion-arousing stimuli.

Cannon-Bard theory
the theory that an emotion-arousing stimulus simultaneously triggers (1) physiological responses and (2) the subjective experience of emotion.

two-factor theory
Schachter's theory that to experience emotion one must (1) be physically aroused and (2) cognitively label the arousal.

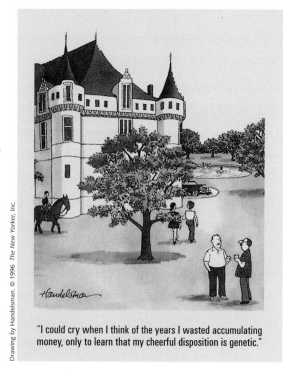

"I could cry when I think of the years I wasted accumulating money, only to learn that my cheerful disposition is genetic."

Drawing by Handelsman. © 1996 The New Yorker, Inc.

"Whenever I feel afraid
I hold my head erect
And whistle a happy tune."

RICHARD RODGERS AND OSCAR HAMMERSTEIN
THE KING AND I
1958

"Every moment
is more intense."

PARALYZED ACTOR CHRISTOPHER REEVE
1995

sible. As James struggled with his own feelings of depression and grief, he came to believe that we can control emotions by going "through the outward motions" of whatever emotion one wants to experience. "To feel cheerful," he advised, "sit up cheerfully, look around cheerfully, and act as if cheerfulness were already there." The last few decades' findings concerning emotional effects of facial expressions (page 402) are precisely what James might have predicted.

Let's check your understanding of the James-Lange and Cannon-Bard theories. Imagine that your brain could not sense your heart pounding or your stomach churning. According to each theory, how would this affect your experienced emotions?

Cannon and Bard would have expected you to experience emotions normally, because they believed emotions occur separately from (though simultaneously with) the body's arousal. James and Lange would have expected greatly diminished emotions because they believed that to experience emotion you must first perceive your body's arousal.

The condition you imagined actually exists in people with severed spinal cords. Psychologist George Hohmann (1966) interviewed 25 soldiers who received such injuries in World War II. He asked them to recall emotion-arousing incidents that occurred before and after their spinal injuries. Those with injuries in the lower part of the spine, who had lost sensation only in their legs, reported little change in their emotions. Those who could feel nothing below the neck reported a considerable decrease in emotional intensity (as James and Lange would have expected). These soldiers said

they might act much the same as before in emotion-arousing situations, but as one confessed about his anger, "It just doesn't have the heat to it that it used to. It's a mental kind of anger." On the other hand, emotions expressed mostly in body areas above the neck are felt more intensely by those with spinal cord injury. Virtually all the men Hohmann interviewed reported increases in weeping, lumps in the throat, and getting choked up when saying good-bye, worshipping, or watching a touching movie.

Although such evidence breathed new life into the James-Lange theory, most researchers agree with Cannon and Bard that our experienced emotions also involve cognition (Averill, 1993). Whether we fear the man behind us on the dark street depends entirely on whether we interpret his actions as hostile or friendly. So with James and Lange we can say that our arousal is an important ingredient of emotion. And with Cannon and Bard we can say that there is more to the experience of emotion than reading our physiology.

Cognition and Emotion

Now, the second and newer controversy: Put simply, what is the connection between what we *think* and how we *feel*? Which is the chicken and which the egg? Do emotions always grow from thoughts? Are our feelings always subject to our mind's appraisal of a situation?

We know that our emotions affect our thinking. When we *feel* like singing "Oh, what a beautiful morning!" we *see* the world and the people around us as wonderful; if the following day we find ourselves singing the blues, we perceive the same world and the same people as less than wonderful.

Can we experience emotion apart from thinking? This issue has practical implications for self-improvement. Can we change our emotions by changing our thinking? Is it true that what we think we become?

Schachter's Two-Factor Theory of Emotion

Most psychologists today believe that our cognitions—our perceptions, memories, and interpretations—are an essential ingredient of emotion. One such theorist is Stanley Schachter, who has proposed a two-factor theory, in which emotions have two ingredients: physical arousal and a cognitive label (Figure 13.15). Like James and Lange, Schachter presumed that our experience of emotion grows from our awareness of our body's arousal. But like Cannon and Bard, Schachter also believed that emo-

Figure **13.15**

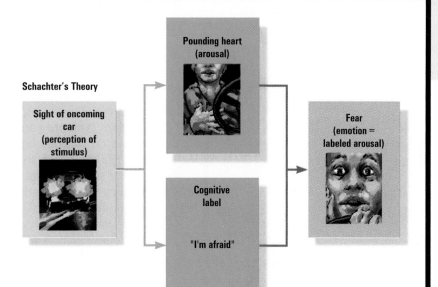

Summary of Schachter's two-factor theory of emotion To experience emotion, we must be aroused and must cognitively label the arousal.

tions are physiologically similar. Thus, in his view, an emotional experience requires a conscious interpretation of the arousal.

Sometimes our arousal response to one event spills over into our response to the next event. Imagine that after an invigorating run you arrive home to find a message that you got the longed-for job. With arousal lingering from the run, would you feel more elated than if you received this news after awakening from a nap?

To find out, Schachter and Jerome Singer (1962) aroused college men with injections of the hormone epinephrine. Picture yourself as one of their subjects: After receiving the injection, you go to a waiting room, where you find yourself with another person (actually an accomplice of the experimenters) who is acting either euphoric or irritated. As you observe this person, you begin to feel your heart race, your body flush, and your breathing become more rapid. If told to expect these effects from the injection, what would you feel? Schachter and Singer's subjects felt little emotion—because they attributed their arousal to the drug. But if told the injection would produce no effects, what would you feel? Perhaps you would react, as another group of subjects did, by "catching" the apparent emotion of the person you are with—becoming happy if the accomplice is acting euphoric, and testy if the accomplice is acting irritated.

This discovery—that a stirred-up state can be experienced as one emotion or another very different one, depending on how we interpret and label it—has been replicated in dozens of experiments. Although emotional arousal is not as undifferenti-

ated as Schachter believed, arousal can intensify just about any emotion (Reisenzein, 1983; Sinclair & others, 1994). Insult people who have just been aroused by pedaling an exercise bike or watching a rock concert film and they will find it easy to misattribute their arousal to the provocation. Their feelings of anger will be greater than those of similarly provoked people who were not previously aroused. Arousal from emotions as diverse as anger, fear, and sexual excitement can spill from one emotion to another (Zillmann, 1986). In anger-provoking situations, sexually aroused people react with more hostility; and the arousal that lingers after an intense argument or a frightening experience may intensify sexual passion (Palace, 1995).

So, arousal fuels emotion and cognition channels it. This can be seen in successful Olympic gymnasts and exam takers—who, more than their less successful competitors, label arousal as energizing, as giving them an edge, rather than as threatening (Raglin, 1992). Professors and public speakers similarly welcome prelecture arousal as meaning they are "up" or "on" rather than flat.

Must Cognition Precede Emotion?

So, to experience an emotion, must we first label our arousal? If Robert Zajonc (pronounced ZI-yence) (1980, 1984a) is right, the answer is no. He argues that our emotional reactions are sometimes quicker than our interpretations of a situation; we therefore feel some emotions *before* we think. For example, in earlier chapters, we noted that when people repeatedly view stimuli flashed too briefly

Figure **13.16**

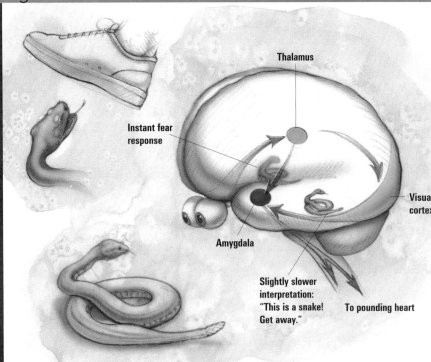

Thalamus

Instant fear response

Amygdala

Visual cortex

Slightly slower interpretation: "This is a snake! Get away."

To pounding heart

The brain's shortcut for emotions Sensory input may be routed both to the cortex and directly to the amygdala for a more instant emotional reaction.

Figure **13.17**

Emotion and cognition feed each other But which is the chicken and which the egg? Lazarus believes that, although emotions influence thinking, our cognitive appraisal of a situation always precedes emotion. Zajonc contends that some of our emotional reactions precede cognitive processing.

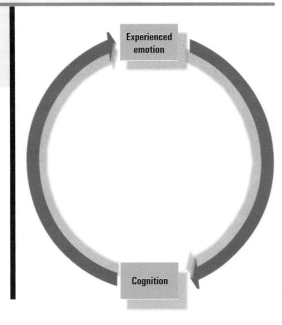

Experienced emotion

Cognition

for them to perceive and recall, they nevertheless come to prefer these stimuli. Without being consciously aware of having seen the stimuli, they rather like them. A subliminally flashed smiling or angry face can also prime us to feel better or worse about a follow-up stimulus (Murphy & others, 1995). (Can you recall liking something or someone immediately, without at first knowing why?)

Research on neurological processes shows how we can experience emotion before cognition. Some neural pathways involved in emotion bypass the cortical areas involved in thinking. One such pathway runs from the eye or ear via the thalamus to the amygdala, an emotional control center (LeDoux, 1994, 1996). This short-cut enables a quick, pre-cognitive emotional response before the intellect intervenes. After the cortex has further interpreted a threat, the thinking brain can take over (Figure 13.16). In the forest, we jump at a nearby twig-cracking sound, leaving the cortex to decide later whether it was made by a predator or just the wind. Such evidence supports Zajonc's belief that *some* of our emotional reactions involve no deliberate thinking, and that cognition is not always necessary for emotion. The heart is not always subject to the mind.

Emotion researcher Richard Lazarus (1984, 1991) disagrees. He concedes that our brains process and react to vast amounts of information without our conscious awareness, and he willingly grants that some emotional responses do not require *conscious* thinking. Nevertheless, he has pointed out, even instantaneously felt emotions require some sort of quick cognitive appraisal of the situation; otherwise, how do we *know* what we are reacting to? The appraisal may be effortless and we may not be conscious of it, but it is still a mental function (Figure 13.17). Emotions arise when we *appraise* an event as beneficial or harmful to our well-being.

Complex emotions, such as guilt, happiness, and love, most clearly arise from our interpretations and expectations. Highly emotional people are intense partly because of their interpretations. They *personalize* events as being somehow directed at them, and they *generalize* their experiences by blowing single incidents out of proportion (Larsen & others, 1987). Whether we attribute a low grade to an unfair exam, bad luck, or our own inability or laziness determines whether we feel irritated or depressed (Weiner, 1985). Attributing failure to our inability erodes motivation: "If I just don't have it, why try?" Attributing failure to unfairness, we instead feel angry.

For us, the important conclusion concerns what Lazarus and Zajonc agree on: Some emotional responses—especially simple likes, dislikes, and fears—involve no conscious thinking. We may fear the spider, even if we "know" it is harmless. After conditioning, Little Albert was afraid of furry objects (Chapter 8). Such responses are hard to alter by changing our thinking.

Other emotions—including moods such as depression and complex feelings such as hatred and love—are greatly affected by our interpretations, memories, and expectations. For these emotions, as we will see in Chapter 16, learning to *think* more positively about ourselves and the world around us makes us *feel* better.

SUMMING UP

The James-Lange and Cannon-Bard Theories One of the oldest theoretical controversies regarding emotion is whether we feel emotion *after* we notice our physiological responses (as James and Lange proposed) or *when* our bodies respond (as Cannon and Bard believed).

Cognition and Emotion A more recent controversy among emotion researchers concerns whether we can experience human emotions apart from cognition. Can we feel before we think? Stanley Schachter's two-factor theory of emotion contends that the cognitive labels we put on our states of arousal are an essential ingredient of emotion. Richard Lazarus agrees that cognition is essential: Many important emotions arise from our interpretations or inferences. Robert Zajonc, however, believes that some simple emotional responses occur instantly, not only outside of conscious awareness but before any cognitive processing occurs. The issue has practical implications: To the degree that emotions are rooted in thinking, we can hope to change them by changing our thinking.

KEY TERMS AND CONCEPTS James-Lange theory, Cannon-Bard theory, two-factor theory

TERMS AND CONCEPTS TO REMEMBER

emotion, p. 393

polygraph, p. 396

catharsis, p. 406

feel-good, do-good phenomenon, p. 407

subjective well-being, p. 407

adaptation-level phenomenon, p. 410

relative deprivation, p. 411

James-Lange theory, p. 413

Cannon-Bard theory, p. 413

two-factor theory, p. 414

CRITICAL THINKING EXERCISE
by Richard O. Straub

Now that you have read and reviewed Chapter 13, take your learning a step further by testing your critical thinking skills on the following scientific problem-solving exercise.

Participants in a recent study were shown an erotic movie while they were in each of three phases of recovery from aerobic exercise. They first pedaled an exercise bicycle intensely enough to produce significant physical arousal. During each of the three recovery phases, the participants were asked (1) whether they still felt physically aroused from the exercise, and (2) how sexually excited by the film they

felt. Their actual physical arousal (heart rate) was measured throughout the experiment. During the first two phases of recovery, all of the participants still showed signs of actual physical arousal, although by the second phase, they said they no longer felt physically aroused from the exercise. By the third phase, they no longer showed signs of physical arousal from the exercise. All participants reported feeling significantly more sexually excited by the film during the second phase of exercise recovery than they did during the first and third phases.

1. How well would the James-Lange theory explain the results of this experiment? What variations in reported feelings of sexual excitement would this theory have predicted in the three phases of exercise recovery?

2. How well would the Cannon-Bard theory explain the results of this experiment? What variations in reported feelings of sexual excitement would this theory have predicted in the three phases of exercise recovery?

3. How well would Schachter's two-factor theory explain the results of this experiment? What variations in reported feelings of sexual excitement would this theory have predicted in the three phases of exercise recovery?

Check your progress on becoming a critical thinker by comparing your answers to the sample answers found in Appendix B.

chapter 14

Personality

Novelist William Faulkner was a master at creating characters with vivid personalities.[1] One of his creations, Ike McCaslin, appears at various ages in more than a dozen novels and short stories. Ike is highly principled, and consistently so. At age 10 he feels a deep reverence for the wilderness and its creatures. At 21 he forfeits a "tainted" inheritance. In his late seventies he counsels his nephew to use his land responsibly. Ike the adult is an extension of Ike the child.

Another Faulkner character, Jason Compson, is a selfish, whining 4-year-old in the opening section of *The Sound and the Fury*, and a selfish, screaming 34-year-old as the novel closes. As head of the Compson household, he verbally abuses family members and household servants. Lying, threatening, conniving, he is a self-centered child who becomes a self-centered adult.

Faulkner's characters, as they appear and reappear throughout his fiction, exhibit the distinctiveness and consistency that define personality. The preceding chapters have emphasized how we are similar—how we all develop, perceive, learn, remember, think, and feel. This chapter emphasizes our individuality. Your individual personality is your characteristic pattern of thinking, feeling, and acting. If your behavior pattern is strikingly distinctive and consistent—if, say, you are always outgoing, whether at a party or in a classroom—people are likely to say that you have a "strong" personality.

> "There is no man who is not, at each moment, what he has been and what he will be."
>
> **OSCAR WILDE (1854–1900)**

Actually, much of this book deals with personality. In earlier chapters, we considered biological influences on personality, personality development across the life span, and personality-related aspects of learning, motivation, and emotion. In later chapters we will study disorders of personality, personality's influence on health, and social influences on personality.

[1]Faulkner scholar Nancy Nicodemus assisted with these examples.

personality
an individual's characteristic pattern of thinking, feeling, and acting.

free association
in psychoanalysis, a method of exploring the unconscious in which the person relaxes and says whatever comes to mind, no matter how trivial or embarrassing.

psychoanalysis
the technique of treating psychological disorders by seeking to expose and interpret unconscious tensions. Freud's psychoanalytic theory of personality sought to explain what he observed during psychoanalysis.

Sigmund Freud (1856–1939)
"I was the only worker in a new field."

In this chapter we explore and evaluate four major perspectives on personality:

- Sigmund Freud's *psychoanalytic* theory, which proposes that childhood sexuality and unconscious motivations influence personality.

- The *trait* perspective, in which researchers identify personality dimensions that account for our consistent behavior patterns.

- The *humanistic* approach, which focuses on our inner capacities for growth and self-fulfillment.

- The *social-cognitive* approach, which emphasizes how we shape and are shaped by our environment.

The Psychoanalytic Perspective

Love him or hate him, Sigmund Freud has influenced Western culture. To recognize his influence, we need to understand Freud's ideas concerning the unconscious, psychosexual stages, and mechanisms for defending against anxiety.

Ask 100 people on the street to name a notable deceased psychologist, suggests Keith Stanovich (1996, p. 1), and "Sigmund Freud would be the winner hands down." Although Freud's current influence in psychological science is slight, his notoriety continues to color people's perceptions of psychology, and his influence lingers in literary interpretation, psychiatry, and pop psychology. So who was Freud, and what did he teach?

Well before entering the University of Vienna in 1873, the youthful Sigmund Freud showed signs of independence and brilliance. He had a prodigious memory. He so loved serious reading that he once ran up a bookstore debt beyond his means, feeding his insatiable interest in plays, poetry, and philoso-

phy. As a teen he often took his evening meal in his tiny bedroom, to lose no time from his studies.

After graduating from medical school, Freud set up a private practice, specializing in nervous disorders. Before long, however, he faced patients whose disorders made no neurological sense. A patient might have lost all feeling in her hand—yet there is no sensory nerve that, if damaged, would numb the entire hand and nothing else. Freud's search for a cause for such disorders set his mind running in a direction that was destined to change human self-understanding. His views, which evolved as he treated patients and analyzed himself, eventually filled 24 volumes that were published between 1888 and 1939. Following his first solo book, *The Interpretation of Dreams* (1900), his ideas gradually began to attract both dedicated followers and intense criticism. For now, let us reserve judgment on Freud's theory and try to see things as he did. It is impossible to summarize 24 volumes in these few pages, but we can highlight Freud's psychoanalytic theory—the first comprehensive theory of personality.

Exploring the Unconscious

Freud wondered whether some neurological disorders might be psychologically rather than physiologically caused. To explore this possibility, he spent several months in Paris studying with a neurologist who was using hypnosis to treat patients suffering from these disorders. On returning to Vienna, Freud began to hypnotize his patients, encouraging them while hypnotized to talk freely about themselves and the circumstances surrounding the onset of their symptoms. Often the patients responded openly, at times becoming quite agitated during the hypnotic experience. Sometimes their symptoms then diminished or even disappeared.

While experimenting with hypnosis, Freud "discovered" the unconscious. Piecing together his patients' accounts of their lives, he decided that the

Freud's consulting room
Freud's office was rich with antiquities from around the world, including artwork related to his ideas about unconscious motives. His famous couch, piled high with pillows, placed patients in a comfortable reclining position facing away from him to help them focus inward.

"Good morning, beheaded—uh, I mean beloved."

loss of feeling in one's hand might be caused by a fear of touching one's genitals; that blindness or deafness might be caused by not wanting to see or hear something that aroused intense anxiety. Given patients' uneven capacity for hypnosis, he turned to free association—in which he merely told the patient to relax and say whatever came to mind, no matter how embarrassing or trivial. Freud believed that free association produced a chain of thought leading into the patient's unconscious, thereby retrieving and releasing painful unconscious memories, often from childhood. Freud called his theory and associated techniques psychoanalysis.

Underlying Freud's psychoanalytic conception of personality was his belief that the mind is like an iceberg—mostly hidden. Our conscious awareness is the part of the iceberg that floats above the surface. Below the surface is the much larger, unconscious region containing thoughts, wishes, feelings, and memories, of which we are largely unaware. Some of these thoughts we store temporarily in a preconscious area, from which we can retrieve them at will into conscious awareness. Of greater interest to Freud was the mass of unacceptable passions and thoughts that he believed we *repress*, or forcibly block from our consciousness because they would be too painful to acknowledge. Freud believed that, although we are not consciously aware of them, these troublesome feelings and ideas powerfully influence us. In his view, our unacknowledged impulses express themselves in disguised forms—the work we choose, the beliefs we hold, our daily habits, our troubling symptoms. In such ways, the unconscious seeps into our thoughts and actions.

For Freud the determinist, nothing was ever accidental. He believed he glimpsed the seepage of the unconscious not only in people's free associations, beliefs, habits, and symptoms but also in their dreams and slips of the tongue and pen while reading, writing, and speaking. Consider his example of a financially stressed patient who, not wanting any large pills, said, "Please do not give me any bills, because I cannot swallow them." Similarly, jokes were a way to express repressed sexual and aggressive tendencies. Freud viewed dreams as the "royal road to the unconscious." The remembered content of dreams (their *manifest content*—see page 218) he believed to be a censored expression of the dreamer's unconscious wishes (the dream's *latent content*). By analyzing people's dreams, Freud believed he could reveal the nature of their inner conflicts and release their inner tensions.

Personality Structure

For Freud, human personality—including its emotions and strivings—arises from a conflict between our aggressive, pleasure-seeking biological impulses and the social restraints against them. In his view, personality results from our efforts to resolve this basic conflict—to express these impulses in ways that bring satisfaction without also bringing guilt or punishment.

Freud theorized that the conflict centers on three interacting systems: id, ego, and superego (Figure 14.1). These abstract psychological concepts are, said Freud, "useful aids to understanding" the mind's dynamics.

The id is a reservoir of unconscious psychic energy that constantly strives to satisfy basic drives to survive, reproduce, and aggress. The id operates on the *pleasure principle*: If unconstrained by real-

unconscious
according to Freud, a reservoir of mostly unacceptable thoughts, wishes, feelings, and memories. According to contemporary research psychologists, information processing of which we are unaware.

preconscious
information that is not conscious but is retrievable into conscious awareness.

id
a reservoir of unconscious psychic energy that, according to Freud, strives to satisfy basic sexual and aggressive drives. The id operates on the pleasure principle, demanding immediate gratification.

"Two passengers leaned against the ship's rail and stared at the sea. 'There sure is a lot of water in the ocean,' said one. 'Yes,' answered his friend, 'we've only seen the top of it.'"

PSYCHOLOGIST GEORGE A. MILLER (1962)

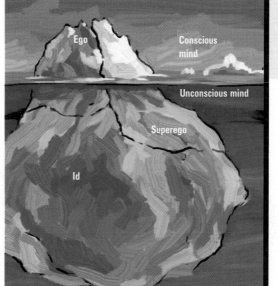

Figure 14.1

Freud's idea of the mind's structure Consciousness is like an iceberg's visible tip. Note that the id is totally unconscious, but ego and superego operate both consciously and unconsciously. (Adapted from Freud, 1933, page 111.)

ego
the largely conscious, "executive" part of personality that, according to Freud, mediates among the demands of the id, superego, and reality. The ego operates on the *reality principle*, satisfying the id's desires in ways that will realistically bring pleasure rather than pain.

superego
the part of personality that, according to Freud, represents internalized ideals and provides standards for judgment (the conscience) and for future aspirations.

psychosexual stages
the childhood stages of development (oral, anal, phallic, latency, genital) during which, according to Freud, the id's pleasure-seeking energies focus on distinct erogenous zones.

Oedipus [Ed-uh-puss] complex
according to Freud, a boy's sexual desires toward his mother and feelings of jealousy and hatred for the rival father.

ity, it seeks immediate gratification. Think of newborn infants, who, governed by the id, cry out for satisfaction the moment they feel a need, caring nothing for the outside world's conditions and demands.

As the ego develops, the young child learns to cope with the real world. The ego operates on the *reality principle*, which seeks to gratify the id's impulses in realistic ways that will bring long-term pleasure rather than pain or destruction. (Imagine what would happen if, lacking an ego, we expressed our unrestrained sexual or aggressive impulses whenever we felt them.) The ego, which contains our partly conscious perceptions, thoughts, judgments, and memories, is the personality "executive." It is a mediator, balancing the impulsive demands of the id, the restraining demands of the superego, and the real-life demands of the external world.

Beginning around age 4 or 5, Freud theorized, a child's ego recognizes the demands of the newly emerging superego. The superego is a voice of conscience that forces the ego to consider not only the real but the ideal. Its sole focus is on how one *ought* to behave. The superego strives for perfection, judging actions and producing positive feelings of pride or negative feelings of guilt. Someone with an exceptionally strong superego may be continually upright yet, ironically, guilt-ridden; another with a weak superego may be wantonly self-indulgent and remorseless. Because the superego's demands often oppose the id's, the ego struggles to reconcile the two. The chaste student who is sexually attracted to someone may satisfy both id and superego by joining a volunteer organization to work with the desired person.

INSTANT CASH

"Fifty is plenty."

"Hundred and fifty."

Drawing by Woodman; © 1987 *The New Yorker Magazine, Inc.*

Personality Development

Analysis of his patients' histories convinced Freud that personality forms during life's first few years. Again and again his patients' symptoms seemed rooted in unresolved conflicts from early childhood. He concluded that children pass through a series of psychosexual stages during which the id's pleasure-seeking energies focus on distinct pleasure-sensitive areas of the body called *erogenous zones* (Table 14.1).

During the *oral stage*, which lasts throughout the first 18 months, the infant's sensual pleasures focus on sucking, biting, and chewing.

During the *anal stage*, from about 18 months to 3 years, the sphincter muscles become sensitive and controllable, and bowel and bladder retention and elimination become a source of gratification.

During the *phallic stage*, from roughly 3 to 6 years, the pleasure zone shifts to the genitals. Freud believed that during this stage boys seek genital stimulation and develop both unconscious sexual desires for their mother and jealousy and hatred for their father, whom they consider a rival. Given these feelings, boys would also feel guilt and a lurking fear of punishment from their father, perhaps by castration. Freud called this collection of feelings the Oedipus complex after the Greek legend of Oedipus, who unknowingly killed his father and married his mother. Although some psy-

Table **14.1**

Freud's Psychosexual Stages

Stage	Focus
Oral (0–18 months)	Pleasure centers on the mouth—sucking, biting, chewing
Anal (18–36 months)	Pleasure focuses on bowel and bladder elimination; coping with demands for control
Phallic (3–6 years)	Pleasure zone is the genitals; coping with incestuous sexual feelings
Latency (6 to puberty)	Dormant sexual feelings
Genital (puberty on)	Maturation of sexual interests

In Freud's view, maladaptive behavior in the adult results from conflicts unresolved during earlier psychosexual stages.

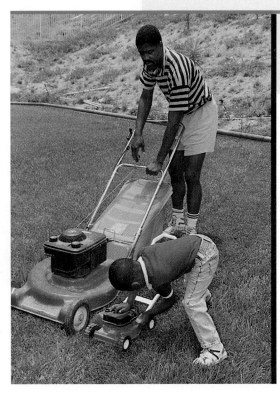

Identification Freud believed that children cope with threatening feelings of competition with their same-sex parent by identifying with that parent.

choanalysts believed that girls experience a parallel *Electra complex*, Freud (1931, page 229) said no: "It is only in the male child that we find the fateful combination of love for the one parent and simultaneous hatred for the other as a rival."

Children eventually cope with threatening feelings, said Freud, by repressing them and by identifying with (trying to become like) the rival parent. It's as if something inside the child decides, "If you can't beat 'em (the parent of the same sex), join 'em." Through this identification process, children's superegos gain strength as they incorporate many of their parents' values. Freud believed that identification with the same-sex parent provides our gender identity—our sense of being male or female.

With their sexual feelings repressed and redirected, children enter a *latency stage*. Freud maintained that during latency, extending from around age 6 to puberty, sexuality is dormant and children play mostly with peers of the same sex.

At puberty, latency gives way to the final stage, the *genital stage*, as the person begins to experience sexual feelings toward others.

In Freud's view, maladaptive behavior in the adult results from conflicts unresolved during earlier psychosexual stages. At any point in the oral, anal, or phallic stage, strong conflict can lock, or fixate, the person's pleasure-seeking energies in that stage. Thus, people who were either orally overindulged or deprived (perhaps by abrupt, early weaning) might fixate at the oral stage. Orally fixated adults are said to exhibit either passive dependence (like that of a nursing infant) or an exaggerated denial of this dependence—perhaps by acting tough and uttering biting sarcasm. They might also continue to seek oral gratification through excessive smoking and eating. Those who never quite resolve the anal conflict, between the desire to eliminate at will and the demands of toilet training, may be either messy and disorganized (*anal expulsive*) or highly controlled and compulsively neat (*anal retentive*). In such ways, believed Freud, the twig of personality is bent at an early age.

Defense Mechanisms

To live in social groups, we cannot act out our sexual and aggressive impulses willy-nilly. We must control them. When the ego fears losing control of the inner war between the demands of the id and the superego, the result is a dark cloud of unfocused anxiety. Anxiety, said Freud, is the price we pay for civilization. Anxiety is hard to cope with, as when we feel unsettled but are unsure why. Freud proposed that the ego protects itself against anxiety with defense mechanisms, which reduce or redirect anxiety in various ways, all of them distorting reality. Some examples:

Repression banishes anxiety-arousing thoughts and feelings from consciousness. According to Freud, repression underlies the other defense mechanisms, all of which disguise threatening impulses and keep them from reaching consciousness. Freud believed that repression explains why we do not remember our childhood lust for our parent of the other sex. However, he also believed that repression is often incomplete, with the repressed urges seeping out in dream symbols and slips of the tongue.

We also cope with anxiety through regression—retreating to an earlier, more infantile stage of development. Thus, when facing the anxious first days of school, a child may regress to the oral comfort of thumb-sucking. Juvenile monkeys, when

identification
the process by which, according to Freud, children incorporate their parents' values into their developing superegos.

gender identity
one's sense of being male or female.

fixation
according to Freud, a lingering focus of pleasure-seeking energies at an earlier psychosexual stage, where conflicts were unresolved.

defense mechanisms
in psychoanalytic theory, the ego's protective methods of reducing anxiety by unconsciously distorting reality.

repression
in psychoanalytic theory, the basic defense mechanism that banishes anxiety-arousing thoughts, feelings, and memories from consciousness.

regression
defense mechanism in which an individual retreats, when faced with anxiety, to a more infantile psychosexual stage where some psychic energy remains fixated.

Regression Faced with a mild stress, children and young monkeys will regress, retreating to the comfort of earlier behaviors.

anxious, retreat to infantile clinging to their mothers or to one another (Suomi, 1987). Even homesick new college students may long for the security and comfort of home.

In reaction formation the ego unconsciously makes unacceptable impulses look like their opposites. En route to consciousness, the unacceptable proposition "I hate him" becomes "I love him." Timidity becomes daring. Feelings of inadequacy become bravado.

"The lady doth protest too much, methinks."

WILLIAM SHAKESPEARE
HAMLET
1600

Projection disguises threatening impulses by attributing them to others. Thus, "He doesn't trust me" may be a projection of the actual feeling "I don't trust him" or "I don't trust myself." An El Salvadoran saying captures the idea: "The thief thinks everyone else is a thief."

The familiar mechanism of rationalization lets us unconsciously generate self-justifying explanations so we can hide from ourselves the real reasons for our actions. Thus, habitual drinkers may say they drink with their friends "just to be sociable." Students who fail to study may rationalize, "All work and no play makes Jack [or Jill] a dull person."

Displacement diverts one's sexual or aggressive impulses toward an object more psychologically acceptable than the one that aroused them. Children who can't express anger against their parents may displace their anger onto the family pet. Students upset over an exam may snap at a roommate.

Note again that all these defense mechanisms function indirectly and unconsciously, reducing anxiety by disguising our threatening impulses. We would never say, "I'm feeling anxious; I'd better project my sexual or hostile feelings onto someone else." Defense mechanisms would not work if we recognized them. As the body unconsciously defends itself against disease, so also, believed Freud, does the ego unconsciously defend itself against anxiety.

Freud's Descendants and Dissenters

Freud's controversial writings soon attracted followers, mostly young, ambitious physicians who formed an inner circle around their strong-minded leader. From time to time sparks flew, and one member or another would leave or be outcast. Even the ideas of the outcasts, however, reflected Freud's influence.

These pioneering psychoanalysts and others, whom we now call neo-Freudians, accepted Freud's basic ideas: the personality structures of id, ego, and superego; the importance of the unconscious; the shaping of personality in childhood; and the dynamics of anxiety and the defense mechanisms. But they veered away from Freud in two important ways. First, they placed more emphasis on the role of the conscious mind in interpreting experience and coping with the environment. And second, they doubted that sex and aggression were all-consuming motivations. Instead, they placed more emphasis on loftier motives and on social interaction, as the following examples illustrate.

Alfred Adler and Karen Horney [HORN-eye] agreed with Freud that childhood is important. But

reaction formation
defense mechanism by which the ego unconsciously switches unacceptable impulses into their opposites. Thus, people may express feelings that are the opposite of their anxiety-arousing unconscious feelings.

projection
the defense mechanism by which people disguise their own threatening impulses by attributing them to others.

rationalization
defense mechanism that offers self-justifying explanations in place of the real, more threatening, unconscious reasons for one's actions.

displacement
defense mechanism that shifts sexual or aggressive impulses toward a more acceptable or less threatening object or person, as when redirecting anger toward a safer outlet.

they believed that childhood *social*, not sexual, tensions are crucial for personality formation. Adler, who himself struggled to overcome childhood illnesses and accidents, said that much of our behavior is driven by an effort to conquer childhood feelings of inferiority, feelings that trigger strivings for superiority and power. (It was Adler who proposed the still-popular idea of the "inferiority complex.") Horney said that childhood anxiety, caused by the dependent child's sense of helplessness, triggers the desire for love and security. In countering Freud's assumptions that women have weak superegos and suffer "penis envy," Horney sought to balance the bias she detected in this masculine view of psychology.

> "The female ... acknowledges the fact of her castration, and with it, too, the superiority of the male and her own inferiority; but she rebels against this unwelcome state of affairs."
>
> SIGMUND FREUD
> *FEMALE SEXUALITY*
> 1931

Unlike other neo-Freudians, Carl Jung—Freud's disciple-turned-dissenter—placed less emphasis on social factors and agreed with Freud that the unconscious exerts a powerful influence. But to Jung (pronounced Yoong), the unconscious contains more than a person's repressed thoughts and feelings. There is also a collective unconscious, he believed, a common reservoir of images derived from our early ancestors' universal experiences. Jung said that the collective unconscious explains why,

for many people, spiritual concerns are deeply rooted and why people in different cultures share certain myths and images, such as mother as a symbol of nurturance.

Since Freud died in 1939, some of his ideas have been incorporated into *psychodynamic theory*. "Most contemporary dynamic theorists and therapists are not wedded to the idea that sex is the basis of personality," notes Drew Westen (1996), "do not talk about ids and egos, and do not go around classifying their patients as oral, anal, or phallic characters." What they do assume, with Freud, is that much of mental life is unconscious, that childhood shapes our personalities and ways of becoming attached to others, and that we often struggle with conflicts among our wishes, fears, and values.

Assessing the Unconscious

Those who study personality or provide therapy need ways to evaluate personality characteristics. Different personality theories have developed different methods of assessment.

Freud's theory maintains that the significant influences on our personalities arise from the unconscious, which contains residues from early childhood experiences. Psychoanalysts therefore dismiss objective assessment tools, such as agree-disagree or true-false questionnaires, as merely tapping the conscious surface. Their tool of choice would be a sort of psychological x-ray—a test that can see through our surface pretensions and reveal our hidden conflicts and impulses.

collective unconscious
Carl Jung's concept of a shared, inherited reservoir of memory traces from our species' history.

Alfred Adler "The individual feels at home in life and feels his existence to be worthwhile just so far as he is useful to others and is overcoming feelings of inferiority" (*Problems of Neurosis*, 1964).

Karen Horney "The view that women are infantile and emotional creatures, and as such, incapable of responsibility and independence is the work of the masculine tendency to lower women's self-respect" (*Feminine Psychology*, 1932).

Carl Jung "We can keep from a child all knowledge of earlier myths, but we cannot take from him the need for mythology" (*Symbols of Transformation*, 1912).

"If a professional psychologist is 'evaluating' you in a situation in which you are at risk and asks you for responses to ink blots ... walk out of that psychologist's office."

ROBYN DAWES
HOUSE OF CARDS: PSYCHOLOGY AND PSYCHOTHERAPY BASED ON MYTH
1994

Projective tests aim to provide such a view by presenting an ambiguous stimulus and then asking test-takers to describe it or tell a story about it. The stimulus has no inherent significance, so any meaning people read into it presumably reflects their interests and conflicts. Henry Murray (1933) demonstrated a possible basis for such a test at a house party hosted by his 11-year-old daughter. Murray got the children to play a frightening game called "Murder." When shown some photographs after the game, the children perceived the photos as more malicious than they had before the game. The children, it seemed to Murray, had *projected* their inner feelings into the pictures.

A few years later, Murray introduced the Thematic Apperception Test (TAT)—a test in which people view ambiguous pictures and then make up stories about them. As you may recall from page 384, one use of the TAT has been to assess achievement motivation. Shown a daydreaming boy, those who imagine him fantasizing an achievement are presumed to be projecting their own goals.

Various projective tests ask test-takers to draw a person, to complete sentences ("My mother . . . "), or to provide the first word that comes to mind after the examiner says a test word. Most widely used is the famous Rorschach inkblot test, introduced in 1921 by Swiss psychiatrist Hermann Rorschach [ROAR-shock]. The test assumes that what we see in its 10 inkblots reflects our inner feelings and conflicts. If we see fierce animals or weapons, the examiner may infer we have aggressive tendencies.

Is this a reasonable assumption? If so, can a psychologist use the Rorschach to understand one's personality and diagnose an emotional disorder?

Recall from Chapter 11's discussion of intelligence tests that the two primary criteria of a good test are reliability (consistency of results) and validity (predicting what it's supposed to). On those criteria, how good is the Rorschach?

Most researchers have considered it not very good (Peterson, 1978). There has been no one accepted system for scoring and interpreting the test. So unless two raters were trained in the same scoring system, their agreement on the results of any given test would be minimal. Nor has the test been very successful at predicting behavior or at discriminating between groups (for example, identifying who is suicidal and who is not).

Although not as popular as it once was, the Rorschach remains one of the most widely used psychological instruments (Piotrowski & Keller, 1989). Some clinicians continue to be confident of the test's validity—not as a device that by itself can provide a diagnosis, but as a source of suggestive leads that supplement other information. Other clinicians believe the test is an icebreaker and a revealing interview technique. A new research-based, computer-aided scoring and interpretation tool is improving agreement among raters and enhancing the test's validity—though not yet with enough evidence to satisfy critics (Exner, 1993; Shontz & Green, 1992; Wood & others, 1996). This scoring system, however, assumes that the blots actually do look like certain things, although the test assumes that they do not (Dawes, 1994). Moreover, Freud himself probably would have been uncomfortable with trying to assign each patient a test score and more interested in the therapist–patient interactions that take place during the test.

(a) The Rorschach test In this projective test, people say what a series of symmetrical inkblots look like. Some who use this test are confident that the interpretation of ambiguous stimuli will reveal unconscious aspects of the test-taker's personality. Others use it as an icebreaker or to supplement other information. **(b) The TAT** This psychologist presumes that the hopes, fears, and interests expressed in this boy's descriptions of a series of ambiguous pictures in the Thematic Apperception Test (TAT) are projections of his inner feelings.

(a)

(b)

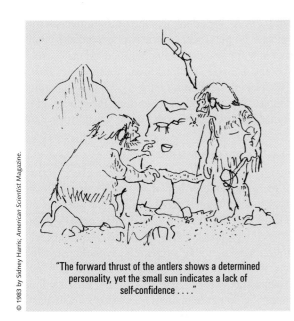

"The forward thrust of the antlers shows a determined personality, yet the small sun indicates a lack of self-confidence . . . ."

Evaluating the Psychoanalytic Perspective

Knowing what you do about Freud's ideas, listen now to his critics. Bear in mind that we critique Freud from the perspective of the late twentieth century, a perspective that is itself subject to revision. Freud died in 1939 without the benefit of all that we have since learned about human development, thinking, and emotion and without today's research tools. To criticize Freud's theories by comparing them with current concepts is like comparing Henry Ford's Model T with today's Escort, say Freud's admirers. To his critics, however, Freud's ideas are psychology's historical equivalent to astronomy's flat-earth theory.

Freud's Ideas in the Light of Modern Research

Recent research contradicts many of Freud's specific ideas. Today's developmental psychologists view our development as lifelong, not fixed in childhood. They also question Freud's idea that conscience and gender identity form as the child resolves the Oedipus complex at age 5 or 6. Children gain their gender identity earlier and become strongly masculine or feminine even without a same-sex parent present (Frieze & others, 1978). Freud's ideas about childhood sexuality arose from his rejection of stories of childhood sexual abuse told by his female patients—stories that some scholars believe he suggested or coerced and then attributed to their own childhood sexual wishes and conflicts (Powell & Boer, 1994). Today, we understand how Freud's questioning might have created false memories, and we also know that childhood sexual abuse does happen. Freud's ideas about the natural superiority of men have been thoroughly discounted.

As we saw in Chapter 7, new ideas about why we dream dispute Freud's belief that dreams disguise and fulfill wishes. Even slips of the tongue can be explained as competition between similar verbal choices in our memory network. Researchers find little support for Freud's idea that people protect themselves against painful self-knowledge by projecting their own unrecognized negative impulses onto others (Holmes, 1978, 1981). And Jerome Kagan (1989b) notes that history has been equally unkind to another of Freud's ideas—that sexual repression causes psychological disorder. From Freud's time to ours, sexual repression has diminished, but psychological disorders have not.

Is Repression a Myth?

Sigmund Freud's entire psychoanalytic theory rests on his assumption that the human mind often *represses* painful experiences, banishing them into unconsciousness. Freud and his legions of followers also assumed that with therapeutic assistance, people could *recover* such experiences years later and gain insight and healing as they do so.

Freud thought that if we could somehow uncover our past experiences, we would find them intact, like long-lost books in a dusty attic. If only we could recover and resolve the painful repressed memories of our childhood, emotional healing would follow. Under Freud's influence, repression has been used to explain hypnotic phenomena and many psychological disorders. It is also one of popular psychology's most widely accepted concepts. In one survey, 88 percent of university students believed that painful experiences commonly get pushed out of awareness and into unconsciousness (Garry & others, 1994).

"Studies have begun to converge toward a verdict . . . : there is literally nothing to be said [for] the entire Freudian system."

FREDERICK CREWS (1996)

To criticize Freud's theories by comparing them with current concepts is like comparing Henry Ford's Model T with today's Escort, say Freud's admirers. To his critics, however, Freud's ideas are psychology's historical equivalent to astronomy's flat-earth theory.

Actually, contend more and more of today's researchers, repression, if it ever occurs, is a rare mental response to terrible trauma. "Repression folklore is . . . partly refuted, partly untested, and partly untestable," says Elizabeth Loftus (1995). Consider: If the human mind indeed commonly banishes painful experiences, how do we explain these odd findings?

- Shouldn't we expect children who have witnessed a parent's murder to repress the experience? But no, one study of sixteen 5- to 10-year-old children who had this horrific experience found that not one repressed the memory (Malmquist, 1986).

- Shouldn't survivors of Nazi death camps have banished the atrocities from consciousness? But no, with rare exceptions they remember all too well—although many do benefit from disclosing and talking through their experiences (Helmreich, 1992, 1994; Pennebaker, 1990).

- Shouldn't we expect children who have been terrorized while their school bus was hijacked or pinned down by sniper fire to repress the experience? But no, in separate incidents all remembered it (Pope & Hudson, 1995).

- Shouldn't we expect victims and observers to black out the image of the horrific collapse of two hotel skywalks in which 114 died and more than 200 were injured? But no, not only do they recall it, nearly 90 percent later said they remembered it repeatedly (Wilkinson, 1983).

- Shouldn't battle-scarred veterans suffer amnesia for their worst experiences? But no, apart from concussion-related amnesia, such forgetting seems not to occur. Folklore regarding recovered battlefield memories is either unconfirmed or related to therapists' use of suggestive techniques, reports David Holmes (1990, 1994).

- Shouldn't people who have kept a diary of everyday life events later recall negative events significantly less well than positive events? But no, "the memory for the two types of events [is] almost the same," report Charles Thompson and his colleagues (1996).

There do appear to be rare exceptions—one death camp survivor reportedly forgot for over thirty years the snatching and shooting of her infant son (Kraft, 1996). Some researchers believe that extreme, prolonged stress, such as some severely abused children experience, might disrupt memory by damaging the hippocampus (Schacter, 1996). But the far more common reality is that negative emotional events are remembered well (Christianson, 1992). In fact, too well: These and other traumatic events, such as rape and torture, haunt survivors, who experience unwanted flashbacks. They are seared onto the soul.

After studying 400 hours of recollections by 120 witnesses to the Holocaust, psychologist Robert

> "Warning. Despite seventy years of research, there is no objective evidence to support the concept of repression."
>
> **DAVID A. HOLMES (1994)**

Kraft (1996) reported that "the nearly universal response is persistent, intrusive, extended, vivid memory for personally-experienced events." "You see the babies," said survivor Sally H. (1979). "You see the screaming mothers. You see hanging people. You sit and you see that face there. It's something you don't forget."

The Unconscious Mind

History has been kinder to Freud's "iceberg" view of the mind, at least in part. We now know that we indeed have limited access to all that goes on in our minds (Erdelyi, 1985, 1988; Kihlstrom, 1990; Lewicki & others, 1992). However, the "iceberg" notion held by today's research psychologists differs from Freud's—so much so, argues Anthony Greenwald (1992), that it is time to abandon Freud's view of the unconscious. As we saw in earlier chapters, many researchers think of the unconscious not as seething passions and repressive censoring but as cooler information processing that occurs without our awareness. To them, the unconscious involves

- the schemas that automatically control our perceptions and interpretations.

- the priming by stimuli which we have not consciously noticed.

- the right-hemisphere activity that enables the split-brain patient's left hand to carry out an instruction the patient cannot verbalize.

- the parallel processing of different aspects of vision and thinking.

- the implicit memories that operate without conscious recall, even among those with amnesia.

- the emotions that activate instantly, before conscious analysis.

- the self-concept and stereotypes that automatically and unconsciously influence how we process information about ourselves and others (Bargh, 1997).

More than we realize, we fly on autopilot. This understanding of unconscious information processing is more like the pre-Freudian view of an underground stream of thought from which spontaneous creative ideas surface.

Recent history has supported Freud's idea that we defend ourselves against anxiety. Again, however, the contemporary idea differs from Freud's. Jeff Greenberg, Sheldon Solomon, and Tom Pyszczynski (1997) believe that one source of anxiety is "the terror resulting from our awareness of vulnerability and death." Experiments testing their *terror-management theory* show that thinking about one's mortality—by writing a short essay on

Traumatic events,
such as rape and torture,
haunt survivors, who
experience unwanted
flashbacks. They are
seared onto the soul.

dying and its associated emotions—provokes enough anxiety to intensify prejudices. Anxiety motivates contempt for others and esteem for oneself. To feel self-esteem is to feel more secure in a threatening world.

Freud's Ideas as Scientific Theory

Psychologists also criticize Freud's theory for its scientific shortcomings. Recall from Chapter 1 that good scientific theories explain observations and offer testable hypotheses. Freud's theory rests on few objective observations and offers few hypotheses to verify or reject. (For Freud, his own recollections and interpretations of patients' free associations, dreams, and slips were evidence enough.)

"Sigmund Freud is an empirical void."

ANONYMOUS

The most serious problem with Freud's theory is that it offers after-the-fact explanations of any characteristic (of one person's smoking, another's fear of horses, another's sexual orientation) yet fails to *predict* such behavior and traits. If you feel angry at your mother's death, you illustrate the theory because "your unresolved childhood dependency needs are threatened." If you do not feel angry, you again illustrate the theory because "you are repressing your anger." That, said Calvin Hall and Gardner Lindzey (1978, p. 68), "is like betting on a horse after the race has been run." After-the-fact interpretation is perfectly appropriate for historical and literary scholarship, which helps explain Freud's currently greater influence on literary criticism than on psychological research. But in science a good theory makes testable predictions.

Yet Freud's supporters point out that to criticize Freudian theory for not making testable predictions is like criticizing baseball for not being an aerobic exercise. Is it fair to fault something for not being what it was never intended to be? Unlike many later psychoanalysts, Freud never claimed that psychoanalysis was predictive science. He merely claimed that, looking back, psychoanalysts could find meaning in our state of mind (Rieff, 1979). Freud's supporters also note that some of his ideas *are* enduring. It was Freud who drew our attention to the unconscious and the irrational, to anxiety and our struggle to cope with it, to the importance of human sexuality, and to the tension between our biological impulses and our social well-being. It was Freud who challenged our self-righteousness, punctured our pretensions, and reminded us of our potential for evil.

Freud's legacy lives on. Some ideas that many people assume to be true—that childhood experiences mold personality, that many behaviors have disguised motives—are Freud's legacy. His early 1900s concepts penetrate our 1990s language. Without realizing their source, we may speak of *ego*, *repression*, *projection*, *complex* (as in "inferiority complex"), *sibling rivalry,* and *fixation*. "Freud's premises may have undergone a steady decline in currency within academia for many years," notes Martin Seligman (1994), "but Hollywood, the talk shows, many therapists, and the general public still love them."

"We are arguing like a man who should say, 'If there were an invisible cat in that chair, the chair would look empty; but the chair does look empty; therefore there is an invisible cat in it.'"

C. S. LEWIS
FOUR LOVES
1958

SUMMING UP

Like intelligence, personality is an abstract concept that cannot be seen, touched, or directly measured. To psychologists, personality is one's relatively distinctive and consistent pattern of thinking, feeling, and acting. We have considered Freud's historically important psychoanalytic perspective first.

Exploring the Unconscious Sigmund Freud's treatment of emotional disorders led him to believe that they sprang from unconscious dynamics, which he sought to analyze through his own free associations and dreams and those of his patients. Freud saw personality as composed of pleasure-seeking psychic impulses (the id), a reality-oriented executive (the ego), and an internalized set of ideals (the superego).

Freud believed that children develop through psychosexual stages, which he labeled the oral, anal, phallic, latency, and genital stages. He suggested that our personalities are influenced by how we have resolved conflicts associated with these stages and whether we have remained fixated at any stage.

Tensions between demands of the id and superego cause anxiety. The ego copes by using defense mechanisms, of which repression is the most basic.

Neo-Freudians Alfred Adler and Karen Horney accepted many of Freud's ideas, as did Carl Jung. But they also argued that we have motives other than sex and aggression, and that the ego's conscious control is greater than Freud supposed.

Assessing the Unconscious Psychoanalytic assessment aims to reveal the unconscious. Although projective tests, such as the Rorschach inkblots, have questionable reliability or validity, many clinicians continue to use them.

Evaluating the Psychoanalytic Perspective Many of Freud's specific ideas are implausible, unvalidated, or contradicted by new research, and his theory offers only after-the-fact explanations. Many researchers now believe that repression rarely, if ever, occurs. Nevertheless, Freud drew psychology's attention to the unconscious, to the struggle to cope with anxiety and sexuality, and to the conflict between biological impulses and social restraints. His cultural impact has been enormous.

KEY TERMS AND CONCEPTS personality, free association, psychoanalysis, unconscious, preconscious, id, ego, superego, psychosexual stages, Oedipus complex, identification, gender identity, fixation, defense mechanisms, repression, regression, reaction formation, projection, rationalization, displacement, collective unconscious, projective test, Thematic Apperception Test (TAT), Rorschach inkblot test

The Trait Perspective

Rather than explaining hidden personality dynamics, trait researchers search for identifiable patterns of behavior or conscious motives that describe basic personality dimensions. Are there stable and enduring traits that underlie our actions? If so, can we devise valid and reliable tests of them for use in personality assessment?

Psychoanalytic theory attempts to explain personality in terms of the dynamics that underlie behavior. It peers beneath the surface in search of hidden motives. In 1919, Gordon Allport, a curious 22-year-old psychology student, interviewed Freud in Vienna and discovered just how preoccupied the founder of psychoanalysis was with finding hidden motives.

> Soon after I had entered the famous red burlap room with pictures of dreams on the wall, he summoned me to his inner office. He did not speak to me but sat in expectant silence, for me to state my mission. I was not prepared for silence and had to think fast to find a suitable conversational gambit. I told him of an episode on the tram car on my way to his office. A small boy about 4 years of age had displayed a conspicuous dirt phobia. He kept saying to his mother, "I don't want to sit there . . . don't let that dirty man sit beside me." To him everything was *schmutzig* (filthy). His mother was a well-starched *Hausfrau*, so dominant and purposive looking that I thought the cause and effect apparent.
>
> When I finished my story Freud fixed his kindly therapeutic eyes upon me and said, "And was that little boy you?" Flabbergasted and feeling a bit guilty, I contrived to change the subject. While Freud's misunderstanding of my motivation was amusing, it also started a deep train of thought (1967, pp. 7–8).

That train of thought ultimately led Allport to do what Freud did not do—to describe personality in terms of fundamental traits—people's characteristic behaviors and conscious motives (such as the professional curiosity that actually motivated Allport to see Freud). Meeting Freud, said Allport, "taught me that [psychoanalysis], for all its merits, may plunge too deep, and that psychologists would do well to give full recognition to manifest motives before probing the unconscious." Allport therefore defined personality in terms of identifiable behavior patterns. He was concerned less with *explaining* individual traits than with *describing* them.

How do psychologists describe and classify personalities? An analogy may help. Imagine that you want to describe and classify apples. Someone might correctly say that every apple is unique. Still, you might find it useful to begin by classifying apples as distinct *types*—Granny Smith, McIntosh, Delicious, and so forth. That is how the ancient Greeks described personality—by classifying people according to four types. Depending on which of one's bodily "humors" (fluids) they believed to predominate, they declared people either melancholic (depressed), sanguine (cheerful), phlegmatic (unemotional), or choleric (irritable).

We now have other ideas of basic personality types. Based on children's physiological and psychological reactivity, Jerome Kagan (1989b) has classified children's temperaments as either shy-inhibited or fearless-uninhibited types. Some health psychologists classify people as intense, *Type A,* or as laid back, *Type B,* personalities (pages 521–522).

Psychologist William Sheldon (1954) classified people by body type. Santa Claus typifies the plump *endomorph*: relaxed and jolly. Superman typifies the muscular *mesomorph*: bold and physically active. Sherlock Holmes typifies the thin *ectomorph*: high strung and solitary. Are different body types actually associated with different personalities? When researchers assess people's body types and personalities separately, there is only a modest linkage. The stereotypes of the chubby, happy-go-lucky person and of the muscular, confident person turn out to be just that—stereotypes that exaggerate a kernel of truth (Tucker, 1983).

More popular today, especially in business and career counseling, is an effort to classify people according to Carl Jung's personality types, based on their responses to 126 questions written by Isabel Briggs Myers (1987) and her mother, Kathleen Briggs. The *Myers-Briggs Type Indicator* is quite simple. It offers choices, such as "Do you usually value sentiment more than logic, or value logic more than sentiment?" Then it counts the test-taker's preferences, labels them as indicating, say, a "feeling" or "thinking" type, and feeds them back to the person in complimentary terms. Feeling types, for example, are told they are sensitive to values and "sympathetic, appreciative, and tactful"; thinking types are told they "prefer an objective standard of truth" and are "good at analyzing."

Whoopi the extravert On stage, Whoopi Goldberg seems as outgoing as her name (which is actually Caryn Johnson) implies. Trait labels such as extraversion can describe our temperaments and typical behaviors.

Most people therefore agree with their announced type profile, which mirrors their declared preferences. They may also accept it as a basis for being matched with work partners and tasks that supposedly suit their temperaments. A National Research Council report, however, noted that the test's use has outrun research on its value as a predictor of job performance, and that "the popularity of this instrument in the absence of proven scientific worth is troublesome" (Druckman & Bjork, 1991, p. 101; see also Pittenger, 1993).

Exploring Traits

If classifying people as one or another distinct personality type fails to fully capture their individuality, how else could we describe their personalities? To return to our apple analogy, we might describe an apple along several trait dimensions—as relatively large or small, red or yellow, sweet or sour. By placing people on several trait dimensions simultaneously, psychologists can describe countless individual personality variations. (Remember from Chapter 5 that variations on just three color dimensions—hue, saturation, and brightness—create many thousands of colors.)

What trait dimensions describe personality? Allport and his associate H. S. Odbert (1936) literally counted all the words in an unabridged dictionary with which one could describe people. The list numbered almost 18,000! How, then, could psychologists condense the list to a manageable number of basic traits?

trait
a characteristic pattern of behavior or a disposition to feel and act, as assessed by self-report inventories and peer reports.

Figure 14.2

Two personality factors

Mapmakers can tell us a lot by using two axes (north-south and east-west). Hans Eysenck and Sybil Eysenck use two primary personality factors—extraversion-introversion and stability-instability—as axes for describing personality variation. Varying combinations define other, more specific traits. Note that the four basic combinations of the two factors resemble the personality types proposed by the ancient Greeks, which are noted in the center of the chart. (From Eysenck & Eysenck, 1963.)

One way has been to propose traits, such as anxiety, that some theory regards as basic. A newer technique is *factor analysis*, the statistical procedure described in Chapter 11 to identify clusters of test items that tap basic components of intelligence (such as spatial ability, reasoning ability, or verbal skill). Imagine that people who describe themselves as outgoing also tend to say that they like excitement and practical jokes and that they do not like quiet reading. Such a statistically correlated cluster of behaviors reflects a basic trait, or factor—in this case, a trait called *extraversion*.

British psychologists Hans Eysenck and Sybil Eysenck [EYE-zink] believe that we can reduce many of our normal individual variations to two or three genetically influenced dimensions, including *extraversion-introversion* and *emotional stability-instability* (Figure 14.2). Their *Eysenck Personality Questionnaire* has been given to people in 35 countries around the world, from China to Uganda to Russia. When people's answers are analyzed, the extraversion and emotionality factors inevitably emerge as basic personality dimensions (Eysenck, 1990, 1992). Extraverts, the researchers contend, seek stimulation because their normal levels of brain arousal are relatively low. Emotionally stable people react calmly because their autonomic nervous systems are not as reactive as those of unstable people.

Many other trait theorists, too, view personality traits as biologically rooted. Jerome Kagan attributes differences in children's shyness and inhibition to their autonomic nervous system reactivity. Studies comparing identical and fraternal twins, comparing identical twins reared apart, and comparing adoptees with their adoptive and biological parents all remind us: Personality forms under the influence of genes (pages 108–111). Our genes have much to say about the temperament and the behavioral style that help define our personality—more, it seems, than the way our parents handled us (although parents also have an influence and are mighty important for other things, such as beliefs and values).

Most researchers believe that the Eysencks' dimensions are important but that they don't tell the whole story of someone's personality. A slightly expanded set of factors—dubbed the *Big Five*—does a better job (Goldberg, 1993; John, 1990; Wiggins, 1996). If a test specifies where you are on the five dimensions of Table 14.2, it has said much of what there is to say about your personality. Around the world, people describe others in terms

Table 14.2

The "Big Five" Personality Factors

Trait Dimension	Description
Emotional stability	Calm versus anxious Secure versus insecure Self-satisfied versus self-pitying
Extraversion	Sociable versus retiring Fun-loving versus sober Affectionate versus reserved
Openness	Imaginative versus practical Preference for variety versus preference for routine Independent versus conforming
Agreeableness	Soft-hearted versus ruthless Trusting versus suspicious Helpful versus uncooperative
Conscientiousness	Organized versus disorganized Careful versus careless Disciplined versus impulsive

Source: Adapted from McCrae & Costa (1986, p. 1002).

roughly consistent with the Big Five—how agreeable they are, how extraverted they are, and so forth. The Big Five is not the last word: Other theorists wonder whether we should add dimensions such as self-consciousness, masculinity-femininity, or positive-negative emotion. But it's currently our best approximation of the basic trait dimensions. If you could ask five questions about the personality of a stranger—say, a blind date you were soon to meet—querying where the person is on these five dimensions would be most revealing.

Assessing Traits

Assessment techniques derived from trait concepts do not reveal the hidden personality dynamics (which is the intent of projective tests). Rather, they profile a person's behavior patterns. Many trait scales provide quick assessments of a single trait, such as extraversion, anxiety, or self-esteem. Alternatively, psychologists can assess several traits at once by administering personality inventories—longer questionnaires on which people respond to items covering a wide range of feelings and behaviors.

The most extensively researched and widely used personality inventory is the Minnesota Multiphasic Personality Inventory (MMPI). Although it assesses "abnormal" personality tendencies rather than normal personality traits, the MMPI illustrates a good way to develop a personality inventory. One of its creators, Starke Hathaway (1960), compared his effort to that of Alfred Binet. Binet,

as you may recall from Chapter 11, developed the first intelligence test by selecting items that discriminated children who would have trouble progressing normally in French schools. The MMPI items, too, were empirically derived. That is, from a large pool of items Hathaway and his colleagues selected those that discriminated particular diagnostic groups.

They initially gave hundreds of true-false statements ("No one seems to understand me"; "I get all the sympathy I should"; "I like poetry") to groups of psychologically disordered patients and to "normal" people. They retained any statement—no matter how silly it sounded—on which the patient group's answer differed from that of the normal group. "Nothing in the newspaper interests me except the comics" may seem senseless, but it just so happened that depressed people were more likely to answer "true." (Nevertheless, pundits have had fun spoofing the MMPI with their own mock items, such as: "Weeping brings tears to my eyes," "Frantic screams make me nervous," and "I stay in the bathtub until I look like a raisin" [Frankel & others, 1983].)

Today's new "MMPI-2," renormed on a full cross-section of Americans and containing revised items, still contains 10 clinical scales (Figure 14.3). It also retains several validity scales, including the so-called lie scale that assesses the extent to which a person is faking to make a good impression (by responding "false" to statements such as "I get angry sometimes"). And it has 15 content scales assessing, for instance, work attitudes, family problems, and anger.

personality inventory
a questionnaire (often with true-false or agree-disagree items) on which people respond to items designed to gauge a wide range of feelings and behaviors; used to assess selected personality traits.

Minnesota Multiphasic Personality Inventory (MMPI)
the most widely researched and clinically used of all personality tests. Originally developed to identify emotional disorders (still considered its most appropriate use), this test is now used for many other screening purposes.

empirically derived test
a test (such as the MMPI) developed by testing a pool of items and then selecting those that discriminate between groups.

Figure **14.3**

Minnesota Multiphasic Personality Inventory (MMPI) test profile High T-scores suggest a psychological disorder; an average score is 50. This graph plots the scores of Ed, a depressed and anxious young man, before and after psychotherapy. (Scores are converted to a "T-scale," such that an average score is called 50 and about two-thirds of people fall between 40 and 60.) (Adapted from Butcher, 1990.)

Hypochondriasis 1
(concern with body symptoms)

Depression 2
(pessimism, hopelessness)

Hysteria 3
(uses symptoms to solve problems)

Psychopathic deviancy 4
(disregard for social standards)

Masculinity/femininity 5
(interests like those of other sex)

Paranoia 6
(delusions, suspiciousness)

Psychasthenia 7
(anxious, guilt feelings)

Schizophrenia 8
(withdrawn, bizarre thoughts)

Hypomania 9
(overactive, excited, impulsive)

Social introversion 10
(shy, inhibited)

Clinically significant range

After treatment (no scores in the clinically significant range)

Before treatment (anxious, depressed, and displaying deviant behaviors)

0   30   40   50   60   70   80

T-score

In contrast to the subjectivity of projective tests, personality inventories are scored objectively—so objectively that a computer can administer and score them. (The computer can also provide descriptions of people who previously responded similarly.) Objectivity does not, however, guarantee validity. For example, sophisticated test-takers can give fake answers to create a good impression if taking the MMPI for employment purposes. (They consistently answer in socially desirable ways, except on those items like "I get angry sometimes," for which nearly anyone would admit to being imperfect.) Moreover, the ease of computerized testing tempts untrained administrators—including many personnel officers, educational admissions officers, and physicians—to use the test in ways for which it has not been validated (Matarazzo, 1983). Nevertheless, for better or worse, the objectivity of the MMPI contributes to its popularity and to its translation into more than 100 languages.

Although self-report personality tests are the most widely used method of assessing traits, psychologist David Funder (1991, 1995) believes that peer reports provide more trustworthy information. Friends who have observed you repeatedly in everyday situations provide the acid test for judging, say, how extraverted you are. Self-reports and peer reports tend to agree (Borkenau & Liebler, 1993). But when they disagree, Funder would put his money on peer reports. If everyone who knows you agrees you are outgoing, then, regardless of what you think, you *are* outgoing.

Evaluating the Trait Perspective

Are our personality traits stable and enduring? Or does our behavior depend on where we are and whom we're with? William Faulkner created characters, like the self-centered Jason Compson, whose personality traits were consistent across various times and places. The Italian playwright Luigi Pirandello had a different view. For him, personality was ever-changing, tailored to the particular role or situation. In one of Pirandello's plays, Lamberto Laudisi describes himself to Signora Sirelli: "I am really what you take me to be; though, my dear madam, that does not prevent me from also being really what your husband, my sister, my niece, and Signora Cini take me to be—because they also are absolutely right!" To which she responds, "In other words you are a different person for each of us."

"There is as much difference between us and ourselves, as between us and others."

MICHEL DE MONTAIGNE
ESSAYS
1588

The Person-Situation Controversy

Who, then, represents human personality, Faulkner's consistent Jason Compson or Pirandello's inconsistent Laudisi? Both. Our behavior is influenced by the interaction of our inner disposition with our environment. Still, the question lingers: Which is *more* important? Are we *more* as Faulkner or as Pirandello imagined us to be? Forced to choose, most people would probably side with Faulkner. Until the late 1960s, most psychologists would have, too. Isn't it obvious that some people are dependably conscientious and others unreliable, some cheerful and others dour, some outgoing and others shy?

In considering this *person-situation controversy*, we seek genuine personality traits that persist over time *and* across situations. If friendliness is a trait, friendly people must act friendly at different times and in places. Do they? In Chapter 4, we considered research that has followed lives through time. We noted that some scholars (especially those who study infants) are impressed with personality change; others are struck by personality stability during adulthood. If people's personalities are assessed in young adulthood and then assessed again several decades later, their characteristics persist. Interests may change—the avid collector of tropical fish may become the avid gardener. Careers may change—the determined salesperson may become a determined social worker. Relationships may change—the hostile spouse may start over with a new partner. But most people recognize their traits as their own, note Robert McCrae and Paul Costa (1994), "and it is well that they do. A person's recognition of the inevitability of his or her one and only personality is . . . the culminating wisdom of a lifetime." Faulkner would not have been surprised.

"Mr. Coughlin over there was the founder of one of the first motorcycle gangs."

The consistency of specific *behaviors* from one situation to the next is another matter. As Walter Mischel (1968, 1984) has pointed out, people do not act with predictable consistency. In one of the first studies to reveal this, Hugh Hartshorne and Mark May (1928) gave thousands of children opportunities to lie, cheat, and steal while at home, at play, and in the classroom. Were some children consistently honest, others dishonest? Generally not. "Most children will deceive in certain situations and not in others," the researchers reported. A child's "lying, cheating, and stealing as measured by the test situations used in these studies are only very loosely related" (p. 411). More than a half-century later, Mischel's studies of college students' conscientiousness revealed a similar finding. There was virtually no relation between a student's being conscientious on one occasion (say, showing up for class on time) and being similarly conscientious on another occasion (say, turning in assignments on time). Pirandello would not have been surprised.

Mischel has also pointed out that people's scores on personality tests only mildly predict their behaviors. For example, people's scores on an extraversion test do not neatly predict how sociable they actually will be on any given occasion. If we remember such results, says Mischel, we will be more cautious about labeling and pigeonholing individuals. We will be more restrained when asked to predict whether someone is likely to violate parole, commit suicide, or be an effective employee. Years in advance, science can tell us the phase of the moon for any given date, but we may never be able to predict how you will feel and act tomorrow.

In defense of traits, Seymour Epstein (1983a,b) maintained that trying to predict a specific act on the basis of a personality test result is like trying to predict your answer to a specific aptitude question on the basis of an intelligence test result. Your answer to any given question is unpredictable because it depends on so many variables (your reading of the question, your understanding of the topic, your concentration level at the moment, luck). Your *average* accuracy over many questions on several tests is more predictable. Similarly, people's *average* outgoingness, happiness, or carelessness over *many* situations is predictable, Epstein observed. When rating someone's shyness or agreeableness, this consistency enables people who know someone well to agree (Kenrick & Funder, 1988). As our best friends can verify, we *do* have personality traits—genetically influenced traits, we now know. Moreover, our traits are socially significant. They influence our health, our thinking, and our job performance (Deary & Matthews, 1993; Hogan & others, 1996).

Consistency of Expressive Style

In unfamiliar, formal situations—perhaps when eating in a strange home—our traits may remain hidden as we attend carefully to social cues. In familiar, informal situations—just hanging out with friends—we feel less constrained, allowing our traits to emerge (Buss, 1989). In such situations, our expressive styles are impressively consistent. Thus, we often form lasting impressions within a few moments of meeting someone and noting the person's animation, manner of speaking, and gestures. Nalini Ambady and Robert Rosenthal (1992, 1993) videotaped 13 Harvard University graduate students teaching undergraduate courses. Observers then viewed three thin slices of each teacher's behavior—mere 10-second clips from the beginning, middle, and end of a class—and rated each teacher's level of confidence, activeness, warmth, and so forth. These behavior ratings, based on 30 *seconds* of teaching from an entire semester, predicted amazingly well the teacher's average student ratings at the semester's end. Observing even thinner slices—three 2-second clips—yielded ratings that still correlated as high as +.72 with the student evaluations. Some people's first impressions, derived from expressive behavior, predicted other people's lasting impressions!

Mere glimpses of someone's behavior can be revealing because of the potency of traits such as expressiveness. Some people are naturally expressive (and therefore talented at pantomime and charades); others are less expressive (and therefore better poker players). To evaluate people's voluntary control over their expressiveness, Bella DePaulo and her colleagues (1992) asked people to *act* as expressive or inhibited as possible while stating opinions. Their remarkable findings: Inexpressive people, even when feigning expressiveness, were less expressive than expressive people acting naturally. Similarly, expressive people, even when trying to seem inhibited, were less inhibited than inexpressive people acting naturally. It's hard to be someone you're not, or not to be what you are.

The irrepressibility of expressiveness explains why we can size up someone's outgoingness within seconds. Imagine yourself as a subject in an experi-

Roughly speaking, the temporary, external influences on behavior are the focus of social psychology, and the enduring, inner influences are the focus of personality psychology. In actuality, behavior always depends on the interaction of persons with situations.

Our expressive styles are impressively consistent. Thus, we often form lasting impressions within a few moments of meeting someone and noting the person's animation, manner of speaking, and gestures.

ment by Maurice Levesque and David Kenny (1993). They seated groups of four university women around a table and asked each woman merely to state her name, year in school, hometown, and college residence. Judging from just these few seconds of verbal and nonverbal behavior, the women were then to guess one another's talkativeness. (Do you think you would be able to make such a guess from so brief a glimpse of someone else's behavior?) When later correlated with how talkative each woman actually was during a series of one-on-one videotaped conversations, the snap judgments proved reasonably accurate. When we judge an expressive trait such as outgoingness, thin slices of behavior can be revealing.

To sum up, we can say that at any moment the immediate situation powerfully influences a person's behavior, especially when the situation makes clear demands. We can better predict drivers' behavior at traffic lights from knowing the color of the lights than from knowing the drivers' personalities. Thus, professors may see a student as subdued (based on classroom behavior), but friends may see her as rather wild (based on party behavior). However, averaging our behavior across many occasions reveals that we do have distinct personality traits. We can also quickly perceive individual differences in some traits, such as expressiveness.

SUMMING UP

Exploring Traits Rather than explain the hidden aspects of personality, trait researchers describe the predispositions that underlie our actions. For example, through factor analysis, researchers have isolated five important dimensions of personality. Genetic predispositions influence most such traits.

Assessing Traits To assess traits, psychologists have devised self-report inventories, such as the empirically derived MMPI-2. Peer reports may provide even more trustworthy clues to a person's behavioral traits.

Evaluating the Trait Perspective Critics of the trait perspective question the consistency with which traits are expressed. Although people's traits persist over time, human behavior varies widely from situation to situation. Despite these variations, a person's *average* behavior across different situations is more consistent.

KEY TERMS AND CONCEPTS trait, personality inventory, Minnesota Multiphasic Personality Inventory (MMPI), empirically derived test

The Humanistic Perspective

Led by Abraham Maslow and Carl Rogers, humanistic psychologists have emphasized the growth potential of healthy people. With personalized methods, they study personality and hope to foster personal growth. Scientific researchers outside the humanistic tradition have picked up on one idea from humanistic theory—that our sense of self is at the center of our personality and outlook.

By 1960, some personality psychologists became discontented with Freud's negativity and with trait psychology's objectivity. In contrast to Freud's study of the base motives of "sick" people, the focus of these *humanistic psychologists* was the strivings of "healthy" people for self-determination and self-realization. In contrast to trait psychologists' profiles, their view emphasized the whole person, beyond encapsulation as so many test scores. Two pioneering theorists illustrate these emphases on human potential and seeing the world through the person's (not the researcher's) eyes: Abraham Maslow (1908–1970) and Carl Rogers (1902–1987).

Exploring the Self

Abraham Maslow's Self-Actualizing Person

Maslow proposed that we are motivated by a hierarchy of needs (page 366). If our physiological needs are met, we become concerned with personal safety; if we achieve a sense of security, we then seek to love, to be loved, and to love ourselves. Having achieved self-esteem, we ultimately seek self-actualization, the process of fulfilling our potential.

Maslow (1970) developed his ideas by studying healthy, creative people rather than troubled clinical cases. He based his description of self-actualization on a study of people who seemed notable for their rich and productive lives—Abraham Lincoln, Thomas Jefferson, and Eleanor Roosevelt among them. These people shared certain characteristics. Maslow reported they were self-aware and self-accepting, open and spontaneous, loving and caring, and not paralyzed by others' opinions. Secure in their sense of who they were, their interests were problem-centered rather than self-centered. Often

Abraham Maslow "Any theory of motivation that is worthy of attention must deal with the highest capacities of the healthy and strong person as well as with the defensive maneuvers of crippled spirits" (*Motivation and Personality*, 1970).

they focused their energies on a particular task, which they regarded as their mission in life. Most enjoyed a few deep relationships rather than many superficial ones. Many had been moved by spiritual or personal *peak experiences* that surpassed ordinary consciousness.

These are mature adult qualities, said Maslow, ones found in those who have learned enough about life to be compassionate, to have outgrown their mixed feelings toward their parents, to have found their calling, to have "acquired enough courage to be unpopular, to be unashamed about being openly virtuous, etc." Maslow's work with college students led him to speculate that those likely to become self-actualizing adults were likable, caring, "privately affectionate to those of their elders who deserve it," and "secretly uneasy about the cruelty, meanness, and mob spirit so often found in young people."

Carl Rogers's Person-Centered Perspective

Fellow humanistic psychologist Carl Rogers agreed with much of Maslow's thinking. Rogers believed that people are basically good and are endowed with self-actualizing tendencies. Each of us is like an acorn, primed for growth and fulfillment, unless thwarted by an environment that inhibits growth. Rogers (1980) surmised that a growth-promoting climate required three conditions—genuineness, acceptance, and empathy.

According to Rogers, people nurture our growth by being *genuine*—by being open with their own feelings, dropping their facades, and being transparent and self-disclosing.

People also nurture growth by being *accepting*—by offering us what Rogers called <u>unconditional positive regard</u>. This is an attitude of grace, an attitude that values us even knowing our failings. Have you ever experienced the relief of having dropped your pretenses, confessed your worst feelings, and discovered that you were still accepted? We sometimes enjoy this gratifying experience in a good marriage, a close family, or an intimate friendship in which we no longer feel a need to explain ourselves and are free to be spontaneous without fear of losing the other's esteem.

Finally, people nurture growth by being *empathic*—by nonjudgmentally reflecting our feelings and meanings. "Rarely do we listen with real understanding, true empathy," said Rogers. "Yet listening, of this very special kind, is one of the most potent forces for change that I know."

Genuineness, acceptance, and empathy are the water, sun, and nutrients that enable people to grow like vigorous oak trees, according to Rogers. For "as persons are accepted and prized, they tend to develop a more caring attitude toward themselves" (Rogers, 1980, p. 116). As persons are empathically heard, "it becomes possible for them to listen more accurately to the flow of inner experiencings."

Rogers believed that genuineness, acceptance, and empathy nurture growth not only in the relationship between therapist and client but also between parent and child, leader and group, teacher and student, administrator and staff member—in fact, between any two human beings. He would have been pleased by a finding published shortly after his death: Preschool children whose parents exhibit such attitudes usually become creative adolescents (Harrington & others, 1987).

self-actualization
according to Maslow, the ultimate psychological need that arises after basic physical and psychological needs are met and self-esteem is achieved; the motivation to fulfill one's potential.

unconditional positive regard
according to Rogers, an attitude of total acceptance toward another person.

The picture of empathy Being open and sharing confidences is easier when the listener shows real understanding. Within such relationships people can relax and fully express their true selves.

self-concept
all our thoughts and feelings about ourselves, in answer to the question, "Who am I?"

self-esteem
one's feelings of high or low self-worth.

For Maslow, and even more for Rogers, a central feature of personality is one's self-concept—all the thoughts and feelings we have in response to the question, "Who am I?" If our self-concept is positive, we tend to act and perceive the world positively. If it is negative—if in our own eyes we fall far short of our "ideal self"—said Rogers, we feel dissatisfied and unhappy. A worthwhile goal for therapists, parents, teachers, and friends is therefore, he said, to help others know, accept, and be true to themselves.

Assessing the Self

Humanistic psychologists sometimes assess personality with questionnaires that evaluate people's self-concepts. One questionnaire, inspired by Carl Rogers, asks people to describe themselves both as they ideally would like to be and as they actually are. When the ideal and the actual self are nearly alike, said Rogers, the self-concept is positive. Thus, to assess his clients' personal growth during therapy, he looked for successively closer ratings of actual and ideal self.

Other humanistic psychologists believe that any standardized assessment of personality is depersonalizing, that even a questionnaire detaches the psychologist from the living human. Rather than forcing the person to respond to narrow categories, these humanistic psychologists believe that interviews and intimate conversation enable a better understanding of each person's unique experiences.

What possible future selves do you envision? To what extent do these imagined selves motivate you now?

Research on the Self

Psychology's concern with people's sense of self dates back at least to William James, who devoted more than 100 pages to the topic in his 1890 *Prin-*

ciples of Psychology. By 1943, Gordon Allport lamented that the self had become "lost to view." Although humanistic psychology's emphasis on the self did not instigate much scientific research, it did help renew the concept of self and keep it alive. Now, more than a century after James, the self is one of Western psychology's most vigorously researched topics. Every year, new studies galore appear on self-esteem, self-disclosure, self-awareness, self-schemas, self-monitoring, and so forth.

One example of the thinking about self is the concept of *possible selves* put forth by Hazel Markus and her colleagues (Inglehart & others, 1989; Markus & Nurius, 1986). Your possible selves include your visions of the self you dream of becoming—the rich self, the thin self, the loved and admired self. They also include the self you fear becoming—the unemployed self, the alcoholic self, the academically failed self. Such possible selves motivate us by laying out specific goals and giving us the energy to work toward them. Olympian Carl Lewis concentrated on the achievements of Olympic hero Jesse Owens to give form to his aspirations. Similarly, University of Michigan students in a combined undergraduate/medical school program earn higher grades if they undergo the program with a clear vision of themselves as successful doctors. The biggest dreams often give birth to the greatest achievements.

Underlying this research is an assumption (shared by humanistic psychologists) that the self, as organizer of our thoughts, feelings, and actions, is a pivotal center of personality. We even remember information better if we encode it in terms of ourselves. Tory Higgins and John Bargh (1987) asked people to consider whether some specific words such as *friendly* described them, or whether the words described someone else. The participants were later better able to recall words they had considered in relation to themselves.

How we *feel* about ourselves is also important. Research studies confirm the benefits of positive self-esteem but also hint at the hazards of pride.

The Benefits of Self-Esteem

High self-esteem—a feeling of self-worth—pays dividends. People who feel good about themselves (who strongly agree with self-affirming questionnaire statements) have fewer sleepless nights, succumb less easily to pressures to conform, are less likely to use drugs, are more persistent at difficult tasks, and are just plain happier (Brockner & Hulton, 1978; Brown, 1991).

People with low self-esteem don't necessarily see themselves as worthless or wicked, but they do

Possible selves By giving them a chance to try out many possible selves, pretend games offer children important opportunities to grow emotionally, socially, and cognitively. Although this young boy may not grow up to be a physician, playing adult roles will certainly bear fruit in terms of an expanded vision of what he might become.

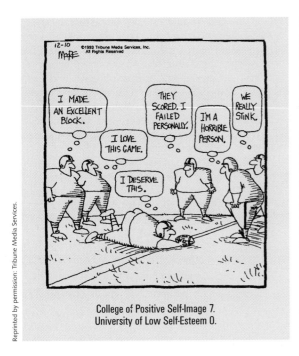

College of Positive Self-Image 7.
University of Low Self-Esteem 0.

lack good things to say about themselves. Such low self-esteem exacts costs. More often than not, unhappiness and despair coexist with low self-esteem. People who feel they are falling short of their hopes are vulnerable to depression. Those whose self-image falls short of what they think they *ought* to be are vulnerable to anxiety (Higgins, 1987). Psychotherapy researcher Hans Strupp (1982) noted, "As soon as one listens to a patient's story, one encounters unhappiness, frustration, and despair. . . . Basic to all these difficulties are impairments in self-acceptance and self-esteem."

Low self-esteem comes in different forms. Those vulnerable to depression often feel they are falling short of their *hopes*. Those vulnerable to anxiety often feel they are falling short of what they *ought* to be (Higgins, 1987). Among those who feel they are falling short, the pain of anticipated social rejection, experienced as low self-esteem, may be adaptive. As with other forms of pain, it may have helped our ancestors survive—by motivating them to behave in ways that sustained their inclusion within a supportive group (Leary & others, 1995). When acting appropriately, they could be comfortable with themselves, knowing they would not be left alone.

The correlational links between low self-esteem and life problems have other possible interpretations. Psychologists William Damon (1995), Robyn Dawes (1994), and Martin Seligman (1994) doubt that self-esteem is really "the armor that protects kids" from life problems. Maybe it's the other way around: Problems and failures may cause low self-esteem. Maybe self-esteem reflects reality.

Maybe feeling good *follows* doing well. Maybe it's a side effect of meeting challenges and surmounting difficulties. If so, they say, the best boost to self-esteem may come less from our repeatedly telling children how wonderful they are than from their own hard-won achievements.

However, an *effect* of low self-esteem appears in experiments. Temporarily deflate people's self-image (say, by telling them they did poorly on an aptitude test or by disparaging their personality) and they will be more likely to disparage other people or to express heightened racial prejudice. People who are negative about themselves also tend to be thin-skinned and judgmental (Baumeister, 1993; Baumgardner & others, 1989; Pelham, 1993). Although some "love their neighbors as themselves," others loathe their neighbors as themselves. In experiments, those made to feel insecure often become excessively critical, as if to impress others with their own brilliance (Amabile, 1983). Such findings are consistent with Maslow's and Rogers' presumptions that a healthy self-image pays dividends. Accept yourself and you'll find it easier to accept others.

Culture and Self-Esteem

Is it true, as so many assume, that ethnic minorities, people with disabilities, and women live handicapped by impoverished self-esteem? The accumulated evidence says no. African-Americans do *not* suffer lower self-esteem. In the words of social psychologists Jennifer Crocker and Brenda Major (1989): "A host of studies conclude that blacks have levels of self-esteem equal to or higher than that of whites." The National Institute of Mental Health's 1980s study of *Psychiatric Disorders in America* similarly reveals that the rates of depression and alcoholism among African- and Hispanic-Americans are roughly comparable to those among other Americans (if anything, America's ethnic minorities suffer slightly less depression—see Table 15.3, page 484).

How could this be? Despite discrimination and lower social status, members of various "stigmatized" groups (people of color, those with disabilities, women) seem to maintain self-esteem in three ways, according to Crocker and Major:

- They value the things at which they excel.
- They attribute problems to prejudice.
- They do what everyone else does—they compare themselves to those in their own group.

These findings help us understand why, despite the realities of prejudice, all such groups report roughly comparable levels of happiness.

self-serving bias
a readiness to perceive oneself favorably.

"To love oneself
is the beginning of
a life-long romance."

OSCAR WILDE
AN IDEAL HUSBAND
1895

"It is only our bad temper
that we put down to being
tired or worried or hungry.
We put our good temper
down to ourselves."

C. S. LEWIS (1898–1963)

The Pervasiveness of Self-Serving Bias

Carl Rogers (1958) once objected to the religious doctrine that humanity's problems arise from excessive self-love, or pride. He noted that most people he had known "despise themselves, regard themselves as worthless and unlovable." Mark Twain had the idea: "No man, deep down in the privacy of his heart, has any considerable respect for himself."

Actually, most of us have a good reputation with ourselves. In studies of self-esteem, even low-scoring people respond in the midrange of possible scores (Baumeister & others, 1989). (A "low" self-esteem person responds to statements such as "I have good ideas" with qualifying adjectives such as *somewhat* or *sometimes*.) Moreover, one of psychology's most provocative yet firmly established recent conclusions concerns our potent self-serving bias—our readiness to perceive ourselves favorably (Brown, 1991; Myers, 1996). Consider these findings:

People accept more responsibility for good deeds than for bad, and for successes than for failures. Athletes often privately credit their victories to their own prowess and their losses to bad breaks, lousy officiating, or the other team's exceptional performance. After receiving poor exam grades, most students in a half-dozen studies criticized the exam, not themselves. Most university students think the Scholastic Assessment Test underestimated their actual ability, although the higher scores they think they deserved would have predicted their later grades less accurately (Shepperd, 1993). On insurance forms, drivers have explained accidents in such words as: "An invisible car came out of nowhere, struck my car, and vanished." "As I reached an intersection, a hedge sprang up, obscuring my vision, and I did not see the other car." "A pedestrian hit me and went under my car." The question "What have I done to deserve this?" is one we ask of our troubles, not our successes—those, we assume we deserve.

Most people see themselves as better than average. This is true for nearly any subjective and socially desirable dimension. In national surveys, most business executives say they are more ethical than their average counterpart. In several studies, 90 percent of business managers and more than 90 percent of college professors rated their performance as superior to that of their average peer. In Australia, 86 percent of people rate their job performance as above average, and only 1 percent as below average. Although the phenomenon is notably less striking in Asia, where people value modesty, self-serving biases have been observed worldwide: among Dutch, Australian, and Chinese students; Japanese drivers; Indian Hindus; and French people of all walks of life. The world, it seems, is Garrison Keillor's Lake Wobegon writ large—a place where "all the women are strong, all the men are good-looking, and all the children are above average."

"The [self-]portraits that we
actually believe, when we are given freedom
to voice them, are dramatically more
positive than reality can sustain."

SHELLEY TAYLOR
POSITIVE ILLUSIONS
1989

Self-serving bias flies in the face of today's pop psychology. "All of us have inferiority complexes," wrote John Powell (1989, p. 15). "Those who seem not to have such a complex are only pretending." But additional findings remove any doubts (Myers, 1996):

- We remember and justify our past actions in self-enhancing ways.

- We exhibit an inflated confidence in the accuracy of our beliefs and judgments.

- We overestimate how desirably *we* would act in situations where most people behave less than admirably.

- We are quicker to believe flattering descriptions of ourselves than unflattering ones, and we are impressed with psychological tests that make us look good.

- We shore up our self-image by *over*estimating how much others support our opinions and share our foibles, and by *under*estimating the commonality of our strengths.

- We exhibit group pride—a tendency to see our group (our school, our country, our race) as superior.

Moreover, pride does often go before a fall. Self-serving perceptions underlie conflicts ranging from other-blaming marital discord to self-promoting ethnic snobbery. It was "Aryan pride" that fueled Nazi atrocities. It was national self-righteousness that led both the Americans and Soviets during the arms race to say, "Your weapons threaten us, ours are only for defense." No wonder religion and literature so often warn against the perils of excessive pride.

PEANUTS

PEANUTS reprinted by permission of UFS, Inc.
© 1989 United Feature Syndicate, Inc.

Still, people object to the idea of self-serving bias. They think of those who do seem to despise themselves, who feel worthless and unlovable. If self-serving bias prevails, why do so many people disparage themselves? For at least two reasons. Sometimes people's self-directed put-downs are subtly strategic: They elicit reassuring strokes. Saying "No one likes me" may at least elicit "But not everyone has met you!" At other times, such as before a game or an exam, self-disparaging comments prepare us for possible failure. The coach who extols the superior strength of the upcoming opponent makes a loss understandable, a victory noteworthy.

Even so, it's true: All of us some of the time, and some of us much of the time, *do* feel inferior—especially when we compare ourselves with those who are a step or two higher on the ladder of status, looks, income, or agility. The deeper and more frequently we have such feelings, the more unhappy, even depressed, we are. But for most people—the 98 percent who at anytime are *not* suffering depression (Diener, 1993; Gotlib, 1992)—thinking has a naturally positive bias.

> "If you compare yourself with others, you may become vain and bitter; for always there will be greater and lesser persons than yourself."
>
> **"DESIDERATA"**
> *FOUND IN OLD ST. PAUL'S CHURCH, LONDON*
> 1692

We can therefore affirm what humanistic psychologists rightly emphasize: For the individual, self-affirming thinking is generally adaptive. To a point, even our positive illusions are beneficial. They maintain our self-confidence, protect against anxiety and depression, and sustain our sense of well-being. "Life is the art of being well-deceived," observed the English essayist William Hazlitt.

Recognizing both the perils of self-righteousness and the dividends of positive self-esteem, psychologists Roy Baumeister (1989), Jonathan Brown (1991), and Shelley Taylor (1989) have all suggested that humans function best with modest self-enhancing illusions. Like the Japanese and European magnetic levitation trains, Brown noted, we function optimally when riding just off the rails—not so high that we gyrate and crash, yet not in such relentlessly close touch that we grind to a halt.

Culture and the Individual Self

If someone were to rip away your social connections, making you a solitary refugee in a foreign land, how much of your identity would remain intact? The answer might depend in large part on whether your culture nurtures the independent self that marks individualism or the interdependent self that marks collectivism.

For individualists, a great deal of their identity would remain intact—the very core of their being, their sense of "me," their awareness of their personal convictions and values. Although individualism varies from person to person, cross-cultural psychologists have mostly studied how it varies by culture, ranging from the extreme collectivism of rural Asia to the extreme individualism of the United States (Hofstede, 1980; Triandis, 1994). Individualistic persons and cultures give priority to personal goals and define their identity mostly in terms of their personal attributes. They strive for personal control and individual achievement.

For collectivists, being set adrift in a foreign land might entail a much greater loss of identity. Cut off from family, groups, and loyal friends, collectivists would lose connections that have defined who they are. In a collectivist culture, a social network provides one's bearings. What's important is not "me" but "we." Collectivists give priority to the goals of their groups—often their family, clan, or work group—and define their identity accordingly. By their group identifications, collectivists gain a sense of belonging, a set of values, a network of caring individuals, an assurance of security.

Compared with American students, students in Japan, China and India are much less likely to complete the sentence "I am . . ." with personal traits ("I am sincere," "I am confident") and are much more likely to declare their social identities ("I am a Keio University student," "I am the third son in my family") (Cousins, 1989; Dhawan & others, 1995; Triandis, 1989a,b). For Westerners, individual identity is primary; for Asians, collective identity is more often primary.

The contrast between more individualistic and collectivistic cultures appears in people's names. Individualist cultures give priority to personal identity, by putting the personal name first ("Christine Brune"). Collectivist cultures often give priority to

individualism
giving priority to one's own goals over group goals, and defining one's identity in terms of personal attributes rather than group identifications.

collectivism
giving priority to the goals of one's group (often one's extended family or work group) and defining one's identity accordingly.

Like athletes who take more pleasure in their team's victory than in their own performance, collectivists find satisfaction in advancing their groups' interests, even at the expense of personal needs.

In a collectivist culture, a social network provides one's bearings. What's important is not "me" but "we."

Collectivism By identifying with family and other groups, these yak herders in India gain a sense of "we," a set of values, a network of care.

No wonder, says Harry Triandis (1989b), that modern world colonization was led not by Asians, who were reluctant to cut social and family ties, but by the more individualist Europeans. And no wonder that countries colonized by Europeans willing to leave friends and family are today highly individualistic.

one's family identity ("Hui Harry"). Family loyalty also appears in popular Chinese songs, which much more often than Western popular songs express positive feelings for one's parents. To those who are from individualistic cultures, a typical Chinese song may sound quaint (Rothbaum & Xu, 1995):

> *I am mamma's short poem*
> *Composed of mother's painstaking effort,*
> *Mamma has suffered so much pain for me . . .*
> *How much I wish there would be good news tomorrow*
> *To repay mother's deep feeling for me.*

To a rural Chinese person, songs like "I Gotta Be Me" would seem as odd.

Being more self-contained, individualists easily move in and out of social groups. They feel rela-

tively free to switch churches, leave one job for another, or even to leave their extended families and migrate to a new place. Marriage is for as long as they both shall love. In contrast, collectivists may act shy in new groups and are more easily embarrassed (Singelis & Sharkey, 1995). They have deeper, more stable attachments to their familiar groups and friends. Relationships are long-term. Thus, loyalties run strong between employer and employees.

Because they value communal solidarity, people in collectivist cultures place a premium on maintaining harmony and allowing others to save face. Direct confrontation and blunt honesty are rare, as are expressions of personal egotism. What people say reflects not only what they feel (their inner attitudes) but also what they presume others feel (Kashima & others, 1992). Elders and superiors command respect. To preserve group spirit, people avoid touchy topics, defer to others' wishes, and display a polite, self-effacing humility (Kitayama & Markus, in press; Markus & Kitayama, 1991). People remember those who have done them favors and make reciprocation a social art. The collectivist self is not independent but interdependent (Table 14.3). Among collectivists, especially those influenced by the Confucian idea of self as a node in "a web of interrelatedness" (Kim & Lee, 1994), no person is an island.

Individualism and collectivism each offers benefits—at a cost. People in competitive, individualistic cultures have more personal freedom, take more pride in personal achievements, are less geographically bound to their families, and enjoy more pri-

Table 14.3

Value Contrasts Between Individualism and Collectivism

Concept	Individualism	Collectivism
Self	Independent (identity from individual traits)	Interdependent (identity from belonging)
Life task	Discover and express one's uniqueness	Maintain connections, fit in
What matters	Me—personal achievement and fulfillment; rights and liberties	We—group goals and solidarity; social responsibilities and relationships
Coping method	Change reality	Accommodate to reality
Morality	Defined by individuals (self-based)	Defined by social networks (duty-based)
Relationships	Many, often temporary or casual; confrontation acceptable	Few, close and enduring; harmony valued
Attributing behavior	Behavior reflects one's personality and attitudes	Behavior reflects social norms and roles

Source: Adapted from Thomas Schoeneman (1994) and Harry Triandis (1994).

vacy. Their less-unified cultures offer a smorgasbord of life-styles and invite individuals to construct their own identities. Innovation and creativity are celebrated, and human rights are respected. Such may help explain Ed Diener, Marissa Diener, and Carol Diener's (1995) finding that people in individualistic cultures report greater happiness than do those in collectivist cultures. When individualists pursue their own ends and all goes well, life can seem rewarding.

But such benefits can come at the price of more frequent loneliness, more divorce, more homicide, and more stress-related disease (Popenoe, 1993; Triandis et al., 1988). Collectivists demand less romance and personal fulfillment in marriage, which puts the marriage relationship under less pressure (Dion & Dion, 1993). In one survey, "keeping romance alive" was rated as important to a good marriage by 78 percent of American women and 29 percent of Japanese women (*American Enterprise*, 1992).

In recent decades, Western individualism has increased, and the priority placed on social obligations and family ties has decreased (Yankelovich, 1993). Martin Seligman (1988) has argued that "rampant individualism carries with it two seeds of its own destruction. First, a society that exalts the individual to the extent ours now does will be ridden with depression. . . . Second, and perhaps most important, is meaninglessness [which occurs when there is no] attachment to something larger than you are."

Evaluating the Humanistic Perspective

One thing said of Freud can also be said of the humanistic psychologists: Their impact has been pervasive. Their ideas have influenced counseling, education, child-rearing, and management. They have also influenced—sometimes in ways they did not intend—much of today's popular psychology.

Through popular psychology many of us absorb some of what Maslow and Rogers taught—that a positive self-concept is the key to happiness and success, that acceptance and empathy help nurture positive feelings about oneself, and that people are basically good and capable of self-improvement. One study found that, by a 4-to-1 margin, Americans believe "human nature is basically good" rather than "fundamentally perverse and corrupt" (NORC, 1985). Humanistic psychologists can also take satisfaction in the changed response to one of the MMPI items: Among those in the 1930s normal standardization sample, only 9 percent agreed

"We do pretty well when you stop to think that people are basically good."

that "I am an important person"; in the mid-1980s, more than half agreed (Holden, 1986b). Responding to a 1989 Gallup poll, 85 percent of Americans rated "having a good self-image or self-respect" as *very* important; 0 percent rated it unimportant. And 89 percent of people responding to a 1992 *Newsweek* Gallup poll rated self-esteem as very important for "motivating a person to work hard and succeed." Humanistic psychology's message has been heard.

Perhaps one reason that message has been so well received is that its emphasis on the individual self reflects and reinforces Western cultural values. As self-reliant individualism has grown, with increased priority given to personal identity and aspirations, the popular media have celebrated the rugged individual. Movie plots feature rugged heroes who, true to themselves, buck social convention or take the law into their own hands. Popular songs proclaim that "I Did It My Way" and remind us that to love yourself is "The Greatest Love of All" (Schoeneman, 1994).

The prominence of the humanistic perspective also set off a backlash of criticism. First, said the critics, its concepts are vague and subjective. Consider the description of self-actualizing people as open, spontaneous, loving, self-accepting, and productive. Is this really a scientific description? Or is it merely a description of Maslow's personal values and ideals? What Maslow did, noted M. Brewster Smith (1978), was to offer impressions of his own personal heroes. Imagine another theorist who began with a different set of heroes—perhaps Napoleon,

Alexander the Great, and John D. Rockefeller, Sr. This theorist would likely describe self-actualizing people as "undeterred by the needs of others," "motivated to achieve," and "obsessed with power."

Second, some object to the idea that, as Carl Rogers put it, "The only question which matters is, 'Am I living in a way which is deeply satisfying to me, and which truly expresses me?'" (quoted by Wallach & Wallach, 1985). These critics have argued that the individualism encouraged by humanistic psychology—trusting and acting on one's feelings, being true to oneself, fulfilling oneself—may promote self-indulgence, selfishness, and an erosion of moral restraints (Campbell & Specht, 1985; Wallach & Wallach, 1983). Indeed it is those who focus not on themselves but beyond themselves who are most likely to experience social support, to enjoy life, and to cope effectively with stress (Crandall, 1984).

Humanistic psychologists rebut such objections. They counter that belligerence, hostility, and insensitivity are often traceable to a poor self-concept. Moreover, they argue, a secure, nondefensive self-acceptance is actually the first step toward loving others.

A final accusation leveled against the humanistic psychologists is that of failing to appreciate the reality of our human capacity for evil. Faced with assaults on the environment, overpopulation, and threats of nuclear war, we may develop apathy from either of two rationalizations. One is a naive optimism that denies the threat ("People are basically good; everything will work out"). The other is a dark despair ("It's hopeless; why try?"). Action requires enough realism to fuel concern and enough optimism to provide hope. Humanistic psychology, say the critics, encourages the needed hope but not the equally necessary realism about evil.

However, even within humanistic psychology there is debate over whether people are basically good. Carl Rogers clearly thought so. Although aware of the "incredible amount" of cruel, destructive behavior in the world, he did "not find that this evil is inherent in human nature." Given growth-promoting conditions, "I have never known an individual to choose the cruel or destructive path" (Rogers, 1981). Evil, in his view, springs not from human nature but from toxic cultural influences, including "the constricting, destructive influence of our educational system, the injustice of our distribution of wealth, [and] our cultivated prejudices against individuals who are different."

Fellow humanistic psychologist Rollo May dissented from Rogers's optimism. Of course the cultural context matters, he said. But "Who makes up the culture except persons like you and me? The culture is evil as well as good because we, the human beings who constitute it, are evil as well as good." May agreed with critics who see people joining the humanistic movement seeking "a community of like-minded persons who also are playing possum to the evils about us." Accepting the reality of human evil requires "the age-old religious truths of mercy and forgiveness," he said, "and it leaves no place for self-righteousness" (May, 1982).

SUMMING UP

Humanistic psychologists have sought to turn psychology's attention from baser motives and environmental conditioning to the growth potential of healthy people, as seen through the individual's own experiences.

Exploring the Self Abraham Maslow believed that if basic human needs are fulfilled, people will strive to actualize their highest potential. To describe self-actualization, he studied some exemplary personalities and summarized his impressions of their qualities. To nurture growth in others, Carl Rogers advised being genuine, accepting, and empathic. In such a climate, people can develop a deeper self-awareness and a more realistic and positive self-concept.

Assessing the Self Humanistic psychologists assess personality through questionnaires on which people report their self-concept and through seeking to understand others' subjective personal experiences in therapy. Research on the self documents the importance of high self-esteem and the potency of self-serving bias. Individuals and cultures vary in giving priority to "me" or "we"—to personal control and individual achievement or to social connections and solidarity. Self-reliant *individualism* defines identity in terms of personal goals and attributes; socially connected *collectivism* gives priority to group goals and to one's social identity and commitments.

Evaluating the Humanistic Perspective Humanistic psychology's critics complain that its concepts are vague and subjective, its values individualistic and self-centered, and its assumptions naively optimistic. Nevertheless, humanistic psychology helped to renew psychology's interest in the self.

KEY TERMS AND CONCEPTS self-actualization, unconditional positive regard, self-concept, self-esteem, self-serving bias, individualism, collectivism

The Social-Cognitive Perspective

The social-cognitive perspective applies principles of learning, thinking, and social influence. How might such principles work together to influence behavior in particular situations?

Our fourth major perspective on personality derives from psychological principles of learning, cognition, and social behavior. Called the *social-cognitive perspective* by psychologist Albert Bandura (1986), and the *cognitive social learning perspective* by others, its proponents emphasize the importance of external events. Like learning theorists, they believe that we learn many of our behaviors either through conditioning or by observing others and modeling our behavior after theirs. They also emphasize the importance of mental processes: What we think about our situations affects our behavior. So instead of focusing solely on how our environment controls us (behaviorism), social-cognitive theorists focus on how we and our environment interact: How do we interpret and respond to external events? How do our schemas, our memories, and our expectations influence our behavior patterns?

Exploring Behavior in Situations

Reciprocal Influences

Bandura (1986) called the process of interacting with our environment reciprocal determinism. "Behavior, internal personal factors, and environmental influences," he said, "all operate as interlocking determinants of each other" (Figure 14.4). For example, children's TV-viewing habits (past behavior) influence their viewing preferences (personal factor), which influence how television (environmental factor) affects their current behavior. The influences are mutual.

Consider three specific ways in which persons and environments interact:

1 **Different people choose different environments.** The school you attend, the reading you do, the television programs you watch, the music you listen to, the friends you associate with—all are part of an environment you have chosen, based partly on your dispositions. *You choose it and it shapes you.*

2 **Our personalities shape how we interpret and react to events.** Anxious people, for example, are more likely to be attuned to potentially threatening events than are nonanxious people (Eysenck & others, 1987). Thus, anxious people perceive the world as more threatening, and they react accordingly.

3 **Our personalities help create situations to which we react.** Many experiments reveal that how we view and treat people influences how they in turn treat us. If we expect someone to be angry with us, we may give the person a cold shoulder, touching off the very behavior we expect.

In such ways, we are both the products and the architects of our environments. If all this has a familiar ring, it may be because it parallels and reinforces a pervasive theme in psychology and in this book: Behavior emerges from the interplay of external and internal influences. Boiling water turns an egg hard and a potato soft. A threatening environment turns one person into a hero, another into a scoundrel. *At every moment*, our behavior is determined by our genes, our experiences, and our personalities.

Personal Control

One important aspect of personality is our sense of personal control—whether we learn to see ourselves as controlling, or as controlled by, our environments. Psychologists have two basic ways to study the effect of personal control (or any personality factor). One: *Correlate* people's feelings of control with their behaviors and achievements. Two: *Experiment*, by raising or lowering people's sense of control and noting the effects. Let's take these one at a time.

Locus of Control

Consider your own feelings of control. Do you feel that your life is beyond your control? That the

reciprocal determinism
the interacting influences between personality and environmental factors.

personal control
our sense of controlling our environments rather than feeling helpless.

Figure **14.4**

Reciprocal determinism The social-cognitive perspective proposes that our personalities are shaped by the interaction of personal/cognitive factors (our thoughts and feelings), our environment, and our behaviors.

Internal personal/ cognitive factors (liking high-risk activities)

Behavior (learning to bungee jump)

Environmental factors (bungee-jumping friends)

external locus of control
the perception that chance or outside forces beyond one's personal control determine one's fate.

internal locus of control
the perception that one controls one's own fate.

learned helplessness
the hopelessness and passive resignation an animal or human learns when unable to avoid repeated aversive events.

Creators Syndicate, Inc. © Leigh Rubin/Funny Times.

world is run by a few powerful people? That getting a good job depends mainly on being in the right place at the right time? Or do you more strongly believe that what happens to you is your own doing? That the average person can influence government decisions? That being a success is a matter of hard work, not luck?

Hundreds of studies have compared people who differ in their perceptions of control. On the one side are those who have what psychologist Julian Rotter called an external locus of control—the perception that chance or outside forces determine their fate. On the other are those who perceive an internal locus of control and believe that to a great extent they control their own destinies. In study after study, "internals" achieve more in school, act more independently, and feel less depressed than do "externals" (Findley & Cooper, 1983; Lefcourt, 1982; Presson & Benassi, 1996). Moreover, they are better able to delay gratification and cope with various stresses, including marital problems (Miller & others, 1986).

Learned Helplessness Versus Personal Control

Helpless, oppressed people often perceive control to be external, and this perception may deepen their feelings of resignation. This is precisely what researcher Martin Seligman (1975, 1991) and others found in experiments with both animals and people. When dogs were strapped in a harness and given repeated shocks, with no opportunity to avoid them, they learned a sense of helplessness. When later placed in another situation where they *could* escape the punishment by merely leaping a hurdle, they cowered without hope. Faced with repeated traumatic events over which they have no control, people, too, come to feel helpless, hopeless, and depressed. This passive resignation is called learned helplessness (Figure 14.5). In contrast, animals able to escape the shocks in the first situation learn personal control and easily escape shocks in the new situation.

Control affects well-being   Nursing home residents who can arrange their own possessions, control other aspects of their daily lives, and pursue their own interests are more vigorous and happy than those who do not have these opportunities.

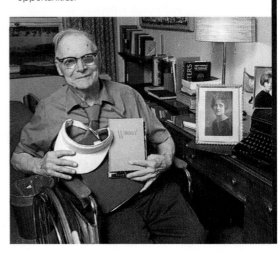

In concentration camps, in prisons, even in factories, colleges, and well-meaning nursing homes, people given little control experience a similar lowering of morale and increased stress. Part of the shock we feel in an unfamiliar culture is a sense of diminished control when we are unsure of how people in the new environment will respond (Triandis, 1994). Measures that increase control—allowing prisoners to move chairs and control room lights and the TV, having workers participate in decision making, offering nursing home patients choices about their environment—noticeably improve health and morale (Miller & Monge, 1986; Ruback & others, 1986; Wener & others, 1987). In one famous study of nursing home patients, 93 percent of those encouraged to exert more control became more alert, active, and happy (Rodin, 1986). As researcher Ellen Langer (1983, p. 291) concluded, "Perceived control is basic to human functioning." "For the young and old alike," she argued, we should create environments that enhance a sense of control and personal efficacy.

The verdict of these studies is reassuring: People thrive under conditions of democracy, personal freedom, and empowerment. Small wonder that the citizens of stable democracies report higher levels of happiness (Inglehart, 1990). Shortly before the democratic revolution in the former East Germany, psychologists Gabriele Oettingen and Martin Seligman (1990) compared the telltale body language of working-class men in East and West Berlin bars. Compared with their counterparts on the other side of the Wall, the empowered

Figure 14.5

Learned helplessness   When animals and people experience no control over repeated bad events, they often learn helplessness.

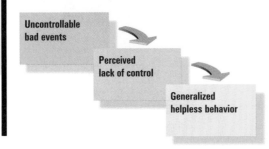

West Berliners much more often laughed, sat upright rather than slumped, and had upward- rather than downward-turned mouths. To paraphrase the Roman philosopher Seneca, happy are those who choose their own path.

Optimism

One measure of how helpless or effective you feel is where you stand on the trait dimension of optimism-pessimism. How do you characteristically explain negative and positive events? Perhaps you have known students whose *attributional style* is negative—who attribute poor performance to their lack of ability ("I can't do this") or to situations beyond their control ("bad" teachers, textbooks, or exam questions). Such students are more likely to persist in getting low grades than are students who adopt the more hopeful attitude that effort, good study habits, and self-discipline can make a difference (Noel & others, 1987; Peterson & Barrett, 1987).

In one study of optimism and behavior, Seligman and Peter Schulman (1986) compared sales made by new life insurance representatives who were more or less optimistic in their outlooks. Those who put an optimistic spin on setbacks—by seeing them as flukes or as suggesting a new approach rather than viewing them as signs of incompetence—sold more policies during their first year and were half as likely to quit. Seligman's finding came to life for him when Bob Dell, one of the optimistic recruits who began selling for Metropolitan Life after taking Seligman's optimism test, later dialed him up and sold him a policy.

Health, too, benefits from a basic optimism. As we will see in Chapter 17, a depressed hopelessness dampens the body's disease-fighting immune system. In repeated studies, optimists have been found to outlive pessimists or to live with fewer illnesses.

If positive thinking in the face of adversity pays dividends, so, too, can a dash of realism. Anxiety over contemplated failure can actually fuel energetic efforts to avoid the dreaded fate (Cantor & Norem, 1989; Goodhart, 1986; Showers, 1992). Overconfident students often perform less well than their equally able peers who, fearing they are going to bomb on the upcoming exam, proceed to study furiously and get fabulous grades. Edward Chang (1996) reports that, compared to European-American students, Asian-American students express somewhat greater pessimism—which he suspects helps explain their considerable academic achievements. Success requires enough optimism to provide hope, but also enough pessimism to prevent complacency.

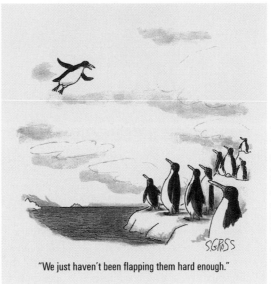

"We just haven't been flapping them hard enough."

Drawing by Gross; © 1995 *The New Yorker Magazine, Inc.*

Excessive optimism can also blind us to real risks. Neil Weinstein (1980, 1982, 1996) has shown how our natural positive-thinking bias can promote "an unrealistic optimism about future life events." Most college students perceive themselves as less likely than their average classmate to develop drinking problems, drop out of school, or have a heart attack by age 40. Most late adolescents see themselves as much less vulnerable than their peers to the AIDS virus (Abrams, 1991).

Given such illusory optimism, documented in nearly 200 research reports, people may fail to take sensible precautions. Most young Americans know that half of U.S. marriages end in divorce, but they are confident that *theirs* will not (Lehman & Nisbett, 1985). Most cigarette smokers smoke high-tar brands, but only 17 percent believe their brand to have a more hazardous tar level than most others (Segerstrom & others, 1993). Compared with other women at their university, sexually active undergraduate women—especially those who do *not* consistently use effective contraception—perceive themselves as *less* vulnerable to unwanted pregnancy (Burger & Burns, 1988). Those who optimistically venture into ill-fated relationships, deny the effects of smoking, or engage in unprotected sex remind us that, like pride, blind optimism may go before a fall.

"O God, give us grace to accept with serenity the things that cannot be changed, courage to change the things which should be changed, and the wisdom to distinguish the one from the other."

REINHOLD NIEBUHR
"THE SERENITY PRAYER"
1943

Success requires enough optimism to provide hope, but also enough pessimism to prevent complacency.

THINKING CRITICALLY ABOUT

Pseudo-Assessment—How to Be a "Successful" Astrologer or Palm Reader

How should we evaluate alternative ways of assessing personality? Does the alignment of the stars and planets at the time of one's birth give a clue? Is one's handwriting revealing? Do our palms expose deep secrets?

While astronomers scoff at the naiveté of astrology, psychologists ask a different question: Does it work? Are birth dates correlated with character traits? Given someone's birth date, can astrologers surpass chance when asked to identify the person from a short lineup of different personality descriptions? Can people pick out their own horoscopes from a lineup of horoscopes? The consistent answers have been: no, no, no, and no (British Psychological Society, 1993; Carlson, 1985). Graphologists, who make predictions from handwriting samples, have similarly been found to do no better than chance when trying to guess people's occupations, based on several pages of their handwriting (Beyerstein & Beyerstein, 1992; Dean & others, 1992).

How, then, do astrologers and the like persuade thousands of newspapers worldwide and millions of people to buy their advice? Ray Hyman (1981), palm reader turned research psychologist, has revealed the suckering methods of astrologers, palm readers, and crystal-ball gazers.

Their first technique, the "stock spiel," builds on the observation that each of us is in some ways like no one else and in other ways like everyone. That some things are true of us all enables the "seer" to offer statements that seem impressively accurate: "I sense that you're nursing a grudge against someone; you really ought to let that go." "You worry about things more than you let on, even to your best friends." "You are adaptable to social situations and your interests are wide-ranging."

Such generally true statements can be combined into a personality description. Imagine that you take a personality test and then receive the following character sketch:

> You have a strong need for other people to like and to admire you. You have a tendency to be critical of yourself. . . . You pride yourself on being an independent thinker and do not accept other opinions without satisfactory proof. You have found it unwise to be too frank in revealing yourself to others. At times you are extraverted, affable, sociable; at other times you are introverted, wary, and reserved. Some of your aspirations tend to be pretty unrealistic. (Forer, 1949)

In experiments, college students have received stock assessments like this one, drawn from statements in a newsstand astrology book. When they think the bogus feedback was prepared just for them and when it is generally favorable, they nearly always rate the description as either "good" or "excellent." Peter Glick and his co-workers (1989) found that even skeptics of astrology, when given a flattering description attributed to an astrologer, begin to think that "maybe there's something to this astrology business after all."

French psychologist Michael Gauguelin placed an ad in a Paris newspaper offering a free personal horoscope. Ninety-four percent of those receiving the horoscope later praised the description as accurate. Actually, all had received the horoscope of France's Dr. Petiot, a notorious mass murderer (Kurtz, 1983).

This acceptance is called *the Barnum effect*, named in honor of master showman P. T. Barnum's dictum, "There's a sucker born every minute." So powerful is the Barnum

SPECIAL BULLETIN! THIS JUST IN! THE FAULT IS NOT IN OURSELVES, BUT IN OUR STARS.

HEY! DID YOU HEAR THAT!

WE'RE OFF THE HOOK!

Drawing by Bruce Eric Kaplan; © 1992 The New Yorker Magazine, Inc.

effect that, given a choice between this stock spiel and an individualized personality description actually based on a real test, most people choose the phony description as being more accurate. Astrologers and palm readers sprinkle their assessments with stock statements.

Even some popular psychological labels are made plausible by Barnum statements. Mary Beth Logue and her colleagues (1992) report that adult children of alcoholics rate descriptions of their supposed traits ("You are sensitive to the difficulties of others" or "You sometimes project a front, hiding your true feelings") as accurate. But people who are *not* children of alcoholics rate the same statements as descriptive of *themselves*.

A second technique used by seers is to "read" our clothing, physical features, nonverbal gestures, and reactions to what they are saying. Imagine yourself as the character reader who was visited by a young woman in her late twenties or early thirties. Hyman described the woman as "wearing expensive jewelry, a wedding band, and a black dress of cheap material. The observant reader noted that she was wearing shoes which were advertised for people with foot trouble." Do these clues suggest anything?

Drawing on these observations, the character reader proceeded to amaze his client with his insights. He assumed that the woman had come to see him, as did most of his female customers, because of a love or financial problem. The black dress and the wedding band led him to reason that her husband had died recently. The expensive jewelry suggested that she had been financially comfortable during marriage, but the cheap dress suggested that her husband's death had left her impoverished. The therapeutic shoes signified that she was now standing on her feet more than she was used to, implying that she had been working to support herself since her husband's death.

If you are not as shrewd as this character reader (who correctly guessed that the woman was wondering if she should remarry in hope of ending her economic hardship), no matter, according to Hyman. Just tell people what they want to hear. Memorize some Barnum statements from astrology and fortune-telling manuals and use them liberally. Tell people it is their responsibility to cooperate by relating your message to their specific experiences. Later they will recall that you predicted the specifics. Phrase statements as questions, and when you detect a positive response assert the statement strongly. Be a good listener, and later, in different words, reveal to people what they earlier revealed to you. If you dupe them, they will come.

Better yet, beware of fortune-tellers, who, by exploiting people with these techniques, become fortune-takers.

Assessing Behavior in Situations

Social-cognitive researchers explore the effect of differing situations on people's behavior patterns and attitudes. They study, for example, how viewing aggressive or nonaggressive models affects behavior. They assess the impact of dehumanizing situations on people's attitudes. And they examine the consistency of people's personalities in varying circumstances.

An ambitious example of such research, and one that predates social-cognitive theory, is the U.S. Army's World War II strategy for assessing candidates for spy missions. Rather than using paper-and-pencil tests, army psychologists subjected the candidates to simulated undercover conditions. They tested their ability to handle stress, solve problems, maintain leadership, and withstand intense interrogation without blowing their covers. Although time-consuming and expensive, the assessment of behavior in a realistic situation helped predict later success on real spy missions (OSS Assessment Staff, 1948).

Business, military, and educational organizations are continuing this strategy in their evaluations of several hundred thousand persons each year in some 2000 assessment centers (Bray & Byham, 1991). AT&T observes prospective managers doing simulated managerial work. Many colleges assess potential faculty members' teaching abilities by observing them teach. The army assesses its soldiers by observing them during military exercises.

These procedures exploit the principle that the best means of predicting people's future behavior is not a personality test or an interviewer's intuition. Rather, it is their past behavior patterns in similar situations (Mischel, 1981). As long as the situation and the person remain much the same, the best predictor of future job performance is past job performance; the best predictor of future grades is past grades; the best predictor of future aggressiveness is past aggressiveness; the best predictor of drug use in young adulthood is drug use in high school. If you can't check the person's past behavior, the next-best thing is to create an assessment situation that simulates the task demands so you can see how the person handles them.

Evaluating the Social-Cognitive Perspective

The social-cognitive perspective on personality sensitizes researchers to how situations affect, and are affected by, individuals. More than the other perspectives, we can also credit it with building from psychological research on learning and cognition.

One criticism is that the theory focuses so much on the situation that it fails to appreciate the person's inner traits. Where is the person in this view of personality, ask the dissenters (Carlson, 1984); and where are human emotions? True, the situation guides our behavior. But in many instances our unconscious motives, our emotions, and our pervasive traits shine through, say the critics. Consider Percy Ray Pridgen and Charles Gill, who faced the same situation: They jointly won a $90 million lottery jackpot (Harriston, 1993). Upon learning the winning numbers, Pridgen began trembling uncontrollably, then huddled with a friend behind a bathroom door while confirming the win, then sobbed. Gill told his wife and then went to sleep.

And that brings us back to where we began our review of these personality theories: Each perspective summarized in Table 14.4 can teach us something. The psychoanalytic perspective draws our attention to the unconscious and irrational aspects of human existence. The trait perspective systematically describes and classifies important personality components. The humanistic perspective reminds us of the importance of our sense of self and of our potential for self-actualization. The social-cognitive perspective applies psychology's basic concepts of learning and thinking and teaches us that we always act in the context of situations that we help to create.

Seldom in life does a single perspective on any issue give us a complete picture of another human being. Human personality reveals its different aspects when we view it from different perspectives. Each perspective enlarges our vision of the whole person.

> "Nature is always more subtle, more intricate, more elegant than what we are able to imagine."
>
> **CARL SAGAN**
> *"SCIENCE—WHO CARES?"*
> 1991

Table **14.4**

The Four Perspectives on Personality

Perspective	Behavior Springs From	Assessment Techniques	Evaluation
Psychoanalytic	Unconscious conflicts between pleasure-seeking impulses and social restraints	Projective tests aimed at revealing unconscious motivations	A speculative, hard-to-test theory with enormous cultural impact
Trait	Expressing biologically influenced dispositions, such as extraversion or introversion	(a) Personality inventories that assess the strengths of different traits (b) Peer ratings of behavior patterns	A descriptive approach criticized as sometimes underestimating the variability of behavior from situation to situation
Humanistic	Processing conscious feelings about oneself in the light of one's experiences	(a) Questionnaire assessments of self-concept (b) Empathic interviews	A humane theory that reinvigorated contemporary interest in the self; criticized as subjective and sometimes naively self-centered and optimistic
Social-cognitive	Reciprocal influences between people and their situations, colored by perceptions of control	(a) Questionnaire assessments of people's feelings of control (b) Observations of people's behavior in particular situations	An interactive theory that integrates research on learning, cognition, and social behavior; criticized as underestimating the importance of emotions and enduring traits

SUMMING UP

Exploring Behavior in Situations The social-cognitive perspective applies principles of learning, cognition, and social behavior to personality, with particular emphasis on the ways in which our personalities influence and are influenced by our interaction with the environment. It assumes reciprocal determinism—that personal-cognitive factors combine with the environment to influence people's behavior. By studying variations among people in their perceived locus of control and in their experiences of learned helplessness, researchers have found that a sense of personal control helps people to cope with life.

Assessing Behavior in Situations Social-cognitive researchers observe how people's behaviors and beliefs both affect and are affected by their situations. They have found that the best way to predict someone's behavior in a given situation is to observe that person's behavior pattern in similar situations.

Evaluating the Social-Cognitive Perspective Although faulted for slighting the importance of unconscious dynamics, emotions, and inner traits, the social-cognitive perspective builds on psychology's well-established concepts of learning and cognition and reminds us of the power of social situations.

KEY TERMS AND CONCEPTS reciprocal determinism, personal control, external locus of control, internal locus of control, learned helplessness

TERMS AND CONCEPTS TO REMEMBER

CRITICAL THINKING EXERCISE
by Richard O. Straub

Now that you have read and reviewed Chapter 14, take your learning a step further by testing your critical thinking skills on the following perspective-taking exercise.

Darren is a first-year college student who has a biting, sarcastic manner. He has a pessimistic outlook on life and feels that the world is run by a few powerful people. When he received a poor grade on a recent exam, Darren blamed the instructor and claimed the test was unfair. He stopped attending lectures, gave up studying for the course, and will probably drop it. He is experiencing similar difficulties in his other courses.

Darren always dreamed of doing well in college. Now he is despondent over his failure and believes his professors hate him. Most of all, he is concerned that if he fails in school his parents will no longer love him.

1. How might Darren's problems be explained from the psychoanalytic perspective?

2. How might Darren's problems be explained by a trait theorist?

3. How might Darren's problems be explained by a humanistic theorist?

4. How might Darren's problems be explained by a social-cognitive theorist?

5. Which perspective most closely represents your own belief about Darren's problems? Why?

Check your progress on becoming a critical thinker by comparing your answers to the sample answers found in Appendix B.

chapter

15

Psychological Disorders

I felt the need to clean my room at home in Indianapolis every Sunday and would spend four to five hours at it. I would take every book out of the bookcase, dust and put it back. At the time I loved doing it. Then I didn't want to do it anymore, but I couldn't stop. The clothes in my closet hung exactly two fingers apart. . . . I made a ritual of touching the wall in my bedroom before I went out because something bad would happen if I didn't do it the right way. I had a constant anxiety about it as a kid, and it made me think for the first time that I might be nuts.

MARC, SUFFERING OBSESSIVE-COMPULSIVE DISORDER
(FROM SUMMERS, 1996)

Whenever I get depressed it's because I've lost a sense of self. I can't find reasons to like myself. I think I'm ugly. I think no one likes me. . . . I become grumpy and short-tempered. Nobody wants to be around me. I'm left alone. Being alone confirms that I am ugly and not worth being with. I think I'm responsible for everything that goes wrong.

GRETA, SUFFERING DEPRESSION
(FROM THORNE, 1993, P. 21)

Voices, like the roar of a crowd came. I felt like Jesus; I was being crucified. It was dark. I just continued to huddle under the blanket, feeling weak, laid bare and defenseless in a cruel world I could no longer understand.

STUART, SUFFERING SCHIZOPHRENIA
(FROM EMMONS & OTHERS, 1997)

People are fascinated by the exceptional, the unusual, and the abnormal. "The sun shines and warms and lights us and we have no curiosity to know why this is so," observed Ralph Waldo Emerson, "but we ask the reason of all evil, of pain, and hunger, and [unusual] people."

Why a fascination with disturbed people? Perhaps in them we see something of ourselves. At various moments, all of us feel, think, or act as disturbed people do much of the time. We, too, get anxious, depressed, withdrawn, suspicious, deluded, or antisocial, although less intensely and enduringly. Studying psychological disorders may therefore at times evoke an eerie sense of self-recognition that illuminates our own personality dynamics. "To study the abnormal is the best way of understanding the normal," proposed William James (1842–1910).

Another reason for our curiosity is that so many of us have felt, either personally or through friends or family members, the bewilderment and pain of a psychological disorder. In all likelihood, you or someone you care about has been disabled by unexplained physical symptoms, overwhelmed by irrational fears, or paralyzed by the feeling that life is not worth living. Each year there are nearly 1.9 million inpatient admissions to U.S. mental hospitals and psychiatric units (Bureau of the Census, 1996). Some 2.4 million others, often troubled but not disabled, seek help as outpatients from mental health organizations and clinics. Many more—15 percent of Americans, according to one government study—are judged to need such help, as have twice that many at some time in their lives (Robins & Regier, 1991). Such problems are not peculiar to the United States. No known culture is free of the two terrible maladies this chapter examines in depth—depression and schizophrenia (Draguns, 1990a,b). Some 400 million people worldwide suffer psychological disorders, according to the World Health Organization's mental health director (Sartorius, 1994). As members of the human family, few of us go through life unacquainted with the reality of psychological disturbance.

> "We are all mad at some time or another."
>
> BATTISTA MANTUANUS
> *ECLOGUES*
> 1500

Perspectives on Psychological Disorders

Where should we draw the line between normality and disorder? Should we think of psychological disorders as genuine illnesses or as socially defined categories? How are disorders classified and labeled? Why do some psychologists criticize diagnostic labels?

Most people would agree that someone who is too depressed to get out of bed for weeks at a time suffers a psychological disorder. But what about those who, having experienced a loss, are unable to resume their usual social activities? Where should we draw the line between normality and abnormality? How should we *define* psychological disorders? Equally important, how should we *understand* disorders—as sicknesses that need to be diagnosed and cured, or as natural responses to a troubling environment? Finally, how might we *classify* psychological disorders? Can we do so in a way that allows us to help disturbed people and not merely stigmatize them with labels?

A benign obsession Although British street cleaner Snowy Farr's eccentric behavior may indeed be atypical, clinicians would not label it disordered because it is neither particularly disturbing nor maladaptive.

Defining Psychological Disorders

Mental health workers label behavior psychologically disordered when they judge it *atypical, disturbing, maladaptive,* and *unjustifiable.* The emotions and perceptions of Marc, Greta, and Stuart are "*ab*normal" (atypical). Being different from most other people in one's culture is *part* of what it takes to define a psychological disorder. As the reclusive poet Emily Dickinson observed in 1862,

> *Assent—and you are sane—*
> *Demur—you're straightaway dangerous—*
> *and handled with a Chain.*

But there is more to a disorder than being atypical. Olympic gold medalists are abnormal in their physical abilities, and they are heroes. To be considered disordered, an atypical behavior must also be one that other people find *disturbing.*

Standards of acceptability for behaviors vary. In some cultures, people routinely behave in ways (such as going about naked) that in other cultures would be grounds for arrest. In at least one cultural context—wartime—even mass killing may be viewed as heroic. One person's homicidal "terror-ist" is another person's "freedom fighter." Standards of acceptability also vary over time. Sex experts William Acton, writing in the late 1800s, and William Masters and Virginia Johnson, writing in the late 1900s, all knew that some women have orgasms during intercourse while others don't (Wakefield, 1992). For Acton, orgasm was the disorder (resulting from overstimulation); for Masters and Johnson, lack of orgasm was the disorder (resulting from inadequate stimulation). Nearly three decades ago, the American Psychiatric Association dropped homosexuality as a disorder (because it was no longer believed connected with psychological problems). Later it added tobacco dependence (because it deemed smoking both addictive and self-destructive).

Atypical and disturbing behaviors are more likely to be considered disordered when judged as harmful. Indeed, many clinicians define disorders as behaviors that are *maladaptive*—as when a smoker's nicotine dependence produces physical damage. Accordingly, even typical behaviors, such as the occasional despondency that many college students feel, may signal a psychological disorder if they become disabling. Thus, maladaptiveness is a key element in defining a disorder: The behaviors must be distressing or disabling or put one at greatly increased risk of suffering or death.

Finally, abnormal behavior is most likely to be considered disordered when others find it rationally *unjustifiable*. Stuart claimed to hear voices and people presumed he was deranged. But actress Shirley MacLaine could wear a crystal on her neck and say, "See the outer bubble of white light watching you. It is part of you," and not be considered disordered because enough people took her seriously (Friedrich, 1987).

"If a man is in a minority
of one, we lock him up."

OLIVER WENDELL HOLMES (1841–1935)

exorcising the demon. Until the last two centuries, "mad" people were sometimes caged in zoolike conditions or given "therapies" appropriate to a demon. A disordered person might have been beaten, burned, or castrated. The therapy might have included pulling teeth, removing lengths of intestines, or cauterizing the clitoris. Some even had their own blood removed and replaced with transfusions of animal blood (Farina, 1982).

The Medical Perspective

In response to such brutal treatment, reformers such as Philippe Pinel (1745–1826) in France insisted that madness was not demonic possession but a sickness in response to severe stresses and inhumane conditions. For Pinel and other reformers, treatment meant boosting patients' morale by unchaining them, talking with them, and replacing brutality with gentleness, isolation with activity, and filth with fresh air and sun.

When it was later discovered that an infectious brain disease, syphilis, produced a disordered mind, people also came to believe in physical causes for disorders and to search for medical treatments. Today, this medical perspective is familiar to us in the medical terminology of the mental *health* movement: A mental *illness* (also called a psycho*pathology*) needs to be *diagnosed* on the basis of its *symptoms* and *cured* through *therapy*, which may include *treatment* in a psychiatric *hospital*. In the 1800s, the assumption of this medical model—that psychological disorders are sicknesses—provided the impetus for much-needed reform. The "sick" were unchained and hospitals replaced asylums.

The medical perspective has gained credibility from recent discoveries. As we will see, genetically influenced abnormalities in brain structure and biochemistry contribute to a number of disorders. Two of the most troubling, depression and schizophrenia, are often treated medically. As we will also see, psychological factors, such as traumatic stress, also play an important role.

psychological disorder
a condition in which behavior is judged atypical, disturbing, maladaptive, and unjustifiable.

medical model
the concept that diseases have physical causes that can be diagnosed, treated, and, in most cases, cured. When applied to psychological disorders, the medical model assumes that these "mental" illnesses can be diagnosed on the basis of their symptoms and cured through therapy, which may include treatment in a psychiatric hospital.

Understanding Psychological Disorders

To explain puzzling behavior, people in earlier times often presumed that strange forces—the movements of the stars, godlike powers, or evil spirits—were at work. "The devil made him do it," you might have said, if you had lived during the Middle Ages. The cure might have been to get rid of the evil force—by placating the great powers or

The medical perspective has gained credibility from recent discoveries. As we will see, genetically influenced abnormalities in brain structure and biochemistry contribute to a number of disorders.

bio-psycho-social perspective
a contemporary perspective which assumes that biological, sociocultural, and psychological factors combine and interact to produce psychological disorders.

"Who in the rainbow can draw the line where the violet tint ends and the orange tint begins? Distinctly we see the difference of the colors, but where exactly does the one first blendingly enter into the other? So with sanity and insanity?"

HERMAN MELVILLE
BILLY BUDD, SAILOR
1924

The Bio-Psycho-Social Perspective

Today's psychologists contend that *all* behavior, whether called normal or disordered, arises from the interaction of nature (genetic and physiological factors) and nurture (past and present experiences). To presume that a person is "mentally ill" attributes the condition solely to an internal problem—to a "sickness" that must be found and cured. Maybe there *is* no deep, internal problem. Maybe there is instead a growth-blocking difficulty in the person's environment, in the person's current interpretations of events, or in the person's bad habits and poor social skills.

When Native Americans were banished from their ancestral lands, forced into poverty on barren reservations, and deprived of personal control, the result was a rate of alcoholism more than five times that of other Americans (May, 1986). Because only some Native Americans become alcoholic, the medical model would attribute such alcoholism to individual "sickness." A contemporary psychological perspective would emphasize the interaction between an individual's vulnerability and a hope-eroding environment.

Evidence of environmental effects comes from links between disorder and culture. As we noted earlier, some major disorders such as depression and schizophrenia are universal. From Asia to Africa and across the Americas, the core symptoms of schizophrenia include irrationality and incoherent speech (Brislin, 1993; Draguns, 1990b). Other disorders are culture-bound (Beardsley, 1994; Carson & others, 1988). Different cultures have different sources of stress and produce different ways of coping. Anorexia nervosa and bulimia, for example, are disorders mostly of Western cultures (page 379). *Susto*, marked by severe anxiety, restlessness, and fear of black magic, is a disorder found in Latin America. *Taijin-kyofusho*, which combines social anxiety with easy blushing and fear of eye contact, appears in Japan. Such disorders may share an underlying dynamic (anxiety), yet culturally differ in symptoms (eating problem or type of fear).

Most mental health workers today assume that disorders are indeed influenced by genetic predispositions and physiological states. And by inner psychological dynamics. And by social and cultural circumstances. To get the whole picture, we need an interdisciplinary bio-psycho-social perspective (Figure 15.1).

"It's no measure of health to be well adjusted to a profoundly sick society."

KRISHNAMURTI (1895–1986)

Figure 15.1

The bio-psycho-social perspective. Today's psychology studies how biological, psychological, and social factors interact to produce specific psychological disorders.

CLOSE-UP

The Insanity Defense on Trial

The definition of psychological disorders does not include the term *insanity*. That is because *sane* and *insane* are *legal*, not psychological, terms. They are also either/or categories. You can be a little depressed or greatly depressed; you cannot be a little insane.

The British created the insanity defense in 1843 after a deluded Scotsman, Daniel M'Naghten, tried to shoot the prime minister (who he thought was persecuting him) and killed the prime minister's secretary by mistake. A furor erupted after M'Naghten was acquitted as insane and sent to a mental hospital rather than to prison. When the M'Naghten verdict was upheld, an insanity rule emerged. It limited the insanity defense to cases where persons were judged not to have known what they were doing or not to have known that the action was wrong. Shakespeare's Hamlet anticipated the defense. If I wrong someone when not myself, he explains, "then Hamlet does it not, Hamlet denies it. Who does it then? His madness."

By the time John Hinckley, Jr., came to trial in 1982 for shooting then-President Ronald Reagan and his press secretary, the insanity defense had been broadened. The prosecution had to prove that Hinckley was sane. This meant his having "a substantial capacity" not merely to "know" his act was wrong but to "appreciate" its wrongfulness and to act accordingly.

The prosecution was unable to prove sanity to the jurors' satisfaction. So Hinckley, like M'Naghten, was sent to a mental hospital. And, as in the M'Naghten case, the public was outraged. One newspaper

headlined "Hinckley Insane, Public Mad." The outrage was partly because Hinckley, like others declared not guilty by reason of insanity, will be released when declared sane and no longer dangerous—conceivably earlier, though quite possibly later, than he would have been released from a prison.

Some news commentators complained that the heinousness of a crime had become the very basis for evading responsibility for it, "like the person who kills his parents and demands mercy because he is an orphan." Are "sick crimes" necessarily the products of sick minds that need treatment, not punishment? Was there a serious point to the joke that "Anyone crazy enough to want to kill the president must be crazy"? Was Jeffrey Dahmer, who in 1991 admitted murdering 15 young men and eating parts of their bodies, necessarily insane? Are the genuinely bad truly mad? If so, said one commentator, then modern society has become like Aldous Huxley's nightmarish *Brave New World*, in which the correct response when someone commits a crime is, "I did not know he was ill." (Juries rejected Dahmer's insanity plea and found him guilty. Lorena Bobbitt, however, was acquitted by reason of temporary insanity for cutting off her sleeping husband's penis after he raped her while drunk.)

In defense of the insanity plea, psychologists note that, actually, such a plea is entered in only about 1 percent of felony cases (Callahan & others, 1991). Even then, it is unsuccessful three times out of four. When the insanity plea is successful, the judge and prosecution usually concur that the deranged

person was not responsible. So, the most important issues that involve psychology and law are not the rare disputes over insanity. They are instead the far more frequent cases concerning child custody (judging who will be the better parent), involuntary commitment to mental hospitals, and predictions about a criminal's future behavior made at the time of sentencing or parole.

In Canada, and now in three-fourths of the U.S. states, the insanity defense survives in a restricted format that shifts the burden of proving insanity to the defense (Ogloff & others, 1993). Now defendants must show that they did not understand the wrongfulness of their acts.

Some states have instituted a verdict of "guilty but mentally ill." This verdict recognizes a need for treatment but holds people responsible and sends them to prison if they are judged recovered before their sentence is over (Rosenfeld, 1987). Jurors find the verdict a viable option. In mock trials, defendants who otherwise would have been judged either innocent or not guilty by reason of insanity are often judged guilty but mentally ill (Savitsky & Lindblom, 1986).

Is this man sane? A posed self-portrait of John W. Hinckley, Jr., former President Reagan's would-be assassin.

Classifying Psychological Disorders

In biology and the other sciences, classification creates order. To classify an animal as a mammal says a great deal—that it is warm-blooded, has hair or fur, and nourishes its young with milk. In psychiatry and psychology, too, classification orders and describes clusters of symptoms. To classify a person's disorder as "schizophrenia" suggests that the person talks incoherently, halluci-nates or has delusions (bizarre beliefs), shows ei-ther little emotion or inappropriate emotion, or is socially withdrawn. Thus, the diagnostic term pro-vides a handy shorthand for describing a complex disorder.

In psychiatry and psychology, diagnostic classi-fication ideally aims to describe a disorder, to predict its future course, to imply appropriate treat-ment, and to stimulate research into its causes. In-deed, to study a disorder we must first name and describe it. The current authoritative scheme for classifying psychological disorders is the Ameri-can Psychiatric Association's *Diagnostic and Statistical Manual of Mental Disorders* (Fourth Edition), nicknamed DSM-IV. This 1994 volume and accompanying case illustrations provide the basis for much of the material in this chapter. DSM-IV was developed in coordination with the tenth edition of the World Health Organization's *International Classification of Diseases* (ICD-10).

The very idea of "diagnosing" people's prob-lems in terms of their "symptoms" presumes a mental "illness." Some practitioners are not en-thralled with this medical terminology, but most find DSM-IV a helpful and practical tool. It is also a financially necessary one: Most North American health insurance companies require a DSM-IV di-agnosis before they will pay for therapy.

DSM-IV describes disorders and their preva-lence without presuming to explain their causes. Thus, the once-popular term *neurosis* is no longer a diagnostic category—because neurosis was Freud's idea of the process by which unconscious conflicts cope with anxiety. DSM-IV does mention neurotic disorders—psychological disorders that, although distressing, still allow one to think ratio-nally and function socially. But even this term is so vague that psychologists now use it minimally, usually as a contrast to the more bizarre and debili-tating psychotic disorders, marked by irrationality.

DSM-IV groups some 230 psychological disor-ders and conditions into 17 major categories of "mental disorder." There are diagnoses for almost every conceivable complaint. In fact, some critics have faulted the manual for bringing "almost any kind of behavior within the compass of psychiatry" (Eysenck & others, 1983). These critics point to behaviors ranging from irrational fear of humilia-tion and embarrassment (social phobia) to persis-tently breaking rules at home or school (conduct disorder).

For the DSM-IV categories to be valid, they must first be reliable. If one psychiatrist or psy-chologist diagnoses someone as having, say, "cata-tonic schizophrenia," what are the chances that another mental health worker will independently give the same diagnosis? With the DSM-IV's diag-nostic guidelines, the chances are good. The guide-lines work by asking clinicians a series of objective questions about observable behaviors, such as, "Is the person afraid to leave home?" In one study, 16 psychologists used this structured-interview proce-dure to diagnose 75 psychiatric patients as suffer-ing from (1) depression, (2) generalized anxiety, or (3) some other disorder (Riskind & others, 1987). Without knowing the first psychologist's diagno-sis, another psychologist viewed a videotape of each interview and offered a second opinion. For 83 percent of the patients, the two opinions agreed.

Labeling Psychological Disorders

Most clinicians believe that classification helps in describing, treating, and researching the causes of psychological disorders. Critics, however, say that these labels are at best arbitrary and at worst value judgments that masquerade as science. It is better, they say, to study the roots of specific symptoms,

"I'm always like this, and my family was wondering if you could prescribe a mild depressant."

© 1992 by Sidney Harris.

such as delusions or hallucinations, than to study catchall categories, such as schizophrenia (Persons, 1986). Moreover, once we label a person, we view that person differently (Farina, 1982). Labels create preconceptions that can bias our perceptions and interpretations.

In the most controversial demonstration of the biasing power of diagnostic labels, David Rosenhan (1973) and seven of his friends and Stanford University colleagues went to mental hospital admissions offices, complaining of "hearing voices" that were saying "empty," "hollow," and "thud." Apart from this complaint and giving false names and occupations, they truthfully answered all the questions. All eight were diagnosed as mentally ill.

That these normal people were misdiagnosed is not surprising. As one psychiatrist noted, if someone swallowed blood, went to an emergency room, and spat it up, would we fault the doctor for diagnosing a bleeding ulcer? What followed the diagnosis was more startling. After admission, the "patients" exhibited no further symptoms. Yet the clinicians were able to "discover" the causes of their disorders after analyzing their (quite normal) life histories. One person was said to be reacting to mixed emotions about his parents. Furthermore, before being released (an average of 19 days later), the "patients'" normal behaviors, such as taking notes, were often misinterpreted as symptoms.

Other studies confirm that labels affect how we perceive one another. Ellen Langer and her colleagues (1974, 1980) had people rate an interviewee they thought was either normal (a job applicant) or out of the ordinary (a psychiatric or cancer patient). All raters saw the identical videotape. Those who watched unlabeled interviewees perceived them as normal; those who watched supposed patients perceived them as "different from most people." Therapists (who thought they were evaluating a psychiatric patient) perceived the interviewee as "frightened of his own aggressive impulses," a "passive, dependent type," and so forth. A label can serve a useful purpose. But as Rosenhan discovered, it can also have "a life and an influence of its own."

Labels can also stigmatize people in others' eyes. U.S. Senator Thomas Eagleton experienced this in 1972, when he was dumped as the Democratic party's vice-presidential candidate after it was discovered he had been treated for depression with electroconvulsive therapy. The same stigma surfaced when a female associate of psychologist Stewart Page (1977) called 180 people in Toronto who were advertising furnished rooms for rent. When she merely asked if the room was still available, the answer was nearly always yes. When she

said she was about to be released from a mental hospital, the answer three times out of four was no (as it was when she said she was calling for her brother who was about to be released from jail). When some of those who answered no were called by a second person who simply asked if the room was still available, the advertiser nearly always revealed that it was. Surveys in Western Europe have uncovered similar attitudes toward those labeled mentally ill. But as people come to understand psychological disorders as diseases of the brain, not failures of character, the stigma seems to be lifting (Solomon, 1996). More and more public figures are feeling free to "come out" and speak with candor about their struggles with disorders such as depression.

If people also form their impressions of psychological disorder from the media, then lingering stereotypes are hardly surprising. Television researcher George Gerbner (1985) reported that 1 in 5 prime-time and daytime programs depicts a psychologically disordered person, and 7 in 10 of such programs portray this character as violent or criminal. Movies, too, stereotype mental patients, sometimes as homicidal (Anthony Hopkins's role in *Silence of the Lambs*), or as freaks (Woody Allen as *Zelig*) (Hyler & others, 1991; Wahl, 1992). Schizophrenia patients with positive symptoms are indeed more likely than other people to commit violent crime, and some disordered people are amoral and antisocial (Eronen & others, 1996; Monahan, 1992; Silverton, 1988). However, at least 9 in 10 disordered people are *not* dangerous; instead, they are anxious, depressed, or withdrawn.

Labels not only bias perceptions, they can also change reality. When teachers are told certain students are "gifted," when students expect someone to be "hostile," or when interviewers check to see whether someone is "extraverted," they may act in ways that elicit the very behavior expected (Snyder, 1984). Someone who was led to think you are

> Labels not only bias perceptions, they can also change reality. When teachers are told certain students are "gifted," when students expect someone to be "hostile," or when interviewers check to see whether someone is "extraverted," they may act in ways that elicit the very behavior expected.

> "One of the unpardonable sins, in the eyes of most people, is for a man to go about unlabelled. The world regards such a person as the police do an unmuzzled dog, not under proper control."
>
> **T. H. HUXLEY**
> *EVOLUTION AND ETHICS*
> 1893

anxiety disorders
psychological disorders characterized by distressing, persistent anxiety or maladaptive behaviors that reduce anxiety.

generalized anxiety disorder
an anxiety disorder in which a person is continually tense, apprehensive, and in a state of autonomic nervous system arousal.

phobia
an anxiety disorder marked by a persistent, irrational fear and avoidance of a specific object or situation.

obsessive-compulsive disorder
an anxiety disorder characterized by unwanted repetitive thoughts (obsessions) and/or actions (compulsions).

nasty may treat you coldly, provoking you to respond as a nasty person would. Labels can serve as self-fulfilling prophecies.

But let us also remember the benefits of diagnostic labels. As Robert Spitzer (1975), a chief author of the current diagnostic system explained, "There is a purpose to psychiatric diagnosis. It is to enable mental health professionals to (a) communicate with each other about the subject matter of their concern, (b) comprehend the pathological processes involved in psychiatric illness, and (c) control psychiatric outcomes."

SUMMING UP

Psychological disorders fascinate us, partly because most of us will at some time experience or witness them close at hand.

Defining Psychological Disorders Between normality and abnormality there is not a gulf, but a fine and somewhat arbitrary line. Where we draw the line depends on how atypical, disturbing, maladaptive, and unjustifiable a person's behavior is.

Understanding Psychological Disorders The medical model's assumption that psychological disorders are mental illnesses has displaced earlier views that demons and evil spirits were to blame. However, critics question the medical model's labeling of psychological disorders as sicknesses. Most mental health workers today adopt a bio-psycho-social perspective. They assume that disorders are influenced by genetic predispositions, physiological states, psychological dynamics, and social circumstances.

Classifying Psychological Disorders Many psychiatrists and psychologists believe that a system for naming and describing psychological disorders facilitates treatment and research. The current edition of the *Diagnostic and Statistical Manual of Mental Disorders* (DSM-IV) provides an authoritative classification scheme.

Labeling Psychological Disorders Diagnostic labels facilitate mental health professionals' communications and research. Critics point out that we pay a price for these benefits. Labels also create preconceptions that bias our perceptions of people's past and present behavior and unfairly stigmatize them.

KEY TERMS AND CONCEPTS psychological disorder, medical model, bio-psycho-social perspective, DSM-IV, neurotic disorder, psychotic disorder

Anxiety Disorders

Anxiety becomes disabling when people are unexplainably and uncontrollably tense (general anxiety disorder), irrationally fearful of something (a phobia), or troubled by repetitive thoughts and actions (obsessive-compulsive disorder). What do these disorders look like in real people? What causes them?

Anxiety is part of life. When speaking in front of a class, when peering down from a ledge, when waiting to play in a big game, any one of us might feel anxious. At one time or another, most of us feel enough anxiety that we fail to make eye contact or we avoid talking to someone—"shyness" we call it. Fortunately for most of us, our occasional uneasiness is not intense and persistent. If it becomes so, we may have one of the anxiety disorders, marked by distressing, persistent anxiety or maladaptive behaviors that reduce anxiety. In this section we focus on generalized anxiety disorder, in which a person feels unexplainably tense and uneasy; phobias, in which a person has a disruptive, irrational fear of a specific object or situation; and obsessive-compulsive disorder, in which a person is troubled by repetitive thoughts and/or actions.

Generalized Anxiety Disorder

Tom, a 27-year-old electrician, seeks help, complaining of dizziness, sweating palms, heart palpitations, and ringing in his ears. He feels edgy and sometimes finds himself shaking. With reasonable success he hides his symptoms from his family and co-workers. Nevertheless, he has had few social contacts since the symptoms began two years ago. Worse, he occasionally has to leave work. His family doctor and neurologist can find no physical problem.

Tom's unfocused, out-of-control, negative feelings suggest a generalized anxiety disorder. The symptoms of this disorder are commonplace; their persistence is not. The sufferers are continually tense and jittery, worried about bad things that might happen, and experience all the symptoms of autonomic nervous system arousal (racing heart, clammy hands, stomach butterflies, sleeplessness). The tension and apprehension may leak out through furrowed brows, twitching eyelids, or fidgeting. One of the worst characteristics of a generalized

CLOSE-UP

The Wounds of War—Post-Traumatic Stress Disorder

During the fighting in Vietnam, Jack's platoon was repeatedly under fire. In one ambush, his closest friend was killed while standing a few feet away. Jack himself killed a young Vietcong soldier by bludgeoning him with a rifle butt. Years later, images of these events intrude as flashbacks and nightmares. He still jumps at the sound of a cap gun or the backfire of a car. When annoyed by family or friends, he lashes out in ways he seldom did before Vietnam. To calm his continuing anxiety, he drinks more than he should.

Such has been the experience of many combat veterans and sexual assault victims. Traumatic stress—experiencing or witnessing severely threatening, uncontrollable events with a sense of fear, helplessness, or horror—can produce a *post-traumatic stress disorder*, symptoms of which include haunting memories and nightmares, social withdrawal, and anxiety or depression (Goodman & others, 1993; Kaylor & others, 1987; Wilson & others, 1988). After witnessing atrocities or living in life-threatening circumstances, children of the world's war zones and violent neighborhoods show similar symptoms (Garbarino & others, 1991). Their sense of basic trust erodes; many experience fearful wariness, troubled sleep, nightmares, and a sense of hopelessness about their future. This "learned helplessness" predisposes children who repeatedly suffer abuse to more often experience post-traumatic stress if assaulted as adults (Mineka & Zinbarg, in press).

To pin down the frequency of post-traumatic stress disorder, the U.S. Centers for Disease Control (1988) compared 7000 Vietnam combat veterans with 7000 noncombat veterans who served during the same years. Combat stress more than doubled a veteran's risk of alcohol abuse, depression, or anxiety.

Studies of U.S. and Israeli soldiers reveal that the more terrifying and prolonged the battle experience, the greater the psychological casualties (King & King, 1991; Solomon, 1990). The roughly 15 percent rate of post-traumatic stress symptoms among all Vietnam veterans was halved among those who never saw combat and tripled among those who experienced heavy combat. More than a decade after the war, one study located 2095 identical twins among Vietnam-era veterans (Goldberg & others, 1990). Compared with co-twins who served noncombat roles in Vietnam, those who experienced heavy combat were 5.4 times more likely to be suffering post-traumatic stress disorder.

Researchers have also found that psychological disorders and suicide attempts were most common among vets who felt responsible for a trauma, because they had either killed someone or failed to prevent a death (Fontana & others, 1992). Many still experience nightmares, have trouble sleeping and concentrating, and find themselves easily startled. This is especially so for those exposed to savage mutilation, torture, or the sight of a friend's death. Much as they might wish to avoid or suppress the memory, it intrudes.

Despite such symptoms, some psychologists believe post-traumatic stress disorder is a fad diagnosis. The disorder, these skeptics say, actually is infrequent (Young, 1995). Most combat-stressed veterans live productive lives. Most rescuers, such as all the Sioux City fire fighters who rescued people and charred bodies from a flaming 1989 DC-10 crash, cope well afterwards (Redburn & others, 1993). Most political dissidents who survive many dozens of torture episodes do *not* later exhibit post-traumatic stress disorder (Mineka & Zinbarg, in press). And, although suffering some lingering stress symptoms, most American Jews who survived the Holocaust trauma—starvation, beatings, lost freedom, the murders of loved ones—went on to live productive lives. In fact, compared with other American Jews of the same age, these survivors have been *less* likely to have seen a psychotherapist (18 percent versus 31 percent) and *more* likely to have had stable marriages (83 percent versus 62 percent). Moreover, virtually none has committed criminal acts. Researcher William Helmreich (1992, p. 276) reflects on their successes:

The story of the survivors is one of courage and strength, of people who are living proof of the indomitable will of human beings to survive and of their tremendous capacity for hope. It is not a story of remarkable people. It is a story of just how remarkable people can be.

<u>panic disorder</u>
an anxiety disorder marked by a minutes-long episode of intense dread in which a person experiences terror and accompanying chest pain, choking, or other frightening sensations.

anxiety disorder is that the person cannot identify, and therefore cannot avoid, the cause of these persistent, unpleasant symptoms. To use Freud's term, the anxiety is "free-floating."

As some 1 in 75 people with <u>panic disorder</u> know, anxiety may at times suddenly escalate into a terrifying *panic attack*—a minutes-long episode of intense fear that something horrible is about to happen to them. Heart palpitations, shortness of breath, choking sensations, trembling, or dizziness typically accompany the panic. The experience is unpredictable and so frightening that the sufferer often comes to fear the fear itself and to avoid situations where panic has struck. *Agoraphobia* is fear or avoidance of situations in which escape or help might not be available when panic strikes. Given such fear, people may avoid being outside the home, being in a crowd, or traveling in a plane or train or on an elevator.

Phobias

Phobias *focus* anxiety on some specific object, activity, or situation. (See Figure 15.2 for one ranking of some common and less common fears.) Phobias— irrational fears that disrupt behavior—are a common psychological disorder that people often accept and live with. Some *specific phobias* are incapacitating, however. Marilyn, a 28-year-old homemaker, so

fears thunderstorms that she feels anxious as soon as a weather forecaster mentions possible storms later in the week. If her husband is away and a storm is forecast, she sometimes stays with a close relative. During a storm, she hides from windows and buries her head to avoid seeing the lightning. She is otherwise healthy and happy.

Other people suffer from irrational fears of specific animals or insects, or of such things as heights, blood, or tunnels. Sometimes it is possible to avoid the fear-arousing stimulus: One can hide during thunderstorms or avoid high places. With a *social phobia*, an intense fear of being scrutinized by others, the anxious person will avoid potentially embarrassing social situations. The person may avoid speaking up, eating out, or going to parties— or will sweat, tremble, or have diarrhea when doing so. Compared with the other disorders discussed in this chapter, phobias appear at a younger age—often by the early teens (Burke & others, 1990).

Obsessive-Compulsive Disorder

As with generalized anxiety and phobias, we can see aspects of our own behavior in the obsessive-compulsive disorder. We may at times be obsessed with senseless or offensive thoughts that will not

Figure **15.2**

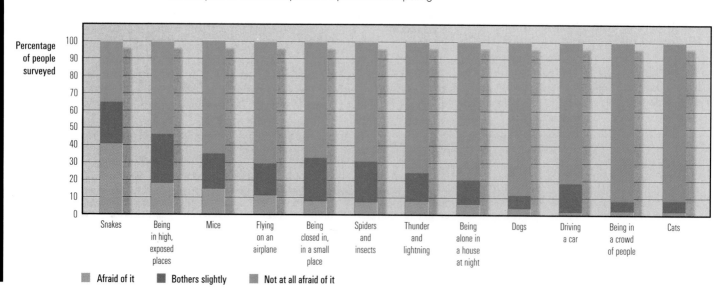

Some common and uncommon fears This national survey ranked the relative fear levels of Americans to some sources of anxiety. A fear becomes a phobia if it provokes a compelling but irrational desire to avoid the dreaded object or situation. (From *Public Opinion*, 1984.)

Percentage of people surveyed

Snakes | Being in high, exposed places | Mice | Flying on an airplane | Being closed in, in a small place | Spiders and insects | Thunder and lightning | Being alone in a house at night | Dogs | Driving a car | Being in a crowd of people | Cats

■ Afraid of it   ■ Bothers slightly   ■ Not at all afraid of it go away. Or we may engage in compulsive, rigid behavior—rechecking a locked door, stepping over cracks in the sidewalk, or lining up our books and pencils "just so" before studying.

Obsessive thoughts and compulsive behaviors cross the fine line between normality and disorder when they become so persistent that they interfere with the way we live or when they cause distress. Checking to see that the door is locked is normal; checking the door 10 times is not. Hand washing is normal; hand washing so often that one's skin becomes raw is not. (Table 15.1 offers more examples.) At some time during their lives, often during their late teens or twenties, 2 to 3 percent of people cross that line from normal preoccupations and fussiness to debilitating disorder (Karno & others, 1988). The obsessive thoughts become so haunting, the compulsive rituals so senselessly time-consuming, that effective functioning becomes impossible.

One such person was billionaire Howard Hughes. Hughes would compulsively dictate the same phrases over and over again. Under stress, he developed an obsessive fear of germs. He became reclusive and insisted that his assistants carry out elaborate hand-washing rituals and wear white gloves when handling documents he would later touch. He ordered tape around doors and windows and forbade his staff to touch or even look at him. "Everybody carries germs around with them," he explained. "I want to live longer than my parents, so I avoid germs" (Fowler, 1986).

"He always times '60 Minutes.'"

Explaining Anxiety Disorders

Freud assumed that, beginning in childhood, intolerable impulses, ideas, and feelings get repressed, and that this submerged mental energy sometimes produces mystifying symptoms such as anxiety.

Common Obsessions and Compulsions Among People With Obsessive-Compulsive Disorder
Table **15.1**

Thought or Behavior	Percentage* Reporting Symptom
Obsessions (repetitive thoughts)	
Concern with dirt, germs, or toxins	40
Something terrible happening (fire, death, illness)	24
Symmetry, order, or exactness	17
Compulsions (repetitive behaviors)	
Excessive hand washing, bathing, tooth brushing, or grooming	85
Repeating rituals (in/out of a door, up/down from a chair)	51
Checking doors, locks, appliances, car brake, homework	46

*Seventy children and adolescents reported their symptoms.
Source: Adapted from Rapoport, 1989.

However, today's psychologists have turned away from Freud to two contemporary perspectives—learning and biological.

The Learning Perspective

Fear Conditioning
Researchers have linked general anxiety with classical conditioning of fear. In the laboratory, they have created chronically anxious rats by giving them unpredictable electric shocks (Schwartz, 1984). Like the rape victim who reported feeling anxious when entering her old neighborhood (page 253), the animals are apprehensive in their lab environment. For many victims of post-traumatic stress disorder, anxiety swells with any reminder of their trauma. Such experiences might help explain why anxious people are hyperattentive to possible threats (Mineka & Sutton, 1992).

When experimental shocks become predictable—when preceded by a particular conditioned stimulus—the animals' fear focuses on *that* stimulus and they relax in its absence. So it can happen with human fears. My car was once struck by another whose driver missed a stop sign. For months afterward, I felt a twinge of unease with the approach of any car from a side street. Perhaps Marilyn's phobia was similarly conditioned during a terrifying or painful experience associated with a thunderstorm.

Stimulus Generalization

Conditioned fears may remain long after we have forgotten the experiences that produced them (Jacobs & Nadel, 1985). Moreover, some fears arise from stimulus generalization. A person who fears heights after a fall may be afraid of airplanes without ever having flown.

Reinforcement

Avoiding or escaping the feared situation reduces anxiety, thus reinforcing the phobic behavior. Feeling anxious or fearing panic attacks, a person may go or stay inside (Antony & others, 1992). Compulsive behaviors similarly reduce anxiety. If washing your hands relieves your feelings of unease, you will likely wash your hands again when the feelings return.

Observational Learning

Someone might also learn fear through observational learning—by observing others' fears. As we saw in Chapter 13, wild monkeys transmit their fear of snakes to their offspring; human parents similarly transmit their fears to their children.

The Biological Perspective

Evolution

Human behavior was road tested in the stone age. Compulsive acts therefore typically exaggerate behaviors that contributed to our species' survival. Grooming gone wild becomes hair pulling. Washing up becomes ritual hand washing. Checking territorial boundaries becomes checking and rechecking a door known to be locked (Rapoport, 1989).

We humans also seem biologically prepared to fear dangers faced by our ancestors. Most phobias therefore focus on objects that presented occasional threats: spiders, snakes, closed spaces, heights, storms. It is easy to condition and hard to extinguish fears of such stimuli (Davey, 1995; Ohman, 1986). Many of our modern fears may also have an evolutionary explanation. Fear of flying may come from our biological past, which predisposes us to fear confinement and heights.

Moreover, consider what people tend *not* to learn to fear. World War II air raids produced remarkably few lasting phobias. As the air blitz continued, the British, Japanese, and German civilian populations became not more panicked, but more indifferent to planes that were not in their immediate neighborhood (Mineka & Zinburg, 1996). Evolution does not prepare us to learn fears of bombs dropping from the sky.

Genes

Some people more than others seem genetically predisposed to particular fears and high anxiety. Identical twins often develop similar phobias, in some cases even when raised separately (Carey, 1990; Eckert & others, 1981). One pair of 35-year-old identical female twins independently developed claustrophobia. They also became so fearful of water that each would gingerly wade backward into the ocean, only up to the knees. Among monkeys, fearfulness runs in families. Individual monkeys react more strongly to stress if their close biological relatives are anxiously reactive (Suomi, 1986). Among humans, vulnerability to anxiety disorder rises when the afflicted relative is an identical twin (Barlow, 1988; Kendler & others, 1992; Roy & others, 1995).

Physiology

Generalized anxiety disorder, panic, and even obsessions and compulsions are biologically measurable as an overarousal of brain areas involved in impulse control and habitual behaviors. PET scans of persons with obsessive-compulsive disorder reveal unusually high activity in an area of the frontal lobes just above the eyes (Figure 15.3) and in a more primitive area deep in the brain (Rauch & Jenike, 1993; Resnick, 1992). Some antidepressant drugs dampen this activity by affecting the availability of the neurotransmitter serotonin. This helps control obsessive-compulsive behavior.

SUMMING UP

Anxiety is part of our everyday experience. It is classified as a psychological disorder only when it becomes distressing or persistent or is characterized by maladaptive behaviors intended to reduce it. The section covered three types of anxiety disorders.

Generalized Anxiety Disorder Those who suffer a generalized anxiety disorder may for no clear reason feel uncontrollably tense and uneasy, an anxiety that can escalate into a panic attack.

Phobias Those with phobias may be irrationally afraid of a specific object or situation.

Obsessive-Compulsive Disorder Persistent and repetitive thoughts and actions characterize obsessive-compulsive disorder.

An emotional high Although we humans seem biologically predisposed to fear heights—certainly an adaptive response—this construction worker seems fearless. The biological perspective helps us understand why most people would be terrified in this situation.

Figure **15.3**

A PET scan of the brain of a person with obsessive-compulsive disorder The scan reveals an abnormally high metabolic activity (red areas) in the frontal lobes, seen at the top of the photo. This is visible in a region of the left hemisphere's frontal lobe involved in directing attention.

Explaining Anxiety Disorders The psychoanalytic perspective views anxiety disorders as the discharging of repressed impulses. The learning perspective sees them as a product of fear conditioning, stimulus generalization, reinforcement, and observational learning. The biological perspective considers possible evolutionary, genetic, and physiological influences.

KEY TERMS AND CONCEPTS anxiety disorders, generalized anxiety disorder, phobia, obsessive-compulsive disorder, panic disorder

Dissociative Disorders

Most controversial of all disorders are those in which conscious awareness is said to become dissociated (separated) from previous memories, thoughts, and feelings. What are these disorders, and why are they controversial?

Among the most intriguing disorders are the rare dissociative disorders, in which a person appears to experience a sudden loss of memory or change in identity. When a situation becomes too stressful, people are said to dissociate themselves from it. Their conscious awareness becomes separated from painful memories, thoughts, and feelings. (Note that this explanation presumes the existence of repressed memories, which have recently been questioned, as discussed in Chapters 9 and 14.)

Certain symptoms of dissociation are not so rare. Now and then, many people may have a sense of being unreal, of being separated from one's body, of watching oneself as in a movie. Facing trauma, such detachment may actually protect a person from being overwhelmed by emotion. Only when such experiences are severe and prolonged do they suggest a dissociative disorder.

Dissociative Amnesia

Amnesia, the failure to recall events, can be caused by head injuries or alcoholic intoxication. But dissociative amnesia, some psychologists believe, usually begins as a response to intolerable psychological stress. One 18-year-old victim was rescued from his sailboat by the Coast Guard and brought to a hospital. He knew he had gone sailing with friends and that he was a college student, but he said he could not recall what had happened to his friends. Moreover, he kept forgetting he was in a hospital; each reminder surprised him. Later, aided by a drug that relaxed him, he formed a memory: A ferocious storm had washed his companions overboard.

As this case illustrates, the forgetfulness of amnesia is selective: The young man seemed to forget what was intolerably painful (although traumatic experiences usually produce intrusive memories). Those with amnesia may be somewhat disoriented and may forget who they are, but they will remember how to drive, count, and talk. Typically, the amnesia vanishes as abruptly as it began and rarely recurs.

Dissociative Fugue

Like amnesia, dissociative fugue (pronounced fewg, meaning "flight") involves presumed forgetting, but it also involves fleeing one's home and identity for days, months, or years. Gene Smith, a mid-level manager, had been passed over for promotion, faulted by his supervisor, and rejected by his 18-year-old son, who during a violent argument called him a "failure." Two days later, Smith disappeared. A month later and 200 miles away, police brought a man who said he was "Burt Tate" to the emergency room. Tate had been hurt in a fight at a diner, where he had been working as a short-order cook since drifting into town a month earlier. He claimed not to recall where he had lived or worked before that. He admitted that was strange but did not seem upset by it. After a missing-person check,

dissociative disorders *disorders in which conscious awareness becomes separated (dissociated) from previous memories, thoughts, and feelings. See dissociative amnesia, dissociative fugue, and dissociative identity disorder.*

dissociative amnesia *loss of memory. Dissociative amnesia is selective memory loss often brought on by extreme stress.*

dissociative fugue *[fewg] a dissociative disorder in which flight from one's home and identity accompanies amnesia.*

dissociative identity disorder a rare dissociative disorder in which a person exhibits two or more distinct and alternating personalities. Formerly called multiple personality disorder.

Mrs. Smith confirmed that Burt Tate was Gene Smith. Though noticeably anxious when faced with his wife, he denied recognizing her. When "awakening" from a fugue state, people such as Gene Smith remember their old identities but typically deny remembering what occurred during the fugue. Skeptics wonder if such patients may be feigning memory loss for strategic reasons.

Dissociative Identity Disorder

Even more mysterious and controversial is the massive dissociation of self from ordinary consciousness in those with multiple personality disorder, now called dissociative identity disorder. These people have two or more distinct personalities that alternately control the person's behavior. One is usually restrained and dull, another more impulsive and uninhibited. The person with this disorder may be prim and proper one moment and loud and flirtatious the next. Each personality has its own voice and mannerisms, and the original one typically denies awareness of the other(s).

Although people diagnosed as having multiple personalities are usually not violent, there have been cases in which the person reportedly became dissociated into a "good" and a "bad" or aggressive personality—a modest version of the Dr. Jekyll/Mr. Hyde split immortalized in Robert

The "Hillside Strangler" Kenneth Bianchi is shown here at his trial.

Louis Stevenson's story. Freud would have said that, rid of the original "good" personality's awareness, the wanton second personality is free to discharge forbidden impulses. One unusual case that for a time seemed to support this interpretation involved Kenneth Bianchi, who was on trial for the "Hillside Strangler" rapes and murders of 10 California women. During a hypnosis session with Bianchi, psychologist John Watkins (1984) "called forth" a hidden personality: "I've talked a bit to Ken, but I think that perhaps there might be another part of Ken that I haven't talked to, another part that maybe feels somewhat differently from the part that I've talked to. . . . Would you talk with me, Part, by saying, 'I'm here'?" Bianchi answered "Yes" and engaged in the following interchange:

Watkins: Part, are you the same thing as Ken, or are you different in any way?

Bianchi: I'm not him.

Watkins: You're not him? Who are you? Do you have a name?

Bianchi: Steve. You can call me Steve.

When speaking as Steve, Bianchi stated that he hated Ken because Ken was nice and that he (Steve), aided by a cousin, had murdered women. He also claimed that Ken knew nothing about his existence and that Ken was innocent of the murders.

Was Bianchi's second personality a ruse, simply a way of disavowing responsibility for his actions? (Bianchi, who was later convicted, was a practiced liar who had read about multiple personality in psychology books.) Exploring our capacity for personality shifts, Nicholas Spanos (1986, 1994, 1996) asked college students to pretend they were accused murderers being examined by a psychiatrist. When given the same hypnotic treatment Bianchi received, most spontaneously expressed a second personality.

This discovery made Spanos wonder: Are dissociative identities simply a more extreme version of our normal human capacity to vary the "selves" we present—as when displaying a goofy, loud-mouthed self while hanging out with friends, and a subdued, respectful self around grandparents? Are clinicians who discover multiple personalities merely triggering fantasy-prone people's enactment of a role? If so, can such people then convince themselves of the authenticity of their own

"Pretense may become reality."

CHINESE PROVERB

role enactments? Are they like actors, who commonly report "losing themselves" in their roles? (Recall from Chapter 7 that Spanos also raised these questions about the hypnotic state. Given that most multiple personality patients are highly hypnotizable, whatever explains one condition—dissociation or role playing—may help explain the other.)

Those who accept dissociative identity as a genuine disorder find support in the distinct brain and body states associated with differing personalities (Putnam, 1991). Handedness, too, sometimes switches with personality (Henninger, 1992). In one study, ophthalmologists detected shifting visual acuity and eye-muscle balance as patients switched personalities. Such changes did not occur among control subjects trying to simulate multiple personality (Miller & others, 1991).

Skeptics nevertheless find it suspicious that the disorder has just recently become rather popular. In North America, the number of diagnoses exploded from only two reported cases per decade from 1930 to 1960 to more than 20,000 in the 1980s (McHugh, 1995a). The average number of personalities displayed also has mushroomed—from 3 to 12 per patient (Goff & Sims, 1993). This is just what one would expect after the role of multiple personality was well publicized in books and films of that time, including *The Three Faces of Eve* and *Sybil*. Moreover, most clinicians have never encountered a case of dissociative identity and the disorder is almost nonexistent outside North America, although in other cultures some people are said to be "possessed" by an alien spirit (Aldridge-Morris, 1989; Kluft, 1991). In Britain, the diagnosis—which some consider "a wacky American fad" (Cohen, 1995)—is rare. In India and Japan it is essentially nonexistent.

To skeptics, these findings point to a cultural phenomenon—a disorder created by therapists in a particular social context (Merskey, 1992). Skeptics note how some therapists go fishing for it: "Have you ever felt like another part of you does things you can't control? Does this part of you have a name? Can I talk to the angry part of you?" Once patients permit a therapist to "talk to the part of you that says those angry things," they have begun acting out the fantasy. Moreover, say skeptics, "It is no coincidence" that multiple personality studies began among hypnosis practitioners (Goff, 1993).

With the dissociative disorders, as with the anxiety disorders, the psychoanalytic and learning perspectives view the symptoms as ways of dealing with anxiety. Psychoanalysts see them as defenses against the anxiety caused by the eruption of unacceptable impulses. Learning theorists see them as behaviors reinforced by anxiety reduction.

Others view dissociative disorders as what psychiatrist Frank Putnam (1995) calls "posttraumatic disorders"—a natural, protective response to "histories of childhood trauma." People diagnosed as having dissociative identity disorder are mostly women who reportedly suffered physical, sexual, or emotional abuse as children (Gleaves, 1996). Perhaps, then, multiple personalities are the desperate efforts of the traumatized to flee inward. Perhaps alternative personalities allow traumatic repressed memories to resurface. Maladaptive as they may be, perhaps such psychological disorders express our human struggle to cope with the stresses of life.

Or perhaps, say skeptics, the condition is either contrived by fantasy-prone, emotionally variable people, or constructed out of the therapist-patient interaction. "This epidemic will end in the way that the witch craze ended in Salem," predicts psychiatrist Paul McHugh (1995b). "The [multiple personality] phenomena will be seen as manufactured, the 'repressed memory' explanation will be recognized as misguided, and psychiatrists will become immunized against the practices that generated these artifacts."

> "Though this be madness, yet there is method in 't."
>
> **WILLIAM SHAKESPEARE**
> *HAMLET*
> 1600

SUMMING UP

Under stress, a person's conscious awareness may become dissociated (separated) from previous memories, thoughts, and feelings. *Dissociative amnesia* involves selective forgetting, usually in response to stress. *Dissociative fugue* involves not only forgetting one's identity but also fleeing one's home. Most mysterious of all dissociative disorders are cases of *dissociative identity disorder*. The afflicted person is said to have two or more distinct personalities, with the original typically unaware of the other(s). Skeptics question whether this disorder may be a cultural phenomenon, finding it suspicious that the disorder has recently become popular.

KEY TERMS AND CONCEPTS dissociative disorders, dissociative amnesia, dissociative fugue, dissociative identity disorder

mood disorders
psychological disorders characterized by emotional extremes. See major depressive disorder, mania, and bipolar disorder.

major depressive disorder
a mood disorder in which a person, for no apparent reason, experiences two or more weeks of depressed moods, feelings of worthlessness, and diminished interest or pleasure in most activities.

mania
a mood disorder marked by a hyperactive, wildly optimistic state.

bipolar disorder
a mood disorder in which the person alternates between the hopelessness and lethargy of depression and the overexcited state of mania. Formerly called manic-depressive disorder.

For some people, recurring depression during winter's dark months constitutes a seasonal affective disorder. For others, winter darkness means more blue moods: "Have you cried today?" Percent of Americans answering yes.

	Men	Women
August	4%	7%
December	8%	21%

Source: TIME/CNN survey, 1994

Mood Disorders

In the Western world, more and more youth and younger adults have been suffering depression. What forms does depression take? What might explain depression and its rising incidence?

The emotional extremes of mood disorders come in two principal forms: (1) *major depressive disorder*, in which the person experiences prolonged hopelessness and lethargy until eventually rebounding to normality; and (2) *bipolar disorder* (formerly called *manic depressive disorder*), in which the person alternates between depression and *mania*, an overexcited, hyperactive state.

Major Depressive Disorder

Perhaps you know what depression feels like. If you are like most college students, at some time during this year—more likely the dark months of winter than the bright days of summer—you will probably experience a few of the symptoms of depression (Beck & Young, 1978). You may feel deeply discouraged about the future, dissatisfied with your life, or isolated from others. You may lack the energy to get things done or even to force yourself out of bed; be unable to concentrate, eat, or sleep normally; or even wonder if you would be better off dead. Perhaps academic success came easily to you in high school, and now you find that disappointing grades jeopardize your goals. Perhaps you feel lonely and isolated as a "nontraditional" student—returning after attending to other work or family commitments. Perhaps social difficulties, such as loneliness or the breakup of a romance, have plunged you into despair. And maybe your brooding has at times only worsened your self-torment.

If so, you are not alone. Depression is the "common cold" of psychological disorders—an expression that effectively describes its pervasiveness, but not its seriousness. Although phobias are more common, depression is the number one reason why people seek mental health services.

Depression can be an appropriate response to profoundly sad events, such as a significant loss or bereavement. To feel bad in reaction to painful events is to be in touch with reality. In such times, depression is like a car's low-oil-pressure light—a signal that warns us to stop and take protective measures. Depression is a sort of psychic hibernation: It slows us down, avoids attracting predators, and evokes support. To grind to a halt and ruminate, as depressed people do, is to reassess one's life when feeling threatened. Biologically speaking, the purpose of life is not happiness but survival and reproduction. From this perspective, there is sense to suffering.

But when does this response become seriously maladaptive? The line separating life's normal "downs" from major depression is difficult to define. Joy, contentment, sadness, and despair are different points on a continuum, points at which any of us may be found at any given moment. On that continuum, between the temporary blue moods we all experience and the crushing impact of major depression, is a condition called *dysthymic disorder*—a down-in-the-dumps mood that fills most of the day, nearly every day, for two years or more. Although less disabled than people with major depression, those with dysthymic disorder tend to experience chronic low energy and self-esteem, have difficulty concentrating or making decisions, and sleep and eat too much or too little.

Major depressive disorder occurs when signs of depression (including lethargy, feelings of worthlessness, or loss of interest in family, friends, and activities) last two weeks or more without any notable cause. The difference between a blue mood after bad news and a mood disorder is like the difference between gasping for breath for a few minutes after a hard run and being chronically short of breath.

> "My life had come to a sudden stop. I was able to breathe, to eat, to drink, to sleep. I could not, indeed, help doing so; but there was no real life in me."
>
> **LEO TOLSTOY**
> *MY CONFESSION*
> 1887

Bipolar Disorder

With or without therapy, episodes of major depression usually end. Depressed people typically rebound—usually by returning to their previous behavior patterns. However, some people rebound to or from the opposite emotional extreme—a euphoric, hyperactive, wildly optimistic state of mania. If depression is living in slow motion, mania is fast forward. Alternation between depression and mania signals bipolar disorder. During the manic phase of bipolar disorder, the person is typically overtalkative, overactive, elated (though easily irritated if crossed), has little need for sleep, and shows fewer sexual inhibitions. Speech is loud, flighty, and hard to interrupt.

CLOSE-UP

Suicide

*"But life, being weary of these worldly bars,
Never lacks power to dismiss itself."*
WILLIAM SHAKESPEARE
JULIUS CAESAR
1599

Each year some three-quarters of a million wearied, despairing people worldwide will say no to life by electing a permanent solution to what may be a temporary problem (Retterstøl, 1993). In retrospect, families and friends may recall signs they believe should have fore-warned them—verbal hints, giving away possessions, or withdrawal and preoccupation with death. Most people who kill themselves have been depressed. One-third have tried suicide before.

Few people who talk of suicide or think suicidal thoughts (a number that includes one-third of all adolescents and college students) actually attempt suicide, and few of those who attempt it succeed in killing themselves (Centers for Disease Control, 1989; Westefeld & Furr, 1987). Still, most individuals who do commit suicide have talked of it. And any who do threaten suicide are at least sending a signal of their desperate or despondent feelings.

To find out who commits suicide, researchers have compared the suicide rates of different groups.

- **National Differences** The suicide rates of England, Italy, and Spain are little more than half those of Canada, Australia, and the United States; Austrian, Danish, and Finnish suicide rates are nearly double (U.S. Bureau of the Census, 1996).

- **Racial Differences** In the United States, whites are twice as likely as blacks to kill themselves (Bureau of the Census, 1996).

- **Gender Differences** Women are much more likely than men to attempt suicide. Depending on the country, however, men are two to four times more likely to succeed (Figure 15.4). (Men are more likely to use foolproof methods, such as firing a bullet into the head, the method of choice in 6 of 10 U.S. suicides.)

- **Age Differences** Due partly to improved reporting (Gist & Welch, 1989), the known suicide rate among 15- to 19-year-olds has more than doubled in the United States since 1950. It now nearly equals the traditionally higher suicide rate among adults (Figure 15.5). In Canada, the suicide rate among 15- to 18-year-olds has increased sixfold since 1955 (NFFRE, 1996).

- **Other Group Differences** Suicide rates are much higher among the rich, the nonreligious, and those who are single, widowed, or divorced (Hoyer & Lund, 1993; Stack, 1992; Stengel, 1981). In both the United States and Australia, the teen suicide surge is almost entirely among males (Hassan & Carr, 1989).

People who commit suicide often do so not while in the depths of depression, when energy and initiative are lacking, but when they begin to rebound and become capable of following through. Teenage suicides may follow a traumatic event, such as a romantic breakup or a guilt-provoking antisocial act; they are often linked with drug and alcohol abuse (Fowler & others, 1986; Kolata, 1986). Compared with people who suffer no disorder, alcoholics are roughly 100 times more likely to commit suicide, as some 3 percent of them do (Murphy & Wetzel, 1990). Even among those who have attempted suicide, alcoholics are five times more likely than non-alcoholics eventually to kill themselves (Beck & Steer, 1989). Among the elderly, suicide is sometimes chosen as an alternative to future suffering. In people of all ages, suicide is not necessarily an act of hostility or revenge, as many people think, but may be a way of switching off unendurable pain (Shneidman, 1987).

Social suggestion may trigger the final act. Following highly publicized suicides and TV programs featuring suicide, known suicides increase. So do fatal auto "accidents" and private airplane crashes.

Figure **15.4**

Suicide rates by gender and age In the United States, suicide rates are higher among males than among females. The highest rates of all are found among older men. (From Bureau of the Census, 1996.)

Suicides per 100,000 people

The higher suicide rate among men greatly increases in late adulthood

70
60
50
40
30
20
10
0

15–24 25–34 35–44 45–54 55–64 65–74 75–84 85+

Age

■ Males   ■ Females

Figure **15.5**

Increasing rates of teen suicide Teen suicide has soared since 1960. (From National Center for Health Statistics.)

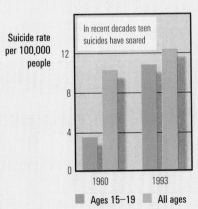

In recent decades teen suicides have soared

Suicide rate per 100,000 people

12

8

4

0

1960   1993

■ Ages 15–19   ■ All ages

One of mania's maladaptive symptoms is grandiose optimism and self-esteem, which may lead to reckless spending and investment sprees. Although people in a manic state find advice irritating, they need protection from their own poor judgment. In milder forms, however, the energy and free-flowing thinking of mania can fuel creativity. Bipolar disorder is especially common among creative artists (Jamison, 1993, 1995). George Frideric Handel (1685–1759), who many believe suffered a mild form of bipolar disorder, composed his nearly four-hour-long *Messiah* during three weeks of intense, creative energy (Keynes, 1980). Creative professionals who rely on precision and logic (people like architects, designers, and journalists) are less vulnerable to bipolar disorder than are those who rely on emotional expression and vivid imagery (people like poets, novelists, and entertainers), reports Arnold Ludwig (1995).

"All the people in history,
literature, art, whom I most admire:
Mozart, Shakespeare, Homer,
El Greco, St. John, Chekhov,
Gregory of Nyssa, Dostoevsky,
Emily Brontë: not one
of them would qualify for a
mental-health certificate."

MADELEINE L'ENGLE
A CIRCLE OF QUIET
1972

It is as true of emotions as all else: What goes up comes down. Before long, the elated mood either returns to normal or plunges into a brief depression. Though as maladaptive as major depression, bipolar disorder is much less common, occurring in about 1 percent of the population. Unlike major depression, bipolar disorder afflicts as many men as women.

Explaining Mood Disorders

Because depression profoundly affects so many people, it has been the subject of thousands of studies. Psychologists are working to develop a theory of mood disorders that will suggest ways to treat or prevent them. Researcher Peter Lewinsohn and his colleagues (1985) summarized the facts that any theory of depression must explain. Among them are the following:

- **Many behavioral and cognitive changes accompany depression.** Depressed people are inactive and unmotivated. They also are especially sensitive to negative happenings, expect negative outcomes, and are more likely to recall negative information. When the depression lifts, these behavioral and cognitive accompaniments disappear.

- **Depression is widespread.** Its commonality suggests that its causes, too, must be common.

- **Compared with men, women are twice as vulnerable to major depression, even more so if they have been depressed before** (Figure 15.6). In general, women are most vulnerable to passive disorders—internalized states, such as depression, anxiety, and inhibited sexual desire. Men's disorders are more active—alcohol abuse, antisocial conduct, lack of impulse control (see Table 15.3, page 484). Curiously, among college students the gender difference in depression is quite small (Regeth & Lewis, 1995).

- **Most major depressive episodes last less than 3 months.** Although therapy can speed recovery, most people suffering major depression return to normal without professional help. The plague of depression comes and, a few weeks or months later, it usually goes.

- **Stressful events related to work, marriage, and close relationships often precede depression.** A family member's death, a wage cut, or a physical assault increase one's risk of depression (Shrout & others, 1989). National samples of Israelis, whose tiny nation is a living stress laboratory, revealed greater feelings of depression after the outbreak of the 1982 Israel-Lebanon war (Hobfoll & others, 1989). Note, too, the high rate of depression among people in strife-torn Beirut (Figure 15.6).

Figure 15.6

Gender and depression
Interviews with 38,000 adults in ten countries confirm what many smaller studies have found: women have double men's risk of major depression. Note, too, that lifetime risk of depressions varies by culture—from 1.5 percent in Taiwan to 19 percent in Beirut. (Data from Weissman & others, 1996).

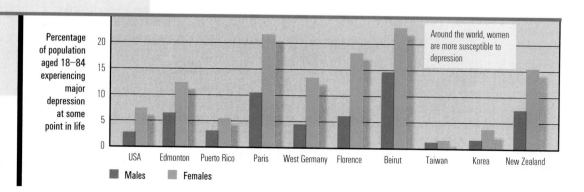

To these facts we can add one more: With each new generation, the rate of depression is increasing and the disorder is striking earlier (now often in the late teens). It's true not only in Canada and the United States but also in Germany, Italy, France, Lebanon, New Zealand, Taiwan, and Puerto Rico (Cross-National Collaborative Group, 1992). In North America, today's young adults are three times as likely as their grandparents to report recently—or ever—suffering depression (despite the grandparents' having had many more years at risk). In one National Institute of Mental Health study of 18,244 Americans, only 1 percent of those born before 1905 had suffered major depression by age 75. Of those born since 1955, 6 percent had been depressed by age 25. The increase appears genuine, *not* primarily a result of younger adults' greater willingness to admit depression. The increasing rate of depression appears in a dramatic rise in the proportion of psychiatric patients with mood disorders. In a survey of North American psychiatric teaching hospitals, mood disorder diagnoses rose from 10 percent of patients in 1972 to 44 percent in 1990 (Stoll & others, 1993).

As you might expect, researchers understand and interpret these facts in ways that reflect their different perspectives. To explain depression, psychoanalytic theory applies Freud's ideas about the importance of early childhood experiences and unconscious impulses. It suggests that depression occurs when significant losses evoke feelings associated with losses experienced in childhood. Loss of a romantic relationship or a job might evoke feelings associated with the loss of the intimate relationship with one's mother. Alternatively, unresolved anger toward one's parents might be turned inward against the self. Today's bio-psycho-social perspective is replacing these Freudian explanations of depression with biological and cognitive explanations.

The Biological Perspective

Most of the mental health research dollars of late have funded explorations of biological influences on mood disorders. Depression is a whole-body disorder, involving genetic predispositions, biochemical imbalances, melancholy mood, and negative thoughts.

Genetic Influences

We have long known that mood disorders run in families. The risk of major depression and bipolar disorder increases if you have a parent or sibling who became depressed before age 30 (Pauls & others, 1992; Weissman & others, 1986). If one identi-

cal twin is diagnosed as suffering major depressive disorder, the chances are about 1 in 2 that at some time the other twin will be, too. If one identical twin has bipolar disorder, the chances are 7 in 10 that the other twin will at some point be diagnosed similarly. Among fraternal twins, the corresponding odds are just under 1 in 5 (Tsuang & Faraone, 1990). The greater similarity of identical twins' depressive tendencies even occurs among twins reared apart (DiLalla & others, 1996). Moreover, adopted people who suffer a mood disorder often have close biological relatives who suffer mood disorders, become alcoholic, or commit suicide (Wender & others, 1986).

A search for the genes that put people at risk for depression is now under way. At least fifteen groups worldwide are sleuthing the genes that make one vulnerable to bipolar disorder (Veggeberg, 1996). To tease out which genes are implicated, researchers use *linkage analysis*. First, they find families that have had the disorder across several generations. Then they draw blood from both affected and unaffected family members and examine their DNA, looking for differences.

The Depressed Brain

Genes act by directing biochemical events that, down the line, influence behavior. The biochemical key is the neurotransmitters, those messenger molecules that shuttle signals between nerve cells. Norepinephrine, a neurotransmitter that increases arousal and boosts mood, is overabundant during mania and scarce during depression. A second

With each new generation, the rate of depression is increasing and the disorder is striking earlier (now often in the late teens).

About 50 percent of those who recover from depression will suffer another episode within two years. Recovery is more likely to be enduring the longer patients stay well, the fewer their previous episodes, the less stress they experience, and the more social support they have (Belsher & Costello, 1988).

Gene-hunters' pursuit of bipolar-DNA links Linkage studies seek to identify aberrant genes in family members suffering the disorder. The Pennsylvania Amish—an isolated population sharing a common life-style and some vulnerability to the disorder—have been among the volunteer subjects.

Figure **15.7**

The ups and downs of bipolar disorder PET scans show that brain energy consumption rises and falls with the patient's emotional switches. Red areas are where the brain rapidly consumes glucose. (Courtesy of Drs. Lewis Baxter and Michael E. Phelps, UCLA School of Medicine.)

| **Depressed state** | **Manic state** | **Depressed state** |
| (17-May-83) | (18-May-83) | (27-May-83) |

neurotransmitter, serotonin, also appears scarce during depression. Drugs that alleviate mania reduce norepinephrine; drugs that relieve depression tend to increase norepinephrine or serotonin supplies by blocking either their reuptake (as Prozac, Zoloft, and Paxil do with serotonin) or their chemical breakdown. Repetitive physical exercise, such as jogging, also increases serotonin and helps reduce depression (Jacobs, 1994).

Using the new scanning machines, researchers are spotting neurological signs of depression. In recent studies, the brains of depressed people have been found to be less active, indicating a slowed-down state (Figure 15.7). The left frontal lobe, which is active during positive emotions, is likely to be inactive (Davidson, 1992). MRI scans have even shown the frontal lobes to be 7 percent smaller in severely depressed patients (Coffey & others, 1993).

The Social-Cognitive Perspective

Some people slide into depression for no obvious reason, even when life has been going well. Often, however, biological factors are linked with psychological reactions to experience (Figure 15.8). The

Figure **15.8**

Depression—an ailing mind in an ailing body Altering any one component of the chemistry-cognition-mood circuit can alter the others.

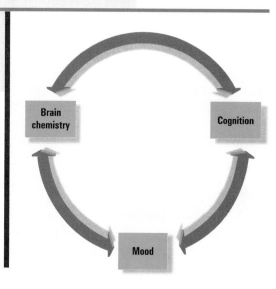

mind's negative thoughts somehow influence biochemical events that in a vicious cycle amplify depressing thoughts.

Recent research reveals how *self-defeating beliefs* feed the vicious cycle. Depressed people view life through dark glasses. Their intensely negative assumptions about themselves, their situations, and their futures lead them to magnify bad experiences and minimize good ones. Listen to Norman, a Canadian college professor recalling his depression:

> I [despaired] of ever being human again. I honestly felt subhuman, lower than the lowest vermin. Furthermore, I was self-deprecatory and could not understand why anyone would want to associate with me, let alone love me. . . . I was positive that I was a fraud and a phony and that I didn't deserve my Ph.D. I didn't deserve to have tenure; I didn't deserve to be a Full Professor. . . . I didn't deserve the research grants I had been awarded; I couldn't understand how I had written books and journal articles that I had and how they had been accepted for publication. I must have conned a lot of people. (Endler, 1982, pp. 45–49)

Self-defeating beliefs may arise from *learned helplessness*. As we saw in Chapter 14, both dogs and humans act depressed, passive, and withdrawn after experiencing uncontrollable painful events. Women more often than men have been abused or made to feel helpless, which may help explain why women have been twice as vulnerable to depression as have men (Nolen-Hoeksema, 1990, and see page 470). (Another explanation is that men more often suppress their negative feelings, act them out, or drown them in alcohol.)

Negative Thoughts Feed Negative Moods

Why do life's unavoidable failures lead some people, but not others, to become depressed? The difference lies partly with people's *attributions* of blame. We have some choice of whom or what to blame for our failures. If you fail a test and blame yourself, you may feel stupid and depressed. If you externalize the blame—perhaps attributing your failure to an unfair test—you are more likely to feel angry.

"A recipe for severe depression is preexisting pessimism encountering failure," notes Martin Seligman (1991, p. 78). Depression is often brought on by stressful experiences—losing a job, getting divorced or rejected, physical trauma—anything that disrupts your sense of who you are and why you are a worthy human being (Hamilton & others, 1993; Kendler & others, 1993). Such brooding after failure can be adaptive; insights gained during times of depressed inactivity may later enable better strategies for interacting with the world. But depression-prone people respond to bad events in an especially self-focused, self-blaming way (Pyszczynski & others, 1991; Wood & others, 1990a,b). Their self-esteem fluctuates more rapidly up with boosts and down with threats (Butler & others, 1994). When down, their brooding amplifies negative feelings, which in turn trigger depression's other cognitive and behavioral symptoms.

This phenomenon also helps explain women's doubled risk of depression. When trouble strikes, women tend to think, men tend to act. A woman may ruminate and act anxious or depressed, whereas a man may distract himself by drinking, delving into work, and playing and watching sports (Seligman, 1994).

None of us is immune to the dejection, diminished self-esteem, and negative thinking brought on by rejection or defeat. As Edward Hirt and his colleagues (1992) demonstrated, even small losses can temporarily sour our thinking. They studied some avid Indiana University basketball fans who seemed to regard the team as an extension of themselves. After the fans were depressed by watching their team lose, or elated by a victory, the researchers asked them to predict the team's future performance, and their own. After a loss, the fans offered bleaker assessments not only of the team's future, but also of their own likely performance at throwing darts, solving anagrams, and getting a date. When things aren't going our way, it may seem as though they never will. For the truly depressed, these feelings persist for weeks on end.

Depressed people tend to explain bad events in terms that are *stable* ("It's going to last forever"), *global* ("It's going to affect everything I do"), and *internal* ("It's all my fault"). Lyn Abramson, Gerald Metalsky, and Lauren Alloy (1989) theorize that the result of these pessimistic, overgeneralized, self-blaming attributions is a depressing sense of hopelessness. If you tend to see bad grades, social rejection, and work problems as inevitable and your own fault, and if you ruminate about such things, then when bad events happen you will experience a bad case of the blues.

In research demonstrating this effect, Susan Nolen-Hoeksema and Jannay Morrow (1991) happened to assess Stanford University students' moods and ruminations 2 weeks before the 1989 earthquake devastated much of their area. Those identified as prone to brood over negative events showed more symptoms of depression both 10 days and 7 weeks after the earthquake. If you have an optimistic way of interpreting events, a failure or stress is unlikely to provoke depression (Seligman, 1991). Even if you do get depressed, you are more likely to recover quickly (Metalsky & others, 1993; Needles & Abramson, 1990).

Martin Seligman (1991, 1995) has argued that depression is common among young Westerners because of epidemic hopelessness, which stems from the rise of individualism and the decline of commitment to religion and family. When facing failure or rejection, contends Seligman, the self-focused individual takes on personal responsibility for problems and has nothing to fall back on for hope. In non-Western cultures, where close-knit relationships and cooperation are the norm, major depression is less common and less tied to self-blame over personal failure. In Japan, for example, depressed people instead tend to report feeling shame over letting others down (Draguns, 1990a).

Negative Moods Feed Negative Thoughts

There is, however, a chicken-and-egg problem with the social-cognitive explanation of depression. Self-defeating beliefs, self-blame, and negative at-

"I have learned to accept my mistakes by referring them to a personal history which was not of my making."

B. F. SKINNER (1983)

tributions surely do support depression. But do they *cause* depression, any more than a speedometer's reading 70 mph causes a car's speed? Peter Barnett and Ian Gotlib (1988) note that such cognitions are *indicators* of depression. Depressing thoughts *coincide* with a depressed mood. But before or after being depressed, people's thoughts are less negative. Perhaps this is because, as we noted in our discussion of mood-congruent memory (pages 290–291), a depressed mood triggers negative thoughts. If you temporarily put people in a bad or sad mood, their memories, judgments, and expectations are suddenly more pessimistic.

Joseph Forgas and his associates (1984) provided a striking demonstration of the mood effect. Subjects who had been put in a good or bad mood via hypnosis then watched a videotape of themselves talking with someone the day before. The happy subjects detected in themselves more instances of positive behavior than of negative; the unhappy subjects more often saw themselves behaving negatively (Figure 15.9). Thus, even when viewing themselves on videotape, people judge themselves more negatively when feeling depressed.

Depression's Vicious Cycle

So, there is two-way traffic between depressed mood and negative thinking. Depression causes self-focused negative thinking, and a self-focused, self-blaming style of explaining events puts one at risk for depression when bad events strike.

Another source of depression's vicious cycle is its social consequences. Being withdrawn, self-focused, and complaining elicits rejection (Gotlib

> "Man never reasons so much and becomes so introspective as when he suffers, since he is anxious to get at the cause of his sufferings."
>
> LUIGI PIRANDELLO
> *SIX CHARACTERS IN SEARCH OF AN AUTHOR*
> 1922

Figure **15.9**

The mood effect A happy or depressed mood strongly influences people's rating of their own behavior. In this experiment, those in a hypnotically induced good mood detected many more positive than negative behaviors. The reverse was true for those in a bad mood. (From Forgas & others, 1984.)

Figure **15.10**

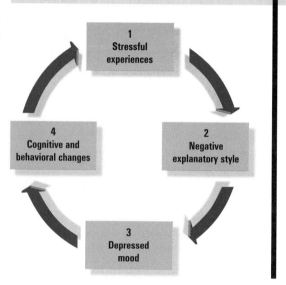

The vicious cycle of depression This cycle can be broken at any point. The next chapter describes some therapeutic techniques. (Adapted from Lewinsohn & others, 1985.)

& Hammen, 1992; Segrin & Dillard, 1992). In one study, researchers Stephen Strack and James Coyne (1983) noted that "depressed persons induced hostility, depression, and anxiety in others and got rejected. Their guesses that they were not accepted were not a matter of cognitive distortion." Weary of the depressed person's fatigue, hopeless attitude, and lethargy, a spouse may threaten to leave or a boss may begin to question the person's competence. Indeed, depressed people are at high risk for divorce and job loss—events that only compound their depression. Misery may love another's company, but company does not love another's misery.

We can now assemble the pieces of the depression puzzle (Figure 15.10): (1) Stressful events interpreted through (2) a ruminating, pessimistic explanatory style create (3) a hopeless, depressed state that (4) hampers the way the person thinks and acts. This, in turn, fuels (1) more negative experiences. It's a cycle we can all recognize. Bad moods feed on themselves: When we *feel* down we *think* negatively and remember bad experiences. On the brighter side, we can break the cycle of depression at any of these points—by moving to a different environment, by reversing our self-blame and negative attributions, by turning our attention outward, or by engaging in more pleasant activities and more competent behavior.

CLOSE-UP

Loneliness

Loneliness—the painful awareness that one's social relationships are deficient—is both a contributor to depression and its own problem. The deficiency stems from a mismatch between one's actual and desired social contacts. One person may feel lonely when isolated and another may feel lonely in a crowd.

Aloneness often breeds loneliness. People who are alone—unmarried, unattached, and often young—are more likely to feel lonely. Dutch psychologist Jenny de Jong-Gierveld (1987) has speculated that the emphasis on individual fulfillment and the downgrading of stable relationships and commitment to others are "loneliness-provoking factors."

People commonly experience one or more of four types of loneliness (Beck & Young, 1978). To be lonely is to feel *excluded* from a group you would like to belong to; to feel *unloved* and uncared about by those around you; to feel *constricted* and unable to share your private concerns with anyone; or to feel *alienated*, or different, from those in your community.

Like depressed people, lonely people tend to blame themselves, attributing their deficient social relationships to their own inadequacies (Snodgrass, 1987). There may be a basis for this self-blame:

Chronically lonely people tend to be shy, self-conscious, and lacking in self-esteem, and to be perceived as less socially competent and attractive (Cheek & Melchior, 1990; Lau & Gruen, 1992; Vaux, 1988). They often find it hard to introduce themselves, make phone calls, and participate in groups (Rook, 1984; Spitzberg & Hurt, 1987). In addition, their belief in their social unworthiness restricts their noticing and remembering positive feedback and from taking steps that would reduce their loneliness (Frankel & Prentice-Dunn, 1990). Thus, factors that work to create and maintain the cycle of depression can also produce a cycle of loneliness.

Winston Churchill called depression a "black dog" that periodically hounded him. Poet Emily Dickinson was so afraid of bursting into tears in public that she spent much of her adult life in seclusion (Patterson, 1951). Abraham Lincoln was so withdrawn and brooding as a young man that his friends feared he might take his own life (Kline, 1974). As each of these lives reminds us, people can and do struggle through depression. Most regain their capacity to love, to work, and even to succeed at the highest levels.

SUMMING UP

Major Depressive Disorder In major depression, the person—without apparent reason—descends for weeks or months into deep unhappiness, lethargy, and feelings of worthlessness before rebounding to normality. Although less disabling, dysthymic disorder is marked by chronic low energy and poor self-esteem.

Bipolar Disorder In the less common bipolar disorder, the person alternates between the hopelessness and lethargy of depression and the hyperactive, wildly optimistic, impulsive phase of mania.

Explaining Mood Disorders Current research on depression is vigorously exploring two sets of influences. The first focuses on genetic predispositions and neurotransmitter abnormalities. The second views the cycle of depression from a social-cognitive perspective, in light of cyclic self-defeating beliefs, learned helplessness, negative attributions, and aversive experiences.

KEY TERMS AND CONCEPTS mood disorders, major depressive disorder, mania, bipolar disorder

schizophrenia
a group of severe psychotic disorders characterized by disorganized and delusional thinking, disturbed perceptions, and inappropriate emotions and actions.

delusions
false beliefs, often of persecution or grandeur, that may accompany psychotic disorders.

Schizophrenia

Schizophrenia is a psychotic disorder in which a person loses contact with reality, experiencing grossly irrational ideas or distorted perceptions. What forms does schizophrenia take? And what are its possible causes?

If depression is the common cold of psychological disorders, chronic schizophrenia is the cancer. About 1 in 100 people will develop schizophrenia, joining the millions across the world who have suffered one of humanity's most dreaded disorders. It typically strikes during adolescence or young adulthood. It knows no national boundaries, and it affects males and females about equally.

Symptoms of Schizophrenia

Literally translated, schizophrenia means "split mind." It refers not to a multiple-personality split but rather to a split from reality that shows itself in disorganized thinking, disturbed perceptions, and inappropriate emotions and actions.

Disorganized Thinking

Imagine trying to communicate with Maxine, a young woman whose thoughts spill out in no logical order. Her biographer, Susan Sheehan (1982, p. 25; 1995), observed her saying aloud to no one in particular,

"This morning, when I was at Hillside [Hospital], I was making a movie. I was surrounded by movie stars. The X-ray technician was Peter Lawford. The security guard was Don Knotts. That Indian doctor in Building 40 was Lou Costello. I'm Mary Poppins. Is this room painted blue to get me upset? My grandmother died four weeks after my eighteenth birthday."

As this strange monologue illustrates, the schizophrenia patient's thinking is fragmented, bizarre, and distorted by false beliefs, called delusions ("I'm Mary Poppins"). Jumping from one idea to another may occur even within sentences, creating a sort of "word salad." One young man begged for "a little more allegro in the treatment," and suggested that "liberationary movement with a view to the widening of the horizon" will "ergo extort some wit in lectures." Those with paranoid tendencies may have delusions of persecution or grandeur.

Many psychologists believe disorganized thoughts result from a breakdown in selective attention. Recall from Chapter 6 that we normally have a remarkable capacity for selective attention—for, say, giving our undivided attention to one voice at a party while filtering out competing sensory stimuli. Schizophrenia sufferers have impaired attention (Gjerde, 1983). Thus, an irrelevant stimulus or an extraneous part of the preceding thought easily distracts them. Minute stimuli, such as the grooves on a brick or the inflections of a voice, may distract attention from the whole scene or from the speaker's meaning. As one former schizophrenia patient recalled, "What had happened to me . . . was a breakdown in the filter, and a hodge-podge of unrelated stimuli were distracting me from things which should have had my undivided attention" (MacDonald, 1960, p. 218).

Art by people diagnosed with schizophrenia Commenting on the kind of art work shown here, poet John Ashbery wrote: "The lure of the work is strong, but so is the terror of the unanswerable riddles it proposes."

Disturbed Perceptions

A person with schizophrenia may perceive things that are not there.

Such hallucinations (sensory experiences without sensory stimulation) are usually auditory. The person may hear voices that make insulting statements or give orders. The voices may tell the patient that she is bad or that he must burn himself with a cigarette lighter. Less commonly, people see, feel, taste, or smell things that are nonexistent. Such hallucinations have been compared to dreams breaking into waking consciousness. When the unreal seems real, the resulting perceptions are at best bizarre and at worst terrifying.

Inappropriate Emotions and Actions

The emotions of schizophrenia are often utterly inappropriate. Maxine's emotions seemed split off from reality. She laughed after recalling her grandmother's death. On occasion, she became angry for no apparent reason or cried when others laughed. Other victims of schizophrenia sometimes lapse into *flat affect*, a zombielike state of apparent apathy.

Motor behavior also may be inappropriate. The person may perform senseless, compulsive acts, such as continually rocking or rubbing an arm. Those who exhibit *catatonia* may remain motionless for hours on end and then become agitated.

As you can imagine, disorganized thinking, disturbed perceptions, and inappropriate emotions and actions disrupt social relationships. During their most severe periods, people with schizophrenia live in a private inner world, preoccupied with illogical ideas and unreal images. Although some people suffer from schizophrenia only intermittently, others remain socially withdrawn and isolated throughout much of their lives. Rarely is schizophrenia a one-time episode that is "cured," never to return.

Types of Schizophrenia

We have described schizophrenia as if it were a single disorder. Actually, it is a cluster of disorders that have common features but also some distinguishing symptoms. Schizophrenia patients with *positive symptoms* are disorganized and deluded in their talk or are prone to inappropriate laughter, tears, or rage. Those with *negative symptoms* have toneless voices, expressionless faces, or mute and rigid bodies. Because schizophrenia is more than one disorder (Table 15.2), there could be more than one cause.

Sometimes, as in the case of Maxine, schizophrenia develops gradually, emerging from a long history of social inadequacy (which partially explains why those predisposed to schizophrenia often end up in the lower socioeconomic levels, or even as homeless people). Other times it appears suddenly, seemingly as a reaction to stress. There is a rule that holds true around the world (World Health Organization, 1979): When the schizophrenia is a slow-developing process (called *chronic*, or *process*, schizophrenia), recovery is doubtful. When, in reaction to particular life stresses, a previously well-adjusted person develops schizophrenia rapidly (*acute*, or *reactive*, schizophrenia), recovery is much more likely. Those with chronic schizophrenia often exhibit the negative symptom of withdrawal. The outlook is better for those exhibiting positive symptoms—they more often have a reactive condition that responds to drug therapy (Fenton & McGlashan, 1991, 1994; Fowles, 1992).

Understanding Schizophrenia

Schizophrenia is not only the most dreaded psychological disorder but also one of the most heavily researched. Most new research studies link schizophrenia with brain abnormalities and genetic predispositions.

hallucinations
false sensory experiences, such as seeing something without any external visual stimulus.

Subtypes of Schizophrenia		Table 15.2
Paranoid:	Preoccupation with delusions or hallucinations	
Disorganized:	Disorganized speech or behavior, or flat or inappropriate emotion	
Catatonic:	Immobility (or excessive, purposeless movement), extreme negativism, and/or parrotlike repeating of another's speech or movements	
Undifferentiated or residual:	Schizophrenia symptoms without fitting one of the above types	

Brain Abnormalities

The idea that imbalances in brain chemistry might underlie schizophrenia has long intrigued scientists. Strange behaviors, they knew, could have strange chemical causes. The saying "mad as a hatter" refers to the psychological deterioration of British hatmakers whose brains, it was later discovered, were slowly poisoned as they moistened the brims of mercury-laden felt hats with their lips (Smith, 1983). As we saw on page 234, scientists are beginning to understand the mechanism by which chemicals such as LSD produce hallucinations. These discoveries hint that schizophrenia symptoms might have a biochemical key.

Dopamine Overactivity

One such key to schizophrenia involves the neurotransmitter dopamine. When researchers examined patients' brains after death, they found an excess of receptors for dopamine—in fact, a sixfold excess for the so-called D4 dopamine receptor (Seeman & others, 1993; Wong & others, 1986). Such a high level may intensify brain signals, the researchers speculate, creating schizophrenia's positive symptoms. As we might therefore expect, drugs that block dopamine receptors often lessen schizophrenia symptoms. Drugs that increase dopamine levels, such as amphetamines and cocaine, sometimes intensify schizophrenia symptoms (Swerdlow & Koob, 1987). Such dopamine overactivity may be what makes schizophrenia victims overreact to irrelevant external and internal stimuli.

Brain Anatomy

Modern brain-scanning techniques reveal that many people with chronic schizophrenia have abnormal brain tissue. Some have abnormally low brain activity in the frontal lobes (Pettegrew & others, 1993; Resnick, 1992). One recent study took PET scans of brain activity while people were hallucinating (Silbersweig & others, 1995). When they heard a voice or saw something, the brain became vigorously active in several core regions, including the thalamus, which transmits sensory signals up to the cortex.

Enlarged, fluid-filled areas and a corresponding shrinkage of cerebral tissue seems characteristic of schizophrenia, especially in men (Cannon & Marco, 1994; Elkis & others, 1995). The greater the shrinkage, the worse the thought disorder tends to be (Shenton & others, 1992). The thalamus, too, is smaller than normal, which may explain why people with schizophrenia have difficulty filtering sensory input and focusing attention (Andreasen & others, 1994). The bottom line of various brain studies, reports Nancy Andreasen (1997), is that schizophrenia involves not a single brain abnormality but problems with several brain regions and their interconnections.

Naturally, scientists wonder what causes these brain abnormalities. One possibility is a prenatal problem. People conceived during the peak of the Dutch wartime famine later displayed a doubled rate of schizophrenia (Susser & others, 1996). A midpregnancy viral infection that might impair fetal brain development is another possible culprit (Waddington, 1993). Can you imagine some ways to test this fetal virus idea?

Scientists exploring this possibility have asked the following questions:

- **Are people at increased risk of schizophrenia if, during the middle of their fetal development, their country experienced a flu epidemic?** The repeated answer is yes (Mednick & others, 1994; Murray & others, 1992; Wright & others, 1995).

- **Are those born during the winter and spring months—after the fall-winter flu season—also at increased risk?** The answer is yes, at 5 to 15 percent increased risk (Pulver & others, 1992; Torrey & others, 1977, 1993, 1996; Wright & Murray, 1993).

- **In the southern hemisphere, where the seasons are the reverse of the northern hemisphere, are the months of above-average schizophrenia births similarly reversed?** Again, the answer is yes. In Australia, for example, people born between August and October are at greater risk—unless they migrated from the northern hemisphere, in which case their risk is greater if born between January and March (McGrath & others, 1995).

- **As infectious disease rates have declined, has there been a correlated decline in the later incidence of schizophrenia?** Once again, the answer is yes (Eagles, 1991).

Although schizophrenia has other causes as well (as genetics research makes plain), these converging lines of evidence suggest that prenatal viral infections do play a contributing role.

Genetic Factors

Might people also inherit a predisposition to certain brain abnormalities? The evidence strongly suggests that some do. The 1-in-100 odds of any person's being diagnosed with schizophrenia become 1 in 10 among those who have an afflicted sibling or parent, and close to 1 in 2 among those who have an afflicted identical twin (Figure 15.11). Although barely a dozen such cases are known, it appears that an identical twin of a schizophrenia victim retains that 1-in-2 chance, whether the twins are reared together or apart (Plomin & others, 1997).

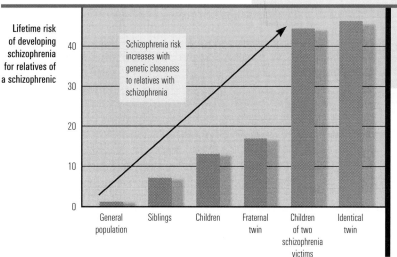

Figure **15.11**

Risk of developing schizophrenia
The lifetime risks of developing schizophrenia vary with one's genetic relatedness to someone having this disorder. (From family and twin studies conducted between 1920 and 1987 in Europe—Irving Gottesman, 1991.)

Curiously, though, even with identical twins there may be a prenatal environmental component. About 60 percent of identical twins share the same placenta. (They usually also have opposite, mirror-imaged, handedness to their co-twin.) If you have an identical twin with schizophrenia, and if you shared a placenta, you are also more likely to share the disorder. Twins who have the same placenta are more likely to experience the same prenatal viruses (Davis & others, 1995a,b). So it's possible that shared germs as well as shared genes produce identical twin similarities.

Adoption studies, however, confirm that the genetic link is real (Gottesman, 1991). Children adopted by someone who develops schizophrenia seldom "catch" the disorder. Rather, adopted children have an elevated risk if a biological parent is diagnosed with schizophrenia. Moreover, several linkage studies have implicated chromosomes 6 and 22 as the site of genes that makes some people susceptible to schizophrenia (DeAngelis, 1997; Lander & Kruglyak, 1995).

The genetic contribution to schizophrenia is beyond question. But the genetic role is not so straightforward as the inheritance of eye color. After all, about half the twins who share identical genes with a schizophrenia victim do *not* develop the disorder. Thus, behavior geneticists Susan Nicol and Irving Gottesman (1983) concluded that some people "have a genetic predisposition to the disorder but that this predisposition by itself is not sufficient for the development of schizophrenia."

Given the genetic influences upon disorders such as schizophrenia and bipolar disorder, might scientists develop genetic tests that reveal who is at risk? If so, will people in the future subject their embryos to genetic testing (and gene repair or abortion if they are at risk for a psychological or physical malady)? Or might they take their egg and sperm to the genetics lab for screening before combining them to produce an embryo? Or might children be tested for genetic risks and given appropriate preventive treatments? Although there is a growing possibility of such a test, the patterns of inheritance seem too complex to expect that a single gene abnormality will prove predictive (Gottesman, 1993). But given the explosion in gene and brain research technologies, scientists are optimistic that schizophrenia will be much better understood by the time we reach the new millenium.

Psychological Factors

If, by themselves, genetically predisposed physiological abnormalities do not cause schizophrenia, neither do psychological factors alone. It remains true, as Nicol and Gottesman (1983) have noted, that "No environmental causes have been discovered that will invariably, or even with moderate probability, produce schizophrenia in persons who are not related to a schizophrenic."

Nevertheless, if genes predispose some people to *react* to particular experiences by developing schizophrenia, then there must be identifiable triggering experiences. Researchers have asked: Can stress trigger schizophrenia? Can difficulties in family communications be a contributing factor?

The answer to each question is a strong maybe. The psychological triggers of schizophrenia have proved elusive, partly because they may vary with the type of schizophrenia and its speed of onset—whether it is a slow-developing, chronic schizophrenia, or a sudden, acute reaction to stress. It is true that young people with schizophrenia tend to have

Schizophrenia in twins   When twins differ, only the one afflicted with schizophrenia typically has enlarged, fluid-filled cranial cavities (Suddath & others, 1990). The difference between the twins implies that some nongenetic factor, such as a virus, is also at work.

Schizophrenia

No schizophrenia

CLOSE-UP

Experiencing Schizophrenia

These recollections by a person who recovered from schizophrenia illustrate some of the thoughts and feelings of those who suffer the positive symptoms of schizophrenia. Note the hallucinations and the delusions of persecution and grandeur.

One night I was invited to listen to a talk by a worker in the foreign service. I was suspicious of him and thought he thought I was a Communist spy. I didn't say anything. I just leaned over and stared at him.

I thought the Government was spying on my room with a telescope in a building across the street. I thought people were loading down my food in the cafeteria with salt. In criminology class I thought the professor and the other students were laughing about me. I thought they were directing the poisoning of my food in the cafeteria. When I went to the cafeteria my hand shook as the waitress poured what I thought was poisonous coffee into my cup. I thought everyone in the cafeteria knew I was going to die. They all thought it was too bad but I was so evil it was necessary.

On a Saturday I drank lemonade to try to neutralize the poison. Then I would take showers to try to sweat the poison out. I was so nervous I could hardly think. I thought I might only have hours left to live. I thought of taking a bus home to my parents. But no, I thought, it was too late for that.

One day when my strange behavior landed me in a jail cell, the walls began to buzz like bees. I felt there were thousands of bees in the walls buzzing. The buzzing went on and on. There was no relief. It was maddening. Finally, I felt my father's hand rest on my head and I felt peace.

When someone asks me to explain schizophrenia I tell them, you know how sometimes in your dreams you are in them yourself and some of them feel like real nightmares? My schizophrenia was like I was walking through a dream. But everything around me was real. At times, today's world seems so boring and I wonder if I would like to step back into the schizophrenic dream, but then I remember all the scary and horrifying experiences. (Excerpted and paraphrased with permission from Stuart Emmons, Craig Geisler, Kalman J. Kaplan, and Martin Harrow, *Living with Schizophrenia*. Muncie, IN: Taylor & Francis, 1997.)

---

unusually disturbed communications with their parents. But is this a cause or a result of their disorder? It is true that stressful experiences, biochemical abnormalities, and schizophrenia's symptoms often occur together. But as the bio-psycho-social perspective emphasizes, the traffic between brain biochemistry and psychological experiences runs both ways, so cause and effect are difficult to sort out. It is true that schizophrenic withdrawal often occurs in adolescence or early adulthood, coinciding with the stresses of having to become independent, assert oneself, and achieve social success and intimacy. So is schizophrenia the maladaptive coping reaction of biologically vulnerable people?

Hoping to identify the psychological causes of schizophrenia, several investigators are now following the development of "high-risk" children, such as those born to a parent with schizophrenia (Erlenmeyer-Kimling & others, 1995; Olin & Mednick, 1996). By comparing the experiences of high-risk and low-risk children who do and do not develop schizophrenia, these researchers are seeking the early warning signs of schizophrenia. So far, these signs seem to include the following:

- A mother whose schizophrenia was severe and long-lasting
- Birth complications and low birth weight
- Separation from parents
- Short attention span and poor muscle coordination
- Disruptive or withdrawn behavior
- Emotional unpredictability
- Poor peer relations

Most of us can relate more easily to the ups and downs of mood disorders than to the strange thoughts, perceptions, and behaviors of schizophrenia. Sometimes our thoughts do jump around, but we do not talk nonsensically. Occasionally we feel unjustly suspicious of someone, but we do not fear that the world is plotting against us. Often our perceptions err, but rarely do we see or hear things that are not there. We have felt regret after laughing at someone's misfortune, but we rarely giggle in response to bad news. At times we just want to be alone, but we do not live in social isolation. However, millions of people around the world do talk strangely, suffer delusions, hear nonexistent voices, see things that are not there, laugh or cry at inappropriate times, or withdraw into private imaginary worlds. Because this is true, the quest to solve the cruel puzzle of schizophrenia continues.

The Genain quadruplets
The odds of any four people picked at random all being diagnosed with schizophrenia are 1 in 100 million. But Nora, Iris, Myra, and Hester Genain have the disease. Two of the sisters have more severe forms of the disorder than the others, suggesting the influence of environmental as well as biological factors.

SUMMING UP

Schizophrenia typically strikes during adolescence. It affects men and women about equally, and it seems to occur in all cultures.

Symptoms of Schizophrenia Schizophrenia shows itself in disorganized thinking (nonsensical talk and delusions, which may stem from a breakdown of selective attention); disturbed perceptions (including hallucinations); and inappropriate emotions and actions. It is rarely a one-time episode.

Types of Schizophrenia Schizophrenia is a set of disorders that emerge either gradually from a chronic history of social inadequacy (in which case the outlook is dim) or suddenly in reaction to stress (in which case the prospects for recovery are brighter).

Understanding Schizophrenia As they have for depression, researchers have linked certain forms of schizophrenia with brain abnormalities, such as enlarged, fluid-filled cerebral cavities or increased receptors for the neurotransmitter dopamine. Twin and adoption studies also point to a genetic predisposition that, in conjunction with environmental factors, may bring about a schizophrenia disorder.

KEY TERMS AND CONCEPTS schizophrenia, delusions, hallucinations

Personality Disorders

Some maladaptive behavior patterns impair people's social functioning without anxiety, depression, or delusions. For society the most troubling of these is the antisocial personality disorder.

Personality disorders are inflexible and enduring patterns of behavior that impair one's social functioning. A person with a *histrionic personality disorder* displays shallow, attention-getting emotions. Histrionic individuals go to great lengths to gain others' praise and reassurance. Those with *narcissistic personality disorder* exaggerate their own importance, aided by success fantasies. They find criticism hard to accept, often reacting with rage or shame. Those with *borderline personality disorder* have an unstable identity, unstable relationships, and unstable emotions. If personality is one's enduring pattern of thinking, feeling, and acting, then a markedly unstable sense of self defines a "borderline personality."

The most frequent of these disorders, and the most troubling to society, is the antisocial personality disorder. The person (formerly called a *sociopath* or a *psychopath*) is typically a male whose lack of conscience becomes plain before age 15, as he begins to lie, steal, fight, or display unrestrained sexual behavior. About half of such children become antisocial adults—unable to keep a job, irresponsible as a spouse and parent, and assaultive or otherwise criminal (Farrington, 1991). When the antisocial personality combines a keen intelligence

Does a full moon trigger "madness" in some people? James Rotton and I. W. Kelly (1985) examined data from 37 studies that related lunar phase to crime, homicides, crisis calls, and mental hospital admissions. Their conclusion: There is virtually no evidence of "moon madness." Nor does lunar phase correlate with suicides, assaults, emergency room visits, or traffic disasters (Byrnes & Kelly, 1992; Kelly & others, 1990; Martin & others, 1992).

personality disorders
psychological disorders characterized by inflexible and enduring behavior patterns that impair social functioning.

antisocial personality disorder
a personality disorder in which the person (usually a man) exhibits a lack of conscience for wrongdoing, even toward friends and family members. May be aggressive and ruthless or a clever con artist.

with amorality, the result may be a charming and clever con artist—or worse.

Despite their antisocial behavior, most criminals do not fit the description of antisocial personality disorder. Most criminals show responsible concern for their friends and family members. Antisocial personalities feel little and fear little. In extreme cases, the results can be tragic. Henry Lee Lucas reported that at age 13 he strangled a woman who refused to have sex with him. He at one time confessed to having bludgeoned, suffocated, stabbed, shot, or mutilated some 360 women, men, and children during his 32 years of crime. During the last 6 years of his reign of terror, Lucas teamed with Elwood Toole, who reportedly slaughtered about 50 people whom he "didn't think was worth living anyhow." It ended when Lucas confessed to stabbing and dismembering his 15-year-old common-law wife, who was Toole's niece.

The antisocial personality expresses little regret over violating others' rights. "Once I've done a crime, I just forget it," said Lucas. Toole was equally matter-of-fact: "I think of killing like smoking a cigarette, like another habit" (Darrach & Norris, 1984).

As with mood disorders and schizophrenia, the antisocial personality disorder is woven of biological as well as psychological strands. Although there is no single gene that codes for a complex behavior such as crime, twin and adoption studies reveal that biological relatives of certain individuals are at increased risk for criminality (Brennan & Mednick, 1993; DiLalla & Gottesman, 1993; Lyons & others, 1995). Their genetic vulnerability appears as a fearless approach to life. When they await aversive events, such as electric shocks or loud noises, they show little autonomic nervous system arousal (Hare, 1975). Even as youngsters, before committing any crime, they react with lower levels of stress hormones than do others their age (Figure 15.12).

Some studies have detected the early signs of antisocial behavior in children as young as ages 3 to 6 (Caspi & others, 1996; Tremblay & others, 1994). Boys who later became aggressive or antisocial as adolescents tended, as young children, to have been impulsive, uninhibited, unconcerned with social rewards, and low in anxiety. If channeled in more productive directions, such fearlessness may lead to courageous heroism or adventurism. Lacking a sense of social responsibility, the same disposition produces a cool con artist or killer (Lykken, 1995).

Perhaps a biologically based fearlessness, as well as early environment, helps explain the reunion of long-separated sisters Joyce Lott, 27, and Mary Jones, 29—in a South Carolina prison where both were sent on drug charges. After a newspaper story about their reunion, their long-lost half-brother Frank Strickland called. He explained it would be a while before he could come see them—because he, too, was in jail, on drug, burglary, and larceny charges (Shepherd & others, 1990).

Genetics alone is hardly the whole story of crime, however. Relative to 1960, the average American in 1995 was twice as likely to be murdered, four times as likely to report being raped, four times as likely to report being robbed, and five times as likely to report being assaulted (FBI *Uniform Crime Reports*). Violent crime is also surging in other Western nations. Yet the human gene pool has hardly changed. Or consider the British social

Figure **15.12**

Cold-blooded arousability and risk of crime Levels of the stress hormone adrenaline were measured in two groups of 13-year-old Swedish boys. In both stressful and nonstressful situations, those who were later convicted of a crime (as 18- to 26-year-olds) showed relatively low arousal. (From Magnusson, 1990.)

Figure **15.13**

Bio-psycho-social roots of crime   Danish male babies whose backgrounds were marked *both* by obstetrical complications and social stresses associated with poverty were twice as likely to be criminal offenders by ages 20 to 22 as those in either the biological or social risk groups. (From Raine & others, 1996.)

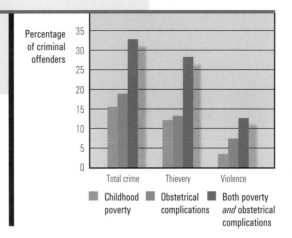

experiment begun in 1787, exiling 160,000 criminals to Australia. The descendants of these exiles, carrying their ancestors' supposed "criminal genes," have helped create a civilized democracy whose crime rate is slightly *lower* than Britain's (Reddy, 1996; *World Atlas*, 1993). Genetic predispositions do put some individuals more at risk for antisocial conduct than others; biological as well as environmental influences explain why 5 to 6 percent of offenders commit 50 to 60 percent of crimes (Lyman, 1996). But we must look to sociocultural factors to explain the modern epidemic of violence.

A recent study of criminal tendencies among young Danish men illustrates the usefulness of a complete bio-psycho-social perspective. A research team led by Adrian Raine (1996) checked criminal records on nearly 400 men at ages 20 to 22, knowing that all had experienced either biological risk factors at birth, such as premature birth, or had come from family backgrounds marked by poverty and family instability. At doubled risk of crime compared to either of these groups were those in a "biosocial" group whose lives were marked by *both* the biological and social risk factors (Figure 15.13).

SUMMING UP

Personality disorders are enduring, maladaptive patterns of behavior that impair social functioning. For society, the most troubling of these is the remorseless and fearless antisocial personality.

KEY TERMS AND CONCEPTS   personality disorders, antisocial personality disorder

Rates of Psychological Disorders

How prevalent are the different psychological disorders? Does risk of a specific disorder vary with one's ethnicity or gender?

How prevalent are the various disorders discussed in this chapter? Who is most vulnerable to them? At what times of life? To answer such questions, the U.S. National Institute of Mental Health (NIMH) undertook during the 1980s a short census of psychological disorders. In five different regions of the country researchers conducted lengthy, structured interviews with a representative sample of people—all told, nearly 20,000 people—and then projected their findings to the entire U.S. population. After asking hundreds of questions that probed for symptoms—"Has there ever been a period of two weeks or more when you felt like you wanted to die?"—the researchers estimated both the current and the lifetime prevalence of various disorders.

How many people suffer, or have suffered, a psychological disorder? More than most of us suppose. Reporting on the NIMH study, Lee Robins and Darrel Regier (1991, p. 329) noted that "one or more of the psychiatric disorders . . . had been experienced at some time in their lives by 32 percent of American adults, and 20 percent had an active disorder." These surprisingly high rates reflect the inclusion of institutionalized as well as community samples, and surely also reflect how well many people manage to hide disorders such as a phobia, alcohol abuse, or depression. Table 15.3 shows the relative prevalence of most of the disorders we

Table 15.3

Percentage of Americans Who Have Ever Experienced Psychological Disorders

Disorder	Ethnicity			Gender		Totals
	White	Black	Hispanic	Men	Women	
Alcohol abuse or dependence	13.6%	13.8%	16.7%	23.8%	4.6%	13.8%
Generalized anxiety	3.4	6.1	3.7	2.4	5.0	3.8
Phobias	9.7	23.4	12.2	10.4	17.7	14.3
Obsessive-compulsive disorder	2.6	2.3	1.8	2.0	3.0	2.6
Mood disorder	8.0	6.3	7.8	5.2	10.2	7.8
Schizophrenic disorders	1.4	2.1	0.8	1.2	1.7	1.5
Antisocial personality disorder	2.6	2.3	3.4	4.5	0.8	2.6

Source: Data from Robins & Regier, 1991. Similar gender differences, though with somewhat higher rates of disorder, come from the U.S. National Comorbidity Survey (Kessler & others, 1994).

have considered among three ethnic groups and among men and women.

The incidence of serious psychological disorders is doubly high among those below the poverty line (Centers for Disease Control, 1992). Like so many other correlations, the poverty-disorder association raises a chicken-and-egg question: Does poverty cause disorders? Or do disorders cause poverty? It's both, though the answer varies with the disorder. Schizophrenia understandably leads to poverty. Yet the stresses and demoralization of poverty can also precipitate disorders, especially depression in women and substance abuse in men (Dohrenwend & others, 1992).

Those who experience a psychological disorder usually do so by early adulthood. "Over 75 percent of our sample with any disorder had experienced its first symptoms by age 24," reported Robins and Regier (1991, p. 331). The symptoms of antisocial personality disorder and of phobias appear earliest, by a median age of 8 and 10, respectively. Symptoms of alcohol abuse, obsessive-compulsive disorder, bipolar disorder, and schizophrenia appear at a median age near 20. Major depression often hits somewhat later, at a median age of 25. Such findings make clear the need for research and treatment to help the growing number of peo-

ple, especially youth and young adults, who suffer the bewilderment and pain of a psychological disorder.

Although mindful of the pain, we can also be encouraged by the many successful people—including Leonardo da Vinci, Isaac Newton, and Leo Tolstoy—who pursued brilliant careers while enduring psychological difficulties. The bewilderment, fear, and sorrow caused by psychological disorders are real. But, as the next chapter shows, hope is also real.

SUMMING UP

A 1980s National Institute of Mental Health survey of nearly 20,000 institutionalized and community residents revealed that 1 in 3 U.S. adults had experienced a psychological disorder and that 1 in 5 were currently experiencing a disorder. The three most common were phobias and mood disorder (with women outnumbering men 2 to 1) and alcohol abuse or dependence (with men outnumbering women 5 to 1).

TERMS AND CONCEPTS TO REMEMBER

CRITICAL THINKING EXERCISE
by Richard O. Straub

Now that you have read and reviewed Chapter 15, take your learning a step further by testing your critical thinking skills on the following perspective-taking exercise.

Since her divorce three months ago, 65-year-old Phyllis has constantly felt tired, has had difficulty sleeping and eating, and has lost all interest in her family, friends, and usual activities. Once proud of her accomplishments and optimistic about her future, Phyllis now believes that everything she has ever done, or will do, is worthless. Although her husband was far from a perfect partner, Phyllis is convinced that the divorce really was her fault. Her once-close friends, weary of Phyllis's self-absorbed and hopeless attitude, have stopped calling her. The family physician referred Phyllis to a psychiatrist, who prescribed an antidepressant. The drug seemed to help somewhat, but Phyllis, worried that she would become addicted, stopped taking it regularly. Phyllis's son-in-law is concerned about her dejected attitude. Her daughter, however, insists that there is no cause for alarm. She says that her mother is simply growing old—that the listlessness is reminiscent of her maternal grandmother's behavior at the same age.

1. Should Phyllis's daughter be more concerned about her mother's behavior, or is she correct in attributing it to aging? Explain your reasoning.

2. How might Phyllis's behavior be classified by a clinical psychologist?

3. How might Phyllis's behavior be explained according to (a) the biological, and (b) the social-cognitive perspectives?

4. Which diagnostic perspective most closely represents your own belief about Phyllis's condition? Why?

Check your progress on becoming a critical thinker by comparing your answers to the sample answers found in Appendix B.

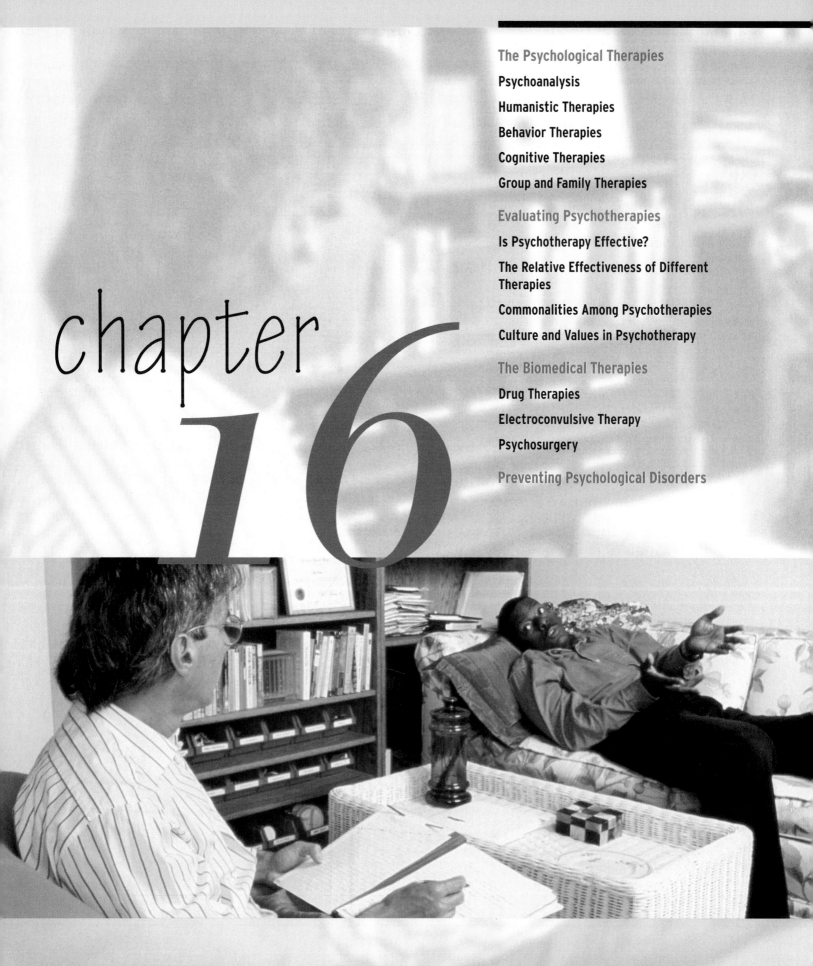

chapter

16

Therapy

The history of treating psychological disorders reveals how mystifying and intractable these problems are. We can now state with certainty the chemical composition of Jupiter's atmosphere. But in understanding and treating what is much closer to home—the psychological disorders described in Chapter 15—we are only beginning to make real progress. Consider: In the 2200 years since Eratosthenes correctly estimated the Earth's circumference, we have charted the heavens, explored the solar system, reconstructed the basic history of life on Earth, cracked the genetic code, and eliminated or found cures for all sorts of diseases. Meanwhile, we have treated psychological disorders with a bewildering variety of methods, harsh and gentle: by cutting holes in the head and by giving warm baths and massages; by restraining, bleeding, or "beating the devil" out of people; by placing them in sunny, serene environments; by administering drugs and electric shocks; and by talking—talking about childhood experiences, about current feelings, about maladaptive thoughts and behaviors.

The transition from brutal to gentler treatments occurred thanks to the efforts of reformers such as Philippe Pinel in France and Dorothea Dix in the United States, Canada, and Scotland. Both advocated the construction of mental hospitals offering more humane methods of treatment. As we shall see, the introduction of therapeutic drugs and community-based treatment programs has, however, largely emptied mental health hospitals since the mid-1950s.

Today's favored treatment depends on the therapist's viewpoint. Those who believe that psychological disorders are learned will tend to favor psychological therapies. Those who view disorders as biologically rooted are likely to advocate medication as well. Those who believe that disorders are responses to social conditions will, in addition, want to reform the "sick" environment.

We can classify therapies into two main categories: The *psychological therapies* involve structured interaction (usually verbal) between a trained professional and a client with a problem. The *biomedical therapies* directly affect the nervous system.

The history of treatment   William Hogarth's (1697–1764) engraving (left) of St. Mary of Bethlehem hospital in London (commonly called Bedlam) depicts the treatment of mental disorders in the eighteenth century. Visitors paid to gawk at the patients as if they were viewing zoo animals. The chair on the right was designed by Benjamin Rush (1746–1813) "for the benefit of maniacal patients." Rush, a founder of the movement for more humane treatment of the mentally ill, believed that they required restraint to regain their sensibilities.

Dorothea Dix (1802–1887)
"I. . . call your attention to the state of the Insane Persons confined within this Commonwealth, in cages."

The Psychological Therapies

What are the aims and methods of each major type of psychotherapy? And how does each apply the personality theory that underlies it?

Psychological therapy, or psychotherapy, is "a planned, emotionally charged, confiding interaction between a trained, socially sanctioned healer and a sufferer" (Frank, 1982). From among the 250 or more types of psychotherapy (Parloff, 1987), we will consider the most influential. These derive from psychology's major personality theories: psychoanalytic, humanistic, behavioral, and cognitive. We will also consider the use of these techniques in group therapies.

Each technique is distinctive, but there are common threads. Therapists who view disorders as an interplay of bio-psycho-social influences may welcome a combination of treatments. Indeed, half of all psychotherapists describe themselves as taking an eclectic approach—as using a blend of therapies (Beitman & others, 1989; Castonguay & Goldfried, 1994). Depending on the client and the problem, an eclectic therapist will use a variety of techniques.

Psychoanalysis

Although most of today's therapists do not practice therapy as Sigmund Freud did, his psychoanalytic techniques survive. Psychoanalysis is part of our modern vocabulary, and its assumptions influence many other therapies.

Aims

As we noted when considering Freud's theory in Chapters 14 and 15, psychoanalysis assumes that many psychological problems are fueled by childhood's residue of supposedly repressed impulses and conflicts. Psychoanalysts try to bring these repressed feelings into conscious awareness where the patient can deal with them. By gaining insight into the origins of the disorder—by fulfilling the ancient imperative to "know thyself" in a deep way—the patient "works through" the buried feelings. The theory presumes that healthier, less anxious living becomes possible when patients release the energy they had previously devoted to id-ego-superego conflicts.

Methods

Psychoanalysis is historical reconstruction. Its goal is to unearth the past in hope of unmasking the present. But how?

When Freud discarded hypnosis as unreliable, he turned to *free association*. Imagine yourself as a patient using the free association technique. The analyst invites you to relax, perhaps by lying on a couch. He or she will probably sit out of your line of vision, helping you focus attention on your internal thoughts and feelings. Beginning with a childhood memory, a dream, or a recent experience, you say aloud whatever comes to your mind from moment to moment. It sounds easy, but soon you notice how often you edit your thoughts as you speak, omitting material that seems trivial, irrelevant, or shameful. Even in the safe presence of the analyst, you may pause momentarily before uttering an embarrassing thought. You may make a joking remark or change the subject to something less threatening. Sometimes your mind may go blank

Classical psychoanalysis The placement of the analyst's chair out of view is thought to minimize distraction and make it easy for the patient—relaxed on a couch—to verbalize whatever comes to mind.

or you may find yourself unable to remember important details.

To the psychoanalyst, these blocks in the flow of your free associations indicate resistance. They hint that anxiety lurks and that you are repressing sensitive material. The analyst will want to explore these sensitive areas by making you aware of your resistance and by interpreting their underlying meaning. The analyst's interpretations—suggestions of underlying wishes, feelings, and conflicts—aim to provide people with *insight*. If offered at the right moment, the analyst's interpretation—of, say, your not wanting to talk about your mother—may illuminate what you are avoiding. You may then discover what your resistances mean and how they fit with other pieces of your psychological puzzle.

Freud believed that another clue to repressed impulses is our dreams' *latent content* (page 218). Thus, after inviting you to report a dream, the analyst may offer a dream analysis, suggesting its hidden meaning.

During many such sessions you will probably disclose more of yourself to your analyst than you have ever revealed to anyone. Because psychoanalytic theory emphasizes the formative power of childhood experiences, much of what you reveal will pertain to your earliest memories. You will also probably find yourself experiencing strong positive or negative feelings for your analyst. Such feelings may express the dependency or mingled love and anger that you earlier experienced toward family members or other important people in your life. When this happens, Freud would say you are actually *transferring* your strongest feelings from

those other relationships to the analyst. Analysts and other therapists believe that this transference exposes long-repressed feelings, giving you a belated chance to work through them with your analyst's help. By examining your feelings toward the analyst you may also gain insight into your current relationships.

Note how much of psychoanalysis is built on the assumption that repressed memories exist. That assumption, as we noted in Chapter 9, is now questioned. This challenge to an assumption that is basic to so much of professional and popular psychology is provoking intense debate.

Critics also say that psychoanalysts' interpretations are hard to refute. If, in response to the analyst's suggested interpretation, you say, "Yes! I see now," your acceptance confirms the analyst's interpretation. If you emphatically say, "No! That doesn't ring true," your denial may be taken to reveal more resistance, which would also confirm the interpretation. Psychoanalysts acknowledge that it's hard to prove or disprove their interpretations. But they insist that interpretations often are a great help to patients.

Traditional psychoanalysis is slow and expensive. It requires up to several years of several sessions a week with a highly trained and well-paid analyst. (Three times a week for just two years at $100 or more per hour comes to about $30,000.) Only those with a high income can afford such treatment.

Although there are relatively few traditional psychoanalysts, psychoanalytic assumptions influence many therapists, especially those who make *psychodynamic* assumptions. Psychodynamic therapists try to understand patients' current symptoms

psychotherapy
an emotionally charged, confiding interaction between a trained therapist and someone who suffers from psychological difficulties.

eclectic approach
an approach to psychotherapy that, depending on the client's problems, uses or integrates techniques from various forms of therapy. (Also called *psychotherapy integration*.)

psychoanalysis
Sigmund Freud's therapeutic technique. Freud believed the patient's free associations, resistances, dreams, and transferences—and the therapist's interpretations of them—released previously repressed feelings, allowing the patient to gain self-insight.

resistance
in psychoanalysis, the blocking from consciousness of anxiety-laden material.

interpretation
in psychoanalysis, the analyst's noting supposed dream meanings, resistances, and other significant behaviors in order to promote insight.

transference
in psychoanalysis, the patient's transfer to the analyst of emotions linked with other relationships (such as love or hatred for a parent).

"I haven't seen my analyst in 200 years. He was a strict Freudian. If I'd been going all this time, I'd probably almost be cured by now."

WOODY ALLEN, AFTER AWAKENING FROM SUSPENDED ANIMATION IN "SLEEPER"

Psychodynamic therapists try to understand patients' current symptoms by exploring their childhood experiences. They probe for supposed repressed, emotion-laden information.

by exploring their childhood experiences. They probe for supposed repressed, emotion-laden information. They seek to help people gain insight into the unconscious roots of problems and work through newly resurrected feelings. Although influenced by Freud's psychoanalysis, these therapists may talk to people face to face (rather than out of the line of vision), once a week (rather than several times weekly), and for only a few weeks or months (rather than several years).

No brief therapy excerpt can exemplify the lengthy process of probing the past. But we can illustrate psychodynamic therapists' goal of enabling insight via their interpretations. In the following interaction, therapist David Malan responds to all that he has heard from a depressed patient by suggesting insights into her problems. Note how Malan interprets the woman's earlier remarks and suggests that her relationship with him reveals a characteristic pattern of behavior (1978, pp. 133–134).

Malan: I get the feeling that you're the sort of person who needs to keep active. If you don't keep active, then something goes wrong. Is that true?

Patient: Yes.

Malan: I get a second feeling about you and that is that you must, underneath all this, have an awful lot of very strong and upsetting feelings. Somehow they're there but you aren't really quite in touch with them. Isn't this right? I feel you've been like that as long as you can remember.

Patient: For quite a few years, whenever I really sat down and thought about it I got depressed, so I tried not to think about it.

Malan: You see, you've established a pattern, haven't you? You're even like that here with me, because in spite of the fact that you're in some trouble and you feel that the bottom is falling out of your world, the way you're telling me this is just as if there wasn't anything wrong.

Humanistic Therapies

As we noted in Chapter 14, the humanistic perspective emphasizes people's inherent potential for self-fulfillment. Not surprisingly, then, humanistic therapists aim to boost self-fulfillment by helping people grow in self-awareness and self-acceptance. Unlike psychoanalytic therapists, humanistic therapists tend to focus on

- the *present* and *future* instead of the past. They explore feelings as they occur, rather than achieving insights into the childhood origins of the feelings.

- *conscious* rather than unconscious thoughts.

- taking immediate *responsibility* for one's feelings and actions rather than uncovering hidden determinants.

- promoting *growth* and fulfillment instead of curing illness. Thus, those in therapy are "clients" rather than "patients."

Person-Centered Therapy

The most widely used humanistic technique is Carl Rogers' (1961, 1980) person-centered therapy. A person-centered therapist focuses on the client's conscious self-perceptions rather than on the therapist's own interpretations. The therapist listens, without judgment or interpretation, and refrains from directing the client toward certain insights. This strategy has earned person-centered therapy the label *nondirective* therapy.

Believing that most people already possess the resources for growth, Rogers encouraged therapists to exhibit *genuineness, acceptance*, and *empathy*. When therapists drop their facades and genuinely express their true feelings, when they enable their clients to feel unconditionally accepted, and when they empathically sense and reflect their clients' feelings, the clients may increase in self-understanding and self-acceptance. As Rogers (1980, p. 10) explained,

Face-to-face therapy   In this type of therapy session the couch has disappeared. But the influence of psychoanalytic theory probably has not, especially if the therapist probes for the origin of the patient's symptoms by seeking information from the patient's childhood.

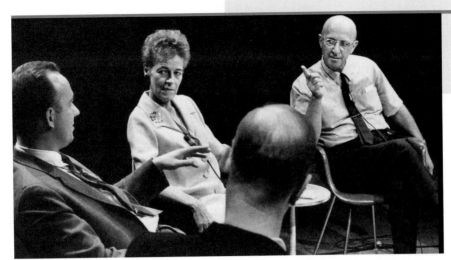

Active listening The late Carl Rogers (right) empathizes with a client during a group therapy session.

Hearing has consequences. When I truly hear a person and the meanings that are important to him at that moment, hearing not simply his words, but him, and when I let him know that I have heard his own private personal meanings, many things happen. There is first of all a grateful look. He feels released. He wants to tell me more about his world. He surges forth in a new sense of freedom. He becomes more open to the process of change.

I have often noticed that the more deeply I hear the meanings of the person, the more there is that happens. Almost always, when a person realizes he has been deeply heard, his eyes moisten. I think in some real sense he is weeping for joy. It is as though he were saying, "Thank God, somebody heard me. Someone knows what it's like to be me."

"Hearing" refers to Rogers' technique of active listening—echoing, restating, and seeking clarification of what the person expresses (verbally or nonverbally) and acknowledging the expressed feelings. Active listening is now an accepted part of therapeutic counseling practices in many schools, colleges, and clinics. The counselor listens attentively and interrupts only to restate and confirm the client's feelings, to accept what the client is expressing, or to seek clarification. In counseling a male client, Rogers illustrates active listening:

> *Unlike psychoanalytic therapists, humanistic therapists tend to focus on the present and future instead of the past.*

Client: I just ain't no good to nobody, never was, and never will be.

Rogers: Feeling that now, hm? That you're just no good to yourself, no good to anybody. Never will be any good to anybody. Just that you're completely worthless, huh?— Those really are lousy feelings. Just feel that you're no good at all, hm?

Client: Yeah. (Muttering in low, discouraged voice) That's what this guy I went to town with just the other day told me.

Rogers: This guy that you went to town with really told you that you were no good? Is that what you're saying? Did I get that right?

Client: M-hm.

Rogers: I guess the meaning of that if I get it right is that here's somebody that—meant something to you and what does he think of you? Why, he's told you that he thinks you're no good at all. And that just really knocks the props out from under you. (Client weeps quietly.) It just brings the tears. (Silence of 20 seconds)

Client: (Rather defiantly) I don't care though.

Rogers: You tell yourself you don't care at all, but somehow I guess some part of you cares because some part of you weeps over it. (Meador & Rogers, 1984, p. 167)

> *"We have two ears and one mouth that we may listen the more and talk the less."*
>
> ZENO (335–263 B.C.)
> *DIOGENES LAERTIUS*

person-centered therapy
a humanistic therapy, developed by Carl Rogers, in which the therapist uses techniques such as active listening within a genuine, accepting, empathic environment to facilitate clients' growth.

active listening
empathic listening in which the listener echoes, restates, and clarifies. A feature of Rogers's person-centered therapy.

"You say, 'Off with her head,' but what I'm hearing is, 'I feel neglected.'"

Gestalt therapy
developed by Fritz Perls; combines the psychoanalytic emphasis on bringing unconscious feelings to awareness and the humanistic emphasis on getting "in touch with oneself"; aims to help people become more aware of and able to express their feelings, and to take responsibility for their feelings and actions.

behavior therapy
therapy that applies learning principles to the elimination of unwanted behaviors.

As this brief excerpt illustrates, the person-centered counselor seeks to provide a psychological mirror that helps clients see themselves more clearly. But can a therapist be a perfect mirror, without selecting and interpreting what is reflected? Rogers conceded that one cannot be *totally* nondirective. Nevertheless, he believed that the therapist's most important contribution is to accept and understand the client. Given a nonjudgmental, grace-filled environment that provides *unconditional positive regard*, people internalize unconditional positive self-regard; they may accept even their worst traits and feel valued and whole.

If you want to listen more actively in your own relationships, three hints may help:

1 *Paraphrase.* Check your understandings by summarizing the speaker's words in your own words.

2 *Invite clarification.* "What might be an example of that?" may encourage the speaker to say more.

3 *Reflect feelings.* "That must be frustrating," might mirror what you're sensing from the speaker's body language and intensity.

Gestalt Therapy

Another influential humanistic therapy, developed by Fritz Perls (1969), blends the psychoanalytic emphasis on bringing unconscious feelings and conflicts into awareness with the humanistic emphasis on getting in touch with oneself and taking responsibility for oneself in the present. Perls's Gestalt therapy aims to make people self-aware by breaking through their defenses and helping them sense and express their moment-to-moment feelings. "All therapy that has to be done can only be done in the now," said Perls (1970). "Nothing exists except in the now."

Eavesdropping on a Gestalt therapy session, we might hear the therapist using any one of several techniques for getting people to express their real feelings and to "own responsibility" for them. One way is to train people to speak in the first person (Passons, 1975, p. 79):

Client: When you go skiing you feel healthy and vigorous. You have this sense of excitement.

Therapist: Sue, try saying the same thing only substituting the word "I" for "you."

Client: Why?

Therapist: Because I believe you're saying something about yourself except you're not sounding that way.

Client: When I'm skiing I feel healthy and excited.

Therapist: Do you hear the difference?

Client: Yes. The second one is what I really meant.

To encourage people to take responsibility for their feelings, the Gestalt therapist might get them to change their verbs—to say, for instance, "I want" instead of "I need," "I choose to" instead of "I have to," and "I won't" instead of "I can't" (Passons, 1975, p. 82):

Client: Every day I just sit there and feel like a stooge. I just can't speak up in that class.

Therapist: You say you can't.

Client: That's right. I've tried and I know I should, I mean I know the stuff, that's not the problem. I just can't get the words out.

Therapist: Try saying "I won't talk" instead of "I can't talk."

Client: I won't talk in that class.

Therapist: Let yourself feel how you are refusing to talk.

Client: I guess I am holding myself back a little.

Therapist: What are your objections to speaking up?

Client: Well, everyone else in there seems to be talking just to talk. I don't like doing that.

Gestalt therapists also capitalize on the power of actions to affect thoughts and feelings (more on this in Chapter 18). The therapist may ask people to role-play different aspects of their relationships or to act out suppressed feelings. Gestalt therapists encourage people to be true to themselves by becoming more aware of, and more expressive of, their feelings.

Behavior Therapies

All the therapies we have considered so far assume that, for nonpsychotic people at least, psychological problems diminish as self-awareness grows. The psychoanalyst expects problems to subside as people gain insight into their unresolved and unconscious tensions. So does the humanistic therapist, as people "get in touch with their feelings." Behavior therapists, however, doubt that self-awareness is the key. They assume that the problem behaviors *are* the problems. You can, for example, become aware of why you are highly anxious during exams and still be anxious. Instead of trying to alleviate distressing behaviors by resolving a presumed underlying problem, behavior therapy applies well-established learning principles to eliminate the unwanted behavior. To treat phobias or sexual dysfunctions, behavior therapists do not delve deep below the surface looking for inner causes. Rather, they try to replace problem thoughts and maladaptive behaviors with more constructive ways of thinking and acting.

Classical Conditioning Techniques

One cluster of behavior therapies derives from principles developed in Pavlov's conditioning experiments (pages 246–250). As Pavlov and others showed, we learn various behaviors and emotions through classical conditioning. So, are maladaptive symptoms conditioned responses? If, say, a claustrophobic fear of elevators is a learned response to the stimulus of being in an enclosed space, then might one unlearn the fear by counterconditioning the fear response? Counterconditioning pairs the trigger stimulus with a new response that is incompatible with fear. For example, if we repeatedly pair the enclosed space of the elevator with a relaxed response, the fear response may be displaced.

One classical conditioning therapy was developed by learning theorist O. H. Mowrer for chronic bed-wetters. The child sleeps on a liquid-sensitive pad connected to an alarm. Moisture on the pad triggers the alarm, awakening the child. With repetition, this association of urinary relaxation with awakening stops the bed-wetting. In three out of four cases the treatment is effective and the success provides a boost to the child's self-image (Christophersen & Edwards, 1992; Houts & others, 1994).

Two specific counterconditioning techniques are *systematic desensitization* and *aversive conditioning*.

Systematic Desensitization

Picture this scene reported in 1924 by Mary Cover Jones, an associate of the behaviorist John B. Watson: Three-year-old Peter is petrified of rabbits and other furry objects. (Unlike Little Albert's laboratory-conditioned fear of white rats, described in Chapter 8, Peter's fear arose during the course of his life at home and is more intense.) Jones aims to replace Peter's fear of rabbits with a conditioned response that is incompatible with fear. Her strategy is to associate the fear-evoking rabbit with the pleasurable, relaxed response associated with eating.

As the hungry child begins eating his midafternoon snack, Jones introduces a caged rabbit on the other side of the huge room. Peter hardly notices as he eagerly munches his crackers and drinks his milk. On succeeding days, she gradually moves the rabbit closer and closer. Within two months, Peter tolerates the rabbit in his lap and strokes it while he eats. Moreover, his fear of other furry objects subsides as well, having been "countered," or replaced, by a relaxed state that cannot coexist with fear (Fisher, 1984; Jones, 1924).

Unfortunately for those who might have been helped by her counterconditioning procedures,

Jones's story of Peter and the rabbit did not immediately become part of psychology's lore. It was not until more than 30 years later that psychiatrist Joseph Wolpe (1958, 1982) refined her technique into what has become the most widely used method of behavior therapy: systematic desensitization. Wolpe assumed, as did Jones, that you cannot simultaneously be anxious and relaxed. Therefore, if you can repeatedly relax when facing anxiety-provoking stimuli, you can gradually eliminate your anxiety. The trick is to proceed gradually.

Let's see how this might work with a common phobia. Imagine yourself afraid of public speaking. A behavior therapist might first ask your help in constructing a hierarchy of anxiety-triggering speaking situations. Your anxiety hierarchy could range from mildly anxiety-provoking situations, such as speaking up in a small group of friends, to panic-provoking situations, such as having to address a large audience.

The therapist would then train you to relax. Using *progressive relaxation*, you learn to relax one muscle group after another, until you achieve a drowsy state of complete relaxation and comfort. Then the therapist asks you to imagine, with your eyes closed, a mildly anxiety-arousing situation: You are having coffee with a group of friends and

counterconditioning
a behavior therapy procedure that conditions new responses to stimuli that trigger unwanted behaviors; based on classical conditioning. Includes systematic desensitization and aversive conditioning.

systematic desensitization
a type of counterconditioning that associates a pleasant, relaxed state with gradually increasing anxiety-triggering stimuli. Commonly used to treat phobias.

THE FAR SIDE

Professor Gallagher and his controversial technique of simultaneously confronting the fear of heights, snakes, and the dark.

are deciding whether to speak up. If imagining the scene causes you to feel any anxiety, you signal your tension by raising your finger, and the therapist instructs you to switch off the mental image and go back to deep relaxation.

This imagined scene is repeatedly paired with relaxation until you can feel no trace of anxiety while imagining it. The therapist progresses up your anxiety hierarchy, using the relaxed state to desensitize you to each imagined situation. After several therapy sessions, you practice the imagined behaviors in actual situations, beginning with relatively easy tasks and gradually moving to more anxiety-filled ones (Figure 16.1). Conquering your anxiety in an actual situation, not just in your imagination, raises your self-confidence (Foa & Kozak, 1986; Williams, 1987). Eventually, you may even become a confident public speaker.

More aggressive than systematic desensitization is "flooding," an extinction procedure that forces a person to confront feared stimuli. When dogs are forced to face situations in which they have previously received shocks, it floods them with fear, which then begins to extinguish. People, too, when guided to experience or vividly imagine feared situations often come to realize that no real danger exists.

Therapists sometimes combine systematic desensitization with other techniques. For clients with phobias, they may have someone model appropriate behavior in a fear-arousing situation. If you were afraid of snakes, you would first observe someone handling a snake. Then you would be coaxed in gradual steps to approach, touch, and handle it yourself (Bandura & others, 1969). By applying this principle of observational learning, therapists have helped people overcome disruptive fears of snakes, spiders, and dogs.

Notice that the systematic desensitization and modeling procedures make no attempt to help you achieve insight into your fear's underlying cause. If you are afraid of heights, the therapist will not spend much time probing when you first experienced this fear or what may have caused it. Nor do behavior therapists worry that eliminating your fear of heights will leave an underlying problem that may now be expressed as, say, a fear of elevators. On the contrary, they find that overcoming maladaptive behaviors helps people feel better about themselves.

Aversive Conditioning

In systematically desensitizing a patient, the therapist seeks to substitute a positive (relaxed) response for a negative (fearful) response to a harmless stimulus. In aversive conditioning, the therapist tries to replace a positive response to a harmful stimulus with a negative (aversive) response. Thus, aversive conditioning is the reverse of systematic desensitization.

The procedure is simple: It associates unpleasant feelings with the unwanted behavior. In treating an alcoholic, aversion therapists offer appealing drinks laced with a drug that produces severe nausea. By

Figure **16.1**

Systematic desensitization of a phobia Beverly, who is terribly afraid of spiders, is gradually able to relax—as shown by her decreasing pulse rate—first at the sight of a spider, then in the presence of a toy spider, a dead spider, and a live one. (Adapted from Gilling & Brightwell, 1982.)

Pulse rate in beats per minute

Time

Figure 16.2

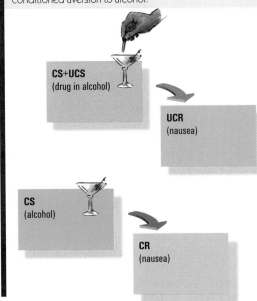

Aversion therapy for alcoholics After repeatedly imbibing an alcoholic drink mixed with a drug that produces severe nausea, some patients develop at least a temporary conditioned aversion to alcohol.

CS+UCS
(drug in alcohol)

UCR
(nausea)

CS
(alcohol)

CR
(nausea)

linking the drinking of alcohol with violent nausea, the therapist seeks to transform the alcoholic's reaction to alcohol from positive to negative (see Figure 16.2, and recall the taste-aversion experiments with rats and coyotes in Chapter 8). Similarly, by giving child molesters electric shocks as they view photos of nude children, aversion therapists aim to eliminate the molesters' sexual response to children. And by giving withdrawn and self-abusing autistic children harmless "aversives," such as a spray of cold water in the face, therapists hope to suppress self-injury while reinforcing more appropriate behavior. Because this therapy involves an unpleasant experience, it is practiced sparingly, with the appropriate consent. Arthur Wiens and Carol Menustik (1983) studied 685 alcoholic patients who completed an aversion therapy program at a Portland, Oregon, hospital. One year later, after returning for several booster treatments of alcohol-sickness pairings, 63 percent were still successfully abstaining. But after three years, only 33 percent had remained abstinent.

Does aversive conditioning work? In the short run it may. But, as we saw in Chapter 8, the problem is that cognition influences conditioning. People know that outside the therapist's office they can drink without fear of nausea or engage in sexually deviant behavior without fear of shock. The person's ability to discriminate between the aversive conditioning situation and all other situations can limit the treatment's effectiveness.

Operant Conditioning

As we saw in Chapter 8, voluntary behaviors are strongly influenced by their consequences. This simple fact enables behavior therapists to reinforce desired behaviors and to withhold reinforcement for undesired behaviors. Using operant conditioning to solve specific behavior problems has raised hopes for some cases thought to be hopeless. Retarded children have been taught to care for themselves. Socially withdrawn autistic children have learned to interact. People with schizophrenia have been helped to behave more rationally in their hospital ward.

In extreme cases, the treatment must be intensive. For 19 withdrawn, uncommunicative, 3-year-old autistic children in one study, it involved a 2-year, 40-hour-a-week shaping program by their parents (Lovaas, 1987). The combination of positive reinforcement of desired behaviors and the ignoring or punishing of aggressive and self-abusive behaviors worked wonders. By first grade, 9 of the 19 children were functioning successfully in school and exhibiting normal intelligence. Only 1 of 40 comparable children who did not undergo this treatment showed similar improvement.

The rewards used to modify behavior vary. With some people the reinforcing power of attention or praise is sufficient. Others require more concrete rewards, such as food. In institutional settings, therapists may create a token economy. When patients display appropriate behavior, such as getting out of bed, washing, dressing, eating, talking coherently, cleaning up their rooms, or playing cooperatively, they receive a token or plastic coin. Later, they can exchange their accumulated tokens for various rewards, such as candy, television watching, trips to town, or better living quarters. Therapists use tokens as positive reinforcers to shape behavior in the step-by-step manner de-

token economy
an operant conditioning procedure that rewards desired behavior. A patient exchanges a token of some sort, earned for exhibiting the desired behavior, for various privileges or treats.

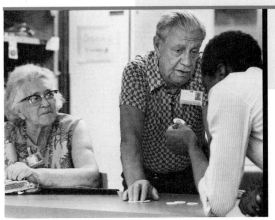

Token reinforcement Operant conditioning has proved to be a powerful tool in teaching people with severe mental disabilities. At the Brooklyn Development Center (New York), clients receive tokens for learning, maintaining, or improving a skill. They can then take the tokens to the center's "store," where volunteers "sell" them different items.

scribed on pages 255–256. Token economies have been successfully applied in various settings (classrooms, hospitals, homes for the delinquent) and among members of various populations (disturbed children, those with mental disability, schizophrenia patients).

Critics of such *behavior modification* express two concerns. One concern is practical: What happens when the reinforcers stop, as when the person leaves the institution? Might the person have become so dependent on the extrinsic rewards that the appropriate behaviors quickly disappear? If so, how can behavior therapists make the appropriate behaviors durable? First, they may wean patients from the tokens by shifting them toward rewards, such as social approval, that are more typical of life outside the institution. They may also train patients to behave in ways that are intrinsically rewarding. For example, as a withdrawn person becomes more socially competent, the intrinsic satisfactions of social interaction may help the person maintain the behavior.

The second concern is ethical: Is it right for one human to control another's behavior? Those who set up token economies typically deprive people of something they desire and then decide which behaviors they will reinforce. To critics, the whole behavior modification process has an authoritarian taint. Advocates reply that control already exists; rewards and punishers are already maintaining destructive behavior patterns. So why not reinforce adaptive behavior instead? They argue that treatment with positive rewards is more humane than being institutionalized or punished, and that the right to effective treatment and to an improved life justifies temporary deprivation.

Cognitive Therapies

We have seen how behavior therapists treat specific fears and problem behaviors. But how do they deal with major depression or general anxiety? One can reinforce healthier behaviors and train people to avoid "high-risk" situations. Still, when anxiety has no focus, making a hierarchy of anxiety-triggering situations is difficult. The cognitive revolution that has so changed psychology during the last four decades has influenced how therapists treat these less clearly defined psychological problems (Figure 16.3).

The cognitive therapies assume that our thinking colors our feelings (Figure 16.4). Between the event and our response falls the mind. As we noted in Chapter 15, self-blaming and overgeneralized explanations of bad events are an integral part of the vicious cycle of depression. The depressed person interprets a suggestion as criticism, disagreement as dislike, praise as flattery, friendliness as pity. Ruminating on such thoughts sustains the bad mood. (That explains why distracting oneself, perhaps by getting absorbed in a task, can alleviate a bad mood [Erber & Tesser, 1992; Lyubomirsky & Nolen-Hoeksema, 1994].) If depressing thinking patterns are learned, then surely they can be replaced. Thus, cognitive therapists try in various ways to teach people new, more constructive ways of thinking.

Rational-Emotive Therapy

According to Albert Ellis (1962, 1987, 1993), the creator of rational-emotive therapy (also called *rational-emotive behavior therapy*), many prob-

Figure 16.3

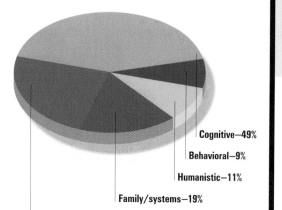

The cognitive revolution Half of all faculty in accredited clinical psychology Ph.D. programs now align themselves with a cognitive or cognitive-behavioral therapy orientation. (Data from Mayne & others, 1994.)

Cognitive—49%

Behavioral—9%

Humanistic—11%

Family/systems—19%

Psychoanalytic/psychodynamic—28%

Figure 16.4

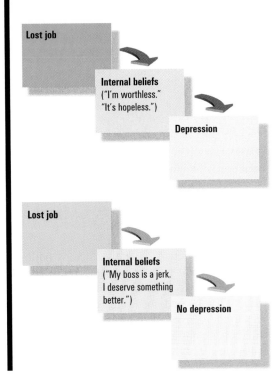

A cognitive perspective on psychological disorders
The person's emotional reactions are produced not directly by the event but by the person's thoughts in response to the event.

The depressed person interprets a suggestion as criticism, disagreement as dislike, praise as flattery, friendliness as pity.

lems arise from irrational thinking. For example, he describes a disturbed woman and suggests how therapy might challenge her illogical, self-defeating assumptions (1984, p. 198):

> [She] does not merely believe it is *undesirable* if her love partner is rejecting. She tends to believe, also, that (1) it is *awful*; (2) she *cannot stand* it; (3) she *should not*, must not be rejected; (4) she will *never* be accepted by any desirable partner; (5) she is a *worthless person* because one lover has rejected her; and (6) she *deserves to be damned* for being so worthless. Such common covert hypotheses are nonsensical. . . . They can be easily elicited and demolished by any scientist worth his or her salt; and the rational-emotive therapist is exactly that: an exposing and nonsense-annihilating scientist.

Does this sound like the opposite of the warm, caring, reflective acceptance of feelings expressed by Carl Rogers? It very nearly is. Ellis intends to "make mincemeat" of people's illogical ideas—that we must be loved by everyone, that we must be thoroughly competent and successful at everything, that it is a disaster when things do not go as we

wish. Change people's thinking by revealing the "absurdity" of their self-defeating ideas, he believes, and you will change their self-defeating feelings and actions. Let's eavesdrop as tart-tongued Ellis exhibits his confrontational style with a 25-year-old female client who suffers feelings of guilt, unworthiness, and depression (1989, p. 219):

Ellis: The same crap! It's always the same crap. Now if you would look at the crap—instead of "Oh, how stupid I am! He hates me! I think I'll kill myself!"—then you'd get better right away.

Client: You've been listening! (laughs)

Ellis: Listening to what?

Client: (laughs) Those wild statements in my mind, like that, that I make.

Ellis: That's right! Because I know that you have to make those statements—because I have a good theory. And according to my theory, people couldn't get upset unless they made those nutty statements to themselves. . . . Even if I loved you madly, the next person you talk to is likely to hate you. So I like brown eyes and he likes blue eyes, or something. So you're then dead! Because you really think: "I've got to be accepted! I've got to act intelligently!" Well, why?

Client: (very soberly and reflectively) True.

Ellis: You see?

Client: Yes.

Ellis: Now, if you will learn that lesson, then you've had a very valuable session. Because you don't have to upset yourself. As I said before: If I thought you were the worst [expletive] who ever existed, well that's my opinion. And I'm entitled to it. But does it make you a turd?

Client: (reflective silence)

Ellis: Does it?

Client: No.

Ellis: What makes you a turd?

Client: Thinking that you are.

Ellis: That's right! Your belief that you are. That's the only thing that could ever do it. And you never have to believe that. See? You control your thinking. I control my thinking—my belief about you. But you don't have to be affected by that. You always control what you think.

cognitive therapy
therapy that teaches people new, more adaptive ways of thinking and acting; based on the assumption that thoughts intervene between events and our emotional reactions.

rational-emotive therapy
a confrontational cognitive therapy, developed by Albert Ellis, that vigorously challenges people's illogical, self-defeating attitudes and assumptions. Also called rational-emotive behavior therapy by Ellis, emphasizing a behavioral "homework" component.

Cognitive Therapy for Depression

Like Ellis, cognitive therapist Aaron Beck was originally trained in Freudian techniques. As Beck analyzed his depressed patients' dreams, he found recurring negative themes of loss, rejection, and abandonment that extended into their waking thoughts. So in his form of cognitive therapy, Beck and his colleagues (1979) seek to reverse clients' catastrophizing beliefs about themselves, their situations, and their futures. Beck shares with Ellis the goal of getting depressed people to take off the dark glasses through which they view life. But his technique is a kinder, gentler questioning that aims to help people discover their irrationalities (Beck & others, 1979, pp. 145–146):

Patient: I agree with the descriptions of me but I guess I don't agree that the way I think makes me depressed.

Beck: How do you understand it?

Patient: I get depressed when things go wrong. Like when I fail a test.

Beck: How can failing a test make you depressed?

Patient: Well, if I fail I'll never get into law school.

Beck: So failing the test means a lot to you. But if failing a test could drive people into clinical depression, wouldn't you expect everyone who failed the test to have a depression? . . . Did everyone who failed get depressed enough to require treatment?

Patient: No, but it depends on how important the test was to the person.

Beck: Right, and who decides the importance?

Patient: I do.

Beck: And so, what we have to examine is your way of viewing the test (or the way that you think about the test) and how it affects your chances of getting into law school. Do you agree?

Patient: Right.

Beck: Do you agree that the way you interpret the results of the test will affect you? You might feel depressed, you might have trouble sleeping, not feel like eating, and you might even wonder if you should drop out of the course.

Patient: I have been thinking that I wasn't going to make it. Yes, I agree.

Beck: Now what did failing mean?

Patient: (tearful) That I couldn't get into law school.

Beck: And what does that mean to you?

Patient: That I'm just not smart enough.

Beck: Anything else?

Patient: That I can never be happy.

Beck: And how do these *thoughts* make you feel?

Patient: Very unhappy.

Beck: So it is the meaning of failing a test that makes you very unhappy. In fact, believing that you can never be happy is a powerful factor in producing unhappiness. So, you get yourself into a trap—by definition, failure to get into law school equals "I can never be happy."

A newer variety of cognitive therapy builds on the finding that depressed people do not exhibit the self-serving bias common in nondepressed people (page 473). Instead, they often attribute their failures to themselves and attribute their successes to external circumstances. Thus, Adele Rabin and her colleagues (1986) explained to 235 depressed adults the advantages of interpreting events as nondepressed people do. She then trained them to reform their habitually negative patterns of thinking and labeling. For example, she gave the patients homework assignments that required them to record each day's positive events and to write down how they contributed to each. Compared with depressed people who remained on a waiting list, those who went through the positive thinking exercises became much less depressed (Figure

Figure **16.5**

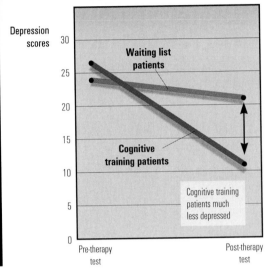

Cognitive therapy for depression   After undergoing a program that trained them to think more like nondepressed people—by noticing and taking personal credit for good events and by not taking blame for or overgeneralizing from bad events—patients' depression dropped dramatically. (From Rabin & others, 1986.)

and to practice the more positive approach in everyday settings.

Because we often think in words, getting people to change what they say to themselves is an effective way to change their thinking. Perhaps you can identify with the anxious students who before an exam make matters worse with self-defeating thoughts: "This exam is probably going to be impossible. All these other students seem so relaxed and self-confident. I wish I were better prepared. Anyhow, I'm so nervous I'll forget everything." To change such negative patterns, Donald Meichenbaum (1977, 1985) offers "stress inoculation training." He trains people to restructure their thinking in stressful situations. Sometimes it may be enough simply to say more positive things to oneself: "Relax. The exam may be hard, but it will be hard for everyone else, too. I studied harder than most people. Besides, I don't need a perfect score to get a good grade."

Group and Family Therapies

Except for traditional psychoanalysis, the therapies we have considered may also occur in therapist-led small groups. Although it does not provide the same degree of therapist involvement with each client, group therapy saves therapists' time and clients' money—and usually is no less effective than individual therapy (Fuhriman & Burlingame, 1994). More important, the social context allows people both to discover that others have problems similar to their own and to try out new ways of behaving. As you have perhaps experienced, receiving honest feedback—being reassured that you look poised even though you feel anxious and self-conscious, for example—can be very helpful. And it can be a relief to find that you are not alone—to learn that others, despite their apparent composure, share your problems and your feelings of loneliness, inadequacy, or anger.

16.5). The more people change their negative thinking styles, the more their depression lifts (Seligman, 1989).

Changed thinking after cognitive therapy also reduces the risk of relapse (Hollon & others, 1992). Changed thinking *before* depression hits can also help "vaccinate" those at risk. Teams led by Martin Seligman (1996; Gillham & others, 1995) are helping at-risk children—those who have suffered mild depression or whose parents are in conflict—learn how to dispute their pessimistic, negative thoughts and to think and act more positively. Once children experience a depressive episode, it often becomes their way of reacting to bad events. But not so for the 10- to 12-year-old children in one of the Seligman team's studies. Two years after receiving cognitive training, the participants were half as likely as those in a control group to be moderately or severely depressed. "Our results suggest," conclude the hopeful researchers, "that children can be taught cognitive and social skills that will buffer them against the alarmingly high rate of depression that occurs during puberty."

Cognitive therapists often combine the reversal of self-defeating thinking with efforts to modify behavior. *Cognitive-behavior therapy* aims to make people aware of their irrational negative thinking, to replace it with new ways of thinking and talking,

Such has been the experience of a wide range of people, from cancer patients to dieters to recovering alcoholics (Yalom, 1985). Many participate in *self-help* and *support groups*—for substance abusers, divorced people, gamblers, the bereaved, and those simply seeking personal growth. In an individualistic age, with more and more people living or feeling alone, the popularity of support groups also reflects a longing for community and connectedness. More than 100 million Americans belong to small religious, interest, or self-help groups that meet regularly—and nine in ten report that group members "support each other emotionally" (Gallup, 1994). The grandparent of self-help

family therapy
therapy that treats the family as a system. Views an individual's unwanted behaviors as influenced by or directed at other family members; encourages family members toward positive relationships and improved communication.

groups, Alcoholics Anonymous (AA), reportedly has 60,000 chapters in 112 countries. Its famous 12-step strategy, emulated by many other self-help groups, asks members to admit their powerlessness, to seek help from a higher power and from one another, and (the twelfth step) to take the message to others in need of it. In one 8-year, $27 million investigation, alcoholics seeking treatment reduced their drinking sharply and to roughly the same degree whether randomly assigned to a therapy based on AA principles and AA participation, or to cognitive-behavior therapy or a "motivational therapy" (Project Match, 1997).

One special type of group interaction, family therapy, assumes that no person is an island. We live and grow in relation to others, especially our families. We struggle to differentiate ourselves from our families but we also need to connect with them emotionally. Some of our problem behaviors arise from the tension between these two tendencies, which often creates family stress. Thus, patients often come to therapists seeking help in their relationships with family members.

Unlike most psychotherapy, which focuses on what happens inside the person's own skin, family therapists work with family groups to heal relationships and to mobilize family resources. Their aim is to help family members discover the role they play within their family's social system. A child's rebellion, for example, affects and is affected by other family tensions. Family therapists also attempt—usually with some success, research suggests (Hazelrigg & others, 1987; Shadish & others, 1993)—to open up communication within the family or to help family members discover new ways of preventing or resolving conflicts.

Family therapy   This type of therapy often acts as a preventive mental health strategy. The therapist helps family members understand how the ways they relate to each other create problems. The treatment emphasis is not on changing the individuals but rather on changing their relationships and interactions.

SUMMING UP

Treatment for psychological disorders encompasses both the psychological therapies, involving structured interactions, and the biomedical therapies, which alter neural functions. The major psychotherapies derive from the familiar psychoanalytic, humanistic, behavioral, and cognitive perspectives on psychology.

Psychoanalysis   Psychoanalysts try to help people gain insight into the unconscious origins of their disorders and to work through the accompanying feelings. To do so, an analyst draws on techniques such as free association and dream analysis, and interprets resistance and the transference to the therapist of long-repressed feelings. Like psychoanalytic theory, psychoanalysis is criticized for assuming repression, for after-the-fact interpretations, for being time-consuming and costly. Although traditional psychoanalysis is not practiced widely, its influence can be seen in the work of psychodynamic therapists who explore childhood experiences, who assume that defense mechanisms repress emotion-laden information, and who seek to help their (nonpsychotic) clients achieve insight into the root of their problems.

Humanistic Therapies   Unlike psychoanalysts, humanistic therapists focus on clients' current conscious feelings and on their taking responsibility for their own growth. Carl Rogers, in his person-centered therapy, used active listening to express genuineness, acceptance, and empathy. With Gestalt therapy, Fritz Perls sought to break down people's defenses and to make them accept responsibility for their feelings.

Behavior Therapies   Behavior therapists worry less about promoting self-awareness and more about directly modifying problem behaviors. Thus, they may countercondition behaviors through systematic desensitization or aversive conditioning. Or they may apply operant conditioning principles with behavior modification techniques, such as token economies.

Cognitive Therapies   The cognitive therapies, such as Albert Ellis's rational-emotive therapy and Aaron Beck's cognitive therapy for depression, aim to change self-defeating thinking by training people to look at themselves in new, more positive ways.

Group and Family Therapies Many therapeutic techniques can also be applied in a group context. Self-help and support groups, such as AA, engage many millions of people. Family therapy treats the family as an interactive system from which problems may arise.

KEY TERMS AND CONCEPTS psychotherapy, eclectic approach (psychotherapy integration), psychoanalysis, resistance, interpretation, transference, person-centered therapy, active listening, Gestalt therapy, behavior therapy, counterconditioning, systematic desensitization, aversive conditioning, token economy, cognitive therapy, rational-emotive therapy (rational-emotive behavior therapy), family therapy

Evaluating Psychotherapies

Does psychotherapy work? More specifically, do particular therapies work for particular problems? How might psychology's critical thinking methods provide answers?

Advice columnist Ann Landers frequently advises her troubled letter writers to get professional help. One response urged the writer "not to give up. Hang in there until you find [a psychotherapist] who fills the bill. It's worth the effort." She advised the same day's second letter writer, "There are many excellent mental health facilities in your city. I urge you to make an appointment at once" (Farina & Fisher, 1982). Therapy advocate Tipper Gore (1994) would concur: "We have ways to help. . . . The data show high levels of success in treating large numbers of people suffering [mental illnesses]." Many people share Ann Landers' and Tipper Gore's confidence in psychotherapy's effectiveness. The National Institute of Mental Health estimates that 15 percent of Americans seek help for psychological and addictive disorders each year (Figure 16.6).

Before 1950, the main mental health providers were psychiatrists. Since then, the demand has outgrown the psychiatric profession, and most psychotherapy is now done by clinical and counseling psychologists; clinical social workers; pastoral, marital, abuse, and school counselors; and psychiatric nurses. Much of it is done through *community mental health* programs, which provide outpatient therapy, crisis phone lines, and halfway houses for those making the transition from hospitalization to independent living. Is the faith that Ann Landers and millions of others worldwide place in these therapists justified?

Is Psychotherapy Effective?

The question, though simply put, is not simply answered. For one thing, measuring therapy's effectiveness is not like taking your body's temperature. If you and I were to undergo psychotherapy, how would we gauge its effectiveness? By how we feel about our progress? How our therapist feels about it? How our friends and family feel about it? How our behavior has changed?

Clients' Perceptions

If clients' testimonials were the only yardstick, we could strongly affirm the effectiveness of psychotherapy. Three out of four clients report themselves satisfied, and one in two say they are "very satisfied" (Lebow, 1982). When 2900 readers of *Consumer Reports* (1995; Kotkin & others, 1996; Seligman, 1995) reported on their experiences with mental health professionals, 89 percent were at least "fairly well satisfied." Nine in ten who recalled feeling *fair* or *very poor* when beginning therapy now were feeling *very good, good,* or at least *so-so.* We have their word for it—and who should know better?

We should not dismiss these testimonials lightly. People enter therapy because they are suffering, and most leave feeling better about themselves. But there are several reasons why client testimonials do not persuade psychotherapy's skeptics:

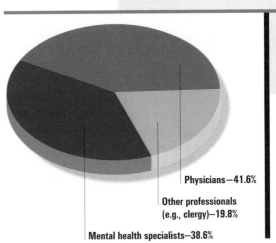

Figure **16.6**

To whom do people turn? The National Institute of Mental Health reports that 19 million Americans a year seek help for psychological difficulties. About two in five seek out a mental health worker, such as a psychologist or psychiatrist. (Data from Regier & others, 1993.)

Physicians—41.6%

Other professionals (e.g., clergy)—19.8%

Mental health specialists—38.6%

CLOSE-UP

A Consumer's Guide to Psychotherapists

When should a person seek the help of a mental health professional? Life for everyone is marked by a mix of serenity and stress, blessing and bereavement, good moods and bad. It is only when troubling thoughts and emotions interfere with normal living that we should consider talking to a professional. The American Psychological Association offers these common trouble signals:

- Feelings of hopelessness
- Deep and lasting depression
- Self-destructive behavior such as alcohol and drug abuse
- Disruptive fears
- Sudden mood shifts
- Thoughts of suicide
- Compulsive rituals such as hand washing
- Sexual difficulties

If you are looking for a therapist, you may wish to shop around by having a preliminary consultation with two or three therapists. You can describe your problem and learn each therapist's treatment approach. You can ask questions about the therapist's values, credentials (see Table 16.1), and fees. And you can assess your feelings about each therapist.

Table 16.1

Therapists and Their Training

Type	Description
Psychiatrists	Physicians who specialize in the treatment of psychological disorders. Not all psychiatrists have had extensive training in psychotherapy, but as M.D.s they can prescribe medications. Thus, they tend to see those with the most serious problems. Many have a private practice.
Clinical psychologists	Most are psychologists with a Ph.D. and expertise in research, assessment, and therapy, supplemented by a supervised internship. About half work in agencies and institutions, half in private practice.
Clinical or psychiatric social workers	A two-year Master of Social Work graduate program plus postgraduate supervision prepares some social workers to offer psychotherapy, mostly to people with everyday personal and family problems. About half have earned the National Association of Social Workers' designation of clinical social worker.
Counselors	Marriage and family counselors specialize in problems arising from family relations. Pastoral counselors provide counseling to countless people. Abuse counselors work with substance abusers and with spouse and child abusers and their victims.

- **People often enter therapy in crisis.** When, with the normal ebb and flow of events, the crisis passes, people may attribute their improvement to the therapy.

- **Clients may need to believe the therapy was worth the effort.** To admit investing time and money in something ineffective is like admitting to having one's car serviced repeatedly by a mechanic who never fixed it. Self-justification is a powerful human motive.

- **Clients generally like their therapists and speak kindly of them.** Even if the clients' problems remain, say the therapy critics, "they work hard to find something positive to say. The therapist had been very understanding, the client had gained a new perspective, he learned to communicate better, his mind was eased, anything at all so as not to have to say treatment was a failure" (Zilbergeld, 1983, p. 117).

Such testimonials can be misleading. As earlier chapters document, we are prone to selective and biased recall and to making judgments that confirm our beliefs. Consider a massive experiment with over 500 Massachusetts boys, aged 5 to 13 years, many of whom seemed bound for delinquency. By the toss of a coin, half the boys were assigned to a five-year treatment program. Counselors visited them twice a month. They were involved in community programs such as the Boy Scouts. And, as the need arose, they received academic tutoring, medical attention, and family assistance. Some 30 years after the end of the program, Joan McCord (1978,

1979) located 97 percent of the participants. To assess the treatment's impact, she sent them questionnaires and checked public records from courts, mental hospitals, and other sources.

Assessing the treatment program with client testimonials yielded encouraging results. Many of the men offered glowing reports. Some noted that had it not been for their counselors, "I would probably be in jail"; "My life would have gone the other way"; or "I think I would have ended up in a life of crime." The court records offered apparent support for these testimonials. Even among the "difficult" boys in the program, 66 percent had no official juvenile crime record.

But recall psychology's most powerful weapon for sorting reality from wishful thinking: the *control group*. For every boy who was counseled there was a similar boy in a control group who was not. McCord tracked down these untreated people and found that among the predelinquent boys in the control group, *70 percent* had no juvenile record. Moreover, on some measures, such as a record of having committed a second crime, alcoholic tendencies, death rate, and job satisfaction, the untreated men exhibited slightly *fewer* problems. The glowing testimonials of those treated had been deceiving.

Clinicians' Perceptions

If clinicians' perceptions accurately reflected therapeutic effectiveness, we would have even more reason to celebrate. Case studies of successful treatment abound. Furthermore, every therapist treasures compliments from clients as they say goodbye or later express their gratitude. The problem is that clients justify entering psychotherapy by emphasizing their woes, justify leaving therapy by emphasizing their well-being, and stay in touch only if satisfied. Therapists are aware of failures, but they are mostly the failures of *other* therapists—those whose clients, having experienced only temporary relief, are now seeking a new therapist for their recurring problems. Thus, the same person with the same recurring difficulty—the same old weight problem, depression, or marital difficulty—may represent "success" stories in several therapists' files.

Because people enter therapy when they are extremely unhappy, and usually leave when they are less extremely unhappy, most therapists as well as clients testify to therapy's success—regardless of the treatment. Although "treatments" have varied widely, from chains to counseling, every generation views its own approach as more enlightened. Testimonials, therefore, do not prove effectiveness.

Outcome Research

How, then, can we objectively measure the effectiveness of psychotherapy? What types of people and problems are best helped, and by what type of psychotherapy? The questions have both academic and personal relevance. If you or someone you care about feels anxious or depressed, or suffers some psychological disorder, how likely is it that psychotherapy will help?

In hopes of better assessing psychotherapy's effectiveness, psychologists have turned to controlled research studies. Similar research in the 1800s transformed medicine from concocted treatments (bleeding, purging, infusions of plant and metal substances) into a science. The transformation occurred when skeptical physicians began to realize that many patients got better on their own, that most of the fashionable treatments were doing no good, and that sorting sense from nonsense required closely following illnesses—with and without a particular treatment. Typhoid fever patients, for example, often improved after a treatment such as bleeding. That convinced most physicians that the treatment worked. It was not until a control group was given mere bed rest—and 70 percent were observed to improve after five weeks of fever—that physicians were shocked to learn that their treatments were, at best, worthless (Thomas, 1992).

In psychology, the opening volley in what became a spirited debate over such research was fired by British psychologist Hans Eysenck (1952). He summarized studies showing that after undergoing psychotherapy, two-thirds of those suffering nonpsychotic disorders improve markedly. To this day, no one disputes that optimistic estimate.

So why are we still debating psychotherapy's effectiveness? Because Eysenck also reported similar improvement among *untreated* persons, such as those who were on waiting lists. With or without psychotherapy, he said, roughly two-thirds improved noticeably. Time was a great healer.

The avalanche of criticism prompted by Eysenck's conclusions revealed shortcomings in his analyses. Also, Eysenck could find only 24 studies of psychotherapy outcomes to analyze in 1952. Today, there are hundreds. The best of these studies randomly assign people on a waiting list to therapy or to no therapy. Afterward, researchers evaluate everyone, using tests and the reports of friends and family or of psychologists who don't know whether therapy was given. The results of such studies are then digested by a technique called <u>meta-analysis</u>, a procedure for statistically combining the results of many different studies as

meta-analysis
a procedure for statistically combining the results of many different research studies.

"Fortunately, [psycho]analysis is not the only way to resolve inner conflicts. Life itself still remains a very effective therapist."
KAREN HORNEY
OUR INNER CONFLICTS
1945

if they had come from one huge study with thousands of participants.

In the first reported meta-analysis of psychotherapy outcome studies, Mary Lee Smith and her colleagues (1980) combined the results of 475 investigations. For psychotherapists, the welcome result was that "the evidence overwhelmingly supports the efficacy of psychotherapy" (p. 183). Figure 16.7 depicts their finding—that the average therapy client ends up better off than 80 percent of the untreated individuals on waiting lists. The claim is more modest than it first appears—by definition, about 50 percent of untreated people also are better off than the average untreated person. Nevertheless, Smith and her collaborators concluded that "psychotherapy benefits people of all ages as reliably as schooling educates them, medicine cures them, or business turns a profit" (p. 183).

Newer research summaries confirm this optimism (Lipsey & Wilson, 1993). In one ambitious study, the National Institute of Mental Health compared three depression treatments: cognitive therapy, interpersonal therapy (which focuses on social relations), and a standard drug therapy. Twenty-eight experienced therapists at research sites in Norman, Oklahoma; Washington, DC; and Pittsburgh, Pennsylvania, were trained in one of the three methods and randomly assigned their share of the 239 depressed patients who participated. Patients in all three groups improved more than did those in a control group who received merely an inert medication and supportive attention, encouragement, and advice. Among patients who completed a full 16-week treatment program, the depression had lifted for slightly more than half of those in each treatment group—but for only 29 percent of those in the control group (Elkin & oth-

ers, 1989). This verdict echoes the results of the earlier outcome studies: *Those not undergoing therapy improved, but those undergoing therapy improved more.*

Often, however, the improvement was not permanent. Only one in four patients undergoing psychotherapy and one in six undergoing drug therapy both recovered and experienced no relapse within 18 months (Shea & others, 1992). So, extravagant expectations that psychotherapy will transform your life and personality seem unwarranted. Still, Eysenck's pessimism also seems unwarranted. *On average*, psychotherapy is somewhat effective—and is also cost-effective when compared with the greater costs of medical care for psychologically related ailments (Turkington, 1987). The annual cost of psychological disorders and substance abuse—including crime, accidents, lost work, and treatment—is staggering. Thus, as an investment in prenatal and well-baby care *reduces* long-term costs, so will an investment in almost any effective treatment for psychological problems. Anything that boosts employees' psychological well-being will reduce medical costs, improve work efficiency, and diminish absenteeism. Studies by health insurers show that mental health treatment can more than pay for itself with reduced medical costs (American Psychological Association, 1991).

But note that "on average" refers to no one therapy in particular. It is like saying, "Surgery is somewhat effective," or like reassuring lung-cancer patients that "on the average" medical treatment of health problems is effective. What people want to know is not the effectiveness of therapy in general but the effectiveness of particular treatments for their particular problems.

In general, therapy is most effective when the problem is clear-cut (Singer, 1981). Those who suffer phobias, who are unassertive, or who are frustrated by sexual performance problems can hope for improvement. Those who suffer chronic schizophrenia or who wish to change their whole personality are unlikely to benefit from psychotherapy alone (Zilbergeld, 1983). The more specific the problem, the more hope there is.

The Relative Effectiveness of Different Therapies

People considering therapy want to know *which* psychotherapy will be most effective for their problem. The meta-analysis conducted by Mary Lee Smith and her colleagues (1977, 1980) allowed a comparison of the effectiveness of differ-

Figure **16.7**

Treatment versus no treatment
These two normal distribution curves based on data from 475 studies show the improvement of untreated people and psychotherapy clients. The outcome for the average therapy client surpassed that for 80 percent of the untreated people. (Adapted from Smith & others, 1980.)

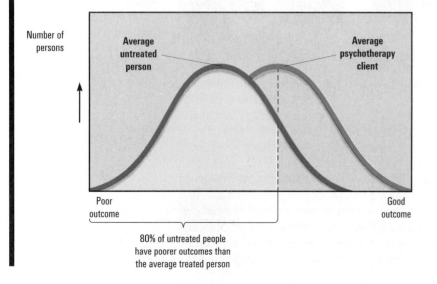

ent therapies. What do you suppose they found? Did one therapeutic technique get the best results? Did people benefit more from group or individual therapy? From sustained or short-term therapy? From therapy with experienced or novice therapists?

Despite claims of superiority by advocates of different types of therapy, Smith's comparison of therapies revealed no clear winner. No one type of therapy proved consistently superior. (*Consumer Reports* [1995] readers likewise were equally satisfied no matter what type of therapy they received and whether treated by a psychiatrist, psychologist, or social worker.) Moreover—and more astonishing—it made no discernible difference whether the therapy was group or individual or how well trained and experienced the therapist was. It seemed as though the dodo bird in *Alice in Wonderland* was right: "Everyone has won and all must have prizes."

Some therapies are, however, well suited to particular disorders. With specific behavior problems such as phobias, compulsions, or sexual dysfunctions, behavioral conditioning therapies achieve especially favorable results (Bowers & Clum, 1988; Giles, 1983). With depression, the cognitive therapies prove most successful (Dobson, 1989; Shapiro & Shapiro, 1982). Just as physicians offer particular treatments for specific medical problems, rather than treating every complaint with the same drug or surgical procedure, so psychotherapists increasingly offer particular treatments for specific psychological problems.

"Different sores have different salves."

ENGLISH PROVERB

Commonalities Among Psychotherapies

Some clinicians suggest a reason why no one therapeutic method proves generally superior or inferior to another. Despite their differences, each therapy's effectiveness may derive from underlying commonalities. Jerome Frank (1982), Marvin Goldfried (Goldfried & Padawer, 1982), and Hans Strupp (1986) studied common ingredients of various therapies and suggested that they all offer at least three benefits: hope for demoralized people; a new perspective on oneself and the world; and an empathic, trusting, caring relationship. These "nonspecific" factors aren't all that therapy offers, but they are important aspects (Barker & others,

Consumer Reports readers ... were equally satisfied no matter what type of therapy they received and whether treated by a psychiatrist, psychologist, or social worker.

1988; Jones & others, 1988; Roberts & others, 1993). They are part of what the growing numbers of self-help and support groups offer their members. And they have been part of what traditional healers offer (Jackson, 1992). Healers—special people to whom others disclose their suffering—have for centuries listened to understand and to empathize, reassure, advise, console, interpret, or explain.

Hope for Demoralized People

People who seek therapy typically feel anxious, depressed, devoid of self-esteem, and incapable of turning things around. What any therapy offers is the expectation that, with commitment from the patient, things can and will get better. Apart from the particular therapeutic technique, this belief may itself promote improved morale, new feelings of self-efficacy, and diminished symptoms (Prioleau & others, 1983). This benefit of a person's belief in a treatment is the *placebo effect*. As we saw in Chapter 1, a placebo is an inert treatment often used as a control treatment in drug experiments. The placebo has no effect apart from a person's belief in it. In psychotherapy experiments, the placebo treatment may be listening to inspirational tapes, attending group discussions, or taking a fake pill.

"I utilize the best from Freud, the best from Jung, and the best from my Uncle Marty, a very smart fellow."

"All successful therapy has two things in common: It is forward-looking and it requires assuming responsibility. Therapy that reviews childhood endlessly has a century-long history of being ineffective. All therapy that works for depression, anxiety, and sexual problems focuses on exactly what is going wrong now and on how to correct it."

MARTIN E. P. SELIGMAN
WHAT YOU CAN CHANGE AND WHAT YOU CAN'T
1994

The finding that improvement is greater for placebo-treated people than for untreated people (although not as great as for those receiving actual psychotherapy) suggests that one reason therapies help is that they offer hope. Said differently, therapy outcomes vary with the client's attitude—the client's motivation, confidence, and commitment. Each therapy, in its individual way, may harness the client's own healing powers. And that, says psychiatrist Jerome Frank, helps us understand why all sorts of treatments—including some folk healing rites known to be powerless apart from the patient's belief—may in their own time and place produce cures. Until the 1800s, most medicines and the healers who prescribed them owed their good reputations to natural recoveries—and to placebo effects. (In the next chapter we will explore the power and the limits of this mind-over-body factor.)

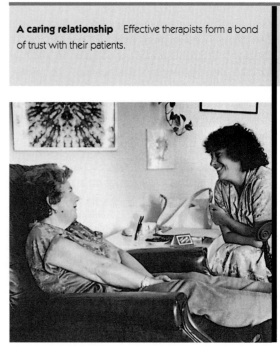

A caring relationship Effective therapists form a bond of trust with their patients.

A New Perspective

Every therapy offers people a plausible explanation of their symptoms and an alternative way of looking at themselves or responding to their worlds. Therapy also offers new experiences that help people change their views of themselves and their behaviors. Armed with a believable fresh perspective, they may approach life with a new attitude.

An Empathic, Trusting, Caring Relationship

To say that all therapies are about equally effective is not to say all *therapists* are equally effective. Regardless of their therapeutic technique, effective therapists are empathic people who seek to understand another's experience; whose care and concern the client feels; and whose respectful listening, reassurance, and advice earn the client's trust and respect. In the National Institute of Mental Health depression treatment study, the most effective therapists were those who were perceived as most empathic and caring, and who established the closest therapeutic bonds with their clients (Blatt & others, 1996). Indeed, some believe that warmth and empathy are hallmarks of healers everywhere, whether psychiatrists, witch doctors, or shamans (Torrey, 1986).

The notion that all therapies offer *hope* through the *fresh perspective* offered by a *caring person* gains support from a meta-analysis of 39 studies. Each study compared treatment offered by professional therapists with treatment offered by lay people. These lay people included friendly professors, people who had had a few hours' training in empathic listening skills, and college students supervised by a professional clinician. The result? The "paraprofessionals," as we call these briefly trained people, typically proved as effective as the professionals (Christensen & Jacobson, 1994). Although most of the problems they treated were mild, trained paraprofessionals were—believe it or not—as effective as professionals even when dealing with more disturbed adults, such as those diagnosed as seriously depressed.

To recap, people who seek help usually improve. So do many of those who do not undergo psychotherapy, and that is a tribute to our human resourcefulness and to our capacity to care for one another. Nevertheless, though the therapist's orientation and experience appear not to matter much, those who receive some psychotherapy usually improve more than those who do not. Mature, articulate people with specific emotional or behavioral problems often improve the most.

Part of what all therapies offer is hope, a fresh way of looking at life, and an empathic, caring relationship. That may explain why the empathy and friendly counsel of paraprofessionals are often as helpful as professional psychotherapy. And that may also explain why people who feel supported by close relationships—who enjoy the fellowship and friendship of caring people—are less likely to need or seek therapy (Frank, 1982; O'Connor & Brown, 1984).

Culture and Values in Psychotherapy

All therapies offer hope, and nearly all therapists attempt to enhance their clients' sensitivity, openness, personal responsibility, and sense of purpose (Jensen & Bergin, 1988). But on certain matters of moral and cultural diversity, therapists may differ from one another and from their clients (Kelly, 1990). In Canada and the United States, for example, about 1 in 25 people declare themselves atheists or agnostics, as do (depending on the survey) one-fifth to one-half of psychiatrists and clinical psychologists (Gallup, 1993; Jensen, 1991; Lukoff & others, 1992). In Britain, two-thirds of psychiatrists say they are atheists (Neeleman & Persaud, 1995). That raises an issue: What values prevail in psychotherapy? What values *should* prevail? Should it matter that highly religious persons prefer religiously similar therapists (Worthington & others, 1996)?

Albert Ellis, the rational-emotive therapist, and Allen Bergin, co-editor of the *Handbook of Psychotherapy and Behavior Change*, illustrate how sharply values can differ. Ellis (1980) assumes that "no one and nothing is supreme," that "self-gratification" should be encouraged, and that "unequivocal love, commitment, service, and . . . fidelity to any interpersonal commitment, especially marriage, leads to harmful consequences." Bergin (1980) assumes the opposite—that "because God is supreme, humility and the acceptance of divine authority are virtues," that "self-control and committed love and self-sacrifice are to be encouraged," and that "infidelity to any interpersonal commitment, especially marriage, leads to harmful consequences." Bergin and Ellis disagree more radically than most therapists regarding what values are healthiest. In so doing, however, they illustrate what they agree on: that psychotherapists' personal beliefs and values influence their practice. Knowing that clients tend to adopt their therapists' values (Worthington & others, 1994), Bergin and Ellis also agree that therapists should divulge their values more openly.

Value differences also can become significant when a therapist from one culture meets a client from another. In North America, Europe, and Australia, for example, most therapists reflect their culture's individualism (by giving priority to personal desires and identity). Clients who are immigrants from Asian countries, which expect people to be mindful of others' expectations, may therefore have difficulty with therapies that require them to think independently. Such differences help explain the reluctance of some minority populations to use mental health services (Sue, 1990). Recognizing that therapists and clients may differ in values, in communication styles, and in language, many therapy training programs are now providing training in cultural sensitivity and recruiting members of underrepresented culture groups.

SUMMING UP

Because the positive testimonials of clients and therapists cannot prove that therapy is actually effective, psychologists have conducted hundreds of studies of psychotherapy's outcomes. Meta-analyses of these studies reveal that (1) people who remain untreated often improve; (2) those who receive psychotherapy are more likely to improve, regardless of what kind of therapy they receive and for how long; (3) mature, articulate people with specific behavior problems often receive the greatest benefits from therapy; but (4) placebo treatments or the sympathy and friendly counsel of paraprofessionals also tend to produce more improvement than occurs with untreated people.

Different types of psychotherapy offer certain commonalities, such as new hope and a fresh perspective. Therapists do, however, differ in the values that influence their aims.

KEY TERMS AND CONCEPT meta-analysis

The Biomedical Therapies

Psychotherapy is one way to treat psychological disorders. The other is physically changing the brain's functioning—by altering its chemistry with drugs, by overloading its circuits with electroconvulsive shock, or by disconnecting its circuits through psychosurgery.

Drug Therapies

By far the most widely used biomedical treatments today are the drug therapies. When introduced in the 1950s, drug therapy greatly reduced the need

Figure **16.8**

The emptying of U.S. mental hospitals After the widespread introduction of antipsychotic drugs, starting in about 1955, the number of residents in state and county mental hospitals declined sharply. But in the rush to deinstitutionalize the mentally ill, many people who were ill-equipped to care for themselves were left homeless on city streets. (Data from the National Institute of Mental Health and Bureau of the Census, 1996.)

> "The mentally ill were out of the hospital, but in many cases they were simply out on the streets, less agitated but lost, still disabled but now uncared for."
>
> **LEWIS THOMAS**
> *LATE NIGHT THOUGHTS ON LISTENING TO MAHLER'S NINTH SYMPHONY*
> *1983*

for psychosurgery or hospitalization. Discoveries in psychopharmacology (the study of drug effects on mind and behavior) revolutionized the treatment of severely disordered people, liberating hundreds of thousands from confinement in mental hospitals. Thanks to drug therapy—and to political and legal efforts to minimize involuntary hospitalization and to return hospitalized people to their communities, aided by community mental health programs—the resident population of state and county mental hospitals in the United States today is but 20 percent of what it was 40 years ago (Figure 16.8).

For those still unable to care for themselves, however, release from hospitals has meant not liberation but homelessness. If home is the place where, as Robert Frost said, when you go there, they have to take you in, then some 200,000 disordered Americans and many thousands of Europeans have no place to call home (Fichter & others, 1996; Leshner, 1992). Studies suggest that about one-third of the homeless suffer disabling psychological disorders (Fischer & Breakey, 1991; Levine & Rog, 1990; McCarty & others, 1991). And that doesn't include alcohol or drug abuse, which also plague at least one in three homeless people. Unlike the homeless on the 1950s skid rows in major cities, 3 percent of whom were female, 25 percent of today's homeless are female (Rossi, 1990).

With almost any new treatment, including drug therapy, there is a first wave of enthusiasm as many people apparently improve. But that enthusiasm often diminishes after researchers subtract the rate of (1) normal recovery among untreated persons and (2) recovery due to the placebo effect, which arises from the positive expectations of patients and mental health workers alike. So, to evaluate the effectiveness of any new drug, researchers use the *double-blind technique*. Half the patients re-

ceive the drug, the other half a similar-appearing placebo. Neither the staff nor the patients know who gets which. In double-blind studies, several types of drugs have proved useful in treating psychological disorders.

Antipsychotic Drugs

The revolution in drug therapy for psychological disorders began when it was accidentally discovered that certain drugs, used for other medical purposes, also calmed psychotic patients. These antipsychotic drugs, such as chlorpromazine (sold as Thorazine), provide most help to people experiencing the positive symptoms of auditory hallucinations and paranoia, by dampening their responsiveness to irrelevant stimuli (Lenzenweger & others, 1989). Schizophrenia patients with the negative symptoms of apathy and withdrawal often do not respond well to these antipsychotic drugs. A newer drug, clozapine (marketed as Clozaril), does sometimes enable "awakenings" in such people. It also sometimes helps those who have positive symptoms but haven't responded to other drugs. Although clozapine has a toxic effect on white blood cells in 1 or 2 percent of cases—thus necessitating regular blood tests—it is currently the most effective schizophrenia treatment (Skelton & others, 1995). Researchers are testing possible cousin drugs that would offer the same benefits without the blood problem.

The molecules of antipsychotic drugs are similar enough to molecules of the neurotransmitter dopamine to occupy its receptor sites and block its activity (Pickar & others, 1984; Taubes, 1994). (Clozapine also blocks serotonin activity.) The finding that most antipsychotic drugs block dopamine receptors reinforces the idea that an overactive dopamine system contributes to schizophrenia.

psychopharmacology
the study of the effects of drugs on mind and behavior.

Antipsychotics such as Thorazine are powerful drugs that can produce sluggishness, tremors, and twitches similar to those of Parkinson's disease, which is marked by too little dopamine (Kaplan & Saddock, 1989). (Clozapine, thankfully, has few such side effects.) What is an effective dose for some people may be an overdose for others. Asians, for example, seem to require lower doses than do Caucasians (Holden, 1991). By carefully monitoring the dosage and its effects, therapist and patient tread the fine line between relieving the symptoms and causing extremely unpleasant side effects. In this way, and with the help of supportive people, hundreds of thousands of people with schizophrenia who had been consigned to the back wards of mental hospitals have returned to jobs and to near-normal lives.

Antianxiety Drugs

Among the most heavily prescribed and abused drugs are the antianxiety agents, such as Valium and Librium. Like alcohol, these drugs depress central nervous system activity. Because they reduce tension and anxiety without causing excessive sleepiness, they have been prescribed even for minor emotional stresses. Used in combination with other therapy, an antianxiety drug can help a person learn to cope with frightening situations and fear-triggering stimuli.

The criticism sometimes made of the behavior therapies—that they reduce symptoms without resolving underlying problems—is also made of antianxiety drugs. Unlike the behavior therapies, they may even be used as a continuing treatment. Routinely "popping a Valium" at the first sign of tension can produce psychological dependence on the drug. When heavy users stop taking the drug, they may experience increased anxiety and insomnia, driving them back to the drug for relief.

Antidepressant Drugs

As the antianxiety drugs calm anxious people down, the antidepressants sometimes lift depressed people up. The boost is due partly to a nice placebo effect—the new hope that patients gain when taking a drug they believe will help them—and partly to the drug's physical effect (Sapirstein & Kirsch, 1996).

Most of these drugs increase the availability of the neurotransmitters norepinephrine or serotonin, which elevate arousal and mood and appear scarce during depression. Consider fluoxetine, which 20 million users worldwide know as Prozac, the world's most widely prescribed psychiatric drug (Horgan, 1996). Prozac blocks the reabsorption and removal of serotonin from synapses (Figure 16.9). Prozac, and its cousins Zoloft and Paxil, are therefore called serotonin-reuptake-inhibitor drugs. Other antidepressants work by blocking the reabsorption of both norepinephrine and serotonin or by inhibiting an enzyme that breaks down neurotransmitters such as serotonin. These drugs, however, have more potential side effects, such as dry mouth, weight gain, or dizzy spells.

Herself renewed Thanks to clozapine, Daphne Moss went "from hating the sunshine in the morning to loving it." No longer suffering from the paranoid delusion that her parents were witches, Moss began teaching school and living independently.

Figure **16.9**

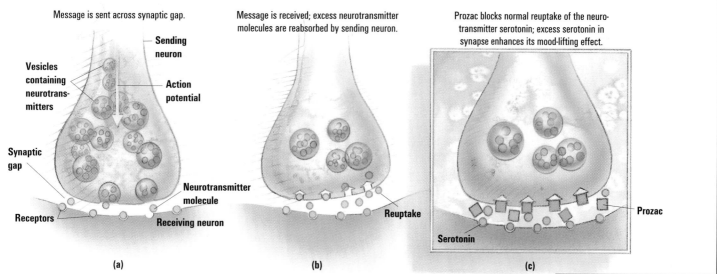

Message is sent across synaptic gap.

Message is received; excess neurotransmitter molecules are reabsorbed by sending neuron.

Prozac blocks normal reuptake of the neurotransmitter serotonin; excess serotonin in synapse enhances its mood-lifting effect.

Sending neuron

Vesicles containing neurotransmitters

Action potential

Synaptic gap

Neurotransmitter molecule

Receptors

Receiving neuron

Reuptake

Prozac

Serotonin

(a)

(b)

(c)

Biology of antidepressants
Neurotransmitters carry a message across a synapse.

lithium
a chemical that provides an effective drug therapy for the mood swings of bipolar (manic-depressive) disorders.

electroconvulsive therapy (ECT)
a biomedical therapy for severely depressed patients in which a brief electric current is sent through the brain of an anesthetized patient.

The medical use of electricity is an ancient practice. Physicians treated the Roman Emperor Claudius (10 B.C.–A.D. 54) for headaches by pressing electric eels to his temples.

Patients who begin taking antidepressants do not wake up the next day singing "Oh, what a beautiful morning!" Although the influence of antidepressants on neurotransmission occurs within hours, their full psychological effect often requires four weeks, sometimes aided by cognitive therapy to help the patient reverse a now-habitual negative thinking style. Moreover, after allowing for natural recovery ("spontaneous remission") and placebo effect, the drug effect is often modest (Greenberg & others, 1992, 1994). Aerobic exercise, which helps calm anxious people and energize depressed people, does about as much good, and with positive side effects (see page 529).

Although the drug effects are less exciting than many news stories would have us believe, they also are less frightening than other stories have suggested. Some people taking Prozac, for example, have committed suicide, but their numbers seem fewer than we would expect from millions of depressed people not taking the medication. Prozac users who commit suicide are like cellular phone users who get brain cancer. Given the millions of people taking Prozac and using cellular phones, alarming anecdotes tell us nothing. The question critical thinkers want answered is this: Do these groups suffer an elevated *rate* of suicide and brain cancer? The answer in each case appears to be no (Paulos, 1995; Tollefson & others, 1993, 1994).

For those suffering the manic-depressive mood swings of a bipolar disorder, the simple salt lithium can be an effective mood stabilizer. An Australian physician, John Cade, discovered this in the 1940s when he administered lithium to a severely manic patient. Although his reason for doing so was misguided—he thought lithium had calmed excitable guinea pigs when actually it made them sick—Cade found that in less than a week the patient became perfectly well (Snyder, 1986). With continued lithium use, the emotional highs and lows typically level. After suffering mood swings for years, about seven in ten people with bipolar disorder benefit from a long-term daily dose of this cheap salt (Solomon & others, 1995).

Electroconvulsive Therapy

A more controversial brain manipulation occurs through shock treatment, or electroconvulsive therapy (ECT). When ECT was first introduced in 1938, the wide-awake patient was strapped to a table and jolted with roughly 100 volts of electricity to the brain, producing racking convulsions and brief unconsciousness. ECT therefore gained a barbaric image that lingers to the present. Today, however, patients first receive a general anesthetic so they are not conscious, and a muscle relaxant to prevent injury from convulsions. Then a psychiatrist momentarily electrically shocks the unconscious patient's brain. Within 30 minutes the patient awakens and remembers nothing of the treatment or of the hours preceding it.

Psychiatrists usually limit ECT to severely depressed patients. (It is usually ineffective in treating other psychological disorders.) After three such treatments each week for two to four weeks, 80 percent or more of depressed people improve

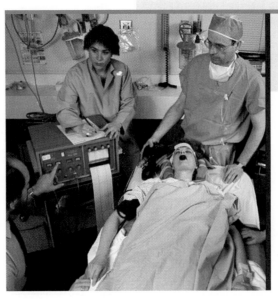

Electroconvulsive therapy Although ECT is controversial, it is the preferred treatment for depression that does not respond to drug therapy.

markedly and without discernible brain damage (Bergsholm & others, 1989; Coffey, 1993). "A miracle had happened in two weeks," reported noted research psychologist Norman Endler (1982) after ECT alleviated his deep depression. A 1985 panel of the National Institutes of Health, as well as newer research reviews, confirm that ECT is an effective treatment for severely depressed patients who have not responded to drug therapy (Consensus Conference, 1985; Parker & others, 1992). Thus, reports the American Psychiatric Association (1990), ECT has regained respectability as a "major treatment" for depression.

How does ECT work? After more than 50 years, no one knows for sure (Kapur & Mann, 1993). Perhaps electrical shock increases the release of norepinephrine, a neurotransmitter that elevates arousal and mood and seems in short supply during depression. Or perhaps the shock-induced seizures cause the brain to react by calming neural centers where overactivity produces depression.

Although ECT is credited with saving many from suicide, its Frankenstein-like image continues. No matter how impressive the results, the idea of electrically shocking people into convulsions still strikes many as barbaric, especially given our ignorance about why ECT works. Moreover, ECT-treated patients, like other formerly depressed patients, are vulnerable to relapse (Table 16.2). Nevertheless, electroconvulsive therapy is, in the minds of many psychiatrists and patients, a lesser evil than depression's misery, anguish, and risk of suicide. One recipient likened ECT to smallpox vaccine, which was saving lives before we knew how it worked.

Psychosurgery

Because its effects are irreversible, psychosurgery —surgery that removes or destroys brain tissue to change behavior—is the most drastic and the least-used biomedical intervention. In the 1930s, Portuguese physician Egas Moniz developed what became the best-known psychosurgical operation: the lobotomy. Moniz found that cutting the nerves connecting the frontal lobes with the emotion-controlling centers of the inner brain calmed uncontrollably emotional and violent patients. After shocking the patient into a coma, a neurosurgeon would hammer an icepicklike instrument through each eye socket into the brain, then wiggle it to sever connections running up to the frontal lobes. If a bit crude, the whole procedure was at least easy and cheap, taking only about 10 minutes. During the 1940s and 1950s, tens of thousands of severely disturbed people were "lobotomized," and Moniz was honored with a Nobel prize (Valenstein, 1986).

Although the intention was simply to disconnect emotion from thought, the effect was often more drastic: The lobotomy produced a permanently lethargic, immature, impulsive personality. During the 1950s, after some 35,000 people had been lobotomized in the United States alone, calming drugs became available and psychosurgery was largely abandoned. Today, lobotomies are almost never performed. Other psychosurgery is used only in extreme cases. For example, if a patient suffers uncontrollable seizures, surgeons can deactivate the specific nerve clusters that cause or transmit the convulsions. Because such beneficial opera-

psychosurgery
surgery that removes or destroys brain tissue in an effort to change behavior.

lobotomy
a now-rare psychosurgical procedure once used to calm uncontrollably emotional or violent patients. The procedure cut the nerves that connect the frontal lobes to the emotion-controlling centers of the inner brain.

Comparing Treatments for Depression

Table **16.2**

	Cognitive Therapy	Antidepressant Drugs	Electroconvulsive Therapy
Percent marked improvement	60–80%	60–80%	80%
Relapse rate	moderate	moderate to high	moderate to high
Side effects	none	moderate	severe
Time scale	months	weeks	days
Overall	very good	useful to very good	useful to very good

Source: Adapted from Seligman (1994).

tions are irreversible, however, neurosurgeons perform them only as a last resort.

The effectiveness of the biomedical therapies reminds us of a fundamental lesson: We find it convenient to talk of separate psychological and physiological influences, but everything psychological is physiological. Every thought and feeling depends on the functioning brain. Every creative idea, every moment of joy or anger, every period of depression emerges from the electrochemical activity of the living brain. But the influence is two-way. Thus, when therapy calms obsessive-compulsive behavior, PET scans reveal a calmer brain (Schwartz & others, 1996).

Mind-body interaction. The biomedical therapies assume that mind and body are a unit: Affect one and you will affect the other.

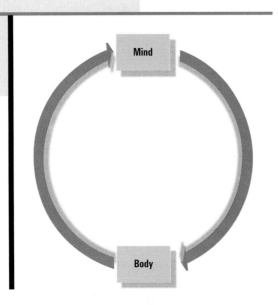

SUMMING UP

Drug Therapies The most widely used biomedical therapies are the antipsychotic, antianxiety, and antidepressant drugs.

Electroconvulsive Therapy Although controversial, ECT is an effective treatment for many severely depressed people who do not respond to drug therapy.

Psychosurgery Neurosurgeons rarely perform brain surgery to alleviate specific problems, because the effects of radical psychosurgical procedures such as lobotomy are irreversible and potentially drastic.

KEY TERMS AND CONCEPTS psychopharmacology, lithium, electroconvulsive therapy (ECT), psychosurgery, lobotomy

Preventing Psychological Disorders

There is an alternative perspective on alleviating disorder: Rather than treat the "sick" person, change the "sick" social contexts that breed disorder.

Psychotherapies and biomedical therapies tend to locate the cause of psychological disorders within the disordered person. We infer that people who act cruelly must be cruel and that people who act "crazy" must be "sick." We attach labels to such people, thereby distinguishing them from "normal" folks. It follows, then, that we try to treat "abnormal" people by giving them insight into their problems, by changing their thinking, or by controlling them with drugs.

There is an alternative viewpoint: We could interpret many psychological disorders as understandable responses to a disturbing and stressful society. According to this view, it is not just the person who needs treatment, but also the person's social context. Better to prevent a problem by reforming a sick situation than to wait for a problem to arise and then treat it.

A story about the rescue of a drowning person from a rushing river illustrates this viewpoint: Having successfully administered first aid to the first victim, the rescuer spots another struggling person and pulls her out, too. After a half dozen repetitions, the rescuer suddenly turns and starts running away while the river sweeps yet another floundering person into view. "Aren't you going to rescue that fellow?" asks a bystander. "Heck no," the rescuer replies. "I'm going upstream to find out what's pushing all these people in."

Preventive mental health is upstream work. It seeks to prevent psychological casualties by identifying and alleviating the conditions that cause them. George Albee (1986) believes there is abundant evidence that poverty, meaningless work, constant criticism, unemployment, racism, and sexism undermine people's sense of competence, personal control, and self-esteem. Such stresses increase their risk of depression, alcoholism, and suicide.

"It is better to prevent than to cure."

PERUVIAN FOLK WISDOM

Albee contends that those who care about preventing psychological casualties should therefore support programs that alleviate poverty, discrimination, and other demoralizing situations. We eliminated smallpox not by treating the afflicted but by inoculating the unafflicted. We conquered yellow fever by controlling mosquitos. Prevention of psychological problems means empowering those who have learned an attitude of helplessness, changing environments that breed loneliness, renewing the disintegrating family, and bolstering parents' and teachers' skills at nurturing children's self-esteem. Indeed, "Everything aimed at improving the human condition, at making life more fulfilling and meaningful, may be considered part of primary prevention of mental or emotional disturbance" (Kessler & Albee, 1975, p. 557).

There is more to the psychological disorders story than bad environments. Anxiety disorders, major depression, bipolar disorder, and schizophrenia are known biological events. Yet Albee reminds us again of one of this book's themes: *A human being is an integrated bio-psycho-social system.* For years we have trusted our bodies to

physicians and our minds to psychiatrists and psychologists. That neat separation no longer seems valid. Chemical imbalances can produce schizophrenia and depression. And anger, depression, and stress, as the next chapter shows, can threaten our physical health. *"Mens sana in corpore sano,"* says an ancient Latin adage: A healthy mind in a healthy body.

> "Mental disorders arise from physical ones, and likewise physical disorders arise from mental ones."
>
> THE MAHABHARATA
> C. A.D. 200

SUMMING UP

Advocates of preventive mental health argue that many psychological disorders could be prevented. Their aim is to change oppressive, esteem-destroying environments into more benevolent, nurturing environments that foster individual growth and self-confidence.

TERMS AND CONCEPTS TO REMEMBER

psychotherapy, p. 488

eclectic approach, p. 488

psychoanalysis, p. 488

resistance, p. 489

interpretation, p. 489

transference, p. 489

person-centered therapy, p. 490

active listening, p. 491

Gestalt therapy, p. 492

behavior therapy, p. 492

counterconditioning, p. 493

systematic desensitization, p. 493

aversive conditioning, p. 494

token economy, p. 495

cognitive therapy, p. 496

rational-emotive therapy, p. 496

family therapy, p. 500

meta-analysis, p. 503

psychopharmacology, p. 508

lithium, p. 510

electroconvulsive therapy (ECT), p. 510

psychosurgery, p. 511

lobotomy, p. 511

CRITICAL THINKING EXERCISE
by Richard O. Straub

Now that you have read and reviewed Chapter 16, take your learning a step further by testing your critical thinking skills on the following practical problem-solving exercise.

Deborah is very satisfied with the large amount of time and money she has invested in psychotherapy. When she began

therapy, her life was in crisis and she was desperate for help in overcoming her depressed, pessimistic attitude. After shopping around, she finally found an understanding cognitive therapist who made her feel she could get her life back on track. After three months of psychotherapy, Deborah is once again enjoying her life and attributes her recovery to the psychotherapy.

Vincent is a middle-aged manager of an auto parts store. He is under a lot of pressure at work, has a very negative attitude about life, and "blows up" frequently at minor family annoyances. Although he admits that he is depressed and complains to his family a lot, he doesn't feel there is anything wrong with him. His family disagrees and is concerned that he is increasingly showing signs of psychologically disordered behavior. At their insistence, Vincent reluctantly agrees to see a psychotherapist. He picks a name at random from the phone book and grudgingly endures several weeks of "overpriced gibberish" to appease his family. Despite the good efforts of the psychotherapist, who attempts to countercondition Vincent's maladaptive behaviors, Vincent shows no improvement following psychotherapy.

1. Assuming their initial problems were equally serious, what could account for Deborah's and Vincent's very different experiences with psychotherapy?

2. Deborah now swears by cognitive therapy, while Vincent is very critical of behavior therapy. Are their recommendations acceptable as scientific evidence regarding the effectiveness of psychotherapy? Why or why not?

Check your progress on becoming a critical thinker by comparing your answers to the sample answers found in Appendix B.

chapter

17

Stress and Health

No one needs to be told that psychological states cause physical reactions. Nervous about an important exam, we feel stomach butterflies. Anxious over a public speaking assignment, we frequent the bathroom. Smoldering over a conflict with a family member, we develop a splitting headache. If such stress endures, it may also bring on (in those physiologically predisposed) skin rashes, asthma attacks, or high blood pressure.

Many people are less aware of how behavior kills. Our behaviors influence whether we will become victims of one of today's four leading causes of serious illness and death: heart disease, cancer, stroke, and chronic lung disease (Figure 17.1). The National Academy of Sciences' Institute of Medicine (1982) traced half the mortality from the 10 leading causes of death to people's behavior—to cigarette smoking, alcohol abuse, unprotected sex, ignoring doctors' orders, insufficient exercise, use of illicit drugs, and poor nutrition. If we could understand and modify these behavioral sources of illness, we might lessen people's suffering and increase their life expectancy and quality of life. To pursue these goals, psychologists and physicians created the interdisciplinary field of behavioral medicine, integrating behavioral and medical knowledge.

Health psychology provides psychology's contribution to behavioral medicine. Its numbers include many of the 3500 psychologists now on the faculties of Canadian and U.S. medical schools (Michaelson, 1993). Health psychologists ask: How do our perceptions of a situation determine the stress we feel? How do our emotions and personality influence our risk of disease? How do people decide they are sick, and when do they seek treatment? What attitudes and behaviors help prevent illness and promote health and well-being? How can we reduce or control stress?

Figure **17.1**

The four leading causes of death in the United States in 1900 and 1991 With the conquering of the major infectious diseases, diseases that are influenced by behavior have now emerged as the major causes of death. (From National Center for Health Statistics.) The story is much the same in Canada, Australia, New Zealand, and most European countries. (From World Health Statistics Annual.)

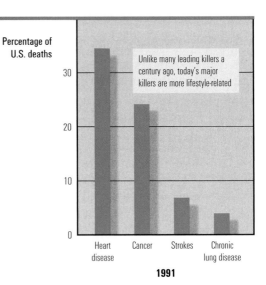

Worldwide, reports the World Health Organization, nearly a quarter of health care contacts are prompted by psychological problems (Sartorius, 1994).

behavioral medicine
an interdisciplinary field that integrates behavioral and medical knowledge and applies that knowledge to health and disease.

health psychology
a subfield of psychology that provides psychology's contribution to behavioral medicine.

stress
the process by which we perceive and respond to certain events, called *stressors*, that we appraise as threatening or challenging.

Stress and Illness

What is stress? To what extent, and by what mechanisms, does stress contribute to heart disease, infectious diseases, and cancer? What types of people are most at risk for stress-related ailments?

Walking along the path toward his Rocky Mountain campsite, Karl hears a rustle at his feet. As he glimpses a rattlesnake, his body mobilizes for fight or flight: His muscles tense, his adrenaline flows, his heart pounds. Flee he does, racing to the security of camp. Once there, Karl's muscles gradually relax and his heart rate and breathing ease.

Karen leaves her suburban apartment one morning and, delayed by road construction, arrives at the parking lot of the commuter train station just in time to see the 8:05 pull away. Catching the next train, she arrives in the city late and elbows her way through crowds of rush-hour pedestrians. Once at her bank office, she apologizes to her first client, who wonders where Karen has been and why his quarterly investment report is not ready. Karen does her best to mollify the client. Afterward, she notices her tense muscles, clenched teeth, and churning stomach.

Karl's response to stress saved his life; Karen's, if chronic, could increase her risk of heart disease, high blood pressure, and other stress-linked health problems. Moreover, feeling under pressure, she might sleep and exercise less and smoke and drink more, further endangering her long-term health.

Stress and Stressors

Stress is a slippery concept. People sometimes use the word *stress* to describe threats or challenges ("Karen was under a lot of stress"), other times to describe our responses ("When Karl saw the rattler he experienced acute stress"). Most psychologists would define Karen's missed train as a "stressor," Karl's physical and emotional responses as a "stress reaction," and the process by which Karen and Karl related to their environments as stress. Thus, stress is not just a stimulus or a response. It

Figure **17.2**

The stress process How we react to stressors depends on who we are and how we appraise and cope with them. For example, criticism that an easygoing optimist perceives as a challenge may seem a dire threat to a temperamental pessimist.

is the process by which we appraise and cope with environmental threats and challenges (Figure 17.2).

When perceived as challenges, stressors can have positive effects by arousing and motivating us to conquer problems. Championship athletes, successful entertainers, and great teachers and leaders all thrive and excel when aroused by a challenge. But more often stressors threaten our resources—our status and security on the job, our loved ones' health or well-being, our deeply held beliefs, our self-image (Hobfoll, 1989). And when such stress is severe or prolonged, it may also harm.

The Stress Response System

Although medical interest in stress dates back to Hippocrates (460–377 B.C.), it was not until the 1920s that physiologist Walter Cannon (1929) confirmed that the stress response is part of a unified mind–body system. He observed that extreme cold, lack of oxygen, and emotion-arousing incidents all trigger an outpouring of epinephrine (adrenaline) and norepinephrine (noradrenaline). These stress hormones enter the bloodstream from sympathetic nerve endings in the inner part of the adrenal glands. As we saw in Chapter 13's discussion of emotional arousal, this is but one part of the sympathetic nervous system's response. When alerted by any of a number of brain pathways, the sympathetic nervous system increases heart rate and respiration, diverts blood to skeletal muscles, and releases fat from the body's stores—all to prepare the body for what Cannon called *fight or flight*. All in all, this stress response struck Cannon as wonderfully adaptive. Physiologists have also identified a second stress response system (Figure 17.3). On orders from the cerebral cortex (via the hypothalamus and pituitary gland), the outer (cortex) part of the adrenal gland secretes the stress hormone cortisol.

Canadian scientist Hans Selye's (1936, 1976) 40 years of research on stress extended Cannon's findings and helped make stress a major concept in both psychology and medicine. The story of how Selye arrived at his concept of the stress response is one worth remembering in times of intellectual discouragement. Hoping to discover a new sex hormone, Selye injected rats with ovarian hormone extract. He detected three effects: enlargement of the adrenal cortex, shrinkage of the thymus gland (which contains disease-fighting white blood cells), and bleeding ulcers. Because no known hormone had ever produced such symptoms, Selye was elated. "At the age of 28, I seemed to be already on the track of a new hormone."

The faces of stress Challenging positive events, such as graduating into the working world, can be stressful. But most stresses arise from negative events, such as a loved one's death.

Figure **17.3**

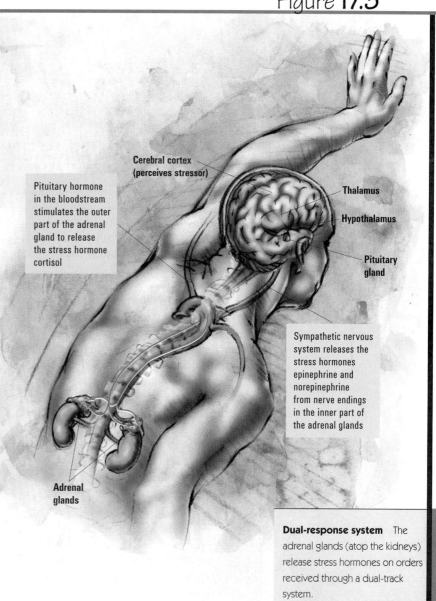

Pituitary hormone in the bloodstream stimulates the outer part of the adrenal gland to release the stress hormone cortisol

Cerebral cortex (perceives stressor)

Thalamus

Hypothalamus

Pituitary gland

Sympathetic nervous system releases the stress hormones epinephrine and norepinephrine from nerve endings in the inner part of the adrenal glands

Adrenal glands

Dual-response system The adrenal glands (atop the kidneys) release stress hormones on orders received through a dual-track system.

general adaptation syndrome (GAS)
Selye's concept of the body's adaptive response to stress as composed of three stages—alarm, resistance, exhaustion.

Before long, Selye's elation became disappointment. When he injected the rats with other fluids, he observed the same adrenal enlargement, thymus shrinkage, and bleeding ulcers. Alas, Selye concluded, the effects were *not* due to a new hormone:

All my dreams of discovering a new hormone were shattered. All the time and all the materials that went into this long study were wasted. . . . I became so depressed that for a few days I could not do any work at all. I just sat in my laboratory, brooding. . . . The ensuing period of introverted contemplation turned out to be the decisive factor in my whole career; it pointed the way for all my subsequent work. . . . As I repetitiously continued to go over my ill-fated experiments and their possible interpretation, it suddenly struck me that one could look at them from an entirely different angle. If there was such a thing as a single nonspecific reaction of the body to damage of any kind, . . . the general medical implications of the syndrome would be enormous! (1976, pp. 24–26)

To verify his hunch, Selye studied animals' reactions to various other stressors, such as electric shock, surgical trauma, and immobilizing restraint. He discovered that the body's adaptive response to stress was so general—like a single burglar alarm that sounds no matter what intrudes—that he called it the general adaptation syndrome (GAS).

Selye saw the GAS as having three phases (Figure 17.4). Let's say you suffer a physical or emotional trauma. In Phase 1, you experience an *alarm reaction* due to the sudden activation of your sympathetic nervous system. Your heart rate zooms. Blood is diverted to your skeletal muscles. You feel the faintness of shock. With your resources mobilized, you are now ready to fight the challenge during Phase 2, *resistance*. Your temperature, blood pressure, and respiration remain high, and there is a sudden outpouring of hormones. If persistent, the stress may eventually deplete your body's reserves during Phase 3, *exhaustion*. With exhaustion, you are more vulnerable to illness or even, in extreme cases, collapse and death.

Newer research reveals subtle differences in the body's reactions to different stressors. Nevertheless, few medical experts today quarrel with Selye's basic point: Prolonged stress can produce physical deterioration. Several recent studies have taken MRI brain scans of people who have experienced a prolonged flood of stress hormones, due to sustained child abuse, combat, or an endocrine disease (Sapolsky, 1996). Most have a shrunken hippocampus, the inner brain structure vital to laying down explicit (declarative) memories. Such findings lead to the practical concerns of today's health psychologists: What causes stress? What are the effects of stress? And how can we alleviate those effects?

Stressful Life Events

How stressed we feel depends on how we appraise events. One person alone in a house dismisses its creaking sounds and experiences no stress; someone else suspects an intruder and becomes alarmed. One person regards a new job as a welcome challenge; someone else appraises it as risking failure. Research has focused on our responses to three types of stressors: catastrophes, significant life changes, and daily hassles.

Figure **17.4**

Selye's general adaptation syndrome After a trauma, the body enters an alarm phase of temporary shock. From this it rebounds, as stress resistance rises. If the stress is prolonged, wear and tear may lead to exhaustion.

The body's resistance to stress can only last so long before exhaustion sets in

Stress resistance

↑ **Stressor occurs**

Phase 1
Alarm reaction
(mobilize
resources)

Phase 2
Resistance
(cope with stressor)

Phase 3
Exhaustion
(reserves
depleted)

Catastrophes

Catastrophes are unpredictable, large-scale events such as war and natural disasters that nearly everyone appraises as threatening. Although people often provide one another with aid and comfort after such events, the health consequences can be significant. Three examples:

- On the day of its 1994 earthquake, Los Angeles experienced a fivefold increase in sudden-death heart attacks—especially in the first two hours after the quake and near its epicenter. Physical exertion (running, lifting debris) was a factor in only 13 percent of the deaths, leaving stress as the likely trigger for the others (Muller & Verrier, 1996).

- In the year following the crash of a 747 jumbo jet at Lockerbie, Scotland, police officers—after being pressed into recovering human remains and patrolling the disaster zone—suffered a 38 percent increase in short-term illnesses (Paton, 1992).

- In the Republic of Belarus, where the worst fallout rained down from the nearby Chernobyl nuclear disaster, those who left their native homes and friends and those who stayed to live in a threatening environment all suffered severe stress. Stress-related ailments such as hypertension and heart disease reportedly tripled (Kolominsky & Parkhomenko, 1993).

Do community disasters usually produce effects this great? After digesting data from 52 such studies of catastrophic floods, hurricanes, and fires, Anthony Rubonis and Leonard Bickman (1991) found the typical effect more modest but nonetheless genuine. In disaster's wake, rates of psychological disorders, such as depression and anxiety, rose an average 17 percent. The nuclear accident at Three Mile Island produced similar stress symptoms in area residents (Baum & Fleming, 1993). Refugees fleeing their homeland also suffer increased rates of psychological disorder. Their stress stems from the trauma of uprooting and family separation and from the challenges of adjusting to a foreign culture, with its new language, ethnicity, climate, and social norms (Williams & Berry, 1991). In all these cases, the health consequences often come only after prolonged stress.

Significant Life Changes

The second type of life event stressor is a significant personal life change—the death of a loved one, the loss of a job, a marriage or divorce. Some psychologists study the health effects of life changes by following people over time to see if such events precede illnesses. Others compare the life changes recalled by those who have or have not suffered a specific health problem, such as a heart attack. A review of these studies commissioned by the National Academy of Sciences revealed that

Toxic stress   Researchers have found that catastrophes such as flooding increase psychological disorders.

people recently widowed, fired, or divorced are more vulnerable to disease (Dohrenwend & others, 1982). A Finnish study of 96,000 widowed people confirmed the phenomenon: Their risk of death doubled in the week following their partner's death (Kaprio & others, 1987). Experiencing a cluster of crises puts one even more at risk.

Why, then, do some people feel stressed after a major life change while others do not? What matters more than the situation itself is our appraisal of it. Retirement may be viewed by one person as a time to relax and enjoy, by another person as a threat to identity and income. Having an abortion creates stress for women who morally oppose abortion and who lack their partner's or parents' support. Yet most women who appraise abortion differently do not experience severe distress after abortion (Adler & others, 1990; Major & others, 1990; Russo, 1992). The events of our lives flow through a psychological filter. Stress arises less from events per se than from how we appraise them.

People recently widowed, fired, or divorced are more vulnerable to disease.

Daily Hassles

As we noted in Chapter 13, our happiness stems less from enduring good fortune than from our response to daily events—an A on an exam, a gratifying letter, your team's winning the big game.

The principle works for negative events, too. Everyday annoyances may be the most significant sources of stress (Kohn & Macdonald, 1992; Lazarus, 1990; Ruffin, 1993). These daily hassles include rush-hour traffic, aggravating housemates, long lines at the bank or store, too many things to

No end in sight "It's not the large things that send a man to the madhouse . . . no, it's the continuing series of small tragedies . . . not the death of his love but the shoelace that snaps with no time left" (Charles Bukowski, cited by Lazarus in Wallis, 1983).

do, and misplacing things. Although some people can simply shrug them off, others are "driven up the wall" by such inconveniences. Thus, 6 in 10 people say they feel "great stress" at least once a week (Harris, 1987).

Over time, these little stressors can add up and take a toll on health and well-being. Among urban ghetto residents, many of whom endure the daily stresses that accompany poverty, unemployment, solo parenting, and overcrowding, hypertension (high blood pressure) rates are high. From 1990 to 1993, following the collapse of socialism in the former Soviet Union, Russia experienced mushrooming divorce, murder, suicide, and rates of stress-related disease—and life expectancy for Russian men plummeted nearly 5 years to 58.9 years (Holden, 1996). In contrast to these high-stress groups, there is a *low* rate of heart attacks among those who live the relatively peaceful monastic life (Henry & Stephens, 1977).

Persistent on-the-job hassles can lead to a condition of mental, physical, and emotional exhaustion called burnout (Maslach, 1982). Teachers, nurses, social workers, and police officers—indeed, anyone facing persistent work hassles—may become worn down by the never-ending stress of their job. The result may be a sharp drop in performance caused by the fatigue of physical exhaustion, the depression of emotional exhaustion, and the cynicism of mental exhaustion.

Perceived Control

Catastrophes, important life changes, and daily hassles and conflicts are especially stressful when we appraise them as both negative *and* uncontrollable. If two rats receive simultaneous shocks, but one of them can turn a wheel to stop the shocks, the helpless rat becomes more susceptible to ulcers and lowered immunity to disease (Laudenslager & Reite, 1984) (Figure 17.5).

So it goes in humans: Perceiving a loss of control, we are vulnerable to ill health. As we noted in Chapter 14, elderly nursing home patients who have little perceived control over their activities tend to decline faster and die sooner than do those given more control over their activities (Rodin, 1986). Given control over their work environments—by being able to adjust office furnishings and control interruptions and distractions—workers, too, experience less stress (O'Neill, 1993).

A related factor that influences our stress vulnerability is optimism. Psychologists Michael Scheier and Charles Carver (1992) report that optimists—people who agree with statements such as, "In uncertain times, I usually expect the best"—cope better with stressful events and enjoy better health.

Figure **17.5**

"Executive" rat   "Subordinate" rat   Control rat

To shock control   To shock source   No connection to shock source

Health consequences of a loss of control The "executive" rat at the left can switch off the tail shock by turning the wheel. Because it has control over the shock, it is no more likely to develop ulcers than is the unshocked control rat on the right. The "subordinate" rat in the center receives the same shocks as the executive rat. But because the subordinate rat has no control over the shocks, it is more likely to develop ulcers. (Adapted from Weiss, 1977.)

Figure **17.6**

Toxic hopelessness Compared to Finnish middle-aged men scoring low in hopelessness, those scoring high were 2 to 4 times more vulnerable to a heart attack over the ensuing six years and 3 to 4 times more likely to die. (Data from Everson & others, 1996.)

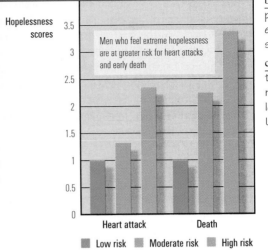

Hopelessness scores

Men who feel extreme hopelessness are at greater risk for heart attacks and early death

Heart attack   Death

■ Low risk   ■ Moderate risk   ■ High risk

burnout
physical, emotional, and mental exhaustion brought on by persistent job-related stress.

coronary heart disease
the clogging of the vessels that nourish the heart muscle; the leading cause of death in the United States.

During the last month of a semester, students previously identified as optimistic report less fatigue and fewer coughs, aches, and pains. Optimists also respond to stress with smaller increases in blood pressure, and they recover faster from heart bypass surgery. One study that followed 2428 middle-aged Finnish men for up to 10 years discovered that the number of deaths among men with a bleak, hopeless outlook was more than double that found among their optimistic counterparts (Figure 17.6).

Why do perceived loss of control and pessimism predict health problems? Animal studies show—and human studies confirm—that losing control provokes an outpouring of stress hormones. When rats cannot control shock or when humans feel unable to control their environment, cortisol levels rise and immune responses drop (Rodin, 1986). Captive animals therefore experience more stress and are more vulnerable to disease than are wild animals (Roberts, 1988). The crowding that occurs in high-density neighborhoods, prisons, and college dorms is another source of diminished feelings of control—and of increased levels of stress hormones and blood pressure (Fleming & others, 1987; Ostfeld & others, 1987).

Stress, Personality, and Heart Disease

Although infrequent before this century, coronary heart disease—the narrowing of the vessels that nourish the heart muscle—became by the 1950s North America's leading cause of death. In addition to family history of the disease, many behavioral and physiological factors increase the risk of heart disease—smoking, obesity, high-fat diet, physical inactivity, elevated blood pressure, and elevated cholesterol level. The psychological factors of stress and personality also play a big role.

In 1956, cardiologists Meyer Friedman, Ray Rosenman, and their colleagues stumbled upon an indication of how big a role (Friedman & Ulmer, 1984). While studying the eating behavior of white, San Francisco Junior League women and their husbands, Friedman and Rosenman discovered that the women consumed as much cholesterol and fat as their husbands did, yet they were far less susceptible to heart disease. Was it because of their female sex hormones? No, the researchers surmised, because African-American women with the same sex hormones but facing more stress are as prone to heart disease as their husbands are.

The Junior League president thought she knew the answer. "If you really want to know what is going to give our husbands heart attacks, I'll tell you. It's stress," she said sadly, "the stress they have to face in their businesses, day in, day out. Why, when my husband comes home at night, it takes at least one martini just to unclench his jaws."

To test the idea that stress increases vulnerability to heart disease, Friedman and Rosenman measured the blood cholesterol level and clotting speed of 40 tax accountants. From January through March, both of these coronary warning indicators were completely normal. Then, as the accountants began scrambling to finish their clients' tax returns before the April 15 filing deadline, their cholesterol and clotting measures rose to dangerous levels. In May and June, with the deadline past, the measures returned to normal. The researchers' hunch had paid off: Stress predicted heart attack risk.

Type A
Friedman and Rosenman's term for competitive, hard-driving, impatient, verbally aggressive, and anger-prone people.

Type B
Friedman and Rosenman's term for easygoing, relaxed people.

The stage was set for Friedman and Rosenman's classic 9-year study of more than 3000 healthy men aged 35 to 59. At the start of the study, they interviewed each man for 15 minutes about his work and eating habits. During the interview, they noted the man's manner of talking and other behavioral patterns. Those who seemed the most reactive, competitive, hard-driving, impatient, time-conscious, supermotivated, verbally aggressive, and easily angered they called Type A. A roughly equal number who were more easygoing they called Type B. Which group do you suppose turned out to be the most coronary-prone?

> When harassed, given a challenge, or threatened with a loss of control, Type A individuals are more physiologically reactive. Their hormonal secretions, pulse rate, and blood pressure soar, while Type Bs remain calm.

In both India and America, Type A bus drivers are literally hard-driving: They brake, pass, and honk their horns more often than their more easygoing Type B colleagues (Evans & others, 1987).

By the time the study was complete, 257 of the men had suffered heart attacks, 69 percent of whom were Type A. Moreover, not one of the "pure" Type Bs—the most mellow and laid-back of their group—had suffered a heart attack.

As often happens in science, this exciting discovery provoked enormous public interest. But after the honeymoon period, in which the finding seemed definitive and revolutionary, other researchers began asking, Is the finding reliable? If so, what is the toxic component of the Type A profile: The time-consciousness? The competitiveness? The anger?

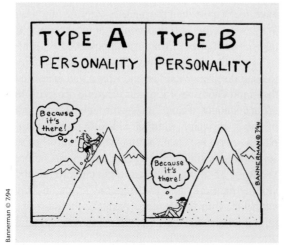

Type A people may be more prone to heart disease for at least two reasons. First, such individuals smoke more, sleep less, and drink more caffeinated drinks, all of which are associated with coronary risk (Hicks & others, 1982, 1983). Second, their temperament may contribute directly to heart disease. In relaxed situations, the arousal of Type As and Type Bs is no different. But when harassed, given a challenge, or threatened with a loss of control, Type A individuals are more physiologically reactive. Their hormonal secretions, pulse rate, and blood pressure soar, while Type Bs remain calm (Lyness, 1993). For example, when Redford Williams (1989) asked Duke University men to do simple math problems (with a prize for the fastest), the Type A students' stress-hormone levels rose to more than double those of their Type B classmates. These hormones accelerate the buildup of plaques (scarlike masses formed by cholesterol deposits) on the artery walls, producing atherosclerosis, or "hardening" of the arteries. Atherosclerosis also makes reactive people vulnerable to high blood pressure, a risk factor for strokes and heart attacks (Schneiderman & others, 1989).

These findings suggest that reactive Type A individuals are more often "combat ready." When harassed or challenged, their active sympathetic nervous system redistributes bloodflow to the muscles and away from internal organs such as the liver, which removes cholesterol and fat from the blood. Thus, their blood may contain excess cholesterol and fat that later get deposited around the heart. Further stress—sometimes conflicts triggered by their own abrasiveness—may trigger the altered heart rhythms that, in those with weakened hearts, can cause sudden death (Kamarck & Jennings, 1991). In such ways, the hearts and minds of people interact.

Newer research reveals that the Type A's toxic core is not a fast-paced life but rather is negative emotions—especially the anger associated with an aggressively reactive temperament (Miller & others, 1996; Williams, 1993). The effect of an anger-prone personality appears most noticeably in studies in which interviewers assess verbal assertiveness and emotional intensity. (If you pause in the middle of a sentence, an intense, anger-prone person may jump in and finish it for you.) Among young and middle-aged adults, those who react with anger over little things are the most coronary-prone. One study followed Duke University law students over 25 years. Those inclined to be hostile and cynical were five times more likely than their gentler, trusting classmates to die by middle age (Williams, 1989). As Charles Spielberger and Perry London (1982) put it, rage "seems to lash back and strike us in the heart muscle."

Anger isn't the only toxic emotion. Depression, too, can be lethal. Centers for Disease Control researchers studied adults who were feeling a sense of hopelessness or at least mild depression. Compared with those without such feelings, these downhearted people were more vulnerable to heart disease in the ensuing 12 years. This was true even after controlling for differences in age, sex, smoking, and other factors linked to heart ailments (Anda & others, 1993). In the years following a heart attack, depressed people have a quadrupled risk of further heart problems (Eaton & others, 1996; Frasure-Smith & others, 1995). The depression that follows a spouse's death similarly increases one's risk of having a heart attack or stroke (National Academy of Sciences, 1984).

The toxic effects of negative emotions help explain why about a quarter of medical inpatients suffer a mood or anxiety disorder, and why 4 in 10 chronically ill patients suffer or have suffered a psychiatric disorder (Cohen & Rodriguez, 1995; Katon & Sullivan, 1990). Negative emotions have physical consequences, and may also lead to poor health practices and health-related decisions. (Of course, the correlation between physical and psychological disorder may also reflect the effect of illness. Sickness, pain, and disability can impact one's hormones and neurotransmitters and have a demoralizing impact on one's abilities and self-esteem.)

Stress and Resistance to Disease

Not so long ago, the term *psychosomatic* described psychologically caused physical symptoms. To lay people, the term implied that the symptoms were unreal—they were "merely" psychosomatic. To avoid such connotations and to describe better the genuine physiological effects of psychological states, most experts today refer instead to psychophysiological illnesses. These illnesses, which include certain forms of hypertension and headaches, are stress-related. A person under stress may retain excess sodium and fluids, which, together with constriction of the arteries' muscle walls, contributes to increased blood pressure (Light & others, 1983).

Stress and the Immune System

Evidence that psychophysiological ailments are real comes from hundreds of new experiments that reveal the nervous and endocrine systems' influence on the immune system. The immune system is a complex surveillance system that defends the body by isolating and destroying bacteria, viruses, and other foreign substances. It includes two types of white blood cells, called lymphocytes. *B lymphocytes* form in the *b*one marrow and release antibodies that fight bacterial infections. *T lymphocytes* form in the *t*hymus and other lymphatic tissue and attack cancer cells, viruses, and foreign substances—even "good" ones, such as transplanted organs. Another agent of the immune system is the *macrophage* ("big eater"), which identifies, pursues, and ingests harmful invaders. Age, nutrition, genetics, body temperature, and stress all influence the immune system's activity.

The immune system can err in two directions. Responding too strongly, it may attack the body's own tissues, causing arthritis or an allergic reaction. Or it may underreact, allowing, say, a dormant herpes virus to erupt or cancer cells to multiply. Women are immunologically stronger than men (Morell, 1995). This makes them less susceptible to infections. But it also makes them more susceptible to self-attacking diseases, such as lupus and multiple sclerosis.

The immune system is not a headless horseman. Rather, it exchanges information with the brain and the hormone-secreting endocrine system. The brain regulates the secretion of stress hormones, which in turn suppress the disease-fighting lymphocytes. Thus, when animals are physically restrained, given unavoidable electric shocks, or subjected to noise, crowding, cold water, social defeat, or maternal separation, their immune systems become less active (Maier & others, 1994). One study monitored immune responses in 43 monkeys over 6 months (Cohen & others, 1992). Twenty-one were stressed by being housed with new roommates—three or four new monkeys—each month. (To empathize with the monkeys, recall the stress of leaving home to attend school or summer camp, and imagine having to repeat this experience weekly.) Compared with monkeys left in stable groups, the socially disrupted monkeys developed suppressed immune systems.

psychophysiological illness
literally, "mind–body" illness; any stress-related physical illness, such as hypertension and headaches. Note: This is distinct from *hypochondriasis*—misinterpreting normal physical sensations as symptoms of a disease.

lymphocytes
the two types of white blood cells that are part of the body's immune system: *B lymphocytes* form in the bone marrow and release antibodies that fight bacterial infections; *T lymphocytes* form in the thymus and, among other duties, attack cancer cells, viruses, and foreign substances.

The immune system in action
A large macrophage (at top) is about to trap and ingest a tiny bacterium (lower right). Macrophages constantly patrol the body in a search for invaders, such as this *Escherichia coli* bacterium, and for debris, such as worn-out red cells.

Does stress similarly depress the immune system of humans? Consider:

- Accumulating evidence shows that stress lowers the body's resistance to upper respiratory infections as well as to herpes (Cohen, 1996).

- In three separate *Skylab* missions, the immune systems of the astronauts showed reduced effectiveness immediately after the stress of reentry and splashdown (Kimzey, 1975; Kimzey & others, 1976).

- Marital spats are not good for health. As 90 healthy newlywed couples spent a half-hour discussing problem areas in their marriage, some became angrier than others—and suffered more immune system suppression during the next day (Kiecolt-Glaser & others, 1993).

- Students' disease-fighting mechanisms are weaker during high-stress times, such as exam weeks, and on days when they are upset (Jemmott & Magloire, 1988; Stone & others, 1987). In one experiment, a stressful experience increased the severity of symptoms experienced by volunteers who were knowingly infected with a cold virus (Dixon, 1986). In another, 47 percent of subjects living stress-filled lives developed colds after a virus was dropped in their noses, but only 27 percent of those living relatively free of stress caught colds (Cohen & others, 1991, 1993, 1995).

- The National Academy of Sciences (1984) reports that the grief and depression that follow the death of a spouse decrease immune defenses (which helps explain the increase in disease among those recently widowed). In fact, depression of any sort tends to suppress the immune system (Herbert & Cohen, 1993; Weisse, 1992). Thus, in one study of leukemia patients preparing to undergo bone marrow transplants, 12 of 13 depressed patients died within one year. Among the many more who were not depressed, 39 percent were still alive after two years (Colon & others, 1991).

The stress effect on immunity makes physiological sense (Maier & others, 1994). Stress, as we have seen, involves an aroused fight-or-flight response. Stress diverts energy to the muscles and brain, mobilizing the body for action. The immune response to disease is a competing energy system. It takes energy to fight infections, produce inflammations, and maintain fevers. Thus, when diseased, the body reduces muscular energy output by inactivity and increased sleep. Stress diverts energy from the disease-fighting system, rendering the person more vulnerable to illness.

Stress and Cancer

Stress and negative emotions such as depression also have been linked to cancer. To explore a possible connection between stress and cancer, experimenters have implanted tumor cells into rodents or given them cancer-producing substances. Those rodents also exposed to uncontrollable stress, such as inescapable shocks, were more prone to cancer (Sklar & Anisman, 1981). With their immune systems weakened by stress, their tumors developed sooner and grew larger.

Several investigators have reported that people, too, are at increased risk for cancer a year or so after experiencing depression, helplessness, or bereavement. For example, cancer occurs more often than usual among those widowed, divorced, or separated. One study of the husbands of women with terminal breast cancer pinpointed a possible reason: During the first two months after their wives' deaths, the bereaved men's lymphocyte responses dropped (Schleifer & others, 1979).

Another study gave a personality test to 2018 middle-aged men employed by the Western Electric Company in 1958. During the next 20 years, 7 percent of those not depressed and 12 percent of those somewhat depressed died of cancer (Persky & others, 1987). A large Swedish study revealed that people with a history of workplace stress had 5.5 times greater risk of colon cancer than those who reported no such problems (Courtney & others, 1993). In both studies, the cancer difference was not attributable to differences in age, smoking, drinking, or physical characteristics.

Supporting survival Can support groups help reduce cancer-enhancing emotional distress? One experiment has suggested that they can. Other research, currently under way, will reveal whether this finding is replicable.

"When the heart is at ease, the body is healthy."

CHINESE PROVERB

"A cheerful heart is a good medicine, but a downcast spirit dries up the bones."

PROVERBS 17:22

What is more, ever-nice cancer patients who bottle up their negative emotions have less chance of survival than do those who verbalize their feelings (O'Leary, 1990; Temoshok, 1992). A UCLA survey of 649 cancer specialists, who had treated more than 100,000 cancer patients, supported the idea that patients' attitudes matter. Four in five of these physicians rated "a positive approach to the challenge of the illness" and a "strong will to live" as important contributors to longevity (Cousins, 1989).

In the first weeks after receiving their diagnosis, cancer patients and those carrying the AIDS virus are understandably anxious and depressed (Andersen, 1989; Antoni & others, 1991). Might promoting their fighting spirit aid their survival? Can hope boost the body by alleviating negative emotions that suppress the cancer-fighting immune system?

With cancer patients, several studies suggest yes. Mastectomy patients who display a determination to conquer their breast cancer survive longer than do those who are stoic or feel hopeless (Hall & Goldstein, 1986; Pettingale & others, 1985). A study of 86 women undergoing breast cancer therapy at Stanford University Medical School found that those who participated in weekly group therapy survived an average of 37 months, double the 19-month average survival rate among the randomly assigned nonparticipants (Spiegel & others, 1989). The investigator, psychiatrist David Spiegel (1993), was stunned. He expected the support groups to alleviate cancer-related emotional distress, but he was intending to show that more positive emotions would not influence the course of cancer. At least half a dozen research teams are now repeating his study. If Spiegel's finding proves reliable, it will surely reinforce efforts to train physicians to communicate with patients in ways that minimize resignation and sustain hope.

One danger in publicizing reports on attitudes and cancer is that they may lead some patients to blame themselves for their cancer—"If only I had been more expressive, relaxed, and hopeful." A corollary danger is a "wellness macho" among the healthy, who credit their health to their healthy character and lay a guilt trip on the ill: "She has cancer? That's what you get for holding your feelings in and being so nice." Dying thus becomes the ultimate failure.

"I didn't give myself cancer."

MAYOR BARBARA BOGGS SIGMUND
(1939–1990)
PRINCETON, NEW JERSEY

In noting the link between emotions and cancer, we must remember that stress does not create cancer cells. Rather, it affects their growth by weakening the body's natural defenses against a few proliferating, malignant cells. Although a relaxed, hopeful state may enhance these defenses, we should be aware of the thin line that divides science from wishful thinking. The physiological processes at work in advanced cancer or AIDS are not likely to be derailed by avoiding stress or by a relaxed but determined spirit (Kessler & others, 1991).

By studying the interplay among emotions, the brain, and the immune system, health psychologists seek the wisdom needed to distinguish between pseudoscientific hocus-pocus and the genuine effects of emotions on health.

We must also remember that our emotional reactivity is partly inherited (recall pages 96–97). As theologian Reinhold Niebuhr recognized in his "serenity prayer," we would do well to accept those things about ourselves that we cannot change, to change those things that we can, and to seek wisdom to discern the difference. By studying the interplay among emotions, the brain, and the immune system, health psychologists seek the wisdom needed to distinguish between pseudoscientific hocus-pocus and the genuine effects of emotions on health.

Conditioning the Immune System

A hay fever sufferer sees the flower on the restaurant table and, not realizing it is plastic, begins to sneeze. Such experiences hint that stress is not the only psychological influence on the body's ailments. Simple classical conditioning may be an added influence. This raises an intriguing question: If conditioning affects the body's overt physiological responses, might it affect the immune system as well?

When organic causes of illness are unknown, it is tempting to invent psychological explanations. Before the germ that causes tuberculosis was discovered, personality explanations of TB were popular (Sontag, 1978).

THINKING CRITICALLY ABOUT

Handedness and Health—The Case of the Disappearing Southpaws

While studying handedness, psychologist Stanley Coren (1993) stumbled upon a rather stunning fact of life: With age, the percentage of left-handers declines dramatically. In his initial sample of 5147 people, he found that left-handers were 14.6 percent of 10-year-olds, 4.6 percent of 50-year-olds, and less than 1 percent of those over age 80 (Figure 17.7). Other researchers around the world have confirmed Coren's finding: Left-handers disappear with age.

One cannot resist asking, Why? Intrigued, Coren and fellow sleuth Diane Halpern (1991; Halpern & Coren, 1988, 1991, 1993) set out in search of an answer. (If you were they, what explanations might have come to mind?)

Perhaps, Coren and Halpern first thought, childhood coercion causes natural lefties to become right-handed as they age. (Many older people can recall having their left hands slapped, tied down, or even balled into a fist with surgical tape when they tried to use it.) If today's parents and teachers are more accepting of left-handedness than were those earlier in this century, the result might be more young left-handers.

If indeed the vanishing southpaws are a historical rather than an age-driven phenomenon, then left-handedness should be increasing along with its acceptance. But no—North American and European studies suggest that during this century left-handers have increased only from about 6 percent of the population to 10 percent (Porac & others, 1980). This small increase hardly explains the much greater percentage of left-handers among the very young. Examining handed-ness in art works over centuries, Coren and his colleagues again were amazed by the stability of left-handedness. In art works dated from 15,400 to 3000 B.C., 10 percent of the people were depicted as left-handed. In modern art works, 11 percent were left-handers.

If childhood coercion doesn't explain the disappearance of left-handers, might the world's being designed for right-handers make it easier for lefties to learn *gradually* to use their right hands? But again, no—preschoolers who switch handedness complete the process before adolescence. Handedness rarely switches after age 8 or 9, and even before then it occurs only for specific coerced actions (such as eating or writing). So simple learning just doesn't explain the slow and gradual disappearance of left-handers.

"Truth is arrived at by the painstaking process of eliminating the untrue," said Sherlock Holmes. "When you have eliminated the impossible, whatever remains, *however improbable*, must be the truth." But what else remains? Coren and Halpern then dared to think the unthinkable: that left-handers die younger. "That can't be true," skeptical colleagues replied when Coren first voiced the idea. "If true, surely someone would have noticed by now. Besides, my paternal grandmother was left-handed and lived to 91. And what about lefties Benjamin Franklin (who lived to 84), Charlie Chaplin (88), and Pablo Picasso (92)?"

As we have seen many times, vivid anecdotes ("I know a person who . . .") are no substitute for conclusions based on large and representative samples. Examples do not prove a generality, nor do counterexamples of short-lived left-handers, such as Babe Ruth (53), Marilyn Monroe (36), and Alexander the Great (33). So, to explore their morbid idea, Coren and Halpern first reflected on the lefties' known health risks. Left-handers are more likely to have experienced birth stress, such as prematurity or the need for assisted respiration.

Figure **17.7**

The disappearing southpaws
The percentage of left-handers decreases sharply in samples of older people. (Adapted from Coren, 1993.)

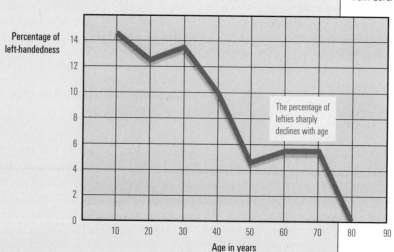

Percentage of left-handedness

The percentage of lefties sharply declines with age

Age in years

Right-hander

Left-hander

The southpaw's hazardous life   In the book *The Left-Hander Syndrome*, Stanley Coren illustrates risks posed by a world made for right-handers. When left-handers use a drill press, their left arm may obscure their view.

They also endure more headaches, have more accidents (partly because of right-handed equipment), have more knee and joint problems, use more tobacco and alcohol, and suffer more immune system problems (including allergies such as asthma, eczema, and hay fever).

These handedness differences aren't huge (individual differences are much greater). But might they, like sex differences in health risks, add up to differing life spans? When Coren and Halpern studied a random sample of recently deceased people of all ages they felt they were on to something. On average, right-handers lived eight or nine years longer. When Coren, Halpern, and other researchers excluded children, by comparing left-handed and right-handed former baseball and cricket players, they found the life-span difference reduced—three years, Coren now estimates—but still apparent (Aggleton & others, 1993; Rogerson, 1994; Seppa, 1997).

This stunning finding triggered an avalanche of publicity, much of it distorted, which in turn triggered nasty letters ("You have some gall to publicly ridicule people you have just condemned to an early death"), newspaper columns ("dear professor . . . we strongly suggest that you beware of sinister lefties bearing grudges—and chain saws"), and phone messages ("You right-handers think that you'll live longer than left-handers but you won't if we kill you first") (Halpern & others, 1996). The finding also stimulated some follow-up research that produced no life-expectancy advantage for right-handers (Harris, 1993). One National Institute of Aging research team followed 3800 East Boston adults for six years and found that, at any age, left-handers were *not* more likely to die (Salive & others, 1993). Coren (1993) is not convinced. He responds that six years is not long enough to catch a statistically significant handedness effect in a sample this small.

The unfinished case of the disappearing southpaws illustrates the very heart of science. Science dares to ask researchable questions, even those with unsettling implications. It welcomes new ideas, but it also subjects them to skeptical scrutiny. In the court of scientific judgment, researchers must state their case and expose themselves to counterexamination from opposing views. The process is imperfect. During heated debate, scientists sometimes forget their own ideals. Yet, over time, science has a way of unmasking error and taking us closer to truth. As it does so, explaining the absence of old left-handers, perhaps it will also point the way to safer, more comfortable environments for left-handed people.

Psychologist Robert Ader and immunologist Nicholas Cohen (1985) discovered that the answer is yes. Ader came upon this discovery while researching taste aversion in rats. He paired the rats' drinking of saccharin-sweetened water with injections of a drug that happened to suppress immune functioning. After repeated pairings, sweetened water alone triggered immune suppression, as if the drug had been given (Figure 17.8). Such conditioned immune suppression can triple an animal's likelihood of growing a tumor when fed a carcinogen (Blom & others, 1995).

Many questions about the role of the immune system and how to harness its healing potential remain unanswered. If it is possible to condition the immune system's suppression, should it not also be possible to condition its enhancement? Might this be one way in which placebos—treatments that have no biochemical effect—promote healing? Can a placebo sometimes elicit the same healthful state produced by an actual drug? Research now under way may soon answer such questions.

Figure **17.8**

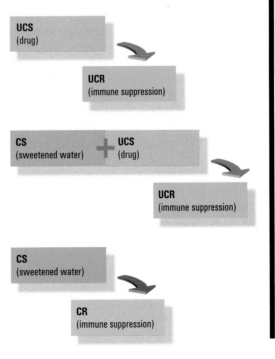

The conditioning of immune suppression   After Ader and Cohen associated sweetened water with a drug that causes immune suppression in rats, the inert substance alone triggered the conditioned immune response.

Figure **17.9**

Negative emotions can have a variety of health-related consequences This is especially so when experienced by "disease-prone" angry, depressed, or anxious persons.

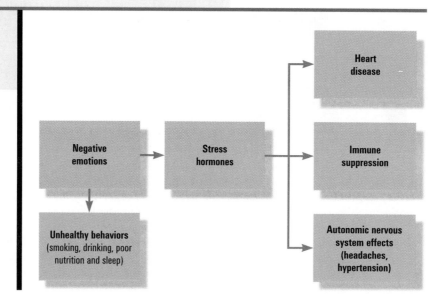

For now, we can view the toll that stress sometimes takes on our resistance to disease as a price we pay for the adaptive benefits of stress (Figure 17.9). Stress invigorates our lives by arousing and motivating us. An unstressed life would hardly be challenging or productive. Moreover, spending our resources in fighting or fleeing an external threat aids our immediate survival. But it does so at the cost of diminished resources for fighting internal threats to our body's health. When the stress is momentary, the cost is negligible. When uncontrollable aggravations persist, however, the cost may become considerable.

On the up side, we can celebrate the self-healing powers of people who maintain a sense of control and a positive approach to life. Facing surmountable challenges and striving for realistic goals may at first be fatiguing. But in the long run, self-confidence, stability, and future stress resistance come not from avoiding challenges but from conquering them (Friedman, 1991; Taylor & Armor, 1996).

All this new behavioral medicine research provides yet another reminder of one of contemporary psychology's overriding themes. Mind and body continuously interact. Everything psychological is simultaneously physiological. And because psychological states are physiological events, they influence other parts of our physiological system. As the Indian sage Santi Parva recognized more than 4000 years ago, "Mental disorders arise from physical causes, and likewise physical disorders arise from mental causes."

SUMMING UP

People's behaviors and stress responses are major influences on health and disease. Health psychology contributes to the interdisciplinary field of behavioral medicine, which provides new avenues for the prevention and treatment of illness. Among health psychology's concerns are the effects of stress, the seeking and following of medical treatment, and the promotion of healthier living.

Stress and Stressors Walter Cannon viewed stress, the process by which we appraise and respond to events that challenge or threaten us, as a "fight or flight" system. Hans Selye saw it as a three-stage (alarm/resistance/exhaustion) general adaptation syndrome. Modern research on stress assesses the health consequences of catastrophic events, significant life changes, and daily hassles. Events are stressful when we perceive them as both negative and uncontrollable.

Stress, Personality, and Heart Disease Coronary heart disease, the number one cause of death, has been linked with the competitive, hard-driving, impatient, and (especially) anger-prone Type A personality. Under stress, the body of a reactive, hostile person secretes more of the hormones that accelerate the buildup of plaque on the heart's artery walls.

Stress and Resistance to Disease Stress diverts energy from the immune system, making a person more vulnerable to infections and malignancy. Although stress does not cause diseases such as cancer, it may influence the disease's progression. New experiments show that conditioning also influences the immune system's responses.

KEY TERMS AND CONCEPTS behavioral medicine, health psychology, stress, general adaptation syndrome (GAS), burnout, coronary heart disease, Type A, Type B, psychophysiological illness, lymphocytes

Promoting Health

Health promotion involves not only treating illness but also implementing strategies that help prevent illness or enhance wellness. What tactics can people use to reduce stress-related ailments? What influences health-destructive behaviors such as smoking? And how effective are programs that aim to help people stop smoking or lose weight?

Traditionally, people have sought out medical doctors for the diagnosis and treatment of disease. That, say the advocates of behavioral medicine, is like ignoring a car's maintenance and going to a mechanic only when the car breaks down. Now that we realize that our attitudes and behaviors affect our health, attention is focusing more and more on health maintenance—on ways of coping with stress, preventing illness, and promoting well-being.

Coping With Stress

Coping with stress can mean confronting or escaping the problem and taking steps to prevent its recurrence. Coping can involve fight or flight, repelling the challenge or avoiding it, solving the problem or mentally distancing oneself from it. Yet stressors are an unavoidable part of life. This fact, coupled with the growing awareness that recurring stress correlates with heart disease, lowered immunity, and other bodily ailments, gives us a clear message. If the stress cannot be eliminated by changing or ignoring the situation, we had best learn to manage it. Stress management includes aerobic exercise, biofeedback, relaxation, and social support.

Aerobic Exercise

Aerobic exercise is sustained exercise that increases heart and lung fitness. Clearly, such exercise strengthens the body. Does it also boost the spirit?

Exercise and Mood

Many studies suggest that aerobic exercise can reduce stress, depression, and anxiety. One-third of U.S. adults exercise regularly, and studies indicate that they also cope better with stressful events, exhibit more self-confidence, and are less often depressed than those who exercise less (Brown, 1991; Hogan, 1989; *Prevention*, 1995). But if we state this observation the other way around—that stressed and depressed people exercise less—cause and effect become unclear.

Experiments resolve the ambiguity by randomly assigning stressed, depressed, or anxious people either to aerobic exercise treatments or to other treatments. In one such experiment, Lisa McCann and David Holmes (1984) assigned one-third of a group of mildly depressed female college students to a program of aerobic exercise and another third

aerobic exercise
sustained exercise that increases heart and lung fitness; may also alleviate depression and anxiety.

The women in the aerobic exercise program reported the greatest decrease in depression. Many of them had, quite literally, run away from their troubles.

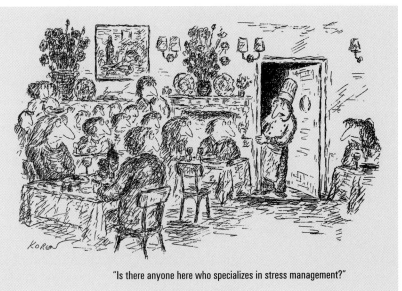

"Is there anyone here who specializes in stress management?"

Figure **17.10**

Aerobic exercise and depression
Mildly depressed college women who participated in an aerobic exercise program showed markedly reduced depression, compared with those who did relaxation exercises or received no treatment. (From McCann & Holmes, 1984.)

Exercise and Health

Other research reveals that exercise also benefits health.

- One sixteen-year study of 17,000 middle-aged Harvard alumni found that those who exercised regularly were likely to live longer (Paffenbarger & others, 1986).

- A study of 15,000 Control Data Corporation employees found that those who exercised had 25 percent fewer hospital days than those who didn't (Anderson & Jose, 1987).

- A digest of data from 43 studies revealed that, compared with inactive adults, people who exercise suffer half as many heart attacks (Powell & others, 1987).

By one estimate, moderate exercise adds two years to one's expected life. "Perhaps God does not subtract the time spent exercising from your allotted time on earth," jests Martin Seligman (1994, p. 193). The "mood boost" is reaping dividends. So off your duffs, couch potatoes!

Biofeedback and Relaxation

When a few psychologists started experimenting with ways to train people to bring their heart rate and blood pressure under conscious control, many of their colleagues thought them foolish. These functions are, after all, controlled by the autonomic ("involuntary") nervous system. Then, in the late 1960s, experiments by respected psychologists began to make the doubters wonder. Neal Miller,

to a treatment of relaxation exercises; the remaining third, a control group, received no treatment. As Figure 17.10 shows, 10 weeks later the women in the aerobic exercise program reported the greatest decrease in depression. Many of them had, quite literally, run away from their troubles.

More than 100 other studies confirm that exercise reduces depression and anxiety (Long & van Stavel, 1995; Petruzzello & others, 1991; Scott & Pepperell, 1992). Repeated surveys, some by government health agencies, reveal that Canadians and Americans are more self-confident, self-disciplined, and psychologically resilient if physically fit (Stephens, 1988). Even a ten-minute walk stimulates two hours of increased well-being by raising energy levels and lowering tension (Thayer, 1987, 1993).

Researchers are now wondering *why* aerobic exercise alleviates the effects of stress and negative emotions. They know that exercise strengthens the heart and lowers both blood pressure and the blood pressure reaction to stress (Perkins & others, 1986; Roviario & others, 1984). Exercise also orders up chemicals from our body's internal pharmacy by increasing production of mood-boosting neurotransmitters such as norepinephrine, serotonin, and the endorphins. Perhaps the emotional benefits of exercise are a side effect of increased body arousal and warmth or of the muscle relaxation and sounder sleep that occur afterward. Or perhaps a sense of accomplishment and an improved physique enhance one's emotional state.

The mood boost Aerobic exercise such as jogging appears to counteract depression partly by increasing arousal (replacing depression's low-arousal state) and by doing naturally what Prozac does—increasing the brain's serotonin activity (Jacobs, 1994).

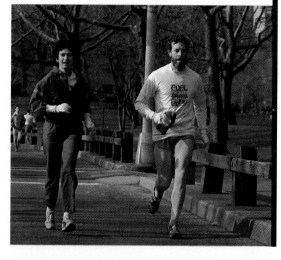

Figure **17.11**

Biofeedback systems Biofeedback systems—such as this one, which records tension in the forehead muscle of a headache sufferer—allow people to monitor their subtle physiological responses.

Patient observes signal

biofeedback
a system for electronically recording, amplifying, and feeding back information regarding a subtle physiological state, such as blood pressure or muscle tension.

for one, found that rats could modify their heartbeat if given pleasurable brain stimulation when their heartbeat increased or decreased. Later research revealed that some paralyzed humans could also learn to control their blood pressure (Miller & Brucker, 1979).

Miller was experimenting with biofeedback, a system of recording, amplifying, and feeding back information about subtle physiological responses. Biofeedback instruments have been likened to a mirror (Norris, 1986). The instruments no more control one's body than a mirror combs one's hair. Rather, by reflecting the results of a person's own efforts, they allow the person to assess which techniques are most effective in controlling a particular physiological response.

In the example in Figure 17.11, a sensor records tension in the forehead muscle of a person with chronic headaches. A computer processes this physiological information and instantly feeds it back to the person in some easily understood image. As the person relaxes the forehead muscle, the pointer on the display screen may go lower, or a light may grow brighter. The patient's task is to learn to control the pointer or the light and thereby learn to control the tension in the forehead muscle and the accompanying headaches.

Initially, biofeedback researchers and practitioners reported that people could learn to increase their production of alpha brain waves, warm their hands, and lower their blood pressure—all signs of a more relaxed state. These reports triggered both excitement and some 4000 studies, including more than 400 in Russia (Sokhadze & Shtark, 1991). After a decade of study, researchers stepped back to assess the results and decided the initial claims for biofeedback were overblown and oversold (Miller,

1985). Biofeedback does enable some people to influence their finger temperature and forehead-muscle tension, and it can help somewhat in reducing the intensity of migraine headaches and chronic pain (King & Montgomery, 1980; Qualls & Sheehan, 1981; Turk & others, 1979). (Biofeedback works best on tension headaches, declared a 1995 National Institutes of Health panel.) But other, simpler methods of relaxation, which require no expensive equipment, produce many of the same benefits.

If relaxation is an important part of biofeedback, then might relaxation exercises alone be a natural antidote to stress? Cardiologist Herbert Benson (1976 to 1996) became intrigued with this possibility when he found that experienced meditators could decrease their blood pressure, heart rate, and oxygen consumption and raise their fingertip temperature. You can experience the essence of this *relaxation response*, as Benson calls it, right now: Assume a comfortable position, breathe deeply, and relax your muscles from foot to face. Now, concentrate on a single word or a phrase. (About 80 percent of Benson's patients choose to focus on a favorite prayer.) Close your eyes and let other thoughts drift away when they intrude as you repeat your phrase continually for 10 to 20 minutes. Simply by setting aside a quiet time or two each day, many people report enjoying greater tranquility. Stress worsens pain, infertility, and insomnia, and it also suppresses the immune system. Meditative relaxation counteracts all these effects, Benson reports. One astonishing study assigned 73 residents of homes for the elderly either to daily meditation or to none. After three years, one-fourth of the nonmeditators had died, while all the meditators were still alive (Alexander & others, 1989).

Meditation—a modern phenomenon with a long history: "Sit down alone and in silence. Lower your head, shut your eyes, breathe out gently, and imagine yourself looking into your own heart. . . . As you breathe out, say 'Lord Jesus Christ, have mercy on me.' . . . Try to put all other thoughts aside. Be calm, be patient and repeat the process very frequently."

GREGORY OF SINAI
DIED 1346

Learning the "relaxation response" Relaxation training is a component of many stress-reduction programs. At Boston's Deaconess Hospital, hypertension patients learn meditation techniques that counteract stress.

If Type A heart attack victims could be taught to relax, might their risk of another attack be reduced? To find out, Meyer Friedman and his colleagues randomly assigned hundreds of middle-aged heart attack survivors in San Francisco to one of two groups. The first group received standard advice from cardiologists concerning medications, diet, and exercise habits. The second group received similar advice plus continuing support and counseling on life-style modification—how to slow down and relax by walking, talking, and eating more slowly; by smiling at others and laughing at themselves; by admitting mistakes; by taking time to enjoy life; and by renewing their religious faith. As Figure 17.12 indicates, during the ensuing three years, the second group experienced half as many repeat heart attacks as the first group. This, wrote the exuberant Friedman, is an unprecedented, spectacular reduction in heart attack recurrence. A smaller-scale British study similarly divided heart attack–prone people into control and life-style modification groups (Eysenck & Grossarth-Maticek, 1991). During the next thirteen years, it also found a 50 percent reduction in death rate among those trained to alter their thinking and life-style.

It remains for other researchers to do the painstaking work of identifying which of Friedman's dozens of stress-reduction drills are beneficial. Even while Friedman was collecting his data, other investigators were studying specific stress buffers. For example, laughter seems to work in ways similar to exercise—it arouses us, massages muscles, and then leaves us feeling relaxed (Robinson, 1983). This may help explain findings that stressful life events are less disturbing to good-humored people (Lefcourt & Davidson-Katz, 1991; Nezu & others, 1988). Although it would probably be an overstatement to suggest that "laughter is the best medicine," there is reason to suspect that those who laugh, last.

> "There ain't much fun in medicine, but there's a heck of a lot of medicine in fun."
>
> HUMORIST JOSH BILLINGS (1818–1885)

Social Support

Linda and Emily had much in common. When interviewed for a study conducted by UCLA social psychologist Shelley Taylor (1989), both Los Angeles women had married, raised three children, suffered comparable breast tumors, and recovered from surgery and six months of chemotherapy. But there was a difference. Linda, a widow in her early fifties, was living alone, her children scattered in Atlanta, Boston, and Europe. "She had become odd in ways that people sometimes do when they are isolated," reported Taylor. "Having no one with whom to share her thoughts on a daily basis, she unloaded them somewhat inappropriately with strangers, including our interviewer."

Figure **17.12**

Recurrent heart attacks and life-style modification The San Francisco Recurrent Coronary Prevention Project offered survivors of heart attacks counseling from a cardiologist. Those who were also guided in modifying their Type A life-style suffered fewer repeat heart attacks. (From Friedman & Ulmer, 1984.)

Percentage of patients with recurrent heart attacks (cumulative average)

Control patients

Modifying life-style reduced recurrent heart attacks

Life-style modification patients

Year

Interviewing Emily was difficult in a different way. Phone calls interrupted. Her children, all living nearby, were in and out of the house, dropping things off with a quick kiss. Her husband called from his office for a brief chat. Two dogs roamed the house, greeting visitors enthusiastically. All in all, Emily "seemed a serene and contented person, basking in the warmth of her family."

Three years later, the researchers tried to reinterview the women. Linda, they learned, had died two years before. Emily was still lovingly supported by her family and friends and was as happy and healthy as ever.

Because no two cancers are identical, we can't be certain that different social situations led to Linda's and Emily's fates. But they do illustrate a conclusion drawn from several large studies: Social support—feeling liked, affirmed, and encouraged by intimate friends and family—promotes happiness and health.

If this result seems obvious, imagine why close relationships could contribute to *illness*. Relationships are often fraught with stress, especially in crowded living conditions lacking privacy (Evans & others, 1989). "Hell is others," wrote Jean-Paul Sartre. Peter Warr and Roy Payne (1982) at the University of Sheffield asked a representative sample of British adults what, if anything, had emotionally strained them the day before. "Family" was their most frequent answer. Even when well-meaning, family intrusions can be stressful. And stress, as we have seen, contributes to heart disease, hypertension, and a suppressed immune system.

On balance, however, close relationships more often contribute to health and happiness. Asked what prompted yesterday's times of pleasure, the same British sample, by an even larger margin, again answered "family." For most of us, family relationships provide not only our greatest heartaches but also our greatest comfort and joy.

Moreover, seven massive investigations, each following thousands of people for several years, reveal that close relationships affect health. Compared with those having few social ties, people are less likely to die prematurely if supported by close relationships with friends, family, or fellow members of church, work, or other support groups (Cohen, 1988; House & others, 1988; Nelson, 1988).

Some recent examples:

- Recall the study mentioned earlier in this chapter that followed leukemia patients preparing to undergo bone marrow transplants. Two years later, only 20 percent of those who said they had little social support from their family or friends were still alive. Among those who felt strong emotional support, the 2-year survival rate was 54 percent (Colon & others, 1991).

- A study of 1234 heart attack patients found nearly a doubled rate of a recurring attack within 6 months among those living alone (Case & others, 1992).

- A study of 1965 heart disease patients revealed a 5-year survival rate of 82 percent among those married or having a confidant, but only 50 percent among those not (Williams & others, 1992).

- A 70-year study following 1528 California children with high IQ scores found that those whose parents did not divorce during their childhood outlived children of divorce by about 4 years (Schwartz & others, 1995). Controlling for the family's economic status and the child's personality did little to diminish the family-stability factor.

There are several possible reasons for the link between social support and health. Perhaps people with strong social ties eat better and exercise more because their partners guide and goad them into adhering to treatment regimens. Perhaps they smoke and drink less, which would help explain the repeated finding that religiously active people enjoy better health (See Close-Up: Spirituality, Religion, and Health). Perhaps such relationships help us evaluate and overcome stressful events, such as social rejection. Perhaps they help bolster our self-esteem. When we are wounded by someone's dislike or by the loss of a job, a friend's advice, assistance, and reassurance may be good medicine (Cutrona, 1986; Rook, 1987). Given lots of social support, spouses of cancer patients exhibit stronger immune functioning (Baron & others, 1990). Many studies further reveal that social support calms the cardiovascular system and lowers stress hormones (Uchino & others, 1996).

Humans aren't the only source of stress-buffering comfort. After stressful events, Medicare patients who have a dog or other companionable pet are less likely to visit their doctor (Siegel, 1990).

"I get by with a little help from my friends."

JOHN LENNON AND PAUL MCCARTNEY
SGT. PEPPER'S LONELY HEARTS CLUB BAND
1967

Friendships are good medicine
Several long-term studies of thousands of people have found that individuals with close supportive relationships are less likely than socially isolated people to die prematurely.

"Woe to one who is alone and falls and does not have another to help."

ECCLESIASTES 4:10

CLOSE-UP

Spirituality, Religion, and Health

Throughout history, humans have suffered ills and have sought healing. In response, the two healing traditions—religion and medicine—historically have joined hands in care of the sick. Religious and healing efforts were often conducted by the same person; the priest was also the medicine man. Hospitals were first established in monasteries, then spread by missionaries.

As medical science matured, however, healing and religion diverged. Rather than asking God to spare their children from smallpox, people began vaccinating them. Rather than seeking a spiritual healer when burning with bacterial fever, they turned to antibiotics.

This wall of separation between religion and medicine is now breaking down again. "Spirituality" has made a comeback. Pollster George Gallup (1994) detects "the search for spiritual moorings" as a "dominant trend" in the mid 1990s. At one point, six of the ten best-selling American books explored spiritual matters. Since 1995, Harvard Medical School has been attracting some 1000 health professionals from across North America to its annual conferences on "Spirituality and Healing in Medicine." New books such as *Religion and the Clinical Practice of Psychology* (American Psychological Association, 1996) and *Religion and Health* (Oxford University Press, forthcoming) are appearing. Detecting a renewed convergence of religion and medicine, *Time* devoted a 1996 cover story to "Faith and Healing."

Is there fire underneath all this smoke? Do religion and spirituality actually relate to health, as polls show 4 in 5 Americans believe (Matthews, 1997)? Some 200 studies have sought to correlate "the faith factor" with health and healing (Koenig, 1997; Matthews & Larson, 1997). Among the suggestive findings are these:

- An Israeli research team compared the death rates of 3900 people living either in one of 11 religiously orthodox or 11 matched, nonreligious collective settlements (kibbutz communities). Jeremy Kark and his collaborators (1996) report that "belonging to a religious collective was associated with a strong protective effect" that was not explained by age or economic differences. Over the 16-year study period, those belonging to the religious communities were, in every age group, about half as likely to have died.

- An earlier study of 91,909 persons in one Maryland county found that those who attended religious services weekly died less often during the study period than those who did not—53 percent less often from coronary disease, 53 percent less often due to suicide, and 74 percent less often from cirrhosis (Comstock & Partridge, 1972).

- A Dartmouth Medical School team followed 232 people who had open heart surgery (Oxman & others, 1995). In the ensuing six months, 12 percent of those who never or rarely attended religious services died, as did 5 percent of those who attended more often, and 0 percent of those who said they were "deeply religious."

Such findings demand explanation. In part, they seem due to the healthier life-styles of religiously active people—who smoke and drink less (Levin, 1994, 1996). Health-oriented, vegetarian Seventh Day Adventists have longer life expectancy (Berkel & de Waard, 1983). Religiously orthodox Israelis eat somewhat less fat than their nonreligious compatriots.

But such differences are not great enough to explain the dramatically reduced mortality in the religious kibbutzim, argued the Israeli researchers. There seems to have been additional stress protection and enhanced well-being in the religious communities, possibly resulting from a coherent worldview, an amplified sense of belonging, highly stable marriages (divorce is almost nonexistent), and the rest and meditation associated with frequent prayer and Sabbath observance. In North America the more than 350,000 local faith communities are each support networks for their active participants, for whom faith is also a source of solace and hope during times of stress.

Although the religion-health correlations typically leave cause and effect ambiguous, Harold Pincus (1997), deputy medical director of the American Psychiatric Association, believes that these findings "have made clear that anyone involved in providing health care services . . . cannot ignore . . . the important connections between spirituality, religion, and health."

Close relationships also provide the opportunity to confide painful feelings. In one study, health psychologists James Pennebaker and Robin O'Heeron (1984) contacted the surviving spouses of people who had committed suicide or died in car accidents. Those who bore their grief alone had more health problems than those who openly expressed it. Talking about our troubles can be "open heart therapy."

Actively suppressing thoughts can cause them to bubble up intrusively, preoccupying the person (Wegner, 1990). Disclosing suppressed thoughts may stop the cycle. In a simulated confessional, Pennebaker asked volunteers to share with a hidden experimenter some upsetting events that had been preying on their minds. He asked some of the volunteers to describe a trivial event before they divulged the troubling one. Physiological measures revealed that their bodies remained tense the whole time they talked about the trivial event; they relaxed only when they later confided the cause of their turmoil. Even writing about personal traumas in a diary can help. When volunteers in other experiments did this, they had fewer health problems during the ensuing four to six months (Pennebaker, 1990). As one subject explained, "Although I have not talked with anyone about what I wrote, I was finally able to deal with it, work through the pain instead of trying to block it out. Now it doesn't hurt to think about it."

Suppressed traumas sometimes eat away at us and affect our physical health. Consider:

- When Pennebaker surveyed more than 700 undergraduate women, he found that about 1 in 12 reported a traumatic sexual experience in childhood. Compared with women who had experienced nonsexual traumas, such as parental death or divorce, the sexually abused women—especially those who had kept their secret to themselves—reported more headaches and stomach ailments.

- After the 1989 San Francisco Bay Area earthquake, residents talked nonstop about the upheaval for about two weeks. Then the talking died down as people tired of hearing others' opinions and feelings. ("Thank you for not sharing your earthquake experience," read one popular T-shirt.) But for another month people kept thinking about the quake. During this inhibition phase—when people kept ruminating but with less disclosure of their anxieties and feelings—hostility, nightmares, and health problems peaked (Pennebaker & Harber, 1993).

- Pennebaker and his colleagues (1989) also invited 33 Holocaust survivors to spend two hours recalling their experiences. Many did so in intimate detail never before disclosed. Most watched and showed family and friends a videotape of their recollections in the weeks following. Again, those who were most self-disclosing had the most improved health 14 months later. Although talking about a stressful event can temporarily arouse people, it calms them in the long run (Mendolia & Kleck, 1993). Confiding is good for the soul.

Figure **17.13**

```
┌──────────────────┐
│    Life events   │
└──────────────────┘
          │
          ▼
┌──────────────────────────┐
│    Personal appraisal    │
├─────────────┬────────────┤
│  Challenge  │   Threat   │
└─────────────┴────────────┘
          +
┌──────────────────────────┐
│     Personality type     │
├─────────────┬────────────┤
│  Easygoing  │   Hostile  │
│ Nondepressed│  Depressed │
│  Optimistic │ Pessimistic│
└─────────────┴────────────┘
          +
┌──────────────────────────┐
│     Personal habits      │
├─────────────┬────────────┤
│  Nonsmoking │   Smoking  │
│Regular exer.│  Sedentary │
│Good nutrition│Poor nutrition│
└─────────────┴────────────┘
          +
┌──────────────────────────┐
│  Level of social support │
├─────────────┬────────────┤
│Close, endur.│   Lacking  │
└─────────────┴────────────┘
          │
          ▼
┌──────────────────────────┐
│     Tendency toward      │
├─────────────┬────────────┤
│   Health    │   Illness  │
└─────────────┴────────────┘
```

Coping with stress Life events can be debilitating or not. It all depends on how we appraise them and whether the stresses are buffered by a stress-resistant disposition, healthy habits, and enduring social support.

Sustained emotional reactions to stressful events can be debilitating. However, the level of stress experienced depends on the person and the environment. Nothing is stressful until we appraise it as such. Thus, our personalities and interpretations influence how we react emotionally when stressful things happen. Moreover, the toxic impact of stressful events can be buffered by a relaxed, healthy life-style and by the comfort and aid provided by supportive friends and family (Figure 17.13).

Modifying Illness-Related Behaviors

Researchers are persuaded that health-promotion programs cost far less than it now costs to treat diseases. With combined expenditures of more than $1 trillion annually (not counting lost workdays), Canada now spends 10 percent and the United States 14 percent of its gross domestic product on health care (Census Bureau, 1996). Moreover, among patients visiting their primary care physicians with typical complaints such as fatigue, headache, chest or abdominal pain, dizziness, constipation, and insomnia, fewer than 20 percent have a clear organic problem. Medical researchers presume many of these problems involve "psychosocial factors" (Kroenke & Mangelscorff, 1989). Thus, even modestly successful health-promotion programs could save more money than they cost.

In the United States, two-thirds of organizations with more than 50 employees now offer some sort of health-promoting program, most of which began during the 1980s (Gebhardt & Crump, 1990; Roberts & Harris, 1989). Such programs commonly provide health assessments and support fitness training, quitting smoking, and stress management. The workplace is an ideal location for the promotion of health and vitality because most employees are there regularly. In addition, employers can actively encourage healthy behaviors by providing social support, arranging for competition among work groups, and awarding bonuses or days off for sticking to an exercise or smoking-cessation regimen.

Are such programs effective? Several careful evaluations revealed that they can be. At Prudential Insurance Company, for example, a fitness program reduced sick days by 20 percent and major medical costs by 46 percent. Thus, the company saved $1.93 for every dollar it spent operating the program (Bowne & others, 1984). Control Data Corporation also found that its StayWell health program improved employee health and the company's balance sheet. Compared with other Control Data sites, sites that implemented the program reported decreases in smoking by 20 percent, in the number of overweight employees by 25 percent, and in the number of nonexercising employees by 32 percent—with corresponding reductions in health care claims and sick leave (Jose & Anderson, 1991). Other studies reveal decreases in seeking expensive medical care for minor illnesses, acute asthma, and arthritis (Sobel, 1993).

How might such programs modify health-related behaviors such as smoking and eating habits? Let's see.

Smoking

Each year throughout the world, the tobacco industry kills some 3 million of its best customers—equivalent to 20 loaded jumbo jets daily (Peto & others, 1992, 1994). And the worst is yet to come. Given present trends, estimated a 1994 World Health Organization report, *half a billion* people alive today will be killed by tobacco. A teen-to-the-grave smoker has a 50 percent chance of being killed by the habit and often dies an agonizing, premature death. With these odds, getting hooked can only be viewed as a deeply dumb, or at least tragically naive, thing to do (even if one doesn't mind bad breath, yellowed teeth, and earlier wrinkles and graying). Smoke a cigarette and nature will charge you 12 minutes off your life expectancy (*Discover*, 1996). Thus, the elimination of smoking would do more to increase life expectancy than would any other preventive measure. Smoking's destructiveness has prompted psychologists to study why people start smoking, why they keep smoking, and how we might prevent smoking or help people to quit.

When and Why Do People Start Smoking?

Smoking is a "pediatric disease." It usually begins during early adolescence and is especially common among those who get low grades, who feel less competent and in control of their future, and whose friends, parents, and siblings smoke (Chassin & others, 1987; Schulenberg & others, 1994). If the cigarette manufacturers haven't attracted your business by now, the odds are overwhelming that they never will.

We can understand adolescents' vulnerability to the allure of smoking with the help of social-cognitive theory, which explains how we learn behaviors through the models we imitate and the social rewards we receive (pages 265–266, 445). Teenage smokers have traditionally been perceived

The United States spends nearly three times more per person on health care than does Great Britain (partly because the average income of a U.S. doctor is nearly four times that of a British doctor). In the United States, average life expectancy is 76; in Britain it is also 76 (Bureau of the Census, 1996).

Smokers repay society for the health, disability, and fire risk costs of their habit by dying earlier, saving Social Security and retirement pension payments (Manning & others, 1989).

Among teens whose parents and best friends are nonsmokers, the smoking rate is close to zero.

as tough, precocious, and sociable (Barton & others, 1982). Indeed, teen smokers are a somewhat rebellious, risk-taking group. The National Center for Health Statistics (1995) reports they are twice as likely as nonsmokers to have had sex, three times as likely to drink alcohol, and 17 times more likely to use marijuana.

Self-conscious adolescents, who think the world is watching their every move, may begin smoking to imitate cool models, to receive the social reward of being accepted by them, and to project a mature image (Covington & Omelich, 1988). Teens who start smoking typically also have friends who model smoking, suggest its pleasures, and offer cigarettes (Eiser, 1985; Evans & others, 1988). Among teens whose parents and best friends are nonsmokers, the smoking rate is close to zero (Moss & others, 1992).

Why Do People Continue Smoking?

Three in four smokers have tried to stop (Niemi & others, 1989). However, once addicted to nicotine it is hard to quit, because tobacco products are as addictive as heroin and cocaine. As with other addictions, the smoker becomes *dependent*; each year fewer than 1 in 10 smokers who want to quit do so. The smoker also develops *tolerance*, eventually needing larger and larger doses to get the same effect. Those who initially are most sensitive to nicotine—and most likely to feel sick or dizzy on first smoking—tend to develop tolerance quickly and to become most strongly addicted (Pomerleau & others, 1993). A final reason smokers do not stop is that quitting causes *withdrawal* symptoms. The craving, insomnia, anxiety, and irritability that accompany nicotine withdrawal are aversive states that a cigarette relieves (Figure 17.14). Cigarettes provide nicotine with the same rushed delivery method as does crack cocaine, and after an hour or a day without smoking, the habitual smoker finds a cigarette powerfully reinforcing. Given low-nicotine cigarettes, the smoker will smoke more of them to maintain a roughly constant level of nicotine in the blood.

Smoking reinforces by both terminating the aversive craving and offering a pleasurable lift. Nicotine triggers the release of epinephrine and norepinephrine, which in turn diminish appetite and boost alertness and mental efficiency. More important, nicotine also stimulates the central nervous system to release neurotransmitters that calm anxiety and reduce pain sensitivity. For example, nicotine, like cocaine, increases dopamine—cocaine does so by blocking its reuptake, nicotine by stimulating its release (Nowak, 1994). Anxious or

Nic-a-teen Aware that virtually all smokers start as teenagers—and that sales would plummet if no teens were enticed to smoke—tobacco companies have targeted teens. By portraying tough, appealing, socially adept smokers, they entice teens to imitate. They are supported by the resurgence of Hollywood's modeling of smoking. With such stars as Vanessa Williams, Winona Rider, Sharon Stone, Bruce Willis, and Arnold Schwarzenegger all looking cool or rebellious while dragging on a cigarette or cigar, teens in the mid 1990s were getting the message and becoming addicted in increasing numbers.

depressed people therefore often find it especially hard to forgo smoking's rewards (Mansnerus, 1992). These rewards of smoking, combined with the relief smoking provides from the unpleasantness of withdrawal, keep people smoking even when they wish they could stop—indeed, even when they know they are committing slow-motion suicide.

Figure **17.14**

Where there's smoke . . . : the physiological effects of nicotine
Nicotine reaches the brain within 7 seconds, twice as fast as intravenous heroin. Within minutes, the amount in the blood soars. Nicotine stimulates neurons by mimicking the action of the neurotransmitter acetylcholine and produces the effects shown here.

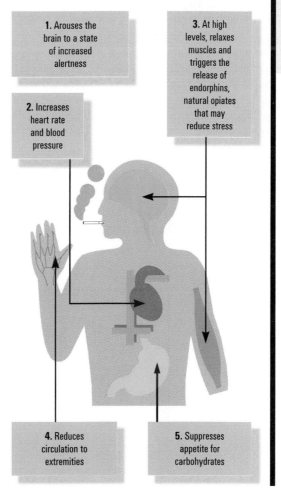

1. Arouses the brain to a state of increased alertness

2. Increases heart rate and blood pressure

3. At high levels, relaxes muscles and triggers the release of endorphins, natural opiates that may reduce stress

4. Reduces circulation to extremities

5. Suppresses appetite for carbohydrates

A correlation–causation question: What does the close link between teen smoking and friends' smoking more reflect? Peer influence, or teens seeking similar friends?

Figure 17.15

Teen smoking comeback
Although adult smoking has dropped sharply over the last quarter-century, especially among educated people, smoking has made a partial comeback among U.S. teens. (Data from Johnston & others, 1996.)

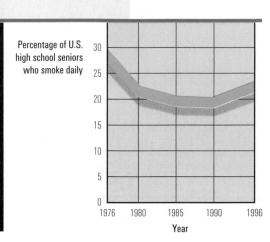

How Effective Are Programs to Stop Smoking?

Efforts to help people stop smoking include public health warnings, counseling, drug treatments, hypnosis, aversive conditioning (for example, having people sicken themselves by rapidly smoking cigarette after cigarette), operant conditioning, cognitive therapy, and support groups. These treatments are often effective in the short run. But the bad news is that all but one-fifth of the participants eventually succumb to the habit again (Schelling, 1992). With a pack of cigarettes seldom more than five minutes away, a single moment of weakness is enough to break the resolve. (If one could buy cigarettes only by mail order, allowing time for renewed resolve, efforts to quit would succeed far more often.)

Better news comes from a Centers for Disease Control report that half of Americans who have ever smoked have quit. More than 90 percent did so on their own, often after repeated attempts. Because so many people have stopped or not started smoking, the percentage of Americans who smoke is down to 25 percent, well below the 42 percent rate in 1965. Time was when public places were aswirl with tobacco smoke. Among high school dropouts and those of lower socioeconomic levels, smoking rates remain higher. But among college students and graduates, smoking has become gauche rather than cool; nearly 9 in 10 are nonsmokers. The drop has been most pronounced in the male smoking rate, which now barely exceeds women's smoking rate. Thanks in part to such trends, the death rate due to coronary heart disease has declined by about 30 percent since the mid-1960s.

For the tobacco industry, the news is not all bad. Teen smoking has rebounded during the mid-1990s (Figure 17.15). And despite the declining cigarette sales among educated adults in Western countries and the new restrictions on cigarette advertising, sales, and smoking, per-person cigarette consumption worldwide is near an all-time high. With relatively low per-person consumption rates, countries like Kenya and Zimbabwe are developing markets. In other developing countries where smoking is on the increase, British and U.S. tobacco companies are more than making up for declining domestic production (Shenon, 1994). In so doing, they are putting hundreds of millions of unsuspecting people at risk for ill health and premature death.

How Can We Prevent Smoking?

It is vastly easier never to begin smoking than to stop once addicted. Drawing on social psychological analyses of why youngsters start smoking, several research teams have devised strategies for averting the behavior patterns that lead to smoking (Evans & others, 1984; Murray & others, 1984). In one such study, a research team led by Alfred McAlister (1980) had high school students "inoculate" seventh-graders against peer pressure to smoke. The older peers taught the youngsters to respond to ads implying that liberated women smoke by saying, "She's not really liberated if she is hooked on tobacco." They also role-played calling someone a "chicken" for not trying a cigarette and responding with statements like, "I'd be a real chicken if I smoked just to impress you." After several sessions during the seventh and eighth grades, these students were only half as likely to begin smoking as were those in a control group at a neighboring junior high school, even though the parents of both sets of students had the same smoking rate (Figure 17.16).

This experiment and others like it have generated curricular programs that teachers can implement easily and inexpensively. According to a National Cancer Institute panel, the key ingredients of such programs are information about the effects of smoking; information about peer, parent, and media influences; and training in refusal skills, through modeling and role playing. The informational ingredients can also be offered through the mass media, which Australia has effectively used to discourage smoking across educational levels (Macaskill & others, 1992). To be permanently effective, such programs may require follow-up booster sessions in later years (Murray & others, 1989). Nevertheless, the plummeting rate of smoking in the general population suggests that smoking prevention programs are succeeding.

There is one other way to discourage smoking: Make it more immediately costly. Recall from

Figure 17.16

Results of a smoking "inoculation" program After participating in a smoking prevention program that prepared them to cope with smoking ads and peer pressure, junior high school students were much less likely to begin smoking than were students at a matched control school. (Data from McAlister & others, 1980.)

Chapter 8 that the most effective rewards and punishments are immediate. When the delayed rewards of exercise compete with the immediate discomfort of doing so, the immediate consequences often win out. Likewise, we can *know* that in the long run smoking is often suicidal, yet many people continue to smoke. If we could only raise the immediate costs, consumption would surely decline.

Consider one such cost: the tax paid per pack. The 1993 taxes varied considerably, from $3.68 per pack in Denmark and $3.01 per pack in Canada to $0.56 per pack in the United States and $0.24 per pack in the Philippines. Raising taxes (and therefore prices) cuts consumption—by about 4 percent for each 10 percent rise, according to the Centers for Disease Control (Brown & others, 1993). The effect is even greater among teenagers—the age when 90 percent of smokers start their habit. Canada raised its average tax more than sevenfold since 1980, and smoking declined there dramatically (Brown & others, 1993). When a pack of cigarettes costs more than five Canadian dollars—as it did until a recent tax revolt in Canada—many younger people will choose not to start a pack-a-day habit.

Nutrition

Is the way you feel and act affected by what you eat? The discovery that specific neurotransmitters affect emotion and behavior has fueled speculation: Might eating foods that provide the biochemical building blocks for those neurotransmitters affect mood and behavior? For example, the body synthesizes the neurotransmitter serotonin from the amino acid tryptophan. Several studies have found that high-carbohydrate foods (such as bread, potatoes, and pasta) increase the relative amount of tryptophan reaching the brain via the bloodstream. That, in turn, raises the level of serotonin, which makes us feel relaxed, sleepy, and less sensitive to pain (Spring, 1988). And that helps explain why people feeling tense or in a bad mood, including those on nicotine withdrawal, often snack on carbohydrate-rich foods for a mood lift (Christensen, 1993). When we instead desire food for thought, a high-protein meal improves concentration and alertness. Deprived of adequate protein, malnourished young children may suffer enduring cognitive deficits (Lozoff, 1989).

Other nutritional issues are now the subject of vigorous research and debate:

- Are children and prisoners hyped by a diet high in sugar and calmed by one that is low in sugar? Researchers doubt this folk wisdom (Spring & others, 1987). They have, however, found that well-nourished children are more active and happy at play (Espinoza & others, 1992).

- What are the links between diet and high blood pressure? Hypertensive people tend to have higher than normal salt intake and lower than normal calcium intake (Feinleib & others, 1984; McCarron & others, 1984).

- Does skipping breakfast matter? Three studies by Bonnie Spring and her colleagues (1992) suggest it does. Those who eat a balanced breakfast are, by late morning, more alert and less fatigued.

Obesity and Weight Control

People wonder: Why do some people gain while others eat the same amount and remain slim? Why do so few overweight people win the battle of the bulge? And what hope is there for the one-third of Americans who, according to the National Center for Health Statistics, are overweight?

Government guidelines encourage a body mass index (BMI) under 25.

$$BMI = \frac{\text{weight in kg (pounds} \times .45)}{\text{squared height in meters}}$$
(inches divided by 39.4)

In the U.S., 59 percent of men and 49 percent of women have BMIs over 25. Some experts define obesity as a BMI of 30 or more (Haney, 1996).

First, the good news about fat. Fat is an ideal form of stored energy that provides the body with a high-caloric fuel reserve to carry it through periods when food is scarce—a common occurrence in the feast-or-famine existence of our prehistoric ancestors. Eating three or more meals every day is a relatively recent phenomenon and a luxury hundreds of millions of people still do not enjoy. In circumstances of alternating feast and famine, overeating and storing the excess as fat is adaptive; it prepares the body to withstand famine. This may explain why in most developing societies today, as in Europe in earlier centuries—in fact, wherever people face famine—obesity is a sign of affluence and social status (Furnham & Baguma, 1994).

Cultures without a thin-ideal for women also are cultures without eating disorders. For example, Ghanians idealize a larger body size than do Americans—and experience fewer eating disorders (Cogan & others, 1996). The same differences exist between African-American and European-American women (Parker & others, 1995).

The bad news is that in those parts of the world where food and sweets are now abundantly available, the adaptive tendency to store fat has become maladaptive. Being slightly overweight poses no health risks. But the National Institutes of Health reports that genuine obesity increases the risk of diabetes, high blood pressure and heart disease, gallstones, arthritis, and certain types of cancer. This is more true for apple-shaped people who carry their weight in pot bellies than for pear-shaped people with ample hips and thighs (Greenwood, 1989). In some animals, a restricted-calorie diet prolongs youthful vitality and life expectancy (Weindruch, 1996).

Obesity is not just a threat to physical health. Being perceived as obese can affect how you are treated and how you feel about yourself. People often stereotype the obese as slow, lazy, and sloppy (Crandall, 1994, 1995; Ryckman & others, 1989). Widen people's images on a video monitor (making them look fatter) and they suddenly seem less sincere and friendly, and meaner and more obnoxious (Gardner & Tockerman, 1994).

The obese—sometimes victims of ridicule and job discrimination—know the stereotype. In studies of patients who were especially unhappy with their weight—those who had lost an average of 100 pounds after short-cutting digestion with intestinal bypass surgery—4 in 5 said their children had asked them not to attend school functions. Nine in 10 said they would rather have a leg amputated than be obese again (Rand & Macgregor, 1990, 1991). Another study followed 370 obese 16- to 24-year-olds (Gortmaker & others, 1993). When restudied seven years later, two-thirds of the women were still obese. They also were less likely to be married, and they were making less money than a comparison group of some 5000 other women. Even after correcting for aptitude test scores, race, and parental income, the obese women's incomes were $7000 a year below average.

Rubens' *The Garden of Love* In other times and places, fatter bodies have been idealized.

In most developing societies today, as in Europe in earlier centuries—in fact, wherever people face famine—obesity is a sign of affluence and social status.

Bob REALIZED THAT INSIDE EVERY FAT PERSON WAS a SKINNY PERSON WHO ATE an INCREDIBLE AMOUNT.

The stereotype of fat people as gluttons.

In one clever experiment, Regina Pingitore and her colleagues (1994) videotaped job interviews in which professional actors appeared as either normal-weight applicants or as overweight applicants. In one condition, they wore makeup and prostheses that made them look 30 pounds heavier. When appearing overweight, the same person, using the same lines, intonation, and gestures, was rated as less worthy of hiring. The weight bias was especially strong against women applicants (Figure 17.17).

The Physiology of Obesity

Many people think fat people are gluttons. They see obesity as a matter of choice or as reflecting a personality problem—as a maladjusted way of reducing anxiety, dealing with guilt, or gratifying an "oral fixation." If being obese signifies either a lack of self-discipline or a personality problem, then who would want to hire, date, or associate with such people? And if obese people believe such things about themselves, how could they feel anything but unworthy and undesirable? (Surprisingly, in studies to date, obese people have not suffered a notably higher rate of depression—Friedman & Brownell, 1995.)

Research on the physiology of obesity challenges the image of fat, weak-willed gluttons. Con-

sider the arithmetic of weight gain: People get fat by consuming more calories than they expend, and the energy equivalent of a pound of fat is 3500 calories. Dieters have therefore been told that they will lose a pound for every 3500-calorie reduction in their diet. Surprise: This conclusion turns out to be false. To see why, consider the physiology of fat.

Fat Cells

The immediate determinants of body fat are the size and number of fat cells. A typical adult has about 30 billion of these miniature fuel tanks, half of which lie near the skin's surface. A fat cell can vary from relatively empty, like a deflated balloon, to overly full. In an obese person, fat cells may swell to two or three times their normal size and then divide. Once the number of fat cells increases—due to genetic predisposition, early childhood eating patterns, or adult overeating—it never decreases. On a diet, fat cells may shrink, but they do not disappear (Sjöstrum, 1980).

The unyielding nature of our fat cells is but one way in which, once we become fat, our bodies maintain fat. Another way is that fat tissue has a low metabolic (energy expenditure) rate. Compared with other tissue, fat takes less food energy to maintain. Thus, once we become fat, we require less food to maintain our weight than we did to attain it.

Set Points and Metabolism

There is another reason why most obese people find it so difficult to lose weight permanently. Their bodies' "weight thermostats" are set to maintain body weight within a higher-than-average range. When weight drops below the set-point range, hunger increases and metabolism decreases.

Figure **17.17**

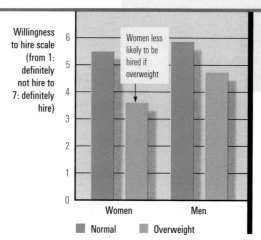

Gender and weight discrimination When women applicants were made to look overweight, university students were less willing to think they would hire them. Among men applicants, weight mattered less. (Data from Pingitore & others, 1994).

Figure **17.18**

The effects of a severe diet on obese patients' body weight and metabolism After 7 days on a 3500-calorie diet, six obese patients were given only 450 calories a day for the next 24 days. Body weight declined only 6 percent and then leveled off, because metabolism dropped about 15 percent. (From Bray, 1969.)

Caloric intake in calories per day — Calorie intake plunges

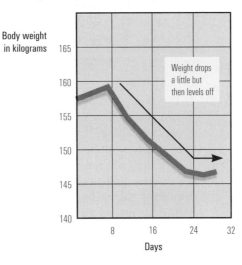

Body weight in kilograms — Weight drops a little but then levels off

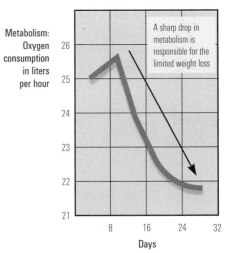

Metabolism: Oxygen consumption in liters per hour — A sharp drop in metabolism is responsible for the limited weight loss

As many a dieter can testify, the drop in resting metabolic rate can be particularly frustrating. After the rapid weight losses that occur during the initial three weeks or so of a rigorous diet, further weight loss comes slowly. In one classic experiment (Bray, 1969), obese patients whose daily food intake was reduced from 3500 to 450 calories lost only 6 percent of their weight—partly because their metabolic rates dropped about 15 percent (Figure 17.18). Thus, the body adapts to starvation by burning off fewer calories, and to extra calories by burning off more. That is why reducing your food intake by 3500 calories may not reduce your weight by 1 pound. And that is why when a diet ends and the body is still conserving energy, amounts of food that only maintained weight before the diet may now increase it.

Individual differences in resting metabolism explain why—contrary to the stereotype of the overweight glutton—it is possible for two people of the same height, age, and activity level to maintain the same weight, even if one of them eats much more than the other does. Or why it is possible for a person to eat less than another similarly active person, yet weigh more. This appears true despite findings that people—obese people, especially—tend to overestimate their physical activity and underestimate their caloric intake (Brownell & Wadden, 1992; Lichtman & others, 1992).

The Genetic Factor

Studies of adoptees and twins reveal a genetic influence on body weight. Consider:

- Despite shared family meals, the body weights of adoptive siblings are uncorrelated with one another and with their adoptive parents. Rather, people's weights resemble those of their biological parents (Grilo & Pogue-Geile, 1991).

- Identical twins have closely similar weights, even when reared apart (Plomin & others, 1997; Stunkard & others, 1990). Being overweight is therefore *not* simply a matter of scarfing too many hot fudge sundaes. And losing weight is not simply a matter of mind over platter.

Recent experiments reveal a mechanism for weight control. As a normal mouse's fat cells become bloated, its genes produce a protein, leptin. To estimate body fat, the brain monitors leptin levels in the blood. Increased leptin therefore signals the brain to curb eating and increase activity. So researchers injected obese mice, which produce less leptin, with daily doses of leptin. The mice then ate less, became more active, and lost weight (Halaas & others, 1995). This discovery excites wondering: Might injections of leptin similarly serve as virtual fat for humans, fooling the brain into making a fat body thinner? Or, as newer research suggests, are the leptin receptors of obese humans insensitive to leptin (Considine & others, 1996)? If so, might a slightly different drug be designed that activates

Identical twins have closely similar weights, even when reared apart. Being overweight is therefore *not* simply a matter of scarfing too many hot fudge sundaes.

Fat-signaling hormone The obese mouse at left has a defective gene for producing the fat-signaling hormone, leptin. When the genetically similar mouse at right was treated with leptin, it shed 40 percent of its body weight.

- U.S. models of a generation ago weighed 8 percent less than the average woman; today they weigh 23 percent less—which makes the average model thinner than 95 percent of women (Wolf, 1991). Most of today's models and actresses have hardly more than half the 22 to 26 percent body fat of an average woman (Brownell, 1991). When young women view magazine pictures of ultra-thin models, they report increased feelings of shame, guilt, and body dissatisfaction (Stice & Shaw, 1994).

- In 1950, department-store mannequins looked nearly like real women. Since then, they have lost about 3 inches around their hips, which now average only 31 inches—quite unlike today's average young adult woman's 37 inches. In fact, women with as little body fat as these mannequins likely would not menstruate (University of California, 1993).

- While the average North American woman weighs more than her counterpart of 40 years ago and obesity rates are increasing, today's average Miss America contestant weighs about 15 pounds less.

insensitive leptin receptors? Or might we look forward to a drug that blocks hypothalamic receptors that activate eating (Gerald & others, 1996)? Given the huge potential market for such drugs, the race to define them is on.

Genes aren't the whole story behind obesity, however. Diet or exercise rather than genes must explain why obesity is six times more common among lower-class than among upper-class women, more common among Americans than among Europeans, and more common among Americans today than in 1900. (Compared with their counterparts in the early 1900s, people are eating a higher-fat diet and expending fewer calories.) Ironically, the growing pudginess of Americans coincides with an increasing idealization of the thin-and-fit look. Consider:

Losing Weight

Perhaps you shake your head in sympathy with obese people: "Slim chance they (or we) have of becoming and staying thin. If they lose weight on a diet, their metabolism slows and their hungry fat cells cry out, 'Feed me!'" Indeed, the condition of an obese person's body reduced to average weight is much like that of a semistarved body. Held under normal set point, each body "thinks" it is starving. Having lost weight, formerly obese people look normal, but their fat cells may be abnormally small, their metabolism slowed, and, like the semistarved subjects we met in Chapter 12, their minds obsessed with food.

All this explains why most people who succeed on a weight-loss program eventually gain nearly all of the weight back (Garner & Wooley, 1991; Wing & Jeffery, 1979). One study followed 207 obese patients who had lost large amounts of weight during a 2-month hospital fast (Johnson & Drenick, 1977). Half gained back all the lost weight within 3 years, and virtually all were again obese within 9 years. Programs that modify life-style and ongoing

"After years of research, after tens of millions of dieters, after tens of billions of dollars, no one has found a diet that keeps the weight off in any but a small fraction of dieters."

MARTIN E. P. SELIGMAN
WHAT YOU CAN CHANGE AND WHAT YOU CAN'T
1994

The lean look Contemporary clothing ads and films present an ideal of thinness that most women cannot attain. The message is so pervasive in our culture that even those of flawless appearance are often worried about their bodily "imperfections."

Having lost weight, formerly obese people look normal, but their fat cells may be abnormally small, their metabolism slowed, and, like the semistarved subjects we met in Chapter 12, their minds obsessed with food.

eating behavior have better carryover to postdiet weight management. Yet participants in these programs, too, typically regain much of their lost weight (Figure 17.19). When cultural ideals of slimness collide with hunger, hunger usually wins. Commercial weight-loss programs can justifiably proclaim that they help people lose weight, *temporarily*. For most people, however, the only long-term result is a thinner wallet.

Nonetheless, the battle of the bulge rages as intensely as ever. It is especially intense in North America, where weight concern and dieting are a greater preoccupation than in, say, Australia or developing countries (Rothblum, 1990; Tiggemann & Rothblum, 1988). Americans spend $30 billion a year trying to lose weight (Gura, 1997). In one poll, 32 percent of men and 44 percent of women said they were trying to lose weight (Castro, 1991). Asked if they would rather "be five years younger or weigh 15 pounds less," 29 percent of men and 48 percent of women would prefer losing the weight (*Responsive Community*, 1996). The gender difference is even larger for teenagers: 15 percent of boys and 44 percent of girls are trying to lose weight (Centers for Disease Control, 1991).

With fat cells, set points, metabolism, and genetic factors all tirelessly conspiring to make losing weight a big problem, what advice can psychology offer to those who wish to shed excess pounds? The most important advice seems to be that we should begin a diet only if we feel motivated and self-disciplined enough to restrict our eating or exercise permanently. For most people, permanent weight loss requires making a career of staying thin—a lifelong change in eating habits combined with gradually increased exercise. In fact, sustained exercise can be a weapon against the body's normal metabolic slowdown when dieting. One of the few predictors of successful long-term weight loss is exercise during and after dieting (Brownell & Wadden, 1991, 1992; Foreyt & others, 1996).

Although preserving weight loss is a constant challenge, Stanley Schachter (1982) has been less pessimistic than most obesity researchers about the likelihood of doing it successfully. He recognizes the overwhelming rate of failure among people in structured weight-loss programs. But he also notes that these are a special group of people, probably people who have been unable to help themselves.

Janet Polivy and Peter Herman (1987) believe that widespread, chronic dieting among basically normal-weight girls and women represents the seeds of eating disorders on a massive scale.

Bottom Liners

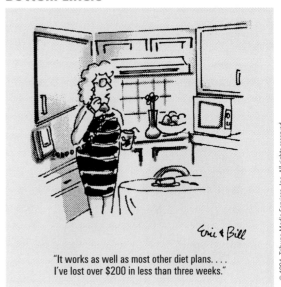

"It works as well as most other diet plans. . . . I've lost over $200 in less than three weeks."

Figure **17.19**

Weight-loss programs and weight change Behavior management weight-loss programs promote weight loss, but most lost weight is regained. (From Brownell & Jeffery, 1987.)

Weight change in pounds

Starting point

Normal trend for untreated obese people: Gradually rising weight

After participation in behavioral program: Much of initial weight loss regained

Post treatment   1   2   3   4   5

Years of follow-up

CLOSE-UP

Helpful Hints for Dieters

Minimize exposure to tempting food cues. Keep tempting foods out of the house or out of sight. Stay out of the sweets shops. Go to the supermarket only on a full stomach.

Take steps to boost your metabolism. Inactive people are often overweight (Figure 17.20). Sustained exercise, such as brisk walking, running, and swimming, not only empties fat cells, builds muscle, and makes you feel better, it can also temporarily speed up metabolism (Kolata, 1987; Thompson & others, 1982).

Modify both your metabolic rate and your hunger by changing the food you eat Findings suggest that complex carbohydrates (pasta, grains, potatoes) increase metabolism and are less readily converted to body fat than are the same calories eaten as fats (Rodin, 1979, 1985). Complex carbohydrates and fructose (the sugar in fruits) stimulate less of the hunger-producing insulin jump than does refined sugar (sucrose).

Don't starve all day and eat one big meal at night. This eating pattern, common among overweight people, slows metabolism.

Beware of the binge. Among people who consciously restrain their eating, drinking alcohol or feeling anxious or depressed can unleash the urge to eat (Herman & Polivy, 1980). Once the diet is broken, the person often thinks "what the heck" and then binges (Polivy & Herman, 1985, 1987): A lapse becomes a full collapse. Remember, most people occasionally lapse. Remind yourself that you've succeeded before and continue with your plan.

Set realistic goals. Targeting an ambitiously low weight usually dooms a dieter to eventual defeat. Setting a realistic objective—such as walking several times a week—can promote effort and persistence.

Percentage obese — *The more TV people watch, the more apt they are to be obese*

Hours of TV watched per day

(y-axis: 0, 5, 10, 15, 20, 25)
(x-axis: 0–1, 1–2, 2–3, 3–4, 4–5, More than 5)

Figure 17.20

Couch potatoes beware: a correlational study of TV watching and obesity In one study of 6671 12- to 17-year-olds, obesity was more common among those who watched the most television (Dietz & Gortmaker, 1985). Of course, overweight people may avoid activity, preferring to sit and watch TV. But the association between TV watching and obesity remained when many other factors were controlled, suggesting that inactivity and snacking while watching TV do contribute to obesity. Also, as life-styles have become more sedentary and TV watching has increased, so has the percentage of overweight people in Britain, North America, and elsewhere (Vines, 1995).

Moreover, the failure rates recorded for these programs are based on single attempts at weight loss. Perhaps when people try repeatedly to lose weight, more of them do eventually succeed. When Schachter interviewed a haphazard sample of people, he found that one-fourth of them had at one time been significantly overweight and had tried to slim down. Of these, 6 out of 10 had *succeeded*: They weighed at least 10 percent less than their maximum prediet weight (an average loss of 35 pounds) and were no longer obese. And a 1993 survey of 90,000 *Consumer Reports* readers found 25 percent of dieters claiming enduring weight loss.

Two other studies reveal less encouraging results: Fewer than a third of formerly overweight people were no longer overweight (Jeffery & Wing, 1983; Rzewnicki & Forgays, 1987). But the findings do hint that prospects for losing weight may be somewhat brighter than the dismal conclusions drawn from following patients who undergo a single weight-loss program. If all this has a familiar ring, recall that stop-smoking programs tend to be (1) effective in the short run and (2) ineffective in the long run, but that (3) many people are former smokers.

There is, however, another option for overweight people, the one chosen by 13 percent of the people Schachter interviewed—simply to accept one's weight. We all do well to note what researchers have *not* identified as causes of obesity: guilt, hostility, oral fixation, or any similar personality maladjustment. Nor is obesity simply a matter of a lack of willpower. If dieters are more likely to binge when under stress or after breaking their diets, this may be largely a consequence of their constant dieting. "Fat is not a four-letter word," proclaims the National Association to Aid Fat Acceptance, so "a waist is a terrible thing to mind." Although such statements disregard the health risks linked with significant obesity, they do convey a valid point: It is surely better to accept oneself as a little chubby than to diet and binge, and feel continually out of control and guilty. Fans loved Oprah Winfrey before she lost 67 pounds.

They loved her after she put them back on. They loved her when she shed them again. And they will love her still, chubby or not.

While working to clarify the precise relationships among diet, behavior, and health, health psychologists continue their efforts to persuade people to adopt healthier life-styles. Doing so is quite a challenge, however. Happy people tend to see themselves as relatively invulnerable to health problems, especially those that might arise from their own actions (Salovey & Birnbaum, 1989; Weinstein, 1987). They also typically believe their own life-style is healthier than other people's—that they drink less alcohol, consume less fat and cholesterol, and get more exercise. Often they are fooling themselves. Furthermore, many individuals who admit to behaviors known to increase health risks will deny that the behaviors actually make them personally more vulnerable to illness or injury. Unlike people who are told they have normal blood pressure, those told they have high blood pressure tend to dismiss its seriousness (Croyle & Ditto, 1990). Smokers may delude themselves by saying that their exercising counteracts the negative effects of smoking.

Because of people's optimistic denials of health risks, the first hurdle health-promotion programs must surmount is to get people to realize their vulnerability to stress- and behavior-related health problems. Only then will people make an effort to control stress, stop smoking, moderate their drinking, eat wisely, exercise regularly, and even buckle their seat belts.

The weight she was. Oprah Winfrey's yo-yo dieting illustrates both the difficulty of keeping weight off and the contemporary obsession with women's weight.

1984–1987	About 200 pounds
1988–1989:	Loses 67 pounds
1990:	Regains 70 pounds
1992:	Peaks at 235 pounds
1993:	Loses 72 pounds
1994:	Loses 15 pounds more; runs 26.2-mile marathon
1995:	66 percent of McCall's (August) readers think *this time* she'll not regain the weight

Note what researchers have
not identified as causes of obesity:
guilt, hostility, oral fixation, or any
similar personality maladjustment.
Nor is obesity simply a matter
of a lack of willpower.

SUMMING UP

Preventing illness and promoting health through stress management and behavior change is far better than attempting to treat problems after they occur.

Coping With Stress Among the components of stress-management programs are training in aerobic exercise, biofeedback, and relaxation. Although the degree of mind control over the body that can be gained through biofeedback has fallen short of early expectations, it sometimes helps people control tension headaches and high blood pressure. Simple relaxation exercises offer some of the same benefits. Counseling Type A heart attack survivors to slow down and relax has helped them lower their rate of recurring attacks. Social support also helps people cope, partly by buffering the impact of stress.

Modifying Illness-Related Behaviors The largest preventable cause of death in North America is cigarette smoking, a fact that motivates psychologists to study the social influences that cause adolescents to start smoking, the negative and positive reinforcers that maintain the habit, and possible ways to stop and prevent smoking.

Researchers are now exploring how certain foods, by providing the building blocks for specific neurotransmitters, affect mood and behavior.

Fat is a concentrated fuel reserve stored in fat cells. The number and size of these cells, influenced by genetics, determine one's body fat. Obese people find it difficult to lose weight permanently because the number of fat cells is not reduced by a diet, because the energy expenditure necessary for tissue maintenance is lower in fat than in other tissues, and because the overall metabolic rate decreases when body weight drops below the set point. Thus, the professional consensus: with dieting you can lose weight, but you will probably regain it. Those who nevertheless wish to diet should minimize exposure to food cues, boost energy expenditure through exercise, and make a lifelong change in eating patterns.

KEY TERMS AND CONCEPTS   aerobic exercise, biofeedback

TERMS AND CONCEPTS TO REMEMBER

behavioral medicine, p. 515

health psychology, p. 515

stress, p. 516

general adaptation syndrome (GAS), p. 518

burnout, p. 520

coronary heart disease, p. 521

Type A, p. 522

Type B, p. 522

psychophysiological illness, p. 523

lymphocytes, p. 523

aerobic exercise, p. 529

biofeedback, p. 531

CRITICAL THINKING EXERCISE
by Richard O. Straub

Now that you have read and reviewed Chapter 17, take your learning a step further by testing your critical thinking skills on the following practical problem-solving exercise.

Janet and Sheila have been good friends since meeting in their introductory psychology class as first-year students. Although they are about the same height and age, their weights differ. Janet, whose parents are both obese, has always been between normal weight and 25 percent above normal. Acquaintances assume she is lazy and gluttonous, but Janet's friends know that she is neither. Sheila's weight is normal, as are her parents'.

As a final project in their health psychology class, Janet and Sheila decided to make themselves the subjects of an experiment. For a month, they ate the same total number of calories per day, spread across several small, healthy meals that were low in fat and included whole grains, fruits, and vegetables. They also added a brisk, 30-minute walk to their daily routines. At the end of the month, Janet and Sheila weighed themselves for the first time since the experiment began. Although Janet was pleased to find that she had lost some weight, Sheila had lost more. When they presented their findings to the class, several students speculated that perhaps Janet simply hadn't employed the willpower that Sheila had, and that was why Sheila lost more weight.

1. What factors in Janet's background might have contributed to her obesity?

2. What factors in Sheila's background might have contributed to her being of normal weight?

3. Why did Sheila lose more weight than Janet, even though they consumed the same number of calories, ate the same types of food, and did the same amount of exercise?

Check your progress on becoming a critical thinker by comparing your answers to the sample answers found in Appendix B.

chapter 18

Social Psychology

"We cannot live for ourselves alone," remarked the novelist Herman Melville, for "our lives are connected by a thousand invisible threads." Social psychologists explore these connections by scientifically studying how we *think about, influence*, and *relate to* one another.

Social Thinking

How do we explain people's behavior? How do we form our beliefs and attitudes? How does what we think affect what we do?

Especially when the unexpected occurs, we analyze why people act as they do. Does her warmth reflect romantic interest in me, or is that how she relates to everyone? Does his absenteeism signify laziness or a stressful work atmosphere?

Attributing Behavior to Persons or to Situations

After studying how people explain others' behavior, Fritz Heider (1958) proposed an attribution theory. Heider noted that people usually attribute others' behavior either to their internal dispositions or to their external situations. A teacher, for example, may wonder whether a child's hostility reflects an aggressive personality (*a dispositional attribution*) or whether the child is reacting to stress or abuse (*a situational attribution*).

In class, we notice that Julie doesn't say much; over coffee, Jack talks nonstop. Attributing their behaviors to their personal dispositions, we decide that Julie is shy and Jack is outgoing. Because people do have enduring personality traits, such attributions are sometimes valid. However, we often overestimate the influence of personality and underestimate the influence of situation. In class, Jack may be as quiet as Julie. Catch Julie at a party and you may hardly recognize your quiet classmate. Underestimating such situational influences is known as the fundamental attribution error.

social psychology
the scientific study of how we think about, influence, and relate to one another.

attribution theory
the theory that we tend to give a causal explanation for someone's behavior, often by crediting either the situation or the person's disposition.

fundamental attribution error
the tendency for observers, when analyzing another's behavior, to underestimate the impact of the situation and to overestimate the impact of personal disposition.

An experiment by David Napolitan and George Goethals (1979) illustrates the phenomenon. They had Williams College students talk, one at a time, with a young woman who acted either aloof and critical or warm and friendly. Beforehand, they told half the students the woman's behavior would be spontaneous. They told the other half the truth—that she had been instructed to *act* friendly (or unfriendly). What effect do you suppose this information had?

None. The students disregarded the information. If the woman acted friendly, they inferred she really was a warm person. If she acted unfriendly, they inferred she really was a cold person. In other words, they attributed her behavior to her personal disposition *even when told that her behavior was situational*—that she was merely acting that way for purposes of the experiment.

The fundamental attribution error is almost irresistible. In a high school play I once attended, a talented 16-year-old girl convincingly played the part of a bitter old woman—so convincingly that, although I reminded myself of the fundamental attribution error, I still assumed that the young actress was typecast because she was well-suited for the part. Meeting her later at a cast party, I discovered she actually has a very pleasant disposition. I then remembered that several months earlier I had seen her play the part of a charming child in *The Sound of Music.* Leonard Nimoy of "Star Trek" fame would not have been surprised by my error. He titled one of his books *I Am Not Spock.*

You, too, have surely committed the fundamental attribution error. In judging, say, whether your psychology instructor is shy or outgoing, you have perhaps by now inferred that he or she has an outgoing personality. But you know your instructor only from the classroom, a situation that demands outgoing behavior. Catch the instructor in a different situation and you might be surprised (as some of my students are when confronting me in a pickup basketball game). Outside their assigned roles, professors seem less professorial, presidents less presidential, servants less servile.

The instructor, on the other hand, observes his or her own behavior in many different situations—in the classroom, in meetings, at home—and so might say, "Me, outgoing? It all depends on the sit-

uation. In class or with good friends, yes, I'm outgoing. But at conventions I'm really rather shy."

So, when explaining *our own* behavior, we are sensitive to how our behavior changes with the situations we encounter. When explaining *others'* behavior, particularly after observing them in only one type of situation, we often commit the fundamental attribution error: We disregard the situation and leap to unwarranted conclusions about their personality traits. We do so partly because we have learned to focus our attention more on the person than on the situational context. Meanwhile, the person's own attention focuses more on the situation to which he or she is reacting. Reverse the perspectives of actor and observer—by having each view a videotape replay of the situation from the other's perspective—and this reverses the attributions (Lassiter & Irvine, 1986; Storms, 1973). By seeing the world from the actor's perspective, the observers better appreciate the situation. Given an observer's point of view, the actors better appreciate their own personal style.

The Effects of Attribution

In everyday life we often struggle to explain others' actions. To what should we attribute them? A jury must decide whether a shooting was malicious or in self-defense. An unhappy wife and husband each ponder why the other behaves so selfishly. An interviewer must judge whether the applicant's geniality is genuine. When we make such judgments, our attributions—either to the person or to the situation—have important consequences (Fincham & Bradbury, 1993; Fletcher & others, 1990). Happily married couples attribute their spouse's tart-tongued remark to a temporary situation ("She must have had a bad day at work"). Unhappily married persons attribute the same remark to a

Recall from Chapter 14 that personality psychologists study the enduring, inner determinants of behavior that help to explain why different people act differently in a given situation. Social psychologists study the social influences that help explain why the same person will act differently in different situations.

Outside their assigned roles, professors seem less professorial, presidents less presidential, servants less servile.

"Otis, shout at that man to pull himself together."

mean disposition ("Why did I marry such a hostile person?").

Or consider the political effects of attribution: How do you explain poverty or unemployment? Researchers in Britain, India, Australia, and the United States (Furnham, 1982; Pandey & others, 1982; Wagstaff, 1982; Zucker & Weiner, 1993) report that political conservatives tend to attribute such social problems to the personal dispositions of the poor and unemployed themselves: "People generally get what they deserve. Those who don't work are often freeloaders. People who take initiative can still get ahead." "Society is not to blame for crime, criminals are," said one U.S. presidential candidate (Dole, 1996). Political liberals (and social scientists) are more likely to blame past and present situations: "If you or I had to live with the same poor education, lack of opportunity, and discrimination, would we be any better off?"

In evaluating employees, managers must also make attributions. They are likely to attribute the poor performance of workers to personal factors, such as low ability or lack of motivation. Workers who are doing poorly on a job recognize situational influences: inadequate supplies, poor working conditions, difficult co-workers, impossible demands (Rice, 1985).

The practical point to remember: Our attributions—to individuals' dispositions or to their situations—have real consequences (Figure 18.1).

Attitudes and Actions

Social psychology's single most important concept has been that of *attitudes*. Attitudes are beliefs and feelings that predispose our reactions to objects, people, and events. If we *believe* that someone is mean, we may *feel* dislike for the person and *act* unfriendly. "Change the way people think," said South African civil rights martyr Steve Biko, "and things will never be the same."

Do Our Attitudes Guide Our Actions?

Although most persuasive appeals assume that changed attitudes can indeed change behavior, dozens of studies during the 1960s challenged this idea (Wicker, 1971). Moreover, studies of people's attitudes and behaviors regarding cheating, religion, and racial minorities revealed that folks often talk and act a different game.

But the seeming hypocrisy did startle social psychologists, most of whom shared Biko's belief that there is a close connection between thought and action, character and conduct, private words and public deeds. So they conducted many follow-up studies during the 1970s and 1980s (Kraus, 1991; Wallace & others, 1996). These studies reveal that our attitudes *will* guide our actions if:

attitude
a belief and feeling that predisposes one to respond in a particular way to objects, people, and events.

> "Thinking is easy, acting difficult, and to put one's thoughts into action, the most difficult thing in the world."
>
> GERMAN POET GOETHE (1749–1832)

Figure 18.1

Situational attribution
"Maybe that driver is ill."

Tolerant reaction
(proceed cautiously, allow driver a wide berth)

Negative behavior

Dispositional attribution
"Crazy driver!"

Unfavorable reaction
(speed up and race past the other driver, craning to give them a dirty look)

Attributions and attitudes How we explain someone's behavior affects how we react to it.

Figure 18.2

- **Outside influences on what we say and do are minimal.** Social pressures may blur the underlying connection between our attitudes and actions by affecting either what we say or what we do (Figure 18.2). In 1990, four weeks before a congressional election, President Bush and political leaders from both parties asked members of the U.S. House of Representatives to pass a compromise deficit-reducing budget. Privately, most members of Congress agreed that the painful cuts and tax increases were essential to the nation's health: Among those retiring or unopposed for reelection, and thus facing little external pressure, 86 percent voted for the bill. For others, voting their privately held attitude was more difficult. Among the 36 representatives who were about to face angry voters in close races back home, there were no profiles in courage: All 36 voted against it.

- **The attitude is specifically relevant to the behavior.** People readily profess *general* attitudes that contradict their behavior. They proclaim love while yelling at their mate, cherish honesty while cheating on their income tax returns, and value good health while smoking and not exercising. Attitudes about the specific act do, however, guide action. Attitudes toward exercise predict exercising behavior.

- **We are keenly aware of our attitudes.** When we mindlessly follow habit or social expectations, our attitudes lie dormant. If something makes us self-conscious or reminds us of how we feel, we are truer to our convictions. For example, Martha Powell and Russell Fazio (1984) report that repeating an attitude makes it come to mind more quickly. Moreover, attitudes that come quickly to mind are more likely to guide our behavior (Fazio, 1990). When we know and are conscious of what we believe, we are true to ourselves.

Do Our Actions Affect Our Attitudes?

So, people will stand up for what they believe under certain circumstances: when other influences are minimal, when the attitude is specific to the behavior, and when they are mindful of their attitudes. Attitudes will affect behavior. Now consider a more surprising principle: People also come to believe in what they have stood up for. Many streams of evidence confirm that *attitudes follow behavior*. Here are two.

foot-in-the-door phenomenon the tendency for people who have first agreed to a small request to comply later with a larger request.

The Foot-in-the-Door Phenomenon

During the Korean War, many captured U.S. soldiers were imprisoned in war camps run by Chinese communists. Without using brutality, the captors secured hundreds of their prisoners' collaboration in various activities. Some merely ran errands or accepted favors. Others made radio appeals and false confessions. Some others informed on fellow prisoners and divulged military information. When the war ended, 21 prisoners chose to stay with the communists. More returned home "brainwashed"—convinced that communism was a good thing for Asia.

A key ingredient of the Chinese "thought-control" program was its effective use of the foot-in-the-door phenomenon—a tendency for people who agree to a small request to comply later with a larger one. The Chinese harnessed this phenomenon by gradually escalating their demands on the prisoners, beginning with harmless requests (Schein, 1956). Having "trained" the prisoners to speak or write trivial statements, the communists then asked them to copy or create something more important, noting, perhaps, the flaws of capitalism. The prisoners then participated in group discussions, wrote self-criticisms, or uttered public confessions. Once they had done so, perhaps to gain privileges, the prisoners then often adjusted their beliefs toward consistency with their public acts.

Attitudes follow behavior.   Cooperative actions, such as those performed by people on sports teams, feed mutual liking. Such attitudes, in turn, promote positive behavior.

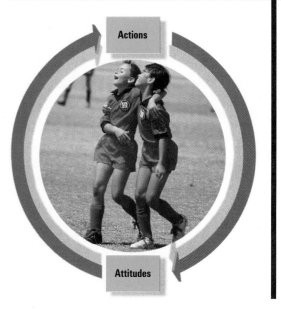

The point is simple, says Robert Cialdini (1993): To get people to agree to something big, "Start small and build." And be wary of those who would exploit you with the tactic. This chicken-and-egg spiral of actions feeding attitudes feeding actions enables behavior to escalate. A trifling act makes the next act easier. Succumb to a temptation and you will find the next temptation harder to resist.

Dozens of experiments have simulated part of the war prisoners' experience, by coaxing people into acting against their attitudes or violating their moral standards. The nearly inevitable result: Most subjects begin to rationalize their behavior by persuading themselves that they were justified in saying or doing what they did. If induced to speak or write on behalf of a point of view they have doubts about, they begin to believe their own words. Saying becomes believing. Similarly, subjects induced to harm an innocent victim—by making cutting comments or by delivering electric shocks—typically begin to disparage their victim.

"If the King destroys a man,
that's proof to the King it must
have been a bad man."

THOMAS CROMWELL
IN ROBERT BOLT'S A MAN FOR ALL SEASONS
1960

Fortunately, the attitudes-follow-behavior principle works as well for good deeds as for bad. The foot-in-the-door tactic helps boost charitable contributions, blood donations, and product sales. In one experiment, researchers posing as safety-drive volunteers asked Californians to permit the installation of a large, poorly lettered "Drive Carefully" sign in their front yards. Only 17 percent consented. Other home owners were first approached with a small request: Would they display a 3-inch-high "Be a Safe Driver" sign? Nearly all readily agreed. When reapproached two weeks later to allow the large, ugly sign in their front yards, 76 percent consented (Freedman & Fraser, 1966).

In the years immediately following the introduction of school desegregation and the passage of the Civil Rights Act of 1964, white Americans expressed diminishing racial prejudice. And as Americans in different regions came to act more alike—thanks to more uniform national standards against discrimination—they began to think more alike. Experiments confirm that moral action has positive effects on the actor, and that doing favors for another person often leads to greater liking of the person. We love people for the good we do them as well as for the good they do us. Evil acts shape the self, but so do moral acts.

Role Playing Affects Attitudes

In psychology, as in the theater, a role refers to a cluster of prescribed actions—the behaviors we expect of those who occupy a particular social position. When you adopt a new role—when you become a college student, marry, or begin a new job—you strive to follow the social prescriptions. At first, the behaviors may feel phony, because you are *acting* the role. The first weeks in the military feel artificial—as if one is pretending to be a soldier. The first weeks of a marriage may feel like "playing house." Before long, however, your behavior no longer feels forced. What began as play-acting in the theater of life becomes *you*.

Researchers have confirmed this effect by assessing people's attitudes before and after they adopt a new role. Sometimes this occurs in laboratory situations, sometimes in everyday situations, such as before and after taking a job. In one laboratory study, college students volunteered to spend time in a simulated prison devised by psychologist Philip Zimbardo (1972). Some he randomly designated as guards; he gave them uniforms, billy clubs, and whistles and instructed them to enforce certain rules. The remainder became prisoners; they were locked in barren cells and forced to wear humiliating outfits. After a day or two of self-consciously "playing" their roles, the simulation became real—too real. Most of the guards developed disparaging attitudes, and some devised cruel and degrading routines. One by one the prisoners either broke down, rebelled, or became passively resigned, causing Zimbardo to call the study off after only six days.

role
a set of expectations about a social position, defining how those in the position ought to behave.

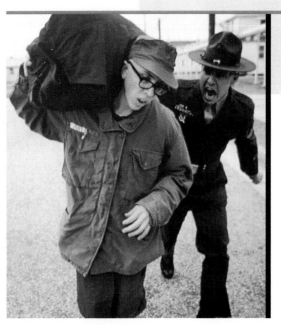

Social roles are powerful Initially both the obedient recruit and the abusive sergeant may have consciously adopted the behavior expected of them. In time, they may become the characters they are playing.

cognitive dissonance theory
the theory that we act to reduce the discomfort (dissonance) we feel when two of our thoughts (cognitions) are inconsistent. For example, when we become aware that our attitudes and our actions clash, we can reduce the resulting dissonance by changing our attitudes.

"Sit all day in a moping posture, sigh, and reply to everything with a dismal voice, and your melancholy lingers.... If we wish to conquer undesirable emotional tendencies in ourselves, we must ... go through the outward movements of those contrary dispositions which we prefer to cultivate."

WILLIAM JAMES
PRINCIPLES OF PSYCHOLOGY
1890

Meanwhile, in real life, the military junta then in power in Greece was training another group of men to become torturers (Staub, 1989). The men's indoctrination into their roles occurred in small steps. First, the trainee stood guard outside the interrogation cells—the "foot in the door." Next, he stood guard inside. Only then was he ready to become actively involved in the questioning and torture. As the nineteenth-century writer Nathaniel Hawthorne noted, "No man, for any considerable period, can wear one face to himself and another to the multitude without finally getting bewildered as to which may be true." Behavior affects attitudes. What we do, we gradually become.

Why Do Our Actions Affect Our Attitudes?

Without doubt, then, actions can affect attitudes, sometimes turning prisoners into collaborators, doubters into believers, or mere acquaintances into friends. But why? One explanation is that we feel motivated to justify our actions. When aware that our attitudes and actions don't coincide, we experience tension, called *cognitive dissonance*. To relieve this tension, according to the cognitive dissonance theory proposed by Leon Festinger, people often bring their attitudes into line with their actions. It's as if people rationalize, "If I chose to do it (or say it), I must believe in it." The less coerced and more responsible we feel for a troubling act, the more dissonance we feel. The more dissonance we feel, the more motivated we are to find consistency, such as by changing our attitudes to help justify the act.

Dozens of experiments have confirmed cognitive dissonance by making people feel responsible for behavior that is inconsistent with their attitudes and that has foreseeable consequences. As a subject in one of these experiments, you might agree for a measly $2 to help a researcher by writing an essay that supports something you don't believe in (perhaps a tuition increase). Feeling responsible for the statements (which are not consistent with your attitudes), you likely would feel dissonance, especially if you thought an administrator would

be reading your essay. How would you reduce the uncomfortable dissonance? One way would be to start believing your phony words. Let your pretense become your reality.

The attitudes-follow-behavior principle has some heartening implications. Although we cannot directly control all our feelings, we can influence them by altering our behavior. If we are unloving, we can become more loving by behaving as if we were so—by doing thoughtful things, expressing affection, giving affirmation. If we are down in the dumps, we can do as cognitive therapists advise and talk in more positive, self-accepting ways with fewer self–put-downs. *The point to remember: Changing our behavior can change how we think and feel. Just do it.*

Although we cannot directly control all our feelings, we can influence them by altering our behavior. If we are unloving, we can become more loving by behaving as if we were so—by doing thoughtful things, expressing affection, giving affirmation.

SUMMING UP

Social psychology is the study of how people think about, influence, and relate to one another.

Attributing Behavior to Persons or to Situations We generally explain people's behavior by attributing it either to internal dispositions or to external situations. In accounting for others' actions, we often underestimate the influence of the situation, thus committing the fundamental attribution error. When we explain our own behavior, however, we more often point to the situation and not to ourselves.

Attitudes and Actions Attitudes predict behavior only under certain conditions, as when other influences are minimized, when the attitude is specific to the behavior, and when people are aware of their attitudes. Studies of the foot-in-the-door phenomenon and of role playing reveal that our actions can also modify our attitudes, especially when we feel responsible for those actions. Cognitive dissonance theorists explain that behavior shapes attitudes because people feel discomfort when their actions go against their feelings and beliefs; they reduce the discomfort by bringing their attitudes more into line with what they have done.

KEY TERMS AND CONCEPTS social psychology, attribution theory, fundamental attribution error, attitude, foot-in-the-door phenomenon, role, cognitive dissonance theory

Social Influence

How do we influence each other? How are we affected by pressures to conform and obey, by group interaction, and by cultural influences?

Social psychology's great lesson is the enormous power of social influence on our attitudes, beliefs, decisions, and actions. This influence can be seen in our conformity, compliance, and group behavior. Suicides, bomb threats, airplane hijackings, and UFO sightings all have a curious tendency to come in clusters. Armed with principles of social influence, advertisers and salespeople aim to sway our decisions to buy, to donate, to vote. Isolated with others who share their grievances, dissenters may gradually become rebels and rebels may become terrorists. During a lengthy stay in another part of the the world, we may struggle with the new cultural norms. Let's examine the pull of these social strings. How strong are they? How do they operate?

Conformity and Obedience

Behavior is contagious. One person giggles, coughs, or yawns, and others in the group are soon doing the same. A cluster of people stands gazing upward, and passersby pause to do likewise. Laughter, even canned laughter, can be infectious. Bartenders and street musicians know to "seed" their tip cups with money to suggest that others have given.

Sometimes the effects of suggestibility are more serious. Sociologist David Phillips and his colleagues (1985, 1989) found that known suicides increase following a highly publicized suicide. So do fatal auto accidents and private airplane crashes (some of which disguise suicides)—and they do so only in areas where the suicide is publicized. Following film star Marilyn Monroe's suicide on August 6, 1962, the number of August suicides in the United States exceeded the usual count by 200. In Germany and the United States, suicide increases have also followed fictional suicides on soap operas and on dramas dealing with suicide (Gould & Shaffer, 1986; Hafner & Schmidtke, 1989; Phillips, 1982). Such copycat suicides help explain the clusters of teenage suicides that occasionally occur in some communities.

Group Pressure and Conformity

Suggestibility is a subtle type of conformity—adjusting our behavior or thinking to bring it into line with some group standard. To study conformity, Solomon Asch (1955) devised a simple test. As a participant in the study, you arrive at the experiment location in time to take a seat at the end of a row where five people are already seated. The experimenter asks which of three comparison lines is identical to a standard line (Figure 18.3). You see clearly that the answer is line 2 and await your turn to say so after the others. Your boredom with this experiment begins to show when the next set of lines proves equally easy.

Now comes the third trial, and the correct answer seems just as clear-cut, but the first person gives what strikes you as a wrong answer: "Line 3." When the second person and then the third and fourth give the same wrong answer, you sit up straight and squint. When the fifth person agrees with the first three, you feel your heart begin to pound. The experimenter then looks to you for your answer. Torn between the unanimity of your five fellow subjects and the evidence of your own eyes, you feel tense and much less sure of yourself than you were moments ago. You hesitate before answering, wondering whether you should suffer the discomfort of being viewed as an oddball. What answer do you give?

conformity
adjusting one's behavior or thinking to coincide with a group standard.

Standard line　　Comparison lines　1　2　3

Figure 18.3

Asch's conformity experiments
Which of the three comparison lines is equal to the standard line? What do you suppose most people would say after hearing five others say, "Line 3"? In this photo from one of Asch's experiments, the subject (center) shows the severe discomfort that comes from disagreeing with the responses of other group members.

In the experiments conducted by Asch and others after him, thousands of college students have experienced this conflict. Answering such questions alone, they erred less than 1 percent of the time. But it was a different story when several others—confederates working for the experimenter—answered incorrectly. Asch reports that more than one-third of the time his "intelligent and well-meaning" college subjects were then "willing to call white black" by going along with the group.

Conditions That Strengthen Conformity

Asch's procedure became the model for later investigations. Although experiments have not always found such a high degree of blind conformity, they reveal that conformity increases when:

- we are made to feel incompetent or insecure.
- the group has at least three people. (Further increases in the group size yield not much more conformity.)
- the group is unanimous. (The support of a single fellow dissident greatly increases our social courage.)
- we admire the group's status and attractiveness.
- we have made no prior commitment to any response.
- others in the group observe our behavior.
- our culture strongly encourages respect for social standards.

Thus, we might predict the behavior of Joe, an eager but insecure new member of a prestigious fraternity: Noting that the 40 other members appear unanimous in their plans for an upcoming fund-raiser, Joe is unlikely to voice his dissent.

Figure 18.4

Informational influence Sample task: After seeing Slides 1 and 2, participants judged which person in Slide 2 was the same as the person in Slide 1. (Adapted from Baron, Vandello, & Brunsman, 1996.)

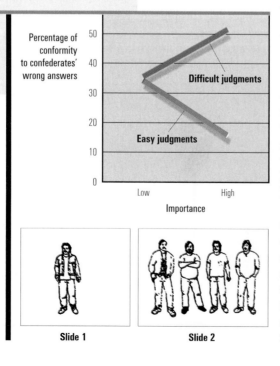

Reasons for Conforming

Why do we clap when others clap, eat as others eat, believe what others believe, even see what others see? Frequently, it is to avoid rejection or to gain social approval. In such cases, we are responding to what social psychologists call normative social influence. We are sensitive to social norms—understood rules for accepted and expected behavior—because the price we pay for being different may be severe. Marco Lokar knows. During the 1991 Persian Gulf War, Lokar, an Italian, was the only Seton Hall University basketball player who chose not to display an American flag on his uniform. As the team traveled about, the fans' abusive responses to his nonconforming behavior became unbearable, so he quit the team and returned to Italy.

> "Have you ever noticed how one example—good or bad—can prompt others to follow? How one illegally parked car can give permission for others to do likewise? How one racial joke can fuel another?"
>
> **MARIAN WRIGHT EDELMAN**
> *THE MEASURE OF OUR SUCCESS*
> 1992

But respecting norms is not the only reason we conform: The group may provide valuable information. Only a very stubborn person will *never* listen to others. When we accept others' opinions about reality, we are responding to informational social influence . "Those who never retract their opinions love themselves more than they love truth," observed Joseph Joybert, an eighteenth-century French essayist.

Robert Baron and his colleagues (1996) cleverly demonstrated informational influence. Although common sense might predict that we would conform less on really important issues, they showed that conformity can *increase* when being right matters. Baron and his co-researchers modernized the Asch experiment by showing University of Iowa students a slide of a stimulus person, followed by a slide of a four-person lineup (Figure 18.4). Their experiment made the task either easy (viewing the lineup for five seconds) or difficult (viewing the lineup for but half a second). It also construed their judgments as either unimportant (just a preliminary test of some eyewitness identification procedures) or as important (establishing norms for an eyewitness accuracy test, with a $20 award to the most accurate participants). The conformity test then exposed individual students to the judgments of two supposed fellow subjects who gave a wrong answer. When the accuracy of their judgments seemed important, people rarely conformed when the task was easy. But they conformed half the time when the task was difficult. When we are unsure what is right, and being right matters, we become more open to others' opinions.

We perceive social influence as negative or positive depending on our values. When influence supports what we approve, we applaud those who are "open-minded" and "sensitive" enough to be "responsive." When influence supports what we disapprove, we scorn the "submissive conformity" of those who comply with others' wishes. As we saw in Chapter 14, cultures vary in the value they place on individualism or collectivism. Western Europeans and those in most English-speaking countries tend to prize individualism more than conformity and obedience. In experiments conducted in 17 countries, conformity rates have been lower in individualistic cultures (Bond & Smith, 1996).

Obedience

Social psychologist Stanley Milgram (1965, 1974) knew that people often comply with social pressures. But how would they respond to outright commands? To find out, he undertook what have become social psychology's most famous and controversial experiments. Imagine yourself as one of the nearly 1000 participants in Milgram's 20 experiments.

Responding to an advertisement, you come to Yale University's psychology department to participate in an experiment. Professor Milgram's assistant explains that the study concerns the effect of punishment on learning. You and another person draw slips out of a hat to see who will be the "teacher" (which your slip says) and who will be the "learner." The learner is then led to an adjoining room and strapped into a chair that is wired through the wall to an electric shock machine. You sit down in front of the machine, which has switches labeled with voltages. Your task: to teach and then test the learner on a list of word pairs. You are to punish the learner for wrong answers by delivering brief electric shocks, beginning with a switch labeled "15 Volts—Slight Shock." After each error by the learner, you are to move up to the next higher voltage. With each flick of a switch, lights flash, relay switches click on, and an electric buzzing fills the air.

If you comply with the experimenter's instructions, you hear the learner grunt when you flick the third, fourth, and fifth switches. After you activate

Why do we clap when others clap, eat as others eat, believe what others believe, even see what others see? Frequently, it is to avoid rejection or to gain social approval.

the eighth switch (labeled "120 Volts—Moderate Shock"), the learner shouts that the shocks are painful. After the tenth switch ("150 Volts—Strong Shock"), he cries, "Experimenter, get me out of here! I won't be in the experiment anymore! I refuse to go on!" You draw back when you hear these pleas, but the experimenter prods you: "Please continue—the experiment requires that you continue." If you still resist, he insists, "It is absolutely essential that you continue," or "You have no other choice, you *must* go on."

If you obey, you hear the learner's protests escalate to shrieks of agony as you continue to raise the shock level with each succeeding error. After the 330-volt level, the learner refuses to answer and soon falls silent. Still, the experimenter pushes you toward the final, 450-volt switch, ordering you to ask the questions and, if no correct answer is given, to administer the next shock level.

How far do you think you would follow the experimenter's commands? When Milgram surveyed people before conducting the experiment, most declared they would stop playing such a sadistic role soon after the learner first indicated pain and certainly before he shrieked in agony. This also was the prediction made by each of 40 psychiatrists whom Milgram asked to guess the outcome. When Milgram actually conducted the experiment with men aged 20 to 50, he was astonished to find that 63 percent complied fully—right up to the last switch.

Did the "teachers" figure out the hoax—that no shock was being delivered? Did they guess that the learner was a confederate who only pretended to feel the shocks? Did they realize that the experiment was really testing their willingness to comply with commands to inflict punishment? No, the teachers typically displayed genuine agony: They sweated, trembled, laughed nervously, and bit their lips.

Milgram's use of deception and stress triggered a debate over his research ethics. In his own defense, Milgram pointed out that, after the participants learned of the deception and actual research purposes, virtually none regretted taking part. When 40 of the "teachers" who had agonized most

Stanley Milgram (1933–1984) The late social psychologist's obedience experiments now "belong to the self-understanding of literate people in our age" (Sabini, 1986).

Milgram discovered that subtle details of a situation powerfully influence people. When he varied the social conditions, the proportion of fully compliant subjects varied from 0 to 93 percent.

were later interviewed by a psychiatrist, none appeared to be suffering emotional aftereffects. All in all, said Milgram, the experiments provoked less stress than university students experience when facing and sometimes failing big exams (Blass, 1996).

Perhaps the participants obeyed because the learners' protests were not convincing. To preclude this possibility, Milgram repeated the experiment, with 40 new teachers. This time his confederate mentioned a "slight heart condition" while being strapped into the chair, and then he complained and screamed more intensely as the shocks became more punishing. Still, 65 percent of the new teachers complied fully (Figure 18.5).

In later experiments, Milgram discovered that subtle details of a situation powerfully influence people. When he varied the social conditions, the proportion of fully compliant subjects varied from 0 to 93 percent. Obedience was highest when:

- the person giving the orders was close at hand and perceived to be a legitimate authority figure.

- the authority figure was supported by a prestigious institution. (Milgram got somewhat less compliance when he dissociated his experiments from Yale University.)

- the victim was depersonalized or at a distance, even in another room. (Similarly, in combat with an enemy they can see, many soldiers either do not fire their rifles or do not aim them properly. Such refusals to kill are rare among those who operate the more distant weapons of artillery or aircraft [Padgett, 1989].)

- there were no role models for defiance; that is, no other subjects were seen disobeying the experimenter.

The power of legitimate, close-at-hand authorities is dramatically apparent in stories of those who complied with orders to carry out the atrocities of the Holocaust, and those who didn't. In the summer of 1942 nearly 500 middle-aged German reserve police officers were dispatched to Jozefow, Poland, in German-occupied territory. On July 13, the group's visibly upset commander informed his recruits, mostly family men, that they had been ordered to round up the village's Jews, who were said to be aiding the enemy. Able-bodied men were to be sent to work camps, and all the rest were to be shot on the spot. Given a chance to refuse participation in the executions, only about a dozen immediately refused. Within 17 hours, the remaining 485 officers killed 1500 helpless women, children, and

Figure **18.5**

Milgram's follow-up obedience experiment In a repeat of the earlier experiment, 65 percent of the adult male "teachers" fully obeyed the experimenter's commands to continue. This was despite the "learner's" earlier mention of a heart condition and despite hearing cries of protest after 150 volts and agonized protests after 330 volts. (Data from Milgram, 1974.)

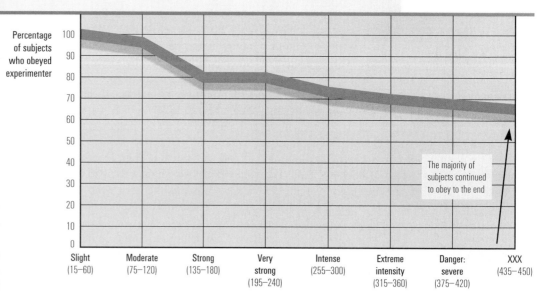

The majority of subjects continued to obey to the end

Percentage of subjects who obeyed experimenter

Shock levels in volts

Slight (15–60)	Moderate (75–120)
Strong (135–180)	Very strong (195–240)
Intense (255–300)	Extreme intensity (315–360)
Danger: severe (375–420)	XXX (435–450)

elderly by shooting them in the back of the head as they lay face down. Faced with the pleadings of the victims, and seeing the gruesome results, some 20 percent of the officers did eventually dissent, managing either to miss their victims or to wander away and hide until the slaughter was over (Browning, 1992). But in real life, as in Milgram's experiments, the disobedient were the minority.

Meanwhile, in the French village of Le Chambon, French Jews destined for deportation to Germany were being sheltered by villagers who openly defied orders to cooperate with the "New Order." The villagers' ancestors had themselves been persecuted and their pastors had been teaching them to "resist whenever our adversaries will demand of us obedience contrary to the orders of the Gospel" (Rochat, 1993). Ordered by police to give a list of sheltered Jews, the head pastor modeled defiance: "I don't know of Jews, I only know of human beings." Without realizing how long and terrible the war would be, or how much punishment and poverty they would suffer, the resisters made an initial commitment to resist. Supported by their beliefs, their role models, their interaction with one another, and their own initial acts, they remained defiant to the war's end.

Lessons From the Conformity and Obedience Studies

What do the Asch and Milgram experiments teach us about ourselves? How does judging the length of a line or flicking a shock switch relate to everyday social behavior? Recall from Chapter 1 that psychological experiments aim not to re-create the literal behaviors of everyday life but to capture and explore the underlying processes that shape those behaviors. Asch and Milgram devised experiments in which the subjects had to choose between holding to their own standards and being responsive to others, a dilemma we all face frequently.

"Drive off the cliff, James, I want to commit suicide."

Drawing by Mel Yauk.

In Milgram's experiments, subjects were also torn between what they should respond to—the pleas of the victim or the orders of the experimenter. Their moral sense warned them not to harm another, but it also prompted them to obey the experimenter and to be a good research participant. With kindness and obedience on a collision course, obedience usually won.

These experiments demonstrate that social influences can be strong enough to make people conform to falsehoods or capitulate to cruelty. "The most fundamental lesson of our study," Milgram noted, is that "ordinary people, simply doing their jobs, and without any particular hostility on their part, can become agents in a terrible destructive process" (1974, p. 6). Milgram entrapped his subjects not by asking them first to zap "learners" with enough electricity to make their hair stand on end. Rather, he exploited the foot-in-the-door effect, beginning with a little tickle of electricity and escalating step by step. In the subjects' minds, the little action became justified, making the next act tolerable. In Jozefow, in Le Chambon, and in Milgram's experiments, those who resisted often did so early. With the first acts of compliance or resistance, attitudes began to follow and justify behavior.

So it happens when people succumb, gradually, to evil. In any society, great evils sometimes grow out of people's compliance with little evils. The Nazi leaders suspected that most German civil servants would resist shooting or gassing Jews directly, but they found them surprisingly willing to handle the paperwork of the Holocaust (Silver & Geller, 1978). Likewise, when Milgram asked 40 men to administer the learning test while someone else did the shocking, 93 percent complied. Contrary to our images of devilish villains, evil doesn't require monstrous characters; it's enough to have ordinary people corrupted by an evil situation.

Standing up for democracy
Some individuals—roughly one in three in Milgram's experiments—resist social coercion, as did this unarmed man in Beijing, by single-handedly challenging an advancing line of tanks the day after the 1989 Tiananmen Square uprising was crushed.

"I was only following orders."

ADOLF EICHMANN
DIRECTOR OF NAZI DEPORTATION OF JEWS TO CONCENTRATION CAMPS

THINKING CRITICALLY ABOUT

Social Influence

Many social influences are so subtle that we don't notice them. Or if we do, we think ourselves immune. "Yes, TV affects others," most people say, "but not me." Peer examples don't intimidate us. Role models don't sway us. Ads don't persuade us. For we are not slaves to fads, fashions, and opinions; we are true to ourselves.

Or so we think. The reality, as social influence research has a thousand times demonstrated, is that the influence others have on us, and we on them, is real, though often unnoticed. The extent to which influences go unnoticed, even by those looking for them, appears in studies of "facilitated communication" with autistic children. *Autism*, a pervasive disorder that appears during the preschool years, is marked by apparent indifference to others, minimal intelligible speech, and restricted interests and activities. Hoping to break down the walls that isolate such children, a facilita-

tor holds or steadies the arm of an autistic child, who uses one finger to type words on a keyboard.

The technique is said to have produced breathtaking results with thousands of children, who suddenly begin typing intelligible words (sometimes elaborate sentences) which supposedly report their experiences and feelings. In several dozen cases where a person other than the parent was a facilitator, children have typed accusations of sexual abuse by their parents.

These spectacular findings and serious accusations led some people to question who was doing the communicating and the accusing—the child or the facilitator? To find out, Douglas Wheeler and his colleagues (1993) had 12 autistic children view pictures of everyday objects (a shoe, a book, a comb) and then type what they saw. When their facilitators saw the same picture, the children often typed the correct answer. When the facilita-

tors saw a different picture, or no picture, the children were *never* correct (Figure 18.6).

More than two dozen other experiments have produced similar results, some by not allowing the facilitator to see the keyboard (Jacobson & others, 1995). Facilitated communication proponents reply (as have ESP proponents) that the pressure of the testing situation obliterates the delicate phenomenon. But to the researchers, the more logical conclusion is the one reluctantly drawn by some of the shocked facilitators: The communication comes not from the child but from the facilitator (who misattributes the action to the child). The results stunned the well-meaning facilitators. Until the controlled experiment, they had no awareness of their influence on the child's movements. In this situation, as in so many others, human influence is subtle, unnoticed, even disbelieved, yet very real.

Child   **Facilitator**

Figure **18.6**

Testing facilitated communication The child responds after the facilitator and child see the same or different pictures. (Adapted from Wheeler & others, 1993.)

Group Influence

How do groups affect our behavior? To find out, social psychologists study the various influences that operate in the simplest of groups—one person in the presence of another—and those that operate in more complex groups, such as families, teams, and committees.

Individual Behavior in the Presence of Others

Appropriately, social psychology's first experiments focused on the simplest of all questions about social behavior: How are we influenced by the mere presence of others—by people watching us or joining us as we engage in various activities?

Social Facilitation

Having noticed that cyclists' racing times were faster when they competed against each other than when competing with a clock, Norman Triplett (1898) guessed that the presence of others boosts performance. To test his hypothesis, Triplett had adolescents wind a fishing reel as rapidly as possible. He discovered that they wound faster in the presence of someone who worked simultaneously on the same task. This stronger performance in the presence of others is known as social facilitation. For example, after a light turns green, drivers take about 15 percent less time to travel the first 100 yards when another car is beside them at the intersection than when they are alone (Towler, 1986). But on tougher tasks (learning nonsense syllables or solving complex multiplication problems), people perform less well when observers or others working on the same task are present.

Further studies revealed why others' presence sometimes helps and sometimes hinders performance (Guerin, 1986; Zajonc, 1965). When observed by others, people become aroused. This arousal strengthens the most likely response—the correct one on an easy task, an incorrect one on a difficult task. Thus, when observed, people perform well-learned tasks more quickly and accurately and unmastered tasks less quickly and accurately. James Michaels and his associates (1982) found that expert pool players who made 71 percent of their shots when alone made 80 percent when four people came to watch them. Poor shooters, who made 36 percent of their shots when alone, made only 25 percent when watched. The energizing effect of an enthusiastic audience probably contributes to the home advantage enjoyed by various sports teams. Studies of more than 80,000

college and professional athletic events in Canada, the United States, and England reveal that home teams win about 6 in 10 games (somewhat fewer for baseball and football, somewhat more for basketball and soccer—see Table 18.1).

The point to remember: What you do well, you are likely to do even better in front of an audience, especially a friendly audience; what you normally find difficult may seem impossible when others are watching.

Social facilitation also helps explain a funny effect of crowding: Comedy records that are mildly amusing to people in an uncrowded room seem funnier to people in a densely packed room (Aiello & others, 1983; Freedman & Perlick, 1979). As comedians and actors know, a "good house" is a full one. The arousal triggered by crowding amplifies other reactions, too. If sitting close, participants in experiments like a friendly person more, an unfriendly person less (Schiffenbauer & Schiavo, 1976; Storms & Thomas, 1977).

Home Advantage in Major Team Sports

Sport	Games Studied	Home Team Winning Percentage
Baseball	23,034	53.5%
Football	2,592	57.3
Ice hockey	4,322	61.1
Basketball	13,596	64.4
Soccer	37,202	69.0

From Courneya & Carron, 1992

Table **18.1**

Social facilitation Skilled athletes often find they are "on" before an audience. What they do well, they do even better when people are watching.

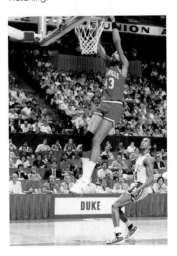

Social Loafing

The social facilitation experiments test the effect of others' presence on performance on an individual task, such as shooting pool. What happens to performance when people perform the same task as a group? In a team tug-of-war, for example, do you suppose the effort that a person puts forth would be more than, less than, or the same as the effort he or she would exert in a one-on-one tug-of-war?

To find out, Alan Ingham and his fellow researchers (1974) asked blindfolded University of Massachusetts students to "pull as hard as you can" on a rope. When Ingham fooled the students into believing three others were also pulling behind them, they exerted only 82 percent as much effort as when they knew they were pulling alone.

social loafing
the tendency for people in a group to exert less effort when pooling their efforts toward attaining a common goal than when individually accountable.

deindividuation
the loss of self-awareness and self-restraint occurring in group situations that foster arousal and anonymity.

group polarization
the enhancement of a group's prevailing attitudes through discussion within the group.

To describe the diminished effort by those submerged in a group, Bibb Latané and his colleagues (1981; Jackson & Williams, 1988) coined the term social loafing. In 78 experiments conducted in the United States, India, Thailand, Japan, China, and Taiwan, social loafing occurred on various tasks, though it was especially common among men in individualistic cultures (Karau & Williams, 1993). For example, blindfolded subjects seated in a group clapped or shouted as loud as they could while listening through headphones to the sound of loud clapping or shouting. When told they were doing it with the others, the subjects produced about one-third less noise than when they thought their individual efforts were identifiable.

Why? First, people acting as part of a group feel less accountable and therefore worry less about what others think. Second, they may view their contribution as dispensable (Harkins & Szymanski, 1989; Kerr & Bruun, 1983). As many leaders of organizations know, if group members share equally in the group's benefits regardless of how much they contribute, they may slack off and "free-ride" on the other group members' efforts.

Deindividuation

So, the presence of others can arouse people (as in the social facilitation experiments) or can diminish their feelings of responsibility (as in the social loafing experiments). Sometimes the presence of others both arouses people *and* diminishes their sense of responsibility. The result can be uninhibited behavior ranging from a food fight in the dining hall or screaming at a basketball referee to vandalism or rioting. Abandoning normal restraints to the power of the group is termed deindividuation. To be deindividuated is to be less self-conscious and less restrained when in a group situation.

Deindividuation often occurs when group participation makes people feel aroused and anonymous. In one experiment, New York University women dressed in depersonalizing Ku Klux Klan-style hoods delivered twice as much electric shock to a victim as did identifiable women (Zimbardo, 1970). (As in all such experiments, the "victim"

did not actually receive the shocks.) Similarly, tribal warriors who depersonalize themselves with face paints or masks are more likely than those with exposed faces to kill, torture, or mutilate captured enemies (Watson, 1973). Whether in a mob, at a rock concert, at a dance, or at worship, to lose self-consciousness (to become deindividuated) is to become more responsive to the group experience.

Effects of Group Interaction

We have examined the conditions under which the presence of others can

- make easy tasks easier and difficult tasks harder.
- tempt people to free-ride on the efforts of others and motivate them to cycle faster.
- enhance humor and fuel mob violence.

Research shows how group interaction, too, can have both bad and good effects.

Group Polarization

Educational researchers have noted that, over time, initial differences between groups of college students often grow. If the first-year students at College *X* tend to be more intellectually oriented than those at College *Y*, that difference will probably be amplified by the time they are seniors. Similarly, if the political conservatism of students who join fraternities and sororities is greater than that of students who do not, the gap in the political attitudes of the two groups will probably widen as they progress through college (Wilson & others, 1975).

This enhancement of a group's prevailing tendencies—called group polarization—occurs when people within a group discuss attitudes that most of them favor or oppose. For example, George Bishop and I discovered that when highly prejudiced high school students discussed racial issues, their attitudes became more prejudiced. When low-prejudice students discussed the same issues, they became more tolerant (Figure 18.7).

Group polarization can have beneficial results, as when it amplifies a sought-after spiritual awareness or strengthens the resolve of those in a self-help group. But it can also have dire consequences. From their analysis of terrorist organizations around the world, psychologists Clark McCauley and Mary Segal (1987) note that the terrorist mentality does not erupt suddenly. Rather, it arises among people who have come together because of a grievance and who become more and more extreme as they interact in isolation from moderating influences.

> Whether in a mob, at a rock concert, at a dance, or at worship, to lose self-consciousness (to become deindividuated) is to become more responsive to the group experience.

Groupthink

Does group interaction ever distort important group decisions? Social psychologist Irving Janis thought so when he first read historian Arthur M. Schlesinger, Jr.'s, account of how U.S. President John F. Kennedy and his advisers blundered into an ill-fated plan to invade Cuba with 1400 CIA-trained Cuban exiles. When the invaders were easily captured and soon linked to the U.S. government, Kennedy wondered aloud, "How could we have been so stupid?"

To find out, Janis (1982) studied the decision-making procedures that led to the fiasco. He discovered that the high morale of the recently elected president and his advisers fostered a sense that the plan would succeed. To preserve the good group feeling, dissenting views were suppressed or self-censored, especially after the president voiced his enthusiasm for the scheme. Since no one spoke sharply against the idea, everyone assumed there was a consensus of support for it. To describe this harmonious but unrealistic group thinking, Janis coined the term groupthink.

Janis and others then examined other historical fiascos—the failure to anticipate the 1941 Japanese attack on Pearl Harbor, the escalation of the Vietnam War, the U.S. Watergate cover-up, the Chernobyl nuclear reactor accident (Reason, 1987), and the U.S. space shuttle *Challenger* explosion (Esser & Lindoerfer, 1989). They discovered that in these cases, too, groupthink was fed by overconfidence, conformity, self-justification, and group polarization. Buoyed by a string of successful space shuttle launches, the NASA (National Aeronautics and Space Administration) management team approached the 1985 *Challenger* mission brimming with confidence but frustrated by launch delays. When the rocket booster's engineers opposed the launch because of dangers posed by freezing temperatures, group pressures to go ahead effectively silenced their warnings. Unless the engineers could *prove* that the rocket seals would not hold, the management group would not agree to another delay. Moreover, managers shielded the NASA executive who made the final "Go" decision from information about the warnings. Wrongly assuming that support was unanimous, he launched the *Challenger* on its one-way flight to annihilation.

Despite such fiascos and tragedies, Janis also knew that, with some types of problems, two heads are better than one. So he also studied instances in which U.S. presidents and their advisers collectively made good decisions. Examples were the Truman administration's formulation of the Marshall Plan, which offered assistance to Europe after World War II, and the Kennedy administration's actions to keep the Soviets from installing missiles in Cuba. In such instances—and in the business world, too, Janis believed—groupthink is prevented by a leader who welcomes various opinions, invites experts' critiques of developing plans, or even assigns people to identify possible problems. As the suppression of dissent bends a group toward bad decisions, so open debate often shapes good decisions.

groupthink
the mode of thinking that occurs when the desire for harmony in a decision-making group overrides a realistic appraisal of alternatives.

"One's impulse to blow the whistle on this nonsense was simply undone by the circumstances of the discussion."

ARTHUR M. SCHLESINGER, JR. (1965, P. 255)

"Truth springs from argument among friends."

PHILOSOPHER DAVID HUME (1711–1776)

Figure **18.7**

Group polarization   If a group is like-minded, discussion strengthens its prevailing opinions. Talking over racial issues increased prejudice in a high-prejudice group of high school students and decreased it in a low-prejudice group. (Data from Myers & Bishop, 1970.)

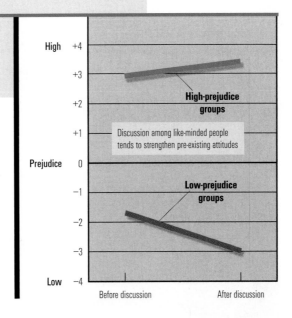

High +4
        +3
        +2   **High-prejudice groups**
        +1
              Discussion among like-minded people
              tends to strengthen pre-existing attitudes
Prejudice 0
        −1   **Low-prejudice groups**
        −2
        −3
Low   −4

Before discussion   After discussion

culture
the enduring behaviors, ideas, attitudes, and traditions shared by a large group of people and transmitted from one generation to the next.

In affirming the power of social influence, we must not overlook our power as individuals. *Social control* (the power of the situation) and *personal control* (the power of the individual) interact. People aren't billiard balls. When feeling pressured, we may react by doing the opposite of what is expected, thereby reasserting our sense of freedom (Brehm & Brehm, 1981). Moreover, many of the situations that influence us are ones we helped create. If we expect people to be uncooperative and hostile, we may treat them in ways that elicit such behavior. Thus, our expectations may become *self-fulfilling prophecies*. In one experiment, men talked more charmingly by phone to women they believed to be beautiful. This led the women to respond more warmly—confirming the men's idea that attractive people are likeable (Snyder & others, 1977).

Minority Influence

The power of committed individuals also appears in their influence over their groups. Social history is often made by a minority that sways the majority. Were this not so, communism would be an obscure theory, Christianity would be a small Middle Eastern sect, and Rosa Parks's refusal to sit at the back of the bus would not have ignited the civil rights movement. Technological history, too, is often made by innovative minorities who overcome the majority's resistance to change. To many folks, the railroad was a nonsensical idea; some farmers feared that train noise would prevent hens from laying eggs. People derided Robert Fulton's steamboat as "Fulton's Folly." As Fulton later said, "Never did a single encouraging remark, a bright

hope, a warm wish, cross my path." Much the same reaction greeted the printing press, the telegraph, the incandescent lamp, and the typewriter (Cantril & Bumstead, 1960).

To better understand how minorities can sway majorities, European social psychologists led by Serge Moscovici (1985) have investigated groups in which one or two individuals consistently express a controversial attitude or an unusual perceptual judgment. They have repeatedly found that a minority that unswervingly holds to its position is far more successful in swaying the majority than is a minority that waffles. Holding consistently to a minority opinion will not make you popular, but it may make you influential. This is especially so if your self-confidence stimulates others to consider why you react as you do. Although people often follow the majority view publicly, they may privately develop sympathy for the minority view. Even when a minority's influence is not yet visible, it may be persuading some members of the majority to rethink their views (Wood & others, 1994). Thus, the combined powers of social thinking and social influence are enormous; but so are the powers of the committed individual.

Cultural Influences

The readers of this book are a diverse community, reaching from Africa to Australia and from Singapore to Sweden. Our varying cultures exert a powerful, long-lasting influence on our behaviors, ideas, attitudes, and traditions. Riding along with a unified culture is like riding a bike with the wind: As the wind carries us along, we hardly notice it's there. When we try riding *against* it we feel its force, as when moving to or visiting another part of the world. Face to face with a different culture, people become aware of the cultural winds. Visiting Europe, most North Americans are struck by the smallness of the cars, the left-handed use of the fork, the uninhibited attire on the beaches. Stationed in Saudi Arabia, European and American soldiers alike realized the liberality of their home cultures. Visiting North America, visitors from some cultures struggle to understand why people wear their dirty *street* shoes in the house, or why people find it fun to eat a picnic lunch out in the bush amid flies and ants.

Gandhi As the life of Mahatma Gandhi powerfully testifies, a consistent and persistent minority voice can sometimes sway the majority. The nonviolent appeals and fasts of the Hindu nationalist and spiritual leader were instrumental in winning India's independence from Britain in 1947.

"Live with vultures, become a vulture; live with crows, become a crow."

LAOTIAN PROVERB

Cultural norms for greeting A Palestinian, Khalil al-Qot, kisses his father after being freed from a South Lebanon jail.

Cultural Norms

All cultural groups evolve norms—their rules for accepted and expected behavior. Muslims use only the right hand's fingers for eating. The Japanese have norms for taking shoes off, for giving and opening gifts, and for showing respect to one's social superiors.

Sometimes social expectations seem oppressive. "Why should it matter how I dress?" However, norms also grease the social machinery. Prescribed, well-learned behaviors free us from self-preoccupation. Knowing when to clap or bow, which fork to pick up first at the dinner party, and

Culture influences personal space Behavior that is seen as appropriate in one culture may violate the norms of another group. In Arab countries, such as Saudi Arabia, people typically require less personal space than do members of some European and North American groups.

what sorts of gestures and compliments are appropriate, we can relax and enjoy one another without fear of embarrassment or insult. Likewise, having a well-understood norm for greeting people in one's culture—by shaking hands or kissing each cheek—precludes awkward moments deciding whether to lead with one's hand or cheek.

When cultures collide, their differing norms often bemuse or befuddle. If someone invades our personal space—the portable buffer zone we like to maintain around our bodies—we feel uncomfortable. Scandinavians, most Americans, and the British prefer more personal space than do Latin Americans, Arabs, and the French (Sommer, 1969). At a social gathering, a Mexican seeking a comfortable conversation distance may waltz around a room with a backpedaling American. (You can demonstrate this at a party by playing space invader as you talk with someone.) To the American, the Mexican may seem intrusive; to the Mexican, the American may seem cold and standoffish.

Cultures also vary in their expressiveness. People whose roots are in northern European cultures often perceive people from Mediterranean cultures as warm and charming but inefficient. The Mediterraneans, in turn, see the northern Europeans as efficient but cold and preoccupied with punctuality (Triandis, 1981).

Cultures vary in their pace of life, too. The British businessperson may feel frustrated by a Latin American client who arrives 30 minutes late for lunch. People from time-conscious Japan—where bank clocks keep exact time, pedestrians walk briskly, and postal clerks fill requests speedily—may find themselves growing impatient when visiting Indonesia, where clocks keep less exact time and the pace of life is slower (Levine, 1990). In adjusting to their host countries, U.S. Peace Corps volunteers reported that, after the language difference, two of their greatest culture shocks were the slower pace of life and the differing punctuality of the people (Spradley & Phillips, 1972).

personal space the buffer zone we like to maintain around our bodies.

An exercise in culture People in individualistic Western cultures sometimes see the Japanese as straitjacketed by their culture's norms. But from the Japanese perspective, the same tradition expresses a "serenity that comes to people who know exactly what to expect from each other"(Weisz & others, 1984).

Norms . . . grease the social machinery . . . Having a well-understood norm for greeting people in one's culture—by shaking hands or kissing each cheek—precludes awkward moments deciding whether to lead with one's hand or cheek.

gender role
a set of expected behaviors for males and for females.

Gender Roles

A whole set of norms defines our culture's gender roles—our expectations about the way men and women behave. Traditionally, men initiate dates, drive the car, and pick up the check; women cook the meals, buy and care for the children's clothes, and do the shopping. In the United States, for example, married mothers do 90 percent of the laundry and 13 percent of the car maintenance (Acock & Demo, 1994). And, I don't have to tell you which parent, about 90 percent of the time in two-parent families, stays home with a sick child, arranges for the baby-sitter, or calls the doctor (Maccoby, 1995). Such formulas smooth social relations, saving awkward decisions about who does what. But they do so at a cost: If we deviate from such conventions, we may feel anxious.

Gender roles are not rigidly fixed by evolution, because they vary across cultures and over time.

Evolution may predispose men to the assertiveness and toughness that serve their reproductive goals, and women to the interpersonal skills that serve their reproductive goals (Archer, 1996). But we know that gender roles are not rigidly fixed by evolution, because they vary across cultures and over time. In nomadic societies of food-gathering people, there is minimal division of labor by sex. Thus, boys and girls receive much the same upbringing. In agricultural societies, women stay close to home, working in the fields and staying with the children; men often roam more freely, herding cattle or sheep. Such societies typically socialize children into distinct gender roles (Segall & others, 1990; Van Leeuwen, 1978).

Gender roles have tended not to offer equal rights and power. "There are no human societies in which women dominate men," notes Felicia Pratto (1996). As of 1997, women were 11.7 percent of the world's national legislators (Briscoe, 1997). They were also 3 percent of United Nations ambassadors, less than 1 percent of the presidents and prime ministers of the world's countries, and 0 percent of the Nobel awardees in economics since the prize began in 1901 (Sivard, 1995). Even in Israel's communal farms, the kibbutzim, where children were reared together—dressed, bathed, and given toys without regard to gender—boys grew up to do mostly masculine things and to dominate the leadership roles. Girls, though legally equal, played more with dolls and in adulthood sought more contact with children (Wilson, 1993).

Yet among the industrialized countries, gender roles vary. Women fill 48 percent of managerial positions in Switzerland, 28 percent in Austria, 17 percent in the United States, 3 percent in Ghana, and 2 percent in South Korea (Triandis, 1994). In North America, medicine and dentistry have been predominantly male occupations; in Russia, most medical doctors are women, as are most dentists in Denmark.

Gender roles vary over time as well as across cultures:

- As we began this century only one country—New Zealand—granted women the right to vote. As we end it, only one democracy—Kuwait—did not (Briscoe, 1995).

- In 1938, only one in five Americans approved of "a married woman earning money in business or industry if she has a husband capable of supporting her"; by 1996, four in five approved (Niemi & others, 1989; NORC, 1996).

- In the flick of an apron, the number of U.S. college women hoping to be full-time homemakers plunged during the late 1960s and early 1970s (Figure 18.8).

- Since 1968, women's assertiveness has also increased (Twenge, 1996).

- In developing countries, too, gender roles are changing. Between 1970 and 1992, girls' enrollment in schools rose from 38 to 68 percent, shrinking the gender gap (UNICEF, 1996).

Cultural influences are huge, but cultures can change.

Figure **18.8**

Changing attitudes about gender roles U.S. college students' endorsement of the traditional view of women's role has declined dramatically. Men's and women's attitudes have also converged. (From Sax & others, 1996; Dey & others, 1991.)

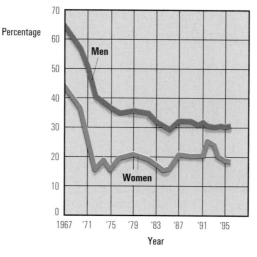

Percentage agreeing
"The activities of married women are best confined to home and family"

Percentage

Men

Women

Year

"So—against odds, women inch forwards."

ELEANOR ROOSEVELT
1946

prejudice
an unjustifiable (and usually negative) attitude toward a group and its members. Prejudice generally involves stereotyped beliefs, negative feelings, and a predisposition to discriminatory action.

stereotype
a generalized (often overgeneralized) belief about a group of people.

SUMMING UP

Conformity and Obedience As suggestibility studies demonstrate, when we are unsure about our judgments, we are likely to adjust them toward the group standard. Solomon Asch found that under certain conditions people will conform to a group's judgment even when it is clearly incorrect. We may conform either to gain social approval (normative social influence) or because we welcome the information that others provide (informational social influence). In Milgram's famous experiments, people torn between obeying an experimenter and responding to another's pleas usually chose to obey orders, even though obedience supposedly meant harming the other person. Such is the potency of social influence.

Group Influence Experiments on social facilitation reveal that the presence of either observers or co-actors can arouse individuals, boosting their performance on easy tasks but hindering it on difficult ones. When people pool their efforts toward a group goal, social loafing may occur as individuals free-ride on others' efforts. When a group experience arouses people and makes them anonymous, they may become less self-aware and self-restrained, a psychological state known as deindividuation.

Within groups, discussions among like-minded members often produce group polarization, an enhancement of the group's prevailing attitudes. This is one cause of groupthink, the tendency for harmony-seeking groups to make unrealistic decisions after suppressing unwelcome information.

The power of the group is great, but so is the power of the person. Even a small minority sometimes sways a group, especially when it expresses its views consistently.

Cultural Influences Cultural rules for accepted and expected behavior vary in ways that befuddle people interacting with members of unfamiliar cultures. Cultures differ, for example, in their requirements for personal space, their expressiveness, their pace of life, and the strength of their role expectations. They also differ in their gender roles—the behaviors expected of males and females. Cultures themselves change over time.

KEY TERMS AND CONCEPTS conformity, normative social influence, norm, informational social influence, social facilitation, social loafing, deindividuation, group polarization, groupthink, culture, personal space, gender role

Social Relations

What makes us harm or help or fall in love? How can we transform the closed fists of aggression into the open arms of compassion?

Having sampled how we *think* about and *influence* one another, we come finally to social psychology's third focus—how we *relate* to one another. We will ponder the bad and the good: from prejudice, aggression, and conflict to attraction, altruism, and peacemaking.

Prejudice

Prejudice means prejudgment. It is an unjustifiable and usually negative attitude toward a group—typically a different cultural, ethnic, or gender group. Like all attitudes, prejudice is a mixture of beliefs (often overgeneralized and called stereotypes), emotions (hostility, envy, or fear), and predispositions to action (to discriminate). To *believe* that overweight people are gluttonous, to *feel* antipathy for an overweight person, and to be hesitant to hire or date an overweight person is to be prejudiced.

Does perception change with race?
The Italian clothing manufacturer Benetton asked this question with altered photographs in their company magazine. Skin color and facial features are, however, mere frosting on the physiological cake. On average, any two randomly chosen humans are 99.8 percent alike in the alphabetic sequence in their genetic code. Only 6 percent of their 0.2 percent difference is racial; 9 percent represents ethnic difference within races (for example, between French and Italians); 85 percent is individual differences within one's group (Hoffman, 1994; Vines, 1995).
Courtesy of COLORS Magazine.

Like other forms of prejudgment, prejudices are schemas that influence how we notice and interpret events. In one study, most whites perceived a white man shoving a black man as "horsing around." The same shove by the black man to the white was more often seen as "violent" (Duncan, 1976). Our preconceived ideas about people bias our impressions of their behavior. Prejudgments color perceptions.

Figure **18.9**

Prejudice over time Americans today express much less racial and gender prejudice than they did two and three decades ago. (Niemi & others, 1989; T. Smith, personal communications.)

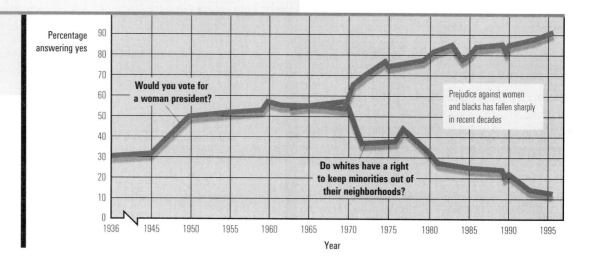

Would you vote for a woman president?

Prejudice against women and blacks has fallen sharply in recent decades

Do whites have a right to keep minorities out of their neighborhoods?

"Unhappily the world has yet to learn how to live with diversity."

POPE JOHN PAUL II
ADDRESS TO THE UNITED NATIONS
1995

A Gallup poll (1993) question—"In your view, does the increasing diversity that immigrants bring to this country mostly *improve* American culture or mostly *threaten* American culture?"—brought these responses:

Mostly improve	35%
Mostly threaten	55%
Other response	10%

How prejudiced are people? To find out, we can assess what they say and what they do. To judge by what Americans say, racial and gender attitudes have changed dramatically in the last half-century (Figure 18.9). Nearly everyone agrees that children of all races should attend the same schools and that women and men should receive the same pay for the same job.

As blatant prejudice wanes, subtle prejudice lingers. In socially intimate settings (dating, dancing, marrying), many people admit they would feel uncomfortable with someone of another race. (Although the percentage of interracial marriages in the United States has increased sixfold since 1960, this still represents only 2.4 percent of all married couples.) This fact helps explain why, in a survey of students at 390 colleges and universities, 53 percent of African-American students felt excluded from school activities (Hurtado & others, 1994). (Similar feelings were reported by 24 percent of Asian-Americans, 16 percent of Mexican-Americans, and 6 percent of European-Americans.) On NBA basketball teams, where 81 percent of the 1995 players and all the top 20 scorers were African-American, a similar majority–minority dynamic can lead some white minority players to feel lonely or disrespected (Schoenfeld, 1995).

But lest we think blatant prejudice is behind us, we should be aware that prejudice has occasionally resurfaced since the late 1980s, in public settings as well as in private. European and North American cities and campuses have experienced significant increases in "hate talk" and "hate crimes" (slurs, vandalism, and physical violence) against immigrants, blacks, and homosexuals (Herek, 1989, 1990; Levine, 1990). Elsewhere, hate has raged openly—between Israel's Palestinians and Jews, Bosnia's Serbs and Muslims, Rwanda's Tutsis and Hutus.

Around the world, gender prejudice and discrimination persist, too. Worldwide, two-thirds of children without basic schooling are girls. Thus, there are some 350 million illiterate men and 600 million illiterate women (United Nations, 1991, 1993). In Saudi Arabia, women are not allowed to drive. In Western countries, we pay more to those (usually men) who take care of our garbage than to those (usually women) who take care of our children. Despite gender equality in intelligence scores, people perceive their fathers as more intelligent than their mothers (Furnham & Rawles, 1995).

Nowhere are female infants left out on a hillside to die of exposure, as was the practice in ancient Greece. Yet even today boys are often valued more than their sisters. During the 1970s Bangladesh famine, preschool girls were more malnourished than boys were, and in many developing countries death rates are higher for girls than for boys (Bairagi, 1987). Because testing now enables sex-selective abortions, South Korean male births exceed female births by 14 percent (instead of the normal 5 percent). In China, male births during 1992 exceeded female births by 18 percent. In five of China's provinces there are now 120 boys for every 100 girls (Kristof, 1993). Sex-selective neglect and abortions have resulted in China and India together having 76 million fewer females than they should have (Klasen, 1994). (You read that right: 76 *million* "missing women.")

Why does prejudice arise? Inequalities, social divisions, and emotional scapegoating are partly responsible. But so are the natural cognitive mechanisms by which we simplify our worlds.

Social Inequalities

When some people have money, power, and prestige and others do not, the "haves" usually develop attitudes that justify things as they are. In the extreme case, slave owners perceived slaves as innately lazy, ignorant, and irresponsible—as having the very traits that "justified" enslaving them. More commonly, women are perceived as unassertive but sensitive and therefore suited for the caretaking tasks they often perform (Hoffman & Hurst, 1990). In short, prejudice rationalizes inequalities.

Discrimination also increases prejudice through the reactions it provokes in its victims, another example of a self-fulfilling prophecy. In his classic 1954 book, *The Nature of Prejudice*, Gordon Allport noted that being a victim of discrimination can produce either self-blame or anger. Both reactions may create new grounds for prejudice through the classic *blame-the-victim* dynamic. If the circumstances of ghetto life breed a higher crime rate, someone can then use the higher crime rate to justify continuing the discrimination that helped to create the ghetto.

"You cannot oppress people for over three centuries and then say it is all over and expect them to put on suits and ties and become decent attaché-carrying citizens and go to work on Wall Street."

SHELBY STEELE
"THE NEW SEGREGATION"
1992

Us and Them: Ingroup and Outgroup

The social definition of who you are—your ethnicity, gender, religion, academic major—also implies who you are not. Mentally drawing a circle that defines "us" excludes "them." Such group identifications typically promote an ingroup bias—a favoring of one's own group. Even an arbitrary us-them dis-

"All good people agree,
And all good people say
All nice people, like us, are We
And everyone else is They.
But if you cross over the sea
Instead of over the way
You may end by (think of it)
looking on We
As only a sort of They."

RUDYARD KIPLING
"WE AND THEY"
1926

The social definition of who you are—your ethnicity, gender, religion, academic major—also implies who you are not. Mentally drawing a circle that defines "us" excludes "them."

tinction—created by grouping people with the toss of a coin—leads people to show favoritism to their own group when dividing rewards (Tajfel, 1982; Wilder, 1981).

The urge to distinguish enemies from friends predisposes prejudice against strangers. To Greeks of the classical era, all non-Greeks were "barbarians." Most citizens in the coalition of countries fighting in the 1991 Persian Gulf War felt more pain over the few hundred dead Allied soldiers than over the reported 100,000 Iraqi dead. In Africa, where some 700 traditional societies cluster into fewer than 50 nations, people typically like and admire their own group and direct their hostility toward other groups (Segall & others, 1990). Most children believe their school is better than the other schools in town. Even chimpanzees have been seen to wipe clean the spot where they were touched by a chimp from another group (Goodall, 1986).

Scapegoating

Prejudice springs not only from the divisions of society but also from the passions of the heart. Prejudice may express anger: When things go wrong, finding someone to blame can provide a target for one's anger. Evidence for this scapegoat theory of prejudice comes from high prejudice levels among economically frustrated people and from experiments in which a temporary frustration intensifies prejudice. Nazi leader Hermann Rausching once explained the Nazis' need to scapegoat: "If the Jew did not exist, we should have to invent him" (quoted by Koltz, 1983). Passions produce prejudice.

In addition to providing a handy emotional outlet for anger, despised outgroups can also boost ingroup members' self-esteem. In experiments, students who experience failure or are made to feel insecure will often restore their self-esteem by disparaging a rival school or another person (Cialdini & Richardson, 1980; Crocker & others, 1987). To boost our own sense of status, it helps to have others to denigrate. For this reason, a rival's misfortune sometimes provides a twinge of pleasure.

"If the Tiber reaches the walls, if the Nile does not rise to the fields, if the sky doesn't move or the Earth does, if there is famine, if there is plague, the cry is at once: 'The Christians to the lion!'"

TERTULLIAN
APOLOGETICUS
A.D. 197

ingroup bias
The tendency to favor one's own group.

scapegoat theory
The theory that prejudice provides an outlet for anger by providing someone to blame.

Do racial stereotypes influence perceptions? Augustana College's (Illinois) black students' and white students' reactions to the O.J. Simpson "not guilty" criminal trial verdict mirrored the nation's racial difference in perceptions of his guilt or innocence (based partly on stereotypes of white police officers as honest or as oppressive).

Cognitive Roots of Prejudice

Prejudice springs from the divisions of society, the passions of the heart, and also from the mind's natural workings. Stereotyped beliefs are a by-product of how we cognitively simplify the world.

Categorization

One way we simplify our world is to categorize things. A chemist classifies molecules as organic and inorganic. A mental health professional classifies people's psychological disorders by types. In categorizing people into groups we often stereotype them. Stereotypes may contain a germ of truth, yet they also bias our perceptions. Jeff Stone and his colleagues (1997) demonstrated this by having Princeton University students listen to a radio broadcast of a university basketball game, evaluating the performance of one player. Those introduced to him with a photo of a black player gave him a better performance evaluation than did those who had been shown a photo of a white player.

Categorization also biases our perceptions of diversity. Although we view ourselves as individuals, we overestimate the similarity of people within

Do people of another race look alike? Foreign sunbathers on Bali's beaches may think they do. Balinese masseuses wear identifying numbers on their hats, enabling visitors to recognize them easily.

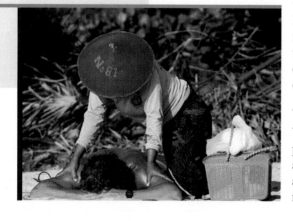

groups other than our own. "They"—the members of some other group—seem to look and act alike, but "we" are diverse (Bothwell & others, 1989). If we could see ourselves from a penguin's perspective, we would all look alike—much as penguins all look alike to us (though not to their fellow penguins). We are keenly sensitive to differences within our group, less so to differences within other groups. To those in one ethnic group, members of another often seem more alike in appearance, personality, and attitudes than they are.

Vivid Cases

As noted in Chapter 10's discussion of the availability heuristic, we often judge the frequency of events by instances that readily come to mind. If asked whether black men jump higher than white men, those who think of Michael Jordon may overgeneralize that "yes, white men can't jump."

In an experiment with University of Oregon students, Myron Rothbart and his colleagues (1978) showed how we overgeneralize from vivid, memorable cases. They divided the students into two groups and showed them information about 50 men. The first group's list included 10 men arrested for nonviolent crimes, such as forgery. The second group's list included 10 men arrested for violent crimes, such as assault. When both groups later recalled how many men on their list had committed any sort of crime, the second group overestimated how many there were. Vivid (violent) cases, being readily available to memory, influence our judgments of a group.

The Just-World Phenomenon

We noted earlier that people often justify their prejudice by blaming its victims. Bystanders may also blame victims, by assuming the world is just and that people get what they deserve. In experiments, merely observing someone receive painful shocks has led many people to think less of the victim (Lerner, 1980). This just-world phenomenon reflects an idea we commonly teach our children—that good is rewarded and evil is punished. From this it is a short leap to assume that those who succeed must be good and those who suffer must be bad. Such reasoning enables the rich to see their own wealth, and the poor's misfortune, as justly deserved. As one German civilian is said to have remarked when visiting the Bergen-Belsen concentration camp shortly after World War II, "What terrible criminals these prisoners must have been to receive such treatment."

Hindsight bias is also at work here (Carli & Leonard, 1989). Have you ever heard people say that rape victims, abused spouses, or people with AIDS got what they deserved? An experiment by Ronnie Janoff-Bulman and her collaborators (1985) illustrates victim-blaming. When given an account of a date that ended with the woman's being raped, people perceived the woman as partly to blame. In hindsight, they thought, "She should have known better." (Victim-blaming also reassures people that it couldn't happen to them.) Others who were given the same account, without the rape, did not perceive the woman as inviting rape. Only when victimized was she faulted for her behavior.

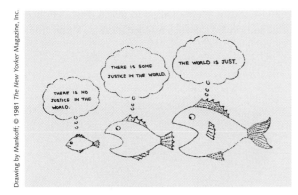

Aggression

The most destructive force in our social relations is aggression. In psychology, *aggression* has a more precise meaning than it does in everyday usage. The assertive, persistent salesperson is not aggressive. Nor is the dentist who makes you wince with pain. But the person who passes along a vicious rumor about you and the attacker who mugs you are aggressive. Aggression is any physical or verbal behavior intended to hurt or destroy, whether done out of hostility or as a calculated means to an

end. Many of the 110 million war-related deaths during this century were cool and calculated. So were some of the 21,597 murders and 1.1 million assaults recorded in the United States during 1995, but more were hostile outbursts.

A rising tide of violence, especially violence by youth, plagues many countries. Most readers living outside the United States can, however, take comfort that their risk of being murdered is *much* lower than for Americans—one-fourth less if you are a Canadian or an Australian, one-fifth less if you are a New Zealander, and, on average, one-sixth less if you are a European (United Nations, 1992).

Why are some countries, and some individuals, so violence-prone? And why have violence rates increased in so many countries?

Time and again, we have seen that behavior emerges from the interaction of biology and experience. Research on aggression reinforces that theme. For a gun to fire, the trigger must be pulled; with some people, as with hair-trigger guns, it doesn't take much to trip an explosion. Let us look first at biological factors that influence our thresholds for aggressive behavior. Then we'll examine the psychological factors that pull the trigger.

The Biology of Aggression

According to one view, argued by Sigmund Freud and others, our species has a volcanic potential to erupt in aggression. Freud thought that we harbor not only positive survival instincts but also a self-destructive "death instinct" that we usually displace toward others as aggression or release in socially approved activities such as painting or sports.

Although aggression varies too widely from culture to culture and person to person to be considered an unlearned instinct, biology does influence aggression. Stimuli that influence aggressive behavior operate through our biological system. We can look for biological influences at three levels—genetic, neural, and biochemical. Our genes engineer our individual nervous systems, which operate electrochemically.

Genetic Influences

Animals have been bred for aggressiveness—sometimes for sport, sometimes for research. Twin studies suggest that genes influence human aggression as well (Raine, 1993; Rushton & others, 1986). If one identical twin admits to "having a violent temper," the other twin will often independently admit the same. Fraternal twins are much less likely to respond similarly.

just-world phenomenon
the tendency of people to believe the world is just and that people therefore get what they deserve and deserve what they get.

aggression
any physical or verbal behavior intended to hurt or destroy.

In the last 25 years in the United States, guns have caused 800,000 suicidal, homicidal, and accidental deaths. Compared with people of the same sex, race, age, and neighborhood, those who keep a gun in the home (ironically, often for protection) are 2.7 times more likely to be murdered—nearly always by a family member or close acquaintance (Kellermann & others, 1993).

Neural Influences

Animal and human brains have neural systems that produce aggressive behavior when stimulated (Moyer, 1983). Consider:

- The domineering leader of a caged monkey colony had a radio-controlled electrode implanted in a brain area that, when stimulated, inhibits aggression. When researchers placed the button that activates the electrode in the colony's cage, one small monkey learned to push it every time the boss became threatening.

- A mild-mannered woman had an electrode implanted in her brain's limbic system (in the amygdala) by neurosurgeons seeking to diagnose a disorder. Because the brain has no sensory receptors, she was unable to feel the stimulation. But at the flick of a switch she snarled, "Take my blood pressure. Take it now," and then stood up and began to strike the doctor.

- Intensive evaluation of 15 death-row inmates revealed that all 15 had suffered a severe head injury. Researcher Dorothy Lewis and her colleagues (1986) infer that many condemned criminals suffer unrecognized neurological disorders.

So, does the brain have a "violence center" that produces aggression when stimulated? Actually, no one spot in the brain controls aggression, because aggression is a complex behavior that occurs in particular contexts. Rather, the brain has neural systems that facilitate aggression, making it more likely, given provocation and no deterrents.

Biochemical Influences

Hormones, alcohol, and other substances in the blood influence the neural systems that control aggression. A raging bull will become a gentle Ferdinand when castration reduces its testosterone level. The same is true of castrated mice. When injected with testosterone, the castrated mice again become aggressive. However, the traffic between hormones and behavior is two-way. Testosterone heightens dominance and aggressiveness, but dominating or defeating behavior also boosts testosterone levels (Gladue & others, 1989).

Although humans are less sensitive to hormonal changes, violent criminals tend to be muscular young males with lower-than-average intelligence scores, low levels of the neurotransmitter serotonin, and higher-than-average testosterone levels (Dabbs, 1992; Pendick, 1994; Wilson & Herrnstein, 1985). Drugs that sharply reduce their testosterone levels subdue their aggressive tendencies. With age, testosterone levels—and aggressiveness—diminish. Among teenage boys and adult men, high testosterone levels correlate with delinquency, hard drug use, and aggressive-bullying responses to frustration (Berman & others, 1993; Dabbs & Morris, 1990; Olweus & others, 1988).

Deindividuation + competition + alcohol = aggression
A 1985 riot at a soccer game in Brussels left 38 dead and 437 injured. Aroused by the competition and loaded with alcohol, English fans lost all restraint when provoked by Italian fans. They attacked the Italians, who retreated and were then crushed against a wall.

For both biological and psychological reasons, alcohol unleashes aggressive responses to frustration (Bushman, 1993; Ito & others, 1996; Taylor & Chermack, 1993). (Just *thinking* you've imbibed alcohol has some effect; but so, too, does unknowingly ingesting alcohol slipped into a drink.) Police data and prison surveys reinforce conclusions from

"It's a guy thing."

"We could avoid two-thirds of all crime simply by putting all able-bodied young men in cryogenic sleep from the age of 12 through 28."

DAVID T. LYKKEN
THE ANTISOCIAL PERSONALITIES
1995

experiments on alcohol and aggression. Aggression-prone people are more likely to drink, and to become violent when intoxicated (White & others, 1993). People who have been drinking commit about 50 percent of sexual assaults and other violent crimes (Abbey & others, 1993, 1996; Seto & Barbaree, 1995).

"He that is naturally addicted to Anger, let him Abstain from Wine; for it is but adding Fire to Fire."

SENECA
DE IRA
A.D. 49

The Psychology of Aggression

Biological factors influence the ease with which the aggression trigger pulls. But what psychological factors do the pulling?

Aversive Events

Although suffering sometimes builds character, it may also bring out the worst in us. Studies in which animals or humans experience unpleasant events reveal that those made miserable often make others miserable (Berkowitz, 1983, 1989).

Being blocked short of a goal also increases people's readiness to aggress. This phenomenon is called the frustration-aggression principle: Frustration creates anger, which may in some people generate aggression, especially in the presence of an aggressive cue, such as a gun. Frustrations are instances of aversive events. Like frustration, other aversive stimuli—physical pain, personal insults, foul odors, hot temperatures, cigarette smoke, and a host of others—can also evoke hostility. For example, violent crime and spouse abuse occur more in summer than winter, in hot years than in cooler years, in hot cities than in cooler cities, and on hotter days than on colder days (Anderson, 1989, and Figure 18.10).

Learning to Express and Inhibit Aggression

Aggression may be a natural response to aversive events, but learning can alter natural reactions. Animals naturally eat when they are hungry. But if appropriately rewarded or punished, they can be taught either to overeat or to starve.

Aggressive reactions are more likely in situations where experience has taught us that aggression pays. Children whose aggression successfully intimidates other children may become more aggressive. Aggressive behavior can be learned through direct rewards. Animals that have fought successfully to get food or mates become increasingly ferocious. Aggression can also be learned through observation. Children who grow up observing aggressive models often imitate the behaviors they see. Parents of delinquent youngsters typically discipline with beatings, thus modeling aggression as a method of dealing with problems (Patterson & others, 1982, 1992). They also frequently cave into (reward) their children's tears and temper tantrums.

Different cultures model, reinforce, and evoke differing tendencies toward violence. For example, crime rates are higher in countries marked by a great disparity between rich and poor (Triandis, 1994). Richard Nisbett (1993) and Dov Cohen (1996) show how cultures can also differ within a country. They analyzed violence among whites in

frustration-aggression principle *the principle that frustration—the blocking of an attempt to achieve some goal—creates anger, which can generate aggression.*

\ *"Why do we kill people who kill people to show that killing people is wrong?"*

NATIONAL COALITION TO ABOLISH THE DEATH PENALTY
1992

Figure **18.10**

Murders and rapes per day in Houston, Texas

8.0 — 7.5 — 7.0 — 6.5 — 6.0

As temperature soars, so does aggression

40–68   69–78   79–85   86–91   92–99
Temperature in degrees Fahrenheit

Uncomfortably hot weather and aggressive reactions Between 1980 and 1982 in Houston, murders and rapes were more common on days over 91°F, as shown in the graph. This finding is consistent with those from laboratory experiments in which people working in a hot room reacted to provocations with greater hostility. (From Anderson & Anderson, 1984.)

Children who grow up observing aggressive models often imitate the behaviors they see. Parents of delinquent youngsters typically discipline with beatings, thus modeling aggression as a method of dealing with problems.

southern U.S. towns settled by Scottish-Irish herders whose tradition emphasized "manly honor," the use of arms to protect one's flock, and a history of coercive slavery. To this day, their cultural descendants have triple the homicide rates and are more supportive of physically punishing children, of warfare initiatives, and of uncontrolled gun ownership than are whites in New England towns settled by Puritan, Quaker, and Dutch farmer-artisans.

Social influence also appears in high violence rates among cultures and families that experience minimal father care (Triandis, 1994). For example, the U.S. Bureau of Justice Statistics reports that 70 percent of imprisoned juveniles did not grow up with two parents (Beck & others, 1988). (Because an absent parent is usually a father, most grew up with minimal father care.) The correlation between father absence and violence in the United States holds for all races, income levels, and locations (Prothrow-Stith, 1991; Staub, 1993). The correlation also appears over time. In 1960, just over 1 in 10 children did not live with two parents, and only 16,000 juveniles were arrested for violent crime. In 1995, more than 3 in 10 children did not live with two parents, and a similar-sized juvenile population produced more than 100,000 arrests for violent crime.

That many individuals lead gentle, even heroic, lives amid social stresses reminds us that individuals differ. The person matters. That people differ over time and place reminds us that environments differ. Situations matter. Aggressive behavior, like all behavior, arises from the interaction of persons and situations.

Once established, however, aggressive behavior patterns are difficult to change. To foster a kinder, gentler world we had best model and reward sensitivity and cooperation from an early age, perhaps by training parents how to discipline without modeling violence. Modeling violence—screaming and hitting—is precisely what exasperated parents often do. Parent-training programs advise a more positive approach. They encourage parents to reinforce desirable behaviors and to frame statements positively ("When you finish loading the dishwasher, you can go play," rather than "If you don't load the dishwasher, there'll be no playing.") One "aggression-replacement program" that brought down re-arrest rates of juvenile offenders and gang members taught the youth and their parents communication skills, trained them in how to control anger, and encouraged more thoughtful moral reasoning (Goldstein & Glick, in press).

Television Watching and Aggression

Parents are hardly the only aggression models. During their first 18 years, most children spend more time watching television than they spend in school. In the United States, the average household has a TV on 51 hours a week (Elliot, 1996). In urban homes across the world, including those of South America and Asia, television is now commonplace. In Beijing, for example, the percentage of homes with television skyrocketed from 32 percent in 1980 to 95 percent by the end of the decade (Lull, 1988). With more than 1 billion TV sets now in homes around the world, CNN reaching 150 countries, and MTV videos seen from Alaska to Bangladesh, television is creating a global pop culture (Lippman, 1992). One can watch American programs in Perth or Prague and hear Madonna and Pearl Jam from New Delhi to Newfoundland.

So near, but . . . Being blocked from achieving a goal can trigger aggression. This is especially likely when the frustration can be blamed on the "other."

But television does not reflect the world we live in. On evening dramas broadcast in the United States during the 1980s and early 1990s and often exported to the rest of the world, only one-third of the characters were women. Fewer than 3 percent were visibly old. One percent were Hispanic. Only 1 in 10 was married (Gerbner, 1993).

In 1993, U.S. network programs offered about 3 violent acts per hour during prime time, and 18 per hour during children's Saturday morning programs (Gerbner & others, 1994). During the last 20 years the average child has viewed some 8000 TV murders and 100,000 other acts of violence before finishing elementary school (Huston & others, 1992). If one includes cable programming and video rentals, the violence numbers escalate. (Popular rental films like *Die Hard 1*, with its 264 deaths, are much more violent than major network programs.) Half of television's violent interactions don't show the harm done to victims and 6 in 10 don't show the victims' pain (Mediascope, 1995).

This is life as rendered by a rather peculiar storyteller, one who reflects the culture's mythology but not its reality. In U.S. action-oriented crime shows (the shows most often exported to the world market), TV cops fire their guns in almost every episode; in Chicago, the average police officer has fired a gun once every 27 years (Radecki, 1989).

Does viewing televised aggression influence some people to commit aggression? Was the judge who in 1993 tried two British 10-year-olds for their murder of a 2-year-old right to suspect that one possible influence was the aggressors' exposure to "violent video films"? To answer such questions, researchers have conducted correlational and experimental studies (Hearold, 1986; Wood & others, 1991).

Correlational studies link young children's viewing of violence and their combativeness as teenagers and young adults (Eron, 1987; Turner & others, 1986). In the United States and Canada, a doubling of homicide rates between 1957 and 1974 coincided with the introduction and spread of television.

Moreover, census regions that were late in acquiring television showed the homicide jump correspondingly later. Among white South Africans, who were first introduced to television in 1975, a similar near-doubling of the homicide rate did not begin until after 1975 (Centerwall, 1989). "There is absolutely no doubt," concluded the 1993 American Psychological Association Commission on Violence and Youth, "that higher levels of viewing violence on television are correlated with increased acceptance of aggressive attitudes and increased aggressive behavior."

But as we know from Chapter 1, correlation does not imply causation. So these correlational studies do not prove that viewing violence *causes* aggression (Freedman, 1988; McGuire, 1986). Maybe aggressive children prefer violent programs. Maybe children of neglectful or abusive parents are both more aggressive and more often left in front of the TV. Or maybe television simply reflects, rather than affects, violent trends.

To pin down causation, experimenters have randomly assigned some viewers to view violence and others to view entertaining nonviolence. Does viewing murder and mayhem make people react more cruelly when irritated? "The consensus among most of the research community," reported the National Institute of Mental Health (1982), "is

TV's greatest effect may stem from what it displaces. Children and adults who spend four hours a day watching television spend four fewer hours in active pursuits—talking, studying, playing, reading, or socializing with friends. What would you have done with your extra time if you had never watched television, and how might you therefore be different?

THE FAR SIDE

In the days before television

that violence on television does lead to aggressive behavior by children and teenagers who watch the programs." The violence effect stems from a combination of factors—from *arousal* by the violent excitement, from the strengthening of violence-related *ideas*, from the erosion of one's *inhibitions*, and from *imitation* (Geen & Thomas, 1986). One research team observed a sevenfold increase in violent play immediately after children viewed the "Power Rangers" (Boyatzis & others, in press). Boys' aggressive acts often precisely imitated the characters' flying karate kicks and other violent acts.

Television's unreal world, in which acts of aggression greatly outnumber acts of affection, can also affect our *thinking* about the real world. Those who avidly watch prime-time crime regard the world as more dangerous (Gerbner & others, 1993; Heath & Petraitis, 1987; Singer & Singer, 1986). Prolonged exposure to violence also desensitizes viewers; they become more indifferent to it when later viewing a brawl, whether on TV or in real life (Rule & Ferguson, 1986). While spending three evenings watching sexually violent movies, male viewers in one experiment became progressively less bothered by the raping and slashing. Three days later, they also expressed less sympathy for domestic violence victims than did research participants who had not been exposed to the films, and they rated the victims' injuries as less severe (Mullin & Linz, 1995). Indeed, as Edward Donnerstein and his co-researchers (1987) suggested, an evil psychologist could hardly imagine a better way to make people indifferent to brutality than to expose them to a graded series of scenes, from fights to killings to the mutilations in slasher movies. Watching cruelty fosters indifference.

Sexual Aggression and the Media

A woman's risk of rape has varied across cultures and times (Koss & others, 1994). Over the last 30 years, America's reported rape rate has quadrupled. Recent surveys of both women and men reveal that unreported rapes—four in five committed by dates or acquaintances—greatly outnumber those reported (Schafran, 1995). In other surveys, about one-fifth of women report that a man has forced them to do something sexually, about one-half report some form of unwanted sexual coercion, and most report experiencing verbal sexual harassment (Craig & others, 1989; Laumann & others, 1994; Sandberg & others, 1985). Similar levels of sexual coercion have been reported in Canadian, Australian, and New Zealand surveys (Koss & others, 1994; Patton & Mannison, 1995).

What factors might explain the modern epidemic of sexual aggression? Alcohol consumption—often linked with aggression—has not increased. We do know that sexually coercive men typically are sexually unrestrained and hostile in their relationships with women (Figure 18.11). Might changes in the media have contributed to such tendencies?

Figure **18.11**

Men who sexually coerce women The recipe for coercion against women combines an impersonal approach to sex with a hostile masculinity. (Adapted from Malamuth, 1996.)

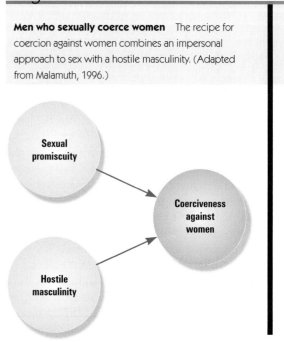

Coinciding with the increase in sexual aggression has been, thanks to the home video business, easier access to *R*-rated "slasher films" and *X*-rated films. Content analyses reveal that *X*-rated films mostly depict quick, casual sex between strangers, but that scenes of rape and sexual exploitation of women by men are also common (Cowan & others, 1988; NCTV, 1987; Yang & Linz, 1990).

Rape scenes often portray the victim at first fleeing and resisting her attacker, then becoming aroused and finally driven to ecstasy. Most men are not sexually aroused (as measured by a "penile plethysmograph") while viewing rape depictions. But convicted rapists are. So are normal men if they have been drinking or if, after being aroused by exercise, a woman's insults anger them (Barbaree & Marshall, 1991). In less graphic form, the same unrealistic script—she resists, he persists, she melts—is commonplace in TV scenes and in romance novels. The woman who first thwarts the insistent man ends up passionately kissing him. In *Gone with the Wind*, Scarlett O'Hara is carried to bed screaming and wakes up singing. Most rapists accept this "rape myth"—the idea that some women invite or enjoy rape and get "swept away" while being "taken" (Brinson, 1992). (In actuality, rape is not only traumatic, it also frequently harms women's reproductive and sexual health—Golding, 1996.)

Do images of sexual exploitation influence sexual aggression? When interviewed, Canadian and U.S. sex offenders (rapists, child molesters, and serial killers) do report a greater-than-usual appetite for sexually explicit and sexually violent materials—materials typically labeled as "pornography" (Marshall, 1989; Ressler & others, 1988). For example, the Los Angeles Police Department reports that pornography was "conspicuously present" or used in 62 percent of its extrafamilial child sexual abuse cases during the 1980s (Bennett, 1991). But are the sexual offenders merely, as sex researcher John Money (1988) suspects, using pornography "as an alibi to explain to themselves and their captors what otherwise is inexplicable"?

Laboratory experiments reveal that repeated viewing of *X*-rated films (even if nonviolent) makes one's own partner seem less attractive (page 377), makes women's friendliness seem more sexual, and makes sexual aggression seem less serious (Harris, 1994). In one such experiment, Dolf Zillmann and Jennings Bryant (1984) showed undergraduates six brief, sexually explicit films a week for six weeks. A control group viewed nonerotic films during the same six-week period. Three weeks later, both groups read a newspaper report about a man convicted but not yet sentenced for raping a hitchhiker. When asked to suggest an appropriate prison term, those who had viewed sexually explicit films recommended sentences half as long as those recommended by the control group.

In search of possible media effects on men's willingness to aggress against women, experimenters examined the effect of film viewing on men's acceptance of the rape myth. Neil Malamuth and James Check (1981) compared reactions of University of Manitoba men who were shown either two nonsexual movies or two movies depicting a man sexually overpowering a woman. A week later, when surveyed by a different experimenter, those who had seen the films with mild sexual violence were more accepting of violence against women and reported themselves a little more likely to rape if assured they could get away with it. Further experiments showed that viewing slasher movies, such as *The Texas Chainsaw Massacre*, can also lead viewers to trivialize rape.

Other experiments have explored the effect of violent versus nonviolent films on men's willingness to deliver supposed electric shocks to women who earlier provoked them. (Although such experiments cannot study actual sexual violence, they can assess a man's willingness to hurt a woman.) These experiments suggest that it's not eroticism but depictions of sexual *violence* (whether in *R*-rated slasher films or *X*-rated films) that most directly affect men's acceptance and performance of aggression against women. A 1986 conference of 21 social scientists, including many of the researchers who conducted these experiments, produced a consensus (Surgeon General, 1986): "Pornography that portrays sexual aggression as pleasurable for the victim increases the acceptance of the use of coercion in sexual relations." Contrary to much popular opinion, viewing such depictions does not provide an outlet for bottled-up impulses. Rather, "in laboratory studies measuring short-term effects, exposure to violent pornography increases punitive behavior toward women."

Repeated viewing of X-rated films (even if nonviolent) makes one's own partner seem less attractive, makes women's friendliness seem more sexual, and makes sexual aggression seem less serious.

Pornography means different things to different people. Following Webster's dictionary, some define pornography as erotic depictions intended to excite sexual arousal. Others define it as sexual materials that exploit, degrade, or subordinate women.

In follow-up studies, Zillmann (1989) found that after massive exposure to X-rated sexual films, men and women became more accepting of extramarital sex, of women's sexual submission to men, and of a man's seducing a 12-year-old girl. As people heavily exposed to televised crime perceive the world as more dangerous, so people heavily exposed to pornography see the world as more sexual.

conflict
a perceived incompatibility of actions, goals, or ideas.

social trap
a situation in which the conflicting parties, by each rationally pursuing their self-interest, become caught in mutually destructive behavior.

U.S. First Lady Hillary Rodham Clinton and others have also worried about media models of an "impulsive sexuality" that encourage uncommitted sex (a predictor of sexual violence) and father-absent families (a predictor of juvenile violence).

"If we expect families to teach children not to solve their problems with guns and violence, we need cultural and media signals and public policies that demonize rather than glamorize and support violence."

CHILDREN'S DEFENSE FUND
1992

"What we're trying to do is raise the level of awareness of violence against women and pornography to at least the level of awareness of racist and Ku Klux Klan literature."

GLORIA STEINEM (1988)

TV Violence, Pornography, and Society

Significant behaviors such as violence usually have many determinants, making any single explanation an oversimplification. Asking what causes violence is therefore like asking what causes cancer. Those who study the effects of asbestos exposure on cancer rates may remind us that asbestos is indeed a cancer cause, but only one among many. Likewise, report Neil Malamuth and his colleagues (1991, 1995), several factors can create a predisposition to sexual violence; they include not only the media but also child abuse, dominance motives, and disinhibition by alcohol. Still, if media depictions of violence can disinhibit and desensitize; if viewing sexual violence fosters hostile, domineering attitudes and behaviors; and if viewing pornography leads viewers to trivialize rape, devalue their partners, and engage in uncommitted sex, then media influence is not a minor issue.

Social psychologists attribute the media's influence partly to the *social scripts* they provide. When we find ourselves in new situations, uncertain how to act, we rely on social scripts provided by our culture. After so many episodes of "Power Rangers," followed by Sylvester Stallone and Arnold Schwarzenegger action films, youngsters may acquire a script—a mental tape for how to act—that gets played when they face real-life conflicts. Challenged, they may "act like a man" by intimidating or eliminating the threat. Likewise, after viewing 15 sexual innuendoes and acts per primetime TV hour—nearly all involving impulsive, short-term relationships—youths may acquire sexual scripts they later enact in real-life relationships (Sapolsky & Tabarlet, 1991).

Might public consciousness be raised by making people aware of the information you have just been reading? In the 1940s, movies often depicted African-Americans as childlike, superstitious buffoons. Today, such images are offensive. In the 1960s and 1970s, entertainment from Beatles' music to movies such as *Easy Rider* glamorized drug use. Responding to a tidal change in cultural attitudes, the entertainment industry now more often portrays drugs as dangerous. Even gratuitous cigarette smoking largely disappeared until the 1990s, whereupon its reappearance was accompanied by a new surge in teen smoking rates. Responding to growing public concern about violence and the media, television violence levels declined in the early 1990s (Gallup, 1993; Gerbner & others, 1993). The growing sensitivity to violence has raised hopes that, without violating artistic freedom, society might someday look back with embarrassment on the days when movies "enter-tained" people with scenes of torture, mutilation, and sexual coercion.

Conflict

We live in surprising times. With astonishing speed, democratic movements have swept away totalitarian rule in Eastern European countries, and hopes for a new world order have displaced the Cold War chill. Yet world spending for arms and armies continues to drain $2 billion per day from spending for housing, nutrition, education, and health. Knowing that, as the UNESCO motto declares, wars begin in human minds, psychologists have wondered what causes destructive conflict? How might the perceived threats of social diversity be replaced by a spirit of cooperation?

To a social psychologist, a conflict is a seeming incompatibility of actions, goals, or ideas. The elements of conflict are much the same at all levels, from nations in an arms race to cultural disputes within a society to individuals in marital strife. In each situation, people become enmeshed in a destructive social process that produces results no one wants. Among these destructive processes are social traps and distorted perceptions.

Social Traps

In some situations, we can enhance our collective well-being by pursuing our personal interests. As capitalist Adam Smith wrote in *The Wealth of Nations* (1776), "It is not from the benevolence of the butcher, the brewer, or the baker that we expect our dinner, but from their regard to their own interest." In other situations, the parties involved may become caught up in mutually harmful behavior as they pursue their own ends. Such situations are social traps.

Consider the simple game matrix in Figure 18.12, which is similar to those used in experiments with thousands of people. In this game, both sides can win or both can lose, depending on the players' individual choices. Pretend that you are Person 1, and that you and Person 2 will each receive the amount shown after you separately choose either *A* or *B*. (You might invite someone to look at the matrix with you and take the role of Person 2.) Which do you choose—*A* or *B*?

As you ponder the game, you will discover that you and Person 2 are caught in a dilemma. If you both choose *A*, you both benefit, making $5 each. Neither of you benefits if you both choose *B*, for neither of you make anything. Nevertheless, on any single trial you serve your own interests if you

Figure **18.12**

Social trap game matrix By pursuing our self-interest and not trusting others, we can end up losers. To illustrate this, imagine playing the game above. The pink triangles show the outcomes for Person 1, which depend on the choices made by both persons. If you were Person 1, would you choose A or B? (This game is called a "non–zero-sum game" because the outcomes need not add up to zero; both sides can win or both can lose.)

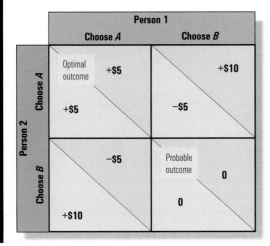

choose *B*: You can't lose, and you might make $10. But the same is true for the other person. Hence, the social trap: As long as you both pursue your own immediate best interest and choose *B*, you will both end up with nothing—the typical result—when you could have made $5.

Many real-life situations similarly pit people's individual interests against their communal well-being. Individual whalers reason that the few whales they take will not threaten the species and that if they didn't take them others would anyway. The result: A species of whales becomes endangered. The individual car owner and home owner reasons, "It would cost me comfort or money to buy a more fuel-efficient car and furnace. Besides, the fossil fuels I burn don't add much to the greenhouse gases." When others reason similarly, the collective result threatens disaster—global warming.

Social traps challenge us to find ways of reconciling our right to pursue our personal well-being with our responsibility for the well-being of all. Psychologists are therefore exploring ways to convince people to cooperate for their mutual betterment—through agreed-upon *regulations*, through better *communication*, and through promoting *awareness* of our responsibilities toward community, nation, and the whole of humanity (Dawes, 1980; Linder, 1982; Sato, 1987). Under such conditions, people more often cooperate, whether playing laboratory games or playing the real game of life.

Enemy Perceptions

Psychologists have noted a curious tendency for those in conflict to form diabolical images of each other. These distorted images are so similar that we call them *mirror-image perceptions*: As we see them—as untrustworthy and evil intentioned—so they see us. Thus, during the early 1980s, the U.S. government viewed the Communist support of guerrillas trying to overthrow the government of El Salvador as evidence of an "evil empire" at work. Meanwhile, the Soviets saw the U.S. support of guerrillas trying to overthrow the government of Nicaragua as the work of "imperialist warmongers." As enemies change, so do perceptions. In American minds and media, the "bloodthirsty, cruel, treacherous" Japanese of World War II later became our "intelligent, hardworking, self-disciplined, resourceful allies" (Gallup, 1972).

We have considered the psychological roots of biased perceptions. The *self-serving bias* leads each party to accept credit for good deeds and to shuck the blame for bad deeds (Chapter 14). Although two nations admit to a buildup of military forces, the *fundamental attribution error* leads each to see the other's actions as arising from an aggressive disposition, and to view its own buildup as necessary self-defense. Information about each other's actions is then filtered, interpreted, and remembered through preconceived *stereotypes*. Group interaction among like-minded policymakers may

"Why do you see the speck that is in your brother's eye, but do not notice the log that is in your own eye?"

JESUS
LUKE 6:41–42

A social trap In the Atlantic waters off Newfoundland, those who fished knew that their individual catch was their livelihood and, by itself, hardly depleted the whole fish population. Such reasoning by everyone, including outsiders, depleted fish stocks. The result: Newfoundland's fishing fleet sits idle and an economy is in ruins during a 1990s fishing moratorium. This unemployed fisherman has been forced to use his boat for firewood.

mere exposure effect
the phenomenon that repeated exposure to novel stimuli increases liking of them.

polarize these tendencies, leading to *groupthink*, whereby each sees its own group as more moral, thereby justifying retaliation. In Soviet-U.S. relations, such biases resulted in the social perceptions that fueled the arms race: Each side (1) wished for mutual arms reduction, but (2) wanted above all to avoid disarming while the other armed, and (3) perceived the other side as wanting above all to gain an arms advantage (Plous, 1993).

Another result of such perceptions is a vicious cycle of hostility. If Victor believes Samantha is annoyed with him, he may snub her, causing her to act in ways that justify his perception. As with individuals, so with countries. Perceptions confirm themselves by influencing the other country to react in ways that seem to justify them. The self-fulfilling prophecy rides again.

Now that we've pondered the bad side of our social relations—prejudice, aggression, and conflict—let's focus on the positive side of social relations—attraction, altruism, and peacemaking.

Attraction

Pause a moment and think about your relationships with two people—a close friend, and someone who has stirred in you feelings of romantic love. What factors lead to friendship and romance? What factors help us sustain these relationships?

We endlessly wonder how we can win others' affection and what makes our own affections flourish or fade. Do birds of a feather flock together, or do opposites attract? Does familiarity breed contempt or liking? Does absence make the heart grow fonder, or is out of sight out of mind? Social psychology suggests some answers.

The Psychology of Attraction

What is the psychological chemistry that binds two people together in that special sort of friendship that helps one cope with all other relationships? Consider three ingredients of our liking for one another.

Proximity

Before friendships become close, they must begin. Proximity—geographic nearness—is perhaps the most powerful predictor of friendship. Proximity provides opportunities for aggression, but much more often it breeds liking. Study after study reveals that people are most likely to like, and even to marry, those who live in the same neighborhood, who sit nearby in class, who work in the same office, who share the same parking lot. Look around.

Familiarity breeds acceptance When this rare white penguin was born in the Sydney, Australia, zoo, his tuxedoed peers ostracized him. Zookeepers thought they would need to dye him black to gain acceptance. But after three weeks of contact, the other penguins came to accept him.

Why is proximity so conducive to liking? Obviously, part of the answer is the greater availability of those we often meet. But there is more to it than that. For one thing, repeated exposure to novel stimuli—be they nonsense syllables, musical selections, geometric figures, Chinese characters, human faces, or the letters of our own name—increases our liking for them (Moreland & Zajonc, 1982; Nuttin, 1987). This phenomenon, which is now exploited by advertisers, we call the mere exposure effect. Within certain limits (Bornstein, 1989), familiarity breeds fondness. Richard Moreland and Scott Beach (1992) demonstrated this by having four equally attractive women silently attend a 200-student class for zero, 5, 10, or 15 class sessions. At the end of the class, students were shown slides of each

The mere exposure effect The mere exposure effect applies even to ourselves. Because the human face is not perfectly symmetrical, the face we see in the mirror is not the same as the one our friends see. Most of us prefer the familiar mirror image, while our friends like the reverse (Mita & others, 1977). The Prime Minister Jim Bolger known to New Zealanders is shown at left. The person Bolger sees in the mirror each morning is shown at right, and that's the photo he would probably prefer.

woman and asked to rate their attractiveness. The most attractive? The ones they'd seen most often. The phenomenon will come as no surprise to the young Taiwanese man who wrote more than 700 letters to his girlfriend, urging her to marry him. She did marry—the mail carrier (Steinberg, 1993).

For our ancestors, the mere exposure phenomenon was adaptive. What was familiar was generally safe and approachable. What was unfamiliar was more often dangerous and threatening. Robert Zajonc (in press) concludes that evolution has hardwired into us the tendency to bond with those who are familiar and to be wary of those who are unfamiliar. Gut-level prejudice against those culturally different may thus be a primitive, automatic emotional response (Devine, 1995).

Physical Attractiveness

Once proximity affords you contact, what most affects your first impressions: the person's sincerity? Intelligence? Personality? Hundreds of experiments reveal that it is something far more superficial: appearance.

For people taught that "beauty is only skin deep" and that "appearances can be deceiving," the power of physical attractiveness is unnerving. In one early study, Elaine Hatfield and her co-workers (Walster & others, 1966) randomly matched new University of Minnesota students for a "Welcome Week" dance. Before the dance, all took a battery of personality and aptitude tests. On the night of the blind date, the couples danced and talked for more than two hours and then took a brief intermission to rate their dates. What determined whether they liked each other? So far as the researchers could determine, only one thing mattered: physical attractiveness (which had been rated by the researchers beforehand). Both the men and the women liked good-looking dates best. Although women are more likely than men to *say* that another's looks don't affect them, a man's looks do affect

women's behavior (Feingold, 1990; Sprecher, 1989; Woll, 1986).

People's physical attractiveness has wideranging effects. It predicts their dating frequency, their feelings of popularity, and others' initial impressions of their personalities. We perceive attractive people, even children and those of our own sex, to be happier, more sensitive, more successful, and more socially skilled, though not more honest or compassionate (Eagly & others, 1991; Feingold, 1992; Hatfield & Sprecher, 1986). Attractive and well-dressed people are more likely to make a favorable impression on potential employers (Cash & Janda, 1984; Solomon, 1987). To judge from their gazing times, even babies prefer attractive over unattractive faces (Langlois & others, 1987).

That looks are important may seem unfair and unenlightened. Two thousand years ago the Roman statesman Cicero felt the same way: "The final good and the supreme duty of the wise person is to resist appearance." Cicero might be reassured by two other findings about attractiveness.

First, people's attractiveness is surprisingly unrelated to their self-esteem and happiness (Diener & others, 1995; Major & others, 1984). One reason may be that, except after comparing themselves with superattractive people, few people view themselves as unattractive (Thornton & Moore, 1993). (Thanks, perhaps, to the mere exposure effect, most of us become accustomed to our faces.) Another reason is that strikingly attractive people are sometimes suspicious that praise may be simply a reaction to their looks. When less attractive people are praised for their work, they are more likely to accept it as sincere (Berscheid, 1981).

Cicero might also find comfort in knowing that attractiveness judgments are relative. The standards by which judges crown "Miss Universe" hardly apply to the whole planet. Rather, beauty is in the eye of the culture—most accepted standards of beauty are influenced by one's place and time.

In the eye of the beholder
Conceptions of attractiveness vary by culture and across time. What may be deemed attractive in one culture may seem strange or unattractive in another. And the current concept of beauty in Kenya, Morocco, and the United States may well change in the future.

Hoping to look attractive, people in different cultures have pierced their noses, lengthened their necks, bound their feet, dyed their skin and hair, gorged themselves to achieve a full figure or liposuctioned fat to achieve a slim one, strapped on leather garments to make their breasts seem smaller or surgically filled their breasts with silicone and put on Wonder Bras to make them look bigger.

Figure **18.13**

Worldwide mating preferences
David Buss and an international team of collaborators surveyed the mating preferences of 10,047 people in 37 countries. Men everywhere preferred attractive physical features suggesting youth and health—and reproductive potential. Women everywhere preferred men with resources and social status. (From Buss, 1994b.) This gender difference, evolutionary psychologists believe, is the result of natural selection favoring those whose choices help perpetuate their genes.

Hoping to look attractive, people in different cultures have pierced their noses, lengthened their necks, bound their feet, dyed their skin and hair, gorged themselves to achieve a full figure or liposuctioned fat to achieve a slim one, strapped on leather garments to make their breasts seem smaller or surgically filled their breasts with silicone and put on Wonder Bras to make them look bigger. In North America, the ultra-thin ideal of the Roaring Twenties gave way to the soft, voluptuous Marilyn Monroe ideal of the 1950s, to be replaced by the lean, athletic ideal of the 1990s.

Some aspects of attractiveness, however, do cross place and time. It comes as no surprise to evolutionary psychologists that men in 37 cultures, from Australia to Zambia, judge women as more attractive if they have a youthful appearance (Figure 18.13). These psychologists say that men drawn to healthy, fertile-appearing women have stood a better chance of sending their genes into the future.

From yesterday's stone age figurines to today's *Playboy* centerfolds and Miss America winners—and regardless of cultural variations in ideal weight—men feel most attracted to women whose waists are roughly a third narrower than their hips—a sign of youthful fertility (Singh, 1993).

Women also feel attracted to healthy-looking men, but especially to those who seem mature, dominant, and affluent (Singh, 1995a). Such attributes connote, say the evolutionary psychologists, a capacity to support and protect (Buss, 1996; Schmitt & Buss, 1996). Henry Kissinger, an adviser to U.S. presidents, had the same idea: "Power is the world's greatest aphrodisiac." Evolutionary psychologists also are unsurprised that each sex tends to advertise the qualities that maximize its odds of attracting desirable partners: women by spending time and money on appearance, men by trying to establish their status and dominance. In singles ads, for example, women tend to offer looks and seek status; men do the reverse (Rajecki & others, 1991).

People also seem to prefer physical features—noses, legs, physiques—that are neither unusually large or small. In one clever demonstration of this, Judith Langlois and Lori Roggman (1990) digitized the faces of up to 32 college students and used a computer to average them. Students judged the averaged, composite faces as more attractive than 96 percent of the individual faces. Being truly average is not optimally beautiful (Perrett & others, 1994), but it is to be more attractive than most. One reason is that averaged faces are symmetrical, and people with symmetrical faces and bodies are more sexually attractive (Singh, 1995b; Thornhill & Gangestad, 1995). So sensitive is our radar for facial attractiveness that we can judge someone's looks after but a 0.15 second glimpse (Zajonc, in press).

Cultural standards aside, attractiveness also depends on our feelings about the person. In a Rodgers and Hammerstein musical, Prince Charming asks Cinderella, "Do I love you because you're beautiful, or are you beautiful because I love you?" Chances are it is both. As we see someone again and again, and come to like them, their physical imperfections grow less noticeable and their attractiveness grows more apparent (Beaman & Klentz, 1983; Gross & Crofton, 1977). As Shakespeare put

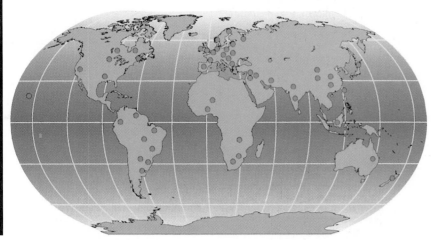

"Love is a dirty trick played on us to achieve the continuation of the species."

NOVELIST W. SOMERSET MAUGHAM (1874–1965)

Sexy symmetry Actor Denzel Washington, recently judged "The Sexiest Man Alive" by *People* magazine, has an almost perfectly symmetrical face. By drawing lines between facial midpoints and paired features, researchers can gauge symmetry.

it in *A Midsummer Night's Dream*, "Love looks not with the eyes, but with the mind." Until you got to know him, E.T. was as ugly as Darth Vader.

Similarity

Let's say that proximity has brought you into contact with someone and that your appearance has made a favorable first impression. What now influences whether acquaintances develop into friends? For example, as you get to know someone better, is the chemistry better if you are opposites or if you are alike?

It makes a good story—extremely different types living in harmonious union: Rat, Mole, and Badger in *The Wind in the Willows*, Frog and Toad in Arnold Lobel's books. The stories delight us by expressing what we seldom experience, for we tend *not* to like dissimilar people (Rosenbaum, 1986). In real life, opposites retract. Birds that

"Pardon me, but I can't help noticing that we share similar tastes in tropical-fruit-flavored chewing gum."

flock together usually *are* of a feather. Friends and couples are far more likely to share common attitudes, beliefs, and interests (and, for that matter, age, religion, race, education, intelligence, smoking behavior, and economic status) than are randomly paired people. Much as you and I may dismiss such differences, seeing ourselves as one human family in a global village, we can't hang out with 6 billion people. Moreover, the greater people's likeness, the more their liking endures (Byrne, 1971). Journalist Walter Lippmann was right to suppose that love is best sustained "when the lovers love many things together, and not merely each other." Similarity breeds content.

Proximity, attractiveness, and similarity are not the only determinants of attraction. We also like those who like us, especially when our self-image is low. When we believe someone likes us, we respond to them more warmly, which leads them to like us even more (Curtis & Miller, 1986). To be liked is powerfully rewarding.

Indeed, a simple reward theory of attraction—that we will like those whose behavior is rewarding to us and that we will continue relationships that offer more rewards than costs—can explain all the findings we have considered so far. When a person lives or works in close proximity with someone else, it costs less time and effort to develop the friendship and enjoy its benefits. Attractive people are aesthetically pleasing, and associating with them can be socially rewarding. Those with similar views reward us by validating our own.

Romantic Love

Occasionally, people progress quickly from initial impressions to friendship to the more intense, complex, and mysterious state of romantic love. Elaine Hatfield (1988) distinguishes two types of love: temporary passionate love and a more enduring companionate love.

Passionate Love

Noting that arousal is a key ingredient of passionate love, Hatfield suggests that the two-factor theory of emotion (page 414) can help us understand this intense positive absorption in another. The theory assumes that (1) emotions have two ingredients—physical arousal plus cognitive appraisal—and that (2) arousal from any source can enhance one emotion or another, depending on how we interpret and label the arousal.

In tests of this theory, college men have been aroused by fright, by running in place, by viewing erotic materials, or by listening to humorous or repulsive monologues. They are then introduced to

passionate love
An aroused state of intense positive absorption in another, usually present at the beginning of a love relationship.

"Love has ever in view the absolute loveliness of that which it beholds."

GEORGE MACDONALD
UNSPOKEN SERMONS
1867

HI & LOIS

Companionate Love

Inevitably, the passion of romantic love subsides. The intense absorption in the other, the thrill of the romance, the giddy "floating on a cloud" feeling fades. JUST MARRIED becomes just married. Recognizing the short duration of passionate love, some societies have deemed such feelings an irrational reason for marrying. Better, such cultures say, to choose (or have someone choose for you) a partner with compatible backgrounds and interests. Non-Western cultures, where people rate love as less important for marriage decisions, indeed have lower divorce rates (Levine & others, 1995).

an attractive woman and asked to rate her (or their girlfriend). Unlike unaroused men, those who are stirred up attribute some of their arousal to the woman or girlfriend and feel more attracted to her (Carducci & others, 1978; Dermer & Pyszczynski, 1978; White & Kight, 1984).

Outside the laboratory, Donald Dutton and Arthur Aron (1974, 1989) went to two bridges across British Columbia's rocky Capilano River. One was a swaying footbridge 230 feet above the rocks; the other was a low, solid bridge. An attractive young female accomplice intercepted men coming off each bridge, sought their help in filling out a short questionnaire, and then offered her phone number in case they wanted to hear more about her project. Far more of those who had just crossed the high bridge—which left their hearts pounding—accepted the number and later called the woman. To be revved up and to associate some of that arousal with a desirable person is to feel the pull of passion. As lovers who take a thrilling roller coaster ride together know, adrenaline makes the heart grow fonder.

> "When two people are under the influence of the most violent, most insane, most delusive, and most transient of passions, they are required to swear that they will remain in that excited, abnormal, and exhausting condition continuously until death do them part."
>
> **GEORGE BERNARD SHAW**
> *MAN AND SUPERMAN*
> 1903

So, are the French correct in saying that "love makes the time pass and time makes love pass"? Or can friendship and commitment keep a relationship going after the passion cools? Hatfield notes that if love matures it becomes a steadier <u>companionate love</u>—a deep, affectionate attachment. There may be adaptive wisdom to this change from passion to affection. Passionate love often produces children, whose survival is aided by the parents' waning obsession with one another. Social

Passionate love to companionate love The quality of love changes as a relationship matures from passionate absorption to affectionate attachment.

psychologist Ellen Berscheid and her colleagues (1984) note that the failure to appreciate passionate love's limited half-life can doom a relationship: "If the inevitable odds against eternal passionate love in a relationship were better understood, more people might choose to be satisfied with the quieter feelings of satisfaction and contentment."

One key to a gratifying and enduring relationship is equity: Both partners receive in proportion to what they give. When equity exists—when both partners freely give and receive, when they share decision making—their chances for sustained and satisfying companionate love are good (Gray-Little & Burks, 1983; Van Yperen & Buunk, 1990). Mutually sharing self and possessions, giving and getting emotional support, promoting and caring about one another's welfare, are at the core of every type of loving relationship (Sternberg & Grajek, 1984). It's true for lovers, for parent and child, and for intimate friends.

> "When a match has
> equal partners then I fear not."
>
> **AESCHYLUS**
> *PROMETHEUS BOUND*
> 478 B.C.

Another vital ingredient of loving relationships is intimacy. A strong friendship or marriage permits self-disclosure, a revealing of intimate details about ourselves—our likes and dislikes, our dreams and worries, our proud and shameful moments. "When I am with my friend," noted the Roman statesman Seneca, "me thinks I am alone, and as much at liberty to speak anything as to think it." Self-disclosure breeds liking, and vice versa (Collins & Miller, 1994). As one person reveals a little, the other reciprocates, the first person reveals more, and on and on, as friends or lovers move to deeper

intimacy. Given self-disclosing intimacy plus mutually supportive equality, the odds favor enduring companionate love.

Altruism

Altruism—an unselfish regard for others' welfare—is another powerful example of positive social interactions. Altruism became a major concern of social psychologists after an especially vile act of sexual violence. A knife-wielding stalker repeatedly stabbed Kitty Genovese, then raped her as she lay dying outside her Queens, New York, apartment at 3:30 A.M. on March 13, 1964. "Oh, my God, he stabbed me!" Genovese screamed into the early-morning stillness. "Please help me!" Windows opened and lights went on as 38 of her neighbors heard her screams. Her attacker fled and then returned to stab her eight more times and rape her again. Not until he departed for good did anyone so much as call the police, at 3:50 A.M.

Bystander Intervention

Reflecting on the Genovese murder and other such tragedies, most commentators lamented the bystanders' "apathy" and "indifference." Rather than blaming them, social psychologists John Darley and Bibb Latané (1968b) attributed onlooker inaction to an important situational factor—the presence of others. Given the right circumstances, they suspected, most of us might behave similarly.

After staging emergencies under various conditions, Darley and Latané assembled their findings into a decision scheme: We will help only if the situation enables us first to *notice* the incident, then to *interpret* it as an emergency, and finally to *assume responsibility* for helping (Figure 18.14).

companionate love
the deep affectionate attachment we feel for those with whom our lives are intertwined.

equity
a condition in which people receive from a relationship in proportion to what they give to it.

self-disclosure
revealing intimate aspects of oneself to others.

altruism
unselfish regard for the welfare of others.

> "Probably no single incident has caused social psychologists to pay as much attention to an aspect of social behavior as Kitty Genovese's murder."
>
> **R. LANCE SHOTLAND (1984)**

Figure **18.14**

The decision-making process for bystander intervention Before helping, one must first notice an emergency, then correctly interpret it, and then feel responsible. (From Darley & Latané, 1968b.)

| Notices incident? | →Yes→ | Interprets incident as emergency? | →Yes→ | Assumes responsibility? | →Yes→ | Attempts to help |

No → **No help**   No → **No help**   No → **No help**

At each step, the presence of other bystanders turns people away from the path that leads to helping. In the laboratory and on the street, people in groups of strangers are more likely than solitary individuals to keep their eyes on what they are doing or where they are going. If they notice an unusual situation, they may infer from the blasé reactions of the other passersby that the situation is not an emergency. "The person lying on the sidewalk must be drunk," they think, and move on.

But sometimes, as with the Genovese murder, the emergency is unambiguous and people still fail to help. The witnesses looking out through their windows noticed the incident, correctly interpreted the emergency, yet failed to assume responsibility. To find out why, Darley and Latané (1968a) simulated a physical emergency in their laboratory. University students participated in a discussion over an intercom. Each student was in a separate cubicle, and only the person whose microphone was switched on could be heard. One of the students was an accomplice of the experimenters. When his turn came, he called for help and made sounds as though he were having an epileptic seizure.

How did the other students react? As Figure 18.15 shows, those who believed they were the only person who could hear the victim—and therefore thought they bore total responsibility for helping—usually went to his aid. Those who thought others could also hear were more likely to react as did Kitty Genovese's neighbors. When more people shared responsibility for helping, any single listener was less likely to help.

In hundreds of additional experiments, psychologists have studied the factors that influence bystanders' willingness to relay an emergency phone call, aid a stranded motorist, donate blood, pick up dropped books, contribute money, and give time. For example, Latané, James Dabbs (1975), and 145 collaborators took 1497 elevator rides in three cities and "accidentally" dropped coins or pencils in front of 4813 fellow passengers. The women coin-droppers were more likely to receive help than were the men—a gender difference often reported by other researchers (Eagly & Crowley, 1986). But the major finding was the bystander effect: Any particular bystander was less likely to give aid with other bystanders present. When one other person was on the elevator, those who dropped the coins were helped 40 percent of the time. When there were six passengers, help came less than 20 percent of the time.

From their observations of behavior in tens of thousands of such "emergencies," altruism researchers have discerned some additional patterns. The *best* odds of our helping someone occur when

- we have just observed someone else being helpful.
- we are not in a hurry.
- the victim appears to need and deserve help.
- the victim is in some way similar to us.
- we are in a small town or rural area.
- we are feeling guilty.
- we are focused on others and not preoccupied.
- we are in a good mood.

This last result, that happy people are helpful people, is one of the most consistent findings in all of psychology. No matter how people are cheered—whether by being made to feel successful and intelligent, by thinking happy thoughts, by finding money, or even by receiving a posthypnotic suggestion—they become more generous and more eager to help (Carlson & others, 1988).

"Oh, make us happy and you make us good!"

ROBERT BROWNING
THE RING AND THE BOOK
1868

The Psychology of Helping

So *why* do we help? One widely held view is that self-interest underlies all human interactions: Our constant goal is to maximize rewards and minimize costs. Accountants call it cost–benefit analysis. Philosophers call it utilitarianism. Social

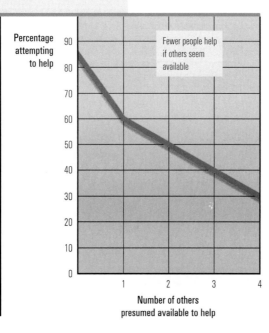

Figure **18.15**

Responses to a simulated physical emergency When people thought they alone heard the calls for help from a person they believed to be having an epileptic seizure, they usually helped. But when they thought four others were also hearing the calls, fewer than a third responded. (From Darley & Latané, 1968a.)

Percentage attempting to help

Fewer people help if others seem available

Number of others presumed available to help

psychologists call it social exchange theory. If you are pondering whether to donate blood, you may weigh the costs of doing so (time, discomfort, and anxiety) against the benefits (reduced guilt, social approval, good feelings). If the anticipated rewards of helping exceed the anticipated costs, you help.

Social expectations also influence helping. They prescribe how we ought to behave, often to our mutual benefit. Through socialization, we learn the *reciprocity norm*, the expectation that we should return help, not harm, to those who have helped us. In our relations with others of similar status, the reciprocity norm compels us to give (in favors, gifts, or social invitations) about as much as we receive. With young children and others who cannot give as much as they receive, we also learn a *social responsibility norm*—that we should help those who need our help, even if the costs outweigh the benefits. In repeated Gallup surveys, people who each week attend church or synagogue services often exhibit the social responsibility norm: They report volunteering more than twice as many hours in helping the poor and infirm than do those who rarely or never attend religious services (Hodgkinson & Weitzman, 1992). They also give away three times as much money.

Peacemaking

How can we transform antagonisms fed by prejudice, aggression, and various conflicts into constructive attitudes that promote peace? Such transformations are most likely in situations characterized by cooperation, communication, and conciliation.

Cooperation

Does it help to put two conflicting parties into close contact so they might get to know and like each other? It depends. When the contact is non-competitive and between parties of equal status, such as fellow store clerks, it may help. Initially prejudiced co-workers of different races have, in such circumstances, usually learned to accept one another. Among Europeans, friendly contact with ethnic minorities leads to less prejudice (Pettigrew, 1969, 1997). However, mere contact is sometimes not enough. In most desegregated middle and junior high schools in the United States, white and black students resegregate themselves in the lunchrooms and on the school grounds (Schofield, 1986).

Mere contact was not enough to defuse intense conflicts instigated by researcher Muzafer Sherif (1966). He placed 22 Oklahoma City boys in two separate areas of a Boy Scout camp. He then put the two groups through a series of competitive activities, with prizes going to the victors. Before long, each group became intensely proud of itself and hostile to the other group's "sneaky," "smart-alecky stinkers." Food wars broke out during meals. Cabins were ransacked. Fistfights had to be broken up by members of the camp staff. When Sherif brought the two groups together, they avoided one another, except to taunt and threaten.

Nevertheless, within a few days Sherif transformed these young enemies into jovial comrades by giving them superordinate goals—shared goals that overrode their differences and that could be achieved only through cooperation. A planned disruption of the camp water supply necessitated that all 22 boys work together to restore water. Renting a movie in those pre-VCR days required their pooled resources. A truck stalled until all the boys pulled and pushed together to get it moving. Having used isolation and competition to make strangers into enemies, Sherif used shared predicaments and goals to reconcile the enemies and make them friends. What reduced conflict was not contact itself, but *cooperative* contact.

Extending these findings, Samuel Gaertner and his co-workers (1989) report that cooperation has especially positive effects when it leads people to define a new, inclusive group that dissolves their former subgroups. Seat the members of two groups not on opposite sides, but alternately around the table. Give them a new, shared name. Have them work together. Such experiences change "us and them" into "we." People once perceived as in another group now are part of one's own group.

During the 1970s, several teams of educational researchers simultaneously wondered: If cooperative contacts between members of rival groups encourage positive attitudes, could we apply this principle in multicultural schools? Could we promote interracial friendships by replacing competitive classroom situations with cooperative ones? And could cooperative learning maintain or even enhance student achievement? Many experiments confirm that in all three cases, the answer is yes (Johnson & Johnson, 1989, 1994; Slavin, 1989). Members of interracial groups who work together on projects and play together on athletic teams typically come to feel friendly toward those of the other race. So do those who engage in cooperative classroom learning. So encouraging are these results that more than 25,000 teachers have introduced interracial cooperative learning into their classrooms (Kohn, 1987). Working with fellow students in all their diversity sets the stage, declared

social exchange theory
the theory that our social behavior is an exchange process, the aim of which is to maximize benefits and minimize costs.

superordinate goals
shared goals that override differences among people and require their cooperation.

"You cannot shake hands with a clenched fist."

INDIRA GANDHI (1971)

Superordinate goals override differences Cooperative efforts to achieve shared goals are an effective way to break down social barriers.

"I am prepared this day to declare myself a citizen of the world, and to invite everyone everywhere to embrace this broader vision of our interdependent world, our common quest for justice, and ultimately for Peace on Earth."

FATHER THEODORE HESBURGH
THE HUMAN IMPERATIVE
1974

GRIT
Graduated and Reciprocated Initiatives in Tension-Reduction— a strategy designed to decrease international tensions.

the Carnegie Council on Adolescent Development (1989), for "adult work life and for citizenship in a multicultural society."

The power of cooperative activity to make friends of former enemies has led psychologists to urge increased international exchange and cooperation (Klineberg, 1984). As we engage in mutually beneficial trade, as we work to protect our common destiny on this fragile planet, and as we become more aware that our hopes and fears are shared, we can change misperceptions into a solidarity based on common interests. Although we will never love all our differences or be pals with everyone, we can, as we work toward shared goals, grow to accept and value human diversity.

Communication

In the social trap game matrix we considered earlier, people usually are distrustful and pursue their individual interests as a defense against exploitation. But when allowed to discuss the dilemma and negotiate, cooperation increases (Jorgenson & Papciak, 1981).

When conflicts become intense, a third-party mediator—a marriage counselor, labor mediator, diplomat, community volunteer—may facilitate communication (Rubin & others, 1994). Mediators help each party to voice its viewpoint and to understand the other's. By helping each side think about the other's underlying needs and goals, the mediator aims to replace a competitive *win-lose* orientation with a cooperative *win-win* orientation that aims at a mutually beneficial resolution. A classic example concerns the two friends who, after quarreling over an orange, agreed to split it, whereupon one squeezed his half for juice while the other used the peel from her half to make a cake. If only the two had understood each other's motives, they could have hit on the win-win solution of one having all the juice, the other all the peel.

Such understanding and cooperative resolution is most needed, yet least likely, in times of anger or crisis (Bodenhausen & others, 1994; Tetlock, 1988). When conflicts intensify, images become more stereotyped, communication becomes more difficult, and judgments become more rigid. Iraq's President Saddam Hussein, America's friend while attacking Iran in the 1980s, became to U.S. President George Bush "another Hitler" after attacking oil-producing Kuwait in 1990. To Hussein, Bush became "Satan in the White House."

Neutral third parties may also suggest proposals that would be dismissed if offered by either side. People often "reactively devalue" a concession offered by an adversary ("if they're willing to give that up, they must not value it"); the same concession may seem less like a token gesture when suggested by a third party. Lee Ross and Constance Stillinger (1991) showed how this works. They found that a nuclear disarmament proposal that Americans dismissed when attributed to the Soviet Union seemed more acceptable when attributed to a neutral third party.

Conciliation

When tension and suspicion peak, cooperation and communication may become impossible. Each party is likely to threaten, coerce, or retaliate. In the weeks before the Persian Gulf War, President Bush threatened, in the full glare of publicity, to "kick Saddam's ass." Saddam Hussein communicated in kind, threatening to make Americans "swim in their own blood."

Under such conditions, is there an alternative to war or surrender? Social psychologist Charles Osgood (1962, 1980) has advocated a strategy of "Graduated and Reciprocated Initiatives in Tension-Reduction," nicknamed GRIT. In applying GRIT, one side first announces its recognition of mutual interests and its intent to reduce tensions. It then initiates one or more small, conciliatory acts. Without weakening one's retaliatory capability, this modest beginning opens the door for reciprocation by the other party. Should the enemy respond with hostility, one reciprocates in kind. But so, too, with any conciliatory response. Thus, President Kennedy's gesture of stopping atmospheric nuclear tests began a series of reciprocated conciliatory acts that culminated in the 1993 atmospheric test-ban treaty.

In laboratory experiments, GRIT has been the most effective strategy known for increasing trust and cooperation (Lindskold & others, 1978–1988). Even during intense personal conflict, when communication has been nonexistent, a small conciliatory gesture—a smile, a touch, a word of apology—may work wonders. Conciliations allow both parties to begin edging down the tension ladder to a safer rung where communication and mutual understanding can begin.

And how good that such can happen, for civilization advances not by cultural isolation—maintaining walls around ethnic enclaves—but by tapping the knowledge, the skills, and the arts that are each culture's legacy to the whole human race. Thomas Sowell (1991) notes that, thanks to cultural sharing, every modern society is enriched by a cultural mix. We have China to thank for paper and printing, and for the magnetic compass that opened the great explorations. We have Egypt to thank for trigonometry. We have the Islamic world and India's Hindus to thank for our Arabic numerals, which, except for numbering kings and queens, really are superior to the Roman numerals they replaced. While celebrating and claiming these cultural legacies, we can also welcome the enrichment of today's social diversity. We can view ourselves as individual instruments in a human orchestra. And we can therefore affirm our own culture's heritage while building bridges of communication, understanding, and cooperation across cultural traditions.

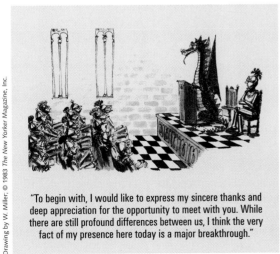

"To begin with, I would like to express my sincere thanks and deep appreciation for the opportunity to meet with you. While there are still profound differences between us, I think the very fact of my presence here today is a major breakthrough."

Drawing by W. Miller; © 1983 The New Yorker Magazine, Inc.

SUMMING UP

Prejudice Prejudice often arises as those who enjoy social and economic superiority attempt to justify the status quo. Even the temporary assignment of people to groups can cause an ingroup bias. Once established, the inertia of social influence can help maintain prejudice. Prejudice may also serve the emotional functions of draining off the anger caused by frustration and of boosting self-esteem.

Newer research reveals how our ways of processing information—for example, by overestimating similarities when we categorize people or by noticing and remembering vivid cases—work to create stereotypes. In addition, favored social groups often rationalize their higher status by the just-world phenomenon.

Aggression Aggressive behavior, like all behavior, is a product of nature and nurture. Although psychologists dismiss the idea that aggression is instinctual, aggressiveness is genetically influenced. Moreover, certain areas of the brain, when stimulated, activate or inhibit aggression, and these neural areas are biochemically influenced.

A variety of psychological factors also influence aggression. Aversive events heighten people's hostility. Such stimuli are especially likely to trigger aggression in those rewarded for their own aggression or those who have learned aggression from role models or observed violent media portrayals of aggressive models. Such factors desensitize people to cruelty and prime them to behave aggressively when provoked.

Conflict Conflicts between individuals and cultures often arise from malignant social processes. These include social traps, in which each party, by protecting and pursuing its self-interest, creates an outcome that no one wants. The spiral of conflict also feeds and is fed by distorted mirror-image perceptions, in which each party views itself as moral and the other as untrustworthy and evil-intentioned.

Attraction Three factors are known to influence our liking for one another. Proximity—geographical nearness—is conducive to attraction, partly because mere exposure to novel stimuli enhances liking. Physical attractiveness influences social opportunities and the way one is perceived. As acquaintanceship moves toward friendship, similarity of attitudes and interests greatly increases liking.

We can view passionate love as an aroused state that we cognitively label as love. The strong affection of companionate love, which often emerges as a relationship matures, is enhanced by an equitable relationship and by intimate self-disclosure.

Altruism In response to incidents of bystander non-intervention in emergencies, social psychologists undertook experiments that revealed a bystander effect: Any given bystander is less likely to help if others are present. The bystander effect is especially apparent in situations where the presence of others inhibits one's noticing the event, interpreting it as an emergency, or assuming responsibility for helping. Many factors, including mood, also influence willingness to help someone in distress.

Social exchange theory proposes that our social behaviors—even our helpful acts—maximize our benefits (which may include our own good feel-ings) and minimize our costs. Our desire to help is also affected by social norms, which prescribe reciprocating the help we have received and being socially responsible toward those in need.

Peacemaking Enemies sometimes become friends, especially when the circumstances favor cooperation to achieve superordinate goals, understanding through communication, and reciprocated conciliatory gestures.

KEY TERMS AND CONCEPTS prejudice, stereotype, ingroup bias, scapegoat theory, just-world phenomenon, aggression, frustration-aggression principle, conflict, social trap, mere exposure effect, passionate love, companionate love, equity, self-disclosure, altruism, bystander effect, social exchange theory, superordinate goals, GRIT

TERMS AND CONCEPTS TO REMEMBER

CRITICAL THINKING EXERCISE
by Richard O. Straub

Now that you have read and reviewed Chapter 18, take your learning a step further by testing your critical thinking skills on the following pattern recognition exercise (adapted from Zechmeister & Johnson, 1992).

Write down three characteristics or descriptions that you associate with each of the following groups of people.

Physicians:

Athletes:

Artists:

Vegetarians:

College Students:

Lawyers:

With which of these groups do you most closely identify? With which do you least identify? The group with which you most closely identify can be considered one of your ingroups; the one that you feel most unlike is one of your outgroups.

1. Was it easier to come up with descriptions for your ingroup or for your outgroup?

2. Are your descriptions of your ingroup and outgroup equally favorable? If not, why do you think this is so?

3. In the answer key you will find ingroup and outgroup descriptions made by a group of college students. Before looking at it, decide whether your ingroup or your outgroup descriptions are more likely to match those of the other college students. How would you explain this phenomenon?

Check your progress on becoming a critical thinker by comparing your answers to the sample answers found in Appendix B.

FOR FURTHER INFORMATION

More information on **culture and muticultural experience** can be found on the following pages:

More information on **the psychology of women and men** can be found on the following pages:

appendix A

Statistical Reasoning

Science fiction writer H. G. Wells predicted that "statistical thinking will one day be as necessary for efficient citizenship as the ability to read and write." That day has arrived. Today's statistics are tools that help us see and interpret what the unaided eye might miss.

Unaided by statistics, top-of-the-head estimates often misread reality and mislead the public. Someone throws out a big round number, which others echo. Before long the big round number becomes a public myth. A few examples:

- 1 percent of Americans (2.6 million) are homeless. Or is it 300,000, as earlier estimated by the federal government? Or 600,000, as estimated by the Urban Institute (Crossen, 1994)?

- 10 percent of people are homosexual. Or is it 2 to 3 percent, as suggested by various national surveys (Chapter 12)?

- We ordinarily use but 10 percent of our brain. Or is it closer to 100 percent? (Which 90 percent, or even 10 percent, would you be willing to sacrifice?)

- Two-thirds of married men and half of married women have had an affair. Or is it more like only 1 in 7, as suggested in careful surveys in several countries (Chapter 1)?

The point to remember: Doubt big, round, un-documented numbers.

Describing Data

Researchers or not, we all make observations or gather data that we must organize and interpret. Let's see how we might effectively do this.

Distributions

Laura is a college admissions officer. Attempting to predict which currently enrolled students succeed at her school, she sorts through their high school grades, aptitude scores, biographical statements, recommendation letters, and subsequent college grades. But there is too much information to remember. Moreover, she knows that impressions are swayed by remembered information, often the vivid or extreme instances. So she starts by laying out the basic data on a small random sample of students (Table A.1).

She is first interested in how these students did in high school. She therefore displays the applicants' precollege grade-point averages as a bar graph (Figure A.1). By showing the number of GPAs within a particular interval as a bar, Laura

Table A.1

Laura's Sample Data

Student	Precollege GPA	College GPA	SAT	Family Income
Andrea	2.1	1.6	950	$ 15,000
Bubba	2.9	2.8	720	20,000
Cindy	3.7	3.6	1350	30,000
Dang Cho	3.1	3.9	1100	20,000
Ezekiel	3.4	3.1	1100	40,000
Fiona	2.9	2.6	775	20,000
Gamal	2.7	3.3	750	25,000
Hope	2.0	2.4	800	45,000
Huong	3.5	2.7	1010	70,000
Jae-Min	3.9	3.5	1375	475,000
Kraig	3.4	3.7	820	30,000
Larry	3.1	2.5	1105	15,000
Malachi	3.4	3.3	800	50,000
Manuel	3.3	3.3	1120	25,000
Maria	3.5	3.6	900	710,000
Mark	3.6	4.0	1370	45,000
Nicole	2.9	2.2	875	35,000
Nobuyuki	3.2	2.1	1180	25,000
Ralph	2.7	2.8	1065	35,000
Renae	3.9	3.3	1130	20,000
Rochelle	2.3	2.5	725	30,000
Rowland	2.8	2.5	700	40,000
Tammy	3.0	3.5	1270	20,000
Tiffany	3.1	2.7	810	25,000
Timothy	3.5	2.9	900	90,000
Todd	3.8	3.2	940	20,000
Wilbur	2.6	2.1	750	30,000
Xandria	3.5	3.3	1020	20,000
Xin	4.0	3.8	1400	45,000
Yolanda	3.1	2.8	900	30,000

Figure **A.1**

Bar graph High school
GPAs of 30 students.

Number of students

GPAs: 2.01–2.40 2.41–2.80 2.81–3.20 3.21–3.60 3.61–4.0

percentile rank
the percentage of the scores in a distribution that fall below a given score.

mode
the most frequently occurring score in a distribution.

mean
the arithmetic average of a distribution, obtained by adding the scores and then dividing by the number of scores.

median
the middle score in a distribution; half the scores are above it and half are below it.

can see approximately where any particular student's GPA falls relative to the others. She can also express any student's ranking as a <u>percentile rank</u>, which states the percentage of scores that fall below a particular score. A student whose percentile rank is 99 has a GPA that exceeds those of 99 percent of all the students. (You can never have a percentile rank of 100. Your score can never exceed those of 100 percent of the people because you are one of them.)

A note of caution: Take care when reading statistical graphs (Figure A.2). Depending on what people want to emphasize, they can design the graph to make the same difference look small or big. *The point to remember:* When looking at statistical graphs in books and magazines and on television ads and news broadcasts, think critically. Always read the scale labels and note their range.

Central Tendencies

Laura wonders: What are typical precollege grades and family income levels among her college's students? That is, what is a representative or *central tendency*? For any distribution of scores there are three commonly used measures of the central tendency. The simplest is the <u>mode</u>, the most frequently occurring score. The most commonly reported is the <u>mean</u>, or arithmetic average—the total sum of all the scores divided by the number of scores. (From calculating your grade-point average, you are familiar with the mean.) The <u>median</u> is the middle score—the 50th percentile; if you arrange all the scores in order from the highest to the lowest, half will be above the median and half will be below it.

Figure **A.2**

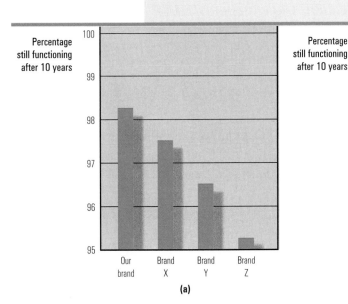

Percentage still functioning after 10 years

Our brand / Brand X / Brand Y / Brand Z

(a)

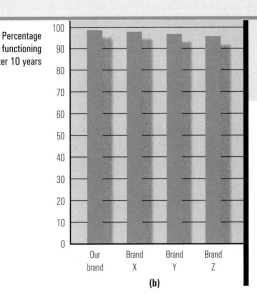

Percentage still functioning after 10 years

Our brand / Brand X / Brand Y / Brand Z

(b)

Read the scale labels An American truck manufacturer offered graph (a)—with actual brand names included—to suggest the much greater durability of its trucks. Note, however, how the apparent difference shrinks as the vertical scale changes in graph (b).

range
the difference between the highest and lowest scores in a distribution.

standard deviation
a measure of score variability; computed by (1) calculating the deviation of each score from the mean, (2) squaring those deviations, (3) finding their average, and (4) finding the square root of this average.

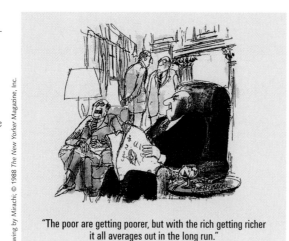

"The poor are getting poorer, but with the rich getting richer it all averages out in the long run."

Drawing by Mirachi; © 1988 *The New Yorker Magazine, Inc.*

If Microsoft founder Bill Gates were to move to a town with 24,000 penniless people, his 1997 net worth of $24 billion would instantly make its average (mean) resident a millionaire.

The point to remember: Always note which measure of central tendency is reported. Then, if it is a mean, consider whether a few atypical scores could be distorting it.

Measures of central tendency neatly summarize data. Laura can report, for example, that her student sample has a mean precollege GPA of 3.16. But consider what happens to the mean when a distribution is lopsided or *skewed* (rather than symmetrical). As Figure A.3 shows with the family income data, the mode, median, and mean tell different stories. This is because the mean is biased by a few extreme scores (in this case, the two families with very high income). To say her students have a mean family income of $70,000 is true but

misleading. Understanding this, you can see how a British newspaper could accurately run the headline "Income for 62% Is Below Average" (Waterhouse, 1993). Because the bottom *half* of British income earners receive only a *quarter* of the national income cake, most British people, like most people everywhere, make less than the mean.

Variation

Knowing the value of an appropriate measure of central tendency can tell us a great deal. But it also helps to know how similar or diverse the scores are. Thus, Laura wonders: How much do my students vary from one another?

Averages derived from scores with low variability are more reliable than averages based on scores with high variability. Consider a basketball player who scored between 13 and 17 points in each of her first 10 games in a season. Knowing this, we would be more confident that she would score near 15 points in her next game than if her scores had varied from 5 to 25 points.

The range of scores—the gap between the lowest and highest scores—provides only a crude estimate of variation because just one extreme score in an otherwise uniform group will create a deceptively large range. The $695,000 income range in Laura's sample is misleadingly large ($710,000 − $15,000) because all but the two highest incomes range between $15,000 and $90,000.

The more standard measure of how much scores deviate from one another is the standard deviation.

Figure A.3

A skewed distribution This graphic representation of the distribution of incomes illustrates the three measures of central tendency—mode, median, and mean. Note how just a few high incomes make the mean—the fulcrum point that balances the incomes above and below—deceptively high.

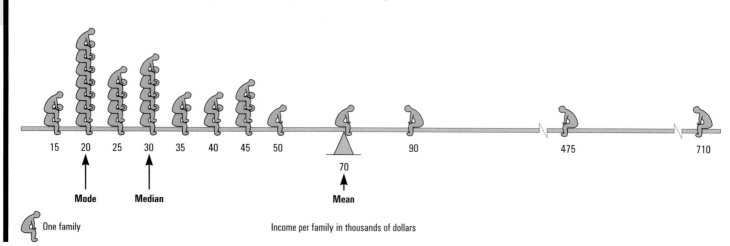

Income per family in thousands of dollars

Standard Deviation

Punting Distance	Deviation From Mean (40 Yards)	Deviation Squared
36	−4	16
38	−2	4
41	+1	1
45	+5	25

Mean = 160/4 = 40   Sum of (deviations)² = 46

$$\text{Standard deviation} = \sqrt{\frac{\text{Sum of (deviations)}^2}{\text{Number of scores}}} = \sqrt{\frac{46}{4}} = 3.4 \text{ yards}$$

It better gauges whether scores are packed together or dispersed, because it uses information from each score. The standard deviation is important and not hard to compute: (1) Calculate the difference, or deviation, between each score and the mean; (2) square these deviations; (3) find their average; and (4) find the square root of this average.

As an example, consider Peter, the punter on his college football team. To keep track of his progress, he records the distance of each of his punts. He does not trust his gut-level impression of how consistent his punting is. After his first football game, Peter therefore calculates the standard deviation for his four punts (Table A.2).

To grasp the meaning of this statistic, Peter would need to understand how scores tend to be distrib-

uted. In nature, large numbers of data—heights, weights, intelligence scores, grades, punt distances (though not incomes)—often form a roughly symmetrical, bell-shaped distribution. Most cases fall near the mean, and fewer cases fall near either extreme. This bell-shaped distribution is so typical that we call the curve it forms the <u>normal curve</u>.

As Figure A.4 shows, a useful property of the normal curve is that roughly 68 percent of the cases fall within 1 standard deviation on either side of the mean (in Peter's case, within 3.4 yards of his 40-yard average). About 95 percent of cases fall within 2 standard deviations. Thus, Chapter 11 notes that about 68 percent of people taking an intelligence test will score within ±15 points of 100. About 95 percent will score within ±30 points.

Figure **A.4**

The normal curve Large samples of data often form a normal, or bell-shaped, curve in which 68 percent of the cases fall within 1 standard deviation of the mean and 95 percent fall within 2 standard deviations. For example, on an intelligence test such as the WAIS, we assign the mean a value of 100 and 1 standard deviation equals 15 points. Therefore 68 percent of the scores fall between 85 and 115, and 95 percent fall between 70 and 130 on this test.

normal curve
a symmetrical, bell-shaped curve that describes the distribution of many types of data; most scores fall near the mean (68 percent fall within 1 standard deviation of it) and fewer and fewer near the extremes. Also called *normal distribution*.

Correlation

In this book we often ask how much two things relate: How closely related are the personality scores of identical twins? How well do intelligence test scores predict achievement? How often does stress lead to disease? To get a feel for whether one set of scores relates to a second set, we can display the data as a scatterplot. Figure A.5(a) depicts the actual relationship between Scholastic Assessment Test scores and college GPAs for Laura's 30 students. Each point on the graph represents these two numbers for one student. Figure A.5(b) is a scatterplot of the relationship between these students' precollege and college GPAs.

The correlation coefficient is a statistical measure of how strongly related any two sets of scores are. Its possible range is as follows:

- **+1.00**, which means that one set of scores increases in direct proportion to the other's increase.

- **0.00**, meaning that the scores are unrelated.

- **−1.00**, which means that one set of scores goes up precisely as the other goes down.

How to Read a Correlation Coefficient

(Note that a correlation's being negative has nothing to do with its strength or weakness; a negative correlation means two things relate inversely. A weak correlation, indicating little or no relationship, is one that has a coefficient near zero.) Now look again at the scatterplots in Figure A.5. Do the correlations look positive or negative?

In each scatterplot in Figure A.5, the upward, oval-shaped slope of the cluster of points as one moves to the right shows that the two sets of scores tend to rise together. This means the correlations are positive: a +.50 correlation for the SAT–college GPA relationship shown in Figure A.5(a), and a

Perfect positive correlation (+1.00)

No relationship (0.00)

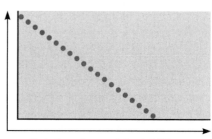

Perfect negative correlation (−1.00)

stronger +.69 for the precollege GPA–college GPA relationship shown in Figure A.5(b). High SAT scores and, especially, high precollege grades, predict high college grades. (The high school–college GPA relationship, incidentally, illustrates the common finding that the best predictor of people's future behavior is usually their behavior in similar situations in the past. The best predictor of future grades is past grades, which reflect both aptitude and motivation. Still, people do sometimes change.)

Statistics can help us see what the naked eye sometimes misses. To demonstrate this for yourself, try to discern what relationship, if any, exists between two sets of scores not yet organized into a scatterplot. Alessandra wonders whether men's heights correlate with their temperaments. She measures the heights of 20 men, has someone else independently assess their temperaments (from zero for extremely calm to 100 for highly reactive), and obtains the data in Table A.3.

With all the relevant data right in front of you, can you tell whether there is (1) a positive correlation between height and reactive temperament, (2) very little or no correlation, or (3) a negative correlation?

Figure A.5

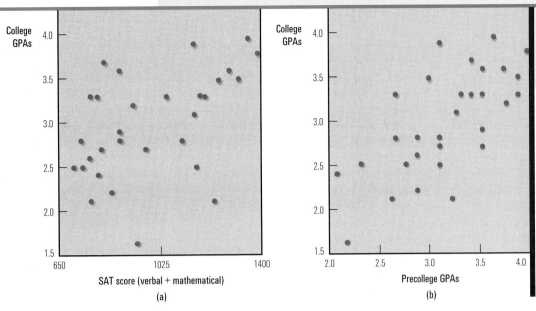

Scatterplots Plot (a) shows, for 30 actual students, the relationship between total Scholastic Assessment Test scores (verbal plus mathematical) and college GPAs. Plot (b) shows the closer relationship between precollege and college GPAs for 30 college students. Each point represents the data for one student.

Comparing the columns in Table A.3, most people detect very little relationship between height and temperament. In fact, the correlation in this imaginary example is moderately positive, +.57, as you could see if you made a scatterplot of the data. If we fail to see a relationship when data are presented as systematically as in this table, how much less likely are we to notice them in everyday life? To see what is right in front of us, we sometimes need statistical illumination. People can easily see evidence of gender discrimination when given statistically summarized information about job level, seniority, performance, gender, and salary. But they often see no discrimination when the same information dribbles in, case by case (Twiss & others, 1989).

The point to remember: Although the correlation coefficient tells us nothing about cause and effect, it *can* help us see the world more clearly by revealing the actual extent to which two things relate.

Correlations not only make visible the relationships that we might otherwise miss, they also restrain our "seeing" nonexistent relationships. As Chapter 1 explained, a perceived correlation that does not really exist is an *illusory correlation.* When we *believe* there is a relationship between two things, we are likely to *notice* and *recall* instances that confirm our belief. If we believe that dreamt events are forecasts of actual events, we may notice and recall confirming instances more than disconfirming instances. The result is an illusory correlation.

Height and Temperament of 20 Men

Table A.3

Subject	Height in Inches	Temperament
1	80	75
2	63	66
3	61	60
4	79	90
5	74	60
6	69	42
7	62	42
8	75	60
9	77	81
10	60	39
11	64	48
12	76	69
13	71	72
14	66	57
15	73	63
16	70	75
17	63	30
18	71	30
19	68	84
20	70	39

regression toward the mean
the tendency for extremes of unusual scores to fall back (regress) toward the average.

> "The real purpose of [the] scientific method is to make sure Nature hasn't misled you into thinking you know something that you actually don't."
>
> **ROBERT PIRSIG,**
> *ZEN AND THE ART OF MOTORCYCLE MAINTENANCE* 1974

Illusory correlations feed an *illusion of control*—that chance events are subject to our personal control. Gamblers, remembering their lucky rolls, may come to believe they can influence the roll of the dice by again throwing gently for low numbers and hard for high numbers. The illusion that uncontrollable events correlate with our actions is also fed by a statistical phenomenon called regression toward the mean. Average results are more typical than extreme results. Thus, after an unusual event, things tend to return toward their average level; extraordinary happenings tend to be followed by more ordinary ones.

Examples are abundant: Basketball players who make or miss all their shots in the first half of the game are likely to "regress" (fall back) to their more usual performance level during the second half. Students who score much lower or higher on an exam than they usually do are likely, when retested, to regress toward their average. Unusual ESP subjects who defy chance when first tested nearly always lose their "psychic powers" when retested (a phenomenon parapsychologists have called the "decline effect").

The point may seem obvious, yet we often miss it. Thus, we sometimes attribute what may be a normal statistical regression (the expected falling back to normal) to something we have done. Consider:

- After a sudden crime wave, the town council initiates a "stop crime" drive and the crime rate then returns to previous levels. The drive may therefore appear more successful than it was.

- Coaches who yell at their players after an unusually bad first half may feel rewarded for having done so when the team's performance improves (returns to normal) during the second half.

- Scientists who win a Nobel prize often have diminished accomplishments thereafter, leading some to wonder whether winning a Nobel hinders creativity.

- Some people also believe there is a "*Sports Illustrated* jinx"—that athletes whose peak performances get them on the cover of the magazine will then suffer a decline in their performance.

In each of these cases, it is possible that the effect is genuine. It is more likely, however, that each represents the natural tendency for behavior to regress from the unusual to the more usual.

Failure to recognize regression is the source of many superstitions and of some ineffective practices as well. When day-to-day behavior has a large element of chance fluctuation, we may notice that others' behavior improves (regresses toward average) after we criticize them for very bad performance, and that it worsens (regresses toward average) after we warmly praise them for an exceptionally fine performance. Ironically, then, regression toward the average can mislead us into feeling rewarded for having criticized others and into feeling punished for having praised them (Tversky & Kahneman, 1974).

The point to remember: When a fluctuating behavior returns to normal, there is no need to invent fancy explanations for why it does so. Regression toward the mean is probably at work.

> "Once you become sensitized to it, you see regression everywhere."
>
> **PSYCHOLOGIST DANIEL KAHNEMAN (1985)**

Statistical Inference

Data are "noisy." One group's average score (women's salaries) could conceivably differ from another's (men's salaries) not because of any real difference but merely due to chance fluctuation in the people sampled. So how confidently can we infer that an observed difference is reliable?

When Is It Safe to Generalize From a Sample?

In deciding whether to generalize from our samples, three principles are worth keeping in mind. Let's look at each in turn.

1 **Representative samples are better than biased samples.** As Chapter 1 explained, the best basis for generalizing is not from the exceptional, memorable cases one finds at the extremes but from a representative sample of cases. No research involves a representative sample of the whole human population. Thus, it pays to keep in mind what population a study has sampled.

2 **Less variable observations are more reliable than those that are more variable.** As we noted in the example of the basketball player whose scores were consistent, an average is more reliable when it comes from scores with low variability.

3 **More cases are better than fewer.** An eager high school senior visits two college campuses, each for a day. At the first, the student randomly attends three classes and discovers each instructor to be witty and engaging. At the next campus, the three sampled instructors seem dull and uninspiring. Returning home, the student tells friends about the "great teachers" at the first school, and the "bores" at the second school. Again, we know it but we ignore it: Small samples provide less reliable estimates of the average than do large samples. The proportion of heads in samples of 10 coin tosses varies more than in samples of 100 tosses.

Said differently, *averages based on more cases are more reliable* (less variable) than averages based on only a few cases. Knowing this, answer a question posed by Christopher Jepson, David Krantz, and Richard Nisbett (1983) to University of Michigan introductory psychology students:

The registrar's office at the University of Michigan has found that usually about 100 students in Arts and Sciences have a 4.00 GPA at the end of their first term at the University. However, only about 10 to 15 students graduate with a 4.00 GPA. What do you think is the most likely explanation for the fact that there are more 4.00 GPAs after one term than at graduation?

How did you answer? Most of the students in the study came up with plausible causes for the drop in GPA, such as, "Students tend to work harder at the beginning of their college careers than toward the end." Fewer than a third recognized the statistical phenomenon clearly at work: Averages based on fewer courses are more variable, which guarantees a greater number of extremely low and high GPAs at the end of the first term.

The point to remember: Don't be overly impressed by a few anecdotes. Generalizations based on only a few cases are unreliable.

When Is a Difference Significant?

We can have most confidence when generalizing from samples that (1) are representative of the population we wish to study, (2) give us consistent rather than highly variable data, and (3) are large rather than small. These principles extend to the inferences we make about differences between groups—as when we generalize from a gender difference in grades in our sample to the whole campus population.

Statistical tests help us decide by indicating the reliability of differences. You needn't understand how they are computed to understand the logic behind them: When *averages* from two samples are each *reliable* measures of their respective populations (as when each is based on many observations that have small variability), then the difference between the samples is likely to be reliable as well. When the *difference* between the averages for the two samples is *large*, we have even more confidence that the difference between them reflects a real difference in their populations.

In short, *when the sample averages are reliable and the difference between them is large*, we say the difference has statistical significance. This simply means that the difference probably reflects a real difference and is not due to chance variation between the samples. In judging statistical significance, psychologists are conservative. They are like juries who must assume innocence unless guilt is proven, because they would rather risk setting free a guilty person than convicting an innocent person. For most psychologists, proof beyond a reasonable doubt means not making much of a finding unless the odds of its occurring by chance are less than 5 percent (an arbitrary criterion).

statistical significance
a statistical statement of how likely it is that an obtained result occurred by chance.

PEANUTS

When reading about research, you should remember that, given large enough or homogeneous enough samples, a difference between them may be "statistically significant" yet have little practical significance. For example, when comparing the intelligence test scores among several hundred thousand first-born and later-born individuals, there is a highly significant tendency for first-born individuals within a family to have higher average scores than their later-born siblings—but only by one or two points (Zajonc & Markus, 1975). Some psychologists therefore advocate alternatives to significance testing (Hunter, 1997). Better, they say, to use other ways to express a finding's magnitude and reliability.

The point to remember: Statistical significance indicates the *likelihood* that a result will happen by chance. It does not indicate the *importance* of the result.

SUMMING UP

To be an educated person today is to be able to apply simple statistical principles to everyday reasoning. One needn't remember complicated formulas to think more clearly and critically about data.

From our consideration of how we can organize and describe data—by constructing distributions and computing measures of central tendency, variation, correlation, and statistical significance—we derived seven important points to remember when assessing studies that use statistical reasoning:

1. Doubt big, round, undocumented numbers.

2. When looking at statistical graphs in books and magazines and on television ads and news broadcasts, think critically: Always read the scale labels and note their range.

3. Always note which measure of central tendency is reported. Then, if it is a mean, consider whether a few atypical scores could be distorting it.

4. Although the correlation coefficient tells us nothing about cause and effect, it *can* help us see the world more clearly by revealing the actual extent to which two things relate.

5. When a fluctuating behavior returns to normal, there is no need to invent fancy explanations for why it does so. Regression toward the mean is probably at work.

6. Don't be overly impressed by a few anecdotes. Generalizations based on only a few cases are unreliable.

7. Statistical significance indicates the *likelihood* that a result will occur by chance. It does not indicate the importance of the result.

TERMS AND CONCEPTS TO REMEMBER

percentile rank, p. 595

mode, p. 595

mean, p. 595

median, p. 595

range, p. 596

standard deviation, p. 596

normal curve, p. 597

scatterplot, p. 598

correlation coefficient, p. 598

regression toward the mean, p. 600

statistical significance, p. 601

appendix B

Sample Answers to Critical Thinking Exercises

Most psychology courses have two major goals: (1) to help you acquire a basic understanding of psychology's knowledge base, and (2) to help you learn to think like a psychologist. The second goal—learning to think like a psychologist—involves critical thinking. Critical thinking can be regarded as a special set of "thinking skills that promote conscious, purposeful, and active involvement of the thinker with new ideas" (Halonen, 1994). Included among these skills are careful observation, asking questions, seeing connections among ideas, and the ability to analyze arguments and the evidence on which they are based.

The critical thinking exercises in this textbook have been designed to help you develop your ability to think critically as you learn about psychology.[1] Each exercise emphasizes one of six categories of critical thinking: *pattern recognition*, *practical problem solving*, *creative problem solving*, *scientific problem solving*, *psychological reasoning*, and *perspective taking*.

As the foundation for all other forms of critical thinking, *pattern recognition* is the ability to use psychological concepts to describe behavior patterns and events, especially when your expectation of what is normal in a certain situation is different from what actually occurs.

When events or behaviors are unexpected, they may constitute a problem. *Practical problem solving* is the ability to use psychological concepts to develop a plan of action that will lead to the problem's solution.

Creative problem solving is the ability to make novel connections between previously unrelated ideas. This type of critical thinking often leads to new insights about behavior and mental phenomena.

Psychologists employ the scientific method to develop comprehensive and systematic explanations of behavior and mental phenomena. At the heart of this is *scientific problem solving*, which seeks to uncover relationships among the many factors, or variables, involved in producing behavior.

Psychological information is transmitted through persuasive arguments that state a relationship be-

[1]The model for these exercises comes from J. S. Halonen (1994), *Critical thinking companion for introductory psychology.* New York: Worth Publishers, Inc.

tween some aspect of behavior, such as intelligence, and another factor, such as age. *Psychological reasoning* is thinking critically about such arguments, especially the evidence on which they are based.

The final category of critical thinking is *perspective taking*, which refers to the ability to recognize the ways in which each person's thinking is shaped by his or her values and past experiences.

You should now be ready to expand your critical thinking skills by completing the exercises prepared for each chapter of your textbook. For some chapters, the exercise presents a hypothetical situation that you will need to think through. For others, you will be asked to evaluate arguments that are derived from actual psychological research. And for still other chapters, your understanding of psychological concepts will be tested by asking you to apply them to a new situation. Carefully read the passage for each exercise and then answer the questions that follow.

Polish your critical thinking skills by applying them to each of your college courses, and to other aspects of life as well. Learn to think critically about advertising, political speeches, and the material presented in popular periodicals.

CHAPTER 1
Thinking Critically With Psychological Science

Scientific Problem Solving

1 *Focal behavior:* Reading ability among first graders.

2 *Hypothesis:* Children who watch *Sesame Street* develop greater reading ability than children who watch cartoons.

3 *Independent variable:* Type of television program (educational versus cartoon).

4 *Dependent variable:* Reading test score.

5 *Controlled variables:*
   (a) Television program content (educational versus noneducational) during the daily, 1-hour period of exposure.
   (b) Ages of subjects.
   (c) Reading ability measured over the same time period.

6 *Uncontrolled variables:*
   (a) Absence of random assignment leaves alternative explanations for reading improvement in the educational television group. As volunteers, the *Sesame Street* subjects may have been more highly motivated to have their children succeed in reading than the cartoon subjects, who were drafted.
   (b) Reading ability of subjects in the two groups was not measured before the experiment began. At the outset, the *Sesame Street* subjects may have

had higher reading scores than the cartoon subjects.

   (c) Knowledge of the teacher's hypothesis (by both students and their parents) may have influenced the results so that the experimental group outperformed the control group.

   (d) Other daily activities, such as reading to parents or watching other television programs, might have differentially influenced the reading skills in the two groups.

7 *Valid test of hypothesis?* No. Since so many variables were not controlled, virtually nothing can be concluded from this study. A more valid test would have *randomly assigned* volunteers, who were *not informed* of the teacher's hypothesis and who had been pretested and matched for comparable reading ability to the two groups.

CHAPTER 2
Neuroscience and Behavior

Pattern Recognition

Lower-Level Brain Structures	How the Structures Are Involved in Musical Performance
Medulla	This structure controls heartbeat, breathing, and other vital systems that keep the musician's body functioning while he or she plays.
Thalamus	By routing sensory information from the musician's eyes, ears, and fingertips to higher brain regions, this structure facilitates the musician's seeing, hearing, touching, decision making, and coordination.
Reticular formation	By helping to control arousal, this structure is crucial in maintaining the musician's attention to the task.
Hippocampus	This structure is involved in the formation of memories for musical theory, as well as of memories of how to play the musical instrument.
Cerebellum	This structure helps coordinate movements involved in playing the instrument.
Motor cortex	This area is involved in organizing the body movements necessary for playing the instrument.
Sensory cortex	This area is involved in processing incoming sensory information from the musician's fingertips.
Association areas	These areas are involved in the planning and decision making in-

Corpus callosum — herent in reading music and playing the instrument.
This area is involved in combining information processed by the left and right hemispheres so that the performance reflects the integrated activity of both sides of the brain.

CHAPTER 3
The Developing Child

Perspective Taking

1   *Eighteen-month-old child's experience of the world:* During Piaget's sensorimotor stage, children understand the world through their senses and actions.

2   *Appropriate activities:* This age group would be most stimulated by a variety of visually interesting toys that foster stacking, banging, rolling, and fitting things together.

3   *Five-year-old-child's experience of the world:* During Piaget's preoperational stage, children understand the world through pretend play that typically is egocentric.

4   *Appropriate activities:* Preoperational children would enjoy activities that are based on pretend play. Dress-up and make-believe games of "go-to-work" and "school" would be appropriate.

5   *Eight-year-old child's experience of the world:* During Piaget's concrete operational stage, children reason logically about concrete events.

6   *Appropriate activities:* Arithmetic games, card games, and other activities based on logical thinking about concrete events would be appropriate activities for this age group.

7   *Twelve-year-old child's experience of the world:* Youngsters who are on the threshold of formal operational thinking reason abstractly about events in their lives.

8   *Appropriate activities:* Problem-solving activities, "who-dunnit?" games, and role-playing games based on hypothetical propositions and deductive reasoning would be stimulating activities for this age group.

CHAPTER 4
Adolescence and Adulthood

Psychological Reasoning

1   Mary's argument is that her father is suffering from Alzheimer's disease, which is causing his memory to lapse occasionally and his thinking to be uncharacteristically slow.

2   The evidence for Mary's argument comes from her daily observations of her father's behavior and the memory "experiment" she conducted.

3   Mary's evidence is not trustworthy for at least three reasons. *First,* informal observations of this type are subjective and unreliable. Since she recently read an article on Alzheimer's disease, Mary may be looking too hard for symptoms of this disorder. Her expectations may bias her observations. *Second,* Mary is comparing her father's performance on the memory "experiment" only with her recollection of his former quick thinking and excellent memory. To be a valid test, Mary would need to have actual data on how her father would have performed on this test *before* he began to display the memory symptoms that are the basis for her concern. *Third,* even if Bentley's thinking ability has changed recently, the cause of the change has not been pinpointed. True experiments rule out the potential effects of other variables. It may be that Bentley's uncharacteristically poor performance is the result of his generally poor health, the medication he is taking for his muscle tremors (which is known to produce Alzheimer's-like symptoms), or his lack of physical and intellectual stimulation since retiring.

(By the way, the answer to Mary's brain teaser—an expanding alphabetical sequence—is *m*.)

CHAPTER 5
Sensation

Psychological Reasoning

1   Several assertions are made: (1) There is an unconscious component of the mind; (2) the unconscious mind is capable of perceiving stimuli that are below the threshold of conscious awareness; (3) subliminal stimuli have motivational power; and (4) subliminal suggestions can persuade a person to quit smoking.

2   The evidence is Carlos's expressed preference for a stimulus (the triangle) to which he had been repeatedly exposed. The evidence is not trustworthy for several reasons. For one, it assumes that Carlos had no initial preference for one geometric form over another. In the absence of some sort of preference pretest, there is no basis to conclude that the subliminal stimulus presentations directly caused his choice of the triangle. Second, the demonstration was based on *visual* stimuli, but the smoking cessation program is based on *auditory* suggestions. There is no evidence that the audio stimuli will be as persuasive as visual stimuli. Moreover, the triangle preference is a trivial choice—probably easier to influence than the drive for nicotine.

3   "Subliminal" merely means that a stimulus is *below* the intensity at which it can be detected half the time. Since Carlos was aware of flashes of light, he may actually have detected the triangle presentations at least part of the time. Thus, his preference for the triangle was not necessarily the result of *unconscious* thought processes, but simply the result of repeated exposure to a specific stimulus. So, it is inappropriate to assume that subliminal visual (or audio) stimuli have an irresistible power to motivate or persuade.

CHAPTER 6
Perception

Practical Problem Solving

Figure-Ground: This grouping principle enables us to perceive any object, called the *figure*, as distinct from its surroundings, called the *ground*. Web text, buttons, and graphics (the "figures") need to be bright and obvious against uncomplicated backgrounds (the "grounds"). Your viewers will miss important information if it has to compete for attention with a background that is either too busy or that does not provide enough contrast with the "figures" (for instance, if colors are too similar, figure can't easily be distinguished from ground).

Similarity: If figures look similar to each other, we group them together. Understanding this principle will help you provide consistency across the pages of a Web site. This should make your viewers feel more comfortable and help them locate what they are looking for more easily. For example, you may want to use the company logo as a consistent element on each page of the Web site. On a more basic level, consistent paragraph formatting, text size, fonts, and color can all be used to increase readability and the ease of navigation through a Web site.

Relative Brightness: Because nearby objects reflect more light to our eyes, dimmer objects seem farther away. You can use this principle to your advantage by effectively using light, shade, and shadow to add the visual appeal of three-dimensional Web graphics and text.

Size-Distance Relationship: Perceiving an object's general size provides us with cues to its distance. As with any two-dimensional representation of depth, Web graphics rely on size constancy and the size-distance relationship to convey the perceptual impression of nearness and farness from the viewer. Effective Web page designs scale the size of graphics to indicate the importance of particular topics. Larger graphics appear closer and more important. Smaller graphics appear farther away and less important.

Culture and Perception: Cultural background influences nearly every aspect of perception, from how our eyes scan a page, to our sensitivity to monocular depth cues, to our emotional response to color. So you will want to pay close attention, for example, to the placement of items at your site. In Western cultures people read from top to bottom and from left to right. You will want to place the more important items near the top of a page, and keep in mind that the top left corner will get the most immediate attention. Well-positioned text and graphic elements capitalize on these tendencies to promote smooth eye flow (top to bottom and left to right) and subordination (read this first, read this next).

The effective use of color also illustrates cultural influences on perception. In the United States, for example, "cool colors" such as blue and green are perceived as soothing, while "warm colors" such as red and orange are perceived as more stimulating. As another example, the color red is often used to indicate danger, while green may represent financial information. So, you will want to incorporate colors into your site *carefully*, based on the messages you wish to convey and the emotional response you wish to evoke.

CHAPTER 7
States of Consciousness

Creative Problem Solving

1. Because insomnia complainers typically overestimate their loss of sleep, you might reasonably doubt the severity of your aunt's problem. In addition, the fact that she apparently is not irritable, unable to concentrate, or suffering from other common effects of sleep deprivation suggests that she may be exaggerating her sleep loss. You might help alleviate your aunt's anxiety by informing her that laboratory studies reveal that insomnia complainers underestimate the amount they sleep by nearly 50 percent. It is likely that she *thinks* she is sleeping very little because she is remembering only her waking moments.

   Being middle-aged, your aunt should be reminded that occasional awakenings are more likely than when she was younger, and that developmental changes in circadian arousal are quite normal. Older adults such as your aunt are more likely to feel at their best during the morning hours, with their alertness and performance efficiency declining as the day wears on.

2. In addition to reassuring your aunt that her problem is probably not worth fretting over, you should advise her that her napping, late-night exercising, and alcohol consumption may be contributing to her perceived sleep problems. To promote better sleep, she should avoid napping during the day, exercise regularly but not in the evening, avoid alcoholic drinks (which suppress REM sleep), and try to maintain a regular sleep/waking schedule.

3. As for your aunt's belief that she has stopped dreaming, you can safely reassure her that even people who claim they never dream will almost always report a dream if they are awakened when their eye movements and bodily arousal indicate REM sleep. And even if she is dreaming less, tell her that she needn't worry that lost

dreams will lead to psychological problems. Freud's theory that dreams provide a psychic safety valve has little support from contemporary psychologists, who emphasize instead the role of REM sleep in information processing.

To prove that she hasn't lost her ability to dream, your aunt might set an alarm to awaken her 15 minutes earlier one morning. Because REM periods are longer near a person's normal waking time, an early alarm is likely to arouse your aunt during a dream and improve her recollection.

4 Freud believed that by fulfilling our unconscious wishes, dreams discharge otherwise unacceptable feelings. According to this theory, a person who could not dream would therefore have no "psychic safety valve." The unresolved inner conflicts presumably would surface in other undesirable ways in the person's behavior and mental processes.

A physiological psychologist would probably emphasize the role of REM sleep in providing the brain with periodic stimulation. The absence of such stimulation might lead to deterioration in the brain's neural circuitry and result in lapses of memory, poor attention span, or other mental difficulties.

A cognitive psychologist would probably point to the role of REM sleep in information processing and memory. Without REM sleep, people might have more difficulty learning new information, retaining and retrieving knowledge, and coping with stressful experiences.

CHAPTER 8
Learning

Pattern Recognition

1 For children who learn to wake up without special training, the sensation of a wet bed or diaper functions as a UCS that elicits awakening, which is the UCR. Bladder tension (unless painful) is an initially neutral stimulus that becomes associated with the UCS. Over time, bladder tension becomes a CS and will cause the child to awaken before the bed or diaper is wet. This learned awakening is the CR.

2 For children who are trained with the special sheet and bell, the UCS is the bell that causes them to wake up; the UCR is waking up in response to the bell; the CS is bladder tension; and the CR is waking up in response to bladder tension.

3 Although the classical conditioning explanation for this example makes sense based on the evidence, an explanation based on operant conditioning is also possible. Although in very young children waking up is normally a reflexive act (and therefore subject to classical conditioning), in older children it might be considered a *voluntary* act (and therefore subject to operant conditioning). Children may learn to wake up because this behavior operates on the environment to produce rewarding stimuli, such as the pleasurable sensation of relieving one's bladder.

CHAPTER 9
Memory

Practical Problem Solving

1 The police are trying to identify the carjacker. For some reason, they suspect that Raymond committed the crime, and they are attempting to obtain more evidence by jogging Naomi's eyewitness memory.

2 Naomi was probably initially unable to identify the gunman because the fleeting glimpse did not allow her to encode the details of his appearance. The confusion of the moment may also have prevented Naomi from rehearsing her mental image of the perpetrator, allowing her memory to decay quickly. Moreover, seeing hundreds of mug-book photographs so soon after the crime could have retroactively interfered with whatever real memory Naomi had of the gunman's appearance. Finally, the mug book may not actually have contained the gunman's photograph.

3 The misleading questioning and repeated exposure to Raymond's photograph may have caused Naomi to misremember the actual event and to reconstruct her memory of it to include Raymond's involvement. Seeing the lineup of men several weeks later, Naomi may have been unable to discriminate her eyewitness memory from her memory of the mug-book photographs. This would also account for Naomi's newfound confidence in the accuracy of her memory.

CHAPTER 10
Thinking and Language

Perspective Taking

1 *Position supported*: B. F. Skinner's

Explanation: Marie's utterances can be explained by three principles of learning: imitation, association, and reinforcement. The first time she said "cow," she may merely have been imitating her mother's utterance. The fact that she later spontaneously identified a cow indicates that she had formed an association between the picture and the word and had been reinforced (by her mother's praise) for demonstrating her new knowledge.

2 *Position supported*: Noam Chomsky's

Explanation: Jack's grammatical error ("goed") is an example of overgeneralizing a grammatical rule (adding *–ed* to form the past tense of a regular verb). Because it is unlikely that Jack has ever heard his parents or teacher make this error, principles of learning cannot explain this utterance. Because all children make this type of error, the existence of a common underlying biological language acquisition device is implicated.

3 *Position supported*: B. F. Skinner's

Explanation: Nicole's deficiency in signing demonstrates the impact of early experience in language development.

4   *Position supported*: Noam Chomsky's

Explanation: Because Malcolm and Maya have presumably been exposed to English for the same number of years, principles of learning cannot explain the difference in their fluency. Chomsky would say that Maya was exposed to English too late in life for her inborn "language acquisition device" to benefit fully.

CHAPTER 11
Intelligence

Creative Problem Solving

1   Carlton considers intelligence to be a measurable, general mental capacity that forms the basis for all cognitive skills. His "intelligence test," however, only measures a collection of proofreading skills.

2   Although Carlton believes that intelligence is a single, *general* entity, he has created a test that taps a collection of *specific* abilities. Moreover, some of these abilities (such as spelling) may have little to do with intelligence. Carlton's problem is that he's confusing general intelligence with aptitude for an everyday task.

3   Carlton would be well advised to test potential employees on the actual skills they will be required to use in their jobs (or their aptitude for learning these skills). The first step would be to identify specific skills for *each job category* and then to devise separate, specialized tests. A test for potential managers, for example, might be based on *practical intelligence* skills, such as how to motivate people, when to delegate tasks, and how to write effective memos. Those whose job it is to find new topics for publication might be tested for skills involving *creative intelligence*. His proofreading test might work quite well for potential copyeditors.

CHAPTER 12
Motivation

Pattern Recognition

1   Assuming that Rochelle and Doreen have roughly equal ability, there must be another explanation for the difference in their school performance. Doreen's high grades, her motivation to select moderately challenging classes where success is attainable yet attributable to her own efforts, and her desire to do *her* best rather than compare herself to others point to a high level of achievement motivation. Rochelle's preference for very easy or very difficult tasks is typical of people with a lower need for achievement. In such situations, failure is either unlikely or unembarrassing because it is attributable to the impossibility of the task rather than the individual's performance. Because birth order correlates with achievement, parental influences may help explain why first-born Doreen apparently has higher achievement motivation than Rochelle. It is possible that Doreen received more attention and encouragement from her parents than did later-born Rochelle.

2   Initially, practicing the guitar was its own reward for Doreen; extrinsic rewards were unnecessary. The monetary reward her parents later provided may have *overjustified* guitar playing, turning it into a form of work and lessening Doreen's intrinsic enjoyment and, thus, her motivation for practicing. Rochelle's primary motive for learning the guitar apparently involved competing with her sister. This is an example of extrinsic motivation rather than motivation to master a skill for its own sake. The monetary reward offered by her parents provided an additional extrinsic incentive, to which Rochelle responded by increasing her practice time. When Doreen began to lose interest in practicing and the monetary reward was withdrawn, the extrinsic basis for Rochelle's motivation was lost. As a result Rochelle lost interest in playing the guitar.

3   The parents would be wise to recognize the different levels of achievement motivation in their daughters and to individualize their treatment in order to capitalize on this difference. As an independent "self-starter," Doreen will probably respond more to rewards that are informative rather than controlling. Praise and encouragement rather than extrinsic rewards will be more effective in boosting Doreen's feelings of competence and intrinsic motivation. For Rochelle, the parents first need to clarify their goal. If they want to do everything in their power to improve Rochelle's proficiency on the guitar, they might capitalize on her competitiveness by placing her in group classes where comparisons with others are inevitable. If they want to cultivate intrinsic motivation, they would do well to encourage greater independence in Rochelle by challenging her to reach her own potential as a musician and frequently praising her for her successes.

CHAPTER 13
Emotion

Scientific Problem Solving

1   The James-Lange theory proposes that the experience of emotion derives from our awareness of our physiological responses to emotion-arousing stimuli. It also equates different emotions with specific body states. Assuming that sexual excitement can be triggered by the physical changes induced by exercise, this theory would predict greater reported feelings of sexual excitement during the first two phases of exercise recovery, when the subjects were actually physically aroused, than during the third phase, when the subjects were no longer aroused. The fact that sexual excitement was low during the first phase of recovery, when physical arousal was high, seems to conflict with the theory.

2   The Cannon-Bard theory proposes that an emotion-arousing stimulus simultaneously triggers physical arousal and the subjective experience of emotion. Assuming that the film was an emotion-arousing stimulus, this theory would predict greater reported feelings of sexual excitement during all three phases of the experiment, because subjects viewed the film in each phase. However, this explanation is inconsistent with the find-

ing that subjects reported being sexually excited only during the second phase of the experiment. The theory offers no explanation of why the emotional experiences of subjects during phases 1 and 2 differed.

3   According to Schachter's two-factor theory, to experience an emotion one must be physically aroused and cognitively label that arousal as an emotion. Of the three theories, this one seems to explain the results of the experiment most fully. During the first phase, subjects were physically aroused, and a potential "emotional" explanation for their arousal (the film) was available. Because they *perceived* that they were still aroused from the exercise, however, subjects during this phase attributed their arousal to the exercise rather than to sexual excitement. By the third phase, the subjects had fully recovered from the exercise and lacked the physical arousal necessary to trigger the emotion-attribution process. In phase 2, the subjects were physically aroused but did not subjectively perceive this arousal. According to the two-factor theory, this unexplained arousal was therefore attributed to sexual excitement from the film.

CHAPTER 14
Personality

Perspective Taking

1   A psychoanalyst might explain Darren's problems as being rooted in unresolved childhood conflicts. His sarcastic manner might indicate that he was orally overindulged as a child and is fixated in the oral stage of psychosexual development. A psychoanalyst might also say that Darren's ego is attempting to defend itself from anxiety by offering a self-justifying explanation for his poor performance on the exam ("the test was unfair") in place of the real, more threatening reason for failure ("I was unprepared").

2   A trait theorist would probably describe Darren's personality in terms of characteristic behaviors and motives. According to the "Big Five" personality factors, for example, Darren might be described as anxious and self-pitying (emotional stability), sober and reserved (extraversion), suspicious and undisciplined (agreeableness and conscientiousness, respectively).

3   A humanistic theorist might explain Darren's pessimism and sarcastic manner as the result of low self-esteem and perhaps not having his basic needs met as his personality was formed. Humanistic theorists might also suggest that Darren has a negative self-concept because his ideal self (a successful college student) differs from his actual self (an academic failure). His unwillingness to accept responsibility for his failure might be described as a self-serving bias.

4   A social-cognitive theorist would probably point to the reciprocal influences among Darren's past behavior, internal personal factors, and external experiences in shaping his personality. His anxiety and unwillingness to accept responsibility for failure suggest that he perceives the world as threatening, and himself as being controlled by his environment. Darren's hopeless atti-

tude and external locus of control may have resulted from repeated experiences with undesirable events over which he had no control.

CHAPTER 15
Psychological Disorders

Perspective Taking

1   Phyllis's daughter should be more concerned; she may by wrongly attributing to old age what is really psychologically disordered behavior. Phyllis's behavior satisfies at least three of the criteria for such a label: It is atypical, disturbing, and maladaptive. Furthermore, although triggered by the stress of her divorce, her symptoms have persisted too long and are too extreme to be considered a normal, justifiable response to a stressful event. Phyllis's daughter is also misinterpreting the biological evidence: The grandmother's similar symptoms and the effectiveness of antidepressant medication are further evidence for a psychological disorder.

2   A clinical psychologist would argue that Phyllis is showing classic symptoms of *major depressive disorder*, including poor appetite, insomnia, lethargy, feelings of worthlessness, and loss of interest in family and friends. He or she would also point out that these symptoms have persisted much longer than would normally be expected following a stressful event.

3   (a) A biologically oriented therapist would cite two pieces of evidence: (1) Since her mother seems to have suffered depression in late middle age, Phyllis may have a genetic predisposition to this condition; and (2) the fact that an antidepressant drug made her feel less depressed suggests Phyllis's depression may be caused by a biochemical imbalance. (b) From the social-cognitive perspective, Phyllis's depression is fueled by a vicious cycle of overgeneralized, self-focused, negative thinking. She has explained a stressful experience (her divorce) in terms that are *stable* and *global* ("Everything I have ever done, or will do, is worthless") and *internal* ("The divorce is my fault"). The hopelessness resulting from these self-blaming attributions has elicited social rejection, has hampered her behavior, and is likely to lead to further negative experiences.

CHAPTER 16
Therapy

Practical Problem Solving

1   There are several possible reasons why psychotherapy was apparently effective for Deborah but not for Vincent. One is that cognitive therapies, such as Deborah's, have proven most successful in treating depression. Behavior therapies, such as the counterconditioning Vincent experienced, have proven to be more effective in treating specific behavior problems, such as phobias, compulsions, or sexual dysfunctions. A second reason is that Deborah actively sought and entered therapy at a

time of personal crisis, while Vincent felt that there was nothing unusual about his behavior or attitude. Deborah's depression may have lifted partly as a result of the passage of time and the lessening of the crisis. A third reason is that Deborah chose her therapist carefully, and she worked with someone who offered her hope that things would improve. Vincent picked his therapist randomly, maintained a skeptical attitude throughout therapy, and never admitted he needed help. Thus, Deborah's belief in her treatment could have created a powerful placebo effect that harnessed her own healing powers and led to improvement. Finally, Deborah invested considerably more time and money in her therapy than Vincent did. This would probably result in a stronger need to justify the therapy and, thus, a more favorable evaluation of its effectiveness.

2   Clients' perceptions of the effectiveness of psychotherapy are not acceptable as scientific evidence. One reason is that people who are suffering nonpsychotic disorders often improve whether or not they receive treatment. Psychotherapy clients who would have improved anyway might misattribute their improvement to therapy. Furthermore, people who go into therapy with the expectation that it will be effective may fall victim to the confirmation bias and remember only information that confirms their expectation.

CHAPTER 17
Stress and Health

Practical Problem Solving

1   Since her parents are both obese, it is likely that Janet inherited a genetic predisposition toward obesity and possibly a lower metabolic rate than Sheila. Janet may also have a higher body weight set point than Sheila.

2   Because her parents are of normal weight, it is likely that Sheila herself is genetically predisposed to be of normal body weight. It is also likely that Sheila has a lower body weight set point and a higher metabolic rate than Janet.

3   The diet Janet and Sheila chose was effective, but more effective for Sheila due to her genetic background. Janet, like her parents, is overweight, so it is likely that her body has a higher percentage of fat than does Sheila's. Because fat tissue has a low metabolic rate (and therefore takes less food energy than other tissues to maintain), Janet's body probably requires fewer calories to maintain its weight than does Sheila's. There is no reason to believe that Janet cheated on her diet for lack of willpower. Those genetically predisposed to obesity can eat the same foods, do the same amount of exercising, and still not lose weight as easily as those of normal body weight.

CHAPTER 18
Social Psychology

Pattern Recognition

1   If, like many people, you found it more difficult to generate descriptions of outgroups, this may be the result of your relatively limited contact with members of such groups.

2   If your ingroup descriptions were more favorable than your outgroup descriptions, you may be expressing a tendency to favor one's own group, called the ingroup bias.

3   When 50 college students were asked to describe each of these groups, their top five descriptions were as follows:

Physicians: (1) intelligent/smart; (2) caring/understanding/compassionate; (3) wealthy/rich; (4) busy/hardworking; (5) well-educated

Athletes: (1) athletic/fit/strong; (2) driven/highly motivated/dedicated; (3) competitive; (4) agile/quick; (5) glorified/famous/popular and egotistical/proud

Artists: (1) creative; (2) bizarre/strange; (3) freespirited/nonconforming/individualistic; (4) liberal/tolerant/open-minded; (5) talented/gifted

Vegetarians: (1) healthy/health-conscious; (2) environmentally or ecologically conscious; (3) limited in diet/picky about food; (4) caring/sensitive; (5) liberal

College Students: (1) fun/wild/exciting; (2) stressed/pressured/fatigued; (3) intelligent/bright; (4) diligent/dedicated/studious; (5) poor/broke and open-minded/tolerant/liberal

Lawyers: (1) articulate/convincing/persuasive; (2) deceptive/dishonest; (3) wealthy/rich; (4) intelligent/smart; (5) strong-willed/powerful and ambitious/success-oriented

If your outgroup descriptions match better with the above than your ingroup descriptions, it may reflect the human tendency to form stereotyped beliefs in order to simplify the world. In categorizing people into groups, we see the members of the outgroup as all alike, whereas the members of the ingroup are viewed as much more diverse.

glossary

absolute threshold the minimum stimulation needed to detect a particular stimulus. (p. 149)

accommodation (1) adapting one's current understandings (schemas) to incorporate new information. (p. 87) (2) the process by which the eye's lens changes shape to focus the image of near objects on the retina. (p. 155)

acetylcholine [ah-seat-el-KO-leen] **(ACh)** a neurotransmitter that, among its functions, triggers muscle contraction. (p. 45)

achievement motivation a desire for significant accomplishment: for mastery of things, people, or ideas; for attaining a high standard. (p. 384)

achievement test a test designed to assess what a person has learned. (p. 342)

acoustic encoding the encoding of sound, especially the sound of words. (p. 275)

acquisition the initial stage of learning, during which a response is established and gradually strengthened. In classical conditioning, the phase in which a stimulus comes to evoke a conditioned response. In operant conditioning, the strengthening of a reinforced response. (p. 248)

action potential a neural impulse; a brief electrical charge that travels down an axon. The action potential is generated by the movement of positively charged atoms in and out of channels in the axon's membrane. (p. 43)

active listening empathic listening in which the listener echoes, restates, and clarifies. A feature of Rogers's person-centered therapy. (p. 491)

acuity the sharpness of vision. (p. 156)

adaptation-level phenomenon our tendency to form judgments (of sounds, of lights, of income) relative to a "neutral" level defined by our prior experience. (p. 410)

adolescence the transition period from childhood to adulthood, extending from puberty to independence. (p. 115)

adrenal [ah-DREEN-el] **glands** a pair of endocrine glands just above the kidneys. The adrenals secrete the hormones epinephrine (adrenaline) and norepinephrine (noradrenaline), which help to arouse the body in times of stress. (p. 51)

aerobic exercise sustained exercise that increases heart and lung fitness; may also alleviate depression and anxiety. (p. 529)

aggression any physical or verbal behavior intended to hurt or destroy. (p. 571)

algorithm a methodical, logical rule or procedure that guarantees solving a particular problem. Contrasts with the usually speedier—but also more error-prone—use of *heuristics*. (p. 307)

alpha waves the relatively slow brain waves of a relaxed, awake state. (p. 212)

altruism unselfish regard for the welfare of others. (p. 585)

Alzheimer's disease a progressive and irreversible brain disorder characterized by gradual deterioration of memory, reasoning, language, and, finally, physical functioning. (p. 132)

amnesia the loss of memory. (p. 286)

amphetamines drugs that stimulate neural activity, causing speeded-up body functions and associated energy and mood changes. (p. 232)

amygdala [ah-MIG-dah-la] two almond-shaped neural clusters that are components of the limbic system and are linked to emotion. (p. 56)

anorexia nervosa an eating disorder in which a normal-weight person (usually an adolescent female) diets and becomes significantly (15 percent or more) underweight, yet, still feeling fat, continues to starve. (p. 371)

antisocial personality disorder a personality disorder in which the person (usually a man) exhibits a lack of conscience for wrongdoing, even toward friends and family members. May be aggressive and ruthless or a clever con artist. (p. 481)

anxiety disorders psychological disorders characterized by distressing, persistent anxiety or by maladaptive behaviors that reduce anxiety. (p. 460)

aphasia impairment of language, usually caused by left hemisphere damage either to Broca's area (impairing speaking) or to Wernicke's area (impairing understanding). (p. 63)

applied research scientific study that aims to solve practical problems. (p. 7)

aptitude test a test designed to predict a person's future performance; *aptitude* is the capacity to learn. (p. 342)

artificial intelligence (AI) the science of designing and programming computer systems to do intelligent things and to simulate human thought processes such as intuitive reasoning, learning, and understanding language. Includes practical applications (chess playing, industrial robots, expert systems) and efforts to model human thinking inspired by our current understanding of how the brain works. (p. 317)

assimilation interpreting one's new experience in terms of one's existing schemas. (p. 87)

association areas areas of the cerebral cortex that are not involved in primary motor or sensory functions; rather, they are involved in higher mental functions such as learning, remembering, thinking, and speaking. (p. 62)

associative learning learning that certain events occur together. The events may be two stimuli (as in classical conditioning) or a response and its consequences (as in operant conditioning). (p. 244)

attachment an emotional tie with another person; shown in young children by their seeking closeness to the caregiver and showing distress on separation. (p. 95)

attitude a belief and feeling that predisposes one to respond in a particular way to people, objects, and events. (p. 551)

attribution theory the theory that we tend to give a causal explanation for someone's behavior, often by crediting either the situation or the person's disposition. (p. 549)

audition the sense of hearing. (p. 164)

automatic processing unconscious encoding of incidental information, such as space, time, and frequency, and of well-learned information, such as word meanings. (p. 273)

autonomic [aw-tuh-NAHM-ik] **nervous system** the part of the peripheral nervous system that controls the glands and the muscles of the internal organs (such as the heart). Its sympathetic division arouses; its parasympathetic division calms. (p. 48)

availability heuristic estimating the likelihood of events based on their availability in memory; if instances come readily to mind (perhaps because of their vividness), we presume such events are common. (p. 311)

aversive conditioning a type of counterconditioning that associates an unpleasant state (such as nausea) with an unwanted behavior (such as drinking alcohol). (p. 494)

axon the extension of a neuron, ending in branching terminal fibers, through which messages are sent to other neurons or to muscles or glands. (p. 42)

babbling stage beginning at 3 to 4 months, the stage of speech development in which the infant spontaneously utters various sounds at first unrelated to the household language. (p. 320)

barbiturates drugs that depress the activity of the central nervous system, reducing anxiety but impairing memory and judgment. (p. 232)

basic research pure science that aims to increase the scientific knowledge base. (p. 7)

basic trust according to Erik Erikson, a sense that the world is predictable and trustworthy; said to be formed during infancy by appropriate experiences with responsive caregivers. (p. 98)

behavior genetics the study of the power and limits of genetic and environmental influences on behavior. (p. 73)

behavior therapy therapy that applies learning principles to the elimination of unwanted behaviors. (p. 492)

behavioral medicine an interdisciplinary field that integrates behavioral and medical knowledge and applies that knowledge to health and disease. (p. 515)

behaviorism the view that psychology (1) should be an objective science that (2) studies behavior without reference to mental processes. Most research psychologists today agree with (1) but not with (2). (p. 246)

belief bias the tendency for one's preexisting beliefs to distort logical reasoning, sometimes by making invalid conclusions seem valid, or valid conclusions seem invalid. (p. 315)

belief perseverance clinging to one's initial conceptions after the basis on which they were formed has been discredited. (p. 315)

binocular cues depth cues, such as retinal disparity and convergence, that depend on the use of two eyes. (p. 186)

bio-psycho-social perspective a contemporary perspective which assumes that biological, sociocultural, and psychological factors combine and interact to produce psychological disorders. (p. 456)

biofeedback a system for electronically recording, amplifying, and feeding back information regarding a subtle physiological state, such as blood pressure or muscle tension. (p. 531)

biological psychology a branch of psychology concerned with the links between biology and behavior. (Some biological psychologists call themselves *behavioral neuroscientists, neuropsychologists, behavior geneticists, physiological psychologists, or biopsychologists.*) (p. 42)

bipolar disorder a mood disorder in which the person alternates between the hopelessness and lethargy of depression and the overexcited state of mania. (p. 468)

blind spot the point at which the optic nerve leaves the eye, creating a "blind" spot because no receptor cells are located there. (p. 156)

bottom-up processing analysis that begins with the sense receptors and works up to the brain's integration of sensory information. (p. 147)

brainstem the oldest part and central core of the brain, beginning where the spinal cord swells as it enters the skull; it is responsible for automatic survival functions. (p. 55)

Broca's area an area of the left frontal lobe that directs the muscle movements involved in speech. (p. 63)

bulimia nervosa an eating disorder characterized by private, "binge-purge" episodes of overeating, usually of highly caloric foods, followed by vomiting or laxative use. (p. 372)

burnout physical, emotional, and mental exhaustion brought on by persistent job-related stress. (p. 520)

bystander effect the tendency for any given bystander to be less likely to give aid if other bystanders are present. (p. 586)

Cannon-Bard theory the theory that an emotion-arousing stimulus simultaneously triggers (1) physiological responses and (2) the subjective experience of emotion. (p. 413)

case study an observation technique in which one person is studied in depth in the hope of revealing universal principles. (p. 18)

catharsis emotional release. In psychology, the catharsis hypothesis maintains that "releasing" aggressive energy (through action or fantasy) relieves aggressive urges. (p. 406)

central nervous system (CNS) the brain and spinal cord. (p. 47)

cerebellum [sehr-uh-BELL-um] the "little brain" attached to the rear of the brainstem; it helps coordinate voluntary movement and balance. (p. 56)

cerebral [seh-REE-bruhl] **cortex** the intricate fabric of interconnected neural cells that covers the cerebral hemispheres; the body's ultimate control and information-processing center. (p. 58)

chromosomes threadlike structures made of DNA molecules that contain the genes. (p. 72)

chunking organizing items into familiar, manageable units; often occurs automatically. (p. 278)

circadian rhythm [ser-KAY-dee-an] the biological clock; regular bodily rhythms (for example, of temperature and wakefulness) that occur on a 24-hour cycle. (p. 210)

classical conditioning a type of learning in which an organism comes to associate stimuli. A neutral stimulus that signals an unconditioned stimulus (UCS) begins to produce a response that anticipates and prepares for the unconditioned stimulus. (Also known as *Pavlovian conditioning*.) (p. 246)

clinical psychology a branch of psychology that studies, assesses, and treats people with psychological disorders. (p. 7)

cochlea [KOHK-lee-uh] a coiled, bony, fluid-filled tube in the inner ear through which sound waves trigger nerve impulses. (p. 165)

cognition (1) all the mental activities associated with thinking, knowing, and remembering. (p. 87) (2) the mental activity associated with processing, understanding, and communicating information. (p. 306)

cognitive dissonance theory the theory that we act to reduce the discomfort (dissonance) we feel when two of our thoughts (cognitions) are inconsistent. For example, when our awareness of our attitudes and of our actions clash, we can reduce the resulting dissonance by changing our attitudes. (p. 554)

cognitive map a mental representation of the layout of one's environment. For example, after exploring a maze, rats act as if they have learned a cognitive map of it. (p. 260)

cognitive therapy therapy that teaches people new, more adaptive ways of thinking and acting; based on the assumption that thoughts intervene between events and our emotional reactions. (p. 496)

collective unconscious Carl Jung's concept of a shared, inherited reservoir of memory traces from our species' history. (p. 425)

collectivism giving priority to the goals of one's group (often one's extended family or work group) and defining one's identity accordingly. (p. 441)

color constancy perceiving familiar objects as having consistent color, even if changing illumination alters the wavelengths reflected by the object. (p. 163)

companionate love the deep affectionate attachment we feel for those with whom our lives are intertwined. (p. 584)

concept a mental grouping of similar objects, events, or people. (p. 306)

concrete operational stage in Piaget's theory, the stage of cognitive development (from about 6 or 7 to 11 years of age) during which children gain the mental operations that enable them to think logically about concrete events. (p. 93)

conditioned response (CR) in classical conditioning, the learned response to a previously neutral conditioned stimulus (CS). (p. 247)

conditioned stimulus (CS) in classical conditioning, an originally neutral stimulus that, after association with an unconditioned stimulus (UCS), comes to trigger a conditioned response. (p. 247)

conduction deafness hearing loss caused by damage to the mechanical system that conducts sound waves to the cochlea. (p. 167)

cones receptor cells that are concentrated near the center of the retina and that function in daylight or in well-lit conditions. The cones detect fine detail and give rise to color sensations. (p. 156)

confirmation bias a tendency to search for information that confirms one's preconceptions. (p. 308)

conflict a perceived incompatibility of actions, goals, or ideas. (p. 578)

conformity adjusting one's behavior or thinking to coincide with a group standard. (p. 555)

consciousness our awareness of ourselves and our environments. (p. 208)

conservation the principle (which Piaget believed to be a part of concrete operational reasoning) that properties such as mass, volume, and number remain the same despite changes in the forms of objects. (p. 91)

content validity the extent to which a test samples the behavior that is of interest (such as a driving test that samples driving tasks). (p. 345)

continuous reinforcement reinforcing the desired response every time it occurs. (p. 257)

control condition the condition of an experiment that contrasts with the experimental treatment and serves as a comparison for evaluating the effect of the treatment. (p. 27)

convergence a binocular cue for perceiving depth; the extent to which the eyes converge inward when looking at an object. (p. 187)

coronary heart disease the clogging of the vessels that nourish the heart muscle; the leading cause of death in the United States. (p. 521)

corpus callosum [KOR-pus kah-LOW-sum] the largest bundle of neural fibers connecting the two brain hemispheres and carrying messages between them. (p. 65)

correlation a statistical measure that indicates the extent to which two factors vary together and thus how well either factor predicts the other. (p. 20)

counterconditioning a behavior therapy procedure that conditions new responses to stimuli that trigger unwanted behaviors; based on classical conditioning. Includes *systematic desensitization* and *aversive conditioning*. (p. 493)

creativity the ability to produce novel and valuable ideas. (p. 351)

criterion the behavior (such as college grades) that a test (such as the SAT) is designed to predict; thus, the measure used in defining whether the test has predictive validity. (p. 345)

critical period an optimal period shortly after birth when an organism's exposure to certain stimuli or experiences produces proper development. (p. 96)

critical thinking thinking that does not blindly accept arguments and conclusions. Rather, it examines assumptions, discerns hidden values, evaluates evidence, and assesses conclusions. (p. 13)

cross-sectional study a study in which people of different ages are compared with one another. (p. 134)

crystallized intelligence one's accumulated knowledge and verbal skills; tends to increase with age. (p. 135)

CT (computed tomograph) scan a series of x-ray photographs taken from different angles and combined by computer into a composite representation of a slice through the body. Also called *CAT scan*. (p. 53)

culture the enduring behaviors, ideas, attitudes, and traditions shared by a large group of people and transmitted from one generation to the next. (pp. 32, 564)

defense mechanisms in psychoanalytic theory, the ego's protective methods of reducing anxiety by unconsciously distorting reality. (p. 423)

deindividuation the loss of self-awareness and self-restraint occurring in group situations that foster arousal and anonymity. (p. 562)

déjà vu that eerie sense that "I've experienced this before." Cues from the current situation may subconsciously trigger retrieval of an earlier experience. (p. 290)

delta waves the large, slow brain waves associated with deep sleep. (p. 212)

delusions false beliefs, often of persecution or grandeur, that may accompany psychotic disorders. (p. 476)

dendrite the bushy, branching extensions of a neuron that receive messages and conduct impulses toward the cell body. (p. 42)

dependent variable the experimental factor—in psychology, the behavior or mental process—that is being measured; the variable that may change in response to manipulations of the independent variable. (p. 28)

depressants drugs (such as alcohol, barbiturates, and opiates) that reduce neural activity and slow body functions. (p. 231)

depth perception the ability to see objects in three dimensions although the images that strike the retina are two-dimensional; allows us to judge distance. (p. 186)

developmental psychology a branch of psychology that studies physical, cognitive, and social change throughout the life span. (p. 77)

difference threshold the minimum difference that a subject can detect between two stimuli 50 percent of the time. We experience the difference threshold as a just noticeable difference. (Also called *just noticeable difference* or *jnd*.) (p. 151)

discrimination in classical conditioning, the ability to distinguish between a conditioned stimulus and other stimuli that do not signal an unconditioned stimulus. In operant conditioning, responding differently to stimuli that signal a behavior will be reinforced or will not be reinforced. (p. 250)

displacement defense mechanism that shifts sexual or aggressive impulses toward a more acceptable or less threatening object or person, as when redirecting anger toward a safer outlet. (p. 424)

dissociation a split in consciousness, which allows some thoughts and behaviors to occur simultaneously with others. (p. 226)

dissociative amnesia loss of memory. Dissociative amnesia is selective memory loss often brought on by extreme stress. (p. 465)

dissociative disorders disorders in which conscious awareness becomes separated (dissociated) from previous memories, thoughts, and feelings. See dissociative *amnesia*, dissociative *fugue*, and *dissociative identity disorder*. (p. 465)

dissociative fugue [fewg] a dissociative disorder in which flight from one's home and identity accompanies amnesia. (p. 465)

dissociative identity disorder a rare dissociative disorder in which a person exhibits two or more distinct and alternating personalities. Also called *multiple personality disorder*. (p. 465)

DNA (deoxyribonucleic acid) a complex molecule containing the genetic information that makes up the chromosomes. (p. 72)

double-blind procedure an experimental procedure in which both the subject and the research staff are ignorant (blind) about whether the subject has received the treatment or a placebo. Commonly used in drug-evaluation studies. (p. 30)

Down syndrome a condition of retardation and associated physical disorders caused by an extra chromosome in one's genetic makeup. (p. 349)

drive-reduction theory the idea that a physiological need creates an aroused tension state (a drive) that motivates an organism to satisfy the need. (p. 364)

DSM-IV the American Psychiatric Association's *Diagnostic and Statistical Manual of Mental Disorders (Fourth Edition)*, a widely used system for classifying psychological disorders. (p. 458)

dualism the presumption that mind and body are two distinct entities that interact. (p. 240)

echoic memory a momentary sensory memory of auditory stimuli; if attention is elsewhere, sounds and words can still be recalled within 3 or 4 seconds. (p. 281)

eclectic approach an approach to psychotherapy that, depending on the client's problems, uses or integrates techniques from various forms of therapy. (Also called *psychotherapy integration*.) (p. 488)

effortful processing encoding that requires attention and conscious effort. (p. 273)

ego the largely conscious, "executive" part of personality that, according to Freud, mediates among the demands of the id, superego, and reality. The ego operates on the *reality principle*, satisfying the id's desires in ways that will realistically bring pleasure rather than pain. (p. 422)

egocentrism in Piaget's theory, the inability of the preoperational child to take another's point of view. (p. 91)

electroconvulsive therapy (ECT) a biomedical therapy for severely depressed patients in which a brief electric current is sent through the brain of an anesthetized patient. (p. 510)

electroencephalogram (EEG) an amplified recording of the waves of electrical activity that sweep across the brain's surface. These waves are measured by electrodes placed on the scalp. (p. 53)

embryo the developing human organism from about 2 weeks after fertilization through the second month. (p. 80)

emotion a response of the whole organism, involving (1) physiological arousal, (2) expressive behaviors, and (3) conscious experience. (p. 393)

emotional intelligence the ability to perceive, express, understand, and regulate emotions. (p. 340)

empirically derived test a test (such as the MMPI) developed by testing a pool of items and then selecting those that discriminate between groups. (p. 433)

encoding the processing of information into the memory system, for example by extracting meaning. (p. 272)

endocrine [EN-duh-krin] **system** the body's "slow" chemical communication system; a set of glands that secrete hormones into the bloodstream. (p. 50)

endorphins [en-DOR-fins] "morphine within"—natural, opiatelike neurotransmitters linked to pain control and to pleasure. (p. 46)

equity a condition in which people receive from a relationship in proportion to what they give to it. (p. 585)

estrogen a sex hormone, secreted in greater amounts by females than by males. In nonhuman female mammals, estrogen levels peak during ovulation, promoting sexual receptivity. (p. 376)

evolutionary psychology the study of the evolution of behavior using the principles of natural selection, which presumably favors behavior tendencies that contribute to the preservation and spread of one's genes. (p. 72)

experiment a research method in which the investigator manipulates one or more factors (independent variables) to observe their effect on some behavior or mental process (the dependent variable) while controlling other relevant factors by random assignment of subjects. (p. 26)

experimental condition the condition of an experiment that exposes subjects to the treatment, that is, to one version of the independent variable. (p. 27)

explicit memory memory of facts and experiences that one can consciously know and "declare." (Also called *declarative memory*.) (p. 286)

external locus of control the perception that chance or outside forces beyond one's personal control determine one's fate. (p. 446)

extinction the diminishing of a conditioned response; occurs in classical conditioning when an unconditioned stimulus (UCS) does not follow a conditioned stimulus (CS); occurs in operant conditioning when a response is no longer reinforced. (p. 248)

extrasensory perception (ESP) the controversial claim that perception can occur apart from sensory input. Said to include *telepathy, clairvoyance,* and *precognition.* (p. 201)

extrinsic motivation a desire to perform a behavior due to promised rewards or threats of punishment. (p. 386)

factor analysis a statistical procedure that identifies clusters of related items (called *factors*) on a test; used to identify different dimensions of performance that underlie one's total score. (p. 338)

false consensus effect the tendency to overestimate the extent to which others share our beliefs and behaviors. (p. 19)

family therapy therapy that treats the family as a system. Views an individual's unwanted behaviors as influenced by or directed at other family members; encourages family members toward positive relationships and improved communication. (p. 500)

fantasy-prone personality someone who imagines and recalls experiences with lifelike vividness and who spends considerable time fantasizing. (p. 209)

farsightedness a condition in which faraway objects are seen more clearly than near objects because the image of near objects is focused behind the retina. (p. 156)

feature detectors nerve cells in the brain that respond to specific features of the stimulus, such as shape, angle, or movement. (p. 159)

feel-good, do-good phenomenon people's tendency to be helpful when already in a good mood. (p. 407)

fetal alcohol syndrome (FAS) physical and cognitive abnormalities in children caused by a pregnant woman's heavy drinking. In severe cases, symptoms include noticeable facial misproportions. (p. 80)

fetus the developing human organism from 9 weeks after conception to birth. (p. 80)

figure-ground the organization of the visual field into objects (the *figures*) that stand out from their surroundings (the *ground*). (p. 185)

fixation (1) the inability to see a problem from a new perspective; an impediment to problem solving. (p. 309) (2) according to Freud, a lingering focus of pleasure-seeking energies at an earlier psychosexual stage, where conflicts were unresolved. (p. 423)

fixed-interval schedule in operant conditioning, a schedule of reinforcement that reinforces a response only after a specified time has elapsed. (p. 258)

fixed-ratio schedule in operant conditioning, a schedule of reinforcement that reinforces a response only after a specified number of responses. (p. 258)

flashbulb memory a clear memory of an emotionally significant moment or event. (p. 270)

fluid intelligence one's ability to reason speedily and abstractly; tends to decrease during late adulthood. (p. 135)

foot-in-the-door phenomenon the tendency for people who have first agreed to a small request to comply later with a larger request. (p. 552)

formal operational stage in Piaget's theory, the stage of cognitive development (normally beginning about age 12) during which people begin to think logically about abstract concepts. (p. 93)

fovea the central focal point in the retina, around which the eye's cones cluster. (p. 157)

framing the way an issue is posed; how an issue is framed can significantly affect decisions and judgments. (p. 314)

fraternal twins twins who develop from separate zygotes. They are genetically no closer than brothers and sisters, but they share the fetal environment. (p. 73)

free association in psychoanalysis, a method of exploring the unconscious in which the person relaxes and says whatever comes to mind, no matter how trivial or embarrassing. (p. 421)

frequency the number of complete wavelengths that pass a point in a given time (for example, per second). (p. 164)

frequency theory in hearing, the theory that the rate of nerve impulses traveling up the auditory nerve matches the frequency of a tone, thus enabling us to sense its pitch. (p. 166)

frontal lobes the portion of the cerebral cortex lying just behind the forehead; involved in speaking and muscle movements and in making plans and judgments. (p. 59)

frustration-aggression principle the principle that frustration—the blocking of an attempt to achieve some goal—creates anger, which can generate aggression. (p. 573)

functional fixedness the tendency to think of things only in terms of their usual functions; an impediment to problem solving. (p. 309)

fundamental attribution error the tendency for observers, when analyzing another's behavior, to underestimate the impact of the situation and to overestimate the impact of personal disposition. (p. 549)

gate-control theory theory that the spinal cord contains a neurological "gate" that blocks pain signals or allows them to pass on to the brain. The "gate" is opened by the activity of pain signals traveling up small nerve fibers and is closed by activity in larger fibers or by information coming from the brain. (p. 172)

gender in psychology, the characteristics, whether biologically or socially influenced, by which people define male and female. (p. 79)

gender identity one's sense of being male or female. (pp. 106, 423)

gender role a set of expected behaviors for males and for females. (p. 566)

gender schema theory the theory that children learn from their cultures a concept of what it means to be male and female and that they adjust their behavior accordingly. (p. 106)

gender-typing the acquisition of a traditional masculine or feminine role. (p. 106)

general adaptation syndrome (GAS) Selye's concept of the body's adaptive response to stress as composed of three stages—alarm, resistance, exhaustion. (p. 518)

general intelligence (*g*) a general intelligence factor that Spearman and others believed underlies specific mental abilities and is therefore measured by every task on an intelligence test. (p. 338)

generalization the tendency, once a response has been conditioned, for stimuli similar to the conditioned stimulus to evoke similar responses. (p. 249)

generalized anxiety disorder an anxiety disorder in which a person is continually tense, apprehensive, and in a state of autonomic nervous system arousal. (p. 460)

genes the biochemical units of heredity that make up the chromosomes; a segment of DNA capable of synthesizing a protein. (p. 72)

gestalt an organized whole. Gestalt psychologists emphasize our tendency to integrate pieces of information into meaningful wholes. (p. 184)

Gestalt therapy developed by Fritz Perls; combines the psychoanalytic emphasis on bringing unconscious feelings to awareness and the humanistic emphasis on getting "in touch with oneself"; aims to help people become more aware of and able to express their feelings, and to take responsibility for their feelings and actions. (p. 492)

glial cells cells in the nervous system that are not neurons but that support, nourish, and protect neurons. (p. 58)

glucose the form of sugar that circulates in the blood and provides the major source of energy for body tissues. When its level is low, we feel hunger. (p. 369)

grammar a system of rules in a language that enables us to communicate with and understand others. (p. 320)

GRIT Graduated and Reciprocated Initiatives in Tension-Reduction—a strategy designed to decrease international tensions. (p. 588)

grouping the perceptual tendency to organize stimuli into coherent groups. (p. 185)

group polarization the enhancement of a group's prevailing attitudes through discussion within the group. (p. 562)

groupthink the mode of thinking that occurs when the desire for harmony in a decision-making group overrides a realistic appraisal of alternatives. (p. 563)

habituation decreasing responsiveness with repeated stimulation. As infants gain familiarity with repeated exposure to a visual stimulus, their interest wanes and they look away sooner. (p. 90)

hallucinations false sensory experiences, such as seeing something in the absence of an external visual stimulus. (pp. 212, 477)

hallucinogens psychedelic ("mind-manifesting") drugs, such as LSD, that distort perceptions and evoke sensory images in the absence of sensory input. (p. 231)

health psychology a subfield of psychology that provides psychology's contribution to behavioral medicine. (p. 515)

heritability the proportion of variation among individuals that we can attribute to genes. The heritability of a trait may vary, depending on the range of populations and environments studied. (pp. 73, 354)

heuristic a rule-of-thumb strategy that often allows us to make judgments and solve problems efficiently; usually speedier but also more error-prone than *algorithms*. (p. 307)

hidden observer Hilgard's term describing a hypnotized subject's awareness of experiences, such as pain, that go unreported during hypnosis. (p. 228)

hierarchy of needs Maslow's pyramid of human needs, beginning at the base with physiological needs that must first be satisfied before higher-level safety needs and then psychological needs become active. (p. 366)

hindsight bias the tendency to believe, after learning an outcome, that one would have foreseen it. (Also known as the I-knew-it-all-along phenomenon.) (p. 14)

hippocampus a neural center located in the limbic system that helps process explicit memories for storage. (p. 287)

homeostasis a tendency to maintain a balanced or constant internal state; the regulation of any aspect of body chemistry, such as blood glucose, around a particular level. (p. 365)

hormones chemical messengers, mostly those manufactured by the endocrine glands, that are produced in one tissue and affect another. (p. 50)

hospice an organization whose largely volunteer staff provides support for dying people and their families either in special facilities or in people's own homes. (p. 142)

hue the dimension of color that is determined by the wavelength of light; what we know as the color names *blue, green*, and so forth. (p. 154)

hypnosis a social interaction in which one person (the hypnotist) suggests to another (the subject) that certain perceptions, feelings, thoughts, or behaviors will spontaneously occur. (p. 221)

hypothalamus [hi-po-THAL-uh-muss] a neural structure lying below (*hypo*) the thalamus; it directs several maintenance activities (eating, drinking, body temperature), helps govern the endocrine system via the pituitary gland, and is linked to emotion. (p. 57)

hypothesis a testable prediction, often implied by a theory. (p. 17)

iconic memory a momentary sensory memory of visual stimuli; a photographic or picture-image memory lasting no more than a few tenths of a second. (p. 281)

id a reservoir of unconscious psychic energy that, according to Freud, strives to satisfy basic sexual and aggressive drives. The id operates on the pleasure principle, demanding immediate gratification. (p. 421)

identical twins twins who develop from a single zygote (fertilized egg) that splits in two, creating two genetic replicas. (p. 73)

identification the process by which, according to Freud, children incorporate their parents' values into their developing superegos. (p. 423)

identity one's sense of self; according to Erikson, the adolescent's task is to solidify a sense of self by testing and integrating various roles. (p. 122)

illusory correlation the perception of a relationship where none exists. (p. 22)

imagery mental pictures; a powerful aid to effortful processing, especially when combined with semantic encoding. (p. 276)

implicit memory retention without conscious recollection (of skills and dispositions). (Also called *nondeclarative memory*.) (p. 286)

imprinting the process by which certain animals form attachments during a critical period very early in life. (p. 96)

incentive a positive or negative environmental stimulus that motivates behavior. (p. 365)

independent variable the experimental factor that is manipulated; the variable whose effect is being studied. (p. 28)

individualism giving priority to one's own goals over group goals, and defining one's identity in terms of personal attributes rather than group identifications. (p. 441)

industrial/organizational psychology a subfield of psychology that studies and advises on workplace behavior. Industrial/organizational (I/O) psychologists help organizations select and train employees, boost morale and productivity, and design products and assess responses to them. (p. 387)

informational social influence influence resulting from one's willingness to accept others' opinions about reality. (p. 556)

ingroup bias The tendency to favor one's own group. (p. 569)

inner ear the innermost part of the ear, containing the cochlea, semicircular canals, and vestibular sacs. (p. 165)

insight a sudden and often novel realization of the solution to a problem; it contrasts with strategy-based solutions. (p. 307)

insomnia a sleep disorder involving recurring problems in falling or staying asleep. (p. 216)

instinct a complex behavior that is rigidly patterned throughout a species and is unlearned. (p. 364)

intelligence the capacity for goal-directed and adaptive behavior. Involves the abilities to profit from experience, solve problems, and reason effectively. (p. 337)

intelligence quotient (IQ) defined originally as the ratio of mental age (*ma*) to chronological age (*ca*) multiplied by 100 (thus, IQ = *ma/ca* × 100). On contemporary intelligence tests, the average performance for a given age is assigned a score of 100. (p. 335)

intelligence test a method for assessing an individual's mental aptitudes and comparing them to those of others, using numerical scores. (p. 334)

intensity the amount of energy in a light or sound wave, which we perceive as brightness or loudness, as determined by the wave's amplitude. (p. 154)

internal locus of control the perception that one controls one's own fate. (p. 446)

interneurons central nervous system neurons that internally communicate and intervene between the sensory inputs and motor outputs. (p. 48)

interposition a monocular cue for perceiving distance; we perceive an object partially blocking our view of another object as more distant. (p. 188)

interpretation in psychoanalysis, the analyst's noting supposed dream meanings, resistances, and other significant behaviors in order to promote insight. (p. 489)

intimacy in Erikson's theory, the ability to form close, loving relationships; a primary developmental task in late adolescence and early adulthood. (p. 123)

intrinsic motivation a desire to perform a behavior for its own sake and to be effective. (p. 386)

iris a ring of muscle tissue that forms the colored portion of the eye around the pupil and controls the size of the pupil opening. (p. 155)

James-Lange theory the theory that our experience of emotion is our awareness of our physiological responses to emotion-arousing stimuli. (p. 413)

just-world phenomenon the tendency of people to believe the world is just and that people therefore get what they deserve and deserve what they get. (p. 571)

kinesthesis [kin-ehs-THEE-sehs] the system for sensing the position and movement of individual body parts. (p. 176)

language our spoken, written, or gestured words and the ways we combine them to communicate meaning. (p. 319)

latent content according to Freud, the underlying but censored meaning of a dream (as distinct from its manifest content). Freud believed that a dream's latent content functions as a safety valve. (p. 218)

latent learning learning that occurs but is not apparent until there is an incentive to demonstrate it. (p. 260)

law of effect Thorndike's principle that behaviors followed by favorable consequences become more likely, and that behaviors followed by unfavorable consequences become less likely. (p. 255)

learned helplessness the hopelessness and passive resignation an animal or human learns when unable to avoid repeated aversive events. (p. 446)

learning a relatively permanent change in an organism's behavior due to experience. (p. 243)

lens the transparent structure behind the pupil that changes shape to focus images on the retina. (p. 155)

lesion [LEE-zhuhn] tissue destruction. A brain lesion is a naturally or experimentally caused destruction of brain tissue. (p. 53)

limbic system a doughnut-shaped system of neural structures at the border of the brainstem and cerebral hemispheres; associated with emotions such as fear and aggression and drives such as those for food and sex. Includes the hippocampus, amydala, and hypothalamus. (p. 56)

linear perspective a monocular cue for perceiving distance; we perceive the converging of what we know to be parallel lines as indicating increasing distance. (p. 189)

linguistic relativity Whorf's hypothesis that language determines the way we think. (p. 328)

lithium a chemical that provides an effective drug therapy for the mood swings of bipolar (manic-depressive) disorders. (p. 510)

lobotomy a now-rare psychosurgical procedure once used to calm uncontrollably emotional or violent patients. The procedure cut the nerves that connect the frontal lobes to the emotion-controlling centers of the inner brain. (p. 511)

longitudinal study research in which the same people are restudied and retested over a long period. (p. 134)

long-term memory the relatively permanent and limitless storehouse of the memory system. (p. 272)

long-term potentiation (LTP) an increase in a synapse's firing potential after brief, rapid stimulation. Believed to be a neural basis for learning and memory. (p. 285)

LSD a powerful hallucinogenic drug; also known as acid (*lysergic acid diethylamide*). (p. 234)

lymphocytes the two types of white blood cells that are part of the body's immune system: *B lymphocytes* form in the *b*one marrow and release antibodies that fight bacterial infections; *T lymphocytes* form in the *t*hymus and, among other duties, attack cancer cells, viruses, and foreign substances. (p. 523)

major depressive disorder a mood disorder in which a person, for no apparent reason, experiences two or more weeks of depressed moods, feelings of worthlessness, and diminished interest or pleasure in most activities. (p. 468)

mania a mood disorder marked by a hyperactive, wildly optimistic state. (p. 468)

manifest content according to Freud, the remembered story line of a dream (as distinct from its latent content). (p. 218)

maturation biological growth processes that enable orderly changes in behavior, relatively uninfluenced by experience. (p. 82)

medical model the concept that diseases have physical causes that can be diagnosed, treated, and, in most cases, cured. When applied to psychological disorders, the medical model assumes that these "mental" illnesses can be diagnosed on the basis of their symptoms and cured through therapy, which may include treatment in a psychiatric hospital. (p. 455)

medulla [muh-DUL-uh] the base of the brainstem; controls heartbeat and breathing. (p. 55)

memory the persistence of learning over time via the storage and retrieval of information. (p. 267)

menarche [meh-NAR-key] the first menstrual period. (p. 117)

menopause the time of natural cessation of menstruation; also refers to the biological changes a woman experiences as her ability to reproduce declines. (p. 128)

mental age a measure of intelligence test performance devised by Binet; the chronological age that most typically corresponds to a given level of performance. Thus, a child who does as well as the average 8-year-old is said to have a mental age of 8. (p. 335)

mental retardation a condition of limited mental ability, as indicated by an intelligence score below 70, that produces difficulty in adapting to the demands of life; varies from mild to profound. (p. 349)

mental set a tendency to approach a problem in a particular way, especially a way that has been successful in the past but may or may not be helpful in solving a new problem. (p. 309)

mere exposure effect the phenomenon that repeated exposure to novel stimuli increases liking of them. (p. 580)

meta-analysis a procedure for statistically combining the results of many different research studies. (p. 503)

metabolic rate the body's base rate of energy expenditure. (p. 370)

middle ear the chamber between the eardrum and cochlea containing three tiny bones (hammer, anvil, and stirrup) that concentrate the vibrations of the eardrum on the cochlea's oval window. (p. 165)

Minnesota Multiphasic Personality Inventory (MMPI) the most widely researched and clinically used of all personality tests. Originally developed to identify emotional disorders (still considered its most appropriate use), this test is now used for many other screening purposes. (p. 433)

misinformation effect incorporating misleading information into one's memory of an event. (p. 295)

mnemonics [nih-MON-iks] memory aids, especially those techniques that use vivid imagery and organizational devices. (p. 277)

modeling the process of observing and imitating a behavior. (p. 265)

monism the presumption that mind and body are different aspects of the same thing. (p. 240)

monocular cues distance cues, such as linear perspective and overlap, available to either eye alone. (p. 186)

mood-congruent memory the tendency to recall experiences that are consistent with one's current good or bad mood. (p. 291)

mood disorders psychological disorders characterized by emotional extremes. See *major depressive disorder*, *bipolar disorder*, and *mania*. (p. 468)

morpheme in a language, the smallest unit that carries meaning; may be a word or a part of a word (such as a prefix). (p. 320)

motivation a need or desire that energizes and directs behavior. (p. 363)

motor cortex an area at the rear of the frontal lobes that controls voluntary movements. (p. 60)

motor neurons the neurons that carry outgoing information from the central nervous system to the muscles and glands. (p. 48)

MRI (magnetic resonance imaging) a technique that uses magnetic fields and radio waves to produce computer-generated images that distinguish among different types of soft tissue; allows us to see structures within the brain. (p. 53)

myelin [MY-uh-lin] **sheath** a layer of fatty cells segmentally encasing the fibers of many neurons; makes possible vastly greater transmission speed of neural impulses. (p. 42)

narcolepsy a sleep disorder characterized by uncontrollable sleep attacks. The sufferer may lapse directly into REM sleep, often at inopportune times. (p. 217)

naturalistic observation observing and recording behavior in naturally occurring situations without trying to manipulate and control the situation. (p. 20)

nature-nurture issue the longstanding controversy over the relative contributions that genes and experience make to the development of psychological traits and behaviors. (p. 6)

near-death experience an altered state of consciousness reported after a close brush with death (such as through cardiac arrest); often similar to drug-induced hallucinations. (p. 238)

nearsightedness a condition in which nearby objects are seen more clearly than distant objects because the lens focuses the image of distant objects in front of the retina. (p. 156)

nerve deafness hearing loss caused by damage to the cochlea's receptor cells or to the auditory nerves. (p. 167)

nerves neural "cables" containing many axons. These bundled axons, which are part of the peripheral nervous system, connect the central nervous system with muscles, glands, and sense organs. (p. 47)

nervous system the body's speedy, electrochemical communication system, consisting of all the nerve cells of the peripheral and central nervous systems. (p. 47)

neural networks (1) interconnected neural cells. With experience, networks can learn, as feedback strengthens or inhibits connections that produce certain results. Computer simulations of neural networks show analogous learning. (p. 50) (2) computer circuits that mimic the brain's interconnected neural cells, performing tasks such as learning to recognize visual patterns and smells. (p. 317)

neuron a nerve cell; the basic building block of the nervous system. (p. 42)

neurotic disorder a psychological disorder that is usually distressing but that allows one to think rationally and function socially. Freud saw the neurotic disorders as ways of dealing with anxiety. (p. 458)

neurotransmitters chemical messengers that traverse the synaptic gaps between neurons. When released by the sending neuron, neurotransmitters travel across the synapse and bind to receptor sites on the receiving neuron, thereby influencing whether it will generate a neural impulse. (p. 44)

night terrors a sleep disorder characterized by high arousal and an appearance of being terrified; unlike nightmares, night terrors occur during Stage 4 sleep, within 2 or 3 hours of falling asleep, and are seldom remembered. (p. 217)

norm an understood rule for accepted and expected behavior. Norms prescribe "proper" behavior. (p. 556)

normal curve the symmetrical bell-shaped curve that describes the distribution of many physical and psychological attributes. Most scores fall near the average, and fewer and fewer scores lie near the extremes. (p. 344)

normative social influence influence resulting from a person's desire to gain approval or avoid disapproval. (p. 556)

object permanence the awareness that things continue to exist even when not perceived. (p. 88)

observational learning learning by observing and imitating the behavior of others. (p. 265)

obsessive-compulsive disorder an anxiety disorder characterized by unwanted repetitive thoughts (obsessions) and/or actions (compulsions). (p. 460)

occipital [ahk-SIP-uh-tuhl] **lobes** the portion of the cerebral cortex lying at the back of the head; includes the visual areas, which receive visual information from the opposite visual field. (p. 59)

Oedipus [ed-uh-puss] **complex** according to Freud, a boy's sexual desires toward his mother and feelings of jealousy and hatred for the rival father. (p. 422)

one-word stage the stage in speech development, from about age 1 to 2, during which a child speaks mostly in single words. (p. 321)

operant behavior behavior that operates on the environment, producing consequences. (p. 255)

operant conditioning a type of learning in which behavior is strengthened if followed by reinforcement or diminished if followed by punishment. (p. 254)

operational definition a statement of the procedures (operations) used to define research variables. (p. 28)

opiates opium and its derivatives, such as morphine and heroin; they depress neural activity, temporarily lessening pain and anxiety. (p. 232)

opponent-process theory the theory that opposing retinal processes (red-green, yellow-blue, white-black) enable color vision. For example, some cells are stimulated by green and inhibited by red; others are stimulated by red and inhibited by green. (p. 162)

optic nerve the nerve that carries neural impulses from the eye to the brain. (p. 156)

overconfidence the tendency to be more confident than correct—to overestimate the accuracy of one's beliefs and judgments. (p. 313)

overjustification effect the effect of promising a reward for doing what one already likes to do. The person may now see the reward, rather than intrinsic interest, as the motivation for performing the task. (p. 261)

panic disorder an anxiety disorder marked by a minutes-long episode of intense dread in which a person experiences terror and accompanying chest pain, choking, or other frightening sensations. (p. 462)

parallel processing processing several aspects of a problem simultaneously; the brain's natural mode of information processing for many functions, including vision. Contrasts with the step-by-step (serial) processing of most computers and of conscious problem-solving. (p. 160)

parapsychology the study of paranormal phenomena, including ESP and psychokinesis. (p. 201)

parasympathetic nervous system the division of the autonomic nervous system that calms the body, conserving its energy. (p. 48)

parietal [puh-RYE-uh-tuhl] **lobes** the portion of the cerebral cortex lying at the top of the head and toward the rear; includes the sensory cortex. (p. 59)

partial reinforcement reinforcing a response only part of the time; results in slower acquisition of response but much greater resistance to extinction than does continuous reinforcement. (p. 257)

passionate love An aroused state of intense positive absorption in another, usually present at the beginning of a love relationship. (p. 583)

perception the process of organizing and interpreting sensory information, enabling us to recognize meaningful objects and events. (p. 147)

perceptual adaptation in vision, the ability to adjust to an artificially displaced or even inverted visual field. (p. 196)

perceptual constancy perceiving objects as unchanging (having consistent lightness, color, shape, and size) even as illumination and retinal images change. (p. 190)

perceptual set a mental predisposition to perceive one thing and not another. (p. 196)

peripheral nervous system (PNS) the sensory and motor neurons that connect the central nervous system (CNS) to the rest of the body. (p. 47)

personal control our sense of controlling our environments rather than feeling helpless. (p. 445)

personal space the buffer zone we like to maintain around our bodies. (p. 565)

person-centered therapy a humanistic therapy, developed by Carl Rogers, in which the therapist uses techniques such as active listening within a genuine, accepting, empathic environment to facilitate clients' growth. (p. 490)

personality an individual's characteristic pattern of thinking, feeling, and acting. (p. 419)

personality disorders psychological disorders characterized by inflexible and enduring behavior patterns that impair social functioning. (p. 481)

personality inventory a questionnaire (often with true-false or agree-disagree items) on which people respond to items designed to gauge a wide range of feelings and behaviors; used to assess selected personality traits. (p. 433)

PET (positron emission tomograph) scan a visual display of brain activity that detects where a radioactive form of glucose goes while the brain performs a given task. (p. 53)

phi phenomenon an illusion of movement created when two or more adjacent lights blink on and off in succession. (p. 190)

phobia an anxiety disorder marked by a persistent, irrational fear and avoidance of a specific object or situation. (p. 460)

phoneme in a spoken language, the smallest distinctive sound unit. (p. 319)

physical dependence a physiological need for a drug, marked by unpleasant withdrawal symptoms when the drug is discontinued. (p. 229)

pitch a tone's highness or lowness; depends on frequency. (p. 164)

pituitary gland the endocrine system's most influential gland. Under the influence of the hypothalamus, the pituitary regulates growth and controls other endocrine glands. (p. 51)

place theory in hearing, the theory that links the pitch we hear with the place where the cochlea's membrane is stimulated. (p. 165)

placebo [pluh-SEE-bo] an inert substance or condition that may be administered instead of a presumed active agent, such as a drug, to see if it triggers the effects believed to characterize the active agent. (p. 30)

plasticity the brain's capacity for modification, as evident in brain reorganization following damage (especially in children) and in experiments on the effects of experience on brain development. (p. 85)

polygraph a machine, commonly used in attempts to detect lies, that measures several of the physiological responses accompanying emotion (such as perspiration, heart rate, blood pressure, and breathing changes). (p. 396)

population all the cases in a group, from which samples may be drawn for a study. (p. 19)

posthypnotic amnesia supposed inability to recall what one experienced during hypnosis; induced by the hypnotist's suggestion. (p. 221)

posthypnotic suggestion a suggestion, made during a hypnosis session, to be carried out after the subject is no longer hypnotized; used by some clinicians to help control undesired symptoms and behaviors. (p. 224)

preconscious information that is not conscious, but is retrievable into conscious awareness. (p. 421)

predictive validity the success with which a test predicts the behavior it is designed to predict; it is assessed by computing the correlation between test scores and the criterion behavior. (Also called *criterion-related validity*.) (p. 345)

prejudice an unjustifiable (and usually negative) attitude toward a group and its members. Prejudice generally involves stereotyped beliefs, negative feelings, and a predisposition to discriminatory action. (p. 567)

preoperational stage in Piaget's theory, the stage (from about 2 to 6 or 7 years of age) during which a child learns to use language but does not yet comprehend the mental operations of concrete logic. (p. 91)

primary reinforcer an innately reinforcing stimulus, such as one that satisfies a biological need. (p. 257)

primary sex characteristics the body structures (ovaries, testes, and external genitalia) that make sexual reproduction possible. (p. 117)

priming the activation, often unconsciously, of particular associations in memory. (p. 289)

proactive interference the disruptive effect of prior learning on the recall of new information. (p. 292)

projection the defense mechanism by which people disguise their own threatening impulses by attributing them to others. (p. 424)

projective test a personality test, such as the Rorschach or TAT, that provides ambiguous stimuli designed to trigger projection of one's inner dynamics. (p. 426)

prosocial behavior positive, constructive, helpful behavior. The opposite of antisocial behavior. (p. 266)

prototype the best example of a category; matching new items to the prototype provides a quick and easy method for including items in a category (as when comparing feathered creatures to a prototypical bird, such as a robin). (p. 306)

psychiatry a branch of medicine dealing with psychological disorders; practiced by physicians who sometimes provide medical (for example, drug) treatments as well as psychological therapy. (p. 7)

psychoactive drug a chemical substance that alters perceptions and mood. (p. 229)

psychoanalysis Sigmund Freud's therapeutic technique. Freud believed the patient's free associations, resistances, dreams, and transferences—and the therapist's interpretations of them—released previously repressed feelings, allowing the patient to gain self-insight. Freud's psychoanalytic theory of personality sought to explain what he observed during psychoanalysis. (pp. 421, 488)

psychological dependence a psychological need to use a drug, such as to relieve negative emotions. (p. 229)

psychological disorder a condition in which behavior is judged atypical, disturbing, maladaptive, and unjustifiable. (p. 454)

psychology the science of behavior and mental processes. (p. 4)

psychopharmacology the study of the effects of drugs on mind and behavior. (p. 508)

psychophysics the study of relationships between the physical characteristics of stimuli, such as their intensity, and our psychological experience of them. (p. 148)

psychophysiological illness literally, "mind–body" illness; any stress-related physical illness, such as hypertension and headaches. Note: This is distinct from *hypochondriasis*—misinterpreting normal physical sensations as symptoms of a disease. (p. 523)

psychosexual stages the childhood stages of development (oral, anal, phallic, latency, genital) during which, according to Freud, the id's pleasure-seeking energies focus on distinct erogenous zones. (p. 422)

psychosurgery surgery that removes or destroys brain tissue in an effort to change behavior. (p. 511)

psychotherapy an emotionally charged, confiding interaction between a trained therapist and someone who suffers from psychological difficulties. (p. 488)

psychotic disorder a psychological disorder in which a person loses contact with reality, experiencing irrational ideas and distorted perceptions. (p. 458)

puberty the period of sexual maturation, during which one first becomes capable of reproducing. (p. 116)

punishment an aversive event that *decreases* the behavior that it follows. (p. 258)

pupil the adjustable opening in the center of the eye through which light enters. (p. 155)

random assignment assigning subjects to experimental and control conditions by chance, thus minimizing preexisting differences between those assigned to the different groups. (p. 27)

random sample a sample that fairly represents a population because each member has an equal chance of inclusion. (p. 19)

rational-emotive therapy a confrontational cognitive therapy, developed by Albert Ellis, that vigorously challenges people's illogical, self-defeating attitudes and assumptions. Also called *rational-emotive behavior therapy* by Ellis, emphasizing a behavioral "homework" component. (p. 496)

rationalization defense mechanism that offers self-justifying explanations in place of the real, more threatening, unconscious reasons for one's actions. (p. 424)

reaction formation defense mechanism by which the ego unconsciously switches unacceptable impulses into their opposites. Thus, people may express feelings that are the opposite of their anxiety-arousing unconscious feelings. (p. 424)

recall a measure of memory in which the person must retrieve information learned earlier, as on a fill-in-the-blank test. (p. 288)

reciprocal determinism the interacting influences between personality and environmental factors. (p. 445)

recognition a measure of memory in which the person need only identify items previously learned, as on a multiple-choice test. (p. 288)

reflex a simple, automatic, inborn response to a sensory stimulus, such as the knee-jerk response. (p. 49)

refractory period a resting period after orgasm, during which a man cannot achieve another orgasm. (p. 375)

regression defense mechanism in which individual retreats, when faced with anxiety, to a more infantile psychosexual stage where some psychic energy remains fixated. (p. 423)

rehearsal the conscious repetition of information, either to maintain it in consciousness or to encode it for storage. (p. 273)

reinforcer in operant conditioning, any event that *strengthens* the behavior it follows. (p. 256)

relative brightness a monocular cue for perceiving distance; dimmer objects appear more distant. (p. 189)

relative clarity a monocular cue for perceiving distance; hazier objects appear more distant. (p. 188)

relative deprivation the perception that one is worse off relative to those with whom one compares oneself. (p. 411)

relative height a monocular cue for perceiving distance; higher objects appear more distant. (p. 188)

relative motion a monocular cue for perceiving distance; when we move, objects at different distances change their relative positions in our visual image, with those closest moving most. (Also called *motion parallax*.) (p. 188)

relative size a monocular cue for perceiving distance; when we assume two objects are the same size, the one that produces the smaller image appears more distant. (p. 188)

relearning a memory measure that assesses the amount of time saved when relearning previously learned information. (p. 288)

reliability the extent to which a test yields consistent results, as assessed by the consistency of scores on two halves of the test, on alternate forms of the test, or on retesting. (p. 345)

REM rebound the tendency for REM sleep to increase following REM sleep deprivation (created by repeated awakenings during REM sleep). (p. 220)

REM sleep rapid eye movement sleep, a recurring sleep stage during which vivid dreams commonly occur. Also known as *paradoxical sleep* because the muscles are relaxed (except for minor twitches) but other body systems are active. (p. 211)

replication repeating the essence of a research study, usually with different subjects in different situations, to see whether the basic finding generalizes to other subjects and circumstances. (p. 17)

representativeness heuristic a rule of thumb for judging the likelihood of things in terms of how well they seem to represent, or match, particular prototypes; may lead one to ignore other relevant information. (p. 310)

repression in psychoanalytic theory, the basic defense mechanism that banishes anxiety–arousing thoughts, feelings, and memories from consciousness. (pp. 294, 423)

resistance in psychoanalysis, the blocking from consciousness of anxiety-laden material. (p. 489)

respondent behavior behavior that occurs as an automatic response to some stimulus; Skinner's term for behavior learned through classical conditioning. (p. 255)

reticular formation a nerve network in the brainstem that plays an important role in controlling arousal. (p. 55)

retina the light-sensitive inner surface of the eye, containing the receptor rods and cones plus layers of neurons that begin the processing of visual information. (p. 155)

retinal disparity a binocular cue for perceiving depth: the greater the disparity (difference) between the two images the retina receives of an object, the closer the object is to the viewer. (p. 187)

retrieval the process of getting information out of memory storage. (p. 272)

retroactive interference the disruptive effect of new learning on the recall of old information. (p. 292)

rods retinal receptors that detect black, white, and gray; necessary for peripheral and twilight vision, when cones don't respond. (p. 156)

role a set of expectations about a social position, defining how those in the position ought to behave. (p. 553)

rooting reflex a baby's tendency, when touched on the cheek, to open the mouth and search for the nipple. (p. 81)

Rorschach inkblot test the most widely used projective test, a set of 10 inkblots, designed by Hermann Rorschach; seeks to identify people's inner feelings by analyzing their interpretations of the blots. (p. 426)

savant syndrome a condition in which a person otherwise limited in mental ability has an amazing specific skill, such as in computation or drawing. (p. 338)

scapegoat theory The theory that prejudice provides an outlet for anger by providing someone to blame. (p. 569)

schema a concept or framework that organizes and interprets information. (p. 87)

schizophrenia a group of severe psychotic disorders characterized by disorganized and delusional thinking, disturbed perceptions, and inappropriate emotions and actions. (p. 476)

secondary reinforcer a conditioned reinforcer; a stimulus that gains its reinforcing power through its association with a primary reinforcer. (p. 257)

secondary sex characteristics nonreproductive sexual characteristics, such as female breasts and hips, male voice quality, and body hair. (p. 117)

selective attention the focusing of conscious awareness on a particular stimulus, as in the cocktail party effect. (p. 181)

self-actualization according to Maslow, the ultimate psychological need that arises after basic physical and psychological needs are met and self-esteem is achieved; the motivation to fulfill one's potential. (p. 436)

self-concept (1) a sense of one's identity and personal worth. (p. 103) (2) all our thoughts and feelings about ourselves, in answer to the question, "Who am I?" (p. 438)

self-disclosure revealing intimate aspects of oneself to others. (p. 585)

self-esteem one's feelings of high or low self-worth. (p. 438)

self-serving bias a readiness to perceive oneself favorably. (p. 440)

semantic encoding the encoding of meaning, including the meaning of words. (p. 275)

semantics the set of rules by which we derive meaning from morphemes, words, and sentences in a given language; also, the study of meaning. (p. 320)

sensation the process by which our sensory receptors and nervous system receive and represent stimulus energies from our environment. (p. 147)

sensorimotor stage in Piaget's theory, the stage (from birth to about 2 years of age) during which infants know the world mostly in terms of their sensory impressions and motor activities. (p. 88)

sensory adaptation diminished sensitivity as a consequence of constant stimulation. (p. 152)

sensory cortex the area at the front of the parietal lobes that registers and processes body sensations. (p. 61)

sensory interaction the principle that one sense may influence another, as when the smell of food influences its taste. (p. 174)

sensory memory the immediate, initial recording of sensory information in the memory system. (p. 281)

sensory neurons neurons that carry incoming information from the sense receptors to the central nervous system. (p. 48)

serial position effect our tendency to recall best the last and first items in a list. (p. 274)

set point the point at which an individual's "weight thermostat" is supposedly set. When the body falls below this weight, an increase in hunger and a lowered metabolic rate may act to restore the lost weight. (p. 370)

sexual disorder a problem that consistently impairs sexual arousal or functioning. (p. 378)

sexual orientation an enduring sexual attraction toward members of either one's own gender (homosexual orientation) or the other gender (heterosexual orientation). (p. 379)

sexual response cycle the four stages of sexual responding described by Masters and Johnson—excitement, plateau, orgasm, and resolution. (p. 375)

shaping an operant conditioning procedure in which reinforcers guide behavior toward closer and closer approximations of a desired goal. (p. 255)

short-term memory activated memory that holds a few items briefly, such as the seven digits of a phone number while dialing, before the information is stored or forgotten. (p. 272)

signal detection theory predicts how and when we detect the presence of a faint stimulus ("signal"). Assumes that there is no single absolute threshold and that detection depends partly on a person's experience, expectation, motivation, and level of fatigue. (p. 149)

skeletal nervous system the division of the peripheral nervous system that controls the body's skeletal muscles. (p. 48)

Skinner box a chamber containing a bar or key that an animal can manipulate to obtain a food or water reinforcer, with attached devices to record the animal's rate of bar pressing or key pecking. Used in operant conditioning research. (p. 255)

sleep apnea a sleep disorder characterized by temporary cessations of breathing during sleep and consequent momentary reawakenings. (p. 217)

social clock the culturally preferred timing of social events such as marriage, parenthood, and retirement. (p. 136)

social exchange theory the theory that our social behavior is an exchange process, the aim of which is to maximize benefits and minimize costs. (p. 587)

social facilitation improved performance of tasks in the presence of others; occurs with simple or well-learned tasks but not with tasks that are difficult or not yet mastered. (p. 560)

social leadership group-oriented leadership that builds teamwork, mediates conflict, and offers support. (p. 388)

social learning theory the theory that we learn social behavior by observing and imitating and by being rewarded or punished. (p. 106)

social loafing the tendency for people in a group to exert less effort when pooling their efforts toward attaining a common goal than when individually accountable. (p. 562)

social psychology the scientific study of how we think about, influence, and relate to one another. (p. 549)

social trap a situation in which the conflicting parties, by each rationally pursuing their self-interest, become caught in mutually destructive behavior. (p. 578)

source amnesia attributing to the wrong source an event that we experienced, heard about, read about, or imagined. (Also called *source misattribution*.) Source amnesia, along with the misinformation effect, is at the heart of many false memories. (p. 296)

spacing effect the tendency for distributed study or practice to yield better long-term retention than is achieved through massed study or practice. (p. 274)

split brain a condition in which the two hemispheres of the brain are isolated by cutting the connecting fibers (mainly those of the corpus callosum) between them. (p. 65)

spontaneous recovery the reappearance, after a rest period, of an extinguished conditioned response. (p. 248)

standardization defining meaningful scores by comparison with the performance of a pretested "standardization group." (p. 344)

Stanford-Binet the widely used American revision (by Terman at Stanford University) of Binet's original intelligence test. (p. 335)

stereotype a generalized (often overgeneralized) belief about a group of people. (p. 567)

stimulants drugs (such as caffeine, nicotine, and the more powerful amphetamines and cocaine) that excite neural activity and speed up body functions. (p. 231)

storage the retention of encoded information over time. (p. 272)

stranger anxiety the fear of strangers that infants commonly display, beginning by about 8 months of age. (p. 94)

stress the process by which we perceive and respond to certain events, called *stressors*, that we appraise as threatening or challenging. (p. 516)

subjective well-being self-perceived happiness or satisfaction with life. Used along with measures of objective well-being (for example, physical and economic indicators) to evaluate people's quality of life. (p. 407)

subliminal below one's absolute threshold for conscious awareness. (p. 149)

superego the part of personality that, according to Freud, represents internalized ideals and provides standards for judgment (the conscience) and for future aspirations. (p. 422)

superordinate goals shared goals that override differences among people and require their cooperation. (p. 587)

survey a technique for ascertaining the self-reported attitudes or behaviors of people, usually by questioning a representative, random sample of them. (p. 19)

sympathetic nervous system the division of the autonomic nervous system that arouses the body, mobilizing its energy in stressful situations. (p. 48)

synapse [SIN-aps] the junction between the axon tip of the sending neuron and the dendrite or cell body of the receiving neuron. The tiny gap at this junction is called the *synaptic gap* or *cleft*. (p. 44)

syntax the rules for combining words into grammatically sensible sentences in a given language. (p. 320)

systematic desensitization a type of counterconditioning that associates a pleasant relaxed state with gradually increasing anxiety-triggering stimuli. Commonly used to treat phobias. (p. 493)

task leadership goal-oriented leadership that sets standards, organizes work, and focuses attention on goals. (p. 388)

telegraphic speech early speech stage in which the child speaks like a telegram—"go car"—using mostly nouns and verbs and omitting "auxiliary" words. (p. 322)

temperament a person's characteristic emotional reactivity and intensity. (p. 96)

temporal lobes the portion of the cerebral cortex lying roughly above the ears; includes the auditory areas, each of which receives auditory information primarily from the opposite ear. (p. 59)

teratogens agents, such as chemicals and viruses, that can reach the embryo or fetus during prenatal development and cause harm. (p. 80)

testosterone the most important of the male sex hormones. Both males and females have it, but the additional testosterone in males stimulates the growth of the male sex organs in the fetus and the development of the male sex characteristics during puberty. (p. 79)

texture gradient a monocular cue for perceiving distance; a gradual change to a less distinct texture suggests increasing distance. (p. 188)

thalamus [THAL-uh-muss] the brain's sensory switchboard, located on top of the brainstem; it directs messages to the sensory receiving areas in the cortex and transmits replies to the cerebellum and medulla. (p. 55)

THC the major active ingredient in marijuana; triggers a variety of effects, including mild hallucinations. (p. 234)

Thematic Apperception Test (TAT) a projective test in which people express their inner feelings and interests through the stories they make up about ambiguous scenes. (p. 426)

theory an explanation using an integrated set of principles that organizes and predicts observations. (p. 17)

Theory X assumes that workers are basically lazy, error-prone, and extrinsically motivated by money and, thus, should be directed from above. (p. 389)

Theory Y assumes that, given challenge and freedom, workers are motivated to achieve self-esteem and to demonstrate their competence and creativity. (p. 389)

threshold the level of stimulation required to trigger a neural impulse. (p. 44)

token economy an operant conditioning procedure that rewards desired behavior. A patient exchanges a token of some sort, earned for exhibiting the desired behavior, for various privileges or treats. (p. 495)

tolerance the diminishing effect with regular use of the same dose of a drug, requiring the user to take larger and larger doses before experiencing the drug's effect. (p. 229)

top-down processing information processing guided by higher level mental processes, as when we construct perceptions drawing on our experience and expectations. (p. 147)

trait a characteristic pattern of behavior or a disposition to feel and act, as assessed by self-report inventories and peer reports. (p. 430)

transduction conversion of one form of energy into another. In sensation, the transforming of stimulus energies into neural impulses. (p. 153)

transference in psychoanalysis, the patient's transfer to the analyst of emotions linked with other relationships (such as love or hatred for a parent). (p. 489)

two-factor theory Schachter's theory that to experience emotion one must (1) be physically aroused and (2) cognitively label the arousal. (p. 414)

two-word stage beginning about age 2, the stage in speech development during which a child speaks mostly two-word statements. (p. 321)

Type A Friedman and Rosenman's term for competitive, hard-driving, impatient, verbally aggressive, and anger-prone people. (p. 522)

Type B Friedman and Rosenman's term for easygoing, relaxed people. (p. 522)

unconditional positive regard according to Rogers, an attitude of total acceptance toward another person. (p. 437)

unconditioned response (UCR) in classical conditioning, the unlearned, naturally occurring response to the unconditioned stimulus (UCS), such as salivation when food is in the mouth. (p. 246)

unconditioned stimulus (UCS) in classical conditioning, a stimulus that unconditionally— naturally and automatically—triggers a response. (p. 246)

unconscious according to Freud, a reservoir of mostly unacceptable thoughts, wishes, feelings, and memories. According to contemporary research psychologists, information processing of which we are unaware. (p. 421)

validity the extent to which a test measures or predicts what it is supposed to. (See also *content validity* and *predictive validity*.) (p. 345)

variable-interval schedule in operant conditioning, a schedule of reinforcement that reinforces a response at unpredictable time intervals. (p. 258)

variable-ratio schedule in operant conditioning, a schedule of reinforcement that reinforces a response after an unpredictable number of responses. (p. 258)

vestibular sense the sense of body movement and position, including the sense of balance. (p. 177)

visual capture the tendency for vision to dominate the other senses. For example, in a movie theater we perceive voices as coming from the images on the screen we see rather than from the projector behind us. (p. 184)

visual cliff a laboratory device for testing depth perception in infants and young animals. (p. 186)

visual encoding the encoding of picture images. (p. 275)

wavelength the distance from the peak of one light or sound wave to the peak of the next. Electromagnetic wavelengths vary from the short blips of cosmic rays to the long pulses of radio transmission. (p. 154)

Weber's law the principle that, to perceive their difference, two stimuli must differ by a constant minimum percentage (rather than a constant amount). (p. 152)

Wechsler Adult Intelligence Scale (WAIS) the WAIS is the most widely used intelligence test; contains verbal and performance (nonverbal) subtests. (p. 343)

Wernicke's area an area of the left temporal lobe involved in language comprehension. (p. 63)

withdrawal the discomfort and distress that follow discontinuing the use of an addictive drug. (p. 229)

X chromosome the sex chromosome found in both men and women. Females have two X chromosomes; males have one. An X chromosome from each parent produces a female. (p. 79)

Y chromosome the sex chromosome found only in males. When paired with an X sex chromosome from the mother, it produces a male child. (p. 79)

Young-Helmholtz trichromatic (three-color) theory the theory that the retina contains three different color receptors—one most sensitive to red, one to green, one to blue—which when stimulated in combination can produce the perception of any color. (p. 161)

zygote the fertilized egg; it enters a 2-week period of rapid cell division and develops into an embryo. (p. 79)

references

Aas, H., & Klepp, K-I. (1992). Adolescents' alcohol use related to perceived norms. *Scandinavian Journal of Psychology, 33,* 315–325. (p. 237)

Abbey, A. (1987). Misperceptions of friendly behavior as sexual interest: A survey of naturally occurring incidents. *Psychology of Women Quarterly, 11,* 173–194. (p. 379)

Abbey, A. (1991). Acquaintance rape and alcohol consumption on college campuses: How are they linked? *Journal of American College Health, 39,* 165–169. (p. 231)

Abbey, A., Ross, L. T., & McDuffie, D. (1993). Alcohol's role in sexual assault. In R. R. Watson (Ed.), *Drug and alcohol abuse reviews, vol 5: Addictive behaviors in women.* Totowa, NJ: Humana Press. (p. 573)

Abbey, A., Ross, L. T., McDuffie, D., & McAuslan, P. (1996). Alcohol and dating risk factors for sexual assault among college women. *Psychology of Women Quarterly, 20,* 147-169. (p. 573)

Abrams, D. (1991). AIDS: What young people believe and what they do. Paper presented at the British Association for the Advancement of Science conference. (p. 447)

Abrams, D. B., & Wilson, G. T. (1983). Alcohol, sexual arousal, and self-control. *Journal of Personality and Social Psychology, 45,* 188–198. (p. 232)

Abramson, L. Y., Metalsky, G. I., & Alloy, L. B. (1989). Hopelessness depression: A theory-based subtype. *Psychological Review, 96,* 358–372. (p. 473)

Acitelli, L. K., & Antonucci, T. C. (1994). Gender differences in the link between marital support and satisfaction in older couples. *Journal of Personality and Social Psychology, 67,* 688-698. (p. 137)

Acock, A. C., & Demo, D. H. (1994). *Family diversity and well-being.* Thousand Oaks, CA: Sage. (p. 566)

Adair, J. G., Paivio, A., & Ritchie, P. (1996). Psychology in Canada. *Annual Review of Psychology, 47,* 341-370. (p. 8)

Adelmann, P. K., Antonucci, T. C., Crohan, S. F., & Coleman, L. M. (1989). Empty nest, cohort, and employment in the well-being of midlife women. *Sex Roles, 20,* 173–189. (p. 138)

Ader, R., & Cohen, N. (1985). CNS–immune system interactions: Conditioning phenomena. *Behavioral and Brain Sciences, 8,* 379–394. (p. 527)

Adler, N. E., David, H. P., Major, B. N., Roth, S. H., Russo, N. F., & Wyatt, G. E. (1990). Psychological responses after abortion. *Science, 248,* 41–44. (p. 519)

Adler, T. (1989, March). FAA establishes unit to study human error. *APA Monitor,* p. 4. (p. 184)

Adolphs, R., Tranel, D., Damasio, H., & Damasio, A. (1994). Impaired recognition of emotion in facial expressions following bilateral damage to the human amygdala. *Nature, 372,* 669-672. (p. 57)

Advertising Age (1958, February 10). "Phone now," said CBC subliminally—but nobody did. P. 8. (p. 150)

Affleck, G., Tennen, H., Urrows, S., & Higgins, P. (1994). Person and contextual features of daily stress reactivity: Individual differences in relations of undesirable daily events with mood disturbance and chronic pain intensity. *Journal of Personality and Social Psychology, 66,* 329–340. (p. 407)

Aggleton, J. P., Kentridge, R. W., & Neave, N. J. (1993). Evidence for longevity differences between left handed and right handed men: An archival study of cricketers. *Journal of Epidemiology and Community Health, 47,* 206–209. (p. 527)

Agnati, L. F., Bjelke, B., & Fuxe, K. (1992). Volume transmission in the brain. *American Scientist, 80,* 362–373. (p. 51)

Ahuja, A. (1996, July 8). Revealed—The truth about false memory syndrome. *The Times of London,* p. 12. (p. 300)

Aiello, J. R., Thompson, D. D., & Brodzinsky, D. M. (1983). How funny is crowding anyway? Effects of room size, group size, and the introduction of humor. *Basic and Applied Social Psychology, 4,* 193–207. (p. 561)

Ainsworth, M. D. S. (1973). The development of infant-mother attachment. In B. Caldwell & H. Ricciuti (Eds.), *Review of child development research* (Vol. 3). Chicago: University of Chicago Press. (p. 96)

Ainsworth, M. D. S. (1979). Infant-mother attachment. *American Psychologist, 34,* 932–937. (p. 97)

Ainsworth, M. D. S. (1989). Attachments beyond infancy. *American Psychologist, 44,* 709–716. (p. 96)

Akin-Ogundeji, O. (1991). Asserting psychology in Africa. *The Psychologist, 14,* 2–4. (p. 8)

Albee, G. W. (1986). Toward a just society: Lessons from observations on the primary prevention of psychopathology. *American Psychologist, 41,* 891–898. (p. 512)

Alcock, J. E. (1981). *Parapsychology: Science or magic?* Oxford: Pergamon. (p. 290)

Alcock, J. E. (1985, Spring). Parapsychology: The "spiritual" science. *Free Inquiry,* pp. 25–35. (p. 204)

Aldrich, M. S. (1989). Automobile accidents in patients with sleep disorders. *Sleep, 12,* 487–494. (p. 217)

Aldridge-Morris, R. (1989). *Multiple personality: An exercise in deception.* Hillsdale, NJ: Erlbaum. (p. 467)

Alexander, C. N., Langer, E. J., Newman, R. I., Chandler, H. M., & Davies, J. L. (1989). Transcendental meditation, mindfulness, and longevity: An experimental study with the elderly. *Journal of Personality and Social Psychology, 57,* 950–964. (p. 531)

Alkon, D. L., Amaral, D. G., Baer, M. F., Black, J., Carew, T. J., Cohen, N. J., Disterhoft, J. F., Eichenbaum, H., Golski, S., Gorman, L. K., Lynch, G., McNaughton, B. L., Mishkin, M., Moyer, J. R. Jr., Olds, J. L., Olton, D. S., Otto, T., Squire, L. R., Staubli, U., Thompson, L. T., & Wible, C. (1991). Learning and memory. *Brain Research Reviews, 16,* 193–220. (p. 284)

Allard, F., & Burnett, N. (1985). Skill in sport. *Canadian Journal of Psychology, 39,* 294–312. (p. 278)

Allen, J. B., Repinski, D. J., Ballard, J. C., & Griffin, B. W. (1996). Beliefs about the etiology of homosexuality may influence attitudes toward homosexuals. Paper presented to the American Psychological Society convention. (p. 382)

Allen, L. S., & Gorski, R. A. (1992). Sexual orientation and the size of the anterior commisure in the human brain. *Proceedings of the National Academy of Sciences, 89,* 7199–7202. (p. 381)

Allman, A. L. (1989). Subjective well-being of students with and without disabilities. Paper presented at the Midwestern Psychological Association convention. (p. 407)

Allport, G. W. (1967). Gordon W. Allport. In E. G. Boring & G. Lindzey (Eds.), *A history of psychology in autobiography* (Vol. V). New York: Appleton-Century-Crofts. (p. 430)

Allport, G. W., & Odbert, H. S. (1936). Trait-names: A psycho-lexical study. *Psychological Monographs, 47*(1). (p. 431)

Altemus, M., Deuster, P. A., Galliven, E., Carter, C. S., & Gold, P. W. (1995). Suppression of hypothalamic-pituitary-adrenal axis responses to stress in lactating women. *Journal of Clinical Endocrinology and Metabolism, 80,* 2954-2959. (p. 99)

Alwin, D. F. (1990). Historical changes in parental orientations to children. In N. Mandell (Ed.), *Sociological studies of child development* (Vol. 3). Greenwich, CT: JAI Press. (p. 105)

Amabile, T. M. (1983). *The social psychology of creativity.* New York: Springer-Verlag. (pp. 352, 439)

Amabile, T. M. (1987). The motivation to be creative. In S. Isaksen (Ed.), *Frontiers in creativity: Beyond the basics.* Buffalo, NY: Bearly Limited. (p. 352)

Amabile, T. M. (1988). From individual creativity to organizational innovation. In K. Gronhaug & G. Kaufmann (Eds.), *Innovation: A crossdisciplinary perspective.* Oslo: Norwegian University Press. (p. 352)

Amabile, T. M., & Hennessey, B. A. (1992). The motivation for creativity in children. In A. K. Boggiano & T. S. Pittman (Eds.), *Achievement and motivation: A social-developmental perspective.* New York: Cambridge University Press. (p. 351)

Amato, P. R., & Keith, B. (1991). Parental divorce and the well-being of children: A meta-analysis. *Psychological Bulletin, 110,* 26–46. (p. 102)

Ambady, N., & Rosenthal, R. (1992). Thin slices of expressive behavior as predictors of interpersonal consequences: A meta-analysis. *Psychological Bulletin, 111,* 256–274. (p. 435)

Ambady, N., & Rosenthal, R. (1993). Half a minute: Predicting teacher evaluations from thin slices of nonverbal behavior and physical attractiveness. *Journal of Personality and Social Psychology, 64,* 431–441. (p. 435)

Ambady, N., Hallahan, M., & Rosenthal, R. (1995). On judging and being judged accurately in zero-acquaintance situations. *Journal of Personality and Social Psychology, 69,* 518-529. (p. 399)

American Psychiatric Association. (1990). *The practice of ECT: Recommendations for treatment, training, and privileging.* Washington, DC: American Psychiatric Press. (p. 510)

American Psychiatric Association. (1994). *Diagnostic and statistical manual of mental disorders (Fourth Edition).* Washington, DC: American Psychiatric Press. (p. 349)

American Psychological Association. (1986). Council of Representatives statement cited by N. Abeles, Proceedings of the American Psychological Association, Incorporated, for the Year 1985: Minutes of the annual meeting of the Council of Representatives August 22 and 25, 1985, Los Angeles, California, and January 31–February 2, 1986, Washington, DC. *American Psychologist, 41,* 633–663. (p. 397)

American Psychological Association. (1991). Medical cost offset. Washington, DC: American Psychological Association Practice Directorate. (p. 504)

American Psychological Association. (1992). Ethical principles of psychologists and code of conduct. *American Psychologist, 47,* 1597–1611. (p. 36)

Anda, R., Williamson, D., Jones, D., Macera, C., Eaker, E., Glassman, A., & Marks, J. (1993). Depressed affect, hopelessness, and the risk of ischemic heart disease in a cohort of U.S. adults. *Epidemiology, 4,* 285–294. (p. 523)

Andersen, B. L. (1983). Primary orgasmic dysfunction: Diagnostic considerations and review of treatment. *Psychological Bulletin, 93,* 105–136. (p. 378)

Andersen, B. L. (1989). Health psychology's contribution to addressing the cancer problem: Update on accomplishments. *Health Psychology, 8,* 683–703. (p. 525)

Andersen, B. L., & Cyranowski, J. M. (1995). Women's sexuality: Behaviors, responses, and individual differences. *Journal of Consulting and Clinical Psychology, 63,* 891-906. (p. 376)

Anderson, C. A. (1989). Temperature and aggression: Ubiquitous effects of heat on occurrence of human violence. *Psychological Bulletin, 106,* 74-96. (p. 573)

Anderson, C. A., & Anderson, D. C. (1984). Ambient temperature and violent crime: Tests of the linear and curvilinear hypotheses. *Journal of Personality and Social Psychology, 46,* 91–97. (p. 573)

Anderson, C. A., Lepper, M. R., & Ross, L. (1980). Perseverance of social theories: The role of explanation in the persistence of discredited information. *Journal of Personality and Social Psychology, 39,* 1037–1049. (p. 315)

Anderson, D. R., & Jose, W. S., II (1987, December). Employee lifestyle and the bottom line: Results from the StayWell evaluation. *Fitness in Business,* pp. 86–91. (p. 530)

Anderson, J. R., & Schooler, L. J. (1991). Reflections of the environment in memory. *Psychological Science, 2,* 396–408. (p. 274)

Anderson, R. C., Pichert, J. W., Goetz, E. T., Schallert, D. L., Stevens, K. V., & Trollip, S. R. (1976). Instantiation of general terms. *Journal of Verbal Learning and Verbal Behavior, 15,* 667-679. (p. 289)

Andersson, B. E. (1989). Effects of public daycare: A longitudinal study. *Child Development, 60,* 857–866. (p. 101)

Andreasen, N. C., & others (1994). Thalamic abnormalities in schizophrenia visualized through magnetic resonance image averaging. *Science, 266,* 294-298. (p. 478)

Angoff, W. H. (1987). The nature-nurture debate, aptitudes, and group differences. Presidential address to American Psychological Association Division 5. (p. 356)

Angoff, W. H. (1988, Winter). A philosophical discussion: The issues of test and item bias. *ETS Developments,* pp. 10–11. (pp. 349, 379)

Antaki, C. (1989, May). A brief account of psychology in Nicaragua. *The Psychologist,* pp. 208–209. (p. 8)

Antoni, M. H., LaPerriere, A., Schneiderman, N., & Fletcher, M. A. (1991). Stress and immunity in individuals at risk for AIDS. *Stress Medicine, 7,* 35–44. (p. 525)

Antony, M. M., Brown, T. A., & Barlow, D. H. (1992). Current perspectives on panic and panic disorder. *Current Directions in Psychological Science, 1,* 79–82. (p. 464)

Antrobus, J. (1991). Dreaming: Cognitive processes during cortical activation and high afferent thresholds. *Psychological Review, 98,* 96–121. (p. 219)

Archer, J. (1996). Sex differences in social behavior: Are the social role and evolutionary explanations compatible? *American Psychologist, 51,* 909-917. (p. 566)

Arendt, H. (1963). *Eichmann in Jerusalem: A report on the banality of evil.* New York: Viking Press. (p. 120)

Aries, E. (1987). Gender and communication. In P. 671ver & C. Henrick (Eds.), *Review of Personality and Social Psychology, 7,* 177–200. (p. 389

Arnold, R. B. (1991, October 7). A star cries incest. *People,* pp. 84–88. (p. 299)

Asch, S. E. (1955). Opinions and social pressure. *Scientific American, 193,* 31–35. (p. 555)

Aserinsky, E. (1988, January 17). Personal communication. (p. 211)

Astin, A. W., Korn, W. S., & Berz, E. R. (1989). *The American freshman: National norms for Fall 1989.* Los Angeles: American Council on Education and UCLA. (p. 139)

Atkinson, R. (1988). *The teenage world: Adolescent self-image in ten countries.* New York: Plenum Press. (p. 105)

Atwell, R. H. (1986, July 28). Drugs on campus: A perspective. *Higher Education & National Affairs,* p. 5. (p. 231)

Averill, J. R. (1983). Studies on anger and aggression: Implications for theories of emotion. *American Psychologist, 38,* 1145–1160. (p. 405)

Averill, J. R. (1993). William James's other theory of emotion. In M. E. Donnelly (Ed.), *Reinterpreting the legacy of William James.* Washington, DC: American Psychological Association. (p. 414)

Avery, R. D., & others (1994, December 13). Mainstream science on intelligence. *Wall Street Journal,* editorial page. (p. 356)

Ax, A. F. (1953). The physiological differentiation of fear and anger in humans. *Psychosomatic Medicine, 15,* 433–442. (p. 398)

Axel, R. (1995, October). The molecular logic of smell. *Scientific American,* pp. 154-159. (p. 175)

Axinn, W. G., & Thornton, A. (1992). The relationship between cohabitation and divorce: Selectivity or causal influence? *Demography, 29,* 357–374. (p. 139)

Azar, B. (1995, May). Several genetic traits linked to alcoholism. *APA Monitor,* pp. 21-22. (p. 237)

Baars, B. J., & McGovern, K. (1994). Consciousness. In V. Ramachandran (Ed.), *Encyclopedia of human behavior.* Orlando, FL: Academic Press. (p. 183)

Babad, E., Bernieri, F., & Rosenthal, R. (1991). Students as judges of teachers' verbal and nonverbal behavior. *American Educational Research Journal, 28,* 211–234. (p. 399)

Bachman, J. G., Johnston, L. D., & O'Malley, P. M. (1987). *Monitoring the future: Questionnaire responses from the nation's high school seniors, 1986.* Ann Arbor, MI: Institute for Social Research, The University of Michigan. (p. 124)

Backman, L., & Dixon, R. A. (1992). Psychological compensation: A theoretical framework. *Psychological Bulletin, 112,* 259–283. (p. 169)

Backus, J. (1977). *The acoustical foundations of music* (2nd ed.). New York: Norton. (p. 166)

Baddeley, A. D. (1982). *Your memory: A user's guide.* New York: Macmillan. (pp. 273, 274)

Badenhoop, M. S., & Johansen, M. K. (1980). Do reentry women have special needs? *Psychology of Women Quarterly, 4,* 591–595. (p. 134)

Bahrick, H. P. (1984b). Semantic memory content in permastore: 50 years of memory for Spanish learned in school. *Journal of Experimental Psychology: General, 111,* 1–29. (p. 283)

Bahrick, H. P., & Hall, L. K. (1991). Lifetime maintenance of high school mathematics content. *Journal of Experimental Psychology: General, 120,* 20–33. (p. 274)

Bahrick, H. P., Bahrick, L. E., Bahrick, A. S., & Bahrick, P. E. (1993). Maintenance of foreign language vocabulary and the spacing effect. *Psychological Science, 4*, 316–321. (p. 288)

Bahrick, H. P., Bahrick, P. O., & Wittlinger, R. P. (1975). Fifty years of memory for names and faces: A cross-sectional approach. *Journal of Experimental Psychology: General, 104*, 54–75. (p. 274)

Bailey, J. M., & Pillard, R. C. (1991). A genetic study of male sexual orientation. *Archives of General Psychiatry, 48*, 1089–1096. (p. 381)

Bailey, J. M., & Pillard, R. C. (1994, January). The innateness of homosexuality. *Harvard Mental Health Letter*, pp. 4–6. (p. 381)

Bailey, J. M., & Pillard, R. C. (1995). Genetics of human sexual orientation. *Annual Review of Sex Research, 6*, 126-150. (p. 381)

Bailey, J. M., & Zucker, K. J. (1995). Childhood sex-typed behavior and sexual orientation: A conceptual analysis and quantitative review. *Developmental Psychology, 31*, 43-55. (p. 379)

Bailey, J. M., Bobrow, D., Wolfe, M., & Mikach, S. (1995). Sexual orientation of adult sons of gay fathers. *Developmental Psychology, 31*, 124-129. (p. 380)

Bailey, J. M., Dunne, M. P., & Martin, N. G. (1997). Sex differences in the distribution and determinants of sexual orientation in a national twin sample. Unpublished manuscript, Northwestern University, Evanston, IL. (p. 381)

Bailey, J. M., Gaulin, S., Agyei, Y, & Gladue, B. A. (1994). Effects of gender and sexual orientation on evolutionarily relevant aspects of human mating psychology. *Journal of Personality and Social Psychology, 66*, 1081–1093. (p. 379)

Bailey, J. M., Pillard, R. C., Neale, M. C., & Agyei, Y. (1993). Heritable factors influence sexual orientation in women. *Archives of General Psychiatry, 50*, 217–223. (p. 381)

Baillargeon, R. (1992). The object concept revisited. In C. Granrud (Ed.), *Visual perception and cognition in infancy. Carnegie-Mellon Symposia on Cognition*, Vol. 23. Hillsdale, NJ: Erlbaum. (p. 89)

Baillargeon, R. (1994). How do infants learn about the physical world? *Current Directions in Psychological Science, 3*, 133-140. (p. 89)

Bairagi, R. (1987). Food crises and female children in rural Bangladesh. *Social Science, 72*, 48–51. (p. 568)

Baker, E. L. (1987). The state of the art of clinical hypnosis. *International Journal of Clinical and Experimental Hypnosis, 35*, 203–214. (p. 224)

Baker-Ward, L., Gordon, B. N., Ornstein, P. A., Larus, D. M., & Clubb, P. A. (1993). Young children's long-term retention of a pediatric examination. *Child Development, 64*, 1519–1533. (p. 298)

Balakrishan, T. R., Rao, K. V., Lapierre-Adamcyk, E., & Krotki, K. J. (1987). A hazard model analysis of the covariates of marriage dissolution in Canada. *Demography, 24*, 395–406. (p. 139)

Baldwin, E. (1993). The case for animal research in psychology. *Journal of Social Issues, 49*(1), 121–131. (p. 35)

Ball, W., & Tronick, E. (1971). Infant responses to impending collision: Optical and real. *Science, 171*, 818–820. (p. 186)

Baltes, P. B. (1993). The aging mind: Potential and limits. *The Gerontologist, 33*, 580–594. (p. 135)

Baltes, P. B. (1994). Life-span developmental psychology: On the overall landscape of human development. Invited address, American Psychological Association convention. (p. 135)

Bandura, A. (1977). *Social learning theory.* Englewood Cliffs, NJ: Prentice-Hall. (p. 266)

Bandura, A. (1982). The psychology of chance encounters and life paths. *American Psychologist, 37*, 747–755. (p. 137)

Bandura, A. (1986). *Social foundations of thought and action: A social-cognitive theory.* Englewood Cliffs, NJ: Prentice-Hall. (p. 445)

Bandura, A., Blanchard, E. B., & Ritter, B. (1969). Relative efficacy of desensitization and modeling approaches for inducing behavioral, affective, and attitudinal changes. *Journal of Personality and Social Psychology, 13*, 173–199. (p. 494)

Bannon, L. (1995, October 25). Beastly gossip. Grand Rapids (Mich.) *Press*, pp. A1, A4 (reprinted from *Wall Street Journal*). (p. 197)

Barbaree, H. E., & Marshall, W. L. (1991). The role of male sexual arousal in rape: Six models. *Journal of Consulting and Clinical Psychology, 59*, 621–630. (p. 577)

Bargh, J. A. (1997). The automaticity of everyday life. In R. S. Wyer, Jr. (ed.), *Advances in social cognition,* vol. 10. Mahwah, NJ: Erlbaum. (p. 428)

Barinaga, M. (1991). How long is the human life-span? *Science, 254*, 936–938. (p. 130)

Barinaga, M. (1992). The brain remaps its own contours. *Science, 258*, 216–218. (p. 85)

Barinaga, M. (1992). How scary things get that way. *Science, 258*, 887–888. (p. 404)

Barinaga, M. (1995). Missing Alzheimer's gene found. *Science, 269*, 817-818. (p. 132)

Barker, S. L., Funk, S. C., & Houston, B. K. (1988). Psychological treatment versus nonspecific factors: A meta-analysis of conditions that engender comparable expectations for improvement. *Clinical Psychology Review, 8*, 579–594. (p. 505)

Barlow, D. H. (1988). *Anxiety and its disorders: The nature and treatment of anxiety and panic.* New York: Guilford. (p. 464)

Barnett, A. (1990). Air safety: End of the golden age? *Chance, 1*(2), pp. 8–12. (p. 312)

Barnett, A. (1996, June 9). Quoted by Adam Bryan, "Fly me; Why no airline brags: "We're the safest." *New York Times*, Section 4, p. 1. (p. 312)

Barnett, P. A., & Gotlib, I. H. (1988). Psychosocial functioning and depression: Distinguishing among antecedents, concomitants, and consequences. *Psychological Bulletin, 104*, 97–126. (p. 474)

Barnier, A. J., & McConkey, K. M. (1992). Reports of real and false memories: The relevance of hypnosis, hypnotizability, and context of memory test. *Journal of Abnormal Psychology, 101*, 521–527. (p. 223)

Baron, J. (1985). *Rationality and intelligence.* New York: Cambridge University Press. (p. 337)

Baron, R. A. (1987). Interviewer's mood and reaction to job applicants: The influence of affective states on applied social judgments. *Journal of Applied Social Psychology, 17*, 911–926. (p. 406)

Baron, R. A. (1988). Negative effects of destructive criticism: Impact on conflict, self-efficacy, and task performance. *Journal of Applied Psychology, 73*, 199–207. (p. 263)

Baron, R. A. (1990). Environmentally induced positive affect: Its impact on self-efficacy, task performance, negotiation, and conflict. *Journal of Applied Social Psychology, 20*, 368–384. (p. 176)

Baron, R. S., Cutrona, C. E., Hicklin, D., Russell, D. W., & Lubaroff, D. M. (1990). Social support and immune function among spouses of cancer patients. *Journal of Personality and Social Psychology, 59*, 344–352. (p. 533)

Baron, R. S., Vandello, J. A., & Brunsman, B. (1996). The forgotten variable in conformity research: Impact of task importance on social influence. *Journal of Personality and Social Psychology, 71*, 915-927. (p. 556)

Barry, D. (1996, August 11). Syndicated column. (p. 116)

Barton, J., Chassin, L., Presson, C. C., & Sherman, S. J. (1982). Social image factors as motivators of smoking initiation in early and middle adolescence. *Child Development, 53*, 1499–1511. (p. 537)

Bartoshuk, L. M. (1993). The wisdom of the body: Using case studies to teach sensation and perception. Paper presented to the National Institute on the Teaching of Psychology, St. Petersburg Beach, Florida. (p. 174)

Baruch, G. K., & Barnett, R. (1986). Role quality, multiple role involvement, and psychological well-being in midlife women. *Journal of Personality and Social Psychology, 51*, 578–585. (p. 140)

Bashore, T. R. (1994). Some thoughts on neurocognitive slowing. *Acta Psychologica, 86*, 295-325. (p. 131)

Bass, E., & Davis, L. (1988). *The courage to heal.* New York: Harper & Row. (p. 299)

Bass, L. E., & Kane-Williams, E. (1993). Stereotype or reality: Another look at alcohol and drug use among African American children. U.S. Department of Health and Human Services, *Public Health Reports, 108* (Supplement 1), 78–84. (p. 237)

Bat-Chava, Y. (1993). Antecedents of self-esteem in deaf people: A meta-analytic review. *Rehabilitation Psychology, 38*(4), 221–234. (p. 168)

Bat-Chava, Y. (1994). Group identification and self-esteem of deaf adults. *Personality and Social Psychology Bulletin, 20*, 494-502. (p. 168)

Bauer, P. J. (1996). What do infants recall of their lives? Memory for specific events by one- to two-year-olds. *American Psychologist, 51*, 29-41. (p. 83)

Baum, A., & Fleming, I. (1993). Implications of psychological research on stress and technological accidents. *American Psychologist, 48*, 665–672. (p. 519)

Baumeister, R. F. (1989). The optimal margin of illusion. *Journal of Social and Clinical Psychology, 8*, 176–189. (p. 314, 441)

Baumeister, R. F. (1993). Understanding the inner nature of low self-esteem: Uncertain, fragile, protective, and conflicted. In R. F. Baumeister (Ed.), *Self-esteem: The puzzle of low self-regard.* New York: Plenum. (p. 439)

Baumeister, R. F., & Leary, M. R. (1995). The need to belong: Desire for interpersonal attachments as a fundamental human motivation. *Psychological Bulletin, 117*, 497-529. (p. 367)

Baumeister, R. F., & Tice, D. M. (1986). How adolescence became the struggle for self: A historical transformation of psychological development. In J. Suls & A. G. Greenwald (Eds.), *Psychological perspectives on the self* (Vol. 3). Hillsdale, NJ: Erlbaum. (p. 115)

Baumeister, R. F., Stillwell, A., & Wotman, S. R. (1990). Victim and perpetrator accounts of interpersonal conflict: Autobiographical narratives about anger. *Journal of Personality and Social Psychology, 59*, 994–1005. (p. 406)

Baumeister, R. F., Tice, D. M., & Hutton, D. G. (1989). Self-presentational motivations and personality differences in self-esteem. *Journal of Personality, 57*, 547–579. (p. 440)

Baumgardner, A. H. (1990). To know oneself is to like oneself: Self-certainty and self-affect. *Journal of Personality and Social Psychology, 58*, 1062–1072. (p. 122)

Baumgardner, A. H., Kaufman, C. M., & Levy, P. E. (1989). Regulating affect interpersonally: When low esteem leads to greater enhancement. *Journal of Personality and Social Psychology, 56*, 907–921. (p. 439)

Baumrind, D. (1982). Adolescent sexuality: Comment on Williams' and Silka's comments on Baumrind. *American Psychologist, 37*, 1402–1403. (p. 383)

Baumrind, D. (1983). Rejoinder to Lewis's reinterpretation of parental firm control effects: Are authoritative families really harmonious? *Psychological Bulletin, 94,* 132–142. (p. 104)

Baumrind, D. (1991). Parenting styles and adolescent development. In J. Brooks-Gunn, R. Lerner, & A. C. Petersen (Eds.), *The encyclopedia of adolescence.* New York: Garland. (p. 104)

Baumrind, D. (1993). The average expectable environment is not good enough: A response to Scarr. *Child Development, 64,* 1299-1353. (p. 111)

Bayley, N. (1949). Consistency and variability in the growth of intelligence from birth to eighteen years. *Journal of Genetic Psychology, 75*, 165–196. (p. 348)

Beaman, A. L., & Klentz, B. (1983). The supposed physical attractiveness bias against supporters of the women's movement: A meta-analysis. *Personality and Social Psychology Bulletin, 9,* 544–550. (p. 582)

Beardsley, L. M. (1994). Medical diagnosis and treatment across cultures. In W. J. Lonner & R. Malpass (Eds.), *Psychology and culture.* Boston: Allyn & Bacon. (p. 456)

Beardsley, T. (1996, July). Waking up. *Scientific American*, pp. 14, 18. (p. 214)

Beauchamp, G. K. (1987). The human preference for excess salt. *American Scientist, 75*, 27–33. (p. 370)

Beck, A. J., Kline, S. A., & Greenfeld, L. A. (1988). Survey of youth in custody, 1987. U.S. Department of Justice, Bureau of Justice Statistics Special Report. (p. 574)

Beck, A. T., & Steer, R. A. (1989). Clinical predictors of eventual suicide: A 5– to 10–year prospective study of suicide attempters. *Journal of Affective Disorders, 17*, 203–209. (p. 469)

Beck, A. T., & Young, J. E. (1978, September). College blues. *Psychology Today*, pp. 80–92. (pp. 514, 522)

Beck, A. T., Rush, A. J., Shaw, B. F., & Emery, G. (1979). *Cognitive therapy of depression.* New York: Guilford Press. (p. 498)

Becklen, R., & Cervone, D. (1983). Selective looking and the noticing of unexpected events. *Memory and Cognition, 11,* 601–608. (p. 182)

Begg, I. M., Needham, D. R., & Bookbinder, M. (1993). Do backward messages unconsciously affect listeners? No. *Canadian Journal of Experimental Psychology, 47,* 1–14. (p. 151)

Beilin, H. (1992). Piaget's enduring contribution to developmental psychology. *Developmental Psychology, 28,* 191-204. (p. 94)

Beitman, B. D., Goldfried, M. R., & Norcross, J. C. (1989). The movement toward integrating the psychotherapies: An overview. *American Journal of Psychiatry, 146,* 138–147. (p. 488)

Bell, A. P. (1982, November/December). Sexual preference: A postscript. (SIECUS Report, 11, No. 2) *Church and Society,* pp. 34–37. (p. 381)

Bell, A. P., Weinberg, M. S., & Hammersmith, S. K. (1981). *Sexual preference: Its development in men and women.* Bloomington: Indiana University Press. (p. 380)

Bell, R. Q., & Harper, L. V. (1977). *Child effects on adults.* Hillsdale, NJ: Erlbaum. (p. 112)

Bell, R. Q., & Waldrop, M. F. (1989). Achievement and cognitive correlates of minor physical anomalies in early development. In M. G. Bornstein & N. A. Krasnegor (Eds.), *Stability and continuity in mental development: Behavioral and biological perspectives.* Hillsdale, NJ: Erlbaum. (p. 348)

Bellugi, U. (1994, August). Quoted in P. Radetsky, "Silence, signs, and wonder". *Discover,* pp. 60-68. (p. 320)

Beloff, J. (1985, Spring). Science, religion and the paranormal. *Free Inquiry,* pp. 36–41 (p. 204)

Belsher, G., & Costello, C. G. (1988). Relapse after recovery from unipolar depression: A critical review. *Psychological Bulletin, 104,* 84–96. (p. 471)

Belsky, J. (1988). The "effects" of infant day care reconsidered. *Early Childhood Research Quarterly* (Vol. III), 235–272. (p. 101)

Belsky, J. (1990). Parental and nonparental child care and children's socioemotional development: A decade in review. *Journal of Marriage and the Family, 52,* 885–903. (p. 100)

Belsky, J. (1994). Effects of infant day care: 1986-1994. Invited address to the British Psychological Society Section on Developmental Psychology. (p. 101)

Belsky, J., Lang, M., & Huston, T. L. (1986). Sex typing and division of labor as determinants of marital change across the transition to parenthood. *Journal of Personality and Social Psychology, 50,* 517–522. (p. 138)

Bem, D. J. (1996). Exotic becomes erotic: A developmental theory of sexual orientation. *Psychological Review, 103,* 320-335. (p. 382)

Bem, D. J., & Honorton, C. (1994). Does psi exist? Replicable evidence for an anomalous process of information transfer. *Psychological Bulletin, 115,* 4–18. (p. 204)

Bem, S. (1993). *The lenses of gender.* New Haven: Yale University Press. (p. 106)

Bem, S. L. (1987). Masculinity and femininity exist only in the mind of the perceiver. In J. M. Reinisch, L. A. Rosenblum, & S. A. Sanders (Eds.), *Masculinity/femininity: Basic perspectives.* New York: Oxford University Press. (p. 106)

Bennett, N. G., Blanc, A. K., & Bloom, D. E. (1988). Commitment and the modern union: Assessing the link between premarital cohabitation and subsequent marital stability. *American Sociological Review, 53,* 127–138. (p. 139).

Bennett, R. (1991, February). Pornography and extrafamilial child sexual abuse: Examining the relationship. Unpublished manuscript, Los Angeles Police Department Sexually Exploited Child Unit. (p. 577)

Bennett, W., & DiIulio, J. (1996). *Body count.* New York: Simon & Schuster. (p. 237)

Benson, H. (1996). *Timeless healing: The power and biology of belief.* New York: Scribner. (p. 531)

Benson, H., & Klipper, M. Z. (1976). *The relaxation response.* New York: Morrow. (p. 531)

Benson, H., & Proctor, W. (1984). *Beyond the relaxation response: How to harness the healing power of your personal beliefs.* New York: Times Books. (p. 531)

Benson, H., & Proctor, W. (1987). *Your maximum mind.* New York: Times Books/Random House. (p. 531)

Benson, P. L. (1992, Spring). Patterns of religious development in adolescence and adulthood. *PIRI Newsletter,* 2–9. (p. 123)

Benson, P. L. (1993, Spring). Patterns of religious development in adolescence and adulthood. *Psychologists Interested in Religious Issues Newsletter, 17,* 2–9. (p. 123)

Benson, P. L., Sharma, A. R., & Roehlkepartain, E. C. (1994). *Growing up adopted: A portrait of adolescents and their families.* Minneapolis: Search Institute. (p. 111)

Berenbaum, S. A., & Hines, M. (1992). Early androgens are related to childhood sex-typed toy preferences. *Psychological Science, 3,* 203–206. (p. 79)

Berenbaum, S. A., Korman, K., & Leveroni, C. (1995). Early hormones and sex differences in cognitive abilities. *Learning and Individual Differences, 7,* 303-321. (p. 358)

Bergin, A. E. (1980). Psychotherapy and religious values. *Journal of Consulting and Clinical Psychology, 48,* 95–105. (p. 507)

Bergin, A. E. (1991). Values and religious issues in psychotherapy and mental health. *American Psychologist, 46,* 394–403. (p. 387)

Bergsholm, P., Larsen, J. L., Rosendahl, K., & Holsten, F. (1989). Electroconvulsive therapy and cerebral computed tomography. *Acta Psychiatrica Scandinavia, 80,* 566–572. (p. 510)

Berk, L. E. (1994, November). Why children talk to themselves. *Scientific American,* pp. 78-83. (p. 93)

Berkel, J., & de Waard, F. (1983). Mortality pattern and life expectancy of Seventh Day Adventists in the Netherlands. *International Journal of Epidemiology, 12,* 455-459. (p. 534)

Berkowitz, L. (1983). Aversively stimulated aggression: Some parallels and differences in research with animals and humans. *American Psychologist, 38,* 1135–1144. (p. 573)

Berkowitz, L. (1989). Frustration-aggression hypothesis: Examination and reformulation. *Psychological Bulletin, 106,* 59–73. (p. 573)

Berkowitz, L. (1990). On the formation and regulation of anger and aggression: A cognitive-neoassociationistic analysis. *American Psychologist, 45,* 494–503. (p. 405)

Berman, M., Gladue, B., & Taylor, S. (1993). The effects of hormones, Type A behavior pattern, and provocation on aggression in men. *Motivation and Emotion, 17*, 125–138. (p. 572)

Berndt, T. J. (1992). Friendship and friends' influence in adolescence. *Current Directions in Psychological Science, 1*, 156–159. (p. 123)

Berscheid, E. (1981). An overview of the psychological effects of physical attractiveness and some comments upon the psychological effects of knowledge of the effects of physical attractiveness. In G. W. Lucker, K. Ribbens, & J. A. McNamara (Eds.), *Psychological aspects of facial form* (Craniofacial growth series). Ann Arbor: Center for Human Growth and Development, University of Michigan. (p. 581)

Berscheid, E. (1985). Interpersonal attraction. In G. Lindzey & E. Aronson (Eds.), *The handbook of social psychology.* New York: Random House. (p. 367)

Berscheid, E., Gangestad, S. W., & Kulakowski, D. (1984). Emotion in close relationships: Implications for relationship counseling. In S. D. Brown & R. W. Lent (Eds.), *Handbook of counseling psychology.* New York: Wiley. (p. 585)

Best, J. A., & Suedfeld, P. (1982). Restricted environmental stimulation therapy and behavioral self-management in smoking cessation. *Journal of Applied Social Psychology, 12*, 408–419. (p. 178)

Beyerstein, B., & Beyerstein, D. (Eds.) (1992). *The write stuff: Evaluations of graphology.* Buffalo, NY: Prometheus Books. (p. 448)

Bhatt, R. S., Wasserman, E. A., Reynolds, W. F., Jr., & Knauss, K. S. (1988). Conceptual behavior in pigeons: Categorization of both familiar and novel examples from four classes of natural and artificial stimuli. *Journal of Experimental Psychology: Animal Behavior Processes, 14*, 219–234. (p. 256)

Bigler, E., D., Johnson, S. C., Jackson, C., & Blatter, D. D. (1995). Aging, brain size, and IQ. *Intelligence, 21,* 109-119. (p. 341)

Binet, A., & Simon, T. (1905; reprinted 1916). New methods for the diagnosis of the intellectual level of subnormals. In A. Binet & T. Simon, *The development of intelligence in children.* Baltimore: Williams & Wilkins. (p. 335)

Binson, D., Michaels, S., Stall, R., Coates, T. J., Gagnon, J.H., & Catania, J. A. (1995). Prevalence and social distribution of men who have sex with men: United States and its urban centers. *Journal of Sex Research, 32,* 245-254. (p. 380)

Bishop, G. D. (1991). Understanding the understanding of illness: Lay disease representations. In J. A. Skelton & R. T. Croyle (Eds.), *Mental representation in health and illness.* New York: Springer-Verlag. (p. 307)

Bjork, R. A. (1978). The updating of human memory. In G. H. Bower (Ed.), *The psychology of learning and motivation* (Vol. 12). New York: Academic Press. (p. 279)

Bjorklund, D. F., & Green, B. L. (1992). The adaptive nature of cognitive immaturity. *American Psychologist, 47,* 46–54. (p. 93)

Blackmore, S. (1991, Fall). Near-death experiences: In or out of the body? *Skeptical Inquirer,* pp. 34–45. (p. 239)

Blackmore, S. (1993). *Dying to live.* Amherst, NY: Prometheus Books. (p. 239)

Blake, J. (1989). Number of siblings and educational attainment. *Science, 245,* 32–36. (p. 385)

Blakemore, C., & Cooper, G. F. (1970). Development of the brain depends on the visual environment. *Nature, 228,* 477–478. (p. 195)

Blanchard, R., & Bogaert, A. F. (1996a). Homosexuality in men and number of older brothers. *American Journal of Psychiatry, 153,* 27-31. (p. 380)

Blanchard, R., & Bogaert, A. F. (1996b). Biodemographic comparisons of homosexual and heterosexual men in the Kinsey interview data. *Archives of Sexual Behavior, 25,* 551-579. (p. 380)

Blanchard, R., Zucker, K. J., Bradley, S. J., & Hume, C. S. (1995). Birth order and sibling sex ratio in homosexual male adolescents and probably prehomosexual feminine boys. *Developmental Psychology, 31,* 22-30. (p. 380)

Blass, T. (1996). Stanley Milgram: A life of inventiveness and controversy. In G. A. Kimble, C. A. Boneau, & M. Wertheimer (Eds.), *Portraits of pioneers in psychology* (Vol. II). Washington, DC, and Mahwah, NJ: American Psychological Association and Lawrence Erlbaum Publishers. (p. 558)

Blatt, S. J., Sanislow, C. A., III, Zuroff, D. C., & Pilkonis, P. (1996). Characteristics of effective therapists: Further analyses of data from the National Institute of Mental Health Treatment of Depression Collaborative Research Program. *Journal of Consulting and clinical Psychology, 64,* 1276-1284. (p. 506)

Blatt, S. J., Zuroff, D. C., Quinlan, D. M., & Pilkonis, P. (1996). Interpersonal factors in brief treatment of depression: Further analyses of the NIMH Treatment of Depression Collaborative Research Program. *Journal of Consulting and Clinical Psychology, 64,* 162-171. (p. 506)

Block, J. (1981). Some enduring and consequential structures of personality. In A. I. Rabin (Ed.), *Further explorations in personality.* New York: Wiley. (p. 143)

Blom, J. M. C., Tamarkin, L., Shiber, J. R., & Nelson, R. J. (1995). Learned immunosuppression is associated with an increased risk of chemically-induced tumors. *Neuroimmunomodulation, 2,* 92-99. (p. 527)

Blom, J. M. C., Tamarkin, L., Shiber, J. R., & Nelson, R. J. (1994). *Learned conditioned immunosuppression is associated with increased risk of chemically-induced tumors.* Unpublished manuscript, Department of Psychology, Johns Hopkins University. (p. 527)

Bloom, B. J. (1964). *Stability and change in human characteristics.* New York: Wiley. (p. 348)

Bloom, B. S. (Ed.). (1985). *Developing talent in young people.* New York: Ballantine. (p. 385)

Bloom, F. E. (1993, January/February). What's new in neurotransmitters. *BrainWork,* pp. 7–9. (p. 44)

Blum, K., Cull, J. G., Braverman, E. R., & Comings, D. E. (1996). Reward deficiency syndrome. *American Scientist, 84,* 132-145. (p. 58)

Bodenhausen, G. V., Sheppard, L. A., & Kramer, G. P. (1994). Negative affect and social judgment: The differential impact of anger and sadness. *European Journal of Social Psychology, 24,* 45–62. (p. 588)

Boesch-Achermann, H., & Boesch, C. (1993). Tool use in wild chimpanzees: New light from dark forests. *Current Directions in Psychological Science, 2*, 18–21. (p. 308)

Boggiano, A. K., Barrett, M., Weiher, A. W., McClelland, G. H., & Lusk, C. M. (1987). Use of the maximal-operant principle to motivate children's intrinsic interest. *Journal of Personality and Social Psychology, 53*, 866–879. (p. 261)

Boggiano, A. K., Harackiewicz, J. M., Bessette, M. M., & Main, D. S. (1985). Increasing children's interest through performance-contingent reward. *Social Cognition, 3*, 400–411. (p. 261)

Bohman, M., & Sigvardsson, S. (1990). Outcome in adoption: Lessons from longitudinal studies. In D. Brodzinsky & M. Schechter (eds.), *The psychology of adoption.* New York: Oxford University Press. (p. 111)

Bolger, N., DeLongis, A., Kessler, R. C., & Schilling, E. A. (1989). Effects of daily stress on negative mood. *Journal of Personality and Social Psychology, 57*, 808–818. (p. 407)

Bonanno, G. A., Keltner, D., Holen, A., & Horowitz, M. J. (1995). When avoiding unpleasant emotions might not be such a bad thing: Verbal-autonomic response dissociation and midlife conjugal bereavement. *Journal of Personality and Social Psychology, 69*, 975-989. (p. 141)

Bond, C. F., Jr., Pitre, U., & Van Leeuwen, M. D. (1991). Encoding operations and the next-in-line effect. *Personality and Social Psychology Bulletin, 17*, 435–441. (p. 274)

Bond, L. (1989). The effects of special preparation on measures of scholastic ability. In R. Linn (ed.), *Educational measurement,* 3rd ed. New York: Macmillan. (p. 346)

Bond, M. H. (1988). Finding universal dimensions of individual variation in multi-cultural studies of values: The Rokeach and Chinese values surveys. *Journal of Personality and Social Psychology, 55*, 1009–1015. (p. 105)

Bond, R., & Smith, P. B. (1996). Culture and conformity: A meta-analysis of studies using Asch's (1952b, 1956) line judgment task. *Psychological Bulletin, 119*, 111-137. (p. 557)

Bonke, B., Schmitz, P. I. M., Verhage, F., & Zwaverling, A. (1986). Clinical study of so-called unconscious perception during general anaesthesia. *British Journal of Anaesthesia, 58*, 957-964. (p. 239)

Boring, E. G. (1930). A new ambiguous figure. *American Journal of Psychology, 42,* 444–445. (p. 196)

Borkenau, P., & Liebler, A. (1993). Convergence of stranger ratings of personality and intelligence with self-ratings, partner ratings, and measured intelligence. *Journal of Personality and Social Psychology, 65*, 546–553. (p. 434)

Bornstein, M. H. (1989). Stability in early mental development: From attention and information processing in infancy to language and cognition in childhood. In M. G. Bornstein & N. A. Krasnegor (Eds.), *Stability and continuity in mental development: Behavioral and biological perspectives.* Hillsdale, NJ: Erlbaum. (p. 96)

Bornstein, M. H., Tamis-LeMonda, C. S., Tal, J., Ludemann, P., Toda, S., Rahn, C. W., Pecheux, M-G., Azuma, H., Vardi, D. (1992). Maternal responsiveness to infants in three societies: The United States, France, and Japan. *Child Development, 63*, 808–821. (p. 107)

Bornstein, M. H., Tal, J., Rahn, C., Galperin, C. Z., Pecheux, M-G., Lamour, M., Toda, S., Azuma, H., Ogino, M., & Tamis-LeMonda, C. S. (1992). Functional analysis of the contents of maternal speech to infants of 5 and 13 months in four cultures: Argentina, France, Japan, and the United States. *Developmental Psychology, 28*, 593–603. (p. 107)

Bornstein, R. F. (1989). Exposure and affect: Overview and meta-analysis of research, 1968–1987. *Psychological Bulletin, 106*, 265–289. (p. 580)

Bornstein, R. F., & Pittman, T. S. (Eds.) (1992). *Perception without awareness: Cognitive, clinical, and social perspectives.* New York: Guilford. (p. 150)

Bornstein, R. F., Galley, D. J., Leone, D. R., & Kale, A. R. (1991). The temporal stability of ratings of parents: Test-retest reliability and influence of parental contact. *Journal of Social Behavior and Personality, 6*, 641–649. (p. 291)

Boroditsky, R., Fisher, W., & Sand, M. (1995, July). Teenagers and contraception. Section of The Canadian Contraception Study. *Journal of the Society of Obstetricians and Gynaecologists of Canada*, Special Supplement, pp. 22-25.

Bothwell, R. K., Brigham, J. C., & Malpass, R. S. (1989). Cross-racial identification. *Personality and Social Psychology Bulletin, 15*, 19–25. (p. 570)

Bothwell, R. K., Deffenbacher, K. A., & Brigham, J. C. (1987). Correlation of eyewitness accuracy and confidence: Optimality hypothesis revised. *Journal of Applied Psychology, 72*, 691–695. (p. 297)

Bouchard, T. J., Jr. (1981, December 6). Interview on *Nova: Twins* [program broadcast by the Public Broadcasting Service]. (p. 109)

Bouchard, T. J., Jr. (1995). Longitudinal studies of personality and intelligence: A behavior genetic and evolutionary psychology perspective. In D. H. Saklofske & M. Zeidner (Eds.), *International handbook of personality and intelligence.* New York: Plenum. (p. 353)

Bouchard, T. J., Jr. (1996a). IQ similarity in twins reared apart: Finding and responses to critics. In R. Sternberg & C. Grigorenko (Eds.), *Intelligence: Heredity and environment.* New York: Cambridge University Press. (p. 353)

Bouchard, T. J., Jr. (1996b). Behavior genetic studies of intelligence, yesterday and today: The long journey from plausibility to proof. *Journal of Biosocial Science, 28*, 527-555. (p. 353)

Bouchard, T. J., Jr., Lykken, D. T., McGue, M., Segal, N. L., & Tellegen, A. (1990). Sources of human psychological differences: The Minnesota study of twins reared apart. *Science, 250*, 223–228. (pp. 21, 109)

Bower, G. H. (1983). Affect and cognition. *Philosophical Transaction: Royal Society of London, Series B, 302*, 387–402. (p. 290)

Bower, G. H. (1986). Prime time in cognitive psychology. In P. Eelen (Ed.), *Cognitive research and behavior therapy: Beyond the conditioning paradigm.* Amsterdam: North Holland Publishers. (p. 289)

Bower, G. H., & Clark, M. C. (1969). Narrative stories as mediators for serial learning. *Psychonomic Science, 14*, 181–182. (p. 277)

Bower, G. H., & Morrow, D. G. (1990). Mental models in narrative comprehension. *Science, 247*, 44–48. (p. 275)

Bower, G. H., Clark, M. C., Lesgold, A. M., & Winzenz, D. (1969). Hierarchical retrieval schemes in recall of categorized word lists. *Journal of Verbal Learning and Verbal Behavior, 8*, 323–343. (p. 279)

Bowers, K. S. (1984). Hypnosis. In N. Endler & J. M. Hunt (Eds.), *Personality and behavioral disorders* (2nd ed.). New York: Wiley. (pp. 222, 224)

Bowers, K. S. (1987, July). Personal communication. (p. 223)

Bowers, K. S. (1990). Unconscious influences and hypnosis. In J. E. Singer (Ed.), *Repression and dissociation: Implications for personality theory, psychopathology, and health.* Chicago: University of Chicago Press. (p. 227)

Bowers, K. S., & LeBaron, S. (1986). Hypnosis and hypnotizability: Implications for clinical intervention. *Hospital and Community Psychiatry, 37*, 457–467. (p. 224)

Bowers, T. G., & Clum, G. A. (1988). Relative contribution of specific and nonspecific treatment effects: Meta-analysis of placebo-controlled behavior therapy research. *Psychological Bulletin, 103*, 315–323. (p. 505)

Bowlby, J. (1973). *Separation: Anxiety and anger.* New York: Basic Books. (p. 100)

Bowlby, J. (1979). *The making and breaking of affectional bonds.* London: Tavistock. (p. 96)

Bowne, D. W., Russell, M. L., Morgan, M. A., Optenberg, S., & Clarke, A. (1984). Reduced disability and health care costs in an industrial fitness program. *Journal of Occupational Medicine, 26*, 809–816. (p. 536)

Boyatzis, C. J., Matillo, G. M., & Nesbitt, K. M. (in press). Effects of the 'Mighty Morphin Power Rangers' on children's aggression with peers. *Child Study Journal.* (p. 576)

Boynton, R. M. (1979). *Human color vision.* New York: Holt, Rinehart & Winston. (p. 162)

Braden, J. P. (1994). *Deafness, deprivation, and IQ.* New York: Plenum. (p. 168, 356)

Bradley, D. R., Dumais, S. T., & Petry, H. M. (1976). Reply to Cavonius. *Nature, 261*, 78. (p. 182)

Bradley-Johnson, S., Johnson, C. M., Shanahan, R. H., Rickert, V. L., & Tardona, D. R. (1984). Effects of token reinforcement on WISC-R performance of black and white, low-socioeconomic second graders. *Behavioral Assessment, 6*, 365–373. (p. 357)

Bradshaw, J. (1990). *Homecoming: Reclaiming and championing your inner child.* New York: Bantam Books. (p. 112)

Brainerd, C. J. (1996). Piaget: A centennial celebration. *Psychological Science, 7*, 191-195. (p. 87)

Brainerd, C. J., Reyna, V. F., & Brandse, E. (1995). Are children's false memories more persistent than their true memories? *Psychological Science, 6*, 359-364. (p. 297)

Brannon, L. A., & Brock, T. C. (1994). Perilous underestimation of sex partners' sexual histories in calculating personal AIDS risk. Paper presented at the American Psychological Society convention. (p. 126, 383)

Bransford, J. D., & Johnson, M. K. (1972). Contextual prerequisites for understanding: Some investigations of comprehension and recall. *Journal of Verbal Learning and Verbal Behavior, 11*, 717–726. (p. 276)

Braskamp, L. A. (1987). Spectrum: Utility for educational selection and organizational development. Paper presented at the American Psychological Association convention. (p. 388)

Braun, S. (1996). New experiments underscore warnings on maternal drinking. *Science, 273*, 738-739. (p. 80)

Bray, D. W., & Byham, W. C. (1991, Winter). Assessment centers and their derivatives. *Journal of Continuing Higher Education*, pp. 8–11. (p. 449)

Bray, G. A. (1969). Effect of caloric restriction on energy expenditure in obese patients. *Lancet, 2*, 397–398. (pp. 542)

Brehm, S., & Brehm, J. W. (1981). *Psychological reactance: A theory of freedom and control.* New York: Academic Press. (p. 564)

Breland, K., & Breland, M. (1961). The misbehavior of organisms. *American Psychologist, 16*, 661–664. (p. 261)

Brennan, P. A., & Mednick, S. A. (1993). Genetic perspectives on crime. *Acta Psychiatrica Scandinavia, Suppl. 370*, 19–26. (p. 482)

Brenner, M. (1973). The next-in-line effect. *Journal of Verbal Learning and Verbal Behavior, 12*, 320–323. (p. 274)

Bretz, R. D. (1989). College grade point average as a predictor of adult success: A meta-analytic review and some additional evidence. *Public Personnel Management, 18*, 11–22. (p. 340)

Brewer, C. (1990). Personal correspondence. (p. 113)

Brewer, C. L. (1996). Personal communication. (p. 5)

Brewer, W. F. (1977). Memory for the pragmatic implications of sentences. *Memory & Cognition, 5*, 673–678. (p. 275)

Brickman, P., Coates, D., & Janoff-Bulman, R. J. (1978). Lottery winners and accident victims: Is happiness relative? *Journal of Personality and Social Psychology, 36*, 917–927. (p. 409)

Briere, J., & Runtz, M. (1993). Childhood sexual abuse: Long-term sequelae and implications for psychological assessment. *Journal of Interpersonal Violence, 8*, 312–330. (p. 298)

Bril, B. (1986). Motor development and cultural attitudes. In H. T. A. Whiting & M. G. Wade (Eds.), *Themes in motor development.* Dordrecht, Netherlands: Martinus Nijhoff. (p. 86)

Brinson, S. L. (1992). The use and opposition of rape myths in prime-time television dramas. *Sex Roles, 27*, 359–375. (p. 577)

Briscoe, D. (1995, August 27). Women's share of power slips since the late 1980s. Associated Press (Grand Rapids [Mich.] *Press*, p. A16). (p. 566)

Briscoe, D. (1997, February 16). Women lawmakers still not in charge. Associated Press (Grand Rapids [Mich.] *Press*, p. A23). (p. 566)

Brislin, R. (1993). *Understanding culture's influence on behavior.* Fort Worth, TX: Harcourt Brace. (p. 456)

British Psychological Society (1993). Ethical principles for conducting research with human participants. *The Psychologist: Bulletin of the British Psychological Society, 6*, 33–36. (p. 36)

British Psychological Society. (1986). Report of the working group on the use of the polygraph in criminal investigation and personnel screening. *Bulletin of the British Psychological Society, 39,* 81–94. (p. 397)

British Psychological Society. (1993). Graphology in personnel assessment. Leicester, England: British Psychological Society. (p. 448)

Broadbent, D. E. (1978). The current state of noise research: Reply to Poulton. *Psychological Bulletin, 85,* 1052–1067. (p. 166)

Brockner, J., & Hulton, A. J. B. (1978). How to reverse the vicious cycle of low self-esteem: The importance of attentional focus. *Journal of Experimental Social Psychology, 14,* 564–578. (p. 438)

Brody, N. (1992). *Intelligence* (2nd ed.). San Diego: Academic Press. (p. 341)

Brodzinsky, D. M., & Schechter, M. D. (Eds.) (1990). *The psychology of adoption.* New York: Oxford University Press. (p. 110)

Broman, S. H. (1989). Infant physical status and later cognitive development. In M. H. Bornstein & N. A. Krasnegor (Eds.), *Stability and continuity in mental development: Behavioral and biological perspectives.* Hillsdale, NJ: Erlbaum. (p. 348)

Bronstein-Burrows, P. (1981). *Introductory psychology: A course in the psychology of both sexes.* Paper presented at the meeting of the American Psychological Association. (p. 581)

Brooks-Gunn, J. (1989). Adolescents as daughters and as mothers: A developmental perspective. In I. Sigel & G. Brody (Eds.), *Family research.* Hillsdale, NJ: Erlbaum. (p. 117)

Brooks-Gunn, J., & Furstenberg, F. F., Jr. (1989). Adolescent sexual behavior. *American Psychologist, 44,* 249–257. (p. 126)

Brothers, J. (1990, February 18). Why wives have affairs. *Parade,* pp. 4–7. (p. 374)

Brown, E. L., & Deffenbacher, K. (1979). *Perception and the senses.* New York: Oxford University Press. (p. 167)

Brown, J. D. (1991). Accuracy and bias in self-knowledge. In C. R. Snyder & D. F. Forsyth (Eds.), *Handbook of social and clinical psychology: The health perspective.* New York: Pergamon Press. (pp. 438, 440, 441)

Brown, J. D. (1991). Staying fit and staying well: Physical fitness as a moderator of life stress. *Journal of Personality and Social Psychology, 60,* 555–561. (p. 529)

Brown, J. L., & Pollitt, E. (1996, February). Malnutrition, poverty and intellectual development. *Scientific American,* pp. 38-43. (p. 355)

Brown, L. R., Kane, H., & Ayres, E. (1993). *Vital signs 1993: The trends that are shaping our future.* New York: Norton. (p. 539)

Brown, R. (1965). *Social psychology.* New York: Free Press. (p. 404)

Brown, R. (1973). *A first language: The early stages.* Cambridge, MA: Harvard University Press. (p. 322)

Brown, R. (1986). Linguistic relativity. In S. H. Hulse & B. F. Green, Jr. (Eds.), *One hundred years of psychological research in America.* Baltimore: Johns Hopkins University Press. (p. 328)

Brown, R., & Kulik, J. (1982). Flashbulb memories. In U. Neisser (Ed.), *Memory observed.* San Francisco: Freeman. (p. 270)

Brown, S. W., Garry, M., Loftus, E., Silver, B., DuBois, K., & DuBreuil, S. (1996). People's beliefs about memory: Why don't we have better memories? Paper presented at the American Psychological Society convention. (p. 283, 294)

Brownell, K. D. (1991). Dieting and the search for the perfect body: Where physiology and culture collide. *Behavior Therapy, 22,* 1–12. (p. 543)

Brownell, K. D., & Jeffery, R. W. (1987). Improving long-term weight loss: Pushing the limits of treatment. *Behavior Therapy, 18,* 353–374. (p. 544)

Brownell, K. D., & Wadden, T. A. (1991). The heterogeneity of obesity: Fitting treatments to individuals. *Behavior Therapy, 22,* 153–177. (pp. 606, 608)

Brownell, K. D., & Wadden, T. A. (1992). Etiology and treatment of obesity: Understanding a serious, prevalent, and refractory disorder. *Journal of Consulting and Clinical Psychology, 60,* 505–517. (pp. 542, 544)

Browning, C. (1992). *Ordinary men: Reserve Police Battalion 101 and the final solution in Poland.* New York: HarperCollins. (p. 559)

Brownmiller, S. (1975). *Against our will: Men, women, and rape.* New York: Simon and Schuster. (p. 377)

Bruner, J. S., & Potter, M. C. (1964). Interference in visual recognition. *Science, 144,* 424–425. (p. 196)

Bryant, F. B., & Brockway, J. H. (in press). Hindsight bias in reaction to the O. J. Simpson verdict. *Basic and Applied Social Psychology.* (p. 14)

Buehler, R., Griffin, D., & Ross, M. (1994). Exploring the "planning fallacy": Why people underestimate their task completion times. *Journal of Personality and Social Psychology,* in press. (p. 314)

Bugelski, B. R., Kidd, E., & Segmen, J. (1968). Image as a mediator in one-trial paired-associate learning. *Journal of Experimental Psychology, 76,* 69–73. (p. 278)

Bugental, D. B. (1986). Unmasking the "polite smile": Situational and personal determinants of managed affect in adult–child interaction. *Personality and Social Psychology Bulletin, 12,* 7–16. (p. 399)

Bullard, T. E. (1987). *UFO abductions: The measure of a mystery. Vol. 2: Catalogue of cases.* Mount Ranier, MD: Fund for UFO Research. Cited by L. S. Newman & R. F. Baumeister (1996). Toward an explanation of the UFO abduction phenomenon: Hypnotic elaboration, extraterrestrial sadomasochism, and spurious memories. *Psychological Inquiry, 7,* 99–126. (p. 224)

Bullough, V. (1990). The Kinsey scale in historical perspective. In D. P. McWhirter, S. A. Sanders, & J. M. Reinisch (Eds.), *Homosexuality/heterosexuality: Concepts of sexual orientation.* New York: Oxford University Press. (p. 379)

Bumpass, L. L., & Sweet, J. A. (1989). National estimates of cohabitation. *Demography, 26,* 615–625. (p. 139)

Buquet, R. (1988). Le reve et les deficients visuels (Dreams and the visually impaired). *Psychanalyse-a-l'Universite, 13,* 319–327. (p. 218)

Bureau of the Census (1993). *Statistical Abstract of the United States 1993.* Washington, DC: U.S. Government Printing Office. (p. 99)

Bureau of the Census (1996). *Statistical abstract of the United States 1996.* Washington, DC: U.S. Government Printing Office. (p. 125, 139, 236, 454, 469, 536)

Burger, J. M. (1987). Increased performance with increased personal control: A self-presentation interpretation. *Journal of Experimental Social Psychology, 23,* 350–360. (p. 389)

Burger, J. M., & Burns, L. (1988). The illusion of unique invulnerability and the use of effective contraception. *Personality and Social Psychology Bulletin,* **14**, 264–270. (p. 447)

Buri, J. R., Louiselle, P. A., Misukanis, T. M., & Mueller, R. A. (1988). Effects of parental authoritarianism and authoritativeness on self-esteem. *Personality and Social Psychology Bulletin, 14,* 271–282. (p. 104)

Burish, T. G., & Carey, M. P. (1986). Conditioned aversive responses in cancer chemotherapy patients: Theoretical and developmental analysis. *Journal of Counseling and Clinical Psychology, 54,* 593–600. (p. 252)

Burke, K. C., Burke, J. D., Regier, D. A., & Rae, D. S. (1990). Age at onset of selected mental disorders in five community populations. *Archives of General Psychiatry, 47,* 511–518. (p. 462)

Busch, C. M., Zonderman, A. B., & Costa, P. T. (1994). Menopausal transition and psychological distress in a nationally representative sample: Is menopause associated with psychological distress? *Journal of Aging and Health, 6,* 209–228. (p. 128)

Bushman, B. J. (1993). Human aggression while under the influence of alcohol and other drugs: An integrative research review. *Current Directions in Psychological Science, 2,* 148–152. (p. 572)

Busnel, M. C., Granier-Deferre, C., & Lecanuet, J. P. (1992, October). Fetal audition. *New York Academy of Sciences, 662,* 118–134. (p. 80)

Buss, A. H. (1989). Personality as traits. *American Psychologist, 44,* 1378–1388. (p. 435)

Buss, D. (1994a). *The evolution of desire.* New York: Basic Books. (pp. 646, 674–675)

Buss, D. (1994b). The strategies of human mating. *American Scientist, 82,* 238–249. (pp. 646, 675)

Buss, D. M. (1991). Evolutionary personality psychology. *Annual Review of Psychology, 42,* 459–491. (p. 33)

Buss, D. M. (1995). Evolutionary psychology: A new paradigm for psychological science. *Psychological Inquiry, 6,* 1–30. (p. 379)

Buss, D. M. (1996). Sexual conflict: Evolutionary insights into feminism and the "battle of the sexes." In D. M. Buss & N. M. Malamuth (Eds.), *Sex, power, conflict: Evolutionary and feminist perspectives.* New York: Oxford University Press. (p. 582)

Butcher, J. N. (1990). *The MMPI-2 in psychological treatment.* New York: Oxford University Press. (p. 433)

Butler, A. C., Hokanson, J. E., & Flynn, H. A. (1994). A comparison of self-esteem lability and low trait self-esteem as vulnerability factors for depression. *Journal of Personality and Social Psychology, 66,* 166–177. (p. 473)

Butler, J., & Rovee-Collier, C. (1989). Contextual gating of memory retrieval. *Developmental Psychobiology, 22,* 533–552. (p. 290)

Butler, R. A. (1954, February). Curiosity in monkeys. *Scientific American,* pp. 70–75. (p. 365)

Butterworth, G. (1992). Origins of self-perception in infancy. *Psychological Inquiry, 3,* 103–111. (p. 103)

Byne, W., & Parsons, B. (1993). Human sexual orientation: The biologic theories reappraised. *Archives of General Psychiatry, 50,* 228–239. (p. 382)

Byrne, D. (1982). Predicting human sexual behavior. In A. G. Kraut (Ed.), *The G. Stanley Hall Lecture Series* (Vol. 2). Washington, DC: American Psychological Association. (pp. 248, 376–377)

Byrne, R. W. (1991, May/June). Brute intellect. *The Sciences,* pp. 42–47. (p. 325)

Byrnes, G., & Kelly, I. W. (1992). Crisis calls and lunar cycles: A twenty-year review. *Psychological Reports, 71,* 779–785. (p. 481)

Cacioppo, J. T., Berntson, G. G., Klein, D. J., & Poehlmann, K. M. (1997). The psychophysiology of emotion across the lifespan. *Annual Review of Gerontology and Geriatrics, 17,* in press. (p. 395)

Cacioppo, J. T., Priester, J. R., & Berntson, G. G. (1993). Rudimentary determinants of attitudes. II: Arm flexion and extension have differential effects on attitudes. *Journal of Personality and Social Psychology, 65,* 5–17. (p. 244)

Cahill, L. (1994). (Beta)-adrenergic activation and memory for emotional events. *Nature, 371,* 702-704. (p. 285)

Callahan, L. A., Steadman, H. J., McGreevy, M. A., & Robbins, P. C. (1991). The volume and characteristics of insanity defense pleas: An eight-state study. *Bulletin of the American Academic of Psychiatry and Law, 19,* 331–338. (p. 457)

Cameron, P., & Biber, H. (1973). Sexual thought throughout the life-span. *Gerontologist, 13,* 144–147. (p. 209)

Campbell, B. A., & Coulter, X. (1976). The ontogenesis of learning and memory. In M. R. Rosenzweig & E. L. Bennet (Eds.), *Neural mechanisms of learning and memory,* pp. 209–235. Cambridge, MA: MIT Press. (p. 83)

Campbell, D. T. (1975). On the conflicts between biological and social evolution and between psychology and moral tradition. *American Psychologist, 30,* 1103–1126. (p. 410)

Campbell, D. T., & Specht, J. C. (1985). Altruism: Biology, culture, and religion. *Journal of Social and Clinical Psychology, 3*(1), 33–42. (p. 444)

Campbell, S. (1986). *The Loch Ness Monster: The evidence.* Willingborough, Northamptonshire, U.K.: Acquarian Press. (p. 197)

Camper, J. (1990, February 7). Drop pompom squad, U. of I. rape study says. *Chicago Tribune,* p. 1. (p. 231)

Campos, J. J., Bertenthal, B. I., & Kermoian, R. (1992). Early experience and emotional development: The emergence of wariness and heights. *Psychological Science, 3,* 61–64. (pp. 186, 404)

Cannon, T. D., & Marco, E. (1994). Structural brain abnormalities as indicators of vulnerability to schizophrenia. *Schizophrenia Bulletin, 20,* 89–102. (p. 478)

Cannon, W. B. (1929). *Bodily changes in pain, hunger, fear, and rage.* New York: Branford. (pp. 368, 517)

Cannon, W. B., & Washburn, A. (1912). An explanation of hunger. *American Journal of Physiology, 29,* 441–454. (p. 368)

Cantor, D. W. (1995, December). Summary of *Report of the Task Force on the Changing Gender Composition of Psychology* (Washington, DC: American Psychological Association Women's Programs Office), *APA Monitor*, p. 15. (p. 8)

Cantor, N., & Kihlstrom, J. F. (1987). *Personality and social intelligence.* Englewood Cliffs, NJ: Prentice-Hall. (p. 340)

Cantor, N., & Norem, J. K. (1989). Defensive pessimism and stress and coping. *Social Cognition, 7*, 92–112. (p. 447)

Cantril, H., & Bumstead, C. H. (1960). *Reflections on the human venture.* New York: New York University Press. (p. 564)

Caplan, N., Choy, M. H., & Whitmore, J. K. (1992, February). Indochinese refugee families and academic achievement. *Scientific American*, pp. 36–42. (pp. 111, 357)

Carducci, B. J., Cosby, P. C., & Ward, D. D. (1978). Sexual arousal and interpersonal evaluations. *Journal of Experimental Social Psychology, 14*, 449–457. (p. 584)

Carey, G. (1990). Genes, fears, phobias, and phobic disorders. *Journal of Counseling and Development, 68*, 628–632. (p. 464)

Carli, L. L., & Leonard, J. B. (1989). The effect of hindsight on victim derogation. *Journal of Social and Clinical Psychology, 8*, 331–343. (p. 571)

Carlson, M. (1995, August 29). Quoted by S. Blakeslee, In brain's early growth, timetable may be crucial. *New York Times*, pp. C1, C3. (p. 98)

Carlson, M., Charlin, V., & Miller, N. (1988). Positive mood and helping behavior: A test of six hypotheses. *Journal of Personality and Social Psychology, 55*, 211–229. (p. 586)

Carlson, R. (1984). What's social about social psychology? Where's the person in personality research? *Journal of Personality and Social Psychology, 47*, 1304–1309. (p. 450)

Carlson, S. (1985). A double-blind test of astrology. *Nature, 318*, 419–425. (p. 448)

Carnegie Council on Adolescent Development. (1989, June). *Turning points: Preparing American youth for the 21st century.* (The report of the Task Force on Education of Young Adolescents.) New York: Carnegie Corporation. (p. 350, 588)

Carr, T. H., Kontowicz, A., & Dagenbach, D. (1987). Subthreshold priming and the cognitive unconscious. Invited paper presented at the Midwestern Psychological Association convention. (p. 150)

Carroll, J. M., & Russell, J. A. (1996). Do facial expressions signal specific emotions? Judging emotion from the face in context. *Journal of Personality and Social Psychology, 70*, 205-218. (p. 401)

Carson, R. C., Butcher, J. N., & Coleman, J. C. (1988). *Abnormal psychology and modern life* (8th ed.). Glenview, IL: Scott, Foresman. (p. 456)

Cartwright, R. D. (1978). *A primer on sleep and dreaming.* Reading, MA: Addison-Wesley. (p. 213)

Caryl, P. G. (1994). Early event-related potentials correlate with inspection time and intelligence. *Intelligence, 18*, 15-46. (p. 341)

Case, R. B., Moss, A. J., Case, N., McDermott, M., & Eberly, S. (1992). Living alone after myocardial infarction: Impact on prognosis. *Journal of the American Medical Association, 267*, 515–519. (p. 533)

Cash, T., & Janda, L. H. (1984, December). The eye of the beholder. *Psychology Today*, pp. 46–52. (p. 581)

Cash, T. F., & Henry, P. E. (1995). Women's body images: The results of a national survey in the U.S.A. *Sex Roles, 33*, 19–28. (p. 372)

Caspi, A., & Herbener, E. S. (1990). Continuity and change: Assortative marriage and the consistency of personality in adulthood. *Journal of Personality and Social Psychology, 58*, 250–258. (p. 144)

Caspi, A., & Moffitt, T. E. (1991). Individual differences are accentuated during periods of social change: The sample case of girls at puberty. *Journal of Personality and Social Psychology, 61*, 157–168. (p. 118)

Caspi, A., Moffitt, T. E., Newman, D. L., & Silva, P. A. (1996). Behavioral observations at age 3 years predict adult psychiatric disorders: Longitudinal evidence from a birth cohort. *Archives of General Psychiatry, 53*, 1033–1039. (p. 482)

Caspi, A., Elder, G. H., Jr., & Bem, D. J. (1987). Moving against the world: Life-course patterns of explosive children. *Developmental Psychology, 23*, 308–313. (p. 144)

Castonguay, L. G., & Goldfried, M. R. (1994). Psychotherapy integration: An idea whose time has come. *Applied & Preventive Psychology, 3*, 159–172. (p. 488)

Castro, J. (1991, October 28). Vox pop. *Time*, p. 23. (p. 544)

Cattell, R. B. (1963). Theory of fluid and crystallized intelligence: A critical experiment. *Journal of Educational Psychology, 54*, 1–22. (p. 135)

Cavalli-Sforza, L., Menozzi, P., & Piazza, A. (1994). *The history and geography of human genes.* Princeton, NJ: Princeton University Press. (p. 357)

Ceci, S. J. (1993). Cognitive and social factors in children's testimony. Master Lecture, American Psychological Association convention. (p. 298)

Ceci, S. J., & Bruck, M. (1993). Child witnesses: Translating research into policy. *Social Policy Report* (Society for Research in Child Development), *7*(3), 1–30. (p. 298)

Ceci, S. J., & Bruck, M. (1995). *Jeopardy in the courtroom: A scientific analysis of children's testimony.* Washington, DC: American Psychological Association. (p. 298)

Ceci, S. J., & Liker, J. K. (1986). A day at the races: A study of IQ, expertise, and cognitive complexity. *Journal of Experimental Psychology: General, 115*, 255–266. (pp. 316, 340)

Ceci, S. J., Huffman, M. L. C., Smith, E., & Loftus, E. F. (1994). Repeatedly thinking about a non-event: Source misattributions among preschoolers. *Consciousness and Cognition, 3*, 388-407. (p. 298)

Centers for Disease Control. (1989). Results from the national adolescent student health survey. *Morbidity and Mortality Weekly Report, 38*(9), 147–150. (p. 469)

Centers for Disease Control. (1989). Weekly report summarized in *Detroit Free Press*, November 25, p. A1. (p. 232)

Centers for Disease Control. (1991). Body-weight perceptions and selected weight-management goals and practices of high school students—United States, 1990. *Morbidity and Mortality Weekly Report, 40*, 741, 747–750. (p. 544)

Centers for Disease Control. (1992, January 3). Sexual behavior among high school students—United States, 1990. *Morbidity and Mortality Weekly Report, 40*, Nos. 51 & 52, 885–888. (p. 126)

Centers for Disease Control. (1992, September 16). Serious mental illness and disability in the adult household population: United States, 1989. *Advance Data* No. 218 from *Vital and Health Statistics*, National Center for Health Statistics. (p. 484)

Centerwall, B. S. (1989). Exposure to television as a risk factor for violence. *American Journal of Epidemiology, 129,* 643–652. (p. 575)

Cerella, J. (1985). Information processing rates in the elderly. *Psychological Bulletin, 98,* 67–83. (p. 132)

Chalmers, R. (1995, September 19). Sizing sizzle of mutuals. *Edmonton Journal,* p. E1. (p. 25)

Chamove, A. S. (1980). Nongenetic induction of acquired levels of aggression. *Journal of Abnormal Psychology, 89,* 469–488. (p. 266)

Chang, E. C. (1996). Cultural differences in optimism, pessimism, and coping: Predictors of subsequent adjustment in Asian American and Caucasian American college students. *Journal of Counseling Psychology, 43,* 113–123. (p. 447)

Chase, M. H., & Morales, F. R. (1983). Subthreshold excitatory activity and motorneuron discharge during REM periods of active sleep. *Science, 221,* 1195–1198. (p. 214)

Chase, W. G., & Simon, H. A. (1973). Perception in chess. *Cognitive Psychology, 4,* 55–81. (p. 278)

Chase-Lansdale, P. L., Cherlin, A. J., Kiernan, K. K. (1995). The long-term effects of parental divorce on the mental health of young adults: A developmental perspective, *Child Development, 66,* 1614–1634. (p. 102)

Chassin, L., Presson, C. C., Sherman, S. J., & McGrew, J. (1987). The changing smoking environment for middle and high school students: 1980–1983. *Journal of Behavioral Medicine, 10,* 581–593. (p. 536)

Chaves, J. F. (1989). Hypnotic control of clinical pain. In N. P. Spanos & J. F. Chaves (Eds.), *Hypnosis: The cognitive-behavioral perspective.* Buffalo, NY: Prometheus Books. (p. 226)

Cheek, J. M., & Melchior, L. A. (1990). Shyness, self-esteem, and self-consciousness. In H. Leitenberg (Ed.), *Handbook of social and evaluation anxiety.* New York: Plenum. (pp. 195, 475)

Cherfas, J. (1990). Two bomb attacks on scientists in the U.K. *Science, 248,* 1485. (p. 36)

Cherlin, A. J., Furstenberg, F. F., Jr., Chase-Landale, P. L., Kiernan, K. E., Robins, P. K., Morrison, D. R., & Teitler, J. O. (1991). Longitudinal studies of effects of divorce on children in Great Britain and the United States. *Science, 252,* 1386–1389. (p. 102)

Chess, S., & Thomas, A. (1987). *Know your child: An authoritative guide for today's parents.* New York: Basic Books. (p. 96)

Chomsky, N. (1959). Review of B. F. Skinner's *Verbal behavior. Language, 35,* 26–58. (p. 322)

Chomsky, N. (1972). *Language and mind.* New York: Harcourt Brace Jovanovich. (p. 319)

Chomsky, N. (1987). Language in a psychological setting. Sophia Linguistic Working Papers in Linguistics, No. 22, Sophia University, Tokyo. (pp. 322–323)

Christensen, A., & Jacobson, N. S. (1994). Who (or what) can do psychotherapy: The status and challenge of nonprofessional therapies. *Psychological Science, 5,* 8–14. (p. 506)

Christensen, L. (1993). Effects of eating behavior on mood: A review of the literature. *International Journal of Eating Disorders, 14,* 171–183. (p. 539)

Christianson, S. A. (1992). Emotional stress and eyewitness memory: A critical review. *Psychological Bulletin, 112,* 284–309. (p. 428)

Christophersen, E. R., & Edwards, K. J. (1992). Treatment of elimination disorders: State of the art 1991. *Applied & Preventive Psychology, 1,* 15–22. (p. 493)

Chugani, H. T., & Phelps, M. E. (1986). Maturational changes in cerebral function in infants determined by ^{18}FDG Positron Emission Tomography. *Science, 231,* 840–843. (p. 87)

Chwalisz, K., Diener, E., & Gallagher, D. (1988). Autonomic arousal feedback and emotional experience: Evidence from the spinal cord injured. *Journal of Personality and Social Psychology, 54,* 820–828. (p. 407)

Cialdini, R. B. (1988). *Influence: Science and practice* (2nd ed.). Glenview, IL: Scott, Foresman. (p. 553)

Cialdini, R. B., & Carpenter, K. (1981). The availability heuristic: Does imagining make it so? In P. H. Reingen & A. G. Woodside (Eds.), *Buyer-seller interactions: Empirical issues and normative issues.* Chicago: American Marketing Association. (p. 313)

Cialdini, R. B., & Richardson, K. D. (1980). Two indirect tactics of image management: Basking and blasting. *Journal of Personality and Social Psychology, 39,* 406–415. (p. 569)

Cipra, B. (1995). Princeton mathematician looks back on Fermat proof. *Science, 268,* 1133–1134. (p. 307)

Clark, R. D., III (1990). The impact of AIDS on gender differences in willingness to engage in casual sex. *Journal of Applied Social Psychology, 20,* 771–782. (p. 379)

Clark, R. D., III, & Hatfield, E. (1989). Gender differences in willingness to engage in casual sex. *Journal of Psychology and Human Sexuality, 2,* 39–55. (p. 379)

Clarke-Stewart, A., Gruber, C. P., & Fitzgerald, L. M. (1994). *Children at home and in day care.* Hillsdale, NJ: Erlbaum. (p. 101)

Coats, E. J., & Feldman, R. S. (1996). Gender differences in nonverbal correlates of social status. *Personality and Social Psychology Bulletin, 22,* 1014–1022. (p. 399)

Coe, W. C. (1989a). Posthypnotic amnesia: Theory and research. In N. P. Spanos & J. F. Chaves (Eds.), *Hypnosis: The cognitive-behavioral perspective.* Buffalo, NY: Prometheus Books. (p. 221)

Coe, W. C. (1989b). Hypnosis: The role of sociopolitical factors in a paradigm clash. In N. P. Spanos & J. F. Chaves (Eds.), *Hypnosis: The cognitive-behavioral perspective.* Buffalo, NY: Prometheus Books. (p. 227)

Coffey, C. E. (Ed.) (1993). *Clinical science of electroconvulsive therapy.* Washington, DC: American Psychiatric Press. (p. 510)

Coffey, C. E., Wilkinson, W. E., Weiner, R. D., Parashos, I. A., Djang, W. T., Webb, M. C., Figiel, G. S., & Spritzer, C. E. (1993). Quantitative cerebral anatomy in depression: A controlled magnetic resonance imaging study. *Archives of General Psychiatry, 50,* 7–16. (p. 472)

Cogan, J. C., Bhalla, S. K., Sefa-Dedeh, A., & Rothblum, E. D. (1996). A comparison study of United States and African students on perceptions of obesity and thinness. *Journal of Cross-Cultural Psychology, 27,* 98–113. (p. 540)

Cohen, D. (1995, June 17). Now we are one, or two, or three. *New Scientist,* pp. 14–15. (p. 467)

Cohen, D. (1996). Law, social policy, and violence: The impact of regional cultures. *Journal of Personality and Social Psychology, 70,* 961–978. (p. 573)

Cohen, S. (1988). Psychosocial models of the role of social support in the etiology of physical disease. *Health Psychology, 7,* 269–297. (p. 533)

Cohen, S. (1996). Psychological stress, immunity, and upper respiratory infections. *Current Directions in Psychological Science, 5,* 86–90. (p. 524)

Cohen, S., & Rodriguez, M. S. (1995). Pathways linking affective disturbances and physical disorders. *Health Psychology, 14,* 374–380. (p. 523)

Cohen, S., Doyle, W. J., Skoner, D. P., Fireman, P., Gwaltney, Jr., J. M., & Newson, J. T. (1995). State and trait negative affect as predictors of objective and subjective symptoms of respiratory viral infections. *Journal of Personality and Social Psychology, 68,* 159–169. (p. 524)

Cohen, S., Kaplan, J. R., Cunnick, J. E., Manuck, S. B., & Rabin, B. S. (1992). Chronic social stress, affiliation, and cellular immune response in nonhuman primates. *Psychological Science, 3,* 301–304. (p. 523)

Cohen, S., Tyrrell, D. A. J., & Smith, A. P. (1993). Negative life events, perceived stress, negative affect, and susceptibility to the common cold. *Journal of Personality and Social Psychology, 64,* 131–140. (p. 524)

Cohen, S., Tyrrell, D. A. J., & Smith, A. P. (1991). Psychological stress and susceptibility to the common cold. *New England Journal of Medicine, 325,* 606–612. (p. 524)

Coile, D. C., & Miller, N. E. (1984). How radical animal activists try to mislead humane people. *American Psychologist, 39,* 700–701. (p. 34)

Cole, N. S. (1995, March 22). Personal correspondence, from Educational Testing Service, Princeton, NJ 08541. (p. 346)

Coleman, J. C. (1980). *The nature of adolescence.* London: Methuen. (p. 116)

Coleman, P. D., & Flood, D. G. (1986). Dendritic proliferation in the aging brain as a compensatory repair mechanism. In D. F. Swaab, E. Fliers, M. Mirmiram, W. A. Van Gool, & F. Van Haaren (Eds.), *Progress in brain research* (Vol. 20). New York: Elsevier. (p. 133)

College Board (1987). *1987 profile of SAT and achievement test takers.* New York: The College Entrance Examination Board. (p. 357)

College Board (1996, August 22). *News from The College Board.* New York: The College Entrance Examination Board. (p. 357)

Colley, A. (1995, August). Psychology, science and women. *The Psychologist,* pp. 346–352. (p. 8)

Collins, N. L., & Miller, L. C. (1994). Self-disclosure and liking: A meta-analytic review. *Psychological Bulletin, 116,* 457–475. (p. 585)

Colombo, J. (1982). The critical period concept: Research, methodology, and theoretical issues. *Psychological Bulletin, 91,* 260–275. (p. 96)

Colon, E. A., Callies, A. L., Popkin, M. K., & McGlave, P. B. (1991). Depressed mood and other variables related to bone marrow transplantation survival in acute leukemia. *Psychosomatics, 32,* 420–425. (pp. 524, 533)

Conley, J. J. (1985). Longitudinal stability of personality traits: A multitrait-multimethod-multioccasion analysis. *Journal of Personality and Social Psychology, 49,* 1266–1282. (p. 144)

Comstock, G. W., & Partridge, K. B. (1972). Church attendance and health. *Journal of Chronic Disease, 25,* 665-672. (p. 534)

Consensus Conference. (1985). Electroconvulsive therapy. *Journal of the American Medical Association, 254,* 2103–2108. (p. 510)

Considine, R. V., Sinha, Madhur, K., Heiman, M. L., & Kriauciunas (1996). Serum immunoreactive-leptin concentrations in normal-weight and obese humans. *New England Journal of Medicine, 334,* 292-295. (p. 542)

Consumer Reports (1995, November). Does therapy help? Pp. 734–739. (p. 501, 505)

Conway, M., & Ross, M. (1984). Getting what you want by revising what you had. *Journal of Personality and Social Psychology, 47,* 738–748. (p. 293)

Cook, E. W., III, Hodes, R. L., & Lang, P. J. (1986). Preparedness and phobia: Effects of stimulus content on human visceral conditioning. *Journal of Abnormal Psychology, 95,* 195–207. (p. 251)

Cook, M., & Mineka, S. (1991). Selective associations in the origins of phobic fears and their implications for behavior therapy. In P. Martin (Ed.), *Handbook of behavior therapy and psychological science: An integrative approach.* New York: Pergamon Press. (p. 404)

Cooper, G. D., Adams, H. B., Scott, J. C. (1988). Studies in REST: I. Reduced environmental stimulation therapy (REST) and reduced alcohol consumption. *Journal of Substance Abuse Treatment, 5,* 61–68. (p. 178)

Cooper, W. H. (1983). An achievement motivation nomological network. *Journal of Personality and Social Psychology, 44,* 841–861. (p. 384)

Coopersmith, S. (1967). *The antecedents of self-esteem.* San Francisco: Freeman. (p. 104)

Corballis, M. C. (1989). Laterality and human evolution. *Psychological Review, 96,* 492–505. (p. 68)

Coren, S. (1993). Failure to find statistical significance in left-handedness and pathology studies: A forgotten consideration. *Bulletin of the Psychonomic Society, 31,* 443–446. (pp. 526, 527)

Coren, S. (1993). *The left-hander syndrome: The causes and consequences of left-handedness.* New York: Vintage Books. (p. 70)

Coren, S. (1996). *Sleep thieves: An eye-opening exploration into the science and mysteries of sleep.* New York: Free Press. (pp. 215, 216)

Coren, S., & Halpern, D. F. (1991). Left-handedness: A marker for decreased survival fitness. *Psychological Bulletin, 109,* 90–106. (p. 526)

Corina, D. P., Vaid, J., & Bellugi, U. (1992). The linguistic basis of left hemisphere specialization. *Science, 255,* 1258–1260. (p. 69)

Costa, P. T., Jr., & McCrae, R. B. (1993). "Set like plaster"? Evidence for the stability of adult personality. In T. Heatherton & J. Weinberger (Eds.), *Can personality change?* Washington, DC: American Psychological Association. (p. 144)

Costa, P. T., Jr., & McCrae, R. R. (1989). Personality continuity and the changes of adult life. In M. Storandt & G. R. VandenBos (Eds.), *The adult years: Continuity and change.* Washington, DC: American Psychological Association. (p. 144)

Costa, P. T., Jr., Zonderman, A. B., McCrae, R. R., Cornoni-Huntley, J., Locke, B. Z., & Barbano, H. E. (1987). Longitudinal analyses of psychological well-being in a national sample: Stability of mean levels. *Journal of Gerontology, 42,* 50–55. (p. 140)

Costanzo, M. (1997). *Just revenge: Costs and consequences of the death penalty.* New York: St. Martins. (p. 38)

Courtney, J. G., Longnecker, M. P., Theorell, T., & de Verdier, M. G. (1993). Stressful life events and the risk of colorectal cancer. *Epidemiology, 4,* 407–414. (p. 524)

Cousins, N. (1989). *Head first: The biology of hope.* New York: Dutton. (p. 525)

Cousins, S. D. (1989). Culture and self-perception in Japan and the United States. *Journal of Personality and Social Psychology, 56,* 124–131. (p. 441)

Covington, M. V., & Omelich, C. L. (1988). I can resist anything but temptation: Adolescent expectations for smoking cigarettes. *Journal of Applied Social Psychology, 18,* 203–227. (p. 537)

Cowan, G., Lee, C., Levy, D., & Snyder, D. (1988). Dominance and inequality in X-rated videocassettes. *Psychology of Women Quarterly, 12,* 299–311. (p. 577)

Cowan, N. (1988). Evolving conceptions of memory storage, selective attention, and their mutual constraints within the human information-processing system. *Psychological Bulletin, 104,* 163–191. (p. 281)

Cowan, N. (1994). Mechanisms of verbal short-term memory. *Current Directions in Psychological Science, 3,* 185–189. (p. 282)

Cowart, B. J. (1981). Development of taste perception in humans: Sensitivity and preference throughout the life span. *Psychological Bulletin, 90,* 43–73. (p. 174)

Craig, M. E., Kalichman, S. C., & Follingstad, D. R. (1989). Verbal coercive sexual behavior among college students. *Archives of Sexual Behavior, 18,* 421–434. (p. 576)

Craig, O., & Shields, J. (1996, July 14). For pity's sake. *The Sunday Times,* Section 3, pages 1–2. (p. 249)

Craik, F. I. M. (1986). A functional account of age differences in memory. In F. Klix & H. Hagendorf (Eds.), *Human memory and cognitive capabilities.* Amsterdam: Elsevier. (p. 135)

Craik, F. I. M., & Tulving, E. (1975). Depth of processing and the retention of words in episodic memory. *Journal of Experimental Psychology: General, 104,* 268–294. (pp. 275, 276)

Craik, F. I. M., & Watkins, M. J. (1973). The role of rehearsal in short-term memory. *Journal of Verbal Learning and Verbal Behavior, 12,* 599–607. (p. 275)

Crain-Thoreson, C., & Dale, P. S. (1992). Do early talkers become early readers? Linguistic precocity, preschool language, and emergent literacy. *Developmental Psychology, 28,* 421–429. (p. 348)

Crandall, C. S. (1988). Social contagion of binge eating. *Journal of Personality and Social Psychology, 55,* 588–598. (p. 372)

Crandall, C. S. (1994). Prejudice against fat people: Ideology and self-interest. *Journal of Personality and Social Psychology, 66,* 882-894. (p. 540)

Crandall, C. S. (1995). Do parents discriminate against their heavyweight daughters? *Personality and Social Psychology Bulletin, 21,* 724–735. (p. 540)

Crandall, J. E. (1984). Social interest as a moderator of life stress. *Journal of Personality and Social Psychology, 47,* 164–174. (p. 444)

Crawford, M., Chaffin, R., & Fitton, L. (1995). *Learning and Individual Differences, 7,* 341-362. (p. 358)

Crews, F. (1996). The verdict on Freud. *Psychological Science, 7,* 63–68. (p. 427)

Crocker, J., & Major, B. (1989). Social stigma and self-esteem: The self-protective properties of stigma. *Psychological Review, 89,* 608–630. (p. 439).

Crocker, J., Thompson, L. L., McGraw, K. M., & Ingerman, C. (1987). Downward comparison, prejudice, and evaluation of others: Effects of self-esteem and threat. *Journal of Personality and Social Psychology, 52,* 907–916. (p. 569)

Crombie, A. C. (1964, May). Early concepts of the senses and the mind. *Scientific American,* pp. 108–116. (p. 155)

Crook, T. H., & West, R. L. (1990). Name recall performance across the adult life-span. *British Journal of Psychology, 81,* 335–340. (p. 133)

Cross-National Collaborative Group (1992). The changing rate of major depression. *Journal of the American Medical Association, 268,* 3098–3105. (p. 471)

Crossen, C. (1994). *Tainted truth: The manipulation of fact in America.* New York: Simon & Schuster. (p. 593)

Crowell, J. A., & Waters, E. (1994). Bowlby's theory grown up: The role of attachment in adult love relationships. *Psychological Inquiry, 5,* 1–22. (p. 96)

Croyle, R. T., & Ditto, P. H. (1990). Illness cognition and behavior: An experimental approach. *Journal of Behavioral Medicine, 13,* 31–52. (p. 546)

CSICOP (1994, December). Psychics fail once again. *Skeptical Briefs,* p. 9. (p. 202)

Csikszentmihalyi, M. (1990). *Flow: The psychology of optimal experience.* New York: Harper & Row. (pp. 309, 412)

Csikszentmihalyi, M., & Larson, R. (1984). *Being adolescent: Conflict and growth in the teenage years.* New York: Basic Books. (p. 141)

Curtis, R. C., & Miller, K. (1986). Believing another likes or dislikes you: Behaviors making the beliefs come true. *Journal of Personality and Social Psychology, 51,* 284–290. (p. 583)

Curtiss, S. (1977). *Genie: A psycholinguistic study of a modern-day "wild child."* New York: Academic Press. (p. 324)

Curtiss, S. (1981). Dissociations between language and cognition: Cases and implications. *Journal of Autism and Developmental Disorders, 11,* 15–30. (p. 324)

Cutler, B. L., & Penrod, S. D. (1989). Forensically relevant moderators of the relation between eyewitness identification accuracy and confidence. *Journal of Applied Psychology, 74,* 650–652. (p. 297)

Cutrona, C. E. (1986). Behavioral manifestations of social support: A microanalytic investigation. *Journal of Personality and Social Psychology, 51,* 201–208. (p. 533)

Dabbs, J. M., Jr. (1992). Testosterone measurements in social and clinical psychology. *Journal of Social and Clinical Psychology, 11,* 302–321. (p. 572)

Dabbs, J. M., Jr., & Morris, R. (1990). Testosterone, social class, and antisocial behavior in a sample of 4,462 men. *Psychological Science, 1,* 209–211. (p. 572)

Dabbs, J. M., Jr., Ruback, R. B., & Besch, N. F. (1987). Male saliva testosterone following conversations with male and female partners. Paper presented at the American Psychological Association convention. (p. 376)

Damasio, H., Grabowski, T., Frank, R., Galaburda, A. M., & Damasio, A. R. (1994). The return of Phineas Gage: Clues about the brain from the skull of a famous patient. *Science, 264,* 1102–1105. (p. 62)

Damon, W. (1995). *Greater expectations: Overcoming the culture of indulgence in America's homes and schools.* New York: Free Press. (p. 87, 439)

Damon, W., & Hart, D. (1982). The development of self-understanding from infancy through adolescence. *Child Development, 53,* 841–864. (p. 103)

Damon, W., & Hart, D. (1988). *Self-understanding in childhood and adolescence.* Cambridge: Cambridge University Press. (p. 103)

Darley, J. M., & Latané, B. (1968a). Bystander intervention in emergencies: Diffusion of responsibility. *Journal of Personality and Social Psychology, 8,* 377–383. (p. 586)

Darley, J. M., & Latané, B. (1968b, December). When will people help in a crisis? *Psychology Today,* pp. 54–57, 70–71. (p. 585)

Darley, J. M., Seligman, C., & Becker, L. J. (1979, April). The lesson of twin rivers: Feedback works. *Psychology Today,* pp. 16, 23–24. (p. 263)

Darrach, B., & Norris, J. (1984, August). An American tragedy. *Life,* pp. 58–74. (p. 482)

Darwin, C. (1859/1988). *The origin of species.* Vol. 15 of *The Works of Charles Darwin,* edited by P. H. Barrett & R. B. Freeman. New York: New York University Press. (p. 73)

Daum, I., & Schugens, M. M. (1996). On the cerebellum and classical conditioning. *Psychological Science, 5,* 58–61. (p. 288)

Davey, G. C. L. (1992). Classical conditioning and the acquisition of human fears and phobias: A review and synthesis of the literature. *Advances in Behavior Research and Therapy, 14,* 29–66. (p. 252)

Davey, G. C. L. (1995). Preparedness and phobias: Specific evolved associations or a generalized expectancy bias? *Behavioral and Brain Sciences, 18,* 289–297. (p. 464)

Davidson, N. E. (1996, September). Is hormone replacement therapy a risk? *Scientific American,* p. 101. (p. 132)

Davidson, R. J. (1991, February 12). Quoted by Daniel Goleman, Feeling cheerful? Thank brain's left lobe. *New York Times,* pp. C1, C10. (p. 398)

Davidson, R. J. (1992). Emotion and affective style: Hemispheric substrates. *Psychological Science, 3,* 39–43. (pp. 398, 472)

Davidson, R. J., Ekman, P., Saron, C. D., Senulis, J. A., & Friesen, W. V. (1990). Approach-withdrawal and cerebral asymmetry: Emotional expression and brain physiology I. *Journal of Personality and Social Psychology, 58,* 330–341. (p. 398)

Davies, D. R., Matthews, G., & Wong, C. S. K. (1991). Aging and work. *International Review of Industrial and Organizational Psychology, 6,* 149–211. (p. 137)

Davies, P. T., & Cummings, E. M. (1994). Marital conflict and child adjustment: An emotional security hypothesis. *Psychological Bulletin, 116,* 387–411. (p. 102)

Davis, J. O., & Phelps, J. A. (1995). Twins with schizophrenia: Genes or germs? *Schizophrenia Bulletin, 21,* 13–18. (p. 479)

Davis, J. O., Phelps, J. A., & Bracha, H. S. (1995). Prenatal development of monozygotic twins and concordance for schizophrenia. *Schizophrenia Bulletin, 21,* 357–366. (p. 479)

Dawes, R. M. (1980). Social dilemmas. *Annual Review of Psychology, 31,* 169–193. (p. 579)

Dawes, R. M. (1994). *House of cards: Psychology and psychotherapy built on myth.* New York: Free Press. (pp. 426, 439)

Dawson, N. V., Arkes, H. R., Siciliano, C., Blinkhorn, R., Lakshmanan, M., & Petrelli, M. (1988). Hindsight bias: An impediment to accurate probability estimation in clinicopathologic conferences. *Medical Decision Making, 8,* 259–264. (p. 14)

Dean, G. A., Kelly, I. W., Saklofske, D. H., & Furnham, A. (1992). Graphology and human judgment. In B. Beyerstein & D. Beyerstein (Eds.), *The write stuff: Evaluations of graphology.* Buffalo, NY: Prometheus Books. (p. 448)

DeAngelis, T. (1988, October). Chinese psychologists focus on the practical. *APA Monitor,* p. 8. (p. 8)

DeAngelis, T. (1997, January). Chromosomes contain clues on schizophrenia. *APA Monitor,* p. 26. (p. 479)

Deardorff, J. (1994, July 28). "It feels like there's a beast inside me." *Chicago Tribune,* p. 1. (p. 372)

Deary, I. J., & Caryl, P. G. (1993). Intelligence, EEG and evoked potentials. In P. A. Vernon (Ed.), *Biological approaches to the study of human intelligence.* Norwood, NJ: Ablex. (p. 341)

Deary, I. J., & Matthews, G. (1993). Personality traits are alive and well. *The Psychologist: Bulletin of the British Psychological Society, 6,* 299–311. (p. 435)

Deary, I. J., & Stough, C. (1996). Intelligence and inspection time: Achievements, prospects, and problems. *American Psychologist, 51,* 599–608. (p. 341)

Deater-Deckard, K., Scarr, S., McCartney, K., & Eisenberg, M. (1994). Paternal separation anxiety: Relationships with parenting stress, child-rearing attitudes, and maternal anxieties. *Psychological Science, 5,* 341–346. (p. 99)

de Boysson-Bardies, B., Halle, P., Sagart, L., & Durand, C. (1989). A cross-linguistic investigation of vowel formats in babbling. *Journal of Child Language, 16,* 1–17. (p. 321)

DeCasper, A. J., & Fifer, W. (1980). Of human bonding: Newborns prefer their mother's voices. *Science, 208,* 1174–1176. (p. 80)

DeCasper, A. J., & Prescott, P. A. (1984). Human newborns' perception of male voices: Preference, discrimination and reinforcing value. *Developmental Psychobiology, 17,* 481–491. (p. 80)

DeCasper, A. J., & Spence, M. J. (1986). Prenatal maternal speech influences newborns' perception of speech sounds. *Infant Behavior and Development, 9,* 133–150. (p. 80)

Deci, E. L., & Ryan, R. M. (1985). *Intrinsic motivation and self-determination in human behavior.* New York: Plenum Press. (p. 386)

Deci, E. L., & Ryan, R. M. (1987). The support of autonomy and the control of behavior. *Journal of Personality and Social Psychology, 53,* 1024–1037. (p. 387)

Deci, E. L., & Ryan, R. M. (1992). The initiation and regulation of intrinsically motivated learning and achievement. In A. K. Boggiano & T. S. Pittman (Eds.), *Achievement and motivation: A social-developmental perspective.* New York: Cambridge University Press. (p. 386)

Deci, E. L., Connell, J. P., & Ryan, R. M. (1989). Self-determination in a work organization. *Journal of Applied Psychology, 74,* 580–590. (p. 389)

de Cuevas, J. (1990, September-October). "No, she holded them loosely." *Harvard Magazine,* pp. 60–67. (p. 322)

de Jong-Gierveld, J. (1987). Developing and testing a model of loneliness. *Journal of Personality and Social Psychology, 53,* 119–128. (p. 475)

Delgado, J. M. R. (1969). *Physical control of the mind: Toward a psychocivilized society.* New York: Harper & Row. (p. 61)

DeLoache, J. S. (1995). Early understanding and use of symbols: The model model. *Current Directions in Psychological Science, 4,* 109–113. (p. 91)

Dement, W. (1990). In the PBS film, *Sleep alert.* Quoted by *Behavior Today,* March 12, p. 8. (p. 214)

Dement, W. C. (1978). *Some must watch while some must sleep.* New York: Norton. (pp. 211, 212, 215, 217)

Dement, W. C., & Wolpert, E. A. (1958). The relation of eye movements, body mobility, and external stimuli to dream content. *Journal of Experimental Psychology, 55,* 543–553. (p. 218)

Dempster, F. N. (1988). The spacing effect: A case study in the failure to apply the results of psychological research. *American Psychologist, 43,* 627–634. (p. 274)

Denes-Raj, V., Epstein, S., & Cole, J. (1995). The generality of the ratio-bias phenomenon. *Personality and Social Psychology Bulletin, 21,* 1083-1092. (p. 314)

Dennett, D. (1996, September 9). Quoted by Ian Parker, Richard Dawkins's evolution. *The New Yorker,* pp. 41–45. (p. 2)

Denton, K., & Krebs, D. (1990). From the scene to the crime: The effect of alcohol and social context on moral judgment. *Journal of Personality and Social Psychology, 59,* 242–248. (p. 231)

D'Eon, J. L. (1989). Hypnosis in the control of labor pain. In N. P. Spanos & J. F. Chaves (Eds.), *Hypnosis: The cognitive-behavioral perspective.* Buffalo, NY: Prometheus Books. (p. 226)

DePaulo, B. M., Blank, A. L., Swaim, G. W., & Hairfield, J. G. (1992). Expressiveness and expressive control. *Personality and Social Psychology Bulletin, 18,* 276–285. (p. 435)

De Pree, M. (1987). *Leadership is an art.* East Lansing, MI: Michigan State University Press. (p. 389)

Deregowski, J. B. (1989). Real space and represented space: Cross-cultural perspectives. *Behavioral and Brain Sciences, 12,* 51–119. (p. 192)

Dermer, M., & Pyszczynski, T. A. (1978). Effects of erotica upon men's loving and liking responses for women they love. *Journal of Personality and Social Psychology, 36,* 1302–1309. (p. 584)

Dermer, M., Cohen, S. J., Jacobsen, E., & Anderson, E. A. (1979). Evaluative judgments of aspects of life as a function of vicarious exposure to hedonic extremes. *Journal of Personality and Social Psychology, 37,* 247–260. (p. 441)

Deutsch, J. A. (1972, July). Brain reward: ESP and ecstasy. *Psychology Today,* pp. 46–48. (p. 58)

Deutsch, M. (1991). Egalitarianism in the laboratory and at work. In R. Vermunt & H. Steensma (Eds.), *Social justice in human relations.* New York: Plenum. (p. 263)

DeValois, R. L., & DeValois, K. K. (1975). Neural coding of color. In E. C. Carterette & M. P. Friedman (Eds.), *Handbook of perception: Vol. V. Seeing.* New York: Academic Press. (p. 162).

Devine, P. G. (1995). Prejudice and outgroup perception. In A. Tesser (Ed.), *Advanced social psychology.* New York: McGraw-Hill. (p. 581)

de Waal, F. B. M. (1995, March). Bonobo sex and society. *Scientific American,* pp. 82–88. (p. 72)

Dey, E. L., Astin, A. W., & Korn, W. S. (1991). *The American freshman: Twenty-five year trends.* Los Angeles: Higher Education Research Institute, UCLA. (pp. 409, 566)

Dhawan, N., Roseman, I. J., Naidu, R. K., Thapa, K., & Rettek, S. I. (1995). Self-concepts across two cultures: India and the United States. *Journal of Cross-Cultural Psychology, 26,* 606–621. (p. 441)

Diaconis, P., & Mosteller, F. (1989). Methods for studying coincidences. *Journal of the American Statistical Association, 84,* 853–861. (p. 24)

Diamond, J. (1986). Variation in human testis size. *Nature, 320,* 488–489. (p. 73)

Diamond, J. (1989, May). The great leap forward. *Discover,* pp. 50–60. (p. 319)

Diamond, R. (1993). Genetics and male sexual orientation (letter). *Science, 261,* p. 1258. (p. 382)

Dickie, J. R. (1987). Interrelationships within the mother-father-infant triad. In P. W. Berman & F. A. Pedersen (Eds.), *Men's transitions to parenthood: Longitudinal studies of early family experience.* Hillsdale, NJ: Erlbaum. (p. 99)

Diener, E. (1993). Most Americans are happy. Unpublished manuscript, University of Illinois. (p. 441)

Diener, E., Diener, M., & Diener, C. (1995). Factors predicting the subjective well-being of nations. *Journal of Personality and Social Psychology, 69*, 851–864. (p. 443)

Diener, E., Emmons, R. A., & Sandvik, E. (1986). The dual nature of happiness: Independence of positive and negative moods. Unpublished manuscript, University of Illinois. (p. 140)

Diener, E., Wolsic, B., & Fujita, F. (1995). Physical attractiveness and subjective well-being. *Journal of Personality and Social Psychology, 69*, 120–129. (p. 581)

Dietz, W. H., Jr., & Gortmaker, S. L. (1985). Do we fatten our children at the television set? Obesity and television viewing in children and adolescents. *Pediatrics, 75*, 807–812. (p. 545)

DiLalla, D. L., Carey, G., Gottesman, I. I., & Bouchard, T. J., Jr. (1996). Heritability of MMPI personality indicators of psychopathology in twins reared apart. *Journal of Abnormal Psychology, 105*, 491–499. (pp. 109, 471)

DiLalla, L. F., & Gottesman, I. I. (1991). Biological and genetic contributors to violence—Widom's untold tale. *Psychological Bulletin, 109*, 125–129. (p. 482)

Dindia, K., & Allen, M. (1992). Sex differences in self-disclosure: A meta-analysis. *Psychological Bulletin, 112*, 106–124. (p. 123)

Dinges, N. G., & Hull, P. (1992). Personality, culture, and international studies. In D. Lieberman (Ed.), *Revealing the world: An interdisciplinary reader for international studies.* Dubuque, IA: Kendall-Hunt. (p. 328)

Dion, K. K., & Dion, K. L. (1993). Individualistic and collectivistic perspectives on gender and the cultural context of love and intimacy. *Journal of Social Issues, 49*, 53–69. (p. 443)

Discover (1996, May). A fistful of risks. Pp. 82-83. (p. 536)

Dixon, B. (1986, April). Dangerous thoughts: How we think and feel can make us sick. *Science, 86*, pp. 63–66. (p. 524)

Dobson, K. S. (1989). A meta-analysis of the efficacy of cognitive therapy for depression. *Journal of Consulting and Clinical Psychology, 57*, 414–419. (p. 505)

Dodd, M. (1996, September 19). $500,000 ball raises skepticism. *USA Today*, p. 9C. (p. 202)

Dohrenwend, B. P., Levav, I., Shrout, P. E., Schwartz, S., Naveh, G., Link, B. G., Skodol, A. E., & Stueve, A. (1992). Socioeconomic status and psychiatric disorders: The causation-selection issue. *Science, 255*, 946–952. (p. 484)

Dohrenwend, B., Pearlin, L., Clayton, P., Hamburg, B., Dohrenwend, B. P., Riley, M., & Rose, R. (1982). Report on stress and life events. In G. R. Elliott & C. Eisdorfer (Eds.), *Stress and human health: Analysis and implications of research* (A study by the Institute of Medicine/National Academy of Sciences). New York: Springer. (p. 519)

Dolan, B. (1991). Cross-cultural aspects of anorexia nervosa and bulimia: A review. *International Journal of Eating Disorders, 10*, 67–78. (p. 373)

Dole, R. (1996, April 20). Quoted by M. Duffy, Look who's talking. *Time*, p. 48. (p. 551)

Dolezal, H. (1982). *Living in a world transformed.* New York: Academic Press. (p. 196)

Domjan, M. (1992). Adult learning and mate choice: Possibilities and experimental evidence. *American Zoologist, 32*, 48–61. (p. 248)

Domjan, M. (1994). Formulation of a behavior system for sexual conditioning. *Psychonomic Bulletin & Review, 1*, 421–428. (p. 248)

Donaldson, M. (1979, March). The mismatch between school and children's minds. *Human Nature,* pp. 60–67. (p. 91)

Donnerstein, E., Linz, D., & Penrod, S. (1987). *The question of pornography.* New York: Free Press. (p. 576)

Dorner, G. (1976). *Hormones and brain differentiation.* Amsterdam: Elsevier Scientific. (p. 382)

Dorner, G. (1988). Neuroendocrine response to estrogen and brain differentiation in heterosexuals, homosexuals, and transsexuals. *Archives of Sexual Behavior, 17*, 57–75. (p. 382)

Dorozyaski, A. (1993, January/February). Maternal alcoholism: Grapes of wrath. *Psychology Today*, p. 18. (p. 81)

Dorris, M. (1989). *The Broken Cord.* New York: HarperCollins. (p. 81)

Doty, R. L., Shaman, P., Applebaum, S. L., Giberson, R., Siksorski, L., & Rosenberg, L. (1984). Smell identification ability: Changes with age. *Science, 226*, 1441–1443. (p. 130)

Draguns, J. G. (1990a). Normal and abnormal behavior in cross-cultural perspective: Specifying the nature of their relationship. *Nebraska Symposium on Motivation 1989, 37*, 235–277. (pp. 454, 473)

Draguns, J. G. (1990b). Applications of cross-cultural psychology in the field of mental health. In R. W. Brislin (Ed.), *Applied cross-cultural psychology.* Newbury Park, CA: Sage. (pp. 454, 456)

Druckman, D., & Bjork, R. A. (1991). *In the mind's eye: Enhancing human performance.* National Academy Press: Washington, DC. (p. 434)

Druckman, D., & Bjork, R. A. (Eds.) (1994). *Learning, remembering, believing: Enhancing human performance.* Washington, DC: National Academy Press. (pp. 222, 223, 226)

Druckman, D., & Swets, J. A. (Eds.). (1988). *Enhancing human performance: Issues, theories, and techniques.* Washington, DC: National Academy Press. (pp. 203, 300)

Drummey, A. B., & Newcombe, N. (1995). Remembering versus knowing the past: Children's explicit and implicit memories for pictures. *Journal of Experimental Child Psychology, 59*, 549–565. (p. 83)

Duclos, S. E., Laird, J. D., Sexter, M., Stern, L., & Van Lighten, O. (1989). Emotion-specific effects of facial expressions and postures on emotional experience. *Journal of Personality and Social Psychology, 57*, 100–108. (p. 402)

Duggan, J. P., & Booth, D. A. (1986). Obesity, overeating, and rapid gastric emptying in rats with ventromedial hypothalamic lesions. *Science, 231*, 609–611. (p. 369)

Duncan, B. L. (1976). Differential social perception and attribution of intergroup violence: Testing the lower limits of stereotyping of blacks. *Journal of Personality and Social Psychology, 34*, 590–598. (p. 567)

Duncan, G. J., Hill, M. S., & Hoffman, S. D. (1988). Welfare dependence within and across generations. *Science, 239,* 467–471. (p. 313)

Duncker, K. (1945). On problem solving. *Psychological Monographs, 58* (Whole no. 270). (pp. 309–310)

Dunn, J., & Plomin, R. (1990). *Separate lives: Why siblings are so different.* New York: Basic Books. (p. 110)

Dunning, D., Griffin, D. W., Milojkovic, J. D., & Ross, L. (1990). *Journal of Personality and Social Psychology, 58,* 568–581. (p. 313)

Dutton, D. G., & Aron, A. (1989). Romantic attraction and generalized liking for others who are sources of conflict-based arousal. *Canadian Journal of Behavioural Sciences, 21,* 246–257. (p. 584)

Dutton, D. G., & Aron, A. P. (1974). Some evidence for heightened sexual attraction under conditions of high anxiety. *Journal of Personality and Social Psychology, 30,* 510–517. (p. 584)

Dweck, C. S., & Elliott, E. S. (1983). Achievement motivation. In P. Mussen & E. M. Hetherington (Eds.), *Handbook of child psychology* (Vol. IV). New York: Wiley. (p. 385)

Dye, D. A., & Reck, M. (1989). College grade point average as a predictor of adult success: A reply. *Public Personnel Management, 18,* 235–241. (p. 340)

Eagles, J. M. (1991). Is schizophrenia disappearing? *British Journal of Psychiatry, 158,* 834–835. (p. 478)

Eagly, A. H., & Johnson, B. T. (1990). Gender and leadership style: A meta-analysis. *Psychological Bulletin, 108,* 233–256. (p. 389)

Eagly, A. H., & Karau, S. J. (1991). Gender and the emergence of leaders: A meta-analysis. *Journal of Personality and Social Psychology, 60,* 685–710. (p. 389)

Eagly, A. H., Ashmore, R. D., Makhijani, M. G., & Kennedy, L. C. (1991). What is beautiful is good, but . . .: A meta-analytic review of research on the physical attractiveness stereotype. *Psychological Bulletin, 110,* 109–128. (p. 581)

Eagly, A. H., & Crowley, M. (1986). Gender and helping behavior: A meta-analytic review of the social psychological literature. *Psychological Bulletin, 100,* 283–308. (p. 586)

Ebbesen, E. B., Duncan, B., & Konecni, V. J. (1975). Effects of content of verbal aggression on future verbal aggression: A field experiment. *Journal of Experimental Social Psychology, 11,* 192–204. (p. 406)

Ebbinghaus, H. (1885). *Über das Gedachtnis.* Leipzig: Duncker & Humblot. Cited in R. Klatzky (1980), *Human memory: Structures and processes.* San Francisco: Freeman. (p. 282)

Eccles, J. S., Jacobs, J. E., & Harold, R. D. (1990). Gender role stereotypes, expectancy effects, and parents' socialization of gender differences. *Journal of Social Issues, 46,* 183–201. (p. 358)

Eckensberger, L. H. (1994). Moral development and its measurement across cultures. In W. J. Lonner & R. Malpass (Eds.), *Psychology and culture.* Boston: Allyn and Bacon. (p. 120)

Eckert, E. D., Heston, L. L., & Bouchard, T. J., Jr. (1981). MZ twins reared apart: Preliminary findings of psychiatric disturbances and traits. In L. Gedda, P. Paris, & W. D. Nance (Eds.), *Twin research: Vol. 3. Pt. B. Intelligence, personality, and development.* New York: Alan Liss. (p. 464)

Ecklund-Flores, L. (1992). The infant as a model for the teaching of introductory psychology. Paper presented to the American Psychological Association annual convention. (p. 80)

Edison, T. A. (1948). *The diary and sundry observations of Thomas Alva Edison,* edited by D. D. Runes. New York: Philosophical Library. Cited by S. Coren (1996). *Sleep Thieves.* New York: Free Press. (p. 214)

Edwards, C. P. (1981). The comparative study of the development of moral judgment and reasoning. In R. H. Munroe, R. L. Munroe, & B. B. Whiting (Eds.), *Handbook of cross-cultural human development.* New York: Garland Press. (p. 120)

Edwards, C. P. (1982). Moral development in comparative cultural perspective. In D. A. Wagner & H. W. Stevenson (Eds.), *Cultural perspectives on child development.* San Francisco: Freeman. (p. 120)

Ehrhardt, A. A. (1987). A transactional perspective on the development of gender differences. In J. M. Reinisch, L. A. Rosenblum, & S. A. Sanders (Eds.), *Masculinity/femininity: Basic perspectives.* New York: Oxford University Press. (p. 793)

Ehrlichman, H., & Halpern, J. N. (1988). Affect and memory: Effects of pleasant and unpleasant odors on retrieval of happy and unhappy memories. *Journal of Personality and Social Psychology, 55,* 769–779. (p. 176)

Eibl-Eibesfeldt, I. (1971). *Love and hate: The natural history of behavior patterns.* New York: Holt, Rinehart & Winston. (p. 401)

Eich, E. (1990). Learning during sleep. In R. B. Bootzin, J. F. Kihlstrom, & D. L. Schacter (Eds.), *Sleep and cognition.* Washington, DC: American Psychological Association. (p. 218)

Eich, E. (1995). Searching for mood dependent memory. *Psychological Science, 6,* 67–75. (p. 290)

Eich, J. E. (1980). The cue-dependent nature of state-dependent retrieval. *Memory and Cognition, 8,* 157–173. (p. 231)

Einstein, G. O., & McDaniel, M. A. (1990). Normal aging and prospective memory. *Journal of Experimental Psychology: Learning, Memory, and Cognition, 16,* 717–726. (p. 133)

Eisenberg, N., & Lennon, R. (1983). Sex differences in empathy and related capacities. *Psychological Bulletin, 94,* 100–131. (p. 124)

Eisenberger, R., & Cameron, J. (1996). Detrimental effects of reward: Reality or myth? *American Psychologist, 51,* 1153–1166. (p. 261)

Eiser, J. R. (1985). Smoking: The social learning of an addiction. *Journal of Social and Clinical Psychology, 3,* 446–457. (p. 537)

Ekman, P. (1994). Strong evidence for universals in facial expressions: A reply to Russell's mistaken critique. *Psychological Bulletin, 115,* 268–287. (p. 400)

Ekman, P., & Friesen, W. V. (1975). *Unmasking the face.* Englewood Cliffs, NJ: Prentice-Hall. (p. 400)

Ekman, P., & O'Sullivan, M. (1991). Who can catch a liar? *American Psychologist, 46,* 913–920. (p. 399)

Ekman, P., Friesen, W. V., O'Sullivan, M., Chan, A., Diacoyanni-Tarlatzis, I., Heider, K., Krause, R., LeCompte, W. A., Pitcairn, T., Ricci-Bitti, P. E., Scherer, K., Tomita, M., & Tzavaras, A. (1987). Universals and cultural differences in the judgments of facial expressions of emotion. *Journal of Personality and Social Psychology, 53,* 712–717. (p. 400)

Ekman, P., Levenson, R. W., & Friesen, W. V. (1983). Autonomic nervous system activity distinguishes among emotions. *Science, 221,* 1208–1210. (p. 402)

Elbert, T., Pantev, C., Wienbruch, C., Rockstroh, B., & Taub, E. (1995). Increased cortical representation of the fingers of the left hand in string players. *Science, 270,* 305–307. (p. 84)

Elkin, I., Shea, T., Watkins, J. T., Imber, S. D., Sotsky, S. M., Collins, J. F., Glass, D. R., Pilkonis, P. A., Leber, W. R., Docherty, J. P., Fiester, S. J., & Parloff, M. B. (1989). National Institute of Mental Health treatment of depression collaborative research program. *Archives of General Psychiatry, 46,* 971–983. (p. 504)

Elkind, D. (1970). The origins of religion in the child. *Review of Religious Research, 12,* 35–42. (p. 118)

Elkind, D. (1978). *The child's reality: Three developmental themes.* Hillsdale, NJ: Erlbaum. (p. 118)

Elkis, H., Friedman, L., Wise, A., & Meltzer, H. Y. (1995). Meta-analyses of studies of ventricular enlargement and cortical sulcal prominence in mood disorders: Comparisons with controls or patients with schizophrenia. *Archives of General Psychiatry, 52,* 735–746. (p. 478)

Elliot, A. (1996, January 18). Personal communication for Nielsen Media Research Director of Communications via e-mail (Anne_Elliot@tvratings.com). (p. 574)

Ellis, A. (1962). *Reason and emotion in psychotherapy.* Secaucus, NJ: Citadel Press. (p. 496)

Ellis, A. (1980). Psychotherapy and atheistic values: A response to A. E. Bergin's "Psychotherapy and religious values." *Journal of Consulting and Clinical Psychology, 48* 635–639. (p. 507)

Ellis, A. (1987). The impossibility of achieving consistently good mental health. *American Psychologist, 42,* 364–375. (p. 496)

Ellis, A. (1993). Changing rational-emotive therapy (RET) to rational emotive behavior therapy (REBT). *The Behavior Therapist, 16,* 257–258. (p. 496)

Ellis, A., & Becker, I. M. (1982). *A guide to personal happiness.* North Hollywood, CA: Wilshire Book Co. (p. 253)

Ellis, H. C., & Ashbrook, P. W. (1989). The "state" of mood and memory research: A selective review. *Journal of Social Behavior and Personality, 4,* 1–21. (p. 290)

Ellis, L., & Ames, M. A. (1987). Neurohormonal functioning and sexual orientation: A theory of homosexuality-heterosexuality. *Psychological Bulletin, 101,* 233–258. (p. 382)

Emde, R. N., Plomin, R., Robinson, J., Corley, R., DeFries, J., Fulker, D. W., Reznick, J. S., Campos, J., Kagan, J., & Zahn-Waxler, C. (1992). Temperament, emotion, and cognition at fourteen months: The MacArthur Longitudinal Twin Study. *Child Development, 63,* 1437–1455. (p. 97)

Emery, Jr., C. E. (1995, September/October). Telephone psychics: Friends or phonies? *Skeptical Inquirer,* pp. 14–17. (p. 201)

Emmons, S., Geisler, C., Kaplan, K. J., & Harrow, M. (1997). *Living with schizophrenia.* Muncie, IN: Taylor and Francis (Accelerated Development). (pp. 453, 480)

Empson, J. A. C., & Clarke, P. R. F. (1970). Rapid eye movements and remembering. *Nature, 227,* 287–288. (p. 219)

Endler, N. S. (1982). *Holiday of darkness: A psychologist's personal journey out of his depression.* New York: Wiley. (pp. 472, 510)

Engen, T. (1987). Remembering odors and their names. *American Scientist, 75,* 497–503. (p. 176)

England, G. W., & Misumi, J. (1986). Work centrality in Japan and the United States. *Journal of Cross-Cultural Psychology, 17,* 396–416. (p. 388)

Epstein, S. (1983a). Aggregation and beyond: Some basic issues on the prediction of behavior. *Journal of Personality, 51,* 360–392. (p. 435)

Epstein, S. (1983b). The stability of behavior across time and situations. In R. Zucker, J. Aronoff, & A. I. Rabin (Eds.), *Personality and the prediction of behavior.* San Diego: Academic Press. (p. 435)

Epstein, S., & Meier, P. (1989). Constructive thinking: A broad coping variable with specific components. *Journal of Personality and Social Psychology, 57,* 332–350. (p. 340)

Erber, R., & Tesser, A. (1992). Task effort and the regulation of mood: The absorption hypothesis. *Journal of Experimental Social Psychology, 28,* 339–359. (p. 496)

Erdelyi, M. H. (1985). *Psychoanalysis: Freud's cognitive psychology.* New York: Freeman. (p. 428)

Erdelyi, M. H. (1988). Repression, reconstruction, and defense: History and integration of the psychoanalytic and experimental frameworks. In J. Singer (Ed.), *Repression: Defense mechanism and cognitive style.* Chicago: University of Chicago Press. (p. 428)

Erel, O., & Burman, B. (1995). Interrelatedness of marital relations and parent-child relations: A meta-analytic review. *Psychological Bulletin, 118,* 108–132. (p. 138)

Ericsson, K. A., & Chase, W. G. (1982). Exceptional memory. *American Scientist, 70,* 607–615. (p. 278)

Erikson, E. H. (1963). *Childhood and society.* New York: Norton. (p. 121)

Erikson, E. H. (1983, June). A conversation with Erikson (by E. Hall). *Psychology Today,* pp. 22–30. (p. 98)

Erlenmeyer-Kimling, L., & others (1995). The New York high-risk project. *Archives of General Psychiatry, 52,* 857–865. (p. 480)

Eron, L. D. (1987). The development of aggressive behavior from the perspective of a developing behaviorism. *American Psychologist, 42,* 435–442. (pp. 146, 636)

Eron, L. D., & Huesmann, L. R. (1984). The control of aggressive behavior by changes in attitudes, values and the conditions of learning. In R. J. Blanchard & C. Blanchard (Eds.), *Advances in the study of aggression* (Vol. 1). Orlando, FL: Academic Press. (p. 144)

Eronen, M., Tihonen, J., & Hakola, P. (1996). Schizophrenia and homicidal behavior. *Schizophrenia Bulletin, 22,* 83–89. (p. 459)

Espinosa, M. P., Sigman, M. D., Neumann, C. G., Bwibo, N. O., & McDonald, M. A. (1992). Playground behaviors of school-age children in relation to nutrition, schooling, and family characteristics. *Developmental Psychology, 28,* 1188–1195. (p. 539)

Esser, J. K., & Lindoerfer, J. S. (1989). Groupthink and the space shuttle *Challenger* accident: Toward a quantitative case analysis. *Journal of Behavioral Decision Making, 2,* 167–177. (p. 563)

ETS (1992). Three reports shed new light on gender differences in testing. *ETS Developments, 37*(3), 4–7. (p. 357)

ETS (1994). *Taking the SAT I reasoning test.* Princeton, NJ: College Board SAT Program. (p. 346)

Evans, C. R., & Dion, K. L. (1991). Group cohesion and performance: A meta-analysis. *Small Group Research, 22,* 175–186. (p. 388)

Evans, G. W., Hygge, S., Bullinger, M. (1995). Chronic noise and psychological stress. *Psychological Science, 6,* 333–338. (p. 166)

Evans, G. W., Palsane, M. N., & Carrere, S. (1987). Type A behavior and occupational stress: A cross-cultural study of blue-collar workers. *Journal of Personality and Social Psychology, 52,* 1002–1007. (p. 522)

Evans, G. W., Palsane, M. N., Lepore, S. J., & Martin, J. (1989). Residential density and psychological health: The mediating effects of social support. *Journal of Personality and Social Psychology, 57,* 994–999. (p. 533)

Evans, R. I., Dratt, L. M., Raines, B. E., & Rosenberg, S. S. (1988). Social influences on smoking initiation: Importance of distinguishing descriptive versus mediating process variables. *Journal of Applied Social Psychology, 18,* 925–943. (p. 537)

Evans, R. I., Raines, B. E., & Hanselka, L. (1984). Developing data-based communications in social psychological research: Adolescent smoking prevention. *Journal of Applied Social Psychology, 14,* 289–295. (p. 538)

Everson, S. A., & others (1996). Hopelessness and risk of mortality and incidence of myocardial infarction and cancer. *Psychosomatic Medicine, 58,* 113–121. (p. 521)

Exner, J. E. (1993). *The Rorschach: A comprehensive system, Vol. 1. Basic foundations* (3rd ed.). New York: Wiley. (p. 426)

Eyer, D. E. (1992). *Mother-infant bonding: A scientific fiction.* New Haven: Yale University Press. (p. 96)

Eysenck, H. J. (1952). The effects of psychotherapy: An evaluation. *Journal of Consulting Psychology, 16,* 319–324. (p. 503)

Eysenck, H. J. (1990, April 30). An improvement on personality inventory. *Current Contents: Social and Behavioral Sciences, 22*(18), 20. (p. 432)

Eysenck, H. J. (1992). Four ways five factors are *not* basic. *Personality and Individual Differences, 13,* 667–673. (p. 432)

Eysenck, H. J., & Grossarth-Maticek, R. (1991). Creative novation behaviour therapy as a prophylactic treatment for cancer and coronary heart disease: Part II—Effects of treatment. *Behaviour Research and Therapy, 29,* 17–31. (p. 532)

Eysenck, H. J., & Kamin, L. (1981). *The intelligence controversy: H. J. Eysenck vs. Leon Kamin.* New York: Wiley. (p. 336)

Eysenck, H. J., Wakefield, J. A., Jr., & Friedman, A. F. (1983). Diagnosis and clinical assessment: The DSM-III. *Annual Review of Psychology, 34,* 167–193. (p. 458)

Eysenck, M. W., MacLeod, C., & Mathews, A. (1987). Cognitive functioning and anxiety. *Psychological Research, 49,* 189–195. (p. 445)

Eysenck, S. B. G., & Eysenck, H. J. (1963). The validity of questionnaire and rating assessments of extraversion and neuroticism, and their factorial stability. *British Journal of Psychology, 54,* 51–62. (p. 432)

Faber, N. (1987, July). Personal glimpse. *Reader's Digest,* p. 34. (p. 351)

Fagan, J. F., III (1992). Intelligence: A theoretical viewpoint. *Current Directions in Psychological Science, 1,* 82–86. (p. 357–391)

Falbo, T., & Polit, D. F. (1986). Quantitative review of the only child literature: Research evidence and theory development. *Psychological Bulletin, 100,* 176–189. (p. 385)

Falbo, T., & Poston, D. L., Jr. (1993). The academic, personality, and physical outcomes of only children in China. *Child Development, 64,* 18–35. (p. 385)

Fallon, A. (1990). Culture in the mirror: Sociocultural determinants of body image. In T. F. Cash & T. Pruzinsky (Eds.), *Body images: Development, deviance, and change.* New York: Guilford Press. (p. 373)

Fallon, A. E., & Rozin, P. (1985). Sex differences in perceptions of desirable body shape. *Journal of Abnormal Psychology, 94,* 102–105. (p. 373)

Fancher, R. E. (1979). *Pioneers of psychology.* New York: Norton. (p. 334)

Fantz, R. L. (1961, May). The origin of form perception. *Scientific American,* pp. 66–72. (p. 81)

Farina, A. (1982). The stigma of mental disorders. In A. G. Miller (Ed.), *In the eye of the beholder.* New York: Praeger. (pp. 455,459)

Farina, A., & Fisher, J. D. (1982). Beliefs about mental disorders: Findings and implications. In G. Weary & H. L. Mirels (Eds.), *Integrations of clinical and social psychology.* New York: Oxford University Press. (p. 501)

Farrell, P. A., Gates, W. K., Maksud, M. G., & Morgan, W. P. (1982). Increases in plasma beta-endorphin/beta-lipotropin immunoreactivity after treadmill running in humans. *Journal of Applied Physiology, 52,* 1245–1249. (p. 46)

Farrington, D. P. (1991). Antisocial personality from childhood to adulthood. *The Psychologist: Bulletin of the British Psychological Society, 4,* 389–394. (p. 481)

Fava, M., Copeland, P. M., Schweiger, U., & Herzog, D. B. (1989). Neurochemical abnormalities of anorexia nervosa and bulimia nervosa. *American Journal of Psychiatry, 146,* 963–971. (p. 372)

Fazio, R. H. (1990). Multiple processes by which attitudes guide behavior: The MODE model as an integrative framework. In M. P. Zanna (Ed.), *Advances in experimental social psychology* (Vol. 23). San Diego, CA: Academic Press. (p. 552)

Feder, H. H. (1984). Hormones and sexual behavior. *Annual Review of Psychology, 35,* 165–200. (p. 376)

Feeney, D. M. (1987). Human rights and animal welfare. *American Psychologist, 42,* 593–599. (p. 35)

Feeney, J. A., & Noller, P. (1990). Attachment style as a predictor of adult romantic relationships. *Journal of Personality and Social Psychology, 58,* 281–291. (p. 98)

Fehr, B., & Russell, J. A. (1991). The concept of love viewed from a prototype perspective. *Journal of Personality and Social Psychology, 60,* 425–438. (p. 306)

Feingold, A. (1990). Gender differences in effects of physical attractiveness on romantic attraction: A comparison across five research paradigms. *Journal of Personality and Social Psychology, 59,* 981–993. (p. 581)

Feingold, A. (1992). Good-looking people are not what we think. *Psychological Bulletin, 111,* 304–341. (p. 581)

Feingold, A., & Mazzella, R. (1996). Gender differences in body image are increasing. *The General Psychologist, 32,* 84–92. (p. 373)

Feinleib, M., Lenfant, C., & Miller, S. A. (1984). Hypertension and calcium. *Science, 226,* 384–385. (p. 539)

Fenton, W. S., & McGlashan, T. H. (1991). Natural history of schizophrenia subtypes: II. Positive and negative symptoms and long-term course. *Archives of General Psychiatry, 48,* 978–986. (p. 477)

Fenton, W. S., & McGlashan, T. H. (1994). Antecedents, symptom progression, and long-term outcome of the deficit syndrome in schizophrenia. *American Journal of Psychiatry, 151,* 351–356. (p. 477)

Ferguson, E. D. (1989). Adler's motivational theory: An historical perspective on belonging and the fundamental human striving. *Individual Psychology, 45,* 354-361. (p. 367)

Fernandez, E., & Turk, D. C. (1989). The utility of cognitive coping strategies for altering pain perception: A meta-analysis. *Pain, 38,* 123–135. (p. 173)

Fernandez-Dols, J-M., & Ruiz-Belda, M-A. (1995). Are smiles a sign of happiness? Gold medal winners at the Olympic Games. *Journal of Personality and Social Psychology, 69,* 1113–1119. (p. 401)

Ferris, C. F. (1996, March). The rage of innocents. *The Sciences,* pp. 22–26. (p. 100)

Fichter, M. M., & Noegel, R. (1990). Concordance for bulimia nervosa in twins. *International Journal of Eating Disorders, 9,* 255–263. (p. 372)

Fichter, M. M., & others (1996). Mental illness in a representative sample of homeless men in Munich, Germany. *European Archives of Psychiatry and Clinical Neuroscience, 246,* 185–196. (p. 508)

Fiedler, F. E. (1981). Leadership effectiveness. *American Behavioral Scientist, 24,* 619–632. (p. 388)

Fiedler, F. E. (1987, September). When to lead, when to stand back. *Psychology Today,* pp. 26–27. (p. 388)

Field, T. (1991). Quality infant daycare and grade school behavior and performance. *Child Development, 62,* 863–870. (p. 101)

Field, T. (1996). Attachment and separation in young children. *Annual Review of Psychology, 47,* 541–561. (p. 101)

Field, T. M., Schanberg, S. M., Scafidi, F., Bauer, C. R., Vega-Lahr, N., Garcia, R., Nystrom, J., & Kuhn, C. M. (1986). Tactile/kinesthetic stimulation effects on preterm neonates. *Pediatrics, 77,* 654–658. (p. 84)

Fincham, F. D., & Bradbury, T. N. (1993). Marital satisfaction, depression, and attributions: A longitudinal analysis. *Journal of Personality and Social Psychology, 64,* 442–452. (p. 560)

Findley, M. J., & Cooper, H. M. (1983). Locus of control and academic achievement: A literature review. *Journal of Personality and Social Psychology, 44,* 419–427. (p. 446)

Fink, G. R., Markowitsch, H. J., Reinkemeier, M., Bruchbauer, Kessler, J., & Heiss, W-D. (1996). Cerebral representation of one's own past: Neural networks involved in autobiographical memory. *Journal of Neuroscience, 16,* 4275–4282. (p. 287)

Finkel, L. H., & Sajda, P. (1994). Constructing visual perception. *American Scientist, 82,* 224–237. (p. 160)

Finucci, J. M., & Childs, B. (1981). Are there really more dyslexic boys than girls? In A. Ansara, N. Geschwind, A. Galaburda, M. Albert, & N. Gartrell (Eds.), *Sex differences in dyslexia.* Towson, MD: The Orton Dyslexia Society. (p. 357)

Fiore, E. (1989). *Encounters: A psychologist reveals case studies of abductions by extraterrestrials.* New York: Doubleday. Cited by L. S. Newman & R. F. Baumeister, (1994). Toward an explanation of the UFO abduction phenomenon: Hypnotic, elaboration, extraterrestrial sadomasochism, and spurious memories. Unpublished manuscript, University of Illinois at Chicago. (p. 224)

Fischer, P. J., & Breakey, W. R. (1991). The epidemiology of alcohol, drug, and mental disorders among homeless persons. *American Psychologist, 46,* 1115–1128. (p. 508)

Fischhoff, B. (1982). Debiasing. In D. Kahneman, P. Slovic, & A. Tversky (Eds.), *Judgment under uncertainty: Heuristics and biases.* New York: Cambridge University Press. (p. 314)

Fischhoff, B., Slovic, P., & Lichtenstein, S. (1977). Knowing with certainty: The appropriateness of extreme confidence. *Journal of Experimental Psychology: Human Perception and Performance, 3,* 552–564. (p. 313)

Fisher, H. E. (1993, March/April). After all, maybe it's biology. *Psychology Today,* pp. 40–45. (p. 137)

Fisher, H. T. (1984). Little Albert and Little Peter. *Bulletin of the British Psychological Society, 37,* 269. (p. 493)

Fisher, R. P., Geiselman, R. E., & Amador, M. (1989). Field test of the cognitive interview: Enhancing the recollection of actual victims and witnesses of crime. *Journal of Applied Psychology, 74,* 722–727. (p. 297)

Fisher, R. P., Geiselman, R. E., & Raymond, D. S. (1987). Critical analysis of police interview techniques. *Journal of Police Science and Administration, 15,* 177–185. (p. 297)

Fitzgerald, R. C. (1970). Reactions to blindness: An exploratory study of adults with recent loss of sight. *Archives of General Psychiatry, 22,* 370–379. (p. 141)

Fleming, I., Baum, A., & Weiss, L. (1987). Social density and perceived control as mediator of crowding stress in high-density residential neighborhoods. *Journal of Personality and Social Psychology, 52,* 899–906. (p. 521)

Fleming, J. H., & Scott, B. A. (1991). The costs of confession: The Persian Gulf War POW tapes in historical an theoretical perspective. *Contemporary Social Psychology, 15,* 127–138. (p. 400)

Fletcher, G. J. O., Fitness, J., & Blampied, N. M. (1990). The link between attributions and happiness in close relationships: The roles of depression and explanatory style. *Journal of Social and Clinical Psychology, 9,* 243–255. (p. 560)

Flynn, J. R. (1987). Massive IQ gains in 14 nations: What IQ tests really measure. *Psychological Bulletin, 101,* 171–191. (p. 344)

Flynn, J. R. (1996). IQ gains over time: Towards finding the causes. Address to conference on "Intelligence on the rise? Secular changes in IQ and related measures," Emory Cognition Project and APA, Emory University, April 12–14. (p. 344)

FMS (1996). *Frequently asked questions about the False Memory Syndrome Foundation* (available at http://www.csicop.org/~fitz/fmsf/faq.html (accessed September 13, 1996). (p. 299)

Foa, E. B., & Kozak, M. J. (1986). Emotional processing of fear: Exposure to corrective information. *Psychological Bulletin, 99,* 20–35. (p. 494)

Folkman, S., Chesney, M., Collette, L., Boccellari, A., & Cooke, M. (1996). Postbereavement depressive mood and its prebereavement predictors in HIV+ and HIV- gay men. *Journal of Personality and Social Psychology, 70,* 336–348. (p. 141)

Foltved, P. (1996). The psychological profession in Denmark. In A. Schorr & S. Saari (Eds.), *Psychology in Europe: Facts, figures, realities.* Gottingen: Hogrefe & Huber. (p. 8)

Fong, G. T., Frantz, D. H., & Nisbett, R. E. (1986). The effects of statistical training on thinking about everyday problems. *Cognitive Psychology, 18,* 253–292. (p. 30)

Fontana, A., Rosenheck, R., & Brett, E. (1992). War zone traumas and posttraumatic stress disorder symptomatology. *Journal of Nervous and Mental Disease, 180,* 748–755. (p. 461)

Foree, D. D., & LoLordo, V. M. (1973). Attention in the pigeon: Differential effects of food-getting versus shock-avoidance procedures. *Journal of Comparative and Physiological Psychology, 85,* 551–558. (p. 561)

Forer, B. R. (1949). The fallacy of personal validation: A classroom demonstration of gullibility. *Journal of Abnormal and Social Psychology, 44,* 118–123. (p. 448)

Foreyt, J. P., Walker, S., Poston, C., II, & Goodrick, G. K. (1996). Future directions in obesity and eating disorders. *Addictive Behaviors, 21,* 767–778. (p. 544)

Forgas, J. P., Bower, G. H., & Krantz, S. E. (1984). The influence of mood on perceptions of social interactions. *Journal of Experimental Social Psychology, 20,* 497–513. (p. 291, 474)

Forgatch, M. S. (1995, March). Reported by W. W. Gibbs, Seeking the criminal element. *Scientific American,* pp. 100–107. (p. 21)

Forge, A., Li, L., Corwin, J. T., & Nevill, G. (1993). Ultrastructural evidence for hair cell regeneration in the mammalian inner ear. *Science, 259,* 1616–1619. (p. 167)

Fortune (1995, March 6). Infomercials 1994: The greatest hits. Page 20. (p. 201)

Fouts, R. S. (1992). Transmission of a human gestural language in a chimpanzee mother-infant relationship. *Friends of Washoe, 12/13,* pp. 2–8. (p. 327)

Fouts, R. S., & Bodamer, M. (1987). Preliminary report to the National Geographic Society on: "Chimpanzee intrapersonal signing." *Friends of Washoe, 7*(1), 4–12. (p. 327)

Fowler, M. J., Sullivan, M. J., & Ekstrand, B. R. (1973). Sleep and memory. *Science, 179,* 302–304. (p. 292)

Fowler, R. C., Rich, C. L., & Young, D. (1986). San Diego suicide study: II. Substance abuse in young cases. *Archives of General Psychiatry, 43,* 962–965. (p. 469)

Fowler, R. D. (1986, May). Howard Hughes: A psychological autopsy. *Psychology Today,* pp. 22–33. (p. 463)

Fowles, D. C. (1992). Schizophrenia: Diathesis-stress revisited. *Annual Review of Psychology, 43,* 303–336. (p. 477)

Fox, J. L. (1984). The brain's dynamic way of keeping in touch. *Science, 225,* 820–821. (p. 61)

Fozard, J. L., & Popkin, S. J. (1978). Optimizing adult development: Ends and means of an applied psychology of aging. *American Psychologist, 33,* 975–989. (p. 130)

Frank, J. D. (1982). Therapeutic components shared by all psychotherapies. In J. H. Harvey & M. M. Parks (Eds.), *The Master Lecture Series: Vol. 1. Psychotherapy research and behavior change.* Washington, DC: American Psychological Association. (pp. 488, 505, 506)

Frank, M. G., & Gilovich, T. (1988). The dark side of self and social perception: Black uniforms and aggression in professional sports. *Journal of Personality and Social Psychology, 54,* 74–85. (p. 27)

Frank, S. J. (1988). Young adults' perceptions of their relationships with their parents: Individual differences in connectedness, competence, and emotional autonomy. *Developmental Psychology, 24,* 729–737. (p. 125)

Frankel, A., & Prentice-Dunn, S. (1990). Loneliness and the processing of self-relevant information. *Journal of Social and Clinical Psychology, 9,* 303–315. (p. 475)

Frankel, A., Strange, D. R., & Schoonover, R. (1983). CRAP: Consumer rated assessment procedure. In G. H. Scherr & R. Liebmann-Smith (Eds.), *The best of The Journal of Irreproducible Results.* New York: Workman Publishing. (p. 433)

Frankenburg, W., Dodds, J., Archer, P., Shapiro, H., & Bresnick, B. (1992). The Denver II: A major revision and restandardization of the Denver Developmental Screening Test. *Pediatrics, 89,* 91–97. (p. 86)

Frasure-Smith, N., Lesperance, F., & Talajic, M. (1995). The impact of negative emotions on prognosis following myocardial infarction: Is it more than depression? *Health Psychology, 14,* 388–398. (p. 523)

Fredrickson, B. L., & Kahneman, D. (1993). Duration neglect in retrospective evaluations of affective episodes. *Journal of Personality and Social Psychology, 65,* 45–55. (p. 277)

Freedman, J. L. (1978). *Happy people.* San Diego: Harcourt Brace Jovanovich. (p. 140)

Freedman, J. L. (1988). Television violence and aggression: What the evidence shows. In S. Oskamp (Ed.), *Television as a social issue.* Newbury Park, CA: Sage. (p. 575)

Freedman, J. L., & Fraser, S. C. (1966). Compliance without pressure: The foot-in-the-door technique. *Journal of Personality and Social Psychology, 4,* 195–202. (p. 553)

Freeman, W. J. (1991, February). The physiology of perception. *Scientific American,* pp. 78–85. (p. 160)

Freud, S. (1931; reprinted 1961). Female sexuality. In J. Strachey (Trans.), *The standard edition of the complete psychological works of Sigmund Freud.* London: Hogarth Press. (pp. 423

Freud, S. (1933). *New introductory lectures on psycho-analysis.* New York: Carlton House. (p. 421)

Freud, S. (1935; reprinted 1960). *A general introduction to psycho-analysis.* New York: Washington Square Press. (p. 137)

Freyd, P. (1996, September 13). Personal correspondence via e-mail. (p. 299)

Friedman, H. S. (1991). *The self-healing personality: Why some people achieve health and others succumb to illness.* New York: Holt. (p. 528)

Friedman, M., & Ulmer, D. (1984). *Treating Type A behavior—and your heart.* New York: Knopf. (pp. 521, 532)

Friedman, M. A., & Brownell, K. D. (1995). Psychological correlates of obesity: Moving to the next research generation. *Psychological Bulletin, 117,* 3–20. (p. 541)

Friedrich, O. (1987, December 7). New age harmonies. *Time,* pp. 62–72. (p. 455)

Frieze, I. H., Parsons, J. E., Johnson, P. B., Ruble, D. N., & Zellman, G. L. (1978). *Women and sex roles: A social psychological perspective.* New York: Norton. (p. 427)

Frijda, N. H. (1988). The laws of emotion. *American Psychologist, 43,* 349–358. (p. 410)

Fritsch, G., & Hitzig, E. (1870; reprinted 1960). On the electrical excitability of the cerebrum. In G. Von Bonin (Trans.), *Some papers on the cerebral cortex.* Springfield, IL: Charles C. Thomas. (p. 60)

Fromkin, V., & Rodman, R. (1983). *An introduction to language* (3rd ed.). New York: Holt, Rinehart & Winston. (pp. 319, 322)

Fry, A. F., & Hale, S. (1996). Processing speed, working memory, and fluid intelligence: Evidence for a developmental cascade. *Psychological Science, 7,* 237–241. (p. 131)

Fryauf-Bertschy, H., & Gantz, B. J. (1994, November/December). Cochlear implants for children: Candidacy and performance results to date. *SHHH Journal,* pp. 20–23. (p. 169)

Fuhriman, A., & Burlingame, G. M. (1994). Group psychotherapy: Research and practice. In A. Fuhriman & G. M. Burlingame (Eds.), *Handbook of group psychotherapy.* New York: Wiley. (p. 499)

Fulker, D. W., DeFries, J. C., & Plomin, R. (1988). Genetic influence on general mental ability increases between infancy and middle childhood. *Nature, 336,* 767–769. (p. 354)

Fuller, M. J., & Downs, A. C. (1990). Spermarche is a salient biological marker in men's development. Poster presented at the American Psychological Society convention. (p. 117)

Funder, D. C. (1987). Errors and mistakes: Evaluating the accuracy of social judgment. *Psychological Bulletin, 101,* 75–90. (p. 316)

Funder, D. C. (1991). Global traits: A neo-Allportian approach to personality. *Psychological Science, 2,* 31–39. (p. 434)

Funder, D. C. (1995). On the accuracy of personality judgment: A realistic approach. *Psychological Review, 102,* 652–670. (p. 434)

Funder, D. C., & Block, J. (1989). The role of ego-control, ego-resiliency, and IQ in delay of gratification in adolescence. *Journal of Personality and Social Psychology, 57,* 1041–1050. (p. 120)

Furlow, F. B., & Thornhill, R. (1996, January/February). The orgasm wars. *Psychology Today,* pp. 42–46. (p. 375)

Furnham, A. (1982). Explanations for unemployment in Britain. *European Journal of Social Psychology, 12,* 335–352. (p. 551)

Furnham, A. (1993). A comparison between psychology and non-psychology students' misperceptions of the subject. *Journal of Social Behavior and Personality, 8,* 311–322. (p. 223)

Furnham, A., & Baguma, P. (1994). Cross-cultural differences in the evaluation of male and female body shapes. *International Journal of Eating Disorders, 15,* 81–89. (p. 540)

Furnham, A., & Rawles, R. (1995). Sex differences in the estimation of intelligence. *Journal of Social Behavior and Personality, 10,* 741–748. (p. 568)

Furnham, A., & Taylor, L. (1990). Lay theories of homosexuality: Aetiology, behaviours, and `cures.' *British Journal of Social Psychology, 29,* 135–147. (p. 382)

Furstenberg, F. F., Jr., Moore, K. A., & Peterson, J. L. (1985). Sex education and sexual experience among adolescents. *American Journal of Public Health, 75,* 1331–1332. (p. 383)

Gabbay, F. H. (1992). Behavior-genetic strategies in the study of emotion. *Psychological Science, 3,* 50–55. (p. 97)

Gabrieli, J. D. E., Desmond, J. E., Demb, J. E., Wagner, A. D., Stone, M. V., Vaidya, C. J., & Glover, G. H. (1996). Functional magnetic resonance imaging of semantic memory processes in the frontal lobes. *Psychological Science, 7,* 278–283. (p. 287)

Gaertner, S. L., Mann, J., Murrell, A., & Dovidio, J. F. (1989). Reducing intergroup bias: The benefits of recategorization. *Journal of Personality and Social Psychology, 57,* 239–249. (p. 587)

Galambos, N. L. (1992). Parent-adolescent relations. *Current Directions in Psychological Science, 1,* 146–149. (p. 124)

Galanter, E. (1962). Contemporary psychophysics. In R. Brown, E. Galanter, E. H. Hess, & G. Mandler (Eds.), *New directions in psychology.* New York: Holt, Rinehart & Winston. (p. 149)

Gallagher, M. (1990). Functional consequences of brain aging: The good news and the bad news. Address to the American Psychological Society convention. (p. 134)

Gallatin, J. (1980). Political thinking in adolescence. In J. Adelson (Ed.), *Handbook of adolescent psychology.* New York: Wiley. (p. 124)

Gallup, G. G., Jr., & Suarez, S. D. (1985). Alternatives to the use of animals in psychological research. *American Psychologist, 40,* 1104–1111. (p. 35)

Gallup, G. G., Jr., & Suarez, S. D. (1986). Self-awareness and the emergence of mind in humans and other primates. In J. Suls & A. G. Greenwald (Eds.), *Psychological perspectives on the self* (Vol. 3.). Hillsdale, NJ: Erlbaum. (p. 103)

Gallup, G. H. (1972). *The Gallup poll: Public opinion 1935–1971* (Vol. 3). New York: Random House. (p. 579)

Gallup, G. H., Jr. (1994, October). Millions finding care and support in small groups. *Emerging Trends,* pp. 2–5. (p. 499)

Gallup, G. H., Jr. (1994, December). A nation in recovery. *PRRC Emerging Trends,* pp. 1–2. (p. 534)

Gallup, G. H., Jr., & Newport, F. (1990, December). Americans now drinking less alcohol. *Gallup Poll Monthly,* pp. 2–6. (p. 201, 225)

Gallup, G. H., Jr., & Newport, F. (1991, Winter). Belief in paranormal phenomena among adult Americans. *Skeptical Inquirer*, pp. 137–146. (p. 201)

Gallup, G. H., Jr., & O'Connell, G. (1986). *Who do Americans say that I am?* Philadelphia, PA: Westminster Press. (p. 239)

Gallup International Institute (1996, February). Parents, grandparents OK with teens. *Youthviews*, p. 3. (p. 124)

Gallup Organization. (1993). Other hemsipheres may think our religion is alien and exotic. *PRRC Emerging Trends, 15,* 1–3. (p. 507)

Gallup Organization. (1996, April). Majority disapprove of homosexual marriages. *Emerging Trends* (Princeton Religion Research Center), p. 2. (p. 382)

Gallup Poll Monthly (1992, October). The first presidential debate: Perot makes best impression; Bush falls short. P. 11. (p. 197)

Gallup Poll Monthly (1993, July). Americans feel threatened by new immigrants. Pp. 2–16. (p. 568)

Gallup Report. (1989, March/April). Commercial aviation. Pp. 32–33. (p. 312)

Garbarino, J., Kostelny, K., & Dubrow, N. (1991). What children can tell us about living in danger. *American Psychologist, 46,* 376-383. (p. 461)

Garcia, J., & Gustavson, A. R. (1997, January). Carl R. Gustavson (1946-1996): Pioneering wildlife psychologist. *APS Observer*, pp. 34–35. (p. 251)

Garcia, J., & Koelling, R. A. (1966). Relation of cue to consequence in avoidance learning. *Psychonomic Science, 4,* 123–124. (p. 250)

Gardner, H. (1983). *Frames of mind: The theory of multiple intelligences.* New York: Basic Books. (p. 338)

Gardner, H. (1993). *Creating minds.* New York: Basic Books. (p. 338)

Gardner, H. (1995). Perennial antinomies and perpetual redrawings: Is there progress in the study of mind? In R. L. Solso & D. W. Massaro (Eds.), *The science of the mind: 2001 and beyond.* New York: Oxford University Press. (p. 337)

Gardner, J. W. (1984). *Excellence: Can we be equal and excellent too?* New York: Norton. (p. 140)

Gardner, R. A., & Gardner, B. I. (1969). Teaching sign language to a chimpanzee. *Science, 165,* 664–672. (p. 26)

Gardner, R. M., & Tockerman, Y. R. (1994). A computer-TV video methodology for investigating the influence of somatotype on perceived personality traits. *Journal of Social Behavior and Personality, 9,* 555–563. (p. 540)

Garfield, C. (1986). *Peak performers: The new heroes of American business.* New York: Morrow. (p. 330)

Garner, D. M., & Wooley, S. C. (1991). Confronting the failure of behavioral and dietary treatments for obesity. *Clinical Psychology Review, 11,* 729–780. (p. 543)

Garnets, L., & Kimmel, D. (1990). Lesbian and gay dimensions in the psychological study of human diversity. Master lecture, American Psychological Association convention. (p. 379)

Garry, M., Loftus, E. F., & Brown, S. W. (1994). Memory: A river runs through it. *Consciousness and Cognition, 3,* 438–451. (p. 427)

Garry, M., Manning, C. G., Loftus, E. F., & Sherman, S. J. (1996). Imagination inflation: Imagining a childhood event inflates confidence that it occurred. *Psychonomic Bulletin & Review, 3,* 208–214. (p. 295)

Gawin, F. H. (1991). Cocaine addiction: Psychology and neurophysiology. *Science, 251,* 1580–1586. (p. 233)

Gazzaniga, M. S. (1967, August). The split brain in man. *Scientific American*, pp. 24–29. (pp. 65, 66)

Gazzaniga, M. S. (1983). Right hemisphere language following brain bisection: A 20–year perspective. *American Psychologist, 38,* 525–537. (p. 66–67)

Gazzaniga, M. S. (1988). *Mind matters: How mind and brain interact to create our conscious lives.* Boston: Houghton Mifflin. (p. 66)

Gazzaniga, M. S. (1988). Organization of the human brain. *Science, 245,* 947–952. (p. 230)

Gazzaniga, M. S. (1992). *Nature's mind: The biological roots of thinking, emotions, sexuality, language, and intelligence.* New York: Basic Books. (pp. 85, 112)

Geary, D. C. (1995). Sexual selection and sex differences in spatial cognition. *Learning and Individual Differences, 7,* 289–301. (p. 358)

Geary, D. C. (1996). Sexual selection and sex differences in mathematical abilities. *Behavioral and Brain Sciences, 19,* 229–247. (p. 358)

Geary, D. C., Salthouse, T. A., Chen, G-P., & Fan, L. (1996). Are East Asian versus American differences in arithmetical ability a recent phenomenon? *Developmental Psychology, 32,* 254–262. (p. 357)

Gebhardt, D. L., & Crump, C. E. (1990). Employee fitness and wellness programs in the workplace. *American Psychologist, 45,* 262–272. (p. 536)

Geen, R. G. (1984). Human motivation: New perspectives on old problems. In A. M. Rogers & C. J. Scheirer (Eds.), *The G. Stanley Hall Lecture Series* (Vol. 4). Washington, DC: American Psychological Association. (p. 384)

Geen, R. G., & Quanty, M. B. (1977). The catharsis of aggression: An evaluation of a hypothesis. In L. Berkowitz (Ed.), *Advances in experimental social psychology* (Vol. 10). New York: Academic Press. (p. 406)

Geen, R. G., & Thomas, S. L. (1986). The immediate effects of media violence on behavior. *Journal of Social Issues, 42*(3), 7–28. (p. 576)

Geldard, F. A. (1972). *The human senses* (2nd ed.). New York: Wiley. (p. 161)

Gelman, D. (1989, May 15). Voyages to the unknown. *Newsweek*, pp. 66–69. (p. 401)

Gelman, R. (1979). Preschool thought. *American Psychologist, 34,* 900–905. (p. 92)

George (1996, December). What does America believe? P. 117. (p. 201)

Gerald, C., Walker, M. W., Criscione, L., & Gustafson, E. L. (1996). A receptor subtype involved in neuropeptide-Y-induced food intake. *Nature, 382,* 168–171. (p. 543)

Geranios, N. K. (1993, September 26). Chimps learn to sign, and in the process, teach humans a little. Associated Press release in Grand Rapids [Mich.] *Press*, p. A18. (p. 326)

Gerard, R. W. (1953, September). What is memory? *Scientific American*, pp. 118–126. (p. 284)

Gerbner, G. (1985). Dreams that hurt: Mental illness in the mass media. Keynote address to the First Rosalynn Carter Symposium on Mental Health Policy, Emory University School of Medicine, Atlanta. (p. 459)

Gerbner, G. (1990). Stories that hurt: Tobacco, alcohol, and other drugs in the mass media. In H. Resnik (Ed.), *Youth and drugs: Society's mixed messages*. Rockville, MD: Office for Substance Abuse Prevention, U.S. Department of Health and Human Services. (p. 237)

Gerbner, G. (1993, June). Women and minorities on television: A study in casting and fate. A report to the Screen Actors Guild and the American Federation of Radio and Television Artists. (p. 575)

Gerbner, G., Morgan, M., & Signorielli, N. (1993). Television violence profile No. 16: The turning point from research to action. Annenberg School for Communication, University of Pennsylvania. (pp. 575, 576, 578)

Gerhart, K. A., Koziol-McLain, J., Lowenstein, S. R., & Whiteneck, G. G. (1994). Quality of life following spinal cord injury: Knowledge and attitudes of emergency care providers. *Annals of Emergency Medicine, 23*, 807–812. (p. 407)

Gerrard, M., & Luus, C. A. E. (1995). Judgments of vulnerability to pregnancy: The role of risk factors and individual differences. *Personality and Social Psychology Bulletin, 21*, 160–171. (p. 126)

Geschwind, N. (1979, September). Specializations of the human brain. *Scientific American*, pp. 180–199. (p. 63–64)

Geschwind, N., & Behan, P. O. (1984). Laterality, hormones, and immunity. In N. Geschwind & A. M. Galaburda (Eds.), *Cerebral dominance: The biological foundations*. Cambridge, MA: Harvard University Press. (pp. 68)

Gfeller, J. D., Lynn, S. J., & Pribble, W. E. (1987). Enhancing hypnotic susceptibility: Interpersonal and rapport factors. *Journal of Personality and Social Psychology, 52*, 586–595. (p. 227)

Giambra, L. M. (1974). Daydreaming across the life span: Late adolescent to senior citizen. *Aging and Human Development, 5*, 115–140. (p. 209)

Gibbons, A. (1992). Chimps: More diverse than a barrel of monkeys. *Science, 255*, 287–288. (p. 308)

Gibbons, F. X. (1986). Social comparison and depression: Company's effect on misery. *Journal of Personality and Social Psychology, 51*, 140–148. (p. 411)

Gibbs, W. W. (1996, June). Mind readings. *Scientific American*, pp. 34–36. (p. 61)

Gibson, E. J., & Walk, R. D. (1960, April). The "visual cliff." *Scientific American*, pp. 64–71. (p. 186)

Gibson, H. B. (1979). The 'Royal Nonesuch' of parapsychology. *Bulletin of the British Psychological Society, 32,* 65–67. (p. 202)

Gibson, H. B. (1995, April). Recovered memories. *The Psychologist*, pp. 153–154. (p. 223)

Giles, D. E., Dahl, R. E., & Coble, P. A. (1994). Childbearing, developmental, and familial aspects of sleep. In J. M. Oldham & M. B. Riba (Eds.), *Review of psychiatry* (Vol. 13). Washington, DC: American Psychiatric Press. (p. 212)

Giles, T. R. (1983). Probable superiority of behavioral interventions—II: Empirical status of the equivalence of therapies hypothesis. *Journal of Behavior Therapy and Experimental Psychiatry, 14*, 189–196. (p. 505)

Gillham, J. E., Reivich, K. J., Jaycox, L. H., & Seligman, M. E. P. (1995). Prevention of depressive symptoms in schoolchildren: Two-year follow-up. *Psychological Science, 6*, 343–351. (p. 499)

Gilligan, C. (1982). *In a different voice: Psychological theory and women's development*. Cambridge, MA: Harvard University Press. (pp. 122, 136)

Gilligan, C., Lyons, N. P., & Hanmer, T. J. (Eds.). (1990). *Making connections: The relational worlds of adolescent girls at Emma Willard School*. Cambridge, MA: Harvard University Press. (pp. 122)

Gilling, D., & Brightwell, R. (1982). *The human brain*. New York: Facts on File. (p. 494)

Gilovich, T. (1991). *How we know what isn't so: The fallibility of human reason in everyday life*. New York: Free Press. (p. 22)

Gilovich, T., & Medvec, V. H. (1995). The experience of regret: What, when, and why. *Psychological Review, 102*, 379–395. (p. 140)

Gilovich, T. D. (1996). The spotlight effect: Exaggerated impressions of the self as a social stimulus. Unpublished manuscript, Cornell University. (p. 92)

Gilovich, T., Vallone, R., & Tversky, A. (1985). The hot hand in basketball: On the misperception of random sequences. *Cognitive Psychology, 17*, 295–314. (p. 25)

Giros, B., Jaber, M., Jones, S. R., Wrightman, R. M., & Caron, M. G. (1996). Hyperlocomotion and indifference to cocaine and amphetamine in mice lacking the dopamine transporter. *Nature, 379*, 606–612. (p. 233)

Gist, R., & Welch, Q. B. (1989). Certification change versus actual behavior change in teenage suicide rates, 1955–1979. *Suicide and Life Threatening Behavior, 19*, 277–288. (p. 469)

Gjerde, P. F. (1983). Attentional capacity dysfunction and arousal in schizophrenia. *Psychological Bulletin, 93*, 57–72. (p. 476)

Gladue, B. A. (1990). Hormones and neuroendocrine factors in atypical human sexual behavior. In J. R. Feierman (Ed.), *Pedophilia: Biosocial dimensions*. New York: Springer-Verlag. (p. 382)

Gladue, B. A. (1994). The biopsychology of sexual orientation. *Current Directions in Psychological Science, 3*, 150–154. (pp. 381, 382)

Gladue, B. A., Boechler, M., & McCaul, K. D. (1989). Hormonal response to competition in human males. *Aggressive Behavior, 15*, 409–422. (p. 572)

Glass, D. C., & Singer, J. E. (1972). *Urban stress*. New York: Academic Press. (p. 166)

Gleaves, D. H. (1996). The sociocognitive model of dissociative identity disorder: A reexamination of the evidence. *Psychological Bulletin, 120*, 42–59. (p. 467)

Glenn, N. D. (1975). Psychological well-being in the postparental stage: Some evidence from national surveys. *Journal of Marriage and the Family, 37,* 105–110. (p. 138)

Glick, P., Gottesman, D., & Jolton, J. (1989). The fault is not in the stars: Susceptibility of skeptics and believers in astrology to the Barnum effect. *Personality and Social Psychology Bulletin, 15,* 572–583. (p. 448)

Godden, D. R., & Baddeley, A. D. (1975). Context-dependent memory in two natural environments: On land and underwater. *British Journal of Psychology, 66,* 325–331. (p. 289)

Goff, D. C. (1993). Reply to Dr. Armstrong. *Journal of Nervous and Mental Disease, 181,* 604–605. (p. 467)

Goff, D. C., & Simms, C. A. (1993). Has multiple personality disorder remained consistent over time? *Journal of Nervous and Mental Disease, 181,* 595–600. (p. 467)

Gold, M., & Yanof, D. S. (1985). Mothers, daughters, and girlfriends. *Journal of Personality and Social Psychology, 49,* 654–659. (p. 124)

Gold, P. E. (1987). Sweet memories. *American Scientist, 75,* 151–155. (p. 285)

Gold, P. E. (1992). A proposed neurobiological basis for regulating memory storage for significant events. In E. Winograd & U. Neisser (Eds.), *Affect and accuracy in recall: Studies of "flashbulb" memories.* New York: Cambridge University Press. (p. 285)

Goldberg, J., True, W. R., Eisen, S. A., & Henderson, W. G. (1990). A twin study of the effects of the Vietnam War on posttraumatic stress disorder. *Journal of the American Medical Association, 263,* 1227–1232. (p. 461)

Goldberg, L. R. (1993). The structure of phenotypic personality traits. *American Psychologist, 48,* 26–34. (p. 432)

Goldfried, M. R., & Padawer, W. (1982). Current status and future directions in psychotherapy. In M. R. Goldfried (Ed.), *Converging themes in psychotherapy: Trends in psychodynamic, humanistic, and behavioral practice.* New York: Springer. (p. 505)

Golding, J. M. (1996). Sexual assault history and women's reproductive and sexual health. *Psychology of Women Quarterly, 20,* 101–121. (p. 577)

Goldman, D. (1996). Why mice drink. *Nature Genetics, 13,* 137–138. (p. 237)

Goldstein, A. P., & Glick, B. (in press). Aggression replacement training: Curriculum and evaluation. *Simulation and Gaming.* (p. 574)

Goleman, D. (1980, February). 1,528 little geniuses and how they grew. *Psychology Today,* pp. 28–53. (pp. 350, 384)

Goleman, D. (1995). *Emotional intelligence.* New York: Bantam. (pp. 340, 398)

Golombok, S., & Tasker, F. (1996). Do parents influence the sexual orientation of their children? Findings from a longitudinal study of lesbian families. *Developmental Psychology, 32,* 3–11. (p. 380)

Golub, S. (1983). *Menarche: The transition from girl to woman.* Lexington, MA: Lexington Books. (p. 117)

Gonsiorek, J. C. (1982). Summary and conclusions. In W. Paul, J. D. Weinrich, J. C. Gonsiorek, & M. E. Hotvedt (Eds.), *Homosexuality: Social, psychological, and biological issues.* Beverly Hills, CA: Sage. (p. 380)

Goodall, J. (1968). The behaviour of free-living chimpanzees in the Gombe Stream Reserve. *Animal Behaviour Monographs, 1,* 161–311. (p. 111)

Goodall, J. (1986). *The chimpanzees of Gombe: Patterns of behavior.* Cambridge, MA: Harvard University Press. (p. 569)

Goodchilds, J. (1987). Quoted by Carol Tavris, Old age is not what it used to be. *The New York Times Magazine: Good Health Magazine,* September 27, pp. 24–25, 91–92. (p. 128)

Goodhart, D. E. (1986). The effects of positive and negative thinking on performance in an achievement situation. *Journal of Personality and Social Psychology, 51,* 117–124. (p. 447)

Goodman, G. S., Rudy, L., Bottoms, B. L., & Aman, C. (1990). Children's concerns and memory: Issues of ecological validity in the study of children's eyewitness testimony. In R. Fivush & J. A. Hudson (Eds.), *Knowing and remembering in young children.* New York: Cambridge University Press. (p. 298)

Goodman, L. A., Koss, M. P., & Russo, N. F. (1993). Violence against women: Mental health effects. Part II. Conceptualizations of posttraumatic stress. Applied & Preventive Psychology, 2, 123–130. (p. 461)

Goodwin, C. J. (1991). Misportraying Pavlov's apparatus. *American Journal of Psychology, 104,* 135–141. (p. 247)

Gopnik, A., & Meltzoff, A. N. (1986). Relations between semantic and cognitive development in the one-word stage: The specificity hypothesis. *Child Development, 57,* 1040–1053. (p. 329)

Goranson, R. E. (1978). *The hindsight effect in problem solving.* Unpublished manuscript, cited by G. Wood (1984), Research methodology: A decision-making perspective. In A. M. Rogers & C. J. Scheirer (Eds.), *The G. Stanley Hall Lecture Series* (vol. 4). Washington, DC: American Psychological Association. (p. 15)

Gore, A., Jr. (1992). *Earth in the balance: Ecology and the human spirit.* Boston: Houghton-Mifflin. (pp. 263, 313)

Gore, T., interviewed by C. Greer (1994, September 11). I know there is help. *Parade,* 4–7. (p. 501)

Gorsuch, R. L. (1988). Psychology of religion. *Annual Review of Psychology, 39,* 201–222. (p. 387)

Gortmaker, S. L., Must, A., Perrin, J. M., Sobol, A. M., & Dietz, W. H. (1993). Social and economic consequences of overweight in adolescence and young adulthood. *New England Journal of Medicine, 329,* 1008–1012. (p. 540)

Gotlib, I. H. (1992). Interpersonal and cognitive aspects of depression. *Current Directions in Psychological Science, 1,* 149–154. (p. 441)

Gotlib, I. H., & Hammen, C. L. (1992). *Psychological aspects of depression: Toward a cognitive-interpersonal integration.* New York: Wiley. (p. 474)

Gottesman, I. I. (1991). *Schizophrenia genesis: The origins of madness.* New York: Freeman. (p. 479)

Gottesman, I. I. (1993). The origins of schizophrenia: Past as prologue. In R. Plomin & G. E. McClearn (Eds.), *Nature, nurture, and psychology.* Washington, DC: American Psychological Association. (p. 479)

Gottman, J. (with N. Silver) (1994). *Why marriages succeed or fail.* New York: Simon & Schuster. (p. 138)

Gould, M. S., & Shaffer, D. (1986). The impact of suicide in television movies: Evidence of imitation. *New England Journal of Medicine, 315,* 690–694. (p. 555)

Gould, S. J. (1981). *The mismeasure of man.* New York: Norton. (pp. 335–336)

Grady, C. L., and others (1995). Age-related reductions in human recognition memory due to impaired encoding. *Science, 269,* 218–221. (p. 279)

Graf, P. (1990). Life-span changes in implicit and explicit memory. *Bulletin of the Psychonomic Society, 28,* 353–358. (p. 133)

Graham, J. W., Marks, G., & Hansen, W. B. (1991). Social influence processes affecting adolescent substance use. *Journal of Applied Psychology, 76,* 291–298. (p. 237)

Gray-Little, B., & Burks, N. (1983). Power and satisfaction in marriage: A review and critique. *Psychological Bulletin, 93,* 513–538. (p. 585)

Greeley, A. M. (1991). *Faithful attraction.* New York: Tor Books. (pp. 20, 138, 324)

Greeley, A. M. (1994, May/June). Marital infidelity. *Society,* pp. 9–13. (p. 20)

Greenberg, J., Solomon, S., & Pyszczynski, T. (1997). Terror management theory of self-esteem and cultural worldviews: Empirical assessments and conceptual refinements. *Advances in social psychology,* in press. (p. 428)

Greenberg, R. P., Bornstein, R. F., Greenberg, M. D., & Fisher, S. (1992). A meta-analysis of antidepressant outcome under "blinder" conditions. *Journal of Consulting and Clinical Psychology, 60,* 664–669. (p. 510)

Greenberg, R. P., Bornstein, R. F., Zborowski, M. J., Fisher, S., & Greenberg, M. D. (1994). A meta-analysis of fluoxetine outcome in the treatment of depression. *Journal of Nervous and Mental Disease, 182,* 547–551. (p. 510)

Greene, R. L. (1987). Effects of maintenance rehearsal on human memory. *Psychological Bulletin, 102,* 403–413. (p. 225)

Greenough, W. T., Black, J. E., & Wallace, C. S. (1987). Experience and brain development. *Child Development, 58,* 539–559. (p. 84)

Greenwald, A. G. (1992). New look 3: Unconscious cognition reclaimed. *American Psychologist, 47,* 766–779. (p. 428)

Greenwald, A. G. (1992). Subliminal semantic activation and subliminal snake oil. Paper presented to the American Psychological Association Convention, Washington, DC. (p. 30)

Greenwald, A. G., & Banaji, M. R. (1995). Implicit social cognition: Attitudes, self-esteem, and stereotypes. *Psychological Review, 102,* 4–27. (p. 208)

Greenwald, A. G., Draine, S. C., & Abrams, R. L. (1996). Three cognitive markers of unconscious semantic activation. *Science, 273,* 1699–1702. (p. 150).

Greenwald, A. G., Spangenberg, E. R., Pratkanis, A. R., & Eskenazi, J. (1991). Double-blind tests of subliminal self-help audiotapes. *Psychological Science, 2,* 119–122. (p. 29)

Greenwood, M. R. C. (1989). Sexual dimorphism and obesity. In A. J. Stunkard & A. Baum (Eds.). *Perspectives in behavioral medicine: Eating, sleeping, and sex.* Hillsdale, NJ: Erlbaum. (p. 540)

Greer, G. (1984, April). The uses of chastity and other paths to sexual pleasures. *MS,* pp. 53–60, 96. (p. 377)

Gregory, R. L. (1978). *Eye and brain: The psychology of seeing* (3rd ed.). New York: McGraw-Hill. (p. 195)

Gregory, R. L., & Gombrich, E. H. (Eds.). (1973). *Illusion in nature and art.* New York: Charles Scribner's Sons. (p. 200)

Gregory, W. L., Cialdini, R. B., & Carpenter, K. M. (1982). Self-relevant scenarios as mediators of likelihood estimates and compliance: Does imagining make it so? *Journal of Personality and Social Psychology, 43,* 89–99. (p. 313)

Greif, E. B., & Ulman, K. J. (1982). The psychological impact of menarche on early adolescent females: A review of the literature. *Child Development, 53,* 1413–1430. (p. 117)

Grenier, G., & Byers, E. S. (1995). Rapid ejaculation: A review of conceptual, etiological, and treatment issues. *Archives of Sexual Behavior, 24,* 447–472. (p. 378)

Griffin, D. R. (1984). Animal thinking. *American Scientist, 72,* 456–464. (p. 317)

Grilo, C. M., & Pogue-Geile, M. F. (1991). The nature of environmental influences on weight and obesity: A behavior genetic analysis. *Psychological Bulletin, 110,* 520–537. (p. 542)

Grobstein, C. (1979, June). External human fertilization. *Scientific American,* pp. 57–67. (p. 79)

Grolnick, W. S., & Ryan, R. M. (1987). Autonomy in children's learning: An experimental and individual difference investigation. *Journal of Personality and Social Psychology, 52,* 890–898. (p. 261)

Grosof, D. H., Shapley, R. M., & Hawken, M. J. (1993). Macaque V1 neurons can signal 'illusory' contours. *Nature, 365,* 550–552. (p. 185)

Gross, A. E., & Crofton, C. (1977). What is good is beautiful. *Sociometry, 40,* 85–90. (p. 582)

Grossberg, S. (1995). The attentive brain. *American Scientist, 83,* 438–449. (p. 198)

Grossman, M., & Wood, W. (1993). Sex differences in intensity of emotional experience: A social role interpretation. *Journal of Personality and Social Psychology, 65,* 1010–1022. (p. 124)

Gruder, C. L. (1977). Choice of comparison persons in evaluating oneself. In J. M. Suls & R. L. Miller (Eds.), *Social comparison processes.* New York: Hemisphere. (p. 411)

Guerin, B. (1986). Mere presence effects in humans: A review. *Journal of Personality and Social Psychology, 22,* 38–77. (p. 561)

Guion, R. M. (1992). Science, pseudoscience, and silly science in applied psychology. Paper presented to the American Psychological Association convention. (p. 23)

Gulevich, G., Dement, W., & Johnson, L. (1966). Psychiatric and EEG observations on a case of prolonged (264 hours) wakefulness. *Archives of General Psychiatry, 15,* 29–35. (p. 215)

Gura, T. (1997). Obesity sheds its secrets. *Science, 275,* 751–753. (p. 544)

Gustavson, C. R., Garcia, J., Hankins, W. G., & Rusiniak, K. W. (1974). Coyote predation control by aversive conditioning. *Science, 184,* 581–583. (p. 251)

Gustavson, C. R., Kelly, D. J., & Sweeney, M. (1976). Prey-lithium aversions I: Coyotes and wolves. *Behavioral Biology, 17,* 61–72. (p. 251)

Guterl, F. (1996, June). Silicon gambit. *Discover,* pp. 48–56. (p. 317)

Guttmacher Institute (1993). *Facts in brief.* New York: Alan Guttmacher Institute. (p. 126)

Guttmacher Institute (1994). *Sex and America's teenagers.* New York: Alan Guttmacher Institute. (pp. 116, 126)

H., Sally (1979, August). Videotape recording number T-3, Fortunoff Video Archive of Holocaust Testimonies. New Haven, CT: Yale University Library. (p. 428)

Haber, R. N. (1970, May). How we remember what we see. *Scientific American,* pp. 104–112. (p. 270)

Hackel, L. S., & Ruble, D. N. (1992). Changes in the marital relationship after the first baby is born: Predicting the impact of expectancy disconfirmation. *Journal of Personality and Social Psychology, 62,* 944–957. (p. 138)

Hafner, H., & Schmidtke, A. (1989). Do televised fictional suicide models produce suicides? In D. R. Pfeffer (Ed.), *Suicide among youth: Perspectives on risk and prevention.* Washington, DC: American Psychiatric Press. (p. 555)

Haier, R. J. (1993). Cerebral glucose metabolism and intelligence. In P. A. Vernon (Ed.), *Biologic approaches to the study of human intelligence.* Norwood, NJ: Ablex. (p. 341)

Halaas, J. L., & others (1995). Weight-reducing effects of the plasma protein encoded by the *obese* gene. *Science, 269,* 543–546. (p. 542)

Halberstadt, J. B., Niedenthal, P. M., & Kushner, J. (1995). Resolution of lexical ambiguity by emotional state. *Psychological Science, 6,* 278–281. (p. 200)

Haldeman, D. C. (1994). The practice and ethics of sexual orientation conversion therapy. *Journal of Consulting and Clinical Psychology, 62,* 221–227. (p. 380)

Hall, C. S. (1984). "A ubiquitous sex difference in dreams" revisited. *Journal of Personality and Social Psychology, 46,* 1109–1117. (p. 218)

Hall, C. S., & Lindzey, G. (1978). *Theories of personality* (2nd ed.). New York: Wiley. (p. 429)

Hall, C. S., & Van de Castle, R. L. (1966). *The content analysis of dreams.* New York: Appleton-Century-Crofts. (p. 218)

Hall, C. S., Dornhoff, W., Blick, K. A., & Weesner, K. E. (1982). The dreams of college men and women in 1950 and 1980: A comparison of dream contents and sex differences. *Sleep, 5,* 188–194. (p. 218)

Hall, G. S. (1904). *Adolescence: Its psychology and its relations to physiology, anthropology, sex, crime, religion and education* (Vol. I). New York: Appleton-Century-Crofts. (p. 116)

Hall, J. A. (1987). On explaining gender differences: The case of nonverbal communication. In P. Shaver & C. Hendrick (Eds.), *Review of Personality and Social Psychology, 7,* 177–200. (pp. 670–671)

Hall, J. A. Y., & Kimura, D. (1994). Dermatoglyphic assymetry and sexual orientation in men. *Behavioral Neuroscience, 108,* 1203–1206. (p. 382)

Hall, N. R., & Goldstein, A. L. (1986, March/April). Thinking well: The chemical links between emotions and health. *The Sciences,* pp. 34–40. (p. 525)

Hall, T. (1987, September 27). Cravings: Does your body know what it needs? *The New York Times Magazine: Good Health Magazine,* pp. 23, 62–65. (p. 369)

Hallinan, J. T. (1997, January 14). State moves to end payments in repressed memory cases. Newhouse News Service relase (*Grand Rapids [Mich.] Press*). (p. 299)

Halpern, D. F. (1991). Cognitive sex differences: Why diversity is a critical research issue. Paper presented to the American Psychological Association convention. (p. 358)

Halpern, D. F., & Coren, S. (1988). Do right-handers live longer? *Nature, 333,* 213. (p. 526)

Halpern, D. F., & Coren, S. (1990). Laterality and longevity: Is left-handedness associated with a younger age at death? In S. Coren (Ed.), *Left-handedness: Behavioral implications and anomalies.* Amsterdam: North-Holland. (p. 68)

Halpern, D. F., & Coren, S. (1991). Lateral preference and life span. *New England Journal of Medicine, 324,* 998. (p. 526)

Halpern, D.F., & Coren, S. (1993). Left-handedness and life span: A reply to Harris. *Psychological Bulletin, 114,* 235–241. (p. 526)

Halpern, D. F., Gilbert, R., & Coren, S. (1996). PC or not-PC? Contemporary challenges to unpopular research. *Journal of Social Distress and the Homeless, 5,* 251–271. (p. 527)

Hamers, J. F., & Blanc, M. H. (1989). *Bilinguality and bilingualism.* Cambridge: Cambridge University Press. (p. 329)

Hamid, A. (1992). The developmental cycle of a drug epidemic: The cocaine smoking epidemic of 1981–1991. *Journal of Psychoactive Drugs, 24,* 337–348. (p. 233)

Hamill, R., Wilson, T. D., & Nisbett, R. E. (1980). Insensitivity to sample bias: Generalizing from atypical cases. *Journal of Personality and Social Psychology, 39,* 578–589. (p. 313)

Hamilton, M. C. (1988). Using masculine generics: Does generic "he" increase male bias in the user's imagery? *Sex Roles, 19,* 785–799. (p. 329)

Hamilton, V. L., Hoffman, W. S., Broman, C. L., & Rauma, D. (1993). Unemployment, distress, and coping: A panel study of autoworkers. *Journal of Personality and Social Psychology, 65,* 234–247. (p. 473)

Hammersmith, S. K. (1982, August). *Sexual preference: An empirical study from the Alfred C. Kinsey Institute for Sex Research.* Paper presented at the meeting of the American Psychological Association, Washington, DC. (p. 380)

Haney, C., & Logan, D. D. (1994). Broken promise: The Supreme Court's response to social science research on capital punishment. *Journal of Social Issues, 50,* 75–101. (p. 38)

Haney, D. Q. (1996, October 16). Fat now outnumber the skinny. Associated Press release (*Anchorage Daily News*). (p. 539)

Hansen, C. H., & Hansen, R. D. (1988). Finding the face-in-the-crowd: An anger superiority effect. *Journal of Personality and Social Psychology, 54,* 917–924. (p. 398)

Hardin, C., & Banaji, M. R. (1993). The influence of language on thought. *Social Cognition, 11,* 277–308. (p. 329)

Hare, R. D. (1975). Psychophysiological studies of psychopathy. In D. C. Fowles (Ed.), *Clinical applications of psychophysiology.* New York: Columbia University Press. (p. 482)

Harkins, S. G., & Szymanski, K. (1989). Social loafing and group evaluation. *Journal of Personality and Social Psychology, 56,* 934–941. (p. 562)

Harlow, H. F., Harlow, M. K., & Suomi, S. J. (1971). From thought to therapy: Lessons from a primate laboratory. *American Scientist, 59,* 538–549. (p. 95)

Harlow, R. E., & Cantor, N. (in press). Still participating after all these years: A study of life task participation in later life. *Journal of Personality and Social Psychology.* (p. 141)

Harrington, D. M., Block, J. H., & Block, J. (1987). Testing aspects of Carl Rogers's theory of creative environments: Child-rearing antecedents of creative potential in young adolescents. *Journal of Personality and Social Psychology, 52,* 851–856. (p. 437)

Harris, B. (1979). Whatever happened to Little Albert? *American Psychologist, 34,* 151–160. (p. 252)

Harris, J. R. (1995). Where is the child's environment: A group socialization theory of development. *Psychological Review, 102,* 458–489. (pp. 111, 125)

Harris, J. R. (1996). Quoted from an article by Jerome Burne for the *Manchester Observer* (via Harris: 72073.1211@CompuServe.com). (p. 111)

Harris, L. (1987). *Inside America.* New York: Random House. (p. 520)

Harris, L. J. (1993). Do left-handers die sooner than right-handers? Commentary on Coren and Halpern's (1991) "Left-handedness: A marker for decreased survival fitness." *Psychological Bulletin, 114,* 203–234. (p. 527)

Harris, R. J. (1994). The impact of sexually explicit media. In J. Brant & D. Zillmann (Eds.), *Media effects: Advances in theory and research.* Hillsdale, NJ: Erlbaum. (p. 577)

Harriston, K. A. (1993, December 24). 1 shakes, 1 snoozes; both win $45 million. *Washington Post* release in *Tacoma News Tribune,* p. A1, A2. (p. 450)

Hart, D. (1988). The development of personal identity in adolescence: A philosophical dilemma approach. *Merrill-Palmer Quarterly, 34,* 105–114. (p. 122)

Hartmann, E. (1981, April). The strangest sleep disorder. *Psychology Today,* pp. 14, 16, 18. (p. 217)

Hartmann, E. (1984). *The nightmare: The psychology and biology of terrifying dreams.* New York: Basic Books. (p. 217)

Hartshorne, H., & May, M. A. (1928). *Studies in deceit.* New York: Macmillan. (p. 435)

Hartup, W. W. (1989). Social relationships and their developmental significance. *American Psychologist, 44,* 120–126. (p. 99)

Harvey, S. M. (1987). Female sexual behavior: Fluctuations during the menstrual cycle. *Journal of Psychosomatic Research, 31,* 101–110. (p. 376)

Hasher, L., & Zacks, R. T. (1979). Automatic and effortful processes in memory. *Journal of Experimental Psychology: General, 108,* 356–388. (p. 273)

Hasher, L., & Zacks, R. T. (1984). Automatic processing of fundamental information: The case of frequency of occurrence. *American Psychologist, 39,* 1372–1388. (p. 273)

Haskins, R. (1989). Beyond metaphor: The efficacy of early childhood education. *American Psychologist, 44,* 274–282. (p. 355)

Hassan, R., & Carr, J. (1989). Changing patterns of suicide in Australia. *Australian and New Zealand Journal of Psychiatry, 23*m 226-234. (p. 469)

Hatfield, E. (1988). Passionate and companionate love. In R. J. Sternberg & M. L. Barnes (Eds.), *The psychology of love.* New Haven: Yale University Press. (p. 583)

Hatfield, E., & Sprecher, S. (1986). *Mirror, mirror . . . The importance of looks in everyday life.* Albany: State University of New York Press. (p. 581)

Hathaway, S. R. (1960). *An MMPI Handbook* (Vol. 1, Foreword). Minneapolis: University of Minnesota Press. (Revised edition, 1972). (p. 433)

Hauser, M. D. (1993). Right hemisphere dominance for the production of facial expression in monkeys. *Science, 261,* 475–477. (p. 66)

Hayes, J. R. (1981). *The complete problem solver.* Philadelphia: Franklin Institute Press. (p. 289)

Hazan, C., & Shaver, P. R. (1994). Attachment as an organizational framework for research on close relationships. *Psychological Inquiry, 5,* 1–22. (p. 100)

Hazelrigg, M. D., Cooper, H. M., & Borduin, C. M. (1987). Evaluating the effectiveness of family therapies: An integrative review and analysis. *Psychological Bulletin, 101,* 428–442. (p. 500)

Hearold, S. (1986). A synthesis of 1043 effects of television on social behavior. In G. Comstock (Ed.), *Public communication and behavior.* New York: Academic Press. (p. 575)

Heath, A. C., Jardine, R., & Martin, N. G. (1989). Interactive effects of genotype and social environment on alcohol consumption in female twins. *Journal of Studies on Alcohol, 50,* 38–48. (p. 237)

Heath, L., & Petraitis, J. (1987). Television viewing and fear of crime: Where is the mean world? *Basic and Applied Social Psychology, 8,* 97–123. (p. 576)

Heatherton, T. F., & Baumeister, R. F. (1991). Binge eating as escape from self-awareness. *Psychological Bulletin, 110,* 86–108. (p. 372)

Hebb, D. O. (1980). *Essay on mind.* Hillsdale, NJ: Erlbaum. 9–16. (pp. 246, 393)

Hedges, L. V., & Nowell, A. (1995). Sex differences in mental test scores, variability, and numbers of high-scoring individuals. *Science, 269,* 41–45. (pp. 357, 358)

Heider, F. (1958). *The psychology of interpersonal relations.* New York: Wiley. (p. 549)

Heiman, J. R. (1975, April). The physiology of erotica: Women's sexual arousal. *Psychology Today,* 90–94. (p. 377)

Heller, W. (1990, May/June). Of one mind: Second thoughts about the brain's dual nature. *The Sciences,* pp. 38–44. (p. 69)

Hellige, J. B. (1993). Unity of thought and action: Varieties of interaction between the left and right cerebral hemispheres. *Current Directions in Psychological Science, 2,* 21–25. (p. 70)

Helmreich, W. B. (1992). *Against all odds: Holocaust survivors and the successful lives they made in America.* New York: Simon & Schuster. (p. 428, 461)

Helmreich, W. B. (1994). Personal correspondence. Department of Sociology, City University of New York. (p. 428)

Hembree, R. (1988). Correlates, causes, effects, and treatment of test anxiety. *Review of Educational Research, 58,* 47–77. (p. 394)

Henley, N. M. (1989). Molehill or mountain? What we know and don't know about sex bias in language. In M. Crawford & M. Gentry (Eds.), *Gender and thought: Psychological perspectives.* New York: Springer-Verlag. (p. 329)

Henninger, P. (1992). Conditional handedness: Handedness changes in multiple personality disordered subject reflect shift in hemispheric dominance. *Consciousness and Cognition, 1,* 265–287. (p. 467)

Henry, J. P., & Stephens, P. M. (1977). *Stress, health, and the social environment.* New York: Springer-Verlag. (p. 520)

Hepper, P. G., Shahidullah, S., & White, R. (1990). Origins of fetal handedness. *Nature, 347,* 431. (p. 68)

Herbert, T. B., & Cohen, S. (1993). Depression and immunity: A meta-analytic review. *Psychological Bulletin, 113,* 472–486. (p. 524)

Herek, G. M. (1989). Hate crimes against lesbians and gay men: Issues for research and policy. *American Psychologist, 44,* 948–955. (p. 568)

Herek, G. M. (1990). The context of anti-gay violence: Notes on cultural and psychological heterosexism. *Journal of Interpersonal Violence, 5,* 316–333. (p. 568)

Herek, G. M., & Capitanio, J. P. (1996). "Some of my best friends": Intergroup contact, concealable stigma, and heterosexuals' attitudes toward gay men and lesbians. *Personality and Social Psychology Bulletin, 22,* 412–424. (p. 382)

Herman, C. P., & Polivy, J. (1980). Restrained eating. In A. J. Stunkard (Ed.), *Obesity.* Philadelphia: Saunders. (p. 545)

Heron, W. (1957, January). The pathology of boredom. *Scientific American,* pp. 52–56. (p. 178)

Herrmann, D. (1982). Know thy memory: The use of questionnaires to assess and study memory. *Psychological Bulletin, 92,* 434–452. (p. 302)

Herrnstein, R. J., & Loveland, D. H. (1964). Complex visual concept in the pigeon. *Science, 146,* 549–551. (p. 255)

Hershenson, M. (1989). *The moon illusion.* Hillsdale, NJ: Erlbaum. (p. 191)

Hertel, P. T. (1994). Depression and memory: Are impairments remediable through attentional control? *Current Directions in Psychological Science, 3,* 190–193. (p. 291)

Hess, D. J. (1993). *Science in the new age: The paranormal, its defenders and debunkers, and American culture.* Madison: University of Wisconsin Press. (p. 203)

Hess, E. H. (1956, July). Space perception in the chick. *Scientific American,* pp. 71–80. (p. 196)

Hetherington, E. M. (1979). Divorce: A child's perspective. *American Psychologist, 34,* 851–858. (p. 105)

Hetherington, E. M., Reiss, D., & Plomin, R. (1993). *The separate social worlds of siblings: The impact of nonshared environment on development.* Hillsdale, NJ: Erlbaum. (p. 110)

Hetherington, E. M., Stanley-Hagan, M., & Anderson, E. R. (1989). Marital transitions: A child's perspective. *American Psychologist, 44,* 303–312. (p. 102)

Hewlett, B. S. (1991). *Intimate fathers.* Ann Arbor, MI: University of Michigan Press (cited by D. Popenoe, The fatherhood problem. Institute for American Values Working Paper No. 40, October, 1993). (p. 99)

Hicks, R. A., & Pellegrini, R. J. (1982). Sleep problems and Type A-B behavior in college students. *Psychological Reports, 51,* 196. (p. 522)

Hicks, R. A., Kilcourse, J., & Sinnott, M. A. (1983). Type A-B behavior and caffeine use in college students. *Psychological Reports, 52,* 338. (p. 522)

Higgins, E. T. (1987). Self-discrepancy: A theory relating self and affect. *Psychological Review, 94,* 319–340. (p. 439)

Higgins, E. T., & Bargh, J. A. (1987). Social cognition and social perception. *Annual Review of Psychology, 38,* 369–425. (p. 438)

Hilgard, E. R. (1986). *Divided consciousness: Multiple controls in human thought and action.* New York: Wiley. (p. 227)

Hilgard, E. R. (1992). Dissociation and theories of hypnosis. In E. Fromm & M. R. Nash (Eds.), *Contemporary hypnosis research.* New York: Guilford. (p. 227)

Hines, M., & Green, R. (1991). Human hormonal and neural correlates of sex-typed behaviors. *Review of Psychiatry, 10,* 536–555. (p. 79)

Hinz, L. D., & Williamson, D. A. (1987). Bulimia and depression: A review of the affective variant hypothesis. *Psychological Bulletin, 102,* 150–158. (p. 372)

Hirst, W., Neisser, U., & Spelke, E. (1978, June). Divided attention. *Human Nature,* pp. 54–61. (p. 227)

Hirt, E. R., Zillmann, D., Erickson, G. A., & Kennedy, C. (1992). Costs and benefits of allegiance: Changes in fans' self-ascribed competencies after team victory versus defeat. *Journal of Personality and Social Psychology, 63,* 724–738. (p. 473)

Hobfoll, S. E. (1989). Conservation of resources: A new attempt at conceptualizing stress. *American Psychologist, 44,* 513–524. (p. 517)

Hobfoll, S. E., Lomranz, J., Eyal, N., Bridges, A., & Tzemach, M. (1989). Pulse of a nation: Depressive mood reactions of Israelis to the Israel-Lebanon war. *Journal of Personality and Social Psychology, 56,* 1002–1012. (p. 470)

Hobson, J. A. (1988). *The dreaming brain.* New York: Basic Books. (p. 219)

Hobson, J. A. (1989). *Sleep.* New York: Scientific American Library. (p. 214)

Hobson, J. A. (1995, September). Quoted by C. H. Colt, The power of dreams. *Life,* pp. 36–49. (p. 220)

Hodgkinson, V. A., & Weitzman, M. S. (1992). *Giving and volunteering in the United States.* Washington, DC: Independent Sector. (p. 587)

Hoebel, B. G., & Teitelbaum, P. (1966). Effects of forcefeeding and starvation on food intake and body weight in a rat with ventromedial hypothalamic lesions. *Journal of Comparative and Physiological Psychology, 61,* 189–193. (p. 369)

Hoffman, C., & Hurst, N. (1990). Gender stereotypes: Perception or rationalization? *Journal of Personality and Social Psychology, 58,* 197–208. (p. 569)

Hoffman, L. W. (1989). Effects of maternal employment in the two-parent family. *American Psychologist, 44,* 283–292. (p. 100)

Hoffman, L. W. (1991). The influence of the family environment on personality: Accounting for sibling differences. *Psychological Bulletin, 110,* 187–203. (p. 110)

Hoffman, P. (1994, November). The science of race. *Discover,* p. 4. (p. 567)

Hofstede, G. (1980). *Culture's consequences: International differences in work-related values.* Beverly Hills: Sage. (pp. 388, 441)

Hogan, J. (1989). Personality correlates of physical fitness. *Journal of Personality and Social Psychology, 56,* 284–288. (p. 529)

Hogan, J. (1995, November). Get smart, take a test. *Scientific American,* pp. 12, 14. (p. 345)

Hogan, R., Hogan, J., & Roberts, B. W. (1996). Personality measurement and employment decisions. *American Psychologist, 51,* 469–477. (p. 435)

Hohmann, G. W. (1966). Some effects of spinal cord lesions on experienced emotional feelings. *Psychophysiology, 3,* 143–156. (p. 414)

Hokanson, J. E., & Edelman, R. (1966). Effects of three social responses on vascular processes. *Journal of Personality and Social Psychology, 3,* 442–447. (p. 406)

Holden, C. (1980a). Identical twins reared apart. *Science, 207,* 1323–1325. (p. 109)

Holden, C. (1980b, November). Twins reunited. *Science, 80,* 55–59. (p. 109)

Holden, C. (1986a). Days may be numbered for polygraphs in the private sector. *Science, 232,* 705. (p. 396)

Holden, C. (1986b). Researchers grapple with problems of updating classic psychological test. *Science, 233,* 1249–1251. (p. 443)

Holden, C. (1991). Alcoholism gene: Coming or going? *Science, 254,* 200. (p. 237)

Holden, C. (1991). New center to study therapies and ethnicity. *Science, 251,* 748. (p. 509)

Holden, C. (1993). Wake-up call for sleep research. *Science, 259,* 305. (p. 214)

Holing, D. (1988, October). Dolphin defense. *Discover,* pp. 70–74. (p. 263)

Hollon, S. D., DeRubeis, R. J., & Seligman, M. E. P. (1992). Cognitive therapy and the prevention of depression. *Applied & Preventive Psychology, 1,* 89–95. (p. 499)

Holmes, D. (1990). The evidence for repression: An examination of sixty years of research. In J. Singer (Ed.), *Repression and dissociation: Implications for personality theory, psychopathology, and health.* Chicago: University of Chicago Press. (p. 428)

Holmes, D. S. (1978). Projection as a defense mechanism. *Psychological Bulletin, 85,* 677–688. (p. 427)

Holmes, D. S. (1981). Existence of classical projection and the stress-reducing function of attributive projection: A reply to Sherwood. *Psychological Bulletin, 90,* 460–466. (p. 427)

Holmes, D. S. (1994). Is there evidence for repression? No. (Unexpurgated version of an article which was rewritten by the *Harvard Mental Health Letter* and published as "Is there evidence for repression? Doubtful," June 1994, pp. 4–6.) (p. 428)

Holtgraves, T., & Skeel, J. (1992). Cognitive biases in playing the lottery: Estimating the odds and choosing the numbers. *Journal of Applied Social Psychology, 22,* 934–952. (p. 23)

Holzman, P. S., & Matthysse, S. (1990). The genetics of schizophrenia: A review. *Psychological Science, 1,* 279–286. (p. 152)

Hooper, J., & Teresi, D. (1986). *The three-pound universe.* New York: Macmillan. (p. 58)

Hooykaas, R. (1972). *Religion and the rise of modern science.* Grand Rapids, MI: Eerdmans. (p. 13)

Horgan, J. (1995, December). A sign is born. *Scientific American,* pp. 18–19. (p. 323)

Horgan, J. (1996, December). Why Freud isn't dead. *Scientific American,* pp. 106–111. (p. 509)

Horn, J. L. (1982). The aging of human abilities. In J. Wolman (Ed.), *Handbook of developmental psychology.* Englewood Cliffs, NJ: Prentice-Hall. (p. 135)

Horne, J. A. (1989). Sleep loss and "divergent" thinking ability. *Sleep, 11,* 528–536. (p. 214)

House, J. S., Landis, K. R., & Umberson, D. (1988). Social relationships and health. *Science, 241,* 540–545. (p. 533)

House, R. J., & Singh, J. V. (1987). Organizational behavior: Some new directions for I/O psychology. *Annual Review of Psychology, 38,* 669–718. (p. 389)

Houts, A. C., Berman, J. S., & Abramson, H. (1994). Effectiveness of psychological and pharmacological treatments for nocturnal enuresis. *Journal of Consulting and Clinical Psychology, 62,* 737–745. (p. 493)

Howe, M. L., & Courage, M. L. (1993). On resolving the enigma of infantile amnesia. *Psychological Bulletin, 113,* 305–326. (p. 82)

Hoyer, G., & Lund, E. (1993). Suicide among women related to number of children in marriage. *Archives of General Psychiatry, 50,* 134–137. (p. 469)

Hubel, D. H. (1979, September). The brain. *Scientific American,* pp. 45–53. (p. 152)

Hubel, D. H., & Wiesel, T. N. (1979, September). Brian mechanisms of vision. *Scientific American,* pp. 150–162. (p. 159)

Hucker, S. J., & Bain, J. (1990). Androgenic hormones and sexual assault. In W. Marshall, R. Law, & H. Barbaree (Eds.), *The handbook on sexual assault.* New York: Plenum. (p. 376)

Hugick, L. (1989, July). Women play the leading role in keeping modern families close. *Gallup Report,* No. 286, pp. 27–34. (p. 123)

Hugo, G. (1987). Aging in the third world. *Social Science, 72,* 57–60. (p. 130)

Hull, J. G., & Bond, C. F., Jr. (1986). Social and behavioral consequences of alcohol consumption and expectancy: A meta-analysis. *Psychological Bulletin, 99,* 347–360. (pp. 231, 232)

Hull, J. G., Young, R. D., & Jouriles, E. (1986). Applications of the self-awareness model of alcohol consumption: Predicting patterns of use and abuse. *Journal of Personality and Social Psychology, 51,* 790–796. (p. 231)

Hulme, C., & Tordoff, V. (1989). Working memory development: The effects of speech rate, word length, and acoustic similarity on serial recall. *Journal of Experimental Child Psychology, 47,* 72-87. (p. 282)

Humphreys, L. G., & Davey, T. C. (1988). Continuity in intellectual growth from 12 months to 9 years. *Intelligence, 12,* 183–197. (p. 348)

Hunt, E. (1983). On the nature of intelligence. *Science, 219,* 141–146. (p. 341)

Hunt, E. (1995). The role of intelligence in modern society. *American Scientist, 83,* 356–368. (p. 340)

Hunt, J. M. (1982). Toward equalizing the developmental opportunities of infants and preschool children. *Journal of Social Issues, 38*(4), 163–191. (p. 354)

Hunt, M. (1974). *Sexual behavior in the 1970s.* Chicago: Playboy Press. (p. 377)

Hunt, M. (1982). *The universe within.* New York: Simon and Schuster. (pp. 315, 316)

Hunt, M. (1990). *The compassionate beast: What science is discovering about the humane side of humankind.* New York: William Morrow. (p. 8)

Hunt, M. (1993). *The story of psychology.* New York: Doubleday. (pp. 2, 41, 119, 122, 253, 350)

Hunter, J. E. (1997). Needed: A ban on the significance test. *Psychological Science, 8,* 3–7. (p. 602)

Hunter, S., & Sundel, M. (Eds.). (1989). *Midlife myths: Issues, findings, and practice implications.* Newbury Park, CA: Sage. (p. 136)

Hurtado, S., Dey, E. L., & Trevino, J. G. (1994). Exclusion or self-segregation? Interaction across racial/ethnic groups on college campuses. Paper presented at the American Educational Research Association annual meeting. (p. 568)

Huston, A. C., Donnerstein, E., Fairchild, H., Feshbach, N. D., Katz, P. A., & Murray, J. P. (1992). *Big world, small screen: The role of television in American society.* Lincoln, NE: University of Nebraska Press. (p. 575)

Hyde, J. S. (1983, November). *Bem's gender schema theory.* Paper presented at GLCA Women's Studies Conference, Rochester, IN. (p. 294)

Hyde, J. S. (1984, July). Children's understanding of sexist language. *Developmental Psychology, 20*(4), 697–706. (p. 329)

Hyde, J. S., & Linn, M. C. (1988). Gender differences in verbal ability: A meta-analysis. *Psychological Bulletin, 104,* 53–69. (p. 357)

Hyde, J. S., Fennema, E., & Lamon, S. J. (1990). Gender differences in mathematics performance: A meta-analysis. *Psychological Bulletin, 107,* 139–155. (p. 357)

Hyler, S., Gabbard, G. O., & Schneider, I. (1991). Homicidal maniacs and narcissistic parasites: Stigmatization of mentally ill persons in the movies. *Hospital and Community Psychiatry, 42,* 1044–1048. (p. 459)

Hyman, I. E., Jr., & Pentland, J. (1996). The role of mental imagery in the creation of false childhood memories. *Journal of Memory and Language, 35,* 101–117. (p. 295)

Hyman, I. E., Jr., Husband, T. H., & Billings, F. J. (1995). False memories of childhood experiences. *Applied Cognitive Psychology, 9,* 181–197. (p. 295)

Hyman, R. (1981). Cold reading: How to convince strangers that you know all about them. In K. Frazier (Ed.), *Paranormal borderlands of science.* Buffalo, NY: Prometheus. (p. 448)

Hyman, R. (1994). Anomaly or artifact? Comments on Bem and Honorton. *Psychological Bulletin, 115,* 19–24. (p. 204)

Hyman, R. (1996, March/April). Evaluation of the military's twenty-year program on psychic spying. *Skeptical Inquirer,* pp. 21–23, 27. (p. 203)

Hyman, R. (1996, March/April). The evidence for psychic functioning: Claims vs. reality. *The Skeptical Inquirer,* pp. 24–26. (p. 204)

Immen, W. (1995, July 16). Canadians ignore 'safe sex' warning. *Toronto Globe and Mail* (reprinted in Grand Rapids [*Mich.*] Press, p. A22). (p. 126)

Ingham, A. G., Levinger, G., Graves, J., & Peckham, V. (1974). The Ringelmann effect: Studies of group size and group performance. *Journal of Experimental Social Psychology, 10,* 371–384. (p. 561)

Inglehart, M. R., Markus, H., & Brown, D. R. (1989). The effects of possible selves on academic achievement—A panel study. In J. P. Forgas & J. M. Innes (Eds.), *Recent advances in social psychology: An international perspective.* New York: Elsevier Science Publishers. (p. 438)

Inglehart, R. (1990). *Culture shift in advanced industrial society.* Princeton, NJ: Princeton University Press. (pp. 138, 140, 141, 367, 446)

Inman, M. L., & Baron, R. S. (1996). Influence of prototypes on perceptions of prejudice. *Journal of Personality and Social Psychology, 70,* 727–739. (p. 307)

Insel, P. M., & Roth, W. T. (1976). *Health in a changing society.* Palo Alto, CA: Mayfield. (p. 128)

Irwin, M., Mascovich, A., Gillin, J. C., Willoughby, R., Pike, J., & Smith, T. L. (1994). Partial sleep deprivation reduces natural killer cell activity in humans. *Psychosomatic Medicine, 56,* 493–498. (p. 214)

Isen, A. M., & Means, B. (1983). The influence of positive affect on decision-making strategy. *Social Cognition, 2,* 28–31. (p. 406)

Isham, W. P., & Kamin, L. J. (1993). Blackness, deafness, IQ, and *g. Intelligence, 17,* 37–46. (p. 330)

ISR (1994, May). High schooler's job may 'cost' too much. *ISR Newsletter,* p. 11 (University of Michigan). (p. 21)

Ito, T. A., Miller, N., & Pollock, V. E. (1996). Alcohol and aggression: A meta-analysis on the moderating effects of inhibitory cues, triggering events, and self-focused attention. *Psychological Bulletin, 120,* 60–82. (p. 572)

Izard, C. E. (1977). *Human emotions.* New York: Plenum Press. (pp. 400, 403)

Izard, C. E. (1994). Innate and universal facial expressions: Evidence from developmental and cross-cultural research. *Psychological Bulletin, 115,* 288–299. (p. 400)

Jackson, J. M., & Williams, K. D. (1988). Social loafing: A review and theoretical analysis. Unpublished manuscript, Fordham University. (p. 562)

Jackson, S. W. (1992). The listening healer in the history of psychological healing. *American Journal Psychiatry, 149,* 1623–1632. (p. 505)

Jacobs, B. L. (1987). How hallucinogenic drugs work. *American Scientist, 75,* 386–392. (p. 234)

Jacobs, B. L. (1994). Serotonin, motor activity, and depression-related disorders. *American Scientist, 82,* 456–463. (pp. 472, 529, 530)

Jacobs, W. J., & Nadel, L. (1985). Stress-induced recovery of fears and phobias. *Psychological Bulletin, 92,* 512–531. (p. 464)

Jacobson, J. W., Mulick, J. A., & Schwartz, A. A. (1995). A history of facilitated communication: Science, pseudoscience, and antiscience. Science working group on facilitated communication. *American Psychologist, 50,* 750–765. (p. 560)

James, W. (1890). *The principles of psychology* (Vol. 2). New York: Holt. (pp. 49, 170, 279, 413)

James, W. (1902; reprinted 1958). *Varieties of religious experience.* New York: Mentor Books. (p. 406)

Jameson, D. (1985). Opponent-colors theory in light of physiological findings. In D. Ottoson & S. Zeki (Eds.), *Central and peripheral mechanisms of color vision.* New York: Macmillan. (p. 163)

Jamison, K. R. (1993). *Touched with fire: Manic-depressive illness and the artistic temperament.* New York: Free Press. (p. 470)

Jamison, K. R. (1995, February). Manic-depressive illness and creativity. *Scientific American,* pp. 62–67. (p. 470)

Janis, I. L. (1982). *Groupthink: Psychological studies of policy decisions and fiascoes.* Boston: Houghton Mifflin. (p. 563)

Janis, I. L. (1986). Problems of international crisis management in the nuclear age. *Journal of Social Issues, 42*(2), 201–220. (p. 310)

Janis, I. L. (1989). *Crucial decisions: Leadership in policymaking and crisis management.* New York: Free Press. (p. 309)

Janoff-Bulman, R., Timko, C., & Carli, L. L. (1985). Cognitive biases in blaming the victim. *Journal of Experimental Social Psychology, 21,* 161–177. (p. 571)

Jarvik, L. F. (1975). Thoughts on the psychobiology of aging. *American Psychologist, 30,* 576–583. (p. 132)

Jeffrey, R. W., & Wing, R. R. (1983). Recidivism and self-cure of smoking and obesity: Data from population studies. *American Psychologist, 38,* 852. (p. 546)

Jelicic, M., De Roode, A., Bovill, J. G., & Bonke, B. (1992). Unconscious learning during anaesthesia. *Anaesthesia, 47,* 835–837. (p. 239)

Jemmott, J. B., III, & Magloire, K. (1988). Academic stress, social support, and secretory immunoglobulin A. *Journal of Personality and Social Psychology, 55,* 803–810. (p. 524)

Jenish, D. (1993, October 11). The king of porn. *Maclean's,* pp. 52–64. (p. 378)

Jenkins, J. G., & Dallenbach, K. M. (1924). Obliviscence during sleep and waking. *American Journal of Psychology, 35,* 605–612. (pp. 292–293)

Jenkins, J. M., & Astington, J. W. (1996). Cognitive factors and family structure associated with theory of mind development in young children. *Developmental Psychology, 32,* 70–78. (p. 92)

Jensen, A. R. (1980). *Bias in mental testing.* New York: The Free Press. (p. 346)

Jensen, A. R. (1983, August). *The nature of the black-white difference on various psychometric tests: Spearman's hypothesis.* Paper presented at the meeting of the American Psychological Association, Anaheim, CA. (p. 359)

Jensen, A. R. (1989). New findings on the intellectually gifted. *New Horizons, 30,* 73–80. (p. 341)

Jensen, A. R. (1993). Psychometric *g* and achievement. In B. R. Gifford (Ed.), *Policy perspectives on educational testing.* Boston: Kluwer. (p. 340)

Jensen, A. R., & Johnson, F. W. (1994). Race and sex differences in head size and IQ. *Intelligence, 18.* (p. 341)

Jensen, J. P., & Bergin, A. E. (1988). Mental health values of professional therapists: A national interdisciplinary survey. *Professional Psychology: Research and Practice, 19,* 290–297. (p. 507)

Jepson, C., Krantz, D. H., & Nisbett, R. E. (1983). Inductive reasoning: Competence or skill. *The Behavioral and Brain Sciences, 3,* 494–501. (p. 601)

Jervis, R. (1985, April 2). Quoted in D. Goleman, Political forces come under new scrutiny of psychology. *The New York Times,* pp. C1, C4. (p. 315)

John, O. P. (1990). The "big five" factor taxonomy: Dimensions of personality in the natural language and in questionnaires. In L. A. Pervin (Ed.), *Handbook of personality: Theory and research.* New York: Guilford Press. (p. 432)

Johnson, C. B., Stockdale, M. S., & Saal, F. E. (1991). Persistence of men's misperceptions of friendly cues across a variety of interpersonal encounters. *Psychology of Women Quarterly, 15,* 463–475. (p. 379)

Johnson, D. (1990). Animal rights and human lives: Time for scientists to right the balance. *Psychological Science, 1,* 213–214. (p. 36)

Johnson, D., & Drenick, E. J. (1977). Therapeutic fasting in morbid obesity. Long-term follow-up. *Archives of Internal Medicine, 137,* 1381–1382. (p. 543)

Johnson, D. W., & Johnson, R. T. (1989). *Cooperation and competition: Theory and research.* Edina, MN: Interaction Book. (p. 587)

Johnson, E. J., & Tversky, A. (1983). Affect, generalization, and the perception of risk. *Journal of Personality and Social Psychology, 45,* 20–31. (p. 406)

Johnson, J. S., & Newport, E. L. (1991). Critical period effects on universal properties of language: The status of subjacency in the acquisition of a second language. *Cognition, 39,* 215-258. (p. 324)

Johnson, M. H. (1992). Imprinting and the development of face recognition: From chick to man. *Current Directions in Psychological Science, 1,* 52–55. (p. 96)

Johnston, L. D. (1996, December 19). Monitoring the future study of drug use. News and Information Services, University of Michigan. (pp. 233, 236)

Johnston, L. D., O'Malley, P., & Bachman, J. (1994, January 27). Drug use rises among American teen-agers. News and Information Services, University of Michigan. (p. 237)

Jones, E. E., Cumming, J. D., & Horowitz, M. J. (1988). Another look at the nonspecific hypothesis of therapeutic effectiveness. *Journal of Consulting and Clinical Psychology, 56,* 48–55. (p. 505)

Jones, M. C. (1924). A laboratory study of fear: The case of Peter. *Journal of Genetic Psychology, 31,* 308–315. (p. 493)

Jones, M. C. (1957). The later careers of boys who were early or late maturing. *Child Development, 28,* 113–128. (p. 117)

Jones, S. S., Collins, K., & Hong, H-W. (1991). An audience effect on smile production in 10–month-old infants. *Psychological Science, 2,* 45–49. (p. 401)

Jones, W. H., Carpenter, B. N., & Quintana, D. (1985). Personality and interpersonal predictors of loneliness in two cultures. *Journal of Personality and Social Psychology, 48,* 1503–1511. (p. 32)

Jorgenson, D. O., & Papciak, A. S. (1981). The effects of communication, resource feedback, and identifiability on behavior in a simulated commons. *Journal of Experimental Social Psychology, 17,* 373–385. (p. 588)

Jorm, A. F., Korten, A. E., & Henderson, A. S. (1987). The prevalence of dementia: A quantitative integration of the literature. *Acta Psychiatrica Scandinavica, 76,* 465–479. (p. 132)

Jose, W. S., II, & Anderson, D. R. (1991). Control data's StayWell program: A health cost management strategy. In S. M. Weiss, J. E. Fielding, & A. Baum (Eds.), *Health at work.* Hillsdale, NJ: Erlbaum. (p. 536)

Kagan, J. (1976). Emergent themes in human development. *American Scientist, 64,* 186–196. (p. 98)

Kagan, J. (1984). *The nature of the child.* New York: Basic Books. (p. 94)

Kagan, J. (1989b). *Unstable ideas: Temperament, cognition, and self.* Cambridge, MA: Harvard University Press. (pp. 427, 431)

Kagan, J. (1990). Interview with M. V. Ellis & E. S. Robbins, In Celebration of nature: A dialogue with Jerome Kagan. *Journal of Counseling and Development, 68,* 623–627. (p. 96)

Kagan, J. (1995). On attachment. *Harvard Review of Psychiatry, 3,* 104–106. (pp. 96, 97)

Kagan, J., Arcus, D., Snidman, N., Feng, W. Y., Hendler, J., & Greene, S. (1994). Reactivity in infants: A cross-national comparison. *Developmental Psychology, 30,* 342–345.

Kagan, J., Snidman, N., & Arcus, D. M. (1992). Initial reactions to unfamiliarity. *Current Directions in Psychological Science, 1,* 171–174. (pp. 96–97)

Kahneman, D. (1985, June). Quoted by K. McKean, Decisions, decisions. *Discover,* pp. 22–31. (p. 600)

Kahneman, D. (in press). Assessments of individual well-being: A bottom-up approach. In D. Kahneman, E. Diener, & N. Schwartz (Eds.), *Understanding well-being: Scientific perspectives on enjoyment and suffering.* New York: Russell Sage Foundation. (p. 172)

Kahneman, D., & Tversky, A. (1972). Subjective probability: A judgment of representativeness. *Cognitive Psychology, 3,* 430–454. (p. 23)

Kahneman, D., & Tversky, A. (1979). Intuitive prediction: Biases and corrective procedures. *Management Science, 12,* 313–327. (p. 313)

Kahneman, D., Fredrickson, B. L., Schreiber, C. A., & Redelmeier, D. A. (1993). When more pain is preferred to less: Adding a better end. *Psychological Science, 4,* 401–405. (p. 172)

Kahneman, D., Knetsch, J. L., & Thaler, R. (1986). Fairness as a constraint on profit seeking: Entitlements in the market. *American Economic Review, 76,* 728–741. (p. 314)

Kail, R. (1991). Developmental change in speed of processing during childhood and adolescence. *Psychological Bulletin, 109,* 490–501. (p. 131)

Kalin, N. H. (1993, May). The neurobiology of fear. *Scientific American,* pp. 94–101. (p. 398)

Kamarck, T., & Jennings, J. R. (1991). Biobehavioral factors in sudden cardiac death. *Psychological Bulletin, 109,* 42–75. (p. 522)

Kaminer, W. (1992). *I'm dysfunctional, you're dysfunctional: The recovery movement and other self-help fashions.* Reading, MA: Addison-Wesley. (p. 230)

Kandel, D. B., & Raveis, V. H. (1989). Cessation of illicit drug use in young adulthood. *Archives of General Psychiatry, 46,* 109–116. (p. 237)

Kandel, E. R., & Schwartz, J. H. (1982). Molecular biology of learning: Modulation of transmitter release. *Science, 218,* 433–443. (p. 284)

Kanekar, S., & Nazareth, A. (1988). Attributed rape victim's fault as a function of her attractiveness, physical hurt, and emotional disturbance. *Social Behaviour, 3,* 37–40. (p. 379)

Kann, L., Warren, W., Collins, J. L., Ross, J., Collins, B., Kolbe, L. J. (1993). Results from the national school-based 1991 Youth Risk Behavior Survey and progress toward achieving related health objectives for the nation. U.S. Department of Health and Human Services, *Public Health Reports, 108* (Supplement 1), 47–55. (p. 237)

Kapitza, S. (1991, August). Antiscience trends in the U.S.S.R. *Scientific American*, pp. 32–38. (p. 204)

Kaplan, H. I., & Saddock, B. J. (Eds.). (1989). *Comprehensive textbook of psychiatry, V.* Baltimore, MD: Williams and Wilkins. (p. 509)

Kaprio, J., Koskenvuo, M., & Rita, H. (1987). Mortality after bereavement: A prospective study of 95,647 widowed persons. *American Journal of Public Health, 77*, 283–287. (p. 519)

Kapur, S., & Mann, J. J. (1993). Antidepressant action and the neurobiologic effects of ECT: Human studies. In C. E. Coffey (Ed.), *The clinical science of electroconvulsive therapy.* Washington, DC: American Psychiatric Press. (p. 510)

Karacan, I., Aslan, C., & Hirshkowitz, M. (1983). Erectile mechanisms in man. *Science, 220*, 1080–1082. (p. 213)

Karacan, I., Goodenough, D. R., Shapiro, A., & Starker, S. (1966). Erection cycle during sleep in relation to dream anxiety. *Archives of General Psychiatry, 15*, 183–189. (p. 213)

Karau, S. J., & Williams, K. D. (1993). Social loafing: A meta-analytic review and theoretical integation. *Journal of Personality and Social Psychology, 65*, 681–706. (p. 562)

Kark, J. D., Shemi, G., Friedlander, Y., Martin, O., Manor, O., & Blondheim, S. H. (1996). Does religious observance promote health? Mortality in secular vs. religious kibbutzim in Israel. *American Journal of Public Health, 86*, 341–346. (p. 534)

Karni, A., & Sagi, D. (1994). Dependence on REM sleep for overnight improvement of perceptual skills. *Science, 265*, 679–682. (p. 219)

Karno, M., Golding, J. M., Sorenson, S. B., & Burnam, A. (1988). The epidemiology of obsessive-compulsive disorder in five US communities. *Archives of General Psychiatry, 45*, 1094–1099. (p. 463)

Kashima, Y., Siegal, M., Tanaka, K., & Kashima, E. S. (1992). Do people believe behaviours are consistent with attitudes? Towards a cultural psychology of attribution processes. *British Journal of Social Psychology, 31*, 111–124. (p. 442)

Kashima, Y., Yamaguchi, S., Kim, U., Choic, S-C., Gelfand, M. J., & Yuki, M. (1995). Culture, gender, and self: A perspective from individualism-collectivism research. *Journal of Personality and Social Psychology, 69*, 925–937. (p. 123)

Kasser, T., & Ryan, R. M. (1996). Further examining the American dream: Differential correlates of intrinsic and extrinsic goals. *Personality and Social Psychology Bulletin, 22*, 280–287. (p. 412)

Kaufman, A. S., Reynolds, C. R., & McLean, J. E. (1989). Age and WAIS-R intelligence in a national sample of adults in the 20– to 74–year age range: A cross-sectional analysis with educational level controlled. *Intelligence, 13*, 235–253. (p. 135)

Kaufman, J., & Zigler, E. (1987). Do abused children become abusive parents? *American Journal of Orthopsychiatry, 57*, 186–192. (p. 100)

Kaufman, L., & Rock, I. (1962). The moon illusion I. *Science, 136*, 953–961. (p. 191)

Kaye, K. L., & Bower, T. G. R. (1994). Learning and intermodal transfer of information in newborns. *Psychological Science, 5*, 286–288. (p. 89)

Kaylor, J. A., King, D. W., & King, L. A. (1987). Psychological effects of military service in Vietnam: A meta-analysis. *Psychological Bulletin, 102*, 257–271. (p. 461)

Keesey, R. E., & Corbett, S. W. (1983). Metabolic defense of the body weight set-point. In A. J. Stunkard & E. Stellar (Eds.), *Eating and its disorders.* New York: Raven Press. (p. 370)

Kellehear, A. (1996). *Experiences near death: Beyond medicine and religion.* New York: Oxford University Press. (p. 239)

Kellerman, J., Lewis, J., & Laird, J. D. (1989). Looking and loving: The effects of mutual gaze on feelings of romantic love. *Journal of Research in Personality, 23*, 145–161. (p. 398)

Kellermann, A. L., Rivara, F. P., Rushforth, N. B., Banton, H. G., Feay, D. T., Francisco, J. T., Locci, A. B., Prodzinski, J., Hackman, B. B., & Somes, G. (1993). Gun ownership as a risk factor for homicide in the home. *New England Journal of medicine, 329*, 1084–1091. (p. 571)

Kelling, S. T., & Halpern, B. P. (1983). Taste flashes: Reaction times, intensity, and quality. *Science, 219*, 412–414. (p. 174)

Kelly, I. W., Laverty, W. H., & Saklofske, D. H. (1990). Geophysical variables and behavior: LXIV. An empirical investigation of the relationship between worldwide automobile traffic disasters and lunar cycles: No relationship. *Psychological Reports, 67*, 987–994. (p. 481)

Kelly, T. A. (1990). The role of values in psychotherapy: A critical review of process and outcome effects. *Clinical Psychology Review, 10*, 171–186. (p. 507)

Kempe, R. S., & Kempe, C. C. (1978). *Child abuse.* Cambridge, MA: Harvard University Press. (p. 100)

Kendall-Tackett, K. A., Williams, L. M., & Finkelhor, D. (1993). Impact of sexual abuse on children: A review and synthesis of recent empirical studies. *Psychological Bulletin, 113*, 164–180. (pp. 100, 300)

Kendler, K. S. (1996). Parenting: A genetic-epidemiologic perspective. *The American Journal of Psychiatry, 153*, 11–20. (p. 105)

Kendler, K. S., Neale, M. C., Kessler, R. C., Heath, A. C., & Eaves, L. J. (1992). Generalized anxiety disorder in women: A population-based twin study. *Archives of General Psychiatry, 49*, 267–272. (p. 464)

Kendler, K. S., Neale, M., Kessler, R., Heath, A., & Eaves, L. (1993). A twin study of recent life events and difficulties. *Archives of General Psychiatry, 50*, 789–796. (p. 108)

Kennell, J. N., & Klaus, M. (1982). *Parent-infant bonding.* St. Louis: C. V. Mosby. (p. 96)

Kenrick, D. T., & Funder, D. C. (1988). Profiting from controversy: Lessons from the person-situation debate. *American Psychologist, 43*, 23–34. (p. 435)

Kenrick, D. T., & Gutierres, S. E. (1980). Contrast effects and judgments of physical attractiveness: When beauty becomes a social problem. *Journal of Personality and Social Psychology, 38*, 131–140. (p. 377)

Kenrick, D. T., & Trost, M. R. (1987). A biosocial theory of heterosexual relationships. In K. Kelly (Ed.), *Females, males, and sexuality.* Albany: State University of New York Press. (p. 379)

Kenrick, D. T., Gutierres, S. E., & Goldberg, L. L. (1989). Influence of popular erotica on judgments of strangers and mates. *Journal of Experimental Social Psychology, 25,* 159-167. (p. 377)

Kerr, N. L., & Bruun, S. E. (1983). Dispensability of member effort and group motivation losses: Free-rider effects. *Journal of Personality and Social Psychology, 44,* 78–94. (p. 562)

Kessler, M., & Albee, G. (1975). Primary prevention. *Annual Review of Psychology, 26,* 557–591. (p. 512)

Kessler, R. C., Foster, C., Joseph, J., Ostrow, D., Wortman, C., Phair, J., & Chmiel, J. (1991). Stressful life events and symptom onset in HIV infection. *American Journal of Psychiatry, 148,* 733–738. (p. 525)

Kessler, R. C., McGonagle, K. A., Zhao, S., Nelson, C. B., Hughes, M., Eshleman, S., Wittchen, H-U., Kendler, K. S. (1994). Lifetime and 12-month prevalence of *DSM-III-R* psychiatric disorders in the United States. *Archives of General Psychiatry, 51,* 8–19. (p. 484)

Kestenbaum, R. (1992). Feeling happy versus feeling good: The processing of discrete and global categories of emotional expressions by children and adults. *Developmental Psychology, 28,* 1132–1142. (p. 398)

Keynes, M. (1980, December 20/27). Handel's illnesses. *The Lancet,* pp. 1354-1355. (p. 470)

Keys, A., Brozek, J., Henschel, A., Mickelsen, O., & Taylor, H. L. (1950). *The biology of human starvation.* Minneapolis: University of Minnesota Press. (p. 368)

Kiecolt-Glaser, J. K., Malarkey, W. B., Chee, M., Newton, T., Cacioppo, J. T., Mao, H-Y., & Glaser, R. (1993). Negative behavior during marital conflict is associated with immunological downregulation. *Psychosomatic Medicine, 55,* 395–409. (p. 524)

Kihlstrom, J. F. (1985). Hypnosis. *Annual Review of Psychology, 36,* 385–418. (pp. 221, 226)

Kihlstrom, J. F. (1990). Awareness, the psychological unconscious, and the self. Address to the American Psychological Association convention. (p. 428)

Kihlstrom, J. F. (1990). The psychological unconscious. In L. A. Pervin (Ed.), *Handbook of personality: Theory and research.* New York: Guilford Press. (p. 428)

Kihlstrom, J. F. (1994). The social construction of memory. Paper presented at the American Psychological Society convention. (p. 291)

Kihlstrom, J. F. (1996). Quoted in *Frequently asked questions about the False Memory Syndrome Foundation* (available at http://www.csicop.org/~fitz/fmsf/faq.html (accessed September 13, 1996). (p. 299)

Kihlstrom, J. F., & McConkey, K. M. (1990). William James and hypnosis: A centennial reflection. *Psychological Science, 1,* 174–177. (p. 228)

Kim, Y., & Lee, S-H. (1994). The Confucian model of morality, justice, selfhood and society: Implications for modern society. In *The universal and particular natures of Confucianism,* The Academy of Korean Studies. (p. 442)

Kimball, M. M. (1989). A new perspective on women's math achievement. *Psychological Bulletin, 105,* 198–214. (p. 357)

Kimble, G. A. (1981). *Biological and cognitive constraints on learning.* In L. T. Benjamin, Jr. (Ed.), *The G. Stanley Hall Lecture Series* (Vol. 1). Washington, DC: American Psychological Association. (p. 250)

Kimzey, S. L. (1975). The effects of extended spaceflight on hematologic and immunologic systems. *Journal of the American Medical Women's Association, 30*(5), 218–232. (p. 524)

Kimzey, S. L., Johnson, P. C., Ritzman, S. E., & Mengel, C. E. (1976, April). Hematology and immunology studies: The second manned Skylab mission. *Aviation, Space, and Environmental Medicine,* pp. 383–390. (p. 524)

King, D. W., & King, L. A. (1991). Validity issues in research on Vietnam veteran adjustment. *Psychological Bulletin, 109,* 107–124. (p. 461)

King, N. J., & Montgomery, R. B. (1980). Biofeedback-induced control of human peripheral temperature: A critical review of the literature. *Psychological Bulletin, 88,* 738–752. (p. 531)

King, P. (1991, March 18). Bawl players. *Sports Illustrated,* pp. 14–17. (p. 411)

Kinnier, R. T., & Metha, A. T. (1989). Regrets and priorities at three stages of life. *Counseling and Values, 33,* 182-193. (p. 116)

Kinsey, A. C., Pomeroy, W., & Martin, C. (1948). *Sexual behavior in the human male.* Philadelphia: Saunders. (p. 374)

Kinsey, A. C., Pomeroy, W., Martin, C., & Gebhard, P. (1953). *Sexual behavior in the human female.* Philadelphia: Saunders. (p. 374)

Kinzl, J. F., Traweger, C., Guenther, V., & Biebl, W. (1994). Family background and sexual abuse associated with eating disorders. *American Journal of Psychiatry, 151,* 1127–1131. (p. 372)

Kirchner, W. H., & Towne, W. F. (1994, June). The sensory basis of the honeybee's dance language. *Scientific American,* pp. 74–80. (p. 325)

Kirk, S. A., & Gallagher, J. J. (1989). *Educating exceptional children.* Boston: Houghton Mifflin. (p. 168)

Kirkpatrick, L. A. (1994). The role of attachment in religious belief and behavior. *Advances in Personal Relationships, 5,* 239–265. (p. 96)

Kirsch, I., & Lynn, S. J. (1995). The altered state of hypnosis. *American Psychologist, 50,* 846–858. (p. 228)

Kisor, H. (1990). *What's that pig outdoors.* New York: Hill and Wang. (p. 168)

Kitayama, S., & Markus, H. R. (in press). Construal of the self as cultural frame: Implications for internationalizing psychology. In J. D'Arms, R. G. Hastie, S. E. Hoelscher, & H. K. Jacobson (Eds.), *Becoming more international and global: Challenges for American higher education.* Ann Arbor: University of Michigan Press. (p. 442)

Kite, M. E., & Johnson, B. T. (1988). Attitudes toward older and younger adults: A meta-analysis. *Psychology and Aging, 3,* 233–244. (p. 133)

Kite, M. E., & Whitley, B. E., Jr. (1996). Sex differences in attitudes toward homosexual persons, behaviors, and civil rights: A meta-analysis. *Personality and Social Psychology Bulletin, 22,* 336–353. (p. 382)

Klasen, S. (1994). "Missing women" reconsidered. *World Development, 22.* (p. 568)

Klayman, J., & Ha, Y-W. (1987). Confirmation, disconfirmation, and information in hypothesis testing. *Psychological Review, 94,* 211–228. (p. 308)

Kleinke, C. L. (1986). Gaze and eye contact: A research review. *Psychological Bulletin, 100,* 78–100. (p. 398)

Kleinmuntz, B., & Szucko, J. J. (1984). A field study of the fallibility of polygraph lie detection. *Nature, 308,* 449–450. (p. 397)

Kleitman, N. (1960, November). Patterns of dreaming. *Scientific American,* pp. 82–88. (p. 211)

Klemm, W. R. (1990). Historical and introductory perspectives on brainstem-mediated behaviors. In W. R. Klemm & R. P. Vertes (Eds.), *Brainstem mechanisms of behavior.* New York: Wiley. (p. 55)

Kline, D., & Schieber, F. (1985). Vision and aging. In J. E. Birren & K. W. Schaie (Eds.), *Handbook of the psychology of aging.* New York: Van Nostrand Reinhold. (p. 131)

Kline, N. S. (1974). *From sad to glad.* New York: Ballantine Books. (p. 475)

Klineberg, O. (1938). Emotional expression in Chinese literature. *Journal of Abnormal and Social Psychology, 33,* 517–520. (p. 400)

Klineberg, O. (1984). Public opinion and nuclear war. *American Psychologist, 39,* 1245–1253. (p. 588)

Kluft, R. P. (1991). Multiple personality disorder. In A. Tasman & S. M. Goldfinger (Eds.), *Review of Psychiatry,* vol. 10. Washington, DC: American Psychiatric Press. (p. 467)

Klüver, H., & Bucy, P. C. (1939). Preliminary analysis of functions of the temporal lobes in monkeys. *Archives of Neurology and Psychiatry, 42,* 979–1000. (p. 56)

Koenig, H. G. (1997). *Is religion good for your health? The effects of religion on physical and mental health.* Binghamton, NY: Haworth Press. (p. 534)

Koestner, R., Franz, C., & Weinberger, J. (1990). The family origins of empathic concern: A 26–year longitudinal study. *Journal of Personality and Social Psychology, 58,* 709–717. (p. 99)

Kohlberg, L. (1981). *The philosophy of moral development: Essays on moral development* (Vol. I). San Francisco: Harper & Row. (p. 119)

Kohler, I. (1962, May). Experiments with goggles. *Scientific American,* pp. 62–72. (p. 196)

Köhler, W. (1925; reprinted 1957). *The mentality of apes.* London: Pelican. (p. 307)

Kohn, A. (1987, October). It's hard to get left out of a pair. *Psychology Today,* pp. 53–57. (p. 587)

Kohn, P. M., & Macdonald, J. E. (1992). The survey of recent life experiences: A decontaminated hassles scale for adults. *Journal of Behavioral Medicine, 15,* 221–236. (p. 519)

Kolata, G. (1986). Youth suicide: New research focuses on a growing social problem. *Science, 233,* 839–841. (p. 469)

Kolata, G. (1987). Metabolic catch-22 of exercise regimens. *Science, 236,* 146–147. (p. 545)

Kolata, G. (1996, May 21). Could it be? Weather has nothing to do with your arthritis pain? *New York Times,* p. C13. (p. 22)

Kolata, G. (1996, December 10). With major math proof, brute computers show flash of reasoning power. *New York Times,* p. C1. (p. 318)

Kolers, P. A. (1975). Specificity of operations in sentence recognition. *Cognitive Psychology, 7,* 289–306. (p. 273)

Kolominsky, Y., & Parkhomenko, V. (1993). Realization of sociopsychological assistance to children and youth of Chernobyl in the Republic of Belarus. Unpublished manuscript, Byelorussian Research Institute for Education, 16 Karolya Street, Minsk. (p. 519)

Koltz, C. (1983, December). Scapegoating. *Psychology Today,* pp. 68–69. (p. 569)

Konishi, M. (1993, April). Listening with two ears. *Scientific American,* pp. 66–73. (p. 167)

Koslowsky, M., & Babkoff, H. (1992). Meta-analysis of the relationship between total sleep deprivation and performance. *Chronobiology International, 9,* 132–136. (p. 214)

Koss, M. P., Heise, L., & Russo, N. P. (1994). The global health burden of rape. *Psychology of Women Quarterly, 18,* 509–537. (p. 576)

Kosslyn, S. M., & Koenig, O. (1992). *Wet mind: The new cognitive neuroscience.* New York: Free Press. (pp. 50, 135, 159, 208)

Kotkin, M., Daviet, C., & Gurin, J. (1996). The *Consumer Reports* mental health survey. *American Psychologist, 51,* 1080–1082. (p. 501)

Kotva, H. J., & Schneider, H. G. (1990). Those "talks"—general and sexual communication between mothers and daughters. *Journal of Social Behavior and Personality, 5,* 603–613. (p. 126)

Kraft, C. (1978). A psychophysical approach to air safety: Simulator studies of visual illusions in night approaches. In H. L. Pick, H. W. Leibowitz, J. E. Singer, A. Steinschneider, & H. W. Stevenson (Eds.), *Psychology: From research to practice.* New York: Plenum Press. (p. 199)

Kraft, R. (1996, December 2, and 1994, July 20). Personal correspondence (from Otterbein College) regarding Holocaust memories. (p. 428)

Kraus, S. J. (1991). Attitudes and the prediction of behavior. Doctoral dissertation, Harvard University. (p. 551)

Kraut, R. E., & Johnston, R. E. (1979). Social and emotional messages of smiling: An ethological approach. *Journal of Personality and Social Psychology, 37,* 1539–1553. (p. 401)

Krebs, D. L., & Van Hesteren, F. (1994). The development of altruism: Toward an integrative model. *Developmental Review, 14,* 103–158. (p. 120)

Krech, D. (1978). Quoted in M. C. Diamond, The aging brain: Some enlightening and optimistic results. *American Scientist, 66,* 66–71. (p. 135)

Kreitner, R. (1992). *Management,* 5th ed. Boston: Houghton Mifflin. (p. 352)

Kristof, N. (1993, July 22). China faces huge surplus of males as scans hold key to missing girls. *The Guardian* (England), p. 22. (p. 568)

Kroenke, K., & Mangelsdorff, A. D. (1989). Common symptoms in ambulatory care: Incidence, evaluation, therapy, and outcome. *American Journal of Medicine, 86*, 262-266. (p. 536)

Krosnick, J. A., & Alwin, D. F. (1989). Aging and susceptibility to attitude change. *Journal of Personality and Social Psychology, 57*, 416–425. (p. 144)

Krosnick, J. A., Betz, A. L., Jussim, L. J., & Lynn, A. R. (1992). Subliminal conditioning of attitudes. *Personality and Social Psychology Bulletin, 18*, 152–162. (p. 150)

Krupa, D. J., Thompson, J. K., & Thompson, R. F. (1993). Localization of a memory trace in the mammalian brain. *Science, 260*, 989–991. (p. 288)

Kübler-Ross, E. (1969). *On death and dying.* New York: Macmillan. (p. 141)

Kuhl, P. K., & Meltzoff, A. N. (1982). The bimodal perception of speech in infancy. *Science, 218*, 1138–1141. (p. 320)

Kurtz, P. (1983, Spring). Stars, planets, and people. *The Skeptical Inquirer,* pp. 65–68. (p. 448)

Kutas, M. (1990). Event-related brain potential (ERP) studies of cognition during sleep: Is it more than a dream? In R. R. Bootzin, J. F. Kihlstrom, & D. Schacter (Eds.), *Sleep and cognition.* Washington, DC: American Psychological Association. (p. 212)

Labouvie-Vief, G., & Schell, D. A. (1982). Learning and memory in later life. In B. B. Wolman (Ed.), *Handbook of developmental psychology.* Englewood Cliffs, NJ: Prentice-Hall. (p. 133)

Lacayo, R. (1995, June 12). Violent reaction. *Time,* pp. 25–39. (p. 19)

Ladd, G. T. (1887). *Elements of physiological psychology.* New York: Scribner's. (p. 207)

Lagerweij, E., Nelis, P. C., van Ree, J. M., & Wiegant, V. M. (1984). The twitch in horses: A variant of acupuncture. *Science, 225*, 1172–1174. (p. 46)

Laird, J. D. (1974). Self-attribution of emotion: The effects of expressive behavior on the quality of emotional experience. *Journal of Personality and Social Psychology, 29*, 475–486. (p. 402)

Laird, J. D. (1984). The real role of facial response in the experience of emotion: A reply to Tourangeau and Ellsworth, and others. *Journal of Personality and Social Psychology, 47*, 909–917. (p. 402)

Laird, J. D., Cuniff, M., Sheehan, K., Shulman, D., & Strum, G. (1989). Emotion specific effects of facial expressions on memory for life events. *Journal of Social Behavior and Personality, 4*, 87–98. (p. 402)

Lambert, W. E. (1992). Challenging established views on social issues: The power and limitations of research. *American Psychologist, 47*, 533–542. (p. 329)

Lambert, W. E., Genesee, F., Holobow, N., & Chartrand, L. (1993). Bilingual education for majority English-speaking children. *European Journal of Psychology of Education, 8*, 3–22. (p. 329)

Lancioni, G. (1980). Infant operant conditioning and its implications for early intervention. *Psychological Bulletin, 88*, 516–534. (p. 82)

Landauer, T. K. (1986). How much do people remember? Some estimates of the quantity of learned information in long-term memory. *Cognitive Science, 10*, 477–493. (p. 282)

Lander, E., & Kruglyak, L. (1995). Genetic dissection of complex traits: Guidelines for interpreting and reporting linkage studies. *Nature Genetics, 11*, 241–247. (p. 479)

Landers, A. (1969, April 8). Syndicated newspaper column. Cited by L. Berkowitz, The case for bottling up rage. *Psychology Today,* September, 1973, pp. 24–31. (p. 405)

Landers, S. (1986, December). Judge reiterates IQ test ban. *APA Monitor,* p. 18. (p. 333)

Landfield, P., Cadwallader, L. B., & Vinsant, S. (1988). Quantitative changes in hippocampal structure following long-term exposure to Delta-9–tetrahydrocannabinol: Possible mediation by glucocorticoid systems. *Brain Research,* Vol. 443, 47–62. (p. 235)

Langer, E. J. (1983). *The psychology of control.* Beverly Hills, CA: Sage. (p. 446)

Langer, E. J., & Abelson, R. P. (1974). A patient by any other name . . . : Clinician group differences in labeling bias. *Journal of Consulting and Clinical Psychology, 42*, 4–9. (p. 459)

Langer, E. J., & Imber, L. (1980). The role of mindlessness in the perception of deviance. *Journal of Personality and Social Psychology, 39*, 360–367. (p. 459)

Langlois, J. H., & Roggman, L. A. (1990). Attractive faces are only average. *Psychological Science, 1*, 115–121. (p. 582)

Langlois, J. H., Roggman, L. A., Casey, R. J., Ritter, J. M., Rieser-Danner, L. A., & Jenkins, V. Y. (1987). Infant preferences for attractive faces: Rudiments of a stereotype? *Developmental Psychology, 23*, 363–369. (p. 581)

Larrance, D. T., & Twentyman, C. T. (1983). Maternal attributions and child abuse. *Journal of Abnormal Psychology, 92*, 449–457. (p. 92)

Larsen, R. J., & Diener, E. (1987). Affect intensity as an individual difference characteristic: A review. *Journal of Research in Personality, 21*, 1–39. (p. 97)

Larsen, R. J., Diener, E., & Cropanzano, R. S. (1987). Cognitive operations associated with individual differences in affect intensity. *Journal of Personality and Social Psychology, 53*, 767–774. (p. 416)

Larsen, R. J., Kasimatis, M., & Frey, K. (1992). Facilitating the furrowed brow: An unobtrusive test of the facial feedback hypothesis applied to unpleasant affect. *Cognition and Emotion, 6*, 321–338. (p. 402)

Larson, R. W., & Bradney, N. (1988). Precious moments with family members and friends. In R. M. Milardo (Ed.), *Families and social networks.* Newbury Park, CA: Sage. (p. 124)

Larzelere, R. E. (1994). Corporal punishment by parents. In M. A. Mason & E. Gambrill (Eds.), *Debating children's lives: Current controversies on children and adolescents.* Thousand Oaks, CA: Sage. (p. 259)

Larzelere, R. E. (1996). A review of the outcomes of parental use of nonabusive or customary physical punishment. *Pediatrics, 78,* 824–828. (p. 259)

Lashley, K. S. (1950). In search of the engram. In *Symposium of the Society for Experimental Biology* (Vol. 4). New York: Cambridge University Press. (p. 284)

Lassiter, G. D., & Irvine, A. A. (1986). Video-taped confessions: The impact of camera point of view on judgments of coercion. *Journal of Personality and Social Psychology, 16,* 268–276. (p. 560)

Latané, B. (1981). The psychology of social impact. *American Psychologist, 36,* 343–356. (p. 562)

Latané, B., & Dabbs, J. M., Jr. (1975). Sex, group size and helping in three cities. *Sociometry, 38,* 180–194. (p. 586)

Lau, S., & Gruen, G. E. (1992). The social stigma of loneliness: Effect of target person's and perceiver's sex. *Personality and Social Psychology Bulletin, 18,* 182–189. (p. 475)

Laudenslager, M. L., & Reite, M. L. (1984). Losses and separations: Immunological consequences and health implications. *Review of Personality and Social Psychology, 5,* 285–312. (p. 520)

Laumann, E. O., Gagnon, J. H., Michael, R. T., & Michaels, S. (1994). *The social organization of sexuality: Sexual practices in the United States.* Chicago: University of Chicago Press. (pp. 374, 379, 380, 576)

Laurence, J-R., & Perry, C. (1988). *Hypnosis, will and memory: A psycho-legal history.* New York: Guilford. (p. 223)

Layton, B. D., & Turnbull, B. (1975). Belief, evaluation, and performance on an ESP task. *Journal of Experimental Social Psychology, 11,* 166–179. (p. 201)

Lazarus, R. S. (1984). On the primacy of cognition. *American Psychologist, 39,* 124–129. (p. 416)

Lazarus, R. S. (1990). Theory-based stress measurement. *Psychological Inquiry, 1,* 3–13. (p. 519)

Lazarus, R. S. (1991). Progress on a cognitive-motivational-relational theory of emotion. *American Psychologist, 46,* 352–367. (p. 416)

Leach, P. (1993). Should parents hit their children? *The Psychologist: Bulletin of the British Psychological Society, 6,* 216–220. (p. 259)

Leach, P. (1994). *Children first.* New York: Knopf. (p. 259)

Leary, M. R., Schreindorfer, L. S., & Haupt, A. L. (1995). The role of low self-esteem in emotional and behavioral problems: Why is low self-esteem dysfunctional? *Journal of Social and Clinical Psychology, 14,* 297–314. (p. 439)

Lebow, J. (1982). Consumer satisfaction with mental health treatment. *Psychological Bulletin, 91,* 244–259. (p. 501)

LeDoux, J. (1994, June). Emotion, memory and the brain. *Scientific American,* pp. 50–57. (p. 416)

LeDoux, J. (1996). *The emotional brain: The mysterious underpinnings of emotional life.* New York: Simon & Schuster. (p. 416)

Lee, G. R., Seccombe, K., & Shehan, C. L. (1991). Marital status and personal happiness: An analysis of trend data. *Journal of Marriage and the Family, 53,* 839–844. (p. 138)

Lefcourt, H. M. (1982). *Locus of control: Current trends in theory and research.* Hillsdale, NJ: Erlbaum. (p. 446)

Lefcourt, H. M., & Davidson-Katz, K. (1991). The role of humor and the self. In C. R. Snyder & D. R. Forsyth (Eds.), *Handbook of social and clinical psychology: The health perspective.* New York: Pergamon Press. (p. 532)

Lehman, D. R., & Nisbett, R. E. (1985). Effects of higher education on inductive reasoning. Unpublished manuscript, University of Michigan. (p. 447)

Lehman, D. R., Lempert, R. O., & Nisbett, R. E. (1988). The effects of graduate training on reasoning: Formal discipline and thinking about everyday-life events. *American Psychologist, 43,* 431–442. (p. 30)

Lehman, D. R., Wortman, C. B., & Williams, A. F. (1987). Long-term effects of losing a spouse or child in a motor vehicle crash. *Journal of Personality and Social Psychology, 52,* 218–231. (p. 141)

Łeibowitz, H. W. (1985). Grade crossing accidents and human factors engineering. *American Scientist, 73,* 558–562. (p. 189)

Leigh, B. C. (1989). In search of the seven dwarves: Issues of measurement and meaning in alcohol expectancy research. *Psychological Bulletin, 105,* 361–373. (p. 232)

Leigh, B. C., Temple, M. T., & Trocki, K. F. (1993). The sexual behavior of US adults: Results from a national survey. *American Journal of Public Health, 83,* 1400–1408. (p. 374)

Leikind, B., & McCarthy, W. J. (1985). An investigation of firewalking. *The Skeptical Inquirer, 10,* 23–34. (p. 173)

Leikind, B., & McCarthy, W. J. (1988). Firewalking. *Experientia, 44,* 310–315. (p. 173)

Leitenberg, H., & Henning, K. (1995). Sexual fantasy. *Psychological Bulletin, 117,* 469–496. (pp. 209, 376, 378)

Lenat, D. B. (1995, September). Artificial intelligence. *Scientific American,* pp. 80–82. (p. 317)

Lenzenweger, M. F., Dworkin, R. H., & Wethington, E. (1989). Models of positive and negative symptoms in schizophrenia: An empirical evaluation of latent structures. *Journal of Abnormal Psychology, 98,* 62–70. (p. 508)

Leo, J. (1991, August 19). No-fault syntax. *U.S. News and World Report,* p. 17. (p. 230)

Lepper, M. R., Ross, L., & Lau, R. R. (1986). Persistence of inaccurate beliefs about the self: Perseverance effects in the classroom. *Journal of Personality and Social Psychology, 50,* 482–491. (p. 316)

Lerner, M. J. (1980). *The belief in a just world: A fundamental delusion.* New York: Plenum Press. (p. 571)

Leshner, A. I. (1992). *Outcasts on main street: Report of the federal task force on homelessness and severe mental illness.* Washington, DC: Interagency Council on the Homeless, Office of the Programs for the Homeless Mentally Ill, National Institute of Mental Health. (p. 508)

LeVay, S. (1991). A difference in hypothalamic structure between heterosexual and homosexual men. *Science, 253,* 1034–1037. (p. 381)

LeVay, S. (1994, March). Quoted in D. Nimmons, Sex and the brain. *Discover,* pp. 64–71. (p. 381)

Levenson, R. W. (1992). Autonomic nervous system differences among emotions. *Psychological Science, 3*, 23–27. (p. 398)

Levenson, R. W., Ekman, P., Heider, K., & Friesen, W. V. (1991). Emotion and autonomic nervous system activity in an Indonesian culture. Unpublished manuscript, University of California, Berkeley. (p. 398)

Levenson, R. W., Ekman, P., Heider, K., & Friesen, W. V. (1992). Emotion and autonomic nervous system activity in the Minangkabau of West Sumatra. *Journal of Personality and Social Psychology, 62*, 972–988. (p. 401)

Lever, J. (1978). Sex differences in the complexity of children's play and games. *American Sociological Review, 43*, 471–483. (p. 123)

Levesque, M. J., & Kenny, D. A. (1993). Accuracy of behavioral predictions at zero acquaintance: A social relations analysis. *Journal of Personality and Social Psychology, 65*, 1178–1187. (pp. 435–436)

Levin, I. P., & Gaeth, G. J. (1988). How consumers are affected by the framing of attribute information before and after consuming the product. *Journal of Consumer Research, 15*, 374–378. (p. 314)

Levin, I. P., Schnittjer, S. K., & Thee, S. L. (1988). Information framing effects in social and personal decisions. *Journal of Experimental Social Psychology, 24*, 520–529. (p. 314)

Levin, J. (1994). Religion and health: Is there an association, is it valid, and is it causal? *Social Science and Medicine, 38*, 1475–1482. (p. 534)

Levin, J. (1996). How religion influences morbidity and health: Reflections on natural history, salutogenesis, and host resistance. *Social Science and Medicine, 43*, 849–864. (p. 534)

Levine, A. (1990, May 7). America's youthful bigots. *U.S. News and World Report*, pp. 59–60. (pp. 655, 668)

Levine, I. S., & Rog, D. J. (1990). Mental health services for homeless mentally ill persons: Federal initiatives and current service trends. *American Psychologist, 45*, 963–968. (p. 508)

Levine, R., Sato, S., Hashimoto, T., & Verma, J. (1995). Love and marriage in eleven cultures. *Journal of Cross-Cultural Psychology, 26*, 554–571. (p. 584)

Levinson, D. J. (1996). *The seasons of a woman's life*. New York: Knopf. (p. 136)

Levinson, D. J., Darow, C. N., Klein, E. B., Levinson, M. H., & McKee, B. (1978). *The seasons of a man's life*. New York: Knopf. (p. 136)

Levitt, E. E. (1986). Coercion, voluntariness, compliance and resistance: The essence of hypnosis twenty-seven years after Orne. Invited address to the American Psychological Association convention. (p. 224)

Levy, B., & Langer, E. (1992). Avoidance of the memory loss stereotype: Enhanced memory among the elderly deaf. American Psychological Association convention, Washington, DC. (p. 169)

Levy, J. (1985, May). Right brain, left brain: Fact and fiction. *Psychology Today*, pp. 38–44. (p. 70)

Lewicki, P., Hill, T., & Czyzewska, M. (1992). Nonconscious acquisition of information. *American Psychologist, 47*, 796–801. (p. 428)

Lewinsohn, P. M., & Rosenbaum, M. (1987). Recall of parental behavior by acute depressives, remitted depressives, and nondepressives. *Journal of Personality and Social Psychology, 52*, 611–619. (p. 291)

Lewinsohn, P. M., Hoberman, H., Teri, L., & Hautziner, M. (1985). An integrative theory of depression. In S. Reiss & R. Bootzin (Eds.), *Theoretical issues in behavior therapy*. Orlando, FL: Academic Press. (pp. 470, 474)

Lewis, C. C. (1981). The effects of parental firm control: A reinterpretation of findings. *Psychological Bulletin, 90*, 547–563. (p. 104)

Lewis, C. S. (1967). *Christian reflections*. Grand Rapids, MI: Eerdmans. (p. 280)

Lewis, D. O., Pincus, J. H., Bard, B., Richardson, E., Prichep, L. S., Feldman, M., & Yeager, C. (1988). Neuropsychiatric, psychoeducational, and family characteristics of 14 juveniles condemned to death in the United States. *American Journal of Psychiatry, 145*, 584–589. (p. 100)

Lewis, D. O., Pincus, J. H., Feldman, M., Jackson, L., & Bard, B. (1986). Psychiatric, neurological, and psychoeducational characteristics of 15 death row inmates in the United States. *American Journal of Psychiatry, 143*, 838–845. (p. 572)

Lewis, M. (1992). Commentary. *Human Development, 35*, 44–51. (p. 291)

Lewontin, R. (1976). Race and intelligence. In N. J. Block & G. Dworkin (Eds.), *The IQ controversy: Critical readings*. New York: Pantheon. (p. 356)

Lewontin, R. (1982). *Human diversity*. New York: Scientific American Library. (pp. 33, 357)

Libet, B. (1985). Unconscious cerebral initiative and the role of conscious will in voluntary action. *Behavioral and Brain Sciences, 12*, 181–187. (p. 208)

Licata, A., Taylor, S., Berman, M., & Cranston, J. (1993). Effects of cocaine on human aggression. *Pharmacology Biochemistry and Behavior, 45*, 549–552. (p. 233)

Lichtman, S. W., Pisarska, K., Berman, E. R., Pestone, M., Dowling, H., Offenbacher, E., Weisel, H., Heshka, S., Matthews, D. E., & Heymsfield, S. B. (1992). Discrepancy between self-reported and actual caloric intake and exercise in obese subjects. *New England Journal of Medicine, 327*, 1893–1898. (p. 542)

Lifton, R. J. (1986). *The Nazi doctors*. New York: Basic Books. (p. 231)

Light, K. C., Koepke, J. P., Obrist, P. A., & Willis, P. W., Jr. (1983). Psychological stress induces sodium and fluid retention in men at high risk for hypertension. *Science, 220*, 429–431. (p. 523)

Linder, D. (1982). Social trap analogs: The tragedy of the commons in the laboratory. In V. J. Derlega & J. Grzelak (Eds.), *Cooperative and helping behavior: Theories and research*. New York: Academic Press. (p. 579)

Lindsay, D. S. (1995). Psychotherapy and memories of childhood sexual abuse. Invited address at the American Psychological Association convention. (p. 300)

Lindskold, S. (1978). Trust development, the GRIT proposal, and the effects of conciliatory acts on conflict and cooperation. *Psychological Bulletin, 85*, 772–793. (p. 589)

Lindskold, S. (1986). GRIT: Reducing distrust through carefully introduced conciliation. In S. Worchel & W. G. Austin (Eds.), *Psychology of intergroup relations* (2nd ed.). Chicago: Nelson-Hall. (p. 589)

Lindskold, S., & Han, G. (1988). GRIT as a foundation for integrative bargaining. *Personality and Social Psychology Bulletin, 14,* 335–345. (p. 589)

Lindskold, S., Han, G., & Betz, B. (1986). Repeated persuasion in interpersonal conflict. *Journal of Personality and Social Psychology, 51,* 1183–1188. (p. 589)

Lindskold, S., Walters, P. S., & Koutsourais, H. (1983). Cooperators, competitors, and response to GRIT. *Journal of Conflict Resolution, 27,* 521–532. (p. 589)

Linn, M. C., & Hyde, J. S. (1991). Trends in cognitive and psychosocial gender differences. In R. M. Lerner, A. C. Petersen, & J. Brooks-Gunn (Eds.), *The encyclopedia of adolescence.* New York: Garland Publishing. (p. 358)

Linville, P. W., Fischer, G. W., & Fischhoff, B. (1992). AIDS risk perceptions and decision biases. In J. B. Pryor & G. D. Reeder (Eds.), *The social psychology of HIV infection.* Hillsdale, NJ: Erlbaum. (p. 314)

Lippman, J. (1992, October 25). Global village is characterized by a television in every home. *Grand Rapids [Mich.] Press* (*Los Angeles Times Syndicate*), p. F9. (p. 574)

Lipsey, M. W., & Wilson, D. B. (1993). The efficacy of psychological, educational, and behavioral treatment: Confirmation from meta-analyses. *American Psychologist, 48,* 1181–1209. (pp. 350, 504)

Livingstone, M., & Hubel, D. (1988). Segregation of form, color, movement, and depth: Anatomy, physiology, and perception. *Science, 240,* 740–749. (p. 160)

Locke, E. A., & Latham, G. P. (1990). Work motivation and satisfaction: Light at the end of the tunnel. *Psychological Science, 1,* 240–246. (p. 388)

Loehlin, J. C., & Nichols, R. C. (1976). *Heredity, environment, and personality.* Austin: University of Texas Press. (pp. 108, 353)

Loewenstein, G., & Furstenberg, F. (1991). Is teenage sexual behavior rational? *Journal of Applied Social Psychology, 21,* 957–986. (p. 257)

Loftus, E. (1995, March/April). Remembering dangerously. *Skeptical Inquirer,* pp. 20–29. (pp. 300, 428)

Loftus, E., & Ketcham, K. (1994). *The myth of repressed memory.* New York: St. Martin's Press. (pp. 283, 284, 297, 301)

Loftus, E. F. (1979). The malleability of human memory. *American Scientist, 67,* 313–320. (p. 295)

Loftus, E. F. (1980). *Memory: Surprising new insights into how we remember and why we forget.* Reading, MA: Addison-Wesley. (p. 223)

Loftus, E. F. (1993). The reality of repressed memories. *American Psychologist, 48,* 518–537. (p. 301)

Loftus, E. F., & Kaufman, L. (1992). Why do traumatic experiences sometimes produce good memory (flashbulbs) and sometimes no memory (repression)? In E. Winograd & U. Neisser (Eds.), *Affect and accuracy in recall: Studies of "flashbulb" memories.* New York: Cambridge University Press. (p. 83)

Loftus, E. F., & Loftus, G. R. (1980). On the permanence of stored information in the human brain. *American Psychologist, 35,* 409–420. (p. 283)

Loftus, E. F., & Palmer, J. C. (1973). Reconstruction of automobile destruction: An example of the interaction between language and memory. *Journal of Verbal Learning and Verbal Behavior, 13,* 585–589. (p. 295)

Loftus, E. F., & Pickrell, J. (1995). The formation of false memories. *Psychiatric Annals, 25,* 720–725. (p. 296)

Loftus, E. F., Coan, J., & Pickrell, J. E. (1996). Manufacturing false memories using bits of reality. In L. Reder (Ed.), *Implicit memory and metacognition.* Mahway, NJ: Erlbaum. (p. 300)

Loftus, E. F., Levidow, B., & Duensing, S. (1992). Who remembers best? Individual differences in memory for events that occurred in a science museum. *Applied Cognitive Psychology, 6,* 93–107. (pp. 295, 298)

Loftus, E. F., Milo, E. M., & Paddock, J. R. (1995). The accidental executioner: Why psychotherapy must be informed by science. *The Counseling Psychologist, 23,* 300–309. (p. 300)

Logothetis, N. K., & Schall, J. D. (1989). Neuronal correlates of subjective visual perception. *Science, 245,* 761–763. (p. 159)

Logue, M. B., Sher, K. J., Frensch, P. A. (1992). Purported characteristics of adult children of alcoholics: A possible "Barnum effect." *Professional Psychology: Research and Practice, 23,* 226–232. (p. 449)

London, P. (1970). The rescuers: Motivational hypotheses about Christians who saved Jews from the Nazis. In J. Macaulay & L. Berkowitz (Eds.), *Altruism and helping behavior.* New York: Academic Press. (p. 266)

Long, B. C., & van Stavel, R. (1995). Effects of exercise training on anxiety: A meta-analysis. *Journal of Applied Sport Psychology, 7,* 167-189. (p. 530)

LoPiccolo, J. L., & Stock, W. E. (1986). Treatment of sexual dysfunction. *Journal of Consulting and Clinical Psychology, 54,* 158–167. (p. 378)

Lord, C. G., Lepper, M. R., & Preston, E. (1984). Considering the opposite: A corrective strategy for social judgment. *Journal of Personality and Social Psychology, 47,* 1231–1247. (p. 315)

Lord, C. G., Ross, L., & Lepper, M. (1979). Biased assimilation and attitude polarization: The effects of prior theories on subsequently considered evidence. *Journal of Personality and Social Psychology, 37,* 2098–2109. (p. 315)

Lorenz, K. (1937). The companion in the bird's world. *Auk, 54,* 245–273. (p. 96)

Lourenco, O., & Machado, A. (1996). In defense of Piaget's theory: A reply to 10 common criticisms. *Psychological Review, 103,* 143–164. (p. 94)

Lovaas, O. I. (1987). Behavioral treatment and normal educational and intellectual functioning in young autistic children. *Journal of Consulting and Clinical Psychology, 55,* 3–9. (p. 495)

Lozoff, B. (1989). Nutrition and behavior. *American Psychologist, 44,* 231–236. (p. 539)

Lu, Z.-L., Williamson, S. J., & Kaufman, L. (1992). Behavioral lifetime of human auditory sensory memory predicted by physiological measures. *Science, 258,* 1668–1670. (p. 281)

Lubart, T. I. (1990). Creativity and cross-cultural variation. *International Journal of Psychology, 25,* 39–59. (p. 351)

Lubinski, D., & Benbow, C. P. (1992). Gender differences in abilities and preferences among the gifted: Implications for the math-science pipeline. *Current Directions in Psychological Science, 1,* 61–66. (pp. 357–358)

Luchins, A. S. (1946). Classroom experiments on mental set. *American Journal of Psychology, 59,* 295–298. (pp. 309–310)

Ludwig, A. M. (1995). *The price of greatness: Resolving the creativity and madness controversy.* New York: Guilford Press. (pp. 380, 470)

Lukoff, D., Lu, F., & Turner, R. (1992). Toward a more culturally sensitive DSM-IV: Psychoreligious and psychospiritual problems. *Journal of Nervous and Mental Disease, 180,* 673–682. (p. 507)

Lull, J. (Ed.). (1988). *World families watch television.* Newbury Park, CA: Sage. (p. 574)

Lummis, M., & Stevenson, H. W. (1990). Gender differences in beliefs and achievement: A cross-cultural study. *Developmental Psychology, 26,* 254–263. (p. 357)

Lumsden, C. J., & Wilson, E. O. (1983). *Promethean fire: Reflections on the origin of mind.* Cambridge, MA: Harvard University Press. (p. 404)

Luria, A. M. (1968). In L. Solotaroff (Trans.), *The mind of a mnemonist.* New York: Basic Books. (p. 270)

Lykken, D. T. (1982, September). Fearlessness: Its carefree charm and deadly risks. *Psychology Today,* pp. 20–28. (p. 405)

Lykken, D. T. (1983, April). Polygraph prejudice. *APA Monitor,* p. 4. (p. 397)

Lykken, D. T. (1992). Science, lies, and controversy: An epitaph for the polygraph. Invited address upon receipt of the Senior Career award for Distinguished Contribution to Psychology in the Public Interest, American Psychological Association convention. (p. 397)

Lykken, D. T. (1995). *The antisocial personalities.* Hillsdale, NJ: Erlbaum. (p. 482)

Lykken, D. T., & Tellegen, A. (1993) Is human mating adventitious or the result of lawful choice? A twin study of mate selection. *Journal of Personality and Social Psychology, 65,* 56–68. (p. 137)

Lykken, D., & Tellegen, A. (1996). Happiness is a stochastic phenomenon. *Psychological Science, 7,* 186-189. (p. 412)

Lykken, D. T., McGue, M., Tellegen, A., & Bouchard, Jr., T. J. (1992). Emergenesis: Genetic traits that may not run in families. *American Psychologist, 47,* 1565–1577. (p. 110)

Lyman, D. R. (1996). Early identification of chronic offenders: Who is the fledgling psychopath? *Psychological Bulletin, 120,* 209–234. (p. 483)

Lynch, G., & Staubli, U. (1991). Possible contributions of long-term potentiation to the encoding and organization of memory. *Brain Research Reviews, 16,* 204–206. (p. 285)

Lyness, S. A. (1993). Predictors of differences between Type A and B individuals in heart rate and blood pressure reactivity. *Psychological Bulletin, 114,* 266–295. (p. 522)

Lynn, M. (1988). The effects of alcohol consumption on restaurant tipping. *Personality and Social Psychology Bulletin, 14,* 87–91. (p. 231)

Lynn, R. (1987). Japan: Land of the rising IQ. A reply to Flynn. *Bulletin of the British Psychological Society, 40,* 464–468. (p. 356)

Lynn, R. (1991, Fall/Winter). The evolution of racial differences in intelligence. *The Mankind Quarterly, 32,* 99–145. (p. 356)

Lynn, S. J., & Rhue, J. W. (1986). The fantasy-prone person: Hypnosis, imagination, and creativity. *Journal of Personality and Social Psychology, 51,* 404–408. (p. 222)

Lynn, S. J., Rhue, J. W., & Weekes, J. R. (1990). Hypnotic involuntariness: A social cognitive analysis. *Psychological Review, 97,* 169–184. (p. 226)

Lyon, D., & Greenberg, J. (1991). Evidence of codependency in women with an alcoholic parent: Helping out Mr. Wrong. *Journal of Personality and Social Psychology, 61,* 435–439. (p. 230)

Lyons, M. J., & others (1995). Differential heritability of adult and juvenile antisocial traits. *Archives of General Psychiatry, 52,* 906–915. (p. 482)

Lytton, H., & Romney, D. M. (1991). Parents' differential socialization of boys and girls: A meta-analysis. *Psychological Bulletin, 109,* 267–296. (p. 106)

Lyubomirsky, S., & Nolen-Hoeksema, S. (1994). The effects of depressive rumination on thinking and problem solving. Unpublished manuscript, Stanford University. (p. 496)

Maas, J. B. (1998). *The sleep advantage: Preparing your mind for peak performance.* New York: Villard. (pp. 214, 215, 217)

Macaskill, P., Pierce, J. P., Simpson, J. M., & Lyle, D. M. (1992). Mass media-led antismoking campaign can remove the education gap in quitting behavior. *American Journal of Public Health, 82,* 96–98. (p. 538)

Maccoby, E. (1980). *Social development: Psychological growth and the parent-child relationship.* New York: Harcourt Brace Jovanovich. (p. 103)

Maccoby, E. E. (1990). Gender and relationships: A developmental account. *American Psychologist, 45,* 513–520. (p. 123)

Maccoby. E. E. (1995). Divorce and custody: The rights, needs, and obligations of mothers, fathers, and children. *Nebraska Symposium on Motivation, 42,* 135–172. (p. 566)

MacDonald, N. (1960). Living with schizophrenia. *Canadian Medical Association Journal, 82,* 218–221. (p. 476)

MacDonald, T. K., Zanna, M. P., & Fong, G. T. (1995). Decision making in altered states: Effects of alcohol on attitudes toward drinking and driving. *Journal of Personality and Social Psychology, 68,* 973–985. (p. 231)

MacDonald, T. K., Zanna, M. P., & Fong, G. T. (1996). Why common sense goes out the window: The effects of alcohol on intentions to use condoms. *Personality and Social Psychology Bulletin, 22,* 763–775. (p. 231)

MacDonald, T. K., Zanna, M. P., & Fong, G. T. (in press). Alcohol and intentions to engage in risky health-related behaviors: Experimental evidence for a causal relationship. In J. Adair & F. Craik

(Eds.), *Advances in psychological science, Vol. 2: Developmental, personal, and social aspects.* East Sussex, UK: Psychology Press. (p. 231)

MacFarlane, A. (1978, February). What a baby knows. *Human Nature,* pp. 74–81. (p. 81)

Macfarlane, J. W. (1964). Perspectives on personality consistency and change from the guidance study. *Vita Humana, 7,* 115–126. (pp. 116, 143)

MacKay, D. G. (1983). Prescriptive grammar and the pronoun problem. In B. Thorne, C. Kramarae, & N. Henley (Eds.), *Language, gender and society.* Rowley, MA: Newbury House. (p. 329)

MacKinnon, D. W., & Hall, W. B. (1972). Intelligence and creativity. *Proceedings, XVIIth International Congress of Applied Psychology* (Vol. 2, pp. 1883–1888). Brussels: Editest. (p. 351)

MacLeod, C., & Campbell, L. (1992). Memory accessibility and probability judgments: An experimental evaluation of the availability heuristic. *Journal of Personality and Social Psychology, 63,* 890–902. (p. 311)

Maehr, M. L., & Braskamp, L. A. (1986). *The motivation factor: A theory of personal investment.* Lexington, MA: Lexington Books. (p. 388)

Magno, J. B. (1989, April 15). The Hospice concept of care: Facing the 1990's. Keynote address to the Association for Death Education and Counseling. (p. 142)

Magnusson, D. (1990). Personality research—challenges for the future. *European Journal of Personality, 4,* 1–17. (p. 482)

Magnusson, D., & Bergman, L. R. (1990). A pattern approach to the study of pathways from childhood to adulthood. In L. N. Robins & M. Rutter (Eds.), *Straight and devious pathways from childhood to adulthood.* Cambridge: Cambridge University Press. (p. 144)

Mahoney, M. J. (1989). Sport psychology. In I. S. Cohen (Ed.), *G. Stanley Hall Lecture Series* (Vol. 9). Washington, DC: American Psychological Association. (p. 79)

Mahowald, M. W., & Ettinger, M. G. (1990). Things that go bump in the night: The parsomias revisted. *Journal of Clinical Neurophysiology, 7,* 119-143. (p. 212)

Maier, S. F., Watkins, L. R., & Fleshner, M. (1994). Psychoneuroimmunology: The interface between behavior, brain, and immunity. *American Psychologist, 49,* 1004–1017. (pp. 523–524)

Major, B., Carrington, P. I., & Carnevale, P. J. D. (1984). Physical attractiveness and self-esteem: Attribution for praise from an other-sex evaluator. *Personality and Social Psychology Bulletin, 10,* 43–50. (p. 581)

Major, B., Cozzarelli, C., Sciacchitano, A. M., Cooper, M. L., Testa, M., & Mueller, P. M. (1990). Perceived social support, self-efficacy, and adjustment to abortion. *Journal of Personality and Social Psychology, 59,* 452–463. (p. 519)

Major, B., Schmidlin, A. M., & Williams, L. (1990). Gender patterns in social touch: The impact of setting and age. *Journal of Personality and Social Psychology, 58,* 634–643. (p. 389)

Malamuth, N. M. (1996). Sexually explicit media, gender differences, and evolutionary theory. *Journal of Communication, 46,* 8–31. (pp. 378, 576)

Malamuth, N. M., & Check, J. V. P. (1981). The effects of media exposure on acceptance of violence against women: A field experiment. *Journal of Research in Personality, 15,* 436–446. (p. 577)

Malamuth, N. M., Linz, D., Heavey, C. L., Barnes, G., & Acker, M. (1995). Using the confluence model of sexual aggression to predict men's conflict with women: A 10-year follow-up study. *Journal of Personality and Social Psychology, 69,* 353–369. (p. 578)

Malamuth, N. M., Sockloskie, R. J., Koss, M. P., & Tanaka, J. S. (1991). Characteristics of aggressors against women: Testing a model using a national sample of college students. *Journal of Consulting and Clinical Psychology, 59,* 670–681. (p. 578)

Malan, D. H. (1978). "The case of the secretary with the violent father." In H. Davanloo (Ed.), *Basic principles and techniques in short-term dynamic psychotherapy.* New York: Spectrum. (p. 490)

Malinosky-Rummell, R., & Hansen, D. J. (1993). Long-term consequences of childhood physical abuse. *Psychological bulletin, 114,* 68–79. (p. 98)

Malkiel, B. (1985). *A random walk down Wall Street* (4th ed.). New York: Norton. (p. 313)

Malkiel, B. G. (1989). Is the stock market efficient? *Science, 243,* 1313–1318. (p. 25)

Malkiel, B. G. (1995, June). Returns from investing in equity mutual funds 1971 to 1991. *Journal of Finance,* pp. 549–572. (pp. 25, 313)

Malloy, E. A., & others (1994, June 7). Report of the Commission on Substance Abuse at Colleges and Universities, reported by *Associated Press.* (p. 231)

Malmquist, C. P. (1986). Children who witness parental murder: Post-traumatic aspects. *Journal of the American Academy of Child Psychiatry, 25,* 320–325. (p. 428)

Malone, T. W., & Lepper, M. R. (1986). Making learning fun: A taxonomy of intrinsic motivations for learning. In R. E. Snow & M. J. Farr (Eds.), *Aptitude, learning, and instruction: III. Cognitive and affective process analysis.* Hillsdale, NJ: Erlbaum. (p. 387)

Manber, R., Bootzin, R. R., Acebo, C., & Carskadon, M. A. (1996). The effects of regularizing sleep-wake schedules on daytime sleepiness. *Sleep, 19,* 432–441. (p. 217)

Mandel, D. (1983, March 13). One man's holocaust: Part II. The story of David Mandel's journey through hell as told to David Kagan. *Wonderland Magazine* (Grand Rapids Press), pp. 2–7. (p. 363)

Mandler, J. M., & McDonough, L. (1995). Long-term recall of event sequences in infancy. *Journal of Experimental Child Psychology, 59,* 457–474. (p. 83)

Manning, W. G., Keefer, E. B., Newhouse, J. P., Sloss, E. M., & Wasserman, J. (1989). The taxes of sin: Do smokers and drinkers pay their way? *Journal of the American Medical Association, 261,* 1604–1609. (p. 536)

Mansnerus, L. (1992, October 4). Smoking: Is it a habit or is it genetic? *New York Times Magazine,* Part 2. (p. 537)

Maquet, P., Peters, J-M., Aerts, J., Delfiore, G., Degueldre, C., Luxen, A., & Franck, G. (1996). Functional neuroanatomy of human rapid-eye-movement sleep and dreaming. *Nature, 383,* 163–166. (p. 220)

Marcel, A. (1983). Conscious and unconscious perception: Experiments on visual masking and word recognition. *Cognitive Psychology, 15,* 197–237. (p. 150)

Marino, L. A., Reiss, D., & Gallup, G. G., Jr. (1994). Mirror self-recognition in bottlenose dolphins: Implications for comparative investigations of highly dissimilar species. In S. P. Parker, R. Mitchell, & M. Boccia (Eds.), *Self-awareness in animals and humans: Developmental perspectives.* New York: Cambridge University Press. (p. 103)

Mark, V., & Ervin, F. (1970). *Violence and the brain.* New York: Harper & Row. (p. 57)

Markowitsch, H. J. (1995). Which brain regions are critically involved in the retrieval of old episodic memory? *Brain Research Reviews, 21,* 117–127. (p. 287)

Markus, G. B. (1986). Stability and change in political attitudes: Observe, recall, and "explain." *Political Behavior, 8,* 21-44. (p. 297)

Markus, H., & Kitayama, S. (1991). Culture and the self: Implications for cognition, emotion, and motivation. *Psychological Review, 98,* 224–253. (pp. 328, 401, 406, 442)

Markus, H., & Nurius, P. (1986). Possible selves. *American Psychologist, 41,* 954–969. (p. 438)

Marlatt, G. A. (1991). Substance abuse: Etiology, prevention, and treatment issues. Master lecture, American Psychological Association convention. (pp. 231, 257)

Marr, D. (1982). *Vision.* San Francisco: W. H. Freeman. (p. 159)

Marschark, M., Richman, C. L., Yuille, J. C., & Hunt, R. R. (1987). The role of imagery in memory: On shared and distinctive information. *Psychological Bulletin, 102,* 28–41. (p. 276)

Marsh, H. W., & Parker, J. W. (1984). Determinants of student self-concept: Is it better to be a relatively large fish in a small pond even if you don't learn to swim as well? *Journal of Personality and Social Psychology, 47,* 213–231. (p. 441)

Marshall, J. C., & Halligan, P. W. (1988). Blindsight and insight in visuo-spatial neglect. *Nature, 336,* 766–767. (p. 160)

Marshall, W. L. (1989). Pornography and sex offenders. In D. Zillmann & J. Bryant (Eds.), *Pornography: Research advances and policy considerations.* Hillsdale, NJ: Erlbaum. (p. 577)

Marteau, T. M. (1989). Framing of information: Its influences upon decisions of doctors and patients. *British Journal of Social Psychology, 28,* 89–94. (p. 314)

Martin, A., Wiggs, C. L., Ungerleider, L. G., & Haxby, J. V. (1996). Neural correlates of category-specific knowledge. *Nature, 379,* 649–652. (p. 54)

Martin, R. J., White, B. D., & Hulsey, M. G. (1991). The regulation of body weight. *American Scientist, 79,* 528–541. (p. 370)

Martin, S. J., Kelly, I. W., & Saklofske, D. H. (1992). Suicide and lunar cycles: A critical review over 28 years. *Psychological Reports, 71,* 787–795. (p. 481)

Martinez, J. L., Jr., Schulteis, G., & Weinberger, S. B. (1991). How to increase and decrease the strength of memory traces. In J. L. Martinez, Jr., & R. P. Kesner (Eds.), *Learning and memory,* 2nd ed. San Diego, CA: Academic Press. (p. 285)

Martyna, W. (1978). What does "he" mean? Use of generic masculine. *Journal of Communication, 28*(1), 131–138. (p. 329)

Maslach, C. (1982). *Burnout: The cost of caring.* Englewood Cliffs, NJ: Prentice-Hall. (p. 520)

Maslow, A. H. (1970). *Motivation and personality* (2nd ed.). New York: Harper & Row. (pp. 366, 436–437)

Maslow, A. H. (1971). *The farther reaches of human nature.* New York: Viking Press. (p. 366)

Masters, M. S., & Sanders, B. (1993). Is the gender difference in mental rotation disappearing? *Behavior Genetics, 23,* 337–341. (p. 358)

Masters, W. H., & Johnson, V. E. (1966). *Human sexual response.* Boston: Little, Brown. (p. 375)

Matarazzo, J. D. (1983). Computerized psychological testing. *Science, 221,* 323. (p. 434)

Matsumoto, D. (1994). *People: Psychology from a cultural perspective.* Pacific Grove, CA: Brooks/Cole. (p. 328)

Matsumoto, D., & Ekman, P. (1989). American-Japanese cultural differences in intensity ratings of facial expressions of emotion. *Motivation and Emotion, 13,* 143-157. (p. 401)

Matsumoto, D., Kudoh, T., Scherer, K., & Wallbott, H. (1988). Antecedents of and reactions to emotions in the United States and Japan. *Journal of Cross-Cultural Psychology, 19,* 267–286. (pp. 401, 403)

Matt, G. E., Vazquez, C., & Campbell, W. K. (1992). Mood-congruent recall of affectively toned stimuli: A meta-analytic review. *Clinical Psychology Review, 12,* 227–255. (p. 290)

Matthews, D. A. (1997). Religion and spirituality in primary care. *Mind/Body Medicine, 2,* 9–19. (p. 534)

Matthews, D. A., & Larson, D. B. (1997). *The faith factor: An annotated bibliography of clinical research on spiritual subjects* (Vols. I–IV). Rockville, MD: National Institute for Healthcare Research and Georgetown University Press. (p. 534)

Matthews, K. A. (1992). Myths and realities of the menopause. *Psychosomatic Medicine, 54,* 1–9. (p. 128)

Maunsell, J. H. (1995). The brain's visual world: Representation of visual targets in cerebral cortex. *Science, 270,* 764–769. (p. 159)

Maurer, D., & Maurer, C. (1988). *The world of the newborn.* New York: Basic Books. (p. 81)

May, C., & Hasher, L. (1997). Circadian arousal and cognition. *Journal of Experimental Psychology: Human Perception and Performance,* in press. (p. 211)

May, C. P., Hasher, L., & Stoltzfus, E. R. (1993). Optimal time of day and the magnitude of age differences in memory. *Psychological Science, 4,* 326–330. (p. 133)

May, P. A. (1986). Alcohol and drug misuse prevention programs for American Indians: Needs and opportunities. *Journal of Studies on Alcohol, 47,* 187–195. (p. 456)

May, R. (1982). The problem of evil: An open letter to Carl Rogers. *Journal of Humanistic Psychology, 22,* 10–21. (p. 444)

Mayer, J. D., & Salovey, P. (1993). The intelligence of emotional intelligence. *Intelligence, 17,* 433–442. (p. 340)

Mayer, J. D., & Salovey, P. (1995). Emotional intelligence and the construction and regulation of feelings. *Applied and Preventive Psychology, 4,* 197–208. (p. 340)

Mayer, J. D., & Salovey, P. (1997). What is emotional intelligence? In P. Salovey & D. Sluyter (Eds.), *Emotional development, emotional literacy, and emotional intelligence*. New York: Basic Books. (p. 340)

Mayne, T. J., Norcross, J. C., & Sayette, M. A. (1994). Admission requirements, acceptance rates, and financial assistance in clinical psychology programs. *American Psychologist, 49,* 806–811. (p. 496)

McAlister, A., Perry, C., Killen, J., Slinkard, L. A., & Maccoby, N. (1980). Pilot study of smoking, alcohol and drug abuse prevention. *American Journal of Public Health, 70,* 719–721. (pp. 538–539)

McBeath, M. K., Shaffer, D. M., & Kaiser, M. K. (1995). How baseball outfielders determine where to run to catch fly balls. *Science, 268,* 569–572. (p. 190)

McBurney, D. H. (1996). *How to think like a psychologist: Critical thinking in psychology*. Upper Saddle River, NJ: Prentice-Hall. (p. 62)

McBurney, D. H., & Collings, V. B. (1984). *Introduction to sensation and perception* (2nd ed.). Englewood Cliffs, NJ: Prentice-Hall. (p. 194)

McBurney, D. H., & Gent, J. F. (1979). On the nature of taste qualities. *Psychological Bulletin, 86,* 151–167. (p. 174)

McCall, R. B. (1994). Academic underachievers. *Current Directions in Psychological Science, 3,* 15–19. (p. 384)

McCall, R. B., & Carriger, M. S. (1993). A meta-analysis of infant habituation and recognition memory performance as predictors of later IQ. *Child Development, 64,* 57–79. (p. 348)

McCall, R. B., Evahn, C., & Kratzer, L. (1992). High school underachievers. Newbury Park, CA: Sage. (p. 357)

McCann, I. L., & Holmes, D. S. (1984). Influence of aerobic exercise on depression. *Journal of Personality and Social Psychology, 46,* 1142–1147. (pp. 529–530)

McCarron, D. A., Morris, C. D., Henry, H. J., & Stanton, J. L. (1984). Blood pressure and nutrient intake in the United States. *Science, 225,* 1392–1398. (p. 539)

McCarthy, P. (1986, July). Scent: The tie that binds? *Psychology Today,* pp. 6, 10. (p. 174)

McCartney, K., Harris, M. J., & Bernieri, F. (1990). Growing up and growing apart: A developmental meta-analysis of twin studies. *Psychological Bulletin, 107,* 226–237. (p. 110)

McCarty, D., Argeriou, M., Huebner, R. B., & Lubran, B. (1991). Alcoholism, drug abuse, and the homeless. *American Psychologist, 46,* 1139–1148. (p. 508)

McCaul, K. D., & Malott, J. M. (1984). Distraction and coping with pain. *Psychological Bulletin, 95,* 516–533. (p. 173)

McCauley, C. R., & Segal, M. E. (1987). Social psychology of terrorist groups. In C. Hendrick (Ed.), *Group processes and intergroup relations*. Beverly Hills, CA: Sage. (p. 562)

McClelland, J. L., & Rumelhart, D. E. (1988). *Explorations in parallel distributed processing: A handbook of models, programs, and exercises*. Cambridge, MA: MIT Press. (p. 317)

McClelland, J. L., McNaughton, B. L., & O'Reilly, R. C. (1995). Why there are complementary learning systems in the hippocampus and neocortex: Insights from the successes and failures of connectionist models of learning and memory. *Psychological Review, 102,* 419–457. (p. 287)

McCloskey, M., Wible, C. G., & Cohen, N. J. (1988). Is there a special flashbulb-memory mechanism? *Journal of Experimental Psychology: General, 117,* 171–181. (p. 270)

McConkey, K. M. (1995). Hypnosis, memory, and the ethics of uncertainty. *Australian Psychologist, 30,* 1–10. (p. 223)

McConnell, A., & Fazio, R. H. (1996). Women as men and people: Effects of gender-marked language. *Personality and Social Psychology Bulletin, 22,* 1004–1013. (p. 329)

McConnell, R. A. (1991). National Academy of Sciences opinion on parapsychology. *Journal of the American Society for Psychical Research, 85,* 333–365. (p. 201)

McCord, J. (1978). A thirty-year follow-up on treatment effects. *American Psychologist, 33,* 284–289. (pp. 502–503)

McCord, J. (1979). Following up on Cambridge-Somerville. *American Psychologist, 34,* 727. (pp. 502–503)

McCormick, C. M., & Witelson, S. F. (1991). A cognitive profile of homosexual men compared to heterosexual men and women. *Psychoneuroendocrinology, 16,* 459–473. (p. 382)

McCrae, R. R., & Costa, P. T., Jr. (1982). Self-concept and the stability of personality: Cross-sectional comparisons of self-reports and ratings. *Journal of Personality and Social Psychology, 43,* 1282–1292. (p. 144)

McCrae, R. R., & Costa, P. T., Jr. (1986). Clinical assessment can benefit from recent advances in personality psychology. *American Psychologist, 41,* 1001–1003. (p. 432)

McCrae, R. R., & Costa, P. T., Jr. (1990). *Personality in adulthood*. New York: Guilford. (pp. 136–137)

McCrae, R. R., & Costa, P. T., Jr. (1994). The stability of personality: Observations and evaluations. *Current Directions in Psychological Science, 3,* 173–175. (pp. 144, 234)

McDonough, L., & Mandler, J. M. (1994). Very long-term recall in infants: Infantile amnesia reconsidered. *Memory, 2,* 339–352. (p. 83)

McFarland, C., & Ross, M. (1987). The relation between current impressions and memories of self and dating partners. *Psychological Bulletin, 13,* 228–238. (p. 297)

McGarry-Roberts, P. A., Stelmack, R. M., & Campbell, K. B. (1992). Intelligence, reaction time, and event-related potentials. *Intelligence, 16,* 289–313. (p. 341)

McGaugh, J. L. (1994). Quoted by B. Bower, Stress hormones hike emotional memories. *Science News, 146,* p. 262. (p. 285)

McGrath, J., Welham, J., & Pemberton, M. (1995). Month of birth, hemisphere of birth and schizophrenia. *British Journal of Psychiatry, 167,* 783–785. (p. 478)

McGrath, M. J., & Cohen, D. G. (1978). REM sleep facilitation of adaptive waking behavior: A review of the literature. *Psychological Bulletin, 85,* 24–57. (p. 219)

McGregor, D. (1960). *The human side of enterprise*. New York: McGraw-Hill. (p. 389)

McGue, M., & Lykken, D. T. (1992). Genetic influence on risk of divorce. *Psychological Science, 3*, 368–373. (p. 108)

McGue, M., Bouchard, T. J., Jr., Iacono, W. G., & Lykken, D. T. (1993). Behavioral genetics of cognitive ability: A life-span perspective. In R. Plomin & G. E. McClearn (Eds.), *Nature, nurture and psychology.* Washington, DC: American Psychological Association. (p. 353)

McGue, M., Pickens, R. W., & Svikis, D. S. (1992). Sex and age effects on the inheritance of alcohol problems: A twin study. *Journal of Abnormal Psychology, 202*, 3–17. (p. 237)

McGuire, W. J. (1986). The myth of massive media impact: Savings and salvagings. In G. Comstock (Ed.), *Public communication and behavior.* Orlando, FL: Academic Press. (p. 575)

McHugh, P. R. (1995a). Witches, multiple personalities, and other psychiatric artifacts. *Nature Medicine, 1*(2), 110–114. (p. 467)

McHugh, P. R. (1995b). Resolved: Multiple personality disorder is an individually and socially created artifact. *Journal of the American Academy of Child and Adolescent Psychiatry, 34*, 957–959. (p. 467)

McHugh, P. R., & Moran, T. H. (1978). Accuracy of the regulation of caloric ingestion in the rhesus monkey. *American Journal of Physiology, 235*, R29–34. (p. 369)

McKinlay, J. B., McKinlay, S. M., & Brambilla, D. J. (1987a). Health status and utilization behavior associated with menopause. *American Journal of Epidemiology, 125*, 110–121. (p. 128)

McKinlay, J. B., McKinlay, S. M., & Brambilla, D. (1987b). The relative contributions of endocrine changes and social circumstances to depression in mid-aged women. *Journal of Health and Social Behavior, 28*, 345–363. (p. 128)

McLennan, W. (1995). *Australian social trends 1995.* Australian Bureau of Statistics. (p. 130)

McMillen, D. L., Smith, S. M., & Wells-Parker, E. (1989). The effects of alcohol, expectancy, and sensation seeking on driving risk taking. *Addictive Behaviors, 14*, 477–483. (p. 232)

McNally, R. J. (1987). Preparedness and phobias: A review. *Psychological Bulletin, 101*, 283–303. (p. 404)

Meador, B. D., & Rogers, C. R. (1984). Person-centered therapy. In R. J. Corsini (Ed.), *Current psychotherapies* (3rd ed.). Itasca, IL: Peacock. (p. 491)

Meaney, M. J., Aitken, D. H., Van Berkel, C., Bhatnagar, S., & Sapolsky, R. M. (1988). Effect of neonatal handling on age-related impairments associated with the hippocampus. *Science, 239*, 766–768. (p. 84)

Mediascope (1995). *National television violence study: Executive Summary, 1994–1995.* Studio City, CA: Mediascope, Inc. (p. 575)

Medical Institute for Sexual Health (1994, April). Condoms ineffective against human papilloma virus. *Sexual Health Update, 2.* (p. 126)

Mednick, S. A., Huttunen, M. O., & Machon, R. A. (1994). Prenatal influenza infections and adult schizophrenia. *Schizophrenia Bulletin, 20*, 263–267. (p. 478)

Meichenbaum, D. (1977). *Cognitive-behavior modification: An integrative approach.* New York: Plenum Press. (p. 499)

Meichenbaum, D. (1985). *Stress inoculation training.* New York: Pergamon. (p. 499)

Meier, R. P. (1991). Language acquisition by deaf children. *American Scientist, 79*, 60–70. (pp. 168, 324)

Meltzoff, A. N. (1988a). Infant imitation and memory: Nine-month-olds in immediate and deferred tests. *Child Development, 59*, 217–225. (p. 265)

Meltzoff, A. N. (1988b). Infant imitation after a 1–week delay: Long-term memory for novel acts and multiple stimuli. *Developmental Psychology, 24*, 470–476. (p. 265)

Meltzoff, A. N. (1988c). Imitation of televised models by infants. *Child Development, 59*, 1221–1229. (p. 265)

Meltzoff, A. N., & Borton, R. W. (1979). Intermodal matching by human neonates. *Nature, 282*, 403-404. (p. 89)

Melzack, R. (1984). The myth of painless childbirth. *Pain, 19*, 321–337. (p. 173)

Melzack, R. (1990, February). The tragedy of needless pain. *Scientific American,* pp. 27–33. (p. 230)

Melzack, R. (1992, April). Phantom limbs. *Scientific American,* pp. 120–126. (p. 171)

Melzack, R. (1993). Distinguished contribution series. *Canadian Journal of Experimental Psychology, 47*, 615-629. (p. 171)

Melzack, R., & Wall, P. D. (1965). Pain mechanisms: A new theory. *Science, 150*, 971–979. (p. 172)

Melzack, R., & Wall, P. D. (1983). *The challenge of pain.* New York: Basic Books. (p. 172)

Mendolia, M., & Kleck, R. E. (1993). Effects of talking about a stressful event on arousal: Does what we talk about make a difference? *Journal of Personality and Social Psychology, 64*, 283–292. (p. 535)

Mento, A. J., Steel, R. P., & Karren, R. J. (1987). A meta-analytic study of the effects of goal setting on task performance: 1966–1984. *Organizational Behavior and Human Decision Processes, 39*, 52–83. (p. 388)

Merikle, P. M., & Daneman, M. (1996). Memory for unconsciously perceived events: Evidence from anesthetized patients. *Consciousness and Cognition, 5*, 525–541. (p. 239)

Merskey, H. (1992). The manufacture of personalities: The production of multiple personality disorder. *British Journal of Psychiatry, 160*, 327–340. (p. 467)

Merton, R. K. (1938; reprinted 1970). *Science, technology and society in seventeenth-century England.* New York: Fertig. (p. 13)

Merton, R. K., & Kitt, A. S. (1950). Contributions to the theory of reference group behavior. In R. K. Merton & P. F. Lazarsfeld (Eds.), *Continuities in social research: Studies in the scope and method of the American soldier.* Glencoe, IL: Free Press. (p. 411)

Mesquita, B., & Frijda, N. H. (1992). Cultural variations in emotions: A review. *Psychological Bulletin, 112*, 179–204. (p. 401)

Messer, W. S., & Griggs, R. A. (1989). Student belief and involvement in the paranormal and performance in introductory psychology. *Teaching of Psychology, 16*, 187–191. (p. 203)

Meston, C. M., Trapnell, P. D., & Gorzalka, B. B. (1996). Ethnic and gender differences in sexuality: Variations in sexual behavior between Asian and non-Asian university students. *Archives of Sexual Behavior, 25,* 33–72. (p. 125)

Metalsky, G. I., Joiner, T. E., Jr., , Hardin, T. S., & Abramson, L. Y. (1993). Depressive reactions to failure in a naturalistic setting: A test of the hopelessness and self-esteem theories of depression. *Journal of Abnormal Psychology, 102,* 101–109. (p. 473)

Metcalfe, J., Funnell, M., Gazzaniga, M. S. (1995). Right-hemisphere memory superiority: Studies of a split-brain patient. *Psychological Science, 6,* 157–164. (p. 66)

Meuwissen, I., & Over, R. (1992). Sexual arousal across phases of the human menstrual cycle. *Archives of Sexual Behavior, 21,* 101–119. (p. 376)

Meyer-Bahlburg, H. F. L. (1995). Psychoneuroendocrinology and sexual pleasure: The aspect of sexual orientation. In P. R. Abramson & S. D. Pinkerton (Eds.), *Sexual nature/sexual culture.* Chicago: University of Chicago Press. (p. 382)

Michaels, J. W., Bloomel, J. M., Brocato, R. M., Linkous, R. A., & Rowe, J. S. (1982). Social facilitation and inhibition in a natural setting. *Replications in Social Psychology, 2,* 21–24. (p. 561)

Michaelson, R. (1993, August). Behavior gets big billing in medical schools today. *The Monitor,* p. 56. (p. 515)

Michel, G. F. (1981). Right-handedness: A consequence of infant supine head-orientation preference? *Science, 212,* 685–687. (p. 68)

Middlebrooks, J. C., & Green, D. M. (1991). Sound localization by human listeners. *Annual Review of Psychology, 42,* 135–159. (p. 167)

Mikulincer, M., Babkoff, H., Caspy, T., & Sing, H. (1989). The effects of 72 hours of sleep loss on psychological variables. *British Journal of Psychology, 80,* 145–162. (p. 214)

Milan, R. J., Jr., & Kilmann, P. R. (1987). Interpersonal factors in premarital contraception. *Journal of Sex Research, 23,* 289–321. (p. 126)

Milgram, S. (1965). Some conditions of obedience and disobedience to authority. *Human Relations, 18,* 57–76. (p. 567)

Milgram, S. (1974). *Obedience to authority.* New York: Harper & Row. (pp. 557–558)

Miller, G. A. (1956). The magical number seven, plus or minus two: Some limits on our capacity for processing information. *Psychological Review, 63,* 81–97. (p. 282)

Miller, G. A. (1962). *Psychology: The science of mental life.* New York: Harper & Row. (p. 421)

Miller, G. A., & Gildea, P. M. (1987, September). How children learn words. *Scientific American,* pp. 94–99. (p. 320)

Miller, J. D., & Pifer, L. (1996). *Science and engineering indicators.* Washington, DC: National Science Foundation. (p. 30)

Miller, K. I., & Monge, P. R. (1986). Participation, satisfaction, and productivity: A meta-analytic review. *Academy of Management Journal, 29,* 727–753. (p. 446)

Miller, N., & Maruyama, G. (1976). Ordinal position and peer popularity. *Journal of Personality and Social Psychology, 33,* 123–131. (p. 385)

Miller, N. E. (1983). Value and ethics of research on animals. Paper presented at the meeting of the American Psychological Association. (p. 35)

Miller, N. E. (1985, February). Rx: biofeedback. *Psychology Today,* pp. 54–59. (p. 531)

Miller, N. E. (1995). Clinical-experimental interactions in the development of neuroscience: A primer for nonspecialists and lessons for young scientists. *American Psychologist, 50,* 901–911. (p. 369)

Miller, N. E., & Brucker, B. S. (1979). A learned visceral response apparently independent of skeletal ones in patients paralyzed by spinal lesions. In N. Birbaumer & H. D. Kimmel (Eds.), *Biofeedback and self-regulation.* Hillsdale, NJ: Erlbaum. (p. 531)

Miller, P. A., Eisenberg, N., Fabes, R. A., & Shell, R. (1996). Relations of moral reasoning and vicarious emotion to young children's prosocial behavior toward peers and adults. *Developmental Psychology, 32,* 210–219. (p. 120)

Miller, P. C., Lefcourt, H. M., Holmes, J. G., Ware, E. E., & Saleh, W. E. (1986). Marital locus of control and marital problem solving. *Journal of Personality and Social Psychology, 51,* 161–169. (p. 446)

Miller, S. D., Blackburn, T., Scholes, G., White, G. L., & Mamalis, N. (1991). Optical differences in multiple personality disorder: A second look. *Journal of Nervous and Mental Disease, 179,* 132–135. (p. 467)

Miller, T. Q., Smith, T. W., Turner, C. W., Guijarro, M. L., & Hallet, A. J. (1996). A meta-analytic review of research on hostility and physical health. *Psychological Bulletin, 119,* 322–348. (p. 522)

Millers, J. G., & Bersoff, D. M. (1995). Development in the context of everyday family relationships: Culture, interpersonal morality and adaptation. In M. Killen and D. Hart (Eds.), *Morality in everyday life: A developmental perspective.* New York: Cambridge University Press. (p. 120)

Mills, M., & Melhuish, E. (1974). Recognition of mother's voice in early infancy. *Nature, 252,* 123–124. (p. 82)

Milner, A. D. (1995). Cerebral correlates of visual awareness. *Neuropsychologia, 33,* 1117–1130. (p. 160)

Mineka, S. (1985). The frightful complexity of the origins of fears. In F. R. Brush & J. B. Overmier (Eds.), *Affect, conditioning and cognition: Essays on the determinants of behavior.* Hillsdale, NJ: Erlbaum. (p. 404)

Mineka, S., & Suomi, S. J. (1978). Social separation in monkeys. *Psychological Bulletin, 85,* 1376–1400. (p. 100)

Mineka, S., & Sutton, S. K. (1992). Cognitive biases and the emotional disorders. *Psychological Science, 3,* 65–69. (pp. 405, 463)

Mineka, S., & Zinbarg, R. (1996). Conditioning and ethological models of anxiety disorders: Stress-in-dynamic-context anxiety models. In D. Hope (ed.), *Perspectives on anxiety, panic, and fear. Nebraska symposium on motivation.* Lincoln, NE: University of Nebraska Press. (pp. 461–464)

Mintz, L. B., & Betz, N. E. (1986). Sex differences in the nature, realism, and correlates of body image. *Sex Roles, 15,* 185–195. (p. 373)

Mirin, S. M., & Weiss, R. D. (1989). Genetic factors in the development of alcoholism. *Psychiatric Annals, 19,* 239–242. (p. 237)

Mischel, W. (1968). *Personality and assessment.* New York: Wiley. (p. 435)

Mischel, W. (1981). Current issues and challenges in personality. In L. T. Benjamin, Jr. (Ed.), *The G. Stanley Hall Lecture Series* (Vol. 1). Washington, DC: American Psychological Association. (p. 449)

Mischel, W. (1984). Convergences and challenges in the search for consistency. *American Psychologist, 39,* 351–364. (p. 435)

Mischel, W., Shoda, Y., & Peake, P. K. (1988). The nature of adolescent competencies predicted by preschool delay of gratification. *Journal of Personality and Social Psychology, 54,* 687–696. (p. 121)

Mischel, W., Shoda, Y., & Rodriguez, M. L. (1989). Delay of gratification in children. *Science, 244,* 933–938. (pp. 121, 257)

Mita, T. H., Dermer, M., & Knight, J. (1977). Reversed facial images and the mere-exposure hypothesis. *Journal of Personality and Social Psychology, 35,* 597-601. (p. 580)

Mitchell, T. R., & Thompson, L. (1994). A theory of temporal adjustments of the evaluation of events: Rosy prospection and rosy retrospection. *Advances in Managerial Cognition and Organizational Information Processing, 5,* 84–114. (p. 277)

MMWR (1995, January 3). Sexual behavior among high school students: United States, 1990. *Morbidity and Mortality Weekly Report, 40,* 885–887. (p. 125)

Monaghan, P. (1992, September 23). Professor of psychology stokes a controversy on the reliability and repression of memory. *Chronicle of Higher Education,* pp. A9–A10. (p. 301)

Monahan, J. (1992). Mental disorder and violent behavior: Perceptions and evidence. *American Psychologist, 47,* 511–521. (p. 459)

Money, J. (1987). Sin, sickness, or status? Homosexual gender identity and psychoneuroendocrinology. *American Psychologist, 42,* 384–399. (pp. 381–382)

Money, J. (1988). *Gay, straight, and in-between.* New York: Oxford University Press. (p. 577)

Money, J., Berlin, F. S., Falck, A., & Stein, M. (1983). *Antiandrogenic and counseling treatment of sex offenders.* Baltimore: Department of Psychiatry and Behavioral Sciences, The Johns Hopkins University School of Medicine. (p. 376)

Moody, R. (1976). *Life after life.* Harrisburg, PA: Stackpole Books. (p. 238)

Mook, D. G. (1983). In defense of external invalidity. *American Psychologist, 38,* 379–387. (p. 32)

Moorcroft, W. (1993). *Sleep, dreaming, and sleep disorders: An introduction* (2nd ed.). Landam, MD: University Press of America. (pp. 211, 214–215)

Moore, D. W. (1993, April). Public polarized on gay issue. *Gallup Poll Monthly,* pp. 30–34. (p. 382)

Moore, T. E. (1988). The case against subliminal manipulation. *Psychology and Marketing, 5,* 297–316. (p. 150)

Moreland, R. L., & Beach, S. R. (1992). Exposure effects in the classroom: The development of affinity among students. *Journal of Experimental Social Psychology, 28,* 255–276. (p. 580)

Moreland, R. L., & Zajonc, R. B. (1982). Exposure effects in person perception: Familiarity, similarity, and attraction. *Journal of Experimental Social Psychology, 18,* 395–415. (p. 580)

Morell, V. (1995). Attacking the causes of "silent" infertility. *Science, 269,* 775–776. (p. 126)

Morell, V. (1995). Zeroing in on how hormones affect the immune system. *Science, 269,* 773–775. (p. 523)

Morelli, G. A., Rogoff, B., Oppenheim, D., & Goldsmith, D. (1992). Cultural variation in infants' sleeping arrangements: Questions of independence. *Developmental Psychology, 26,* 604–613. (p. 105)

Morin, R., & Brossard, M. A. (1997, March 4). Communication breakdown on drugs. *Washington Post,* pp. A1, A6. (p. 125)

Morris, R. L., Dalton, K., Delanoy, D. L., & Watt, C. (1995). Comparison of the sender/no sender condition in the ganzfeld procedure. *Proceedings of the Parapsychological Association 38th Annual Convention,* pp. 244–259. Durham, NC: Parapsychological Association. (p. 204)

Morris. R. L. (1996, September 6). Personal correspondence, citing forthcoming data from Dalton Ph.D thesis. (p. 204)

Morrison, D. C. (1988). Marine mammals join the Navy. *Science,* 242, 1503–1504. (p. 263)

Morrison, D. M. (1985). Adolescent contraceptive behavior: A review. *Psychological Bulletin, 98,* 538–568. (p. 126)

Morton, G. E. (1994). Personal communication. (p. 17)

Moruzzi, G., & Magoun, H. W. (1949). Brain stem reticular formation and activation of the EEG. *Electroencephalography and Clinical Neurophysiology, 1,* 455–473. (p. 55)

Moscovici, S. (1985). Social influence and conformity. In G. Lindzey & E. Aronson (Eds.), *The handbook of social psychology,* 3rd ed. Hillsdale, N.J.: Erlbaum. (p. 564)

Moser, P. W. (1987, May). Are cats smart? Yes, at being cats. *Discover,* pp. 77–88. (p. 158)

Mosher, D. L., & Anderson, R. D. (1986). Macho personality, sexual aggression, and reactions to guided imagery of realistic rape. *Journal of Research in Personality, 20,* 77–94. (p. 231)

Moss, A. J., Allen, K. F., Giovino, G. A., & Mills, S. L. (1992, December 2). Recent trends in adolescent smoking, smoking-update correlates, and expectations about the future. *Advance Data* No. 221 (from Vital and Health Statistics of the Centers for Disease Control and Prevention). (p. 537)

Moss, H. A., & Susman, E. J. (1980). Longitudinal study of personality development. In O. G. Brim, Jr., & J. Kagan (Eds.), *Constancy and change in human development.* Cambridge, MA: Harvard University Press. (p. 144)

Mott, F. L. (1991). Developmental effects of infant care: The mediating role of gender and health. *Journal of Social Issues, 47*(2), 139–158. (p. 100)

Moyer, K. E. (1983). The physiology of motivation: Aggression as a model. In C. J. Scheier & A. M. Rogers (Eds.), *G. Stanley Hall Lecture Series* (Vol. 3). Washington, DC: American Psychological Association. (p. 572)

Muehlenhard, C. L. (1988). Misinterpreted dating behaviors and the risk of date rape. *Journal of Social and Clinical Psychology, 6,* 20–37. (p. 379)

Mukerjee, M. (1997, January). Trends in animal research. *Scientific American,* pp. 86–93. (p. 34)

Muller, J. E., & Verrier, R. L. (1996). Triggering of sudden death—Lessons from an earthquake. *New England Journal of Medicine, 334,* 460–461. (p. 519)

Muller, J. E., Mittleman, M. A., Maclure, M., Sherwood, J. B., & Tofler, G. H. (1996). Triggering myocardial infarction by sexual activity. *Journal of the American Medical Association, 275,* 1405–1409. (p. 375)

Mullin, C. R., & Linz, D. (1995). Desensitization and resensitization to violence against women: Effects of exposure to sexually violent films on judgments of domestic violence victims. *Journal of Personality and Social Psychology, 69,* 449–459. (p. 576)

Murphy, G. E., & Wetzel, R. D. (1990). The lifetime risk of suicide in alcoholism. *Archives of General Psychiatry, 47,* 383–392. (p. 469)

Murphy, S. T., & Zajonc, R. B. (1993). Affect, cognition, and awareness: Affective priming with optimal and suboptimal stimulus exposures. *Journal of Personality and Social Psychology, 64,* 723–739. (p. 150)

Murphy, S. T., Monahan, J. L., & Zajonc, R. B. (1995). Additivity of nonconscious affect: Combined effects of priming and exposure. *Journal of Personality and Social Psychology, 69,* 589–602. (p. 416)

Murphy, T. N. (1982). Pain: Its assessment and management. In R. J. Gatchel, A. Baum, & J. E. Singer (Eds.), *Handbook of psychology and health: Vol. I. Clinical psychology and behavioral medicine: Overlapping disciplines.* Hillsdale, NJ: Erlbaum. (p. 172)

Murray, C., & Herrnstein, R. J. (1994, October 31). Race, genes and I.Q.—An apologia. *New Republic,* pp. 27–37. (p. 356)

Murray, D. M., Johnson, C. A., Luepker, R. V., & Mittelmark, M. B. (1984). The prevention of cigarette smoking in children: A comparison of four strategies. *Journal of Applied Social Psychology, 14,* 274–288. (p. 538)

Murray, D. M., Pirie, P., Luepker, R. V., & Pallonen, U. (1989). Five- and six-year follow-up results from four seventh-grade smoking prevention strategies. *Journal of Behavioral Medicine, 12,* 207–218. (p. 538)

Murray, H. (1938). *Explorations in personality.* New York: Oxford University Press. (p. 384)

Murray, H. A. (1933). The effect of fear upon estimates of the maliciousness of other personalities. *Journal of Social Psychology, 4,* 310–329. (p. 426)

Murray, H. A., & Wheeler, D. R. (1937). A note on the possible clairvoyance of dreams. *Journal of Psychology, 3,* 309–313. (p. 203)

Murray, L., & Trevarthen, C. (1986). The infant's role in mother-infant communications. *Journal of Child Language, 13,* 15–29. (p. 94)

Murray, R., Jones, P., O'Callaghan, E., Takei, N., & Sham, P. (1992). Genes, viruses, and neurodevelopmental schizophrenia. *Journal of Psychiatric Research, 26,* 225–235. (p. 478)

Myers, D. G. (1993). *The pursuit of happiness.* New York: Avon Books. (pp. 407, 412)

Myers, D. G. (1996). *Social psychology,* 5th ed. New York: McGraw-Hill. (p. 440)

Myers, D. G., & Bishop, G. D. (1970). Discussion effects on racial attitudes. *Science, 169,* 78–779. (p. 563)

Myers, D. G., & Diener, E. (1995). Who is happy? *Psychological Science, 6,* 10–19. (p. 412)

Myers, I. B. (1987). *Introduction to type: A description of the theory and applications of the Myers-Briggs Type Indicator.* Palo Alto, CA: Consulting Psychologists Press. (p. 431)

Napolitan, D. A., & Goethals, G. R. (1979). The attribution of friendliness. *Journal of Experimental Social Psychology, 15,* 105–113. (p. 560)

Nash, M. (1987). What, if anything, is regressed about hypnotic age regression? A review of the empirical literature. *Psychological Bulletin, 102,* 42–52. (p. 223)

National Academy of Science. (1984). *Bereavement: Reactions, consequences, and cure.* Washington, DC: National Academy Press. (pp. 523–524)

National Academy of Sciences, Institute of Medicine. (1982). *Marijuana and health.* Washington, DC: National Academic Press. (pp. 235, 515)

National Center for Health Statistics. (1990). *Health, United States, 1989.* Washington, DC: U.S. Department of Health and Human Services. (p. 131)

National Center for Health Statistics. (1991). Family structure and children's health: United States, 1988," *Vital and Health Statistics, Series 10, No. 178,* CHHS Publication No. PHS 91–1506 by Deborah A. Dawson. (pp. 103, 379)

National Center for Health Statistics. (1992, May). *Health United States 1991.* Hyattsville, MD: Department of Health and Human Services Pub. No. (PHS) 92–1232, Table 27. (p. 128)

National Council on the Aging. (1976). *The myth and reality of aging in America.* Washington, DC. (p. 131)

National Institute of Mental Health. (1982). *Television and behavior: Ten years of scientific progress and implications for the eighties.* Washington, DC: U.S. Government Printing Office. (p. 575)

National Institute on Aging. (1993). *In search of the secrets of aging.* Washington, DC: Superintendent of Documents. (p. 129)

National Institute on Drug Abuse. (1991). National Household survey on drug abuse: Population estimates 1991. Rockville, MD: Alcohol, Drug Abuse, and mental Health Administration. (p. 236)

National Institute on Drug Abuse. (1992). National Household survey on drug abuse: Population estimates 1991 (February 27, 1992 replacement pages). Rockville, MD: Alcohol, Drug Abuse, and mental Health Administration. (p. 233)

National Research Council. (1987). *Risking the future: Adolescent sexuality, pregnancy, and childbearing.* Washington, DC: National Academy Press. (p. 126)

National Research Council. (1990). *Human factors research needs for an aging population.* Washington, DC: National Academy Press. (pp. 130–131)

National Safety Council. (1991). *Accident facts.* Chicago: National Safety Council. (p. 312)

Naylor, T. H. (1990). Redefining corporate motivation, Swedish style. *Christian Century, 107,* 566–570. (p. 389)

NCTV News. (1987, July-August). More research links harmful effects to non-violent porn. National Coalition on Television Violence, p. 12. (p. 577)

Needles, D. J., & Abramson, L. Y. (1990). Positive life events, attributional style, and hopefulness: Testing a model of recovery from depression. *Journal of Abnormal Psychology, 99,* 156–165. (p. 473)

Neeleman, J., & Persaud, R. (1995). Why do psychiatrists neglect religion? *British Journal of Medical Psychology, 68,* 169-178. (p. 507)

Neese, R. M. (1991, November/December). What good is feeling bad? The evolutionary benefits of psychic pain. *The Sciences,* pp. 30–37. (pp. 171, 251)

Neisser, U. (1979). The control of information pickup in selective looking. In A. D. Pick (Ed.), *Perception and its development: A tribute to Eleanor J. Gibson.* Hillsdale, NJ: Erlbaum. (p. 182)

Neisser, U. (1981). John Dean's memory: A case study. *Cognition, 9,* 1–22. (pp. 271, 289)

Neisser, U. (1982). Memorists. In U. Neisser (Ed.), *Memory observed: Remembering in natural contexts.* San Francisco: Freeman. (p. 270)

Neisser, U. (1982). Snapshots or benchmarks? In U. Neiser (ed.), *Memory observed: Remembering in natural settings.* San Francisco, CA: W. H. Freeman. (p. 296)

Neisser, U., & Harsch, N. (1992). Phantom flashbulbs: False recollections of hearing the news about *Challenger.* In E. Winograd & U. Neisser (Eds.), *Affect and accuracy in recall: Studies of "flashbulb" memories.* New York: Cambridge University Press. (p. 270)

Neisser, U., Boodoo, G., Bouchard, T. J., Jr., Boykin, A. W., Brody, N., Ceci, S. J., Halpern, D. F., Loehlin, J. C., Perloff, R., Sternberg, R. J., & Urbina, S. (1996). Intelligence: Knowns and unknowns. *American Psychologist, 51,* 77–101. (pp. 348, 356)

Neisser, U., Winograd, E., & Weldon, M. S. (1991). Remembering the earthquake: "What I experienced" vs. "How I heard the news." Paper presented to the Psychonomic Society convention. (p. 285)

Neitz, J., Geist, T., & Jacobs, G. H. (1989). Color vision in the dog. *Visual Neuroscience, 3,* 119–125. (p. 162)

Nelson, K. (1973). Structure and strategy in learning to talk. *Monographs of the Society for Research in Child Development, 38*(1 & 2, Serial No. 149). (p. 321)

Nelson, K. (1993). The psychological and social origins of autobiographical memory. *Psychological Science, 4,* 7–13. (p. 82)

Nelson, N. (1988). *A meta-analysis of the life-event/health paradigm: The influence of social support.* Philadelphia: Temple University Ph.D. dissertation. (p. 533)

Neubauer, P., & Neubauer, A. (1990). *Nature's thumbprint: The new genetics of personality.* Reading, MA: Addison-Wesley. (p. 109)

Neugarten, B. L. (1980, February). Must everything be a midlife crisis? *Prime Time,* pp. 45–48. (p. 143)

Neugarten, B. L., Wood, V., Kraines, R. J., & Loomis, B. (1963). Women's attitudes toward the menopause. *Vita Humana, 6, 140–151.* (p. 128)

Nevin, J. A. (1988). Behavioral momentum and the partial reinforcement effect. *Psychological Bulletin, 103,* 44–56. (p. 257)

Newcomb, M. D., & Bentler, P. M. (1988). Impact of adolescent drug use and social support on problems of young adults: A longitudinal study. *Journal of Abnormal Psychology, 97,* 64–75. (p. 235)

Newcomb, M. D., & Harlow, L. L. (1986). Life events and substance use among adolescents: Mediating effects of perceived loss of control and meaninglessness in life. *Journal of Personality and Social Psychology, 51,* 564–577. (p. 237)

Newell, A. (1988, March 9). Quoted by D. L. Wheeler, From years of work in psychology and computer science, scientists build theories of thinking and learning. *Chronicle of Higher Education,* pp. A4, A6. (p. 17)

Newman, D. L., Caspi, A., Moffit, T. E., & Silva, P. A. (1997). Antecedents of adult interpersonal functioning: Effects of individual differences in age-3 temperament. *Developmental Psychology, 33,* 206–217. (p. 97)

Newman, L. S., & Baumeister, R. F. (1996). Toward an explanation of the UFO abduction phenomenon: Hypnotic elaboration, extraterrestrial sadomasochism, and spurious memories. *Psychological Inquiry, 7,* 99–126. (p. 224)

Newman, L. S., & Ruble, D. N. (1988). Stability and change in self-understanding: The early elementary school years. *Early Child Development and Care, 40,* 77–99. (p. 103)

Newport, E. L. (1990). Maturational constraints on language learning. *Cognitive Science, 14,* 11–28. (p. 324)

Nezu, A. M., Nezu, C. M., & Blissett, S. E. (1988). Sense of humor as a moderator of the relation between stressful events and psychological distress: A prospective analysis. *Journal of Personality and Social Psychology, 54,* 520–525. (p. 532)

NFFRE (1996). Family facts. *Family Matters, 1*(1), 8. Published by National Foundation for Family Research and Education, Calgary, AB T2P 3H5. (p. 469)

Ng, S. H. (1990). Androcentric coding of *man* and *his* in memory by language users. *Journal of Experimental Social Psychology, 26,* 455–464. (p. 329)

Niccols, G. A. (1994). Fetal alcohol syndrome: Implications for psychologists. *Clinical Psychology Review, 14,* 91–111. (p. 80)

NICHD (1996, April 20). Infant child care and attachment security: Results of the NICHD study of early child care. NICHD Early Child Care Research Network Symposium, International Conference on Infant Studies, Providence. (p. 101)

Nickell, J. (1996, May/June). A study of fantasy proneness in the thirteen cases of alleged encounters in John Mack's *Abduction. Skeptical Inquirer,* pp. 18–20, 54. (p. 224)

Nickerson, R. S., & Adams, M. J. (1979). Long-term memory for a common object. *Cognitive Psychology, 11,* 287–307. (p. 280)

Nicol, S. E., & Gottesman, I. I. (1983). Clues to the genetics and neurobiology of schizophrenia. *American Scientist, 71,* 398–404. (p. 479)

Nicolaus, L. K., Cassel, J. F., Carlson, R. B., & Gustavson, C. R. (1983). Taste-aversion conditioning of crows to control predation on eggs. *Science, 220,* 212–214. (p. 251)

Niemi, R. G., Mueller, J., & Smith, T. W. (1989). *Trends in public opinion: A compendium of survey data.* New York: Greenwood Press. (pp. 409, 537, 566, 568)

Nigro, G. (1984). Cited by U. Neisser, The role of invariant structures in the control of movement. In M. Frese & J. Sabini (Eds.), *Goal directed behavior: The concept of action in psychology.* Hillsdale, NJ: Erlbaum. (p. 330)

Nisbett, R., & Ross, L. (1991). *The person and the situation.* New York: McGraw-Hill. (p. 389)

Nisbett, R. E. (1993). Violence and U.S. regional culture. *American Psychologist, 48,* 441–449. (p. 573)

Nisbett, R. E., & Borgida, E. (1975). Attribution and the psychology of prediction. *Journal of Personality and Social Psychology, 32,* 932–943. (p. 316)

Nisbett, R. E., & Ross, L. (1980). *Human inference: Strategies and shortcomings of social judgment.* Englewood Cliffs, NJ: Prentice-Hall. (p. 311)

Nishizawa, S. (1996). The religiousness and subjective well-being of Japanese students. Paper presented at the XXVI International Congress of Psychology. (p. 201)

Noble, E. P. (1993). The D2 dopamine receptor gene: A review of association studies in alcoholism. *Behavior Genetics, 23,* 119–129. (p. 237)

Noel, J. G., Forsyth, D. R., & Kelley, K. N. (1987). Improving the performance of failing students by overcoming their self-serving attributional biases. *Basic and Applied Social Psychology, 8,* 151–162. (p. 447)

Nolen-Hoeksema, S. (1990). *Sex differences in depression.* Stanford, CA: Stanford University Press. (p. 472)

Nolen-Hoeksema, S., & Morrow, J. (1991). A prospective study of depression and post-traumatic stress symptoms following a natural disaster: The 1989 Loma Prieta earthquake. *Journal of Personality and Social Psychology, 61,* 115–121. (p. 473)

NORC (National Opinion Research Center) (1985, October/November). Images of the world. *Public Opinion,* p. 38. (p. 443, 566)

Norman, D. A. (1988). *The psychology of everyday things.* New York: Basic Books. (p. 199)

Norris, P. A. (1986). On the status of biofeedback and clinical practice. *American Psychologist, 41,* 1009–1010. (p. 531)

Norton, K. L., Olds, T. S., Olive, S., & Dank, S. (1996). Ken and Barbie at life size. *Sex Roles, 34,* 287–294. (p. 372)

Notarius, C., & Markman, H. (1993). *We can work it out.* New York: Putnam. (p. 138)

Nowak, R. (1994). Nicotine scrutinized as FDA seeks to regulate cigarettes. *Science, 263,* 1555–1556. (p. 537)

Nuttin, J. M., Jr. (1987). Affective consequences of mere ownership: The name letter effect in twelve European languages. *European Journal of Social Psychology, 17,* 381–402. (p. 580)

Oakhill, J., Garnham, A., & Johnson-Laird, P. N. (1990). Belief bias effects in syllogistic reasoning. In D. J. Gilhooly, M. T. G. Keane, R. H. Logie, & G. Erdos (Eds.), *Lines of thinking* (Vol. 1). Chichester, England: Wiley. (p. 315)

Oakhill, J. V., Johnson-Laird, P. N., & Garnham, A. (1989). Believability and syllogistic reasoning. *Cognition, 31,* 117–140. (p. 315)

O'Connor, P., & Brown, G. W. (1984). Supportive relationships: Fact or fancy? *Journal of Social and Personal Relationships, 1,* 159–175. (p. 506)

Oetting, E. R., & Beauvais, F. (1987). Peer cluster theory, socialization characteristics, and adolescent drug use: A path analysis. *Journal of Counseling Psychology, 34,* 205–213. (pp. 120, 238)

Oettingen, G., & Seligman, M. E. P. (1990). Pessimism and behavioural signs of depression in East versus West Berlin. *European Journal of Social Psychology, 20,* 207–220. (p. 446)

Offer, D., Ostrov, E., Howard, K. I., & Atkinson, R. (1988). *The teenage world: Adolescents' self-image in ten countries.* New York: Plenum. (p. 124)

Ogloff, J. R. P., Roberts, C. F., & Roesch, R. (1993). The insanity defense: Legal standards and clinical assessment. *Applied and Preventive Psychology, 2,* 163–178. (p. 457)

Ohman, A. (1986). Face the beast and fear the face: Animal and social fears as prototypes for evolutionary analyses of emotion. *Psychophysiology, 23,* 123–145. (p. 464)

Olds, J. (1958). Self-stimulation of the brain. *Science, 127,* 315–324. (p. 57)

Olds, J. (1975). Mapping the mind onto the brain. In F. G. Worden, J. P. Swazey, & G. Adelman (Eds.), *The neurosciences: Paths of discovery.* Cambridge, MA: MIT Press. (p. 57)

Olds, J., & Milner, P. (1954). Positive reinforcement produced by electrical stimulation of the septal area and other regions of rat brain. *Journal of Comparative and Physiological Psychology, 47,* 419–427. (p. 57)

O'Leary, A. (1990). Stress, emotion, and human immune function. *Psychological Bulletin, 108,* 363–382. (p. 525)

Olin, S. S., & Mednick, S. A. (1996). Risk factors of psychosis: Identifying vulnerable populations premorbidly. *Schizophrenia Bulletin, 22,* 223–240. (p. 480)

Oliner, S. P., & Oliner, P. M. (1988). *The altruistic personality: Rescuers of Jews in Nazi Europe.* New York: Free Press. (p. 266)

Oliver, M. B., & Hyde, J. S. (1993). Gender differences in sexuality: A meta-analysis. *Psychological Bulletin, 114,* 29–51. (p. 378)

Olshansky, S. J., Carnes, B. A., & Cassel, C. K. (1993, April). The aging of the human species. *Scientific American,* pp. 46–52. (pp. 128–130)

Olweus, D., Mattsson, A., Schalling, D., & Low, H. (1988). Circulating testosterone levels and aggression in adolescent males: A causal analysis. *Psychosomatic Medicine, 50,* 261–272. (p. 572)

O'Malley, P. M., & Bachman, J. G. (1983). Self-esteem: Change and stability between ages 13 and 23. *Developmental Psychology, 19,* 257–268. (p. 122)

O'Neill, M. J. (1993). The relationship between privacy, control, and stress responses in office workers. Paper presented to the Human Factors and Ergonomics Society convention. (p. 520)

Opton, E., Jr. (1979, December). A psychologist takes a closer look at the recent landmark Larry P. opinion. *American Psychological Association Monitor,* pp. 1, 4. (p. 333)

Orne, M. T., & Evans, F. J. (1965). Social control in the psychological experiment: Antisocial behavior and hypnosis. *Journal of Personality and Social Psychology, 1,* 189–200. (p. 224)

Ornstein, R. E. (1991). *The evolution of consciousness: Of Darwin, Freud, and cranial fire.* New York: Prentice-Hall. (p. 58)

Osgood, C. E. (1962). *An alternative to war or surrender.* Urbana: University of Illinois Press. (p. 588)

Osgood, C. E. (1980). *GRIT: A strategy for survival in mankind's nuclear age?* Paper presented at the Pugwash Conference on New Directions in Disarmament. (p. 588)

OSS Assessment Staff. (1948). *The assessment of men.* New York: Rinehart. (p. 449)

Ostfeld, A. M., Kasl, S. V., D'Atri, D. A., & Fitzgerald, E. F. (1987). *Stress, crowding, and blood pressure in prison.* Hillsdale, NJ: Erlbaum. (p. 521)

Oxman, T. E., Freeman, D. H., Jr., & Manheimer, E. D. (1995). Lack of social participation or religious strength and comfort as risk factors for death after cardiac surgery in the elderly. *Psychosomatic Medicine, 57,* 5–15. (p. 534)

Padgett, V. R. (1989). Predicting organizational violence: An application of 11 powerful principles of obedience. Paper presented to the American Psychological Association convention. (p. 558)

Padilla, R. V., & Benavides, A. H. (eds.) (1992). *Critical perspectives on bilingual education research.* Tempe, AZ: Bilingual Press. (p. 329)

Paffenbarger, R. S., Jr., Hyde, R. T., Wing, A. L., & Hsieh, C-C. (1986). Physical activity, all-cause mortality, and longevity of college alumni. *New England Journal of Medicine, 314,* 605–612. (p. 530)

Page, S. (1977). Effects of the mental illness label in attempts to obtain accommodation. *Canadian Journal of Behavioral Science, 9,* 84–90. (p. 459)

Paikoff, R. L., & Brooks-Gunn, J. (1991). Do parent-child relationships change during puberty? *Psychological Bulletin, 110,* 47–66. (p. 124)

Paivio, A. (1986). *Mental representations: A dual coding approach.* New York: Oxford University Press. (p. 276)

Palace, E. M. (1995). Modification of dysfunctional patterns of sexual response through autonomic arousal and false physiological feedback. *Journal of Consulting and Clinical Psychology, 63,* 604–615. (p. 415)

Palladino, J. J., & Carducci, B. J. (1983). "Things that go bump in the night": Students' knowledge of sleep and dreams. Paper presented at the meeting of the Southeastern Psychological Association. (p. 210)

Palmer, S., Schreiber, C., & Box, C. (1991). Remembering the earthquake: "Flashbulb" memory for experienced vs. reported events. Paper presented to the Psychonomic Society convention. (p. 285)

Palumbo, S. R. (1978). *Dreaming and memory: A new information-processing model.* New York: Basic Books. (p. 219)

Pandey, J., Sinha, Y., Prakash, A., & Tripathi, R. C. (1982). Right-left political ideologies and attribution of the causes of poverty. *European Journal of Social Psychology, 12,* 327–331. (p. 551)

Panksepp, J. (1982). Toward a general psychobiological theory of emotions. *Behavioral and Brain Sciences, 5,* 407–467. (p. 398)

Parducci, A. (1995). *Happiness, pleasure, and judgment: The contextual theory and its applications.* Hillsdale, NJ: Erlbaum. (p. 410)

Parke, R. D. (1981). *Fathers.* Cambridge, MA: Harvard University Press. (p. 99)

Parker, G., Roy, K., Hadzi, P. D., Pedic, F. (1992). Psychotic (delusional) depression: A meta-analyis of physical treatments. *Journal of Affective Disorders, 24,* 17–24. (p. 510)

Parker, S., Nichter, M., Nichter, M., & Vuckovic, N. (1995). Body image and weight concerns among African American and white adolescent females: Differences that make a difference. *Human Organization, 54,* 103-114. (p. 540)

Parks, R. W., Loewenstein, D. A., Dodrill, K. L., Barker, W. W., Yoshi, F., Chang, J. Y., Emran, A., Apicella, A., Shermata, W. A., & Duara, R. (1988). Cerebral metabolic effects of a verbal fluency test: A PET scan study. *Journal of Clinical and Experimental Neuropsychology, 10,* 565–575. (p. 341)

Parloff, M. B. (1987, February). Psychotherapy: An import from Japan. *Psychology Today,* pp. 74–75. (p. 488)

Passell, P. (1993, March 9). Like a new drug, social programs are put to the test. *New York Times,* pp. C1, C10. (p. 30)

Passons, W. R. (1975). *Gestalt approaches to counseling.* New York: Holt, Rinehart & Winston. (p. 492)

Pate, J. E., Pumariega, A. J., Hester, C., & Garner, D. M. (1992). Cross-cultural patterns in eating disorders: A review. *Journal of the American Academy of Child and Adolescent Psychiatry, 31,* 802–809. (p. 372)

Paton, D. (1992). Disaster research: The Scottish dimension. *The Psychologist: Bulletin of the British Psychological Society, 5,* 535–538. (p. 519)

Patrick, C. J., & Iacono, W. G. (1991). Validity of the control question polygraph test: The problem of sampling bias. *Journal of Applied Psychology, 76,* 229–238. (p. 397)

Patterson, F. (1978, October). Conversations with a gorilla. *National Geographic,* pp. 438–465. (p. 326)

Patterson, G. R. (1995). Some characteristics of a developmental theory of early-onset delinquency. In M. F. Lenzenweger and J. J. Haugaard (Eds.), *Frontiers of developmental psychopathology.* New York: Oxford University Press, 1995. (p. 111)

Patterson, G. R., Chamberlain, P., & Reid, J. B. (1982). A comparative evaluation of parent training procedures. *Behavior Therapy, 13,* 638–650. (pp. 259, 573)

Patterson, G. R., Reid, J. B., & Dishion, T. J. (1992). *Antisocial boys.* Eugene, OR: Castalia. (p. 573)

Patterson, R. (1951). *The riddle of Emily Dickinson.* Boston: Houghton Mifflin. (p. 475)

Patton, W., & Mannison, M. (1995). Sexual coercion in dating situations among university students: Preliminary Australian data. *Australian Journal of Psychology, 47,* 66–72. (p. 576)

Paulos, J. A. (1995). *A mathematician reads the newspaper.* New York: Basic Books. (p. 510)

Pauls, D. L., Morton, L. A., & Egeland, J. A. (1992). Risks of affective illness among first-degree relatives of bipolar I old-order Amish probands. *Archives of General Psychiatry, 49,* 703–708. (p. 471)

Pavlov, I. P. (1927). In G. V. Anrep (Trans.), *Conditioned reflexes.* London: Oxford University Press. (p. 246)

Pawlik, K., & d'Ydewalle, G. (1996). Psychology and the global commons: Perspectives of international psychology. *American Psychologist, 51,* 488–495. (Updated by e-mail, 8 November 1996.) (pp. 8, 130)

Pedersen, N. L., Plomin, R., McClearn, G. E., & Friberg, L. (1988). Neuroticism, extraversion, and related traits in adult twins reared apart and reared together. *Journal of Personality and Social Psychology, 55,* 950–957. (p. 109)

Pekkanen, J. (1982, June). Why do we sleep? *Science, 82,* p. 86. (p. 215)

Pelham, B. W. (1993). On the highly positive thoughts of the highly depressed. In R. F. Baumeister (Ed.), *Self-esteem: The puzzle of low self-regard.* New York: Plenum. (p. 439)

Pendergrast, M. (1996, May). False memory—forget it. *The Psychologist,* p. 200. (pp. 300–301)

Pendick, D. (1994, January/February). The mind of violence. *Brain Work: The Neuroscience Newsletter,* pp. 1–3, 5. (p. 572)

Penfield, W. (1969). Consciousness, memory, and man's conditioned reflexes. In K. Pribram (Ed.), *On the biology of learning.* New York: Harcourt, Brace & World. (p. 283)

Penfield, W. (1975). *The mystery of the mind.* Princeton, NJ: Princeton University Press. (p. 240)

Pennebaker, J. (1990). *Opening up: The healing power of confiding in others.* New York: William Morrow. (pp. 428, 535)

Pennebaker, J. W., & Harber, K. D. (1993). A social stage model of collective coping: The Loma Prieta earthquake and the Persian Gulf war. *Journal of Social Issues, 49,* 125–145. (p. 535)

Pennebaker, J. W., & O'Heeron, R. C. (1984). Confiding in others and illness rate among spouses of suicide and accidental death victims. *Journal of Abnormal Psychology, 93,* 473–476. (p. 535)

Pennebaker, J. W., Barger, S. D., & Tiebout, J. (1989). Disclosure of traumas and health among Holocaust survivors. *Psychosomatic Medicine, 51,* 577–589. (p. 535)

Peplau, L. A. (1982). Research on homosexual couples: An overview. *Journal of Homosexuality, 8(2),* 3–8. (p. 380)

Peplau, L. A., & Gordon, S. L. (1985). Women and men in love: Gender differences in close heterosexual relationships. In V. E. O'Leary, R. K. Unger, & B. S. Wallston (Eds.), *Women, gender, and social psychology.* Hillsdale, NJ: Erlbaum. (p. 20)

Pepperberg, I. M. (1994). Numerical competence in an African gray parrot (*Psittacus erithacus*). *Journal of Comparative Psychology, 108,* 36–44. (p. 325)

Perkins, H. W. (1991). Religious commitment, Yuppie values, and well-being in post-collegiate life. *Review of Religious Research, 32,* 244-251. (p. 412)

Perkins, K. A., Dubbert, P. M., Martin, J. E., Faulstich, M. E., & Harris, J. K. (1986). Cardiovascular reactivity to psychological stress in aerobically trained versus untrained mild hypertensives and normotensives. *Health Psychology, 5,* 407–421. (p. 530)

Perlmutter, M. (1983). Learning and memory through adulthood. In M. W. Riley, B. B. Hess, & K. Bond (Eds.), *Aging in society: Selected reviews of recent research.* Hillsdale, NJ: Erlbaum. (p. 133)

Perls, F. S. (1969). *Ego, hunger and aggression: The beginning of Gestalt therapy.* New York: Random House. (p. 492)

Perls, F. S. (1970). Four lectures. In J. Fagan & I. L. Shepherd, *Gestalt therapy now.* Palo Alto, CA: Science and Behavior Books. (p. 492)

Perrett, D. I., & Emergy N. J. (1994). Understanding the intentions of others from visual signals: Neurophysiological evidence. *Cahiers de Psychology Cognitive/Current Psychology of Cognition, 13,* 683–694. (p. 159)

Perrett, D. I., Harries, M., Misflin, A. J., & Chitty, A. J. (1988). Three stages in the classification of body movements by visual neurons. In H. B. Barlow, C. Blakemore, & M. Weston Smith (Eds.), *Images and understanding.* Cambridge: Cambridge University Press. (p. 159)

Perrett, D. I., Hietanen, J. K., Oram, M. W., & Benson, P. J. (1992). Organization and functions of cells responsive to faces in the temporal cortex. *Philosophical Transactions of the Royal Society of London: Series B, 335,* 23-30. (p. 159)

Perrett, D. I., May, K. A., & Yoshikawa, S. (1994). Facial shape and judgements of female attractiveness. *Nature, 368,* 239–242. (pp. 159, 582)

Persky, V. W., Kempthorne-Rawson, J., & Shekelle, R. B. (1987). Personality and risk of cancer: 20–year follow-up of the Western Electric study. *Psychosomatic Medicine, 49,* 435–449. (p. 524)

Persons, J. B. (1986). The advantages of studying psychological phenomena rather than psychiatric diagnoses. *American Psychologist, 41,* 1252–1260. (p. 459)

Pert, C. (1986). Quoted in J. Hooper & D. Teresi, *The three-pound universe.* New York: Macmillan. (p. 58)

Pert, C. B. (1986, Summer). The wisdom of the receptors: Neuropeptides, the emotions, and bodymind. *Advances* (Institute for the Advancement of Health), *3,* 8–16. (p. 51)

Pert, C. B., & Snyder, S. H. (1973). Opiate receptor: Demonstration in nervous tissue. *Science, 179,* 1011–1014. (p. 46)

Peschel, E. R., & Peschel, R. E. (1987). Medical insights into the castrati in opera. *American Scientist, 75,* 578–583. (p. 376)

Peters, T. J., & Waterman, R. H., Jr. (1982). *In search of excellence: Lessons from America's best-run companies.* New York: Harper & Row. (p. 263)

Petersen, A. C. (1987, September). Those gangly years. *Psychology Today,* pp. 28–34. (p. 118)

Peterson, C., & Barrett, L. C. (1987). Explanatory style and academic performance among university freshmen. *Journal of Personality and Social Psychology, 53,* 603–607. (p. 447)

Peterson, C., Peterson, J., & Skevington, S. (1986). Heated argument and adolescent development. *Journal of Social and Personal Relationships, 3,* 229–240. (p. 118)

Peterson, I. (1996, February 24). Chess champion sinks Deep Blue's figuring. *Science News,* p. 119. (p. 317)

Peterson, L. R., & Peterson, M. J. (1959). Short-term retention of individual verbal items. *Journal of Experimental Psychology, 58,* 193–198. (p. 281)

Peterson, R. (1978). Review of the Rorschach. In O. K. Buros (Ed.), *The eighth mental measurements yearbook* (Vol. I). Highland Park, NJ: Gryphon Press. (p. 426)

Petitto, L. A., & Marentette, P. F. (1991). Babbling in the manual mode: Evidence for the ontogeny of language. *Science, 251,* 1493–1496. (pp. 321, 324)

Peto, R., & others (1994). *Mortality from smoking in developed countries, 1950–2000: Indirect estimates from national vital statistics.* New York: Oxford University Press. (p. 536)

Peto, R., Lopez, A. D., Boreham, J., Thun, M., & Heath, C., Jr. (1992). Mortality from tobacco in developed countries: Indirect estimation from national vital statistics. *Lancet, 339,* 1268–1278. (p. 536)

Petruzzello, S. J., Landers, D. M., Hatfield, B. D., Kubitz, K. A., & Salazar, W. (1991). A meta-analysis on the anxiety-reducing effects of acute and chronic exercise. *Sports Medicine, 11,* 143–182. (p. 530)

Pettegrew, J. W., Keshavan, M. S., & Minshew, N. J. (1993). 31P nuclear magnetic resonance spectroscopy: Neurodevelopment and schizophrenia. *Schizophrenia Bulletin, 19,* 35–53. (p. 478)

Pettigrew, T. F. (1969). Racially separate or together? *Journal of Social Issues, 25,* 43–69. (p. 587)

Pettigrew, T. F. (1997). Generalized intergroup contact effects on prejudice. *Personality and Social Psychology Bulletin, 23,* 173-185. (p. 587)

Pettingale, K. W., Morris, T., Greer, S., & Haybittle, J. L. (1985, March 30). Mental attitudes to cancer: An additional prognostic factor. *Lancet,* p. 750. (p. 525)

Pfeiffer, E. (1977). Sexual behavior in old age. In E. W. Busse & E. Pfeiffer (Eds.), *Behavior and adaptation in late life* (2nd ed.). Boston: Little, Brown. (p. 132)

Phares, V., & Compas, B. E. (1992). The role of fathers in child and adolescent psychopathology: Make room for Daddy. *Psychological Bulletin, 111,* 387–412. (p. 99)

Phillips, D., & Stipek, D. (1993). Early formal schooling: Are we promoting achievement or anxiety? *Applied and Preventive Psychology, 2,* 141–150. (p. 355)

Phillips, D. P. (1982). The impact of fictional television stories on U.S. adult fatalities: New evidence on the effect of the mass media on violence. *American Journal of Sociology, 87,* 1340–1359. (p. 555)

Phillips, D. P. (1985). Natural experiments on the effects of mass media violence on fatal aggression: Strengths and weaknesses of a new approach. In L. Berkowitz (Ed.), *Advances in experimental social psychology* (Vol. 19). Orlando, FL: Academic Press. (p. 555)

Phillips, D. P., Carstensen, L. L., & Paight, D. J. (1989). Effects of mass media news stories on suicide, with new evidence on the role of story content. In D. R. Pfeffer (Ed.), *Suicide among youth: Perspectives on risk and prevention.* Washington, DC: American Psychiatric Press. (p. 555)

Phillips, J. L. (1969). *Origins of intellect: Piaget's theory.* San Francisco: Freeman. (p. 92)

Piaget, J. (1930). *The child's conception of physical causality.* London: Routledge & Kegan Paul. (p. 88)

Piaget, J. (1932). *The moral judgment of the child.* New York: Harcourt, Brace & World. (p. 119)

Piccione, C., Hilgard, E. R., & Zimbardo, P. G. (1989). On the degree of stability of measured hypnotizability over a 25–year period. *Journal of Personality and Social Psychology, 56,* 289–295. (p. 222)

Pickar, D., Labarca, R., Linnoila, M., Roy, A., Hommer, D., Everett, D., & Payl, S. M. (1984). Neuroleptic-induced decrease in plasma homovanillic acid and antipsychotic activity in schizophrenic patients. *Science, 225,* 954–957. (p. 508)

Pike, K. M., & Rodin, J. (1991). Mothers, daughters, and disordered eating. *Journal of Abnormal Psychology, 100,* 198–204. (p. 372)

Pillemer, D. G. (1995). What is remembered about early childhood events? Invited paper presented to the American Psychological Society convention. (p. 83)

Pincus, H. A. (1997) Commentary: Spirituality, religion, and health: Expanding, and using the knowledge base. *Mind/Body Medicine, 2,* 49. (p. 534)

Pinel, J. P. J. (1993). *Biopsychology,* 2nd ed. Boston: Allyn & Bacon. (p. 370)

Pingitore, R., Dugoni, B. L., Tindale, R. S., & Spring, B. (1994). Bias against overweight job applicants in a simulated employment interview. *Journal of Applied Psychology, 79,* 909–917. (p. 541)

Pinker, S. (1990, September-October). Quoted by J. de Cuevas, "No, she holded them loosely." *Harvard Magazine,* pp. 60–67. (p. 319)

Pinker, S. (1995). The language instinct. *The General Psychologist, 31,* 63–65. (pp. 320, 323, 326, 327)

Piotrowski, C., & Keller, J. W. (1989). Psychological testing in outpatient mental health facilities: A national study. *Professional Psychology: Research and Practice, 20,* 423–425. (p. 426)

Pittenger, D. J. (1993). The utility of the Myers-Briggs Type Indicator. *Review of Educational Research, 63,* 467–488. (p. 431)

Pittman, T. S., Davey, M. E., Alafat, K. A., Vetherill, K. V., & Kramer, N. A. (1980). Informational versus controlling verbal rewards. *Personality and Social Psychology Bulletin, 6,* 228–233. (p. 387)

Pleck, J. H., Sonenstein, F. L., & Ku, L. C. (1993). Masculinity ideology: Its impact on adolescent males' heterosexual relationships. *Journal of Social Issues, 49,* 11–29. (p. 379)

Pliner, P. (1982). The effects of mere exposure on liking for edible substances. *Appetite: Journal for Intake Research, 3,* 283–290. (p. 371)

Pliner, P., & Pelchat, M. L. (1991). Neophobia in humans and the special status of foods of animal origin. *Appetite, 16,* 205–218. (p. 371)

Pliner, P., Pelchat, M., & Grabski, M. (1993). Reduction of neophobia in humans by exposure to novel foods. *Appetite, 20,* 111–123. (p. 371)

Plomin, R. (1986). *Development, genetics and psychology.* Hillsdale, NJ: Erlbaum. (p. 353)

Plomin, R. (1990a). The role of inheritance in behavior. *Science, 248,* 183–188. (p. 110)

Plomin, R., & Bergeman, C. S. (1991). The nature of nurture: Genetic influence on "environmental" measures. *Behavioral and Brain Sciences, 14,* 373–427. (p. 113)

Plomin, R., & Daniels, D. (1987). Why are children in the same family so different from one another? *Behavioral and Brain Sciences, 10,* 1–60. (p. 112)

Plomin, R., DeFries, J. C., McClearn, G. E., & Rutter, M. (1997). *Behavioral genetics.* New York: Freeman. (pp. 72, 73, 381, 478, 542)

Plomin, R., McClearn, G. E., Pedersen, N. L., Nesselroade, J. R., & Bergeman, C. S. (1988). Genetic influence on childhood family environment perceived retrospectively from the last half of the life span. *Developmental Psychology, 24,* 37–45. (p. 113)

Plous, S. (1993). Psychological mechanisms in the human use of animals. *Journal of Social Issues, 49*(1), 11–52. (p. 35)

Plous, S. (1993). The nuclear arms race: Prisoner's dilemma or perceptual dilemma? *Journal of Peace Research, 30,* 163–179. (p. 580)

Plous, S. (1996). A comparison of strategies for reducing interval overconfidence in group judgments. *Journal of Applied Psychology.* (p. 313)

Polich, J. Pollock, V. E., & Bloom, F. E. (1994). Meta-analysis of P300 amplitude from males at risk for alcoholism. *Psychological Bulletin, 115,* 55–73. (p. 237)

Polivy, J., & Herman, C. P. (1985). Dieting and bingeing: A causal analysis. *American Psychologist, 40,* 193–201. (p. 545)

Polivy, J., & Herman, C. P. (1987). Diagnosis and treatment of normal eating. *Journal of Personality and Social Psychology, 55,* 635–644. (p. 545)

Pollard, R. (1992). 100 years in psychology and deafness: A centennial retrospective. Invited address to the American Psychological Association convention, Washington, DC. (p. 329)

Polusny, M. A., & Follette, V. M. (1995). Long-term correlates of child sexual abuse: Theory and review of the empirical literature. *Applied & Preventive Psychology, 4,* 143-166. (p. 100)

Pomerleau, O. F., Collins, A. C., Shiffman, S., & Pomerleau, C. S. (1993). Why some people smoke and others do not: New perspectives. *Journal of Consulting and Clinical Psychology, 61,* 723–731. (p. 537)

Pomeroy, W. B. (1972). *Dr. Kinsey and the Institute for Sex Research.* New York: Harper & Row. (p. 374)

Pons, T. P., Garraghty, P. E., Ommaya, A. K., Kaas, J. H., Taub, E., & Mishkin, M. (1991). Massive cortical reorganization after sensory deafferentation in adult macaques. *Science, 252,* 1857–1860. (p. 85)

Poole, D. A., & Lindsay, D. S. (1995). Interviewing preschoolers: Effects of nonsuggestive techniques, parental coaching and leading questions on reports of nonexperienced events. *Journal of Experimental Child Psychology, 60,* 129–154. (p. 296)

Poole, D. A., Lindsay, D. S., Memon, A., & Bull, R. (1995). Psychotherapy and the recovery of memories of childhood sexual abuse: U.S. and British practitioners' opinions, practices, and experiences. *Journal of Consulting and Clinical Psychology, 63,* 426–437. (p. 299)

Poon, L. W. (1987). Myths and truisms: Beyond extant analyses of speed of behavior and age. Address to the Eastern Psychological Association convention. (p. 132)

Pope, H. G., & Yurgelun-Todd, D. (1996). The residual cognitive effects of heavy marijuana use in college students. *Journal of the American Medical Association, 275,* 521–527. (p. 235)

Pope, H. G., Jr., & Hudson, J. I. (1992). Is childhood sexual abuse a risk factor for bulimia nervosa? *American Journal of Psychiatry, 149,* 455–463. (p. 372)

Pope, H. G., Jr., & Hudson, J. I. (1995). Can memories of childhood sexual abuse be repressed? *Psychological Medicine, 25,* 121–126. (p. 428)

Pope, H. G., Mangweth, B., Negrao, A. B., Hudson, J. I., & Cordias, T. A. (1994). Childhood sexual abuse and bulimia nervosa: A comparison of American, Austrian, and Brazilian women. *American Journal of Psychiatry, 151,* 732–737. (p. 372)

Popenoe, D. (1993). The evolution of marriage and the problem of stepfamilies: A biosocial perspective. Paper presented at the National Symposium on Stepfamilies, Pennsylvania State University. (p. 443)

Porac, C., Coren, S., & Duncan, P. (1980). Life-span age trends in laterality. *Journal of Gerontology, 35,* 715–721. (p. 526)

Porter, D., & Neuringer, A. (1984). Music discriminations by pigeons. *Journal of Experimental Psychology: Animal Behavior Processes, 10,* 138–148. (p. 256)

Posner, M. I., & Carr, T. H. (1992). Lexical access and the brain: Anatomical constraints on cognitive models of word recognition. *American Journal of Psychology, 105,* 1–26. (p. 64)

Powell, J. (1989). *Happiness is an inside job.* Valencia, CA: Tabor. (p. 440)

Powell, J. L. (1988). A test of the knew-it-all-along effect in the 1984 presidential and statewide elections. *Journal of Applied Social Psychology, 18,* 760–773. (p. 14)

Powell, K. E., Thompson, P. D., Caspersen, C. J., & Kendrick, J. S. (1987). Physical activity and the incidence of coronary heart disease. *Annual Review of Public Health, 8,* 253–287. (p. 530)

Powell, M. C., & Fazio, R. H. (1984). Attitude accessibility as a function of repeated attitudinal expression. *Personality and Social Psychology Bulletin, 10,* 139–148. (p. 552)

Powell, R. A., & Boer, D. P. (1994). Did Freud mislead patients to confabulate memories of abuse? *Psychological Reports, 74,* 1283–1298. (p. 427)

Powers, D. E. (1986). Relations of test item characteristics to test preparation/test practice effects: A quantitative summary. *Psychological Bulletin, 100,* 67–77. (p. 346)

Pratkanis, A. R. (1992). The cargo-cult science of subliminal persuasion. *Skeptical Inquirer, 16,* 260–272. (p. 149)

Pratkanis, A. R., & Greenwald, A. G. (1988). Recent perspectives on unconscious processing: Still no marketing applications. *Psychology and Marketing, 5,* 337–353. (p. 150)

Pratkanis, A. R., Eskenazi, J., & Greenwald, A. G. (1994). What you expect is what you believe (but not necessarily what you get): A test of the effectiveness of subliminal self-help audiotapes. *Basic and Applied Social Psychology, 15,* 251–276. (p. 150)

Pratto, F. (1996). Sexual politics: The gender gap in the bedroom, the cupboard, and the cabinet. In D. M. Buss & N. M. Malamuth (Eds.), *Sex, power, conflict: Evolutionary and feminist perspectives.* New York: Oxford University Press. (p. 566)

Prentice, D. A., & Miller, D. T. (1993). Pluralistic ignorance and alcohol use on campus: Some consequences of misperceiving the social norm. *Journal of Personality and Social Psychology, 64,* 243–256. (p. 237)

Prescott, C. A., Hewitt, J. K., Truett, K. R., Heath, A. C., Neale, M. C., & Eaves, L. J. (1994, March). Genetic and environmental influences on lifetime alcohol-related problems in a volunteer sample of older twins. *Journal of Studies on Alcohol,* pp. 184–202. (p. 237)

Presson, P. K., & Benassi, V. A. (1996). Locus of control orientation and depressive symptomatology: A meta-analysis. *Journal of Social Behavior and Personality, 11,* 201–212. (p. 446)

Prevention (1995). Prevention index survey by *Prevention* magazine, summarized by Associated Press, March 6 (Grand Rapids [Mich.] *Press,* p. A1). (p. 529)

Prioleau, L., Murdock, M., & Brody, N. (1983). An analysis of psychotherapy versus placebo studies. *The Behavioral and Brain Sciences, 6,* 275–310. (p. 505)

Pritchard, R. M. (1961, June). Stabilized images on the retina. *Scientific American,* pp. 72–78. (p. 153)

Project Match Research Group (1997). Matching alcoholism treatments to client heterogeneity: Project MATCH posttreatment drinking outcomes. *Journal of Studies on Alcohol, 58,* 7–29. (p. 500)

Project on Redefining the Meaning and Purpose of Baccalaureate Degrees. (1985). *Integrity in the college curriculum.* Washington, DC: Association of American Colleges. (p. 30)

Prothrow-Stith, D. (1991). *Deadly consequences.* New York: HarperCollins. (p. 574)

Public Opinion. (1984, August/September). Phears and Phobias, p. 32. (p. 462)

Public Opinion. (1987, May/June). Teen angels (report of University of Michigan survey), p. 32. (p. 116)

Pugh, G. E. (1977). *The biological origin of human values.* New York: Basic Books. (p. 69)

Pulver, A. E., Liang, K-Y., Brown, C. H., Wolyniec, P., McGrath, J., Adler, L., Tam, D., Carpenter, W. T., & Childs, B. (1992). Risk factors in schizophrenia: Season of birth, gender, and familial risk. *British Journal of Psychiatry, 160,* 65–71. (p. 478)

Putnam, F. W. (1991). Recent research on multiple personality disorder. *Psychiatric Clinics of North America, 14,* 489–502. (p. 467)

Putnam, F. W. (1995). Rebuttal of Paul McHugh. *Journal of the American Academy of Child and Adolescent Psychiatry, 34,* 963. (p. 467)

Pyszczynski, T., Hamilton, J. C., Greenberg, J., & Becker, S. E. (1991). Self-awareness and psychological dysfunction. In C. R. Snyder & D. O. Forsyth (Eds.), *Handbook of social and clinical psychology: The health perspective.* New York: Pergamon. (p. 473)

Qualls, P. J., & Sheehan, P. W. (1981). Electromyograph biofeedback as a relaxation technique: A critical appraisal and reassessment. *Psychological Bulletin, 90,* 21–42. (p. 531)

Quasha, S. (1980). *Albert Einstein: An intimate portrait.* New York: Forest. (p. 348)

Quittner, A. L., Smith, L. B., Osberger, M. J., Mitchell, T. V., & Katz, D. B. (1994). The impact of audition on the development of visual attention. *Psychological Science, 5,* 347-353. (p. 169)

Rabin, A. S., Kaslow, N. J., & Rehm, L. P. (1986). Aggregate outcome and follow-up results following self-control therapy for depression. Paper presented at the American Psychological Association convention. (pp. 498–499)

Radecki, T. (1989, February-March). On picking good television and film entertainment. *NCTV News, 10*(1–2), p. 5. (p. 575)

Raglin, J. S. (1992). Anxiety and sport performance. In J. O. Holloszy (ed.), *Exercise and sports sciences reviews,* vol. 20. Baltimore: Williams & Wilkins. (p. 415)

Raine, A. (1993). *The psychopathology of crime: Criminal behavior as a clinical disorder.* San Diego, CA: Academic Press. (p. 571)

Raine, A., Brennan, P., Mednick, B., & Mednick, S. A. (1996). High rates of violence, crime, academic problems, and behavioral problems in males with both early neuromotor deficits and unstable family environments. *Archives of General Psychiatry, 53,* 544–549. (p. 483)

Rajecki, D. W., Bledsoe, S. B., & Rasmussen, J. L. (1991). Successful personal ads: Gender differences and similarities in offers, stipulations, and outcomes. *Basic and Applied Social Psychology, 12,* 457–469. (p. 582)

Ramey, S. L., & Ramey, C. T. (1992). Early educational intervention with disadvantaged children—To what effect? *Applied and Preventive Psychology, 1,* 131–140. (pp. 84, 355)

Rand, C. S. W., & Macgregor, A. M. C. (1990). Morbidly obese patients' perceptions of social discrimination before and after surgery for obesity. *Southern Medical Journal, 83,* 1390–1395. (p. 540)

Randi, J. (1996, January 15). The 2000 Club. Information available on the World Wide Web at http://www.mamboland.com/randi/randi.html (p. 203)

Rapoport, J. L. (1989, March). The biology of obsessions and compulsions. *Scientific American,* pp. 83–89. (pp. 463–464)

Rauch, S. L., & Jenike, M. A. (1993). Neurobiological models of obsessive-compulsive disorder. *Psychomatics, 34,* 20–32. (p. 464)

Ray, O., & Ksir, C. (1990). *Drugs, society, and human behavior* (5th ed.). St. Louis: Times Mirror/Mosby. (p. 233)

Reason, J. (1987). The Chernobyl errors. *Bulletin of the British Psychological Society, 40,* 201–206. (p. 563)

Reason, J., & Mycielska, K. (1982). *Absent-minded? The psychology of mental lapses and everyday errors.* Englewood Cliffs, NJ: Prentice-Hall. (p. 197)

Redburn, B. G., Gensheimer, L. K., & Gist, R. (1993). Disaster aftermath: Social support among resilient rescue workers. Paper presented at the Fourth Biennial Conference on Community Research and Action, Division 27, American Psychological Association, Williamsburg, VA. (p. 461)

Redelmeier, D. A., & Tversky, D. A. (1996). On the belief that arthritis pain is related to the weather. *Proceedings of the National Academy of Sciences, 93,* 2895-2896. (p. 22)

Reed, T. E., & Jensen, A. R. (1992). Conduction velocity in a brain nerve pathway of normal adults correlates with intelligence level. *Intelligence, 16,* 259–272. (p. 341)

Reeve, C. (1995). ABC 20/20, October 6, 1995, and Associated Press report, October 17, 1995 (*Holland Sentinel,* p. A12). (p. 414)

Regeth, R., & Lewis, M. (1995). Sex differences in depression: A meta-analysis. Paper presented at the American Psychological Society convention. (p. 470)

Regier, D. A., Narrow, W. E., Rae, D. S., Manderscheid, R. W., Locke, B. Z., & Goodwin, F. K. (1993). The de facto U.S. mental and addictive disorders service system: Epidemiologic catchment area prospective 1-year prevalence rates of disorders and services. *Archives of General Psychiatry, 50,* 85–94. (p. 501)

Reisenzein, R. (1983). The Schachter theory of emotion: Two decades later. *Psychological Bulletin, 94,* 239–264. (p. 415)

Reiser, M. (1982). *Police psychology.* Los Angeles: LEHI. (p. 202)

Remley, A. (1988, October). From obedience to independence. *Psychology Today,* pp. 56–59. (p. 105)

Renner, M. J. (1992). Curiosity and exploration. In L. R. Squire (ed.), *Encyclopedia of Learning and Memory.* New York: Macmillan. (p. 365)

Renner, M. J., & Renner, C. H. (1993). Expert and novice intuitive judgments about animal behavior. *Bulletin of the Psychonomic Society, 31,* 551-552. (p. 84)

Renner, M. J., & Rosenzweig, M. R. (1987). Enriched and impoverished environments: Effects on brain and behavior. New York: Springer-Verlag. (p. 83)

Rescorla, R. A. (1988). Pavlovian conditioning: It's not what you think it is. *American Psychologist, 43,* 151–160. (p. 250)

Rescorla, R. A., & Wagner, A. R. (1972). A theory of Pavlovian conditioning: Variations in the effectiveness of reinforcement and nonreinforcement. In A. H. Black & W. F. Perokasy (Eds.), *Classical conditioning II: Current theory.* New York: Appleton-Century-Crofts. (p. 250)

Resnick, S. M. (1992). Positron emission tomography in psychiatric illness. *Current Directions in Psychological Science, 1,* 92–98. (pp. 464, 478)

Responsive Community (1996, Fall). Age vs. weight. Page 83 (reported from a *Wall Street Journal* survey). (p. 544)

Ressler, R. K., Burgess, A. W., & Douglas, J. E. (1988). *Sexual homicide patterns.* Boston: Lexington Books. (p. 577)

Retterstol, N. (1993). *Suicide: A European perspective.* New York: Cambridge University Press. (p. 469)

Reveen, P. J. (1987–88). Fantasizing under hypnosis: Some experimental evidence. *The Skeptical Inquirer, 12,* 181–183. (p. 225)

Reynolds, D. K. (1982). *The quiet therapies.* Honolulu: University of Hawaii Press. (p. 178)

Reynolds, D. K. (1986). *Even in summer the ice doesn't melt: Japan's Morita Therapy.* New York: Morrow (Quill paperback). (p. 178)

Rhodes, S. R. (1983). Age-related differences in work attitudes and behavior: A review and conceptual analysis. *Psychological Bulletin, 93,* 328–367. (p. 131)

Rice, B. (1985, September). Performance review: The job nobody likes. *Psychology Today,* pp. 30–36. (p. 551)

Rice, M. E., & Grusec, J. E. (1975). Saying and doing: Effects on observer performance. *Journal of Personality and Social Psychology, 32,* 584–593. (p. 266)

Richardson, J. (1993). The curious case of coins: Remembering the appearance of familiar objects. *The Psychologist: Bulletin of the British Psychological Society, 6,* 360–366. (p. 280)

Richardson, J. T. E., & Zucco, G. M. (1989). Cognition and olfaction: A review. *Psychological Bulletin, 105,* 352–360. (p. 175)

Rieff, P. (1979). *Freud: The mind of a moralist* (3rd ed.). Chicago: University of Chicago Press. (p. 429)

Ring, K. (1980). *Life at death: A scientific investigation of the near-death experience.* New York: Coward, McCann & Geoghegan. (p. 238)

Ring, K. (1992). *The omega project: Near death experiences, UFO encounters, and mind at large.* New York: Morrow. (p. 239)

Roberts, A. H., Kewman, D. G., Mercier, L., & Hovell, M. (1993). The power of nonspecific effects in healing: Implications for psychosocial and biological treatments. *Clinical Psychology Review, 13,* 375-391. (p. 505)

Roberts, L. (1988). Beyond Noah's ark: What do we need to know? *Science, 242,* 1247. (p. 521)

Roberts, M., & Harris, T. G. (1989). Wellness at work. *Psychology Today,* pp. 54–58. (p. 536)

Robins, L., & Regier, D. (Eds.). (1991). *Psychiatric disorders in America.* New York: Free Press. (pp. 454, 483–484)

Robins, L. N., Davis, D. H., & Goodwin, D. W. (1974). Drug use by U.S. Army enlisted men in Vietnam: A follow-up on their return home. *American Journal of Epidemiology, 99,* 235–249. (p. 230)

Robinson, J. L., Kagan, J., Reznick, J. S., & Corley, R. (1992). The heritability of inhibited and uninhibited behavior: A twin study. *Developmental Psychology, 28,* 1030–1037. (p. 94)

Robinson, V. M. (1983). Humor and health. In P. E. McGhee & J. H. Goldstein (Eds.), *Handbook of humor research: Vol. II. Applied studies.* New York: Springer-Verlag. (p. 532)

Rochat, F. (1993). How did they resist authority? Protecting refugees in Le Chambon during World War II. Paper presented at the American Psychological Association convention. (p. 559)

Rock, I., & Palmer, S. (1990, December). The legacy of Gestalt psychology. *Scientific American,* pp. 84–90. (pp. 184–185)

Rock, I., Hall, S., & Davis, J. (1994). Why do ambiguous figures reverse? *Acta Psychologica, 87,* 33-57. (p. 185)

Rodin, J. (1979). *Obesity theory and behavior therapy: An uneasy couple?* Paper presented at the meeting of the Association for the Advancement of Behavior Therapy. (p. 545)

Rodin, J. (1984, December). A sense of control [interview]. *Psychology Today,* pp. 38–45. (p. 371)

Rodin, J. (1985). Insulin levels, hunger and food intake: An example of feedback loops in body weight regulation. *Health Psychology, 4,* 1–18. (p. 545)

Rodin, J. (1986). Aging and health: Effects of the sense of control. *Science, 233,* 1271–1276. (pp. 446, 520–521)

Rodin, J., & Slochower, J. (1976). Externality in the non-obese: Effects of environmental responsiveness on weight. *Journal of Personality and Social Psychology, 33,* 338–344. (p. 371)

Roediger, H. L., III, and McDermott, K. B. (1995). Creating false memories: Remembering words not presented in lists. *Journal of Experimental Psychology: Learning, Memory, and Cognition, 21,* 803-814. (p. 297)

Roediger, H. L., III, Wheeler, M. A., & Rajaram, S. (1993). Remembering, knowing, and reconstructing the past. In D. L. Medin (Ed.), *The psychology of learning and motivation: Advances in research and theory,* vol. 30. Orlando, FL: Academic Press. (p. 295)

Rogers, C. R. (1958). Reinhold Niebuhr's *The self and the dramas of history:* A criticism. *Pastoral Psychology, 9,* 15–17. (p. 440)

Rogers, C. R. (1961). *On becoming a person: A therapist's view of psychotherapy.* Boston: Houghton Mifflin. (p. 490)

Rogers, C. R. (1980). *A way of being.* Boston: Houghton Mifflin. (pp. 437, 490)

Rogers, C. R. (1981, Summer). Notes on Rollo May. *Perspectives, 2*(1), p. 16. (p. 444)

Rogers, S. (1994). Subliminal advertising: Grand scam of the 20th century. Paper presented to the American Academy of Advertising convention. (p. 190)

Rogers, S. M., & Turner, C. F. (1991). Male-male sexual contact in the U.S.A.: Findings from five sample surveys, 1970–1990. *Journal of Sex Research, 28,* 491–519. (p. 379)

Rogerson, P. A. (1994). On the relationship between handedness and longevity. *Social Biology, 40,* 283–287. (p. 527)

Rohner, R. P. (1986). *The warmth dimension: Foundations of parental acceptance-rejection theory.* Newbury Park, CA: Sage. (p. 107)

Rohner, R. P. (1994). Patterns of parenting: The warmth dimension in worldwide perspective. In W. J. Lonner & R. Malpass (Eds.), *Psychology and culture.* Boston: Allyn & Bacon. (p. 104)

Rook, K. S. (1984). Promoting social bonding: Strategies for helping the lonely and socially isolated. *American Psychologist, 39,* 1389–1407. (p. 475)

Rook, K. S. (1987). Social support versus companionship: Effects on life stress, loneliness, and evaluations by others. *Journal of Personality and Social Psychology, 52,* 1132–1147. (p. 533)

Rorty, M., Yager, J., & Rossotto, E. (1994). Childhood sexual, physical, and psychological abuse in bulimia nervosa. *American Journal of Psychiatry, 151,* 1122-1126. (p. 372)

Rosch, E. (1974). Linguistic relativity. In A. Silverstein (Ed.), *Human communication: Theoretical perspectives.* New York: Halsted Press. (p. 329)

Rosch, E. (1978). Principles of categorization. In E. Rosch & B. L. Lloyd (Eds.), *Cognition and categorization.* Hillsdale, NJ: Erlbaum. (p. 306)

Rosen, R. C., & Leiblum, S. R. (1995). Treatment of sexual disorders in the 1990s: An integrated approach. *Journal of Consulting and Clinical Psychology, 63,* 877-890. (p. 378)

Rosenbaum, M. (1986). The repulsion hypothesis: On the nondevelopment of relationships. *Journal of Personality and Social Psychology,* 51, 1156–1166. (p. 583)

Rosenfeld, S. P. (1987, March 29). Insanity defense is riskier now and can turn winners to losers. Associated Press release (*Grand Rapids Press,* p. A17). (p. 457)

Rosenhan, D. L. (1973). On being sane in insane places. *Science, 179,* 250–258. (p. 459)

Rosenthal, R., Hall, J. A., Archer, D., DiMatteo, M. R., & Rogers, P. L. (1979). The PONS test: Measuring sensitivity to nonverbal cues. In S. Weitz (Ed.), *Nonverbal communication* (2nd ed.). New York: Oxford University Press. (pp. 358, 398)

Rosenzweig, M. R. (1984). Experience, memory, and the brain. *American Psychologist, 39,* 365–376. (p. 83)

Rosenzweig, M. R. (1992). Psychological science around the world. *American Psychologist, 47,* 718–722. (p. 8)

Ross, H. (1975, June 19). Mist, murk, and visual perception. *New Scientist,* pp. 658–660. (p. 184)

Ross, L., & Stillinger, C. (1991). Barriers to conflict resolution. *Negotiation Journal, 7,* 389–404. (p. 588)

Ross, L., Greene, D., & House, P. (1977). The false consensus effect: An egocentric bias in social perception and attribution process. *Journal of Experimental Social Psychology, 13,* 279–301. (p. 19)

Ross, M. (1996). Validating memories. In N. L. Stein, P. A. Ornstein, B. Tversky, & C. Brainerd (eds.), *Memory for everyday and emotional events.* Hillsdale, NJ: Erlbaum. (p. 296)

Ross, M., McFarland, C., & Fletcher, G. J. O. (1981). The effect of attitude on the recall of personal histories. *Journal of Personality and Social Psychology, 40,* 627–634. (p. 293)

Rossi, A. S., & Rossi, P. H. (1993). *Of human bonding: Parent-child relations across the life course.* Hawthorne, NY: Aldine de Gruyter. (p. 123)

Rossi, P. H. (1990). The old homeless and the new homelessness in historical perspective. *American Psychologist, 45,* 954-959. (p. 508)

Rossi, P. J. (1968). Adaptation and negative aftereffect to lateral optical displacement in newly hatched chicks. *Science, 160,* 430–432. (p. 196)

Roth, T., Roehrs, T., Zwyghuizen-Doorenbos, A., Stpeanski, E., & Witting, R. (1988). Sleep and memory. In I. Hindmarch & H. Ott (Eds.), *Benzodiazepine receptor ligans, memory and information processing.* New York: Springer-Verlag. (p. 218)

Rothbart, M., Fulero, S., Jensen, C., Howard, J., & Birrell, P. (1978). From individual to group impressions: Availability heuristics in stereotype formation. *Journal of Experimental Social Psychology, 14,* 237–255. (p. 570)

Rothbaum, F., & Xu, X. (1995). The theme of giving back to parents in Chinese and American songs. *Journal of Cross-Cultural Psychology, 26,* 698-713. (p. 442)

Rothblum, E. D. (1990). Women and weight: Fad and fiction. *Journal of Psychology, 124,* 5–24. (p. 544)

Rothstein, W. G. (1980). The significance of occupations in work careers: An empirical and theoretical review. *Journal of Vocational Behavior, 17,* 328–343. (p. 140)

Rotton, J., & Kelly, I. W. (1985). Much ado about the full moon: A meta-analysis of lunar-lunacy research. *Psychological Bulletin, 97,* 286–306. (p. 481)

Rovee-Collier, C. (1993). The capacity for long-term memory in infancy. *Current Directions in Psychological Science, 2,* 130–135. (p. 290)

Roviaro, S., Holmes, D. S., & Holmsten, R. D. (1984). Influence of a cardiac rehabilitation program on the cardiovascular, psychological, and social functioning of cardiac patients. *Journal of Behavioral Medicine, 7,* 61–81. (p. 530)

Rowe, D. C. (1990). As the twig is bent? The myth of child-rearing influences on personality development. *Journal of Counseling and Development, 68,* 606–611. (pp. 110, 125)

Rowe, D. C. (1994). *The limits of family influence.* New York: Guilford. (p. 125)

Rowe, D. C., Vazsonyi, A. T., & Flannery, D. J. (1995). Ethnic and racial similarity in developmental process: A study of academic achievement. *Psychological Science, 6,* 33-38. (p. 107)

Rowe, D. C., Vazsonyi, A. T., & Flannery, D. J. (1994). No more than skin deep: Ethnic and racial similarity in developmental process. *Psychological Review, 101,* in press. (pp. 107, 359)

Roy, M-A., Neale, M. C., Pedersen, N. L., Mathe, A. A., & Kendler, K. S. (1995). A twin study of generalized anxiety disorder and major depression. *Psychological Medicine, 25,* 1037-1049. (p. 464)

Rozin, P. (1976). The selection of food by rats, humans and other animals. In J. Rosenblatt, R. A. Hinde, C. Beer, & E. Shaw (Eds.), *Advances in the study of behavior,* vol. 6. New York: Academic Press. (p. 371)

Rozin, P., Millman, L., & Nemeroff, C. (1986). Operation of the laws of sympathetic magic in disgust and other domains. *Journal of Personality and Social Psychology, 50,* 703–712. (p. 249)

Ruback, R. B., Carr, T. S., & Hopper, C. H. (1986). Perceived control in prison: Its relation to reported crowding, stress, and symptoms. *Journal of Applied Social Psychology, 16,* 375–386. (p. 446)

Rubin, J. Z., Pruitt, D. G., & Kim, S. H. (1994). *Social conflict: Escalation, stalemate, and settlement.* New York: McGraw-Hill. (p. 588)

Rubin, L. B. (1985). *Just friends: The role of friendship in our lives.* New York: Harper & Row. (p. 124)

Rubin, Z. (1970). Measurement of romantic love. *Journal of Personality and Social Psychology, 16,* 265–273. (p. 398)

Rubonis, A. V., & Bickman, L. (1991). Psychological impairment in the wake of disaster: The disaster-psychopathology relationship. *Psychological Bulletin, 109,* 384–399. (p. 519)

Ruchlis, H. (1990). *Clear thinking: A practical introduction.* Buffalo, NY: Prometheus Books. (p. 307)

Ruffin, C. L. (1993). Stress and health—little hassles vs. major life events. *Australian Psychologist, 28,* 201-208. (p. 519)

Rule, B. G., & Ferguson, T. J. (1986). The effects of media violence on attitudes, emotions, and cognitions. *Journal of Social Issues, 42*(3), 29–50. (p. 576)

Rumbaugh, D. M. (1977). *Language learning by a chimpanzee: The Lana project.* New York: Academic Press. (p. 326)

Rumbaugh, D. M. (1994, February 15). Remarks on *Nova: Can chimps talk?* PBS Television. (p. 327)

Rumbaugh, D. M., & Savage-Rumbaugh, S. (1978). Chimpanzee language research: Status and potential. *Behavior Research Methods & Instrumentation, 10,* 119-131. (p. 327)

Rumbaugh, D. M., & Savage-Rumbaugh, S. (1986). Reasoning and language in chimpanzees. In R. J. Hoage & L. Goldman (Eds.), *Animal intelligence.* Washington, DC: Smithsonian Institution Press. (p. 308)

Rumbaugh, D. M., & Savage-Rumbaugh, S. (1994, January/February). Language and apes. *Psychology Teacher Network,* pp. 2–5, 9. (p. 327)

Rumelhart, D. E. (1989). The architecture of mind: A connectionist approach. In M. Posner (Ed.), *Foundations of cognitive science.* Cambridge, MA: MIT Press. (p. 160)

Rushton, J. P. (1975). Generosity in children: Immediate and long-term effects of modeling, preaching, and moral judgment. *Journal of Personality and Social Psychology, 31,* 459–466. (p. 266)

Rushton, J. P. (1990). Race differences, r/K theory, and a reply to Flynn. *The Psychologist: Bulletin of the British Psychological Society, 5,* 195–198. (p. 356)

Rushton, J. P. (1995). *Race, evolution, and behavior: A life history perspective.* New Brunswick, NJ: Transaction Publishers. (p. 356)

Rushton, J. P., & Ankney, C. D. (1996). Brain size and cognitive ability: Correlations with age, sex, social class, and race. *Psychonomic Bulletin & Review, 3,* 21-36. (p. 341)

Rushton, J. P., Fulker, D. W., Neale, M. C., Nias, D. K. B., & Eysenck, H. J. (1986). Altruism and aggression: The heritability of individual differences. *Journal of Personality and Social Psychology, 50,* 1192–1198. (p. 571)

Russell, B. (1930/1985). *The conquest of happiness.* London: Unwin Paperbacks. (p. 411)

Russell, J. A. (1991). Culture and the categorization of emotions. *Psychological Bulletin, 110,* 426–450. (pp. 400–401)

Russell, J. A. (1995). Facial expressions of emotion: What lies beyond minimal universality. *Psychological Bulletin, 118,* 379-391. (p. 400-401)

Russell, J. A., Lewicka, M., & Niit, T. (1989). A cross-cultural study of a circumplex model of affect. *Journal of Personality and Social Psychology, 57,* 848–856. (p. 403)

Russo, N. F. (1992). Abortion, childbearing, and women's well-being. *Professional Psychology: Research and Practice, 23,* 269–280. (p. 519)

Rutter, M. (1979). Maternal deprivation, 1972–1978: New findings, new concepts, new approaches. *Child Development, 50,* 283–305. (p. 98)

Ryan, E. D. (1980). Attribution, intrinsic motivation, and athletics: A replication and extension. In C. H. Nadeau, W. R. Halliwell, K. M. Newell, & G. C. Roberts (Eds.), *Psychology of motor behavior and sport—1979.* Champaign, IL: Human Kinetics Press. (p. 386)

Ryckman, R. M., Robbins, M. A., Kaczor, L. M., & Gold J. A. (1989). Male and female raters' stereotyping of male and female physiques. *Personality and Social Psychology Bulletin, 15,* 244–251. (p. 540)

Rymer, R. (1993). *Genie: An abused child's flight from silence.* New York: HarperCollins. (p. 324)

Rzewnicki, R., & Forgays, D. G. (1987). Recidivism and self-cure of smoking and obesity: An attempt to replicate. *American Psychologist, 42,* 97–100. (p. 546)

Sacks, O. (1985). *The man who mistook his wife for a hat.* New York: Summit Books. (pp. 65, 286)

Sacks, O. (1990). *Seeing voices: A journey into the world of the deaf.* New York: HarperCollins. (p. 329)

Sacks, O. (1995, January 9). Prodigies. *New Yorker,* pp. 44-65. (p. 339)

Sadato, N., & others (1996). Activation of the primary visual cortex by Braille reading in blind subjects. *Nature, 380,* 526-528. (p. 85)

Saffran, J. R., Aslin, R. N., & Newport, E. L. (1996). Statistical learning by 8-month-old infants. *Science, 274,* 1926-1928. (p. 324)

Sagan, C. (1979a). *Broca's brain.* New York: Random House. (pp. 13, 52)

Sagan, C. (1987, February 1). The fine art of baloney detection. *Parade.* (p. 203)

Sagan, C., & Druyan, A. (1992). *Shadows of forgotten ancestors: A search for who we are.* New York: Random House. (p. 326)

Salive, M. E., Guralnik, J. M., & Glynn, R. J. (1993). Left-handedness and mortality. *American Journal of Public Health, 83,* 265–267. (p. 527)

Salovey, P. (1990, January/February). Interview. *American Scientist,* pp. 25–29. (p. 407)

Salovey, P., & Birnbaum, D. (1989). Influence of mood on health-relevant cognitions. *Journal of Personality and Social Psychology, 57,* 539–551. (pp. 291, 546)

Salovey, P., & Mayer, J. D. (1990). Emotional intelligence. *Imagination, cognition, and personality, 9,* 185-211. (p. 340)

Salthouse, T. A. (1992). *Mechanisms of age-cognition relations in adulthood.* Hillsdale, NJ: Erlbaum. (p. 131)

Salthouse, T. A. (1994). The nature of the influence of speed on adult age differences in cognition. *Developmental Psychology, 30,* 240-259. (p. 131)

Samuels, S., & McCabe, G. (1989). Quoted by P. Diaconis & F. Mosteller, Methods for studying coincidences. *Journal of the American Statistical Association, 84,* 853–861. (p. 24)

Sanchez, R. D., Contri, G. B., & Pardo, I. Q. (1996). Spanish psychologists on the labor market. In A. Schorr & S. Saari (Eds.), *Psychology in Europe: Facts, figures, realities.* Gottingen: Hogrefe & Huber. (p. 8)

Sandberg, G. G., Jackson, T. L., & Petretic-Jackson, P. (1985). *Sexual aggression and courtship violence in dating relationships.* Paper presented at the meeting of the Midwestern Psychological Association. (p. 576)

Sanes, J, Donoghue, J., Thangaraj, V., Edelman, R. R., & Warach, S. (1995). Shared neural substrates controlling hand movements in human motor cortex. *Science, 269,* 1775-1777. (p. 60)

Sapadin, L. A. (1988). Friendship and gender: Perspectives of professional men and women. *Journal of Social and Personal Relationships, 5,* 387–403. (p. 124)

Sapirstein, G., & Kirsch, I. (1996). Listening to Prozac, but hearing placebo? A meta analysis of the placebo effect of antidepressant medication. Paper presented to the American Psychological Association convention. (p. 509)

Sapolsky, B. S., & Tabarlet, J. O. (1991). Sex in primetime television: 1979 versus 1989. *Journal of Broadcasting and Electronic Media, 35,* 505–516. (pp. 126, 578)

Sapolsky, R. (1996). Why stress is bad for your brain. *Science, 273,* 749-750. (p. 518)

Sapolsky, R. M., & Finch, C. E. (1991, March/April). On growing old. *The Sciences,* pp. 30–38. (p. 130)

Sartorius, N. R. (1994). Description of WHO's mental health programme. In W. J. Lonner & R. Malpass (Eds.), *Psychology and culture.* Boston: Allyn and Bacon. (pp. 454, 516)

Sato, K. (1987). Distribution of the cost of maintaining common resources. *Journal of Experimental Social Psychology, 23,* 19–31. (p. 579)

Savage-Rumbaugh, E. S., Murphy, J., Sevcik, R. A., Brakke, K. E., Williams, S. L., & Rumbaugh, D. M., with commentary by Bates, E. (1993). Language comprehension in ape and child. *Monographs of the Society for Research in Child Development, 58* (no. 233), 1–254. (p. 327)

Savitsky, J. C., & Lindblom, W. D. (1986). The impact of the guilty but mentally ill verdict on juror decisions: An empirical analysis. *Journal of Applied Social Psychology, 16,* 686–701. (p. 457)

Sax, L. J., Astin, A. W., Korn, W. S., & Mahoney, K. M. (1996). *The American freshman: National norms for Fall 1996.* Los Angeles, CA: Higher Education Research Institute, UCLA. (pp. 16, 127, 236, 378, 409, 566)

Sayre, R. F. (1979). The parents' last lessons. In D. D. Van Tassel (Ed.), *Aging, death, and the completion of being.* Philadelphia: University of Pennsylvania Press. (p. 132)

Scarr, S. (1984, May). What's a parent to do? [Conversation with E. Hall.] *Psychology Today,* pp. 58–63. (p. 355)

Scarr, S. (1986). *Mother care/other care.* New York: Basic Books. (pp. 100, 355)

Scarr, S. (1989). Protecting general intelligence: Constructs and consequences for interventions. In R. J. Linn (Ed.), *Intelligence:*

Measurement, theory, and public policy. Champaign: University of Illinois Press. (pp. 339, 353–354)

Scarr, S. (1990). Back cover comments on J. Dunn & R. Plomin (1990). *Separate lives: Why siblings are so different.* New York: Basic Books. (p. 113)

Scarr, S. (1993, May/June). Quoted by *Psychology Today,* Nature's thumprint: So long, superparents, p. 16. (p. 112)

Scarr, S., & Weinberg, R. A. (1986). The early childhood enterprise: Care and education of the young. *American Psychologist, 41,* 1140–1146. (pp. 100–101)

Scarr, S., Phillips, D., & McCartney, K. (1990). Facts, fantasies and the future of child care in the United States. *Psychological Science, 1,* 26–35. (p. 102)

Scarr, S., Webber, P. L., Weinberg, R. A., & Wittig, M. A. (1981). Personality resemblance among adolescents and their parents in biologically related and adoptive families. *Journal of Personality and Social Psychology, 40,* 885–898. (p. 110)

Schab, F. R. (1990). Odors and the remembrance of things past. *Journal of Experimental Psychology: Learning, Memory, and Cognition, 16,* 648–655. (p. 176)

Schab, F. R. (1991). Odor memory: Taking stock. *Psychological Bulletin, 109,* 242–251. (p. 176)

Schachter, S. (1982). Recidivism and self-cure of smoking and obesity. *American Psychologist, 37,* 436–444. (p. 544)

Schachter, S., & Singer, J. E. (1962). Cognitive, social and physiological determinants of emotional state. *Psychological Review, 69,* 379–399. (p. 414)

Schacter, D. L. (1992). Understanding implicit memory: A cognitive neuroscience approach. *American Psychologist, 47,* 559–569. (p. 286)

Schacter, D. L. (1996). *Searching for memory: The brain, the mind, and the past.* New York: Basic Books. (pp. 132, 286, 287, 297, 405, 428)

Schacter, D. L., Reiman, E., Curran, T., Yun, L. S., Bandy, D., McDermott, K. B., Roediger, H. L., III (1996). Neuroanatomical correlates of veridical and illusory recognition memory: Evidence from positron emission tomography. *Neuron, 17,* 267–274. (p. 297)

Schafran, L. H. (1995, August 26). Rape is still underreported. *New York Times,* p. I19. (p. 576)

Schaie, K. W. (1987). Old dogs can learn new tricks: Intellectual decline and its remediation in later adulthood. Address to the Eastern Psychological Association convention. (p. 135)

Schaie, K. W. (1994). The life course of adult intellectual abilities. *American Psychologist, 49,* 304–313. (p. 134)

Schaie, K. W., & Geiwitz, J. (1982). *Adult development and aging.* Boston: Little, Brown. (p. 134)

Scheerer, M. (1963, April). Problem solving. *Scientific American,* pp. 118–128. (pp. 309–310)

Scheier, M. F., & Carver, C. S. (1992). Effects of optimism on psychological and physical well-being: Theoretical overview and empirical update. *Cognitive Therapy and Research, 16,* 201–228. (p. 520)

Schein, E. H. (1956). The Chinese indoctrination program for prisoners of war: A study of attempted brainwashing. *Psychiatry, 19,* 149–172. (p. 552)

Schelling, T. C. (1992). Addictive drugs: The cigarette experience. *Science, 255,* 430–433. (p. 538)

Schiavi, R. C., & Schreiner-Engel, P. (1988). Nocturnal penile tumescence in healthy aging men. *Journal of Gerontology: Medical Sciences, 43,* M146–150. (p. 213)

Schiffenbauer, A., & Schiavo, R. S. (1976). Physical distance and attraction: An intensification effect. *Journal of Experimental Social Psychology, 12,* 274–282. (p. 561)

Schlaug, G., Jancke, L., Huang, Y., & Steinmetz, H. (1995). In vivo evidence of structural brain asymmetry in musicians. *Science, 267,* 699–701. (p. 54)

Schleifer, S. J., Keller, S. E., McKegney, F. P., & Stein, M. (1979). *The influence of stress and other psychosocial factors on human immunity.* Paper presented at the 36th Annual Meeting of the American Psychosomatic Society. (p. 524)

Schlesinger, A. M., Jr. (1965). *A thousand days.* Boston: Houghton Mifflin. (p. 563)

Schmidt, F. L., & Hunter, J. E. (1993). Tacit knowledge, practical intelligence, general mental ability, and job knowledge. *Current Directions in Psychological Science, 2,* 8–9. (p. 340)

Schmidt, G., Klusmann, D., Zeitzschel, U., & Lange, C. (1994). Changes in adolescents' sexuality between 1970 and 1990 in West-Germany. *Archives of Sexual Behavior, 23,* 489-513. (p. 126)

Schmitt, D. P., & Buss, D. M. (1996). Strategic self-promotion and competitor derogation: Sex and context effects on the perceived effectiveness of mate attraction tactics. *Journal of Personality and Social Psychology, 70,* 1185-1204. (p. 582)

Schnaper, N. (1980). Comments germane to the paper entitled "The reality of death experiences" by Ernst Rodin. *Journal of Nervous and Mental Disease, 168,* 268–270. (p. 239)

Schneiderman, N., Chesney, M. A., & Krantz, D. S. (1989). Biobehavioral aspects of cardiovascular disease: Progress and prospects. *Health Psychology, 8,* 649–676. (p. 522)

Schnitzer, B. (1984, May). Repunctuated message. *Games,* pp. 57, 62. (p. 317)

Schoeneman, T. J. (1994). *Individualism.* In V. S. Ramachandran (Ed.), *Encyclopedia of Human Behavior.* San Diego: Academic Press. (p. 443)

Schoenfeld, B. (1995, May 14). The loneliness of being white. *New York Times Magazine,* 34-37. (p. 568).

Schofield, J. W. (1986). Black-White contact in desegregated schools. In M. Hewstone & R. Brown (Eds.), *Contact and conflict in intergroup encounters.* Oxford: Basil Blackwell Ltd. (p. 587)

Schonfield, D., & Robertson, B. A. (1966). Memory storage and aging. *Canadian Journal of Psychology, 20,* 228–236. (p. 133)

Schooler, J. W., Gerhard, D., & Loftus, E. F. (1986). Qualities of the unreal. *Journal of Experimental Psychology: Learning, Memory, and Cognition, 12,* 171–181. (p. 295)

Schuckit, M. A., and Smith, T. L. (1996, March). An 8-year follow-up of 450 sons of alcoholic and control subjects. *Archives of General Psychiatry, 53,* 202-210. (p. 237)

Schuerger, J. M., Zarrella, K. L., & Hotz, A. S. (1989). Factors that influence the temporal stability of personality by questionnaire. *Journal of Personality and Social Psychology, 56*, 777–783. (p. 144)

Schwartz, B. (1984). *Psychology of learning and behavior* (2nd ed.). New York: Norton. (pp. 252, 463)

Schwartz, J. E., Friedman, H. S., Tucker, J. S., Tomlinson-Keasey, C., Wingard, D. L., & Criqui, M. H. (1995). Sociodemographic and psychosocial factors in childhood as predictors of adult mortality. *American Journal of Public Health, 85*, 1237-1245. (p. 533)

Schwartz, J. M., Stoessel, P. W., Baxter, L. R., Jr., Martin, K. M., & Phelps, M. E. (1996). Systematic changes in cerebral glucose metabolic rate after successful behavior modification treatment of obsessive-compulsive disorder. *Archives of General Psychiatry, 53*, 109-113. (p. 512)

Schwarz, N., & Clore, G. L. (1983). Mood, misattribution, and judgments of well-being: Informative and directive functions of affective states. *Journal of Personality and Social Psychology, 45*, 513–523. (p. 407)

Schwarz, N., Strack, F., Kommer, D., & Wagner, D. (1987). Soccer, rooms, and the quality of your life: Mood effects on judgments of satisfaction with life in general and with specific domains. *European Journal of Social Psychology, 17*, 69–79. (p. 291)

Sclafani, A. (1995). How food preferences are learned: Laboratory animal models. *Proceedings of the Nutrition Society, 54*, 419-427. (p. 371)

Scott, C., & Pepperell, P. (1992). Exercise and depression: A meta-analysis. Paper presented at the Southwestern Psychological Association convention. (p. 530)

Scott, W. A., Scott, R., & McCabe, M. (1991). Family relationships and children's personality: A cross-cultural, cross-source comparison. *British Journal of Social Psychology, 30*, 1–20. (p. 107)

Scribner, S. (1977). Modes of thinking and ways of speaking: Culture and logic reconsidered. In P. N. Johnson-Laird & P. C. Wason (Eds.), *Thinking: Readings in cognitive science.* New York: Cambridge University Press. (p. 118)

Seeman, P., Guan, H-C., & Van Tol, H. H. M. (1993). Dopamine D4 receptors elevated in schizophrenia. *Nature, 365*, 441–445. (p. 478)

Segall, M. H., Dasen, P. R., Berry, J. W., & Poortinga, Y. H. (1990). *Human behavior in global perspective: An introduction to cross-cultural psychology.* New York: Pergamon. (pp. 93, 192, 378, 566, 569)

Segerstrom, S. C., McCarthy, W. J., Caskey, N. H., Gross, T. D., & Jarvik, M. E. (1993). Optimistic bias among cigarette smokers. *Journal of Applied Social Psychology, 23*, 1606–1618. (p. 447)

Segrin, C., & Dillard, J. P. (1992). The interactional theory of depresion: A meta-analysis of the research literature. *Journal of Social and Clinical Psychology, 11*, 43–70. (p. 474)

Seibert, P. S., & Ellis, H. C. (1991). Irrelevant thoughts, emotional mood states, and cognitive task performance. *Memory and Cognition, 19*, 507–513. (p. 291)

Self, E. A. (1994). Pluralistic ignorance of alcohol attitudes and use among both sexes. Paper presented at the American Psychological Association convention. (p. 237)

Seligman, M. E. P. (1974, May). Submissive death: Giving up on life. *Psychology Today,* pp. 80–85. (p. 394)

Seligman, M. E. P. (1975). *Helplessness: On depression, development and death.* San Francisco: Freeman. (p. 446)

Seligman, M. E. P. (1988, October). Boomer blues. *Psychology Today,* pp. 50–55. (p. 443)

Seligman, M. E. P. (1989). Explanatory style: Predicting depression, achievement, and health. In M. D. Yapko (Ed.), *Brief therapy approaches to treating anxiety and depression.* New York: Brunner/Mazel. (p. 499)

Seligman, M. E. P. (1991). *Learned optimism.* New York: Knopf. (pp. 208, 446, 473)

Seligman, M. E. P. (1994). *What you can change and what you can't.* New York: Knopf. (pp. 372, 406, 429, 439, 473, 511, 530)

Seligman, M. E. P. (1995). The effectiveness of psychotherapy: The *Consumer Reports* study. *American Psychologist, 50*, 965-974. (p. 473, 501)

Seligman, M. E. P. (1996). Predicting and preventing depression. Master Lecture, American Psychological Association convention. (p. 499)

Seligman, M. E. P., & Schulman, P. (1986). Explanatory style as a predictor of productivity and quitting among life insurance sales agents. *Journal of Personality and Social Psychology, 50*, 832–838. (p. 447)

Seligman, M. E. P., & Yellen, A. (1987). What is a dream? *Behavior Research and Therapy, 25*, 1–24. (pp. 211, 220)

Selye, H. (1936). A syndrome produced by diverse nocuous agents. *Nature, 138*, 32. (p. 517)

Selye, H. (1976). *The stress of life.* New York: McGraw-Hill. (pp. 517–518)

Service, R. F. (1994). Will a new type of drug make memory-making easier? *Science, 266*, 218-219. (p. 285)

Seto, M. C., & Barbaree, H. E. (1995). The role of alcohol in sexual aggression. *Clinical Psychology Review, 15*, 545-566. (p. 231, 573)

Shadish, W. R., Montgomery, L. M., Wilson, P., Wilson, M. R., Bright, I., & Okwumabua, T. (1993). Effects of family and marital psychotherapies: A meta-analysis. *Journal of Consulting and Clinical Psychology, 61*, 992-1002. (p. 500)

Shamir, B., House, R. J., & Arthur, M. B. (1993). The motivational effects of charismatic leadership: A self-concept based theory. *Organizational Science,* in press. (p. 389)

Shanks, D. (1993, 30 January). Breaking Chomsky's rules. *New Scientist,* pp. 26–29. (p. 323)

Shapiro, D. A., & Shapiro, D. (1982). Meta-analysis of comparative therapy outcome studies: A replication and refinement. *Psychological Bulletin, 92*, 581–604. (p. 505)

Shaughnessy, J., & Zechmeister, E. (1992). Memory monitoring accuracy as influenced by the distribution of retrieval practice. *Bulletin of the Psychonomic Society, 30*, 125–128. (p. 302)

Shaver, P. R., & Hazan, C. (1993). Adult romantic attachment: Theory and evidence. In D. Perlman & W. Jones (Eds.), *Advances in personal relationships,* vol. 4. Greenwich, CT: JAI. (p. 98)

Shaw, H. L. (1989–90). Comprehension of the spoken word and ASL translation by chimpanzees (Pan troglodytes). *Friends of Washoe, 9*(1/2), 8–19. (p. 327)

Shawitz, B.A., & others (1995). Sex differences in the functional organization of the brain for language. *Nature, 373,* 607-609. (p. 54)

Shea, M. T., Elkin, I., Imber, S. D., Sotsky, S. M., Watkins, J. T., Collins, J. F., Pilkonis, P. A., Beckham, E., Glass, D. R., Dolan, R. T., & Parloff, M. B. (1992). Course of depressive symptoms over follow-up: Findings from the National Institute of mental Health Treatment of Depression Collaborative Research Program. *Archives of General Psychiatry, 49,* 782–787. (p. 504)

Sheehan, S. (1982). *Is there no place on earth for me?* Boston: Houghton Mifflin. (p. 476)

Sheldon, W. H. (1954). *Atlas of man: A guide for somatotyping the adult male of all ages.* New York: Harper & Row. (p. 431)

Shenon, P. (1994, May 15). The world: Asia's having one huge nicotine fit. *New York Times,* 4, p. 1. (p. 538)

Shenton, M. E., Kiknis, R., Jolesz, F. A., & others (1992). Abnormalities of the left temporal lobe and thought disorder in schizophrenia: A quantitative magnetic resonance imaging study. *New England Journal of Medicine, 327,* 604–612. (p. 478)

Shepard, R. N. (1981). Psychophysical complementarity. In M. Kubovy & J. R. Pomerantz (Eds.), *Perceptual organization.* Hillsdale, NJ: Erlbaum. (p. 190)

Shepard, R. N. (1990). *Mind sights.* New York: Freeman. (pp. 36, 191, 198)

Shepherd, C., Kohut, J. J., & Sweet, R. (1990). *More news of the weird.* New York: Penguin/Plume Books. (p. 482)

Shepperd, J. A. (1993). Student derogation of the Scholastic Aptitude Test: Biases in perceptions and presentations of College Board scores. *Basic and Applied Social Psychology, 14,* 455–473. (p. 440)

Sherif, M. (1966). *In common predicament: Social psychology of intergroup conflict and cooperation.* Boston: Houghton Mifflin. (p. 587)

Sherry, D., & Vaccarino, A. L. (1989). Hippocampus and memory for food caches in black-capped chickadees. *Behavioral Neuroscience, 103,* 308–318. (p. 287)

Shettleworth, S. J. (1973). Food reinforcement and the organization of behavior in golden hamsters. In R. A. Hinde & J. Stevenson-Hinde (Eds.), *Constraints on learning.* London: Academic Press. (p. 261)

Shettleworth, S. J. (1993). Where is the comparison in comparative cognition? Alternative research programs. *Psychological Science, 4,* 179–184. (p. 283)

Shimamura, A. P., Berry, J. M., Mangels, J. A., Rusting, C. L., & Jurica, P. J. (1995). Memory and cognitive abilities in university professors: Evidence for successful aging. *Psychological Science, 6,* 271-277. (p. 133)

Shneidman, E. (1987, March). At the point of no return. *Psychology Today,* pp. 54–58. (p. 469)

Shontz, F. C., & Green, P. (1992). Trends in research on the Rorschach: Review and recommendations. *Applied and Preventive Psychology, 1,* 149–156. (p. 426)

Shotland, R. L. (1984, March 12). Quoted by Maureen Dowd, 20 years after the murder of Kitty Genovese, the question remains: Why? *New York Times,* p. B1. (p. 585)

Shotland, R. L. (1989). A model of the causes of date rape in developing and close relationships. In C. Hendrick (Ed.), *Review of Personality and Social Psychology* (Vol. 10). Newbury Park, CA: Sage. (p. 379)

Showers, C. (1992). The motivational and emotional consequences of considering positive or negative possibilities for an upcoming event. *Journal of Personality and Social Psychology, 63,* 474–484. (p. 447)

Shrout, P. E., Link, B. G., Dohrenwend, B. P., Skodol, A. E., Stueve, A., & Mirotznik, J. (1989). Characterizing life events as risk factors for depression: The role of fateful loss events. *Journal of Abnormal Psychology, 98,* 460–467. (p. 470)

Sieff, E. M., Dawes, R. M., & Loewenstein, G. F. (1997). Anticipated versus actual responses to HIV test results. *American Journal of Psychology,* in press. (p. 407)

Siegel, J. M. (1990). Stressful life events and use of physician services among the elderly: The moderating role of pet ownership. *Journal of Personality and Social Psychology, 58,* 1081–1086. (p. 533)

Siegel, L. S., & Hodkin, B. (1982). The garden path to the understanding of cognitive development: Has Piaget led us into the poison ivy? In S. Modgil & C. Modgil (Eds.), *Jean Piaget: Consensus and controversy.* New York: Praeger. (p. 92)

Siegel, R. K. (1977, October). Hallucinations. *Scientific American,* pp. 132–140. (p. 240)

Siegel, R. K. (1980). The psychology of life after death. *American Psychologist, 35,* 911–931. (p. 239)

Siegel, R. K. (1984, March 15). Personal communication. (p. 234)

Siegel, R. K. (1990). *Intoxication.* New York: Pocket Books. (pp. 230, 232–233, 235)

Siegel, R. K. Quoted by J. Hooper (1982, October), Mind tripping. *Omni,* pp. 72–82, 159–160. (p. 234)

Siegler, R. S., & Ellis, S. (1996). Piaget on childhood. *Psychological Science, 7,* 211-215. (p. 87)

Silbersweig, D. A., & others (1995). A functional neuroanatomy of hallucinations in schizophrenia. *Nature, 378,* 176-179. (p. 478)

Silva, A. J., Stevens, C. F., Tonegawa, S., & Wang, Y. (1992). Deficient hippocampal long-term potentiation in alpha-calcium-calmodulin kinase II mutant mice. *Science, 257,* 201–206. (p. 285)

Silva, C. E., & Kirsch, I. (1992). Interpretive sets, expectancy, fantasy proneness, and dissociation as predictors of hypnotic response. *Journal of Personality and Social Psychology, 63,* 847–856. (p. 222)

Silver, M., & Geller, D. (1978). On the irrelevance of evil: The organization and individual action. *Journal of Social Issues, 34,* 125–136. (p. 559)

Silverman, I., & Eals, M. (1992). Sex differences in spatial abilities: Evolutionary theory and data. In J. H. Barkow, L. Cosmides, & J. Tooby (eds.), *The adapted mind: Evolutionary psychology and the generation of culture.* New York: Oxford University Press. (p. 358)

Silverman, K., Evans, S. M., Strain, E. C., & Griffiths, R. R. (1992). Withdrawal syndrome after the double-blind cessation of caffeine consumption. *New England Journal of Medicine, 327,* 1109–1114. (p. 233)

Silverman, P. S., & Retzlaff, P. D. (1986). Cognitive stage regression through hypnosis: Are earlier cognitive stages retrievable? *International Journal of Clinical and Experimental Hypnosis, 34,* 192–204. (p. 223)

Silverton, L. (1988). Crime and the schizophrenia spectrum: A study of three Danish cohorts. In T. E. Moffitt & S. A. Mednick (Eds.), *Biological contributions to crime causation.* New York: Martinus-Nijhoff. (p. 459)

Simek, T. C., & O'Brien, R. M. (1981). *Total golf: A behavioral approach to lowering your score and getting more out of your game.* Huntington, NY: B-MOD Associates. (p. 262)

Simek, T. C., & O'Brien, R. M. (1988). A chaining-mastery, discrimination training program to teach Little Leaguers to hit a baseball. *Human Performance, 1,* 73–84. (p. 262)

Simmons, R. G., & Blyth, D. A. (1987). *Moving into adolescence: The impact of pubertal change and school context.* New York: Aldine De Gruyter. (p. 118)

Simonton, D. K. (1988). Age and outstanding achievement: What do we know after a century of research? *Psychological Bulletin, 104,* 251–267. (p. 136)

Simonton, D. K. (1990). Creativity in the later years: Optimistic prospects for achievement. *The Gerontologist, 30,* 626–631. (p. 136)

Simonton, D. K. (1992). The social context of career success and course for 2,026 scientists and inventors. *Personality and Social Psychology Bulletin, 18,* 452–463. (p. 351)

Simonton, D. K. (1994). *Greatness: Who makes history and why.* New York: Guilford Press. (p. 385)

Simpson, J. A., Rholes, W. S., & Nelligan, J. S. (1992). Support seeking and support giving within couples in an anxiety-provoking situation: The role of attachment styles. *Journal of Personality and Social Psychology, 62,* 434–446. (p. 98)

Sinclair, R. C., Hoffman, C., Mark, M. M., Martin, L. L., & Pickering, T. L. (1994). Construct accessibility and the misattribution of arousal: Schachter and Singer revisited. *Psychological Science, 5,* 15–18. (p. 415)

Singelis, T. M., & Sharkey, W. F. (1995). Culture, self-construal, and embarrassability. *Cross-Cultural Psychology, 26,* 622-644. (p. 442)

Singer, J. L. (1975). Navigating the stream of consciousness: Research in daydreaming and related inner experience. *American Psychologist, 30,* 727–738. (p. 209)

Singer, J. L. (1976, July). Fantasy: The foundation of serenity. *Psychology Today,* pp. 32–37. (p. 210)

Singer, J. L. (1981). Clinical intervention: New developments in methods and evaluation. In L. T. Benjamin, Jr. (Ed.), *The G. Stanley Hall Lecture Series* (Vol. 1). Washington, DC: American Psychological Association. (p. 504)

Singer, J. L. (1986). Is television bad for children? *Social Science, 71,* 178–182. (p. 210)

Singer, J. L., & Singer, D. G. (1986). Family experiences and television viewing as predictors of children's imagination, restlessness, and aggression. *Journal of Social Issues, 42*(3), 7–28. (p. 576)

Singh, D. (1993). Adaptive significance of female physical attractiveness: Role of waist-to-hip ratio. *Journal of Personality and Social Psychology, 65,* 293–307. (p. 582)

Singh, D. (1995a). Female judgment of male attractiveness and desirability for relationships: Role of waist-to-hip ratio and financial status. *Journal of Personality and Social Psychology, 69,* 1089-1101. (p. 582)

Singh, D. (1995b). Female health, attractiveness, and desirability for relationships: Role of breast asymmetry and waist-to-hip ratio. *Ethology and Sociobiology, 16,* 465-481. (p. 582)

Sivard, R. L. (1995). *Women. . . a world survey,* 2nd ed. Washington, DC: World Priorities. (p. 566)

Sivard, R. L. (1996). *World military and social expenditures 1996,* 16th edition. Washington, DC: World Priorities. (p. 566).

Sjostrom, L. (1980). Fat cells and body weight. In A. J. Stunkard (Ed.), *Obesity.* Philadelphia: Saunders. (p. 541)

Skelton, J. A., Pepe, M. M., & Pineo, T. S. (1995). How much better is clozapine? A meta-analytic review and critical appraisal. *Experimental and Clinical Psychopharmacology, 3,* 270-279. (p. 508)

Skinner, B. F. (1953). *Science and human behavior.* New York: Macmillan. (p. 257)

Skinner, B. F. (1956). A case history in scientific method. *American Psychologist, 11,* 221–233. (p. 258)

Skinner, B. F. (1957). *Verbal behavior.* Englewood Cliffs, NJ: Prentice-Hall. (p. 322)

Skinner, B. F. (1961, November). Teaching machines. *Scientific American,* pp. 91–102. (p. 258)

Skinner, B. F. (1983, September). Origins of a behaviorist. *Psychology Today,* pp. 22–33. (pp. 262, 473)

Skinner, B. F. (1986). What is wrong with daily life in the western world? *American Psychologist, 41,* 568–574. (p. 262)

Skinner, B. F. (1988). The school of the future. Address to the American Psychological Association convention. (p. 262)

Skinner, B. F. (1989). Teaching machines. *Science, 243,* 1535. (pp. 258, 262)

Skinner, B. F. (1990). Address to the American Psychological Association convention. (p. 260)

Skinner, M., & Mullen, B. (1991). Facial asymmetry in emotional expression: A meta-analysis of research. *British Journal of Social Psychology, 30,* 113–124. (p. 66)

Sklar, L. S., & Anisman, H. (1981). Stress and cancer. *Psychological Bulletin, 89,* 369–406. (p. 524)

Skov, R. B., & Sherman, S. J. (1986). Information-gathering processes: Diagnosticity, hypothesis-confirmatory strategies, and perceived hypothesis confirmation. *Journal of Experimental Social Psychology, 22,* 93–121. (p. 308)

Slater, A. (1994, February 15). Personal correspondence. (p. 90)

Slater, A., Morison, V., & Somers, M. (1988). Orientation discrimination and cortical function in the human newborn. *Perception, 17,* 597–602. (p. 90)

Slavin, R. E. (1989). Cooperative learning and student achievement. In R. E. Slavin (Ed.), *School and classroom organization.* Hillsdale, NJ: Erlbaum. (p. 587)

Slavin, R. E., & Braddock, J. H., III (1993, Summer). Ability grouping: On the wrong track. *The College Board Review*, pp. 11–18. (p. 350)

Slovic, P. (1987). Perception of risk. *Science, 236,* 280–285. (p. 312)

Slovic, P., & Fischhoff, B. (1977). On the psychology of experimental surprises. *Journal of Experimental Psychology: Human Perception and Performance, 3,* 544–551. (p. 14)

Smart, R. G., Adlaf, E. M., & Walsh, G. W. (1991). The Ontario student drug use survey: Trends between 1977 and 1991. Toronto: Addiction Research Foundation. (p. 236)

Smith, A. (1983). Personal correspondence. (p. 478)

Smith, A. (1987). Personal communication. (p. 85)

Smith, A., & Sugar, O. (1975). Development of above normal language and intelligence 21 years after left hemispherectomy. *Neurology, 25,* 813–818. (p. 85)

Smith, K. H., & Rogers, M. (1994). Effectiveness of subliminal messages in television commercials: Two experiments. *Journal of Applied Psychology, 79,* 866-874. (p. 150)

Smith, M. B. (1978). Psychology and values. *Journal of Social Issues, 34,* 181–199. (p. 443)

Smith, M. L., & Glass, G. V. (1977). Meta-analysis of psychotherapy outcome studies. *American Psychologist, 32,* 752–760. (p. 504)

Smith, M. L., Glass, G. V., & Miller, R. L. (1980). *The benefits of psychotherapy.* Baltimore: Johns Hopkins Press. (p. 504)

Smith, P. B., & Tayeb, M. (1989). Organizational structure and processes. In M. Bond (Ed.), *The cross-cultural challenge to social psychology.* Newbury Park, CA: Sage. (p. 389)

Smith, P. F. (1995). Cannabis and the brain. *New Zealand Journal of Psychology, 24,* 5-12. (p. 235)

Smith, T. W. (1990). Adult sexual behavior in 1989: Number of partners, frequency, and risk. General Social Survey Topic Report No. 18, National Opinion Research Center, University of Chicago. (p. 374)

Smith, T. W. (1997). Personal correspondence. Data from the General Social Survey, National Opinion Research Center, University of Chicago. (p. 409)

Snarey, J. (1987, June). A question of morality. *Psychology Today,* pp. 6–7. (p. 120)

Snarey, J. R. (1985). Cross-cultural universality of social-moral development: A critical review of Kohlbergian research. *Psychological Bulletin, 97,* 202–233. (p. 120)

Snodgrass, M. A. (1987). The relationships of differential loneliness, intimacy and characterological attributional style to duration of loneliness. *Journal of Social Behavior and Personality, 2,* 173–186. (p. 475)

Snodgrass, S. E., Higgins, J. G., & Todisco, L. (1986). The effects of walking behavior on mood. Paper presented at the American Psychological Association convention. (p. 402)

Snyder, F., & Scott, J. (1972). The psychophysiology of sleep. In N. S. Greenfield & R. A. Sterbach (eds.), *Handbook of psychophysiology.* New York: Holt, Rinehart & Winston. (p. 219)

Snyder, M. (1984). When belief creates reality. In L. Berkowitz (Ed.), *Advances in experimental social psychology* (Vol. 18). New York: Academic Press. (p. 459)

Snyder, M., Tanke, E. D., & Berscheid, E. (1977). Social perception and interpersonal behavior: On the self-fulfilling nature of social stereotypes. *Journal of Personality and Social Psychology, 35,* 656–666. (p. 564)

Snyder, S. H. (1984). Neurosciences: An integrative discipline. *Science, 225,* 1255–1257. (p. 44)

Snyder, S. H. (1986). *Drugs and the brain.* New York: Scientific American Library. (p. 510)

Sobel, D. S. (1993). Mind matters, money matters. *Mental Medicine Update Special Report*, pp. 1–8. (p. 536)

Sokhadze, E. M., & Shtark, M. B. (1991). Scientific and clinical biofeedback in the USSR. *Biofeedback and Self-Regulation, 16,* 253–260. (p. 531)

Sokoll, G. R., & Mynatt, C. R. (1984). *Arousal and free throw shooting.* Paper presented at the meeting of the Midwestern Psychological Association. (p. 394)

Solomon, D. A., Keitner, G. I., Miller, I. W., Shea, M. T., & Keller, M. B. (1995). Course of illness and maintenance treatments for patients with bipolar disorder. *Journal of Clinical Psychiatry, 56,* 5-13. (p. 510)

Solomon, J. (1996, May 20). Breaking the silence. *Newsweek,* pp. 20-22. (p. 459)

Solomon, M. (1987, December). Standard issue. *Psychology Today,* pp. 30–31. (p. 581)

Solomon, R. L. (1980). The opponent-process theory of acquired motivation: The costs of pleasure and the benefits of pain. *American Psychologist, 35,* 691–712. (p. 408)

Solomon, Z. (1990). Does the war end when the shooting stops? The psychological toll of war. *Journal of Applied Social Psychology, 20,* 1733–1745. (p. 461)

Sommer, R. (1969). *Personal space.* Englewood Cliffs, NJ: Prentice-Hall. (pp. 21, 565)

Sonenstein, F. L. (1992). Condom use. *Science, 257,* 861. (p. 125)

Sontag, S. (1978). *Illness as metaphor.* New York: Farrar, Straus, & Giroux. (p. 525)

Sowell, T. (1991, May/June). Cultural diversity: A world view. *American Enterprise*, pp. 44–55. (p. 589)

Spanos, N. P. (1982). A social psychological approach to hypnotic behavior. In G. Weary & H. L. Mirels (Eds.), *Integrations of clinical and social psychology.* New York: Oxford. (p. 224)

Spanos, N. P. (1986b). Hypnosis, nonvolitional responding, and multiple personality: A social psychological perspective. *Progress in Experimental Personality Research, 14,* 1–62. (p. 466)

Spanos, N. P. (1987–88). Past-life hypnotic regression: A critical view. *The Skeptical Inquirer, 12,* 174–180. (p. 225)

Spanos, N. P. (1991). Hypnosis, hypnotizability, and hypnotherapy. In C. R. Snyder & D. R. Forsyth (Eds.), *Handbook of social and clinical psychology: The health perspective.* New York: Pergamon Press. (p. 224)

Spanos, N. P. (1994). Multiple identity enactments and multiple personality disorder: A sociocognitive perspective. *Psychological Bulletin, 116,* 143–165. (pp. 227, 466)

Spanos, N. P. (1996). *Multiple identities and false memories: A sociocognitive perspective.* Washington, DC: American Psychological Association Books. (pp. 224, 227, 466)

Spanos, N. P., & Coe, W. C. (1992). A Social-psychological approach to hypnosis. In E. Fromm & M. R. Nash (Eds.), *Contemporary hypnosis research.* New York: Guilford. (p. 226)

Spanos, N. P., Burgess, C. A., & Burgess, M. F. (1994). Past-life identities, UFO abductions, and Satanic ritual abuse: The social construction of memories. *International Journal of Clinical and Experimental Hypnosis, 42,* 433-446. (p. 301)

Spanos, N. P., Menary, E., Gabora, N. J., DuBreuil, S. C., & Dewhirst, B. (1991). Secondary identity enactments during hypnotic past-life regression: A sociocognitive perspective. *Journal of Personality and Social Psychology, 61,* 308–320. (p. 225)

Spanos, N. P., Radtke, L., & Bertrand, L. D. (1985). Hypnotic amnesia as a strategic enactment: Breaching amnesia in highly susceptible subjects. *Journal of Personality and Social Psychology, 47,* 1155–1169. (p. 221)

Spector, P. E. (1986). Perceived control by employees: A meta-analysis of studies concerning autonomy and participation at work. *Human Relations, 39,* 1005–1016. (p. 389)

Spencer, S. J., Steele, C. M., & Quinn, D. M. (1997). Stereotype threat and women's math performance. Unpublished manuscript, Hope College. (p. 359)

Sperling, G. (1960). The information available in brief visual presentations. *Psychological Monographs, 74* (Whole No. 498). (p. 281)

Sperry, R. W. (1956, May). The eye and the brain. *Scientific American,* pp. 48–52. (p. 196)

Sperry, R. W. (1964). *Problems outstanding in the evolution of brain function.* James Arthur Lecture, American Museum of Natural History, New York. Cited by R. Ornstein (1977), *The psychology of consciousness* (2nd ed.). New York: Harcourt Brace Jovanovich. (p. 67)

Sperry, R. W. (1968). Hemisphere deconnection and unity in conscious awareness. *American Psychologist, 23,* 723–733. (p. 66)

Sperry, R. W. (1982). Some effects of disconnecting the cerebral hemispheres. *Science, 217,* 1223–1226. (p. 70)

Sperry, R. W. (1985). Changed concepts of brain and consciousness: Some value implications. *Zygon, 20,* 41–57. (p. 160)

Spiegel, D. (1993). Social support: How friends, family, and groups can help. In D. Goleman & J. Gurin (Eds.), *Mind-body medicine: How to use your mind for better health.* Yonkers, NY: Consumer Reports Books. (p. 525)

Spiegel, D., Bloom, J. R., Kraemer, H. C., & Gottheil, E. (1989, October 14). Effect of psychosocial treatment on survival of patients with metastatic breast cancer. *The Lancet,* pp. 888–891. (p. 525)

Spielberger, C., & London, P. (1982). Rage boomerangs. *American Health, 1,* 52–56. (p. 522)

Spiess, W. F. J., Greer, J. H., & O'Donohue, W. T. (1984). Premature ejaculation: Investigation of factors in ejaculatory latency. *Journal of Abnormal Psychology, 93,* 242–245. (p. 378)

Spitzberg, B. H., & Hurt, H. T. (1987). The relationship of interpersonal competence and skill to reported loneliness across time. *Journal of Social Behavior and Personality, 2,* 157–172. (p. 475)

Spitzer, R. L. (1975). On pseudoscience in science, logic in remission, and psychiatric diagnosis: A critique of Rosenhan's "On being sane in insane places." *Journal of Abnormal Psychology, 84,* 442–452. (p. 460)

Spradley, J. P., & Phillips, M. (1972). Culture and stress: A quantitative analysis. *American Anthropologist, 74,* 518–529. (p. 565)

Sprecher, S. (1989). The importance to males and females of physical attractiveness, earning potential, and expressiveness in initial attraction. *Sex Roles, 21,* 591–607. (p. 581)

Sprecher, S., & Sedikides, C. (1993). Gender differences in perceptions of emotionality: The case of close heterosexual relationships. *Sex Roles, 28,* 511–530. (p. 124)

Spring, B. (1988). Foods, brain and behavior: New links. *Harvard Medical School Mental Health Letter, 4*(7), 4–6. (p. 539)

Spring, B., Chiodo, J., & Bowen, D. J. (1987). Carbohydrates, tryptophan, and behavior: A methodological review. *Psychological Bulletin, 102,* 234–256. (p. 539)

Spring, B., Pingitore, R., Bourgeois, M., Kessler, K. H., & Bruckner, E. (1992). The effects and non-effects of skipping breakfast: Results of three studies. Paper presented at the American Psychological Association convention. (p. 539)

Springer, S. P., & Deutsch, G. (1985). *Left brain, right brain.* San Francisco: Freeman. (p. 68)

Squire, L., & Zola-Morgan, S. (1991). The medial temporal lobe memory system. *Science, 253,* 1380–1386. (p. 287)

Squire, L. R. (1987). *Memory and brain.* New York: Oxford University Press. (pp. 285–286)

Squire, L. R. (1992). memory and the hippcampus: A synthesis from findings with rats, monkeys, and humans. *Psychological Review, 99,* 195-231. (p. 287)

Sroufe, L. A., Fox, N. E., & Pancake, V. R. (1983). Attachment and dependency in developmental perspective. *Child Development, 54,* 1615–1627. (p. 98)

Stack, S. (1992). Marriage, family, religion, and suicide. In R. Maris, A. Berman, J. Maltsberger, & R. Yufit (Eds.), *Assessment and prediction of suicide.* New York: Guilford Press. (p. 469)

Stanford University Center for Narcolepsy (1996). Available: http://www.hia.com/narcoctr/welcome.html (accessed August 26). (p. 217)

Stanovich, K. (1996). *How to think straight about psychology.* New York: HarperCollins. (p. 420)

Statistics Canada (1996). Control and sale of alcoholic beverages 1993/1994. Available at http://:www.statcan.ca/documents/English/MediaRel/Newprod/alcohol.htm (accessed August 31, 1996). (p. 236)

Stattin, H., & Magnusson, D. (1990). *Pubertal maturation in female development.* Hillsdale, NJ: Erlbaum. (p. 118)

Staub, E. (1989). *The roots of evil: The psychological and cultural sources of genocide.* New York: Cambridge University Press. (p. 554)

Staub, E. (1993). Societal-cultural, familial and psychological origins of youth violence. Paper presented at the American Psychological Association convention. (p. 574)

Steele, C. (1990a, May). A conversation with Claude Steele. *APS Observer,* pp. 11–17. (p. 356)

Steele, C. M. (1995, August 31). Black students live down to expectations. *New York Times.* (p. 359)

Steele, C. M. (1997). A threat in the air: How stereotypes shape the intellectual identities and performance of women and African Americans. *American Psychologist, 52,* 613–629. (p. 359)

Steele, C. M., & Aronson, J. (1996). Stereotype threat and the intellectual test performance of African Americans. *Journal of Personality and Social Psychology, 69,* 797-811. (p. 359)

Steele, C. M., & Josephs, R. A. (1990). Alcohol myopia: Its prized and dangerous effects. *American Psychologist, 45,* 921–933. (p. 231)

Stein, J. A., Newcomb, M. D., & Bentler, P. M. (1986). Stability and change in personality: A longitudinal study from early adolescence to young adulthood. *Journal of Research In Personality, 20,* 276–291. (p. 144)

Steinberg, L. (1987, September). Bound to bicker. *Psychology Today,* pp. 36–39. (p. 124)

Steinberg, N. (1993, February). Astonishing love stories (from an earlier United Press International report). *Games,* p. 47. (p. 581)

Stellar, E. (1985). Hunger in animals and humans. Distinguished lecture to the Eastern Psychological Association convention. (p. 370)

Stengel, E. (1981). Suicide. In *The new encyclopaedia britannica, macropaedia* (Vol. 17, pp. 777–782). Chicago: Encyclopaedia Britannica. (p. 469)

Stephens, T. (1988). Physical activity and mental health in the United States and Canada: Evidence from four population surveys. *Preventive Medicine, 17,* 35–47. (p. 530)

Stepp, L. S. (1996, July 2). Universal goals: Family, achievement and dreams. *International Herald Tribune,* p. 2. (p. 124)

Stern, M., & Karraker, K. H. (1989). Sex stereotyping of infants: A review of gender labeling studies. *Sex Roles, 20,* 501–522. (p. 200)

Sternberg, R. J. (1988). Applying cognitive theory to the testing and teaching of intelligence. *Applied Cognitive Psychology, 2,* 231–255. (p. 351)

Sternberg, R. J., & Grajek, S. (1984). The nature of love. *Journal of Personality and Social Psychology, 47,* 312–329. (p. 585)

Sternberg, R. J., & Lubart, T. I. (1991). An investment theory of creativity and its development. *Human Development,* 1–31. (p. 351)

Sternberg, R. J., & Lubart, T. I. (1992). Buy low and sell high: An investment approach to creativity. *Psychological Science, 1,* 1–5. (p. 351)

Sternberg, R. J., & Salter, W. (1982). Conceptions of intelligence. In R. J. Sternberg (Ed.), *Handbook of human intelligence.* New York: Cambridge University Press. (p. 337)

Sternberg, R. J., & Wagner, R. K. (1993). The g-ocentric view of intelligence and job performance is wrong. *Current Directions in Psychological Science, 2,* 1–5. (p. 339)

Sternberg, R. J., Wagner, R. K., Williams, W. M., & Horvath, J. A. (1995). Testing common sense. *American Psychologist, 50,* 912-927. (p. 339)

Stevenson, H. W. (1992, December). Learning from Asian schools. *Scientific American,* pp. 70–76. (p. 357)

Stevenson, H. W., & Lee, S-Y. (1990). Contexts of achievement: A study of American, Chinese, and Japanese children. *Monographs of the Society for Research in Child Development, 55* (Serial No. 221, Nos. 1–2). (p. 350)

Stice, E., & Shaw, H. E. (1994). Adverse effects of the media portrayed thin-ideal on women and linkages to bulimic symptomatology. *Journal of Social and Clinical Psychology, 13,* 288-308. (p. 372, 543)

Stipek, D. (1992). The child at school. In M. H. Bornstein & M. E. Lamb (eds.), *Developmental psychology: An advanced textbook.* Hillsdale, NJ: Erlbaum. (p. 103)

Stock, R. W. (1995, July 13). Reducing the risk for older drivers. *New York Times,* p. C1. (p. 131)

Stockton, M. C., & Murnen, S. K. (1992). Gender and sexual arousal in response to sexual stimuli: A meta-analytic review. Presented at the American Psychological Society convention. (p. 377)

Stoll, A. L., Tohen, M., Baldessarini, R. J., Goodwin, D. C., Stein, S., Katz, S., Geenens, D., Swinson, R. P., Goethe, J. W., & McGlashan, T. (1993). Shifts in diagnostic frequencies of schizophrenia and major affective disorders at six North American psychiatric hospitals, 1972–1988. *American Journal of Psychiatry, 150,* 1668–1673. (p. 471)

Stone, A. A., & Neale, J. M. (1984). Effects of severe daily events on mood. *Journal of Personality and Social Psychology, 46,* 137–144. (p. 407)

Stone, A. A., Cox, D. S., Valdimarsdottir, H., Jandor, L., & Neale, J. M. (1987). Evidence that secretory IgA antibody is associated with daily mood. *Journal of Personality and Social Psychology, 52,* 988–993. (p. 524)

Stone, J., Perry, Z. W., & Darley, J. M. (1997). "White men can't jump": Evidence for the perceptual confirmation of racial stereotypes following a basketball game. *Basic and Applied Social Psychology,* in press. (p. 570)

Stoppard, J. M., & Gruchy, C. D. G. (1993). Gender, context, and expression of positive emotion. *Personality and Social Psychology Bulletin, 19,* 143–150. (p. 124)

Storms, M. D. (1973). Videotape and the attribution process: Reversing actors' and observers' points of view. *Journal of Personality and Social Psychology, 27,* 165–175. (p. 560)

Storms, M. D. (1981). A theory of erotic orientation development. *Psychological Review, 88,* 340–353. (p. 380)

Storms, M. D. (1983). *Development of sexual orientation.* Washington, DC: Office of Social and Ethical Responsibility, American Psychological Association. (p. 380)

Storms, M. D., & Thomas, G. C. (1977). Reactions to physical closeness. *Journal of Personality and Social Psychology, 35,* 412–418. (p. 561)

Strack, F., Martin, L., & Stepper, S. (1988). Inhibiting and facilitating conditions of the human smile: A nonobtrusive test of the facial feedback hypothesis. *Journal of Personality and Social Psychology, 54,* 768–777. (p. 402)

Strack, S., & Coyne, J. C. (1983). Social confirmation of dysphoria: Shared and private reactions to depression. *Journal of Personality and Social Behavior, 44,* 798–806. (p. 474)

Strange, S. L., & Forsyth, D. R. (1993). Long-term benefits of adolescent peer groups. Paper presented at the Eastern Psychological Association convention. (p. 122)

Stratton, G. M. (1986). Some preliminary experiments on vision without inversion of the retinal image. *Psychological Review, 3,* 611–617. (p. 196)

Straub, R. O., Seidenberg, M. S., Bever, T. G., & Terrace, H. S. (1979). Serial learning in the pigeon. *Journal of the Experimental Analysis of Behavior, 32,* 137–148. (p. 326)

Strauman, T. J., Vookles, J., Berenstein, V., Chaiken, S., & Higgins, E. T. (1991). Self-discrepancies and vulnerability to body dissatisfaction and disordered eating. *Journal of Personality and Social Psychology, 61,* 946–956. (p. 373)

Straus, M. A., & Gelles, R. J. (1980). *Behind closed doors: Violence in the American family.* New York: Anchor/Doubleday. (p. 259)

Streissguth, A. P. (1993). Fetal alcohol fact sheet. Fetal Alcohol & Drug Unit, University of Washington, School of Medicine. (p. 81)

Streissguth, A. P., Aase, J. M., Clarren, S. K., Randels, S. P., LaDue, R. A., & Smith, D. F. (1991). Fetal alcohol syndrome in adolescents and adults. *Journal of the American Medical Association, 265,* 1961-1967. (p. 80)

Strentz, H. (1986, January 1). Become a psychic and amaze your friends! *Atlanta Journal,* p. 15A. (p. 202)

Strickland, B. (1992, February 20). Gender differences in health and illness. Sigma Xi national lecture delivered at Hope College. (p. 130)

Striegel-Moore, R. H., Silberstein, L. R., & Rodin, J. (1986). Toward an understanding of risk factors for bulimia. *American Psychologist, 41,* 246–263. (p. 373)

Striegel-Moore, R. H., Silberstein, L. R., & Rodin, J. (1993). The social self in bulimia nervosa: Public self-consciousness, social anxiety, and perceived fraudulence. *Journal of Abnormal Psychology, 102,* 297–303. (p. 372)

Strupp, H. H. (1986). Psychotherapy: Research, practice, and public policy (How to avoid dead ends). *American Psychologist, 41,* 120–130. (p. 505)

Stumpf, H., & Jackson, D. N. (1994). Gender-related differences in cognitive abilities: Evidence from a medical school admissions testing program. *Personality and Individual Differences, 17,* 335-344. (p. 358)

Stunkard, A. J., Harris, J. R., Pedersen, N. L., & McClearn, G. E. (1990). A separated twin study of the body mass index. *New England Journal of Medicine, 322,* 1483–1487. (pp. 373, 542)

Suddath, R. L., Christison, G. W., Torrey, E. F., Casanova, M. F., & Weinberger, D. R. (1990). Anatomical abnormalities in the brains of monozygotic twins discordant for schizophrenia. *New England Journal of Medicine, 322,* 789–794. (p. 479)

Sue, D. W. (1990). Culture-specific strategies in counseling: A conceptual framework. *Professional Psychology: Research and Practice, 21,* 424–433. (p. 507)

Suedfeld, P. (1980). *Restricted environmental stimulation: Research and clinical applications.* New York: Wiley. (p. 178)

Suedfeld, P., & Kristeller, J. L. (1982). Stimulus reduction as a technique in health psychology. *Health Psychology, 1,* 337–357. (p. 178)

Suedfeld, P., & Mocellin, J. S. P. (1987). The "sensed presence" in unusual environments. *Environment and Behavior, 19,* 33–52. (p. 239)

Suinn, R. M. (in press). Mental practice: Where have we been, Where do we go? *Clinical Psychology: Science and Practice.* (p. 330)

Sulloway, F. J. (1990). Orthodoxy and innovation in science: The influence of birth order in a multivariate context. Paper delivered at the American Association for the Advancement of Science annual meeting. (p. 386)

Sulloway, F. J. (1996). *Born to rebel: Birth order, family dynamics, and creative lives.* New York, NY: Pantheon. (p. 386)

Suls, J. M., & Tesch, F. (1978). Students' preferences for information about their test performance: A social comparison study. *Journal of Experimental Social Psychology, 8,* 189–197. (p. 411)

Summers, M. (1996, December 9). Mister clean. *People Weekly,* pp. 139-142. (p. 453)

Sundstrom, E., De Meuse, K. P., & Futrell, D. (1990). Work teams: Applications and effectiveness. *American Psychologist, 45,* 120–133. (p. 389)

Suomi, S. J. (1986). Anxiety-like disorders in young nonhuman primates. In R. Gettleman (Ed.), *Anxiety disorders of childhood.* New York: Guilford Press. (p. 464)

Suomi, S. J. (1987). Genetic and maternal contributions to individual differences in rhesus monkey biobehavioral development. In N. A. Krasnegor & others (Eds.), *Perinatal development: A psychobiological perspective.* Orlando, FL: Academic Press. (p. 424)

Suppes, P. Quoted by R. H. Ennis (1982). Children's ability to handle Piaget's propositional logic: A conceptual critique. In S. Modgil & C. Modgil (Eds.), *Jean Piaget: Consensus and controversy.* New York: Praeger. (p. 93)

Surgeon General. (1986). *The Surgeon General's workshop on pornography and public health,* June 22–24. Report prepared by E. P. Mulvey & J. L. Haugaard and released by Office of the Surgeon General on August 4, 1986. (p. 577)

Susser, E., & others (1996). Schizophrenia after prenatal famine. *Archives of General Psychiatry, 53,* 25-31 (p. 478)

Sweat, J. A., & Durm, M. W. (1993). Psychics: Do police departments really use them? *Skeptical Inquirer, 17,* 148–158. (p. 202)

Swerdlow, N. R., & Koob, G. F. (1987). Dopamine, schizophrenia, mania, and depression: Toward a unified hypothesis of corticostiato-pallido-thalamic function (with commentary). *Behavioral and Brain Sciences, 10,* 197–246. (p. 478)

Symons, C. S., & Johnson, B. T. (1997). The self-reference effect in memory: A meta-analysis. *Psychological Bulletin,* in press. (p. 276)

Taha, F. A. (1972). A comparative study of how sighted and blind perceive the manifest content of dreams. *National Review of Social Sciences, 9*(3), 28. (p. 218)

Tajfel, H. (Ed.). (1982). *Social identity and intergroup relations.* New York: Cambridge University Press. (p. 569)

Talal, N. (1995). Quoted by V. Morell, Zeroing in on how hormones affect the immune system. *Science, 269,* 773-775. (p. 523)

Tang, S-H., & Hall, V. C. (1995). The overjustification effect: A meta-analysis. *Applied Cognitive Psychology, 9,* 365-404. (p. 261)

Tannen, D. (1990). *You just don't understand: Women and men in conversation.* New York: Morrow. (pp. 34, 123)

Tanner, J. M. (1978). *Fetus into man: Physical growth from conception to maturity.* Cambridge, MA: Harvard University Press. (p. 117)

Tassinary, L. G., & Cacioppo, J. T. (1992). Unobservable facial actions and emotion. *Psychological Science, 3,* 28–33. (p. 400)

Tatarkiewicz, W. (1976). *Analysis of happiness.* The Hague: Martinus Nijhoff, 1976. (p. 407)

Taubes, G. (1994). Will new dopamine receptors offer a key to schizophrenia? *Science, 265,* 1034-1035. (p. 508)

Tavris, C. (1982, November). Anger defused. *Psychology Today,* pp. 25–35. (p. 406)

Tavris, C. (1993, January 3). Beware the incest-survivor machine. *New York Times Book Review,* pp. 1, 16–18. (p. 300)

Taylor, S. E. (1989). *Positive illusions.* New York: Basic Books. (pp. 314, 441, 532)

Taylor, S. E., & Armor, D. A. (1996). Positive illusions and coping with adversity. *Journal of Personality, 64,* 873-898. (p. 528)

Taylor, S. P., & Chermack, S. T. (1993). Alcohol, drugs and human physical aggression. *Journal of Studies on Alcohol,* Supplement No. 11, 78–88. (p. 572)

Teevan, R. C., & McGhee, P. E. (1972). Childhood development of fear of failure motivation. *Journal of Personality and Social Psychology, 21,* 345–348. (p. 385)

Temoshok, L. (1992). *The Type C connection: The behavioral links to cancer and your health.* New York: Random House. (p. 525)

Terman, L. M. (1916). *The measurement of intelligence.* Boston: Houghton Mifflin. (p. 336)

Terrace, H. S. (1979, November). How Nim Chimpsky changed my mind. *Psychology Today,* pp. 65–76. (p. 326)

Tesser, A., Forehand, R., Brody, G., & Long, N. (1989). Conflict: The role of calm and angry parent-child discussion in adolescent development. *Journal of Social and Clinical Psychology, 8,* 317-330. (p. 124)

Tetlock, P. E. (1988). Monitoring the integrative complexity of American and Soviet policy rhetoric: What can be learned? *Journal of Social Issues, 44,* 101–131. (p. 588)

Thatcher, R. W., Walker, R. A., & Giudice, S. (1987). Human cerebral hemispheres develop at different rates and ages. *Science, 236,* 1110–1113. (pp. 87, 143)

Thayer, R. E. (1987). Energy, tiredness, and tension effects of a sugar snack versus moderate exercise. *Journal of Personality and Social Psychology, 52,* 119–125. (p. 530)

Thayer, R. E. (1993). Mood and behavior (smoking and sugar snacking) following moderate exercise: A partial test of self-regulation theory. *Personality and Individual Differences, 14,* 97–104. (p. 530)

Thelen, E. (1994). Three-month-old infants can learn task-specific patterns of interlimb coordination. *Psychological Science, 5,* 280-285. (p. 86)

Thelen, E. (1995). Motor development: A new synthesis. *American Psychologist, 50,* 79-95. (p. 86)

Thomas, A., & Chess, S. (1986). The New York Longitudinal Study: From infancy to early adult life. In R. Plomin & J. Dunn (Eds.), *The study of temperament: Changes, continuities, and challenges.* Hillsdale, NJ: Erlbaum. (p. 143)

Thomas, G. V., & Blackman, D. (1991). Are animal experiments on the way out? *The Psychologist, 14,* 208–212. (p. 35)

Thomas, L. (1974). *The lives of a cell.* New York: Viking Press. (p. 176)

Thomas, L. (1983). *The youngest science: Notes of a medicine watcher.* New York: Viking Press. (p. 46)

Thomas, L. (1992). *The fragile species.* New York: Maxwell Macmillan. (p. 503)

Thomas, W. P., & Collier, V. P. (1997). School effectiveness for language minority students. Washington, DC: National Clearinghouse for Bilingual Education. (p. 329)

Thompson, C. P., Frieman, J., & Cowan, T. (1993). Rajan's memory. Paper presented to the American Psychological Society convention. (p. 282)

Thompson, C. P., Vogl, R. J., Walker, W. R., & Wooten, L. (1996). Involuntary memories in depressed and nondepressed individuals. Paper presented to the Psychonomic Society convention. (p. 428)

Thompson, J. K. (1986, April). Larger than life. *Psychology Today,* pp. 38–44. (p. 373)

Thompson, J. K., Jarvie, G. J., Lahey, B. B., & Cureton, K. J. (1982). Exercise and obesity: Etiology, physiology, and intervention. *Psychological Bulletin, 91,* 55–79. (p. 545)

Thompson, L. A., Detterman, D. K., & Plomin, R. (1991). Associations between cognitive abilities and scholastic achievement: Genetic overlap but environmental differences. *Psychological Science, 2,* 158–165. (p. 354)

Thompson, P. (1980). Margaret Thatcher: A new illusion. *Perception, 9,* 483–484. (p. 198)

Thorndike, A. L., & Hagen, E. P. (1977). Measurement and evaluation in psychology and education. New York: Macmillan. (p. 343)

Thorne, J., with Larry Rothstein (1993). *You are not alone: Words of experience and hope for the journey through depression.* New York: HarperPerennial. (p. 453)

Thornhill, R., & Gangestad, G. W. (1994). Human fluctuating asymmetry and sexual behavior. *Psychological Science, 5,* 297-302. (p. 582)

Thornton, B., & Moore, S. (1993). Physical attractiveness contrast effect: Implications for self-esteem and evaluations of the social self. *Personality and Social Psychology Bulletin, 19,* 474–480. (p. 581)

Thorpe, W. H. (1974). *Animal nature and human nature*. London: Metheun. (p. 327)

Tiggemann, M., & Rothblum, E. D. (1988). Gender differences in social consequences of perceived overweight in the United States and Australia. *Sex Roles, 18*, 75–86. (p. 544)

Timmer, S. G., Eccles, J., & O'Brien, K. (1985–1986, Winter). How families use time. *ISR Newsletter* (University of Michigan), pp. 3–4. (p. 101)

Tinbergen, N. (1951). *The study of instinct*. Oxford: Clarendon. (p. 364)

Tirrell, M. E. (1990). Personal communication. (p. 248)

Tolchin, M. (1994, April 17). Major airlines go two years without a fatality. *New York Times* report in *Grand Rapids Press*, p. A10. (p. 312)

Tollefson, G. D., & others (1993). Evaluation of suicidality during pharmacologic treatment of mood and nonmood disorders. *Annals of Clinical Psychiatry, 5*, 209-224. (p. 510)

Tolman, E. C., & Honzik, C. H. (1930). Introduction and removal of reward, and maze performance in rats. *University of California Publications in Psychology, 4*, 257–275. (p. 260)

Tolstoy, L. (1904). *My confessions*. Boston: Dana Estes. (p. 5)

Torrey, E. F. (1986). *Witchdoctors and psychiatrists*. New York: Harper & Row. (p. 506)

Torrey, E. F., Bowler, A. E., Rawlings, R., & Terrazas, A. (1993). Seasonality of schizophrenia and stillbirths. *Schizophrenia Bulletin, 19*, 557–562. (p. 478)

Torrey, E. F., Rawlings, R. R., Ennis, J. M., Merrill, D. D., & Flores, D. S. (1996). Birth seasonality in bipolar disorder, schizophrenia, schizoaffective disorder and stillbirths. *Schizophrenia Research, 21*, 141-149. (p. 478)

Torrey, E. F., Torrey, B. B., & Peterson, M. A. (1977). Seasonality of schizophrenic births in the United States. *Archives of General Psychiatry, 34*, 1065–1070. (p. 478)

Towler, G. (1986). From zero to one hundred: Coaction in a natural setting. *Perceptual and Motor Skills, 62*, 377–378. (p. 561)

Tramontana, M. G., Hooper, S. R., & Selzer, S. C. (1988). Research on the preschool prediction of later academic achievement: A review. *Developmental Review, 8*, 89–146. (p. 348)

Travis, J. (1994). Glia: The brain's other cells. *Science, 266*, 970-972. (p. 58)

Treisman, A. (1987). Properties, parts, and objects. In K. R. Boff, L. Kaufman, & J. P. Thomas (Eds.), *Handbook of perception and human performance*. New York: Wiley. (p. 185)

Tremblay, R. E., Pihl, R. O., Vitaro, F., & Dobkin, P. L. (1994). Predicting early onset of male antisocial behavior from preschool behavior. *Archives of General Psychiatry, 51*, 732-739. (p. 482)

Triandis, H. C. (1981). Some dimensions of intercultural variation and their implications for interpersonal behavior. Paper presented at the American Psychological Association convention. (p. 565)

Triandis, H. C. (1989a). The self and social behavior in differing cultural contexts. *Psychological Review, 96*, 506–520. (p. 441)

Triandis, H. C. (1989b). Cross-cultural studies of individualism and collectivism. In J. J. Berman (Ed.), *Nebraska symposium on motivation 1989* (Vol. 37). Lincoln, NE: University of Nebraska Press. (pp. 441–442)

Triandis, H. C. (1994). *Culture and social behavior*. New York: McGraw-Hill. (pp. 105, 320, 401, 441, 446, 566, 573—574)

Triandis, H. C., Bontempo, R., Villareal, M. J., Asai, M., & Lucca, N. (1988). Individualism and collectivism: Cross-cultural perspectives on self-ingroup relationships. *Journal of Personality and Social Psychology, 54*, 323–338. (p. 443)

Trickett, P. K., & McBride-Chang, C. (1995). The developmental impact of different forms of child abuse and neglect. *Developmental Review, 15*, 311-337. (p. 100)

Trickett, P. K., & Putnam, F. W. (1993). Impact of child sexual abuse on females: Toward a developmental, psychobiological integration. *Psychological Science, 4*, 81–87. (p. 298)

Trimble, J. E. (1994). Cultural variations in the use of alcohol and drugs. In W. J. Lonner & R. Malpass (Eds.), *Psychology and culture*. Boston: Allyn & Bacon. (p. 237)

Triplett, N. (1898). The dynamogenic factors in pacemaking and competition. *American Journal of Psychology, 9*, 507–533. (p. 561)

Trolier, T. K., & Hamilton, D. L. (1986). Variables influencing judgments of correlational relations. *Journal of Personality and Social Psychology, 50*, 879–888. (p. 22)

Tsang, Y. C. (1938). Hunger motivation in gastrectomized rats. *Journal of Comparative Psychology, 26*, 1–17. (p. 369)

Tsuang, M. T., & Faraone, S. V. (1990). *The genetics of mood disorders*. Baltimore, MD: Johns Hopkins University Press. (p. 471)

Tubbs, M. E. (1986). Goal setting: A meta-analytic examination of the empirical evidence. *Journal of Applied Psychology, 71*, 474–483. (p. 388)

Tucker, L. A. (1983). Muscular strength and mental health. *Journal of Personality and Social Psychology, 45*, 1355–1360. (p. 431)

Tulving, E. (1996, August 18). Quoted in J. Gatehouse, Technology revealing brain's secrets. *Montreal Gazette*, p. A3. (p. 287)

Turk, D. C., Meichenbaum, D. H., & Berman, W. H. (1979). Application of biofeedback for the regulation of pain: A critical review. *Psychological Bulletin, 86*, 1322–1338. (p. 531)

Turkheimer, E. (1991). Individual and group differences in adoption studies of IQ. *Psychological Bulletin, 110*, 392–405. (p. 354)

Turkington, C. (1987, August). Help for the worried well. *Psychology Today*, pp. 44–48. (p. 504)

Turnbull, C. (1961). *The forest people*. New York: Simon and Schuster. (p. 192)

Turner, C. W., Hesse, B. W., & Peterson-Lewis, S. (1986). Naturalistic studies of the long-term effects of television violence. *Journal of Social Issues, 42*(3), 7–28. (p. 575)

Tversky, A. (1985, June). Quoted in K. McKean, Decisions, decisions. *Discover*, pp. 22-31. (p. 310)

Tversky, A., & Gati, I. (1978). *Studies of similarity. In E. Rosch & B. Lloyd (Eds.), Cognition and categorization*. Hillsdale, NJ: Erlbaum. Reported by T. Gilovich (1991), *How we know what isn't so: The fallibility of human reason in everyday life*. New York: Free Press. (p. 16)

Tversky, A., & Kahneman, D. (1974). Judgment under uncertainty: Heuristics and biases. *Science, 185,* 1124–1131. (pp. 310, 600)

Twenge, J. M. (1996). Sex differences in personality traits, 1940-1992. Paper presented at the Midwestern Psychological Association convention. (p. 566)

Twiss, C., Tabb, S., & Crosby, F. (1989). Affirmative action and aggregate data: The importance of patterns in the perception of discrimination. In F. Blanchard & F. Crosby (Eds.), *Affirmative action: Social psychological perspectives.* New York: Springer-Verlag. (p. 599)

U.S. Congress, Office of Technology Assessment. (1983, November). *Scientific validity of polygraph testing: A research review and evaluation—A technical memorandum,* p. 4. Washington, DC: U.S. Government Printing Office. (p. 397)

Uchino, B. N., Cacioppo, J. T., & Kiecolt-Glaser, J. K. (1996). The relationship between social support and physiological processes: A review with emphasis on underlying mechanisms and implications for health. *Psychological Bulletin, 119,* 488-531. (p. 533)

Ulrich, R. E. (1991). Animal rights, animal wrongs and the question of balance. *Psychological Science, 2,* 197–201. (p. 34)

Ulrich, R. S. (1984). View through a window may influence recovery from surgery. *Science, 224,* 420–421. (p. 173)

Umilta, C., Simion, F., & Valenza, E. (1996). Newborn's preference for faces. *European Psychologist, 1,* 200-205. (p. 81)

Underwood, B. J. (1957). Interference and forgetting. *Psychological Review, 64,* 49–60. (p. 292)

UNICEF (1996). *The state of the world's children.* New York: Oxford University Press. (p. 566)

United Nations (1991). *The world's women 1970–1990: Trends and statistics.* New York: United Nations. (p. 568)

United Nations (1992). *1991 demographic yearbook.* New York: United Nations. (pp. 137, 571)

United Nations (1993). Children: A basic focus in IYF. *The Family,* No. 3., pp. 1–2. (p. 568)

University of California (1993, December). The new American body. *University of California at Berkeley Wellness Letter,* pp. 1–2. (p. 543)

Urbany, J. E., Bearden, W. O., & Weilbaker, D. C. (1988). The effect of plausible and exaggerated reference prices on consumer perceptions and price search. *Journal of Consumer Research, 15,* 95–110. (p. 314)

Valenstein, E. S. (1986). *Great and desperate cures: The rise and decline of psychosurgery.* New York: Basic Books. (pp. 57, 511)

Vallone, R. P., Griffin, D. W., Lin, S., & Ross, L. (1990). Overconfident prediction of future actions and outcomes by self and others. *Journal of Personality and Social Psychology, 58,* 582–592. (p. 16)

Vance, E. B., & Wagner, N. N. (1976). Written descriptions of orgasm: A study of sex differences. *Archives of Sexual Behavior, 5,* 87–98. (p. 375)

van den Boom, D. (1990). Preventive intervention and the quality of mother-infant interaction and infant exploration in irritable infants. In W. Koops, H. J. G. Soppe, J. L. van der Linden, P. C. M. Molenaar, & J. J. F. Schroots (Eds.), *Developmental psychology behind the dikes: An outline of developmental psychology research in The Netherlands.* The Netherlands: Uitgeverij Eburon. Cited by C. Hazan & P. R. Shaver (1994). Deeper into attachment theory. *Psychological Inquiry, 5,* 68–79. (p. 97)

van der Meer, A. L. H., van der Weel, F. R., & Lee, D. N. (1995). The functional significance of arm movements in neonates. *Science, 267,* 693-695. (p. 86)

VanderStoep, S. W., & Shaughnessy, J. J. (1997). Taking a course in research methods improves reasoning about real-life events. *Teaching of Psychology, 24,* 122-124. (p. 30)

van Drunen, P. (1996). Professional psychology in the Netherlands: History and recent trends. In A. Schorr & S. Saari (Eds.), *Psychology in Europe: Facts, figures, realities.* Gottingen: Hogrefe & Huber. (p. 8)

Van Dyke, C., & Byck, R. (1982, March). Cocaine. *Scientific American,* pp. 128–141. (p. 234)

van IJzendoorn, M. H., & Kroonenberg, P. M. (1988). Cross-cultural patterns of attachment: A meta-analysis of the strange situation. *Child Development, 59,* 147–156. (p. 96)

Van Leeuwen, M. S. (1978). A cross-cultural examination of psychological differentiation in males and females. *International Journal of Psychology, 13,* 87–122. (p. 566)

Van Leeuwen, M. S. (1982). IQism and the just society: Historical background. *Journal of the American Scientific Affiliation, 34,* 193–201. (p. 344)

VanTassel-Baska, J. (1983). Profiles of precocity: The 1982 Midwest Talent Search finalists. *Gifted Child Quarterly, 27,* 139–145. (p. 348)

Van Yperen, N. W., & Buunk, B. P. (1990). A longitudinal study of equity and satisfaction in intimate relationships. *European Journal of Social Psychology, 20,* 287–309. (p. 585)

Vaughn, K. B., & Lanzetta, J. T. (1981). The effect of modification of expressive displays on vicarious emotional arousal. *Journal of Experimental Social Psychology, 17,* 16–30. (p. 403)

Vaux, A. (1988). Social and personal factors in loneliness. *Journal of Social and Clinical Psychology, 6,* 462–471. (p. 475)

Veggeberg, S. K. (1996, March-April). Manic depression: Gene-Hunters' hopes rise. *Brain Work,* pp. 1-2. (p. 471)

Vekassy, L. (1977). Dreams of the blind. *Magyar Pszichologiai Szemle, 34,* 478–491. (p. 218)

Vemer, E., Coleman, M., Ganong, L. H., & Cooper, H. (1989). Marital satisfaction in remarriage: A meta-analysis. *Journal of Marriage and the Family, 51,* 713–725. (p. 138)

Venn, J. (1986). Hypnosis and the Lamaze method: A reply to Wideman and Singer. *American Psychologist, 41,* 475–476. (p. 226)

Vernon, P. A. (1983). Speed of information processing and general intelligence. *Intelligence, 7,* 53–70. (p. 342)

Vetter, B. M. (1989, July 7). Manpower data need an overhaul. *AAAS Observer,* p. 10 (presents NSF estimate of 254,000 psychologists and Bureau of Labor Statistics estimate of 165,000). (p. 8)

Vines, G. (1995, July 22). Fight fat with feeling. *New Scientist*, pp. 14-15. (p. 545)

Vines, G. (1995, July 8). Genes in black and white. *New Scientist*, pp. 34-37. (p. 567)

Vokey, J. R., & Read, J. D. (1985). Subliminal messages: Between the devil and the media. *American Psychologist, 40*, 1231–1239. (pp. 151, 197)

von Békésy, B. (1957, August). The ear. *Scientific American*, pp. 66–78. (p. 165)

von Frisch, K. (1950). *Bees: Their vision, chemical senses, and language*. Ithaca, NY: Cornell University Press. (p. 325)

von Frisch, K. (1974). Decoding the language of the bee. *Science, 185*, 663–668. (p. 325)

von Senden, M. (1932; reprinted 1960). In P. Heath (Trans.), *Space and sight: The perception of space and shape in the congenitally blind before and after operation*. Glencoe, IL: Free Press. (p. 195)

Voyer, D., Voyer, S., & Bryden, M. P. (1995). Magnitude of sex differences in spatial abilities: A meta-analysis and consideration of critical variables. *Psychological Bulletin, 117*, 250-270. (p. 358)

Vreeland, C. N., Gallagher, B. J., III, & McFalls, J. A., Jr. (1995). The beliefs of members of the American Psychiatric Association on the etiology of male homosexuality: A national survey. *Journal of Psychology, 129*, 507-517. (p. 382)

Vygotsky, L. S. (1932, reprinted 1962). *Thought and language* (E. Haufmann & G. Vaker, Eds. & trans.). Cambridge, MA: MIT Press. (p. 92)

Waddington, J. L. (1993). Neurodynamics of abnormalities in cerebral metabolism and structure in schizophrenia. *Schizophrenia Bulletin, 19*, 55–69. (p. 478)

Wagstaff, G. (1982). Attitudes to rape: The "just world" strikes again? *Bulletin of the British Psychological Society, 13*, 275–283. (p. 551)

Wahl, O. F. (1992). Mass media images of mental illness: A review of the literature. *Journal of Community Psychology, 20*, 343–352. (p. 459)

Wakefield, J. C. (1987). The semantics of success: Do masturbation exercises lead to partner orgasm? *Journal of Sex and Marital Therapy, 13*, 3–14. (p. 378)

Wakefield, J. C. (1992). The concept of mental disorder: On the boundary between biological facts and social values. *American Psychologist, 47*, 373–388. (p. 455)

Waldrop, M. M. (1987). The workings of working memory. *Science, 237*, 1564–1567. (p. 279)

Wallace, D. S., Lord, C. G., & Bond, Jr., C. F. (1996). Which behaviors do attitudes predict? Review and meta-analysis of 60 years' research. Unpublished manuscript, Ohio University. (p. 551)

Wallach, M. A., & Wallach, L. (1983). *Psychology's sanction for selfishness: The error of egoism in theory and therapy*. New York: Freeman. (p. 444)

Wallach, M. A., & Wallach, L. (1985, February). How psychology sanctions the cult of the self. *Washington Monthly*, pp. 46–56. (p. 444)

Wallbott, H. G. (1988). In and out of context: Influences of facial expression and context information on emotion attributions. *British Journal of Social Psychology, 27*, 357–369. (p. 200)

Waller, D. (1995, December 11). The vision thing. *Time*, p. 48. (p. 203)

Wallerstein, J. S. (1991). The long-term effects of divorce on children: A review. *Journal of the American Academy of Child and Adolescent Psychiatry, 30*, 349–360. (p. 102)

Wallis, C. (1983, June 6). Stress: Can we cope? *Time*, pp. 48–54. (p. 520)

Wallis, C. (1987, October 12). Back off, buddy: A new Hite report stirs up a furor over sex and love in the '80s. *Time*, pp. 68–73. (p. 20)

Walster (Hatfield), E., Aronson, V., Abrahams, D., & Rottman, L. (1966). Importance of physical attractiveness in dating behavior. *Journal of Personality and Social Psychology, 4*, 508–516. (p. 581)

Warchol, M. E., Lambert, P. R., Goldstein, B. J., Forge, A., & Corwin, J. T. (1993). Regenerative proliferation in inner ear sensory epithelia from adult guinea pigs and humans. *Science, 259*, 1619–1622. (p. 167)

Ward, C. (1994). Culture and altered states of consciousness. In W. J. Lonner & R. Malpass (Eds.), *Psychology and culture*. Boston: Allyn & Bacon. (p. 232)

Warm, J. S., & Dember, W. N. (1986, April). Awake at the switch. *Psychology Today*, pp. 46–53. (p. 149)

Warr, P., & Payne, R. (1982). Experiences of strain and pleasure among British adults. *Social Science and Medicine, 16*, 1691–1697. (p. 533)

Wason, P. C. (1960). On the failure to eliminate hypotheses in a conceptual task. *Quarterly Journal of Experimental Psychology, 12*, 129–140. (p. 308)

Wason, P. C. (1981). The importance of cognitive illusions. *The Behavioral and Brain Sciences, 4*, 356. (p. 16)

Wass, H., Christian, M., Myers, J., & Murphey, M. (1978–1979). Similarities and dissimilarities in attitudes toward death in a population of older persons. *Omega, 9*, 337–354. (p. 141)

Wasserman, E. A. (1993). Comparative cognition: Toward a general understanding of cognition in behavior. *Psychological Science, 4*, 156–161. (p. 256)

Wasserman, E. A. (1995). The conceptual abilities of pigeons. *American Scientist, 83*, 246-255. (p. 306)

Waterhouse, R. (1993, July 19). Income for 62 percent is below average pay. *The Independent*, p. 4. (p. 596)

Waterman, A. S. (1988). Identity status theory and Erikson's theory: Commonalities and differences. *Developmental Review, 8*, 185–208. (p. 122)

Watkins, J. G. (1984). The Bianchi (L. A. Hillside Strangler) case: Sociopath or multiple personality? *International Journal of Clinical and Experimental Hypnosis, 32*, 67–101. (p. 466)

Watson, J. B. (1913). Psychology as the behaviorist views it. *Psychological Review, 20*, 158–177. (pp. 208, 245)

Watson, J. B. (1924). *Behaviorism.* New York: Norton. (p. 252)

Watson, J. B., & Rayner, R. (1920). Conditioned emotional reactions. *Journal of Experimental Psychology, 3*, 1–14. (pp. 252–253)

Watson, R. I., Jr. (1973). Investigation into deindividuation using a cross-cultural survey technique. *Journal of Personality and Social Psychology, 25,* 342–345. (p. 562)

Wayment, H. A., & Peplau, L. A. (1995). Social support and well-being among lesbian and heterosexual women: A structural modeling approach. *Personality and Social Psychology Bulletin, 21,* 1189-1199. (p. 138)

Weaver, J. B., Masland, J. L., & Zillmann, D. (1984). Effect of erotica on young men's aesthetic perception of their female sexual partners. *Perceptual and Motor Skills, 58,* 929–930. (p. 377)

Webb, W. B. (1992). *Sleep: The gentle tyrant.* Bolton, MA: Anker Publishing. (pp. 213, 217)

Webb, W. B., & Campbell, S. S. (1983). Relationships in sleep characteristics of identical and fraternal twins. *Archives of General Psychiatry, 40,* 1093–1095. (p. 216)

Wechsler, D. (1972). "Hold" and "Don't Hold" tests. In S. M. Chown (Ed.), *Human aging.* New York: Penguin. (p. 134)

Wechsler, H., Davenport, A., Dowdall, G., Moeykens, B., & Castillo, S. (1994). Health and behavioral consequences of binge drinking in college. *Journal of the American Medical Association, 272,* 1672-1677. (p. 232)

Wegner, D. M. (1990). *White bears and other unwanted thoughts: Suppression, obsession, and the psychology of mental control.* New York: Penguin Books. (p. 535)

Weinberg, M. S., & Williams, C. (1974). *Male homosexuals: Their problems and adaptations.* New York: Oxford University Press. (p. 380)

Weindruch, R. (1996, January). Caloric restriction and aging. *Scientific American,* pp. 46-52. (p. 540)

Weiner, B. (1985). An attributional theory of achievement motivation and emotion. *Psychological Review, 92,* 548–573. (p. 416)

Weingartner, H., Rudorfer, M. V., Buchsbaum, M. S., & Linnoila, M. (1983). Effects of serotonin on memory impairments produced by ethanol. *Science, 221,* 472–473. (p. 285)

Weinstein, N. (1996, October 4). 1996 optimistic bias bibliography. Distributed via internet from weinstein_c@aesop.rutgers.edu. (p. 447)

Weinstein, N. D. (1980). Unrealistic optimism about future life events. *Journal of Personality and Social Psychology, 39,* 806–820. (p. 447)

Weinstein, N. D. (1982). Unrealistic optimism about susceptibility to health problems. *Journal of Behavioral Medicine, 5,* 441–460. (p. 447)

Weinstein, N. D. (1987). Unrealistic optimism about susceptibility to health problems: Conclusions from a community-wide sample. *Journal of Behavioral Medicine, 10,* 481–500. (p. 546)

Weiss, J. M. (1977). Psychological and behavioral influences on gastrointestinal lesions in animal models. In J. D. Maser & M. E. P. Seligman (Eds.), *Psychopathology: Experimental models.* San Francisco: Freeman. (p. 520)

Weisse, C. S. (1992). Depression and immunocompetence: A review of the literature. *Psychological Bulletin, 111,* 475–489. (p. 524)

Weissman, M. M., & others (1996). Cross-national epidemiology of major depression and bipolar disorder. *Journal of the American Medical Association, 276,* 293-299. (p. 470)

Weissman, M. M., Merikangas, K. R., Wickramaratne, P., Kidd, K. K., Prusoff, B. A., Leckman, J. F., & Pauls, D. L. (1986). Understanding the clinical heterogeneity of major depression using family data. *Archives of General Psychiatry, 43,* 430–434. (p. 471)

Weisz, J. R., Rothbaum, F. M., & Blackburn, T. C. (1984). Standing out and standing in: The psychology of control in America and Japan. *American Psychologist, 39,* 955–969. (p. 565)

Weller, S. (1993). A meta-analysis of condom effectiveness in reducing sexually transmitted HIV. *Social Science and Medicine, 36.* 1635-1644. (p. 126)

Wellman, H. M., & Gelman, S. A. (1992). Cognitive development: Foundational theories of core domains. *Annual Review of Psychology, 43,* 337–375. (p. 89)

Wells, B. L. (1986). Predictors of female nocturnal orgasms: A multivariate analysis. *Journal of Sex Research, 22,* 421–437. (p. 377)

Wells, G., & Murray, D. M. (1984). Eyewitness confidence. In G. L. Wells & E. F. Loftus (Eds.), *Eyewitness testimony: Psychological perspectives.* New York: Cambridge University Press. (p. 297)

Wells, G. L. (1981). Lay analyses of causal forces on behavior. In J. Harvey (Ed.), *Cognition, social behavior and the environment.* Hillsdale, NJ: Erlbaum. (p. 244)

Wender, P. H., Kety, S. S., Rosenthal, D., Schulsinger, F., Ortmann, J., & Lunde, I. (1986). Psychiatric disorders in the biological and adoptive families of adopted individuals with affective disorders. *Archives of General Psychiatry, 43,* 923–929. (p. 471)

Wenderoth, P. (1992). Perceptual illusions. *Australian Journal of Psychology, 44,* 147–151. (p. 185)

Wener, R., Frazier, W., & Farbstein, J. (1987, June). Building better jails. *Psychology Today,* pp. 40–49. (p. 446)

Werker, J. F. (1989). Becoming a native listener. *American Scientist, 77,* 54–59. (p. 321)

West, P. D. B., & Evans, E. F. (1990). Early detection of hearing damage in young listeners resulting from exposure to amplified music. *British Journal of Audiology, 24,* 89–103. (p. 166)

Westefeld, J. S., & Furr, S. R. (1987). Suicide and depression among college students. *Professional Psychology: Research and Practice, 18,* 119–123. (p. 469)

Westen, D. (1996). Is Freud really dead? Teaching psychodynamic theory to introductory psychology. Presentation to the Annual Institute on the Teaching of Psychology, St. Petersburg Beach, Florida. (p. 425)

Wever, E. G. (1949). Theory of hearing. New York: Wiley. (p. 167)

Wheeler, D. L., Jacobson, D. L., Paglieri, R. A., & Schwartz, A. A. (1993). An experimental assessment of facilitated communication. *Mental Retardation, 31,* 49–60. (p. 560)

Whitam, F. L., Diamond, M., & Martin, J. (1993). Homosexual orientation in twins: A report on 61 pairs and three triplet sets. *Archives of Sexual Behavior, 22,* 187-206. (p. 381)

Whitbourne, S. K., Zuschlag, M. K., Elliot, L. B., & Waterman, A. S. (1992). Psychosocial development in adulthood: A 22-year sequential study. *Journal of Personality and Social Psychology, 63,* 260–271. (p. 143)

White, G. L., & Kight, T. D. (1984). Misattribution of arousal and attraction: Effects of salience of explanations for arousal. *Journal of Experimental Social Psychology, 20,* 55–64. (p. 584)

White, H. R., Brick, J., & Hansell, S. (1993). A longitudinal investigation of alcohol use and aggression in adolescence. *Journal of Studies on Alcohol,* Supplement No. 11, 62–77. (p. 573)

White, K. M. (1983). Young adults and their parents: Individuation to mutuality. *New Directions for Child Development, 22,* 61–76. (p. 125)

White, L., & Edwards, J. (1990). Emptying the nest and parental well-being: An analysis of national panel data. *American Sociological Review, 55,* 235–242. (p. 138)

White, P. H., Kjelgaard, M. M., & Harkins, S. G. (1995). Testing the contribution of self-evaluation to goal-setting effects. *Journal of Personality and Social Psychology, 69,* 69-79. (p. 388)

Whitehead, B. D. (1993, April). Dan Quayle was right. *The Atlantic,* pp. 47–84. (p. 98)

Whiten, A., & Byrne, R. W. (1988). Tactical deception in primates. *Behavioral and Brain Sciences, 11,* 233–244, 267–273. (p. 20)

Whiteneck, G. G., & others (1985). A collaborative study of high quadriplegia. Englewood, CO: Rocky Mountain Regional Spinal Cord Injury System for the National Institute of Handicapped Research. (p. 407)

Whiting, B. B., & Edwards, C. P. (1988). *Children of different worlds: The formation of social behavior.* Cambridge, MA: Harvard University Press. (p. 105)

Whitley, B. E., Jr. (1990). The relationships of heterosexuals' attributions for the causes of homosexuality to attitudes toward lesbians and gay men. *Personality and Social Psychology Bulletin, 16,* 369–377. (p. 382)

Whorf, B. L. (1956). Science and linguistics. In J. B. Carroll (Ed.), *Language, thought, and reality: Selected writings of Benjamin Lee Whorf.* Cambridge, MA: MIT Press. (p. 328)

Wickelgren, W. A. (1977). *Learning and memory.* Englewood Cliffs, NJ: Prentice-Hall. (p. 276)

Wicker, A. W. (1971). An examination of the "other variables" explanation of attitude-behavior inconsistency. *Journal of Personality and Social Psychology, 19,* 18–30. (p. 551)

Wickless, C., & Kirsch, I. (1989). Effects of verbal and experiential expectancy manipulations on hypnotic susceptibility. *Journal of Personality and Social Psychology, 57,* 762–768. (p. 222)

Widom, C. S. (1989a). Does violence beget violence? A critical examination of the literature. *Psychological Bulletin, 106,* 3–28. (p. 100)

Widom, C. S. (1989b). The cycle of violence. *Science, 244,* 160–166. (p. 100)

Wiens, A. N., & Menustik, C. E. (1983). Treatment outcome and patient characteristics in an aversion therapy program for alcoholism. *American Psychologist, 38,* 1089–1096. (p. 495)

Wierson, M., & Forehand, R. (1994). Parent behavioral training for child noncompliance: Rationale, concepts, and effectiveness. *Current Directions in Psychological Science, 3,* 146-149. (p. 264)

Wierzbicki, M. (1993). Psychological adjustment of adoptees: A meta-analysis. *Journal of Clinical Child Psychology, 22,* 447–454. (p. 111)

Wiesel, T. N. (1982). Postnatal development of the visual cortex and the influence of environment. *Nature, 299,* 583–591. (p. 195)

Wigdor, A. K., & Garner, W. R. (1982). *Ability testing: Uses, consequences, and controversies.* Washington, DC: National Academy Press. (p. 359)

Wiggins, J. S. (ed.) (1996). *The five-factor model of personality: Theoretical perspectives.* New York: Guilford. (p. 432)

Wilder, D. A. (1981). Perceiving persons as a group: Categorization and intergroup relations. In D. L. Hamilton (Ed.), *Cognitive processes in stereotyping and intergroup behavior.* Hillsdale, NJ: Erlbaum. (p. 569)

Wilkinson, C. B. (1983). Aftermath of a disaster: The collapse of the Hyatt Regency Hotel skywalks. *American Journal of Psychiatry, 140,* 1134-1139. (p. 428)

Williams, C. L., & Berry, J. W. (1991). Primary prevention of acculturative stress among refugees. *American Psychologist, 46,* 632–641. (p. 519)

Williams, J. E., & Best, D. L. (1990). *Measuring sex stereotypes: A multination study.* Newbury Park, CA: Sage. (p. 389)

Williams, L. M. (1994). Recall of childhood trauma: A prospective study of women's memories of child sexual abuse. *Journal of Consulting and Clinical Psychology, 62,* 1167–1176. (p. 299)

Williams, R. (1989). *The trusting heart: Great news about Type A behavior.* New York: Random House. (p. 522)

Williams, R. (1993). *Anger kills.* New York: Times Books. (p. 522)

Williams, R. B., Barefoot, J. C., Califf, R. M., Haney, T. L., Saunders, W. B., Pryor, D. B., Hlatky, M. A., Siegler, I. C., Mark, D. B. (1992). Prognostic importance of social and economic resources among medically treated patients with angiographically documented coronary artery disease. *Journal of the American Medical Association, 267,* 520–524. (p. 533)

Williams, S. L. (1987). Self-efficacy and mastery-oriented treatment for severe phobias. Paper presented to the American Psychological Association convention. (p. 494).

Willingham, W. W., Lewis, C., Morgan, R., & Ramist, L. (1990). *Predicting college grades: An analysis of institutional trends over two decades.* Princeton: Educational Testing Service. (p. 347)

Willmuth, M. E. (1987). Sexuality after spinal cord injury: A critical review. *Clinical Psychology Review, 7,* 389–412. (p. 377)

Wilmut, I., Schnieke, A. E., McWhir, J., Kind, A. J., & Campbell, K. H. S. (1997). Viable offspring derived from fetal and adult mammalian cells. *Nature, 385,* 810-813. (p. 108)

Wilson, J. G. (1993). *The moral sense.* New York: Free Press. (p. 566)

Wilson, J. P., Harel, Z., & Kahana, B. (1988). *Human adaptation to extreme stress: From the Holocaust to Vietnam.* New York: Plenum Press. (p. 461)

Wilson, J. Q., & Herrnstein, R. J. (1985). *Crime and human nature.* New York: Simon and Schuster. (p. 572)

Wilson, R. C., Gaft, J. G., Dienst, E. R., Wood, L., & Bavry, J. L. (1975). *College professors and their impact on students.* New York: Wiley. (p. 562)

Wilson, R. S. (1978). Synchronies in mental development: An epigenetic perspective. *Science, 202,* 939–948. (p. 86)

Wilson, R. S. (1979). Analysis of longitudinal twin data: Basic model and applications to physical growth measures. *Acta Geneticae medicae et Gemellologiae, 28,* 93–105. (p. 86)

Wilson, R. S., & Matheny, A. P., Jr. (1986). Behavior-genetics research in infant temperament: The Louisville twin study. In R. Plomin & J. Dunn (Eds.), *The study of temperament: Changes, continuities, and challenges.* Hillsdale, NJ: Erlbaum. (p. 96)

Wilson, S. C., & Barber, T. X. (1983). The fantasy-prone personality: Implications for understanding imagery, hypnosis, and parapsychological phenomena. In A. A. Sheikh (Ed.), *Imagery: Current theory, research, and applications.* New York: Wiley. (pp. 209, 239)

Wilson, W. R. (1979). Feeling more than we can know: Exposure effects without learning. *Journal of Personality and Social Psychology, 37,* 811–821. (p. 182)

Winckelgren, I. (1992). How the brain 'sees' borders where there are none. *Science, 256,* 1520–1521. (p. 185)

Windholz, G. (1989, April-June). The discovery of the principles of reinforcement, extinction, generalization, and differentiation of conditional reflexes in Pavlov's laboratories. *Pavlovian Journal of Biological Science, 26,* 64–74. (p. 249)

Wing, R. R., & Jeffrey, R. W. (1979). Outpatient treatments of obesity: A comparison of methodology and clinical results. *International Journal of Obesity, 3,* 261–279. (p. 543)

Wingert, P., & Kantrowitz, B. (1990, Winter/Spring). The day care generation. *Newsweek special edition: The 21st century family,* pp. 86–92. (p. 102)

Winn, P. (1995). The lateral hypothalamus and motivated behavior: An old syndrome reassessed and a new perspective gained. *Current Directions in Psychological Science, 4,* 182-187. (p. 370)

Witelson, S. F. (1985). The brain connection: The corpus callosum is larger in left-handers. *Science, 229,* 665–667. (p. 68)

Witelson, S. F., & McCulloch, P. B. (1991). Premortem and postmorten measurement to study structure with function: A human brain collection. *Schizophrenia Bulletin, 17,* 583–591. (p. 341)

Wixted, J. T., & Ebbesen, E. B. (1991). On the form of forgetting. *Psychological Science, 2,* 409–415. (p. 282)

Woehr, D. J., & Cavell, T. A. (1993). Self-report measures of ability, effort, and nonacademic activity as predictors of introductory psychology test scores. *Teaching of Psychology, 20,* 156–160. (p. 9)

Wolf, N. (1991). *The beauty myth: How images of beauty are used against women.* New York: Morrow. (p. 543)

Wolf, R. (1996, May/June). Believing what we see, hear, and touch: The delights and dangers of sensory illusions. *Skeptical Inquirer,* pp. 23-30. (p. 187)

Woll, S. (1986). So many to choose from: Decision strategies in videodating. *Journal of Social and Personal Relationships, 3,* 43–52. (p. 581)

Wolpe, J. (1958). *Psychotherapy by reciprocal inhibition.* Stanford, CA: Stanford University Press. (p. 493)

Wolpe, J. (1982). *The practice of behavior therapy.* New York: Pergamon. (p. 493)

Wong, D. F., & associates. (1986). Positron emission tomography reveals elevated D2 dopamine receptors in drug-naive schizophrenics. *Science, 234,* 1588–1563. (p. 478)

Wong, M. M., & Csikszentmihalyi, M. (1991). Affiliation motivation and daily experience: Some issues on gender differences. *Journal of Personality and Social Psychology, 60,* 154–164. (p. 123)

Wood, C. J, & Aggleton, J. P. (1989). Handedness in `fast ball' sports: Do left-handers have an innate advantage? *British Journal of Psychology, 80,* 227–240. (p. 68)

Wood, G. (1979). The knew-it-all-along effect. *Journal of Experimental Psychology: Human Perception and Performance, 4,* 345–353. (p. 14)

Wood, J. M., Bootzin, R. R., Kihlstrom, J. F., & Schacter, D. L. (1992). Implicit and explicit memory for verbal information presented during sleep. *Psychological Science, 3,* 236–239. (p. 274)

Wood, J. M., Bootzin, R. R., Rosenhan, D., Nolen-Hoeksema, S., & Jourden, F. (1992). Effects of the 1989 San Francisco earthquake on frequency and content of nightmares. *Journal of Abnormal Psychology, 101,* 219–224. (p. 218)

Wood, J. M., Nezworski, M. T., & Stejskal, W. J. (1996). The comprehensive system for the Rorschach: A critical examination. *Psychological Science, 7,* 3-10. (p. 426)

Wood, J. V., Saltzberg, J. A., & Goldsamt, L. A. (1990). Does affect induce self-focused attention? *Journal of Personality and Social Psychology, 58,* 899–908. (pp. 291, 473)

Wood, J. V., Saltzberg, J. A., Neale, J. M., Stone, A. A., & Rachmiel, T. B. (1990). Self-focused attention, coping responses, and distressed mood in everyday life. *Journal of Personality and Social Psychology, 58,* 1027–1036. (p. 473)

Wood, W. (1987). Meta-analytic review of sex differences in group performance. *Psychological Bulletin, 102,* 53–71. (p. 389)

Wood, W., Lundgren, S., Ouellette, J. A., Busceme, S., & Blackstone, T. (1994). Minority influence: A meta-analytic review of social influence processes. *Psychological Bulletin, 115,* 323–345. (p. 564)

Wood, W., Wong, F. Y., & Chachere, J. G. (1991). Effects of media violence on viewers' aggression in unconstrained social interaction. *Psychological Bulletin, 109,* 371–383. (p. 575)

Woodruff-Pak, D. S. (1989). Aging and intelligence: Changing perspectives in the twentieth century. *Journal of Aging Studies, 3,* 91–118. (p. 134)

Woods, N. F., Dery, G. K., & Most, A. (1983). Recollections of menarche, current menstrual attitudes, and premenstrual symptoms. In S. Golub (Ed.), *Menarche: The transition from girl to woman.* Lexington, MA: Lexington Books. (p. 117)

Wooley, S., & Wooley, O. (1983). Should obesity be treated at all? *Psychiatric Annals, 13*(11), 884–885, 888. (p. 372)

World atlas: A multimedia view of the world (1993). A CD-ROM, Macintosh version 3. Novato, CA: Software Toolworks. (p. 483)

World Health Organization.(1979). *Schizophrenia: An international follow-up study.* Chicester, England: Wiley. (p. 477)

Worobey, J., & Blajda, V. M. (1989). Temperament ratings at 2 weeks, 2 months, and 1 year: Differential stability of activity and emotionality. *Developmental Psychology, 25,* 257–263. (p. 96)

Worthington, E. L., Jr. (1989). Religious faith across the life span: Implications for counseling and research. *The Counseling Psychologist, 17,* 555–612. (p. 118)

Worthington, E. L., Jr., Martin, G. A., Shumate, M., & Carpenter, J. (1983). The effect of brief Lamaze training and social encouragement on pain endurance in a cold pressor tank. *Journal of Applied Social Psychology, 13,* 223–233. (p. 173)

Worthington, E. L., Jr., Kurusu, T. A., McCullogh, M. E., & Sandage, S. J. (1996). Empirical research on religion and psychotherapeutic processes and outcomes: A 10-year review and research prospectus. *Psychological Bulletin, 119,* 448–487. (p. 507)

Wortman, C. B., & Silver, R. C. (1989). The myths of coping with loss. *Journal of Consulting and Clinical Psychology, 57,* 349–357. (p. 141)

Wright, P., & Murray, R. M. (1993). Schizophrenia: Prenatal influenza and autoimmunity. *Annals of Medicine, 25,* 497–502. (p. 478)

Wright, P., Takei, N., Rifkin, L., & Murray, R. M. (1995). Maternal influenza, obstetric complications, and schizophrenia. *American Journal of Psychiatry, 152,* 1714-1720. (p. 478)

Wu, T-C., Tashkin, D. P., Djahed, B., & Rose, J. E. (1988). Pulmonary hazards of smoking marijuana as compared with tobacco. *New England Journal of Medicine, 318,* 347–351. (p. 235)

Wulff, D. (1991). *The psychology of religion.* New York: Wiley. (p. 387)

Wyatt, J. K., & Bootzin, R. R. (1994). Cognitive processing and sleep: Implications for enhancing job performance. *Human Performance, 7,* 119–139. (pp. 218, 274)

Wynn, K. (1992). Addition and subtraction by human infants. *Nature, 358,* 749–759. (p. 91)

Wynn, K. (1995). Infants possess a system of numerical knowledge. *Current Directions in Psychological Science, 4,* 172-177. (p. 91)

Wysocki, C. J., & Gilbert, A. N. (1989). *National Geographic* survey: Effects of age are heterogeneous. *Annals of the New York Academy of Sciences, 561,* 12–28. (p. 175)

Yalom, I. D. (1985). *The theory and practice of group psychotherapy* (3rd ed.). New York: Basic Books. (p. 499)

Yang, N., & Linz, D. (1990). Movie ratings and the content of adult videos: The sex-violence ratio. *Journal of Communication, 40*(2), 28–42. (p. 577)

Yankelovich Partners (1995, May/June). Growing old. *American Enterprise,* p. 108. (p. 443)

Yapko, M. D. (1994). Suggestibility and repressed memories of abuse: A survey of psychotherapists' beliefs. *American Journal of Clinical Hypnosis, 36,* 163-171. (p. 223)

Yarmey, A. D. (1991). Voice identification over the telephone. *Journal of Applied Social Psychology, 21,* 1868–1876. (p. 297)

Yarnell, P. R., & Lynch, S. (1970, April 25). Retrograde memory immediately after concussion. *Lancet,* pp. 863–865. (p. 285)

Yarrow, L. J., Goodwin, M. S., Manheimer, H., & Milowe, I. D. (1973). Infancy experience and cognitive and personality development at ten years. In L. J. Stone, H. T. Smith, & L. B. Murphy (Eds.), *The competent infant.* New York: Basic Books. (p. 100)

Yates, A. (1989). Current perspectives on the eating disorders: I. History, psychological and biological aspects. *Journal of the American Academy of Child and Adolescent Psychiatry, 28,* 813–828. (p. 372)

Yates, A. (1990). Current perspectives on the eating disorders: II. Treatment, outcome, and research directions. *Journal of the American Academy of Child and Adolescent Psychiatry, 29,* 1–9. (p. 372)

Young, A. (1995). *The harmony of illusions: Inventing post-traumatic stress disorder.* Princeton: Princeton University Press. (p. 461)

Zajonc, R. B. (1965). Social facilitation. *Science, 149,* 269–274. (p. 561)

Zajonc, R. B. (1980). Feeling and thinking: Preferences need no inferences. *American Psychologist, 35,* 151–175. (p. 415)

Zajonc, R. B. (1984a). On the primacy of affect. *American Psychologist, 39,* 117–123. (p. 415)

Zajonc, R. B. (1984b, July 22). Quoted by D. Goleman, Rethinking IQ tests and their value. *The New York Times,* p. D22. (p. 315)

Zajonc, R. B. (in press). Emotions. In D. Gilbert, S. T. Fiske, & G. Lindzey (eds.), *Handbook of social psychology,* 4th ed. New York: McGraw-Hill. (p. 581, 582)

Zajonc, R. B., & Markus, G. B. (1975). Birth order and intellectual development. *Psychological Review, 82,* 74–88. (p. 602)

Zajonc, R. B., Murphy, S. T., & Inglehart, M. (1989). Feeling and facial efference: Implications of the vascular theory of emotions. *Psychological Review, 96,* 395–416. (p. 402)

Zaslow, M. J. (1991). Variation in child care quality and its implications for children. *Journal of Social Issues, 47*(2), 125–138. (p. 101)

Zechmeister, E. B., & Johnson, J. E. (1992). *Critical thinking: A functional approach.* Pacific Grove, CA: Brooks/Cole. (p. 590)

Zeidner, M. (1990). Perceptions of ethnic group modal intelligence: Reflections of cultural stereotypes or intelligence test scores? *Journal of Cross-Cultural Psychology, 21,* 214–231. (p. 356)

Zelnick, M., & Kim, Y. J. (1982). Sex education and its association with teenage sexual activity, pregnancy, and contraceptive use. *Family Planning Perspectives, 14*(3), 117–126. (p. 383)

Zigler, E. F. (1986, February). Quoted in D. Meredith, Day care: The nine-to-five dilemma. *Psychology Today,* pp. 36–39, 42–44. (p. 101)

Zigler, E. F. (1987). Formal schooling for four-year-olds? No. *American Psychologist, 42,* 254–260. (p. 355)

Zigler, E. F., & Muenchow, S. (1992). *Head start: The inside story of a great American experiment.* New York: Basic Books. (p. 355)

Zilbergeld, B. (1983). *The shrinking of America: Myths of psychological change.* Boston: Little, Brown. (pp. 502, 504)

Zillmann, D. (1986). Effects of prolonged consumption of pornography. Background paper for *The Surgeon General's workshop on* *pornography and public health,* June 22–24. Report prepared by E. P. Mulvey & J. L. Haugaard and released by Office of the Surgeon General on August 4, 1986. (pp. 395, 415)

Zillmann, D. (1989). Effects of prolonged consumption of pornography. In D. Zillmann & J. Bryant (Eds.), *Pornography: Research advances and policy considerations.* Hillsdale, NJ: Erlbaum. (pp. 377, 577)

Zillmann, D., & Bryant, J. (1984). Effects of massive exposure to pornography. In N. Malamuth & E. Donnerstein (Eds.), *Pornography and sexual aggression.* Orlando, FL: Academic Press. (p. 577)

Zimbardo, P. G. (1970). The human choice: Individuation, reason, and order versus deindividuation, impulse, and chaos. In W. J. Arnold & D. Levine (Eds.), *Nebraska Symposium on Motivation, 1969.* Lincoln, NE: University of Nebraska Press. (p. 562)

Zimbardo, P. G. (1972, April). Pathology of imprisonment. *Transaction/Society,* pp. 4–8. (p. 553)

Zucker, G. S., & Weiner, B. (1993). Conservatism and perceptions of poverty: An attributional analysis. *Journal of Applied Social Psychology, 23,* 925–943. (p. 551)

Zuckerman, M. (1979). *Sensation seeking: Beyond the optimal level of arousal.* Hillsdale, NJ: Erlbaum. (p. 365)

credits

photographs

introduction

Opener p. 0 Tom Stewart/The Stock Market; **p. 2** *(left)* Sally Cassidy/The Picture Cube; *(center)* Joe Carini/The Image Works; *(right)* Robert Caputo/Stock, Boston; **p. 3** Wundt, Hall, James, Thorndike, Freud, Binet, Watson: Brown Brothers; Ebbinghaus: The Bettman Archive; Calkins: Wellesley College Archives; Pavlov: Sovfoto; Washburn: National Library of Medicine; **p. 5** Robert Brenner/Photo Edit; **p. 6** Rob Nelson/Black Star; **p. 7** Laura Dwight; **p. 8** *(top)* Laura Dwight/Photo Edit; *(center and bottom)* Treë.

chapter *1*

Opener p. 10 Lawrence Migdale/Stock, Boston; **p. 12** Rob Kinmonth; **p. 14** Jim Pickerell/Stock, Boston; **p. 15** AP/Wide World Photos, Inc.; **p. 18** Susan Kuklin/Photo Researchers; **p. 21** Courtesy of David S. Wilke; **p. 22** *(left)* Michael Newman Jr./Photo Edit; *(right)* David Phillips/Photo Researchers; **p. 24** UPI/Corbis-Bettmann; **p. 26** R. Sidney/The Image Works; **p. 27** Super Stock; **p. 28** Smith/ Monkmeyer; **p. 32** Mark S. Wexler/Woodfin Camp & Associates; **p. 35** Jim Amos/Science Source/Photo Researchers; **p. 36** From *Mind Sights* by Roger N. Shepard. Copyright 1990 by Roger N. Shepard. Reprinted by permission of W. H. Freeman and Company.

chapter *2*

Opener p. 40 C/B Productions/The Stock Market; **p. 43** Oliver Meckes/Ottawa/Photo Researchers; **p. 45** Bob Daemmrich/Stock, Boston; **p. 52** A. Glauberman/Photo Researchers; **p. 53** *(top)* Alexander Tsiaras/Stock, Boston; *(bottom)* Hank Morgan/Rainbow; **p. 54** Daniel R. Weinberger, M.D. CBDB, NIMH; **p. 57** *(top)* Frank Siteman/Stock, Boston; *(bottom)* Pix*ELATION from Fran Heyl Associates; **p. 61** Courtesy of Drs. Jack Belliveau and Bruce Rosen, Massachusetts General Hospital, NMR Center; **p. 62** Hanna Damasio, M.D. University of Iowa and Science; **p. 65** Martin M. Rotker; **p. 68** *(top)* Mel Digiacomo/The Image Bank; *(left)* Reuters/The Bettmann Archive; *(right)* The Platt Collection/Archive Photos; **p. 70** Robert Brenner/Photo Edit.

chapter *3*

Opener p. 76 N. Markus/Photo Researchers; **p. 78** *(left and center)* AP/Wide World Photos, Inc.; *(right)* Lisa Quinones/Black Star; **p. 79** *(left)* Francis Leroy, Biocosmos/Science Photo Library/Photo Researchers; *(right)* Lennart Nilsson/Bonnier Fakta Bokforlag; **p. 80** *(right)* Donald Yeager/Camera MD Studios; *(left, center left and center right)* Petit Format/Science Source/Photo Researchers; **p. 81** *(top)* David Young-Wolff/Photo Edit; *(bottom)* Courtesy of Professor Carlo Umiltá and others/1991 American Psychological Association. Reprinted with permission; **p. 83** Courtesy of Carolyn Rovee-Collier, Rutgers University; **p. 84** *(left and right)* Courtesy of Avi Karni & Leslie Ungerleider, National Institute of Mental Health; **p. 85** Joe McNally; **p. 86** *(left)* Felicia Martinez/Photo Edit; *(center left)* Shackman/ Monkmeyer; *(center right)* Alan Carruthers/ Photo Researchers; *(right)* Bob Daemmrich Photos/Stock, Boston; **p. 88** Bill Anderson/Monkmeyer; **p. 89** *(top)* Patti Putnam/The Stock Market; *(bottom)* Doug Goodman/Monkmeyer; **p. 91** Ontario Science Centre; **p. 95** *(bottom)* Harlow Primate Laboratory, University of Wisconsin; *(top)* Elizabeth Crews/The Image Works; **p. 97** *(top)* B. Mahoney/The Image Works; *(bottom)* Harlow Primate Laboratory, University of Wisconsin; **p. 99** Laura Dwight; **p. 101** Susan Greenwood/The Gamma Liaison Network; **p. 103** Sybil Shackman/Monkmeyer; **p. 104** John Coletti/The Picture Cube; **p. 105** Sybil Shackman/Monkmeyer; **p. 106** Siteman/Monkmeyer; **p. 109** Bob Sacha; **p. 110** Kathleen Marie Menke/Crystal Images/ Monkmeyer; **p. 112** Richard Hutchings/Photo Edit.

chapter *4*

Opener p. 114 Mugshots/The Stock Market; **p. 116** Michael Newman/Photo Edit; **p. 117** J. Gerard Smith/Monkmeyer; **p. 119** *(right)* Charles Harbutt/Actuality; *(bottom)* Matt Herron/Black Star *(left)* Bob Daemmrich/The Image Works; **p. 121** *(center)* John Eastcott/YVA Momatiuk/The Image Works; *(bottom)* Esbin-Anderson/ The Image Works; **p. 122** *(left)* David Vance/The Image Bank; *(right)* David Delossy/The Image Bank; **p. 123** *(left)* Bob Daemmrich/The Image Works; *(right)* David J. Sams/Stock, Boston; **p. 124** Joel Gordon; **p. 130** Michael Newman/Photo Edit; **p. 131** David Wells/The Image Bank; **p. 133** Mary Kate Denny/Photo Edit; **p. 137**

Henley & Savage/Stock, Boston; **p. 138** Tom & Dee Ann McCarthy/Rainbow; **p. 140** *(left)* Joe McNally; *(center)* Bob Daemmrich/The Image Works; *(right)* Charles Harbutt/Actuality; **p. 143** Clyde H. Smith/ Peter Arnold.

chapter 5

Opener p. 146 Paul Barton/The Stock Market; **p. 148** Detail "The Forest Has Eyes" by Bev Doolittle, The Greenwich Workshops, Inc. Trumbull, CT; **p. 149** Carol Lee/Tony Stone Images; **p. 150** Marvin Lyons/The Image Bank; **p. 154** *(left and right)* Thomas Eisner; **p. 156** E.R. Lewis, Y.Y. Zeevi, F.S. Werblin, 1969; **p. 158** Courtesy Dr. Walter Schneider, University of Pittsburgh; **p. 159** *(top)* Fritz Goro, LIFE Magazine, Time Warner, Inc.; *(bottom)* Ross Kinnaird/Allsport; **p. 161** *(top)* Tim Bieber/The Image Bank; *(bottom)* Fritz Goro, LIFE Magazine Time Warner, Inc.; **p. 162** From Richmond Products, Boca Raton, Fl; **p. 163** From Albers, J. (1975). *The Interaction of Color* (revised pocket edition) (Plate VI-**3**). New Haven, Ct: Yale University Press. Photo courtesy of the Josef Albers Foundation.; **p. 164** *(top)* McCarthy/Peter Arnold; *(bottom)* Richard Kaylin/Tony Stone Images; **p. 166** David Barnes/Tony Stone Images; **p. 167** Stan Schroeder/Animals, Animals; **p. 168** Jill Levine; **p. 169** Dave Schlabowske/Time Magazine, Time Warner, Inc.; **p. 170** Bruce Ayres/Tony Stone Images; **p. 171** Michael P. Gadomski/ Photo Researchers; **p. 172** Paul J. Sutton/Duomo; **p. 173** Community News, Christchurch, New Zealand. Photo Courtesy of The Skeptical Inquirer.; **p. 176** B. Daemmrich/The Image Works; **p. 178** *(bottom)* B. Nation/Sygma; *(top)* Joseph McNally/Sygma.

chapter 6

Opener p. 180 Steve Satushek/The Image Bank; **p. 183** *(right and left)* S. Schwartzenberg/The Exploratorium; *(bottom)* Rick Friedman/Black Star, **p. 184** Photos courtesy of Helen E. Ross, from Ross, H.E. (1975). "Mist, murk and visual perception", New Scientist, 66, 658-660.; **p. 186** *(top)* Photo by Walter Wick; *(bottom)* Enrico Ferorelli; **p. 188** *(top)* Otto Greule, Jr./Allsport USA; *(center)* René Magritte, *The Blank Signature*, oil on canvas, National Gallery of Art, Washington. Collection of Mr & Mrs. Paul Mellon. Photo by Richard Carafelli; *(bottom)* Jim Steinberg/Photo Researchers; **p. 189** *(left)* Rainer Grosskopf/Tony Stone Worldwide; *(right)* Photo by George V. Kelvin. All rights reserved; *(bottom)* City Art Gallery, Bristol/The Bridgeman Art Library, Superstock; **p. 191** Alan Choisnet/The Image Bank; **p. 193** E. Schwartzenberg/The Exploratorium; **p. 194** Photo by Walter Wick; **p. 195** Blakemore, C.R., & Cooper, G.F. (1970). "Development of the Brain Depends on the Visual Environment". Nature, 228, 447-448. Reprinted by permission of Nature. Copyright 1970 Macmillan Journals Limited.; **p. 196** Courtesy of Hubert Dolezal; **p. 197** *(top)* From Mind Sights by Robert M. Shepard. Copyright 1990 by Robert N. Shepard. Reprinted by permission by W. H. Freeman & Company; *(left)* Frank Searle, photo Adams/Sygma; *(right)* Dick Ruhl; **p. 204** Alva Bernadine.

chapter 7

Opener p. 206 David M. Grossman; **p. 208** Jeff Greenberg/Photo Edit; **p. 209** Peter Turnley/Black Star; **p. 211** Hank Morgan/Rainbow; **p. 213** Ted Spagna/Science Source/Photo Researchers; **p. 214** Patrick Ward/Discover Magazine; **p. 217** Dan McCoy/Rainbow; **p. 219** *(bottom)* Tom Prettyman/Photo Edit; *(top)* Marc Chagall, *I*

and the Village, 1911. Oil on canvas, 6′ 3 5/8″ x 59 5/8″ (192.1 x 151.4 cm). The Museum of Modern Art, New York. Mrs. Simon Guggenheim Fund. Photograph: The Museum of Modern Art, New York; **p. 221** James Wilson/Woodfin Camp & Associates; **p. 225** Topham/ The Image Works; **p. 226** Joel Gordon; **p. 227** Mimi Forsyth/ Monkmeyer; **p. 228** Courtesy of News and Publications Service, Stanford University; **p. 232** MADD, Minnesota State Office & Clarity Coverdale Rueff, Minneapolis; **p. 234** Ronald K. Siegel; **p. 239** From *Hallucinations* by R.K. Siegel. Copyright 1977 Scientific American, Inc. All rights reserved.

chapter 8

Opener p. 242 Harry Wilks/Stock, Boston; **p. 245** Lawrence Migdale/Stock, Boston; **p. 246** Sovfoto; **p. 250** Courtesy of UCLA Media; **p. 251** C. Parry/The Image Works; **p. 252** Brown Brothers; **p. 255** *(bottom)* Richard Wood/The Picture Cube; *(top)* Fred Bavendam/ Peter Arnold, Inc.; **p. 256** George White/Location Photography; **p. 259** B. Daemmrich/The Image Works; **p. 260** Will & Deni McIntyre/Photo Researchers; **p. 261** Saola/Gamma Liaison; **p. 262** Falk/Monkmeyer; **p. 263** Jeff Greenberg/Photo Edit; **p. 265** From Meltzoff, A.N. (1988). "Imitation of televised models by infants". Child Development, 59, 1221-1229. Photos Courtesy of A.N. Meltzoff & M. Hanak.; **p. 266** *(top)* Courtesy of Albert Bandura, Stanford University; *(bottom)* Bob Daemmrich/The Image Works.

chapter 9

Opener p. 268 John Lewis Stage/The Image Bank; **p. 270** Courtesy of Hersh & Treadgold, Inc., Desktop Paging Software, Inc., and NEC, Inc. ; **p. 271** Fred Ward/Black Star; **p. 272** Gjon Mili, Life Magazine, Time Warner Inc.; **p. 273** *(left)* Hugh Rogers/Monkmeyer; *(right)* C. Parry/The Image Works; **p. 275** Grantpix/Monkmeyer; **p. 283** *(bottom)* Will & Deni McIntyre/Photo Researchers; *(top)* R. J. Erwin/Photo Researchers; **p. 284** Lynn Johnson/Black Star; **p. 285** Fernando Sepe Jr./AP Wide World Photos, Inc.; **p. 287** From "Learning and Memory", 1994. Copyright Cold Springs Laboratories, Courtesy of James Golomb, M.D., Dept. of Neurology, NYU School of Medicine; **p. 288** Seth Poppel/Yearbook Archives; **p. 289** Fred McConnaughey/Photo Researchers; **p. 290** Courtesy of Carolyn Rovee-Collier, Rutgers University; **p. 291** Dan McCoy/Rainbow; **p. 297** *(left)* Reuters/H.O./Archive Photos; *(right)* Reuters/Rick Wilking/Archive Photos; **p. 300** Courtesy of Elizabeth Loftus, University of Washington; **p. 302** Flip Chalfant/ The Image Bank.

chapter 10

Opener p. 304 Photo Edit; **p. 306** Tim Davis/Photo Researchers; **p. 307** *(left)* Daniel J. Cox/Liaison International; *(right)* J. Messerschmidt/The Picture Cube; *(bottom)* Spencer Grant/Liaison International; **p. 308** Baron Hugo Van Lawick National Geographic Society Image Collection; **p. 312** Diedra Laird/The Charlotte Observer; **p. 314** Treë; **p. 315** Stanely Rowin/The Picture Cube; **p. 317** David Swanson/The Gamma Liaison Network; **p. 318** Lloyd DeGrane/NYT Pictures; **p. 319** M. & E. Bernheim/Woodfin Camp & Associates; **p. 320** From *The Wall Street Journal*; **p. 321** Adapted from Werker, J.F. (1989). "Becoming a Native Listener". American Scientist, 77, -59. Reprinted with permission of American Scientist, Journal of Sygma Xi, The Scientific Research Society.

Photos Courtesy of Peter McLeod, Acadia University; **p. 322** David Young-Wolff/Photo Edit; **p. 323** *(left)* Oliver Meckes/Photo Researchers; *(top)* Michael Newman/Photo Edit; *(right)* Crews/The Image Works; **p. 324** *(top)* Shackman/Monkmeyer; *(bottom)* George Ancona in Ancona, G. & Beth, M. (1989) *The Handtalk Zoo*. New York: Macmillan Publishing Company; **p. 325** *(bottom)* Von Frisch, K. (1974). Decoding the language of the bee. *Science 185*, 663–668. Copyright The Nobel Foundation; *(top)* William Munoz; **p. 326** *(top)* Paul Fusco/Magnum Photos; *(bottom)* Language Research Center, Yerkes Regional Primate Research Center; **p. 329** Stephen Dunn/Allsport; **p. 330** *(right)* Elizabeth Crews/The Image Works *(left)* Goodwin/Monkmeyer.

chapter 11

Opener p. 332 Peter Beck/The Stock Market; **p. 334** National Library of Medicine; **p. 335** National Library of Medicine; **p. 336** New Service, Stanford University; **p. 337** *(left)* Victor Englebert/Photo Researchers; *(right)* Jodi Buren/Woodfin Camp & Associates; **p. 339** From Wiltshire, S. (1991) *Floating cities*. London: Michael Joseph Ltd.; **p. 343** Lew Merrim/Monkmeyer; **p. 345** *(left)* Archives of the History of American Psychology/University of Akron; *(right)* Ray Scott/The Image Works; **p. 347** Jim W. Grace/Photo Researchers; **p. 348** Courtesy Dr. Joseph Fagan, Infantest Corp.; **p. 350** *(top)* Greenlar/The Image Works; *(bottom)* Michael O'Neill; **p. 353** Mark Richards/Photo Edit; **p. 355** *(left)* Jacques Chenet/Woodfin Camp & Associates; *(right)* Susan Lapides/Design Conceptions; **p. 357** Jason Goltz; **p. 358** Courtesy Robert Allen Strawn; **p. 360** J. Griffin/The Image Works.

chapter 12

Opener p. 362 David Madison/The Image Bank; **p. 364** *(top)* Bob Daemmrich/The Image Works *(bottom)* Tony Brandenburg/Bruce Coleman, Inc.; **p. 365** *(left)* George Ancona/International Stock; *(right)* Harlow Primate Laboratory, University of Wisconsin; **p. 366** *(left)* Dale Spartas/Liaison International; *(center)* Michael Dwyer/Stock, Boston; *(right)* Wesley Hitt/Liaison International; **p. 367** AP/Wide World Photos, Inc.; **p. 369** Pix*ELATION from Fran Heyl Associates; **p. 370** *(left)* Richard Howard; *(right)* Richard Olsenius/Black Star; **p. 372** Kansas City Star/Sipa Press; **p. 374** Photo by Dellenbeck reprinted by permission of the Kinsey Institute for Research in Sex, Gender, and Reproduction, Inc.; **p. 381** Cynthia Johnson/TIME Magazine, Time Warner, Inc.; **p. 383** Nathaniel Antman/The Image Works; **p. 384** McClelland, D. C., et al (1953). *The achievement motive*. New York: Appleton-Centuy Crofts. Reprinted by permission of Irvington Publishers, New York; **p. 385** Stephen Jaffe/The Gamma Liaison Network; **p. 386** *(top)* *Charles Darwin* (Detail), by John Collier, 1883. London, National Portrait Gallery. Archiv/Photo Researchers, Inc.; *(bottom)* Jack Smith/Associated Press Photo; **p. 388** Fujifotos/The Image Works; **p. 390** Courtesy of Herman Miller Inc.

chapter 13

Opener p. 392 Bob Daemmrich/Stock, Boston; **p. 394** M. Grecco/Stock, Boston; **p. 397** Bernard Gottfryd/Woodfin Camp & Associates; **p. 399** *(top)* Dr. Paul Ekman, University of California at San Francisco; *(bottom)* Culver Pictures; **p. 400** USA Today; **p. 401** Ekman & Matsumoto, Japanese and Caucasian Facial Expressions of Emotions **p. 402** Courtesy of Louis Schakel/Michael Kausman/The New York Times Pictures; **p. 403 Figure 3.8** (a) Tom McCarthy/Rainbow; (b) Patrick Donahue/Photo Researchers; (c) Bob Daemmrich/The Image Works; (d) Merrim/Monkmeyer; (e) Nancy Brown/The Image Bank; (f) Marc Grimberg/The Image Bank; (g) Michael Newman/Photo Edit; **p. 405** Wolfgang Kaehler; **p. 407** Mark Lennihan/AP/Wide World Photos, Inc.; **p. 412** Robert Deutsch/USA Today.

chapter 14

Opener p. 418 Dede Hatch/The Picture Cube; **p. 420** *(left)* Culver Pictures *(right)* Edmund Engelman; **p. 423** Grantpix/Monkmeyer; **p. 424** *(left)* Rick Friedman/Black Star; *(right)* Harlow Primate Laboratory, University of Wisconsin; **p. 425** *(left)* National Library of Medicine; *(center)* The Bettmann Archive; *(right)* Archives of the History of American Psychology; **p. 426** *(right and left)* Merrim/Monkmeyer; **p. 431** AP/Wide World Photos, Inc.; **p. 432** *(right)* Wolf/Monkmeyer *(right)* Robert C. Burke/Liaison International; **p. 437** *(left)* Ted Polumbaum/Life Magazine Time Warner, Inc.; *(right)* Mark Antman/The Image Works; **p. 438** Sybil Shackman/Monkmeyer; **p. 442** B. & C. Alexander/Photo Researchers; **p. 445** Stephen Wade/Allsport USA; **p. 446** *(right)* Joe McNally.

chapter 15

Opener p. 452 David de Lossy/The Image Bank; **p. 454** Tony Ray Jones/Magnum Photos; **p. 457** AP/Wide World Photos, Inc.; **p. 464** John Coletti/ Stock, Boston; **p. 465** Baxter, L. R., et al. (1987). Local cerebral glucose metabolic rates in obsessive-compulsive disorder. *Archives of General Psychology* 44(3), 211–218. Copyright 1987 American Medical Association. ; **p. 466** AP/Wide World Photos, Inc.; **p. 469** Shackman/Monkmeyer; **p. 471** Jerry Irwin Photography; **p. 472** Courtesy of Drs. Lewis Baxter and Michael E. Phelps, UCLA School of Medicine; **p. 474** Sidney/Monkmeyer; **p. 476** *(right)* Berthold, L., *Untitled*. The Prinzhorn Collection, University of Heidelberg; *(left)* August Natterer, *Witch's Head*. The Prinzhorn Collection, University of Heidelberg. Photos: Krannert Museum, University of Illinois at Urbana-Champaign; **p. 479** From Suddath, Richard L., et al. (1990). "Anatomical abnormalities in the brains of monozygotic twins discordant for schizophrenia". The New England Journal of Medicine, 322, 12. 1990 by the Massachusetts Medical Society. Photo courtesy of Daniel R. Weinberger, M.D., NIH-NIMH/NSC.; **p. 481** Courtesy of Genain Family.

chapter 16

Opener p. 486 Michael Newman/Photo Edit; **p. 488** *(top left)* The Granger Collection; *(top right)* The Bettmann Archive; *(middle left)* Culver Pictures; **p. 489** Richard T. Nowitz/Photo Researchers **p. 490** Steve Goldberg/Monkmeyer; **p. 491** Michael Rougier, Life Magazine, Time Warner, Inc.; **p. 495** Joel Gordon; **p. 500** Stacy Pick/Stock, Boston; **p. 506** Mark Antman/The Image Works; **p. 508** Lee Snider/The Image Works; **p. 509** Lynn Johnson/Black Star; **p. 510** James Wilson/Woodfin Camp & Associates.

chapter 17

Opener p. 514 Bob Kirst/Black Star; **p. 517** *(right)* Arlene Collins/Monkmeyer; *(left)* Miro Vintoniv/Stock Boston; **p. 518** Richard Hutchings/Photo Researchers; **p. 519** Charles Bertram/

Gamma Liaison; **p. 520** Peter Glass/Monkmeyer; **p. 523** Lennart Nilsson/Boehringer Ingelheim International GMBH; **p. 524** Gerd Ludwig/Woodfin Camp & Associates; **p. 530** *(top)* P. Fagot/ Explorer/Photo Researchers *(bottom)* LeDuc/Monkmeyer; **p. 531** Dan McCoy/Rainbow; **p. 532** *(top)* Steve Liss/TIME Magazine, Time Warner, Inc.; *(bottom)* Billy E. Barnes/Stock, Boston; **p. 533** Bob Daemmrich/Stock, Boston; **p. 535** John David Mercer/The Gamma Liaison Network; **p. 537** Russel Einhorn/The Gamma Liaison Network; **p. 538** Ullmann/Monkmeyer; **p. 540** *(top)* Lincoln Russell/Stock, Boston; *(bottom) The Garden of Love* (Detail), Peter Paul Rubens, The Prado, Madrid/The Bridgeman Art Library, Superstock; **p. 542** Phyllis Picardi/Stock, Boston; **p. 543** *(top)* Courtesy of John Sholtis, The Rockefeller University, New York, NY; *(bottom)* Michael Newman/Photo Edit; **p. 544** Michael Newman/ Photo Edit; **p. 546** Tony Freeman/Photo Edit.

chapter *18*

Opener p. 548 The Stock Market; **p. 552** D. MacDonald/Photo Edit; **p. 553** Thomas Hopker/Magnum Photos; **p. 555** William Vandivert/Scientific American; **p. 557** Courtesy of CUNY Graduate School and University Center; **p. 558** Copyright 1965 by Stanley Milgram. From the film OBEDIENCE, distributed by Penn State, Media Sales; **p. 559** AP/Wide World Photos, Inc. **p. 564** Margaret Bourke-White, Life Magazine. Copyright Time Warner, Inc.; **p. 565** *(top)* Reuters/Ghassan Zatary/Archive Photos; *(center)* Fujifotos/ The Image Works; *(bottom)* Robert Azzi/Woodfin Camp & Associates; **p. 566** Monkmeyer; **p. 570** *(top)* Larry Fischer/AP/Wide World, Inc.; *(bottom)* Michael S. Yamashita/ Woodfin Camp & Associates; **p. 572** Presse-Sports; **p. 573** Tom Wurl/Stock, Boston; **p. 574** Dion Ogust/The Image Works; **p. 579** Keith Gosse/The Evening Telegram; **p. 580** *(top)* Rex USA ; *(bottom)* Popperfoto/ Archive Photos; **p. 581** *(left)* Margaret Gowan/ Tony Stone Worldwide; *(center)* Victor Englebert/Photo Researchers; *(right)* Nancy Brown/The Image Bank; **p. 583** Albert Sanchez/Outline; **p. 584** *(right)* Barros & Barros/The Image Bank; *(left)* Martin Hooper/The Image Bank; **p. 585** Akos Szilvasi/Stock, Boston; **p. 588** Bob Daemmrich/Stock, Boston.

text and illustration credits

chapter *1*

Fig. 1.2 Adapted with permission of The Free Press, a division of Simon & Schuster from *How We Know What Isn't So: The Fallibility of Human Reason in Everyday Life* by Thomas Gilovich. Copyright © 1991 Thomas Gilovich. **Fig. 1.4** Adapted from Ross, B. (Jan. 1987). In K. McKean, "The orderly pursuit of pure disorder." *Discover*, pp. 72-81. Barry Ross/Copyright © 1987 Discover Magazine **Fig. 1.6** Frank, M.G. & Gilovich, T. (1988). The dark side of self and social perception: Black uniforms and aggression in professional sports. *Journal of Personality and Social Psychology, 54,* 74-85. Copyright © 1988 American Psychological Association. Reprinted by permission. **Fig. 1.8** From *Mind Sights* by Shepard. Copyright © 1990 Roger N. Shepard. Used with permission of W.H. Freeman and Company.

chapter *2*

Fig. 2.17 From *Scientific American*, Oct. 1994, p. 102. Left side © Dana Bums-Pizer. Right side © Judith Glick. **Figs. 2.27 and 2.28** Gazzaniga, M.S. (1983). Right hemisphere language following brain bisection: A 20-year perspective. *American Psychologist, 38,* 525-537.

chapter *3*

Fig. 3.3 Johnson & Morton (1991). *Psychological Review, 98,* 164-181. Copyright © 1991 by the American Psychological Association. Reprinted with permission. **Fig. 3.4** Conel, J.L. (1939-1963). *The postnatal development of the human cerebral cortex (Vols. I-VI).* Reprinted by permission of Harvard University Press. **Fig. 3.6** Adapted from figure in "Brain changes in response to experience" by M.R. Rosenzweig, E.L. Bennett, and M.C. Diamond. Copyright © Ikuyo Tagawa Garber for Bunji Tagawa. **Fig. 3.11** Wynn, K. (1992). Addition and subtraction by human infants. *Nature, 358,* 749-759. Reprinted by permission of Nature. Copyright © 1992 Macmillan Magazines Limited. **Fig. 3.14** Kagan, J. (1976). Emergent themes in human development. *American Scientist, 64,* 186-196. Reprinted by permission of *American Scientist*, Journal of Sigma XI, The Scientific Research Society.

chapter *4*

Fig. 4.1 Reproduced with the permission of the Alan Guttmacher Institute from *Sex and America's teenagers.* Alan Guttmacher Institute, New York, 1994. **Fig. 4.2** Tanner, J.M. (1978). *Fetus into man: Physical growth from conception to maturity.* Cambridge, MA: Harvard University Press. Reprinted by permission. **Fig. 4.5** Bachman, J.G., Johnston, L.D., & O'Malley, P.M. (1987). *Monitoring the future: Questionnaire responses from the nation's high school seniors.* Ann Arbor, MI: Institute for Social Research, The University of Michigan. **Fig. 4.7** Adapted from Insel, P.M. & Roth, W.T. (1976). *Health in a changing society.* Mountain View, CA: Mayfield, p. 98. **Fig. 4.8** Courtesy Ian Worpole/*Scientific American*, April 1993, p. 50. **Fig. 4.9** McLennan, W. (1995). *Australian social trends 1995.* Australian Bureau of Statistics, Cat. no. 4102.0, 1995. Copyright in ABS data resides with the Commonwealth of Australia. Used with permission. **Fig. 4.10** Adapted with permission from Doty, R.L., et al. (1984). Smell identification ability: Changes with age. *Science, 226,* 1441-1443. Copyright © 1984 by the American Association for the Advancement of Science. **Fig. 4.11** Stock, R.W. (1995, July 13). Reducing the risk for older drivers. *New York Times*, p. C1. Copyright © 1995 by The New York Times Co. **Fig. 4.12** Jorm A.F., Korten, A.E., & Henderson, A.S. (1987). The prevalence of dementia: A quantitative integration of the literature. *Acta Psychiatrica Scandinivica, 76,* 465-479. Copyright © 1987 Munksgaard International Publishers, Ltd., Copenhagen, Denmark. **Fig. 4.13** Data from Crook, P.H. & West, R.L. (1990). Name and recall performance across the adult life-span. *British Journal of Psychology, 81,* 335-349. **Fig. 4.14** Schonfield, D. & Robertson, B.A. (1966). Memory Storage and Aging. *Canadian Journal of Psychology, 20,* 228-236. Copyright © 1966. Canadian Psychological Association. Reprinted with permission. **Fig 4.15** Adapted from Schail, K.W. (1994). The life course of adult intellectual abilities. *American Psychologist, 49,* 304–313. Copyright © 1994 American Psychological Association. Adapted by permission. **Fig. 4.16** Adapted from

Kaufman, A.S., Reynolds, C.R., & McLean, J.E. (1989). Age and WAIS-R intelligence in a national sample of adults in the 20 to 74 year age range: A cross-sectional analysis with educational level controlled. *Intelligence, 13*, 235-253. Reprinted with permission from Ablex Publishing Corporation. **Fig. 4.17** McCrae, R.R. & Costa, P.T. Jr. (1990). *Personality in adulthood.* New York: Guilford Press, p. 149. Copyright © 1990 Guilford Press. **p. 139** Bumpass, L.L. & Sweet, J.A. (1989). National estimates of Cohabitation. *Demography, 26*, 615-625. **Fig. 4.18** Data from Inglehart, R. (1990). *Culture shift in advanced industrial society.* Princeton, NJ: Princeton University Press. **Fig. 4.19** Eron, L.D. & Huesmann, R. (1984). The control of aggressive behavior by changes in attitudes, values and the conditions of learning. In R.J. Blanchard & C. Blanchard (Eds.), *Advances in the study of aggression (Vol. 1).* Orlando, FL: Academic Press. **Table 4.1** From *Childhood and Society* by Erik H. Erikson. Copyright 1950, © 1963 by W.W. Norton & Company, Inc., renewed © 1978, 1991 by Erik H. Erikson.

chapter *5*

Fig. 5.2 Copyright © Eric Mose, Jr. *Scientific American*, June 1961, p. 75. **p. 160** Edward S. Gazsi © National Geographic Society. **Fig. 5.19** Data from Bunch and Raiford. From Boring, Langfeld, and Weld *Introduction to Psychology*, 1939, p. 571. **Fig. 5.22** Wysocki, C.J. & Gilbert, A.N. (1989). In C. Murphy & W.S. Cain (Eds.), *Proceedings of the conference on nutrition and the chemical senses in aging* (Annals of the New York Academy of Sciences), Vol. 561. New York: New York Academy of Sciences.

chapter *6*

Fig. 6.1 Bradley, D.R., Dumais, & Petry (1976). Reply to Cavonius. *Nature, 261*, 78. Reprinted with permission from Nature. Copyright © 1976 Macmillan Magazines Limited. **Fig. 6.2** Neisser, U. (1979). The control of information pickup in selective looking. In A.D. Pick (Ed.), *Perception and its development: A tribute to Eleanor J. Gibson.* Hillsdale, NJ: Lawrence Erlbaum. Copyright © 1979 by Lawrence Erlbaum Associates, Inc. **Fig. 6.11** Shepard, R.N. (1981). Psychophysical. In M. Kubovky & J.R. Pomerantz (Eds.), *Perceptual organization* (pp. 279-341). Hillsdale, NJ: Lawrence Erlbaum. Copyright © 1981 by Lawrence Erlbaum Associates. **Fig. 6.13a** From *Mind Sights* by Shepard. Copyright © 1990 by Roger N. Shepard. Used with permission of W.H. Freeman and Company. **Fig. 6.14a** From "Visual Illusions" (November 1968, pp. 66-76) by R.L. Gregory. Copyright © 1968 by Scientific American, Inc. All rights reserved. **Fig. 6.14b** Day, R.H. (1984) The nature of perceptual illusions. *Interdisciplinary Science Reviews, 9*, 47-58. **p. 192** Hunting Scene adapted from Jean B. Deregowski, "Pictorial Perception and Culture," November 1972, p. 83. Copyright 1972 by Scientific American, Inc. All rights reserved. **Fig. 6.17** Blakemore, C.R. & Cooper, G.F. (1970). Development of the brain depends on the visual environment. *Nature, 228*, 447-448. Reprinted with permission from Nature. Copyright © 1970 by Macmillan Journals Limited. **Fig. 6.18** From *Mind Sights* by Shepard. Copyright © 1990 by Roger N. Shepard. Used with permission by W.H. Freeman and Company. **Fig. 6.22** From *Mind Sights* by Shepard. Copyright © 1990 by Roger N. Shepard. Used with permission by W.H. Freeman and Company. **Fig. 6.23** Kraft, C. (1978). A psychological approach to air safety: Simulator studies of visual illusions in night ap-

proaches. In H.L. Pick, H.W. Leibowitz, J.E. Singer, A. Steinschneider, & H.W. Stevenson (Eds.), *Psychology: From research to practice.* New York: Plenum Press. **p. 200** Adapted from Gregory, R.L., & Gombrich, E.H. (Eds.) (1974). *Illusion in nature and art.* New York: Charles Scribner's Sons. Copyright © UNESCO.

chapter *7*

Figs. 7.1 and 7.2 From Dement, W. (1978). *Some must watch while some must sleep.* Stanford, CA: Portable Stanford Book Series, 1972. Reprinted by permission of the Stanford Alumni Association, Stanford University. **Fig. 7.3** Cartwright, R.D. (1978). *A primer on sleep and dreaming.* Reading, MA: Addison-Wesley. **Fig. 7.3** Webb, W.B. (1992). *Sleep: The gentle tyrant, second edition.* Bolton, MA: Anker Publishing. **Fig. 7.4** Adapted with permission of The Free Press, a division of Simon & Schuster from *Sleep thieves: An eye-opening exploration into the science and mysteries of sleep* by Stanley Coren. Copyright © 1996 by Stanley Coren. **Fig. 7.5** Hartmann, E. (1984) *The nightmare: The psychology and biology of terrifying dreams.* Copyright © 1984 by Ernest Hartmann. **Fig. 7.6** Adapted from Snyder, F. & Scott, J. (1972). The psychophysiology of sleep. In N.S. Greenfield and R.A. Steinback (Eds.), *Handbook of psychophysiology.* New York: Holt, Rinehart and Winston. **Fig. 7.11** Johnston, L.D., O'Malley, P.M. & Bachman, J.G. (1996). National survey results on drug use from the *Monitoring the Future Study, 1975-1996, Volume I.* Secondary School Students (Dhhs Pub. No. (ADM)). Rockville, MD: National Institute on Drug Abuse. **Fig. 7.12** From "Hallucinations" by R.K. Siegel. Copyright © 1977 Scientific American, Inc. All rights reserved.

chapter *8*

Fig. 8.4 Adapted from Goodwin, C.J. (1991). Misportraying pavlov's apparatus. *American Journal of Psychology, 104*, 135-141. Copyright © 1991 by the Board of Trustees of the University of Illinois Press. **Fig. 8.9** Copyright Margaret Gladback for Dan Todd. *Scientific American*, Nov. 1961, p. 96 top.

chapter *9*

Fig. 9.3 Data from H. Ebbinghaus, 1885. Reprinted with the permission of Simon & Schuster Inc. from *Your memory: A user's guide* by A.D. Baddeley. Copyright © 1982 by Multimedia Publications (UK) Ltd. **Fig. 9.4** Craik, F.I.M. & Watkins, M.J. (1973). The role of rehearsal in short-term memory. *Journal of Verbal Learning and Verbal Behavior, 12*, 599-607. Reprinted by permission of Academic Press Inc. **Fig. 9.5** Craik, F.I.M. & Tulving, E. (1975). Depth of processing and the retention of words in episodic memory. *Journal of Experimental Psychology: General, 104*, 268-294. Copyright © 1975 American Psychological Association. Reprinted with the permission of the authors. **p. 277** *World military and social expenditures 1966* by Ruth Leger Sivard. Copyright © 1996 by World Priorities, Box 25140, Washington DC, 20007, USA. **Fig. 9.6** From *The psychology of learning and memory* by Douglas L. Hintzman. Copyright © 1978 by W.H. Freeman and Company. Reprinted with permission. **Fig. 9.10** Nickerson, R.S. & Adams M.J. (1979). Long-term memory for a common object. *Cognitive Psychology, 11*, 287-307. Reprinted by permission of Academic Press, Inc. **Fig. 9.12** Peterson, L.R. & Peterson, M.J. (1959). Short-term retention of individual verbal items. *Journal of Experimental Psychology, 58*,

193-198. **Fig. 9.13** Adapted from Ebbinghaus, E. (1885). Über das Gedächtnis. Leipzig: Dunker. *Human memory: Structures and processes, 2/e* by Klatzky. Copyright © 1980 by W.H. Freeman and Company. Used with permission. **Fig. 9.14** Adapted from Bahrick, H.P. (1984). Semantic memory content in permastore: 50 years of memory for Spanish learned in school. *Journal of Experimental Psychology: General, 113*, 1-29. Copyright © 1984 American Psychological Association. Adapted by permission. **Fig. 9.17** Adapted from Bower, G.H. (1986). Prime time in cognitive psychology. In P. Eelen (Ed.), *Cognitive research and behavior therapy: Beyond the conditioning paradigm.* Amsterdam: North Holland Publishers. **Fig. 9.18** Adapted from Godden, D.R. & Baddeley, A.D. (1975). Context-dependent memory in two natural environments: On land and under water. *British Journal of Psychology, 66*, 325-331. **Fig. 9.22** Jenkins, J.G. & Dallenbach, K.M. (1924). Obliviscence during sleep and waking. *American Journal of Psychology, 35*, 605-612. Copyright © 1924 Board of Trustees and the University of Illinois. Reprinted by permission of the University of Illinois Press. **Fig. 9.24** Loftus, E.F. (1979). The malleability of human memory. *American Scientist, 67*, 313-320. Reprinted by permission of *American Scientist*, Journal of Sigma Xi, The Scientific Research Society.

chapter *10*

Figs. 10.1 and 10.4 Copyright © John Alcorn. In "Problem Solving" by M. Scheerer. *Scientific American*, 1963. **Figs. 10.3 and 10.6** Duncker, K. (1945). On problem-solving. *Psychological Monographs, 58* (Whole no. 270). **Fig. 10.7** Adapted from Werker, J.F. (1989). Becoming a native listener. *American Scientist, 77*, 54-59. Reprinted by permission of *American Scientist*, Journal of Sigma Xi, The Scientific Research Society. **Fig. 10.9** Johnson, J.S. & Newport, E.L. (1989). Critical period effects in second language learning: The influence of maturational state on the acquisition of English as a second language. *Cognitive Psychology, 21*, 60-99. Reprinted by permission of Academic Press, Inc. **Fig. 10.10** von Frisch, K. (1974). Decoding the language of the bee. *Science, 185*, 663-668. Copyright © 1974 American Association for the Advancement of Science.

chapter *11*

Fig. 11.1 From *Floating cities* by Stephen Wiltshire (Michael Joseph, 1991, p. 27) copyright © Stephen Wiltshire, 1991. **Fig. 11.2** Deary, I.J., & Stough, C. (1996). Intelligence and inspection time: Achievements, prospects, and problems. *American Psychologist, 51*, 599-608. Copyright © 1996 by the American Psychological Association. Reprinted by permission. **Fig. 11.3** Thorndike et al. *Measurement and evaluation in psychology and education, 5/e*, © 1990, p. 364. Reprinted by permission of Prentice Hall, Upper Saddle River, New Jersey. **Fig. 11.5** Copyright © Dimitry Schidlovsky. In "Get Smart, Take a Test" by J. Hogan (Nov. 1995). *Scientific American*, p. 14. **Table 11.1** American Psychiatric Association (1994). *Diagnostic and statistical manual of mental disorders, Fourth Edition*, Washington, DC: American Psychiatric Association, 1994. **Fig. 11.8** Fulker, D.W., DeFries, J.C. & Plomin, R. (1988). Genetic influence on general mental ability increases between infancy and middle childhood. *Nature, 336*, 767-769. Reprinted by permission of Nature. Copyright © 1988 Macmillan Magazines Limited. **Fig. 11.9** Lewontin, R. (1976). Race and intelligence. In N.J. Block & G. Dworken (Eds.), *The IQ controversy: Critical readings*, New York: Pantheon. Copyright © 1976 N.J. Block & G. Dworken. Reprinted by permission. **Fig. 11.10** Reprinted with permission of authors and publishers from Vandenberg, S.G. & Kuse, A.R. Mental rotations, a group test of three-dimensional spatial visualization. *Perceptual and Motor Skills, 47*, 1978, pp. 599-604. Copyright © Perceptual and Motor Skills, 1978.

chapter *12*

Fig. 12.1 Maslow's hierarchy of needs from *Motivation and Personality (3rd edition)* by Abraham H. Maslow, revised by Robert Frager et al. Copyright © 1954, 1987. by Harper & Row Publishers, Inc. Copyright © 1970 by Abraham H. Maslow. Reprinted by permission of Addison-Wesley Educational Publishers, Inc. **Fig. 12.2** Adapted from Cannon, W.B. (1929). *Bodily changes in pain, hunger, fear, and rage.* New York: Branford. **Fig. 12.4** Scale adapted from "Use of the Danish Adoption Register for the Study of Obesity and Thinness" by A. Stunkard, T. Sorensen, and F. Schulsinger in *The Genetics of Neurological and Psychiatric Disorders*, edited by S. Kety, 1980, p. 119. Copyright 1983 by Raven Press. Adapted by permission of Lippincott-Raven Publishers, Philadelphia, PA. **Fig. 12.5** Adapted from Masters, W.H. & Johnson, V.E. (1966). *Human sexual response.* Boston: Little, Brown & Company. Copyright © 1966 by Masters and Johnson. By permission of Little, Brown & Co. **Fig. 12.6** Byrne, D. (1982). Predicting human sexual behavior. In A.G. Kraut, *The G. Stanley Hall Lecture Series (Vol. 2)*. Copyright © 1982 by the American Psychological Association. Reprinted by permission of the author and publisher.

chapter *13*

Fig. 13.3 Courtesy of David Raskin, University of Utah, as shown in *Science*, June 1982, pp. 24–27. **Fig. 13.4** Kleinmuntz, B. & Szucko, J.J. (1984). A field study of the fallibility of polygraph lie detection. *Nature, 308*, 449-450. Reprinted by permission of Nature. Copyright © 1984 Macmillan Journals Limited. **Fig. 13.10** Sax, L.J. et al. (1996). *The American freshman: National Norms for Fall 1996.* Los Angeles: Higher Education Research Institute, UCLA; Dey, E.L., et al. (1991). *The American freshman: Twenty-five year trends.* Los Angeles: Higher Education Research Institute, UCLA. **Fig. 13.12** Adapted from Solomon, R.L. (1980). The opponent-process theory of acquired motivation: The costs of pleasure and the benefits of pain. *American Psychologist, 35*, 691-712. Copyright © 1980 American Psychological Association. Reprinted by permission of the author.

chapter *14*

Fig. 14.2 Eysenck, S.B.G. & Eysenck, H.J. (1963). The validity of questionnaire and rating assessments of extraversion and neuroticism, and their factorial stability. *British Journal of Psychology, 54*, 51-62. Fig. 1. **Table 14.2** Adapted from McCrae, R. & Costa, P.T. Jr. (1986). Clinical assessment can benefit from recent advances in personality psychology. *American Psychologist, 41*, 1002. Copyright © 1986 American Psychological Association. Adapted by permission. **Fig. 14.3** Adapted from *The MMPI-2 in psychological treatment* by J. N. Butcher. Copyright © 1990 Oxford University Press, Inc. Used with permission of Oxford University Press, Inc.

chapter *15*

Fig. 15.2 Roper report 84-3, February 11-25, 1984. *Public Opinion*, August/September, 25. Reprinted with permission of the American Enterprise Institute for Public Policy Research, Washington, D.C. **Table 15.1** Adapted from Rapoport (1989). The biology of obsessions and compulsions. *Scientific American*, pp. 83-89. **Fig. 15.9** Forgas, J.P., et al. (1984). The influence of mood on perceptions of social interactions. *Journal of Experimental and Social Psychology, 20*, 497-513. Orlando, FL: Academic Press, Journals Division. **Fig. 15.10** Adapted from Lewinsohn, P.M., et al. (1985). An integrative theory of depression. In S. Reiss and R. Bootzin (Eds.), *Theoretical issues in behavior therapy*. Orlando, FL: Academic Press. **Fig. 15.11** Data from *Schizophrenia genesis: The origins of madness* by I.I. Gottesman. Copyright © 1991 by W.H. Freeman and Company. Used with permission. **Fig. 15.12** Adapted from Magnusson, D. (1990). Personality research—challenges for the future. *European Journal of Personality, 4*, 1-17. Copyright © 1990, reprinted by permission of John Wiley & Sons, Ltd. **Fig. 15.13** Adapted from Raine & others, 1996. *Archives of General Psychiatry, 53*, p. 548.

chapter *16*

Fig. 16.1 Gilling, D. & Brightwell, R. (1982). *The human brain*. New York: Facts on File. Reprinted by permission of Little, Brown & Co. (UK). **Fig. 16.5** Rabin, A.S. et al. (1986). Aggregate outcome and follow-up results following self-control therapy for depression. Paper presented at the American Psychological Association convention. **Fig. 16.7** Adapted from Smith, M.L. et al. (1980). *The benefits of psychotherapy* (p. 88) Baltimore, MD: Johns Hopkins University Press. Reprinted by permission.

chapter *17*

Fig. 17.5 Weiss, J.M. (1977). Psychological and behavioral influences on gastrointestinal lesions in animal models. In *Psychopathology: Experimental models* by Maser and Seligman. Copyright © 1977 by Martin E.P. Seligman and Jack Maser. Used with permission of W.H. Freeman and Company. **Fig. 17.7** Adapted with the permission of The Free Press, a division of Simon & Schuster from *The left-hander syndrome: The causes and consequences of left-handedness* by Stanley Coren. Copyright © 1993 by Stanley Coren. **Fig. 17.10** Adapted from McCann, I.L., & Holmes, D.S. (1984). Influence of aerobic exercise on depression. *Journal of Personality and Social Psychology, 46*, 1142-1147. Copyright © 1984 by the American Psychological Association. Adapted by permission of the authors. **Fig. 17.12** From *Treating Type A Behavior and Your Heart* by Meyer Friedman, M.D. and Diane Ulmer, R.N., M.S. Copyright © 1984 by Meyer Friedman. Reprinted by permission of Alfred A. Knopf, Inc. **Fig. 17.18** Bray, G.A. (1969). Effect of caloric restriction on energy expenditure in obese patients. *Lancet, 2*, 397-398. Copyright © 1969 by the Lancet Ltd. **Fig. 17.19** Adapted from Brownell, K.D. & Jeffrey, R.W. (1987). Improving long-term weight loss: Pushing the limits of treatment. *Behavior Therapy, 18*, 353-374. Copyright © 1987 by the Association for Advancement of Behavior Therapy. Reprinted by permission of the publisher. **Fig. 17.20** Dietz, W.H., Jr., & Gortmaker, S.L. (1985). Do we fatten our children at the television set? Obesity and television viewing children and adolescents. Reproduced by permission of *Pediatrics, Vol. 75*, p. 807, copyright 1985.

name index

Guenther, V., 372
Guerin, R. B., 561
Guidice, S., 87
Guijarro, M. L., 522
Guion, R. M., 23
Gulevich, G., 215
Gura, T., 544
Guralnik, J. M., 527
Gurin, J., 501
Gustafson, E. L., 543
Gustavson, C. R., 251
Guterl, F., 317
Gutierres, S. E., 377
Gwaltney, J. M., Jr., 524

Haber, R. N., 270
Hackel, L. S., 138
Hackman, B. B., 571
Hafner, H., 555
Hagen, E. P., 343
Haier, R. J., 341
Hairfield, J. G., 435
Hakola, P., 459
Halaas, J. L., 542
Halberstadt, J. B., 200
Haldane, J. B. S., 152
Haldeman, D. C., 380
Haldeman, R., 271
Hale, S., 131
Hall, C., 218
Hall, C. S., 218, 429
Hall, G. S., 3, 116
Hall, J. A., 124, 358, 389, 398, 399
Hall, J. A. Y., 382
Hall, L. K., 274
Hall, N. R., 525
Hall, S., 185
Hall, T., 369
Hall, V. C., 261
Hall, W. B., 351
Hallahan, M., 399
Halle, P., 321
Hallet, A. J., 522
Halligan, P. W., 160
Hallinan, J. T., 299
Halpern, B. P., 174
Halpern, D. F., 348, 356, 358, 526, 527
Halpern, J. N., 176
Hamburg, B., 519
Hamers, J. F., 329
Hamey, T. L., 533
Hamid, A., 233
Hamill, R., 313
Hamilton, D. L., 22
Hamilton, J. C., 473
Hamilton, M. C., 329
Hamilton, V. L., 473
Hammen, C. L., 474
Hammer, T. J., 123
Hammersmith, S. K., 380
Hammerstein, O., 414, 582
Handel, G. F., 470
Haney, C., 38
Haney, D. Q., 539
Hanselka, L., 538
Hansell, S., 573
Hansen, C. H., 398

Hansen, D. J., 98
Hansen, R. D., 398
Hansen, W. B., 237
Harackiewicz, J. M., 261
Harber, K. D., 535
Hardin, C., 329
Hardin, T. S., 473
Hare, R. D., 482
Harel, Z., 461
Harkins, S. G., 388, 562
Harlow, H. F., 95, 97, 98, 99, 100
Harlow, L. L., 237
Harlow, M. K., 95
Harlow, R. E., 141
Harns, J. R., 542
Harold, R. D., 358
Harper, L. V., 112
Harries, M., 159
Harrington, D. M., 437
Harris, B., 252
Harris, J. K., 530
Harris, J. R., 111, 125, 373
Harris, L., 520
Harris, L. J., 527
Harris, M. J., 110
Harris, R. J., 577
Harris, T. G., 536
Harriston, K. A., 450
Harrow, M., 453, 480
Harsch, N., 270, 295
Hart, D., 103, 122
Hartmann, E., 217
Hartshorne, H., 435
Hartup, W. W., 99
Harvey, S. M., 376
Hasher, L., 133, 211, 273
Hashimoto, T., 584
Haskins, R., 355
Hassan, R., 469
Hatfield, B. D., 530
Hatfield, E., 379, 581, 583
Hathaway, S. R., 433
Hattori, Y., 321
Haupt, A. L., 439
Hauser, M. D., 66
Hautziner, M., 470, 474
Hawken, M. J., 185
Hawkins, W. G., 251
Hawthorne, N., 554
Haxby, J. V., 54
Haybittle, J. L., 525
Hayes, J. R., 289
Hazan, C., 98, 100
Hazelrigg, M. D., 500
Hazlitt, W., 441
Hearold, S., 575
Heath, A., 108
Heath, A. C., 237, 464
Heath, C., Jr., 536
Heath, L., 576
Heatherton, T. F., 372
Heavey, C. L., 578
Hebb, D. O., 246, 393
Hedges, L. V., 357, 358
Heider, F., 549
Heider, K., 398, 400, 401
Heiman, J. R., 377

Heise, L., 576
Heiss, W-D., 287
Heitanen, J. K., 159
Heller, W., 69
Hellige, J. B., 70
Helmreich, W. B., 428, 461
Helson, H., 410
Hembree, R., 394
Henderson, A. S., 132
Henderson, R., 24, 411
Henderson, W. G., 461
Hendler, J., 97
Henley, N. M., 329
Hennessey, B. A., 351
Henning, K., 209, 376, 378
Henninger, P., 467
Henrich, C., 372
Henry VIII, King, 225
Henry, H. J., 539
Henry, J. P., 520
Henry, P. E., 372
Henschel, A., 368
Hepper, P. G., 68
Herbener, E. S., 144
Herbert, T. B., 524
Herek, G. M., 382, 568
Hering, E., 162
Herman, C. P., 545
Herman, P., 544
Heron, W., 178
Herrmann, D., 302
Herrnstein, R. J., 255, 356, 572
Hershenson, M., 191
Hertel, P. T., 291
Hesburgh, T., 588
Heshka, S., 542
Hess, D. J., 203
Hess, E. H., 196
Hesse, B. W., 575
Hester, C., 372
Heston, L. L., 464
Hetherington, E. M., 102, 105, 110, 113
Hetz, B., 589
Hewitt, J. K., 237
Hewlett, B. S., 99
Heymsfield, S. B., 542
Hicklin, D., 533
Hicks, R. A., 522
Higgins, E. T., 373, 438, 439
Higgins, J. G., 402
Higgins, P., 407
Hilgard, E. R., 222, 227, 228
Hill, M. S., 313
Hill, T., 428
Hinckley, J., Jr., 457
Hines, M., 79
Hinz, L. D., 372
Hippocrates, 517
Hirshkowitz, M., 213
Hirst, W., 227
Hirt, E. R., 473
Hite, S., 19, 20
Hitler, A., 11, 313, 588
Hitzig, E., 60
Hlatky, M. A., 533
Hoberman, H., 470, 474
Hobfoll, S. E., 470, 517

Mishkin, M., 85, 284
Misukanis, T. M., 104
Misumi, J., 388
Mita, T. H., 580
Mitchell, T. R., 277
Mitchell, T. V., 169
Mittleman, M. A., 375
Mittlemark, M. B., 538
Mocellin, J. S. P., 239
Moeykens, B., 232
Moffit, T. E., 97
Moffitt, T. E., 118, 482
Mohammed, 178
Molyneux, W., 195
Monaghan, P., 301
Monahan, J., 459
Monahan, J. L., 416
Money, J., 376, 381, 382, 577
Monge, P. R., 446
Moniz, E., 511
Monroe, M., 526, 555, 582
Montaigne, 119
Montgomery, L. M., 500
Montgomery, R. B., 531
Moody, R., 238
Mook, D. G., 32
Moorcroft, W., 211, 214, 215
Moore, D. W., 382
Moore, K. A., 383
Moore, S., 581
Moore, T. E., 150
Morales, F. R., 214
Moran, T. H., 369
Moreland, R. L., 580, 580
Morell, V., 126, 523
Morelli, G., 21
Morelli, G. A., 105
Morgan, M., 576, 578
Morgan, M. A., 536
Morgan, R., 347
Morgan, W. P., 46
Morin, R., 125
Morison, V., 90
Morris, C. D., 539
Morris, R., 572
Morris, R. L., 204
Morris, T, 525
Morrison, D. C., 263
Morrison, D. M., 126
Morrison, D. R., 102
Morrow, D. G., 275
Morrow, J., 473
Morton, G. E., 17
Morton, L. A., 471
Moruzzi, G., 55
Moscovici, S., 564
Moser, P. W., 158
Moses, 12, 178
Mosher, D. L., 231
Moss, A. J., 533, 537
Moss, D., 509
Moss, H. A., 144
Most, A., 117
Mosteller, F., 24
Mott, F. L., 100
Mowrer, O. H., 493
Moyer, J. R., Jr., 284

Moyer, K. E., 572
Mozart, W. A., 470
Muehlenhard, C. L., 379
Mueller, J., 409, 537, 566, 568
Mueller, R. A., 104
Muenchow, S., 355
Mukerjee, M., 34
Mulick, J. A., 560
Mullen, B., 66
Muller, J. E., 375, 519
Mullin, C. R., 576
Murdock, M., 505
Murnen, S. K., 377
Murphey, M., 141
Murphy, G. E., 469
Murphy, J., 327
Murphy, S. T., 150, 402, 416
Murphy, T. N., 172
Murray, C., 356
Murray, D. M., 297, 538
Murray, E., 202
Murray, H., 384
Murray, H. A., 203, 426
Murray, J. P., 575
Murray, L., 94
Murray, R., 478
Murray, R. M., 478
Murrell, A., 587
Must, A., 540
Mycielska, K., 197
Myers, D. G., 407, 412, 440, 563
Myers, I. B., 431
Myers, J., 141
Myers, R., 65
Mynatt, C. R., 394

Nadel, L., 464
Naidu, R. K., 441
Napoleon, 411, 443
Napolitan, D. A., 550
Narrow, W. E., 501
Nash, M., 223
Naveh, G., 484
Naylor, T. H., 389
Nazareth, A., 379
Neale, J. M., 407, 473, 524
Neale, M., 108, 464
Neale, M. C., 237, 381, 464, 571
Neave, N. J., 527
Needham, D. R., 151
Needles, D. J., 473
Neeleman, J., 507
Neese, R. M., 171, 251
Negrao, A. B., 372
Neimi, R. G., 409, 566, 568
Neisser, U., 182, 227, 270, 269, 271, 285, 289, 295, 296, 348, 356
Neitz, J., 162
Nelis, P. C., 46
Nelligan, J. S., 98
Nelson, C. B., 484
Nelson, K., 82, 321
Nelson, N., 533
Nelson, R. J., 527
Nemeroff, C., 249
Nesbitt, K. M., 576
Nesselroade, J. R., 113

Neubauer, A., 109
Neubauer, P., 109
Neugarten, B. L., 128, 143
Neumann, C. G., 539
Neuringer, A., 256
Nevill, G., 167
Nevin, J. A., 257
Newcomb, M. D., 144, 235, 237
Newcombe, N., 83
Newell, A., 17
Newhouse, J. P., 536
Newkirk, I., 35
Newman, D. L., 97, 482
Newman, L. S., 103, 224
Newman, M., 109
Newman, P., 288
Newman, R. I., 531
Newport, E. L., 324
Newport, F., 201, 225
Newson, J. T., 524
Newton, I., 161, 484
Newton, T., 524
Nezu, A. M., 532
Nezu, C. M., 532
Nezworski, M. T., 426
Ng, S. H., 329
Ng, L., 350
Nias, D. K. B., 571
Niccols, G. A., 80
Nichols, R. C., 108, 353
Nichter, M., 540
Nickell, J., 224
Nickerson, R. S., 280
Nicklaus, J., 330
Nicodemus, N., 419
Nicol, S. E., 479
Nicolaus, L. K., 251
Niebuhr, R., 447, 525
Niedenthal, P. M., 200
Niemi, R. G., 537
Nigro, G., 330
Niit, T., 403
Nillson, L., 374
Nimoy, L., 550
Nisbett, R. E., 30, 311, 313, 316, 389, 447, 573, 601
Nishizawa, S., 201
Nixon, R., 271, 274, 275, 400
Noble, E. P., 237
Noegel, R., 372
Noel, J. G., 447
Nolen-Hoeksema, S., 218, 472, 473, 496
Noller, P., 98
Norcross, J. C., 488, 496
Norem, J. K., 447
Norman, D. A., 199
Norris, J., 482
Norris, P. A., 531
Norton, K. L., 372
Nostradamus, 202
Notarius, C., 138
Nowak, R., 537
Nowell, A., 357, 358
Nurius, P., 438
Nuttin, J. M., Jr., 580
Nystrom, J., 84

O'Brien, K., 101

subject index